THE ROYAL ENGINEERS IN EGYPT AND THE SUDAN.

Kitchener of Khartoum

THE ROYAL ENGINEERS
IN
EGYPT AND THE SUDAN.

BY

LIEUT.-COLONEL E. W. C. SANDES,

D.S.O., M.C., R.E. (*Ret.*),

LATE PRINCIPAL, THOMASON CIVIL ENGINEERING COLLEGE, ROORKEE, INDIA,

AND AUTHOR OF

"IN KUT AND CAPTIVITY," "TALES OF TURKEY" AND "THE MILITARY ENGINEER IN INDIA."

The Naval & Military Press Ltd

Published by

The Naval & Military Press Ltd
Unit 5 Riverside, Brambleside
Bellbrook Industrial Estate
Uckfield, East Sussex
TN22 1QQ England

Tel: +44 (0)1825 749494

www.naval-military-press.com
www.nmarchive.com

In reprinting in facsimile from the original, any imperfections are inevitably reproduced and the quality may fall short of modern type and cartographic standards.

To the Memory

of

CHARLES GEORGE GORDON

AND

HORATIO HERBERT KITCHENER.

FOREWORD.

By GENERAL SIR F. REGINALD WINGATE, *Bt.*, G.C.B., G.C.V.O., G.B.E., K.C.M.G., D.S.O., T.D., D.C.L., LL.D., D.L.

THE author of this work, Lieut.-Colonel E. W. C. Sandes, D.S.O., M.C., R.E. (retd.), is eminently fitted for the great task he has undertaken of compiling a history of the Royal Engineers in Egypt and the Sudan. He has already published in 1933 and 1935 two somewhat similar volumes, entitled *The Military Engineer in India*, the Foreword of which was written by that distinguished Veteran Colonel Commandant of the Corps—General Sir Bindon Blood, G.C.B., G.C.V.O., Chief Royal Engineer. When the author informed me that Sir Bindon had read his volumes on India chapter by chapter and had made comments of great value, he hoped that I would do the same for the volume he contemplated writing on the achievements of the Royal Engineers in Egypt and the Sudan. I naturally demurred—feeling that, although I belonged to the Sister Service—the Royal Artillery—what he asked me to undertake would be better carried out by one of his own Corps; but apparently the " Sudan Sappers " he consulted urged that—having regard to my service of 36 years in Egypt and the Sudan, during which I was for 17 years Sirdar of the Army and Governor-General of that country, and for over two years High Commissioner for Egypt (1916–1919)—I should still be approached with a view to reading and criticizing his typescript.

Finally, and with considerable diffidence, I consented, and for upwards of two years the author has sent me each chapter as it was compiled. This led to many letters and interviews between us, and I am only too pleased to state that—in spite of many other preoccupations—the reading of Colonel Sandes' manuscript has given me great interest and satisfaction.

I have now much pleasure in commending this volume to the careful perusal—not only of the Technical Branches of our Combined Services who have or have had direct personal connection with Egypt and the Sudan, but I also commend it unhesitatingly to the general public of our Empire, as well as to students of neighbouring nations who have either a direct or indirect international interest in those countries in the welfare of which Great Britain has been so intimately concerned since 1882 down to the present day.

Beginning from the year 1800, the author has naturally kept in the forefront the undoubtedly great services rendered by the Corps of Royal Engineers—both individually and collectively—and when he deals with such outstanding figures as Gordon, Kitchener and others who rendered conspicuous service either in a military or administrative capacity, he has a great field in which to work. I venture to think that when the reader lays down this book, he will agree with me that Colonel Sandes has carried out his self-imposed task in a manner which reflects the greatest credit on his ability and capacity to produce a most valuable and readable volume—marvellously accurate in detail and written in a fascinating style—showing that he possesses not only a sense of the romance which is invariably connected with the history of Egypt and the Sudan, but that he has also a gift of graphic and humorous story-telling. In a word he has succeeded in clothing the dry bones of official reports with such vivid flesh and blood as to produce a most brilliant and entertaining record. This volume represents an enormous amount of research in widely scattered documents; it represents too the views and experiences of several distinguished brother officers he has consulted; and he has supplemented this vast store of information by personal investigation on the spot, having undertaken a prolonged journey throughout the Sudan and Egypt before he began to write.

The student of military history will find ample food for study and thought, and he will be astounded at the wonderful achievements of those comparatively young Military Engineers, faced with almost insurmountable obstacles and at times with an almost empty exchequer.

When it is realized that the Sudan Railways, Telegraphs, Docks, Canals and Harbours owe their creation almost entirely to the "Sapper," and that exploration and surveying of huge tracts of little known country have been most successfully undertaken by those pioneer Engineers under the leadership of Gordon, Kitchener and other distinguished officers of the Corps, one cannot but be filled with admiration for all that has been achieved during the last fifty years by this splendid band of brothers.

When the brave and resourceful Dervishes had been overcome, and the country resuscitated and made peaceful under British rule, a bond of sympathy, respect and almost affection was established between the inhabitants and their advisers.

I think that those who—like myself—have been thrown into close contact with the Sudanese have found them a really lovable people, and I am bold enough to say that—given present conditions—the peoples of the Anglo-Egyptian Sudan are second to none in loyalty and fidelity.

On the outbreak of the Great War, so spontaneous was the response to my appeal, of which I give an extract in the footnote below,[1] that

---

[1] "God is my witness that we have never interfered with any man in the exercise of his religion. We have brought the Holy Places within a few days' journey of Khartoum. We have assisted the men of religion . . ."

the innumerable letters and telegrams I received from all parts of the Sudan were locally published under the heading *The Sudan Book of Loyalty*.

The Sudan stood fast, and it is with true pride that I have also to place on record my conviction that this loyalty was mainly due to the whole-hearted devotion to duty of the British officers and officials and their native assistants.

This is not the place to describe in any detail the foundations on which we began to rule the country after the Battle of Omdurman and the death of the Khalifa, but it may interest the readers of this Foreword to glance at the following extract from " Instructions from the Council in Calcutta " in 1769 to its officers—who are reminded :—

" Your commission entrusts you with the superintendence and charge of a province, whose rise and fall must considerably affect the public welfare of the whole. The exposing and eradicating of numberless oppressions, which are so grievous to the poor as they are injurious to the Government ; the displaying of those national principles of honour, faith, rectitude, and humility, which should ever characterize the name of an Englishman ; the impressing the lowest individual with these ideas, and raising the heart of the ryot from oppression and despondency to security and joy, are the valuable results which must result to our nation from a prudent and wise behaviour on your part. Versed as you are in the language, depend on none when you yourself can possibly hear and determine. Let access to you be easy, and be careful of the conduct of your dependants. Aim at no undue influence yourself, and check it in all others. Great share of integrity, disinterestedness, assiduity, and watchfulness is necessary not only for your own guidance, but as an example to all others."

The spirit inculcated in these instructions issued a century and a half ago, was also that adopted in the Sudan when we entered upon its administration in 1899. Here again, it is my delight and satisfaction to affirm that British officers and officials employed in those early days of our administration (and happily continuing to the present day) were imbued with that self-same spirit of loyal devotion to duty, of uncomplaining cheerfulness in conditions of loneliness and hardship, in a trying climate and at times involved in struggles with wild savage tribesmen, who were restive under any sort of control. It is to such men that we òwe the present conditions of comparative well-being and prosperity in the Sudan.

All that I have summarized above is brought out in Colonel Sandes' narrative with a wealth of accurate detail and close personal observation which shows his aptitude for his task. Here I may digress for a moment to touch on the author's life and aspects of his personal career which have fitted him to write as authoritatively as he has done, not only on the achievements of the various members of his Corps, but also on the consecutive history of those times, which represent years of research. He has successfully avoided the pitfall of dullness and given an interest and vitality to his story. To put his materials together in so clear and comprehensive a manner is deserving of the highest commendation.

Son of the late Colonel H. T. T. Sandes of the Royal Artillery, he was educated at Monkton Combe School and the Royal Military Academy, Woolwich, whence he was commissioned to the Royal Engineers in 1899. From 1902 to 1910, he served in the Military Works Services in India. From 1910 to 1915, he was Professor of Civil Engineering in the Thomason Civil Engineering College at Roorkee. During the Great War, he commanded the Bridging Train with the 6th Indian Division in Mesopotamia, under the late General Sir Charles Townshend, and was with him during the advance to Ctesiphon and the retreat to Kut el Amarah, during which he bridged the Tigris no less than seventeen times. He was three times mentioned in Despatches, receiving the awards of the D.S.O., M.C. and French Croix de Guerre with palms. He served in the garrison of Kut till its surrender on the 29th April, 1916, and was a prisoner of war in Turkey for two and a half years, when he wrote *In Kut and Captivity*.[1] After his captivity, he returned to India in 1919, and held the appointment of Principal of the Thomason College for over ten years. In 1923, another book came from his fertile pen, entitled *Tales of Turkey*.[2] In 1930, as a Lieut.-Colonel, he retired owing to ill-health and quitted India.

Since his return to England he has been constantly at work, compiling the two volumes of the *Military Engineer in India* to which I have already referred; and now, having published this volume on the achievements of his Corps in Egypt and the Sudan, he is again busy collecting information for a history of the Indian Corps of Sappers and Miners, which, he tells me, may be published by the Institution of Royal Engineers, for the Commandants of the three Corps, within the next five years.

The perusal of the twenty chapters comprising this volume has brought back most vividly to my mind many incidents in my long service in Egypt and the Sudan, some of which I see the author has incorporated in his narrative; but perhaps the most interesting items of our many talks included various incidents, the details of which for obvious reasons could not well be published at present—dealing as they do with the methods, characteristics and idiosyncrasies of prominent personages, the political significance of certain events of historical importance, and the manner in which the respective

---

[1] Published by John Murray in 1919.
[2] Also published by John Murray.

Governments concerned dealt with critical situations which arose from time to time. All these points, and a host of other matters bearing on the narrative, came under review in the course of our conversations—and although I was obliged to place a ban on publication at present of such incidents and my personal connection with them, I felt that it was very advisable that the author should imbibe —so to speak—the atmosphere which is so essential to an accurate appreciation of a situation, and this Colonel Sandes has succeeded in doing.

In this narrative, he has closely adhered to the limits I was obliged to impose on his pen. I refer especially to various incidents connected with the 1884-85 Expedition for the relief of Gordon besieged in Khartoum and the subsequent abandonment of the Sudan;[1]—also our long period of training the Egyptian Army for the task in which it took a prominent and worthy part in the subsequent reconquest of the Sudan. In all these campaigns, I was Lord Kitchener's Confidential Staff Officer and Director of Military Intelligence, and my connection with that very distinguished " Sapper " leader and life-long friend must always remain a treasured memory.

Then there are references to various incidents which were of no mean historical importance, and with which Colonel Sandes has also dealt tactfully and truthfully in so far as hitherto published information or official reports admit. I refer more especially to the British Mission to Abyssinia in 1897; the Fashoda incident in 1898; the defeat and death of the Khalifa in 1899; the beginning and development of Sudan Administration; the outbreak of the Great War and the part played by the Egyptians and Sudanese; the reconquest of Darfur; the rise of the Arab Revolt in Mecca and Medina in 1916; and the effect on the inhabitants of both Egypt and the Sudan of the decisions of the Peace Conference in Paris, 1919.

In all these episodes, and many others, it fell to my lot to take a more or less prominent part, until, on the death of my former chief— Lord Kitchener—I was called upon to fill the place to which (had he lived) he undoubtedly would have returned on the conclusion of the Great War.

The various incidents connected with the tenure of my position as High Commissioner for Egypt from the end of 1916 till early in 1919, still remain to be recorded, but this for the moment is not desirable, for reasons which cannot well be explained here; suffice it to say that, although retired from the Diplomatic Service and from the Active list of the British Army in 1922, and feeling still sufficiently energetic to undertake further work in connection with Africa, where a long

[1] Lieut.-Colonel Milligan, R.A. (retd.), Director of Sudan Surveys, has given much valuable, and hitherto unrecorded, information regarding Gordon's system of defence of Khartoum.

residence in various official positions had given me a general experience which I thought might perhaps be of some small value, I accepted the invitation of that great pioneer and distinguished South African Mining Engineer—Sir Robert Williams, *Bt.*—to join the group of Companies of which he was the originator and very capable Managing Director.[1]

Associated with this British group of Companies is the Union Miniere of the Belgian Congo and the Portuguese Benguela Railway Company. The latter, starting from Lobito Bay—admittedly the finest port and harbour on the West Coast of Africa—traverses the Province of Angola, and entering the Belgian Congo, recently joined the Cape to Cairo Railway at Tenke—a station of the Katanga Railway system. This line, which also owes its inception and completion to Sir Robert Williams, was primarily built for the transport of copper from the Congo, but it must eventually prove of the greatest commercial and strategic value from a Belgian, Portuguese and British point of view.

Although the scope of Colonel Sandes' narrative has only permitted of a comparatively brief reference to the Cape to Cairo Railway scheme—or as some have called it "dream" of that other very distinguished Empire-builder—Cecil Rhodes—nevertheless a further short reference to this subject may not be out of place here.

The development of that great conception dates from the last quarter of the nineteenth century and still remains to be completed; its history is really the history of modern Africa—in a word the spanning of the once "Dark Continent" by rail and telegraph from Cape Town to Cairo.

As the late Viscount Milner so pertinently remarked: "The chief object of the Rhodes line was not so much to connect its one extreme end with the other, as to connect those otherwise isolated points along the great backbone of the Continent from which, later, lines ran to the Coast." Examples of this are to be found not only in the Benguela Railway, but in the Rhodesia, Mashonaland and Beira railways, and in the lines connecting Port Sudan on the Red Sea with the Main Nile at Atbara and with the Blue Nile at Sennar.

The talented authoress of one of the most important studies of the development of lines of communication in Africa aptly summarizes the situation in the following words.[2]

"These Cape to Cairo dreams are closely bound with both economic needs and imperial aspirations. It is this relationship between gigantic economic undertakings and the shaping of

---

[1] Tanganyika Concessions Limited. The Zambesia Exploring Company Limited. Rhodesia—Katanga Company Limited. Kentan Gold Areas Limited. Kimingini Gold Mining Company Limited.

[2] *The Cape to Cairo Dream*, by Lois A. C. Raphael, Ph.D., published by the Columbia University Press, New York, 1936.

imperial policies which makes the story of the influence of Cape to Cairo ideas on British expansion such a significant chapter in the history of British imperialism."

It seems to be generally admitted that if the Cape to Cairo railway is ever brought to completion, it will probably run along the " Great African Watershed," especially along the Nile-Congo Divide. As Sir Robert Williams adumbrated as far back as 1924, mineral discoveries on that Divide, coupled with the Kilo and Moto goldfields of the Belgian Congo, might well result in the eventual junction of the present railway terminus of El Obeid in the Sudan with the Katanga Railway system.

It must, however, be remembered that the locomotive has now to compete with the aeroplane and automobile. A bi-weekly air mail service has been established by the Imperial Airways from the Cape to Alexandria via Uganda and East Africa. There is also an all-British motor route from Cape Town to Juba in the Sudan; and indeed, with the extension of motor highways to link the existing railways, the Cape to Cairo route may quite possibly become important long before the Cape to Cairo railway is a reality.

I have been particularly struck with the modest estimate of the valuable work which Lois Raphael has so successfully accomplished in bringing out her important volume; she writes, " My readers may not agree with my conclusions. I only hope that my errors of judgment and my shortcomings in respect of information may be of some value in provoking others to rectify and round out my narrative. . . ."

In many respects, *The Cape to Cairo Dream* and Colonel Sandes' narrative have much in common in so far as both are largely based on official and other publications. If, as I hope, those who are in a position to implement or criticize the conclusions arrived at, will only do so, they will be contributing valuable service. It is only by such means that—with the efflux of time—true and accurate history can become known to the general public.

REGINALD WINGATE.

London, 1st July, 1937.

PREFACE.

IN October 1933, while engaged in writing the second and final volume of the Corps History for India, entitled *The Military Engineer in India*, I was approached by the Institution of Royal Engineers with a proposal that, on the conclusion of that work, I should compile a history of a similar kind dealing with the achievements of Royal Engineers in Egypt and the Sudan. Unfortunately, I had never served in either of those countries; but feeling confident that other officers would come to my assistance, I agreed to make the attempt.

The collection of information was started in September 1934. From January to March 1935, I toured the Sudan and Egypt, and after my return to England, began to write this book. The task has occupied two years, and though hard and exacting, it has been of absorbing interest. My aim has been to produce an accurate and comprehensive, but essentially readable narrative, avoiding technicalities, and concentrating as much as possible on the work of engineers, and on the men themselves.

Part I deals with the achievements of Royal Engineers in all the campaigns in Egypt and the Sudan from 1800 A.D. to the present day: Part II describes their work in various civil departments during the last half-century. No bibliography is provided as the sources of information are given in footnotes. As regards the spelling of names, I have followed the modern system advocated by the Permanent Committee on Geographical Names. Constant reference to large maps being a weariness of the flesh, I have included in every chapter one or more sketch-maps showing the places mentioned in that chapter, or the dispositions of the forces engaged in a battle, and have supplemented these by small-scale general maps of Egypt and the Sudan at the end of the volume. The 32 sketch-maps were drawn by me, and " faired " at the School of Military Engineering, Chatham.

From beginning to end of this long history, my chief guide and mentor has been General Sir Reginald Wingate, Bt., G.C.B., G.C.V.O., G.B.E., K.C.M.G., D.S.O., the writer of the Foreword. I cannot express adequately my gratitude to him for the unfailing help which he has given. He has read and commented profusely upon every chapter, advising, correcting or amplifying as occasion demanded. It is not too much to say that without the benefit of his matchless knowledge of the Sudan, his deep insight into the affairs of Egypt, and his accurate recollection of the military operations and of the officers and men who took part in them, this history could never have been written, or if written, would have lacked that completeness which every historian strives to attain. Sir Reginald, an officer of the

Royal Artillery, has given whole-hearted assistance in a project of a sister Service. It is a matter of regret to me that the necessity of condensing into a single volume the entire history of Royal Engineer work in Egypt and the Sudan has prevented more than a passing reference to the events of his long and successful administration as Governor-General.

My tour in the Sudan was facilitated by the co-operation of the Government officials under H.E. Sir George Stewart Symes, K.C.M.G., K.B.E., D.S.O., as Governor-General; and my acknowledgments are due in particular to Mr. E. G. Sarsfield-Hall, C.M.G., then Governor of Khartoum, Mr. C. J. Hunter, Deputy General Manager, Sudan Government Railways, and Lieut.-Colonel S. L. Milligan, C.M.G., D.S.O., R.A. (retd.), Director of Survey. Colonel H. L. Bingay, D.S.O., late R.E., Chief Engineer in Egypt, made arrangements for me to see the works in and around Cairo, and to visit the Delta Barrage. Lieut.-Colonel J. R. Marryat, D.S.O., M.C., R.E. (retd.), showed me part of the Delta Light Railway system; and the Suez Canal Company transported me along the Canal in a speed-boat. It was all very enjoyable and highly instructive. Since my return to England, I have received every assistance from the officials of the Sudan Government Office under Mr. A. B. B. Howell, M.B.E., and useful information from Sir George Arthur, Bt., M.V.O., Sir Murdoch MacDonald, K.C.M.G., C.B., M.P., Major-General H. J. Huddleston, C.B., C.M.G., D.S.O., M.C., Dr. Bernard M. Allen and Messrs. Basil Burnett and R. W. S. Weir.

At a very early stage I began to realize that, as the historical works on Egypt and the Sudan do not compare in number with those on India, I should have to rely to a great extent on notes written by brother officers; and accordingly I circularized every Royal Engineer who had served in the Sudan, and many who had served in Egypt. Some of these officers agreed not only to write notes, but to read the typescript of the chapters describing events in which they had taken part, and their suggestions and amendments have tended to reduce the number of errors which are liable to creep into any narrative. Every chapter has been read by at least one, and sometimes by four or five, of these long-suffering critics and advisers. I am deeply indebted to 50 officers and ex-officers of the Corps for notes or the reading of chapters.

It is with regret that I lay down my pen. For the past two years my life has been so bound up with those of Gordon, Kitchener and other heroes of the past that I feel almost that I had known them personally, though Gordon died when I was a child, and on only two occasions did I meet Kitchener. I return now to the study of India and her three famous Corps of Sappers and Miners, and accordingly bid farewell to Egypt and the Sudan.

E. W. C. SANDES.

April 10th, 1937.

CONTENTS.

PART I—MILITARY.

CHAPTER I.

EARLY CAMPAIGNS IN EGYPT.

Turkish Army crosses Sinai in 1800—Lt. Lacy, R.E., accompanies it—Advance on Cairo—Battle of Heliopolis—Defeat and flight of Turks—Military Mission to Constantinople—Capts. Holloway and Fletcher, R.E.—Turkish manners and customs—Expedition to Egypt in 1801 under General Sir R. Abercromby—Major McKerras, R.E., killed—Landing at Abu Qir Bay—Capt. Bryce, R.E., as C.R.E.—Battle of Mandara Tower—Battle of Nikopolis—Death of Abercromby—General Hutchinson takes command—French Army retires on Cairo—General Eyre Coote blockades Alexandria—Hutchinson marches on Cairo—Turks co-operate—Battle of El Khanka—Lacy's account—Hutchinson summons General Belliard to surrender—French Army evacuates Egypt—Indian contingent, under General Baird, arrives too late—Baird's march from Red Sea to Nile—Hutchinson besieges Alexandria—General Menou surrenders—Expedition to Egypt in 1807—General Fraser occupies Alexandria —General Wauchope fails at Rosetta—Disaster to General Stewart—Fraser negotiates with Muhammad Ali for truce—British withdrawal from Egypt—Early projects for ship-canals—Overland route to Suez—Alexandria-Cairo Railway opened in 1856 ... ... PAGE 1

CHAPTER II.

THE EGYPTIAN CAMPAIGN OF 1882.

Extravagance of Khedive Ismail—Intrigues of Arabi Pasha—Alexandria massacres—Bombardment of Alexandria—General Alison occupies city—Expeditionary Force organized under General Sir G. Wolseley—General Graham, v.c. (late R.E.), commands brigade—R.E. units and officers—Major Ardagh, R.E., repairs Alexandria fortifications—Enemy, under Arabi, entrench at Kafr el Dauwar—Expeditionary Force arrives, and sails again for Suez Canal—Wolseley lands force at Ismailia—Murder of Capt. Gill, R.E., and two companions in Sinai Desert—Colonel Warren (late R.E.) investigates—Strategical situation—Graham occupies Nifisha—Wolseley advances along Sweetwater Canal—El Mahuta, El Mahsama and El Qassasin occupied—Removal of obstructions in Sweetwater Canal—Graham repulses counter-attack at El Qassasin—His strategy criticised—Arabi concentrates at Tel el Kebir—He attacks Qassasin again—Arab version of operations—Fortified position at Tel el Kebir—Wolseley's night march—Battle of Tel el Kebir (Sept. 13th, 1882) —Arabi routed—Work of Field and Railway Companies, and Telegraph and Pontoon Troops, R.E.—Indian Sappers and Miners under Colonel " Buster " Browne (late R.(B).E.)—Telegram to Queen Victoria—Indian contingent under General Macpherson—Pursuit of defeated Egyptians—Gallantry of Lt. Burn-Murdoch, R.E., at Zagazig—Cavalry under General Drury Lowe advance to Abbassia outside Cairo—Capt. Watson, R.E., secures surrender of Cairo Citadel garrison—Submission of Arabi—Colonel Wilson (late R.E.) at Arabi's trial—Formation of new Egyptian Army under General Sir E. Wood—Appointment of R.E. officers—Capt. Kitchener, R.E., appointed from Cyprus—R.E. Mess established in Cairo—General remarks on Tel el Kebir Campaign ... 24

CHAPTER III.

OPERATIONS ON THE RED SEA LITTORAL.

Rise of the Mahdi—Disaster to Colonel Hicks' force in Kordofan in 1883—Osman Digna invades Red Sea Littoral—He defeats General Valentine Baker at Et Teb—Suakin and Sheikh Barghut—Fall of Sinkat and Tokar—General Sir

G. Graham, v.c. (late R.E.), leads expedition to Suakin and Trinkitat in February, 1884—Description of Suakin—Graham advances from Trinkitat—Battle of Tamai (March 13th, 1884)—Graham victorious—General Gordon (late R.E.) appeals from Khartoum for help—Mr. Gladstone refuses—Skirmish at Tamanieb—Campaign closes—Major Chermside, R.E., as Governor-General, Red Sea Littoral—Succeeded in 1886 by Colonel Warren and Major Watson, R.E.—17th (Field) Coy., R.E., at Suakin—Urgent appeal from Gordon (November, 1884)—Railway begun from Suakin towards Berber—Large force concentrated at Suakin under Graham—R.E. units and officers—Hashin occupied—Battle of Tofrik (March 22nd, 1885)—Desperate fighting and heavy casualties, but decisive—Work of Balloon Detachment—Osman Digna retreats to Sinkat—10th (Railway) and 17th (Field) Coys., R.E., assist on Suakin-Berber Railway construction—Contractors unsatisfactory—Line reaches Otao—Work stopped—Line dismantled—Nursing sisters at Suakin—Troops withdrawn, except small garrison—Osman Digna returns and besieges Suakin—Defences elaborated—Description of defences and water-supply—Major Watson, R.E., as Governor-General, Red Sea Littoral—Succeeded by Lt.-Colonel Kitchener, R.E., in September, 1886—Kitchener attacks enemy at Handub—Severely wounded (January 17th, 1888)—Invalided to Cairo—Osman Digna resumes siege of Suakin—General Grenfell, with Kitchener as brigade commander, defeats Osman at Gemmaiza (December 20th, 1888)—Successful operations by Colonel Holled-Smith in 1891—Osman driven off finally in 1896—Kitchener's railway schemes—Lt. Gorringe, R.E., at Suakin—Indian troops, under General Egerton, garrison Suakin in 1896 56

CHAPTER IV.

THE NILE EXPEDITION OF 1884—85.

Operations sanctioned for relief of General Gordon—Nile route selected—Lord Wolseley to command force—" Whalers " and *voyageurs*—Plan of operations—Staff—R.E. units and officers—Capt. Kitchener, R.E., as Intelligence Officer—Instructions to Wolseley—Advanced troops occupy Dongola—Wolseley arrives at Wadi Halfa—General advance begins (Nov. 2nd, 1884)—Hauling whalers through cataracts—Rowing and sailing up Nile—Steamers arrive in sections—History of Wadi Halfa-Saras Railway—Gordon's advice regarding railway—Major W. Clarke, R.(B.)E., extends railway southwards (Sept. 1884)—Major Scott, R.E., assumes charge—Line reaches Akasha (Aug. 1885)—Telegraph work under Colonel Webber (late R.E.)—Telegraph experiences of Lt. Stuart and Capt. Bagnold, R.E.—Telegraphs during the evacuation—Capt. Ferrier, R.E., defends Ambigol Wells—Disquieting news of Gordon—Wolseley decides to dispatch Desert Column under General Stewart from Korti to El Metemma, and River Column under General Earle up the Nile—Desert Column marches (Dec. 30th, 1884)—Battle of Abu Klea (Jan. 17th, 1885)—Stewart continues march towards the Nile—Fight near El Metemma—Stewart wounded—Colonel Wilson (late R.E.) takes command—Reaches Nile at Gubat—Major Dorward and Lt. Lawson, R.E., build redoubt—Gordon's steamers appear—Controversy on Wilson's delay at Gubat—Wilson starts upstream in *Bordein*, with *Telahawiya*, to rescue Gordon—In sight of Khartoum (Jan. 28th, 1885)—Gordon dead—Ships turn and steam downstream—*Telahawiya* sinks—*Bordein* runs aground—Party rescued by Lord C. Beresford—General Buller arrives and evacuates Gubat—Desert Column returns to Korti—Adventures of River Column—General Earle killed at Battle of Kirbekan (Feb. 10th, 1885)—General Brackenbury takes command —R.E. Work—River Column returns to Korti—Wolseley ordered to evacuate Sudan (May, 1885)—Buller and Brackenbury execute operation—Wadi Halfa retained as advanced base, with outpost at Kosha—General Grenfell succeeds General Wood as Sirdar, Egyptian Army—Mahdi dies in June, 1885, and is succeeded by Khalifa—General Stephenson defeats dervishes at Kosha and Ginnis (Dec. 1885)—All troops withdrawn to Wadi Halfa—Defences of Wadi Halfa—Colonel Chermside (late R.E.) takes command at Wadi Halfa (Oct., 1886)—Defeats dervishes at Gemai and Saras—Enemy advance again (Sept., 1887)—Repulsed by Lt.-Colonel Wodehouse outside Wadi Halfa—Enemy advance to Nile north of Wadi Halfa (1889)—Grenfell defeats them at Battle of Toski (Aug. 3rd, 1889)—Reputation of Kitchener enhanced by Nile operations 88

CHAPTER V.

GORDON IN KHARTOUM.

General Gordon and Lt.-Colonel Stewart ride from Korosko—Gordon's character—His early career—His appointment as Governor-General of the Sudan—Zubeir, slave-trader—Gordon issues proclamation at Berber—Arrives at Khartoum (Feb. 18th, 1884)—Begins to evacuate Egyptian troops and civilians—Asks Sir E. Baring to send Zubeir and troops—Dervish forces invest Khartoum—Gordon strengthens defences with assistance of Stewart and Power (Correspondent)—Government refuses to send Zubeir or British troops—Gordon appeals to European powers and the Pope—Khartoum defences, arsenal and dockyard—Position of Fort Makran—Other forts—Main entrances in fortified line—Land-mines and entanglements—Telegraph lines—The Palace—Strength of garrison—Gordon rejects summons to surrender—Sends Stewart, Power and Herbin (French Consul) downstream (Sept., 1884)—Mahdi arrives with Slatin (a prisoner) and large enemy reinforcements—Gordon refuses to see Slatin—Final entry in Gordon's diary (Dec. 14th, 1884)—Position desperate—Sickness and starvation—Mahdi prepares to assault—Dervishes outflank fortified line, enter Khartoum, and massacre defenders—Death of Gordon (Jan. 26th, 1885)—Gordon memorials—Statue at Chatham and replica at Khartoum 122

CHAPTER VI.

THE DONGOLA EXPEDITION OF 1896.

Kitchener appointed Sirdar (April, 1892)—Reorganizes and trains Egyptian Army—Stringent economy—Dongola Expedition authorized (March, 1896)—Kitchener selected as commander—Staff—Major Wingate and the Intelligence Department—Problems of supply and transport—Plan of campaign—R.E. officers available—Kitchener's "Band of Boys"—Colonel Hunter moves from Wadi Halfa—He seizes Akasha (March 20th, 1896)—Kitchener leaves Cairo—Dervishes concentrate at Firket and Suarda, and near Kerma—March of 9th Sudanese from Red Sea to Nile—Wadi Halfa and its defences in 1896—Saras—Major Hunter-Weston, R.E., reconnoitres cataracts—Extension southwards of railway and telegraph lines—Hunter reinforced at Akasha—Excellent Intelligence Service—Kitchener masses troops at, and near, Akasha—Night march on Firket—Battle of Firket (June 7th, 1896)—Enemy heavily defeated—Experiences of Lt. Manifold, R.E.—Storms, floods and cholera—Gunboats hauled through cataracts—Gunboat *Zafir* arrives in sections by rail—Assembled at Kosha—Cylinder bursts—Disappointment of Kitchener—Abu Sari occupied (Aug. 23rd)—Battle of Hafir (Sept. 19th)—Gunboats in action—Advance resumed—Dongola occupied (Sept. 24th)—Kitchener and the "Camel Stamp" 147

CHAPTER VII.

RAILWAY AND TELEGRAPH THROUGH THE CATARACTS.

Lt. Girouard, R.E., as Director of Railways—His character and previous career—Lts. Stevenson and Polwhele, R.E., commence railway line from Korosko (Sept. 1895)—Project abandoned (March, 1896)—Wadi Halfa-Saras line repaired and extended—Rail-head reaches Ambigol Wells (May 21st)—Rough track and old rolling-stock—Difficult country—Akasha reached (June 21st)—Progress hindered by cholera epidemic—Polwhele dies of enteric (July 29th)—Rail-head reaches Kosha (Aug. 4th)—Method of track-laying—Violent storms—Miles of track washed away—Kitchener directs repairs—Occupation of Dongola—Railway reaches terminus at Kerma (May, 1897)—Runaway train—R.E. Railway Staff reinforced—Subsequent history of Kerma Railway—Telegraph work—Lt. Manifold, R.E., improvizes equipment—Scarcity of materials and transport—Method of laying bare wire on ground—Railway telephone line—Telegraph keeps pace with troops—Severe damage by storm (Aug. 27th)—Cable laid across Nile at Kerma (Sept. 27th)—Telegraph extended to Ed Debba, Korti and Merowe 173

CHAPTER VIII.

THE ADVANCE TO THE ATBARA.

Kitchener decides to build railway from Wadi Halfa, across Nubian Desert, to Abu Hamed—Line half-way to Abu Hamed (July, 1897)—Dervishes hold El Metemma, Berber and Abu Hamed—Khalifa plans offensive—Massacre by Emir Mahmud at El Metemma—Kitchener resolves to capture Abu Hamed—General Hunter leads flying column up Nile from Kassinger, above Merowe (July 29th, 1897)—Exhausting marches—Hunter captures Abu Hamed (Aug. 7th)—Gunboats follow up cataracts—*Et Teb* capsized—Flotilla reaches Abu Hamed (Aug. 29th)—Experiences of Lt. Manifold, R.E.—Dervishes evacuate Berber—Hunter enters city (Aug. 31st)—Flotilla arrives—Berber occupied (Sept. 3rd)—Desert Railway reaches Abu Hamed (Oct. 31st)—Osman Digna joins Mahmud at El Metemma—Gunboats reconnoitre far up Nile—Kitchener tenders resignation, but withdraws it—Fort established at junction of River Atbara—Kitchener asks for British troops (Jan. 1st, 1898)—British Brigade (Col. Gatacre) and Section of 2nd Coy., R.E., arrive—3 Egyptian brigades, 8 squadrons and 4 batteries available—Scenes in Berber—Strategical errors of Khalifa—Mahmud advances northwards—Crosses desert to River Atbara—Kitchener concentrates force and moves up Atbara—Description by Lt. Manifold, R.E.—Gatacre and British Brigade—Dervish deserters—R.E. officers with force—Mahmud in *zariba* at Nakheila—General Hunter reconnoitres (March 30th)—Kitchener consults Cromer—Composition and strength of force—Hunter reconnoitres again (April 5th)—Night-march on Nakheila—Battle of the Atbara (April 8th, 1898)—Accounts by Lts. Moir and Manifold, R.E.—Desperate fighting—*Zariba* captured—3,000 Dervishes killed—Mahmud, a prisoner—Troops return to Nile camps—Berber *en fête*—Gunboats in sections arrive by rail—Assembled and launched—Railway reaches Fort Atbara 192

CHAPTER IX.

DESERT RAILWAY AND NILE TELEGRAPH.

Selection of Desert Railway route—Lt. Stevenson, R.E., reconnoitres from Korosko to Murrat Wells (Sept. 1895)—Major Talbot, R.E., surveys at Murrat Wells—Stevenson follows Talbot to Wadi Halfa—Kitchener decides to build railway from Halfa direct to Abu Hamed—Work begun (Jan. 1st, 1897)—Reconnaissance from Murrat Wells by Lt. Cator, R.E.—Cator dies of enteric (Feb. 21st)—Gauge of railway—Lt. Girouard, R.E., orders materials in England—Girouard's methods—Water-supply problems and crises—Decrepit locomotives—Additional R.E. officers arrive—Track-laying from Wadi Halfa—Lack of skilled labour and proper materials—Girouard returns from England and assumes charge—Lts. Stevenson and Pritchard, R.E., reconnoitre towards Abu Hamed—They recommend well-digging in two places—Water found later at both places, and nowhere else—Railway Battalion arrives from Kerma line (May, 1897)—Progress accelerated—Lt. Gorringe, R.E., and discovery of water at site of No. 4 Station—Rail-head camp—Rail-head 103 miles from Wadi Halfa (July 23rd)—Occupation of Abu Hamed by General Hunter (Aug. 7th)—Lts. Pritchard and Macauley, R.E., reconnoitre to Abu Hamed—Arab guides verify alignment—Rail-head reaches Abu Hamed (Oct. 31st)—Amusing description of line—Track prolonged 17 miles—Materials exhausted—Work resumed along Nile bank (Jan., 1898)—Rail-head beyond Shereik (March 10th)—Diversion inland—Railway rejoins Nile at Abidiya (May 5th)—Rail-head reaches Fort Atbara, 385 miles from Wadi Halfa (July 3rd)—Bt. Colonel Green, R.E., describes railway—Lts. Girouard and Hall, R.E., improve Luxor-Aswan Railway—Girouard appointed President, Egyptian State Railways—Leaves Sudan (June, 1898)—Succeeded as Director of Railways by Lt. Macauley, R.E.—Telegraph work by Lt. Manifold, R.E.—Cable laid across Nile below 4th Cataract—Bare wire laid on ground to Abu Hamed—Poling of line follows—Desert Railway telegraph provided—Telegraph line reaches Fort Atbara (Jan., 1898)—Manifold rides from Atbara battlefield with telegram for Cromer—Kitchener and Press Correspondents—Berber-Suakin Telegraph—Work of R.E. N.C.O's—Line from Atbara to El Metemma—Failure to lay cable across Nile at Fort Atbara (July 7th)—Temporary connection established upstream—2nd Coy., R.E., and overhead line across Atbara River—Second failure to lay Nile cable (Aug. 11th)—Cable too short—Communication maintained by ferry and heliograph 222

CHAPTER X.

OMDURMAN.

Political situation—Anglo-Egyptian Army heavily reinforced—Formations and commanders—Strength of force—Kitchener sends forward 3rd Egyptian Brigade to below 6th Cataract (July, 1898)—Other brigades follow—1st British Brigade starts (Aug. 13th)—R.E. officers with force—Lt. Gorringe, R.E., and Embarkation Staff—Kitchener employs R.E. subalterns as " gallopers " in battles—Major W. S. Gordon and Lts. Stevenson and E. O. A. Newcombe, R.E., command gunboats—Kitchener leaves Fort Atbara for the front (Aug. 13th)—6th Cataract clear of enemy—Army concentrates south of Cataract (Aug. 26th)—Major Gordon sights Omdurman—Army advances up left bank of Nile—Cavalry scouts see Khalifa's army outside Omdurman (Aug. 31st)—Kitchener halts at Egeiga Village on river bank north of Omdurman (Sept. 1st)—Railway subalterns, R.E., during advance—Telegraph problems of Lt. Manifold, R.E.—Storms damage line—Khalifa's telegraph in Omdurman—Gunboats bombard Dervish defences and Mahdi's tomb—Kitchener reconnoitres from Jebel Surkab—Sees Dervish Army advancing—Dervishes halt—Anglo-Egyptian Army entrenches at Egeiga—Distribution of forces—Battle of Omdurman (Sept. 2nd, 1898)—Dervish attack on Egeiga repulsed—Descriptions by Lts. Manifold and Blakeney, R.E.—Enemy attack mounted troops in Karari Hills—Mounted troops retreat to river, covered by fire of gunboats—Kitchener advances on Omdurman in échelon of brigades—Charge of 21st Lancers—Army of Black Flag attacks MacDonald's brigade—Kitchener reinforces right flank—Narrative of Lt. Pritchard, R.E.—Attack repulsed—Army of Green Flag attacks right rear—Attack repulsed—General retreat of enemy—Tremendous Dervish losses—Anglo-Egyptian casualties small—Bad strategy of Khalifa—Kitchener advances to seize Omdurman—2nd Egyptian Brigade (Maxwell) leads—Brigade enters Khalifa's walled enclosure—Kitchener nearly killed by British shell—Omdurman occupied—Khalifa escapes—Mahdi's tomb destroyed—Mounted troops pursue Khalifa southwards—Pursuit abandoned—Memorial service outside Gordon's Palace in Khartoum (Sept. 4th, 1898)—Honours and rewards—Remarks on Kitchener's strategy, organization and leadership 249

CHAPTER XI.

AFTER OMDURMAN.

Dervish steamer captured—Her crew state that French expedition established on Upper Nile—Kitchener leaves Omdurman for Fashoda (Sept. 10th, 1898)—Lt. E. O. A. Newcombe, R.E., in command of a gunboat—Action at Renk—Naked Shilluks—Kitchener writes to French Commandant, Marchand, announcing approach—Flotilla of gunboats moors at Fashoda (Sept. 19th)—Marchand's reply reaches Kitchener below Fashoda—Kitchener arrives at Fashoda in steamer *Dal*—Interview on *Dal* with Marchand—Colonel Wingate and Commandant Germain also present—Sudanese troops land upstream of fort—Egyptian flag hoisted—Kitchener voyages southwards to Sobat River—Establishes post there—Sudanese and French at Fashoda—Kitchener passes on his return to Omdurman—Search for French launch *Faidherbe*—Expeditions to swamps of Bahr el Jebel and Bahr el Ghazal—Marchand proceeds to Cairo and returns to Fashoda—Strained relations, meanwhile, at Fashoda—Tranquillity restored—French Government agree to evacuate Fashoda—Marchand's expedition leaves for Abyssinia (Dec. 11th, 1898)—General Hunter leads expedition up Blue Nile (Sept. 1898)—Colonel Parsons leads force from Kassala to Gedaref—Parsons besieged by Ahmed Fedil in Gedaref—General Rundle proceeds up Blue Nile—Colonel Collinson relieves Gedaref (Oct. 22nd)—Ahmed Fedil moves southwards—Colonel Lewis follows and defeats him near Roseires (Dec. 26th)—Ahmed Fedil escapes to Khalifa in Kordofan—Kitchener returns to England—Lands at Dover (Oct. 27th)—Attends many public functions—Appeals for funds for Gordon College—Leaves England (Dec. 7th)—Arrives Omdurman (Dec. 28th)—Lt.-Colonel W. Kitchener attempts to capture Khalifa—Marches into Kordofan (Jan. 23rd, 1899)—Locates Khalifa near L. Sherkeila—Retires to Nile—" Sherkeila Reconnaissance " ends (Feb. 5th)—Colonel Wingate becomes Adjutant-General, and Lt.-Colonel Talbot, R.E., Director of Military Intelligence—Lord

Cromer visits Omdurman (Jan. 4th, 1899)—Lord Kitchener appointed Governor-General (Jan. 19th, 1899)—His duties—Kitchener and Cromer—Extension of railway southwards from the Atbara—Lt. Macauley, R.E., places contracts for Atbara Bridge—R.E. Railway Staff—Atbara Bridge opened (Aug. 26th)—Line completed to Halfaya near Khartoum (Dec. 31st)—Kitchener reconnoitres for Nile-Red Sea Railway—Leads expedition against Khalifa north of Fashoda—Sends infantry under Colonel Wingate westwards from Kaka (Oct. 21st)—Khalifa escapes northwards—Expedition returns—Wingate leads final expedition against Khalifa—Marches westwards from Fashashoya (Nov. 1st)—Action at Abu Auda (Nov. 22nd)—Battle of Umm Debeikerat (Nov. 24th, 1899)—Rout of Dervishes—Death of Khalifa and principal Emirs—Major Gorringe, R.E., at Umm Debeikerat—Tribute to Colonel Sir R. Wingate—Lord Kitchener ordered to South African War (Dec. 18th)—Leaves Khartoum (Dec. 21st)—Embarks at Alexandria—Cromer's remarks on Kitchener—History of Kitchener Statue in Khartoum—Colonel Sir R. Wingate appointed Governor-General (Dec. 23rd, 1899)—Lt.-Colonel Gorringe, R.E., captures slave-trader (Jan. 1904)—R.E. officers with " patrols " sent against insurgents—Formation of Sudanese Sapper Section (1912) 278

CHAPTER XII.

FRONTIER DEFENCE IN THE GREAT WAR, 1914—18.

Achievements of Egyptian Army in Great War—Lord Kitchener becomes Secretary of State for War—Colonel Sir Percy Girouard (late R.E.) as Director of Munitions Department—General Sir John Maxwell commands forces in Egypt—Problems of defence—Avenues of approach across Sinai—Fortification of Suez Canal—Inundations—R.E. officers available—Indian Sappers and Miners—Turks near El Qantara (Nov. 20th, 1914)—Large Turkish force near Bitter Lakes (Jan. 25th, 1915)—Djemal Pasha exhorts his troops—General Wilson reinforces Ismailia sector—Turks attempt to cross Suez Canal near Ismailia (Feb. 3rd)—Attempt fails—Gallipoli campaign—R.E. officers from Sudan—Evacuation of Gallipoli—Kitchener orders defence of Suez Canal in depth (Nov. 16th)—General Wright (late R.E.) prepares scheme for 3 defensive lines—General Horne arrives to select lines—Sir M. MacDonald plans roads and water-supply—General Macauley (late R.E.) as Director of Railways—Experiences of Major Grant, R.E., on Suez Canal defences (Jan., 1916)—Changes in higher commands—General Sir A. Murray occupies defences east of Canal with 3 Army Corps—Necessity for piped water-supply—Qatiya seized (April, 1916)—Lt. Wilson, R.E., and Mobile Section, Egyptian M.W.D.—Lt. Ross, R.E.—Victory at Romani (Aug. 4th)—Advance to El Arish—R.E. officers in Palestine and Syria—Lt.-Colonel S. F. Newcombe, R.E., in Arabia and Palestine—Events in the Hedjaz—Railways in Suez Canal zone—Railway across Sinai—Water-supply for Canal defences—Pipe-line across Sinai to Palestine—Road-making—Defence of western frontier—Operations against Senussi—General Wallace concentrates force at Mersa Matruh (Dec., 1915)—Lt. Blunt, R.E., and Camel Troop—General Peyton arrives—General Lukin defeats Senussi near El Barrani (Feb. 26th, 1916)—General Peyton captures Sollum (March 14th)—Duke of Westminster rescues prisoners—Engineer work under Major Griffith, R.E.—Water reconnaissances—Colonel Talbot (late R.E.) conducts political mission—Operations against Senussi in western oases—Campaign in Darfur—Lt. Rainsford-Hannay, R.E., reconnoitres in Kordofan—R.E. officers and Sudanese Sapper Section—Lt.-Colonel Kelly advances into Darfur (March 16th, 1916)—Sultan Ali Dinar—Action at Beringiya (March 22nd)—El Fasher occupied—Engineer work—Water stored in trees—Egyptian Field Company formed—Engineers accompany patrols—Memorial to Lord Kitchener in Khartoum Cathedral 307

CHAPTER XIII.

OPERATIONS SINCE THE GREAT WAR.

Disturbances in Egypt (1919)—Lt. Hart (late R.E.) and Sudanese Sapper Section—Patrols (1921-24)—Mutinies in Khartoum and Atbara (Aug. 1924)—Murder in Cairo of General Sir Lee Stack, Governor-General of the Sudan (Nov. 19th, 1924)—Egyptian troops to leave Sudan—Serious mutiny in Khartoum (Nov. 27th)—Suppressed by General Huddleston—M.W.D.

CONTENTS. xxiii

abolished—Sudan Defence Force formed—Sapper Company and Boys Company PAGE
organized—Units known as "Engineer Troops"—Major Fowle, R.E., as
first Commandant (May, 1925)—Strength of Engineer Troops—Sappers with
patrol in Nuba Mountains (1925–26)—With Lau Nuer Patrol (1927–28)—Gwek
and Pok, magicians—Destruction of Dengkurs Pyramid (Feb. 8th, 1928)—
Organisation of Engineer Troops (1928)—Lt.-Col. Nosworthy, R.E., as 2nd-in-
command, Sudan Defence Force—Nuer Settlement operations (1928–29)—
Sapper Company expanded—Lt.-Col. B. T. Wilson, R.E., succeeds Nosworthy
(Nov., 1929)—Sappers employed on civil engineering work—Engineer Troops'
barracks at Omdurman—Strength of Engineer units (1936)—Modern developments—Dress and equipment—Military Works in Egypt—Chief Engineers
(1919–37)—Staff appointments—Motor convoys—42nd (Field) Coy., R.E., on
Red Sea Coast road construction (1933)—Engineering operations on western
frontier (1935–36)—Roman water-supply system extended at Mersa Matruh—
Aerodrome and barrack construction 339

PART II—CIVIL.

CHAPTER XIV.

IRRIGATION.

Ancient irrigation in Egypt—The Nile—Muhammad Ali and perennial
irrigation—M. Linant de Bellefonds suggests regulating barrages below Cairo—
Muhammad Ali orders building of Nile Barrage—Work commenced (1833)—
Stopped by plague (1835)—Linant departs (1837)—The *Corvée* system of
forced labour—Revised Nile Barrage project by M. Mougel (1843)—Mougel
starts work—Drastic methods of Muhammad Ali—Barrage work suffers—
Muhammad Ali dies (1848)—Abbas Pasha dismisses Mougel (1853)—Mougel
returns—Said Pasha fortifies Nile Barrage area—Rosetta and Damietta works
finished (1861)—Unsound structures—Chaotic state of Egyptian irrigation—
Rosetta Barrage cracks (1867)—Canals silted—Linant suggests abandonment
of Barrage and replacement by pumps (1871)—General Rundall (late R.E.)
recommends reconstruction (1876)—Palestine Canal scheme—Colonel Scott-
Moncrieff (late R.(B).E.) appointed Inspector-General of Irrigation (April,
1883)—Career in India—Arrival from India of Major Ross, R.(B).E., and
Mr. W. Willcocks (Nov. and Dec., 1883)—Ross at work—Pumping proposal
revived—Scott-Moncrieff and Willcocks test and improve Barrage—Arrival
from India of Major Western, R.(B).E., Capt. Hanbury Brown, R.E., and
Messrs. Reid, Foster and Garstin (1884–85)—Careers of Western and Brown—
Scott-Moncrieff becomes Under-Secretary—Western and Reid repair Rosetta
Barrage (1885–89)—Description by Scott-Moncrieff—Western retires (1890)—
Scott-Moncrieff retires (1892)—His achievements in Egypt—His abolition of
the *Corvée*—Hanbury Brown strengthens Nile Barrage works with cement
grouting (1897–1900)—Comment of lady visitor—Supplementary weirs—
Hanbury Brown retires (1904)—Schemes for damming Nile in Middle Egypt—
Western submits Wadi Ryan Reservoir project (1888)—Willcocks sent by
Scott-Moncrieff to examine alternative sites for dams—He suggests dam above
Aswan (1890)—Prepares design (1894)—Prepares revised design (1895)—
Controversy over submersion of Philæ temples—Capt. Lyons, R.E., con-
solidates foundations of temples—Aswan Dam built (1899–1902)—Lyons
accompanies Sir W. Garstin to Upper Nile—Amusing anecdote regarding
river-gauge—Mr. M. MacDonald heightens Aswan Dam (1908–12)—Second
heightening (1929–34)—Barrages at Asyut, Isna and Nag Hamadi—Nile
Projects Commission (1921)—Irrigation Works in the Sudan—Sennar Dam
and Gezira Canal—Capt. Francis, R.E., at Jebel Auliya Dam (1933–35) ... 359

CHAPTER XV.

RAILWAYS.

Sudan Government Railways (1900)—Hardships of travel—Depredations of
white ants—Kitchener reconnoitres for Nile-Red Sea Railway (1899)—Lts.
Longfield and S. F. Newcombe, R.E., reconnoitre up Atbara River (June,
1901)—Arab guide reconnoitres through Sinkat to Suakin—Longfield and

S. F. Newcombe follow—They select alignment through Red Sea Hills—Kamob PAGE
Sanha cutting—They make detailed survey (1902-03)—R.E. Railway Staff—
Preparations for terminus at Suakin—Major Macauley, R.E., (Director)
describes projected line (Oct., 1903)—Rival claims of Sheikh Barghut (Port
Sudan) and Suakin as terminal ports—Railway construction begins from
Suakin (Sept. 1st, 1904)—Labour difficulties—Lt. S. F. Newcombe, R.E.,
starts construction from Atbara end—Lt. Russell, R.E., continues it—Rail-
heads meet (Oct. 15th, 1905)—Branch line to Port Sudan completed (Dec.
31st)—Nile-Red Sea Railway opened (Jan. 27th, 1906)—Capt. E. O. A.
Newcombe, R.E., builds branch line to Kareima, near Merowe (1905-06)—
Amusing incident of Egyptian Station-master—Railway Headquarters trans-
ferred to Atbara—Russell begins to build Atbara Junction—Croton oil for
thieves—S. F. Newcombe reconnoitres for line to Kassala (1906)—Russell
surveys alignment—Major Macauley appointed Director-General, Egyptian
State Railways—Succeeded as Director by Capt. Midwinter, R.E.—S. F.
Newcombe with Lado Enclave Missions (1907-10)—Explores routes in
Abyssinia—Blue Nile Bridge built in Khartoum (1907-09)—White Nile Bridge
built at Kosti (1910)—Construction of Khartoum-El Obeid line (1909-11)—
Lts. S. F. Newcombe and R. Micklem, R.E.—Relaying and renewal operations
—Railway expansion checked by Great War—Construction of Haiya-Kassala
line begins (1923)—Major Lord, R.E., Chief Engineer—Kassala reached (1924)
—Lt.-Col. Midwinter, R.E., retires (1925)—Major E. O. A. Newcombe, R.E., re-
tires (1926)—No R.E. officers remain—Kassala line prolonged to Gedaref (1926-
28)—Opened to Sennar (Feb. 15th, 1929)—Egyptian State Railways—Major
Girouard, R.E., as President (1898-99)—Secures assistance of Capt. Kincaid
and Lts. Blakeney and Hall, R.E.—Prepares extensive programme of work—
Girouard at Board Meeting—Tale of Station-master's cow—Girouard improves
Alexandria Docks—Leaves Egypt (1899)—Succeeded by Major Johnstone, R.E.
—Major Macauley, R.E., succeeds Johnstone (1906)—Farrer and Scotter
Commissions—Egyptian railways under Macauley, with Blakeney and Hall
(1906-14)—Great War activities—General Sir G. Macauley becomes Adviser to
Ministry of Communications (March, 1919)—General Blakeney appointed
General Manager, E.S.R.—Controls railways during disturbances and strikes—
Death of Lt.-Col. Sowerby, R.E. (Jan., 1920)—Blakeney deals with further
strikes (May, 1921)—Macauley and Blakeney retire (1922)—Major McMullen,
R.E., reverts (1930)—R.E. connection with State Railways ceases—History and
description of Delta Light Railways under Lt.-Col. E.L. Marryat, Capt. Kincaid,
Capt. Adams and Lt.-Col. J. R Marryat, R.E. 389

CHAPTER XVI.

TELEGRAPHS.

Lt. Manifold, R.E., completes telegraph to Khartoum (Sept. 7th, 1898)—
Reverts to Home Establishment—Succeeded as Director by Lt. Liddell, R.E.
—Description of telegraph lines—Kitchener tests Liddell—Lts. Roberts and
Douglas, R.E., join Liddell (Jan., 1899)—Kitchener's methods—Line built to
Roseires—Connection across Gezira—Line to Er Renk—Prolongation to
Taufikia—Amusing messages and reports—Omdurman-El Obeid line—*Jehadia*
workmen—Lt. Meyricke, R.E., arrives (Feb. 1901)—Quartermaster and Hon. Lt
Dale, R.E.—Kassala-Sennar line erected (1901-04)—White Nile line built from
Khartoum (1904)—Liddell reconnoitres in Bahr el Ghazal—Marches from
Meshra er Req, through Wau, Tonj and Rumbek to Shambé on Bahr el Jebel—
Mr. Abel Chapman describes *sudd* region—Liddell explores Bahr ez Zeraf—
Accompanies Sir W. Garstin up Bahr el Jebel—Appointed Depy. Inspector-
General, Egyptian State Telegraphs—Leaves Sudan (Sept., 1904)—Succeeded
as Director by Major Turner, R.E.—Dale builds line from Meshra to Tonj
(1905)—Lt. Mackworth, R.E., arrives (Jan., 1905)—Connects Tonj with
Rumbek—Dale builds Bor-Gondokoro line (1906)—Mackworth lays cable
across Bahr el Jebel at Tombé—Dale connects Tombé with Rumbek (1906-07)
—Mackworth reconnoitres northwards from Bor—Wild elephants—
Reconnoitres southwards up Bahr ez Zeraf—Wizardry—Sheikh Din—
Elephants damage line—Donkey-men—Mackworth and Dale complete Bor-
Taufikia connection (1907-08)—Swamps—Dale builds Taufikia-Talodi line
(1907-08)—Linemen attacked by crocodile—Capt. Mackworth succeeded by
Capt. Gandy, R.E. (Jan. 24th, 1909)—Lt. Ferguson, R.E., joins, and Hon. Lt.

Dale reverts (1911)—Major Turner reverts (Sept. 5th, 1912)—Major Moir, R.E., becomes Director—Capt. Gandy invalided (Oct. 23rd, 1912)—Lt. Chenevix-Trench, R.E., joins (Feb. 21st, 1913)—Serjts. Stead and Walshaw, R.E.—Chenevix-Trench introduces Wireless—Establishes stations at Malakal, Nasir and Gambela (1914-15)—Obstruction by Abyssinians—Station established at Port Sudan—Lt.-Col. Moir as Director during Great War—Wireless during Darfur Campaign (1916)—Extension of Wireless—Col. Moir reverts (Sept. 5th, 1922)—El Obeid-Talodi line erected (1925-27)—Further line extensions—Lt.-Col. Edgeworth, R.E. (retd.), appointed Chief Engineer, Sudan Posts and Telegraphs (Dec., 1926)—Improves Wireless—Succeeded (as Director) by Lt.-Col. Tomlin, R.E. (retd.), (Feb., 1931)—Wireless co-operation with aircraft—Connection of Corps with Telegraphy in Egypt—Telegraphy during Nile campaigns—Col. H. F. Turner (late R.E.) reports on civil system (Feb., 1890)—Major Liddell, R.E. (retd.), as Director of Telegraphs (1904-14)—His work during Great War—Inspector-General (1919)—Under-Secretary (1920)—Resigns (1924)   415

CHAPTER XVII.

SURVEY AND EXPLORATION.

Colonel Charles Gordon, and Lts. Watson and Chippindall, R.E., map the Nile from Khartoum to beyond Gondokoro (1874)—Watson and Chippindall invalided (1875)—Gordon surveys almost to Lake Victoria (1876)—Great hardships—He returns to Khartoum (Oct. 1876)—Prepares map—Military surveys by R.E. Officers (1884-92)—Major Talbot, R.E., surveys in Nubian Desert and on Red Sea Littoral (1893)—He surveys with Dongola Expedition and later (1896-98)—Appointed Director of Surveys (Jan. 1st, 1900)—Capt. Austin, R.E., reaches Lake Rudolf from Uganda (1897)—Rodd Mission to Abyssinia—Expedition under Major Austin, R.E., sent to Sudan to demarcate Abyssinian frontier (1899)—Lts. Gwynn and Jackson, R.E., and Major Bright (Rif. Bde.) as members—Gwynn and Jackson survey frontier from Roseires to Sobat River (1900)—Dealings with Abyssinians—They return to England—Gwynn triangulates through Abyssinia (1901)—Austin and Bright survey Sobat River and Baro tributary (1900)—Dinkas, Nuers and Anuaks—They discover French launch *Faidherbe*—Ascend plateau—Detained at Goré—Explore Pibor swamps—Return to Omdurman—They start again with Dr. Garner (Dec. 1900)—Traverse Pibor and Akobo swamps and Boma Plateau—Water famine in desert—They reach Lake Rudolf (April, 1901)—Terrible march towards Uganda—Hostile tribesmen—Heavy casualties—Expedition reaches Uganda Railway (Aug., 1901)—Returns to Sudan *via* Mombasa and Red Sea—Gwynn appointed Assistant Director (Oct. 10th, 1901)—Triangulates along Eritrean frontier and through Suakin to Berber—Reaches Berber (April, 1902)—Demarcates Abyssinian frontier (1903)—Capt. Maud, R.E., with Butter-Maud Survey Expedition in Abyssinia—Gwynn triangulates south of Khartoum (1904)—Surveying by Talbot—Gwynn reverts (July, 1904)—Talbot reverts (April 18th, 1905)—Capt. Pearson, R.E., appointed Director—Lt. Coningham, R.E., joins Sudan Survey—He triangulates in Nubian Desert (1905-06), and in Southern Kordofan and Nuba Mountains (1907-09)—He surveys south of Roseires (1909-10), and in Lado Enclave (1910-11)—Coningham reverts (Jan. 9th, 1912)—Capt. Kelly, R.E., explores Abyssinia (1908-09), Southern Sudan frontier (1910), Sobat region (1911), and Pibor swamps (1912)—With Capt. Huddleston (Dorsets), he traces Sudan-Uganda boundary and enters Abyssinia (1912-13)—Kelly reverts (Nov. 8th, 1913)—Cadastral and Town surveys—Lt. McNeill, R.E., joins (1913)—Outbreak of Great War—R.E. Survey officers leave Sudan—Pearson leads Mission to Lake Tsana in Abyssinia (1916)—Visits Addis Ababa (1917)—Serves in Palestine—Returns to Sudan (1919)—Serves on Anglo-French Boundary Commission (1921-22)—Dies in Western Darfur (Dec. 28th, 1922)—Surveying in Egypt—Lt. de Havilland, M.E., maps Alexandria (1802)—Lt. Mantell, R.E., at Cairo (1882)—Tale of Citadel time-gun—Lt.-Col. Settle, R.E., Surveyor-General (1886-92)—Lt. Lyons, R.E., employed on various Survey duties (1890-96)—Abbassia Observatory story—Lyons appointed Director of Geological Survey (1896) and Director-General of Egyptian Survey (1898)—Tale of Brunner apparatus—Cadastral, meteorological and archæological surveying—Col. Lyons retires (1909)—Major Joly de Lotbiniere, R.E., at Cairo (1906-12)—R.E. connection with Egyptian Survey ceases   441

xxvi   CONTENTS.

CHAPTER XVIII.

WORKS.

History of Khartoum (1822–84)—Death of General Gordon (Jan. 26th, 1885) —Mahdi demolishes town—Kitchener re-occupies it (Sept. 4th, 1898)—He designs a new Khartoum—Union Jack plan—Department of Works under Lt. Gorringe, R.E. (Nov., 1898)—Lt. Done, R.E., as assistant—Gorringe starts rebuilding Gordon's Palace—Lt. Kennedy, R.E., arrives (July, 1899)—Continues work on Palace and other buildings—Kitchener prepares own design for Government Offices—Methods of work and accounts—Kitchener appeals for funds for Gordon College (Nov., 1898)—Selects site in Khartoum—Lord Cromer lays foundation stone (Jan. 5th, 1899)—College opened by Lord Kitchener (Nov. 8th, 1902)—History of College—Sir H. Wellcome, archæologist and philanthropist—Lt.-Col. Friend, R.E., appointed Director of Works (Nov., 1900)—Completes many buildings in Khartoum—Transferred to Egypt (March, 1904)—Construction of river-wall—Several R.E. officers join Works cadre (1903–06)—Rapid growth of Khartoum—Architects engaged—Gordon Statue erected—Principal buildings (1906)—R.E. Mess and members—Department of Works divided into M.W.D. and P.W.D. (Jan. 1st, 1907)—Buildings erected by Gorringe in Sennar Province (1902–04)—Done as Director, M.W.D., and Kennedy as Director, P.W.D.—Lt. Thwaites, R.E., describes tour of inspection and camel-ride—All Saints' Cathedral in Khartoum—Foundation stone laid (1904)—Construction begun (1906)—Consecrated (1912) —Tower added (1929–31)—Lt. Kelly, R.E., reports on Erkowit (1906)—Hill station established there (1907)—Changes in R.E. Staff (1908–16)—Depletion during Great War—Kennedy vacates appointment as Director, P.W.D. (March, 1918)—Major Grant, R.E., as Director of Military Works (1909–14)—He reorganizes the Department—Khartoum in modern times—Work of R.E. officers in out-stations (1919–34)—Military Works Department absorbed into Public Works Department (1925)—Blasting operations in Nile bed (1931–33)—Foundation of Port Sudan (Sheikh Barghut)—Lt. Watson, R.E., notices harbour (1874)—Capt. Kennedy, R.E., reports on its advantages (1904)—Sir R. Wingate recommends it—Commission reports on Suakin and Sheikh Barghut—Kennedy prepares estimates for Sheikh Barghut—Harbour renamed Port Sudan—Lt. Kelly, R.E., appointed Resident Engineer (1904)—He builds Port Sudan—Joined by Lt. Mackintosh, R.E. (1906)—Description of Port Sudan—Kelly and Mackintosh transferred (1908)—Port Sudan opened by Khedive (April 1st, 1909)—Visited by King George V and Queen Mary (Jan. 17th, 1912)—Port Sudan water-supply—Scheme started by Capt. Kennedy, R.E. (1905)—System installed by civil engineers—Supervized by Major Hebbert, R.E. (1927–36)—Public Works in Egypt—Col. Scott-Moncrieff (late R.E.) as Under-Secretary (1883–92)—Lt.-Col Friend, R.E., assists Sir W. Garstin (1904–05)—Military Works in Egypt   470

CHAPTER XIX.

ARCHÆOLOGY AND GEOLOGY.

Capts. Dundas and Squire, R.E., examine inscriptions at Alexandria (1802)—Capts. Wilson and Palmer, R.E., measure base of Great Pyramid (1869)—Col. Sir H. James (late R.E.) discusses dimensions—Descriptions of Great Pyramid—Methods of builders—General Sir C. Warren and Col. Sir C. Watson (late R.E.) discuss Pyramid—Watson on length of cubit—Capt. Wilson, R.E. surveys Jerusalem (1864–65)—He surveys in Palestine with Lt. Anderson, R.E. (1865–66)—Palestine Exploration Fund—Lt. Warren, R.E., undertakes survey of Western Palestine (1867)—His archæological excavations in Jerusalem —Obstruction by Turks—Valuable discoveries—Wilson, Palmer and others explore Sinai (1868–69)—Capt. Stewart, R.E., begins trigonometrical survey of Western Palestine (1871)—Invalided—Lt. Conder, R.E., resumes survey (1872)—Invalided, but returns (1874)—Lt. Kitchener, R.E., arrives (Nov., 1874)—His archæological and survey work—Party attacked by Arabs (July 10th, 1875)—Kitchener rescues Conder—Survey abandoned—Map of Palestine prepared (1876)—Kitchener returns to Palestine (Feb., 1877)—M. Ganneau on Kitchener—Kitchener completes survey of Western Palestine (Sept. 1877)—He surveys in Cyprus (1878–83)—Conder attempts survey of Eastern Palestine with Lt. Mantell, R.E. (1881)—Work stopped by Turks—Archæological notes by Mantell—General Charles Gordon studies biblical archæology at Jerusalem (1883)—Colossus of Rameses II at Memphis near Cairo—Col. Scott-Moncrieff (late R.(B).E.) suggests raising and turning over—General Stephenson furthers project—Major Bagnold, R.E., raises and turns Colossus (1887)—Inscription to Bagnold—Lord Kitchener raises fund for removal of Colossus to Cairo (1913)—Not removed—Work at Abu Simbel—Dangerous rocks reported above façade—Lt. Johnstone, R.E., and section of 24th Coy, R.E., remove rocks (1892)—Capt. Lyons, R.E., clears and repairs Philæ temples (1895-96)—Shows visitors Cairo Museum collections—Studies geology as cadet (1882)—His geological work in Egypt—Becomes Director-General, geological Survey Department 503

CHAPTER XX.

ADMINISTRATION.

Colonel Charles Gordon (late R.E.) appointed Governor, Equatorial Province, Southern Sudan (1873)—Arrives Gondokoro (April, 1874)—Explores in Uganda (1875-76)—Resigns and returns to England—Achievements as Governor—Returns as Governor-General of the Sudan (Feb., 1877)—Proceeds to Abyssinia—Arrives Khartoum (May, 1877)—Reviews his task—Reorganizes administration—Quells insurrection in Darfur—Tours northern districts—Visits Eritrea—Goes to Cairo to give financial advice to Khedive Ismail (1878)—Returns to Khartoum *via* Red Sea—Introduces financial reforms—Lonely existence in Palace—Gessi kills Suleiman in Darfur (July, 1879)—Khedive Ismail deposed—Gordon resigns—Visits Abyssinia at request of Khedive Tewfik—Leaves Egypt (Jan., 1880)—Employed in India, China, Mauritius and South Africa (1880-83)—On leave in Palestine (1883)—Returns to Khartoum (1884)—Major Chermside, Col. Warren, Major Watson and Lt.-Col. Kitchener, R.E., as Governors-General, Red Sea Littoral (1884-88)—Kitchener wounded (Jan., 1888)—Kitchener as Governor-General of the Sudan (1899)—His multifarious duties—His instructions to Governors—His methods—General Sir R. Wingate as Governor-General (1899-1916)—Col. Talbot (late R.E.) acts as Governor-General (1903)—Lt.-Col. Gorringe, R.E., as Governor, Sennar Province (1901-04)—Administration in Egypt—Bt. Col. Stanton, R.E., as British Agent and Consul General (1865-76)—Major Clarke, R.E., inspects Suez Canal (1870)—Recommends purchase—Lt.-Col. Stokes, R.E., as member of Tonnage Commission (1873)—Reports on Suez Canal (1874)—Advises purchase of Khedive Ismail's shares (1875)—Shares purchased—Stokes revisits Canal and makes tonnage agreement—Nominated Director on Board of Management, Suez Canal Company—Assists Sir E. Baring with Canal affairs (1886)—Appointed Vice-President, Suez Canal Company (1887)—Duplication of Canal proposed—Colonel Clarke (late R.E.) advocates widening (1883)—Clarke appointed Vice-President of Consultative Committee (1884)—Widening approved and started—Lord Kitchener as British Agent and Consul General in Egypt—Succeeds Sir Eldon Gorst (Sept., 1911)—Tribute from Sir E. Grey—Ceremonious arrival in Cairo, described by General Blakeney—British prestige restored—Kitchener finds an altered Egypt—Lord Lloyd on Kitchener's administration—The Five Feddan Law introduced—Kitchener's interest in agriculture and the *fellaheen*—Legislative Assembly established—Dispensaries provided—Land reclaimed—Dealings with Khedive Abbas Hilmi—Abbas deposed, and Hussein Kamel appointed Sultan (1914)—Two attempts to assassinate Kitchener—Sir George Arthur on Kitchener's administration—Sir Ronald Storrs on Kitchener's sense of humour—Lord Esher, and General Sir H. Lawson, on Kitchener—Attitude of Kitchener towards women—Traits in his character—Sir George Arthur on Kitchener—Lord Kitchener drowned in H.M.S. *Hampshire* (June 5th, 1916)—Retrospect of R.E. achievements 522

ILLUSTRATIONS.

	FACING PAGE
FIELD-MARSHAL RT. HON. THE EARL KITCHENER OF KHARTOUM AND OF THE VAAL AND ASPALL, K.G., K.P., P.C., G.C.B., O.M., G.C.S.I., G.C.M.G., G.C.I.E., COLONEL COMMANDANT R.E. .. .. *Frontispiece*	
THE BEACH AND SANDHILLS IN ABU QIR BAY	10
LIEUT.-GENERAL SIR GERALD GRAHAM, V.C., G.C.B., G.C.M.G., COL. COMMANDANT R.E.	28
THE SWEETWATER CANAL	34
THE BATTLEFIELD OF TEL EL KEBIR	42
SUAKIN	68
HANDUB	84
THE SECOND CATARACT	92
THE 26TH FIELD COMPANY, R.E., IN WHALERS ON THE NILE	96
DESERT TELEGRAPHS, NEW STYLE, 1886 ..	106
THE RIVER FORT AT GUBAT IN JANUARY, 1885	114
GORDON'S STEAMER, THE *Bordein*, AT KHARTOUM IN 1935 ..	116
MAJOR-GENERAL CHARLES GEORGE GORDON, C.B., LATE ROYAL ENGINEERS	124
THE OLD FORTIFICATIONS SOUTH OF KHARTOUM ..	136
THE DEATH OF GENERAL GORDON	144
THE GORDON STATUE, KHARTOUM	146
SARAS FORT AND THE BATN EL HAGAR DESERT ..	160
KHOR MUSA FORT NEAR WADI HALFA	166
GUNBOAT *Zafir* IN SECTIONS ON THE KERMA RAILWAY ..	168
A DUST-STORM ON THE NILE ..	184
THE KERMA RAILWAY	186
IN THE BATN EL HAGAR	188
SITE OF THE ATBARA *Zariba*	212
MAHMUD, A PRISONER	220
BANK CONSTRUCTION ON THE DESERT RAILWAY	230
SHIFTING CAMP ON THE DESERT RAILWAY	236

ILLUSTRATIONS.

	FACING PAGE
Colonel Sir Edouard Percy Cranwill Girouard, K.C.M.G., D.S.O., late Royal Engineers	242
The Battlefield of Omdurman from Jebel Surkab	260
Kitchener Leading his Victorious Troops from the Battlefield of Omdurman	272
The Gordon Memorial Ceremony at Khartoum	276
The Gunboat *Sultan* on the White Nile	280
Marchand's Boat Approaching the *Dal* below Fashoda	282
The Atbara Bridge	296
The Suez Canal at Tussum	316
Tebeldi Tree, Kordofan Province	336
Wood Pasha Barracks, Omdurman	344
Onbashi (Corporal), Engineer Troops, Sudan Defence Force	354
The Nile Barrage, Rosetta Branch	378
The Aswan Dam	384
On the Desert Railway at Dawn	390
Moghazi Pasha Station	412
Patrolling the Telegraph Line	428
Telegraph Transport crossing a Creek on the Sobat	434
Basha Zodi, an Abyssinian Officer	450
Survey Camp near the Abyssinian Frontier	456
The Palace, Khartoum	476
Gordon Avenue, Khartoum	486
Port Sudan	494
The Colossus of Rameses II at Memphis	512
The Rock Temple of Rameses II at Abu Simbel	516
The River Front at Khartoum	530
Cairo, from the Citadel	540

PLANS AND MAPS.

SKETCH MAPS.

	FACING PAGE
ALEXANDRIA, 1801	12
LOWER EGYPT, COMMUNICATIONS, 1882	32
BATTLE OF TEL EL KEBIR, SEPT. 13TH, 1882	40
SUAKIN DISTRICT IN 1885	58
BATTLE OF ET TEB, FEB. 29TH, 1884	62
BATTLE OF TAMAI, MARCH 13TH, 1884	64
BATTLE OF TOFRIK (OR MCNEILL'S *Zariba*), 2.30 P.M., MARCH 22ND, 1885	72
SUAKIN AND ITS DEFENCES IN 1885	80
NILE, FROM WADI HALFA TO DONGOLA	104
MAIN DEFENCES OF KHARTOUM IN 1884–85	130
NILE, FROM WADI HALFA TO DONGOLA (REPEATED)	152
DEFENCES OF WADI HALFA IN 1896	158
BATTLE OF FIRKET, JUNE 7TH, 1896	164
KERMA RAILWAY AND TELEGRAPH, 1896–97	178
NILE, FROM KERMA TO METEMMA	196
BATTLE OF THE ATBARA, APRIL 8TH, 1898 (TIME 7.40 A.M.)	216
SUDAN GOVERNMENT MILITARY RAILWAYS IN 1900	238
NILE, FROM METEMMA TO KHARTOUM	254
BATTLE OF OMDURMAN, SEPTEMBER 2ND, 1898, FIRST PHASE	264
BATTLE OF OMDURMAN, SEPTEMBER 2ND, 1898, SECOND PHASE	268
BATTLE OF OMDURMAN, SEPTEMBER 2ND, 1898, THIRD PHASE	270
SOUTHERN SUDAN	288
SINAI DESERT IN 1917	312
SUEZ CANAL DEFENCES, 1915–16	314
WESTERN FRONTIER OF EGYPT IN 1916	330
DARFUR AND KORDOFAN IN 1916	334
UPPER NILE	348
NILE BARRAGE IN 1887	368

SKETCH MAPS—*continued.*

	FACING PAGE
SUDAN GOVERNMENT RAILWAYS IN 1930 (SOUTH OF ABU HAMED)	406
SUDAN TELEGRAPH SYSTEM IN 1930	422
EASTERN AND SOUTHERN FRONTIERS OF THE SUDAN	462
KHARTOUM IN 1935	482
PORT SUDAN IN 1929	500

GENERAL MAPS.

EGYPT	*At end*
ANGLO-EGYPTIAN SUDAN	,,

PART I—MILITARY.

THE ROYAL ENGINEERS IN EGYPT AND THE SUDAN

CHAPTER I.

EARLY CAMPAIGNS IN EGYPT.

IN March, 1800, a party of Turks and Arabs traversed the desolate wastes of the Sinai Desert from Syria and straggled into a large camp at Bilbeis, some 30 miles from Cairo. At their head rode Captain Thomas Lacy whose energy and patience were soon to be tested to the utmost in advising the lethargic leader of an Ottoman army. Thus the first Royal Engineer came to Egypt.

England was at war with France. Turkey, her uncertain ally, was ready with promises which were seldom fulfilled. In 1798 Napoleon had captured Alexandria and Cairo, and then, having lost his ships at the Battle of the Nile, found himself isolated in Egypt. He led an expedition into Syria in 1799, but turned back when he failed to reduce Acre. The Turks retorted with an attack on Alexandria, which ended in their defeat with great slaughter. The victorious French were discontented and bordering on mutiny. Napoleon then realized that his dreams of conquest in the East were shattered, and in August, 1799, abandoned his army and returned quietly to France, leaving General Kleber to treat with his enemies. In January, 1800, Kleber signed the Convention of El Arish under which he agreed to evacuate Egypt without delay; but after he had marched some distance from Cairo towards the coast, he heard that the British Government insisted on terms which he considered derogatory to the honour of his country, so he retraced his steps towards the capital. Meanwhile, the main body of the Turkish army, under the Grand Vizier, lay at Bilbeis, and, learning of Kleber's countermarch, the Vizier resolved to forestall the French in Cairo. Such was the situation when Lacy joined the Turks, bearing dispatches from the British Ambassador at Constantinople.

On March 12th, the Ottoman troops marched for six hours and arrived at El Khanka, some 12 miles from Cairo.[1] To their left was a sandy desert; to their right, cultivated land and numerous villages.

---
[1] See the *Sketch Map of Lower Egypt, Communications*, 1882, in Chapter II.

Like a swarm of locusts, the Turks and their Arab satellites moved without order or cohesion, a wild and motley crew who formed an easy prey for the disciplined French. On the 13th the Grand Vizier and his councillors heard, with the greatest alarm, of an impending attack, and sent forward a rabble of 10,000 men as an advanced guard. The situation then appeared so menacing that Lacy volunteered to find his way alone into Cairo to reconnoitre the country and gather information; but the Grand Vizier would not allow him to embark on this dangerous mission, and, to soften his refusal, presented Lacy with a shawl and other rich cloths. During the next few days, the Vizier parleyed with his enemies in the usual Eastern style, hoping to gain time for the concentration of all the Turkish forces in Egypt. At length he was forced to move by the impetuosity of his undisciplined troops, and advancing within sight of Cairo and the Pyramids on March 20th, 1800, he found the French army drawn up for battle on the plain before him.

Lacy, accompanied by some Turkish officers, went forward to reconnoitre. "I placed myself near the right of the enemy's lines," he writes,[1] "and found their chief force compactly drawn up, to the amount of about 7,000 men, with plenty of cavalry and artillery, and seeming to be making dispositions on their left to cut off our advanced parties who were dispersed here and there. Our artillery moved forward at the same time as I did, and were placed in front of the enemy's lines at a distance of about 1,000 yards. As I had placed myself about half-way between these guns and those of the enemy I could perceive that our own did no execution at so great a range, while the enemy's guns, of much larger calibre, threw their shot quite home. The enemy were drawn up in two lines, the right of the second line so far outflanking that of the first that their Artillery from this quarter also had effect upon us. Having finished my observations, I returned to urge the Grand Vizier immediately to form his infantry and to send forward some Artillery to a very advantageous situation near the enemy's right. But the Grand Vizier thought he had done enough for that day, and after inquiring only after the enemy's numbers, seemed determined to return to his Camp at El Hank (El Khanka), supposing no doubt that the enemy would permit us to do so unmolested. Soon after, however, the enemy moved forward, deploying, and extending their front, and with battalions advancing round our right in a position either to cut us off or to drive us immediately to the Desert. When I found it necessary to urge the Grand Vizier either to rally and repel the enemy or instantly to save himself by flight, there was no choice left to him, so we fell back in the greatest disorder and precipitation

---

[1] Letter from Lieut. T. Lacy, R.E., to Major C. Holloway, R.E., dated Jaffa, July 21st, 1800, quoted in the *R.E. Journal*, Vol. XIV, July-Dec., 1911, pp. 94-98. The originals of this letter and other correspondence between Lacy and Holloway are in the R.E. Museum at Chatham.

towards Salahieh (Es Salhiya), the enemy pursuing us as far as Bilbeis. We arrived at Salahieh on March 21st. I recommended them (the Turks) strongly to maintain this post at all events, and to keep open communication with Damiat (Damietta) and to retire thither in case of disaster, but I met with nothing but insult and contempt."

Defeated at the Battle of Heliopolis, the Grand Vizier fled into the desert, directing all his best troops to follow him. Lacy and his servant, mounted on one horse, trailed wearily in pursuit, while the soldiers who had been abandoned fought over the spoils of the camp. The horse soon went lame, but the Grand Vizier offered Lacy no assistance, and had it not been for the humanity of a Mameluke,[1] who mounted Lacy and his servant on a camel and gave them food and drink, there is little doubt that both would have perished. Five thousand men, the remnant of the Turkish army, streamed into Gaza on March 28th, having left their less fortunate comrades to die in the desert or be destroyed by the enemy. Though weak and ill, Lacy was treated with the utmost scorn and indignity, and when the Grand Vizier marched for Jaffa on April 5th, he was left to find his way north as best he could. He arrived in Jaffa on April 9th, seriously ill and likely to be incapacitated for a long period. The first adventure of a Royal Engineer in Egypt was indeed disastrous.

It is necessary now to review the circumstances which led to the dispatch of Captain Thomas Lacy, R.E., to Egypt. From the time of Napoleon's landing in that country, the British Government was anxious about the safety of India. It was evident, also, that if the French should succeed in holding Egypt, they might exercise a dangerous influence at Constantinople and in Russia. The British Government knew that Turkey needed support, and, as early as November, 1798, decided to send a military mission to Constantinople under the command of Brigadier-General Koehler, late R.A., an officer with previous experience of Ottoman diplomacy. "The Defeat and Destruction of the French Army in Egypt," ran the instructions given to Koehler,[2] " and also of their Transports and other Vessels in the Port of Alexandria and elsewhere, will naturally engage Your first Attention. And you will be particularly solicitous to direct the efforts of the Porte in such a manner as may destroy even the Possibility of General Bonaparte's using any part of his Force to the annoyance of the British Dominions in India." A quantity of stores and munitions was allotted to the Mission for transport by sea to Constantinople, and several officers were posted to it to serve under Koehler.

[1] One of a force of light horse, formed of Circassian slaves.
[2] Dispatch from Lord Granville to Brigadier-General Koehler, late R.A., dated November 11th, 1798, quoted in the *R.E. Journal*, Vol. XIV, July-Dec., 1911, pp. 91-93.

Three Royal Engineers were appointed to the Military Mission, those selected being Captain Charles Holloway, Captain-Lieutenant Richard Fletcher and Lieutenant Thomas Lacy.[1] Captains Hope and Fead and Lieutenant Leake, of the Royal Artillery, and Lieutenant Franklin of the East India Company's Army, were added to the cadre, and the staff was completed by the inclusion of Dr. W. Wittman, a few civilians, and 55 non-commissioned officers and men of the Royal Artillery and Royal Military Artificers.[2] Setting out from London on December 3rd, 1798, Koehler, Holloway, Fletcher, Hope, Fead, Franklin and one civilian proceeded by the overland route to Constantinople, while the remainder of the Mission sailed in a transport in the following April. The military officers were given temporary higher rank while employed on special duty, Holloway becoming a Lieutenant-Colonel, Fletcher a Major and Lacy a Captain. The overland party reached Constantinople at the end of March, 1799, after being shipwrecked among ice-floes at the mouth of the Elbe, and those who came by the sea route landed in the middle of June.

Eager to begin their work, the British officers found that they were expected to attend a round of displays and ceremonies, such as that which took place on May 20th when the Grand Vizier took the field at the head of his army. "His Highness the Vizier passed over to Scutari," writes Wittman,[3] "the guns at the Seraglio saluting him on his way. He was attended by the Kaimacan (Lieut.-Colonel, Chief of Staff), Capitan Pacha (Lord High Admiral) and all the great officers of state, preceded by a band of Turkish music, and by a group of gladiators who skirmished as the procession passed along. Some of the troops were enveloped in curious network coats of mail of steel; others wore yellow dresses decorated with ribbons of different colours hanging from their shoulders, and brass helmets on their heads. Others again were clad in parti-coloured dresses. While a part of them were armed with spears or lances from twelve to fourteen feet in length, others carried short, twisted, rifle-barrel guns, the rest muskets, carbines, etc. The whole of them wore swords and pistols in sashes fastened round the waist. The Vizier, the Capitan Pacha, the Kaimacan and other officers were mounted on beautiful horses richly caparisoned. The one which His Highness

---

[1] Major-General Sir Charles Holloway retired in 1824. As a subaltern he took part in the defence of Gibraltar in 1779–82 (see *History of the Corps of Royal Engineers* by Major-General W. Porter, Vol. I, pp. 82–109). Lieut.-Colonel Sir Richard Fletcher Bart, K.C.H., was killed at the storming of San Sebastian in 1813. A Memoir of Sir Richard Fletcher appears in *History of the Corps of Royal Engineers*, Vol. II, pp. 404–406. Captain-Lieutenant Thomas Lacy died on field service at Demerara in 1804.

[2] *Travels in Turkey, Asia Minor, Syria and across the Desert into Egypt during the years 1799, 1800 and 1801*, by Dr. William Wittman (1803), p. 2. A copy of this volume is in the R.E. Library. It has copious marginal notes by Captain T. W. J. Conolly, R.E., in the form of extracts from a manuscript journal in four volumes compiled by Lieut.-Colonel Holloway. These marginal notes describe the part taken by the Royal Engineers in the work of the Military Mission.

[3] *Ibid*, p. 9.

rode made the most magnificent appearance, the embroidered trappings being studded with gems, pearls, etc. A number of dervishes were distributed among the Turkish troops, who are constantly attended, when they go to war, by persons of this character, to exhort them to valour and to kindle up their enthusiasm by shouts and singing." In this manner the Grand Vizier set out for Syria to fight the French, and subsequently advanced to Bilbeis in Egypt after his opponents had retreated and signed the Convention of El Arish. Fletcher accompanied him for a few marches from Constantinople, but then fell ill and returned to the Turkish capital.

In June, 1799, Holloway and Hope were sent to re-design the defences of the Dardanelles. They finished their survey at the end of July, and, with the help of Fletcher, submitted their proposals on September 2nd. These having been approved, the works were taken in hand in November by Fletcher and Lacy and completed within a few weeks. On January 19th, 1800, Koehler, Fletcher and Leake, dressed as Turks, left Constantinople on a tour to Syria and Cyprus, and on January 25th, Lacy started with important dispatches for the Grand Vizier. These were the events which preceded Lacy's appearance at Bilbeis in March, 1800, and his subsequent adventures in the Battle of Heliopolis and the retreat of the Turkish army to Jaffa.

The Grand Vizier having failed miserably, and his troops being in a disorganized state at Jaffa, General Koehler and the remainder of the Military Mission embarked for that place and landed there on July 2nd, 1800. They found the Ottoman camp in a horrible condition. Garbage lay on every side. The tents were pitched in cemeteries where many of the bodies were only partially covered, and carcases of dead animals rotted amongst them. The sea breeze wafted to the camp the putrid odours from the streets of the town. Plague, dysentery and enteric fever ravaged the troops. The British officers did what they could to improve the sanitation of the camp, and Holloway and Fletcher planned fortifications for the town to render it a secure base for the Turkish forces. At every turn they came up against the indolence and apathy of their allies. Pomp and display were more to the Turkish taste than honest labour. At the end of August, after Lacy had marched for El Arish to join an advanced force under Muhammad Pasha, Koehler, Holloway and Fletcher were summoned by the Grand Vizier to the ceremony of laying the first stone of one of the new bastions. Coffee was handed round, prayers were recited, sheep were sacrificed, and then the whole company returned to their tents where Holloway was invested with an ermine pelisse and Fletcher with a silk robe of honour. Whenever reinforcements left the camp for El Arish, their departure was announced by the discharge of muskets loaded with ball ammunition, and bullets flew in all directions. Nevertheless the Engineers managed to make some progress in their work, though they had the misfortune to lose their chief, General Koehler, who died of enteric fever on December 29th. The control of the Mission then devolved on Lieut.-Colonel Holloway, and he at Jaffa, and Captain Lacy at El Arish, continued, until the end of February, 1801, to fortify those localities and urge the Turks to renewed efforts.

When it became known in England that General Menou, the new commander of the French forces in Egypt,[1] had refused to evacuate the country, it was decided that a British expedition should be sent to expel the French; but instant action was impossible because Napoleon, as First Consul, had formed an alliance with Spain and threatened Portugal, and by this move contained a British force which might otherwise have been sent to the Near East. Although information about Egypt and the strength of the enemy was meagre, the French were supposed to number about 10,000 regulars with 5,000 auxiliaries. Actually they numbered more than 30,000 men, 18,000 of whom were available for active operations.[2] In October, 1800, a large British force lay at Gibraltar, and from this it was decided to select 14,000 men with 15 field-guns, under Major-General Sir Ralph Abercromby, for a descent upon Egypt. The expedition sailed in two divisions, and on January 2nd, 1801, the transports lay at anchor in the Bay of Marmaris (Marmorice) on the southern coast of Anatolia, whither they had gone to collect supplies and horses and to co-ordinate plans with the Turks.

The primary objective of Sir Ralph Abercromby was to gain possession of Alexandria, which afforded the only good harbour on the Egyptian coast. Once established there, he could advance safely and rapidly towards Cairo. As an alternative, he proposed to disembark his force at Damietta, and accordingly, after his arrival at Marmaris Bay, he sent General Moore to Jaffa to arrange with the Grand Vizier that the Turks should join in the advance on Cairo while an expedition from India co-operated from Suez. However, the reports which he received concerning the state of the Turkish army at Jaffa, and the obvious ineptitude of the Ottoman Government, decided him to place no reliance on the Turks. He resolved to land at Abu Qir (Aboukir) Bay, east of Alexandria, if such an operation was possible, and meanwhile practised his troops most assiduously in the dangerous manœuvre of disembarking from boats in the face of an enemy.[3]

Although no Engineer units were included in Abercromby's army, there were a number of Royal Engineer officers under Major William

---

[1] General Kleber had been assassinated on June 14th, 1800.
[2] Article entitled, "Egypt," appearing in the *R.E. Journal*, Vol. 12, 1882, p. 205. This serial article is continued through that volume on pp. 187-192, 205-209, 229-231 and 265-268, and gives a concise description of Egypt and its inhabitants, and chronological accounts of all campaigns from 1798 to 1877.
[3] *Passages in the Great War with France*, by Sir Henry Bunbury (1927), p. 59.

McKerras as Commanding Royal Engineer.[1] These were Captain (afterwards Major-General Sir) Alexander Bryce, Captain-Lieutenant (afterwards Major-General) W. H. Ford, Lieutenant (afterwards General) J. F. Birch, Lieutenant (afterwards Lieut.-General Sir) J. R. Arnold, and Lieutenants J. Handfield, C. Hayes, H. F. Brownrigg, J. Squire, C. Graham, G. Kennett, Hon. R. L. Dundas and G. Cardew. Lieutenant J. F. Burgoyne, who was destined to become famous as Field-Marshal Sir John Burgoyne, G.C.B., was originally detailed for the expedition, but was afterwards sent to assist in the blockade of Malta.[2] The strength of the Engineer cadre was sufficient; but all the officers, except McKerras, were under 30 years of age, and consequently they lacked experience.

Major Fletcher, R.E., of the Military Mission, sailed from Jaffa on December 13th, 1800, with dispatches from Lieut.-Colonel Holloway, R.E., for Sir Ralph Abercromby, who was expected shortly at Marmaris Bay; and before the middle of February, when Abercromby had arrived at a correct estimate of the value of the Turks as allies, Fletcher was sent with Major McKerras, R.E., in the sloop *Penelope*, to reconnoitre the coast of Egypt. "When off Alexandria," writes Lieut.-Colonel R. T. Wilson,[3] "they got into the *Peterel*, and in her boat, on the night of February 27th, proceeded into Aboukir Bay to discover the proper point of landing. In vain was McKerras advised not to enter too much into the *cul-de-sac* of the bay. His sense of duty and enterprising spirit urged him to advance, and he even landed on the subsequent ground of debarkation. At dawn of day, as he was returning, a French gunboat, full of soldiers, the commander of which had been informed of their reconnoitring, appeared to windward and instantly bore down, commencing at the same time a fire from her carronade and small arms. A shot soon disabled the English boat from continuing under sail, and, a musket ball having killed McKerras, the master of the boat, as the gunboat came alongside, surrendered her. Major Fletcher and the boat's crew were then all allowed quarter and carried as prisoners into Alexandria and from thence to General Menou at Cairo. The death of McKerras was, as well as the severest private loss, a public misfortune."

This reconnaissance had most unfortunate results. While it indicated to the French the probable point of Abercromby's landing, it added nothing to the available information about Abu Qir Bay. However, it was useless to delay further, so Abercromby sailed from

---

[1] As a Lieutenant, McKerras had served in the defence of Gibraltar, 1779–82. (See *History of the Corps of Royal Engineers*, by Major-General W. Porter, Vol. I, pp. 82–109.)

[2] *History of the Corps of Royal Engineers*, by Major-General W. Porter, Vol. I, p. 230. A Memoir of Field-Marshal Sir John Burgoyne appears in Volume II of that work, pp. 406–408.

[3] *History of the British Expedition to Egypt*, by Lieut.-Colonel Robert T. Wilson (1803), Vol. I, p. 16.

Marmaris Bay on February 23rd, 1801, and succeeded, by a brilliant military operation on March 8th, in landing his whole force at Abu Qir Bay in the face of a determined, forewarned and forearmed enemy. Fortunately, General Menou had neglected to send proper reinforcements to General Friant, the French commander at Alexandria, and thus the force which opposed the British landing mustered only about 1,600 infantry and 200 cavalry with 15 guns.[1] Abercromby, on the other hand, could throw in more than 5,000 infantry, though with very few guns owing to the difficulty of landing them and dragging them through the sand of the narrow peninsula which formed the only road towards the city of Alexandria.

Abu Qir Bay faces east, and measures about two miles from north to south.[2] Upon the northern horn stood the Castle of Abu Qir, with large and small guns enfilading the beach for a distance of one mile, while upon the southern horn was a blockhouse with at least one heavy gun. At about the centre of the bay rose a high sandhill, and to the south of it a confusion of lower sandhills dotted with palm trees and patches of scrub. As the guns of Abu Qir Castle forbade any attempt at landing in the northern sector, it was decided that the high sandhill should be the objective of the right of the British attack. The details of the brilliant feat of March 8th, 1801, are outside the scope of this narrative.[3] It must suffice to say that the British infantry, in lines of boats, approached the shore soon after dawn and were received by heavy cannon and musketry fire. With desperate gallantry, and in spite of heavy losses, they poured on to the beach, swarmed up the sandhills, repelled cavalry charges, and drove the French from the crest. Within a few minutes they had consolidated their position, and in the evening moved forward two or three miles, leaving a detachment to blockade Abu Qir Castle, which held out for a time. There is no record of the part played in these operations by the Engineers, but it is to be presumed that they were fully occupied in arrangements for landing guns, munitions, rations and water, and in consolidating and fortifying the positions won by the infantry. At their head was Captain Alexander Bryce, R.E.,[4] who had succeeded to the post of Commanding Royal Engineer on the death of Major McKerras.

Abercromby's army now stood upon a narrow strip of land with its right flank resting on the sea and its left on the salt lake of Maaddiya (Maadieh).[5] Eleven miles ahead lay Alexandria. The

[1] *A History of the British Army*, by the Hon. J. W. Fortescue, Vol. IV, Part II, p. 818.

[2] See the *Sketch Map of Alexandria*, 1801, which is included in this chapter.

[3] A concise account of the landing at Abu Qir Bay is given in an article entitled, " Over-Sea Expeditions," by Bt. Colonel T. Capper, D.S.O., appearing in the *R.E. Journal*, Vol. II, July-Dec., 1905, pp. 274–281.

[4] There exists in the British Museum a " Plan of the Expedition to Alexandria, 1802," by Major A. Bryce, R.E.

[5] The site of Lake Maaddiya is now a well-drained stretch of fertile land under cultivation.

THE BEACH AND SANDHILLS IN ABU QIR BAY.

The point where the first British troops landed in Egypt in 1801.

[*Photo by the Author.*]

average width of the peninsula was less than two miles, and the ground consisted of undulating sandhills dotted with palm trees. Fortunately the Engineers found water a few feet below the surface, and thus relieved Abercromby of one anxiety ; but the troops were exhausted with marching through heavy sand and dragging their guns into position. The French withdrew to cover Alexandria, and, reinforced by General Lanusse, Friant was soon able to muster about 5,000 men with 21 guns. On March 9th Abercromby advanced to a spot where the peninsula narrowed to less than one mile, and then, having replenished his stores and ammunition, moved forward on the 12th in several columns to a ridge surmounted by a building called the Mandara (Mandora) Tower. The French had taken up a position across the peninsula on high ground a little beyond the western end of Lake Maaddiya, and Abercromby proposed to attack them on the following morning. Lake Maaddiya furnished the British with a means of transport by water, and their armed launches and gunboats had already entered it to support their left flank. It may be explained here that the wide and shallow expanse of this lake communicated with Abu Qir Bay and was consequently flooded with sea-water, and that it was divided by an embankment from a second depression, Lake Maryut (Mariotis), which extended far beyond Alexandria and was almost dry. Along the embankment ran the road from Cairo and Rahmaniya to Alexandria, and also a canal which brought fresh water from the Nile.

The battle which was fought near Mandara Tower on March 13th, 1801, was a stubborn affair. Abercromby advanced with 14,000 men in three columns, his troops struggling laboriously through deep sand under the fire of the French artillery. His plan was to turn the enemy's right, which rested on Lake Maaddiya. The action soon became general, but the British pressure caused the French to retire in the end to the Heights of Nikopolis (Necropolis), about 1,300 yards east of Alexandria, where they intended to make a final stand before taking refuge within the walls of the city.[1] Resuming his advance, Abercromby directed General Hutchinson to lead three brigades over the dried mud along the border of Lake Maryut, until he had turned the enemy's right flank, and then to assault from that direction in conjunction with a frontal attack. The defences on this flank, however, were found to be too strong, and, as his men were suffering heavy casualties from artillery fire, Abercromby decided to break off the action and retire to the original position held by the enemy. The operations of March 13th cost the British some 1,300 casualties. They had out-distanced their meagre transport and had been checked before a seemingly impregnable position,

[1] The walls of Alexandria no longer exist, nor, in 1935, could the author find any traces of the fortifications thrown up by the British and French in the course of their battles. The old battlefields are covered with the roads and buildings of Bulkeley, Ramla and other suburbs of modern Alexandria.

but nevertheless they had established a moral ascendancy over the enemy which helped them in subsequent battles.

Abercromby next proceeded to consolidate his position with the assistance of his Engineers under Captain Bryce. The peninsula at this point was about 1½ miles in width. On the British right was elevated ground crowned by the ruins of a Roman castle; in the centre, a long ridge; and on the left, level ground stretching to the Mahmudiya Canal, which skirted Lake Maryut. Bryce devoted his attention chiefly to the high ground on the right, where he designed a redan, a redoubt and other defences in the neighbourhood of the Roman castle; but many works were thrown up also along the ridge forming the centre of the position, and emplacements for guns were distributed along the whole line. The left was naturally the weakest part of the position, for it was liable to be outflanked through the dry bed of Lake Maryut. Meanwhile, the strength of the enemy had risen to 10,000 men with 46 guns, as General Menou, the French Commander-in-Chief, had succeeded in reaching Alexandria with 6,000 men across the bed of Lake Maryut. Fearing that Abercromby might soon be reinforced from Syria or India, Menou resolved to take the offensive, and by forcing the right and centre of Abercromby's line under cover of a feint against his left, to drive him into Lake Maaddiya. He put this scheme into execution on March 21st, and a desperate battle ensued in which both sides displayed the greatest valour. The French guns were well served, their infantry advanced steadily, their cavalry charged with reckless fury, but all to no purpose. The discipline and fortitude of the British infantry withstood every test, and the French at length gave up the attempt and retired to their position on the Heights of Nikopolis. The numbers engaged on both sides were nearly equal, but the French lost 4,000 men as compared with British casualties amounting to 1,500 killed and wounded. Yet the British suffered an irretrievable loss in the death of their brave and popular commander, for Sir Ralph Abercromby was mortally wounded in the fight and died on March 28th.

On Abercromby's death the command devolved on Major-General Hutchinson, a sound tactician, but unpopular with his men. It seemed probable that a stalemate would result from the Battle of Nikopolis, so the new commander took the right course in fortifying his position to enable him to blockade the city with a limited force while he employed the remainder in offensive operations elsewhere. Four days after the battle he was reinforced by 4,000 Turks and Albanians, who arrived by sea from Jaffa under the leadership of the Capitan Pasha, and he then resolved to capture Rosetta and Fort St. Julien, near the mouth of the western channel of the Nile and some 22 miles east of Abu Qir, and thus to open a river route towards Cairo. Rosetta was taken on April 8th, and Fort St. Julien surren-

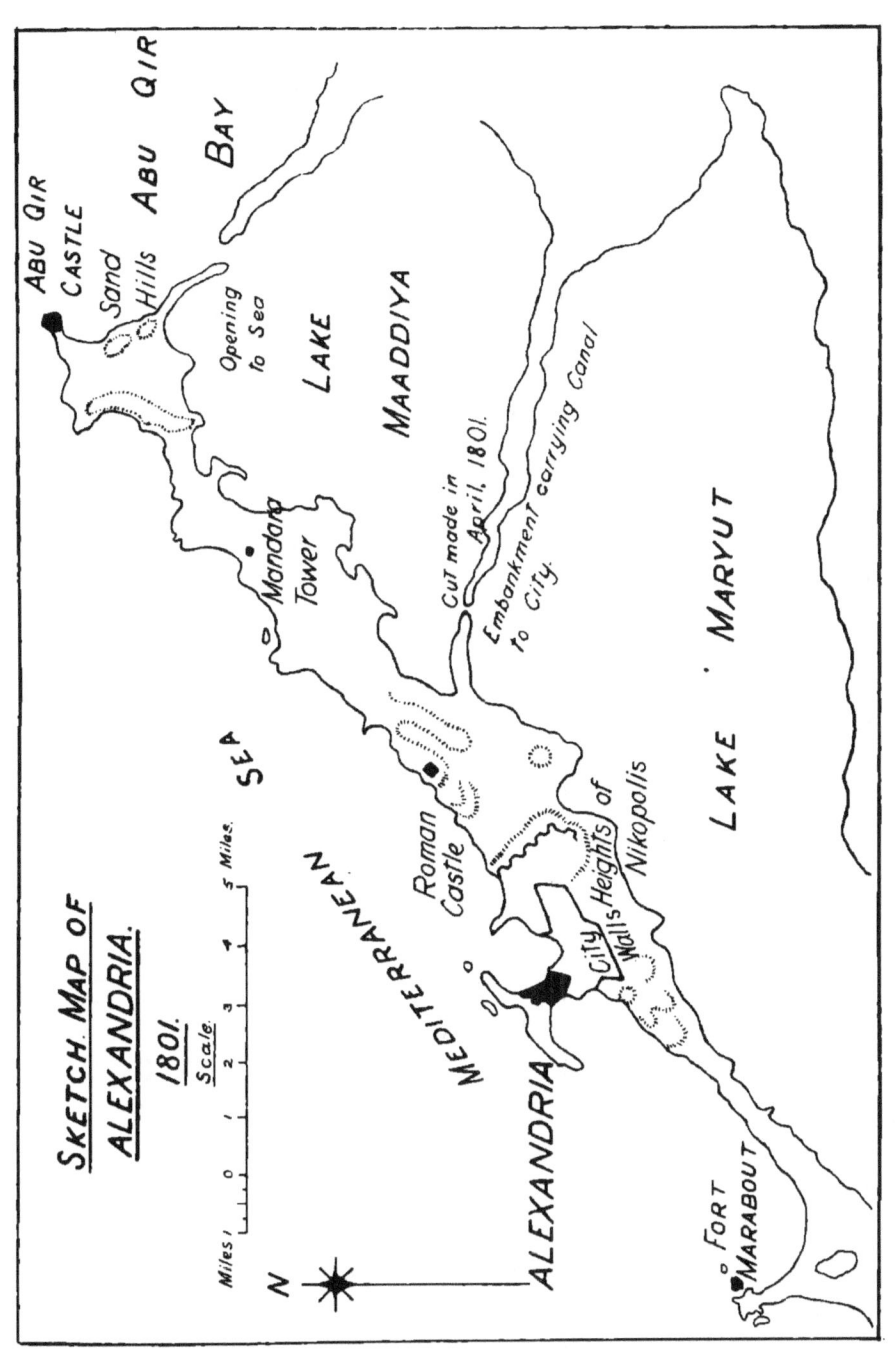

dered on the 19th. British gunboats then sailed up the Nile to co-operate with a force which was assembling at El Hamed above Rosetta. In due course, a column of 5,000 men advanced up the river from El Hamed to El Aft, supported by the Turks and Albanians under the Capitan Pasha, and prepared to attack a body of 4,000 French under General Lagrange. The French, however, retired to a stronger and more important position at Rahmaniya; but even there they made no stand and on May 10th were in full retreat towards Cairo, whither General Hutchinson prepared to follow them in conjunction, as he hoped, with the main body of the Turks from Syria under the Grand Vizier and an Indian contingent from the Red Sea.

Left by Hutchinson to blockade Alexandria, General Eyre Coote had undertaken a most important engineering operation on April 12th and 13th. This was the cutting of the embankment between Lake Maaddiya and the depression of Lake Maryut, thereby admitting the sea to the latter and emptying the canal which carried fresh water to the city. The Royal Engineers, who supervised this work, not only isolated Alexandria, but secured the left flank of the investing army. British and Turkish gunboats patrolled the new expanse of water, and supplies were brought to the front in boats.

News of the advance of the main Turkish army into Egypt reached General Hutchinson at Rahmaniya, and he received, at the same time, a vague report that an Indian contingent had arrived in the Red Sea; but hearing soon afterwards that the French under General Belliard at Cairo were about to issue forth to crush the Grand Vizier on his approach to that city, and that only two companies of infantry from India had landed at Suez, he sent urgent messages to the Grand Vizier to warn him not to fight without British support. Urged continually by Holloway, the Grand Vizier had set out from Jaffa on February 25th, 1801, shortly after Abercromby had sailed from Marmaris Bay. His motley array of some 12,000 men swarmed over the country. In his retinue were several Pashas, a *Tefterdar* or Treasurer, the *Reis Effendi* or Foreign Secretary, Commandants of the Artillery, Bombardiers, Miners, Janissaries and Stores, the *Kadi Asker* or Judge, the *Toutoun Bashi* or Chief of the Tobacco, the *Etchi Bashi* or Chief Cook, the *Samfoongis Bashi* or Principal Dog-keeper, and the *Zahergis Bashi* or Secondary Dog-keeper. It seems that the appointment of *Tournagis Bashi*, or Chief Bird-keeper, was not filled on this occasion.

During the first part of the march from Jaffa to Egypt, Holloway was the only Royal Engineer with the Turkish army, but he was joined by Lacy from El Arish when near Gaza on March 15th. Lacy and a few men of the Royal Artillery and Royal Military Artificers were then detailed to join a force commanded by Muhammad Pasha, and Captain Leake, R.A., was ordered to accompany another commanded by Tahir Pasha. Holloway himself remained at the Grand Vizier's elbow, ready with advice, but greatly annoyed because it was frequently disregarded.

On March 30th, the main body of the Turks entered El Arish. Tahir Pasha, with Leake and 3,000 men, marched for Es Salhiya on April 2nd, and Muhammad Pasha, with Lacy and 8,000 men, followed. Tahir was in Es Salhiya on the 9th, and the Grand Vizier, Holloway and the remainder of the army, on the 27th. While at El Arish a summons of surrender was sent by Holloway to General Belliard at Cairo and was rejected with contempt.[1] When the Grand Vizier's troops entered Es Salhiya, after crossing 150 miles of desert through Qatia and El Qantara, Tahir and Muhammad were at Bilbeis, which Lacy had recently fortified. In due course, the Grand Vizier and Holloway also came to Bilbeis. On May 15th, a courier arrived from General Hutchinson advising the Grand Vizier not to risk an action, but the Turks were so eager to lay their hands on the treasures of Cairo that they could not be restrained. When Belliard advanced from Cairo to attack them with 5,400 men and 24 guns, and was reported to have passed El Khanka, they prepared to fight.[2]

The Battle of El Khanka was fought on May 16th, 1801, at a distance of about 20 miles from the capital. It ended in the retreat of the French ; but this was due more to the fear that Hutchinson might be able to intervene than to any prowess on the part of the Turks, although it seemed to the latter that the French were disorganized and driven back. The following description of the battle is given by Lacy :[3] " On the morning of the 16th, I quitted the Camp at Belbeis, accompanying Mahomed Pacha, who, with the troops under his command, moved forward to support the advanced corps under Tahir Pacha. The enemy were posted near a village and wood half-way distant between Belbeis and El Hank, while Tahir Pacha with his Albanian infantry occupied a village near them, maintaining a brisk cannonading and constant skirmishing. When this had continued nearly an hour, the troops under Mahomed Pacha advanced and the enemy quitted their position. The Corps of Dehlis and Mamalouks had posted themselves upon the hills in the Desert to our left. The enemy then moved towards these hills, the first body of them gaining the heights. While this was effecting, the Grand Vizier arrived with a fresh body which joined Tahir Pacha, whose troops had previously possessed themselves of the position

---

[1] Dispatch dated April 3rd, 1801, from Major Holloway, R.E., to the French Garrison in Cairo, quoted in the *R.E. Journal*, Vol XIV, July-Dec., 1911, p. 99.

[2] A concise account of the Turkish advance from Syria, the Battle of El Khanka, and the occupation of Cairo is given in a report by Lt.-Colonel Holloway, R.E., dated Cairo, August 1st, 1801, quoted in the *R.E. Journal*, Vol. XIV, July-Dec., 1911, pp. 149–156.

[3] Letter from Captain Lacy, R.E., to Major Holloway, R.E., dated Bilbeis, May 17th. 1801. quoted in the *R.E. Journal*, Vol. XIV, July-Dec., 1911, p. 98.

endurance. From Qena they voyaged down the Nile for a distance of 500 miles to Cairo, where they camped on Rhoda Island on August 7th. According to Wilson,[1] the Indians attracted much surprise and admiration :—" The Turks were astonished at the novel spectacle of men of colour being so well disciplined and trained ; indeed the general magnificence of the establishment of the Indian army was so different from what they had been accustomed to see in General Hutchinson's that the contrast could not fail of being striking. Never were finer men seen than those which composed this force." These British and Indian soldiers were veterans of the Mysore and Maratha Wars, and had been trained in a hard school ; but they arrived too late to show their prowess in battle. They left Cairo on August 29th and reached Rosetta on the 31st, and after suffering severely from dysentery and other diseases, returned to India in July, 1802.[2] The campaign had ended at Alexandria shortly before their boats floated into Rosetta. Misfortune followed them from start to finish.

The final hostilities of the campaign of 1801 took place at Alexandria, where General Menou endeavoured in vain to keep a last foothold in Egypt. While Hutchinson was advancing to Cairo, Eyre Coote was blockading Alexandria with 5,000 men. From an engineering point of view the only event of any importance during this blockade occurred in the middle of June when Menou tried to flood a portion of the ground between his fortifications and Eyre Coote's trenches. This scheme was frustrated by Lieutenants Handfield, Hayes and Dundas, the only Royal Engineers then present, who checked the inundation by building a large dam with the help of a battalion of infantry. General Hutchinson arrived on August 15th with a large force, including most of the Engineers except Holloway and Lacy, and began active measures for the reduction of Alexandria with an army of 16,000 men. The capture of Fort Marabout, lying to the west of the city and guarding the only avenue of supply to the garrison, was a necessary preliminary to a complete investment, so Hutchinson detailed 4,000 men under Eyre Coote to commence operations from the west, while a show of attack was made at the same time from the east, where the main body of the British army was assembled. Fort Marabout had been reconnoitred on August 13th by Captain Bryce and another officer, and, on the 17th, Eyre Coote traversed Lake Maryut, landed his men and guns, and with Captain Ford and Lieutenants Graham and Kennett, R.E., to assist him, threw up the necessary siege batteries.

[1] *History of the British Expedition to Egypt*, by Lt.-Colonel R. T. Wilson, Vol. II, p. 39.
[2] Lieut. T. F. De Havilland, of the Madras Engineers, did not rejoin his Corps in India until 1804, for he was captured by a French privateer and held a prisoner until released on parole. While at Alexandria in 1801–02 he prepared a plan of the city and the neighbouring country which is now in the Alexandria Museum (see Chapter XVII).

The British artillery opened a heavy fire, and Fort Marabout surrendered on August 21st. Eyre Coote then fought his way slowly forward, with the help of reinforcements from Hutchinson, until he was close to the western walls of Alexandria.

Meanwhile General Hutchinson, with Captain Bryce as his Commanding Royal Engineer, began his operations from the east, and dug his first parallel on August 17th at a distance of 1,200 yards from the walls. His supply services were strained to their limit. " The transport of provisions and stores was still performed by men," writes Wilson,[1] " General Hutchinson having found himself obliged to order away two regiments of dragoons, the field artillery, as well as the camels, horses and jack-asses to Rosetta on account of the difficulty of procuring forage. These jack-asses were removed to the great joy of everyone but their proprietors. The serenade of at least a thousand such voices, continuing incessantly during the night, was not desirable. Vexatious as the melody was, still there was something ludicrous in such a concert, in which occasionally all the numerous animals, both birds and beasts, joined." Batteries were raised and armed, and on August 26th, a general bombardment was opened on land, while the fire from the Turkish gunboats on Lake Maryut took the French positions in flank. The enemy's fire died away, and a bold reconnaissance by Bryce showed that their guns had been withdrawn. General Menou then sent out a flag of truce, on the 30th the terms of capitulation were signed. On September 3rd, 1801, the British took possession of Alexandria and the last body of French troops quitted Egyptian soil. The unfortunate Major Fletcher, R.E., who had been a prisoner of war since his capture in Abu Qir Bay on February 27th, was able at length to rejoin his comrades and in due course sailed for Europe.

The Egyptian campaign of 1801 ended with brilliant and unexpected success to the British arms, owing partly to the inferior strategy of the French Commander-in-Chief; but England had no intention of annexing Egypt nor even of maintaining a garrison in Alexandria. In March, 1803, the whole of the British troops were withdrawn from that city, and, except for a disastrous venture in 1807, no British soldiers fought on Egyptian soil until 1882. Napoleon afterwards stated that he considered that the evacuation of Alexandria was a grievous error.[2] England, however, preferred to follow her traditional policy of non-interference in the internal affairs of friendly nations.

But Turkey did not remain friendly. She developed strong French proclivities, and in 1807 was in warm alliance with Napoleon. England was then allied with Russia against France, and the

---

[1] *History of the British Expedition to Egypt*, by Lt.-Colonel R. T. Wilson, Vol. II, p. 15.

[2] Article entitled "Napoleon I and Egypt," appearing in the *R.E. Journal*, Vol. 27, 1897, p. 67.

Russians were asking for British assistance. In addition, Napoleon seemed to be contemplating a second descent upon Egypt. Influenced by these factors, the British Government decided to dispatch an expedition to that country and thus not only to checkmate Napoleon's designs, but to distract the attention of the Turks from their operations against the Russians. Accordingly, an expeditionary force of 5,000 men, under Major-General M'Kenzie Fraser, was organized from the troops then garrisoning Sicily against the French and was sent to Alexandria with the hope that its weakness might be remedied by the co-operation of the Mamelukes. By March 18th, 1807, Fraser had landed his troops to the west of Alexandria and was in full occupation of it on the 22nd. He was forbidden to extend his operations beyond the city; yet he was directed, at the same time, to make British influence preponderant throughout the whole country. Regarding this, the Government remarked "How you are to do so, we do not know." Neither did the unfortunate General. The Royal Engineers who set out with Fraser on this wild-goose chase were Captain (afterwards General) F. R. Thackeray, 2nd Captain (afterwards Field-Marshal Sir) J. F. Burgoyne, 2nd Captain W. Nicholas, and Lieutenants G. C. Hoste and E. Parker. Nicholas records that, for the first seven days, he never pulled off his clothes or changed his linen and that he lived on the soldier's ration, and this in days when officers were accustomed to take the field in luxury.[1]

On March 31st, Nicholas set out with a small force under the command of Major-General Wauchope, who was ordered to attack Rosetta. The preliminary operations were successful, but Wauchope afterwards marched his troops into the labyrinth of the town whence they were driven out with the loss of their General and 184 others killed, and 263 men wounded. Muhammad (Mehemet) Ali,[2] the progressive ruler of Egypt, had already defeated the Mamelukes and induced them to side with him against the invaders, so Fraser's hopes of assistance from the Mamelukes were shattered; and being advised that a famine was imminent in Alexandria, he determined to make another attempt to capture Rosetta, which was rich in wheat and rice. He dispatched a force of 2,500 men, under Brigadier-General Stewart, with a large proportion of artillery and engineers' stores for a siege, and with them went Nicholas as a volunteer. The abortive siege of Rosetta lasted from April 7th to April 21st, 1807,

[1] *Royal Military Chronicle*, p. 255.
[2] Muhammad Ali Pasha ruled Egypt from 1805 to 1848 and materially improved the condition of the country. In 1811 he massacred 470 Mameluke chiefs in the citadel at Cairo in order to establish his power. He declared war on the Sultan in 1831 in an endeavour to secure the independence of Egypt; but the European powers intervened and nullified the conquests of his son, Ibrahim, in Syria. Muhammad Ali Pasha was followed by Ibrahim Pasha (1848), Abbas Pasha I (1848–54), Said Pasha (1854–63), Ismail Pasha (1863–79), Muhammad Tewfik Pasha (1879–92), Abbas Pasha Hilmi (1892—1914), Sultan Hussein Kamel (1914–17), H.M. King Fouad I (1917-36) and H.M. King Farouk I (now reigning).

when Stewart abandoned it and fought his way back, with heavy loss, to Alexandria ; but not before a detachment of 800 men had been killed or captured at El Hamed. The wretched prisoners were marched into Cairo along a road lined with poles bearing the heads of their fallen comrades.

General Fraser now found himself isolated in Alexandria, with Muhammad Ali advancing against him at the head of a large army of Turks, Albanians and Mamelukes. He was called upon to defend an extensive perimeter with inadequate numbers, and therefore opened negotiations with the enemy and offered to evacuate Egypt if the British prisoners were restored to him. His immediate anxieties were somewhat relieved by a reinforcement from Malta, but this did not affect the final issue. The British Government had decided that, if Alexandria were held, Sicily must be abandoned, so orders were sent to Fraser on September 3rd to embark his troops. Muhammad Ali collected and restored the prisoners, and the whole British expeditionary force sailed for Sicily on September 19th. All the prestige gained in 1801 was lost in 1807, and France resumed her control of Turkey. This was the end of a rash and disastrous campaign.

There now ensued a very long period during which no Royal Engineers were employed in Egypt ; yet it may be well to outline some of the engineering history of that epoch, and particularly in regard to communications, in order to provide a background for the stirring events which followed.

In 1825, a British engineer, named Alexander Galloway, who had been in the Egyptian service for several years, proposed to Muhammad Ali Pasha that a navigable canal should be dug from the Nile to the Red Sea. Muhammad Ali was then engaged in improving the Mahmudiya Canal between Alexandria and the Rosetta Branch of the Nile, and was much interested in canal construction generally. Galloway's idea was not original. The ancient Egyptians and Persians had already connected the Nile with the Red Sea, and the Roman Emperor Trajan had reopened this waterway in A.D. 100. In 1798, Napoleon had appointed one of his engineers, Monsieur Lepère, to survey for a canal between the Mediterranean and Red Seas ; but the project was abandoned when Lepère declared that the difference in level between the western and eastern waters was too great. Alexander Galloway's proposal of 1825 also came to nothing, though strongly supported by his son Thomas Jefferson Galloway, who succeeded him in 1826. It was not until 1830, when Captain Francis Rawdon Chesney, R.A.,[1] surveyed

---

[1] Captain (afterwards General) F. R. Chesney, R.A., was the uncle of General Sir G. T. Chesney, late R.(B.)E., a celebrated engineer of India. In 1831 Captain F. R. Chesney explored the route to India by way of Syria and the Euphrates, and made three later voyages for the same purpose, but the opposition of Russia prevented the general adoption of this route.

the Isthmus of Suez, that the difference in level between the Mediterranean and Red Seas was found to be much less than Lepère had announced, and this discovery went far towards inducing the enthusiastic Ferdinand de Lesseps to take up the project for a canal at some period after 1836.[1] De Lesseps formed a company in 1854, and, after further investigation, the construction of the Suez Canal was begun at Port Said in 1859. The canal was opened on November 17th, 1869, and soon replaced all other avenues of approach to India from the west.

But for many years before a canal was excavated through the Isthmus of Suez, an overland route was followed by enterprising travellers. Lieutenant Thomas Waghorn, of the Bengal Pilot Service and late of the Royal Navy, the ultimate founder of that route, had urged its advantages in 1827 and traversed it himself in 1829.[2] Passengers and mails were transported from Alexandria to Suez in 1835. They came by sea from Falmouth to Alexandria, whence they were taken in boats along the Mahmudiya Canal to the Nile, and up that river to Cairo. Thence they journeyed in two-wheeled vans across the desert to Suez. A Colonel Barr was sent from India in 1837 to arrange for the building of a series of resthouses or stations in the desert, and found an influential friend in the British Consul-General, Colonel Patrick Campbell.[3] Writing on the subject of the overland journey from Cairo to Suez before the Indian Mutiny, John Tillotson remarks :[4] " The vans or omnibusses employed to take us across the desert contain, when full, six persons; and two, four or sometimes six are despatched at intervals of two or three hours. There are sixteen of the Overland Mail stations,[5] at about five miles from each other. At these places the caravan changes horses, when fresh horses are to be had, or stops to rest when they are not. For miles and miles on every side are vast broad hills and mounds of yellowish sand. The Central Station accommodates travellers with resting places. Good beds, and some hours of rest are allowed. All parties who arrive between six and twelve at night find supper prepared for them ; between twelve and six in

---

[1] Colonel R. H. Vetch, c.b., late R.E., makes the following remarks in his *Life of Lieut.-General Sir Andrew Clarke, G.C.M.G., C.B., C.I.E., Col. Commandant R.E.* (p. 101) :—" Without in any way depreciating the credit due to M. Ferdinand de Lesseps, it is well to point out that the conception of the Canal was a British one. As far back as 1840, Captain James Vetch, f.r.s., R.E., proposed a scheme not essentially different from that eventually carried out, and published a work in 1843 entitled *Inquiry into the Means of Establishing a Ship Canal between the Mediterranean and Red Seas*. He laid his proposals before Lord John Russell's Administration in 1846 ; but the attitude of Lord Palmerston, the Foreign Secretary, was so absolutely opposed to the policy of the canal between the two seas, as one fraught with danger to British interests in the Far East, that Captain Vetch was unable to proceed further in the matter."

[2] The memory of Lieutenant Waghorn is perpetuated by sculptures at Chatham and at Port Tewfik at the southern end of the Suez Canal.

[3] *British Routes to India*, by H. L. Hopkins (1928), p. 228.

[4] *The Overland Route to India*, by John Tillotson, pp. 28-52.

[5] Originally there were seven stations, and also semaphore towers for signalling the mails.

the morning, breakfast ; and for the remainder of the day, dinner. Thus, if one omnibus arrives at half past eleven, its occupants sit down to supper. If another arrives at half past twelve, they sit down to breakfast. . . . The approach to Suez is marked by bold and striking scenery. At last we get into the town. The hotel—a sort of mongrel caravanserai—has not sleeping accommodation for half its guests, and only one bath for the whole. A ship awaits us on the waters of the Red Sea, and we are glad enough to go on board."

The advent of the railway eased the hardships, and shortened the duration, of the overland journey. In 1834, before the arrival of De Lesseps, Thomas Galloway made a survey for the first railway line in Africa—from Cairo to Suez—and his investigations were continued by his brother, John Alexander Galloway. However, the French canal enthusiasts were soon in active opposition to any scheme for a railway, and although materials were collected, they lay rotting on the shore at Alexandria, where a French engineer, De Cérisy, was building a new harbour for Muhammad Ali. About 1847, Lord Palmerston realized that a canal in French hands might be a menace to proper communication with India, so he supported John Galloway's project for a railway. When an International Commission arrived in 1850 to report on the Suez Canal scheme, Abbas Pasha, the Viceroy, consulted Robert Stephenson,[1] one of the members, about the railway project, and appointed him in 1851 as the first Chief Engineer. Construction was begun from Alexandria in the same year.[2] The railway was open to Cairo in 1856, and through to Suez in 1858. It soon proved its value. During the Indian Mutiny, before April, 1858, 5,000 British troops passed along the line from Alexandria to Cairo, and thence to railhead some 25 miles or more from Suez,[3] the charge being £10 for each officer and £5 for each soldier ; but the opening of the Suez Canal in 1869 absorbed much of the railway traffic, and consequently the section from Cairo to Suez was taken up in 1877.[4] For several years after the Canal was opened, the mails were carried by rail from Alexandria to Suez ; but ultimately they were sent by water, and the Cairo-Suez section of the railway ceased to be profitable.

It will be seen that Royal Engineers took no part in the preparation of the overland route or the building of the railway connecting Alexandria with Cairo, and Cairo with Suez ; nor did they share in the construction of the Suez Canal. The civil engineering operations

---

[1] Son of George Stephenson, the father of the locomotive. Robert Stephenson, M.P., died in 1859 and was buried in Westminster Abbey.

[2] The original railway station can still be seen in the Alexandria Docks.

[3] In 1857, the railway extended only to a distance of 58 miles from Cairo. The remaining 25 miles to Suez was covered in vans. The journey from Alexandria to Suez then occupied about 50 hours. One of the engineers employed on the railway in its early days was Capt. H. C. S. Rickards, late 96th and 99th Regiments, who became a Muhammadan and was known as " Abdulla Pasha el Inglisi."

[4] This railway was relaid gradually in later years.

between 1807 and 1882 were executed wholly by civilians employed by the Egyptian Government or the Suez Canal Company, and, as regards military duty, there is no record of the employment of any Royal Engineers in the Egyptian army between these dates. After the American Civil War (1861-65) the Khedive Ismail Pasha had no difficulty in recruiting American Army officers to organize and hold the higher commands in his army, and Prussian officers were available after the Franco-Prussian War.[1] It is true that one or two officers of the Corps surveyed in the Sinai Peninsula and Palestine, that a few helped in the administration of the Suez Canal, that one acted as Consul-General, and that Gordon came to Cairo in 1874 on his way to the Sudan, and again in 1878, at Ismail Pasha's request, to advise him on financial matters; but these services constitute a very small connection with the general development of Egypt, and not until Arabi led the rebellion of 1882 did Royal Engineers appear in force on the banks of the Nile.

[1] *R.E. Journal*, Vol. 12, 1882, p. 192.

ALEXANDRIA.
[*from " The Route of the Overland Mail to India."*

CHAPTER II.

THE EGYPTIAN CAMPAIGN OF 1882.

TOWARDS the close of the year 1875, Ismail Pasha, the Khedive of Egypt, had reached the end of his resources and brought his country to the verge of bankruptcy. His prodigality was unbounded: his power of intrigue, unmatched. It is true that much of the money, which he spent so lavishly, was employed on the construction of railways and canals; but a large part of it was squandered in gratifying his mania for accumulating landed property and building gorgeous palaces. In a belated endeavour to stave off financial ruin he sold to the British Government his shares in the Suez Canal Company, and England thereby acquired an important interest in the Canal, and indirectly in Egypt itself.[1] England had no desire to intervene in Egypt provided that other European powers would follow her example; but investigations revealed that Egyptian affairs were becoming so entangled that the British Consul-General was obliged to press upon the Khedive the necessity of an exhaustive financial inquiry in which Great Britain was bound to be represented, and through which she was drawn ultimately into the Egyptian imbroglio.

Ismail made desperate efforts to raise money by forced loans and pressure on the unfortunate peasantry. The *corvée*, or system of forced labour, was applied with the utmost rigour. Even the Khedive's landed property went into the melting pot. At length, in August, 1878, a Cabinet was formed under Nubar Pasha with an Englishman, Mr. Rivers Wilson, as Minister of Finance, and a Frenchman, M. de Blignières, as Minister of Public Works, and Ismail found himself under what was called the "Dual Control." Neither England nor France could afford to stand aloof while other nations profited by the chaos in Egypt, and England herself could not rest assured while her route to India led through a wilderness of intrigue, corruption and possible war. Ismail, however, had no love for the Dual Control, and to prove that it was a failure, arranged a military outbreak in Cairo in February, 1879. British and French warships then entered the port of Alexandria, Nubar Pasha resigned, and Prince Tewfik, the Khedive's son, became Prime Minister. Intent on giving trouble, Ismail next dismissed Rivers Wilson and de Blignières and proposed to increase his army. As a result,

---

[1] England became the holder of nearly one-half of the Canal stock at a cost of about £4,000,000.

England and France requested the Porte to depose the obstreperous Khedive, and Ismail was exiled to Naples with a numerous retinue and a large harem. On September 4th, 1879, Major Evelyn Baring (afterwards Lord Cromer) and M. de Blignières were appointed Controllers-General, and with Tewfik as Khedive, and Riaz Pasha as Prime Minister, the prospects seemed brighter. The first step of England into the arena of Egyptian politics had been taken, and a definite responsibility incurred.

Although the Egyptian army[1] was composed chiefly of agricultural labourers with no taste for war, it contained a few good fighters from the Sudan. The majority of the officers were of Egyptian or " fellah " origin, whilst others were of Turkish or Circassian extraction, and jealousy between these rival factions led to discontent and insubordination, particularly among the fellah officers, who were despised by the others. Three such officers, Ali Fahmi, Abdel el Al and Ahmed Arabi, joined by Mahmud Sami, a politician, proceeded to form a National Party, Mahmud Sami supplying the requisite cunning, and Ahmed Arabi the energy and power. Colonel Ahmed Arabi, better known as Arabi Pasha, was a burly specimen of the fellah type, with rough-hewn features and a stern demeanour. Strongly opposed to Europeans, poorly educated, ignorant of the finer arts of strategy and tactics, but with a certain quality of sincerity combined with a natural love of intrigue, Arabi possessed a strength of character which brought him rapidly to the front. This was the man who, on September 9th, 1881, instigated a military mutiny against the weak and complacent Tewfik, and then, to safeguard his position, declared that so long as he possessed a drop of blood, or a living breath, both should belong to his beloved sovereign ![2]

A widespread feeling of discontent pervaded not only the Egyptian army but the whole country. The people desired to limit the power of the Khedive and abolish the Anglo-French control. The better educated classes noted the increasing number of European officials, and suspected that Egypt would soon be under foreign domination. The British and French Governments remarked that the Egyptians were improving their coast defences and strengthening their army, and realized that, if the Khedive was to be maintained in power, they would soon be called upon to take active measures in his support, so, on January 8th, 1882, both Governments pledged themselves in a Joint Note to assist the Khedive against all his enemies. Unfortunately this declaration was not backed by a display of force, a fact

[1] The regular army had 36 battalions of infantry, 8 regiments of cavalry, 24 batteries of field artillery, 3 regiments of garrison artillery and 1 battalion of pioneers. In addition there were large irregular forces. The war establishments provided for 53,000 infantry, 3,550 cavalry and 144 field-guns, but these numbers were not available in July, 1882, as the Egyptian Army was supposed to be restricted to a total of 18,000 men. See the *R.E. Journal*, Vol. 12, 1882, p. 192.

[2] *The Egyptian Campaigns*, 1882–1899, by Charles Royle, p. 24.

which Arabi was quick to note. He declared point-blank that any foreign intervention was inadmissible. Bitter opposition arose between Tewfik and his Ministers, among whom was Arabi, who had become Minister of War in May. A few British and French warships were sent to Alexandria, where the European population was seriously alarmed, and on June 7th a Turkish envoy arrived in Cairo, nominally in support of the Khedive, but actually to counteract Anglo-French influence in Egypt.

Convinced of the impotence of the European powers, and inflamed by the truculence of Arabi and the army, the sweepings of Alexandria rose in riot on June 11th, 1882, and rushed through the streets with shouts of "Death to the Christians." The Egyptian troops and police looked on unmoved: occasionally they joined the rioters. Arabi was powerless to control the evil forces which he had let loose. Admiral Sir Beauchamp Seymour, the British naval commander, hesitated to land his men, and, as Lord Salisbury stated in bitter condemnation of Gladstone's pacific policy, British subjects were butchered under the very guns of the fleet. Hundreds of Europeans perished in Alexandria and elsewhere, while others took refuge on ships or in the European consulates. It was not until July 11th that the guns of a powerful British squadron opened a fierce bombardment on the insurgents and, by the following evening, silenced the artillery in the numerous Egyptian forts.[1] Alexandria was then a smoking ruin. Arabi withdrew his forces to a strong position at Kafr el Dauwar, 15 miles away on the neck of land forming the approach to the city, and Alexandria was garrisoned by British sailors and soldiers. Such were the events which preceded the return of Royal Engineers to Egypt in 1882.

Reinforcements arrived gradually from Port Said, Cyprus, and Malta, and when Major-General Sir Archibald Alison, K.C.B., landed on July 17th he could muster nearly 4,000 men to oppose a larger and rapidly increasing force with 36 guns under Arabi Pasha at Kafr el Dauwar. On the 19th, additional troops were ordered from Malta and Cyprus to raise Alison's strength to 15,000 men, and on the following day the Cabinet decided at last to dispatch a powerful expeditionary force to Egypt. At the same time, however, Mr. Gladstone was careful to explain that "England was not at war." The force was fixed at an army corps of 2 divisions, and it was to be under the command of Lieut.-General Sir Garnet Wolseley, G.C.B., with Lieut.-General Sir John Adye, K.C.B., as his Chief of Staff, and Lieut.-Generals G. H. S. Willis, C.B., and Sir Edward Hamley, K.C.M.G., C.B., as Divisional Commanders. The Brigade Commanders of the 1st Division under Willis were Major-General H.R.H. The Duke of Connaught (1st Brigade) and Major-General Gerald

---

[1] A full account of the riots in, and bombardment of, Alexandria is given in *The Egyptian Campaigns*, 1882–1899, by C. Royle, pp. 44–106. The naval dispatches on the bombardment are quoted in the *R.E. Journal*, Vol. 12, 1882, pp. 192–194.

Graham, V.C., C.B., late R.E. (2nd Brigade) ; and of the 2nd Division under Hamley, Major-General Sir Archibald Alison, K.C.B., (1st Brigade) and Major-General Sir Evelyn Wood, K.C.B. (2nd Brigade). Attached to the army corps was a cavalry division under Major-General D. C. Drury Lowe, C.B., and it was arranged that a contingent should be sent from India under Major-General Sir Herbert Macpherson, V.C., K.C.B. The command of the Artillery was given to Brigadier-General W. H. Goodenough, late R.A., and that of the Engineers to Brigadier-General C. B. P. N. H. Nugent, C.B., late R.E. The British Government engaged 71 transports in England and 54 in India to carry the army which, with subsequent reinforcements, was not far short of 40,000 men. The mistakes of 1807 were avoided. The force employed was overwhelming, and the campaign which followed was one of the shortest and most decisive on record. Sir Garnet Wolseley was ordered to support the authority of the Khedive by suppressing the revolt under Arabi, who had been declared a rebel, and his methods and radius of action were unrestricted.

Although the campaign of 1882 in Egypt was an " Infantry " and not an " Engineer " war, the chief interest of Royal Engineers centres naturally on the exploits of Sir Gerald Graham, and on the work of other officers and men of the Corps. Graham had already distinguished himself in many parts of the globe. As a subaltern he had won the Victoria Cross in leading the ladder party in an assault on the Redan at Sevastopol in the Crimea on June 18th, 1855. As a Brevet-Major, in the China War of 1860, he had added to his reputation during the capture of the Taku Forts and the advance on Peking. He was always in the thick of the fight, and was wounded on several occasions. His war services, and his proved ability in both staff and regimental work, secured him such rapid promotion that in 1881 he became a Major-General at the age of 50 years, and in the following year was selected by his personal friend Sir Garnet Wolseley to command a brigade in the field. Some say that Graham was lacking in strategical and tactical ability, although his brigade was allowed to form the spear-point of the thrust towards Cairo. His conduct of operations in the field has been severely, if unjustly, criticized ; but the fact remains that he brought those operations to a successful conclusion. Cool, brave, straightforward and magnificent alike in appearance and character, he inspired admiration which was worth many bayonets.[1]

So numerous were the Royal Engineers who served in Egypt in

---

[1] Memoirs of Lieut.-General Sir Gerald Graham, V.C., G.C.B., G.C.M.G., Col. Commdt. R.E., appear in the *R.E. Journal*, Vol. 30, 1900, pp. 28-34 and 51-62, and in *History of the Corps of Royal Engineers*, by Colonel Sir C. M. Watson, K.C.M.G., C.B., late R.E., Vol. III, pp. 339-350. A full account is given also in *Life, Letters and Diaries of Lieut.-General Sir Gerald Graham, V.C., G.C.B., R.E.*, by Colonel R. H. Vetch, C.B., late R.E.

1882, and afterwards rose to high rank, that it may be well to mention some of their names. The careers of Sir Gerald Graham, V.C., Sir Richard Harrison, Sir James Browne, Sir Charles Wilson, Sir Herbert Chermside, Sir William Nicholson, (afterwards Lord Nicholson of Roundhay), Sir Bindon Blood, Sir Charles Warren, Sir Reginald Hart, V.C., and Sir George Sydenham Clarke (afterwards Lord Sydenham of Combe) are well known to every student of military or political history. Many others, hardly less distinguished, were begun or continued at this time in the sandy deserts around the Nile ; but that of Kitchener in Egypt and the Sudan was yet to come.

The Engineer formations included 6 field companies, 2 field troops and a field park, and these were joined later by 2 companies and a section of Queen's Own (Madras) Sappers and Miners from India.[1] With the 1st Division, under Colonel (afterwards Major-General) J. M. C. Drake as C.R.E., was the 24th Field Company, commanded by Captain C. de B. Carey ; and with the 2nd Division, under Lieut.-Colonel (afterwards Major-General Sir) J. H. M. Maitland, as C.R.E., the 26th Field Company, commanded by Major Bindon Blood, now famous as General Sir Bindon Blood, G.C.B., G.C.V.O., Chief Royal Engineer. The Corps Troops were the " A " or Pontoon Troop, commanded by Major R. J. Bond ; the " C " or Telegraph Troop, commanded by Major Sir A. W. Mackworth, Bart. ; the 8th (Railway) Company, under Captain Sydney Smith ; the 17th Field Company, under Captain (afterwards Major-General) Elliott Wood ; and the 18th Field Company, under Major (afterwards Major-General Sir) W. Salmond. These units were joined subsequently by the 21st Field Company, commanded by Captain A. R. Puzey. Captain (afterwards Major-General Sir) George Barker was Adjutant, R.E., with the 1st Division, and Captain A. O. Green with the 2nd Division. The Field Park was under Captain C. A. Rochfort-Boyd. When the Indian Contingent reinforced the Expeditionary Force on the Suez Canal it brought with it Colonel (afterwards Major-General Sir) James Browne, C.S.I., late Royal (Bengal) Engineers, as C.R.E. ;[2] Major (afterwards General) A. F. Hamilton, Royal (Madras) Engineers, in command of the Queen's Own (Madras) Sappers and Miners ; " A " and " I " Companies of that Corps under Lieutenants C. H. Darling and W. D. Lindley respectively ; and four other Royal Engineers in the persons of Captain William G. (afterwards Field-Marshal Lord) Nicholson, as Field Engineer, Captain H. B. Rich and

---

[1] One section of " E " Company, Madras Sappers and Miners, with instruments and cable for 10 miles of line, was sent from India with the companies.

[2] The romantic, varied and distinguished Indian career of Major-General Sir James ("Buster") Browne is described in *The Life and Times of General Sir James Browne*, R.E., K.C.B., K.C.S.I., by General J. J. McLeod Innes, V.C., late R.E., and also in *The Military Engineer in India*, by Lieut.-Colonel E. W. C. Sandes, D.S.O., M.C., R.E. (retd.), Vols. I and II. A portrait of Sir James Browne is included in Vol. II of the latter work.

LIEUT.-GENERAL SIR GERALD GRAHAM, V.C., G.C.B., G.C.M.G.
COLONEL COMMANDANT ROYAL ENGINEERS.

Lieutenant J. Burn-Murdoch as Assistant Field Engineers, and Lieutenant J. E. Dickie as Superintendent of Army Signalling.[1]

The Royal Engineers holding Staff or special service appointments were Colonel (afterwards General Sir) Richard Harrison, C.B., who was A.A.G. to the Chief of Staff; Lieut.-Colonel (afterwards Major-General) C. E. Webber as A.Q.M.G. for Telegraphy; Major (afterwards Major-General Sir) Thomas Fraser, C.M.G., as a Brigade-Major; Lieutenant E. S. E. Childers as *A.D.C.* to Sir Garnet Wolseley; Major (afterwards General Sir) Reginald C. Hart, V.C., as *A.D.C.* to General Graham; Captain S. Waller as *A.D.C.* to Brigadier-General Nugent; and Lieut.-Colonel H. H. Jones, Major (afterwards Major-General Sir) John C. Ardagh, C.B., Captains C. M. Watson, C. R. Conder, W. J. Gill and G. S. Clarke (afterwards Lord Sydenham of Combe), and Lieutenant V. H. P. Caillard, as special service officers. Colonel (afterwards Lieut.-General Sir) Charles Warren, C.M.G., and Lieutenants E. M. Burton and A. E. Haynes were attached for special duty under Admiral Sir Beauchamp Seymour, the Naval Commander-in-Chief. Lieut.-Colonel (afterwards Major-General) Sir Charles W. Wilson, K.C.M.G., C.B., and Major (afterwards Major-General Sir) H. C. Chermside, C.M.G., were detailed for political duty under Sir Edward Malet, the British Consul-General in Egypt who, with Mr. (afterwards Sir Auckland) Colvin as Controller, had already done fine work for England. Major W. A. J. Wallace, Captain (afterwards Major-General) D. A. Scott, and Lieutenant H. B. Willock were attached as Railway Staff officers, and Lieutenant J. J. Leverson joined the Commissariat staff. After a time, Major-General H. Wray became second-in-command in Alexandria, and Captain Thomas Gracey was posted to the Railway Corps; but neither of these officers saw active service. Nevertheless, it is evident that the Corps of Royal Engineers was very fully represented in most departments of the Army in Egypt, and no less than 77 of its officers received the Egyptian medal at the conclusion of the campaign.[2]

The first Royal Engineer unit to disembark at Alexandria in 1882 was the 17th Field Company, which accordingly had the honour

---

[1] The junior officers of the various units were as follows:—*24th Field Company*, Capt. J. F. Dorward and Lieuts. R. C. Hellard, J. C. L. Campbell and J. C. Tyler; *26th Field Company*, Capt. E. Dickinson, and Lieuts. J. E. Blackburn, W. H. Pollen and M. L. Tuke; "*A*" *Troop*, Lieuts. W. C. Godsal, E. St. C. Pemberton, J. L. Irvine and A. E. Sandbach; "*C*" *Troop*, Capt. M. D. Whitmore and Lieuts. R. L. Hippisley, H. J. Foster, F. G. Bond and R. W. Anstruther; *8th (Railway) Company*, Lieuts. W. S. Vidal, L. J. Dopping-Hepenstal, H. Huleatt and F. W. Bennet; *17th Field Company*, Capt. R. M. Hyslop and Lieuts. F. C. Heath and A. G. Thomson; *18th Field Company*, Capt. C. H. Gordon and Lieuts. A. M. Mantell, S. L. Norris and J. Winn; *21st Field Company*, Lieuts. M. Elrington and S. D. Cleeve; "*A*" *Company Q.O. (Madras) Sappers and Miners*, Lieuts. P. B. Baldwin and H. S. Andrews-Speed; and "*I*" *Company*, of the same Corps, Lieut. H. E. Goodwin. Several of these officers had distinguished careers, *e.g.*, Major-Generals A. E. Sandbach, C.B., D.S.O., Sir Francis G. Bond, K.B.E., C.B., C.M.G., and F. C. Heath-Caldwell, C.B. (formerly F. C. Heath).

[2] A list of these officers is given in the *R.E. Journal*, Vol. 13, 1883, p. 61.

of being the pioneer unit of its Corps in Egypt. This company, more than any other, bore the heat and burden of the day throughout the campaign and is said to have been known as "the maid of all work." Most of the R.E. units did not disembark until they had arrived in the Suez Canal after the transfer of operations to that area. Captain Elliott Wood, R.E., and his men landed at Alexandria on July 17th as part of the advanced force under General Alison, and began at once to consolidate the position under the direction of Major John Ardagh, C.B., R.E., the Commanding Royal Engineer.[1] In the course of a tour of the city walls Ardagh found that a length of 1,000 yards of the original perimeter of 6,500 yards had been demolished at the western end, and that, on the sea-side, the wall had practically disappeared. The old walls had apparently been about 25 feet in height, with towers at intervals overlooking a ditch 40 feet wide and 12 feet deep. Outside the city, and between it and the Mahmudiya Canal, were three masonry works and a few small towers, in addition to an outer line of modern fortifications built by French engineers about 50 years before; and within the city lay the prominent fort of Kom el Dik and the smaller Fort Napoleon. These defences seemed to be satisfactory, but actually they were of little value. Owing to extensive breaches in the walls, and the number of city gates, it was necessary to make the enceinte secure against attack, so Ardagh engaged civilian labour to close the gaps, build up several of the gates and repair the drawbridges of others. He also cut a large gap in the fortifications near the western or El Qabbari Railway Station for seven lines of rails and erected new blockhouses near the canal; and in addition he took steps to preserve the amount of fresh water in the canal by building a dam across the channel.[2] The 17th Company assisted in these operations and put the waterworks at Ramla in a state of defence after they had been occupied by the infantry. Subsequently they took part in an advance to El Mallaha Junction on the Cairo Railway towards Kafr el Dauwar, repairing the line and building defence works.

Arabi's position near Kafr el Dauwar placed the water-supply of Alexandria at his mercy, and he had already dammed the Mahmudiya Canal and admitted sea-water to its lower reaches. General Alison slowly extended his perimeter, but not without frequent skirmishes at night. His task was to hold Alexandria until the

---

[1] A Memoir of Major-General Sir J. C. Ardagh, K.C.M.G., K.C.I.E., C.B., late R.E., is given in *History of the Corps of Royal Engineers*, by Col. Sir C. M. Watson, K.C.M.G., C.B., late R.E., Vol. III, pp. 380–387. When the Expeditionary Force left Alexandria for the Suez Canal, Ardagh remained at Alexandria as Intelligence Officer until he rejoined the Force before the Battle of Tel el Kebir. He had great experience and ability in diplomatic work.

[2] Article entitled "The Land Defences of Alexandria," containing a report by Major J. C. Ardagh, C.B., R.E., appearing in the *R.E. Journal*, Vol. 12, 1882, pp. 235–237. On pp. 237–239 of the same volume is a report on the Sea Defences of Alexandria by Capt. G. S. Clarke, R.E. See also the *Report on the Defences of Alexandria and on the results of the Action of 11th July*, 1882, by Capt. G. S. Clarke, R.E., with plans and photographs (97 pages).

expeditionary force under Sir Garnet Wolseley should arrive; and this concentration having been effected by the middle of August, Wolseley was ready to take the offensive.

The position near Kafr el Dauwar was strategically in an excellent situation for repelling a British invasion through Lower Egypt, and it was also extremely strong. Reconnaissances and reports showed that it had three fortified lines stretching across the narrow neck of dry land which carried the Cairo Railway and the Mahmudiya Canal, the first line being about 2 miles east of El Mallaha Junction, the second 4 miles behind the first, and the third a further 2 miles in rear of the second and a similar distance short of Kafr el Dauwar Station. Some of the parapets were 40 feet in thickness, the ditches were wide and deep, and there were emplacements for 100 guns.[1] Possibly 20,000 Egyptians could have been mustered for the defence. To attack such a position would have been a slow and costly undertaking, but Sir Garnet Wolseley had no intention of doing so. With fine strategic insight he had decided to make his thrust towards Cairo by the shorter and more open route from Ismailia on the Suez Canal. Nevertheless, Alexandria was useful, for it served the double purpose of forming a valuable sea base and at the same time deceiving the enemy as to the probable line of advance.

It is superfluous to describe the political manœuvres which preceded the transfer of the expeditionary force to the Suez Canal. The French Government refused to participate in any operations on land, while other Continental powers held aloof altogether. Turkey, seeing that England was in earnest, desired to land troops in Egypt in order that she might have a voice in the settlement of the affairs of her nominal dependency, but to this England would not agree.[2] De Lesseps protested vehemently against the use of the Suez Canal for warlike operations. He had assured Arabi that if the Egyptians did not interfere with it, the British also would respect it; but his views changed somewhat when he heard, towards the end of July, that Arabi's Council of War proposed to block the waterway. Fortunately the British Navy was able to prevent this disaster by entering and patrolling the Canal.

On August 18th, 1882, Wolseley's transports, carrying the 1st Division, steamed eastwards from Alexandria, followed on the 19th by a stately procession of warships. The objective was said to be Abu Qir Bay and most of the ironclads moored there and ostentatiously prepared for action. But at dawn on the 20th, the whole fleet had vanished. At that moment it was entering the Suez Canal.

---

[1] Paper VI, "Kafr Dowar" by Lieut. S. D. Cleeve, R.E., appearing in *Professional Papers of the Corps of Royal Engineers*, Vol. IX, 1883, pp. 99–106; and sketch entitled "First Position, Kafr Dowar," by the same officer, appearing in the *R.E. Journal*, Vol. 12, 1882, p. 241.

[2] *Modern Egypt*, by the Earl of Cromer (1908), Vol. I, pp. 311–321.

Indeed, the advance guard under General Graham was about to land at Ismailia, which had been seized by the Navy. Suez had been in British hands for nearly three weeks. With the exception of the Serapeum portion between Lake Timsa and the Bitter Lakes, the whole of the Canal was occupied by the evening of the 20th; and on August 21st, Wolseley began to land the main body of his force at Ismailia, while Graham advanced a few miles westwards to Nifisha Junction,[1] which had been bombarded by our warships. Within the next ten days the 2nd Division reinforced the 1st Division on the Suez Canal. The 26th Field Company, under Major Bindon Blood, R.E., had landed in Alexandria on August 24th as part of the 2nd Division, which was then awaiting orders to follow Sir Garnet Wolseley. Learning that General Hamley wished to send a small column to clear the enemy from some outposts near Kafr el Dauwar, and that he lacked mounted infantry, Major Blood volunteered to mount and arm 60 of his Sappers to act as such; but alas, they were ordered to embark for Ismailia before they could show their ability in their new rôle.

Soon after the arrival of the expeditionary force at Ismailia, news was received of the murder of a Royal Engineer, and two other officers, in the Sinai Desert. Professor E. H. Palmer, a well-known Arabic scholar and explorer, had left Suez on August 8th, accompanied by Lieutenant Harold Charrington, R.N., in order to procure camels at Nekhl, half-way between Suez and Aqaba. They were joined by Captain W. J. Gill, R.E., already celebrated as an explorer in China and other countries, who intended to ride northwards to cut the telegraph line between El Qantara and El Arish. Within the next few days, rumours spread that some disaster had overtaken the little party, though no definite confirmation could be obtained. It seems that on August 10th, Palmer, Charrington and Gill were attacked and overpowered by Arabs and, after a day or two in captivity, were put to death in a wild gorge of the Wadi Sudr. It is said that they had to choose between hurling themselves over a cliff or being shot, and that all died bravely. At the end of August, Colonel Charles Warren, late R.E., set out to investigate the murder, but failed in this attempt.[2] In October, however, guided by some of Palmer's camel-men, he succeeded in reaching the scene of the tragedy, where, at the foot of a cliff, he discovered the shattered bodies of two of the officers, riddled with bullets and pierced by

---

[1] See the *Map of Lower Egypt, Communications*, 1882.

[2] Colonel Charles Warren was well fitted for such an investigation. He had surveyed in Palestine and Sinai and was a fine linguist with great experience of the Arab character. Later he led a military expedition in Bechuanaland, became head of the Metropolitan Police in London, and commanded a division in the South African War. He died in 1927 as General Sir Charles Warren, G.C.M.G., K.C.B., F.R.S. A Memoir appears in the *R.E. Journal*, Vol. XLI, 1927, pp. 699–709, and in this will be found a full account of Colonel Warren's search for the victims of the desert tragedy.

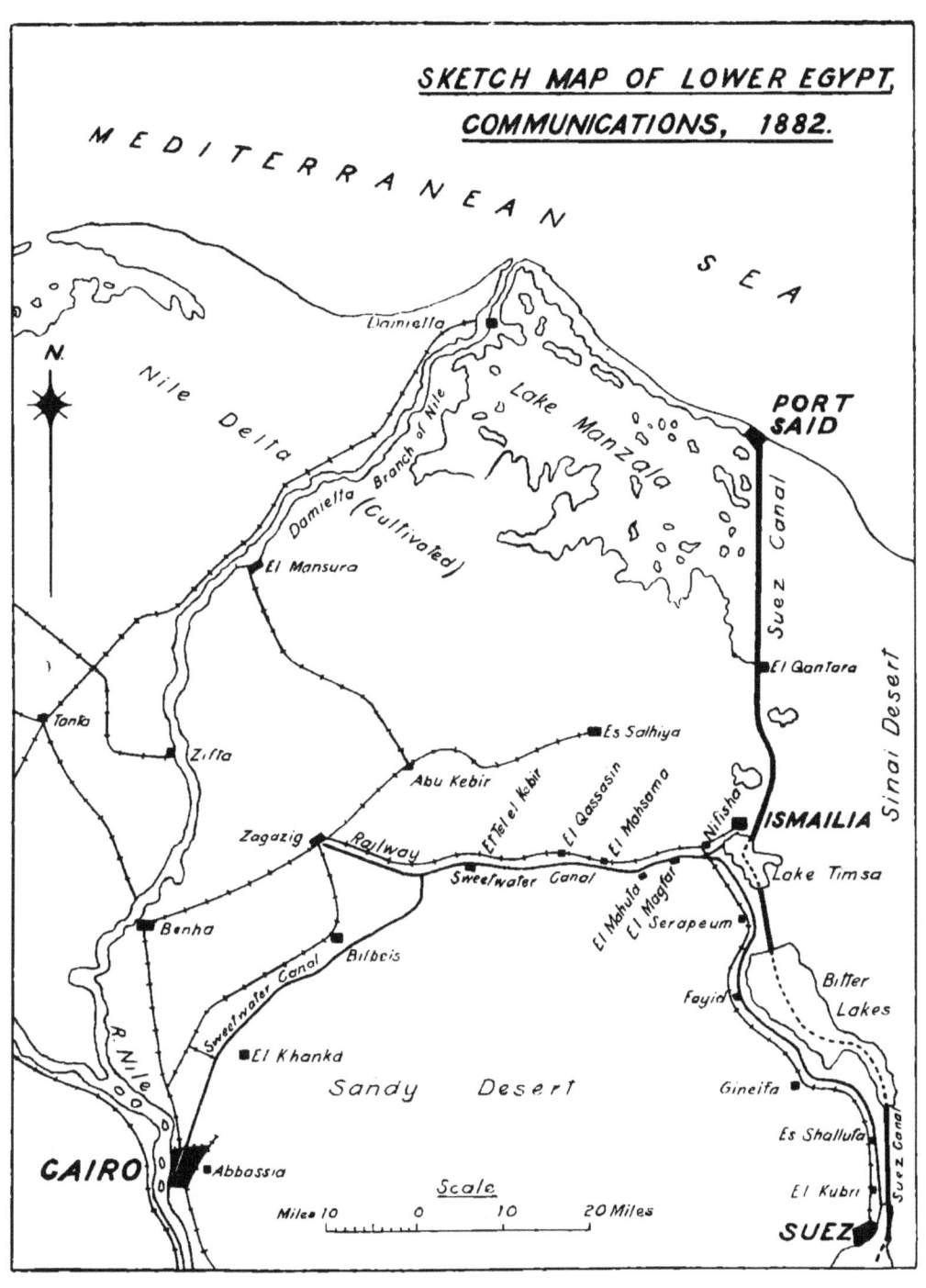

spears. Through the death of Gill, the Corps of Royal Engineers lost a most popular and promising young officer.[1]

Speed was imperative in the advance on Cairo in 1882. Ismailia was supplied with water by a "Sweetwater Canal" which took off from the Nile at Cairo, and it was connected to the capital by a railway. Both canal and railway diverged southwards to Suez from Nifisha Junction, near Ismailia, by way of the western bank of the Maritime or Suez Canal. No means of communication, either by road or railway, existed between Ismailia and Port Said, and fresh water was pumped to Port Said from Ismailia through pipes. The mere occupation of the Suez Canal alone could only be a temporary expedient, because the supply of fresh water along the Canal was under the control of those who held Cairo, and a force holding the Canal was open to attack at any point between El Qantara and Suez. Based on Cairo, Arabi could use the Sweetwater Canal and the railway between the capital and Ismailia, and could empty the canal and destroy the railway, section by section, if he were forced to retire. It was essential that he should not be given time to do so, but should be brought to decisive action and defeated at the earliest possible date. This was no occasion for careful penetration : it demanded bold leadership, backed by overwhelming force. Fortunately, both were available.

When General Graham occupied Nifisha on Monday, August 21st, he had been suffering for more than a week from a violent attack of lumbago which caused him so much pain that he was obliged to have periodical injections of morphia. The malady persisted during the brief campaign, sometimes depriving him of sleep and often torturing him when in the saddle. "Injection of morphia in the back. Sleepless night," he writes on August 23rd. Yet he never relinquished his command, nor failed to make the necessary tactical decisions promptly and coolly. No opposition was encountered in the occupation of Nifisha. Indeed, Graham was met only by an old woman carrying a white flag who described in graphic terms the shelling by the fleet and the flight of the defenders. Transports continued to arrive daily and to land their troops at Ismailia, though with great difficulty as the arrangements were most primitive, and on August 24th Wolseley advanced westwards along the Sweetwater Canal and railway in order to safeguard his precarious water-supply. He found the canal dammed near El Magfar and noticed that the enemy had prepared defences to guard El Mahuta, where they had blocked both the canal and railway. Nevertheless, Wolseley held his ground, though faced by 10,000 Egyptians with 10 guns. "I did not think it in consonance with the traditions of the Queen's Army," he writes, "that we should retire before any

[1] A memoir of Captain W. J. Gill, R.E., appears in the *R.E. Journal*, Vol. 12, 1882, pp. 279–287, and a debate in the House of Commons on the circumstances of the tragedy is recorded on pp. 274 and 275 of the same volume.

number of Egyptian troops."[1] After a heavy bombardment, the Egyptians advanced and manœuvred to attack the centre and right of the British line, and they repeated this threat in the afternoon; but they were careful not to assault, and Wolseley having been reinforced, they withdrew at sunset to their position at El Mahuta.

In these operations General Graham commanded the infantry and artillery, and General Drury Lowe led the cavalry. Graham states in his diary:[2] "*24th August.* Marched out at 5 a.m. Wolseley and Willis both coming. I had 1,000 infantry. York and Lancaster, Royal Marine Artillery, Royal Marine Light Infantry, and two Royal Horse Artillery guns. Saw our cavalry working rapidly on horizon. About 9 a.m. heard firing in front. Message for guns and infantry to move up. I got troops in position. York and Lancaster on left advanced first on dam. . . . Wolseley sent for the Guards, 46th and 60th, and a lot of guns. . . . Before sundown a strong attack was made on our left. . . . Suddenly enemy's attack collapsed. I felt dead tired, and fell asleep on a sandbank."

An advance on the El Mahuta position was undertaken on the 25th, but the enemy refused to fight and abandoned their trenches; and although they offered considerable resistance at El Mahsama, they were soon in full retreat to Tel el Kebir, where they had established a large camp and had begun to make extensive fortifications on the high and barren ground lying to the north of the railway. According to Lord Cromer, a warning had been given to Arabi by a certain Mr. Wilfred Blunt (unfortunately an Englishman) that he would probably be attacked from the direction of Ismailia.[3] El Mahsama was taken by the cavalry, who had been pushed forward in an attempt to cut off the enemy's trains which were being withdrawn along the railway. Seven Krupp guns, quantities of ammunition and stores, and many railway wagons loaded with provisions were captured.[4] The enemy had thrown their dead into the Sweetwater Canal in order to pollute the water. "Beastly place, Mahsama," writes Graham on the 26th. "A lot of dead bodies about. Ordered to occupy Kassassin (El Qassasin), so I moved out at 5 p.m., getting there at 6.30. I took possession of a nice old villa. Found lock and bridges in good order." The lock at El Qassasin had been seized that morning by our cavalry, who were soon reinforced by infantry and artillery. This was a most important move as Wolseley could now control the water in the upper reach

[1] Dispatch by Lieut.-General Sir Garnet Wolseley, dated August 24th, 1882, quoted in the *R.E. Journal*, Vol. 12, 1882, p. 213.
[2] Extracts from General Graham's diary quoted in the *R.E. Journal*, Vol. 30, 1900, p. 52.
[3] *Modern Egypt*, by the Earl of Cromer, Vol. I, p. 323, f.n.1.
[4] Mahmud Fahmi Pasha, Arabi's Chief-of-Staff, who had missed the last train, was also captured. He was strolling on the platform in mufti, wearing a "tarboosh" and carrying a white umbrella. He had acted as Arabi's Chief Engineer, so his capture was an important event.

THE SWEETWATER CANAL. [Photo by the Author.]

of the canal; but in advancing thus far, he had outrun his Commissariat. Railway communication was interrupted in several places, locomotives were not yet available, and no arrangements had been made for mule or camel transport. The troops were forced to live on biscuits, melons, or anything else which they could get, and to drink the muddy and polluted liquid of the so-called Sweetwater Canal along which supplies could not be brought in boats until the obstructions at El Magfar and El Mahuta had been cleared away.

The removal of the dam at El Magfar was a most difficult undertaking. It was composed of alternate layers of strong reeds and sand which had become so solidly compressed below water-level that no tools could make much impression on it. In addition it contained telegraph posts, tied together with wire, and was anchored in position by lines of piles. Throughout August 25th, a party of bluejackets under Lieutenant King-Harman, R.N., worked like beavers on this obstruction. Picks and shovels having proved to be almost useless, King-Harman laid and ignited a number of guncotton charges and by this means secured a narrow passage through the dam which he tried afterwards to widen. The work, however, was continually interrupted by the passage of boats, and, as the level of the water fell, the passage required constant deepening. King-Harman rightly called it a "vile job." The epithets applied to it by his men, who worked up to their necks in water, may be better imagined than described. On the 26th the sailors were reinforced by Captain Elliott Wood, R.E., and 30 Sappers of the 17th Field Company, and together, by exhausting manual labour, they secured a passage suitable for steam cutters early on the 27th. The dam at El Mahuta presented no such problems, for it was composed only of sand. It was about 50 feet thick and 12 feet above the water, and the canal was 70 feet wide. The 17th Field Company under Captain Wood, R.E., and the 24th Field Company under Captain C. de B. Carey, R.E., had little trouble in making a passage through it, assisted as they were by fatigue parties from several battalions.

There were no feats of engineering in the Egyptian campaign comparable with those of the expedition into Abyssinia in 1867,[1] but a host of minor difficulties were met and overcome with commendable patience and ingenuity. As each Field Company arrived at Ismailia it took up its duties without delay. The 17th Field Company was in the van as usual, and landed from Alexandria on August 21st; the 18th, under Major W. Salmond, R.E., came soon afterwards and was kept at Ismailia to act as a reserve and establish an Engineer Park; the 24th joined the 1st Division at El Mahuta on August 26th; but the 26th, under Major Bindon Blood,

---

[1] See *The Military Engineer in India*, by Lt.-Colonel E. W. C. Sandes, D.S.O., M.C., R.E. (retd.), Vol. I, pp. 396–401.

R.E., did not reach the front until a few days before the Battle of Tel el Kebir. The 21st Field Company, under Captain A. R. Puzey, R.E., remained in Alexandria, where it had disembarked on August 8th, and completed the work begun by the 17th Field Company. The achievements of the Railway, Pontoon and Telegraph units of the Royal Engineers, and of the two companies of Madras Sappers and Miners, will be described later. In general it may be said that the Field Companies were concerned mainly with the destruction of obstacles, the fortification of small localities, the improvement of a very defective line of supply, and with arrangements for the comfort and welfare of the troops. In such prosaic duties the units acquitted themselves well, and, indeed, were described as "the pith and directing energy" of the other three arms of the Service.

The Egyptians soon made a serious effort to regain their lost ground by an attack on the advanced force under General Graham at El Qassasin, some 20 miles from Ismailia. The British position was not favourable for defence, divided as it was by the Sweetwater Canal; and on its right the desert rose to a ridge of considerable height, which was too distant to be held, but might yet afford concealment to an outflanking force of the enemy. The first action at El Qassasin, on August 28th, has been so freely criticized that Graham's telegraphic report regarding it may be of interest. On the evening of that day he telegraphed to Sir Garnet Wolseley as follows :—[1] " My force, 1875 men, with 3 guns, with left on canal on Kassassin Lock.[2] About 9.30 a.m. enemy's cavalry showed in our front. At noon, enemy opened fire with two guns, doing no harm. At 3 p.m. enemy seemed to be retiring, so ordered men back to camp for dinner, and cavalry brigade, that had come to my support, returned to Maksanieh (El Mahsama). At 4.30 p.m. enemy's infantry advanced in force, supported by heavy and well-directed artillery fire, endeavouring to overlap my right. Requested cavalry brigade and battalion of Marines to come up from Maksanieh. Pushed forward Marine Artillery Battalion along south bank of canal to take enemy in flank. This movement was admirably executed. At 5 p.m. requested Lowe to attack enemy's left with cavalry, which he did most gallantly. At 6.45 ordered general advance, expecting cavalry about then to attack enemy's left beyond ridge to right. . . . Enemy fell back before us. At 8 p.m. heard result of cavalry charge, and at 8.45, all being quiet, returned to camp." This is the bare tale of the repulse of 9,000 Egyptians with 12 guns by a British force which they outnumbered by three to one.

In view of what followed, it is relevant to remark that, on Septem-

---

[1] Telegraphic dispatch, dated August 28th, 1882, from Major-General Gerald Graham to General Sir Garnet Wolseley, quoted in the *R.E. Journal*, Vol. 12, 1882, p. 214.

[2] Actually the force was astride of the canal, as General Graham admitted in a written dispatch of August 29th. See *R.E. Journal*, Vol. 12, 1882, p. 217.

ber 4th, Sir Garnet Wolseley wrote that the dispositions made by General Graham at the Battle of El Qassasin were all that they should have been, and that his steady advance upon the enemy, when the latter seemed about to drive his attack home, was well conceived and well executed.[1] Yet the writer of a leading article in a London newspaper heaped unmeasured censure on Graham, contending that his dispositions were faulty, and that they supported the current dogma that it was unwise to entrust commands to Engineer officers; he quoted the disaster at Isandhlwana in Zululand as an illustration of the danger to which Graham had exposed his men by advancing so far as El Qassasin. He had the impertinence also to assert that Graham was guilty of errors " which would have been discreditable to the youngest regimental officer." It is true that Graham risked much when he advanced to El Qassasin before concentrating his brigade and supports and without adequate cavalry and artillery. But who can hope to succeed in war unless he is prepared at times to take risks? By his rapid seizure of El Qassasin, Graham paved the way for the decisive victory of Tel el Kebir. It was alleged also that when Graham requested Drury Lowe to lead his cavalry against the enemy's left, he misled him by stating that " he was only just able to hold his own." This was denied emphatically by Graham; and it seems that the young cavalry officer, who delivered the verbal message, altered it to suit his own views on the situation. The British force at El Qassasin was never in serious danger.

Graham was ably defended by General Sir Lintorn Simmons in a speech delivered at Chatham after the end of the campaign.[2] " I have heard it said," remarked Sir Lintorn, " that General Graham neglected to cover his camp sufficiently by outposts; but those who criticize can scarcely have realized his position. His force at first was very small, and, knowing that he might be attacked by very superior numbers, he was compelled to keep his men ready for any emergency, fresh and full of fight. It would probably have required nearly one-third of his force to cover his camp completely, and his men would have been worn out with fatigue by excessive outpost duty. . . . I have also heard remarks from military men criticizing him for not having gone out to meet the enemy and for having allowed his camp to be shelled. I can only say that, with a very small force in an isolated position, it would have been an act of decidedly bad generalship if he had gone out to a distance to attack. What he did was to await the development of the enemy's attack, and then, having secured the co-operation of the cavalry, to make a counter-

[1] Dispatch dated September 4th, 1882, from General Sir Garnet Wolseley, quoted in the *R.E. Journal*, Vol. 12, 1882, p. 217.
[2] This speech, delivered by General Sir J. Lintorn Simmons, G.C.B., G.C.M.G., Col-Commandant R.E., on December 15th, 1882, at a dinner at Chatham to the officers of the Corps who had returned from Egypt, is quoted in the *R.E. Journal*, Vol. 13, 1883, pp. 19-22.

attack. The result was that, after he had made a serious impression and had driven them back for a mile or two, the cavalry completed their discomforture. . . . General Graham has proved that, like Sir Charles Felix Smith in Syria, Lord Napier in Abyssinia and Charles Gordon in China and Egypt, Engineer officers may be as fit for command as officers of any other branch of Her Majesty's service."

With this action at El Qassasin on August 28th, 1882, the first part of the campaign came to an end. A pause ensued in the military operations. The railway was damaged and blocked, and no locomotives were yet available. The troops were suffering from the heat. The army transport was defective, for the carts were found to be unsuitable, and there were few draught animals and pack mules and only 10 camels.[1] Although the Royal Navy was trying to maintain a service of boats on the Sweetwater Canal it was clear that the army could not advance until it was supplied by rail and that no such system could be organized until locomotives were obtained. Much depended, accordingly, on the energy of the 8th (Railway) Company, R.E., in the theatre of war, and on its sources of supply in Alexandria and England.

El Qassasin became a hive of industry. Stores and men were accumulated and all preparations made for a further advance. There was some desultory fighting, but only one real attack by the enemy. Arabi had begun to realize that if he intended to take the offensive he must do so before Wolseley could concentrate his entire force, so he launched Ali Fahmi Pasha against the 1st Division at El Qassasin on September 9th at the head of 17 battalions, 30 guns, several squadrons and some thousands of Bedouin.[2] The Egyptian attack was made from the west by the garrison of Tel el Kebir and from the north by a detachment from Es Salhiya. General Willis was nearly taken by surprise, but he soon repelled the enemy and drove them back towards Tel el Kebir. The 24th Field Company was engaged in this battle. Graham writes in his diary :— " Beginning to arrange my (troops), as on the 28th, when the Philistines are on us. Are they mad ? In five minutes my dispositions are made, and in twenty minutes my troops are out in line of battle. Heavy artillery fire from the enemy as before, but our guns advance with the infantry and before 9 a.m. the enemy are in full retreat. . . . Wolseley tells me he doesn't mean to let Arabi escape him next time ; that he means to smash him altogether and relies on *me* to do it. He doesn't mean him to escape into the delta where he can't get at him. I expect to have to hold him to his works by assaulting in front."

[1] Although Captain C. R. Conder, R.E., had procured an offer of 400 camels from local Arabs and had bought 10 animals on the spot, an Army Order was issued forbidding the purchase of camels. (See *Watson Pasha*, by Stanley Lane-Poole, p. 111.)
[2] Dispatch from General Sir Garnet Wolseley to the Secretary of State for War, dated September 10th, 1882, quoted in the *R.E. Journal*, Vol. 12, 1882, p. 234.

The Egyptian version of the skirmishes which preceded the battle on September 9th is entertaining. "Last evening," it runs,[1] "the Arabs of Sharkiyeh, together with 40 cavalry, advanced against the enemy. They fell in with the English outposts, opened fire and drove them back. At daybreak there advanced a force of the enemy composed of cavalry, infantry and artillery. After an hour's firing on both sides, the Arabs charged forward like lions, and with the greatest courage and bravery drove back the enemy in spite of superior numbers. They pressed them hard, killed about a hundred, and completely dispersed them, carrying off their cattle and about 500 metres of torpedo wire[2] and various instruments of war. Thanks be to Allah, no one on our side was hit." So much for the accuracy of the British rifle fire! The fanciful writer continues :— "On Wednesday last, a detachment of 70 Arabs and 40 cavalry advanced against the enemy. Shaeeb, the well-known horseman, rushed forward on an English sentry and killed him on the spot. Then he charged against the English soldiers and fired a number of bullets at them, shouting out 'Where are you going, Oh! English? Die, you pariah dogs!' Our horsemen then joined him, and charged like those only can charge who do not fear death. The enemy fell back and we surrounded them with a chain of skirmishers. The engagement then became general, including several regiments of cavalry and infantry, until our troops made a general charge and with shouts of victory, drove the enemy back to their tents killing 7 men and 8 horses. The evening was spent in songs of victory." Meanwhile, no doubt, the British mourned their remarkably heavy losses and listened to the sweet music.

The decisive battle at Tel el Kebir on September 13th, 1882, has received so much attention from military historians that it is unnecessary to recapitulate its details. As regards the position held by the Egyptians, it may be said that it was by nature the strongest which could be found between the Suez Canal and Cairo, and that its selection did credit to Arabi's engineers, several of whom had been trained in France. As a battlefield, Tel el Kebir offered one great advantage to the defenders—the bareness of the ground, which would hardly afford cover to a rabbit. The author explored this desolate waste in 1935. Viewed from the centre of the Egyptian front line, the country stretches away to north, east and west as a gently undulating surface of hard sand covered with small stones, falling rapidly to the south until the railway and Sweetwater Canal are reached. The Egyptian lines are still distinctly visible. A little coarse grass grows in some of the old ditches, and in a few hollows;

---

[1] Extracts from the Egyptian newspaper, *El Taif* (The Patrol), dated Sept. 9th, 1882, quoted in an article by Captain A. M. Mantell, R.E., appearing in the *R.E. Journal*, Vol. 13, 1883, p. 230.
[2] Ground cable of the Telegraph Troop, R.E.

but elsewhere not a tree, shrub nor any other form of vegetation breaks the deadly monotony of the barren landscape.

The position occupied by the enemy is shown on the accompanying sketch map of the battlefield. Arabi's engineers had laid out a front line (ABCDEFG), more than 4 miles in length, on the tableland of Tel el Kebir, down its slope to the railway and canal, and for a short distance beyond the canal. A breastwork or parapet was provided which, in some places, was as much as 6 feet high; and in front lay a ditch from 8 feet to 12 feet wide and from 5 feet to 9 feet deep, with vertical escarp and counterscarp. There were no obstacles of any sort in front of the position. It seems that the Egyptians pinned their faith to their parapet and ditch alone, which was unfortunate for them because much of their line was unfinished when attacked and it was too extended to be held properly. The line had a few salients strengthened by small redoubts, and some 1,100 yards in advance lay a polygonal redoubt (H) armed with 8 guns. At least 50 other guns were distributed along the front line. Some distance in rear of it was a second line of defence (KJL) about 2 miles in length, connected to the front line by a trench and parapet (JID) which joined the front line at a redoubt (D) forming the key of the position. The Sweetwater Canal was dammed (at F) and does not appear to have entered into the enemy's scheme of defence as the bridge at Tel el Kebir Village was unprotected. The front line south of the canal (FG), though indefinite, contained a few well-defended posts. From the canal northwards to Redoubt D, the works were strong and well finished, and numerous shelters had been provided behind them; but farther towards the north the works showed increasing haste in execution, and the most northerly section (AB) had hardly been begun. Considerable ingenuity was displayed by the enemy in revetting the interior slopes of their breastworks and batteries with coarse grass, and in building the breastworks with alternate layers of grass and sand. The method of construction is clearly visible to this day.[1] The Egyptian position was certainly formidable. Properly finished, and held by a strong, well-armed and determined garrison, it would have been almost impregnable.

Sir Garnet Wolseley decided to make a frontal attack at dawn, after a night march from El Qassasin. This was a bold stroke, but justified by the circumstances. Though only half as strong as the enemy in numbers, the British force at El Qassasin was superior to them in training and armament. It was essential that Wolseley should engage the Egyptians so closely that they could not retreat into more enclosed country, and that, to ensure this, he should not risk the delay of a flank march into the waterless desert to his right,

[1] Descriptions and plans of the defences at Tel el Kebir are given in articles entitled "The Lines of Tel el Kebir" in the *R.E. Journal*, Vol. XII, 1882, pp. 222 and 223 and "Some Egyptian Field Works" in the same journal, Vol. 13, 1883, pp. 8 and 9.

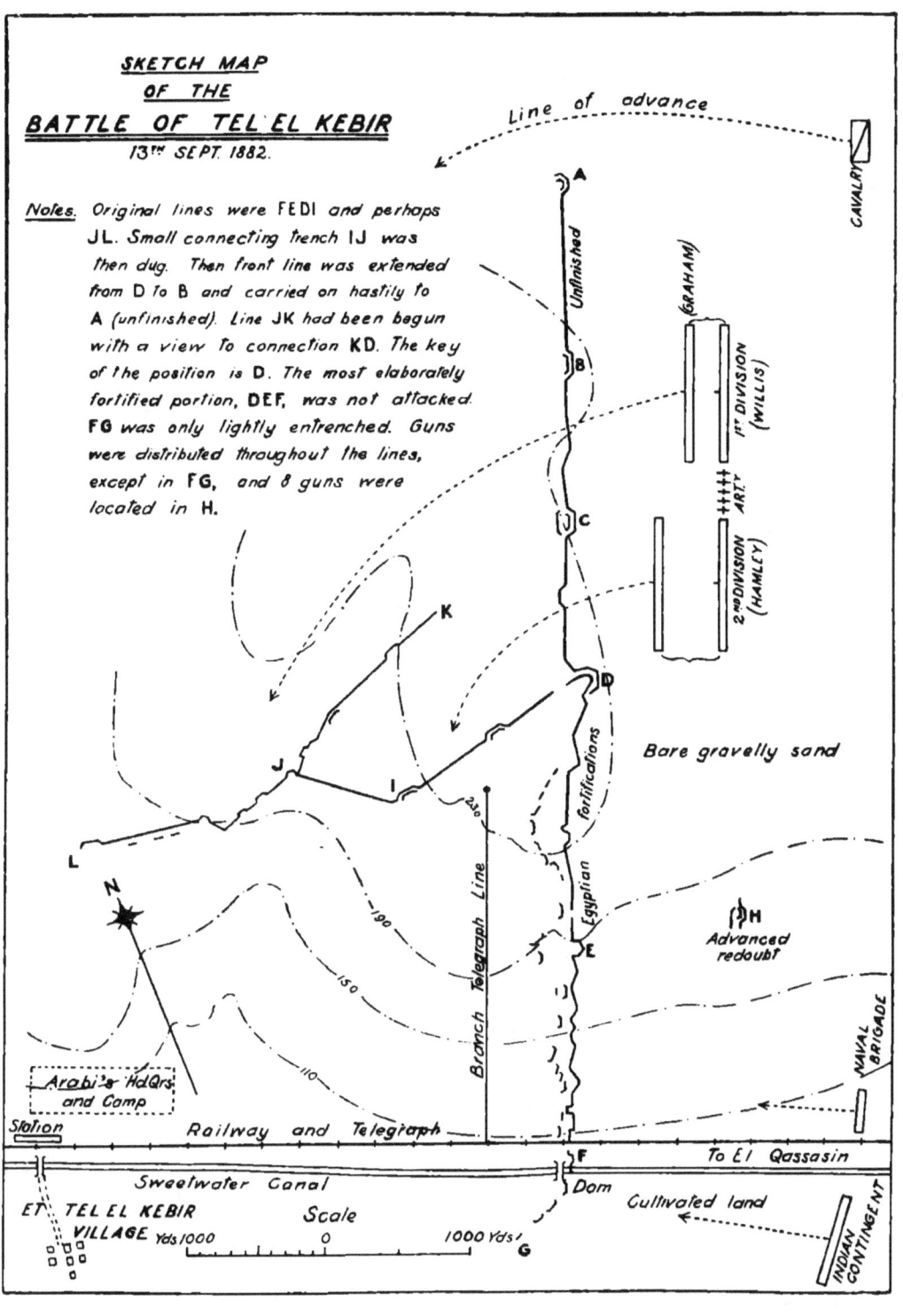

where early discovery might wreck his plans. He must stake all on a surprise and direct assault; and so he struck his camp on the evening of September 12th, leaving his fires burning and the site guarded by some troops under his Chief Engineer, Brigadier-General Nugent, and, at 1.30 a.m. on the 13th, began his celebrated march on Tel el Kebir, an operation executed with wonderful skill and precision.

The 1st and 2nd Divisions marched with the artillery between them, the 1st Division being on the right with Graham's 2nd Brigade leading. The cavalry guarded the right flank. On the extreme left, mostly to the south of the Sweetwater Canal, were the Naval Brigade and the Indian Contingent, which started later than the remainder of the force to avoid giving the alarm to any of the enemy who might be lurking in the villages near the canal. The night being dark, several halts were necessary to correct the formation and direction of the advance; but at early dawn the Egyptian line was approached, and the first assault was delivered by the Highland (1st) Brigade of the 2nd Division, to the north of Redoubt D, against the centre of the line. This brigade reached the enemy's position before Graham's brigade to its north, because the line of march from El Qassasin diverged slightly towards the north and consequently was not exactly perpendicular to the position. The British troops struck the fortifications far north of the canal, and thereby not only avoided the strongest part of them (DEF), but also passed, in ignorance even of its existence, the advanced redoubt which might have disorganized their attack.

Warned too late by their sentries, Arabi's troops manned their parapets and ditches, those in the ditches being often unable to fire except into the air. At 5 a.m., under a hail of bullets, the Highlanders swept through and over them, bayoneting every man who stood his ground, and then, bearing to the left, pushed on to the interior retrenchments and towards the second line. Ten minutes later, Graham carried with a rush the portion of the line lying farther to the north, leading his men in person across the ditch, and then turning also, swept down behind the second line, while the cavalry, on the extreme right, galloped round the north of the position to take up the pursuit. Some of the enemy showed real courage, particularly the Sudanese soldiers who fought grimly to the end; but the most remarkable feature of this brief struggle was the speed with which the bulk of the enemy fled after they met the British bayonets. They faded away and disappeared as miraculously as the desert mirages which they knew so well. A survivor, on reaching his village, described how " the nimble foreigners had scampered over the trenches into the very heart of the camp," adding that Satan must have aided them, for there was no possibility of resistance. " The English," said he, " must already be in Cairo, for they are nimble cunning dogs and sons of dogs."

The Indian Contingent and the Naval Brigade met with little resistance in the neighbourhood of the Sweetwater Canal, for the main attack had succeeded before they became closely engaged. After General Macpherson had ordered his troops to cease fire and charge, Lieutenant J. Burn-Murdoch, R.E., was the first to enter the Egyptian lines in this area. Galloping alone for a distance of nearly 400 yards towards two pits from which guns were about to fire with shrapnel on the attacking Seaforths, he killed the officer in command and drove the crews from their weapons.[1] Wolseley next proceeded to concentrate his troops at Tel el Kebir, preparatory to advancing on Cairo. Meanwhile, the cavalry, under General Drury Lowe, started in pursuit, and were soon followed by the infantry, with the exception of Graham's brigade, which remained for a time at Tel el Kebir. The primary object of the expedition had been accomplished. Arabi's army, of more than 25,000 men, had been defeated and dispersed, and nearly 2,000 Egyptians lay dead on the field of battle, while the total British loss in killed and wounded was only 459 officers and men.[2] Arabi himself was a discredited fugitive, and the rebellion was broken. The brunt of the fighting, as Sir Garnet Wolseley remarked, had fallen to the lot of General Graham, and it could not have been in better hands. In due course the gallant leader of the 2nd Brigade was made a K.C.B. and received the thanks of both Houses of Parliament.

The rapid success which attended Sir Garnet Wolseley's advance from the Suez Canal was attained partly through the strenuous efforts of his technical units, among which the 8th (Railway) Company, R.E., and the Telegraph and Pontoon Troops, R.E., deserve special mention. They transported supplies and food to the fighting forces, and kept them in close contact, and no story of the campaign would be complete without some reference to their work. These units helped to create and operate the intricate system which maintained Wolseley's army in the field.

Prior to the campaign of 1882 there was no Railway unit of the Royal Engineers, but this deficiency was remedied in that year by the Inspector-General of Fortifications, Colonel (afterwards General) Sir Andrew Clarke, K.C.M.G., C.B., C.I.E., late R.E.,[3] who organized a military railway corps to take over the abandoned Egyptian rail-

---

[1] For this gallant act, Burn-Murdoch was strongly recommended for the Victoria Cross by Colonel James Browne, C.R.E., Indian Contingent, but he did not receive it. Though essentially a fighting soldier, he spent the final years of his service on railway work in India. Burn-Murdoch was, perhaps, the only bearded officer in the Army. He had special permission to wear a beard, because of some weakness of the throat which manifested itself during the 2nd Afghan War, and he did so until his death in 1909.

[2] A full account of the operations at Tel el Kebir is given in a dispatch from General Sir Garnet Wolseley, dated Sept. 16th, 1882, quoted in the *R.E. Journal*, Vol. 12, 1882, pp. 234, 235.

[3] The career of Sir Andrew Clarke is described in a volume entitled *The Life of General Sir Andrew Clarke, G.C.M.G., C.B., C.I.E., Colonel Commandant R.E.*, by Colonel R. H. Vetch, C.B., late R.E.

THE BATTLEFIELD OF TEL EL KEBIR.
Showing the existing remains of the Egyptian front line.

[*Photo by the Author.*]

ways and repair the line from the base at Ismailia. He secured the services of Major W. A. J. Wallace, R.E., Manager of the Northern Bengal Railway, who happened to be home on leave from India, as Director of Railways, and put the 8th Field Company, commanded by Captain Sydney Smith, R.E., at his disposal. Permission was obtained from two British railway companies for the 8th Company to work on their lines so that the men might learn as much as possible of traffic control, platelaying, signalling, engine-driving and other duties. The unit then became the " 8th (Railway) Company," and mechanics of all sorts were drafted into it. Rails, sleepers, points and other material for about 5 miles of line were collected, and also some passenger coaches, wagons, and four small tank-engines. On arrival in Egypt these locomotives proved to be too light for the traffic of the army[1] and it was necessary to increase their water capacity by adding tenders with water-tanks. A hand-pump was fitted in each tender to deliver extra water into the engine tank, and the assistant fireman, who was detailed to operate it, had literally to work his passage every trip. The 8th (Railway) Company reached Ismailia on August 23rd and having unloaded its portable stores and equipment as rapidly as possible, set to work to repair a few breaks in the railway and to clear a cutting near El Mahuta which had been blocked by the enemy. Traffic was started with some trucks hauled by horses,[2] and parties were sent to Suez to land one or two Egyptian locomotives from Alexandria and the four tank-engines from England.

On August 27th, amidst the cheers of the troops, the first of the Egyptian locomotives steamed in from Suez with Wallace on the footplate. Attached to it were several wagons carrying a half-company of Madras Sappers and Miners, with Colonel James Browne and Lieutenants C. H. Darling and J. Burn-Murdoch, R.E. An armoured truck, on which was mounted a field-gun manned by sailors, was also included in this train. Four days later, when the El Mahuta cutting had been cleared, a daily train service was started as far as El Qassasin, and at the same time two more locomotives reached Ismailia. Soon there were two trains daily; but they ran with much uncertainty. " To-day," writes Sydney Smith on September 2nd,[3] " Lieutenant Vidal took up the 7 a.m. train with Sir Garnet Wolseley and Staff on board; but on the return journey it came to a standstill about two miles west of Mahouta (El Mahuta) and Sir Garnet and Staff had to make a forced march into camp. I was in charge of the second train, and although we did our best, on

---

[1] It was feared that heavier locomotives could not be landed at Ismailia. Actually none were landed there, but all went to Suez.

[2] 180 tons of ammunition and provisions were conveyed to the front by horse traction before the locomotives arrived.

[3] Report by Captain Sydney Smith, R.E., included in an article, entitled " Diary of the Work Performed by the 8th Company, R.E., in Egypt," which appears in the *R.E. Journal*, Vol. 13, 1883, pp. 4–8.

meeting the other, to get both trains into Mahouta, we could only get within a mile of it, when the engine of my train gave in for want of water. This occurred about 9 p.m. We then walked into Mahouta and the Commissariat sent out five full water-carts. . . . At 1 a.m. Sergeant-Major Loxton appeared on a third engine, and between us we got the trains to Ismailia, arriving there at 6 a.m. on the 3rd."

The history of the railway operations during the early days of September, 1882, is made up of a series of small mishaps. Trains were derailed by sand piled on the line; locomotives broke down; the line was blocked; water was scarce and dirty; errors in traffic control arose through inexperience. Nevertheless, steady progress was made, and on September 5th, Lieutenant H. B. Willock, R.E., brought the four British locomotives from Suez to Ismailia. Three trains ran westwards on the 6th, four on the 7th, and five on the 11th, by which date the military railway corps had no less than nine locomotives. Shortly after the rout of the Egyptians on the 13th, Wallace, Ardagh, Sydney Smith and their men steamed into Tel el Kebir Railway Station on an armoured train, manned by sailors,[1] which was accompanied by a material train. The scene at the station was almost indescribable. Abandoned trains, full of the enemy's ammunition and stores, completely blocked the lines; the permanent way was strewn with dead and wounded; and British soldiers swarmed everywhere, almost mad for want of water. Preceded by Wallace on the " ironclad," Sydney Smith started as soon as possible for Zagazig with the material train, which then collided with a stray camel and suffered a partial derailment. However, Zagazig was reached after dawn on the 14th and was found to be in British hands together with five Egyptian trains and several locomotives. Shortly afterwards Major Wallace proceeded to Cairo to assume supreme charge of the Egyptian railway system. Captain Scott remained at Zagazig, Captain Sydney Smith operated the Ismailia-Zagazig section, and Lieutenants Vidal, Willock and Huleatt were employed on miscellaneous railway duties. Finally, on September 25th, the whole system was handed back to the Egyptian Government, and shortly afterwards the 8th (Railway) Company, R.E., sailed for England.

Rivalling in importance the work of the railway unit was that of " C " (Telegraph) Troop[2] commanded by Major Sir A. W. Mackworth,

---

[1] Two armoured trains were employed during the campaign in Egypt in 1882, one at Alexandria and the other on the Ismailia-Tel el Kebir line. Both were prepared and operated by the Royal Navy. Usually they carried 40-pdr. and 9-pdr. guns, and a few Gatling and Nordenfelt machine-guns. They were used chiefly in support of reconnoitring parties.

[2] " C " (Telegraph) Troop, R.E., was a composite unit formed from a former " C " Troop and two Postal Telegraph Companies (22nd and 34th) R.E. This amalgamation, for war purposes, was the result of the recommendations of a committee presided over by Lieut.-Colonel Richard Harrison, C.B., R.E., in 1881. (See *Report on the British Naval and Military Operations in Egypt*, 1882, by Lieut.-Commander C. F. Goodrich, U.S. Navy, pp. 266-269.)

Bart., R.E., and directed by Lieutenant-Colonel C. E. Webber, R.E., who was A.Q.M.G. for Telegraphy on Sir Garnet Wolseley's Staff. "C" Troop did not land at Ismailia until August 28th, when General Graham was already at El Qassasin, and for a time there was little need for field telegraphy because Wolseley's advance was along a route supplied with three permanent telegraph lines which had been damaged but not destroyed. These lines were repaired by the Troop, and, on the morning of September 1st, Mackworth and his subalterns (R. L. Hippisley, F. G. Bond and H. J. Foster) established telegraphic communication between Ismailia and El Qassasin, thus connecting Graham with Army-Headquarters.[1] Colonel Webber then assumed charge of the permanent lines, and Mackworth was free to devote himself to field telegraphy. R. W. Anstruther, another subaltern of the Troop, opened up the permanent telegraph line from Ismailia to Suez, and Bond was attached to the Cavalry Division with a small party of mounted telegraphists.

Communication was difficult and uncertain. At times there were heavy blocks in the telegraph lines and much impatience on the part of senders. Indeed, one senior officer complained bitterly that he had dispatched three simultaneous messages from Ismailia to El Qassasin, one by boat on the canal, the second by the railway, and the third by telegraph, and that they had arrived at their destination in precisely that order! But "C" Troop was not dismayed. It continued to work with unabated zeal and soon produced order out of chaos.

Field telegraphy is always interesting and often dangerous. During a reconnaissance from El Qassasin on September 8th, when Mackworth, Foster and Bond had paid out $3\frac{1}{2}$ miles of cable, the enemy appeared in force and Mackworth was ordered to cut the cable and retreat. This was done; but in the afternoon he and Foster rode out again with a few men and reeled up the cable to within 400 yards of the enemy's pickets, thus recovering more than 3 miles of valuable line. On the 9th, while the Egyptians were bombarding El Qassasin, a party of telegraphists under Corporal Chapple, R.E., worked steadily in their tent in spite of the shells bursting continually around them and sending splinters through the canvas. Just before dusk on the 12th, a detachment of "C" Troop under Corporal Elsmore, R.E., was employed under the direction of Major Thomas Fraser, R.E., to lay out a line of telegraph poles to give the direction for the advance of the Highland Brigade for a distance of over two miles for the proposed night march on Tel el Kebir. This was a very hazardous mission as the detachment might have been charged at any moment by Egyptian cavalry. While the march was in progress, "C" Troop laid a cable behind the left centre of the British force,

---

[1] Article entitled "The Field Telegraph Corps in Egypt" by Major Sir A. W. Mackworth, R.E., appearing in the *R.E. Journal*, Vol. 12, 1882, pp. 269–272.

and the Indian mule telegraph train, under Lieutenants J. E. Dickie and P. B. Baldwin, R.E., laid another cable behind the Indian Contingent, south of the Sweetwater Canal. The success of Wolseley's operations may be attributed largely to the efficiency of his telegraphic service, both British and Indian; and incidentally it may be remarked that this campaign in Egypt was the first in which Royal Engineers from both England and India fought alongside each other in what may be called a European expedition.

When the Egyptians had fled from the battlefield of Tel el Kebir, Colonel Webber galloped to the telegraph office at the railway station and found it in dire confusion. Arabi's clerks had escaped only ten minutes earlier, and the office was still redolent with their odour. He put the wires in order, intercepted some anxious inquiries from Egyptians at Cairo, and then returned to El Qassasin, where his telegraphers were working desperately with their faces and hands covered with flies. Meanwhile Mackworth had prolonged his cable at a good round trot for a distance of over three miles through the captured position, and had arrived at the railway station. Breaking his way into Arabi's saloon carriage, he established an office there and installed his telegraphers. Messages from Sir Garnet Wolseley, announcing the victory, were then handed to him for dispatch to Queen Victoria, the Secretary of State for War and others. The message to Her Majesty was sent off at 8.30 a.m. and a congratulatory reply was received at 9.15 a.m., this being the first occasion on which a British General was able to telegraph the news of his victory from the actual field of battle. The operator who had the honour of sending and receiving these messages was 2nd Corporal (now Q.M.S. retired) W. F. Seggie, R.E.

After Tel el Kebir, parties of "C" Troop advanced with other formations to Zagazig, Benha, Bilbeis, and finally to Cairo, taking over the Egyptian system as they went, and it is recorded that Lieutenant F. G. Bond, R.E., who was with the cavalry, seized the railway station office at Cairo with only three men. Disarming an Egyptian guard of 20 men, he placed one man as a sentry over them, appointed the second to guard the office, and set the third to telegraph a report to General Drury Lowe. With Cairo, and indeed the whole of Egypt, in British hands, the necessity for military operation of the permanent telegraph lines soon vanished, and "C" Troop duly handed over its work to native personnel and left the country.

There is little to record about doings of "A" (Pontoon) Troop, under Major R. J. Bond, R.E., which landed with "C" Troop on August 28th. As few bridges were needed, the equipment was used mostly for transporting supplies. The traffic on the Sweetwater Canal, by means of naval launches towing boats, was carried on under such difficulties, owing to the shallowness of the water and the remains of two dams, that it was necessary to supplement it by the pontoon rafts of " A " Troop,[1] towed by horses, and nearly 400 tons of stores were conveyed to the front on these rafts before the Battle of Tel el Kebir. Although four bridges were got in readiness to provide communication across the canal during the battle, they were not used because the drawbridge near the village of Tel el Kebir was found to be intact. The bridges accompanied the Indian Contingent in the advance, and one of them, a Blanchard's light infantry bridge, with Lieutenant A. E. Sandbach, R.E., in charge, arrived at the dam in the Egyptian front line within a few minutes of the rout of the defenders. Sandbach hauled his rafts over the dam without dismantling them, and those of the other bridges followed, after which the dam, and a barrier across the railway, were demolished by the 17th and 26th Field Companies, R.E., under Captain Elliott Wood and Major Bindon Blood respectively. A diary kept by Lieutenant J. L. Irvine, R.E., shows the trials which the Pontoon Troop had to endure during the advance from Ismailia. Sunken boats fouled the tow-lines, the rafts foundered under excessive loading or were damaged in negotiating the narrow passages through the dams, and the towing horses often took fright and bolted ; but the unit never failed to " deliver the goods," both literally and figuratively.

The Indian Contingent, under Major-General Sir Herbert Macpherson, V.C., K.C.B., must not be forgotten, for it performed an important, though minor, part in the operations leading up to the decisive battle at Tel el Kebir. Its Sapper units were very early in the field. " I " Company of the Queen's Own (Madras) Sappers and Miners, under Lieutenant W. D. Lindley, R.E., and accompanied by Major A. F. Hamilton, R.E., landed at Suez on August 1st, 1882, with a battalion of infantry. It was followed by " A " Company, under Lieutenant C. H. Darling, on August 23rd, and by a Telegraph section of " E " Company on September 3rd. Like the troops from England, the men of " I " Company wore their usual peace-time uniform, which included a blue serge tunic and black drill trousers. " A " Company, however, were more up-to-date in new khaki uniforms. Opinions differed about dress. While " I " Company complained of sweltering in the sun, " A " Company found that their khaki tunics felt very damp in the morning. The men of " I " Company carried their water in ordinary soda-water bottles covered with leather. " A " Company had copper water-bottles which they soon discarded in favour of Egyptian bottles made of block tin.

It is unfortunate that, though rewarded with a C.B., Colonel James Browne, C.S.I., late R.(B.)E., the famous " Buster " Browne of India, should have had little chance of earning particular distinction as C.R.E. of the Indian Contingent in 1882, for the duties of the

---

[1] " A " Troop had equipment for 100 yards of service pontoon bridge, 80 yards of Blanchard's infantry pontoon bridge, and 20 yards of trestle bridge, in addition to a few Berthon collapsible boats and some trussed baulks.

Contingent were too commonplace to attract special attention, excellently though they were performed. On August 21st half of "I" Company was sent from Suez to Es Shallufa (Chalouf) to stop a breach made by the enemy in the Sweetwater Canal, and afterwards both companies repaired the railway and telegraph lines. General Macpherson advanced without difficulty to Ismailia, but he was soon left with a comparatively small force under his immediate command because he was required to find guards for many posts on the Suez Canal and elsewhere, and most of his cavalry was attached to the British Cavalry Division. "A" and "I" Companies did not reach El Qassasin until September 11th. They took part in the Battle of Tel el Kebir, marched to Zagazig, and finally entrained for Cairo on September 22nd. There they remained until they returned to India in October. The Sappers and Miners from Madras maintained in Egypt the reputation for keenness and efficiency which their Corps had won in many oversea expeditions.[1]

Dramatic events occurred after the Egyptian defeat at Tel el Kebir on September 13th. Arabi and a few of his officers, who reached Cairo by train the same day, are said to have begun preparations for the burning of the city. Wolseley followed up his victory energetically. He selected two avenues of advance ; one along the railway to Zagazig, whence a double line through Benha, and a single line through Bilbeis, led to Cairo ; and a second along the Sweetwater Canal through Bilbeis and past El Khanka. The pursuit was carried out chiefly by the Cavalry Division under Major-General Drury Lowe, who pushed forward a brigade and some mounted infantry under Brigadier-General Wilkinson with Captain C. M. Watson, R.E., as Intelligence Officer.[2] Zagazig was seized in a dashing manner by a squadron of the 6th Bengal Cavalry accompanied by Lieutenant J. Burn-Murdoch, R.E.[3] The men arrived in driblets, as they had galloped for 5 miles on tired horses, and only one trooper was with Burn-Murdoch when he burst into the railway station. "It was very rough on old 'Rocket'," writes Burn-Murdoch,[4] "but he went in rare style, and we got in, tearing along as hard as we could, at about four o'clock. When in sight of the station, which is a great big junction, we saw some 6 engines under steam, getting ready to be off. One of them did get off before

---

[1] An account of the work executed by the Madras Sapper and Miner companies in Egypt is given in an article entitled "The Work of the Detachments of the Queen's Own Sappers and Miners in Egypt," by Major A. F. Hamilton, R.E., appearing in the *R.E. Journal*, Vol. 13, 1883, pp. 67–70.

[2] The pursuit is described in an article entitled "The Cavalry Advance upon Cairo," by Captain C. M. Watson, R.E., appearing in the *R.E. Journal*, Vol. 13, 1883, pp. 29, 30.

[3] General Macpherson sent Burn-Murdoch with the squadron to take charge of the trains which, he had heard, were loading up with retreating Egyptian troops at Zagazig.

[4] Extract from a letter from Lieut. J. Burn-Murdoch, R.E., dated Zagazig, September 15th, 1882, in the possession of the late Colonel P. R. Burn-Clerk-Rattray, C.B.E., late R.E.

we got in, but we nailed all the rest, although three of them were actually on the move. There was no resistance to speak of, a few revolver shots settling the business; but it was rare fun, and 8 locomotives and about 4 trains made up our bag. I then got hold of a train and ran back some 6 miles picking up the infantry who, as you may imagine, were pretty done." It is recorded that, when Burn-Murdoch entered Zagazig railway station he dashed after the leading train, shot the driver when he refused to stop, and leaped on to the footplate. This action had a most salutary effect. Drivers, firemen, guards and hundreds of Egyptian soldiers poured from the trains, and throwing away their arms and belongings, fled across country in a screaming mob. By dark, the entire Indian Contingent was concentrated in and around Zagazig, thanks largely to the timely assistance rendered to the exhausted infantry by Burn-Murdoch.

Wolseley was anxious to save Cairo from the fate which had befallen Alexandria, so he pushed his cavalry ahead with the utmost speed. Watson had orders to guide Wilkinson's brigade along the Sweetwater Canal to Bilbeis ; and having reached that town, on the afternoon of the 13th, without much opposition, he was sent forward with some mounted infantry to seize the railway station and the post and telegraph offices. General Drury Lowe soon joined the advanced troops at Bilbeis and moved thence on Cairo, striking across the desert on September 14th and approaching the suburb of Abbassia by way of the disused railway line from Suez. Both men and horses were exhausted and in no fit state to meet a sudden attack in force, but no enemy appeared.

It seems that the Egyptian garrison of Cairo had been divided into two parts : one, about 7,000 strong, at Abbassia : the other, perhaps 6,000 strong, in the fortified Citadel crowning a rocky eminence in the south-eastern corner of the city and in a fort on the frowning heights of Mokattam beyond it. Judged by the old Egyptian saying that he who holds Cairo holds Egypt, and he who holds the Citadel holds Cairo, it was almost certain that, once the population knew that the Citadel was in British hands, all resistance would collapse ; but before that end could be attained it might be necessary to drive Arabi's thousands from their strongly fortified positions. This was the problem which confronted the advancing cavalry vanguard as it neared Abbassia on September 14th. " Soon we saw the line of the Mokattam Hills, which rise sharply over the city of Cairo," writes Watson,[1] " and then gradually we could make out the dome and minarets of the mosque of Muhammad Ali in the Citadel. An hour more brought us within sight of the great barracks of Abbassia, situated in the desert two miles north-east of the city, around which we could see thousands of Egyptian soldiers. . . .

---

[1] Extracts from the diary of Captain C. M. Watson, R.E., quoted in *Watson Pasha*, by Stanley Lane-Poole, pp. 117, 118.

General Lowe ordered his force to advance by echelons from the left, making as great a show as possible. Then he halted the cavalry and sent Colonel Stewart forward to reconnoitre. Stewart took an escort of 50 men, and accompanied by the Brigade-Major, two other officers and myself, rode towards the barracks and saw an Egyptian squadron coming out to meet us, every man of whom had a white flag. The Abbassia garrison had decided to surrender and were determined to do it in good style ! "

Much relieved by this good fortune, General Lowe then summoned the Governor of Cairo, the Commandant of the Citadel and the Chief of Police, and informed them that the Citadel must be surrendered the same evening. They agreed, and at 8 p.m. Watson was ordered to take over the Citadel from the Egyptian garrison. With only two squadrons of the 4th Dragoon Guards and a party of mounted infantry—some 150 men in all—he skirted the city by the road which passes the Tombs of the Khalifs, and, guided by a few Egyptian officers, entered unopposed through a small gate called the Bab el Wazir. Riding in pitch darkness along a narrow street, and then up a broad road towards the Bab el Gedid or Main Gate of the Citadel, he halted his troops short of the gate and demanded admittance. The Bab el Gedid was held by a strong Egyptian guard, and it was evident that the Citadel had not been vacated, so Watson sent for the Commandant and ordered him peremptorily to parade his whole garrison, disarm them, and march them down to the Kasr el Nil Barracks in the lower part of Cairo, adding that he had brought a large British force to occupy the Citadel and that the keys of all the gates were to be handed over to him at once. The bluff succeeded, the keys were produced, and the Egyptian garrison of at least 4,000 men[1] assembled meekly in the open space lying between the mosques of Muhammad Ali and En Nasr ibn Kalaun in a fortified area outside the Inner Gate of the Citadel. As he was naturally anxious that the Egyptians should not see the weakness of his force, Watson halted his troopers on the road between the Main Gate and another called the Middle Gate, or Bab el Wastani, giving access to the open space already mentioned, and then sent a message to the Egyptians to lay down their arms, march out of the Middle Gate and, turning sharply to their left, proceed down a lane to an outer gate, called the Bab el Azab, at the foot of the hill near the Mahmudiya Mosque in the city. By insistence on this route he avoided actual contact with the enemy. For more than two hours the stream of dejected Egyptians poured from the Middle Gate, and it was midnight before the Dragoon Guards could emerge safely from the shadow of the Main Gate and file into the interior of the fortress.

" While watching the strange procession at the gate," writes

---

[1] Watson estimated the number at 6,000 men, but this was possibly an exaggeration.

Watson, " I thought over the question of the fort on the Mokattam Heights and considered how the Egyptian troops were to be got out of it. A happy thought struck me and I hailed an Egyptian officer on his way out of the Citadel and said I should be much obliged if he would go up to the fort, send the garrison to Kasr el Nil, lock the gate and bring me the keys. He came back in two hours with the keys." It is said that this officer subsequently put in a claim for the British medal! Watson locked all the gates of the Citadel and mounted guards over them; and then, having handed over charge to another British officer, who, incidentally, had to round up hundreds of prisoners released from the jail by the departing Egyptians, he concluded his amazing achievements by riding through the centre of the city, with one of the rebel officers, to report to General Lowe at Abbassia that the Citadel had been occupied without loss and that the population was quiet. The *London Gazette* of October 6th, 1882, assigned the exclusive credit for the capture of the Citadel, not to Watson, but to an officer who was not present at the surrender; indeed, Watson was not even mentioned in dispatches until the omission was rectified in a subsequent Gazette; so it is evident that the fog of war can extend on occasion into the sacred precincts of Whitehall itself.

The Citadel having been secured, the next step was to call upon Arabi to surrender. This he did unconditionally, accompanied by several of his senior officers. The submission of the Egyptian Army in Cairo was followed by other capitulations. On September 16th, Yakub Sami lowered his flag to Major-General Sir Evelyn Wood at Kafr el Dauwar, assuring him that he had always been faithful to the Khedive, and that Arabi was " simply a scoundrel and a monster" who would not listen to his loyal counsels. The garrisons of Abu Qir and Rosetta yielded without protest, and finally, on September 23rd, the Egyptians at Damietta laid down their arms. The last embers of the rebellion had been extinguished.

The arraignment of the ringleaders was naturally one of the first matters to engage the attention of the British and Khedivial Governments, and in addition, there were about 1,200 other political prisoners awaiting trial, some of whom were indicted on the most ludicrous charges, such as " dressing up dogs to imitate Sir Garnet Wolseley and then shooting at them!" However, the minor offences of dog-shooters and others were pardoned, and only the trial of the ringleaders was undertaken. Arabi was arraigned before a court martial which assembled under Raouf Pasha in Cairo on December 4th, 1882. On the President's right sat Major-General Sir Archibald Alison, and on his left that distinguished Royal Engineer, Colonel Sir Charles Wilson, who, as Judge-Advocate-General, was not a member of the court nor concerned in the prosecution or defence, but was there merely to see fair play. Wilson had the full confidence of all members of the tribunal and was frequently consulted by the eminent counsel on both sides. It soon became evident that most of the charges against Arabi could not be sustained, and Wilson reported that if there had been any abuses of the white flag, they had been unintentional, and further that there was no conclusive evidence to connect Arabi with either the massacres at Alexandria or the burning of the city. Nevertheless, as Arabi pleaded guilty to the charge of rebellion, he was condemned to death, the sentence being immediately commuted to one of exile for life, and the same formality was gone through on December 7th and 10th in the trials of his leading associates.

Sir Charles Wilson incurred some hostility through his attitude at the trials, the result of which, though damaging to the popularity and prestige of England, was perhaps the best solution of a difficult problem. Arabi might have prevented the massacres at Alexandria, but this was not sufficient ground for the infliction of the death penalty. It is a fine tribute to Wilson's perfect sense of justice that he performed his thankless task with so much impartiality. He was constantly accosted with the remark, "Well, when are you going to hang Arabi?"[1] Yet he clung to his high ideals, and it was principally through his efforts that Arabi escaped the scaffold and was exiled to Ceylon. There was no proof, said he, that the rebel leader was concerned in murder or massacre, but ample evidence, on the other hand, that he was humane and had tried to save the lives of Europeans. Wilson was a credit to his Corps—a man who did his duty without fear, favour or affection.

While Arabi was awaiting trial, Cairo was given over to festivities and ceremonies. The Khedive returned to the capital, reviewed the British and Indian troops, and distributed honours and rewards, both General Sir Garnet Wolseley and Admiral Sir Beauchamp Seymour receiving from the Sultan of Turkey the Osmanieh Order of the First Class. It is rumoured, however, that at the same time the Sultan bestowed this Order on his bootmaker in Constantinople, a *faux pas* which he attempted to justify by asserting that " after all, he was a very good bootmaker ; "[2] so perhaps Sir Garnet and Sir Beauchamp were not too highly flattered by the mark of foreign favour which was accorded to them. Both were created Peers of the United Kingdom, and each received a grant of £20,000. After the capture of Cairo the old Egyptian Army was disbanded, and the formation of a new Egyptian Army was taken in hand. The officer selected to command it was Major-General Sir Evelyn Wood, V.C., G.C.M.G., K.C.B., with the title of " Sirdar."[3] The army was to consist

---

[1] *The Life of Major-General Sir Charles Wilson, K.C.B., K.C.M.G., F.R.S.*, by Colonel Sir Charles M. Watson, K.C.M.G., C.B., late R.E. (1909), p. 219.

[2] *The Egyptian Campaigns, 1882–1899*, by Charles Royle, p. 199.

[3] It is generally believed that Sir Evelyn Wood was the first Sirdar of the Egyptian Army, but actually Colonel Valentine Baker held the appointment with the old Egyptian Army for a period of three weeks in 1881.

CAPTAIN KITCHENER JOINS THE NEW EGYPTIAN ARMY.

eventually of two brigades of infantry, each of four battalions, one regiment of cavalry, two horse and two camel batteries of artillery, and a camel corps of mounted infantry, and twenty-six British officers were posted originally to it.[1] These officers never held a rank lower than that of *Bimbashi* (Major), nor were they required to serve under Egyptian superiors. Whilst the new Egyptian Army was in process of formation, and for many years later, a British Army of Occupation was maintained in Egypt. At the end of 1882 this army contained 12,000 men; but every effort was made to reduce it, and in 1892 it had shrunk to 3,000 men. As a military force, its presence was then hardly needed; yet, as Sir Alfred Milner remarked,[2] it was still important as the outward and visible sign of the predominance of British influence and of the special interest taken by Great Britain in the affairs of Egypt.[3]

On March 17th, 1883, several Royal Engineers were appointed to the new Egyptian Army. These fortunate officers were Lieut.-Colonel T. Fraser, C.M.G., as Adjutant and Quarter-Master-General with the rank of Colonel; Major C. M. Watson as Surveyor-General, also with the rank of Colonel; Major H. C. Chermside, C.M.G., in command of an infantry battalion with the rank of Lieut.-Colonel; Lieutenant A. M. Mantell as a supernumerary officer with the rank of Major; and lastly, Captain Horatio Herbert Kitchener as second-in-command of a cavalry regiment with the rank of Major.[4] Thus the famous "K. of K." enters this history in the surprising rôle of a leader of light cavalry. He was determined to join the Egyptian service, and he succeeded. Whatever his deficiencies as a horseman, he was equal to any, and superior to most, in endurance, subtlety and courage. Commanding in presence, inscrutable in countenance, Kitchener was designed by Nature to impress his personality on the Eastern mind and to unravel its secrets. Already proficient in the Arabic language, and possessed seemingly of an inborn understanding of Arab mentality, he was soon to be in his element among the mounted tribes of the desert.

The means by which Kitchener obtained his appointment in the Egyptian Army are worthy of record. In June, 1882, while engaged in the survey of Cyprus, he telegraphed to Egypt for permission to join in any military operations which might be undertaken on the Nile. When the rebellion occurred he applied for and obtained a week's sick leave, which it was assumed would be spent in the island. Instead, he boarded the first ship bound for Alexandria and arrived in that port on the day of the fatal riot. He reported himself to

---

[1] Sir Evelyn Wood asked for only 22 British officers.
[2] *England in Egypt*, by Alfred Milner (1894), p. 36.
[3] The British connection with the Egyptian Army lasted until January 12th, 1937, when all British officers left that Service.
[4] "Occasional Notes," *R.E. Journal*, Vol. 13, 1883, pp. 88, 89.

Lieut.-Colonel A. B. Tulloch[1] on board the flagship of Admiral Sir Beauchamp Seymour, saying that he spoke Arabic well and asking whether he could be of any assistance. Tulloch enlisted him for an adventure ashore in which, disguised as Levantines, the two officers travelled by train to Zagazig and returned with notes and sketches of the enemy's dispositions and defences. During the bombardment, Kitchener was present in the Admiral's flagship, and when he missed his return boat to Cyprus, the Admiral telegraphed for an extension of his leave; but as the High Commissioner in Cyprus flatly refused to grant an extension, Kitchener was obliged to return to that island and to answer an accusation of being absent without leave. To the end of his life he maintained that he was justified in proceeding to Egypt because he was free to roam at will from end to end of Cyprus in the course of his survey work and an application for "leave of absence" could only mean permission to quit the island. By the end of 1882, the Survey of Cyprus was nearly finished, and General Sir Evelyn Wood, then in command of the newly formed Egyptian Army, telegraphed to Kitchener asking him to join it. Kitchener declined the invitation; but on the receipt of an offer of the post of second-in-command of an Egyptian cavalry regiment, he notified his acceptance and joined the Egyptian Army on January 4th, 1883.[2]

Perhaps the fact that 45 officers of the Corps, headed by Major-General Graham, V.C., C.B., sat down to dinner in Shepheard's Hotel on September 22nd, 1882,[3] may have suggested the establishment of a Royal Engineers Mess in Cairo. However that may be, it is recorded in August, 1883, that Major K. R. Todd, and Lieutenants Mantell, Tuke and Huleatt had started a Mess at the end of the central wing of the Kasr el Nil Barracks, looking across the Nile towards the Pyramids.[4] Another member soon joined them in the person of Major R. H. Williams, R.E., who, as a student of history and a lover of art, helped to make Egypt and its treasures interesting to the younger officers, and at the same time, by a mild despotism, to maintain the customary standards of smartness and discipline.[5] Thus the representatives of the Corps in Egypt settled

---

[1] Lieut.-Colonel A. B. Tulloch, Welsh Regiment, was Military Staff Officer to the Admiral Commander-in-Chief.

[2] This account is taken from *Life of Lord Kitchener*, by Sir George Arthur, Vol. I, pp. 47–50. A different story was often related by the late Major-General the Hon. E. J. Montagu-Stuart-Wortley, who stated that Kitchener came to see him and when told that there was no vacancy in the Egyptian Army produced papers showing his qualifications in Arabic and Turkish. According to Stuart-Wortley, not until these papers had secured from the Sirdar a promise of an appointment did Kitchener reveal that he was in trouble at Cyprus. In spite of the fact that he was present at the bombardment of Alexandria and carried out Intelligence work ashore, Kitchener was deemed to be ineligible for the Egyptian medal of 1882.

[3] "Occasional Notes," *R.E. Journal*, Vol. 12, 1882, p. 252.

[4] "Occasional Notes," *R.E. Journal*, Vol. 13, 1883, p. 194.

[5] Memoir of Major R. H. Williams, R.E., by Lieut.-General Sir Henry M. Lawson, K.C.B., Col. Commandant R.E., appearing in the *R.E. Journal*, Vol. XVIII, 1929, pp. 107–124.

down as a small but happy coterie with their headquarters in Cairo. The palatial mess-room on the first floor of the Kasr el Nil Barracks, now an officer's quarter, is well worth a visit. What tales it could tell of famous Engineers of the past, if its massive walls could speak! But time has carried most of them away as inexorably as the ancient Nile glides smoothly to its death in the Mediterranean sands.

Viewed in perspective the most remarkable feature of the Egyptian campaign of 1882 is the rapidity with which it was conducted. Only 66 days elapsed between the firing of the first gun at Alexandria and the occupation of Cairo, and the operations between Ismailia and the capital occupied less than four weeks. The Royal Engineers who were privileged to take part in it were called upon to do much heavy work, certainly not of an attractive, much less of a brilliant, nature. Often they laboured under a hot sun, hungry, thirsty and with inadequate material and apparatus; but it is to the credit of Brigadier-General Nugent and his British and Indian officers and men that they turned their limited resources to the best account and so enabled Sir Garnet Wolseley to secure a speedy victory.

DEPARTURE FROM SUEZ.
[*From " The Route of the Overland Mail to India."*]

CHAPTER III.

OPERATIONS ON THE RED SEA LITTORAL.

WHILE Arabi was undermining the loyalty of the Egyptian Army in 1881, there were ominous signs of rebellion in the Sudan, where a religious enthusiast, named Muhammad Ahmed, had proclaimed himself the long-expected Mahdi with a divine mission to reform Islam and destroy all infidels. Repeated attempts to subdue him were made by the Egyptian Governors-General of the Sudan, but these were usually attended by failure and heavy loss, and the Mahdi's following swelled in proportion to his success. At length, in October, 1882, the Governor-General in Khartoum called for large reinforcements, and as the British Government had no desire to undertake any responsibility in the far south, the Egyptian Government was obliged to re-enlist some 10,000 of Arabi's officers and men and to send them by detachments to Suakin on the Red Sea coast and thence across the desert to Berber on the Nile These troops were little more than an armed mob, sullen, badly led, and unable to cope with the fanatical followers of the Mahdi. Failure crowded on failure, and it seemed that the Sudan might be lost unless better leadership were secured, so the Egyptian Government engaged the services of Colonel W. Hicks, a retired officer of the Indian Army who was prepared to take a risk, and sent him with a European staff to the Sudan, where he assumed supreme military command in July, 1883. Two months later, Hicks marched into the Kordofan desert at the head of 10,000 men, and in November encountered a greatly superior force near El Obeid and was utterly destroyed. The panic-stricken Egyptian soldiers were butchered by the fierce dervishes. A few Sudanese in the Egyptian service fought bravely till they fell, and the Europeans charged into the masses of the enemy and so perished to a man. " What can be more melancholy," writes Major F. R. Wingate,[1] " than the history of Hicks' army, collected together in chains from the defeated and disbanded army of Arabi, led into a country they ever regarded as a living grave, by officers they had never seen before, attacked on all sides and massacred ? " Through the annihilation of this army all the country south of Khartoum lay at the Mahdi's mercy, and the capital itself was in deadly peril.

When news of this disaster reached England, the British Government advised the Khedive to abandon all territory south of Aswan

[1] *Mahdiism and the Egyptian Sudan,* by Major F. R. Wingate, D.S.O., R.A., p. 237.

(Assouan), or at least of Wadi Halfa ; but this was most unpalatable to the Egyptian Government who promptly applied to the Porte for a contingent of 10,000 Turkish troops to be sent to Suakin and were as promptly informed that the British Government would not agree to this proposal. It was clear, however, that Great Britain could not abstain for long from armed intervention to guard the frontiers of Egypt, and that, if she did nothing, Turkey might regain her former ascendancy. News had reached Suakin in August, 1883, that emissaries of the Mahdi were raising the tribes around Sinkat, an important town lying some 40 miles inland though more than 60 miles distant from Suakin by road. At their head was a man known as Osman Digna who figures so conspicuously in the operations on the Red Sea littoral that he calls for special notice.

According to Mr. H. C. Jackson,[1] the ancestors of Osman Digna were Kurds from Diabekr who came to Suakin in the sixteenth century. There they settled and intermarried with the Hadendowa and Arteiga tribes. Osman himself was born in Suakin about the year 1840 and was the offspring of a Turk or Levantine and a Hadendowa woman, so that he had much in common with the tribesmen—the " fuzzy-wuzzies " of Kipling's stories. His brothers Ali and Omar, and his cousin Ahmed, were ostensibly honest merchants plying their trade between Suakin and the Arabian coast, but actually they were slave-dealers, in which nefarious occupation they were joined by Osman. As the travelling partner, Osman Digna journeyed to all parts of the Sudan and across the Red Sea, and soon came under the influence of the Mahdi ; and when his slave-dealing business suffered through the interference of British warships, he was particularly ready to throw in his lot with the new prophet. This he did to such good purpose that eventually almost all the tribes in the Eastern Sudan went over to him, and he was acknowledged as an Emir to the Mahdi. Rarely have British troops encountered such an adversary. He was a veritable will-o'-the-wisp, here to-day and gone to-morrow. His followers might be killed or captured ; but Osman himself remained at large until he had kept the Red Sea littoral in a state of ferment for years. There can be little doubt that his operations in that area during 1884 went far to prevent the rescue of Charles Gordon, the hero of Khartoum.

In October, 1883, Osman Digna invested Sinkat, moved down to Tamanieb in the direction of Suakin, and then besieged Tokar, a town which lies 17 miles south of the seaport of Trinkitat ;[2] and on

---

[1] *Osman Digna*, by H. C. Jackson, p. 22. This book gives the full history of Osman Digna and is a valuable commentary on the civil and military history of the Red Sea littoral. The writer of " Occasional Notes," in the *R.E. Journal*, Vol. 17, 1887, p. 135, states that Osman Digna was a Frenchman, Georges Vinet, born at Rouen and brought by his mother to Egypt, where she married a merchant named Osman Digna who bestowed his name on young Vinet, but the facts ascertained by experts disprove this version of Osman's origin.

[2] The *Sketch Map of the Suakin District in* 1885, which is included in this chapter, shows the positions of all places which are mentioned.

November 6th he cut to pieces an Egyptian force sent to the relief of Tokar, among the killed being Captain Moncrieff, R.N., the British Consul at Suakin. Again, on December 2nd, he surrounded and annihilated a small Egyptian force near Tamanieb. Information having been received in Cairo that Osman Digna had concentrated 7,000 men on the Tamanieb road, that Sinkat was encircled by a further 11,000 men, and that 3,000 rebels were at Tokar, the Egyptian Government were at their wits' end to provide reinforcements sufficient to deal with the critical situation which had arisen; but finally they appointed Major-General Valentine Baker, head of the Egyptian Gendarmerie, to raise a force of 4,000 men and take it to Suakin. Valentine Baker, a brother of Sir Samuel Baker,[1] was an experienced campaigner of the Kaffir and Crimean Wars, and he could have had little liking for the prospect before him. However, he collected a staff of 8 British officers, voyaged with his troops to Suakin and farther southwards to Trinkitat, and, on February 4th, 1884, marched out at the head of a rabble of policemen, *fellaheen* and the riff-raff of Cairo and Alexandria to encounter the warlike Sudanese tribesmen of Osman Digna. A battle ensued near the village of Et Teb.[2] The Sudanese displayed the most reckless bravery: the Egyptians, the most craven cowardice. The unwieldy Egyptian square was soon broken, and the enemy swarmed in. As for the Egyptian cavalry, they bolted at the first sight of their foes. Paralysed by fear the infantry threw away their arms and were cut down or stabbed as they ran, nor did the remnants stop until they reached Fort Baker, an outwork of Trinkitat. Though General Baker survived, almost all his officers and no less than 2,400 of his men were killed, and this by a Sudanese force of at most 1,200 tribesmen.

Small wonder that a decision was reached at last that a British force must be sent to defend Suakin, to relieve Tokar, and to crush Osman Digna before he could add the entire Red Sea littoral to the Mahdi's dominions. The prosperity and safety of the administration of the Sudan demanded that a railway should be constructed from the Red Sea to the Nile, and if Suakin were lost, this project must be abandoned, for in 1884 Suakin was the only suitable terminal port. It is true that while Lieutenants C. M. Watson and W. H. Chippindall, R.E., were voyaging down the Red Sea to Suakin in September, 1874, on their way to join Gordon in the distant Equatorial Province beyond Khartoum, Watson was impressed by the advantages of a certain creek which they passed. He wrote in his diary:—[3] "Changed course and stood in for shore to pass reef

---

[1] The explorer who preceded Gordon as Governor of the Equatorial Province on the Upper Nile. (See *Sir Samuel Baker: A Memoir*, by T. Douglas Murray and A. Silva White.)

[2] Et Teb appears as "El Teb" in many histories.

[3] *Watson Pasha*, by Stanley Lane-Poole, pp. 46, 47.

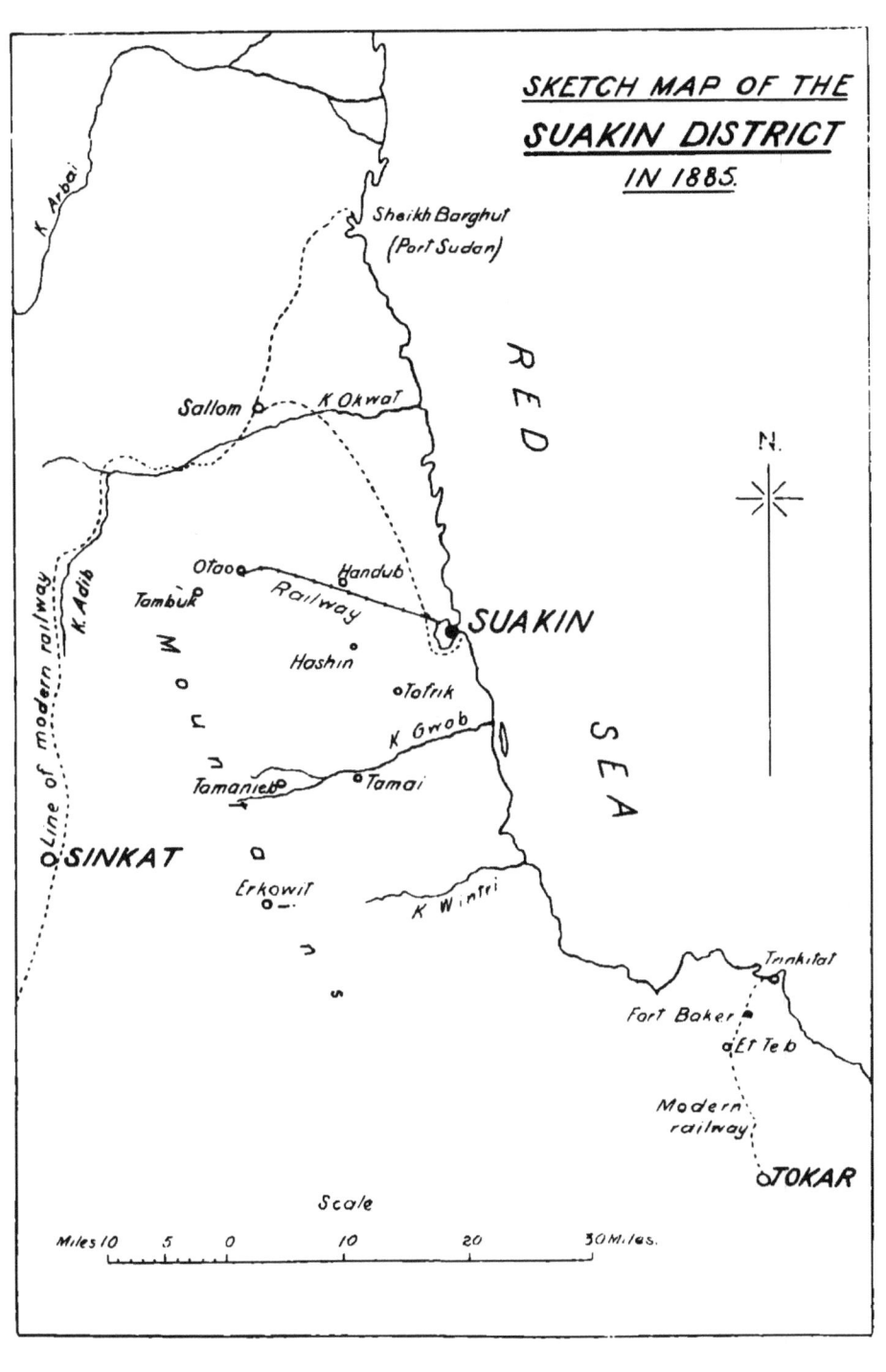

EXPEDITION TO TRINKITAT AND TOKAR UNDER GENERAL GRAHAM.

opposite Sheikh Barud (or Barghut), a port about 30 miles north of Suakin which appears to be a far better harbour than the latter. If a railway is ever made from the Sudan to the Red Sea, it might take its place. It is easier to make, and there is plenty of good anchorage in from 12 to 16 fathoms. . . . Talked to Captain (of the *Hodeida*) about Sheikh Barud, where there is plenty of room for large ships and easy access, night and day, if lighthouses were built ; whereas the harbour of Suakin is small, no water, and impossible to make at night. Pilots think Sheikh Barud (Barghut) the best harbour on the coast. No town there, and no use made of it at present." Nothing, however, was done to develop Sheikh Barghut until the matter was taken up in 1903 by a most distinguished Governor-General of the Sudan, now General Sir Reginald Wingate, Bart., G.C.B., G.C.V.O., G.B.E., K.C.M.G., D.S.O. To him belongs the chief credit for the metamorphosis of silent Sheikh Barghut into thriving Port Sudan. The story of that remarkable achievement appears in a subsequent chapter. For the present it is sufficient to state that, in 1884, Suakin was strategically, economically and politically of the first importance, and that England was forced to intervene to save it from the Mahdi's hordes. When Sinkat fell, Gordon was at Berber on his journey up the Nile to Khartoum as Governor-General of the Sudan, charged with the tasks of extricating the Egyptian garrisons and establishing a settled government.[1] The success of his mission was bound up in the question of prestige, and nothing could be more certain than that all prestige would be lost should Osman Digna become undisputed lord of the Red Sea littoral.

On receipt of the news of the fall of Sinkat, following closely on the disasters to Hicks and Baker, the British Government telegraphed to Lieut.-General Sir Frederick Stephenson, then commanding the Egyptian Army of Occupation, instructing him to organize and dispatch an expedition against Osman Digna for the relief of Tokar. The command of the force was to be entrusted to Major-General Sir Gerald Graham, V.C., K.C.B., late R.E., who was then on his way down the Nile after saying good-bye to Gordon. Graham left Cairo on February 17th, 1884. He reached Suakin on the 22nd and Trinkitat on the 23rd, and by February 25th had landed the greater part of his force and had learnt that Tokar was already in the hands of his enemies. With the fall of Tokar the chief incentive of the expedition was removed, but it was considered advisable to advance as far as Et Teb to protect any fugitives and to bury the bodies of the British officers lying exposed and mutilated on the battlefield. Sir Gerald Graham's command consisted of two brigades of British infantry, under Major-General Sir Redvers Buller, V.C., and Major-General Davis respectively, and, in addition, the 10th and 19th Hussars, two batteries of light artillery, a detachment of mounted

---
[1] *Gordon and the Sudan*, by Dr. Bernard M. Allen, p. 257.

infantry, and the 26th Field Company, R.E., under Major K. R. Todd, with Captain J. F. Dorward and Lieutenants H. M. Lawson, E. M. Burton and M. L. Tuke, R.E. The force numbered about 4,000 men with eight 7-pounder guns and six Gatling machine-guns. Attached to the staff were Lieut.-Colonel J. C. Ardagh, C.B., R.E., as C.R.E. and Chief Intelligence Officer, and Major Elliott Wood, R.E., and Captain A. O. Green, R.E., as Intelligence Officers.

Describing the voyage southwards to Trinkitat, Green remarks:—[1] " As we slowly approached Suakin on February 19th, all were much concerned for the first news we should receive on our arrival. Had Tokar yet fallen ? All we could see of Suakin was its collection of white buildings surrounded by a sandy arid waste, backed up by a distant range of dry and parched mountains. After keeping well in-shore between the coast and its reefs for some 20 miles we headed seawards through a narrow passage, as before reaching Trinkitat the water shoals to three fathoms. About 4 p.m. we changed our course and steered direct for Trinkitat ; but some four miles from its landing, the water shallowed so rapidly, and the reefs became so numerous, that we anchored for the night and sent out steam launches to take soundings." The difficulties of disembarking any large body of troops on this coast are formidable. The western littoral of the Red Sea is very low—a plateau of coral, slightly elevated above the sea in some parts and in others thinly covered by sand. Fringing the shore are submerged coral shelves with outlying reefs which have from two to ten feet of water over them and drop suddenly to great depths. There are many natural inlets, but most of them are small and useless for shipping. A plain from ten to twenty miles in width rises at a gentle slope from the coast to the foot of the rugged mountains which separate the littoral from the Nile basin ; its surface near the sea is almost bare for a mile inland, where stunted bushes are met with, at first in scattered tufts and then in larger numbers. Between Trinkitat and Tokar the bush is mostly a species of tamarisk, while in the plain of Suakin it is thorny mimosa admirably adapted for the formation of *zaribas*. There are no roads in this desert region ; and except during the rainy season, when the mountain gorges or *khors* empty their floods on to the thirsty plain, there is no water other than in the wells of a few oases. Life is hard on the Red Sea coast, and campaigning is still harder.

The picturesque town of Suakin,[2] viewed from the mainland,

[1] " From Cairo to Trinkitat with the Suakin Field Force," by Captain A. O. Green, R.E., appearing in the *R.E. Journal*, Vol. 14, 1884, pp. 75–76 and 99–102.

[2] According to an ancient legend, Suakin was founded by seven beautiful slave-girls (*Sua-gin*) ; but, however that may be, it was certainly used as a port by the Egyptians, and later by the Ptolemies in 250 B.C. It came under the successive control of the Romans, Mamelukes, Arabs and Turks, and in 1865 it was bought from the Turks by the Egyptian Government, together with the more southerly port of Massawa, which is now in Italian Eritrea.

resembles a pearl set in a sapphire ring. The dazzling whiteness of this island city is accentuated by the deep blue of the lagoon in which it stands. Nearer acquaintance dispels much of its glamour, for the streets are narrow and some of the houses dilapidated, but nevertheless Suakin at sunset is a sight not easily forgotten. Actually there are two islands in the lagoon or harbour, the town being situated on the southern island and covering every inch of it. The northern is known as Quarantine (or Condenser) Island. On the mainland is the suburb of El Geif (El Kaff), connected to Suakin Island by a causeway. The harbour is very secure, though with a narrow and dangerous entrance between coral reefs. In 1884 it was capable of accommodating the transports of an expedition of considerable size ; but the growth of the reefs, and the increase in the tonnage of ships, have since reduced its utility. Suakin is now a dying city. Though it presents a brave face to the world, it is being killed by Port Sudan. Unutterable peace and uncanny quiet pervade its once busy thoroughfares Its days are uneventful. Its short twilights deepen into tranquil nights.

> " Here while the still evening falls
> And the grey light grows less,
> Peace builds within the shadowy walls
> Of ancient quietness."

On the arrival of Graham's expedition at Trinkitat in February, 1884, the chief problems for the Engineers were to provide means for landing the troops and stores and to arrange for a supply of fresh water. Assisted by the Royal Navy, the 26th Field Company set to work to build piers, and afterwards this unit constructed troughs and tanks to hold the 13,000 gallons of water which were needed daily for the men and animals. All fresh water was obtained from the condensing machinery of the troopships. Not a drop was available on land. Two battalions struggled across 3 miles of morass to Fort Baker, which Lieutenant H. M. Lawson, R.E., put in a state of defence. The fort was garrisoned by four companies, and Major Elliott Wood, R.E., laid a brushwood causeway between it and Trinkitat. On February 28th, Graham concentrated his striking force at the fort.

At dawn on February 29th, the British advanced in square formation, officers in the centre, guns and Gatlings at the corners, cavalry and mounted infantry thrown out to the front and flanks and guarding the rear. No transport was taken. The route was somewhat to the left of the site of Baker's defeat, but the cavalry scouts on the right flank were obliged to traverse that area. The air was polluted with the smell of decomposed bodies which lay in heaps, stripped and savagely mutilated, on the spot where Baker's square had been destroyed. The enemy were found to be entrenched on the left front, their defences consisting of shallow earthworks facing west by north and defended on the south-west side by two small guns and a howitzer captured from Baker. Towards the north-east side was another battery of two guns, two howitzers and a Gatling, and half-way between the batteries a disused building prepared for defence. Large rifle-pits were scattered around the position, behind which lay the village and wells of Et Teb. At 11.0 a.m., having approached the left front of the enemy's position, Graham determined to turn that flank and marched farther to his right under a heavy fire; then, after his artillery had silenced the first hostile battery, he changed front to his left, stormed the enemy's left flank, carried the entrenchments in gallant style, and turned the captured guns of the first battery on to those of the second. The fighting was bitter and hand-to-hand. For a time the defenders of the rifle-pits and the solitary building clung to their positions with desperate energy, asking and receiving no quarter. The British cavalry executed a gallant charge and suffered severely, but by 2 p.m. the whole position was taken and the Sudanese were streaming away towards Tokar. Out of a total strength of perhaps 6,000 men the enemy lost over 2,000 in killed alone as compared with the British casualties of 34 killed and 155 wounded, among the latter being Captain A. O. Green, R.E. During the attack the 26th Field Company was inside the square in rear of the Gordon Highlanders who formed the front face.

The victory at Et Teb went far to wipe out the disgrace of Baker's failure, and Baker himself was there to share in it. Many and bloody are the tales of this battle. It was almost impossible to take prisoners because the enemy's wounded and dying, expecting torture and mutilation, attempted to kill all who approached them. Early in the battle a lone warrior, spear in hand, hurled himself against our square. With a mighty leap he cleared the front rank only to be caught adroitly on the bayonet of a soldier behind. "How's that, sir?" said the man, turning to his officer. "Well caught," replied the latter. The Sudanese were unspeakably cruel to our wounded and it was necessary to punish them; but their extraordinary bravery called forth the highest admiration.

After the battle, the 26th Field Company built a small redoubt for a temporary garrison at Et Teb and helped to draw water from the wells, and on March 1st the unit accompanied General Graham and the main body in an advance to Tokar, which had been abandoned by the enemy. The troops remained for 3 days at Tokar and got back to Trinkitat on March 5th. By March 9th, Graham had vacated Trinkitat and had concentrated his force at Suakin, where the 26th Field Company occupied themselves in building piers. On the same day, Graham sent the Black Watch to occupy a *zariba* about eight miles distant on the road to Sinkat; but before doing

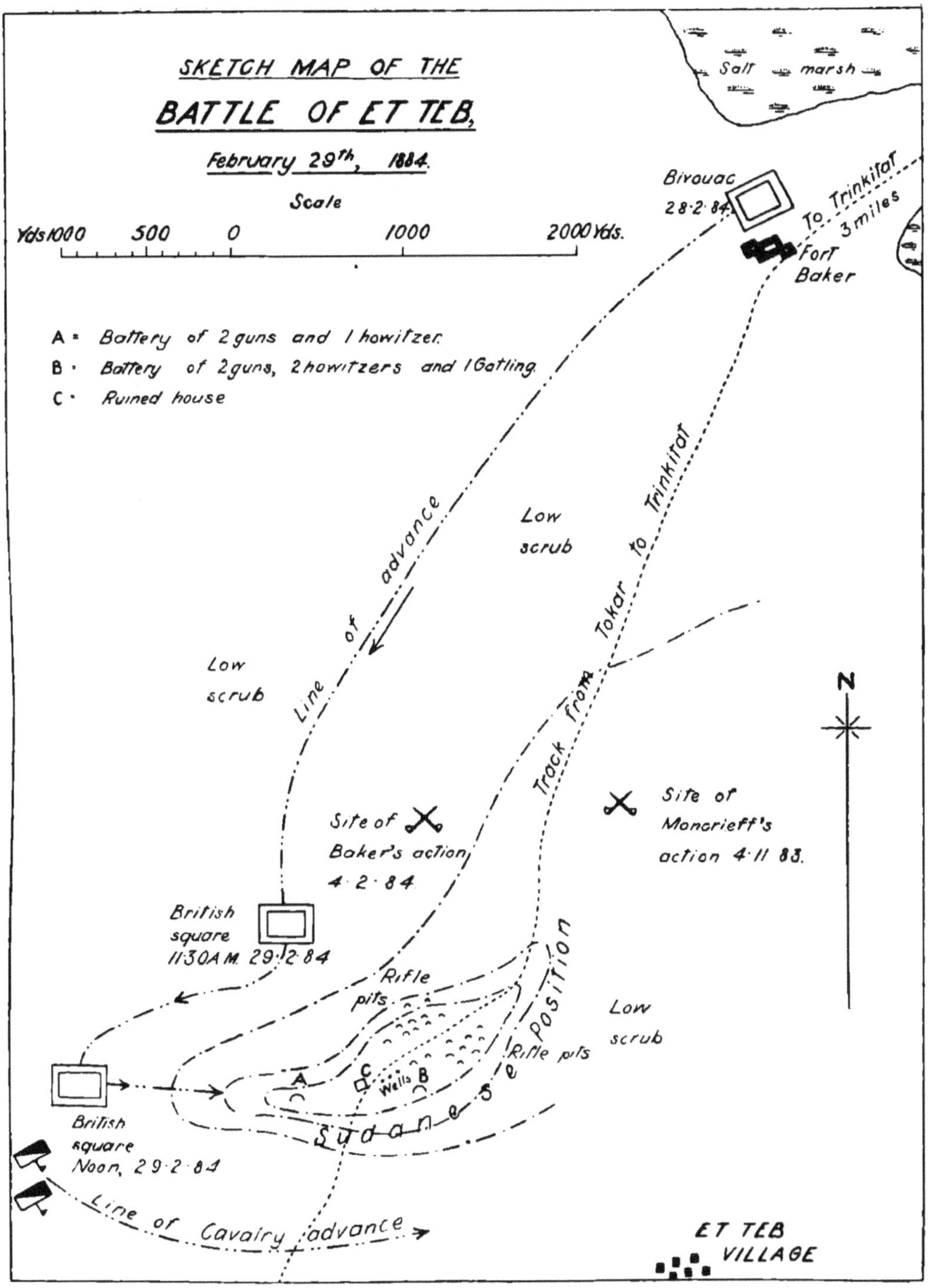
SKETCH MAP OF THE
BATTLE OF ET TEB,
February 29th, 1884.
Scale
Yds 1000 500 0 1000 2000 Yds.
A = Battery of 2 guns and 1 howitzer.
B = Battery of 2 guns, 2 howitzers and 1 Gatling.
C = Ruined house
Salt marsh
Bivouac 28·2·84.
To Trinkitat 3 miles
Fort Baker
Line of advance
Low scrub
Track from Tokar to Trinkitat
Low scrub
Site of Baker's action 4·2·84
Site of Moncrieff's action 4·11·83.
N
British square 11.30 A.M. 29·2·84
Rifle pits
Rifle pits
Sudanese position
Low scrub
A
C
Wells
B
British square Noon, 29·2·84
Line of Cavalry advance
ET TEB VILLAGE

so, he addressed the officers and men and informed them that their advance had been very slow at Et Teb and that much ammunition had been wasted. He added, however, that in order to show that he had not lost confidence in the battalion, he would place it in the front during the coming operations.[1] This speech, whether justified or not, had most unfortunate results within the next few days, for the Black Watch resolved that the speed of their advance should never be criticized in future.

Sir Gerald Graham lost no time in resuming the offensive against Osman Digna's forces. On March 12th, 1884, having concentrated 4,000 men at the *zariba* on the Sinkat road, he set out towards the south-west. His two brigades marched, each in rectangular formation, in echelon from the left, the 2nd Brigade under General Davis leading, with the 1st Brigade under General Buller on its right rear. This disposition was preferable to a single unwieldy square, for the units of each brigade were arranged so that they could form square rapidly, and the squares could support each other by fire. The brigades plodded steadily onwards through thorny scrub until they bivouacked for the night about half a mile short of a deep ravine called the Khor Gwob, some 13 miles south-west of Suakin. The 26th Field Company, R.E., made a *zariba* around the camp, south of a rocky ridge called Tesela Hill, and the tired infantry slept within its walls. The cavalry and mounted infantry rode back some miles to water their horses and re-appeared on the following morning.

At 8 a.m. on March 13th, Graham moved out with his whole force to attack the enemy who were in position near the village and wells of Tamai beyond the ravine. As before, the two brigades advanced in squares in echelon from the left, with Davis' 2nd Brigade leading and the cavalry and mounted infantry on the left flank. Thousands of Sudanese were visible on the far side of the ravine and it was known that the ravine itself was occupied. When Davis had approached within 200 yards of the edge, a series of irregular rushes were made on his square, but all were repulsed by steady fire. Graham was with Davis, and it seems that he had assumed direct command, for at 9 a.m. he ordered the Black Watch to charge. Possibly he thought that one such charge would decide the battle. Certainly he under-estimated the determination of the enemy. The Black Watch formed the left front of the 2nd Brigade square, and remembering the General's remarks at Suakin, they advanced rapidly to the edge of the ravine, followed by the 65th Regiment which formed the remainder of the front face. The square was now open. Under cover of thick smoke, hundreds of Sudanese emerged from the ravine, assailed the right front and flank of the

---

[1] *The Egyptian Campaigns*, 1882–1899, by C. Royle, p. 291. At the battle of Et Teb the Gordons had formed the front face, and the Black Watch the rear face, of the square.

2nd Brigade, entered the square, and bore it back in wild confusion. The Marines in the rear face tried vainly to stem the tide, though they and many of the gallant Highlanders checked it to some extent by forming into small groups and disputing every inch of ground as they retreated. Had it not been for the timely support of Buller's 1st Brigade the 2nd Brigade might have shared the fate of Baker's force at Et Teb.

Buller's square was too far from the ravine to be reached by a sudden rush, and it remained in proper formation. Not a Sudanese warrior could live against the fire of its Martini rifles, Gatlings and guns. Covered by this fire, and the dismounted action of the cavalry and mounted infantry on the left, the remnants of the 2nd Brigade rallied and reformed. Buller then advanced a short distance towards the ravine so that he could enfilade the enemy in front of the 2nd Brigade and, supported in this way by the 1st Brigade, the 2nd Brigade went forward once more to the ravine and recaptured some abandoned guns. It was now the turn of the 1st Brigade. Onward, down and across the ravine went Buller's men, and by 11.40 a.m. the Sudanese camp and village at Tamai were in Graham's hands. The strength of the enemy was reckoned at about 9,000 men, of whom 2,000 were killed, and the British casualties were 109 killed and 102 wounded. No Sudanese prisoners were taken as the wounded would not surrender. The 26th Field Company, R.E., was in the rear face of Buller's square and consequently saw little fighting; but its steady fire was useful in warding off a threatened attack on the *zariba* in rear. On the day after the battle, the company assisted in the destruction of the enemy's village and camp, and the whole force then returned to Suakin.

Sir Gerald Graham was blamed for his tactics at Tamai. Charles Royle observes :—[1] " Of the nature of the surprise intended for him at the ravine, Graham had ample warning beforehand. Nevertheless, he moved his men almost up to the brink of the spot where the enemy lay in ambush and very nearly brought about a disaster. As to the order given to a part of the front rank to charge, it is unnecessary to say anything in its condemnation. The charge was made at nothing. The front rank of the square doubled, while the sides and rear followed in quick time. It was, as a critic remarked, taking the lid off the box." Obviously, Graham was guilty of errors of judgment in approaching too near the edge of the ravine and in ordering the Black Watch to charge, but due allowance should be made for the fact that he was himself in the thick of the fight and could see little. His errors on this occasion may be forgiven in view of his sound tactics in other battles.

The victory at Tamai on March 13th, 1884, opened the road from Suakin to Berber on the Nile, and a fleeting opportunity for rescuing

[1] *The Egyptian Campaigns*, 1882–1899, by C. Royle, p. 302.

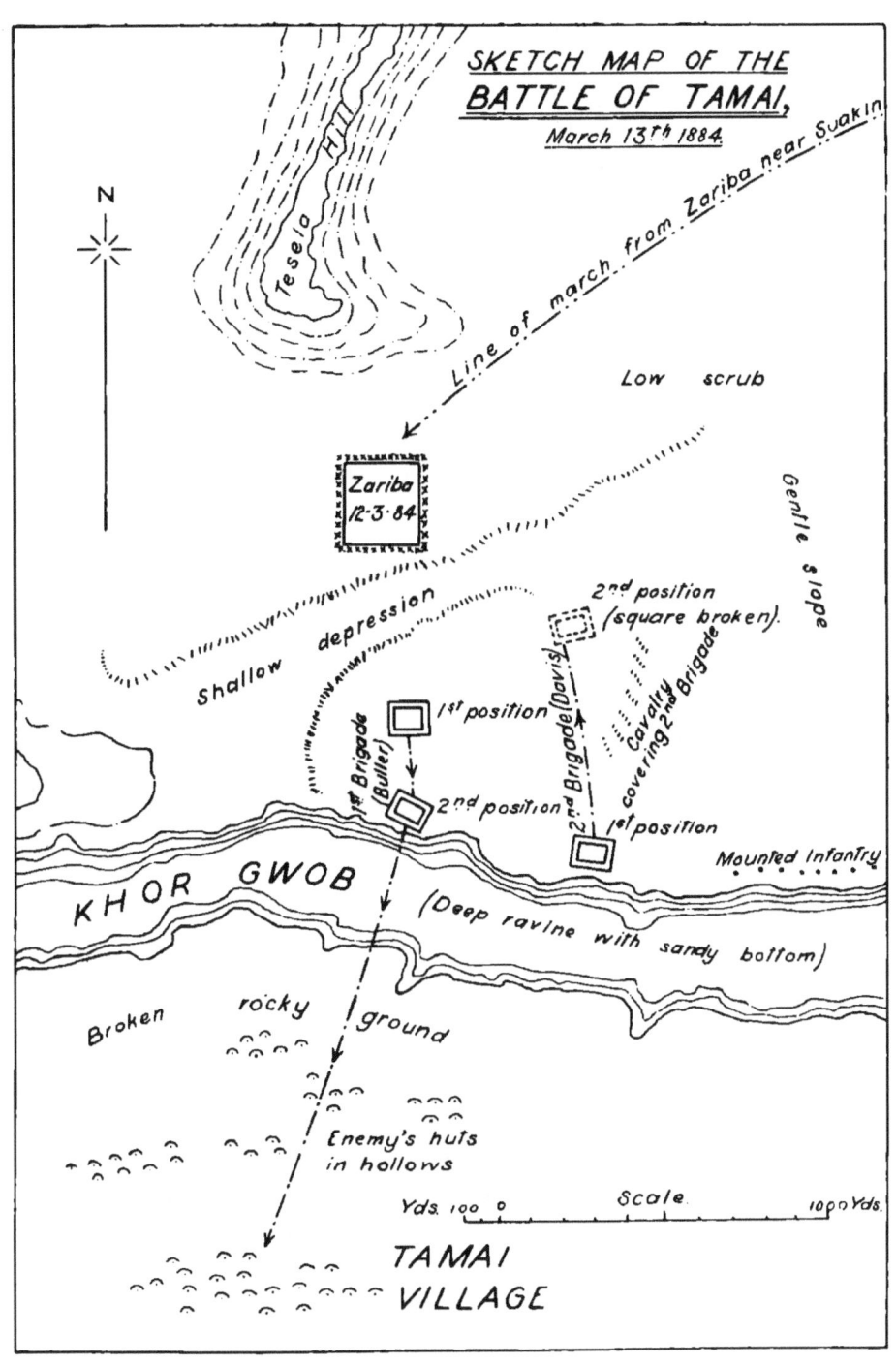

Gordon at Khartoum was perhaps within England's grasp. As early as March 5th, both Graham and Lieut.-Colonel Ardagh, R.E., his Chief Intelligence Officer, had foreseen this possibility, and Graham had telegraphed to Major-General Sir Frederick Stephenson suggesting that Gordon should be asked whether he would recommend an advance along the Berber road. This was done, and Gordon replied that it was most important that the success near Suakin should be followed up by sending a small force to Berber. However, in transmitting the reply to England, General Stephenson intimated that he was not prepared to recommend an advance to Berber owing to the scarcity of water on the road. Sir Evelyn Baring, Her Majesty's representative in Cairo, supported Graham and Gordon. He telegraphed on March 16th that it was of the utmost importance not only to open up the road between Suakin and Berber, but to come to terms with the tribes between Berber and Khartoum, and on the 24th he stated that he thought that an effort should be made to help Gordon from Suakin, for both Generals Stephenson and Sir Evelyn Wood, whilst admitting the extraordinary risks, considered that such an undertaking was possible. After the battle at Tamai, Graham was positive that he could get troops through to the Nile and was most anxious to make the attempt forthwith as the hot weather was approaching; but Gladstone's careful and idealistic Government, which had rejected every proposal emanating from Gordon or favoured by him, refused permission. So Gordon was sacrificed in January, 1885, and Graham wrote:[1] " Though not allowed the honour of being Gordon's deliverer, though sorrowing with all England, with the added grief of one who has lost a dear friend, it is yet some small consolation to me to know that Gordon, in the midst of his bitter reflections when alone at Khartoum, acquitted me, and the gallant little force I had the honour to command, of all unreadiness or disinclination to advance to his rescue." Graham always regretted that, instead of telegraphing for permission to dispatch troops to Berber, he had not sent them on his own responsibility and afterwards requested the approval of Government.

Had Graham been prepared to start soon after the Battle of Tamai, with large numbers of camels and experienced camel-men, *while Berber was still held by an Egyptian garrison*, he might have got through; but under the existing circumstances, as the preparations for such a march, and the collection of camels, would have occupied a considerable time, it is doubtful whether, with the meagre knowledge which he possessed, the plan was feasible. A dash for Berber might have been made at enormous risk; and if connection between Suakin and Berber had been established, it is possible that

---

[1] *Last Words with Gordon*, by Lieut.-General Sir Gerald Graham, V.C., G.C.M.G., K.C.B., late R.E., p. 52.

Khartoum and Gordon might have been saved. Then came the fall of Berber on May 26th, an event which, as Jackson remarks,[1] gave a new lease of life to the moribund forces of Osman Digna. From that moment, the Egyptian Government had practically no foothold on the Nile from Khartoum to Wadi Halfa, and Graham would have courted disaster if he had advanced with a force large enough to meet and overcome the dervish masses which could have been hurled against it at any point on the river. For safe progress, the construction of a railway would have been necessary, step by step with the advancing army, and such construction would necessarily have been slow in difficult country. Modern experience in desert warfare seems to confirm these opinions.

Determined to make as brave a show as possible, whatever the future might hold, Graham occupied his remaining time at Suakin in reconnaissances and skirmishes, while Brigadier-General H. Stewart, his cavalry commander, prepared a scheme for the advance of mounted troops to Berber. Stewart reconnoitred, with Major Elliott Wood, R.E., to Handub, ten miles north-west of Suakin, to Otao, a further eight miles westwards, and to the Tamanieb valley. On March 25th Graham led his two brigades against a hostile gathering at Tamanieb, drove the enemy away, and burnt their village. The 26th Field Company built *zaribas* at several places, and Wood examined the nature of the water in the wells at Tamanieb, Handub and Otao. However, by March 28th, Graham had returned to Suakin and had received instructions that the campaign was to be brought to a close. Leaving two British battalions to assist in garrisoning the town, he embarked the remainder of his force, sailed for Egypt on April 3rd, and finally proceeded to England, where he was thanked by Parliament and promoted to the rank of Lieutenant-General.

The rapidity of the campaign of 1884 on the Red Sea littoral is one of its most striking features, for the operations lasted barely five weeks. Much was accomplished in that short period; but although Osman Digna was subdued he was not crushed, and the political effects of the British withdrawal were deplorable. As later events proved, the departure of Graham from Suakin in 1884 sealed the fate of Gordon at Khartoum.

When the last transport had disappeared below the northern horizon the little garrison settled down to hold what it had got and to add to the defences of the town. Among the British officers was Major H. C. Chermside, C.M.G., R.E., in command of the Egyptian troops, who had been acting for some weeks as Political Officer.[2] He assumed the chief military command on May 10th, 1884, and was

---

[1] *Osman Digna*, by H. C. Jackson, p. 84.
[2] The career of Lieut.-General Sir Herbert C. Chermside, G.C.M.G., C.B., Col. Commandant R.E., appears in a Memoir by Major-General J. A. Ferrier, C.B., D.S.O., late R.E., in the *R.E. Journal*, Vol. XLIV, 1930, pp. 336–345.

appointed Governor-General of the Red Sea littoral in the following October. As most of the littoral was at that time in the hands of Osman Digna the title was certainly misleading. Chermside, as a Lieut.-Colonel, held the appointment until relieved, on February 8th, 1886, by Brevet-Colonel Sir Charles Warren, G.C.M.G., late R.E., who had been engaged on important political work in South Africa. During his tenure as Governor-General, Chermside undertook negotiations with King John of Abyssinia for the relief and withdrawal of some Egyptian garrisons scattered in out-stations adjoining the Abyssinian frontier. This was in pursuance of a treaty signed at Adowa on June 3rd, 1884, by which King John was to receive certain concessions after he had helped to evacuate the garrisons. The Abyssinian ruler dispatched a force from Adowa on the day after Gordon's death in Khartoum, and in due course three garrisons were relieved, so Chermside's political work had good effect. His administration of Suakin may have erred on the side of severity, for he was no believer in kid-glove methods. Rigid discipline was the order of the day. For instance, it is said that, as a precaution against spies, every native entering the town was obliged to wear a sack over his head.[1] Sir Charles Warren favoured a milder rule and won the confidence of the inhabitants; but he left Suakin on March 15th, 1886, after a few weeks as Governor-General, to become Chief Commissioner of Police in London and was succeeded on May 3rd by Major C. M. Watson, R.E., the captor of the Cairo Citadel. Such frequent changes, though unsettling to the inhabitants, were unavoidable owing to the kaleidoscopic alterations in the strategic and political problems of the Sudan. Four Royal Engineers in succession were Governors-General in Suakin—Chermside, Warren, Watson and Kitchener—and each pursued his own policy. Nevertheless, the cumulative effect of their labours in the early days went far to secure for England a peaceful and prosperous Red Sea littoral after the destruction of the Khalifa's power in 1899.

The decision that an attempt to rescue Gordon should be made by the Nile route, rather than from Suakin, was reached towards the end of August, 1884. Until then, controversy raged as to the relative advantages of the alternative routes, and, as Suakin might still be required as a base for an expeditionary force and as the starting point of a railway to Berber, the 17th Field Company, R.E., under Lieut.-Colonel Elliott Wood, R.E., was sent from Egypt in June, 1884, to make the necessary preparations. So once again the 17th Company was first in the field. It disembarked at Suakin on July 1st. Wood was short of officers; at first he had only Lieutenant A. Graham Thompson, R.E.; but Lieutenant F. C. Heath, R.E., arrived at the end of the month and, in February, 1885, Lieutenant A. A. M.

---

[1] *Watson Pasha*, by Stanley Lane-Poole, p. 186, footnote 2.

Layard, R.E.,[1] to replace Lieutenant W. B. Askwith who was killed soon after his arrival by the accidental explosion of a landmine.[2] The company worked under war conditions for the enemy were all around Suakin. Piers for ships and boats, hutments and blockhouses were constructed ; water-supply and light railway systems were taken in hand, and landmines laid. On March 6th, 1885, Wood was able to report that five piers, suitable for large ships, were ready on Quarantine Island, that nine smaller piers had been made elsewhere, that five miles of 18-in. gauge railway line had been laid, and that Quarantine Island had been connected to the mainland by a causeway 500 yards in length.[3] Many wells had been dug, acres of land had been reclaimed from the sea, and the building of a stone hospital was progressing. Undeterred by the intense heat, the 17th Company worked from dawn till sunset. Without their labours the second British expedition to Suakin would have been unable to take the field.

On November 18th, 1884, the British Government received from Lord Wolseley, then in command of the Nile expedition, a telegraphic summary of a letter from Gordon of November 4th in which the latter wrote that only with great difficulty could he hold out for more than 40 days. The receipt, on December 30th, of Gordon's further letter of December 14th, in which he warned Wolseley not to leave Berber untaken in his rear and described the pitiful conditions at Khartoum, emphasized the need of action from Suakin towards Berber in order to secure the flank of the Nile column. It was not, however, until after the receipt, in February, 1885, of the news of the fall of Khartoum that the Government decided definitely to dispatch a second expedition to Suakin, and having informed Lieut.-General Sir Gerald Graham, V.C., K.C.B., that he was selected to command it, asked him whether the railway, which it was proposed to build between Suakin and Berber, should be constructed by military labour or by contract. Graham preferred military labour. Major-General Sir Andrew Clarke, K.C.M.G., C.B., C.I.E., the Inspector-General of Fortifications, was in favour of a metre-gauge line and advised that it should be constructed by engineers and workmen from the Public Works Department of India, but this was opposed by the India Office. Ultimately, on February 17th, a contract was signed with Messrs. Lucas and Aird for the construction of a 4 ft. 8½ in. gauge railway from Suakin to Berber.[4] The contractors were to be responsible for labour, materials and construction, but were subject to the general control of Graham.

---

[1] Son of the diplomat and archæologist, Sir A. H. Layard, who unearthed at Nineveh in 1846 the colossal human-headed bulls now in the British Museum.

[2] Lieut.-Colonel Wood, R.E., subsequently dismantled all the remaining mines at great risk to himself.

[3] See *Sketch Map of Suakin and its Defences in* 1885, included in this chapter.

[4] The contractors were to receive a commission of 2 per cent. upon all expenditure, subject to a limit of £20,000, and a further £20,000 on the satisfactory completion of the line to Berber.

SUAKIN.

(By kind permission of the Controller, Sudan Government Office.)

They were authorized to collect the necessary plant and material in England and to ship them from London and Hull, and each vessel was to contain everything needed for the construction of five miles of railway. This plan was adopted so that if any ship was lost or delayed, the contractors would know that a further consignment for five miles of line should be sent in replacement. On paper, the scheme appeared sound : in practice, it proved a failure for the ships were not laden as intended.

Sir Gerald Graham's instructions were that on arrival with his troops at Suakin he should take command of the garrison and make the best possible arrangements, before the hot weather set in, to organize a field force, with the necessary transport, for the destruction of the power of Osman Digna. He was told that he must rely chiefly on Messrs. Lucas and Aird's railway for carrying supplies, and that consequently he should help that firm as much as possible and devote particular attention to pushing on the railway, section by section, towards Berber and to the completion of the 18-in. gauge railway system in and around Suakin. Lord Hartington, the Secretary of State, impressed on him the important part which the railway might play, not only in connection with operations near Suakin, but with the supply and reinforcement of Lord Wolseley's army when it reached Berber during its advance up the Nile. On February 27th, Hartington wrote to Graham " When the first and essential operation of crushing Osman Digna and clearing the country sufficiently to make it safe for the construction of the railway is accomplished, the next most important duty will be the pushing on of the railway, and I request that you will facilitate and aid this object by every means in your power."

On March 12th, 1885, Graham arrived at Suakin, where his troops had already begun to assemble, and the construction of the railway was begun on the day after he landed. By the 17th he had 491 officers, 10,222 non-commissioned officers and men, 1,616 horses, 2,759 camels, 791 mules and 2,629 followers. Reinforcements continued to arrive, and before he took the field he had about 13,000 fighting men, with 11,000 followers (labourers, camel-drivers, muleteers, etc.) to oppose Osman Digna's forces of 7,000 men at Tamai, 3,000 men at Hashin (six miles west of Suakin) and a small garrison at Tokar. With an army twice as powerful as that which he had commanded in 1884, Graham was set to complete the task which he might have finished in the previous year if his proposals had been approved by a strong Government. His appointment was freely criticized. His detractors pointed to the narrow margin by which he had escaped disaster at Tamai. But Wolseley had confidence in his ability, and public opinion was satisfied. It was right that, as the leader of the main expedition against the Madhi, Wolseley should have on his left flank a commander of his own choice.

The British force, assembling at Suakin, consisted of two infantry brigades—the 1st (Guards) Brigade under Major-General A. J. Lyon-Fremantle, and the 2nd Brigade under Major-General Sir John C. McNeill, V.C., K.C.B.; four squadrons of cavalry; three batteries of artillery; four companies of mounted infantry; and two field companies, a railway company, two telegraph sections and a balloon detachment of the Royal Engineers. An Indian Contingent, under the command of Brigadier-General J. Hudson, C.B., was also present; it included a regiment of cavalry, three battalions of infantry and a company of Madras Sappers and Miners. At the end of March, an Australian Contingent arrived, adding a further battalion of infantry, and two batteries of artillery, to the establishment.[1] The Guards Brigade was one of the finest in the British Army, and Sir Gerald Graham was soon so well provided with men and material that he felt justified in taking the field before the last transports had arrived.

Under the direction of Colonel (afterwards Lieut.-General Sir) James B. Edwards, C.B., as Commanding Royal Engineer, were the 17th Field Company, R.E., commanded by Lieut.-Colonel Elliott Wood; the 24th Field Company, R.E. commanded by Colonel (afterwards General Sir) E. P. Leach, V.C.; the 10th (Railway) Company, R.E., commanded by Major W. H. Rathborne; the 2nd and 3rd Sections of the Telegraph Battalion, R.E., under Lieutenant H. E. M. Lindsay and Captain C. F. C. Beresford respectively; a Balloon Detachment under Major J. F. B. Templer (K.R.R.C.)[2] with Lieutenant R. J. H. L. Mackenzie; and "F" Company, Madras Sappers and Miners, under Captain C. B. Wilkieson. Many other Royal Engineers held staff or administrative appointments. For a short time, Brigadier-General C. B. Ewart was in charge of the engineering works at the base and on the line of communications, being succeeded in this post by Lieut.-Colonel F. A. Le Mesurier. Major H. C. Chermside, C.M.G., was Governor-General of the Red Sea littoral; Major H. F. Turner, Director of Telegraphs; Major G. E. Grover, Chief Intelligence Officer; and Majors W. E. Peck, A. de V. Brooke and A. J. Hepper, Special Service Officers. Major H. W. Smith (afterwards Smith-Rewse) was Brigade-Major, R.E., and Captain G. Sydenham Clarke (afterwards Baron Sydenham of Combe) Intelligence Officer. An Indian Labour Corps was commanded by Captain T. P. Cather, a Survey Detachment by Lieutenant F. B. Longe, a Mounted Detachment by Lieutenant A. E. Sandbach, and a Field Park by Captain S. A. E. Hickson. Including Sir Gerald Graham no less than 47 officers of the Corps

---

[1] The occasion is remarkable as the first on which Dominion troops co-operated with the Home Army on an expedition overseas.
[2] Major J. F. B. Templer was a militia officer, belonging to the 7th Battalion, King's Royal Rifle Corps, who had specialized in balloon work. He was attached to the Royal Engineers to command the Balloon Detachment.

landed in Suakin before the end of April, 1885.[1] This was a liberal number for a campaign against a few thousands of savages, but it should be remembered that important engineering work was to accompany and follow the military operations against Osman Digna, not only in railway construction but in the general development of Suakin as the port of entry to the Sudan.

As the enemy's detachment at Hashin threatened the right flank of any column moving south-westwards against Tamai, Graham decided to begin operations by dispersing it and occupying both Hashin and Handub. After a reconnaissance on March 19th, he advanced against Hashin on the 20th with 10,000 men. The infantry reached some foothills near Hashin at 8.25 a.m., and the 17th and 24th Field Companies, R.E., and " F " Company, Madras Sappers and Miners, built four strong posts and afterwards a *zariba*. Meanwhile, the enemy retired to a steep hill in rear, from which they were driven after a stiff fight. Leaving a garrison of infantry to guard Hashin, and part of the 17th Field Company to improve its defences, Graham then returned to Suakin.

Having dealt with the force at Hashin, Graham turned his attention to Osman Digna's stronghold at Tamai. For reasons of supply, it was necessary to establish intermediate posts in that direction, and on March 22nd, he dispatched a force under Major-General Sir John McNeill, V.C., K.C.B., towards Tamai with orders to make and garrison two *zaribas*, one at five miles' and the other at eight miles' distance from Suakin. McNeill marched accordingly with two squadrons of cavalry, two battalions of British infantry (Berkshires and Royal Marines), three battalions of Indian infantry (15th Sikhs, 17th Bengal Native Infantry and 28th Bombay Native Infantry), four Gardner machine-guns, manned by the Royal Navy, the 24th Field Company, R.E., under Colonel Leach, V.C., R.E., " F " Company, Madras Sappers and Miners, under Captain Wilkieson, R.E., and the 2nd Telegraph Section, R.E., under Lieutenant Lindsay, R.E.,—in all, about 4,000 men. A large convoy of camels accompanied the force, and Lieut.-Colonel Elliott Wood, R.E., guided it. Major H. F. Turner, R.E., superintended the laying of a telegraph line by the Telegraph Section as the troops advanced, a maddening business as the line was continually knocked down by camels. The whole force was to march to the more distant site and

---

[1] The remaining R.E. officers were as follows:—*17th Field Company*, Lieuts. F. C. Heath, A. G. Thompson and A. A. M. Layard (in place of Lieut. W. B. Askwith, accidentally killed); *24th Field Company*, Capt. E. Dickinson, and Lieuts. F. D. F. MacCarthy, C. Godby and R. U. H. Buckland; *10th (Railway) Company*, Capts. H. G. Kunhardt, G. H. Sim and W. A. E. St. Clair, and Lieuts. F. A. Molony and H. Bonham-Carter; *2nd Telegraph Section*, Lieut. F. G. Bowles; *" F " Company, Madras Sappers and Miners*, Captain F. J. Romilly and Lieut. E. M. B. Newman (replaced later by Capts. C. H. Darling and W. D. Lindley and Lieut. A. C. MacDonnell); *Indian Labour Corps*, Lieuts. J. A. Tanner, Godfrey Williams and C. D. Learoyd; *Water-supply Work*, Capt. C. Mc G. Bate; *In charge of Stores*, Quartermaster A. T. Lewis.

construct a *zariba*. This enclosure was then to be garrisoned by the Berkshires, Royal Marines and the 24th Field Company, R.E., while the Indian units retraced their steps to the five miles' point, where they were to build another *zariba*, and after leaving the 15th Sikhs to garrison it, return to Suakin.

Open country soon gave place to mimosa bush, and progress was necessarily slow as the troops had to march in square formation. McNeill had been warned by Major Chermside, R.E., that he might be attacked at any time. By noon, having got no farther than Tofrik, six miles from Suakin, he realized that he could not reach the eight miles' point and build a *zariba* there before dusk, so he telegraphed to Graham and received permission to make a *zariba* instead at Tofrik. The plan adopted for the Tofrik *zariba* was to form three separate squares of mimosa thorn fence, placed diagonally like the squares on a chess-board—a large central square to contain the transport animals, followers and stores, and two flanking squares, of smaller size, to hold the fighting troops and machine-guns. Attention was devoted first to building the flanking squares under the protection of a screen of infantry pickets and cavalry vedettes in the surrounding bush. Infantry working parties proceeded to clear the bush near the *zariba* while the engineer units assisted them and also laid out and built the defences. To expedite the work, all the troops so engaged piled arms.

When the small enclosures were sufficiently advanced the Marines occupied the northern flanking square with two Gardner guns, and some of the Berkshires the southern flanking square with the other two Gardners. As the bush was thickest on the north and west, the defences on these sides were finished first; but at 2 p.m., when many of the troops were at dinner, the central square was still open to the east and south and partly also to the west and north. The camels and mules, having been unloaded in the central square, were collected to the east of it, and near them were two companies of Berkshires. The 17th Bengal Native Infantry were mostly to the south of the unfinished central square, and the other two Indian battalions to the west and north of it. The heat was oppressive, the men were tired, and there was yet no proper field of fire around the incomplete defences.

At 2.30 p.m. a cavalry soldier reported that the enemy were advancing, and orders were given for the working and covering parties to come in; but before they could be collected the cavalry galloped towards the *zariba* with the Sudanese swarming at their heels. The attack was delivered mainly on the southern and eastern sides and into the midst of the transport animals and non-combatants. Enveloped in clouds of dust, and filling the air with savage cries, the Sudanese surged onwards in a vast impetuous mass. Our working parties rushed for their arms; some men found them, others did not.

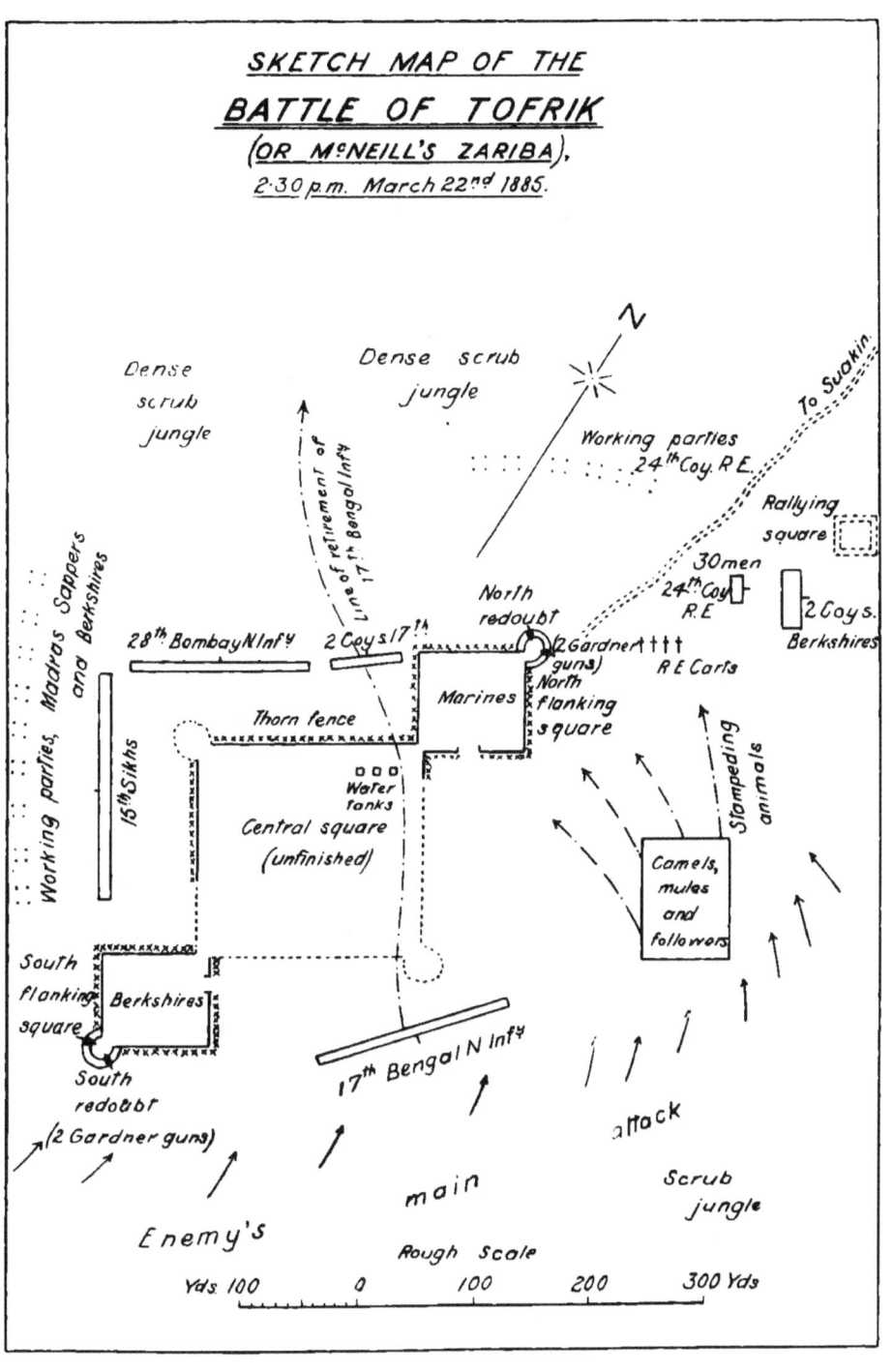

Thrown into disorder by the cavalry riding through them, the 17th Bengal Native Infantry fired a volley, broke their ranks, and rushed towards the central square. The two companies of Berkshires, forming square to the north of the transport animals, stood firm, but the enemy were soon among the camels and mules, and an avalanche of Sudanese, Bengal Infantry, followers and animals burst through the central square in a stabbing and hacking mob and carried many of the Royal Engineers and Madras Sappers with them. A party of the 24th Field Company, under Lieutenant F. D. F. MacCarthy, R.E., swept away like straws in a wind, managed to fight their way back and rejoined their comrades. Another party, under Lieutenant C. Godby, R.E., joined the rallying square of the Berkshires outside the *zariba* and helped to repel the assault. "For the next few minutes," writes Godby,[1] "we were infantry pure and simple: targets in plenty: range, three to thirty yards: ammunition, not marksmanship, required." The situation was saved chiefly by the Marines and those of the Berkshires who were securely entrenched with their Gardner guns in the flanking squares, although their fire killed hundreds of our stampeding camels. Both the 24th Field Company, R.E., and "F" Company, Madras Sappers and Miners, suffered severely. When the attack began, Captain F. J. Romilly, R.E., was superintending the Madras Sappers who were loading their equipment on mules, and the retreating Bengal Infantry carried these Sappers with them across the unfinished angle of the central square. Captain C. B. Wilkieson, R.E., severely wounded in the leg, saw a Sudanese warrior run alongside Romilly's horse and spear the rider through the side and heart. The man was shot immediately afterwards. It seems that Romilly was attempting to save the life of a brother officer. Lieutenant E. M. B. Newman, R.E., was killed by a swordsman. The swords used by the enemy were murderous weapons, five feet in length and with edges sharpened like razors, and Newman's left arm was severed and the top of his head sliced clean off. His opponent was soon among the dead.[2]

The battle at Tofrik on March 22nd, 1885, was finished in 20 minutes, a brief period crowded with instances of cool bravery, wild bewilderment, and fanatical desperation. When the smoke cleared away, the place was a shambles. Dead bodies of men and animals lay in heaps on every side. The British lost about 100 men killed and 140 wounded, and no less than 900 camels perished. At least 1,000 of the enemy lay motionless around and within the *zariba*.

[1] Notes by Brigadier-General C. Godby, C.B., C.M.G., D.S.O., late R.E., sent to the author on October 24th, 1934.
[2] There are many excellent accounts of the Battle of Tofrik. A very complete and descriptive account appears in *The Egyptian Campaigns, 1882–1899*, by C. Royle, pp. 416–429, and others appear in an article entitled "Suakin, 1885, Field Operations" in the *R.E. Journal*, Vol. 16, 1886, pp. 97–101, and in a Report entitled "Appendix to Diary for March, 1885. Action at Zereba (Tofrik), 22nd March, 1885," by Colonel E. P. Leach, V.C., R.E., included in the Official Report on the Royal Engineers at Suakin.

The Sudanese fought, as usual, with extraordinary courage. Braving our rifle fire, charging on to the points of our bayonets, hurling themselves into or over our thorny defences, they showed an absolute disregard for death. The action at McNeill's *zariba*, as it is sometimes called, was a bloody affair, but it had good results. The Sudanese began to lose confidence in Osman Digna, who had told them that our bullets were made of water and could do them no harm. News of the battle was telegraphed to Suakin, and Graham rode out on the 23rd at the head of a strong force which safeguarded the position. For the next eight days, the 24th Field Company was busy in clearing the battlefield and rebuilding the *zariba* on a smaller scale to suit a garrison of one battalion. Water was scarce, and the heat terrific. Men collapsed in dozens from sunstroke.

For several days after March 23rd, the military operations were confined to the dispatch of convoys to Tofrik and their defence against sporadic attacks. However, a convoy which marched on the 25th was unmolested, for it was accompanied by a new " engine of war," the captive balloon, which brought astonishment and fear into the Sudanese heart. Major J. F. B. Templer, K.R.R., in charge of the Balloon Detachment, writes :—[1] " We began to fill at 9 p.m. and marched to the *rendez-vous* outside Suakin at daybreak. I sent Mackenzie up to a height of 400 feet and he worked at that altitude until he got all the outside country well searched. I then pulled him down to 300 feet and worked him from the inside of the square for the seven miles' march. We could see everything. I had to keep Mackenzie up for eight hours and then sent up Sapper Wright (rigger) who did well for two hours." The balloon was filled from gas cylinders and was towed by a rope attached to a wagon drawn by horses in the centre of the moving square. Templer had much difficulty in getting the team to move steadily over the uneven ground and thus to avoid breaking the rope. Mackenzie wrote messages on small pieces of paper, attached them to loops of rope, and allowed the loops to slide down the towing rope. On arrival at the Tofrik *zariba* the balloon was hauled down, packed, and taken back to Suakin. When MacKenzie was asked what he would do if the square below him was attacked and overwhelmed he replied that he had thought of this when in the air and had decided that he would come down, anchor at 50 feet from the ground, and defend his anchorage until the balloon was rescued. Fortunately, he never found himself in such a horrible predicament.

The " balloonatics," as the facetious called them, were useful on other occasions though not always successful. They accompanied Graham's force to Tofrik on April 2nd, and inflated their balloon before the march was resumed towards Tamai ; but a strong wind

---

[1] Article entitled, " Balloon Work on Active Service " appearing in the *R.E. Journal*, Vol. 15, 1885, p. 119.

made the balloon so unmanageable that MacKenzie could not remain in the basket, and the balloon was blown to the ground and torn on a mimosa bush. Afterwards, it split in half and collapsed. However, on April 24th, at Tambuk beyond Handub, a small balloon named ' The Fly ' was inflated and sent up to an altitude of 1,200 feet so that the observers could watch the roads leading into the mountains towards Sinkat. " The Fly has been working capitally," writes Templer. " I have sent two friendly Arabs up. They make excellent scouts as they see in the most extraordinary manner. I shall try to bring ' Mahomet ' home when we come as he will make a good aeronaut. On his first ascent, he sang all the way up and reported splendidly, but when he came down he told the General he did not like it at all." On the following day, the Fly ascended to more than 2,000 feet and a view was obtained to a distance of 28 miles. The new engine of war proved its value in the Eastern Sudan as it did in Bechuanaland with Major-General Sir Charles Warren.[1]

There is little more to record of the military operations on the Red Sea littoral in the spring of 1885. Graham marched with a strong force from Suakin on April 2nd to attack Osman Digna at Tamai, taking with him the 17th Field Company, R.E., and picking up the 24th Field Company and other troops at Tofrik, so that he was able to continue with 8,000 fighting men and 4,000 animals. Before dusk he halted, and his engineer troops searched for water and assisted the infantry in making a second *zariba*. On the 3rd, he advanced again towards the villages at Tamai which had long been Osman Digna's headquarters. It soon became evident that there would be no resistance, and the force proceeded through the villages, which were found to be deserted. The wells were almost dry. This failure of the water-supply may have been the cause of Osman Digna's departure, but it precluded any further advance by Graham, so he destroyed the enemy's huts and stores and retraced his steps to Suakin, which he reached on April 4th. Offensive operations were now practically at an end. Most of the tribes had deserted Osman Digna, and that elusive leader was well on his way to Sinkat. It was safe to devote particular attention to pushing on the construction of the Suakin-Berber railway, so the garrison of Tofrik was withdrawn, and Handub, ten miles west of Suakin, was occupied without opposition on April 8th.

The construction of the so-called Suakin-Berber railway, which was carried no farther than Otao, $18\frac{3}{4}$ miles from the coast, was a fiasco which cost the Government more than £865,000. The railway started from Quarantine Island in Suakin harbour, and during the early part of March, 1885, before the fight at Tofrik,

---

[1] A brief history of military ballooning is included in *History of the Corps of Royal Engineers*, by Major-General W. Porter, late R.E., Vol. II, pp. 189–195.

sidings were prepared on the island and a line was laid along the causeway to the mainland. About 2½ miles of 4 ft. 8½ in. gauge track were completed by March 22nd. Work was then stopped until April 6th when Graham had returned from Tamai and it was safe to extend the railway beyond the protection of the outer defences. The 10th (Railway) Company, under Major W. H. Rathborne, R.E., landed on April 7th, and a party under Captains H. G. Kunhardt and W. A. E. St. Clair and Lieutenant F. A. Molony, R.E., was detailed to survey and stake out the line whilst the remainder of the company worked on the 18-in. gauge railway system around the town. Handub having been occupied, the Guards Brigade and the 17th Field Company, R.E., cleared a road through the bush for a width of 100 yards along the proposed alignment, and the Indian Labour Corps, under Captain T. P. Cather, R.E., worked on Quarantine Island and afterwards moved out along the line to assist in platelaying.

Although the construction of the railway was supposed to be in the hands of Messrs. Lucas and Aird, it was carried out almost entirely by Government labour and under Government officers. The only work executed by the contractors' employees was the running of trains and the fishing and spiking of rails, for which navvies were sent from England. These men had no previous experience of the East or the Army. They drank their beer, wore bowler hats,[1] and drew at least 12s. a day in pay while they remained above ground, which, in many cases, was not for long. The line to and beyond Handub was laid out by officers and men of the Royal Engineers: the formation was cleared and levelled by Madras Sappers and Indian coolies under Royal Engineer officers: the material was unloaded from ships, and the trains were loaded and unloaded by Indian coolies who were directed by Royal Engineer officers: even the necessary road transport was found by Government. Yet the supply of material and the entire administration of the line was in the hands of the contractors. Constant delays occurred at railhead through lack of material, and the trains were rarely loaded with proper quantities of each kind of material. Sometimes rails would be deficient ; at other times, sleepers. Only 16 miles of line were completed in 23 working days from April 6th to 30th. The Suakin-Berber railway furnished a striking example of the evils of dual control.

Graham took every precaution to ensure the safe progress of the undertaking and made several reconnaissances beyond railhead.[2] On April 16th, he occupied Otao, nearly eight miles west of Handub,

---

[1] They were supplied with pith helmets but often preferred to wear their customary headgear.

[2] A small "mounted division" from the 11th Field Company, R.E., at Cairo, served with the mounted infantry in these reconnaissances. It was commanded by Lieut. A. E. Sandbach, R.E. (See *R.E. Journal*, Vol. 15, 1885, p. 156.)

when the railway was still one mile short of the latter place. On the 19th, he was at Tambuk, five miles beyond Otao, when railhead was three miles beyond Handub. Although an armoured train was prepared by the 10th (Railway) Company and patrolled the line at night, the enemy contrived to do some damage by setting fire to sleepers and cutting down the telegraph line. Construction was easy as there were no bridges and the grades were gentle, yet progress was slow because of the confusion at Suakin. No depot of material was ever formed there. The rails, bolts and nuts were found to be of many different patterns. Until Handub was reached, all water had to be brought in tanks from Suakin. The line was never used to supply the troops, and afterwards, when an attempt was made to work to a timetable, it failed for want of an efficient Traffic Manager. The Suakin-Berber railway got no farther than Otao, where it arrived on April 30th.[1]

The hot weather had come, and rumours spread that the campaign was to end. As it was necessary to keep the troops in good health and spirits, the Indian Contingent, under Brigadier-General Sir John Hudson, K.C.B., organized a gymkhana. Lieutenant Lindsay and Captain Beresford, R.E., won prizes in the mounted events, and the rank and file enjoyed themselves in many amusing competitions on foot. An eye-witness of the festivities records:—[2] " Four ladies graced the course, two from the *Jumna* (officers' wives from India for home) and two of the nursing sister ladies. All, from Sir Gerald Graham to the junior bugler, saluted these sisters with respect, the General going out of his way to secure them good places and standing by them till the meeting was brought to an end. None but those who have lain sick or wounded in a hot tent, swarming with flies, can recognize the change which these true Sisters of Mercy have brought about in our hospital arrangements. Ladies by birth and education, they cheerfully expose themselves to danger and hardship, shrinking from nothing that their fathers and brothers face." The nursing sisters who worked in the sweltering climate of the Red Sea littoral in 1885 set a noble example which was followed by those of their profession who tended the sick and wounded on the Tigris during the Great War.

Lord Wolseley arrived at Suakin on May 2nd, a few days after Graham had been warned that his force was to be broken up. There was a possibility of trouble with Russia. The British Government had decided to abandon the Sudan and to discontinue the construction of the railway to Berber, and consequently a large force was no longer needed at Suakin. The ships laden with material were to be

---

[1] The construction of the Suakin-Berber Railway is dealt with in the *R.E. Journal*, Vol. 15, 1885, pp. 52, 135, and 155-156, and in Vol. 16, 1886, pp. 97-100. Also in *Royal Engineers at Suakin. Further Report*, 1885, pp. 21-22 and 31-43. A complete history of this undertaking appears also in *The Sudan Railways*, by Lieut.-Colonel W. E. Longfield, R.E. (*retd.*).

[2] *R.E. Journal*, Vol. 15, 1885, p. 135.

sent back to England, and the line dismantled as the troops retired; so the garrisons of Otao and Handub were recalled, and the storeships, which had been lying for weeks in the harbour at Suakin, steamed out to sea. Graham left Suakin on May 17th, and his force was withdrawn until only a small garrison remained. Most of the railway material and other engineering plant found its way to England where it was said to be useful for the relief of officers who had cut their estimates too fine; but some of it lay rotting for years along the road to Otao and on Quarantine Island as a testimony to the waste and extravagance of war. The author explored this neighbourhood in 1935. Nothing was then visible of the derelict Suakin-Berber line except a length of 100 yards of embankment at Handub and the foundations of a railway blockhouse built at that place by the 24th Field Company, R.E. Iron perishes rapidly in the salt air of the Red Sea coast, and sleepers make valuable building material.

Lieut.-General Sir Gerald Graham, V.C., reached England in June, 1885. Once again he received the thanks of both Houses of Parliament. He was made a G.C.M.G., and after some years on half-pay, retired from the Army. Although his conduct of the operations around Suakin was good, the results were frankly disappointing. Tamai, Handub and other places had been taken and held for a time; the enemy had been repulsed with slaughter at Tofrik; a few miles of railway had been laid; Suakin had been strengthened and improved. Nevertheless, Osman Digna was still at large; the route to Berber remained unopened; the garrison of Kassala[1] was still besieged; and Government had spent £3,000,000 with little to show for it. Graham did not wish to withdraw when his task was only half-finished, but circumstances were too strong for him. Osman wrote to the Mahdi " God struck fear into the hearts of the English and they went away." The power of the dervishes was supreme in the land and British prestige at a low ebb.

England, however, has a way of withdrawing only to return. She did so in Bengal, in Burma, in Afghanistan; and she followed her custom in the Sudan. Although there was much hostile talk on the Red Sea littoral, some of the tribes remained friendly in spite of their dismay at the British retreat after the campaign of 1885. It is said that an Arab Sheikh of Egypt once signed a petition for the withdrawal of the British from that country. The Sheikh, who was known to be friendly, was asked why he had signed. He smiled and answered " It is all empty words. I often say to my camel, if in some trifling way he taxes my patience, ' Curses on you! May Allah strike you dead, O son of a pig!' If I thought it would really happen I should be silent; but I know that the beast will remain

[1] Kassala is an important town about 250 miles east of Khartoum and near the boundary between the Sudan and the Italian territory of Eritrea. The garrison was obliged to surrender to the dervishes on June 30th, 1885.

unharmed." The advantages of British rule were apparent to many of the inhabitants of the Red Sea coast, and England kept a firm hold on Suakin until she could regain the Sudan for Egypt and break the Dervish domination.

When General Graham's division had gone, General Hudson was left at Suakin in command of a force of one British battalion, an Indian Contingent, and several Egyptian units—in all about 6,000 men. After the hot weather the garrison was reduced. "F" Company, Madras Sappers and Miners, returned to India in November, 1885, and by the following May all the British and Indian units had quitted the Red Sea.[1] Suakin was then held by only 2,500 Egyptian soldiers. Osman Digna was besieging it and had re-occupied Tamai, Hashin and Handub. Day after day the enemy's scouts approached the Suakin forts. Night after night they fired into the defended area. However, no serious damage was done, for the town was well protected. So much, at least, had been secured by Graham's expeditions. For a time the only Royal Engineers in Suakin were the Governor-General, Lieut.-Colonel H. C. Chermside, C.M.G., and Captain C. McG. Bate in charge of the water-supply; but "B" Company, Madras Sappers and Miners, under Captain F. W. T. Attree, arrived in February to continue the improvements to the harbour, fortifications and water-supply.

Prior to 1881, Suakin was almost undefended, but some works were commenced in that year by Colonel Harrington and carried on by Major-General Valentine Baker and Colonel Hallam Parr.[2] These works were afterwards strengthened, and in some cases reconstructed, by Egyptian troops under Lieut.-Colonel Chermside, R.E., and by the spring of 1885, thanks to the efforts of the 17th Field Company, R.E., Suakin was protected on the mainland by an inner cordon of small forts or redoubts, connected by a high mud wall or parapet, and by an outer cordon of detached works. No attempt was made to fortify Quarantine Island, which was covered with railway lines, workshops, hospitals, barracks and other buildings and was the site of a large water-condensing installation.[3] Quarantine Island was, in fact, the base of all operations and movements. The first work on the right or north flank of the inner cordon was the Island or Water Fort in the harbour. Then, in succession, came the Gezira, Yamin, Lansari (Ansari), Urbani and Wastaniya Redoubts; Forts Carysfort, Euryalus and Commodore; the Gedida Redoubt and Fort Turk; the Arab and Sphinx Redoubts and Camel Post; and on the water's edge at the southern end of the line, the Left Redoubt. Within this cordon was an area containing the suburb of

---

[1] *Watson Pasha*, by Stanley Lane-Poole, p. 182.
[2] Article entitled "The Suakin Expedition" appearing in the *R.E. Journal*, Vol. 16, 1886, pp. 43–45.
[3] A plan of Quarantine Island in 1886 appears in the *R.E. Journal*, Vol. 16, 1886, opposite page 172. The island is now called "Condenser Island."

El Geif (El Kaff) from which Suakin could be reached by a causeway built in earlier days by Charles Gordon.[1]

At the northern end of the outer cordon of defence was the Sandbag Redoubt, overlooking an entrenched camp. This work was followed in a southerly direction by four small Egyptian redoubts which carried the line to the important Right and Left Water Forts (Forts Shata and Gemmaiza), distant about 1,200 yards from the inner cordon. The Water Forts were originally earthworks constructed by Valentine Baker, but they had been provided with masonry towers by Chermside, and being situated on an embankment, had a good field of fire. They guarded the Shata wells which supplied the town with water. The southern sector of the outer cordon was composed of three more Egyptian redoubts and finished at the important Fula Redoubt on a mound due south of Suakin. Between the inner and outer cordons was H Redoubt, north-west of the Yamin Redoubt. This, again, was originally an earthwork made by Baker, but was subsequently altered into a strong masonry blockhouse forming part of an entrenched camp.[2]

Other redoubts, and small blockhouses called "pepper-boxes," were added during 1885 and 1886 when some of the older works were abandoned and demolished. As the railway was extended from Quarantine Island, new redoubts or blockhouses were built for its defence; for example, a powerful work called Fort Hashin, some 1,300 yards west of the Sandbag Redoubt. No defences were built on Graham's Point on the southern side of the harbour entrance, where the terminus of the railway line is now located, nor on the northern side of the entrance. It is unnecessary to enter into further detail. The accompanying map of Suakin will suffice to show the general defensive system. The searchlights on the inner redoubts, and on the warships which secured the flanks, were useful in preventing a surprise assault by night or the passage of spies into the defended area. Indeed, by the end of 1885, Suakin was safeguarded from all chance of capture and could be held easily by an Egyptian garrison commanded by British officers.[3]

The supply of pure water to the garrison and to the inhabitants of the town and its suburb, El Geif, was always a difficult problem. Sanitary conditions were deplorable, and dysentery and cholera were endemic before the British occupation. In 1884, the main supply was from the Shata wells, guarded by the Right and Left Water Forts, and the water was carried to the town and suburb in skins by

---

[1] Gordon is said also to have been responsible for the construction of some defence walls. The causeway leads to the "Gordon Gate" of the town.

[2] The construction of the Sandbag and H Redoubts by the 17th Field Company, R.E., is described, with sketches, in the *R.E. Journal*, Vol. 15, 1885, p. 10. The designs for these and other redoubts and blockhouses were prepared by Lieut.-Colonel Elliott Wood, R.E., who commanded the 17th Company.

[3] A good general description of the gradual elaboration of the defences of Suakin is given in *Osman Digna*, by H. C. Jackson, pp. 125–129.

women and donkeys. Lieut.-Colonel Elliott Wood, R.E., sank more than 50 wells around Suakin, but obtained water which was fit only for washing, and in March, 1885, he handed over the water-supply of Suakin to the Commissariat Department. When the military operations were extended to advanced posts such as Handub, Otao and Tambuk, the water-supply at each post was opened up by the 17th Field Company and developed by the 24th Field Company, and except at Tambuk, a good yield was obtained from ordinary wells, though the water was slightly brackish. Tube wells could not be driven in the hard soil.[1] Towards the close of 1885, Captain C. McG. Bate, R.E., completed the installation of two quadruple condensers on Quarantine Island, supplying fresh water through a 4-in. main to El Geif and beyond it. This relieved the burden on the condensing plants of the ships, but the Shata supply was still needed.[2] The civil population were supplied, on payment, with a limited quantity of drinking water from the new condensing plant and carried the remainder, as before, from the Shata Wells. The condensing installation on Quarantine Island included a masonry water-tower, the ruins of which are still visible from the wide verandah of the interesting old "Muhafsa," the Governor-General's Palace, built on the very edge of the blue lagoon which encircles Suakin town. Some years ago a patriotic British journalist described the "War Memorial" on the island. It was actually the derelict water-tower of the condensing installation!

In 1894, the water-supply of Suakin was greatly improved. Lieutenant (now Lieut.-General Sir) G. F. Gorringe, R.E.,[3] who was at that time in charge of both military and civil works in addition to being Brigade Major, was directed by the Governor, Colonel Archibald Hunter, D.S.O., to lay a pipe-line from the Shata wells into El Geif and to order a pulsometer pump from England. Gorringe used old pipes which he dug up from the system laid in 1884 for the Suakin-Berber Railway, and in due course installed the pulsometer. Further work on the supply system was executed in 1896 by Major Suene Grant, R.E., assisted by Lieutenants A. Gardiner and R. B. D. Blakeney, R.E. The water from several wells beyond the Shata oasis was pumped by a pulsometer into a group of large iron tanks holding a total quantity of about 23,000 gallons, and was led thence through a 4-in. main to reservoirs in El Geif. The rusted remains of the iron tanks and the pulsometer

---

[1] Article entitled "Suakin Water Supply" appearing in the *R.E. Journal*, Vol. 16, 1886, pp. 116-118.
[2] See the Report on the Suakin Waterworks by Captain C. McG. Bate, R.E., dated January 12th, 1886, appearing in the *R.E. Journal*, Vol. 16, 1886, pp. 166-168, with a plan of Quarantine Island opposite p. 172.
[3] Lieut. G. F. Gorringe, R.E., was stationed in Suakin from January, 1893, to November, 1895. He relieved Lieut. R. S. Curtis, R.E., who came to Suakin from the 26th Field Coy., R.E., in 1890. Gorringe was relieved at Suakin by Lieut. M. G. E. Manifold, R.E., who remained until he joined the Dongola Expedition in the spring of 1896.

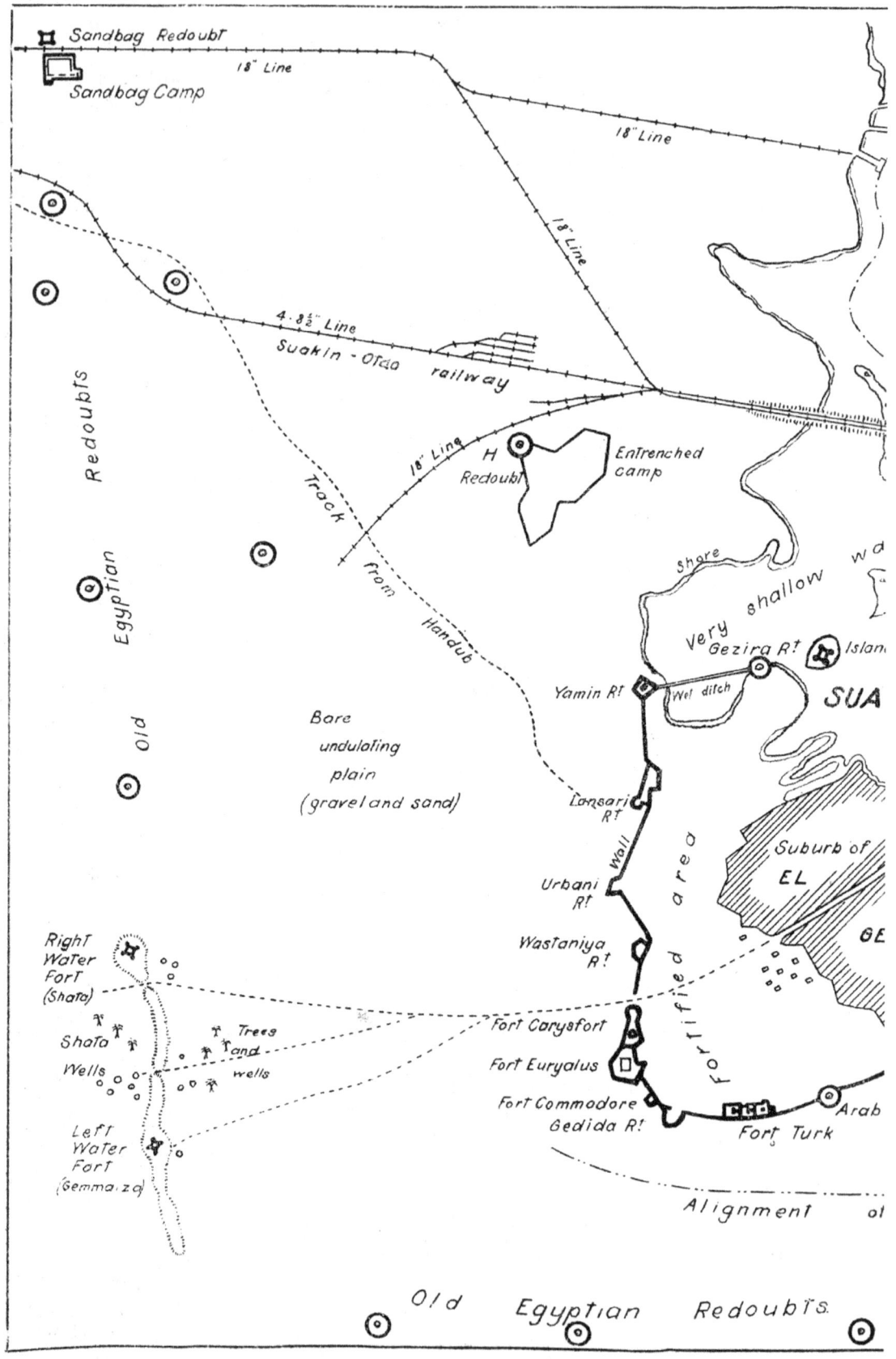

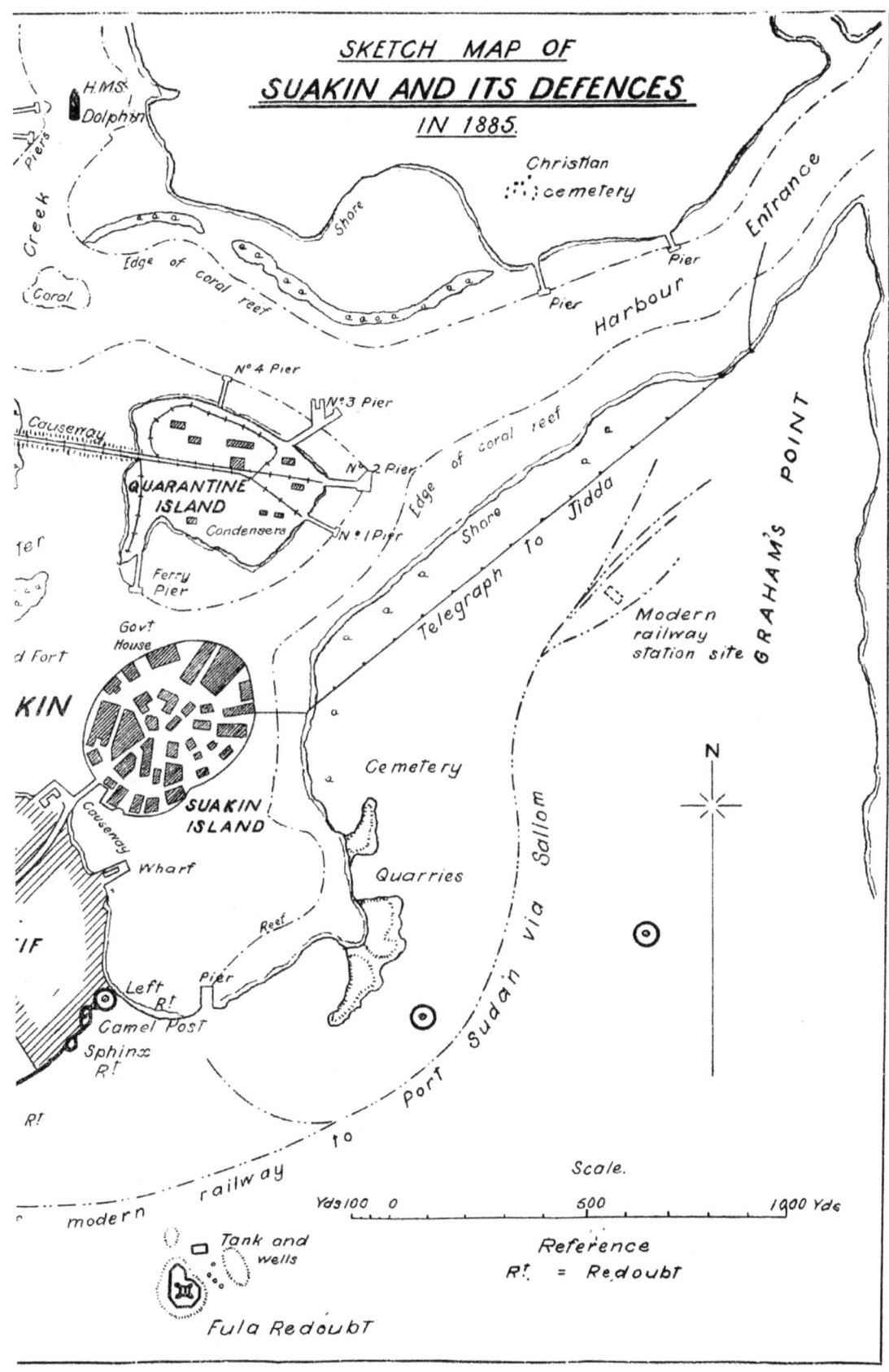

pump can still be seen beyond the Shata oasis. Water is now supplied through the 4-in. main from a masonry tank at the old Shata wells and by animal transport, and the piped water is known to the inhabitants as " Pulsometer." The Eastern mind is essentially conservative. Not a soul can explain why the water should bear this curious name, for none but an engineer could recognize the rusted pulsometer pump.

When Major C. M. Watson, R.E., became Governor-General of the Red Sea littoral on May 3rd, 1886, he assumed both military and civil control as his predecessor, Colonel Sir Charles Warren, had done, but he relinquished the military command on June 8th. His duties were responsible, difficult, and often peculiar. For instance, he acted on one occasion as a matrimonial agency. Having learnt that many of the Sudanese soldiers were still unprovided with wives, he assembled a number of freed slave-girls in his office and asked them whether they would marry the soldiers. Twelve daring maidens stepped forward without a blush and were sent forthwith to the barracks to choose their husbands; but two coyly remarked that it would be more proper for the soldiers to come to ask them. Watson tried to follow Warren's policy of winning the confidence and adherence of the local tribes by pacific measures. " If Government were to declare that the war was at an end, and to reopen trade," he wrote, " it is possible that, after a time, the country would settle down." To encourage trade, he opened markets on the sea-coast at Rawaya and Sheikh Barghut (now Port Sudan) and interviewed many of the local Sheikhs. Unfortunately, however, he did not confine himself strictly to civil administration. He informed the Government that, if trade were revived, the garrison of Suakin could be reduced, and his advice to the Sheikhs induced them to embark on a series of military operations by which they cleared the enemy from the country north of Suakin and blockaded Osman Digna at Tamai. Like Sir Charles Warren, Watson was a champion of the Suakin-Berber route to the Sudan in place of the Nile route, and did not hesitate to express his preference. His views, and the results of his policy, were freely criticized, and he fell into disfavour not only with the Egyptian Government, but with Lord Salisbury and the Home Government.

Suddenly, in August, 1886, Watson was informed that his successor as Governor-General had already been appointed, and, in consequence, he tendered his resignation and sailed soon afterwards for England. His successor at Suakin was his brother officer, Lieut.-Colonel H. H. Kitchener, C.M.G., R.E., who had distinguished himself in the Nile Expedition. It is only fair to Kitchener to state that he lost no time in writing personally to Watson to explain that when he had accepted the post at Suakin he had assumed that Watson had already resigned; and further that, when he had proposed to withdraw his acceptance after he had ascertained that Watson had *not* resigned, he was told that, if he did so, Watson would not benefit because another officer would be appointed in his place. Accordingly Kitchener became Governor-General in September, 1886, and ruled the Suakin region successfully until the beginning of 1888. Although Watson never returned to Egypt nor the Sudan, he continued to take a keen interest in the affairs of both countries and became a doughty champion of Colonel Sir Charles Wilson when the latter was attacked for his failure to rescue Gordon. The fact that he was subsequently offered a responsible post in East Africa[1] shows that his Governor-Generalship at Suakin was approved by many, though condemned by some. He was, perhaps, too sympathetic to excel as the ruler of the savage and wild inhabitants of the Red Sea coast in 1886.

Under Kitchener, nothing of importance occurred on the Red Sea littoral until the end of 1887, when Osman Digna, attracted by the news that the garrison of Suakin had been reduced, and joined by many of the hitherto friendly tribes, established himself at Handub, advanced on Suakin, and attacked the Water Forts. Kitchener, however, was not perturbed, for he had built not only the Ansari barracks for the troops, but also a wall around the town and its suburbs which, with the outlying forts, made them secure against attack and controlled the traffic of natives through the main gates. He applied to Cairo for permission to drive Osman from Handub, but was told that he must on no account take out the garrison of Suakin and should be content merely to reconnoitre. Not to be balked, he decided to advance in support of a Camel Corps of friendly Arabs, and did so at the head of a small force of mounted regular troops, reinforced by the bandsmen of all the military bands in Suakin![2] This mixed assembly captured Handub on January 17th, 1888; but the friendlies then began to loot, and being counter-attacked by Osman, fled towards Suakin, covered by the regulars. This skirmish was of little importance except that, during the fighting, Kitchener was wounded so severely in the neck that he was compelled to go to Cairo for treatment and, after his recovery, was succeeded as Governor-General by Lieut.-Colonel (afterwards Major-General Sir) C. Holled-Smith, K.R.R.[3] His rule at Suakin was thus brought to an untimely end. It is related that while Kitchener was talking to a friend in the hospital at Cairo, he had a fit of coughing and said that he had swallowed something. A doctor was summoned, who, suspecting that it was the bullet, administered a purgative. On the following morning Queen Victoria

---

[1] Watson did not accept the post.
[2] Notes by Lieut.-General Sir George Gorringe, K.C.B., K.C.M.G., D.S.O., Col. Commandant R.E., sent to the author on January 28th, 1936.
[3] Colonel Holled-Smith was confirmed as Governor-General on September 13th, 1888, and Colonel Kitchener was appointed Adjutant-General of the Egyptian Army.

wired for precise details of the patient's condition and progress, and the doctor, no doubt a frugal Scotsman, sat down to draft a reply. " Kitchener passed good night," wrote he, and paused for a moment. He scanned the draft with disapproving eye. It gave no details. It was incomplete. Then with happy inspiration he added the magic words " and bullet."

Emboldened by their success on January 17th, 1888, Osman Digna's forces began to show increased activity around Suakin, and early in March, they closed on the town and fired heavily into it. After this, they blockaded it until September, when they threatened a serious attack. The garrison was strengthened, and by the middle of December a force of 750 British and 4,000 Egyptian and Sudanese troops was concentrated at Suakin under the leadership of Major-General F. W. Grenfell, C.B., Sirdar of the Egyptian Army, with Colonels H. H. Kitchener (late R.E.) and C. Holled-Smith as brigade commanders. Lieut.-Colonel (afterwards Lieut.-General Sir) H. H. Settle, C.B., R.E., was Grenfell's Chief Staff Officer. The operations were brief and decisive. Grenfell led his force out of Suakin on December 20th, and, having routed the enemy, pursued them towards Handub. Captain A. C. Foley, R.E., shared in this fight, which is known as the " Battle of Gemmaiza," and Lieutenant (afterwards Major-General Sir) R. U. H. Buckland, R.E., was mentioned in General Grenfell's dispatches. Kitchener handled his Sudanese brigade with skill and precision. The defeat of Osman Digna's followers was complete and England's prestige on the Coast was enhanced ; but it fell when the British troops re-embarked after the battle and the friendly tribes realized that no further action was contemplated. Although Kitchener remained for a time at Suakin in command of a garrison of 2,000 men, he was instructed to maintain a purely defensive attitude and did so.[1]

Royal Engineers had little concern in the desultory fighting which took place from time to time near the Red Sea after 1888. Their services were in urgent demand on the Nile. Osman Digna continued to haunt the region between Handub and Tokar until early in 1891, when Colonel Holled-Smith occupied both places and Osman fled towards Kassala. Holled-Smith took Handub on January 27th, and on February 15th concentrated nearly 2,000 men at Trinkitat for an advance on Tokar. The only Royal Engineers who took part in this operation were Lieut.-Colonel H. H. Settle, as Chief of Staff, and Lieutenant (afterwards Major-General Sir) R. S. Curtis as a staff officer. As Osman Digna was at Afafit, a short distance beyond Tokar, Holled-Smith set out to occupy the latter place on the 19th. His cavalry seized its ruined Government

---

[1] These, and other, operations in the Suakin region are fully dealt with in *Mahdiism and the Egyptian Sudan*, by Major F. R. Wingate, D.S.O., R.A., A.A.G. for Intelligence, Egyptian Army.

HANDUB.

[*Photo by the Author.*]

buildings, and his infantry arrived at 10 a.m. With Colonel Settle, Major Wingate, R.A., Lieutenant Curtis and others of his staff, he then reconnoitred the position and observed the enemy, about 6,000 strong, advancing through the bush. No time was to be lost. The infantry took up a semi-circular line of defence and received the attack with a heavy fire which soon led to the repulse of Osman's force. Charged by the cavalry, the enemy finally fled in confusion, and Holled-Smith, after halting for a time at Tokar, went forward to Afafit where he was received with joy by the inhabitants.[1]

In 1892, however, Osman Digna returned and caused some trouble near Suakin; and in 1895 he raided Tokar from the Erkowit Hills in which he had taken refuge with a few followers. Accordingly, in April, 1896, a small force was dispatched from Suakin to deal with him, and succeeded in driving him back into the hills after some skirmishes at the Khor Wintri. Osman Digna's followers then became demoralized, and dispersed to their homes or followed him to the battlefields on the Nile. Thus ended the last fight in the neighbourhood of Suakin. The Khalifa having been defeated and killed at Umm Debeikerat by Colonel Wingate in November, 1899, Osman Digna was run to earth and captured in the Gemilab Hills, 100 miles south of Suakin, early in 1900.[2] He died a few years ago at Wadi Halfa.

After Kitchener had become Sirdar of the Egyptian Army in April, 1892, he devoted close attention to the possibility of an advance into the Sudan from the Red Sea littoral. Acting under his orders, Lieutenant G. F. Gorringe, R.E., built a causeway during 1893-94 from the port of Trinkitat across the swamps to the mainland, being given to understand that it was intended for a tramway to Tokar for supply purposes. Actually, Kitchener had in mind the construction of a railway from Suakin past Trinkitat and up the Khor Baraka to Kassala, and proposed to use Trinkitat as an intermediate point for unloading material, and commencing work up the Khor Baraka, while the first section of the line was being built at the same time through Et Teb from the base at Suakin. It seems that, at this period, Kitchener also had a scheme for a railway past Sheikh Barghut to Sinkat and thence to Berber, for he sent Colonel Archibald Hunter and Captain Henderson, R.N., to reconnoitre the harbour at Sheikh Barghut for this purpose, and Gorringe accompanied them. The foresight shown by Kitchener is

---

[1] A full account of the capture of Tokar and the occupation of Afafit in February, 1891, is given in *Mahdiism and the Egyptian Sudan*, by Major F. R. Wingate, D.S.O., R.A., pp. 492-505. An account appears also in *Osman Digna* by H. C. Jackson, pp. 144, 145, in which mention is made of the valuable Intelligence work of Major Wingate.

[2] The capture of Osman Digna is described in *Osman Digna*, by H. C. Jackson, pp. 164, 165.

exemplified in these preparations. To use a modern *cliché*, he "explored every avenue" before he reached a decision.

While at Suakin, Gorringe was called upon by the Sirdar and Colonel Hunter to exercise the strictest economy in the erection of buildings. The rails of the old Suakin-Berber line were used for roofing, and the Works Department lived, in fact, on the wastage of 1884. "Much of the work which I was ordered to carry out between January, 1893 and November, 1895," writes General Gorringe,[1] "though nominally to improve the accommodation for the troops, was really, in Kitchener's mind, preparation for an advance from Suakin. For example, I was ordered to build a new prison. I suggested a site, away from the water's edge. The Sirdar did not approve, and another site was selected where dhows could come alongside. I was told to make large, roomy buildings as he wanted the convicts to be comfortable. This I did. At his next inspection he came to see the finished work, and then remarked, 'I don't like this building for the convicts. They must build another prison on more healthy ground *outside the walls*. What you have built will make an excellent *Nuzl* (Supply and Ordnance Store).' Needless to say, that is what he intended from the first; but, having no funds, he had the building erected by convict labour for practically nothing!"

During the Dongola Expedition of 1896, every available Egyptian soldier was needed on the Nile, so a contingent from India was sent to hold Suakin in replacement of the Egyptian garrison. This force of 4,000 men was commanded by Colonel (afterwards Lieut.-General Sir) C. C. Egerton, and included the 1st Company, Madras Sappers and Miners, under Lieutenant G. A. F. Sanders, R.E.[2] No fighting took place, but a great deal of hard work was done in temperatures rising to 119 degrees in the shade and dust-storms as black as night. The Sappers landed in June and returned to India in December.[3] They improved the accommodation and water-supply at Suakin and Trinkitat, and laboured also at Tokar and other places. As Major Suene Grant, their Commanding Royal Engineer, once stated,

[1] Notes by Lieut.-General Sir George Gorringe, K.C.B., K.C.M.G., D.S.O., Col.-Commandant R.E., sent to the author on January 28th, 1936.

[2] The subalterns were Lieutenants J. R. Chancellor, H. A. Cameron and C. F. Anderson, R.E. Lieutenants A. G. Bremner and A. Gardiner, R.E., were present as Assistant Field Engineers. Lieut. J. R. Chancellor, R.E. (now Lieut.-Colonel Sir John Chancellor, G.C.M.G., G.C.V.O., D.S.O.) had a distinguished administrative career. After service in the Dongola Expedition (1896) and on the Indian Frontier (1897–98), he held several military Staff appointments and then entered the field of civil administration. He was Governor and Commander-in-Chief of Mauritius, 1911–16; of Trinidad and Tobago, 1916–21; and of Southern Rhodesia, 1923–28. Finally, he was High Commissioner and Commander-in-Chief in Palestine from 1928 to 1931.

[3] The only R.E. officer at Suakin when the contingent began to arrive in May, 1896, was Lieut. R. B. D. Blakeney, who repaired the old landing stages and piers erected in 1885, and prepared barrack accommodation for the troops. Soon afterwards, Blakeney left Suakin to join the Dongola Expedition, travelling *via* Quseir to Qift on the Nile, whither Lieut. M. G. E. Manifold had preceded him in March.

"Nothing seemed to be able to get along without the Madras Sappers having a say in the matter." The same remark might apply to the officers and men of the Royal Engineers who fought in the *zaribas* of 1884 and 1885, changed defenceless Suakin into a fortress, and assisted so ably in the subsequent pacification and general development of the Red Sea littoral.

THE RED SEA.
from "The Route of the Overland Mail to India."

CHAPTER IV.

THE NILE EXPEDITION OF 1884–85.

When Allah made the Sudan, he laughed—Arab proverb.

ENTRUSTED with the impossible task of evacuating the Egyptian garrisons which were threatened by the Mahdi's hordes, General Gordon ascended the Nile from Cairo, and having arrived in Khartoum on February 18th, 1884, was soon invested by the rebels. "Even if I was mean enough to escape," he wrote, "I have no power to do so." He could hold Khartoum for a time, and in the early days he was hoping that a few British or Indian troops might be sent up from Suakin to Berber to assist him in conducting the evacuation; but when he learned that the Government had forbidden General Graham to detach any troops to Berber, he realized that he was cut off. On April 18th, he wrote to Sir Evelyn Baring :—" I shall hold out here as long as I can, and if I can suppress the rebellion, I shall do so. If I cannot, I shall retire to the Equator." Forced to action at last by political expediency and public opinion, the British Government began preparations for the dispatch of an expedition to Khartoum; but it was not until August 5th that Gladstone moved a vote of credit to undertake operations for the relief of Gordon " in case it might be necessary."

Opinions differed as to the best route. Sir Evelyn Baring, and Generals Stephenson and Graham, maintained that it would be preferable to incur the enormous risks of a desert march of 280 miles from Suakin to Berber, and up the Nile for a further 200 miles to Khartoum, rather than to send a force from Cairo for a distance of 1,650 miles through the many cataracts which obstruct the river. Their proposals were rejected. The Government could not, or would not, understand that time was precious and that risks must be taken, and they superseded General Stephenson by Lord Wolseley, a champion of the Nile route. Wolseley based his calculations on his experience of river transport under very different conditions in Canada. He had never seen the cataracts of the Nile beyond the bounds of Egypt. He had never encountered a Dervish. Yet his opinion was accepted in preference to that of Graham. The fateful die was cast. Gordon was already doomed.

Before his successful leadership of the Red River Expedition in 1871, Wolseley had become an enthusiastic waterman. He loved to negotiate the Canadian rapids and to watch the skill of the native boatmen called "voyageurs," and later, when employed at the War Office, his favourite pastime was to shoot the largest weirs of the Thames in a birch-bark canoe.[1] The Red River Expedition from Lake Superior to Lake Winnipeg and up the Red River to Fort Garry, a distance of 600 miles, had proved to his satisfaction that troops could be transported rapidly and cheaply in boats. "The experience I had had in canoe work and in the woods during my seven or eight years' service in Canada helped me greatly," he wrote.[2] "All the officers soon became expert in making portages[3] and in mending their boats, and no one more so than my very able friend and valued comrade Redvers Buller. It was here I first made his acquaintance." Another trusted assistant on the Red River was Lieutenant (afterwards General Sir) William F. Butler, 69th Regiment, whom Wolseley selected in 1884 to supervise the whaler fleet on the Nile.

However, there was little resemblance between the problems of ascending the Red River and the Nile. On the Red River, portages could be arranged by felling trees on the spot and making long slides over which the boats could be pushed; moreover, the rocks were easily seen and avoided, as the water was clear. On the Nile the banks were precipitous or of shifting sand; there was no timber except palm trees, and the rocks were hidden in muddy water. The climate, the nature of the enemy, the size of the force, the urgency of the situation—all were different. Experience gained on the Red River was no sure guide for operations on the Nile. Several officers were consulted about the Nile route. The Royal Navy reported against the proposed expedition in boats. Lieut.-Colonel J. C. Ardagh, C.B., R.E., a supporter of the alternative Suakin-Berber route, was posted at once as Commandant of the Base at Cairo, and was kept there, doing excellent work, throughout the campaign. Backed by the report of a Committee consisting of Major-General Sir Redvers Buller, V.C., Major-General Sir John McNeill, V.C., and Colonel W. F. Butler,[4] Lord Wolseley had little difficulty in securing the adoption of the Nile route. No Royal Engineer served on that Committee, though engineering problems might be involved; and Colonel Butler, who admitted that he had never seen the Nile above Cairo, advanced the opinion that "water was water, and rock was rock, whether they lay in America or Africa." Wolseley himself had made his choice on April 8th, 1884, when he wrote "Remembering the great superiority of river over land transport, the ease with which stores of all kinds can be carried in boats, and the vast saving

[1] *The Life of Lord Wolseley*, by Major-General Sir F. Maurice and Sir George Arthur, p. 50.
[2] *The Story of a Soldier's Life*, by Field-Marshal Viscount Wolseley, O.M., K.P., G.C.B., G.C.M.G., Vol. II, p. 177.
[3] Carrying goods or boats across the space between two waterways, or preparing the ground for this work.
[4] This Committee assembled on July 29th, 1884.

that there would be in expense, I have no hesitation whatever in saying that the river route from Wadi Halfa to Khartoum is infinitely preferable to any other." The pity of it is that boats had to be built to enable the troops to follow that route, and that the whole expedition was kept back to wait for the boats.

The Nile route having been selected, preparations were begun for the provision of the necessary river transport. It was clear that large boats could not be hauled quickly through the worst cataracts, and it was soon found that the supply of small native craft would be very limited. Indeed, Major-General Sir Evelyn Wood, V.C., G.C.M.G., K.C.B., as G.O.C. Line of Communications, succeeded in buying only 50 half-decked boats called *nuggars*, and 68 other craft, to meet the needs of the expedition when it got beyond the reach of the existing fleet of Nile river-steamers.[1] Evidently, it would be necessary to send specially designed boats from England. It was decided that each must be large enough to carry 12 men with food supplies for 100 days, strong enough to withstand the battering of the cataracts and the extremes of the climate, light enough to be carried overland, and staunch enough to weather the squalls which sweep the Nile. Experiments were made in England, a type was approved, and 800 boats called " whalers " were ordered from a number of firms. Each whaler was about 30 feet in length and $6\frac{1}{2}$ feet in beam and drew less than 2 feet of water even when fully loaded with $2\frac{1}{2}$ to 3 tons. As her weight was only 9 cwt. she could be carried over portages of moderate length to avoid particularly bad cataracts, and she could be manœuvred easily by her crew of 2 boatmen and 10 soldiers. Each boat was fitted with 12 oars and 2 masts with big lug sails. So well did the British firms rise to the occasion that although they did not receive their orders until August 12th, 1884, they completed and shipped 400 whalers by the middle of September, and by October 3rd the last of the 800 boats had left England. At Alexandria they were disembarked and loaded on trains under the superintendence of Major-General W. O. Lennox, V.C., C.B., late R.E.,[2] who dispatched them to railhead at Asyut (Assiut), a distance of 229 miles from Cairo. Thence they were towed in barges to Aswan (Assuan), a further 318 miles, where they were launched and towed, " tracked "[3] or poled through the First Cataract. Their stores were conveyed round the cataract to Esh Shallal (near Philae) by a short line of railway. From Esh Shallal the boats were towed by steamers to Wadi Halfa on the frontier, a distance of 210 miles, the whole arrangements being in the hands of Messrs. Thomas Cook

---

[1] *History of the Sudan Campaign*, by Colonel H. E. Colvile, C.B., Grenadier Guards, Part I, p. 72.

[2] As a subaltern, Lennox was the first R.E. officer to gain the Victoria Cross. He did so at Sebastopol on November 20th, 1854. He distinguished himself afterwards at Lucknow during the Indian Mutiny. (See *The Military Engineer in India*, by Lieut.-Colonel E. W. C. Sandes, D.S.O., M.C., R.E. (retd.), Vol. I, pp. 355, 360, 361.)

[3] Towed by a line from the shore.

and Sons, owners of the steamers, who had contracted for the transport of the entire expedition as far as Saras above the Second Cataract.[1] To assist in the navigation of the Nile beyond Wadi Halfa, 380 "voyageurs," including about 100 Red Indians and half-breeds, were engaged in Canada, and 300 Kroomen were obtained from West Africa to carry stores round the cataracts. All the river-steamers on the Egyptian portion of the Nile were requisitioned for the transport of troops, stores and boats.[2] Nevertheless it was not until November 1st, 1884, that the first few whaler boats, propelled by British crews and guided by "voyageurs," set forth from Gemai after entering the Sudan and passing the Second Cataract, and having loaded up with stores at Saras, began to penetrate the black wilderness of the Batn el Hagar or "Belly of Rocks."

Apart from questions of time and space, the Nile route had certain strategic advantages. For instance, it provided a line of communication which could be covered properly by an advancing or retreating force. An expedition from Suakin through Berber might be driven off its line of communication if forced to retreat northwards. But Lord Wolseley should have used the camel instead of the whaler.

The original plan of campaign was simple. A strong column of infantry in boats was to work up the river from above Wadi Halfa, accompanied by mounted troops and transport on the banks. If the column was delayed, a Camel Corps was to leave the Nile at Korti and strike across the Bayuda Desert to the river-bank at El Metemma—a short cut across a great bend. Having arrived there, a small detachment was to be dispatched to Khartoum in steamers sent down by Gordon, and these troops would sustain the defence until the arrival of the main body in the spring of 1885, when the Mahdi could be driven off. Wolseley, however, was misinformed regarding the number of camels which could be procured for his advance; he imagined that there was a scarcity when actually there was none.[3] It seems that the agents of Messrs. Thomas Cook and Sons could have obtained from the Arabs of the Dongola region enough camels to render the use of "whalers" unnecessary. If the original contract given to that firm had been extended from Saras to Korti, Khartoum might have been relieved and Gordon saved. The efforts of the Engineers to short-circuit the cataracts above Wadi Halfa by a railway, and to keep the whalers in repair, could not remedy this initial and fundamental error.

[1] The construction of the whalers, and their voyage up the Nile, are described fully in *The Campaign of the Cataracts*, by Colonel Sir W. F. Butler, K.C.B. (1887).
[2] In addition, eight steam-pinnaces, and two stern-wheel paddle-boats, were sent from England.
[3] Article by Colonel Mason Bey appearing in the *United States Army and Navy Journal*, quoted under the title "The Soudan Campaign on the Nile," in the *R.E Journal*, Vol. 22, 1892, pp. 31–33.

It was intended originally that the Nile Expeditionary Force, or the " Gordon Relief Column " as it was sometimes called, should consist of not more than 5,000 men, but this number was increased later to 7,000. The troops in Egypt were reinforced by a Naval Brigade, two battalions of British infantry from India, four battalions from Gibraltar, Malta, Cyprus and Barbadoes, two companies of Royal Engineers from England, some batteries of Royal Artillery, and the necessary Commissariat and Medical formations, so that Lord Wolseley had 14,000 men under his command from which to select his striking force. Although it was destined to play the chief part in the operations against the Mahdi, this striking force was much weaker than that of General Graham on the Red Sea littoral, for its strength was governed by problems of supply and transport. It could rarely be operated in regular brigades because the troops arrived piecemeal through the cataracts. A Camel Corps was in the process of formation, and it was necessary to make up columns as the situation demanded. The Nile campaign was loosely woven and elastic. Deliberate and ordinary methods were out of the question.

Lord Wolseley's staff, headed by Major-General Sir Redvers Buller, V.C., K.C.B., consisted of more than 100 officers. Captain Lord Charles Beresford, R.N., was in command of the Naval Brigade; Colonel H. Brackenbury, C.B., was Deputy Adjutant-General, Lieut.-Colonel J. F. Maurice, R.A., was Assistant Adjutant and Quarter-Master-General, and Colonel W. F. Butler, C.B., Assistant Adjutant-General in charge of the boat service; Major-General W. Earle, C.B., C.S.I., and Brigadier-General Sir Herbert Stewart, K.C.B., held command of troops. On the line of communication, under Major-General Sir Evelyn Wood, V.C., G.C.M.G., K.C.B., was Brigadier-General F. W. Grenfell. Lieutenant (now General Sir) F. R. Wingate, R.A., was Aide-de-Camp to Sir Evelyn Wood. Colonel F. G. Burnaby, Royal Horse Guards, was one of 39 Special Service officers, and Lieutenant E. J. M. Stuart-Wortley, K.R.R., was the leader of an Arab corps in the Libyan Desert to the west of the Nile. These few names are taken at random from a long list because they figure in this narrative.[1]

A large number of Royal Engineer officers took part in the Nile Expedition, either on the Staff or with the three companies and the Telegraph section of the Corps which were included. Colonel Sir Charles W. Wilson, K.C.M.G., C.B., was Chief Intelligence Officer, and Colonel C. E. Webber, C.B., Director of Telegraphs. The Commanding Royal Engineer was Major W. H. Mulloy. Captain H. H. (afterwards Field-Marshal Earl) Kitchener was an Intelligence officer usually to be found at or beyond the farther outpost up the Nile. Kitchener, assisted by Lieutenant (afterwards General Sir

---

[1] A list of the Staff is given in Appendix 36 of the official *History of the Sudan Campaign*, by Colonel H. E. Colvile, C.B., Grenadier Guards, Part I, pp. 270-274.

THE SECOND CATARACT.

Looking down the Nile towards Wâdi Halfa from Abu Sir Rock.

[*Photo by the Author.*]

Leslie) Rundle, R.A., was in charge of an Arab corps guarding the approaches from the Nubian Desert to the east of the river. Lieutenant E. S. E. Childers was an Aide-de-Camp to Lord Wolseley. On the line of communication were Colonel (afterwards General Sir) Richard Harrison, C.B., as Colonel on the Staff; Lieut.-Colonel (afterwards Major-General Sir) Thomas Fraser, C.M.G., as Assistant Adjutant-General; and Lieut.-Colonel (afterwards Major-General Sir) J. C. Ardagh, C.B., as Commandant of the Base. Captain (afterwards Lieut.-General Sir) H. H. Settle was appointed as a Special Service Officer, and Major H. Wilberforce Clarke (Royal (Bengal) Engineers) and Captain H. A. Yorke as Railway Staff Officers. In various employments were Major W. F. Spaight, Captains D. C. Courtney, R. M. Barklie, H. P. Leach, J. E. Blackburn and F. S. Leslie, and Lieutenants T. B. Shaw, A. R. M. Sankey, R. P. Littledale, W. F. Hawkins, H. N. Dumbleton, M. Nathan, W. F. H. S. Kincaid, C. A. Leahy and W. Du C. Luard.

The 8th (Railway) Company, R.E., the 11th and 26th Field Companies, R.E., and the 4th Section of the Telegraph Battalion, R.E., undertook the engineering and communication work of the expedition. The Railway unit was commanded by Major (afterwards Major-General) D. A. Scott, who was assisted by Captains G. F. Wilson and P. G. Von Donop, Lieutenants W. S. Vidal and A. W. Roper, and Lieutenant (afterwards Major-General) J. A. Ferrier. With the 11th Company, under Major G. T. Plunkett, were Captain G. A. Cockburn, Lieutenants A. H. Kenney and H. B. N. Adair, and Lieutenant (afterwards Major-General) A. E. Sandbach.[1] The 26th Company was commanded by Lieut.-Colonel K. R. Todd, the company officers being Major J. F. Dorward, Lieutenants M. L. Tuke and E. M. Burton, and Lieutenant (afterwards Lieut.-General Sir) H. M. Lawson. With the Telegraph Section under Captain F. W. Bennet were Captains C. K. Wood and A. H. Bagnold, Lieutenants G. A. Tower and C. Hill, and Lieutenant (afterwards Major-General Sir) Andrew M. Stuart. In all, 48 officers of the Corps were engaged in the Nile Expedition during the winter of 1884–85, though some were not present at the outset. A similar number subsequently assisted Sir Gerald Graham on the Red Sea littoral. Lord Wolseley, though remaining firmly wedded to the Nile route, soon realized its difficulties and arranged for the provision of a large cadre of engineers to overcome them.

The first Royal Engineer to prospect towards the south was Captain H. H. Kitchener. At the end of July, 1884, he set out from Korosko, dressed as an Arab and with a native escort of only 20 men, and, on August 2nd, sent news of his safe arrival at Dongola, where he was to ascertain the precise attitude, towards the British,

---

[1] In April, 1885, Lieut. A. E. Sandbach, R.E., took one section of the 11th Field Company to Suakin. The 11th Company was then in Cairo. (See Chapter III.)

of the Mudir or Governor of the Province, who was known to be in close touch with the Mahdi.[1] Kitchener had volunteered for this dangerous mission after an Egyptian officer had demanded, and had been refused, a reward of £10,000 for the same service.[2] On August 8th, it was decided that some British troops should be sent beyond Wadi Halfa, and Kitchener realized at once that Ed Debba, at the bend of the Nile, would not only become an important starting point for any overland expedition towards Khartoum, but was also the best base for his intelligence and reconnaissance work, so he went there with an escort of 100 Arabs and examined and reported upon four possible routes,[3] recommending finally the route from Ed Debba to Khartoum which involved a desert journey of some 250 miles.

At Ed Debba, Kitchener was an important link between Gordon and the outer world, and he carried his life in his hands. It is said that he was present one day at the execution of a supposed spy who was tortured so horribly that Kitchener thereafter carried a small bottle of poison about with him. His courage and resource are shown by an incident which is vouched for by one of his relatives. Two Arab spies had been caught and confined in a tent. They pretended to be deaf, and Kitchener could get nothing from them. Another spy was captured soon afterwards and promptly pushed into the tent. The three started to talk, freely exchanging confidences. The third spy then demanded to be taken to headquarters. He was Kitchener himself. His talent for disguise was so extraordinary that on one occasion a soldier flung a stone at him, thinking he was an Arab who had no business to be prowling around. Bennet Burleigh, correspondent of the *Daily Telegraph*, who had also made his way up to Ed Debba in advance of the troops, paints an interesting picture of Kitchener at this period. " To my astonishment and delight," he says, " I found one Englishman within the mud walls of Debbeh—Captain Kitchener, R.E. He gave me a hearty welcome and added to my debt of gratitude by producing two bottles of claret, his whole store, which we drank most loyally at dinner. For weeks he had not heard the English tongue spoken, and naturally he was glad to see a countryman able to tell him something of what was happening outside the Sudan. In manner he is good-natured, a listener rather than a talker, but readily pronouncing an opinion if it is called for."[4] Kitchener's presence in Ed Debba helped to ensure the loyalty of the province of Dongola, and his work at this outpost laid the foundations of his remarkable career.

[1] *Life of Lord Kitchener*, by Sir George Arthur, Vol. I, p. 72.
[2] Speech by H.R.H. The Duke of Cambridge at a complimentary dinner to Major-General Sir H. H. Kitchener and the R.E. officers of the Dongola Expedition as reported in the *R.E. Journal*, Vol. 26, 1896, pp. 255–256.
[3] Ed Debba to Khartoum; Ambukol (near Korti) to El Metemma; Ambukol to Bishara (south of El Metemma); and Merowe to Berber. See the general map, entitled *The Anglo-Egyptian Sudan*, at the end of this volume.
[4] *Field-Marshal Lord Kitchener*, by E. S. Grew, Vol. I, p. 116.

PREPARATIONS AT WADI HALFA.

Throughout the early part of September, 1884, British troops were advancing steadily up the Nile towards Dongola by way of Asyut, Aswan and Wadi Halfa. The instructions given to Lord Wolseley were that the primary object of the expedition was to rescue Gordon from Khartoum, and that, when that had been accomplished, no further offensive operations should be undertaken. Every effort was made to push the expedition southwards before the Nile flood began to subside, and even before Wolseley left England, Sir Evelyn Wood had voyaged up the river with Commander T. F. Hammill, R.N., to superintend the initial operations. Preceded by Generals Earle and Sir Herbert Stewart, Wolseley started from Cairo on September 27th and arrived at Wadi Halfa on October 5th. Meanwhile Stewart had continued his journey upstream and had occupied Dongola with a small force on September 30th. The advanced base at Wadi Halfa presented a scene of great activity and much confusion. "The shore," writes Butler,[1] "was covered with the vast preparation of the coming campaign. Under a sun which still blazed fiercely overhead, soldiers, sailors, black men and yellow men, horses, camels, steam-engines, heads of departments, piles of food and forage, newspaper correspondents, sick men, Arabs and generals seemed to be all thrown together as though the goods station of a London terminus, a couple of battalions of infantry, the War Office, and a considerable portion of Woolwich Arsenal had been thoroughly shaken together and then cast forth upon the desert."

Wadi Halfa in October, 1884, was a poor place—a few buildings of sun-dried brick and a cluster of mud hovels sheltering beneath a fringe of palm-trees on the right bank of the river. From it a line of railway, in a shocking state of disrepair, led southwards through the rocky Batn el Hagar for a distance of $33\frac{1}{2}$ miles to Saras. The chequered history of that line will be dealt with later. For the present it is sufficient to remark that it was a mournful example of Ismail Pasha's extravagance and incapacity. Until November the railway played a negligible part in the transport of men and stores. Its single workable locomotive could barely drag one train daily to Saras on rails half-covered with sand and over bridges which threatened to collapse. Everything depended for a time on the success of the whalers. The first of these boats had been hauled through the "Great Gate"[2] of the Second Cataract on September 25th, and others followed it or were carried round the rapids. Nevertheless, they arrived so slowly at their dockyard and place of assembly at Gemai above the broken waters that it was not until November 2nd that Wolseley was able to begin a general advance on Dongola by embarking a battalion of the South Staffordshire Regiment in

[1] *The Campaign of the Cataracts*, by Colonel Sir W. F. Butler, K.C.B., p. 119.
[2] The most restricted parts of all the cataracts were called "gates."

whalers at Saras. Wolseley himself reached Dongola on the 3rd, and his infantry followed him, strung out in long processions of boats, sailed or rowed over open water and hauled by exhausted men through eleven large or small cataracts north of Kerma.[1] From Kerma, all was plain sailing to Dongola.[2] The advance was continued on December 2nd, when the expeditionary force in boats and a few small steamers[3] began to move southwards to Ed Debba and then gradually eastwards round the bend of the Nile to Korti, where Wolseley landed on December 16th. Fifty boats had been lost in the cataracts. The men were in good spirits, but very tired, and, as regards clothing, they resembled Falstaff's ragged regiment rather than picked British troops.

Due credit for the safe arrival of so many of the whalers at Korti should be given to the carpenters of the 11th and 26th Field Companies working under Lieutenant A. H. Kenney, R.E. After the first whalers had negotiated the Second Cataract, Kenney and 22 carpenters of the 11th Company were sent to Gemai to repair them. Other boats soon arrived and all had to be beached, turned over, caulked, white-leaded, and painted. There were countless cracks to cover and holes to mend, and most of the rudders required strengthening. After the Sappers had done their work, the Naval Brigade fitted the whalers with masts and sails, and by November 22nd, when 23 carpenters of the 26th Company were helping Kenney's original repair party, 450 whalers had been overhauled and sent upstream.[4]

The following extracts from an account by Captain J. E. Blackburn, R.E., show the difficulties and dangers encountered by the expedition in ascending the Nile to Ed Debba and Korti:—[5] " On November 1st, 1884, the first portion of the Nile Expedition, which went forward in whalers, left Gemai ; it consisted of the detachment of the 26th Company, R.E., which had been told off to accompany

---

[1] The cataracts are at Semna, Atiri, Ambigol, Tanjur, Ukma (Okmeh), Akasha, Dal, Amara, Abu Sari (Absarat), Kagbar (Kaibar) and Hannek. The Hannek Cataract is also known as the " Third Cataract." A detailed description of all these cataracts is given in the official *History of the Soudan Campaign*, by Colonel H. E. Colvile, C.B., Grenadier Guards, Part I, pp. 117–120.

[2] Sometimes called " New Dongola " to distinguish it from Old Dongola near Ed Debba farther up the Nile.

[3] Six small steamers were hauled safely through the " Great Gate " of the Second Cataract and were of immense importance in the subsequent transport arrangements. Indeed, the whole plan of campaign would have been upset without them. It appears that Commander Hammill was told by a cowardly interpreter that the Sheikh of the Cataract had announced that, owing to a sudden fall in the Nile level, no ships could be got through the Great Gate. The Sheikh denied this story, and to prove that there was sufficient depth, jumped into the roaring torrent and was swept unharmed over the submerged rocks.

[4] " Diary of an Officer with the Khartoum Expedition," appearing in the *R.E. Journal*, Vol. 15, 1885, pp. 13–14.

[5] Article entitled " From Gemai to Debbeh in a Whaler," by Captain J. E. Blackburn, R.E., appearing in the *R.E. Journal*, Vol. 15, 1885, pp. 23–26. Extracts from this article appear also in the *History of the Corps of Royal Engineers*, by Major-General W. Porter, Vol. II, pp. 74–78. The wording of the extracts now given has been altered in a few places to save space.

THE 26TH FIELD COMPANY, R.E., IN WHALERS ON THE NILE.
Leaving Saras for Dal, November 2, 1884.

[*From the original pencil sketch by Melton Prior.*]

this part of the expedition. The party, which included Major Dorward, Lieutenant Lawson, 46 N.C.O's and men, a native *reiss* (pilot) and five Canadians, embarked in five whalers and reached Sarras (Saras) by 1 p.m. Here the afternoon was spent in loading up the boats with Engineer equipment, 20 days' 'Nile boat provisions' and 10 days' ordinary rations, making a total weight of a little under 7,000 lbs. in each boat. On November 2nd the party was joined by Captain Blackburn, R.E., and a start was made for Dal. For about a mile we sailed merrily along when, owing to our first experience of a small rapid, we met with our first accident. A collision occurred, the result being that a rudder was broken off. We found that it had already been damaged and roughly repaired. Later we were informed by Colonel Butler that, owing to the hurry in which we were fitted out, our boats had never been thoroughly overhauled. In the course of the day we had our first experience of towing or 'tracking,' and the first four boats halted for the night about one mile short of Semneh (Semna). All the boats reached Semneh by 11.30 a.m. on the 3rd, and here we had our first " portage " —unloading our boats, loading up all stores on camels, carrying them thus for about half a mile to the top of the cataract, and there again reloading. This work was decidedly laborious, the more so as hands were sore and limbs stiff from yesterday's and the morning's rowing. Colonel Harrison, R.E., who had seen us off at Sarras, turned up at Semneh to see how we were getting on. By 11.30 a.m. on the 4th, we had got through a long succession of lower rapids and up to Ambigol, the last rapid having been very stiff and taking three boats' crews to haul up each boat. On the 6th, we reached Lower Tanjour (Tanjur), said to be half an hour's sailing from the cataract."

In the Tanjur Cataract several of the whalers were holed by rocks, and the crews had a hard time ; but the boats negotiated the Third or Hannek Cataract and some minor rapids and arrived at Abu Fatima, below Kerma, on the 29th. At Abu Fatima, Blackburn found Captain D. C. Courtney and Lieutenant W. F. H. S. Kincaid, R.E.; also Captain H. P. Leach, R.E., on his way to Dongola with transport camels.[1] The five whalers, under Major Dorward, R.E., sailed for Dongola on November 30th, accompanied fortunately by one Canadian, for at that time the " voyageurs " were forbidden usually to go beyond Abu Fatima. Kincaid had joined the boat expedition, which duly arrived in Dongola on December 2nd. There the travellers heard for the first time of the £100 prize offered for the quickest

[1] In notes sent to the author on September 28th, 1934, Colonel W. F. H. S. Kincaid, C.B., late R.E., remarks that, early in September, 1884, he received orders to accompany Major D. C. Courtney, R.E., up the Nile from Cairo to report on the cataracts beyond Saras and to select portage routes round them. They reconnoitred and reported on the cataracts throughout October, 1884, and remained at Abu Fatima until the first whalers arrived on November 29th. Lieut. H. P. Leach, R.E., had been appointed to command the 9th Company, Camel Transport Corps, but was employed on Engineer duties in addition to transport work. Major D. C. Courtney, R.E., was occupied usually in surveying the Nile and the adjacent country.

E

passage from Gemai to Ed Debba and determined to set up an unbeatable record. In this, however, they were unsuccessful because of the accidents and delays which they had experienced during the first part of their journey. They were the pioneers of the river route, and pioneers are always martyrs. Nevertheless, by reaching Handak Camp on December 4th, they covered the 42 miles from Dongola in less than 48 hours. " Everyone was greatly excited at our arrival," remarks Blackburn, " we being the first whalers seen in these waters. On the 5th we came to Old Dongola, and at 8.30 p.m. on the 6th, one boat reached Debbeh where we were rapturously received by the Royal Sussex as the first whaler of the expedition. The other four boats halted for the night and arrived on Sunday, December 7th. So ended our journey from Sarras to Debbeh. At the time of writing (9th) the first boats of the South Staffordshires are in sight, being two days and some hours behind our last boat. As yet there are no British troops farther up the Nile than Debbeh."

There was not much work for the detachment of the 26th Field Company while at Ed Debba, as a fort had already been laid out by Kitchener and was making good progress in the hands of the Royal Sussex Regiment, so the aquatic Marathon was resumed on December 13th when 14 South Staffordshire whalers competed against five Sapper boats. Hard rowing was the order of the day, but the Sapper crews always drew away from the infantry and led them till the evening. At last, on the afternoon of December 15th, Korti was reached and the tired men disembarked and enjoyed a much needed rest. " On Christmas Day," writes Blackburn,[1] " we had our R.E. Dinner at which Sir C. Wilson, Major Kitchener, whom we found at Korti on our arrival, Childers, Slade (R.A.), and Piggott, Reuter's news agent, were our guests : other R.E's included Major Dorward, Lawson, Kincaid, Stuart of the Telegraph Battalion, and myself. We had a jolly dinner and afterwards adjourned to the camp fire where there were some very good songs."

Many tales were told in the flickering light of camp fires ; and the Telegraph officers, being behind the scenes, were always sure of an appreciative audience. One story relates to the Mudir or Egyptian Governor of Dongola. This vain and fanatical official was concerned in the collection of camels and supplies for the military authorities and made frequent use of the telegraph line. An excellent arrangement, apparently, and one which was calculated to ensure brevity of correspondence. But there was a fly in the ointment. The Mudir insisted on heading every telegram with an entire chapter from the Koran![2] Another tale illustrates Egyptian methods of administration. A telegraph line from Cairo to Wadi Halfa was cut, and the

[1] Article entitled " From Debbeh to Hamdab with the Nile Column," by Captain J. E. Blackburn, R.E., appearing in the *R.E. Journal*, Vol. 15, 1885, pp. 50–52.
[2] *History of the Corps of Royal Engineers*, by Major-General W. Porter, late R.E., Vol. II, p. 157.

fault was discovered in the capital itself. The Inspector-General thereupon assembled his native engineers who, having told him that they knew the culprit but could get no proof, were warned that unless the man was in prison within 24 hours they would all be dismissed. Within the stipulated period he was duly arrested, tried and imprisoned. He had been found guilty of "stealing a pig from a Christian" and was sent to jail for 12 months! There is a story also of a Telegraph officer who came across the following message from one General to another on the eve of a great native festival:—" You say that Ibrahim Bey wants to be allowed to fire a salute at *Ramadam*. Stop. I don't care a Damadam."

Attempts were made in 1884 to coax two stern-wheel paddle steamers through the cataracts, and thousands of men were employed in hauling them against swift currents pouring between sharp rocks. The *Ghizeh* was brought in 700 pieces to Semna by barges and assembled and launched at that place, thus avoiding the Second and Semna Cataracts. She was 80 feet in length, 18 feet in beam, and could carry 500 men. However, she survived only as far upstream as the Tanjur Cataract, where she foundered. The other steamer, the *Nassif el Kheir*, was hauled through the Semna Cataract and gave some assistance in transport work over a short length of river. A twin-screw vessel, the *Montgomery*, negotiated the Semna Cataract under steam and helped in local river-transport operations, and a steam pinnace was carried by rail to Saras and launched above the worst part of the Second Cataract. Nevertheless, it may be said that steam transport failed miserably on the Nile above Wadi Halfa in 1884 and 1885,[1] a failure which increased the burden on the railway engineers, whose efforts to provide a satisfactory line from Wadi Halfa to Akasha in the direction of Dongola may now be described. By such a line of railway communication it was hoped to avoid the Second Cataract and those between Semna and Akasha, and to reach a portion of the Nile which, though obstructed here and there by rapids, is more easily navigable than the lower reaches.

When the leading troops arrived in Wadi Halfa in 1884, they found that the existing railway line to Saras was almost worthless as a means of transporting men and stores. The history of this first Sudan Railway, or "Sudan Military Railway" as it afterwards became, is interesting. In 1860, Said Pasha proposed to connect

[1] The failure was due to the state of the Nile, the urgency of the situation, and lack of experience. On three previous occasions, paddle steamers had been sent from Egypt to Khartoum, and nine of these had travelled by river. During the vice-royalty of Said Pasha (1854-63), four steamers ascended the Nile to Khartoum. In 1869, six steamers, including the celebrated *Bordein* and the *Telahawiya* reached Khartoum by the Nile, and three others were taken in sections across the Nubian Desert. These nine vessels were for the use of Sir Samuel Baker in his expedition up the White Nile. Finally, in 1877, four steamers, including the *Abbas*, reached Khartoum in sections by the Suakin-Berber route. (See "The Campaign of Gordon's Steamers," by Colonel Sir Charles Watson, K.C.M.G., C.B., late R.E., appearing in the *R.E. Journal*, Vol. 18, 1888, pp. 211–216.)

the Sudan with Egypt by a railway, and Mougel Bey, a French engineer, reported on the scheme. His estimate was so excessive that the project was shelved until it was revived and enlarged in later years by Ismail Pasha. During 1865 and 1866 two British engineers made rough surveys for a railway from Wadi Halfa to Khartoum, with branch lines eastwards to Massawa on the Red Sea coast and westwards into the Kordofan and Darfur deserts. Their labours were wasted; but some detailed surveys, executed by Mr. J. Fowler in 1871 and 1872, resulted in an elaborate project for a railway from Wadi Halfa along the east bank of the Nile to Koya (140 miles), thence by the west bank to Ed Debba, and finally across the Bayuda Desert to El Metemma, which faces the important caravan centre of Shendi on the Nile. The scheme having met with the approval of Ismail Pasha in 1873, a British firm undertook to build the first 100 miles of 3 ft. 6 in. gauge railway from Wadi Halfa to Kerma at the head of the Third or Hannek Cataract, the consulting engineer of the Egyptian Government being Shahin Pasha, an Egyptian who had been trained in France.[1] Modifications and alterations of the scheme followed; but by 1877, the line had reached Saras (33½ miles), and the formation, exclusive of bridges, was complete for a further 21 miles to a point eight miles short of Ambigol. A sum of £450,000 had then been spent, and the work was stopped on the advice of General Gordon.

Several important items had been omitted from the estimates, and Gordon, as Governor-General of the Sudan, rightly objected to Ismail's ambitious project for which there was no money. " As it is impossible to carry on the construction of the line on the grand scale," he wrote, " we should sell or send back to Cairo everything which could be used there and which will not be wanted at Wadi Halfa. I am of opinion that for an expenditure of £20,000 in all, I could in time carry the railway from Halfa to Amara."[2] He went on to propose that the Nile route beyond Amara should be opened up by a chain of river steamers plying to Khartoum, and that, ultimately, tram lines should be built round the difficult cataracts at Kagbar, Hannek, Merowe and Abu Hamed for the transport of passengers and goods from steamer to steamer.[3] Such a service would have been laborious to maintain and commercially unsound, and nothing more was heard of Gordon's proposals after he had returned to England in 1879. The short length of completed railway from Wadi Halfa to Saras rotted and mouldered until 1884. The

[1] The author is indebted for this information to El Lewa Muhammad Fadil Pasha, an Egyptian officer and railway engineer of great experience in early railway operations in the Sudan, whom he interviewed in Cairo in February, 1935.

[2] See the *Sketch Map of the Nile from Wadi Halfa to Dongola*, included in this chapter.

[3] Gordon proposed that, to save expense, only one crew should be employed and should shift from steamer to steamer. He estimated that the entire cost of his scheme would be £70,000 as against £1,000,000 required to complete the railway to El Metemma. (See *The War in Egypt and the Sudan*, by Thomas Archer, Vol. I, p. 188.)

establishment dwindled to a dozen mechanics ; the buildings fell to ruin ; sand drifted slowly over the rails ; and the only result achieved by a mint of squandered money was a weekly train which meandered slowly over the uneven rails when a locomotive could be found which was capable of drawing it. There is little doubt that Gordon was justified in advising the Egyptian Government to stop construction in 1878 ; but, in so doing, he signed his own death warrant. A railway to El Metemma, though the target of every savage in the Bayuda Desert, would surely have saved Khartoum from destruction, for it is easier to repair a desert line than to build one ; the cuttings and embankments, at least, are ready for use, and probably much of the permanent way may be serviceable.

In 1884, the 8th Company, R.E., then stationed at Chatham, had been recognized for some time as a Railway unit, and in June of that year its two half-companies were attached as separate "sections" to the London, Chatham and Dover Railway for training in construction and traffic duties. The Construction Section was supervised by Captain G. F. Wilson and Lieutenant W. S. Vidal, and the Traffic Section by Captain P. G. Von Donop and Lieutenants J. A. Ferrier and A. W. Roper, R.E., the whole being under Major D. A. Scott, R.E., who had some experience of railway work in India. It was intended originally that the unit should be sent to build the Suakin-Berber Railway (as Messrs. Lucas and Aird and the 10th (Railway) Company, R.E., did in the spring of 1885), but the withdrawal of General Graham's force in 1884 caused this proposal to be dropped. However, when the Nile Expedition began to come under discussion, the 8th Railway Company was well trained and fully capable of constructing, repairing and operating a line. The unit left England in September, 1884, reached Egypt in due course, ascended the Nile to Aswan, where Captain (afterwards Lieut.-Colonel Sir) Horatio A. Yorke, R.E., had already improved the short railway line round the First Cataract to Esh Shallal, and arrived at Wadi Halfa between October 4th and 6th.[1]

Early in September, 1884, the railway to Saras had been taken over for the Sudan Government by Major H. Wilberforce Clarke, Royal (Bengal) Engineers, who had begun platelaying at Saras with old material which he found at that place.[2] Assisted only by some British and Egyptian infantry and a number of native labourers, and by the 4th Battalion, Egyptian Army, who repaired the old formation ahead, Clarke worked slowly towards the south, leaving the Wadi Halfa-Saras line as he found it. However, within a few days after the arrival of the 8th (Railway) Company, Colonel Richard Harrison reorganized the management of the railway. Scott

---

[1] "The 8th Company, Royal Engineers," appearing in the *R.E. Journal*, Vol. 15, 1885, p. 82.

[2] "The Sudan Military Railway," by Lieut. M. Nathan, R.E., appearing in *Professional Papers of the Royal Engineers*, Vol. XI, 1885, p. 36.

was appointed Managing Director; G. F. Wilson, Superintendent of Works; Von Donop, Assistant Director; and Mr. N. M. Carnell, Traffic Manager. Carnell left for India on November 10th, when Von Donop became Traffic Manager, and Ferrier was made Assistant Director and Locomotive Superintendent. Clarke remained in charge of the extension of the line beyond Saras until his departure at the end of November, when Scott took over both the open line and extension work.

In a comprehensive history of the Sudan railways, Lieut.-Colonel W. E. Longfield, R.E. (retd.), writes:—[1]" It is doubtful whether, at the outset of the expedition, the military authorities were fully aware of the bad condition of the railway. It appears to have been assumed that the railway from Wadi Halfa to Saras could be used to carry the boats—upon which everything depended—round the worst part of the Second Cataract; but it was found that neither the permanent way nor the rolling stock was in a condition to meet such a demand. Nevertheless, in spite of this, efforts were made to extend the line beyond Saras without first ensuring that the section of the line from Halfa to Saras was safe and workable.... It was not until Lord Wolseley himself had taken the matter in hand and insisted on the Halfa-Saras line being first made good, that work on the extension was stopped and Major Scott and his staff were able to take systematic steps to put the Halfa-Saras section, and the rolling stock, into working order.... The permanent way material for the extension had not even been dispatched from Cairo and could not possibly arrive in time to affect the essential transport of the force, and the first 35 miles of the line were in no condition to form part of the Line of Communication.... The arrival of the Railway Company and the immediate reorganization of the management by Colonel Harrison created a speedy improvement. By the middle of November, two trains daily were being run to Saras, troops and supplies were being transported to rail-end, and boat stores for more than 700 boats had been deposited at Saras. When it is remembered that three locomotives and some twenty or thirty trucks were the only rolling stock available, the work done by the Railway Company must be considered satisfactory.... After the main body of the Relief Expedition had passed on to the south, the work of the railway, in the transport of men and stores, became less strenuous, and the Railway Staff at Halfa were able to devote their energies to improving the condition of the line and carrying on the extension of the railway southward from Saras."

The extension progressed slowly but steadily during December, 1884, and January and February, 1885. On December 4th the line was open to a point six miles beyond Saras; on January 18th it

[1] Extracts from a typescript lent to the author by Lieut.-Colonel W. E. Longfield in 1935.

extended to Murrat (Moghrat) Wells Station, a further seven and a half miles ; and on February 21st, a station was opened at Ambigol Road, 17 miles from Saras and $50\frac{1}{2}$ miles from Wadi Halfa. The Nile Expedition had then entered on another phase. Khartoum had fallen ; an autumn campaign was in prospect, and a further extension of the railway was essential. Captain Wilson surveyed southward across the desert to Abu Sari and recommended that the line should be taken direct to Akasha instead of following the river, thus avoiding the rocky country near the Nile. Accordingly, an extension towards Firket was put in hand, and by the end of May, 1885, the formation reached to within ten miles of that place. Platelaying proceeded slowly in rear. Ambigol Wells Station ($64\frac{1}{2}$ miles) was established on June 13th, and Tanjur Road Station (75 miles) on July 12th, in spite of the fact that our troops were already withdrawing from the Sudan. Although Dongola had been evacuated on July 5th it was considered that a railway connection to Akasha was needed in case that place should be held as an outpost, so the line was continued and reached Akasha Station ($87\frac{1}{4}$ miles) early in August when the formation had been prepared almost to Firket. Most of the construction was carried out by Captain Wilson and Lieutenant Vidal, R.E., assisted at times by Lieutenants Hawkins, Roper, Nathan and Luard, R.E. Work ceased finally on August 23rd. A corps of 350 Indian platelayers, who had rendered good service under Captain H. D. Olivier, R.E., returned to Bombay, and several Royal Engineer officers left the railway. Olivier remained for a time as Managing Director and then handed over charge to Captain J. A. Ferrier, R.E., on whom fell the chief burden of the railway work during the evacuation.

It cannot be said that the Sudan Military Railway played an important part in the advance of Lord Wolseley's force up the Nile in 1884 ; but it was certainly valuable during the evacuation in 1885. The work accomplished by the Engineer officers and men included the repair and maintenance of $33\frac{1}{2}$ miles of existing railway, the construction of nearly 54 miles of new line through barren country, the transport of 9,000 troops round the worst part of the Second Cataract in ascending the Nile and round almost the whole of it in descending that river, and the carriage of 40,000 tons of stores and munitions. The Engineers were hampered throughout by lack of railway material because all available river transport was employed in forwarding other stores. To give them their due, Major D. A. Scott and the 8th (Railway) Company, R.E., accomplished as much as could be expected under the circumstances.

Telegraph work in the Nile Expedition was as important as railway construction and operation, though, from a technical point of view, it was simple owing to the dryness of the climate. Its special features were the length of the line and the extra responsibility involved through the lack of an adequate postal service. All communications requiring action or early reply were sent by wire. The telegraphists and linemen on the Nile were not exposed to risks such as those run by their brethren on the Red Sea littoral, where the Hadendowa tribesmen sometimes tied an unfortunate lineman to a telegraph pole and burnt him, first placing the ends of the cut wires in the victim's ears in the hope that they would make him "talk like the telegraph" and so disclose the British plans. Yet the operations on the Nile were difficult, if not dangerous, because of the distances to be covered, the lack of material, and the inefficiency of the Egyptian telegraph system which extended into the Sudan.

Under Ismail Pasha the Egyptian telegraphs had been positively Gilbertian. It was decreed, for example, that all telegraph lines must end in the Khedive's Palace at Cairo. In 1884 the telegraph poles north of Wadi Halfa were ant-eaten and rickety, the insulators cracked, and the instruments antiquated. Everything was dirty and incomplete. At Aswan, the first task of Lieutenant A. H. Bagnold, R.E., was to replace an enormous overhead span across the river by an armoured cable, so he secured the only available theodolite in order to measure the width. The instrument had no cross-hairs! Then a brother officer came to the rescue. Producing a very long fair hair, he said with becoming gravity, "I found this in a clothes-brush which I borrowed from my sister before I left England." So all was well. When viewed through the object glass the hair resembled a ship's cable, but it answered its purpose. The Telegraph engineer is always ready to improvise. In London, in 1858, a line was replaced in a long underground pipe of small section by attaching a fine wire to a rat, inserting the rat in the pipe and adding a ferret behind it.[1] Ingenuity almost equal to this was shown on the banks of the Nile by our military telegraphists in 1884 and 1885.

In September, 1884, Colonel C. E. Webber, C.B., late R.E., was appointed Director of Army Telegraphs, Nile Expedition,[2] and proceeded to Egypt where No. 4 Section, Telegraph Battalion, R.E., was arriving by detachments. As already recorded, the unit was commanded by Captain F. W. Bennet, R.E. Five other officers of the Corps—Captains C. K. Wood and A. H. Bagnold and Lieutenants A. M. Stuart, G. A. Tower and C. Hill—served with it during the campaign.[3] Up to the time of Colonel Webber's arrival, Lieut.-Colonel Elliott Wood, R.E., had been in charge of the military telegraphy on the Egyptian system, and had made arrangements

---

[1] "Occasional Notes," *R.E. Journal*, Vol. 14, 1884, p. 240.
[2] Colonel Webber remained as Director until May, 1885, when he was succeeded by Lieut.-Colonel H. F. Turner, R.E.
[3] Lieut. F. G. Bowles, R.E., served with the 4th Section in 1886 during the Mahdist invasion.

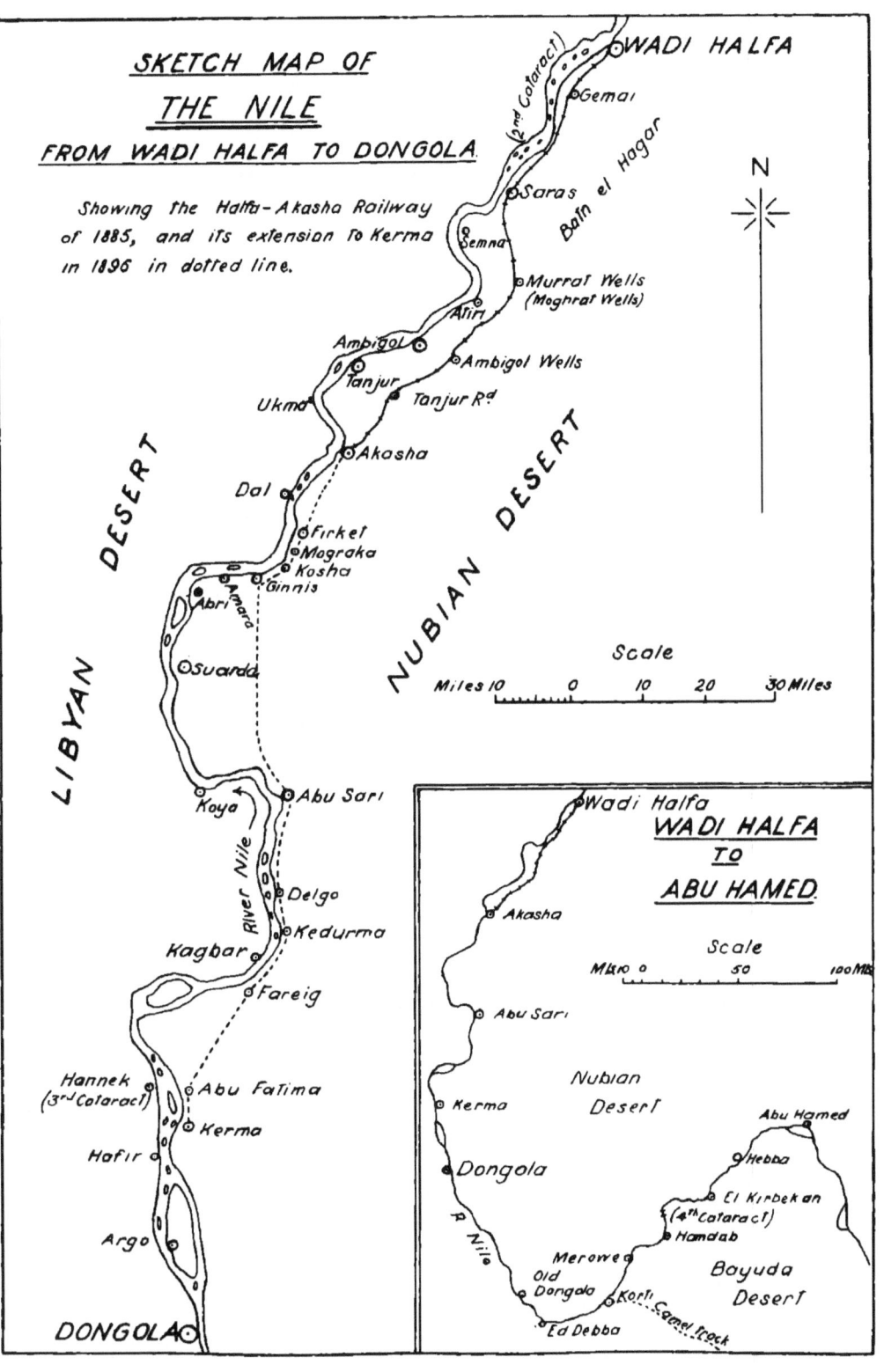

for the immediate needs of the expeditionary force in the face of much opposition from senior Egyptian officials. Permission was obtained to use one wire as far as Wadi Halfa for military work, but the maintenance of the whole system remained in the hands of the Egyptian Government. Such administrative matters, however, are outside the scope of this narrative, which is concerned mainly with operations in the field. The true history of the Nile Expedition is written in the 70,000 messages which passed in seven months through military hands over a system extending eventually for a distance of 1,150 miles from Cairo in the north to Hamdab, beyond Merowe, in the south, to which place the line was carried by Lieutenant A. M. Stuart, R.E., in January, 1885. The late Major-General Sir Andrew Stuart, K.C.M.G., C.B., recorded some interesting details of his adventurous voyage up the Nile and his extension of the telegraph. Describing the carriage of telegraph stores overland he remarked :—[1] " The transport consisted of donkeys, and the method of loading wire on to them was to stand the hind feet in the coil and lift it up on to the saddle over the tail. The back view of a convoy thus loaded resembled a number of footballs." Fourteen years later, after the Omdurman Campaign, Lieutenant J. S. Liddell, R.E., was racking his brains as to the best way to load coils of telegraph wire on to donkeys when Major-General Kitchener rode up and showed him how to do it. Liddell was much impressed, for apparently he did not know of the system adopted during the Nile Expedition.

Many were the trials of the Telegraph officers on field service in 1884. The general transport difficulties south of Wadi Halfa hindered the forwarding of equipment, and no provision had been made for special transport. The equipment itself was often unsuitable. There was so much theft that linemen sometimes preferred to keep their ladders in native cemeteries where, they said, they were safe under the guardianship of the Spirits. Thousands of messages were transmitted in Arabic, and hundreds in cipher. The accounts were complicated. Press correspondents were pertinacious and pushing : staff officers, irritable and insistent. All the Press correspondents, except one, sent long daily messages to their papers. The exception sent only a brief summary of events ; yet his account was as complete as, if not superior to, the others. It was whispered that the necessary " corroborative detail " was added in the London office.

No. 4 Telegraph Section, R.E., voyaged gradually up the Nile during October and November and entered the Sudan at Wadi Halfa, where a temporary cable was laid across the river. The existing main line of telegraph passed up the west bank of the Nile, from a village opposite Wadi Halfa, for a distance of 230 miles to Dongola

[1] Extract from a typed narrative entitled " Telegraphs of the Nile Expedition," written by Major-General Sir Andrew Stuart in 1935, and sent to the author for his perusal. The typescript has been used frequently in writing this account.

and onwards to Ed Debba and Merowe. Stuart pushed forward through Dal to Dongola, establishing an office at Dal on his way, and arriving in Dongola on the same day as Lord Wolseley. The line south of Dongola had been injured by the enemy. In some places the wire had been cut up and thrown into the river, the iron bases of the poles smashed, and the wrought-iron tops carried away.[1] Kitchener and the Mudir of Dongola had repaired the telegraph connection between Ed Debba and Merowe by collecting any of the iron tops which could be found and mounting them on branches of trees, but the line was in a very shaky condition.[2] On the east bank there was a telegraph line along the railway from Wadi Halfa to Saras, and this was prolonged to Akasha, with branch lines to Semna and Ambigol. A branch line was laid also from the Egyptian main line at Dongola northwards along the west bank to Abu Fatima, across the river, and again northwards to Kagbar. On the whole, it may be said that a satisfactory connection was established between all places along the left or west bank of the Nile as far south as Hamdab, and that, on the east bank, the section between Wadi Halfa and Akasha was well supplied with lines.

Wooden telegraph poles were used extensively in Egypt, but they had been replaced in the Sudan by iron poles because white ants have a particular liking for wood. There was another reason, however, for the substitution of metal. The Bedouin, who were employed to guard the lines, had a fixed idea that Allah had put the wooden poles in the desert for the use of the faithful. What with building huts and making coffee it was not long before the wire lay on the ground, and when the unbelievers found that the wire continued to function in this lowly state so long as there was no rain, they actually laid some field-lines across the desert with bare wires held down by stones. Great was the disgust of the Bedawi at such a scurvy trick!

The reticence and discretion shown by the Sapper telegraphists in withholding secret news from earnest inquirers was worthy of the highest praise. For instance, when the River Column under General Brackenbury was recalled at the beginning of the evacuation in 1885, the fact was known to every telegraphist for two days before the troops or newspaper correspondents became aware of it. Secret messages were usually in code; but on one occasion, during the autumn of 1885, Captain A. H. Bagnold, R.E., was asked by General Stephenson at Cairo to transmit a secret message in clear to an officer at Wadi Halfa who had no access to the code book at that place. The message was very important, but required only a simple

---

[1] "The Telegraphs of the Nile Expedition," a Paper read by Major-General C. E. Webber, C.B., late R.E., appearing in the *Journal of the Society of Telegraph-Engineers and Electricians*, Vol. XIV, 1885, pp. 452–474.

[2] *Report on Army Telegraphs, Nile Expedition,* 1885, by Captain F. W. Bennet, R.E., p. 1.

DESERT TELEGRAPHS, NEW STYLE, 1886.

reply in the affirmative or negative. "It so happened," writes Bagnold,[1] "that I had, at Wadi Halfa, a telegraph clerk, Sapper John Conolly, who could send so fast that often the other clerks on the line could not read his sending, and as a Morse reader by sound he could receive and write down clearly as fast as any of his fellows could send clearly. I asked him on the wire, 'How many words a minute can you take down?' and he replied 'Anything you like to send provided that the sending is good.' I told him that I should want him on the line at 9.0 p.m. My instrument mechanic and I rigged up a Morse Inker as an automatic transmitter, the contact being made between a piece of platinum wire and the milled roller which normally propelled the Morse paper strip on which messages were received. I then marked out the message accurately in Morse characters on a strip and cut them out carefully with a penknife and a sharp bradawl. Running the strip through the Inker, I succeeded in arranging that its speed could be varied between 30 and 50 words a minute. At the appointed time I cleared the Cairo office and the line, leaving only Sergeant W. F. Seggie, R.E., in the office, and I instructed Halfa to leave only Conolly in that office. We passed the strip through at 47 words a minute and asked Conolly if he had got the message. He replied 'Some of it. Try again.' We passed the strip through again, reducing speed a little, and Conolly said 'Not all.' Again the strip went through at a slightly less speed and Conolly was satisfied. The message was delivered by Conolly himself at Halfa, and in subsequent conversation with clerks on the line, I ascertained that they knew nothing of its contents. I believe this is the earliest instance of automatic transmission by the Telegraph organization of any Army."

During the evacuation of the Sudan, when the British troops were retiring before the advancing armies of the Khalifa, invaluable work was performed by the officers and men of the Telegraph Section under the general supervision of Lieut.-Colonel H. F. Turner, R.E., at that time Director of Army Telegraphs with the Nile Expeditionary Force.[2] A line of telegraph was urgently needed between Abu Fatima and Kagbar on the east bank, because the permanent line to the west of the Nile in that section was far out in the desert, so a bare copper wire was laid across the stony waste by Captain G. A. Tower, R.E. The troops used it as a guide by night, picking it up and allowing it to run through their hands as they plodded along. When the dervishes reached Abri near Amara in December, 1885, the most advanced telegraph office on the east bank was at Akasha, where the railway ended; but a fortified post had been established at Ginnis beyond Kosha, and communication

---

[1] Notes by Colonel A. H. Bagnold, C.B., C.M.G., late R.E., sent to the author in July, 1935. These notes have been used extensively in writing this account.

[2] Lieut.-Colonel H. F. Turner, R.E., was Director of Army Telegraphs from May 27th to July 31st, 1885.

with it was needed. Accordingly, Lieutenant A. M. Stuart, R.E., ran a bare wire for 30 miles through Firket and Mograka to Ginnis. The dervishes did not know of its existence until they attacked Mograka and stumbled over the wire. A connection was also made by bare wire from the west bank opposite Akasha to the permanent line at Ukma, thus giving Akasha two lines into Wadi Halfa ; and when 700 dervishes attacked the post at Ambigol Wells, north of Akasha, tearing up the railway line, pulling down the field telegraph, and shouting to Captain J. A. Ferrier, R.E., and his little garrison of 50 Berkshires, "Railway finish. Telegraph finish. *You* finish," they never dreamed that Akasha was still in telegraphic connection with headquarters. For three days, Ferrier made a most gallant defence,[1] and drove his assailants away before the relieving forces arrived on December 4th, 1885. These few examples must suffice to illustrate the achievements of the Telegraph personnel in the Nile Campaign. A portion of the 4th Telegraph Section, R.E., returned to England in August, 1885, with Bennet, Tower and Hill; but Bagnold and Stuart, with the remainder of the unit, continued to operate the Sudan lines until these were handed back to the Egyptian Government in 1887.

When Lord Wolseley reached Dongola on November 3rd, 1884, he had not yet realized the urgency of his mission. While at Wadi Halfa in October, he had heard of a disaster to three officers who had been allowed by Gordon to voyage downstream from Khartoum because the situation at that place was becoming critical and few written messages seemed to reach Kitchener, the nearest political officer. Lieut.-Colonel J. H. D. Stewart, 11th Hussars, with Mr. Frank Power and M. Herbin, the British and French Consuls, had left Khartoum on September 10th, and running the gauntlet of Berber[2] and Abu Hamed, had been wrecked in the *Abbas*, about 50 miles below the latter place, and treacherously murdered. The tidings carried by this forlorn hope never reached Wolseley, who was aware only that Gordon had telegraphed on July 13th that he could hold out for four months, and consequently he continued his plans for a methodical and deliberate advance such as Kitchener executed in the campaign of 1897–98. As Winston Churchill puts it, he excluded the idea of a wild glorious rush, which might result in astonishing success or terrible disaster.[3] Then came disquieting rumours that all was not well with Gordon, though Kitchener telegraphed from Korti that he had learnt from spies that Gordon had said " he could hold Khartoum for years." The necessity of pushing forward immediately was made clear to Wolseley at last by a letter, dated November 4th and received on November 17th, in which Gordon wrote " We can hold out forty days with ease ; after

---

[1] For this exploit, Capt. Ferrier was awarded the D.S.O. when this Order was founded in 1886.
[2] Berber had fallen to the dervishes on May 26th, 1884.
[3] *The River War*, by the Rt. Hon. Winston Churchill, c.h., M.P., p. 60.

that it will be difficult. . . . Since 10th March, we have had up to date, exclusive of Kitchener's of 14th October, only two dispatches. . . . I have sent out a crowd of messengers in all directions for eight months. I should take the road from Ambukol to Metammah, where my steamers wait for you." A safe limit having now been fixed by Gordon at 40 days, or up to December 14th, a general advance from Dongola was begun on December 2nd, and by Christmas Day most of Wolseley's force was concentrated at Korti beyond Ambukol.

As Gordon was known to be short of supplies and the hot weather would soon be approaching, Wolseley adopted a new plan of campaign. He decided to divide his striking force. A mobile "Desert Column" on camels would cross the Bayuda Desert to El Metemma, as suggested by Gordon, occupying the oases of Gakdul and Abu Klea on the way, and establishing contact with Gordon's steamers at the end of its march; and a "River Column" would fight its way up the Nile, capture Abu Hamed, open up the desert route to Korosko as an additional line of communication, drive the rebels from Berber, and join hands with the Desert Column at El Metemma.[1] Brigadier-General Sir Herbert Stewart was appointed to command the Desert Column, and Major-General Earle, the River Column. Colonel F. G. Burnaby, late Royal Horse Guards, was posted to the Desert Column to become Commandant at El Metemma, and Colonel Sir Charles Wilson was sent with it as Chief Intelligence Officer. Captain Lord Charles Beresford, R.N., was also attached to it. The only Royal Engineer officers with this column were Sir Charles Wilson, Major Dorward and Lieutenant Lawson, and for a time, Major Kitchener, Captain Leach and Lieutenant Burton. Four others—Major Courtney, Captain Blackburn and Lieutenants Kenney and Kincaid—were posted to the River Column. Wilson and Kitchener were "politicals"; Leach and Burton, "camelmen"; Kenney, a boat repairer; and Courtney, a surveyor. The entire responsibility for any engineering work fell on Dorward and Lawson with the Desert Column, and on Blackburn and Kincaid with the River Column; and Dorward and Lawson were accompanied by only 26 N.C.O's and men of the 26th Field Company, R.E., mounted on riding camels and with a few baggage camels for their Engineer equipment.[2] The 48 officers of the Corps on service in the Sudan had dwindled to ten officers selected for the final and vital operations towards Khartoum. This was the penalty imposed by the enormous line of communication along the Nile.

On December 30th, 1884, Sir Herbert Stewart set out from Korti at the head of the Desert Column to attack and occupy El Metemma. The column consisted of three Camel Regiments, a small Naval

---

[1] See the general map, entitled *The Anglo-Egyptian Sudan*, at the end of this volume
[2] "Desert Notes from Korti to El Goubat," by Lieut. H. M. Lawson, R.E., appearing in the *R.E. Journal*, Vol. 15, 1885, p. 71.

Brigade, three 7-pounder guns, 500 infantry, and Dorward's detachment of Royal Engineers, with the necessary medical and transport details—in all about 1,100 officers and men—and Kitchener marched with it as Intelligence Officer. Grassy country was soon reached, and the column made such good progress that it arrived at the oasis of Gakdul Wells on January 2nd. It had then covered about 100 miles and was half-way across the Bayuda Desert. Leaving the Guards Camel Regiment and the Royal Engineers (including Kitchener) at Gakdul, Stewart started back at once for Korti with the remainder of the troops and the transport. Owing to the inadequate number of camels. it was necessary to collect supplies at Gakdul before a further advance could be made. Stewart left Korti again on January 8th, 1885, with about 2,000 officers and men, and arrived at Gakdul on the 12th, accompanied by Sir Charles Wilson.

Gakdul was a curious spot. " Leaving the plain," writes Wilson,[1] " we turned up a wide valley with good grass, and then swinging left, passed through a narrow opening into a sort of punch-bowl, or crater-like place into which three or four ravines drained. Two stone forts had been built,[2] the ground laid out for us to camp on, paths made and signboards put up. Dorward and Lawson, R.E., had been working hard at the watering arrangements. They had made a small canal into which water was pumped for the camels, and a reservoir of biscuit-tins for the men. I passed the afternoon with Kitchener, who had established himself in a cave on the side of the hill. He was very sore at an order I brought him to return to Korti with Stanley Clarke's[3] convoy. Gakdul is not a pleasant place. It is a regular frying-pan ; the rocks get heated up and there is no breeze ; but about 2 a.m. a hurricane comes down the hills and nearly pulls the blanket off one. . . . Stuart-Wortley[4] has joined me for service at Khartoum with Gordon. Burnaby has also come in with a convoy." Captain H. P. Leach and Lieutenant E. M. Burton, R.E., were at Gakdul Wells, engaged in the camel transport duties which kept them moving up and down the line of communication.

On January 14th, 1885, Sir Herbert Stewart resumed his march towards the oasis of Abu Klea with 1,600 officers and men and 2,900 camels, and on the evening of the 16th, he bivouacked within three miles of the Abu Klea wells after covering more than 40 miles from Gakdul. He was then confronted by a dervish army in a partially entrenched position barring his way to the wells, so he made a

[1] *From Korti to Khartum*, by Colonel Sir Charles W. Wilson, K.C.B., K.C.M.G., F.R.S., late R.E., pp. 12–13.
[2] A third fort had also been constructed from boxes of Commissariat stores. The engineering work executed at Gakdul is described in a report by Major Dorward, R.E., entitled " Work done at Jakdul Wells," appearing as Appendix 42 in the official *History of the Sudan Campaign*, by Colonel H. E. Colvile, C.B., Part II, pp.251–253.
[3] Colonel Stanley Clarke commanded a Camel Regiment.
[4] Lieutenant E. J. M. Stuart-Wortley, King's Royal Rifle Corps.

zariba and prepared to fight on the morrow. The enemy's drums, called *noggara*, sent their sinister sound over the night air. There is a tale of these drums which is worth repeating. During the expedition under Holled-Smith against Tokar in 1891, a report was sent to Cairo that, as Osman Digna's men had been beating their *noggara* for several days, it was evident that warlike preparations were in progress. The report was duly telegraphed to England; but the message which reached an astonished Home Government ran: " The fierce and formidable tribe, the Noggara, have been continuously beaten during the last few days."[1]

The British were early astir on the morning of January 17th, and at ten o'clock their square advanced over rough and uneven ground, leaving a small garrison to protect the baggage and camels in the *zariba*. Within an hour, the square was opposite the left flank of the dervish position and threatening to enfilade it. Then our skirmishers were seen running in at full speed and followed by an avalanche of at least 5,000 savages. The yells of the dervishes as they swarmed towards the waiting square were like the roar of the sea. Wave after wave went down before the fire of Martinis and Gardners, and their banners sank to the blood-stained ground; but still they came on, regardless of death, and broke at last into the square, where for ten minutes bayonet met spear in a whirlwind of dust and smoke. Burnaby fell dead; Wilson shot a man who was rushing to spear Stewart; but not a dervish who entered the square survived to tell the tale. Abu Klea was perhaps the most savage and bloody action ever fought by British troops in the Sudan. By 3.30 p.m. the enemy were in full retreat, leaving 1,200 dead and wounded on the field. Our cavalry pushed forward to the wells and were followed in due course by the infantry. In spite of heavy losses, the men were in great spirits, but they suffered severely from the bitter cold during the ensuing night. Abu Klea was a decisive victory. Yet it hastened the fall of Khartoum, for the news of the battle convinced the Emir Abd el Kerim, one of the Mahdi's Generals, that Gordon's defences should be carried without delay, and, after a period of uncertainty, he managed to dissuade the Mahdi and the other khalifas and emirs from raising the siege, and withdrawing to Kordofan, as they had intended. " If we succeed and enter Khartoum," said he, " the English will not dare to come on; and if we fail, we shall still have time to retreat." After a council on January 25th, the Mahdi sent word to all his camps that he had seen a vision in which the Prophet had assured him that God had put the lives of all the garrison of Khartoum into his hands and that the attack should take place on the following day.

The Sappers, under Dorward and Lawson, saw little of Abu Klea

---

[1] *The Egyptian Soudan. Its Loss and Recovery*, by Lieuts. H. S. L. Alford and W. D. Sword, p. 77.

for they were with the transport in the *zariba*. Lawson writes :—[1] " Between the hours of 7 and 10 a.m. the Sappers were employed in constructing a fort of saddles and biscuit-boxes, at times under a hot cross-fire. Just before the square moved out we were told off to a biscuit-box fort on the left of the *zariba*, which we were ordered to garrison. How anxiously we watched the square in its advance until the falling ground hid it from our sight. In a few minutes, however, the boom-boom of the 7-pounder, the charge downhill of a motley crowd of Arabs in the direction we knew the square to be in, and followed by their hastier return, told us the crisis had come and gone. Not till 11 o'clock that night did we hear the full news and details of the fight." Wilson was the only Royal Engineer in the battle at Abu Klea, and at the end of it he was so exhausted that he was obliged to lie for some time in the shade of a kneeling camel. Little did he think that he would soon be called upon to command the column and to bear the full responsibility of the attempt to rescue Gordon. His instructions were simple.[2] He was to proceed, as an Intelligence Officer, to El Metemma, and then, with Captain Lord Charles Beresford, R.N., and three young military officers and a small detachment of British infantry, to Khartoum in one or more of Gordon's steamers, which were to be placed under Beresford's command. On arrival at Khartoum, he could, if he thought fit, march the detachment through the city to impress upon the populace the proximity of Wolseley's army. He was to give a letter to Gordon, discuss the situation with him, and tell him of the progress of General Earle's column up the Nile, and, having done so, he was to return to El Metemma and then to Korti. He was also to report fully to Wolseley whenever possible. It is worthy of particular note that he received no orders to rescue Gordon. .

On the day after the battle at Abu Klea, Sir Herbert Stewart resumed his march towards the Nile, proposing to strike it about three miles upstream of El Metemma and then to capture that town ; but he was delayed by difficult country, and at daybreak on January 19th, having covered nearly 30 miles, he was still four miles from the river and crowds of the enemy were issuing from El Metemma to attack him. He had tried to accomplish a surprise advance to the Nile, but the noise made during the night march by the struggling camels and their drivers had risen to the sky as a loud continuous roar and defeated his object. The column reached open ground, where the troops halted on a gravelly knoll around which they proceeded to form a *zariba* of camel-saddles and biscuit-boxes to protect the transport. Meanwhile, the enemy worked round them and kept up a desultory fire. The Sappers built two small redoubts

[1] " Desert Notes from Korti to El Goubat," by Lieut. H. M. Lawson, R.E., appearing in the *R.E. Journal*, Vol. 15, 1885, pp. 71–73.
[2] The instructions are quoted in full in the official *History of the Sudan Campaign*, by Col. H. E. Colvile, C.B., Part II, pp. 8–9.

of saddles and boxes, for the defence of the enclosure, one within it and the other on an adjacent knoll, and while they were so engaged, Sir Herbert Stewart was seriously wounded.[1] As Colonel Burnaby had been killed at Abu Klea, the chief command then fell to Sir Charles Wilson as the next senior officer, and the latter, after consultation with Stewart, decided to force his way at once to the river through the horde of dervishes who occupied a ridge between him and the water. At 3 p.m. the British square began its advance, Lawson marching with it and Dorward remaining in the *zariba*. "I fully felt the gravity of the situation," writes Wilson,[2] " but from the moment I entered the square I felt no anxiety as to the result. I asked Boscawen[3] to take executive command and told Verner[4] to give the square its direction." The square of 900 British soldiers approached the ridge, and 800 dervishes charged down upon it only to be mown down by the steady fire of rifles and guns. With great difficulty our troops reached the Nile after darkness had fallen, and bivouacked near the little village of Abu Kru, also called Gubat, which lies a short distance upstream of El Metemma. The transport, and its guard, came in on the following day, when Dorward and Lawson began to fortify the village. The camels were so weak that they could hardly crawl to the water, the cavalry horses had been ridden to a standstill, the infantry were exhausted, and the leader of the expedition in hospital; yet the Nile had been attained, and the victory of Abu Kru added to that of Abu Klea.

Writing of Sir Charles Wilson's dash for the Nile, Royle remarks :—[5] " It was one of the most hazardous of military operations and has been condemned by nearly all professional critics. He not only divided his already reduced forces in the face of the enemy, but cut himself off from his baggage, artillery and supplies. On the other hand, there was an absolute necessity for gaining a position on the river with the least possible delay, and, if a further justification were wanted, Sir Charles can point to the complete success which attended the movement." Wilson afterwards advanced on El Metemma, but decided not to attempt an assault. Instead, he consolidated his position at Gubat, where Dorward and Lawson began to construct an entrenched redoubt with the assistance of the infantry. This work was not completed until February 11th, on which day Sir Redvers Buller arrived as the successor of Sir Herbert Stewart, and with him, Kitchener and Burton as Intelligence and Transport officers.

While Wilson was reconnoitring towards El Metemma on January

---

[1] The wound proved to be mortal, for Major-General Sir Herbert Stewart died on February 16th.
[2] *From Korti to Khartum*, by Colonel Sir Charles W. Wilson, K.C.B., K.C.M.G., F.R.S., late R.E., p. 353.
[3] Lieut.-Colonel the Hon. E. E. T. Boscawen, Coldstream Guards.
[4] Captain W. W. C. Verner, Rifle Brigade.
[5] *The Egyptian Campaigns*, 1882–1899, by Charles Royle, p. 353.

21st, 1885, four of Gordon's steamers, under Nushi Pasha, were seen coming down the Nile. From their commander, Wilson learnt of their remarkable adventures during the previous four months.[1] Nushi Pasha showed Wilson several letters written by Gordon on December 14th. In one, addressed to the Chief of Staff, Gordon expressed his conviction that the position was extremely critical and that Khartoum might fall within a few days ; in another,[2] to his friend Major Charles Watson, R.E., he wrote, " I think the game is up. . . . We may expect a catastrophe in the town in or after ten days' time ; " and in a third, to Nushi Pasha, he urged the latter to ask the British commander to hasten.[3] Nushi also showed Wilson a tiny scrap of paper on which Gordon had scrawled " Khartoum all right. Could hold out for years. 14th December, 1884." This fiction was a ruse intended to deceive the enemy if the paper fell into their hands ; but unfortunately it was allowed to percolate to England where it misled the British public most effectively because Gladstone's Government suppressed the more serious news.

Realizing the urgency of the case, Sir Charles Wilson's first resolve was to start at once for Khartoum ; yet it was not until the morning of January 24th that he set out from Gubat with Captains F. R. Gascoigne and L. J. Trafford, Lieutenant E. J. M. Stuart-Wortley, 20 men of the Royal Sussex Regiment, and 240 Sudanese and Egyptian soldiers, to run the gauntlet of the dervishes in the small paddle-steamers *Bordein* and *Telahawiya*. Why did he delay his departure for nearly three days ? According to his own account[4] he heard that large dervish forces were advancing on Gubat from the north and south, and he felt bound to reconnoitre in both directions before leaving his small command. On the 22nd, he went downstream in the *Telahawiya* and found no threat from the north, and his cavalry reported that there was no danger from the south. On the 23rd, as Lord Charles Beresford was in hospital and the Naval Brigade depleted, he was obliged to man his two selected ships with Sudanese collected from all four vessels ; and it was necessary also to overhaul the worn machinery of the ships and to add protection against bullets. He knew that Khartoum was still holding out, and there was nothing to show that a delay of a day or two would

---

[1] These adventures are described by Colonel Sir Charles M. Watson, K.C.M.G., C.B., late R.E., in an article entitled " The Campaign of Gordon's Steamers," appearing in the *R.E. Journal*, Vol. 18, 1888, pp. 211-217. The most complete account is given, however, in the diary of Nushi Pasha himself.

[2] The original envelope of this letter is in the R.E. Museum at Chatham. It is addressed " Colonel Watson, C.M.G., R.E., Cairo." The original letter itself is in a large album in the Museum, entitled " *Cairo, 1883-1886*," containing letters, photos, cards, etc., collected by Sir Charles and Lady Watson during Sir Charles Watson's service in the Egyptian Army. Other letters from Gordon are also in this album.

[3] *Gordon and the Sudan*, by Dr. Bernard M. Allen, pp. 424-425.

[4] Statement by Sir Charles Wilson, dated Korti, March 23rd, 1885, quoted in an article entitled " The Attack on Sir Charles Wilson, K.C.M.G., C.B., F.R.S., in the *Fortnightly Review*," appearing in the *R.E. Journal*, Vol. 15, 1885, pp. 128-129.

THE RIVER FORT AT GUBAT IN JANUARY, 1885.

Lieut. H. M. Lawson, R.E. (standing third from left), directing entrenching work by the Royal Sussex Regiment.

affect the issue. This, in brief, was Wilson's explanation to Lord Wolseley; but the Commander-in-Chief remarked thereon:[1] " He might have started on the afternoon of the 21st and did not start till the morning of the 24th." Wilson stood condemned, and, as events proved, the delay was fatal. Yet if he had started on the 21st in ill-protected, hurriedly equipped, poorly provisioned and badly engined vessels, would he have reached Khartoum?[2]

Dr. Bernard Allen writes:—[3] " Admirable as he was in his own field as head of the Intelligence Department, Sir Charles Wilson was not fitted either by experience or by temperament to grapple with a critical emergency. He had never held command in the field,[4] and he lacked that force of character and driving power which would enable him to override the inclination shown by his naval colleague to delay the departure of the steamers. . . . The present writer, after a detailed study of the documentary evidence, formed the opinion that it was probably Lord Charles Beresford's influence which induced Sir Charles Wilson to delay the departure. Subsequently this opinion was completely confirmed by a first-hand account of the incidents at Metemma given to the present writer by Major-General the Hon. E. J. Montagu-Stuart-Wortley." Who knows what passed between Beresford and Wilson? Beresford was determined to go, and Wilson may have thought that a small delay was warranted if Beresford's services could be secured thereby. If Wilson is blamed for the delay at Gubat, what of the much greater delay due to the insufficient camel transport provided for Stewart's journey across the Bayuda Desert? Charles Watson wrote[5] that it would have made no difference if the steamers had left Gubat three days earlier, for in that case Khartoum would have fallen three days sooner. On the other hand, both Slatin and Ohrwalder, who were prisoners in the Mahdi's camp at the time, were of opinion that, if Wilson had started at once, the whole aspect of affairs might have been changed. Be that as it may, it is a fact that the Nile Expedition failed mainly because it started too late and took too long on the road.

Few stories are so dramatic as that told by Wilson in *From Korti to Khartum*. His little party struggled up the Nile in ships which

---

[1] Public Record Office Papers, W.O., 32–127.

[2] Sir Charles Wilson's refutation, point by point, of the allegations made against him by the correspondent of the *Daily Chronicle*, writing in the *Fortnightly Review*, appears in an article entitled " Sir Charles Wilson and the *Fortnightly Review*," in the *R.E. Journal*, Vol. 15, 1885, pp. 168, 169 ; and an able defence of Wilson is made in an article by Colonel Sir C. M. Watson, K.C.M.G., C.B., late R.E., entitled " Lord Cromer and Sir Charles Wilson," which appears in the *R.E. Journal*, Vol. VII, Jan.-June, 1908, pp. 293–300.

[3] *Gordon and the Sudan*, by Dr. Bernard M. Allen (1931), pp. 426 and 453.

[4] It is noteworthy that at Abu Kru, as already related, Wilson handed over the executive military command to another officer as soon as it devolved upon him.

[5] " Lord Cromer and Sir Charles Wilson," by Colonel Sir Charles M. Watson, K.C.M.G., C.B., late R.E., appearing in the *R.E. Journal*, Vol. VII, Jan.-June, 1908, pp. 293–300.

would have been sent to the bottom by any well-directed shell. The *Bordein* and *Telahawiya* had each an open wooden turret for one gun in the bow, and another amidships between the paddle-boxes. Behind the funnel and main hatchway was a deck-house on top of which the guard of a few British soldiers was sheltered by walls of boiler-plate. Round the sides of the ship the bulwarks were reinforced with boiler-plates fixed to wooden stanchions and surmounted by horizontal wooden beams to give head-cover and provide a continuous loophole above the plates.[1] Every hole and corner of the vessels was filled with fuel, supplies and ammunition. The old " penny steamers " of the Thames were converted into armed blockade runners.

Little opposition was encountered during the voyage upstream, though the natural difficulties were formidable as the Nile was exceptionally low, and on the morning of January 28th, Khartoum was in sight above the trees on Tuti Island. A native on the bank shouted that the city had been taken and Gordon killed, and Wilson noticed many wrecked houses and some of Gordon's boats at the water's edge. These signs, and the absence of any of Gordon's steamers, combined with a regular fusillade which was beginning from the Omdurman side and from Tuti Island, seemed to confirm the sad news. At length, when the Palace could be seen, it was evident that the Egyptian flag no longer floated over it. Khasm el Mus, the Arab captain of the *Bordein*, was sure that some disaster had happened. Nevertheless, the ships held on past Tuti Island until they reached the junction of the Blue and White Niles. The roll of musketry from each side was mingled with the roar of concealed guns. Hundreds of dervishes were seen standing under their banners at the point where the rivers join, and thus the last doubt was dispelled. Wilson reluctantly gave the order to go about and the ships ran at full speed down the Nile. It seemed almost impossible that either should escape ; but at 4 p.m. after hours of severe fighting and many casualties, they passed beyond the range of the enemy's guns.

The *Bordein* and *Telahawiya* approached the Sixth Cataract. On January 29th, the *Telahawiya* struck a rock and sank at Jebel Rowiyan above the Sabaluka Gorge, all on board being transferred to the *Bordein* : on the 31st the *Bordein* grounded at Mirnat Island, some 40 miles above Gubat, and could not be refloated. Wilson and his party took refuge on the island while Stuart-Wortley, in a small boat, ran past an enemy's battery and summoned help from Gubat. Lord Charles Beresford then led a rescue party upstream in the *Safiya* and, after a stiff fight, brought Wilson and his men to Gubat

---

[1] The bulwark protection provided by Gordon took the form of a breastwork of timber astern of the paddle-boxes, and loopholed iron plates forward of them. (See the illustration showing the *Bordein* as reconditioned in 1935.) Wilson replaced the timber by iron.

GORDON'S STEAMER, THE "BORDEIN," AT KHARTOUM IN 1935.

Moored opposite the Palace on January 26th, 1935, on the occasion of the 50th anniversary of Gordon's death.

[*Photo by the Author.*]

on February 4th.[1] Wilson left Gubat on the 6th and in due course reached Korti, where he reported to Wolseley. Whatever his defects as a military commander he had proved that he could keep a cool head in many desperate situations. At Khartoum he took his ships into the very jaws of death, but all to no purpose. Gordon was dead, and the heart went out of the Nile Expedition. Threatened by the advance of a large dervish army, Sir Redvers Buller evacuated Gubat and retired to Abu Klea.[2] He was surrounded at that place, but the enemy soon drew off in expectation of a strong attack by Sir Evelyn Wood, who had been sent with a few troops from Korti to Gakdul Wells to carry out the withdrawal. Buller was able to resume his retreat to Gakdul Wells, and early in March, 1885, the Desert Column was back once more in Korti. The Mahdi reigned supreme from the Bayuda Desert to the far south, from the Red Sea Hills to Darfur.

While the Desert Column was marching and fighting its way to Gubat, the Nile or River Column under Major-General W. Earle, C.B., C.S.I., was moving upstream from Korti towards Abu Hamed, the infantry in some 200 whalers and the mounted troops along the banks. This column saw little fighting except on one occasion. It began to leave Korti on December 28th, 1884, passed through Merowe, remained at Hamdab from January 3rd to 24th, 1885, and after ascending the Fourth Cataract, reached Birti. There, on February 4th, Earle heard of the fall of Khartoum and received orders to halt. However, he was allowed to resume his advance on February 8th, and on the 10th encountered 2,000 dervishes in a position at El Kirbekan. Earle turned the enemy's flank and repelled a furious charge, but unhappily he was killed when victory had been won. His successor, Brigadier-General H. Brackenbury, C.B., continued the forward movement on the following day. On February 17th, Brackenbury was at Es Salamat, and on the 20th at El Hebba close to the scene of the murder of Colonel Stewart and his companions. The wreck of the *Abbas* lay on a rock, and some relics of the victims were found in a house. The mounted troops having crossed the river, the column advanced until the evening of February 23rd, when it was only 26 miles from Abu Hamed; but on the following day it was ordered back to Merowe, where it arrived

[1] In running the gauntlet of a dervish battery at Wad Habashi below Mirnat Island, the *Safiya* was disabled by a shot which penetrated her boiler; but the hole was mended under great difficulties by Mr. Benbow, R.N., her Chief Engineer, so that she was able to carry Wilson's party to Gubat. Later, she was abandoned to the enemy, and was not recaptured until the time of the advance southwards after the Battle of Omdurman in September, 1898. The plate fixed over the hole by Benbow in 1885 was then found to be still in position, and it was removed and sent as a memento to Lord Charles Beresford. It is now in the Royal Naval Museum at Greenwich.

[2] It was intended originally that Buller should move down the Nile to Berber to meet the River Column while reinforcements from England landed at Suakin and marched to join them. An order for 10,000 umbrellas was placed in England for the use of these reinforcements!

on March 5th. Thence it moved downstream to Korti and joined hands with the travel-stained Desert Column.

The engineering duties with the River Column were shared by Captain J. E. Blackburn and Lieutenants W. F. H. S. Kincaid and A. H. Kenney, R.E. Major D. C. Courtney, R.E., was also with the column for a time and surveyed the country around the Fourth Cataract, north of Hamdab. Blackburn had 22 N.C.O's and men of the 26th Field Company R.E., and Kenney ten men of the 11th Field Company. "Our rate of progress was very slow," writes Blackburn,[1] "for some time not more than three miles a day. The first day's cataract work illustrates pretty nearly our everyday experience—the same monotonous grind, walking over slippery and sharp-pointed rocks or through deep sand, hauling on ropes, wading in water, and cutting pathways up the steep banks. Of engineering work there was little. Camp and *zariba* building, a little demolition and a good deal of boat patching made up the sum total. Kenney and his men did by far the lion's share of the latter. Hut building and defence works have been our lot since stopping at Merowe." The Engineers with the River Column had little chance of glory. Intended to be the main advance on Khartoum in support of the thrust across the Bayuda Desert, this column did not attain even its first object, the capture of Abu Hamed, for it was not allowed to make the attempt.

Towards the end of March, 1885, the force at Korti began to retire on Dongola, leaving a rearguard for a time at Merowe. There was a Russian scare on the Afghan border[2] and withdrawal from the Sudan was probable. Wolseley wished to hold on to Dongola and continue the campaign, but he was forbidden to do so. Complete evacuation was ordered on May 11th and was soon in progress, the forts and large buildings being destroyed as the troops retired. Sir Redvers Buller superintended the arrangements until June 17th, when he handed over the command of the rearguard to General Brackenbury, but much responsibility fell on Colonel (afterwards Lieut.-General Sir) Robert Grant, late R.E., who was made Commandant of the Abu Fatima District around Kerma and was required to evacuate the troops in that area. Brackenbury left Dongola on July 5th, bringing with him all whalers, steamers and stores, and the transport by water from Abu Fatima to Akasha was managed by Captain H. H. Settle, R.E. At about this period, an Egyptian or Nile Frontier Force of British and Egyptian troops was formed under Major-General Sir Francis W. Grenfell, K.C.B., who had succeeded Sir Evelyn Wood as Sirdar of the Egyptian Army.

[1] Extracts from an article entitled "With the Nile Column from January 17th to March 7th, 1885," by Captain J. E. Blackburn, R.E., appearing in the *R.E. Journal*, Vol. 15, 1885, pp. 151–155. See also "From Debbeh to Hamdab with the Nile Column" and "Journal of the 4th Section of the 11th (Field) Company, R.E.," appearing in the same volume, pp. 50–52 and 85.
[2] The "Panjdeh" incident.

Grenfell established his headquarters at Aswan, and Brigadier-General W. F. Butler, C.B., assumed command of an advanced brigade at Wadi Halfa with outposts at Kosha, 42 miles south of the railway terminus at Akasha. The Mahdi had died in June, and Lord Wolseley had returned to England in the same month. The Nile Expedition was at an end.

However, the Khalifa Abdullahi, who, on the Mahdi's death, became his successor, had already decided to invade Egypt, and towards the end of November, 1885, a dervish army appeared a few miles south of Ginnis and attacks were made on British posts at Kosha and Mograka. General Sir Frederick Stephenson then came up from Cairo, and on December 30th, at the head of two British brigades, attacked and defeated the enemy at Kosha and the neighbouring village of Ginnis. Major A. J. Hepper was the Commanding Royal Engineer in these operations, and Captain J. E. Blackburn, R.E., was present with a section of the 11th Field Company. It is recorded that after the Battle of Ginnis, a plan of the British fort at Kosha was found in the dervish camp. The plan was a drawing such as a young child might have produced, but it was headed with the awe-inspiring announcement: " This is the Fort of the Infidels, the Enemies of God, the Liars, God curse them ! "[1] The action at Ginnis was a serious check to the Khalifa, and thereafter his forces remained inactive for several months at Kerma.

Early in 1886, it was decided that the Egyptian Frontier Force should retire into Egypt, and this movement was completed by the middle of April. Egyptian troops were allotted for the defence of Wadi Halfa and Korosko, while the British troops were withdrawn to Aswan or still farther to the north. Major A. J. Hepper, R.E., began to fortify Wadi Halfa, and by the end of the month he had enclosed the landing stage with loopholed mud walls and had converted the railway workshop into a defensible post. Throughout the remainder of 1886, the fortifications grew steadily, and they were continued in later years. The entire town was enclosed by a bastioned mud wall, with detached forts as an outer line of defence, and Fort Khor Musa was built some five miles upstream in line with a small redoubt on the river-bank and another on an island. Meanwhile the Khalifa, having announced that he was about to take " Constantinople, Mecca and other parts of the world," advanced his troops in June, 1886, occupied Akasha, and destroyed the railway from that place as far as Ambigol Wells. In the autumn he prepared to besiege Wadi Halfa, and at the same time to cut its communications by sending a column through the western desert to reach the Nile at Argin, a few miles below the town. Lieut.-Colonel H. C. Chermside, C.B., C.M.G., R.E., took command of the troops at Wadi Halfa on October 20th, a few days after the enemy under Nur

[1] The plan is reproduced in the *R.E. Journal*, Vol. 16, 1886, page 104.

el Kanzi had advanced through Saras to Gemai, which is only 22 miles from Halfa. The situation was threatening; but Chermside moved out with his cavalry and camel corps, supported by an armoured train, and having driven the enemy from Gemai and Saras, returned to Halfa. He was not disturbed again until Nur el Kanzi pushed an advanced guard to Gemai once more on April 27th, 1887. On this occasion Chermside made a night march, cleared Gemai, seized the railway station and some commanding positions around Saras with his cavalry, and attacked with his infantry. He killed Nur el Kanzi and annihilated the dervishes. This was his last military exploit in the Sudan, for he left the country a few months later and terminated his service with the Egyptian Army in May, 1888, to resume his Consular duties, first in Kurdistan and then in Constantinople. The small affair at Saras on April 28th, 1887, is remarkable as the first occasion on which Egyptian regular troops fought the dervishes without British or other support.[1] Chermside's victory helped to raise the *morale* of the Egyptian Army, for it showed the native troops that the Khalifa's warriors were not invincible.

It is impossible in this brief narrative to follow in detail the ebb and flow of the dervish invasion. The enemy reoccupied Saras in September, 1887, and pushed forward to Gemai; then they attacked Khor Musa and were repulsed by Lieut.-Colonel J. H. Wodehouse, R.A. Afterwards, they concentrated at Saras, with Gemai as an advanced post. However, on August 29th, 1888, they made a night attack and succeeded in entering one of the Khor Musa forts, from which they were expelled by reinforcements under Wodehouse.[2] In the spring of 1889 they planned to invade Egypt and isolate Wadi Halfa by sending a force through the western desert to a point on the Nile 25 miles north of Aswan. The Emir Wad en Nejumi marched to Argin, below Wadi Halfa, and attacked it on July 1st, only to be driven away from the Nile by Wodehouse. Afterwards, Major-General Sir Francis Grenfell, K.C.B., Sirdar of the Egyptian Army, came up from Cairo to superintend the operations. Wad en Nejumi was marching northwards past Abu Simbel, followed step by step by a column under Wodehouse, and Kitchener, then Adjutant-General, had concentrated a column of all arms at Toski, about 60 miles downstream of Wadi Halfa, to oppose him. Two brigades of Egyptian infantry and a regiment of British cavalry having arrived, and a brigade of British infantry being on its way

---

[1] It is interesting to note that a uniform case, believed to be Gordon's, was found in the dervish camp, after the battle, filled with Arabic documents. It was presented in later years by Lieut.-General Sir H. C. Chermside, G.C.M.G., C.B., to the R.E. Museum at Chatham, where it can now be seen with many other Gordon relics. In 1935, the author saw Gordon relics also in the museums at Omdurman and Wadi Halfa. Others may be found in museums in London. Gordon's bible was presented to Her Majesty Queen Victoria and is now in Windsor Castle.

[2] These and other operations during the dervish invasion are described fully in *Mahdiism and the Egyptian Sudan*, by Major F. R. Wingate, D.S.O., R.A.

from Aswan, Grenfell attacked and defeated Wad en Nejumi in a decisive battle at Toski on August 3rd, 1889. In this action, Kitchener was in command of the mounted troops, and, by skilful manœuvring of his squadrons, lured the dervish forces to destruction. Wad en Nejumi was killed and his force almost annihilated. Several Royal Engineers, besides Kitchener, took part in these operations. Major A. G. Clayton and Captain A. C. Foley were present with a section of the 24th Field Company. Lieut.-Colonel H. H. Settle and Lieutenant C. Godby were on Grenfell's staff, and Lieutenant W. S. Gordon commanded the artillery detachment with Kitchener's mounted troops.[1]

The Battle of Toski marked the turning point in the tide of the Mahdist invasion. The dervish hordes retreated sullenly towards the south. Peace descended on Egypt. Not until Kitchener had succeeded Grenfell as Sirdar in April, 1892,[2] was that calm disturbed, and then only by a few raids towards Wadi Halfa in 1893 and 1895. The enemy were exhausted, and the Egyptian Government was fully occupied in pacifying and developing the Red Sea littoral and setting its own house in order. The time was not yet ripe for an attempt to re-occupy the Sudan, though Kitchener, feeling that at any moment circumstances might necessitate a sudden move, made every preparation for such an eventuality.

Many reputations were lost during the Nile Campaign and its aftermath, but that of Kitchener was firmly established. Nevertheless, his first step to fame did not come until 1894, when, as Sirdar of the Egyptian Army, he received the K.C.M.G. in recognition of the able assistance which he gave to Lord Cromer in dealing, promptly and effectively, with a difficult contretèmps, known as the " Frontier Incident," which occurred at Wadi Halfa. Kitchener had his failings, but they were far outweighed by his sterling attributes. He possessed determination, strength, sagacity, and experience both in civil and military administration. He had shown daring and enterprise in war, and was a master in overcoming the natural obstacles inseparable from campaigning in savage countries. He loved the desert, and was respected by its wildest tribes. He inspired his subordinates with trust and confidence. These were the qualities which brought him to the front and enabled him to reconquer the Sudan.

---

[1] *Mahdiism and the Egyptian Sudan*, by Major F. R. Wingate, D.S.O., R.A. (1891), pp. 602, 603, 605. Lieutenant W. S. Gordon, R.E., was a nephew of General Gordon. He had been transferred to the Royal Engineers from the Royal Marine Artillery. The artillery commander for the whole force was Major H. M. Rundle, D.S.O., R.A.

[2] In the meantime, Kitchener had been Adjutant-General in Cairo, and Inspector-General of the Egyptian Police, which he re-organized very successfully.

CHAPTER V.

GORDON IN KHARTOUM.

To Major-General Charles George Gordon, C.B. Who at all times and everywhere gave his support to the weak, his substance to the poor, his sympathy to the suffering, his heart to God. Born at Woolwich, 28th January, 1833. Slain at Khartoum, 26th January, 1885. He saved an Empire by his warlike genius. He ruled vast provinces with justice, wisdom and power; and lastly, obedient to his Sovereign's command, he died in the heroic attempt to save men, women and children from imminent and deadly peril. "Greater love hath no man than this, that a man lay down his life for his friends."—

Inscription on the Gordon Memorial in St. Paul's Cathedral, London.

THE scene is the Nubian Desert at Korosko on the Nile: the date, February 2nd, 1884. Gordon and Stewart are setting out for distant Khartoum, and Gerald Graham is there to bid them good-bye. The desert is a sea of black volcanic hills and blacker ravines. With a shake of the hand, and a " God bless you " from Graham, the travellers mount and ride to the head of the line of swaying camels, Stewart with a revolver, Gordon unarmed. They thread their way along a sandy valley. Graham, gazing after them, expects a wave of the hand; but Gordon never looks back; his thoughts are far ahead. The caravan turns the dark corner of one of the hills and is gone. Sadly, Graham returns to his steamer with a presentiment that he will never see Gordon again. Nor did he. The man who was to make history had started on his last journey.[1]

Let us observe Gordon as he was at this time. Compact in build and of medium height, his figure and gait expressed unbounded vitality, resolution and strength. Few could ride fast and far enough to outstrip him in the desert. He carried his 51 years with remarkable buoyancy. Time had streaked with grey the curly brown hair of his youth and had traced deep lines across a wide forehead and around a well-shaped mouth. His face, though not beautiful, was arresting. Its serene and quiet aspect was unruffled except for an occasional wave of impatience or anger, which swept across it and was gone like a wind over a mountain lake. The steadfast and fearless gaze of his blue-grey eyes showed the upright spirit within. This was a man born to inspire trust and confidence.

Gordon's character was a tangled skein which few could unravel. " Pray do not suppose," said William Edward Forster in March,

---

[1] The scene is described by Lieut.-General Sir Gerald Graham, V.C., G.C.M.G., K.C.B., in his book *Last Words with Gordon*, p. 35.

1884,[1] "that I disparage the qualities of this wonderful man. I know no man like him. I go further than that. I believe him to be a hero. As a personal administrator he has the intuitions of genius. He is utterly regardless of all personal considerations. He despises money. He cares nothing for fame; he cares nothing for pleasure, for life or for death. He seems to have no temptations. Perhaps he may have one temptation. If you will read his striking journals and letters, you will feel—I do not know why—that perhaps he is weary of life. Well, he says so; and I confess it sometimes occurs to me that it would be the greatest possible delight to him to be a martyr. Undoubtedly he is a deeply religious man. In this world, God's guidance and government are to him the strongest and greatest realities of life, and so we find this, that, while personally one of the humblest of men, thinking nothing of his own qualities, he has the power of unlimited self-confidence in himself to be God's instrument. He gets out of difficulties in a way no other man could. No wonder that, with all those qualities, those savages look upon him, not as a man, but as a demi-god."

A modern author, John Buchan, is more critical. In estimating Gordon's character he writes:—[2] "He had a mind which was a strange blend of crudity and power. He had little knowledge of the world outside his profession; his education had been slight[3] and was not supplemented by later study except constant reading of the Bible; his views on ordinary questions, economic, educational and political, were often shrewd but not based on any considered philosophy of life, and the cosmogony in which he believed was mediæval in its simplicity. He had a quick eye for facts, and his judgment on matters with which he was acquainted was mostly sound and penetrating, but on other subjects few men could talk wilder nonsense. Like Cromwell, he relied more on instinct than on reason; his first summing up of a situation, his first impression of a man, was commonly his last. His heart was tender, and he hated all cruelty and injustice; but his temper was often out of control, and he was capable of great harshness. His humility with his Maker did not make him humble before his fellow-mortals. He was not an easy man to work with for he had moods of extreme irritability and petulance. With a deep love and charity towards mankind, he could be grossly uncharitable in his behaviour to individuals. His habits were temperate, indeed ascetic, for he had trained his body

---

[1] Extracts from an address by Mr. W. E. Forster in a debate in the House of Commons on March 10th, 1884, quoted in *Gordon and the Sudan*, by Dr. Bernard M. Allen (1931), p. 301. The author has made extensive use of Dr. Bernard Allen's valuable and comprehensive history in writing this chapter. It is the most complete and accurate account yet published of Gordon's work in Africa.

[2] Extracts from *Gordon at Khartoum*, by John Buchan (1934), pp. 45-53. John Buchan is now Lord Tweedsmuir, Governor-General of Canada.

[3] A matter of opinion. Gordon, as a cadet at Woolwich, gained a commission in the Royal Engineers in competition against the cream of the public schools of England.

to need little nourishment and little sleep. He made sparing use of wine and spirits,[1] but he smoked incessantly. The smug gentility of Victorian England he had at all times detested, and he carried his dislike so far as to be scornful even of ordinary etiquette. He had that scorn of death which comes from an abiding sense of the littleness of life. He longed for the joy of battle even when he knew the ultimate triviality of the issue. The convictions of the quietist could not bridle the instincts of the born man of action. He accepted in the simplest sense every word of the Bible as a direct revelation. His belief in predestination was no blind fatalism, for, though he knew that his life was in God's hands, he omitted no precaution to ensure the success of his work and his own health and safety. To learn to wait in patience was the chief discipline of his life. He prayed at all times, for in prayer he felt himself at one with God, and through prayer he could benefit the world."

The opinion of Lord Cromer is worth quoting. Major Sir Evelyn Baring, as he then was, had little in common with the daring and somewhat unconventional soldier with whom he was associated, yet he shows a singular sense of fairness and toleration. " A wave of Gordon *cultus* passed over England in 1884," writes Cromer in 1908.[2] " During this stage of natural excitement anyone who had attempted to judge General Gordon's conduct by the canons of criticism which are ordinarily applied to human action, would have failed to obtain a hearing. Whatever may have been General Gordon's defects, the main lines of his character were really worthy of admiration. I do not speak so much of his high courage and fertility of military resource, though in these respects he was remarkable,[3] but of his moral qualities. His religious convictions, though eccentric, were sincere. No one could doubt the remarkable purity of his private life, or his lofty disinterestedness as regards objects, such as money and rank.[4] His aims were unquestionably high and noble. He was thoroughly unconventional. He chafed under discipline and was never tired of pouring forth the vials of his wrath on the official classes. ' I must say,' he wrote, ' I hate our diplomatists. I think, with few exceptions, they are arrant humbugs; and I expect they know it.' . . . Impulsive flightiness was the main defect of General Gordon's character."

[1] The insinuation made by Mr. Lytton Strachey, in his book *Eminent Victorians* (1918), that Gordon drank to excess under the influence of the African climate, is disproved completely by Dr. Bernard Allen in *Gordon and the Sudan*, pp. 83–96, where the subject is dealt with at length.

[2] Extracts from *Modern Egypt*, by the Earl of Cromer, Vol. I, pp. 429–439.

[3] A tribute to Gordon's capacity as a soldier is given by Colonel Sir William Butler in his book *Charles George Gordon*, p. 128. " There is a peculiar trait in Gordon's method of war," he writes. " Above every other English soldier of his time he possessed the power of catching the weak point of his adversary. It is the root and foundation of successful offensive warfare. Turenne, Frederick, Napoleon, Stonewall Jackson possessed this power. With it, almost everything is possible to a commander."

[4] In these and some other respects, Gordon's character resembled that of the late Lawrence of Arabia.

MAJOR-GENERAL CHARLES GEORGE GORDON, C.B.,
LATE ROYAL ENGINEERS.

[*Portrait as a Colonel by Géruzet Frères, Brussels, March, 1880.*]

GORDON APPOINTED GOVERNOR-GENERAL OF THE SUDAN.

In general it may be said that Gordon excelled as a soldier and military engineer. He seems to have been eternally at war with himself in an endeavour to follow an ideal. He craved insistently for action and more action ; yet he longed for periods of contemplation, whose monotony, nevertheless, he could not endure. He shunned feminine society, despised celebrity,[1] and loved power. He strove to be humble and was very sympathetic to Eastern ideas and customs. Though merciful to the weak, he could be ruthless to his enemies. A keen sense of humour supported him in anxious moments. Quick-tempered and excitable, outspoken and critical, he made many enemies. Lastly, he was extraordinarily brave and deeply religious. A fascinating, yet contradictory, character. A man perhaps without counterpart in history.[2]

Gordon was selected in 1884 for service in the Sudan largely because of his previous experience in that country, but also because the British public clamoured for his appointment. Gazetted to the Royal Engineers on June 23rd, 1852, he had served with distinction in the Crimea, and in 1860 had gone to China and shared in the advance on Peking. During the spring of 1862, he was summoned to Shanghai to check the advance of the Taiping rebels, and was appointed in March, 1863, to command 3,000 Chinese desperadoes whom he welded into an " ever victorious army " and led in many desperate fights. The Emperor made Gordon one of his generals and wished to load him with gifts and honours, few of which Gordon would accept. The British Government showed its appreciation by promoting him to the rank of Colonel and making him a Companion of the Bath. In 1865 he returned to England as " Chinese Gordon." Then he vanished from the public eye, and for several years devoted himself to the most prosaic of regimental duties and to philanthropic work amongst the poor. Emerging from seclusion in 1874, he was selected to succeed Sir Samuel Baker in the Sudan, and proceeding by Suakin and Berber to Khartoum, journeyed southwards as far as Gondokoro in the Equatorial Province. He laboured unceasingly in the heart of Africa until he had extended a chain of posts along the Upper Nile and had opened a line of regular connection to Lakes Victoria and Albert. Incidentally, he made the first detailed survey of a long stretch of the Nile between the two lakes and established friendly relations with the King of Uganda.

In the autumn of 1876, Gordon returned to England ; but the Khedive was so impressed by the value of his work in the far south that, in February, 1877, he appointed him Governor-General of the whole Sudan—an area of about 1,000,000 square miles. Gordon

---

[1] He detested dining out if there was a chance of his being "lionized." (See " Reminiscences of General Gordon " in the *R.E. Journal*, Vol. 15, 1885, p. 12.)

[2] A study of Gordon's character is given in *Gordon. An Intimate Portrait*, by H. E. Wortham ; but it can be realized more clearly by a perusal of Gordon's journals than by any other means. (See *The Journals of Major-General C. G. Gordon, C.B., at Khartoum*, edited by A. Egmont Hake (1885).)

ruled this vast territory until 1879, his main preoccupation being to combat the slave-trade. He also revolutionized the administration, abolished wholesale flogging, checked bribery, arranged for a water-supply at Khartoum, and established a proper arsenal and dockyard.[1] By 1878, however, he had fallen into disfavour with the Egyptian Government, and so, when Ismail Pasha was deposed in the following year, he relinquished his Governor-Generalship, went on a mission to King John of Abyssinia, and returned once more to England. Persuaded by his friends to accept the post of Private Secretary to a new Viceroy of India, he visited that country in 1880, but resigned the appointment soon after his arrival. Next he went to China, then to Mauritius, and in 1882, as a Major-General, to South Africa. Again he vanished for a time, for he spent the year 1883 in the study of Biblical archæology and topography in Palestine. He had not been too successful of late, and thought that his work for England was done. Towards the close of the year, he went to Brussels at the request of the King of the Belgians, and having decided to fulfil a promise to serve him in the Upper Congo, he sent in the resignation of his commission to the War Office.

The British Government, however, did not accept the resignation. Instead, they asked Gordon to return to the Sudan to withdraw the Egyptian garrisons, whose safety was threatened by the Mahdi's hordes, and to substitute for Egyptian rule a suitable form of administration. This he agreed to do. On January 18th, 1884, accompanied by Lieut.-Colonel J. D. H. Stewart of the 11th Hussars, he left London in the Continental Express. Again he was the hero of the hour. Lord Wolseley carried his solitary kitbag, Lord Granville took his ticket, and the Duke of Cambridge held open the carriage door for him, and so he started on his fateful journey to Khartoum. In Cairo, he interviewed Sir Evelyn Baring and received his final instructions. There also he renewed his acquaintance with Zubeir Pasha, a former slave-dealer of the Bahr el Ghazal Province of the Sudan, who had been interned in the Egyptian capital for the last six years and was his sworn enemy. Zubeir had been valuable to Egypt, but had become too powerful. In spite of his unscrupulous character, he had many fine attributes. Gordon had ruined Zubeir's slave-trade and had been responsible for the death of his rebel son, Suleiman; yet he had so high an opinion of Zubeir's ability, strength and influence with the nomad tribes that he wished to take him with him to Khartoum.[2] This project was vetoed by Baring, so Gordon and Stewart, accompanied by Sir

---

[1] These civil activities of Gordon's early service in the Sudan are dealt with in Chapter XX.
[2] Zubeir was the greatest slave-trader of the Sudan from 1856 to 1876. In 1874, he attacked Darfur, killed the Sultan, and with the help of the Egyptian Governor of Khartoum, conquered the province. In 1878, the Italian, Gessi, one of Gordon's lieutenants, led an expedition against Zubeir's son, Suleiman, who was organizing a rebellion in Darfur against the Khedive, and killed him.

Gerald Graham, left Cairo and travelled by rail and steamer to Korosko, whence, as already related, they set out on February 2nd to cross the Nubian Desert to Abu Hamed on the road to Berber and Khartoum.[1]

In due course the travellers reached Berber, Gordon carrying with him a *firman* or decree, appointing him Governor-General of the Sudan, and two proclamations, one of which announced the proposed evacuation of the country. He was at liberty to withhold the proclamations if he thought fit; but, unfortunately, he showed the proclamation of withdrawal to the notables of Berber. Further, he announced that, as Egypt was about to evacuate the Sudan, she could not give effect to her treaty undertaking to abolish slavery in the country by 1889, and that slavery would consequently continue there, a statement which was misinterpreted in England as condoning the slave-trade. Gordon felt that, unless he told the Berber chiefs that he had been sent to evacuate the Sudan, they would, as soon as they found that he was sending down the Egyptians from Khartoum, conclude that he had been keeping them in the dark as to his intentions. Sir Gerald Graham considered that Gordon adopted the right course in being perfectly open with them. There is no doubt, however, that the publication of the news of the withdrawal induced many waverers to flock to the Mahdi's standards and resulted eventually in the fall of Berber and the massacre of its inhabitants. " Hussein Pasha's defence appears to have been half-hearted," writes Major Wingate,[2] " though there is no doubt that he did make a stand. Unnerved by the fatal proclamation which gave the Sudan away, he evidently despaired of success." To this, Father Ohrwalder adds :—[3] " Gordon committed a mistake by which he gave the death-blow to himself and his mission." However, the unfortunate effects of the announcement of withdrawal were not immediately apparent, and Gordon and Stewart voyaged upstream to Khartoum, where they were received on February 18th with the acclamations of the entire population.

At Khartoum, Gordon found Colonel de Coetlogon, one of Hicks Pasha's officers who, happily for himself, had been left in charge of

---

[1] Gordon's career, prior to the siege of Khartoum is described in many volumes and articles. An excellent history of his work in China is given in *Gordon in China*, by Dr. Bernard M. Allen (1933), and this part of his career is dealt with in less detail in the general Memoir which appears in the *History of the Corps of Royal Engineers*, by Major-General W. Porter, Vol. II, pp. 500–529. A Memoir appears also in the *R.E. Journal*, Vol. 15, 1885, pp. 47–50, and another by Dr. Bernard Allen in Vol. XLVII, March, 1933. Much information can be gained also from Gordon's Journals (1885) and his letters to his sister (1888), and from the volumes which have been referred to already in this narrative. Particular phases of Gordon's career appear in a number of historical and biographical works. An interesting article by J. Elizabeth Garcia, entitled " Recollections of General Gordon in South Africa," was published in *The National Review* in January, 1936.

[2] *Mahdiism and the Egyptian Sudan*, by Major F. R. Wingate, D.S.O., R.A., p. 121.

[3] *Ten Years' Captivity in the Mahdi's Camp*, by Joseph Ohrwalder, p. 123. Father Ohrwalder, a missionary, was for many years a prisoner of the dervishes. He escaped in 1891.

the garrison when his commander marched to destruction in the desert. El Obeid having capitulated to the Mahdi on January 17th, 1883, the Khedive had determined to organize a counter-stroke and, after a delay of several months, had sent Colonel Hicks into the wilds of Kordofan at the head of 10,000 men to attack the enemy in their strongholds. This Egyptian force was annihilated in the early days of November, 1883, and the guns, rifles and ammunition so obtained, added to those already secured at El Obeid, converted the Mahdi's rabble into a powerful army. Assisted by de Coetlogon and Stewart, Gordon proceeded to cleanse the Augean stable of Khartoum. He granted interviews to all who had grievances, burnt the implements of corporal punishment and the Government books which recorded unjust debts, and liberated many innocent prisoners. The inhabitants rejoiced that he had returned to save them from the oppression of Egyptian officialdom and the cruelties of the Mahdi. Gordon, on his part, was confident that his presence alone would suffice to extinguish the rebellion. He had no desire to fight; and when he despatched de Coetlogon to Cairo on February 20th, 1884, he gave him an open letter in which he stated that Khartoum was as safe as Cairo or Kensington Park![1]

So confident was Gordon that he telegraphed to Baring that he was proceeding forthwith to send his Egyptian soldiers downstream as well as the women, children and officials, and he actually began this evacuation. Some of the inhabitants were alarmed at the reduction of the garrison; but Gordon was resolved that, if it were humanly possible to do so, he would carry out his orders and evacuate the 21,000 troops and 11,000 civilians in the Sudan. He implored the British Government to allow the ex-slave-dealer Zubeir to be sent to the Sudan to rule it as Governor-General after the evacuation. According to Gordon, and in the opinion also of Baring, who had now come round to Gordon's view, Zubeir was the only man with the necessary strength of character for such a task; but before the end of February, Gordon learnt that the Government would not agree. Although he tried his best to arrange terms with the Mahdi for the peaceful departure of the whole garrison, the dervish leader rejected his overtures with contempt. He was thwarted at every turn. At the same time, by alluding to some armed reconnaissances as "attacks" and "expeditions," by advancing a new proposal that 3,000 troops should be retained in the Sudan to keep order, and by asserting that, if Egypt was to be kept quiet, "the Mahdi must be smashed up," Gordon conveyed to the Home Government the impression that he was bent on aggression when actually he had no such design. He asked that a small flying column of British or Indian troops should be detached from the large force which the Government had dispatched to the Red Sea littoral under General

[1] *Gordon and the Sudan*, by Dr. Bernard M. Allen, p. 275.

Graham, and be sent up from Suakin to hold Berber and impress the wavering tribes in that region. In the belief that this would be done, he announced that these troops were actually on their way to Khartoum. He telegraphed several times daily to Baring, revealing his latest ideas as they occurred to him. This was his usual custom; but it caused some confusion in the mind of the British representative at Cairo as in one message Gordon suggested sending troops up the Nile to Dongola. Baring wanted carefully considered plans and not trains of thought.

Doubt began to displace confidence in Gordon's mind. On March 1st he wired " I will do my best to carry out my instructions, but I feel a conviction that I shall be caught in Khartoum." The task seemed already beyond the power of any one man. In Gordon's eyes, Baring appeared obstructive, and Gladstone's Government suspicious and even hostile. By March 8th, the situation had become critical, and Gordon dispatched a series of urgent telegrams which indicated that Khartoum would soon be surrounded. He told Baring that the Mahdi had raised the tribes and was about to cut the road to Berber and destroy the telegraph. In face of the approaching storm, he suggested that an Egyptian force should advance through Dongola to Berber. " We have provisions for six months," he added. The British Government, however, refused to send any troops to Berber, and repeated their refusal to employ Zubeir. They were averse, also, to dispatching an Egyptian force up the Nile. Their attention was fixed on Sir Gerald Graham's operations south of Suakin. They distrusted Gordon and appeared to think that he was disregarding his instructions. Then, on March 12th, 4,000 dervishes cut the telegraph line at Halfaya, nine miles downstream from Khartoum, and stopped all river traffic. Thereafter, the Mahdi's forces closed in on Gordon from every side. The siege of Khartoum had begun.

When Gordon reached Khartoum in February, he found it not wholly unprotected, for it was shielded on the north and west sides by the Blue and White Niles respectively, and on the south and east sides by a line of fortification designed to extend from river to river. This line had been planned and constructed by Abd el Kader Pasha, the energetic Governor-General who replaced the ineffective Raouf Pasha in the spring of 1882. Having served with the French in Mexico, and under Sir Samuel Baker in the Sudan, Abd el Kader had probably acquired some knowledge of fortification; and when news of the Arabi rebellion in Egypt was added to that of several recent victories of the Mahdi in the Sudan, he lost no time in strengthening the defences of Khartoum and asking for large reinforcements. His line of fortification was located about one mile distant from the town and formed an arc some four miles in length, protecting it on the east and the south. It consisted of a ditch and

F

parapet, with bastions at intervals, and three or four entrances unprovided with proper gates. The ditch was made of such a width that no one could jump across it.[1] Assuming that 20,000 soldiers could have been assembled to hold Khartoum, and that it was essential to save the town from bombardment, the situation and extent of the defensive line selected by Abd el Kader is not open to much criticism; but the line was far too long to be held safely by any garrison which Gordon could muster in 1884. Yet Gordon had no time to lay out and fortify a more restricted line nearer to the town. Stewart must have seen Abd el Kader's works when he was in Khartoum from December 16th, 1882, to March 8th, 1883, as one of three officers sent to assist the Egyptian Governor-General, so Gordon was probably aware of the nature of Abd el Kader's line. On his arrival, he wished to abandon that line, but was persuaded by the inhabitants not to do so. The northern end of the line was fixed securely on the high left bank of the Blue Nile; but the other or western end was "in the air," for it rested on the shelving and indefinite right bank of the White Nile.

Colonel de Coetlogon, arriving with Hicks Pasha in March, 1883, was confronted with the problem of the western end of the fortified line, part of which was flooded during the summer and then uncovered as the water receded. Major (now General Sir Reginald) Wingate writes:—[2] "Hussein Pasha Sirri and Colonel de Coetlogon busied themselves in putting in order such defences as were possible for an area at once extensive and, what made more difficulty, of greatly varying extent. De Coetlogon personally attended to a work of great importance. He drove a deep ditch and parapet 1,530 yards long across a level space or plain left dry by the subsidence of the river." Frank Power, correspondent of *The Times*, who came to Khartoum in August, 1883, and remained there when Hicks marched to destruction, states that de Coetlogon had almost finished the excavation of the ditch at the beginning of January, 1884.[3] The whole of Abd el Kader's works had been allowed to fall into a sad state of dilapidation, for Power says of Khartoum (on January 1st and 2nd, 1884) "It is an open town, with gardens, fields, etc., and not a bit of defence till Colonel Coetlogon commenced the ditch. . . . We have paved the bottom of the ditch and side of the fortification with spear-heads, and have strewn the ground for 100 yards in front with iron 'crows' feet,' things that have three short spikes up, however they are thrown, and then beyond, for 500 yards, broken bottles (you know the Mahdi's men are all in bare feet). At intervals

---

[1] Evidence of Mikhail Bey Daud at the court martial of Colonel Hassan Benhassaoui in June, 1887, quoted in *Mahdiism and the Egyptian Sudan*, by Major F. R. Wingate, D.S.O., R.A., p. 561.
[2] *Mahdiism and the Egyptian Sudan*, by Major F. R. Wingate, D.S.O., R.A., p. 107.
[3] *Letters from Khartoum. Written during the Siege by the late Frank Power, H. B. M.'s Acting Consul, Correspondent of The Times*, edited by his brother Arnold Power (1885), pp. 67, 69.

we have put tin biscuit-boxes full of powder, nails, bullets, at two feet under the ground, with electric wires to them, so *Messieurs* the rebels will have a *mauvais quart d'heure* before they get to the ditch." De Coetlogon and Power not only strengthened and repaired the fortifications but took steps to see that they were properly guarded, for during a surprise visit before dawn on January 3rd, they had discovered that most of the defenders were asleep. Although only 2,000 men were available until December 26th, 1883, to hold the four miles of ramparts,[1] in January, 1884, the total amounted to 8,000 men after some outlying garrisons had marched in. In general it may be said that, when Gordon arrived, the defences were of some value, though held by an insufficient number of inferior troops. They were weakest at the western end, where a retrenchment parallel to the White Nile, above high-water level, was required to guard that flank when the river subsided. At the moment, this may not have been evident ; and when, late in the siege, the need for a retrenchment became clear, the garrison was too feeble to complete the work, although a beginning was made.

So magnetic and attractive was Gordon's personality, that when Power had only known the defender of Khartoum for four days he wrote :—[2] " Gordon is a most lovable character—quiet, mild, gentle and strong ; he is so humble too. The way he pats you on the shoulder when he says, ' Look here, dear fellow, now what do you advise ? ' would make you love him. When he goes out of doors there are always crowds of Arab men and women at the gate to kiss his feet, and twice to-day the furious women, wishing to lift his feet to kiss them, threw him over. He appears to like me and already calls me Frank. He likes my going so much amongst the natives, for not to do so is a mortal sin in his eyes. He is indeed, I believe, the greatest and best man of this century."

De Coetlogon having left Khartoum, Gordon, Stewart and Power settled down, as happily as they might, to organize the defence of the town. On March 6th, a new French Consul arrived—Monsieur Herbin, ex-editor of an Anglophobe newspaper in Cairo, called the *Bosphore Egyptien*—but they saw nothing of him nor wished to do so. " He has not yet called on any of us at the Palace," remarks Power.[3] On the 14th, Power wrote :—[4] " Hicks Pasha's defeat not only entailed a loss of life, but deprived General Gordon of all those who have ever shown any ability in the public departments. Here he must do everything himself. If General Gordon succeeds in extricating the garrison at Halfaya, that is about all he can do before an English force arrives. With the material in his hands,

---

[1] *Letters from Khartoum*, p. 59.
[2] *Ibid.*, pp. 96, 97.
[3] *Ibid.*, p. 101.
[4] Extract from a typescript entitled " Frank Power's telegrams and letters from Khartoum," lent to the author by Dr. Bernard Allen in August, 1935.

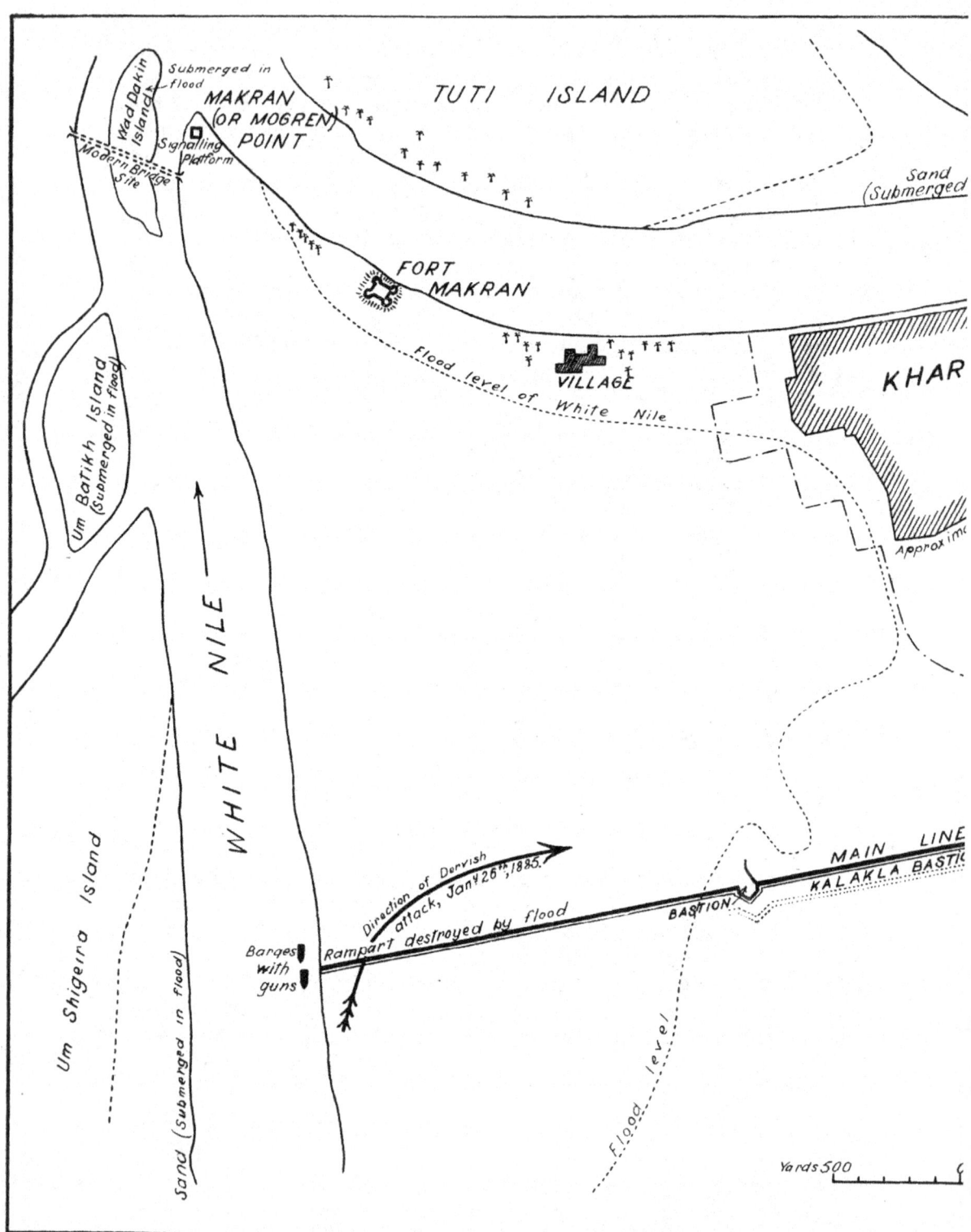

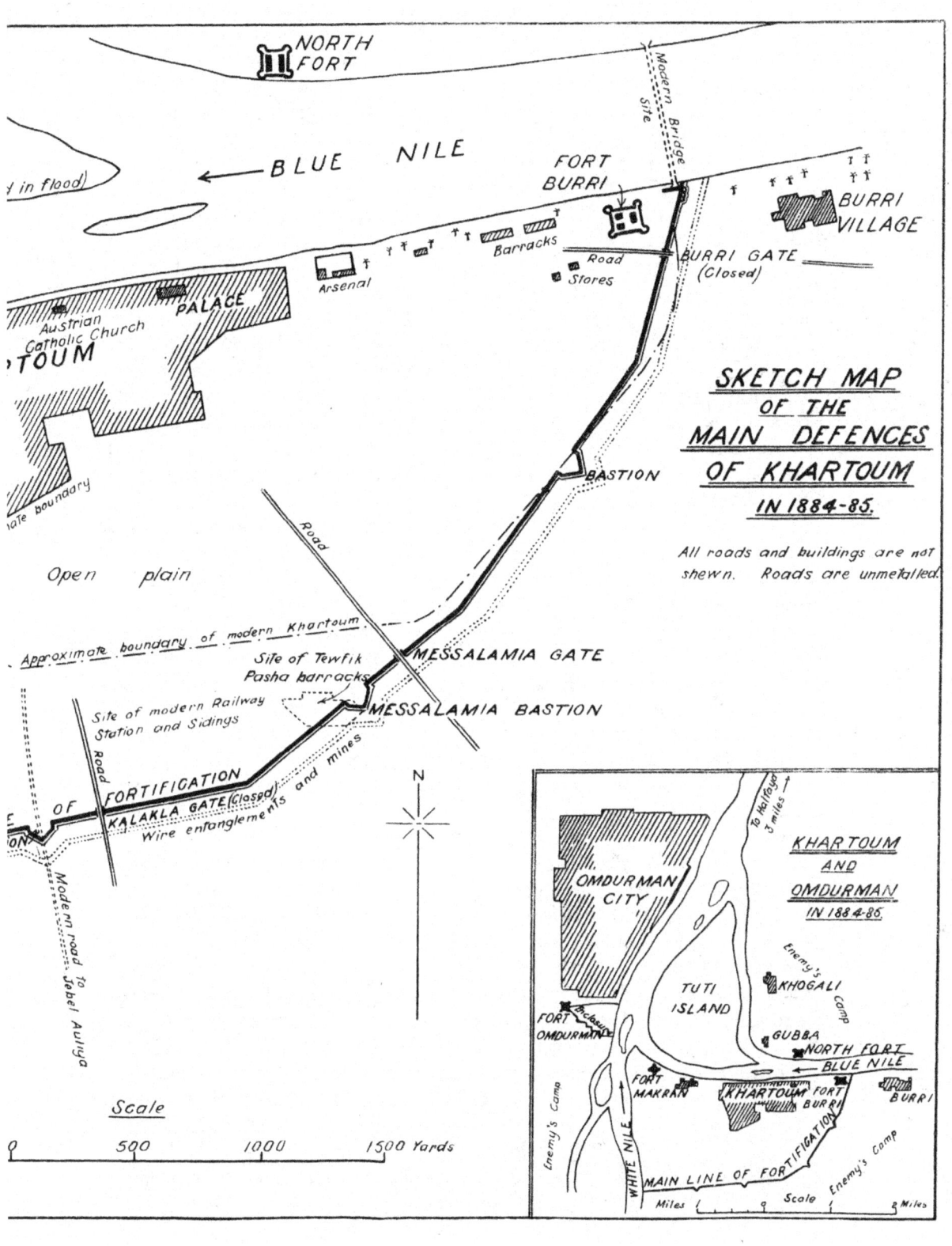

General Gordon could do little or nothing against the vastness of the enemy now fronting Khartoum.[1] In order to prevent anxiety in England, if postal communication be stopped, I may say that there is no danger of Khartoum itself falling." But, on the 23rd, he added, " We are daily expecting British troops. We cannot bring ourselves to believe that we are to be abandoned by the Government. Our existence depends on England."

An Arab arrived in Khartoum on April 9th with a message from Baring to Gordon. " So far as I know," it ran, " there is no intention on the part of the Government to send an English force to Berber." This was a cruel blow, though Gordon had already received a like message from Giuseppe Cuzzi, the British Consul at Berber. Clearly, he could expect no help from England. He must act on his own responsibility. He replied in the following terms :— " As far as I can understand, the situation is this : you state your intention of not sending any relief force up here or to Berber, and you refuse me Zubeir. I consider myself free to act according to circumstances. I shall hold on here as long as I can, and, if I can suppress the rebellion, I shall do so. If I cannot, I shall retire to the Equator and leave you the indelible disgrace of abandoning the garrisons of Sennar, Kassala, Berber and Dongola, with the certainty that you will eventually be forced to smash up the Mahdi under great difficulties if you would retain peace in Egypt." Gordon then decided to make his final appeals for outside assistance. He had already suggested that Turkey should be invited to send troops to the Sudan, and on April 12th he made a further proposal that the country should be transferred to the Sultan. A few days later, he appealed to the Consuls of several of the European powers, and to the Pope, to afford financial help towards a Turkish expedition, and to the Sultan himself to send 3,000 men, but none of these messages got through. That they should ever have been written was, indeed, a bitter reproach to Gladstone's Government.

Gordon now abandoned the pen for the sword. Through the exercise of his personal authority and prestige, he succeeded in enrolling a number of volunteers and in building up a force of negro troops.[2] Under a black Commander-in-Chief, Farag Pasha, these men proved highly efficient and were the only troops on whom he could depend. Undaunted by the news, at the end of April, of the surrender of an outlying garrison on the Blue Nile, and at the end of May, of the fall of Berber, which severed his last connection with the outer world, Gordon redoubled his efforts to improve the defences of Khartoum. How well he succeeded is shown by the fact that he

[1] Gordon succeeded in bringing in the Halfaya garrison ; but his troops under Stewart were defeated ignominiously at Halfaya on the 16th, and Stewart was wounded. The Egyptians were cowardly, and two Pashas were afterwards tried by court martial and shot. The affair proved the unreliability of most of Gordon's soldiers. No blame attached to Stewart.

[2] *Gordon and the Sudan*, by Dr. Bernard M. Allen, p. 356.

held the town for a further eight months against the overwhelming masses which the Mahdi brought against him.

There are frequent references, in contemporary accounts and modern historical works, to Gordon's use of wire entanglements, "crows' feet," mines, and bullet-proof plating for ships, and it is surprising to find that materials for such protective measures should have been available in a town situated in the wilds of Africa; but the fact that they were ready for use when required was due mainly to the energy and foresight of Gordon himself in establishing an arsenal, in combination with a dockyard, during his previous terms of service in the Equatorial Province and as Governor-General. " The Arsenal does great credit to Gordon, by whom it was founded," wrote the Italian explorer, Matteucci, in 1877.[1] " It is a great brick structure on the banks of the Nile, a scene of great activity. It was established in order to repair the Nile steamers. But for lack of basic materials, it could construct new steamers. The workmen consist of blacks, under the direction of Lorenzo Spada, an able Italian." The combined arsenal and dockyard lay on the left bank of the Blue Nile, about 600 yards upstream of the Governor's Palace.[2] It was in existence in 1875, for in that year Gessi, who was Gordon's representative in Khartoum, put together the steamer *Ismailia*, which Samuel Baker had brought out with him in sections in 1869.[3] As the dockyard branch of the arsenal could not undertake new construction, Gordon had ordered four small steamers to be sent out in sections from England in 1877. Two of them were assembled in the dockyard in the following year, one being the ill-fated *Abbas* in which Stewart, Power and Herbin were wrecked in 1884.[4] The sections of the other two steamers were stored in the arsenal until they were assembled, and the ships launched under the names of the *Husseiniya* and *Zubeir*, during the latter part of the siege. The dockyard had slips up which small vessels could be hauled.

It seems that the main store of ammunition was kept in the arsenal until Gordon moved it into the Austrian Catholic Church during the siege. The church was a large stone building, downstream of the Palace, and consequently more distant from the northern end of the fortified line than the arsenal. While Governor-General from 1877 to 1879, Gordon had accumulated arms, ammunition and materials of war in the arsenal, and further additions were made by Abd el Kader, who sent a French merchant to Cairo in September, 1882, expressly to obtain arms and ammunition from the Egyptian

---

[1] *Sudan e Gallas*, By Dr. P. Matteucci (1879).
[2] See the map of Khartoum by Borelli Bey in his book *La Chute de Khartoum. Procès du Colonel Hassan-Benhassaoui, Juin-Juillet,* 1887 (published in 1893), and also the map of Khartoum and Omdurman in *Fire and Sword in the Sudan*, by Slatin Pasha.
[3] The *Ismailia* was at Khartoum throughout the siege.
[4] The other steamer was the *Muhammad Ali*, which was captured by the dervishes on the Blue Nile in 1884.

Government.[1] Had it not been for Gordon's foresight and the energy displayed by Abd el Kader, the defences of Khartoum would have been carried easily by the Mahdi. As it was, the dervish leader developed such a wholesome fear of Gordon's mines, entanglements and other obstacles that he was deterred from attempting an assault until an easy path was opened for him by the treacherous Nile.

The general arrangement of the defences of Khartoum is shown in the sketch map which is included in this chapter. The system comprised a continuous line of rampart and ditch from the Blue to the White Nile, and four strong points called " forts." On the left bank of the Blue Nile, upstream of Khartoum and close within the northern end of the main line of rampart, lay Fort Burri; on the opposite bank, and almost facing the Palace, was the North Fort; a short distance downstream of the town, at the point where the Blue and White Niles meet when in flood, was the Makran (or Mogren) Fort; and across the White Nile, 1,200 yards back from the river-bank,[2] Fort Omdurman. Little is known about the design of these forts, as all were destroyed before Kitchener recaptured Khartoum in 1898, but some of them were strongly-built stone or brick houses, or groups of houses, enclosed by a rampart and ditch. In his Journals, written during the siege, Gordon gives a sketch of the North Fort.[3] It consisted of two flat-roofed double-storeyed buildings, loopholed on each floor and 60 yards apart. A telegraph office was situated in one of the buildings, which had been a Governor's residence.[4] Around them was a parapet, and, outside the parapet, a ditch on three sides and the river on the fourth. The normal garrison of the North Fort was 700 " Bashi-Bazouks,"[5] but in October, 1884, it amounted to 1,300 men.[6] Fort Burri also was composed of a group of houses within an entrenchment.[7] Fort Makran was an enclosure on a mound. Fort Omdurman, however, according to a plan drawn by Gordon,[8] was a solid structure specifically designed for defence, being a large square building with four flanking bastions. It was situated at the apex of a triangular enclosure having the river as its base. The sides of the

---

[1] Letter from G. Shweinfurth, written in 1882 and quoted in the Italian journal *Esploratore*.

[2] *The Journals of Major-General C. G. Gordon, C.B., at Kartoum*, edited by A. Egmont-Hake (1885), p. 329.

[3] *Ibid.*, p. 266.

[4] Evidence of Ali Hassan Effendi. *La Chute de Kartoum*, by Borelli Bey, p. 158.

[5] A name applied indiscriminately to any irregular soldiers, whether Egyptian, Arab or Turkish.

[6] *The Journals of Major-General C. G. Gordon, C.B., at Kartoum*, edited by A. Egmont-Hake, p. 258.

[7] An untelegraphed message from Frank Power is quoted in a footnote on page 198 of *Mahdiism and the Egyptian Sudan*, by Major F. R. Wingate, D.S.O., R.A. It runs as follows :—" We have, besides the line of fortifications, four fortified posts. Mukran at the juncture of the two Niles, Omdurman opposite, a fortified house on the Blue Nile vis-à-vis to the Palace, and Burri, a fortified village on the extreme left of our line of fortifications."

[8] *The Journals of Major-General C. G. Gordon, C.B., at Kartoum*, p. 321.

enclosure were formed by entrenchments, the southern side being zigzagged and the northern curved. Near the river, the enclosed ground was not visible from the fort. The enclosure was necessary to ensure that reinforcements and supplies might reach the fort safely from Khartoum across the White Nile. Although Fort Omdurman was a valuable outpost, its isolated position caused Gordon much anxiety.

The site of Fort Makran has been a matter of some controversy. In a map headed " Kartoum, 1884," said to have been drawn from rough sketches made by Gordon, the Makran or Mogren Fort is shown on the right bank of the White Nile *at the end of the fortified line*—an impossible position in which it would be partially submerged at high Nile. In another map, which appears in Borelli Bey's book *La Chute de Khartoum*, it is shown once again as being on the bank of the White Nile; but in this case it is placed nearly two miles behind the fortified line. Finally, there is Rudolf Slatin's map, " Khartum and Omdurman," in his book *Fire and Sword in the Sudan*, which shows Fort Makran close to the bank of the Blue Nile and downstream of the western boundary of the town. This is the position given in the map headed " Khartum and Environs " in Major (now General Sir Reginald) Wingate's great work *Mahdiism and the Egyptian Sudan*, and it is approximately correct. The authority of the " Kartoum, 1884 " map is doubtful; and no reliance whatever can be placed on Borelli's map, which was prepared by a Court Martial Prosecution anxious to prove at all costs that Khartoum was betrayed. The contradictory opinions regarding the position of Fort Makran may also be explained partly by the fact that the fort was actually on the bank of the White Nile *when the river was in full flood*. In such a condition, the river inundated the shelving right bank to a maximum width of more than one mile, and so reached the fort. Sir Reginald Wingate writes:—[1] " While in Khartoum I often walked from the Palace to the ruins of the old Makran Fort at the junction of the two Niles, and when the rivers were in full flood, the water of *both* rivers swirled through the broken-down walls of the fort, which was some distance up the Blue Nile at extreme low water." A careful examination of the remains of the Gordon defences, and of any evidence concerning them, was made in October, 1935, by Lieut.-Colonel S. L. Milligan, C.M.G., D.S.O., Director of Survey, and Mr. E. G. Sarsfield-Hall, C.M.G., Governor of Khartoum. In a letter dated November 5th, referring to the Makran Fort and other defences, Colonel Milligan writes :— " As regards Makran or Mogren Fort, there was a very large mound fort at the western end of Mogren Village. It was almost certainly on the site of the three or four westernmost existing houses, very near

---

[1] Letter from General Sir Reginald Wingate to the author, dated September 6th, 1935.

the site of a subsequent dervish fort. The mound fort had a loop-holed parapet round the top, which was reached by a stairway of mud steps. It mounted a gun and was also used as a signal station when the rising river covered the station at the extreme point. There appears to have been no proper trench system in connection with this fort. The dervishes made use of the earth from the mound when they built their mud fort. The latter was demolished recently when the road leading to the new Omdurman Bridge was constructed."

During the siege, Gordon made several small batteries and entrenched posts, which were sometimes called "forts." He wished to maintain an active defence and succeeded remarkably well. On October 12th, he wrote in his Journals:—[1] "Went over to Goba,[2] and chose positions for the Shaggeyeh tribe. If we evacuate Halfeyeh we shall have to give up three outer forts and one central one (Seyd Mahomet Osman's house)." On November 14th, he added:—[3] "The Arabs, some 400 rifles, line a trench opposite the *Husseinyeh*: we have erected a parapet on our side opposite her. . . . We have put a gun of the steamer *Ismailia* on the bank of the Nile to cover the approach to the *Husseinyeh*." The ship had run aground in the White Nile near the junction with the Blue Nile, and the works which Gordon built were on the ground north of Fort Makran, which would be under water when the rivers rose.[4] Borelli's map shows a battery also at the south or upstream end of Tuti Island, designed to engage the enemy in the vicinity of Goba.

The main line of defence, as already explained, stretched for about four miles from the Blue to the White Nile. Few traces of this line are visible at the present day.[5] Wind, rain, flood and the hand of the builder have done their work. The cross-section of the fortifications varied according to the ground; but usually it provided a ditch, six feet to eight feet deep and ten feet wide at the bottom, with steeply sloping sides. The ditch was separated from a parapet, seven feet high and fourteen feet thick at the crest, by a berm three feet wide. The defenders stood on a raised step from four to fourteen feet in width, and fired over the crest of the parapet. There is no reliable record of the use of any form of revetment. The parapet

---

[1] *The Journals of Major-General C. G. Gordon, C.B., at Kartoum*, p. 184.

[2] The village of Goba (Gubba) lay downstream of the North Fort on the right bank of the subsidiary channel of the Blue Nile skirting Tuti Island. Downstream of Goba was another village called Hogali (Khogali) which figures also in the siege operations.

[3] *The Journals of Major-General C. G. Gordon, C.B., at Kartoum*, pp. 327, 330.

[4] According to Colonel Milligan, the inhabitants of Khartoum say that Gordon began the building of a fort at the extreme end of Makran Point. Its brick walls were carried up to a height of a few feet, but the work was then abandoned and the incomplete structure was used as a signalling platform when the Nile level was low.

[5] In January, 1935, the author explored the line in company with Mr. E. G. Sarsfield-Hall, C.M.G., Governor of Khartoum. A rounded bank, from 3 feet to 6 feet in height along some stretches of the southern alignment, was all that could be seen. There was no ditch.

THE OLD FORTIFICATIONS SOUTH OF KHARTOUM.
Remains of the Kalakla Bastion in 1935.

[*Photo by the Author.*]

was of earth, though a certain amount of stone is visible in places. Overhead cover was not provided; but it seems that Gordon built a loopholed wall about five feet high along the top of the parapet in certain sections.[1] The curving alignment was broken by four small pointed bastions,[2] each mounting two or three small guns, and occasionally by traverses or "buttresses," which were higher than the ordinary parapet.[3] About 100 yards outside the ditch, Gordon laid wire entanglements, and also rows of land-mines where the ground was not too wet. In addition, he widened the ditch by about two feet, and deepened it so that in some places a man could not get out of it except by standing on the shoulders of another.[4] The ditch was, indeed, a formidable obstacle with its accessories of entanglements and mines. Gordon employed large gangs of civilian labourers in addition to soldiers, and completed most of the earthwork by the end of March, 1884. Beyond each flank[5] of the fortified line, he moored barges carrying guns, and built structures 20 feet high on them to give two tiers of fire.

There were three main entrances through the fortifications. In the northern curtain, south of Fort Burri, was the Bab el Burri or Burri Gate; in the next curtain south-westwards, and east of the Messalamia Bastion, the Bab el Messalamia; and in the next curtain westwards, and about 200 yards east of the Kalakla Bastion, the Bab el Kalakla.[6] The Burri and Kalakla entrances had no bridges, though the piers remained; but an iron drawbridge existed at the

---

[1] Evidence of Sergeant Hussein Yusuf Agur at the court martial in Cairo:—"Men in one rank. Every man opposite his loophole . . . 1½ metres apart; one man to each loophole." *Mahdiism and the Egyptian Sudan*, by Major F. R. Wingate, D.S.O., R.A., p. 568.

[2] Seven small rectangular bastions are shown in Borelli's map, and four very large and elongated ones in Slatin's map. The investigations conducted in 1935 proved that the bastions are incorrectly shown in both maps, and that in Slatin's map the southern line of the fortifications is located too far south of Khartoum. The four small pointed bastions are shown in their correct positions in the sketch map included in this chapter. Reading from east to west they were an unnamed bastion midway between Fort Burri and the Messalamia Bastion, the Messalamia Bastion itself, the Kalakla Bastion, and another unnamed bastion, of very small dimensions, situated close above the high-water level of the Nile. No trace exists of Fort Burri or the fortified line in its vicinity. The outbuildings of the Gordon Memorial College now cover the site of Fort Burri. The unnamed bastion, between that fort and the Messalamia Bastion, has been obliterated by a railway line. The Messalamia Bastion was demolished when the Tewfik Pasha Barracks were built. An unmetalled road to Gebel Auliya now runs through the remains of the Kalakla Bastion (see illustration). The site of the other unnamed bastion near high-water level is occupied by the oil presses of the Noxious Trades Area. It may be well to remark that, about 85 yards south of, and parallel to, the southern face of the old fortifications (in the position of the fortified line as shown on Slatin's map) exist the remains of a drainage channel and a Decauville Railway embankment which may be mistaken in future years for the southern face itself or for an outer line of defence. There was no such outer line.

[3] Letter from Dr. Bernard Allen to the author, dated September 3rd, 1935, giving the results of an interview at Khartoum in 1930 with an old merchant, George Yusuf Abagi.

[4] Evidence of Sergeant Hussein Yusuf Agur. *Mahdiism and the Egyptian Sudan*, by Major F. R. Wingate, D.S.O., R.A., p. 571.

[5] Some say beyond the western flank only.

[6] Evidence of Mikhail Bey Daud. *Mahdiism and the Egyptian Sudan*, p. 561.

main entrance, the Bab el Messalamia. Gordon provided iron gates for all the entrances and repaired the gateways. A blockhouse, or "fortin," was constructed at the Kalakla entrance. During the siege, Gordon blocked both the Burri and Kalakla entrances and used only the Messalamia gateway for his sorties.[1]

The extensive employment of land-mines is an interesting feature of the defence. They were percussion mines—notably a very large number of Krupp 20-pound shells—and were fired, singly or in groups, by fuses. "Land-mines are the things for defence in future" wrote Gordon to Baring on July 30th.[2] "We have covered the works with them and they have deterred all attacks and done much execution." But mines can be dangerous to friend as well as foe. On May 1st, Frank Power records that "the officer commanding the Engineers, having put down a mine of 78 pounds of powder, trod on it and with six soldiers was blown to pieces."[3] However, on May 7th, 115 rebels perished by the explosion of nine mines during an attack. As regards the means of ignition, Gordon writes on September 10th, "The matches used for mines are all finished, and we are obliged to go back to powder hose and unite the mines in families of ten. . . . It is extraordinary that after a good deal of rain and three months' exposure, the domestic match-box should retain its vitality."[4] There were many failures in the mining operations, and straying animals sometimes caused premature explosions. The Krupp shells were not very effective. "I dug up a shell yesterday which was at the foot of a lay figure[5] on the north side," writes Gordon on October 12th,[6] "and I see now that the reason of the shells not proving fatal is that they are buried too deep. Were I to put them out again, I would lay the shells on the surface, hiding the fuses or ignitors." Bordeini Bey, a merchant of Khartoum, records that Gordon frequently went downstream in a boat and buried mines in any place frequented by the enemy. He attached red flags to the mines, and when the rebels seized the flags they were blown up.[7] Sometimes the rebels drove cattle into the mine-fields. On November 8th,

---

[1] These details are gathered from a translation of *The Sudan under Gordon and Kitchener*, by Ibrahim Fauzi Bey; from evidence recorded in *La Chute de Khartoum* by Borelli Bey, and from statements made to Dr. Bernard Allen in Khartoum in 1930.

[2] Letter headed "Land Torpedoes," by Major J. T. Bucknill, R.E., appearing in the *R.E. Journal*, Vol. 14, 1884, p. 283.

[3] *Letters from Khartoum*, p. 108.

[4] *The Journals of Major-General C. G. Gordon, C.B., at Kartoum*, p. 5. A fragment of a diary by Lieut.-Colonel J. D. H. Stewart, found at El Hebba where he was murdered, shows that the fuse was removed from a shell, the top flattened, and the tube filled with powder. A number of matches, wrapped with powder and quick-match in a covering of emery-paper, were then tied on to the flattened head of the fuse so that they ignited if a man stepped on them. (See *Journal of the Royal United Service Institution*, Vol. 43, Part 2, 1899, pp. 947, 1036.)

[5] To hide the weakness of the garrison, Gordon made extensive use of dummy soldiers behind the parapets.

[6] *The Journals of Major-General C. G. Gordon, C.B., at Kartoum*, p. 183.

[7] *Mahdiism and the Egyptian Sudan*, by Major F. R. Wingate, D.S.O., R.A., p. 165.

Gordon writes:[1] "The Arabs have collected in the vicinity of Omdurman Fort a heap of cows who seem drawing down towards the fort. I expect they will drive the cows on to the fort and try and explode the mines." This they did, but without much success. So late in the siege as December 11th, Gordon was still laying mines. It is clear that he must have formed a corps of engineers to help him. These men probably came from the arsenal and dockyard. Unhappily it was impossible, because of the damp ground, to mine the area in front of the fortified line near the White Nile in which mines were most needed.

Communication was maintained by a system of telegraph lines, connecting the Palace to the forts and the fortified line, and extending throughout the whole length of the position from river to river. A submarine cable prolonged the telegraph from Fort Burri to the North Fort,[2] and another carried it through the White Nile to Fort Omdurman. Visual signalling was difficult on account of the haze and mirage and the intervening palm-trees. The Palace roof offered an excellent platform for observation when the weather was clear, and Gordon installed a telescope on it. An old photograph shows that the Palace was a long, double-storeyed, flat-roofed building, about 40 feet in height,[3] lying close to the river-bank. At each end were projecting wings. The lower storey was strongly built and heavily buttressed, and in the upper storey, in which Gordon lived and which was reached by an outside stairway, there were nine large windows in each of the longer faces. At the back lay a small garden, bordered by a dozen large palm-trees, and beyond the trees, cultivated ground. Gordon states that the roof was a flimsy structure, supported on strutted wooden beams, so it is remarkable that it could carry the 20-pounder gun which he mounted there to answer the enemy's artillery across the Blue Nile during the latter part of the siege.

From the roof of the Palace, Gordon kept a vigilant watch on the weary and lazy garrisons of his forts. "No sentries at the North Fort or Bourré" he writes.[4] "These people are enough to break one's heart. . . . The North Fort hate my telescope. Day and night I work them. . . . Sentries off the roof of the North Fort again. Sent over to have them flogged." Gordon was essentially a humane man, but no other form of punishment was possible. He was feeling the terrific tension of the final months of the siege. "You can scarcely imagine the state one gets in when one is constantly hearing explosions. What with guns, mines and musketry, one's nerves get strained and nothing can drop without one thinking it is an explosion." His hair changed from grey to white, and he became a

---
[1] *The Journals of Major-General C. G. Gordon, C.B., at Kartoum,* p. 391.
[2] *Ibid.,* p. 222.
[3] *Ibid.,* p. 377.
[4] *Ibid.,* pp. 222, 265, 271.

prematurely aged man. Yet his undaunted spirit drove his tired body forward, and he inspired his motley force with some of his own courage.

The defensive system at Khartoum was well organized and the guns distributed to the best advantage. The garrison amounted to some 2,400 Egyptian and Sudanese regular troops and 5,000 irregulars, armed mostly with Remington rifles, and the artillery included two Krupp guns (20-pounders), 11 " mountain " guns (7-pounders), and 16 other small guns and howitzers of various sorts.[1] There were also one or two Gardner or Nordenfelt machine-guns. The supply of ammunition was ample. The artillery was at least equal to that of the Mahdi ; and so well were the guns served that it was not until late in the siege that the Palace itself came under artillery fire.

The duties which Gordon carried out during the siege were so numerous and varied that it is wonderful that any one man could perform them. He was Governor, Judge, Commander-in-Chief, Admiral, Chief Engineer and Commissariat Officer. Everything was referred to him. Every order emanated from him. Yet he found time to superintend the armouring of his river steamers and to visit the fortifications, on horseback or on foot, at frequent intervals. He directed personally the laying of mines and entanglements, watched the progress of repairs, and, once in each month, saw that the soldiers received their pay. During one of these visits to the front line, he was furious on finding that 300 yards of wire entanglement had been removed near the White Nile, and as a punishment, ordered that the pay of the Egyptian officers in that sector should be stopped until the cost of new pickets and wire had been defrayed. Severity was necessary to keep the troops in hand. At the same time, Gordon was always ready to listen to the poorest and neediest of the inhabitants, and to help them so far as his means would allow.

The tragic story of the siege of Khartoum has been told too often to need repetition in detail. The Mahdi's hordes closed in ; scarcity changed slowly to starvation, and hope to despair. At the end of June, Gordon rejected with scorn a demand that he should surrender and renounce his faith. In July and August things went better for the defence, and Muhammad Ali, an able subordinate, won a victory on the Blue Nile, only to be destroyed later in an ambush. Then Gordon decided to make a last effort to let the world know the true state of affairs ; and so, in September, he allowed Stewart, Power and Herbin to attempt to run the gauntlet in the steamer *Abbas*. Thereafter, he was alone.

The Mahdi, at the head of vast reinforcements, descended on Khartoum, bringing with him his prisoner, Rudolf Slatin.[2] This

---

[1] *The Journals of Major-General C. G. Gordon, C.B., at Kartoum*, p. 525.
[2] Afterwards Colonel (Hon. Major-General) Sir Rudolf Baron von Slatin, G.C.V.O., K.C.M.G., C.B., who was Inspector-General in the Sudan for many years under General Sir Reginald Wingate as Governor-General. Sir Rudolf died in 1932.

Austrian ex-officer had first set out to explore the Sudan in 1874 and had returned early in 1879, on Gordon's invitation, in the service of the Khedive. When the Mahdi rebelled, Slatin was Governor of Darfur, and, forced to surrender, he was kept a prisoner in Omdurman until, through the good offices of Colonel Wingate, he managed to escape in 1895 to Egypt. Slatin, at the Mahdi's instigation, wrote to Gordon and advised him to surrender. He also addressed a short letter to him in French and a long one in German.[1] In the former, he said that he wished to join Gordon in Khartoum. In the latter, he told of his campaign in Darfur, the circumstances of his surrender, and his reasons for having become, ostensibly, a Muhammadan. " I am ready, with or under you, for either victory or death " he added. Gordon sent back the messenger without a word. His puritan spirit would allow him no dealings with apostasy in any guise. He refused to receive Slatin, and he rejected another summons from the Mahdi. The dervish leader then proceeded to press the siege with greater vigour.

Alone in his palace overlooking the Blue Nile, Gordon wrote his famous Journals. Deprived of all intercourse with his fellow countrymen, this relaxation helped him to retain his equilibrium and perhaps his sanity. The Journals are a moving record of their author's innermost thoughts and unflinching determination. " I am sure I should like that fellow Egerton " runs an entry in September.[2] " There is a light-hearted jocularity about his communications. . . . He wishes to know *exactly* ' day, hour and minute ' that he (Gordon) expects to be in ' difficulties as to provisions and ammunition '. . . . It is as if a man on the bank, having seen his friend in the river already bobbed down two or three times, hails, ' I say, old fellow, let us know when we are to throw you the lifebuoy. I know you have bobbed down two or three times, but it is a pity to throw you the lifebuoy until you really are *in extremis*. . . .' I altogether decline the imputation that the projected expedition has come to relieve me. It has come to *save our national honour* in extricating the garrisons, etc., from a position (in which) our action in Egypt has placed these garrisons. I was relief expedition No. 1. They are relief expedition No. 2. . . . I am not the *rescued lamb*, and I will not be." At the end of November appears the following :—[3] " I declare *positively* and *once for all that I will not leave the Soudan until every one who wants to go down is given the chance to do so* unless a government is established which relieves me of the charge : therefore, if any emissary or letter comes up here ordering me to come down, *I will not obey it but will stay here and fall with the town*

---

[1] *Fire and Sword in the Sudan*, by Rudolf Slatin Pasha, pp. 320, 321.

[2] *The Journals of Major-General C. G. Gordon, C.B., at Kartoum*, pp. 74, 93. Entry dated September 23rd, 1884. Mr. E. H. Egerton was officiating for Sir Evelyn Baring in Cairo, and had sent two cipher messages to Gordon.

[3] *Modern Egypt*, by the Earl of Cromer, Vol. I, p. 564. Entry of November 29th, 1884.

and run all risks." On December 13th, he writes :—[1] " If some effort is not made before ten days' time, the town will fall. It is inexplicable, this delay ; " and on the following day he makes his final historic entry :—[2] " Now *mark this*, if the Expeditionary Force, and I ask no more than two hundred men, does not come in ten days, *the town may fall :* and I have done my best for the honour of our country. Goodbye. C. G. Gordon."

The position was desperate. Fort Omdurman had been isolated since November 3rd,[3] and the enemy had captured the enclosure between the fort and the river on the 12th. Having sent all his largest steamers downstream, Gordon was unable to re-open communication, and the starving garrison of the fort was battered slowly into submission. Although Gordon tried to relieve the pressure by costly sorties, Fort Omdurman fell on January 15th, 1885. Easy communication across the White Nile was then possible between the Mahdi's army around Omdurman and Wad en Nejumi's army fronting the fortified line which shielded Khartoum. Food was scarce, so Gordon issued a proclamation allowing the civil population to go over to the Mahdi. Many of the inhabitants availed themselves of this permission ; but 14,000 civilians remained in the town to be fed from the rapidly dwindling supplies. Crops were gathered from Tuti Island, and every house in Khartoum was searched. As the days dragged on, the soldiers and inhabitants were reduced to eating donkeys, dogs, cats, rats, gum and the pith from palms. Many died from dysentery, enteritis and starvation. With swollen limbs, and bodies racked with pain, the soldiers were too weak and ill even to move about the fortifications. Gordon visited them daily under a fire which none of the inhabitants would brave. " He was almost superhuman in his efforts to keep up our hope," writes Father Ohrwalder, then a prisoner in the Mahdi's camp.[4] " Every day, and many and many a time during the day, did he look towards the north, from the roof of the palace, for the relief which never arrived." News of the rebel defeat at Abu Klea came to the Mahdi on January 20th, and he thought of raising the siege ; but being dissuaded by his generals, he fired a salute of 101 guns to give the impression that Abu Klea had been a victory, and resolved to transfer his men across the White Nile to join Wad en Nejumi in a general assault before help could reach Gordon.

The capitulation of Fort Omdurman had enabled the Mahdi to mount guns on the left bank of the White Nile to enfilade the western end of Gordon's fortifications. The Egyptian guns, on armoured

---
[1] *The Journals of Major-General C. G. Gordon, C.B., at Kartoum,* p. 394.
[2] *Ibid.,* p. 395.
[3] " The Fall of Khartoum," by Major H. H. Kitchener, R.E., appearing in the *R.E. Journal,* Vol. 15, 1885, pp. 270–272. The same report appears in the official *History of the Sudan Campaign,* by Colonel H. E. Colvile, C.B., Grenadier Guards, Part II, pp. 270–276.
[4] *Ten Years' Captivity in the Mahdi's Camp,* by Father Ohrwalder, p. 132.

barges anchored in the river, could not subdue the enemy's fire. The North Fort also was under severe bombardment from Khojali, and the Palace itself was hit many times from across the Blue Nile. For several months, the level of the White Nile had been falling steadily, and as it fell, the fortified line south of Khartoum had been prolonged in wake of the receding water; but the work became more costly as the enemy's fire increased, and after the fall of Fort Omdurman it was impossible. The Nile, however, did not recede regularly. In January a sandbank appeared some 300 yards from the eastern shore, opposite the end of the fortifications, and remained separated from the mainland by a stretch of shallow water. A traitor, Omar Ibrahim, noted the fact. Here lay the road into Khartoum; no trenches, no mines, no entanglements could be placed to block it. He stole away to Omdurman, and on January 25th the Mahdi began to pass his troops across the Nile.

The whole story of the fall of Khartoum, after a seige lasting 317 days, will never be known, but a general idea may be gathered from the often conflicting accounts of native witnesses. Before dawn, on Sunday, January 26th, 1885, under cover of a fierce and general bombardment, the enemy turned the right flank of Gordon's defences by way of the sandbank, and then, rushing along the fortified line, bore down all resistance. Most of the defenders, under Farag Pasha, were incapable of fighting, though the Sudanese soldiers resisted and died bravely at their posts. In the general confusion, no telegraphic report was sent to Gordon—a matter of little importance, for nothing and nobody could have stemmed the tide. A number of dervishes made their way across the plain to the town, intent on robbery and massacre, and a small party passed through it to the Palace. Gordon met them proudly at the head of the stairway, in uniform,[1] with a sword at his belt and a revolver in his hand. He fell at once beneath their spears; and so, at the hour of dawn, a great spirit passed to a happier life. His murderers cut off Gordon's head and carried it in triumph to Omdurman, leaving his body to be stabbed and mangled by every savage who passed.

In the Mahdi's camp at Omdurman, the captive Slatin, heavily fettered in his miserable tent, listened to the bombardment, and when the sun had risen, crawled out to gather news. Advancing towards him were three black soldiers, one of them carrying something wrapped in a bloody cloth, while behind followed a weeping crowd. The man undid the cloth and showed the head of Gordon. The blue eyes were half-opened; the mouth perfectly natural; the hair of the head, and the short whiskers, almost white. " Is not this the head of your uncle, the unbeliever ? " jeered the black, holding up the head. " What of it ? " replied Slatin quietly. " A brave soldier, who

---

[1] Some say that he was dressed in white.

fell at his post. Happy is he to have fallen. His sufferings are over."

* * * * *

Though Charles George Gordon died more than half a century ago, his fame still lives, and his memory is perpetuated in bronze, stone and stained glass throughout the length and breadth of the British Empire. No trace exists of the stairway at Khartoum on which he met his end, for the old palace was destroyed by the dervishes, and a new one took its place after the British re-occupation in 1898; but the site of his death at the head of the stair is marked by a tablet high up in the wall of a corridor within the present building.[1]

The finest memorial to Gordon stands in front of the School of Military Engineering at Chatham. This is a bronze statue representing him on a riding camel and wearing the uniform and *tarbush* of an Egyptian general. It is the work of Mr. E. Onslow Ford, R.A., and was unveiled by H.R.H. the Prince of Wales (afterwards King Edward VII) on May 19th, 1890, in the presence of a large gathering of distinguished officers of the Corps.[2] Gordon is depicted carrying the historical rattan in his right hand, and with his left he is reining up the camel, an action which throws the animal's head back and gives it a fine poise. The statue is more than 12 feet in height and is mounted on a pedestal of Portland stone. Around three sides of the bronze base are the names of places with which Gordon was identified, and in front the one word "Gordon." The inscription on the pedestal runs:— "Charles George Gordon, Royal Engineers, Companion of the Bath, Major-General of the British Army, Mandarin of China, Pasha of Turkey, Governor-General of the Soudan. Born at Woolwich, 28th January, 1833; killed at Khartoum, 26th January, 1885. Erected by the Corps of Royal Engineers, 1890."

Before this statue was erected, another had been unveiled in Trafalgar Square in London. This statue of Gordon faces the Nelson Monument and Whitehall, and shows him in British uniform, wearing a patrol jacket. The rattan is under his left arm, which is folded, while the right hand is raised to the chin in a manner suggestive of thoughtful contemplation. Beneath the elbow of the right arm is a Bible, firmly clasped in the left hand, and over the shoulders a field-glass is slung. The left foot rests on a broken mortar. Bronze panels on the limestone pedestal represent Charity and Justice, Fortitude and Faith. The Trafalgar Square statue is by Mr. Hamo Thornycroft, R.A., and was unveiled on October 16th, 1888.

[1] The tablet can be seen near the western end of the large transverse corridor on the ground floor of the Palace. It is about 11 feet from the floor and bears the simple inscription "Charles George Gordon. Died 26th Jan., 1885."

[2] A full account of the ceremony, and an illustration showing the statue and the officers present, appears in the *R.E. Journal*, Vol. 20, 1890, pp. 123-127.

THE DEATH OF GENERAL GORDON.

[*From the painting by G. W. Joy, etched by Herbert Dicksee.*]

A recumbent figure in bronze by Mr. Edgar Boehm, R.A., can be seen in a recess of the north aisle in St. Paul's Cathedral in London. It was presented in 1887 by Sir Henry William Gordon, K.C.B., a brother of Charles Gordon, and the cenotaph bears the moving inscription which forms the opening of this chapter. The original plaster cast of the monument in St. Paul's was transferred to the R.E. Museum at Chatham in 1892.[1] Another memorial, presented by the Corps of Royal Engineers, exists in Westminster Abbey in the form of a bronze head in high relief surmounting a shield. It occupies a space within a trefoil of arcading over a belfry door to the north of the west entrance, and was unveiled on June 9th, 1892.[2] Southampton has a memorial in Queen's Park—a cluster of stone columns unveiled in October, 1885[3]—and Rochester Cathedral has stained glass windows unveiled by Lord Wolseley in August, 1888. Bronze busts exist in the Royal Engineers' Mess at Chatham and the Royal Artillery Mess at Woolwich, and other memorials in many churches, institutions and public buildings in Great Britain. In addition, a large bronze statue, by Thorneycroft, was erected in Melbourne in 1889.[4]

Perhaps the most interesting of the memorials to be found outside Great Britain is the bronze replica of the Chatham statue which stands in Gordon Avenue behind the Palace in Khartoum. This was produced from the original cast by Mr. E. Onslow Ford, R.A., and was unveiled by the Duke of Cambridge in St. Martin's Place in London on July 15th, 1902. Lord Kitchener, who had just arrived from South Africa, remarked after the ceremony that although he had originated the idea of erecting a Gordon memorial at Khartoum, Lord Glenesk of the *Morning Post* had made it possible by the money collected in response to an appeal to the public. The statue remained for a short time in St. Martin's Place, on the site now occupied by the monument to Nurse Cavell, and, in October, 1902, was shipped in the S.S. *Cedardine* for transport to Alexandria. The *Cedardine* collided with another ship in the Thames, and the statue was submerged for 24 hours. Having been transferred to the S.S. *Lesbian*, it reached Alexandria in November, and, after a long and adventurous journey by rail and river, it was erected on a stone pedestal in Khartoum in 1903.

On January 26th, 1935, the author was present at a ceremony in Khartoum marking the fiftieth anniversary of Gordon's death. It was brief and unostentatious, as Gordon himself would have desired. The Governor-General, the chief civil and military officers, the

---

[1] The monument in St. Paul's Cathedral is referred to in *R.E. Journals*, Vol. 16, 1886, p. 10, and Vol. 22, 1892, p. 137. The cast is now in the Hall of the S.M.E. Main Building at Chatham.

[2] The memorial in Westminster Abbey is described and illustrated in the *R.E. Journal*, Vol. 22, 1892, p. 156.

[3] See *R.E. Journal*, Vol. 15, 1885, p. 282.

[4] See *R.E. Journal*, Vol. 18, 1888, p. 175.

dignitaries of the various Churches, leading European and Sudanese officials and residents, and representatives of the troops, advanced in succession to the statue, placed their wreaths at the base of the pedestal, saluted, and in silence resumed their places. The tribute of Alfred Tennyson leapt to the mind :—

> "*Warrior of God, man's friend, not laid below,*
> *But somewhere dead far in the waste Soudan,*
> *Thou livest in all hearts, for all men know*
> *This earth has borne no simpler, nobler man.*"

GOVERNMENT HOUSE, KHARTOUM.

THE GORDON STATUE, KHARTOUM.

[By permission of Karakashian Bros., Ltd.,
Tropical Photo Stores, Khartoum.]

CHAPTER VI.

THE DONGOLA EXPEDITION OF 1896.

DURING the years which followed the tragedy of Khartoum, the British public demanded insistently that Gordon should be avenged; but before that object could be achieved by the reconquest of the Sudan, it was necessary to create an efficient army in Egypt and a solvent Treasury. After the lesson learnt in the hard school of the Nile Expedition, the British Government had no desire to finance another venture against the Mahdists, and was resolved that any action which might be taken should emanate from Egypt and should be paid for by Egypt. It was fortunate for that country that, on the recommendation of the British Agent and Consul-General (Sir Evelyn Baring),[1] Colonel H. H. Kitchener, C.B., C.M.G., late R.E., was appointed Sirdar, or Commander-in-Chief, of the Egyptian Army in April, 1892, and was able to devote his great energies to training and equipping the men who were destined to bring light and liberty into the darkness and misery of the Sudan.

Economy was never irksome to the new Sirdar who, with his eyes fixed on the future, set himself to mould the material which he had at hand and to husband his resources. Nothing was discarded until it fell almost to pieces. Equipment was repaired again and again; Europe was scoured for cheap fabrics for clothing; factories which were established in Cairo produced articles at one-half the price of imported goods. As Director of Stores in the Egyptian capital, Captain W. S. Gordon, R.E.,[2] gave shape to these measures of economy, and in so doing helped to build up the military machine. By sending numbers of men to the reserve before their time, a body was created from which new battalions could be formed rapidly in case of emergency.[3] The training and discipline of the troops knew no relaxation. With Lieut.-Colonel H. M. L. Rundle, D.S.O., R.A., as his Adjutant-General, the Sirdar welded his little army into an efficient organization of 14 battalions of infantry (eight Egyptian and six Sudanese), three batteries of light artillery, four squadrons of

---

[1] Major Sir Evelyn Baring, G.C.M.G., K.C.B., K.C.S.I., C.I.E., R.A. (retd.), was created a Baron in June, 1892, under the title of Lord Cromer. He became a Viscount in 1899, and an Earl in 1901.
[2] A nephew of General Charles Gordon and familiarly known as "Monkey" Gordon. (See p. 121, f.n. 1.)
[3] Three battalions were thus formed when the Dongola Expedition was undertaken.

cavalry and a few supply and transport cadres.[1] Yet although this army might be called upon to operate in difficult country, it contained no unit of Engineer troops. Kitchener, himself an Engineer, knew well that such units are costly to train and to maintain. If the need should arise, he hoped that he could borrow them. Nevertheless, economy was never enforced at the expense of health or efficiency. Under Kitchener's rule, the Egyptian conscript soldiers developed such smartness and confidence that they bore no resemblance to the rabble who fled at Et Teb. The martial Sudanese were taught discipline and restraint; the peaceful Egyptians were transformed into soldiers. Both learned to respect and trust the young British officers who were selected so carefully by Kitchener himself to train the Egyptian Army in peace and lead it in war.[2]

As an illustration of Kitchener's economical methods and foresight, it may be permissible to quote a story related by Sir George Arthur.[3] Some battalion commanders at Suakin came to the Sirdar in August, 1893, and asked that, for convenience of accounts, issues of clothing to their men should be made in January and July instead of in March and September. "Very good," said Kitchener, and ordered that the next issue should be made in January—thus avoiding an issue in September. In the following June, the disappointed commanders decided to apply for a reversion to the old system. Again they approached the Sirdar who, having considered their request during July and August, agreed to it in September and informed them that as, under the old system, the next issue would not be due until March, *two* issues of clothing had thus been saved, one in each year. The story illustrates the lengths to which Kitchener was prepared to go in his campaign of economy, a campaign forced upon him by the poverty of the country and the necessity for accumulating reserves for the task which he had always in view.

By 1895, it seemed that the reconquest of the Sudan might soon be taken in hand, but the Egyptian Government had other views. For some time they had been considering a project for damming the Nile at Aswan, and it appeared that it would be wise to avoid the expense

---

[1] On his appointment as Sirdar, Kitchener reorganized the Headquarter Staff. He abolished the appointment of Quarter-Master-General (previously held by Lt.-Col. H. H. Settle, R.E.) and became his own Q.M.G. The Director of Military Intelligence (Major F. R. Wingate, R.A.), Chief Engineer (Capt. C. Godby, R.E.), Financial and Military Secretaries, Directors of Stores and Supplies, P.M.O., and the D.A.A.G. "B" (Lieut. H. G. Lyons, R.E.), worked directly under him. The Adjutant-General was assisted by an A.A.G. and a D.A.A.G. "A." The D.A.A.G. "B" dealt with all Q.M.G. questions except those concerning the Intelligence, Stores, Supplies and Medical departments, most of the routine papers being taken to the A.G. for signature. Thus the Sirdar was able to give his instructions to the D.A.A.G. "B" on all questions in which he was personally interested, while the A.G. relieved him of all "A" matters, such as discipline, recruiting, etc.

[2] Kitchener interviewed every candidate for the Egyptian Army, and usually did so in a small room facing the top of the grand staircase in the Junior United Service Club in London. Selected officers joined as *Bimbashis* (Majors) on a two years' contract at £E. 540 per annum, though at first Kitchener allowed them only £E. 440 per annum. (£E.1 =approx. £1 0s. 6d.)

[3] *Life of Lord Kitchener*, by Sir George Arthur, Vol. 1, p. 171, footnote 2.

of military operations until that work had been executed and increased revenue was available through the extension of irrigation. A friendly struggle developed between Kitchener for war, and William Garstin, the Egyptian engineer, for water—and Garstin won. Had it not been for certain political events, and the advent of a strong Conservative Government under Lord Salisbury, it is possible that the Dongola Expedition might have been postponed for several years while the Aswan dam was under construction. However, rumours began to reach London that the French from Equatorial Africa were making their way towards the upper waters of the Nile. The Italians had advanced from Massawa, on the Red Sea coast, to Kassala, and not only were they hard pressed by the Abyssinians under Menelik but in danger also from the Khalifa Abdullahi and his dervishes in the Sudan. Under these circumstances, it was suggested that a "demonstration" up the Nile by the Egyptian Government might be a suitable diversion in the interests of a friendly power. Then came the crushing disaster to the Italian forces under General Baratieri at the first battle of Adowa on March 1st, 1896[1]—a defeat which remained unavenged until the Italian success under General de Bono at the same place on October 6th, 1935—and so a suitable pretext for immediate action was furnished to Salisbury's Government. It was advisable to save the Italians at Kassala from the dervishes, and also to safeguard the frontiers of Egypt. At 3 a.m. on March 13th, a telegram announcing the Government's decision was handed to Kitchener, who roused Sir Evelyn Baring and accompanied him to the Palace to break the news to the Khedive. Kitchener, though taken by surprise, was fully prepared. He understood that the campaign was to be conducted with the utmost economy. Indeed, a sum of only £E.500,000 was voted from the General Reserve Fund of the Egyptian Government to cover the cost of the operations; but, for a time, financial stringency was subordinated to strategical considerations, and after the successful conclusion of the campaign, the British Exchequer met the whole cost of the venture.[2]

It was decided that Egyptian troops alone should be employed in the Nile Valley; but as an indication that British help would be forthcoming in case of need, one battalion of British Infantry—the 1st Battalion, North Staffordshire Regiment—was sent from Cairo to Wadi Halfa. Arrangements were made to relieve the Egyptian garrison of Suakin by a contingent from India, and thus to allow the

[1] An interesting article by Captain F. D. Irvine, R.E., on the Italians in Abyssinia appears, under the title of "The Italian Operations in Abyssinia, 1894 to 1896," in the *R.E. Journal*, Jan.-June, 1909, Vol. IX, pp. 13–22. Another, by Lieut. J. F. Shaw, R.A., entitled "The Italian Reverse at Adowa," appears in the *Journal of the Royal United Service Institution*, Vol. 58, Jan.-June, 1914, pp. 237–256.

[2] The sum was voted on the undertaking that, if it were exceeded, the vote would be cancelled. However, Baring and Kitchener had taken steps to induce the British Government to pay for the expedition. Ultimately, the cost was shown to have exceeded the sum voted, and so the British Exchequer paid.

entire Egyptian Army to be concentrated for the advance on Dongola. While the details of the campaign were left to Kitchener's discretion, the general scheme of operations was discussed fully by Kitchener and Baring before the troops took the field, and it was agreed that the main object was to bring hostilities to a close in the shortest possible time by the advance of a small and mobile force. Thus began a very peculiar campaign. Kitchener was under the absolute control of Baring, or Lord Cromer as he may now be called. The British War Office held aloof and accepted no responsibility. Cromer could approve or disapprove every plan suggested by Kitchener, and could grant or refuse all his demands for men, materials, stores or money. It was fortunate, indeed, that the British Agent and the Sirdar worked in complete harmony, and were thus able to carry to a successful conclusion a makeshift campaign which is unrecorded in any official history.

When the Dongola Expedition was sanctioned, it was by no means certain that Kitchener would be in chief command. It was stated in certain circles in England that he was unpopular with his officers, and that he did not inspire his troops with confidence; but his detractors overlooked the facts that he was an adept in Eastern warfare, that he had made the Egyptian Army what it was, and that his supersession must lead inevitably to his resignation. The following comments appeared in an article in the *Pall Mall Gazette* on March 24th, 1896:—[1] "There are very grave doubts whether the control of the military operations on the Egyptian frontier should be entrusted to Sir Herbert Kitchener,[2] and it is already rumoured that some senior and more distinguished officer will shortly be sent out. Sir Herbert Kitchener is still a very young man, a Major only in the English Army, and he has never yet had an independent command of troops in the field. For the present, he may be left to the supervision of General Knowles, commanding in Cairo,[3] an excellent soldier; but if the coming campaign expands into a big business, it will be necessary to give the command to either Sir Redvers Buller, Sir Evelyn Wood or Sir Francis Grenfell. The first would no doubt have the preference, and his appointment would find most favour both in the army and with the public at large." To which a reply was published on March 27th from Lieut. General Sir John Stokes, K.C.B., late R.E. :— " Sir. In your issue of yesterday you questioned whether, by reason of his youth, and as he is only a Major in Her Majesty's Army, Sir Herbert Kitchener is competent to take command of such an expedition as that now

---

[1] Extracts from this article, and a copy of the reply from Lieut.-General Sir John Stokes, K.C.B., late R.E., appear in an article entitled " The Command in Egypt," in the *R.E. Journal*, Vol. 26, 1896, pp. 256–257.

[2] Colonel Kitchener had become Brig.-General Sir H. H. Kitchener, K.C.M.G., C.B.

[3] Major-General C. B. Knowles, C.B., late R.A., commanded the British Army of Occupation. For a few days, all instructions for the impending campaign were sent to General Knowles, instead of to Kitchener.

on the march to Dongola; and you suggested that one of the officers now holding three of the highest staff appointments at the Horse Guards should be sent to command the expedition. As regards the first two points, Sir Herbert Kitchener is forty-six years of age, or four years older than the Duke of Wellington when he finished his military career on the field of Waterloo, and he is a Colonel in the Army and *A.D.C.* to Her Majesty. As to your suggestion that the officer who has successfully commanded the Egyptian Army for the last three years should be superseded when that army takes the field, I trust that, in justice to the distinguished officer, whose career in Egypt for the last fourteen years has been marked by unbroken success, and who has a unique experience of campaigning in that country, you will insert this letter in your next issue." Happily, through Lord Cromer's influence, Kitchener did not suffer the fate of General Stephenson before the Nile Expedition. The proposal that the British War Office should send an officer from the Home Establishment, to command an Egyptian Army in a campaign for which it assumed no responsibility, was the height of absurdity.

Kitchener was fortunate in his assistants. With Brevet-Colonel (afterwards General Sir) H. M. L. Rundle, C.M.G., D.S.O., R.A., as his Chief of Staff, Brevet Colonel (afterwards General Sir) Archibald Hunter, D.S.O., Royal Lancaster Regiment, in command of the troops at Wadi Halfa and south of that place,[1] and Major (now General Sir) F. R. Wingate, D.S.O., R.A., as his Chief Intelligence Officer, he was well served. " Underlying all the Sirdar's preparations," writes Sir George Arthur,[2] " was the military intelligence wrought by Colonel Wingate—with but slender financial resources—into a subtle system, perfected in every detail. His secret service honeycombed the Sudan, and in the guise of merchants, holy men, artisans, wandering beggars, and even women, his spies penetrated the fastnesses of Dervishdom and brought back inside information acquired at first hand and derived from paid and unpaid agents in Omdurman and elsewhere. Among the latter the most important were a few white men and women left in the capital, some Greek and Austrian priests and nuns captured in Gordon's time, the German prisoner Neufeld, and, more especially, Slatin Bey[3]. . . . Thanks to the Intelligence Department, we were admirably primed as to what was going on inside the enemy's lines, whether on the Nile or in the countries far beyond." Aided by this wonderful system, Kitchener was enabled to make his dispositions with certainty and to strike at an opportune moment.

The main body of the dervish garrison of the Dongola province was known to be in Dongola itself; but it was reported that a force

[1] Subsequently from Saras southwards.
[2] *Life of Lord Kitchener*, by Sir George Arthur, Vol. I, p. 180.
[3] After his escape from the Khalifa in 1895, Slatin served under Colonel Wingate in the Intelligence Department in Egypt and the Sudan.

of perhaps 3,000 men was farther north at Suarda, with advanced posts at Firket and Akasha.[1] Evidently the first object should be to defeat the enemy between Suarda and Akasha, if possible by a surprise attack; but this would involve an advance of about 100 miles from the Egyptian outpost at Saras, with concomitant difficulties of supply. Fifteen thousand camels would be needed for the transport of one month's supplies over such a distance for a force of 10,000 men,[2] and a further advance would be almost impossible for a considerable period. The chief problem of the Dongola Expedition was the question of supply. Kitchener solved it by taking every advantage of river transport, difficult though it was; this he supplemented by camel transport, and, most important of all, by extending the Wadi Halfa-Saras Railway as he progressed.

It was decided that the first move should be to send forward a small force to seize Akasha, where a fortified camp would be formed to cover the railway construction. Supplies for a further advance would then be accumulated at that place by camel convoys following the river route, along which fortified posts would be established. Meanwhile, reinforcements and supplies would be hurried up the Nile from Egypt, and when sufficient supplies were available at Wadi Halfa and Saras, the greater part of the Egyptian Army would be concentrated at those places. It was arranged that 2,000 camels should be purchased and dispatched to the Egyptian frontier to operate as a Transport Corps under Lieut.-Colonel Frederick Walter Kitchener, West Yorkshire Regiment, a younger brother of Sir Herbert Kitchener; also that friendly tribesmen should be organized to act as scouts in the Libyan and Nubian Deserts, and that reconnaissances should be sent out from Murrat Wells, a fortified post on the Korosko-Abu Hamed route in the Nubian Desert. Shielded by Akasha, the railway and telegraph would be pushed forward to the limit of safety; and when the time was ripe, Sir Herbert Kitchener would concentrate his striking force and drive the enemy from Firket and Suarda. The railway could then be extended to Firket, while camel convoys worked between railhead and the force.[3] When

[1] See the *Sketch Map of the Nile from Wadi Halfa to Dongola*, included in Chapter IV and repeated in this chapter.
[2] *Sudan Campaign*, 1896–1899, by "An Officer" (Lieut. H. L. Pritchard, R.E.), p. 11.
[3] In a note sent to the author on May 12th, 1936, Lieut.-General Sir George Gorringe, K.C.B., K.C.M.G., D.S.O., Col. Commandant R.E., remarks:—
" The problems of supply and transport required most careful consideration. We had not only to move the troops gradually up to Akasha, together with their ammunition and equipment, but to feed them *en route*, and to collect at Akasha sufficient supplies to maintain them there until the date of the advance, and for a period after the advance until further supplies could arrive. All this had to be done by camel transport. Owing to the low state of the river, only the smaller boats could be used above Wadi Halfa. These were taken gradually upstream, and were eventually utilized when the camel transport was unable to maintain the supplies at Firket and Suarda. The line of supply had then to be altered. Where it was possible to use the small boats, they were distributed into sections, depots were formed, and camel transport was operated between the depots. This system involved most careful control, which it fell to my lot to undertake. Daily reports from each depot were telegraphed to me, and I ordered what was to be forwarded each day."

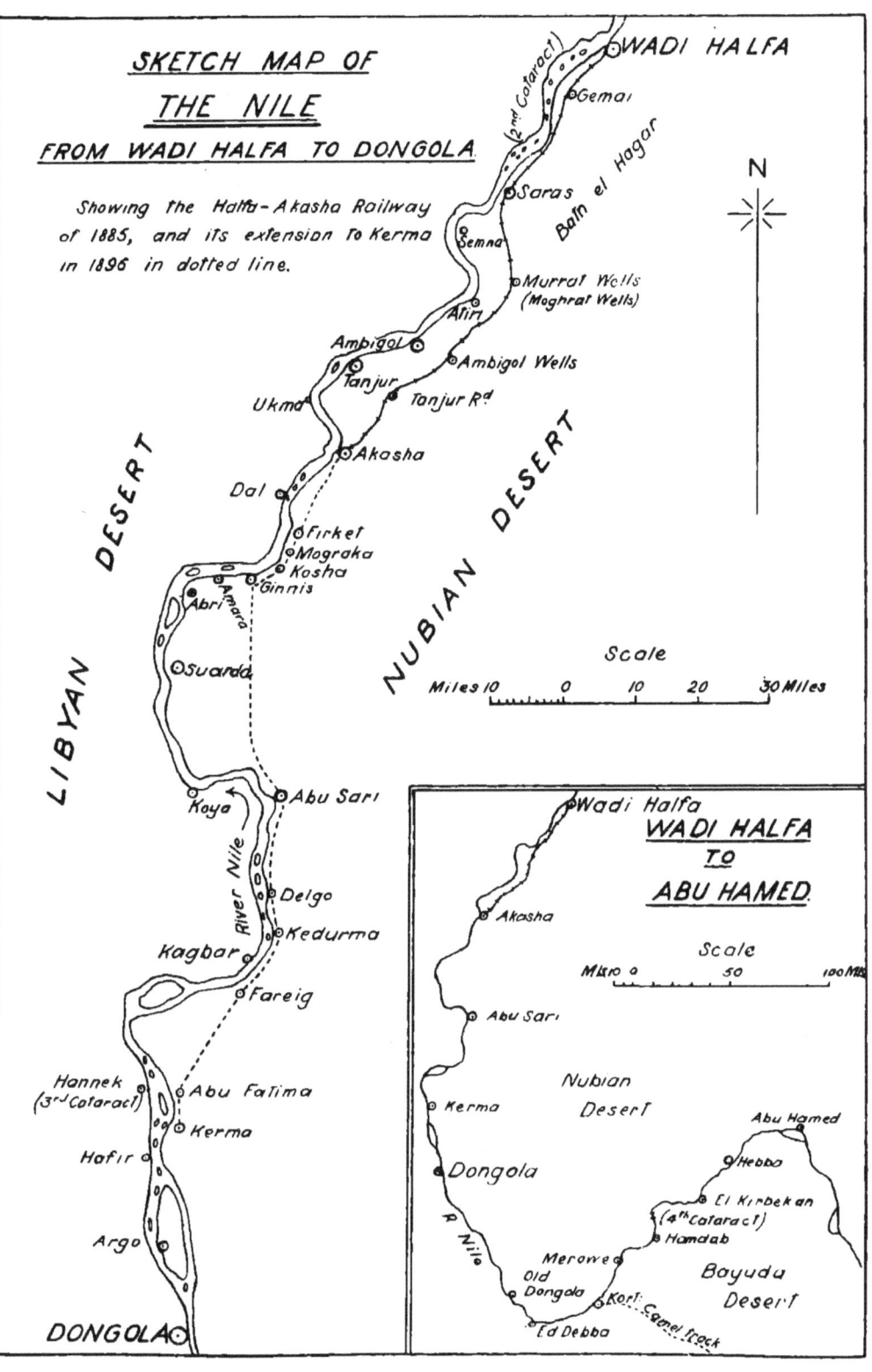

the Nile rose, the reserve of supplies accumulated at Firket could be carried in sailing-boats up to Dongola in the wake of the army. Gunboats of shallow draught would assist and guard the river traffic, and take part in all battles. The railway was to be constructed and operated by a Railway Battalion of 700 armed men assembled at Aswan and sent up to Wadi Halfa. A Maxim Battery of four machine-guns, formed from the combined machine-gun sections of the North Staffords and Connaught Rangers, would add to the fire-power of the infantry. These were some of the details of the scheme evolved by Kitchener and carried out with conspicuous success by his staff and subordinate commanders.

Throughout the Sudan campaigns of 1896–98, military operations were determined largely by questions of supply, dependent on the rise and fall of the Nile and the consequent variation in the extent of the cataracts. Kitchener's main principle of supply was to use boats on the river between the cataracts, wherever and whenever possible, and to build a railway round each cataract as he came to it. He made his advances at high Nile, because at that period he could drag ships and boats up the cataracts, and having done so, he prolonged his railway to the farthest point of his advance, preparatory to another forward movement. For instance, when he brought his railway to Firket he had a long stretch of water ahead of him on which his boats could work up to the foot of the next cataract, and when he carried the railway to Kerma he had turned all the cataracts in the Dongola province. Similarly, as will appear later, he avoided the obstacle presented by the Fourth Cataract at low water by constructing a railway across the Nubian Desert to Abu Hamed, and overcame the difficulties of the Fifth Cataract below Berber by prolonging that railway to the junction of the Atbara River. Thence he had clear water up to the Sixth Cataract, midway between Metemma and Omdurman, and brought his campaign to a successful conclusion without the necessity of extending the railway to circumvent that final obstacle.

For engineering work during the Dongola Expedition, Kitchener had to rely chiefly on the officers of the Royal Engineers who were serving in the Egyptian Army. When the campaign started, only six of these officers were available for military duty; but others joined the cadre, and during part of the campaign there were ten such officers at the front or on the line of communication. They were Captains W. S. Gordon and W. F. H. S. Kincaid, and Lieutenants G. F. Gorringe, E. P. C. Girouard, A. G. Stevenson, M. G. E. Manifold, H. L. Pritchard, R. Polwhele, R. B. D. Blakeney and E. H. S. Cator.[1]

---

[1] Captain W. S. Gordon was usually at Cairo as Director of Stores; Captain W. F. H. S. Kincaid was occupied mostly in Staff work at the front; and Lieutenant G. F. Gorringe was also employed mainly on the Staff on " Q " duties in connection with supplies. Consequently, the bulk of the engineering work fell on the remaining R.E. officers.

The eight subalterns became known as "Kitchener's Band of Boys"—a very happy band who did credit to their chief. Captain and Brevet Major A. G. Hunter-Weston, to be found usually on the Staff, and Lieutenant G. E. Elkington, with one section of the 2nd (Fortress) Company, R.E., from Cairo, also served with the Expedition. Thus, only 12 officers of the Corps took part in the military operations under Kitchener in 1896. There were others, however, who were concerned indirectly with them. Major the Hon. Milo G. Talbot, then D.A.A.G. in the Intelligence Department of the War Office, had induced Kitchener to obtain permission for him to join the expedition as a Special Service Officer for survey and intelligence work. He continued a triangulation of the Nile basin which he had begun in 1893 under the auspices of his personal friend, Major Wingate, and reconnoitred occasionally for railway routes. In so doing, he added to the brilliant reputation which he had gained in surveying on the north-west frontier of India and in Afghanistan.[1] Lieutenants G. A. F. Sanders, H. A. Cameron, J. R. Chancellor and C. F. Anderson served with the 1st Company, Madras Sappers and Miners, in the garrison of Suakin and earned the Dongola medal, but they did not leave the Red Sea littoral.[2] The survivors of Kitchener's "Band of Boys" are Lieut.-General Sir George Gorringe, K.C.B., K.C.M.G., D.S.O., Colonel Commandant R.E., Major-General H. L. Pritchard, C.B., C.M.G., D.S.O., Colonel Commandant R.E., Major-General A. G. Stevenson, C.B., C.M.G., D.S.O., Colonel Commandant R.E., Major-General Sir M. Graham E. Bowman-Manifold, K.B.E., C.B., C.M.G., D.S.O., and Brigadier-General R. B. D. Blakeney, C.M.G., D.S.O. Colonel Sir Percy Girouard, K.C.M.G., D.S.O., the railway expert and Colonial Governor, died in 1932.[3] Of the others, Lieut.-General Sir Aylmer Hunter-Weston, K.C.B., D.S.O., Colonel Commandant R.E., and Colonel W. F. H. S. Kincaid, C.B., are still with us. It is evident that Kitchener's care in choosing his officers was well justified.

The Sirdar expected much from his subordinates in the Egyptian Army, and he got it; but he made it his business never to lose sight of a man who had served him well. He was a firm friend, if a hard master. "I remember" writes Colonel Sir Henry Lyons,[4] "that he said one day that if you give a man rather more to do than you think he can do, nine times out of ten he will do it. We knew that he was

---

[1] See *The Military Engineer in India*, by Lieut.-Colonel E. W. C. Sandes, D.S.O., M.C., R.E. (retd.), Vol. I, p. 391, and Vol. II, pp. 216 and 236–238. A Memoir of Colonel the Hon. Milo G. Talbot, C.B., late R.E., appears in the *R.E. Journal*, Vol. XLVI, 1932, pp. 138–150.

[2] See Chapter III.

[3] A Memoir of Colonel Sir Edouard Percy Cranwill Girouard, K.C.M.G., D.S.O., late R.E., appears in the *R.E. Journal*, Vol. XLVII, 1933, pp. 323–343.

[4] Extract from notes sent to the author by Colonel Sir Henry Lyons, F.R.S., late R.E., in 1934. During the Dongola Expedition, Sir Henry, then a Captain, was in charge of the Geological Survey of Egypt with his headquarters at Aswan.

perfectly ready to undertake himself any task that he gave. Also, he did not mind criticism. For instance, I remarked on one occasion that it was hard on villagers living near the frontier that he would not arm them so that they could defend themselves against raiding dervishes. " Do you think so ? " he replied. " Well, when I was at Suakin in 1886, we had Osman Digna and a large dervish force in front of us, and, in between, a body of 2,000 friendly Arabs to whom I gave rifles. That night two dervishes rode over to the friendlies and asked them how they dared to take arms from the infidel. They ordered them to load the rifles and bring them to the dervish lines, which they did. Since then I have not armed friendlies."

The Dongola Expedition, and the Omdurman Campaign which followed it, consisted of the building of railways with attendant military operations rather than of military operations with attendant railway construction. Second only to the railways in importance were the telegraphs by which, in a roadless country, all communication was maintained. As the railway and telegraph operations were so important, they will be dealt with in a separate chapter. For the present, it is necessary to follow the fortunes of the troops in the field.

The campaign opened on March 16th, 1896, when Colonel Archibald Hunter, in command of the southern outposts beyond Wadi Halfa, dispatched a small force of all arms from Saras to seize Akasha, and thus began the invasion of territory which had been abandoned to the dervishes since 1885. Atiri was reached on the 18th, Tanjur on the 19th, and on the 20th the column marched into Akasha. No opposition was encountered, and, in fact, very few dervishes were seen. The occupation was announced to the Sirdar at Cairo, and as soon materials became available, Lieutenant M. G. E. Manifold, R.E., rapidly extended the telegraph to the new advanced post. Akasha was a melancholy sight. The mud huts of the deserted village were crumbling to dust, and here and there lay the ruins of the old British buildings and defences of the Nile Campaign. The rails of the former line from Saras had been thrown down the low embankments. Everything bespoke the hideous desolation of war, followed by years of neglect and misrule. But all was soon changed. The troops set to work with a will to clear the site, build a new fort and prepare an entrenched camp. The line of communication along the bank of the Nile from Saras was opened up and strengthened by the establishment of fortified posts at Semna, Atiri and Tanjur; and the desert on both sides of the Nile was patrolled by friendly Arabs, mounted on swift camels and armed with Remington rifles. Garrisoned by three battalions of infantry, with a battery of artillery, some cavalry and a company of the Camel Corps, Akasha was secure against a dervish attack.

On the day following the occupation of Akasha by Hunter's

troops, Kitchener, Wingate and Slatin left Cairo for Wadi Halfa. When the concentration at Akasha was completed, they were followed by the 1st Battalion, North Staffordshire Regiment and a section of the 2nd (Fortress) Company, R.E., under Lieutenant G. E. Elkington. Several Egyptian battalions had already been hurried up the Nile by rail and in the river-steamers of Messrs. Thomas Cook and Sons. The North Staffords were detailed to garrison Wadi Halfa, while most of the Egyptian units, including six battalions already at Wadi Halfa, passed on to the various posts between that place and Akasha. The Railway Battalion, under an Egyptian officer, came up from Aswan to begin the reconstruction of the line from Saras onwards. Two Railway Officers, Lieutenants A. G. Stevenson and R. Polwhele, R.E., arrived from Korosko. Kitchener himself reached Wadi Halfa on March 29th and, except for tours of inspection, remained there throughout the month of April to superintend the arrangements for the extension of the railway and the accumulation of supplies.[1] It was not until the end of May that he felt justified in transferring his headquarters to Akasha, though he visited that place frequently during the month.

News of the rapid movement of the Egyptian Army, and of reinforcements on their way from Suakin, having been carried to the Khalifa at Omdurman, the dervishes began to mass in greater force at Firket, Suarda, and still farther south at Abu Fatima, near Kerma. They were under the Emir Hammuda, with the Emir Osman Azrak as his lieutenant, and were strengthened from time to time by contingents sent forward by Wad el Bishara, the Emir of Dongola. The dervishes of 1896 were very different in appearance from those of 1884. In the time of Gordon, their coats were a mere collection of patches; but the Khalifa now clothed them in short-sleeved *jibbas* or smocks of coarse white cotton, on which square pieces of coloured cotton fabric were sewn with some semblance of regularity. The colour varied according to the tribe of the wearer. The dervishes wore large white turbans and cut their hair short. Emirs could be distinguished from the rank and file by the greater length and ornamentation of their *jibbas*, and by the fact that they were always mounted. In character, the enemy had not altered appreciably, and they retained all their old dash and fire; but their spears and Remington rifles were no match for the hard-hitting Martini-Henry rifles of the Egyptian Army of 1896.

The 9th Sudanese Battalion, which came from Suakin, made a fine march across the desert on its way to the front. This unit embarked on March 20th and sailed for Quseir (Kosseir), the scene of Major-General David Baird's concentration of the Indian contingent for the march to the Nile in June, 1801.[2] Following Baird's

[1] *The River War*, by the Rt. Hon. Winston Churchill, p. 128.
[2] See Chapter I.

route from Quseir towards Qena (Kena),[1] the 9th Sudanese covered a distance of 120 miles across desolate country in less than five days and struck the Nile at Qift (Kift), north of Luxor. Lieutenant M. G. E. Manifold, R.E., who accompanied this battalion from Suakin, records that the first halt was at an oasis called " Bir Inglesi," a name attributed to Baird's troops. The men marched with great swing and endurance, and on one day travelled a distance of 30 miles. It is interesting to note that when Major-General Sir Graham Bowman-Manifold, the Lieutenant Manifold of 1896, repeated the desert journey between the Red Sea and the Nile in 1927, he accomplished it by car in eight hours.[2]

Wadi Halfa in 1896 bore little resemblance to the mud village of 1885. It had expanded enormously and had barrack accommodation for 4,000 men.[3] Hilliard Atteridge, of the *Daily Chronicle*, writes :—[4] " If the importance of the place could be measured by its river frontage, Wadi Halfa would be one of the most considerable cities on the Nile. It extends for rather more than three miles along the eastern bank of the river, but there are some breaks in continuity. Nowhere is it more than four hundred yards wide : often it is only forty. At its north end is Tewfikiya (formerly known as Dabarosa), a group of fairly well-built houses with a handsome mosque and minaret, the whole surrounded by a slight enclosing wall. South of Tewfikiya runs a suburb of scattered mud huts and straw shelters with little gardens between them ; and then one reaches the cantonment, rather less than a mile long, barrack huts, officers' cottages along the river front, a hospital, some workshops, stores and offices, with railway sidings at the south end of the place. The cantonment is protected by a ditch and mud wall, with heavy Krupp pieces on little bastions where the ends of the rampart rest upon the river, and five small detached forts strengthen the land front. On the top of a sandy ridge on the other side of the Nile there are three blockhouses. South of the cantonment there is another mile and a half of Arab mud-walled houses. A caravan track runs south beside the railway. Beyond the line is one large group of native houses ; then comes an expanse of undulating sand, bounded eastward by a low range of red, rocky hills traversed by numerous *khors* (ravines). During the weeks I lived in my cottage on the river bank, the frontier garrison was a busy place. As each steamer arrived with its attendant barges, it was rapidly unloaded, generally by fatigue parties of Egyptian soldiers, sometimes by gangs of

[1] This route was the normal one for troops moving on relief between the Halfa District and Suakin.
[2] Notes by Major-General Sir M. G. E. Bowman-Manifold, K.B.E., C.B., C.M.G., D.S.O., sent to author in September, 1934.
[3] *Letters from the Sudan*, by E. F. Knight, Special Correspondent of *The Times*, p. 18.
[4] *Towards Khartoum. The Story of the Sudan War of 1896*, by Captain A. Hilliard Atteridge, London Irish Rifles, Special Correspondent of the *Daily Chronicle*, pp. 92–94.

convicts. Every morning one or two heavy train-loads of stores went off to Saras. At the arsenal workshops in the cantonment, engines were being repaired, and large trucks, brought piecemeal on the steamers, were being put together. Camels were being collected, and transport companies organized and marched up by the desert track beside the railway to strengthen the convoys from Saras. Troops were passing through to the front. The Sirdar had his headquarters near the railway station, and there was little rest in the various offices where his staff were at work. At Major Wingate's house on the river bank there was a coming and going of picturesque Arab agents bringing information, and of newspaper correspondents anxious to get their share of it."

The capacious building, which had been the railway station before the dervishes destroyed the greater part of the line to the south, had become a military hospital. All the other buildings were single-storeyed and without a pane of glass in their windows. The principal group of houses, offices and quarters was known as the "Commanderia," and in it was the "Sirdaria," Kitchener's residence, a long, low building on the river-bank which fronted a small garden surrounded by a high wall. In the scorching heat and roaring dust-storms of summer, Wadi Halfa fully deserved the name of " B—— Hell-Fire " bestowed upon it by the North Staffords.[1] They felt that the Arab saying " the ground is like fire and the wind like flame " was no exaggeration.

Portions of the Wadi Halfa defences still remain. The author visited three of the detached forts—Nos. 2, 3 and 4—in 1935. Their high mud walls were in varying stages of decay, and owed their survival to the fact that the official annual rainfall of Wadi Halfa is *nil*. No trace existed of Fort No. 1, but some of the foundations of Fort No. 5 could be seen in a garden on the river-bank. The wire entanglements, which in 1896 ran down the bank into the water at this point and also at the southern end of the wall enclosing the cantonment, had vanished, and the alignment of the wall itself was marked only in certain sections by a low embankment. The remains of the South Gate and an adjacent bastion were visible outside the entrance to the modern Wadi Halfa Hotel.[2] Five miles upstream, the ruins of the massive structure known as Fort Khor Musa made a conspicuous landmark ; and the crumbling walls of the adjacent redoubts on the river-bank, and on an island which, with Khor Musa, formed the outermost defences of Wadi Halfa towards the south, could still be seen.

Saras was an important outpost in 1896, for it was the point

[1] *The Egyptian Sudan. Its Loss and Recovery*, by Lieutenants H. S. L. Alford and W. D. Sword, p. 81.
[2] The Wadi Halfa Hotel is one of four excellent establishments controlled by the Sudan Government Railways and maintained by them in the interests of Government officers and tourists. The others are the Port Sudan Hotel, the Grand Hotel, Khartoum, and an hotel at Juba on the Upper Nile.

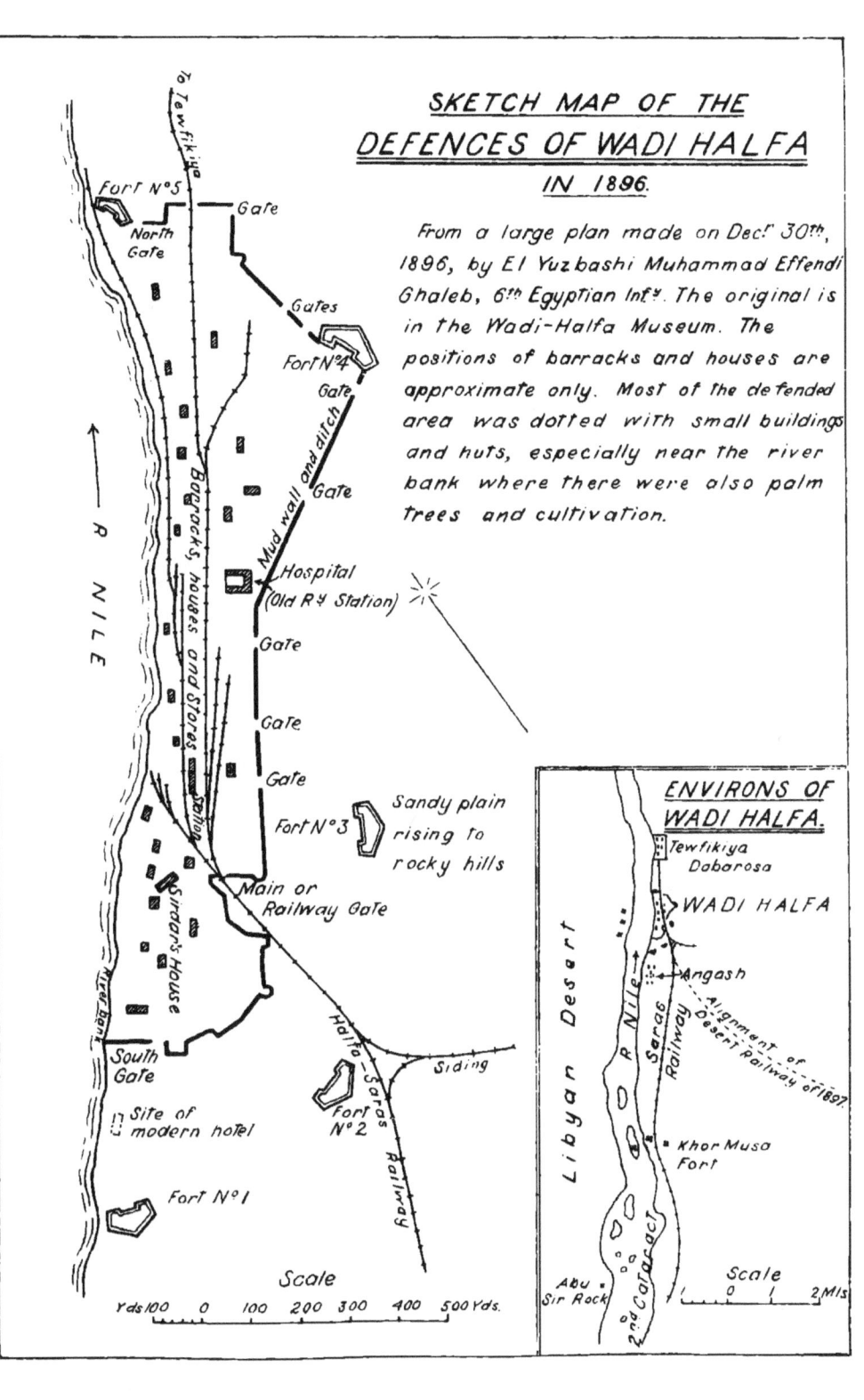

from which the offensive was launched, and also the original terminus of the railway and a depot for supplies. Its position, about 30 miles south of Wadi Halfa, is marked by a great crag of black rock overlooking the Nile and the sombre wilderness of the Batn el Hagar. The 12th Dynasty fortress, which once crowned the rock, had been remodelled in 1894 and contained barracks and other buildings for the troops, and quarters for Colonel Archibald Hunter, who commanded the district known as " Saras and the South."[1] Stone walls had been built from the northern and southern ends of the crag to the Nile, and the space thus enclosed provided camping accommodation for some thousands of men and animals. A cavalry camping ground near the railway, about one mile to the north, was used when necessary. Wire entanglements to the landward side of the crag, and in front of the stone walls, made Saras secure from a sudden assault. On the south side, a railway siding ran down to the river so that engines could get water, and it was from this point that Lieutenants A. G. Stevenson and R. Polwhele, R.E., began to reconstruct the railway towards Akasha.

A problem which demanded immediate attention was that of river transport above the Second Cataract, and, on his arrival at Wadi Halfa, Major A. G. Hunter-Weston, R.E., was sent by Kitchener to reconnoitre the various rapids and to determine whether steamers could be taken through them, and if so, by what means. He was directed to report also as to whether any engineering work would be necessary to improve the channels. Hunter-Weston, like Milo Talbot, was one of a band of " Special Service Officers," chosen by Kitchener and kept more or less under his own hand for any duty which might arise. Although he had never soldiered in the Sudan, he had graduated in the excellent school of the North-West Frontier of India, having served with the Bengal Sappers and Miners and on the staff during the Miranzai and Waziristan Expeditions under Sir William Lockhart in 1891 and 1894.[2] " I started my work alone," he writes,[3] " assisted by such of the natives as were likely to have special knowledge of the subject. As I was a fairly good swimmer and had had experience of using *mashaks* (inflated skins) in India, I was able to carry out the reconnaissance to Kitchener's satisfaction. My costume was simple, artistic and well suited to the purpose, for it consisted only of a large helmet, a sun-umbrella and my birthday suit ! The simplicity of this attire, however, evoked considerable merriment in the Force, and in due course a picture of the cataracts appeared in the London illustrated

---

[1] Colonel Hunter moved his headquarters to Saras when Kitchener established his headquarters at Wadi Halfa. All the necessary engineering and other stores had already been ordered up.

[2] *The Military Engineer in India*, by Lieut.-Colonel E. W. C. Sandes, D.S.O., M.C., R.E. (retd.), Vol. I, pp. 432, 440.

[3] Letter from Lieut.-General Sir Aylmer Hunter-Weston, K.C.B., D.S.O., M.P., Col. Commandant R.E., to the author, dated October 15th, 1935.

papers with crocodiles in the background and me in my artistic costume in the foreground." The information collected in this preliminary survey of the cataracts was handed over to Commanders the Hon. S. C. G. Colville and C. H. Robertson, and Lieutenant (afterwards Admiral of the Fleet Earl) Beatty, R.N., and assisted them in making the arrangements for hauling many vessels through the swirling waters.

Having surveyed and reported upon the cataracts, Hunter-Weston joined Kitchener's staff at Akasha and was concerned in all the preparations for the next advance. "During the lulls in our work," he writes, "I had the unusual experience of passing the Qualifying Examination for the Staff College—a very irregular examination, I am afraid, but Kitchener was not a man to be tied by red tape. From time to time I was given a paper, and without any preparation —for there were no text books—I had to try to answer the questions while sitting in a small tent, covered with sweat, at a table, covered with dust, on which the sweat dropped and formed mud. However, under these very unusual circumstances I managed to qualify, and being given a nomination, joined the Staff College in January, 1897, thus, to my great disgust, missing Khartoum." Kitchener had insisted that Hunter-Weston should join and graduate as soon as possible at the Staff College. The episode is quoted in these pages as an instance of the real and personal interest which the Sirdar took in the career of each of his officers.

During the month of May, 1896, Kitchener consolidated his position at Akasha, brought up more troops and improved his communications. The camel track from Saras southwards to Ambigol was converted into a road[1] so that convoys could move with greater rapidity; but the most important engineering work was the extension of the railway, which was carried out with the utmost energy by the Railway Battalion, at first under Lieutenant A. G. Stevenson, R.E., and later under Lieutenant E. P. C. Girouard, R.E.[2] By the end of the month, the line had been rebuilt as far as Ambigol Wells, about 64 miles from Wadi Halfa, leaving only 23 miles to be constructed before Akasha was reached. Lieutenant M. G. E. Manifold, R.E., improved the telegraph system, and Lieutenant G. F. Gorringe, R.E., accelerated the supply services. The tents of the British officers at Akasha were pitched in a dry ravine, where there was some green turf and a few trees, so that life was not unbearable in spite of day temperatures ranging up to 124 degrees in the shade. The heat was so great that boot-nails became loose in the leather and fell out continually. Manifold messed with the

---

[1] *Letters from the Sudan*, by E. F. Knight, p. 102.
[2] Charles Royle, in his book *The Egyptian Campaigns, 1882—1899*, p. 506, states that the railway was constructed under the combined direction of Girouard and Nicour Bey, the French Chief Engineer of the Egyptian Railways. This is incorrect. Nicour Bey had no part in the direction of the work.

SARAS FORT AND THE BATN EL HAGAR DESERT.

[*Photo by the Author.*]

officers of the 12th Sudanese, a battalion commanded by Major (afterwards Major-General) C. V. F. Townshend, C.B., the defender of Chitral in 1895 and of Kut el Amara in 1915–16.[1]

At the end of May, the garrison of Akasha consisted of the 9th, 11th, 12th and 13th Sudanese, a squadron of Egyptian cavalry, a British Maxim Battery of four machine-guns and an Egyptian battery of 7-pounder Krupp " mountain " guns. The month had not been without incident. The dervish cavalry reconnoitred continually down the left bank of the Nile. On the 1st, there was an exciting skirmish near the camp between dervish horsemen and Egyptian cavalry under Major B. F. Burn-Murdoch, 1st Dragoons; and on the 21st, a demonstration from Firket by 2,000 infantry and 300 cavalry was foiled by the same officer. The Intelligence Department knew everything that happened in Hammuda's army. On the eve of attack, Major Wingate was able to issue to each British officer a plan of the dervish camp, a list of the Emirs and the troops under their command, and a memorandum on their organization and their usual dispositions and tactics. The enemy were mostly Baggara Arabs; but there were a certain number of Jaalin from the region of Berber, Danagla of the Dongola province, and Sudanese who were enrolled as " Jehadia "[2] and were regularly drilled and armed with rifles. Of these opponents, by far the most fierce, war-like, vicious and treacherous were the cattle-owning Baggara, the " Red Indians of the Sudan,"[3] a tribe to which the Khalifa himself belonged.

Though unfavourably situated for defence, being overlooked on three sides by rugged hills, Akasha was soon so strongly fortified that Hammuda could not hope to capture it by a surprise assault. Most of the troops and transport occupied an area on the right bank of the river, enclosed by a continuous breastwork of rails, small girders or stones, strengthened by wide belts of thorn. Three blockhouses, an old fort, and a battery for two guns were in this line, and the Maxim Battery was sited behind a sandbag breastwork to sweep a large ravine leading into the hills. Three other blockhouses on the right bank, and one on the left, formed an outer ring of observation and defence. Ranging marks were laid out, and every advanced post was well supplied with water and ammunition.[4]

The time had now arrived for Kitchener to pounce upon the force of 3,000 men under Hammuda at Firket, 16 miles upstream of Akasha. The 10th Sudanese joined him on June 2nd, and on the 4th, the troops in the posts downstream began to move to the front.

[1] *The Military Engineer in India*, by Lieut.-Colonel E. W. C. Sandes, D.S.O., M.C., R.E. (retd.), Vol. I, pp. 440 and 485. A full account of the defence of Kut el Amara is given in *In Kut and Captivity* by the same author.
[2] Men engaged to fight in a " Jehad " or Religious War.
[3] *Mahdiism and the Egyptian Sudan*, by Major F. R. Wingate, D.S.O., R.A., p. 9.
[4] A plan of the defences of Akasha in 1896 appears in the *Journal of the Royal United Service Institution*, Vol. 41, Part I, Jan.-June, 1897, p. 681, in connection with a lecture on the Dongola Expedition by Capt. A. H. Atteridge, London Irish Rifles.

The greatest care was taken that the enemy's scouts should not see these reinforcements, which came by rail to Ambigol Wells, marched westwards to the Nile, and ascended it only as far as Ukma, two miles short of Akasha. Colonel Archibald Hunter had already reconnoitred the river route towards Firket, and the cavalry had ridden over most of the desert route along the line of the projected railway. It was known that no less than 57 Emirs were in the enemy's camp, so that the destruction of Hammuda's force would be a crushing blow which might soon bring the campaign to an end.

The enemy played into Kitchener's hands by continuing to hold Firket, and as Winston Churchill remarks,[1] they dallied and faltered on the fatal ground until sudden, blinding, inevitable catastrophe fell upon them from all sides at once and swept them out of existence as a military force.

Kitchener concentrated at Akasha three brigades of infantry, seven squadrons of cavalry, eight companies of the Camel Corps, three batteries of artillery[2] and a Maxim Battery—about 9,000 men in all. The only British soldiers were those manning the four Maxim guns and a few on specialist duties. The 1st Brigade under Major D. F. Lewis, Cheshire Regiment, consisted of the 3rd and 4th Egyptians and the 10th Sudanese; the 2nd Brigade under Major H. A. MacDonald, Royal Fusiliers,[3] included the 9th, 11th, 12th and 13th Sudanese; and the 3rd Brigade under Major J. G. Maxwell, Black Watch,[4] was composed of the 2nd, 7th and 8th Egyptians. Major B. F. Burn-Murdoch, 1st (Royal) Dragoons, commanded the cavalry, and Major R. J. Tudway, Essex Regiment, the Camel Corps. As before remarked, no Engineer units were present; but Kitchener ensured that as many Engineer officers as possible were attached to the staff whenever military operations were contemplated, and these outings came to be known as "week-ends at the front." Thus, in addition to Major Hunter-Weston, Captain Kincaid and Lieutenant Gorringe who held staff appointments, Lieutenants Stevenson, Manifold, Polwhele and Cator reverted from technical to military duty, being made Special Service Officers or "gallopers" to brigade commanders.

It was decided that the advance from Akasha should commence on June 6th, 1896, by both the river and desert routes. The main body, under Colonel Hunter, accompanied by the Sirdar himself, would follow the track along the right bank of the Nile, while a Desert Column of 2,000 mounted men, under Major Burn-Murdoch, made a wide detour inland and came down upon the enemy's flank and rear. It was hoped that, with the aid of friendly Arabs on the other side of the Nile, the dervishes at Firket would be not only

---

[1] *The River War*, by the Rt. Hon. Winston Churchill, M.P., p. 128.
[2] One Horse Battery, and two Field Batteries with teams of mules.
[3] Afterwards Major-General Sir Hector MacDonald, K.C.B., D.S.O.
[4] Afterwards General Sir John Maxwell, K.C.B., K.C.M.G., C.V.O., D.S.O.

defeated, but hemmed in and destroyed. The essence of the operation was absolute secrecy, silence, and perfect timing. Burn-Murdoch's mobile column, consisting of the cavalry, the Camel Corps, a battery of Horse Artillery and two machine-guns, was strengthened by the 12th Sudanese Infantry mounted on camels; and its commander was instructed to occupy the hills to the southeast of Firket village by 4.30 a.m. on June 7th and to dispose his force facing the Nile, with the cavalry on the left, the Camel Corps in the centre and the 12th Sudanese, acting as infantry, on the right.

Marshalled by Hunter-Weston, the two columns moved out of Akasha during the afternoon of June 6th, and by 9 p.m. the River Column had traversed 12 miles of rough ground and bivouacked on a sandy plain. Not a sound had broken the stillness of the night; and within three miles of the enemy, the troops lay down to snatch a few hours of sleep. Meanwhile, the Desert Column was threading its way through a wilderness of rock, yet with such precision that it reached its appointed post in good time and was ready to play its part at the hour fixed for the attack. Below it, but hidden from view, was Firket, a straggling village of mud-walled houses and straw huts (*tukuls*) extending for some distance along the river-bank. The dervishes were holding the northern end strongly, and had prepared defences also along some ridges of rock which ran from the village up to the desert hills. To the north, towered the heights of Jebel Firket, between which and the river lay Kitchener's line of approach.

The River Column resumed its march at 2.30 a.m. on June 7th through most difficult country with several narrow defiles, but at length it skirted the base of Jebel Firket and was able to deploy gradually for the attack. The plan was simple. The 1st Brigade under Lewis, moving nearest to the river-bank, was to push forward towards the northern end of the village, while on its left MacDonald, with three battalions of the 2nd Brigade, was to attack the enemy on the rocky ridges. The 3rd Brigade, under Maxwell, would be held in reserve at the outset so that it might be ready to fill any gap in the line or to reinforce any point where unexpected resistance was encountered.

At 5 a.m. an enemy outpost on a spur of the Firket Mountain discovered the River Column and opened fire, but too late. The 2nd Brigade returned the fire and continued towards the ridges, while the 1st Brigade swung half-right to assault the end of the village. Drums beat, and the dervishes poured out to man their outer defences. MacDonald soon cleared the enemy from the ridges, and Maxwell came up with the 3rd Brigade to fill the widening gap between MacDonald and Lewis, who was forcing his way through the village at the head of the 1st Brigade. The dervishes in Firket fought with the courage of despair, frequently charging single-handed into the masses of Egyptian infantry and stabbing right and left until they died. Nothing could exceed the ferocity of the Baggara. Though desperately wounded, they would not surrender, but preferred to feign death until they could summon up enough strength to stab an enemy in the back before they expired. Hut after hut had to be cleared at the point of the bayonet, and the nature of the resistance is shown by the fact that 80 Baggara corpses were found, after the battle, in one hut alone. However, by 7.20 a.m. all was over. The enemy had lost 1,000 men killed or wounded, and 500 of the less desperate characters were prisoners. The cavalry then took up the pursuit of the remaining half of Hammuda's force and continued it for a distance of about 30 miles to Suarda, which they occupied in due course. Unfortunately, many dervishes made good their escape under cover of the high right bank or by crossing the shallow Nile; but nevertheless, Firket was a decisive victory and brought the end of the Dongola Campaign within sight. Though a small affair, it was classed as a general action, and a special clasp was awarded for it.

Writing of his experiences as a "galloper," Major-General Sir M. G. E. Bowman-Manifold says:—[1] "The long, snaky column of troops crawled along until 4.30 a.m., when we got on to a plain about three-quarters of a mile wide. Firket Mountain, a very scarped rock, was on our left, and the Nile on our right. Here, the 1st and 2nd Brigades got into line and the day began to dawn. I was sent to gallop for Lewis Bey, commanding the 1st Infantry Brigade. The 2nd Brigade, all blacks, under MacDonald, was on our left. I had plenty of hard riding, some of it very difficult. At first we moved along very quietly. Then a horse neighed and I heard Hunter say 'That's given the show away,' but apparently it did not alarm the outposts, for another ten minutes elapsed before we were fired on. To begin with, the fire was from only ten or twelve men; but a whole army soon poured out and lined the ridges beyond Firket Mountain. Our flanks were well protected, resting on the mountain and the river. Before we fired a shot, we heard the Desert Column open fire from the far side of Firket. Men and horsemen were running about, waving flags and firing. The rattle of fire from both sides was deafening, and soon our men began to be hit. One could see our fire rolling over the dervish horsemen like rabbits. Our mule batteries were very smart, firing over the heads of the infantry as they advanced. Houses in the village were soon ablaze, and the Egyptians kept advancing continuously. Their steadiness was wonderful; only the blacks were a little excited. All along the river was a thick grove of palm-trees with houses under them, and here very heavy fighting took place. My horse was hit at about 250 yards' range.[2] A

[1] Extract from a letter by Lieut. M. G. E. Manifold, R.E., dated Firket, June 13th, 1896.
[2] Manifold was riding at the time with Kincaid.

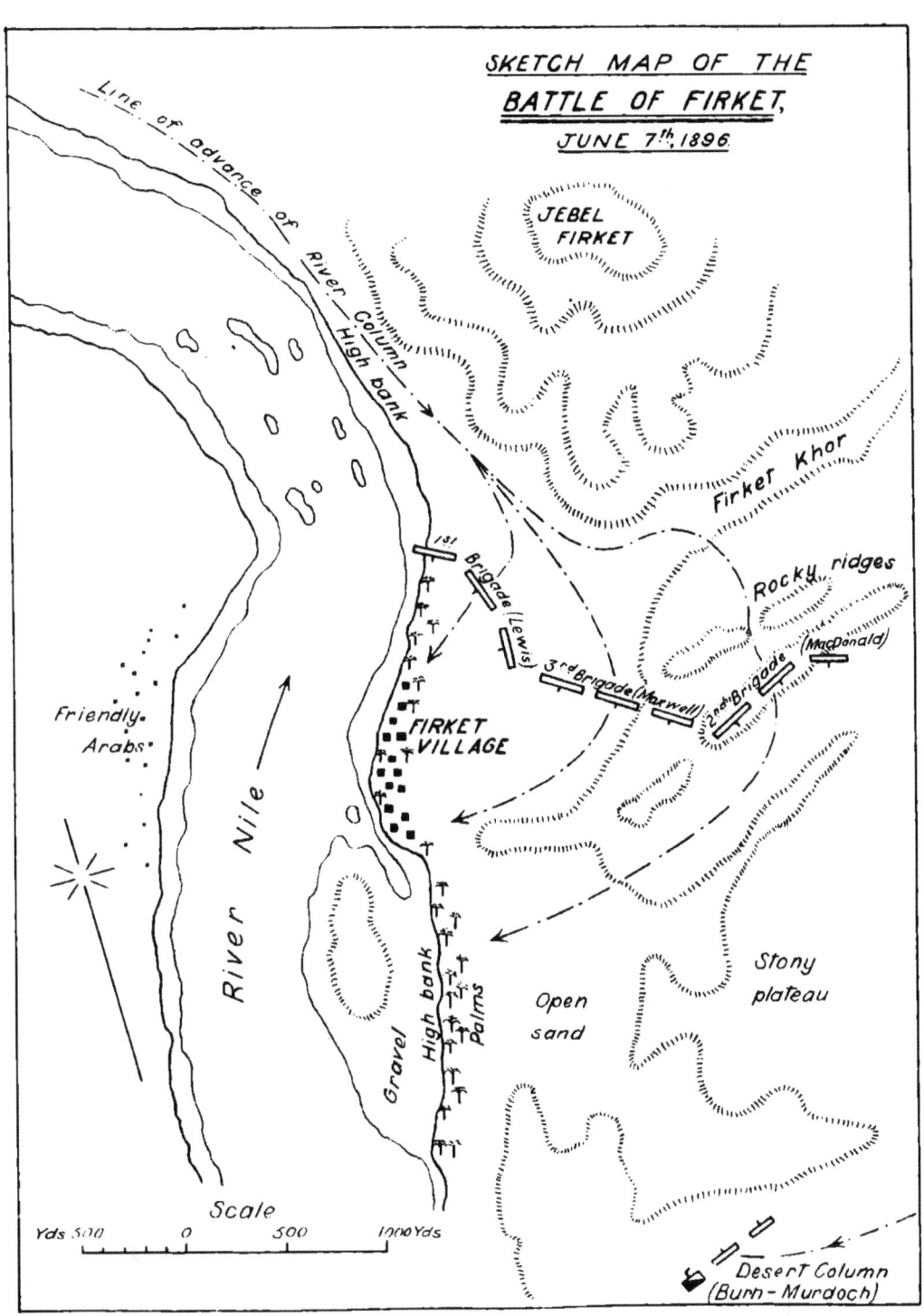

party of horsemen attempted to charge out from behind the houses, but they never reached more than 50 yards. The line moved gradually on through the village, and the dervishes ran into the arms of the cavalry. Some got across the river and were met by our friendly Arabs. All the prisoners were identified; also the dead. I started back at 5 p.m. with Stevenson and Polwhele and rode into Akasha early next morning. There I got 30 camels and began my return journey to Firket at 2 p.m., laying the telegraph line, and having halted by the river at night, pushed into the Sirdar's camp on June 9th."

The results of the Battle of Firket were important. In 24 hours, more than 50 miles of the Nile Valley had been cleared of the enemy; the Egyptian troops had proved their valour; Kitchener had fully justified the confidence placed in him by Cromer; the line of communication through the difficult Batn el Hagar was rendered secure from attack; and Suarda, for years the starting-point of cruel raids, was in the Sirdar's hands. But the moral effect of the victory was incalculable. At least 40 leading Emirs, including Osman Azrak, were among the slain. The news spread far and wide. Many waverers deserted from the Khalifa's banners, and the prisoners of Firket enlisted forthwith in the Egyptian Army and became useful soldiers of the Khedive.

The successful night march on Firket has been compared to that on Tel el Kebir in 1882, but actually there was little resemblance between them. Although Wolseley at Tel el Kebir had to handle much larger forces than Kitchener at Firket, he could move over open ground in battle formation. Kitchener, on the other hand, was obliged to advance in column through narrow defiles, and it was only through perfect organization and march discipline, exact calculation of time and distance, and the excellence of his Intelligence information that he was able to surprise and defeat Hammuda.

The victory of June 7th, 1896, was followed by an interval of three months during which one misfortune succeeded another and no further advance could be undertaken. Storm, flood and sickness tested the troops to the uttermost. The enemy were discouraged after Firket, and it might have been possible to push on at once towards Dongola, but Kitchener rightly decided that it would be safer to wait until the railway was close behind him and a rise in the Nile had allowed his steamers to join him. MacDonald's brigade and some artillery having reinforced the mounted troops at Suarda on June 9th, this place became the advanced post of the Expedition, with a garrison of 2,000 men, supported by the main body of 7,000 men, who remained for a few weeks longer at Firket. Cholera was the first unwelcome visitor, and at the end of June there were cases at Wadi Halfa. The North Staffords were moved southwards to Gemai, where the dread disease overtook them and spread to Saras, Ambigol, Akasha and Firket. On July 5th, the camp at Firket was abandoned,[1] and the garrison moved six miles upstream to Kosha, but cholera soon appeared there also in a most virulent form. No man knew whether he might see the rise of another sun. Death stalked through the army and claimed many of the bravest and best. The troops were moved out into the desert, where they lived in straw *tukuls* in temperatures mounting to 129 degrees in the shade; but still the disease persisted, and by the time that it subsided, in the middle of August, more than 900 soldiers and camp followers had died.[2] Enteric fever also claimed its victims. Among these was Lieutenant R. Polwhele, R.E., who succumbed at Wadi Halfa on July 29th. Polwhele was a most popular young officer, who had been employed for several months on the railway construction, and it was literally devotion to duty that killed him. When removed to the base at Wadi Halfa, he was already in a dying condition. Overworked though he was, he had allowed himself no rest in the scorching heat of summer, and so he fell an easy prey to a disease which was little understood at that period.

Lieutenant M. G. E. Manifold, R.E., extended the telegraph to Suarda, and on August 4th, Lieutenant E. P. C. Girouard, R.E., managed to bring the railway to Kosha,[3] but otherwise the stars in their courses seemed to fight against Kitchener. Violent duststorms, followed by torrential rain, occurred at the end of July and early in August in a country where rain is almost unknown; and on August 25th, the bad weather culminated in a storm which swept away part of the railway line near Saras. Every ravine was filled with a rushing torrent; tents and huts collapsed in a sea of liquid mud; telegraphic communication was interrupted; the movement of troops became impossible. The Nile itself behaved unexpectedly, for it rose unusually late, and consequently it was not until the middle of August that attempts could be made to drag ships through the Second Cataract. Lieutenant G. E. Elkington and a section of the

---

[1] The locality was insanitary owing to the number of dervish corpses and dead camels.

[2] Of the Egyptians, 260 soldiers and 640 camp followers died. Only 19 British soldiers succumbed to the disease. It is said that Colonel Rundle kept a bottle of "Cholera Mixture" for his Staff. The ingredients were brandy, chlorodyne and Worcester sauce in equal parts. Anyone feeling symptoms of cholera was required to drink a tumblerful. No one drank, and no one died!

[3] When the railway reached Firket, small boats were employed for carrying supplies as far as Suarda. Until the Nile rose, steamers and large boats could not pass the cataracts. As the force was dependent on railway, boat and camel transport for its supplies, it was essential to extend the railway as rapidly as possible, and for this railway material was needed. Consequently, the amount of supplies sent forward had to be limited, especially when the camel transport began to break down, and it fell to Lieut. G. F. Gorringe, R.E., to decide what should or should not be sent to the front. He was empowered by Kitchener to issue orders, for the Chief of Staff, direct to all commanders of depots on the line of communication north of Wadi Halfa, and to control what came up by rail—a most responsible charge for a junior officer, and one which was executed with remarkable precision and ability.

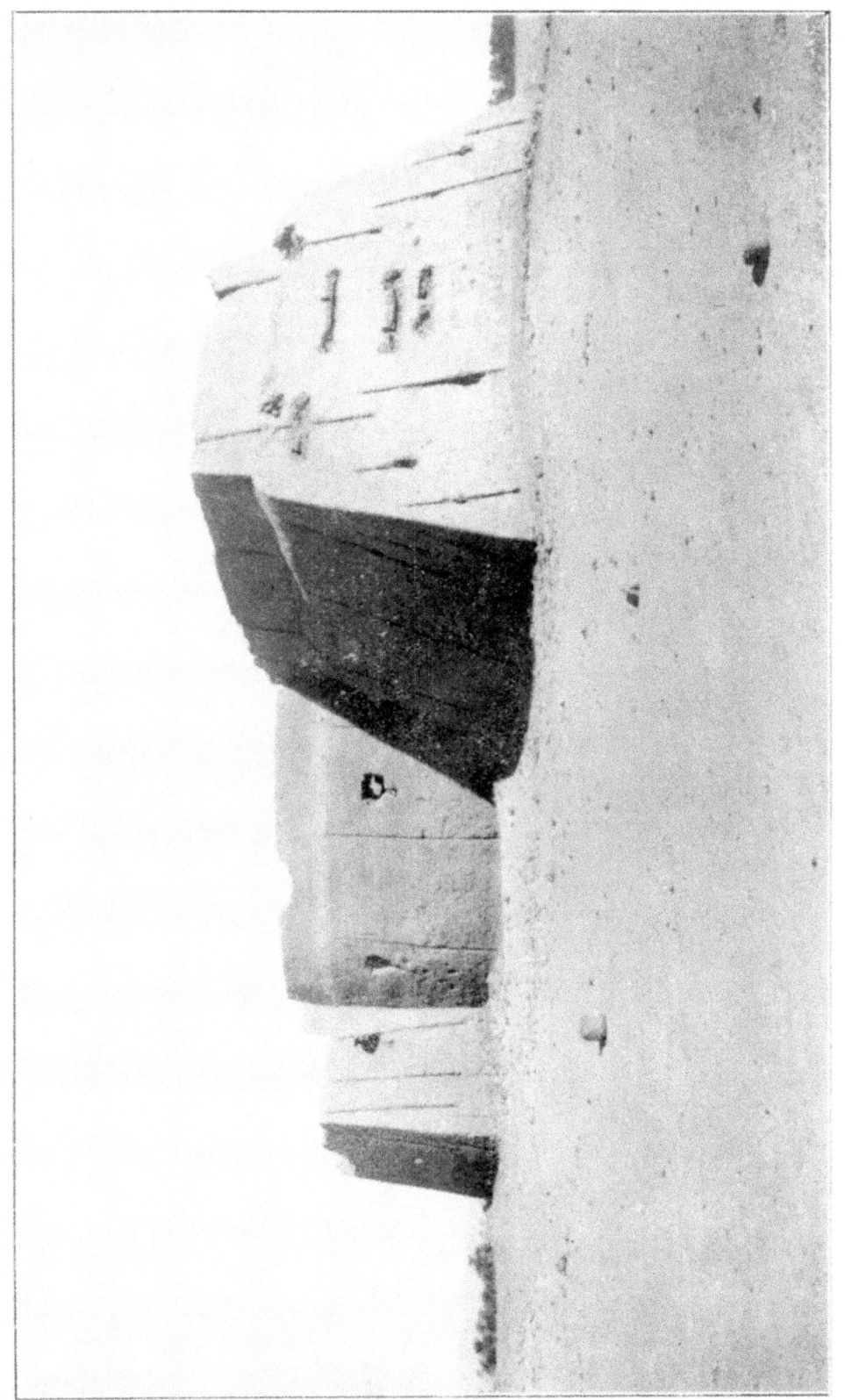

KHOR MUSA FORT, NEAR WADI HALFA.

[*Photo by the Author.*]

2nd (Fortress) Company, R.E., from Cairo, had been occupied for several weeks[1] in rounding off dangerous corners and clearing away obstructive rocks with the aid of guncotton; and on August 14th, the first gunboat, the *Metemma*, was hauled through the " Great Gate " by five immense cables, on each of which 400 men pulled with all their might. Three more gunboats—the *Tamai*, *Abu Klea* and *Et Teb*—and three unarmed steamers—the *Kaibar*, *Akasha* and *Dal*—followed on successive days, and on August 23rd all seven vessels arrived safely at Kosha. Captain W. F. H. S. Kincaid, R.E., worked with the Royal Navy and the infantry in these aquatic exploits.

Meanwhile, another important naval project was in the process of execution. This was the transport overland of a new gunboat, and her launching above the Second Cataract. She arrived, of course, in pieces. " Just before sunset on August 14th," writes E. F. Knight at Kosha,[2] " we heard the whistle of a locomotive and perceived, rolling slowly across the desert towards the camp, a train with four trucks bearing what appeared to be four huge square iron cases, painted red, each as big as a two-storeyed house and towering high above the engine. We knew these to be the first four sections of the new gunboat that had been constructed in England for the Egyptian Government."[3]

The sections of this ship, the *Zafir*, reached Alexandria on July 23rd and were conveyed up the Nile, by water and rail, under arrangements made by Captain W. S. Gordon, R.E., in consultation with Commander the Hon. S. C. G. Colville, R.N., and at length, after being transhipped seven times and travelling more than 4,000 miles, they were brought to Kosha by the Dongola Railway. Each section was a box, about 24 feet by 14 feet by 4 feet in dimensions, weighted with rail-fastenings, and standing on edge on a long flat truck to which it was lashed down. Lieutenant A. G. Stevenson, R.E., who brought the train from Wadi Halfa, said that he had been two days on the road, travelling at a maximum speed of only five miles an hour. The journey had been full of exciting incidents, especially on sharp curves, where the top-heavy loads tilted to an alarming angle. Each truck carried an anchor, which could be thrown out into the desert in case a gale should threaten to overturn the entire train.

The *Zafir* had been designed by Kitchener himself in collaboration with Major Burn-Murdoch. The plans had been completed by Mr. E. B. Thubron, a British engineer in Cairo. The ship was built in England in ten sections by British engineering firms. She was a stern paddle-wheel vessel, 140 feet in length, 24 feet in beam, and drawing

---

[1] This detachment of Royal Engineers arrived in Firket on July 20th, 1896.
[2] *Letters from the Sudan*, by E. F. Knight, Special Correspondent of *The Times*, p. 223.
[3] The remaining six sections of the gunboat followed in another train.

only two feet of water. With her three decks (carrying a 12-pounder gun, two 6-pounder guns, a small howitzer, 12 Maxims and a searchlight), her conning tower, and her rows of loopholed steel shutters, she promised to be a notable addition to the fleet. Kitchener was very proud of her and intended to make full use of her powerful armament. She was to be followed shortly by two sister ships, the *Nazir* and the *Fateh*.[1]

But the work of reassembling the *Zafir* was retarded by lack of expert direction and supervision. The chief engineer of the British firm had died as a result of an accident in Egypt; the second engineer had succumbed to cholera at Wadi Halfa. A junior employé alone remained to superintend the difficult operation, so Elkington and his Sappers were called in to help Colville and his sailors in the temporary dockyard at Kosha. "It was like putting a Chinese puzzle together without knowing the key" writes Pritchard.[2] "Several stores and pieces of the gunboat had got mixed with railway stores, so frantic wires flew between Kosha and Halfa. On one occasion, Halfa declared they had sent off a particular nut, while Kosha declared they had not received it. The inference was that it had fallen off in transit on the railway, so cavalry were sent patrolling along the line to find the nut. Strange to say, it was found." When the hull was ready, it was launched, and the machinery, conning tower and armament were lifted by great shears and put on board. By tremendous exertions, the *Zafir* was finished in time to take part in the renewed offensive which Kitchener had in view, and on the afternoon of September 11th the river-bank was lined with spectators to witness her trial trip. Colville took command, Kitchener embarked, and the moorings were cast off; but hardly had the stern wheel begun to revolve than there was a loud explosion. A cylinder had burst, and the *Zafir* was out of action until another could be obtained. This was the climax to the Sirdar's misfortunes. He was bitterly disappointed, and it was not till evening that he resumed his final preparations for an immediate advance to Dongola.

Already the leading troops were far up the river. MacDonald's brigade had marched up the right bank from Suarda to Abu Sari, which it occupied on August 23rd. In spite of the havoc wrought by the storm on the 25th, it was followed, on the 27th, by Lewis's brigade from Kosha along a more direct route through the desert. This brigade was caught in a terrific dust-storm, and although water depots had been laid out at intervals, the men were so overcome by heat, thirst and exhaustion that 1,700 out of 3,000 collapsed before Abu Sari was reached and several died. For a time, the 1st Brigade

---

[1] A detailed description of the *Zafir* and her sister ships is given in Appendix IV of *Letters from the Sudan*, by E. F. Knight, pp. 354-356.
[2] *Sudan Campaign*, by "An Officer" (Lieut. H. L. Pritchard, R.E.), p. 46.

GUNBOAT "ZAFIR" IN SECTIONS ON THE KERMA RAILWAY.
At Wadi Halfa before dispatch to Kosha.

[By kind permission of Major-General H. L. Pritchard, C.B., C.M.G., D.S.O.,
Colonel Commandant R.E.]

was unfit to take the field, and its desert journey came to be spoken of as the "Death March."

Reinforced by the arrival of the North Staffords from Gemai on September 15th, the Dongola Expeditionary Force amounted to nearly 15,000 men. In addition to the British battalion, there were the three brigades which had fought at Firket, a fourth brigade of three Egyptian battalions (1st, 5th and 15th) under Major E. F. David, R.M.L.I., four batteries of artillery, the Maxim Battery and a large Camel Corps. Most of the troops advanced southwards in brigade formations along the desert route, and subsequently by the river-bank, but some made the journey in river steamers protected by the gunboats which patrolled the Nile. They passed through Abu Sari, Delgo, Kedurma and Kagbar, and concentrated gradually at Fareig. Opposed to them at Kerma, 22 miles to the south, was the Emir Wad Bishara with only 5,600 men and a few small brass cannon. On September 18th, Kitchener advanced on Kerma; but Wad Bishara wisely declined a general action and transferred his force across the Nile to an entrenched position on the left bank at Hafir, a short distance upstream of Kerma. This was a masterly manœuvre, for it obliged Kitchener to open the way to Dongola by the action of his gunboats and artillery alone, without the aid of his infantry. The broad Nile ran swiftly between the opposing forces.

The action which was fought at Hafir on September 19th, 1896, is probably unique, for the Egyptian infantry sat idle on the sands under a burning sun and watched a spirited battle between their artillery and gunboats and the dervishes across the river. The flanks of the enemy's position rested on deep morasses extending inland from the Nile, and the defenders were posted behind a long line of loopholed mud walls. Their guns fired from earthen emplacements, and their snipers from the tops of palm-trees. At 6.30 a.m., the Egyptian artillery opened a heavy bombardment but did little damage, so the gunboats advanced under Commander Colville, R.N., and, steaming up to the enemy's position, poured in a concentrated fire at close range. The dervishes replied with good effect. Bullets rattled like hail on the armour-plating on the ships, and Colville and several men were wounded. A bullet passed through Beatty's helmet; another grazed his leg. The gunboats steamed up and down the river and continued the engagement for three hours, but they could not subdue the enemy's fire, and it was not until our artillery and machine-guns had come into action on an island in midstream that the dervish guns were silenced and their musketry fire died down. The gunboats then made another attempt to pass the hostile fortifications, and having succeeded in running the gauntlet, steamed onwards to Dongola, which they reached before sunset. Wad Bishara evacuated Hafir during the night, and on

September 20th, the Egyptian force crossed the Nile in the boats which the dervishes had abandoned.[1]

Several Royal Engineers served under Kitchener at the Battle of Hafir and earned the clasp which was awarded for it. Captain W. F. H. S. Kincaid was on General Hunter's staff, and Lieutenant G. F. Gorringe on the Sirdar's staff; and Lieutenants E. P. C. Girouard, M. G. E. Manifold, H. L. Pritchard, R. B. D. Blakeney and E. H. S. Cator were fortunate enough to be allowed to leave their normal technical duties to become "gallopers" or Special Service Officers, as Stevenson, Manifold, Polwhele and Cator had done at Firket. The Sirdar was ever mindful of his chosen "Band of Boys."

Little more remains to be recorded of the Dongola Expedition. The advance was resumed on September 23rd, along the left bank of the Nile, and the enemy retreated before it. The gunboats, among which was the reconditioned *Zafir* with Lieutenant G. E. Elkington and his R.E. Section on board, preceded the army and bombarded the defences of Dongola. No serious resistance was encountered, and, on the evening of the 24th, Kitchener received the surrender of the town. His infantry bivouacked in and around it, while the cavalry took up the pursuit of the mounted dervishes, who were riding across the desert towards Omdurman. Dongola was in ruins. Every building was gutted; every street choked with vegetation. The evils of the Khalifa's rule were never more clearly exemplified. While the troops were cleaning and improving the town, the gunboats proceeded as far as Merowe to harry Wad Bishara's infantry in their retreat up the Nile to Berber, and they were followed by MacDonald's brigade, which occupied Ed Debba, Korti and Merowe. Kitchener visited these advanced posts to receive the surrender of the various Sheikhs, and then, having handed over command to Hunter in October, went with Girouard to England on a short visit to lay his plans for a more ambitious campaign before the British Government while Girouard purchased railway material. Pacification and reorganization of the Dongola Province proceeded hand in hand. Manifold prolonged the telegraph to Merowe and into the Fourth Cataract, and in May, 1897, the Dongola Railway reached its southern terminus at Kerma.

There is a tale that, while Kitchener was in England, he was

[1] A tale was circulated afterwards that Colonel Rundle, becoming impatient, sent a message to General Hunter requesting information as to progress of the crossing, to which Hunter replied "See Hymn 221. Verse 3." This, being found, read "Part of the host have cross'd the flood, and part are crossing now." The true version, however, as related to the author by Lieut.-General Sir George Gorringe, who was in charge of the operation, is that the troops crossed in the early morning, and were followed throughout the day, the next night and the next day by the transport. About 3 a.m., when everyone was hot and weary, and a mass of mules and camels was still waiting to cross, Colonel Rundle and Veterinary-Captain G. R. Griffith came to see how the operation was progressing, and Griffith asked Rundle what it reminded him of. He received a curt reply; and it was then that Griffith suggested the very appropriate hymn.

commanded to Windsor Palace for a couple of days and directed to bring with him a collection of relics of the Dongola Campaign which Queen Victoria wished to see. After dinner, he was asked by Her Majesty to relate the histories of all the articles. Now it so happened that Kitchener had never seen most of these things; but nevertheless, he rose to the occasion and discoursed fluently for three-quarters of an hour on the stories attached to every sword, spear, drum and suit of mail. However, as he was undressing that night, an Equerry knocked at his door and said " Her Majesty asks that you will kindly write down all that you have told her." The unfortunate Sirdar and the Equerry sat up most of the night trying to recollect what had been said, for they knew that the Queen had an excellent memory.

Kitchener was thorough in everything that he undertook, and no detail was too small to escape his notice. Towards the end of 1896, he decided that the Sudan should have its own postage stamp and directed his staff to obtain a design from a British artist, who happened to be touring the Nile. The artist produced a beautiful design, showing the great rock-temple of Abu Simbel, and said that his fee would be 25 guineas; but Kitchener would not agree to such an expenditure and ordered Lieutenant E. A. Stanton, Oxfordshire Light Infantry, to prepare an alternative design. "I want you to go on drawing designs till you produce something I like," said he, "but remember that there is to be no caricature of myself nor anybody else in it. Good morning." He added that the design must be ready within five days. Having racked his brains for a suitable subject, Stanton finally induced a local Sheikh to pose on a camel. The sketch was submitted to Kitchener, who remarked "That's not so bad. I think it will do. Good morning," and the stamps appeared a few months later. Pleased with his success, Stanton wrote to Kitchener's Aide-de-Camp that he would much appreciate a set of stamps signed by the Sirdar, to which he received a reply that the Sirdar had said "Certainly. Provided that he pays for the stamps." As the cost was only 4s. 6d., Stanton rightly guessed that this was an example of the Sirdar's humour, and in due course he received a complete set, signed to the effect that he had designed them.[1]

In Kitchener's own words, the results of the Dongola Expedition were to stop the constant dervish raids on the villages between Aswan and Wadi Halfa, to add some 450 miles of the Nile Valley to Egyptian territory, and to relieve the suffering population of Dongola from the barbarous and tyrannical rule of savage and fanatical Baggaras. The success which attended it was attained at an extraordinarily small expenditure in lives and money. During a campaign

---

[1] Article entitled "The Sudan Camel Stamp," by Colonel E. A. Stanton, C.M.G., appearing in the *R.E. Journal*, Vol. XLVII, July-Dec., 1933, pp. 486, 487.

which lasted six months, the Egyptian Army lost only 530 soldiers, of whom 47 were killed and 122 wounded. Money was saved by employing the troops on most arduous physical labour in the cataracts and on the railway without extra pay; but there was little grumbling because all knew that the Sirdar spared himself no more than he spared others. The strictest economy prevailed in every department of the Army, and thus, at a cost of only £E.715,000,[1] Kitchener restored to Egypt her lost province of Dongola, using for the purpose the instrument which he himself had fashioned.

[1] *Modern Egypt*, by the Earl of Cromer, Vol. II, p. 91.

ENCAMPMENT BY NIGHT.
[*from " The Route of the Overland Mail to India."*]

CHAPTER VII.

RAILWAY AND TELEGRAPH THROUGH THE CATARACTS.

THE story of how a few subalterns of the Royal Engineers carried the railway and telegraph up the Nile towards Dongola in 1896 is a record of many dangers and hardships and much strenuous endeavour. Lieutenants E. P. C. Girouard, A. G. Stevenson, M. G. E. Manifold, H. L. Pritchard, R. Polwhele, R. B. D. Blakeney and E. H. S. Cator were the men who did it. They had youth, courage and endurance, and to these they added unswerving devotion to their work and unstinted admiration of their leader, Kitchener, both as a soldier and an engineer. Girouard headed the Railway contingent : Manifold played a lone hand in Telegraphs. Buoyed up by enthusiasm, and untrammelled by red tape, the " Band of Boys " accomplished, time after time, the seemingly impossible.

Outstanding amongst them was Percy Girouard, Director of Railways at the age of 29 years. " Gerry " was a French Canadian with the adventurous blood of the early settlers in his veins. Educated at Kingston College, Canada, and trained in the rough but splendid school of the Canadian Pacific Railway, he was very unconventional and quite unawed by Generals and their gilded staffs. It is related, for instance, that on his first interview with the Adjutant-General at the War Office, he offered him his left hand to shake. The Adjutant-General enquired sympathetically whether he had hurt his right hand. Fixing his monocle securely, Girouard replied with a strong Canadian accent " No. Only a *seegar*," and produced from behind his back a well-licked stump.[1] He was the personification of cheerfulness, obviously revelling in the mastery of every difficulty, and he never spared himself nor paid any regard to his health. Often he would visit railhead in the Sudan and find one of his subalterns in despair ; but with a pat on the back he soon restored confidence, and with unerring instinct he would indicate how the problem should be solved. Such was the loyalty and affection which he inspired in British and Egyptians alike that his presence alone was worth a battalion of workers. He would brook no interference with his subordinates and would always support them in any dispute.

Between Kitchener and Girouard there was a bond of mutual

[1] The story was told to the author by Brig.-General R. B. D. Blakeney, C.M.G., D.S.O., late R.E., in 1934, and it appears in an article by that officer entitled " K. and Gerry," in *The National Review*, January, 1936.

sympathy and understanding. The Canadian was a man after the Sirdar's own heart, and his keen sense of humour found its echo in his reputedly stern and silent commander. Yet, before they joined forces for the Dongola Expedition in 1896, they had never met. Girouard passed through Halifax, Nova Scotia, in that year on his way to England, having been posted to Mauritius to raise a native company of Engineers. Kitchener had heard of him, and stopped him in London; he interviewed him, and promptly annexed him. If Girouard had gone to Mauritius, would he ever have had his railway opportunity? Certainly, Dongola would not have been occupied by the Egyptian Army in September. The Sirdar loved a man who was not afraid to speak his mind, and he learned many home truths from his Canadian assistant. For instance, on one occasion, Kitchener was impatient because a crazy old engine was not pulling his heavily-laden train fast enough, so he mounted the footplate, shunted the train himself, left part of it behind, and told the driver to "Go like hell." He reached his destination in record time, over a corkscrew line on which the train rocked like a ship at sea. On arrival he emerged saying "What a dreadful journey we have had, Girouard! A dreadful journey! Terrible, terrible!" There was a pause while Girouard adjusted his eyeglass. Then he faced Kitchener. "You will break the record *and* your own neck one day" he replied.[1] An explosion followed; but Girouard did not care. He was no respecter of persons.[2]

Girouard did not arrive at Wadi Halfa until the end of March, 1896, when Stevenson and Polwhele had been busy for six months on railway preparations farther down the Nile. Their work was in connection with a scheme for building a line from Korosko southeastwards across the Nubian Desert, for a distance of more than 100 miles, to the oasis of Murrat Wells (not the Murrat Wells of the

[1] Notes by Brig.-General R. B. D. Blakeney, C.M.G., D.S.O., late R.E., sent to the author on July 20th, 1934.

[2] A Memoir of Colonel Sir E. Percy C. Girouard, K.C.M.G., D.S.O., late R.E., by Major-General H. L. Pritchard, C.B., C.M.G., D.S.O., late R.E., appears in the *R.E. Journal*, Vol. XLVII, Jan.-June, 1933, pp. 323-343. Girouard had a most varied and successful career. After the Dongola Expedition he built the desert railway to Abu Hamed, and prolonged it almost to Berber during the Omdurman campaign. Then he went to Egypt to supervise the construction of a line from Luxor to Aswan. In June, 1898, he was appointed "President of the Egyptian State Railways and Alexandria Harbour," and so missed the Battle of Omdurman in September. Having evolved a scheme for the reorganization of the Egyptian railways, he proceeded to America and England in 1899 to order material, and while he was in England in October, he accepted the appointment of Director of Railways for the South African War and served with distinction throughout that campaign. Afterwards, he became Commissioner of Railways in South Africa, but resigned that appointment at the end of 1904. A few years later he appeared in a new field, for in February, 1907, he was made High Commissioner and Commander-in-Chief of Northern Nigeria, and in September, 1909, Governor and Commander-in-Chief of the East Africa Protectorate. Soon he changed his profession once more, for in July, 1912, he accepted the post of Managing Director of Messrs. Armstrong, Whitworth, Ltd. During the Great War he worked for a time as Director of the Munitions Department at the War Office, but returned later to the north to control the output of Armstrong, Whitworth, Ltd. He died on September 26th, 1932. A portrait of Sir Percy Girouard appears in Chapter IX.

Kerma Railway) whence it might be possible to operate successfully against the dervishes, in conjunction with a force on the Nile, and subsequently to prolong the railway to the Nile at Abu Hamed. By cutting across the desert, Abu Hamed could be reached with 240 miles of line, whereas the length required along the Nile route from Wadi Halfa would be nearly 600 miles.[1] In the summer of 1895, Lord Cromer had not yet decided to postpone military operations in favour of the Aswan Dam project, and Kitchener hoped that his plans might be approved if he could show that he was already in possession of a strategic railway leading towards Murrat Wells. Consequently, he resolved to push on steadily with this project, and on September 15th, Stevenson and Polwhele arrived at Korosko to lay out the necessary sidings and to reconnoitre the route towards the desert outpost, which was held securely by four companies of Egyptian infantry under a British officer.[2]

According to Lieut.-Colonel Longfield, the labour at the disposal of Stevenson and Polwhele at Korosko consisted of a party of 200 convicts—mostly brigands—from Lower Egypt; and the first task which these men were set was the building of their own prison.[3] Meanwhile, the two officers were reconnoitring and surveying the route, and when the prison was ready, a shunting engine and some railway material were sent down from Wadi Halfa, and the ex-brigands began to lay out the base and make an embankment into the desert. There was little money, however, because the decision to build the Aswan Dam had at last been made. The death blow to the Korosko-Murrat scheme was delivered after a report was received from Stevenson and Major the Hon. M. G. Talbot, R.E. The Dongola Expedition was sanctioned in March, 1896, and all railway material was then needed at Saras for an extension up the Nile. The rails were pulled up, and Stevenson left Korosko at once for Wadi Halfa, whither he was followed by Polwhele and the convicts after they had loaded the shunting engine and material on to barges.

At this time, the railway from Wadi Halfa was in working order for a distance of only 33 miles to Saras. Beyond that place, it had been torn up as far as the former terminus at Akasha, another 54 miles; but the embankments remained, and the rails were close at hand. Most of the sleepers had been removed or burnt. In some stretches, however, the dervishes had turned the line over bodily in lengths of several hundreds of yards, and in these places the sleepers

---

[1] See the general map, entitled *The Anglo-Egyptian Sudan*, at the end of this volume.

[2] Murrat Wells was a sandy valley overlooked by rugged ridges of volcanic rock, on which were three small forts armed with 7-pounder guns. The wells were shallow, but the yield was sufficient to water 5,000 camels. A complete description of this oasis is given by E. F. Knight in *Letters from the Sudan*, pp. 42–69. The possession of Murrat Wells was essential to secure the flank of any advance up the Nile.

[3] Extract from *The Sudan Railways*, by Lieut.-Colonel W. E. Longfield, R.E. (retd.). Colonel Longfield's narrative has been used frequently in writing this chapter.

lay on top of the rails.[1] The wreckers had not troubled to heat and twist the rails to render them unusable, but had been content to throw them down the embankments, where they had lain for years without rusting. All the fastenings had been removed for use as spear-heads or for household purposes. The huts and houses of Wadi Halfa, Gemai, Saras and other places were full of rails, sleepers, bolts, nuts and fishplates which Kitchener proceeded to recover. The available locomotives and rolling stock consisted of two decrepit engines[2] and a few old trucks; the machine shops at Wadi Halfa were inadequate; stores and tools were deficient; there was no skilled labour; and as the gauge of the railway was 3 ft. 6 in., additional locomotives and rolling stock could be obtained only from South Africa, which had the same gauge, or by special order from England. Inferior sleepers were procured at first from stocks set aside for the Luxor-Aswan line, and afterwards from Turkey, and fastenings were made in the workshops of Cairo and Alexandria; but the best that could be done for the "Loco and Traffic Departments" was to patch up, as well as possible, the old contraptions on wheels which lurched and rattled along the uneven line through the Batn el Hagar.

While these preliminary measures were being taken, orders had been placed for material, stores, rolling stock and machine-tools; and foremen and artisans were engaged in Egypt. Local labour having proved unsuitable, a Railway Battalion was recruited from the donkey-boys of Cairo, the *fellahin* of Egyptian country districts, and the labourers of towns. It was mustered at Aswan under Egyptian officers and sent up to Wadi Halfa, and then to Saras, to work on the railway extension. Progress at first was slow, but it accelerated as the men learned their duties. Under Polwhele at rail-head,[3] four and a half miles of track had been laid beyond Saras by April 15th,[4] and six miles by April 23rd, when rail-head was advancing at the rate of 1,000 yards a day. As Colonel Hunter had occupied Akasha on March 20th, his troops were able to screen the railway operations. Nevertheless, as a precaution against raids, the 7th Egyptian Infantry, under Lieut.-Colonel Fathi Bey, was detailed to act as a rail-head guard and picketed the surrounding heights as the work progressed.

At the beginning of April, 1896, the Railway staff of Royal Engineer officers was augmented by the arrival of Cator, who was followed by Pritchard.[5] Girouard as Director, and Stevenson as

---

[1] *Letters from the Sudan*, by E. F. Knight, p. 107.
[2] There were eight locomotives at Wadi Halfa, but six of these were incomplete or out of repair.
[3] Stevenson had returned to Wadi Halfa.
[4] *Towards Khartoum*, by A. H. Atteridge, p. 88.
[5] In a letter dated April 5th, 1896, Manifold writes: "Cator has joined and has gone on to Saras. I hear Pritchard is likely to come out here. Gorringe is D.A. and Q.M.G."

Locomotive Superintendent, had their headquarters at Wadi Halfa; but Girouard, in particular, was travelling continually up and down the line in a small carriage, which he had fitted up as an office. Polwhele, as already stated, was always at rail-head in charge of construction. Pritchard was sent up to rail-head during survey operations, and sometimes to join in construction work, and Cator assisted him in both pursuits.[1] Blakeney arrived in Wadi Halfa from Suakin at the beginning of July, and relieved Girouard of most of the traffic work until he went to rail-head after Polwhele had died. Occasional assistance was given by Captain W. F. H. S. Kincaid and Lieutenant G. E. Elkington in the supervision of working parties of Egyptian troops, and on one occasion by Lieutenant M. G. E. Manifold in construction work at rail-head.

On May 4th, rail-head reached Murrat (Moghrat) Wells, about 14 miles south of Saras, and was advancing at a maximum rate of 1,200 yards a day; but when Girouard and Pritchard joined Polwhele for a time, the rate was increased to one mile daily, so that by May 21st, the track was laid to Ambigol Wells, 64 miles from Wadi Halfa and 31 miles from Saras. The Railway Battalion had become highly efficient, and a proper supply of material was maintained at rail-head. Stevenson had a thankless task in endeavouring to patch up his old locomotives, for most of them had no brake-blocks and ran away down every hill, incurring fresh damage almost as soon as the traces of the last accident had been obliterated.

Since the railway could not be prolonged more than a few miles beyond Ambigol Wells while Wad Bishara held Firket, Kitchener decided to make the former place a temporary terminus until the dervishes had been driven back. The journey to Ambigol Wells was difficult and even dangerous. "The permanent way could not be called suitable for high speed," writes Longfield.[2] "It was, in fact, a continual succession of sharp curves and steep gradients; and often the trains, after failing to surmount an incline, had to roll back to the foot and gather breath, as it were, for a renewed attempt. Heated axles were then, and for years afterwards, a common cause of delay; more serious and, luckily, more unusual, was a breakdown caused by the engine suddenly losing one of its wheels." One such accident resulted in a whole day being wasted, and Kitchener, who had recently congratulated Girouard on the rapid advance of his rail-head gangs, wired "Am bitterly disappointed at your miserable progress." Girouard was furious at this unmerited reproach until he discovered that it was not meant to be taken seriously.

Troops were soon pouring into Ambigol Wells for the advance on

---

[1] Letter to the author from Major-General H. L. Pritchard, C.B., C.M.G., D.S.O., dated Sept. 12th, 1934.
[2] *The Sudan Railways*, by Lieut.-Colonel W. E. Longfield, R.E. (retd.).

Firket. "The night of June 4th was one to be remembered," continues Longfield. "It is difficult to convey an adequate impression of what a congested station in the Sudan was like on a hot night in June during the expedition. Every siding was filled with trucks. There were no signals. The Egyptian N.C.O's, who were acting as shunters, were liable at any moment to give the wrong signal, and the engine-drivers might easily misinterpret the correct one. A pointsman might turn over his lever at a wrong moment, and the driver of one engine might act on the signal intended for his fellow. A move too far in the wrong direction would derail the trucks over the end of the siding into deep sand, or would split and cripple the siding points. All the probabilities had to be foreseen. The space between the sidings was deep sand, cumbered with piles of stores and equipment. It was pitch dark, and the thermometer stood at anything over 100 degrees. In these nightmare conditions, the detrainment of troops, the shunting of trains and the clearing of the station were carried out."

From Saras to Ambigol Wells, and on to Firket, the country was a wilderness of black rock through which the railway turned and twisted in an extraordinary manner to avoid large cuttings and embankments. Hardly anywhere was there a straight or level piece of line. Every obstacle was turned; every spur which ran out from the black and red volcanic rocks on either side was out-flanked by a sharp bend, where in England it would have been attacked directly by a cutting. As the greater part of the track was laid in watercourses, it was liable to be washed away in any sudden storm; but the adoption of a safer alignment was out of the question in 1896, when money was scarce and speed of construction essential. Girouard and his staff were fortunate that they had not to deal with the still worse section, north of Saras, traversed by the Egyptian line of 1874–78. Some of the cuttings between Saras and Wadi Halfa were 40 feet deep and taken through solid rock; the gradients were as steep as 1 in 60; many of the curves had a radius of only 500 feet; and there were no less than 24 bridges in a length of 33 miles.[1]

As the line grew longer, it became necessary to recruit and train an entire Traffic Staff, and for this purpose recourse was had to the Egyptian Army and its Reserves. Native officers and non-commissioned officers were appointed as station-masters, and intelligent men from the ranks were converted into shunters, guards and pointsmen. Traffic was controlled by telephone, so two "schools" were opened in Wadi Halfa, where 20 prospective clerks acquired the rudiments of knowledge under the shade of a couple of palm trees.[2] They could read and write their own names, and that was neces-

---

[1] Paper read by Major G. B. Macauley, R.E., before the International Engineering Congress in Glasgow in 1901.
[2] *The River War*, by the Rt. Hon. Winston Churchill, M.P., p. 165.

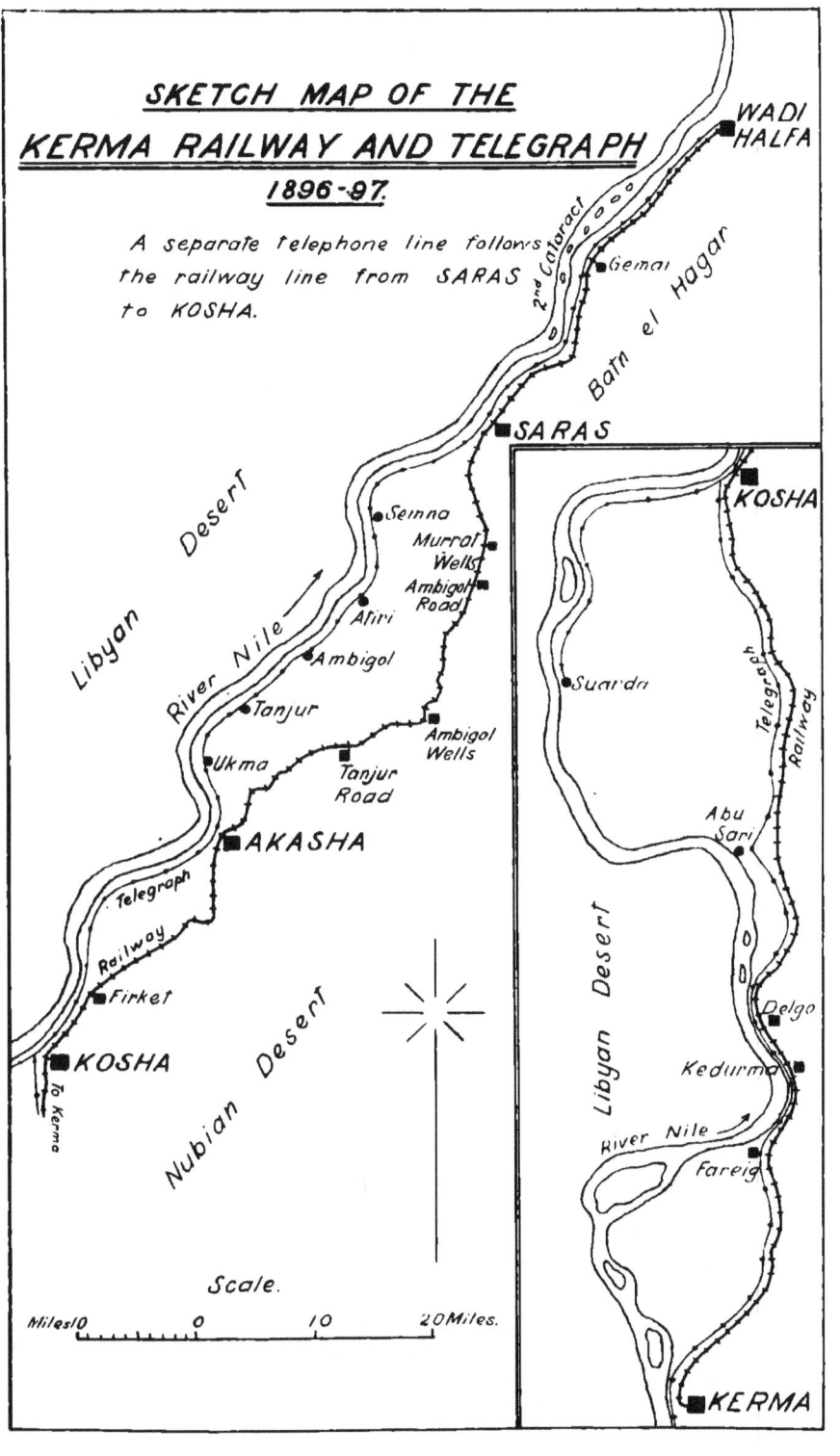

sarily accepted as a sufficient qualification for initiation into the mysteries of the line-clear system.

After the Battle of Firket on June 7th, there was no longer any need for a rail-head guard. Accordingly, the 7th Egyptians became available for construction work, and the railway began to forge ahead rapidly towards Akasha, Firket and Kosha. Although MacDonald's brigade had occupied Suarda, no general advance was possible until more river-transport could be collected when the Nile had risen. Meanwhile, the accumulation of supplies at Kosha and Suarda depended largely on the railway, which was prolonged at the rate of more than a mile a day along the old embankment laid in 1885, and brought into Akasha, 87 miles from Wadi Halfa, on June 21st.[1] From Akasha onwards it was necessary to make the embankments and provide rails, so the work was heavier than before. Fortunately, ten miles of rails had been lying at Wadi Halfa since 1886, and these were sent at once to the front, while troops from Firket assisted in the earthwork.

The conditions under which the line was extended towards Kosha are described in graphic terms by Brigadier-General Blakeney. " Kitchener," he says,[2] " had bought a mixed assortment of rails, some from Syria, some from other light railways, which did not make the work of track-laying any easier.[3] There were two shifts, on one of which an Egyptian battalion (the 7th) did most of the heavy work, the other shift being the hastily raised Railway Battalion. Spiking and linking up the rails was done by some antiquated Sudanese. There were very few trained plate-layers. At first, the railway resembled parallel corkscrews and a right of way. For a time, owing to shortage of material, only two bolts were put into each fishplate, and when one of these worked loose it was no uncommon thing to have to clear a train-wreck. The Sapper subalterns became experts at this business. The engines suffered from every locomotive complaint, the only part that was never known to go wrong being the whistle. Comfort there was none. The subalterns had to supervise both shifts, and then be regaled during the night by dreadful telephones, staffed by Egyptians who tried to talk all at once. They became proficient in Arabic swear-words, though their mother tongue stood them in good stead on emergency."

Early in July, the progress of the railway was hindered by the epidemic of cholera which spread rapidly up the Nile, one of the first victims being Mr. Vallom, Superintendent of the Railway Workshops at Wadi Halfa. Vallom had held this post for 11 years, and it was largely due to his skill and energy that some of the

[1] *Towards Khartoum*, by A. H. Atteridge, p. 271.
[2] These rails were so unsuitable that, afterwards, a large consignment of rails was secured from the Luxor-Aswan line to complete the railway to Kosha.
[3] Extract from notes by Brig.-General R. B. D. Blakeney, C.M.G., D.S.O., late R.E., sent to the author on July 20th, 1934.

locomotives and rolling stock had been kept in running order. The native staff at rail-head was decimated by the disease, and the Egyptian troops and camp followers suffered heavily. Several cases of enteric fever occurred. Polwhele complained of feeling ill, but insisted on remaining at his post; and not until three weeks later, when the 100th mile had been reached, did he relinquish the struggle and allow himself to be sent to hospital in Wadi Halfa, where he died of enteric on July 29th. So mercilessly had he worked himself that he had no power to resist the onset of the disease. Another popular officer, " Roddy " Owen,[1] had succumbed to cholera on the 11th, and several more had followed him. Gloom settled over the Dongola Expedition. In the hope of shaking off the scourge, rail-head camp was moved each day, thus adding a new burden to the already overworked gangs.

The rigid quarantine regulations, which the situation demanded, also interfered with the progress of the railway. A. H. Atteridge writes :—[2]" Owen went on with me from Ambigol Wells to Akasha (on July 2nd) and it was dark when we reached the *khor* by which the railway enters the Akasha valley. A little before coming to the triangle,[3] the train was stopped, and as I climbed from the railway carriage, I saw dimly a white tent among the rocks, and a young British officer came out of it saying, ' I am sorry for your sake that you have stopped, but I am glad for my own. I have been 24 hours in quarantine and it's luck to have another white man come in.' He was Lieutenant Blakeney, of the Royal Engineers, who had already done five days' quarantine in a cholera camp on the river between Aswan and Wadi Halfa and was now doing a second quarantine at Akasha.[4] Blakeney and I had some dinner outside the tent, and as we finished it, an orderly brought orders that we were to go back as far as Ambigol Wells by a train that would leave Akasha at 5 a.m., and complete our quarantine there. So we resolved to make the best of our bad luck and turned in for the night, sleeping inside the tent on the ground. Just after midnight, a storm burst upon us, and I was aroused by Blakeney shaking me and asking me to help him to save the tent. The wind was roaring through the *khor*, carrying quantities of sand and making the night pitch dark. I held the tent-pole up, while Blakeney and his Arab servant secured the pegs. After about ten minutes, Blakeney called out,

---

[1] Major E. R. Owen, Lancashire Fusiliers, commanding the Arab irregulars. " Roddy" Owen was one of the best gentleman riders of his day, and had won the Grand National, on " Father O'Flynn," in 1892. He served in Uganda in 1894, and in the Chitral Expedition in 1895.

[2] *Towards Khartoum*, by A. H. Atteridge, p. 282.

[3] A triangular lay-out of tracks for reversing trains.

[4] Blakeney had come from Suakin, marching with the 1st Egyptian Infantry across the desert from Quseir to Qift (on the Nile below Luxor), early in June. He was kept in quarantine at Faris, above Aswan, for some days, and then went up to Wadi Halfa, and so to Akasha, only to be sent back for further quarantine to Ambigol Wells, as recorded by Atteridge. He was unable to join the railway staff at rail-head until July 6th.

'You can let go now,' but he had hardly done speaking when the pole seemed to spring out of the ground and knocked me down, with the folds of the tent on top of me. I struggled out from under the tent and we both threw ourselves on top of the bellying canvas, calling to our servant to add his weight to ours. We crouched like this in the dark *khor* for a quarter of an hour, the wind whirling and driving along showers of sand and rolling pebbles, while all along the hollow of the railway track we could hear the cries of Arabs, Berberis and negroes of the Railway Battalion in distress like ourselves. Then the wind began to go down a little, and we put some stones on the tent. Still later we lay down among the canvas folds and got some sleep. The storm was over in an hour."

On August 4th, the railway reached Kosha, 105 miles from Wadi Halfa and 72 miles from Saras, where track-laying had begun some four months earlier. The country from Firket was easier than in the Batn el Hagar, being a wide sandy plain with a considerable amount of cultivation and many date palms near the river-bank. The Nile had now risen, and it was possible to haul ships through the cataracts. Kosha had already been fortified, and it was soon provided with railway sidings, and a miniature dockyard to receive the sections of the gunboat *Zafir*. As the terminus of the railway for the final advance on Dongola, it was of the utmost importance.

The prolongation of the railway to Kosha at such an early date was a very fine performance. For a time, after Polwhele had been invalided to Wadi Halfa, Pritchard was the only officer left at rail-head, and he was handicapped by the fact that he could not speak Arabic. Blakeney, moving from one repair camp to another, had his hands full. Cator was far from well. Elkington, who might have been able to give some assistance on the railway, was confined to his bed.[1] Stevenson could not leave his locomotives. The situation was so critical that Girouard himself started from the base to take charge at rail-head, only to go down at once with sunstroke so that he was incapacitated for a fortnight.

Manifold then stepped into the breach with an offer to the Sirdar to leave his telegraphs and help Pritchard to bring the railway in to Kosha. This he was allowed to do, and in a letter written from rail-head on July 31st, 1896, he says:—" We lay anything from a quarter of a mile to one and a half miles a day, depending on the number of trains of material that arrive. The general idea of the work is that a train-load comes up and goes to the end of the line, as far as is safe. A gang of men unload sleepers, walk out in front, and throw them down roughly in place on the bank. Another gang carry rails, and throw them down roughly in place on the sleepers. This is an amusing sight. The rail gangs are Sudanese pensioners,

[1] Lieut. G. E. Elkington, R.E., contracted cholera and made an amazing recovery; but his constitution was undermined, and he died at Bloemfontein on Jan. 12th, 1901, during the South African War.

mostly old men, and they abuse each other all the time for not taking fair shares; and generally, after they have dropped the rail, they have to be separated by a spare gang from a sort of Donnybrook! Next come a gang of men with fishplates, which join the rails together. Then a man with a piece of chalk, marking the positions of the sleepers on the rail—a soft job. After him, a few men moving the sleepers correctly under the chalk marks. Then come 12 'workshops,' each consisting of five men—two with crowbars as levers, two with hammers, and one with a gauge to measure the correct width between the rails. The crowbar-men lever the sleeper up, sitting on the end of the bar. After a man has sat on a crowbar for four months he wears out his breeches, so you can tell a crowbarman at a glance as generally he has no breeches left. The hammermen knock in the spikes, and then the hardest worked man of the lot, who carries the gauge, measures to see if they have done right. You can always tell a gauge-man: his clothes are so good. The line is now laid, but it looks rather inebriated, and so a real *Osta*, or plate-layer, comes along with a party who move the whole thing sideways, one way or the other, until it is fairly straight. Then, as about 50 yards or so are finished, the material train moves over the line. Behind the train come the remainder of the men, and a huge lever, with two men to sit on it, which is used to level the rails. Then about 20 men with shovels, who throw on the ballast; and another 20 with beaters, who pack it well into the sleepers. Finally there comes another *Osta*, who finishes up the straightening. It all goes like clockwork, and Pritchard and I have only to ride up and down and shout '*Shogloo*,' or 'get on,' and vary it by separating the old Sudanese when they have dropped a rail."

"Yesterday was an extraordinary day," continues Manifold. "I saw a black cloud coming up, and after about an hour we heard a commotion. All the camp fell down, and our servants' tent went up like Elijah in a whirlwind. Pritchard and I ran out and held on to our tent-ropes for half an hour, and I noticed my stable going for a sail into the desert. Next, it rained in buckets; all the telephones stopped working, and the steam came out of the ground and hit us in the eye. We gasped for breath. The wind came again and blew down anything it had forgotten to blow down before, and then we had dinner consisting of sandy soup and dusty meat. After that, a hot night with no wind at all until we were blown out of bed at four o'clock in the morning. And now, three trains have arrived together and we are going to do a day's work. Oh, it is a lovely spot!"

A general advance southwards from Kosha was begun on August 23rd by the movement of MacDonald's brigade from Suarda to Abu Sari, and from that date, the uninterrupted supply of stores and munitions along the railway, to replenish the stocks already accumulated at Kosha, became of supreme importance. The railway embankment between Wadi Halfa and Akasha, though unprovided with bridges, had stood undamaged for ten years, and there was no reason to suppose that, in an almost rainless country, it would be breached by storm and flood during the Dongola Expedition; but a series of storms during August, 1896, culminated in a gale which swept away whole sections of the line. On the evening of the 27th, news came to Kosha that 12 miles of railway had been destroyed between Saras and Murrat Wells, and that the line near Ambigol Wells was damaged. It was estimated that 5,000 men would have to be employed for three weeks to repair the havoc wrought in a few hours, and this at a time when the Nile would soon be due to fall and ships would be unable to pass up the Second Cataract. Unless the railway could be reopened within the next few days, Kitchener might be forced to postpone his advance on Dongola for a whole year. Realizing this fact, he promptly took charge of the situation and set out to superintend the work of repair.

Although the line between Akasha and Kosha had been damaged, a train got through to Kosha at about midnight, and, with two others already there, was loaded with troops, tools, water and rations and started for Akasha at 1 a.m. with the Sirdar on board. At the crest of a long descent into Akasha, the boiler of the engine was burnt out, and as the steam-brakes were consequently out of action, the train was only prevented by its hand-brakes from dashing to destruction. Again, in attempting to cross a partially repaired breach at Ambigol Wells, the engine of the Sirdar's train threatened to overturn, and for seven hours remained balanced precariously above the flood. On the following day, about 3,500 Egyptian soldiers were at work under the personal direction of the Sirdar. It is said that they laboured so well with the *fass*, or mattock, that a facetious R.E. subaltern was heard to murmur a parody of his Corps motto.[1] In just retribution for such sacrilege, news arrived that six miles of line had been washed away at Akasha, and that one of the two remaining engines had been caught and capsized. The surviving locomotive could hardly crawl for want of cleaning and repair, and its driver had jaundice.[2] Away went Kitchener to direct the work at Akasha. Girouard and Stevenson both came up to lend a helping hand, and Stevenson remained with the railway repair gangs for the next three weeks. The line presented a fantastic appearance. In one place an embankment 24 feet high had been washed away for a distance of about 30 yards, and the track hung like a suspension bridge above the water.[3] Accidents were reported all along the line; some through flood, others through the carelessness or inexperience of engine-drivers, and others again through the

---

[1] "*Quo fass et maktaf ducunt,*" said the subaltern. (*Maktaf*—a basket.)
[2] *Sudan Campaign,* 1896—1899, by "An Officer" (Lieut. H. L. Pritchard, R.E.), p. 52.
[3] Letter from Lieut. A. G. Stevenson, R.E., dated Sept. 20th, 1896.

dilapidation of the locomotives and rolling stock; but by the unremitting toil of all the available troops, the railway was restored to running order by September 6th, and a desperate situation was saved. Never did Kitchener's training as an engineer stand him in better stead than on the Nile in the autumn of 1896.

The successful action at Hafir on September 19th, having opened the way to Dongola, Kitchener occupied that town on the 24th and sent MacDonald forward to Ed Debba, Korti and Merowe. The railway was left far behind, and all the Royal Engineers who could be spared from it were at the front. However, with the Nile subsiding rapidly, transport by river was becoming more difficult; and although a force sufficient to hold the advanced posts could be supplied during the season of low Nile by river and camel transport alone, it was evident that no major operations from Dongola could be contemplated unless these services were supplemented by a railway extending at least to Kerma, whence the Nile is navigable at all seasons to the foot of the Fourth Cataract. Accordingly, in view of a possible advance beyond Merowe, track-laying was resumed on October 9th, 1896, along the 98-mile stretch from Kosha to Kerma, Blakeney being in charge at rail-head. New engines and trucks had arrived. They were worked mercilessly—so mercilessly, in fact, that at times only three engines out of eight were in a condition to move.[1] The problem of feeding the army, without interfering with railway construction, was extremely difficult, and on three occasions, construction had to be stopped while supplies were rushed forward; but the country presented few natural obstacles, and the Railway Battalion having become experts to a man, good progress was made. The line was taken straight across the flat desert to Delgo, 174 miles from Wadi Halfa, to avoid a large bend in the Nile, and thence up the river-bank for about ten miles. At this point, the river makes another considerable bend, so the railway was laid direct to its terminus at Kerma, 203 miles from Wadi Halfa; but before Kerma was reached at the beginning of May, 1897, Girouard had turned his attention to a greater enterprise—the project for building a line through the Nubian Desert.

The work during the final stages of the Kerma Railway was not without exciting incidents. One night, Blakeney had retired to bed, after supervising the shunting of trucks at a dangerous loop near a long down-grade, when he heard the engine moving again and ran out to see the cause. He found that the Egyptian shunter had begun to re-sort a train without orders, and had moved on to the main line several trucks, including one carrying two enormous water-tanks and a guard of soldiers. The engine had been backed too far, with the result that the trucks had taken charge and the

---

[1] These eight engines included four different types, mostly obsolete, and there was great difficulty and delay in getting replacements.

A DUST-STORM ON THE NILE.

shunter was running after them, calling on Allah and trying to stop them with one hand. Without hesitation, the engine-driver started on his locomotive to chase the runaways down the 14-mile descent to Kosha, and Blakeney was left to decide what to do. Either, he could have the trucks turned into a siding at Kosha, which was already occupied by other rolling stock, a course which would probably entail the death of the soldiers riding on the leading truck, or he could order their diversion into another siding, laid towards the river-bank, where they would play havoc with a gunboat which was being assembled there by Lieutenant David Beatty, R.N. Alternatively, he might have the runaways turned on to the main line, where they would probably meet a material train in a head-on collision. He chose the first course, telephoned his orders to the sleepy little Egyptian stationmaster at Kosha, and sat down forlornly on his camp bed to await the result. After what appeared to be an interminable interval, the telephone bell rang and he asked excitedly for news. A long and disjointed tale was poured into his ear, from which it transpired that, although the pointsman at Kosha had disobeyed his instructions to divert the runaways into the occupied siding, and had attempted instead to turn them towards the river, he had contrived to block that outlet with a barrier of thorn bushes. " Well, what has happened ? " inquired Blakeney, on tenterhooks. " Sare," drawled the stationmaster, " the trucks have arrived." " Yes, yes. But what about the soldiers ? " The answer came slowly over the wire. " Sare. They are *still* sleeping."[1]

During the period which followed the occupation of Dongola, there were several additions to the cadre of Engineer officers. Lieutenants G. B. Macauley, H. A. Micklem, G. C. M. Hall, E. C. Midwinter and E. O. A. Newcombe, R.E.[2], arrived in the Sudan to strengthen the staff and fill the vacancies caused by the deaths of Polwhele and Cator.[3] Girouard went to England and America to buy material and could not spare much time for the affairs of the Kerma railway. Pritchard, joined by Hall, surveyed the alignment from Kosha to Kerma. Blakeney built the sections of the line from Kosha to Abu Sari and from Fareig to Kerma, the intermediate portion being constructed by Newcombe.[4] Macauley was usually to be found at Wadi Halfa in connection with the new line towards

---

[1] This tale appears also in an article by Brig.-General R. B. D. Blakeney, C.M.G., D.S.O., late R.E., entitled " K. and Gerry," published in *The National Review*, January, 1936.
[2] The survivors of this reinforcement are Brig.-General Sir George Macauley, K.C.M.G., K.B.E., C.B., Lieut.-Colonel Sir Edward Midwinter, K.B.E., C.B., C.M.G., D.S.O., Major E. O. A. Newcombe, D.S.O., and Lieut.-Colonel H. A. Micklem, C.B., C.M.G., D.S.O. Lieut.-Colonel G. C. M. Hall, C.M.G., C.B.E., D.S.O., died in December, 1930.
[3] Lieut. E. H. S. Cator, R.E., died of enteric fever in February, 1897, after a reconnaissance in the Nubian Desert.
[4] Letter from Brig.-General R. B. D. Blakeney, C.M.G., D.S.O., late R.E., to the author, dated November 9th, 1935.

Abu Hamed; but he was for a time in charge of the Works Department at Kerma and was also an assistant to Girouard. Stevenson was Traffic Manager and Locomotive Superintendent, and was afterwards helped by Newcombe. Midwinter worked under Macauley on the Abu Hamed line, and Micklem took over the control of the Works Department from Gorringe, who was then free to devote his energies to staff work.

Invaluable experience was gained during the railway extension up the Nile in 1896, experience without which Girouard and his staff could never have built the subsequent line from Wadi Halfa to Abu Hamed at the speed which they attained. As to the Kerma line, long sections of it were taken up to provide material for the railway across the Nubian Desert and beyond, and the residue fell gradually into disuse. The line was closed officially in 1904; but until 1908, excursions were run twice daily from Wadi Halfa over the few miles to Gemai, a favourite place for picnics. All traffic then ceased, for the trade requirements of the district did not warrant the running expenses. Up to 1924, old sleepers were being torn up by Arabs, and floated down to Wadi Halfa for sale to the Railway Department as firewood; but to-day, the route of the Kerma Railway is marked only by a few broken bridges and a line of crumbling embankment, which forms a precarious road for motor-cars, and occasionally by some twisted rails, half-covered with sand. These are the last melancholy relics of a great achievement.

The telegraph work of the Dongola Expedition was in the hands of Lieutenant M. G. E. Manifold, R.E., who arrived in Wadi Halfa from Suakin at the beginning of April, 1896, and was ordered to lay a line from Saras to Akasha, a distance of 55 miles, in extension of an existing line along the railway from Wadi Halfa to Saras.[1] In the usual cheerful manner with which he disarmed comment, Kitchener told Manifold that an engineer and a construction party, on loan from the Egyptian State Telegraphs, were on their way up the Nile with everything that was necessary. On April 14th, the party arrived, and Manifold found that it consisted of Mr. Paoletti, a Maltese engineer, about 20 linemen, and a carpenter. With them came 20 miles of assorted wire, a number of light 16 feet poles, and a consignment of small " Bobbin " insulators,[2] but not an instrument of any sort. Manifold returned to Kitchener, who informed him that he should use some obsolete telephones, which were amongst the railway stores. However, he managed to convince the Sirdar that

[1] In describing the Telegraph operations of the Dongola Expedition, the author has made extensive use of notes kindly sent to him on September 17th, 1934, by Major-General Sir M. G. E. Bowman-Manifold, K.B.E., C.B., C.M.G., D.S.O., and letters written by that officer as a subaltern in 1896. A valuable article by the same officer appears under the title of " The Field Telegraph, Dongola Expedition, 1896," in the *R.E. Journal*, Vol. 27, Jan.-June, 1897, pp. 3–5. This also has been used.

[2] These porcelain insulators were designed to be fastened with screws to the sides of the poles.

THE KERMA RAILWAY.
Between Gemai and Saras.

[*Photo by the Author.*]

a few Morse telegraph instruments were essential, and also men to operate them, and a request for the services of four trained telegraphists was accordingly dispatched to the Egyptian State Telegraphs in Cairo. The Sirdar would not entertain any proposal to provide special " air-line," or field-cable at £25 per mile, and he restricted the order for instruments to the number required for the line to Akasha only. When the larder is almost empty it is necessary to live from hand to mouth.

Pending the arrival of the Morse instruments, Manifold contrived, with the assistance of two R.E. plumbers from the 2nd (Fortress) Company, to make a couple of vibrator (" buzzer ") instruments from some old bells, a sheet of brass and a biscuit tin, and also to patch up some of the antiquated magneto-bell telephones, hidden away among the railway stores. With Paoletti and the linemen and stores, he left Wadi Halfa for Saras by train on April 15th to lay a field telegraph wire along the line of march of the army, and a railway telephone wire (later increased to two) along the railway line. The laying of the field wire was taken in hand first. The men and stores were divided between an advanced party under Manifold to lay the wire on the ground as rapidly as possible, and a rear party under Paoletti to erect the poles. Transport was so scarce that only 12 camels could be allotted to the wire party and ten to the pole party; but nevertheless, leaving Saras on the 17th, the wire party brought the line through 53 miles of rough country to Akasha by April 20th, and finished with only 30 yards of wire in hand.

Writing of the start from Saras, Manifold says :— " We paraded at 5 a.m., and began to lay the line on the ground. At rail-head, five miles on, I got an escort of 20 men from Fathi Bey[1] and, at 1 p.m., halted in the hills and rested under the shade of my umbrella for one and a half hours. The road had been awful in places—boulders, and almost impassable. We laid at one mile an hour. The natives drank gallons of water. I had a sausage for lunch, and it became cooked in the shade of my umbrella. We reached Wadi Atiri about 5.30 p.m., after a fearful descent from the hills, and at 6 p.m. I joined up the " buzzer " and sent a message reporting the line open. Thirteen miles of such heavy line in this country is good going for one day. I left Paoletti at Saras to follow on, putting up the poles." The method of laying was simple. A revolving drum having been unloaded from a camel and placed on the ground, a man took the end of the wire and walked away with it. After he had gone 50 yards, another man picked up the wire near the drum, and then another, and so on until 500 yards had been pulled out by ten men. In open desert country, a camel replaced the men.

After the line had reached Akasha, telephones from the railway

---

[1] Lieut.-Colonel Fathi Bey, commanding the 7th Egyptian battalion, which formed the rail-head guard.

were put in circuit and gave good results. The extraordinary dryness of the country made it possible to work the 53 miles of bare wire, lying on the ground, without any appreciable loss of current. Poling of the line to Akasha was not completed until the end of May, owing to the scarcity of transport; and for six weeks, parts of the line lay unprotected on the rocky ground and exposed to rough usage by camel convoys. Morse signalling could not be undertaken, because neither instruments nor clerks were available. Manifold's demands for more Egyptian telegraphists were met in Cairo by advertising in the local Arabic Press, and a heterogeneous collection of Levantines was sent up the Nile. Active service in the Sudan, at £12 per month, had little attraction for these men, and they envied the stout-hearted employés of the Egyptian State Telegraphs, who received £20 per month.

The provision of a railway telephone line from Saras southwards was taken in hand on May 11th. A line was laid on the ground to Murrat Wells, and onwards to Ambigol Wells, and communication was begun with instruments made from parts of old telephones discovered in Wadi Halfa. In addition, a wire was added to the existing Wadi Halfa-Saras line. Girouard had secured the Sirdar's approval for a separate railway telephone system, although Manifold did not want to expend 85 miles of wire on it and had no liking for telephones. Eventually, some new telephones arrived from Egypt, and communication along the railway was improved.

On June 2nd, an intensely hot day, when the thermometer registered 130 degrees in his tent, Manifold opened a special telegraph office for the Sirdar at Ukma near Akasha. The Sirdar was impatient to know the meaning of a cypher message from Lord Cromer. Major Wingate had the key, and no one knew where he was.[1] "There was a great scurry," says Manifold, " and we telegraphed everywhere to ask about Wingate. That night, the line was broken by camels. About 10 p.m., I was turned out of bed to hunt Wingate again, and next morning I was at Ukma at dawn to find the Sirdar still Wingate-hunting. I started to go back towards Saras, met Wingate at last, and rode into Ambigol about 2.30 p.m. The last ten miles were almost impossible—no air, no direct sun, but a haze. My jacket and saddle were soaking with sweat. Twice I stopped under a tree, and drank some warm water and ate a biscuit. Ambigol was deserted except for some Arabs.[2] I sent for several buckets of water and had three poured over my head, and then went out and put the line right. Suddenly, thunder began; then a fearful whirlwind of dust, and then tremendous rain. My line was blown flat as far as

---

[1] Message from the Sirdar to Bimbashi Manifold, dated 2nd/3rd June, 1896. " Dear Manifold. This line has broken down again. For God's sake do something to get into communication with Wingate, wherever he is, and get the message from Lord Cromer deciphered. H.H.K."

[2] The troops were moving southwards for the Battle of Firket on June 7th, 1896.

IN THE BATN EL HAGAR.
On the alignment of the old Kerma Railway.

[*Photo by the Author.*]

I could see. After mending it, I rode into Ambigol Wells, a hot, steamy ride, and I was wet inside and out. Pritchard gave me some soup, and I went to bed and slept, and then had dinner. About 11 p.m., the train came in with the news that the telegraph line was all washed down between Wadi Halfa and Saras."

Great pressure was thrown on the Telegraph staff after the Battle of Firket, in which Manifold acted as a " galloper."[1] Nearly 12,000 words passed over the wire from Akasha, including the Sirdar's official narrative of the operations and his recommendations thereon. It is curious that this dispatch was never published, although it was forwarded to the British Government by Lord Cromer. Manifold was not allowed to lay a line to Firket during the battle, but an office was established there on June 9th. "This is not a bad place," he writes on June 17th, "but the braying of the donkeys is almost intolerable. Our camp extends for about two and a half miles along the river bank, and every quarter of an hour a *feu-de-joie* of brays goes down the line." On July 1st, he adds, "I have a complete set of telephones from station to station all along the railway between Wadi Halfa and Akasha, 87 miles, eight stations. They work beautifully, and all the telegraphs also are in good working order. The great anxiety now is the cholera. To-day, there is a case at Wadi Halfa. It is pretty warm here—118 degrees in my tent."

The telegraph line was prolonged to Kosha, and, when transport became available, to Suarda. At the end of July, four non-commissioned officers arrived from the 1st Division Telegraph Battalion, R.E., at Aldershot. These men—Sergeants Kilburn and Brewster and Corporals Dennett and Hensler, R.E.—were invaluable, for they had energy and initiative and understood their work.[2] Paoletti was able to return to Cairo with some of his linemen, whose duties could now be carried out by locally trained men. The telegraph and telephone lines suffered severely during the bad weather in August. At one time there were 60 miles of telephone line to be re-erected, all of which had been working perfectly on the previous day. On the 23rd, Manifold completed the laying of a telegraph line from Kosha across the desert to Abu Sari, visiting Pritchard and Cator in their railway survey camp soon after his start. "You can wash your hands before dinner, if you like," said Pritchard. "Cator and I share that basinful. It is rather thick, but it has only done duty since yesterday."

The storm on August 27th, which was the occasion of the " death

---

[1] See Chapter VI. Mounted messengers, attached to brigade commanders in action, were called " gallopers." They were usually young officers selected by the Sirdar.

[2] Corporal Dennett's services in the Sudan were of outstanding merit. As will appear later, he supervised most of the poling construction work from Dongola to Berber, and ultimately to Khartoum. On terminating his military service, he joined the Sudan Postal Telegraph Department, and rose to be a Superintending Engineer before his retirement in 1921.

march" of the 1st Brigade, caused great dislocation of the telegraph system. The poles were removed from several miles of line by a torrent flowing down a *khor* from Murrat Wells, and a rush of water at Atiri led to a complete interruption of both vibrator and sounder signals between Saras and Akasha for two days. Altogether, seven miles of telegraph, and twelve miles of telephone line, were overturned by these floods. However, the damage was repaired; and on September 7th, the line was taken to Delgo in preparation for the general advance on Dongola. On the 13th, an office was opened at Kedurma; on the 14th, another at Fareig; and on the 19th, during the action at Hafir, the telegraph reached Kerma. No less than 100 miles of bare wire lay on the ground; yet the sounder signals came through perfectly, though the vibrator signals were unsatisfactory. The line stretched for 215 miles to Wadi Halfa, and the circuit was worked direct to that place.

After the action at Hafir on September 19th, 1896, Kitchener transferred his troops across the Nile and advanced up the left bank. Consequently, it was necessary for the telegraph to follow him by means of a submarine cable through the river and a land line towards Dongola. Two cables had been prepared in Egypt for crossings at points where the width of the Nile, at that season, was estimated to be about three-quarters of a mile; but one was damaged in transit up the river, and the other did not arrive at Kerma until September 26th. It seems that Kitchener himself had determined the length of this cable by map measurement, without due allowance for sagging and the effect of current, with the result that it proved to be too short. Possibly, he may have been influenced, as he so often was, by considerations of economy. " I got orders to lay the cable àt Kerma, instead of at Dongola;" writes Manifold, "and as I was of opinion that the cable was not long enough, I went up to report. I saw the Sirdar, who said that it would be better to cross at Kerma, so at 5 a.m. on the 27th, I started making arrangements. A steamer and troops had been placed at my disposal for laying the cable, and we crossed over and made the shore-end fast to a tree, and anchored the tree. I decided to run the cable over the bow of the ship, and gave orders to the native *Rheis*, or Master, to go stern first, straight across the stream, so that he might avoid cutting the cable with the stern wheel. Of course, the idiot went bow first! Also he did not go straight across, but allowed the current to carry him downstream. The cable flew out like lightning. Two of my R.E. stood in the coil and cleared it as it strained. They had to twist each coil over their heads, and a slip might have been fatal. I stood in the bow, where the line went into the water, and a man poured water continually on the fender, over which the cable ran, to prevent it from catching fire. I told the *Rheis* to make for an island about 100 yards from the mainland, and there I landed the remainder of the cable and put it in a boat to complete the crossing, but the end failed to reach the other side by about 70 yards."

Connection was completed by running an overhead line from the shore to the mast of the boat, and afterwards, a line was taken up the river bank for a distance of 35 miles to Dongola, where an office was opened. It was then found that through communication was still possible with Wadi Halfa, 250 miles distant, although 130 miles of bare wire lay on the ground.

At the beginning of November, during Kitchener's absence in England, Manifold extended the telegraph to Ed Debba, and finally he prolonged it, through Korti and Merowe, to Kassinger, at the foot of the Fourth Cataract. Young telegraphists were recruited in Cairo at £E.3 a month, and trained by Corporal Hensler, R.E., in a telegraph school at Wadi Halfa, and as these youths gradually replaced some of the highly paid telegraphists of the Egyptian State Telegraphs, a greater measure of economy was secured.

The total length of the telegraph and telephone lines erected along the Nile during 1896 was 630 miles. Manifold had to travel far and fast to supervise the work of his partially trained men. Indeed, between March, 1896, and his departure on leave in January, 1897, he covered more than 5,000 miles by land and water. His trials were many and varied ; but, in the end, he had the satisfaction of knowing that, through his wanderings in the wilderness, he had succeeded in providing an efficient line of telegraphic communication in the reconquered province of Dongola.

CHAPTER VIII.

THE ADVANCE TO THE ATBARA.

TO Kitchener, the occupation of Dongola was but the prelude to an advance on Omdurman. His ultimate objective was clear, and indeed it was impossible to imagine that any sure halting-place could be found between Wadi Halfa and the Khalifa's capital. The problems which confronted him were both strategical and political. He must select a suitable line of advance, and also secure the consent of the British Government to his proposals, for it was evident that a campaign into the far south would be beyond the resources of the Egyptian Government alone. Accordingly, having consolidated his position south of Dongola, he set himself to decide whether he was on the right road to Omdurman, and, finding that he was on the wrong road, he determined to make a fresh start by building a railway from Wadi Halfa or Korosko across the Nubian Desert to Abu Hamed.[1] He considered and rejected the alternative of transferring his base to the Red Sea littoral and constructing a railway from Suakin to Berber, for such a line would be costly, difficult to build, and exposed to frequent attack. On the other hand to advance from his present position beyond Dongola would necessitate not only the construction of a railway from Korti through the Bayuda Desert in the face of hostile action from Metemma, but also the bridging of the Nile in order to continue the line on the left bank. Influenced by the situations of the cataracts as much as by the dispositions of the enemy, Kitchener preferred to incur the grave risks of launching out into the uncharted and waterless desert between Wadi Halfa and Abu Hamed. Eminent railway engineers, and distinguished soldiers, advised him that his project was foolhardy. How could he keep his men and his locomotives supplied with water? The dervishes awaited him at the end of his long journey and could bar his approach to the Nile. Nevertheless, on January 1st, 1897, shortly after he had returned from England, the first sleepers of the historic Desert Railway were laid at Wadi Halfa.

The representations of Lord Cromer, and of Kitchener himself, had convinced the British Government that the reconquest of the Sudan could not be delayed.[2] Hesitation would be attributed to fear. The

---

[1] According to Lieut.-General Sir George Gorringe, K.C.B., K.C.M.G., D.S.O., Col.-Commandant R.E., who was on Lord Kitchener's staff, the Sirdar reached this decision as early as April, 1896, when he evacuated the railway plant from Korosko.
[2] It was known that a French expedition under Commandant Marchand was already in movement up the Ubangi River, a tributary of the Congo.

success of the Dongola Expedition must be followed up, and the offensive sustained until the Dervish armies were defeated and scattered to the four winds. These opinions brought an announcement from the Chancellor of the Exchequer[1] in the House of Commons on February 5th, 1897. Egypt, he said, could never be held to be permanently secure so long as a hostile Power was in occupation of the Nile valley up to Khartoum, and the duty of giving a final blow to the baleful power of the Khalifa devolved on England.[2] With the guarantee of help from the British Government, success was assured ; but it is doubtful if it would have been attained so quickly had it not been for the defective strategy and overweening confidence of the Dervish leaders, who quarrelled incessantly and neglected heaven-sent opportunities. The rank and file of the dervishes, though magnificent fighters, could not retrieve the strategical errors of the Khalifa and his Generals.

The story of the Desert Railway to Abu Hamed is told in the next chapter. For the present, it is sufficient to remark that its progress at first was slow. Indeed, by the end of April, 1897, only 34 miles of track had been laid out of 230 miles needed to reach Abu Hamed.[3] Thereafter, the work went forward more rapidly, and, by the middle of July, rail-head was about 100 miles from Wadi Halfa. Until Girouard and his staff had completed the Kerma Railway on May 4th, the Desert Railway suffered through lack of expert supervision and labour ; but with the subsequent transfer of all available officers and men from the Kerma line, and the arrival of new engines at Wadi Halfa, the railway towards Abu Hamed soon reached a point which justified Kitchener in opening his military campaign. In his own words : " On July 15th, the construction of the railway from Wadi Halfa having been pushed almost half-way across the desert towards Abu Hamed, I deemed it inadvisable to continue the work until the dervishes had been expelled from that position, which information led me to believe the Khalifa was about to reinforce."[4]

The most important strategic outposts of the Dervish army were Metemma and Berber, and it was improbable that these key-positions would be abandoned without a severe struggle. The enemy's advanced position at Abu Hamed, downstream of Berber, was not essential to his scheme of defence and consequently was not likely to be strongly held.[5] However, it was clear that Abu Hamed must

---

[1] Sir Michael Hicks-Beach.
[2] *Modern Egypt*, by the Earl of Cromer, Vol. II, p. 94.
[3] Lieut.-General Sir George Gorringe remarks that it was necessary to give preference to the Kerma Railway in order that the supplies required for an advance from Merowe should be concentrated there. He adds that the only material available for the Desert Railway was that which could be spared from the material needed for the Kerma line. (Notes sent to the author on August 1st, 1936.)
[4] Dispatch from Major-General Sir Herbert Kitchener, K.C.B., K.C.M.G., to Major-General Sir Francis Grenfell, G.C.M.G., K.C.B., G.O.C., in Egypt, dated December 9th, 1897.
[5] See the *Sketch Map of the Nile from Kerma to Metemma*, which is included in this chapter.

H

be seized before the Desert Railway could approach it, so Kitchener proceeded to carry out this project by dispatching a mobile column from the neighbourhood of Merowe up the right bank of the Nile. Since the completion of the Kerma Railway in May, it had been possible to make full use of that line in accumulating stores and supplies in the region of Dongola while awaiting the rise of the Nile during July and August which would enable ships to pass the cataracts. These stores were sufficient for the lightly-equipped expedition which was intended to take Abu Hamed by a surprise assault before it could be reinforced from Berber.

Encouraged by the fact that the Egyptian army had halted at Merowe, the Khalifa was known to be planning a counter-offensive, and Kitchener feared that one of his first moves would be to reinforce Abu Hamed. The Dervish army at Omdurman had been drilled, reorganized, and strengthened by contingents from outlying districts, and the Emir Mahmud, at the head of 10,000 men, had been summoned from the wilds of Kordofan. This young and ambitious leader was anxious to show his prowess in battle, and at the end of May he was allowed to march northwards to Metemma to quell a revolt of the Jaalin Arabs, who garrisoned that town for the Khalifa. The Jaalin fortified and defended Metemma against Mahmud but could not resist his assault, and the fall of the town on July 1st was followed by a terrible massacre of 2,000 of the garrison. Such of the Jaalin as escaped declared their allegiance to Egypt, and being supplied with rifles, became valuable allies.[1] They rallied at Gakdul Wells in the Bayuda Desert and helped to guard Ed Debba, Korti and Merowe from raids. Nevertheless, with Mahmud and his powerful and aggressive army installed within easy reach of Berber and Abu Hamed, Kitchener could afford to delay no longer. He must capture Abu Hamed before the fleeting chance was gone. If he failed in the attempt, his railway would be cast away in the Nubian Desert.

The officer selected by Kitchener to lead the all-important expedition up the Nile to Abu Hamed was his right-hand man, Major-General (afterwards General Sir) Archibald Hunter, D.S.O., a soldier whose natural daring was tempered with the caution engendered by long experience. " If the Sirdar is the brain of the Egyptian Army," wrote G. W. Steevens in 1898,[2] " General Hunter is its sword-arm. For fourteen years he has been in the front of all the fighting on the southern border. From the feather in his helmet to the spurs on his heels, he is all energy. Every movement is vivacious. He is one of the finest leaders of troops in the army, and never fails to plan and execute a masterly victory." With Archibald Hunter, was Lieut.-Colonel (afterwards Major-General) Hector MacDonald, C.B.,

[1] Rifles and ammunition had been dispatched to the Jaalin at Metemma to enable them to resist any Dervish attack, but unfortunately they did not reach Metemma before the assault.
[2] *With Kitchener to Khartoum*, by G. W. Steevens, pp. 54-56.

D.S.O., Royal Fusiliers, an officer who had risen from the ranks by sheer merit and had fought in Afghanistan, at Majuba, and in many battles in the Sudan. Nothing could daunt " Old Mac." The greater the emergency, the more surely and skilfully did he handle his troops.

The date fixed for Hunter's start from Kassinger above Merowe was kept a profound secret, so it was an occasion for general surprise when, on July 29th, 1897, he set out at the head of a " flying column " consisting of an infantry brigade (3rd Egyptians, and 9th, 10th and 11th Sudanese) under MacDonald, a mule battery of six Krupp 12-pounders, four machine-guns, a few cavalry scouts and 1,300 camels. Before darkness fell, he had plunged with his 2,700 men into a miserable wilderness of rock and sand which stretched for a distance of 132 miles to Abu Hamed. " His line of advance lay along the river bank," says Winston Churchill,[1] " but no road relieved the labour of the march. Sometimes trailing across a broad stretch of white sand in which the soldiers sank to their ankles; sometimes winding over a pass or through a gorge of sharp-cut rocks, which, even in the moonlight felt hot with the heat of the previous day—always in a long, jerky and interrupted procession of men and camels—the column toiled painfully like the serpent to whom it was said ' On thy belly shalt thou go and dust shalt thou eat.' "

So careful had the Sirdar been to conceal his intentions that, although he had promised Lieutenant G. F. Gorringe, R.E., that the latter should accompany Hunter in the advance, he kept him at work on a well at No. 4 Station on the Desert Railway until the last possible moment, so that Gorringe reached Merowe two days after Hunter had started and had great difficulty in overtaking the column. " Before I left Merowe," writes Sir George Gorringe,[2] " the Sirdar confided his plans to me, which I was required to keep absolutely secret. They were to seize Abu Hamed, to build a fort there in the strongest possible position which could be held by one battalion and a battery, and then to bring back Hunter and the three Sudanese battalions to Merowe to take part in an advance from that place across the desert to the Nile near Metemma, where he hoped that the Jaalin would have been able to put up a sufficient resistance until reinforced. He anticipated that the Khalifa, on hearing of the capture of Abu Hamed, would reinforce Berber and endeavour to retake Abu Hamed. Meanwhile, he (Kitchener) would cross the desert and get behind them. The garrison at Abu Hamed was, in fact, to form a bait to entice the Khalifa to divide his forces."

Halting during the heat of the day, and marching by night along

---

[1] *The River War*, by the Rt. Hon. Winston Churchill, M.P., p. 191.
[2] Notes by Lieut.-General Sir George Gorringe, K.C.B., K.C.M.G., D.S.O., Col.-Commandant R.E., sent to the author on August 1st, 1936.

the route taken by General Earle in 1885,[1] the flying column under General Hunter passed through Mushra el Abiad, Shebabit, Abu Haraz, Hosh el Geref, Salmi, Dakhfili and other desolate spots in the region of the Fourth Cataract. Near Hebba, lay the hull of the ill-fated *Abbas*, the steamer in which Stewart, Power and Herbin had tried to run the gauntlet of the Dervish positions in 1884. Men and animals were exhausted when they arrived at El Kab on August 4th. Then, with Hunter only 35 miles away, the Dervish garrison of Abu Hamed awoke at last to their danger and summoned help from Berber. On the following day, Hunter covered 14 miles; and early on the 6th, when at Ginefab, he learnt that a large body of the enemy was hurrying northwards from Berber. He redoubled his efforts in the race for Abu Hamed, and on the same evening arrived at a place called Wadib Gerub within striking distance of the village. The flying column had covered no less than 118 miles in seven and a half days at the hottest time of the year.

Only two Royal Engineers were privileged to share in this remarkable feat of endurance—Major W. F. H. S. Kincaid and Lieutenant G. F. Gorringe, D.S.O., both of whom were serving on General Hunter's staff—but following behind the flying column was another officer of the Corps, Lieutenant M. G. E. Manifold, unwinding through the wilderness a slender wire on which the very existence of the force might depend.

At 2 a.m. on August 7th, 1897, Hunter completed a circuitous march of 16 miles and found himself at dawn on high ground overlooking the Nile and the straggling village of Abu Hamed. Not a sign of the enemy was visible, so Kincaid was sent forward to reconnoitre. Riding to the edge of the crater-like depression in which the village lay, he noticed some trenches within about 80 yards of him which appeared to be empty, and taking out his notebook, began to write a report. Instantly he was fired upon; and Hunter and his staff, who arrived soon afterwards, were met by a furious volley, which fortunately was aimed too high. The infantry were deployed only 200 yards from the Dervish trenches and just out of sight over the rim of the crater, and there they remained while the artillery bombarded the enemy for half an hour. The battalions were in a crescent formation, partly encircling the village, and it is said that MacDonald, in order to keep them occupied while awaiting the order to assault, made them " dress on markers," as if on a ceremonial parade.[2]

The enemy lay silent in their trenches during the artillery bombardment, which unfortunately did little damage because the guns could not be depressed sufficiently to hit their targets, and at 6.30 a.m., Hunter ordered a general advance. The dervishes held

[1] See Chapter IV.
[2] *Sudan Campaign,* 1896—1899, by " An Officer " (Lieut. H. L. Pritchard, R.E.), p. 108.

their fire until the attackers were almost upon them, and then opened with heavy volleys which did considerable execution. The Sudanese infantry, however, could not be checked. They rushed the trenches, poured like an avalanche into the village, and fought their way through it at the point of the bayonet. Among those of the garrison who surrendered was their commander, Muhammad Zain; but for the most part, the dervishes preferred to charge into the masses of Sudanese infantry and so perish, fighting to the last.

On joining the column, Lieutenant G. F. Gorringe, R.E., had been appointed as Provost-Marshal, and after the battle he assisted Captain C. Fergusson and the 10th Sudanese[1] in clearing Abu Hamed of dervishes who refused to surrender. "Each house had only one entrance," writes Sir George Gorringe,[2] "and from the inside, the Dervishes were able to cause many casualties among the 10th Sudanese until we evolved a plan to deal with them. Fortunately, all the doors faced in the same direction, and opposite each was a small hole, close under the roof, for ventilation. Fergusson kept his men back in a position from which they could cover the doors by rifle fire, while a party under my command collected straw, and rushing up on the other side, set it alight and pushed it through the ventilation holes so that the roofs caught fire. Some of the enemy ran out and were shot down; others perished in the houses. The method was drastic, but it saved many casualties among our own men. Afterwards, the most pressing work was to clear the place of Dervish corpses. Our own dead were buried; but I decided to make the Dervish prisoners throw their dead into the swift current of the river as the ground was rocky and hard, tools were scarce, and our men were exhausted. This was done, and the first intimation which Kitchener had of the fight was when he looked out of his tent at Merowe, two days later, and saw a procession of corpses floating downstream. Anxiously, he sent out a Staff officer in a boat to ascertain what they were, and was much relieved when they proved to be Dervishes in their *jibbas*. It was then clear that we had won the battle."

The welcome news of the capture of Abu Hamed was carried swiftly by camel to rail-head in the Nubian Desert and sent by code telegram to Kitchener at Merowe.[3] Protected on the southern flank by a strong patrol of the Camel Corps, stationed at Gakdul Wells in the Bayuda Desert under the command of Major R. J.

[1] Owing to casualties, Capt. Fergusson was in command of the 10th Sudanese.
[2] Notes by Lieut.-General Sir George Gorringe sent to the author on August 1st, 1936.
[3] In a letter to the author, dated April 10th, 1936, Brig.-General R. B. D. Blakeney, C.M.G., D.S.O., late R.E., remarks:—" I was at rail-head when the camel man arrived. We were not unprepared for the news. Vultures, who had not been seen since before the Battle of Hafir, passed through rail-head camp towards the south on the day before the fight at Abu Hamed. They did the same before the Battle of the Atbara, and they were in full force to the north of Karari on the day before the Battle of Omdurman."

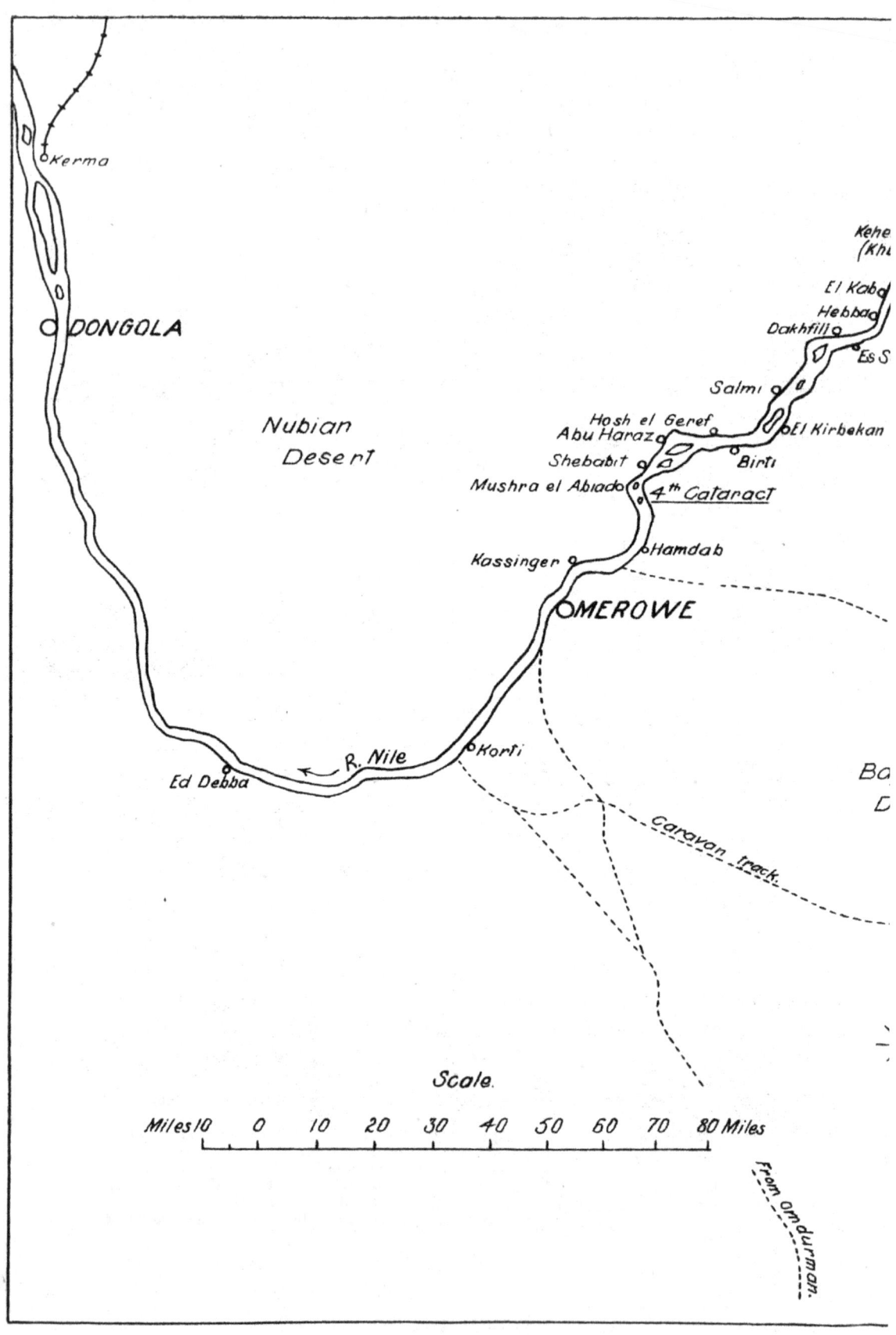

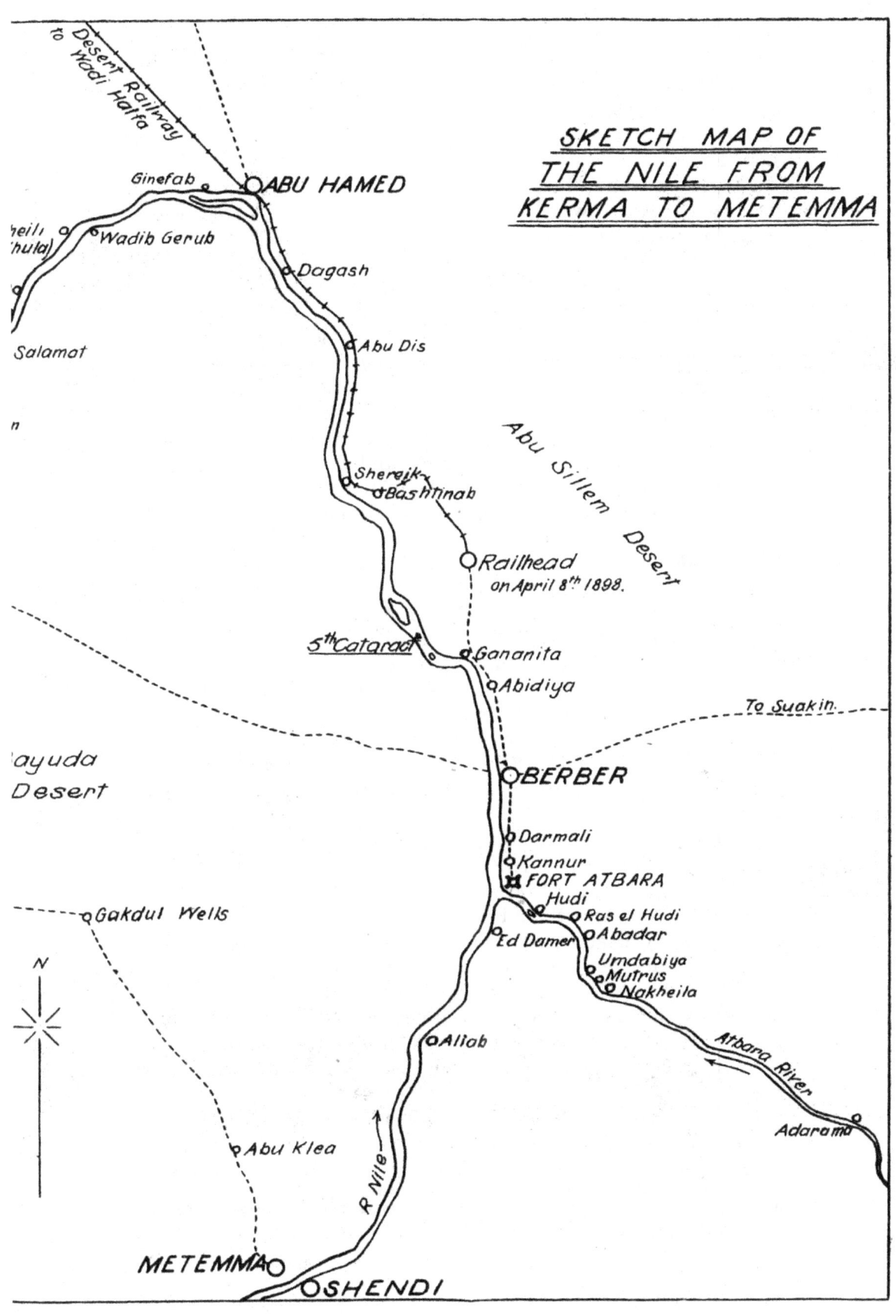

Tudway, Essex Regiment, and also by remnants of the Jaalin, who had rallied there after their flight from Metemma, the gunboats had already begun the passage of the Fourth Cataract from Kassinger. The Desert Railway crept forward once more, and Girouard was able to send Pritchard and Macauley to reconnoitre the unknown tract between rail-head and the Nile. Everything and everybody converged at top speed on Abu Hamed. But could that place be reached before Hunter's isolated brigade was overwhelmed ? On this depended not only the fate of the brigade, but possibly the result of the campaign.

Until the Desert Railway reached Abu Hamed, the only available line of communication to that place was by the Nile ; and the passage of the gunboats through the Fourth Cataract, though under the able direction of Commander Colin Keppel, D.S.O., R.N.,[1] proved to be an extremely difficult and hazardous operation. Two of the smaller and older gunboats, the *Tamai* and *Et Teb*, started upstream from Kassinger on August 4th, when Hunter had covered nearly 100 miles towards Abu Hamed. The *Tamai* was commanded by Lieutenant the Hon. A. Hood, R.N., and the *Et Teb* by Lieutenant (afterwards Admiral of the Fleet Earl) Beatty, R.N. Entering the rapids on the 5th, the *Tamai* failed to surmount them. The *Et Teb* next attempted the passage, and with her stern-wheel churning the water to foam, and hundreds of men hauling on cables attached to her, she succeeded in ascending a short distance ; but her bows were swept round by the current, and as the men on the hawsers continued to pull, she heeled over and capsized, throwing Beatty and most of his crew into the swirling waters. However, all except one man were picked up by the *Tamai*, though two of the crew had the unpleasant experience of being imprisoned for a time in the capsized gunboat.

Nevertheless, these misfortunes did not deter the Royal Navy. Although the level of the Nile was still too low for safety, one of the small gunboats, the *Metemma*, was hauled through the Fourth Cataract on August 13th and was followed by the *Tamai* on the 14th. On August 19th and 20th the three large gunboats—*Zafir, Fateh* and *Nasir*—accomplished the passage, and on the 23rd, the unarmed steamer *Dal*. By August 29th, the whole flotilla had reached Abu Hamed, while far behind were hundreds of heavily laden native boats, struggling through the rapids under the supervision of a special staff of British infantry officers. It is related that, during the passage of the Fourth Cataract by the gunboats, one of the native steersmen, overwhelmed by his responsibilities, developed the dangerous habit of leaving his wheel at critical moments and

---

[1] Winston Churchill in *The River War* (p. 196), states that Major David (Major E. F. David, R.M.L.I.) was in charge of the operation. He was in charge at the outset ; but afterwards the responsibility for the passage of the gunboats rested with Commander Keppel, R.N., as Senior Naval Officer.

falling on his knees to pray, until Keppel explained to him that the correct times for prayer were before and after a crisis and not exactly when it occurred.[1]

Many exciting episodes on the river were observed by Lieutenant M. G. E. Manifold, R.E., while laying his telegraph along the line of the Fourth Cataract. On August 18th, he writes from Mushra el Abiad :— " I have just come back from the Cataract, where I saw the big gunboat *Nasir* steaming up and watched to see how she would go, knowing what it was like from my experience yesterday in the *Fateh*. She ascended the worst place quite easily, and then, to my surprise, took a new route. The *Rheis* (steersman) hesitated and started turning too late, and so her stern crashed into the bank. Then she pushed off, turned round and tried to steam down again, but in so doing, went with a loud scrunch on to and over another rock. Finally, they got her to an island in the middle of the Cataract, and they are trying to repair the damage." And on the 19th, he continues :— " To-day, I have seen the passing of a big gunboat over the Cataract. The 7th Egyptians were there to haul on the ropes. Their costume was a *tarbush* and the rags they call shirts. It was really a splendid sight to see 300 men take to the water together and swim across a rapid, each with his shirt as a turban round his *tarbush*. Much time is spent in getting the ropes into position. There is usually a very long towing rope from the bows, manned by 400 or 500 men, and one or two steadying ropes, held by 150 men or so, to keep the ship's head from swinging. When the ropes are in position, and the men ready, the bugle sounds the advance, and the men begin to pull, while steam is turned on and the great stern-wheel revolves. The towing rope is really only a safeguard, for these boats can stem the stream easily, but the side ropes are of great use. It is very exciting to see the boat steered just clear of a great rock, or stopped before harm is done."

The zeal, energy and skill displayed by Commander Keppel and his officers brought a congratulatory message from Kitchener, which was worded in a rather frivolous manner. To this, Keppel replied " All dining together to celebrate occasion. Main brace being spliced. Your orders respecting tactics will be adhered to. At present the fleet, though disposed to port, has none."

The sudden advance of the Egyptian vanguard to Abu Hamed disheartened and perturbed the enemy. Fugitives poured into Berber, and in the absence of support from Mahmud at Metemma, the Emir of Berber evacuated the town on August 24th and marched south. The news was brought to Hunter at Abu Hamed on the 27th, two days before the gunboats began to arrive, and as soon as the first ship, the *Zafir*, had reached him, he boarded her and set off

---

[1] *Sudan Campaign, 1896—1899*, by "An Officer" (Lieut. H. L. Pritchard, R.E.), p. 115.

upstream with a small party of Ababda tribesmen, riding on camels alongside him on the bank. About 30 miles below Berber, the gunboat struck a rock and could proceed no farther; but the escort, under Ahmed Bey Khalifa, rode on and entered Berber on August 31st.

Lieutenants G. F. Gorringe and W. A. S. Kincaid, R.E., were with Hunter in the damaged *Zafir*, which fortunately had on board a few bags of cement. The ship was beached, and Gorringe repaired her by building a concrete block, in wooden boxing, against the side and bottom, stayed to the steel framing of the ship. As the *Zafir* had been constructed in sections, it was possible, after 48 hours of strenuous labour, to pump the water out of the flooded section. The voyage was then resumed to Berber, where the ship arrived shortly after the Ababda Arabs. Gorringe had seen a ship repaired in this manner by a salvage official near Suakin.

It seems that the Khalifa Abdullahi had expected that Kitchener would attempt to advance from Korti across the Bayuda Desert against Metemma—as Kitchener had actually contemplated—and thence up the Nile on Omdurman, so he would not allow Mahmud to weaken the garrison of Metemma by reinforcing Berber; and even when he heard of the fall of Abu Hamed, he clung to the idea that Kitchener would make for Metemma and not for Berber. The Khalifa knew, and Kitchener did not, that navigation of the Nile in the region of the Fifth Cataract below Berber would soon be difficult for shipping, and he decided that, as it was either too late or too dangerous to reinforce Berber adequately, he would order the evacuation of that town and be content to concentrate his main army at Omdurman with a strong outpost under Mahmud at Metemma. This he proceeded to do, and thereby missed an opportunity such as falls to few commanders in the field.

The astounding news of the evacuation of Berber placed Kitchener in a quandary. The bait was tempting, but dare he take it? To supply the outpost at Abu Hamed, until the railway reached it, was no easy task.[1] How much more difficult would it be to carry stores and provisions to Berber, nearly 130 miles farther up the Nile! In any case the force at Berber would have to be small, its communications would be constantly threatened, and it might be required to fight for its existence against vastly superior numbers. On the other hand, the possession of Berber was of extreme importance. It was the centre of many trade routes, including the route to Suakin, and the moral effect of its occupation would be incalculable. Strategically, it was the most vital point between Wadi

---

[1] Until the project for a direct advance from Merowe to Metemma had been abandoned, few camels could be spared for transporting supplies from Merowe to Abu Hamed. Kitchener had arranged, however, for two camel convoys to proceed from Korosko through Murrat Wells. The first, an Arab convoy, perished in a dust-storm. The second, an Egyptian Army Transport convoy, reached Abu Hamed by the strictest water discipline.

Halfa and Omdurman. Influenced by these considerations and by the rapid progress of the railway towards Abu Hamed, Kitchener decided to risk a further advance if he could obtain the consent of Lord Cromer, and on September 3rd, having secured permission,[1] he ordered the occupation of Berber. Hunter was already there with the *Zafir*, and took formal possession of the town on September 5th, after the *Fateh*, *Nasir* and *Tamai* had arrived from Abu Hamed with 350 men of the 9th Sudanese battalion. The Nile being still navigable for steamers, some of the gunboats proceeded upstream to Ed Damer, beyond the junction of the Atbara River, to harry the retreating dervishes and capture their boats ; and on the 10th, Kitchener himself arrived in Berber by the desert route from Merowe to inspect the troops and their defences.

Sir George Gorringe describes an incident which occurred when the Sirdar was received on parade by the officers at Berber.[2] As already mentioned, Kitchener had confided his secret plans to Gorringe at Merowe, and had told him that he relied upon him to carry out his instructions that a fort to hold one battalion and a battery was to be built at Abu Hamed in the best tactical position to withstand an assault. Gorringe had accordingly reconnoitred the ground and had submitted his proposals to General Hunter, who had objected to them because he considered that it would be easier to build a fort on lower ground nearer to the river. Gorringe had then informed Hunter that he had received direct confidential orders and must adhere to his recommendation, in which he was supported by Kincaid, so the fort was built on the site which he had selected. When Kitchener came to Gorringe in the line of officers at Berber, he turned to Hunter and said, "I think that a good site was selected for the fort. Don't you agree, Hunter ?" History does not relate what Hunter replied, but he bore no ill-will against Gorringe, of whom he had formed the highest opinion since the successful repair of the *Zafir*.

After leaving Berber, Kitchener proceeded downstream to Abu Hamed and awaited the approach of the railway. Abu Hamed was reinforced, MacDonald's brigade was sent up to Berber, and a Camel Corps post was established at Dakhila, a small village at the confluence of the Atbara with the Nile.[3] This was a period of great anxiety. Even after the railway reached Abu Hamed on October 31st, 1897, Lord Cromer had grave misgivings. "Sir Herbert Kitchener's force depended entirely on the desert railway for its supplies," he writes.[4] " I was rather haunted with the idea that some European adventurer, of the type familiar in India a century and

---

[1] *The River War*, by the Rt. Hon. Winston Churchill, p. 200.
[2] Notes by Lieut.-General Sir George Gorringe sent to the author on August 1st, 1936.
[3] Afterwards the site of the fort and encampment of Atbara.
[4] *Modern Egypt*, by the Earl of Cromer, Vol. II, p. 94, footnote.

more ago, might turn up at Khartoum and advise the Dervishes to make frequent raids across the Nile below Abu Hamed, with a view to cutting the communication of the Anglo-Egyptian force[1] with Wadi Halfa. This was unquestionably the right military operation to have undertaken; neither, I think, would it have been very difficult of accomplishment.[2] Fortunately, however, the Dervishes were themselves devoid of all military qualities, with the exception of undaunted courage, and did not invite any European assistance. They therefore failed to take advantage of the opportunity presented to them. To myself, it was a great relief when the period of suspense was over. I do not think that the somewhat perilous position in which Sir Herbert Kitchener's army was unquestionably placed for some time was at all realized by the public in general." Nevertheless, the completion of the Desert Railway to Abu Hamed minimized the immediate dangers to which the Egyptian army was exposed, for it shortened the duration of the journey from Wadi Halfa from 18 days by the Nile route to 24 hours across the Nubian Desert.

While Hunter was making his remarkable advance up the Nile, the elusive Osman Digna had collected 5,000 men at a village called Adarama on the Atbara River, about 90 miles above its junction with the Nile. However, the occupation of Berber by the Egyptians made his isolated position precarious, and although he hated Mahmud, he decided to join forces with him at Metemma. After raiding the Egyptian communications north of Berber, he began his journey on September 23rd, and crossing the Atbara with the greatest difficulty, made his way by easy stages northwards and then westwards to the Nile.[3] This manœuvre had important results, for it left the Eastern Sudan clear of the enemy and enabled Kitchener to take steps to re-open the route from Berber to Suakin, which had been closed for many years.

During October, 1897, the flotilla of gunboats was very active in spite of the increasing difficulty of navigation on the Nile. On several occasions, Commander Keppel, R.N., took the *Zafir*, *Fateh* and *Nasir* southwards to test the attitude of the riverain tribes and to reconnoitre Metemma. The town stood some distance from the river bank, on which mud forts, armed with light guns, had been built at intervals for a distance of one and a half miles. On October 16th and 17th, the gunboats were in action against the forts. These reconnaissances, and another on November 3rd, when the flotilla

---

[1] As will appear later, the Egyptian Army under Kitchener had then been reinforced by a brigade of British troops.

[2] Most military critics disagree with this opinion. Before Abu Hamed was occupied, the Desert Railway was exposed to raids; but with Hunter at that place, and the Nile patrolled, there was little risk.

[3] In the absence of proper boats, the crossing occupied Osman Digna for nearly one month. A small flying column under General Hunter reconnoitred to Adarama in November, and destroyed the village, but failed to catch Osman.

proceeded as far south as the foot of the Sixth Cataract, were useful in keeping the Sirdar fully informed of the state of the enemy's defences, but they drew no reply from Mahmud, who was still forbidden to attack.

After the consolidation of the position at Berber, the Egyptian Government had time to review the general situation and arrived at the conclusion that the time was fast approaching when it would have to ask for the assistance of British troops. The question then arose as to whether Kitchener should command the Anglo-Egyptian army at the front. Major-General Sir Francis Grenfell, G.C.M.G., K.C.B., had arrived in Egypt on October 8th to command the Army of Occupation, and as he was senior to the Sirdar it seemed probable that he might supersede him. Kitchener's health was beginning to fail. He was harassed and anxious about financial questions and was pressed repeatedly by Sir Elwin Palmer, the Director-General of Finance, to effect further economies in the conduct of the campaign. On October 6th, he had written to the Under-Secretary for Finance[1] " The strain on all of us and on the troops is very great. . . . You have no idea what continual anxiety, worry and strain I have through it all. I do not think I can stand much more and I feel sometimes so completely done up that I can hardly go on and wish I were dead. . . . Before next year's work in the field begins I must get some leave or I shall break down, for I have had none now for three years." Outwardly, he remained the same man of iron ; inwardly, he felt the insistent urge to rest.

As time went on, the strain increased rather than diminished, and at length on October 18th, when difficult questions about finding a garrison for Kassala,[2] and meeting the cost of that project, had been added to his other worries, Kitchener was driven to tender his resignation to Lord Cromer. " I do not know that the gravity of the situation is fully realized," he telegraphed.[3] " Holding our long line, which is liable to attack at many points, leaves me with a small force at Berber, a place most difficult to defend, and without supports. We have in front of us a force of Dervishes of better fighting qualities and far greater numerical strength than we have ever met before. In face of this, the financial authorities appear to be unable to grant what I think necessary for military efficiency and to carry

[1] Sir Clinton Dawkins. The letter is quoted in *Life of Lord Kitchener*, by Sir George Arthur, Vol. I, p. 217.

[2] The town of Kassala, about 250 miles east of Khartoum, had been captured by the dervishes from the Egyptians in 1885. In 1893, the Dervish garrison of Kassala marched against Agordat. They were unsuccessful, and in the following year the Italians retaliated by taking Kassala. In 1896, after their defeat at Adowa, the Italians offered to return Kassala to Egypt. The offer was accepted, and it was arranged that an Egyptian garrison should take over the town. An Egyptian force, under Lieut.-Colonel C. S. B. Parsons, R.A., was sent to Massawa on the Red Sea coast in November, 1897, and marched thence to Kassala, where it arrived in December. The formal transfer of the town to the Egyptian Government was made on Christmas Day.

[3] *Life of Lord Kitchener*, by Sir George Arthur, Vol. I, p. 219.

out the military programme.[1] My estimate of the situation and military requirements may be wrong, but feeling, as I do, my inability to cope with the difficulties and the grave responsibilities of the position in which I find myself, I beg to tender my resignation to your Lordship."[2] Cromer was surprised at this ultimatum, but he had too high an opinion of Kitchener to desire at that moment to lose his services. The Sirdar was summoned to Cairo where, with Cromer and Grenfell to support him, he was able to smooth away all financial and other difficulties and regain his health and spirits. He returned to the front in the middle of December with the assurance that the campaign would be continued with the assistance of British troops when required and that no instructions whatever had been received regarding his supersession.[3]

It has been suggested that although Kitchener meant his telegram to be taken seriously he knew that his resignation would not be accepted[4]—that, in fact, his application to resign was a gesture of protest against financial inflictions. Be that as it may, the fact that he was prepared to stake his career in Egypt against what he considered to be unwarranted interference with his conduct of affairs shows the strength of the man. As a Government tests the confidence of a nation by inviting a General Election, so Kitchener made sure of the attitude of his superiors towards him before embarking on a more extended campaign in which he would need their unfailing support. His doubts were resolved, and he was able to set about his task with greater freedom and renewed vigour.

Lack of material interfered so much with the extension of the railway from Abu Hamed towards Berber that by the end of 1897 only 17 miles of line had been opened for traffic. Transport by the river was difficult ; and the steady fall of the Nile during November, with the consequent appearance of an impassable rapid south of Berber, had forced the Sirdar to decide whether he should keep his gunboats in an exposed, but useful, position upstream of the obstacle or in a safe but almost useless position below it. He chose the more dangerous alternative, and ordered the preparation of a small

---

[1] Sir Elwin Palmer wished to restrict Kitchener to a definite sum (£200,000) for all expenses, foreseen and unforeseen. According to Kitchener, this was insufficient, even without the extra expenses which might be incurred on account of Kassala.

[2] The telegrams passing between Kitchener and Cromer were coded and decoded by Lieut. G. F. Gorringe, R.E., who was living with the Sirdar during the temporary absence of Capt. Watson, the A.D.C. " I well remember the state of mind he was in," writes Sir George, " when he handed me, for coding, the telegram in which he resigned. That evening I induced him to come out duck shooting with me, a thing he rarely did, and it took his mind off his worries."

[3] Nevertheless, Lord Cromer had so little in common with Kitchener that he wrote to Lord Salisbury on December 16th, 1897, " Kitchener's main idea now seems to be to get away from Egypt and obtain some English military command in order to qualify for higher positions later. I would rather he did not go just yet, as, whatever may be his defects, he is unquestionably the best man I know to command the Egyptian Army for the present. However, no one is indispensable, and if he really wishes to go, I do not want to stand in his way."

[4] *Kitchener*, by Brig.-General C. R. Ballard, C.B., C.M.G., p. 78.

dockyard and the building of an entrenchment at the camel post of Dakhila, where the Atbara joins the Nile. This was the beginning of the Atbara Fort, designed and built by Lieutenant G. F. Gorringe, R.E., a work which was destined, within the next few months, to screen the concentration of British and Egyptian troops for the operations against Mahmud.

As time went on, the Atbara entrenchment was lengthened northwards and its defences became more formidable. A newspaper correspondent writes,[1] "To find so strong a place in the wilderness was a revelation. The wall was six feet high, firmly built of sun-dried mud, and round it a six-foot ditch. On the inside was a parapet, gun-platforms with a couple of Maxims in each, a couple of guard-houses at the two main gates, and a couple of blockhouses outside. Across the Atbara was a small fort, and at the angle of the rivers a covered casemate gallery. On the other side of the Nile was a smaller fort, walled and ditched likewise. Under the walls of Fort Atbara a forest of stumps showed where the field of fire had been cleared for over a mile in every direction, and upright and regular among the stumps you could see a row of stakes, each of which marked a range. The fort, though it dominated the country for miles, was itself hardly visible." Forts were provided on both banks of the Nile at Atbara in order to check Dervish raids; and as a further precaution, Kitchener consented on this occasion to the arming of the Nile villagers with Remington rifles. Being very nervous, the villagers were inclined to open fire first and inquire afterwards; and on the day after the issue of the rifles, when Hunter and his staff rode from Berber to Atbara, they were under fire the whole way.

On his return to Wadi Halfa from Cairo on December 18th, 1897, Kitchener received important news in confirmation of previous rumours that the Khalifa was meditating a general advance. The Dervish leader had apparently satisfied himself that the "Turks" would not attack Omdurman on a falling Nile and thought that he might be able to overwhelm the small garrison of Berber while the railway was yet far away. The Sirdar's reply was to push Lewis's brigade, and a battery of artillery, up to the Atbara entrenchment, to strengthen and enlarge that work, and to send forward to Berber every available man from the garrisons of Merowe, Korti and Ed Debba. The infantry and guns descended the Nile to Kerma, and continued northwards by rail to Wadi Halfa. Thence they travelled by the Desert Railway to Abu Hamed, and onwards for 12 miles to rail-head near Dagash. They arrived at their destination in four days, whereas Hunter had taken eight days to reach Abu Hamed—facts which prove, as Winston Churchill remarks,[2] that in certain circumstances two sides of a triangle may be shorter than the third.

[1] *With Kitchener to Khartoum*, by G. W. Steevens, p. 76.
[2] *The River War*, by the Rt. Hon. Winston Churchill, M.P., p. 213.

The cavalry and camelry marched across the bend of the Nile along the desert route to Berber.

Lord Cromer had encouraged Kitchener to ask for British troops directly he thought that their presence was necessary, and on January 1st, 1898, he received from the Sirdar an historic telegram which, in his opinion, virtually sealed the fate of the Sudan. "General Hunter," it ran, "reports confirming the news of a Dervish advance. I think that British troops should be sent to Abu Hamed, and that reinforcements should be sent to Egypt in case of necessity. The fight for the Sudan would appear to be likely to take place at Berber."[1]

No time was lost. On January 2nd, orders were issued to the 1st Battalion, Royal Warwickshire Regiment, at Alexandria, and to the 1st Battalions of the Lincolnshire Regiment and Cameron Highlanders at Cairo, to proceed immediately to Wadi Halfa. Instructions were cabled also to the 1st Battalion, Seaforth Highlanders, at Malta, and to the 5th Battalion, Northumberland Fusiliers, at Gibraltar, to move to Egypt. So promptly were these orders executed that the Lincolns, Warwicks and Camerons arrived in Wadi Halfa at the end of the third week in January to form a British brigade, and soon afterwards the Seaforths were at Aswan and the Northumberlands at Cairo. With the British brigade came an artillery detachment armed with Maxim guns, and also one section of the 2nd (Fortress) Company, R.E., under Lieutenant J. P. Moir.

It is indeed remarkable that in a campaign such as that up to the Atbara, the only regular unit available for general engineering duties should have been so diminutive; but the Egyptian Army could not afford the luxury of a Field Company, and the Army of Occupation itself was restricted to a single Fortress Company and a detachment of a Railway Company.[2] There were many men, however, among the Egyptian battalions, who would have been called "Pioneers" in a British unit, and in each Egyptian battalion there was at least one officer with experience in building construction. While at Suakin from 1893 to 1895, Lieutenant G. F. Gorringe, R.E., had employed such officers and men in the repair and erection of barracks; and during the campaigns of 1896-98, and subsequently in the rebuilding of Khartoum, they worked under his supervision and produced excellent results. After the Dongola Expedition, Gorringe suggested to the Sirdar that tradesmen of suitable age might be enlisted for construction and repair duties, and two

[1] A few days later, Kitchener, with extraordinary foresight, dispatched another telegram to Cromer in which he stated that, for the final advance on Omdurman, he would need an additional brigade of British infantry, a regiment of British Cavalry and a battery of field artillery. His forecast proved to be wonderfully accurate.

[2] The 2nd (Fortress) Company, R.E., and a detachment of the 8th (Railway) Company, R.E. The 2nd Company was commanded by Major L. A. Arkwright, R.E., with Lieutenants D. A. Friederichs and J. P. Moir, R.E., as Company Officers. The detachment of the 8th Company was commanded by Lieutenant E. C. Midwinter, R.E., and was employed on the Desert Railway and its extension southwards.

"Works Department" Companies of these men were formed in Egypt and brought up the Nile to Wadi Halfa at the beginning of 1897. These were the men who assisted Gorringe in building the extension of the workshops at Halfa, and in constructing and repairing bridges on the Kerma line, and were employed under him after the Battle of Omdurman.

In command of the British brigade on the Nile, was Colonel (afterwards Lieut.-General Sir) William F. Gatacre, C.B., D.S.O., a man of great strength and courage and so consumed by energy that he was known to his hard-worked troops as "Old Back-acher." Gatacre had distinguished himself in operations on the North-West Frontier of India and in Burma, and came to the Sudan from Aldershot with a fine reputation as a tireless and resourceful leader. He was well fitted for the task in hand, though he and his men were at some disadvantage through their inexperience of conditions in the Sudan.

At the end of January, 1898, the general situation was that the Egyptian Army, of three infantry brigades, eight squadrons of cavalry and four batteries of artillery, held various posts along the Nile, chiefly from Fort Atbara to Abu Hamed, with a main concentration at Berber, and that the British brigade under Gatacre was in camp at Abu Dis, 30 miles south of Abu Hamed. The Suakin-Berber route had been opened, and its oases were held by armed posts. An Egyptian garrison, under Lieut.-Colonel Parsons, defended Kassala. As a result of a Mission under Mr. Rennell Rodd to Abyssinia in 1897, King Menelik had agreed to remain neutral.[1] Rail-head had reached Abu Dis, and the Egyptian line from Cairo had been extended to Aswan. Large quantities of material were stored at Berber. The main Dervish army, perhaps 40,000 strong, was with the Khalifa at Omdurman, and a further 20,000 men with Mahmud and Osman Digna at Metemma; but in spite of the rumours of a general Dervish advance, there was yet no sign of it in the region of the Egyptian post at Fort Atbara.

The British units in camp at Abu Dis were armed with ·303 Lee-Metford rifles. In many respects, the heavy Martini-Henry bullet of the Egyptian Army was superior at close quarters to the Lee-Metford; but the ·450 Martini rifle had no magazine, and consequently its rate of fire was slow. Nevertheless, the accuracy of the British and Egyptian fire always transcended that of the dervishes and stopped their most desperate assaults, and this, apart from tactical and strategical superiority, gave Kitchener his unfailing victories against superior numbers.

In February, 1898, the important town of Berber, renowned for its camels, leather and salt, had become a centre of excitement and

---

[1] Colonel Wingate accompanied this Mission, and assisted in the negotiations at Addis Ababa. During his absence from April to September, 1897, his duties as Director of Military Intelligence were performed by Major the Hon. M. G. Talbot, R.E., with his headquarters at Cairo.

animation. Along its main thoroughfare, wide and sandy, jostled a throng of British, Egyptian and Sudanese soldiers, intermingled with merchants, wild tribesmen of the desert, camels and donkeys. Many of its mud hovels bore the enticing notice " Officers' Club and Mineral Waters," and there the rash could sample liquors other than water and listen to a limpid stream of modern Greek from an unshaved proprietor. To the south of vociferous New Berber lay the acres and acres of Old Berber, silent and in ruins, a sun-dried skeleton of a city, peopled only by the ghosts of the thousands who perished by the sword in the Dervish invasion of 1884. During the concentration of 1898, New Berber flourished and expanded ; then the tide of war rolled on towards the far south, and it relapsed into its normal lazy existence beneath a burning sun. The traders counted their gains : the dogs searched the refuse. There was little insobriety among the Anglo-Egyptian troops because, as in the Nile Expedition of 1885, the use of alcohol, and even of beer, was prohibited ; and when " Old Back-acher," addressing his British battalions, complimented them very correctly on the absence of crime " and of drunkenness," he provoked roars of laughter in which, disciplinarian though he was, he could not help joining.

The Khalifa now committed another serious strategical error. Although he had refused to allow Mahmud to march against Berber when the Egyptian forces were weak and scattered, he permitted him to advance in February against a reinforced and concentrated army. On the 10th, Mahmud began to cross the Nile from Metemma to Shendi, observed but not seriously hindered by Keppel's gunboats, for this was the very movement which the Sirdar desired. It was an essential part of Kitchener's strategy to draw Mahmud from his fortified position. With the Nile between the opposing forces, and Mahmud entrenched at Metemma and able to retreat rapidly on Omdurman, Kitchener might have to repeat on a grander scale the action of Hafir and the pursuit to Dongola ; but with the enemy in the open country, and on the right bank of the Nile, the scales were weighted heavily in his favour. The British brigade had arrived ; the railway had reached Shereik, only 70 miles short of Berber ; and a strong garrison was posted at Atbara Fort. Mahmud completed the crossing on February 25th, and then found himself in an angle formed by the Nile and the Atbara from which he could not retreat without giving battle. The British brigade moved up to Berber, where it was received with enthusiasm on March 2nd, and on the 4th it bivouacked at Kannur (Kenur) within ten miles of Atbara Fort.

Leaving a small garrison near Shendi to guard his women and supplies, Mahmud started on March 12th to descend the Nile to Aliab[1] with the plain intention of making a direct attack on Atbara

---

[1] Aliab, and all places mentioned in connection with the campaign on the Atbara River, are shown on the inset of the *Sketch Map of the Battle of the Atbara*, which is included in this chapter.

Fort; but the close attention of the gunboats on the river, the reports of spies, and some hesitation on the part of Osman Digna, induced him on the 18th to leave the Nile at Aliab and strike north-eastwards into the desert towards the village of Hudi on the Atbara. By crossing the Atbara at Hudi, and turning the Sirdar's left, he hoped that he might be able to operate against Berber from the desert and to cut the Anglo-Egyptian line of communication—an excellent plan against a purely passive defence. But Kitchener was not disposed to remain passive. Summoning his troops from Darmali and other camps between the Atbara and Berber, he had concentrated almost his entire force at Kannur by March 16th.[1] Under the Egyptian flag—a white star and crescent on a red ground— he marched on the 20th with 12,000 men to Hudi, thus forestalling Mahmud. There he was joined by Lewis's brigade from Atbara Fort, and settled down for the night in a strong *zariba*.

The news was carried to Mahmud who, faced with the alternatives of attacking the Anglo-Egyptian army, which he knew now to be formidable and well-armed, or making a further detour to reach water, changed the direction of his march still more to the right, and striking due east, reached the Atbara close below the village of Nakheila, about 30 miles up the river. His plan had failed. To avoid Kitchener's army by a circuitous march on Berber was now impossible; the distance was too great and water too scarce. Short of supplies, his force dwindling through desertions, unable to retreat, unwilling to advance, Mahmud and his 12,000 followers entrenched themselves on the right bank of the Atbara and awaited attack. On March 21st, Kitchener marched up the river for a further distance of seven miles to Ras el Hudi, where he camped in a *zariba* and paused in the hope that sickness, starvation and desertion would play havoc with the dervishes and force them in desperation to advance against him.

Extracts from the letters of Lieutenant M. G. E. Manifold, R.E., throw interesting sidelights on the movement up the Atbara. Writing from Ras el Hudi he says, " On Saturday we got news (at Kannur) that Mahmud had left the Nile for the Atbara and that Berber was his objective. On Sunday I was up at 5.30 a.m. and found 'Saat-el'[2] (Kitchener) wandering about in full kit. I followed him to Church Parade, and afterwards walked back with him, and he said, ' I think Mahmud may try to avoid us, so we had better go up to him.' The whole force moved off at 11 a.m. Saat-el having told me to open a telegraph office at Atbara and afterwards to rejoin him, it was not until 3 p.m. that I started to ride to Hudi. The force had gone by a

[1] The Seaforths had arrived from Aswan, and had joined the British brigade. Kitchener had kept only one Egyptian brigade at Atbara Fort in order to entice Mahmud to attack him in that strong position. It is presumed that Mahmud learnt at Aliab that there was a large concentration at Kannur in rear of the fort.

[2] " *Sa'at el Sirdar* " (His Excellency the Sirdar). The prefix " Sa'at el " is accorded to all senior officers having the title of Sirdar, Pasha or Bey.

short cut across the desert (11 miles) and I found them at 4.30 p.m. just settling down. The dust was awful. Everyone was black. The whole crowd of 15,000 were in an oblong, one mile long by a quarter-mile wide. I had brought no camp bed, and even the Sirdar lay on the ground. At dark it got very cold. When the table had been laid for dinner at 7.30 p.m., Cecil (Lord Edward) said in a hoarse voice, 'The worst has happened. *He* has gone to sleep.' We recalled occasions on which the Sirdar had slept until 9.30 and had then said it was 'too late to dine,' so it was a great relief when we heard a voice say, 'Watson. Isn't dinner ready?' and we all trooped in. We were up in bitter cold at 5 a.m., had breakfast, moved off at 7.30, and are now at Ras el Hudi. No news of Mahmud. The Atbara is a clear stream, very thickly wooded, and the water quite blue, but at present only in pools."

The narrative is resumed on March 22nd:— "About 8.30 a.m. I went out with Saat-el, and Hunter met him and asked if he could spare some officers to act as 'gallopers,' so I was told to report myself to MacDonald. Saat-el's mess consists of himself, Watson, Cecil, Rawlinson, Gallwey, Wingate, Blunt, A'Court, Rhodes and myself."[1]

On March 24th, Manifold writes:—"Saat-el has heard rumours of the hardships of the British brigade who, having expected that the march would be across a fearful desert, carried on their camels scarcely anything but water and left most of the other necessaries behind. Not a man had more than one blanket. We heard heart-breaking accounts of one mess, who had eaten all their rations at lunch so had to go without dinner, and of another where the Colonel was found cutting up his bully beef with a piece of hoop-iron. To-day, Saat-el sent for Gatacre and told him to arrange for ten camels to go to Atbara and Kannur to fetch stores. Gatacre replied that he considered that his troops 'had everything they wanted'; but Saat-el thought otherwise."

Letters dated the 25th and 26th record:— "Our chief excitement has been the arrival of two deserters, black, lean, hungry and weak. Saat-el examined one who told us that Mahmud's men had had a bad time when crossing the desert and many were now dying for want of food. At lunch, Saat-el sent some soup to the man, and so on at each course, ending with preserved apricots, and finally asked him whether he got the like from Mahmud. After lunch, Watson (the A.D.C.) being absent, Saat-el said, 'Get Bimbashi Watson's bad cigarettes,' selected one, and sent it to the dervish.

[1] Captain J. K. Watson, D.S.O., K.R.R.C.; Major Lord E. H. Cecil, Grenadier Guards; Captain Sir H. S. Rawlinson, Bt., Coldstream Guards; Lieut.-Colonel T. J. Gallwey, C.B., R.A.M.C.; Lieut.-Colonel F. R. Wingate, C.B., D.S.O., R.A.; Captain C. E. G. Blunt, A.S.C.; Major C. A'Court, Rifle Brigade; Colonel F. W. Rhodes, D.S.O., late 1st Dragoons (Correspondent of *The Times*); and Lieutenant M. G. E. Manifold, R.E. The names of several of these officers, notably Rawlinson and Wingate, are familiar to students of military history. Colonel Frank Rhodes figured in the Jameson raid in South Africa, and Major A'Court became Colonel C. A'Court Repington, the author and critic.

Watson was very indignant on his return as his cigarettes are the best available and very precious now. However, the deserter declined to smoke as the dervishes do not allow smoking. . . . After breakfast to-day, I was told to join MacDonald. I have a little bush with two sticks and a piece of canvas to give shade; the neighbourhood is not sheltered like the thicket in which Saat-el lives, and everyone else has a big umbrella with an extra stick and spike to put into the ground. The dust here is red, as soft as flour, and ankle deep. . . . Gatacre, commanding the British brigade, has asked for four coils of wire to make a trip-line outside his *zariba* in case he is attacked by night."

The trip-line was provided and soon fulfilled its purpose. On the 28th, it was laid by Lieutenant J. P. Moir, R.E., along the front and flanks of the British *zariba* and about 50 yards outside it; and before dawn on the 30th, General Hunter and some of his staff, cantering gaily out at the head of a reconnoitring force, encountered the obstacle and bit the dust.[1] A veil may be drawn over this scene; but the unfortunate Manifold was not allowed to forget that he had supplied the wire and was thus indirectly responsible for the downfall of the great.

Very few officers of the Royal Engineers were privileged to take part in the military operations on the Atbara River which culminated in the Battle of the Atbara. Major W. F. H. S. Kincaid, was on General Hunter's staff, and Lieutenant G. F. Gorringe on the Sirdar's staff. Lieutenant M. G. E. Manifold, as already related, was attached as a "galloper" to MacDonald's 2nd Infantry Brigade, and Lieutenant J. P. Moir was present with a section of the 2nd (Fortress) Company, R.E. Towards the end of 1898, several other officers received decorations or promotions "in recognition of services in Egypt and the Sudan, including the battles of the Atbara and Khartoum,"[2] but they were employed only on the line of communication while the Atbara campaign was in progress. They were engaged chiefly on railway construction and operation, and a few were occupied with Staff, Supply, or Intelligence work. At this stage, the maintenance and improvement of the line of communication were of such paramount importance that Kitchener could not afford to follow his usual practice of bringing almost all his young specialists to the front to participate in the fighting.

Every artifice was employed to draw Mahmud from Nakheila. On March 25th, a small expedition under Commander Keppel, R.N.,

---

[1] Lieut. J. P. Moir, R.E., in a report dated April 11th, 1898 (quoted in the *R.E. Journal*, Vol. 28, 1898, p. 123), states that the accident occurred when General Hunter was returning to camp.

[2] Majors the Hon. M. G. Talbot, A. E. Sandbach and W. S. Gordon; and Lieutenants A. G. Stevenson, R. B. D. Blakeney, H. A. Micklem, E. C. Midwinter and G. B. Macauley among the Railway officers. Decorations or promotions were awarded later to Lieut. E. P. C. Girouard and other Royal Engineers without specifying particular battles.

was sent up the Nile in three gunboats to raid Shendi. The troops landed and destroyed the defences, while the gunboats pursued the enemy up to the Sixth Cataract. The expedition then returned northwards, bringing with it some hundreds of Jaalin women who had become the wives of the dervishes after the massacre at Metemma. It was hoped that this exploit would rouse Mahmud to attack; but the only result was that a large number of his followers deserted him in order to learn what had befallen their beloved in Egyptian hands and were sadly disappointed to find that they had already consoled themselves with new husbands.

On March 30th, Hunter led a reconnaissance in force against Nakheila, taking with him eight squadrons of cavalry, two battalions of infantry, a battery of artillery, and four Maxims. He examined the Dervish *zariba* from some high ground within 300 yards of the defences; but the enemy would neither open fire nor emerge, so he withdrew to Ras el Hudi. He reported that, so far as he had been able to ascertain, the Dervish position was exceedingly strong, and that the enemy were lying thickly in their rifle-pits and trenches which, in some places, were in three lines behind a formidable barrier of thorn bushes. Experiments of all kinds were then put in hand to deal with the obstacles anticipated at Nakheila. Moir was ordered to make hand-grenades of gun cotton, and explosive charges for use against stockades. He produced hooks from telegraph wire, and grapnels from pick-heads, and experimented with these, and with leather gloves and blankets, in pulling away the thorn bushes of a *zariba*. Not meeting with much success, he made a number of ladders to enable stormers to climb over the fence.[1] As it happened, all this labour was thrown away, for the obstacles at Nakheila proved to be very weak.

Hunter's report seems to have produced in Kitchener a state of temporary indecision most unusual in a man of his determination. "I am rather perplexed by the situation here," he wired to Lord Cromer on April 1st.[2] "Yesterday I discussed it with Gatacre and Hunter. The former was inclined to attack Mahmud's present position; the latter to wait here. We should have great advantage of ground if Mahmud would advance; but if he retires without our attacking him the opportunity will have been lost of dealing a blow by which future resistance in the Sudan would probably be considerably affected. I have little doubt of the success of our attack on his present entrenched position, though it would probably entail considerable loss. I have decided not to change my present policy for three days, before which something definite will, I hope, be known. I shall be glad to learn your views on the subject."

[1] Report by Lieut. J. P. Moir, R.E., dated April 11th, 1898, appearing in an article, entitled "The Sudan Campaign," in the *R.E. Journal*, Vol. 28, 1898, p. 123.
[2] *Modern Egypt*, by the Earl of Cromer, Vol. II, p. 98.

SITE OF THE ATBARA ZARIBA.

Showing existing remains of Dervish trenches.

[*Photo by the Author.*]

It is somewhat difficult to understand the reasons which induced Kitchener to consult Lord Cromer on a question of pure strategy. Possibly, as Sir George Arthur suggests,[1] he thought that, as he had British troops under his command, he should obtain the approval of General Sir Francis Grenfell, to whom, as commander of the British Army of Occupation, Cromer would naturally refer for advice. Lord Wolseley, the Commander-in-Chief in England, strongly disapproved of the telegram. He was well aware that Cromer, though originally a soldier, had never held an important military command in the field and was nearly one thousand miles distant from the Atbara River.

The British Consul-General himself was placed in a most difficult position. He knew that Hunter was a fighting General, and that he was experienced in desert warfare and had seen Mahmud's defences. Accordingly, after consultation with Sir Francis Grenfell, he sent a guarded reply to Kitchener on April 2nd enumerating the arguments for and against an immediate attack and advising him to await developments. However, before this message could reach the Sirdar, the latter had dispatched a second telegram to Cromer (on April 3rd) announcing that he, Hunter and Gatacre had now agreed that an attack on Mahmud's position was advisable, and that he proposed to make it on April 6th unless the reply to his first telegram was unfavourable to such a project; but later in the day, having received that reply, he wired that he would postpone the attack and content himself with moving nearer to the Dervish *zariba*.

Meanwhile Cromer, having received the telegram announcing that Hunter was now in favour of attacking, wired to Kitchener that he withdrew any opposition to an immediate offensive. He added that it was very difficult for him to express an opinion of any value, and that he left the final decision entirely to Kitchener, who could count on his support. The Sirdar then telegraphed on April 4th, "I propose to advance more slowly, and with greater deliberation than was originally my intention, and to make as sure as it is possible to do, by careful reconnaissances, of the success of an attack. I shall not commit myself to a general attack until the right moment has, in my opinion, arrived." So the matter was settled. The fate of the Sudan might depend on the result of the operations on the Atbara. With the caution which always tempered his strategy, Kitchener proceeded to put his fortune to the test.

The Anglo-Egyptian force, assembled at Ras el Hudi, consisted of about 14,000 men with 24 guns and 12 machine-guns. It comprised the British Brigade (Royal Warwicks, Lincolns, Seaforths and Camerons) under Major-General W. F. Gatacre; an Egyptian Division of three infantry brigades, under Major-General A. Hunter;

---

[1] *Life of Lord Kitchener*, by Sir George Arthur, Vol. I, p. 225.

eight squadrons of Egyptian cavalry, under Lieut.-Colonel R. G. Broadwood, 12th Lancers; six companies of the Camel Corps, under Major R. J. Tudway, Essex Regiment; a section of the 2nd (Fortress) Company, R.E., under Lieutenant J. P. Moir, R.E.; and, under Lieut.-Colonel C. J. Long, R.A., four mule batteries of Egyptian artillery,[1] one British and two Egyptian Maxim batteries,[2] and a Rocket Detachment commanded by Lieutenant D. Beatty, R.N. The force contained a greater proportion of Sudanese than in the final advance on Dongola in 1896. The 1st Infantry Brigade, under Lieut.-Colonel J. G. Maxwell, Black Watch, had three Sudanese and one Egyptian battalions; the 2nd Brigade, under Lieut.-Colonel H. A. MacDonald, Royal Fusiliers, was similarly constituted; and the 3rd Brigade, under Lieut.-Colonel D. F. Lewis, Cheshire Regiment, had three Egyptian battalions.[3] Thus the native infantry comprised six Sudanese and five Egyptian battalions, as compared with five Sudanese and eight Egyptian battalions employed in 1896. Strengthened by the British Brigade and by additional artillery, the army on the Atbara was much superior in fighting power to the force which had ascended the Nile towards Dongola, but the delay at Ras el Hudi did it no good. The British troops in particular began to suffer from the heat, bad food, and exposure; sanitary conditions were deteriorating, and dysentery and enteric fever made their appearance. Realizing this, the Sirdar struck his camp on April 4th and moved upstream for a further distance of five miles to Abadar.

A final effort was made on April 5th to entice Mahmud from his trenches. Once more Hunter rode to Nakheila with the mounted troops, a battery of artillery and some machine-guns, but on this occasion without infantry support. Kincaid, as usual, was on his Staff as Assistant Adjutant General. They were kept under observation by Dervish cavalry, but continued their march until they could look down upon the enemy's *zariba*. Large bodies of Dervish horsemen then galloped out and tried to cut off their retreat, and infantry also swarmed from the *zariba*, so Hunter retired on Abadar, screened by Broadwood's cavalry, who fought and defeated their pursuers in a spirited action. The dervishes soon returned to Nakheila, and it was realized that the ruse had failed. Although additional information had been obtained, the general situation was unchanged; so on April 6th, Kitchener resumed his forward movement by marching his whole force for a distance of seven miles upstream to Umdabiya, within seven and a half miles of the enemy, and there he made his final preparations for attack.

[1] One " Horse " artillery, and three field artillery, batteries.
[2] Each with 4 maxims.
[3] *1st Brigade*, 8th Egyptians and 12th, 13th and 14th Sudanese; *2nd Brigade*, 2nd Egyptians, and 9th, 10th and 11th Sudanese; *3rd Brigade*, 3rd, 4th and 7th Egyptians.

It was decided that the assault on the position at Nakheila should take place on Friday, April 8th, though Kitchener, who had a strong vein of superstition, was doubtful whether that day would be propitious until he discovered that it would be Good Friday and therefore, presumably, a good day for liberating the northern Sudan from the oppression of the dervishes.[1] Towards sunset on the 7th, four lightly-equipped brigades of infantry paraded and marched into the desert, where they formed into column of brigade squares, the British leading, and moving south-eastwards to a spot called Mutrus, halted at 8 p.m. within three miles of the Dervish position. They were guided with great precision by Captain H. G. Fitton, Royal Berkshire Regiment, who marched by star observations. Officers and men had a frugal meal, while the transport fetched some water from the river, and all except the pickets lay down on the stony ground to snatch a few hours of sleep. "Ah ! Tam," murmured a drowsy and sentimental Highlander. "How many thousands there are at home a-thinkin' o' us the nicht," to which "Tam" replied, "Right, Sandy. But how many *millions* there are that don't care a damn." Conversation languished, and the tired men slept until they were roused before 1 a.m. to resume their march. An hour later, the cavalry and guns started from the Umdabiya camp to overtake them, leaving the camp fires burning, and the camp itself empty except for half a battalion of infantry as a guard over the baggage.

In dead silence, under the light of a bright moon, the four great squares plodded slowly forward through the desert, parallel to the river, until the glow of the Dervish camp fires was sighted and the wheel-tracks of Hunter's reconnaissances discovered, when the direction of the march was changed towards the *zariba*, and about 4 a.m., after the arrival of the mounted troops and artillery, the infantry halted and deployed into attack formation. They advanced through the scattered bush and scrub, which fringes the Atbara River, and emerged on to open ground overlooking the shallow crater-like depression near the river bank in which, at a distance of less than half a mile, lay Mahmud's stronghold. With the exception of one or two mounted scouts, there was no sign of the enemy. The Anglo-Egyptian force spread in a great arc along the plateau, Gatacre's British brigade on the left, MacDonald in the centre, and Maxwell's brigade curving forward on the right. In rear of the left flank were the mounted troops ; and in reserve behind the left-centre of the line, Lewis's brigade guarding the transport and water and prepared to repel any attack from the left flank. Between Gatacre's and MacDonald's brigades were two batteries of artillery, and two others were with Maxwell's brigade on the right. The Rocket Detachment had a roving commission ; at first it was on the left

[1] *Life of Lord Kitchener*, by Sir George Arthur, Vol. I, p. 225.

flank, but afterwards moved to the right. Two Maxim batteries were on the left flank of the infantry, and one with the cavalry.[1]

At 6 a.m., when there was sufficient light, the artillery moved to the front, and within a few minutes opened a heavy cross-fire. Trees and bushes were set alight by shells and rockets; smoke rolled in clouds over the enemy's trenches; straw huts blazed furiously, and earth and stones flew in all directions; but still the dervishes lay prone in their deep excavations and gave not a sign of life, except on one occasion when hundreds of horsemen scrambled into their saddles and galloped out of the enclosure to the Egyptian left front, where they were engaged by Broadwood's cavalry and machine-guns. At 7.15 a.m., the troops took up their assault formations near the edge of the crater. The bombardment ceased at 7.40 a.m., the General Advance was sounded, and shortly after 8 a.m. on April 8th, 1898, with bands playing, pipes skirling and shouts of "Remember Gordon," the lines and columns of infantry, led by their officers on foot, bore down upon the Dervish *zariba*.[2]

Many accounts have been written of the Battle of the Atbara, but a few extracts from the reports and letters of Royal Engineer officers may be added to them.

Lieutenant J. P. Moir, who was present with a section of the 2nd (Fortress) Company, R.E., writes:—[3] "We advanced in attack formation to 600 yards, where we halted and all the transport was sent back behind Colonel Lewis's brigade, except ammunition mules and camels carrying ladders, blankets, gloves and other appliances for getting over the *zariba*. The batteries opened a terrific bombardment, but not a shot did the enemy fire. It appears that Mahmud, finally recognizing that his Remington elephant guns and Ismail's brass muzzle-loaders were useless at ranges over 500 yards, had given orders to his men to reserve their fire, and they did so. The artillery bombardment ceased at 7.40 a.m. and we formed for an attack. The Camerons (79th) formed the first line and advanced in

[1] The general dispositions are shown in the *Sketch Map of the Battle of the Atbara*, which is included in this chapter.

[2] The Sirdar's official dispatch, describing the operations (dated April 10th, 1898), is quoted in *Sirdar and Khalifa*, by Bennet Burleigh, pp. 286-299. The British Brigade advanced with the Camerons in line in front, and behind them the Lincolns, Seaforths and Warwicks in column of companies. It was intended that the Camerons should open gaps in the *zariba* fence through which the other battalions should pass and then deploy to sweep through the Dervish camp. Gatacre adopted this plan because he expected that the fence would prove a formidable obstacle, but in the confusion of the assault it could not be carried out. The Egyptian brigades attacked in their usual formation. The official dispatch records that each had 2 battalions in the front line, and two in support in the form of a central assaulting column in double companies; but Lieut. Pritchard, R.E., states that MacDonald had 3 battalions in the front line and 1 battalion in support. Maxwell needed 1 battalion to guard the extreme right flank, to which 1 squadron of cavalry was also sent. The massed formation adopted by the supporting battalions of the British Brigade, and the fact that they ceased fire to charge the defences led to heavy casualties. The Egyptian front line never ceased fire, and so escaped with a smaller percentage of casualties in entering the *zariba*.

[3] Report by Lieut. J. P. Moir, R.E., appearing in the *R.E. Journal*, Vol. 28, 1898, pp. 123-125.

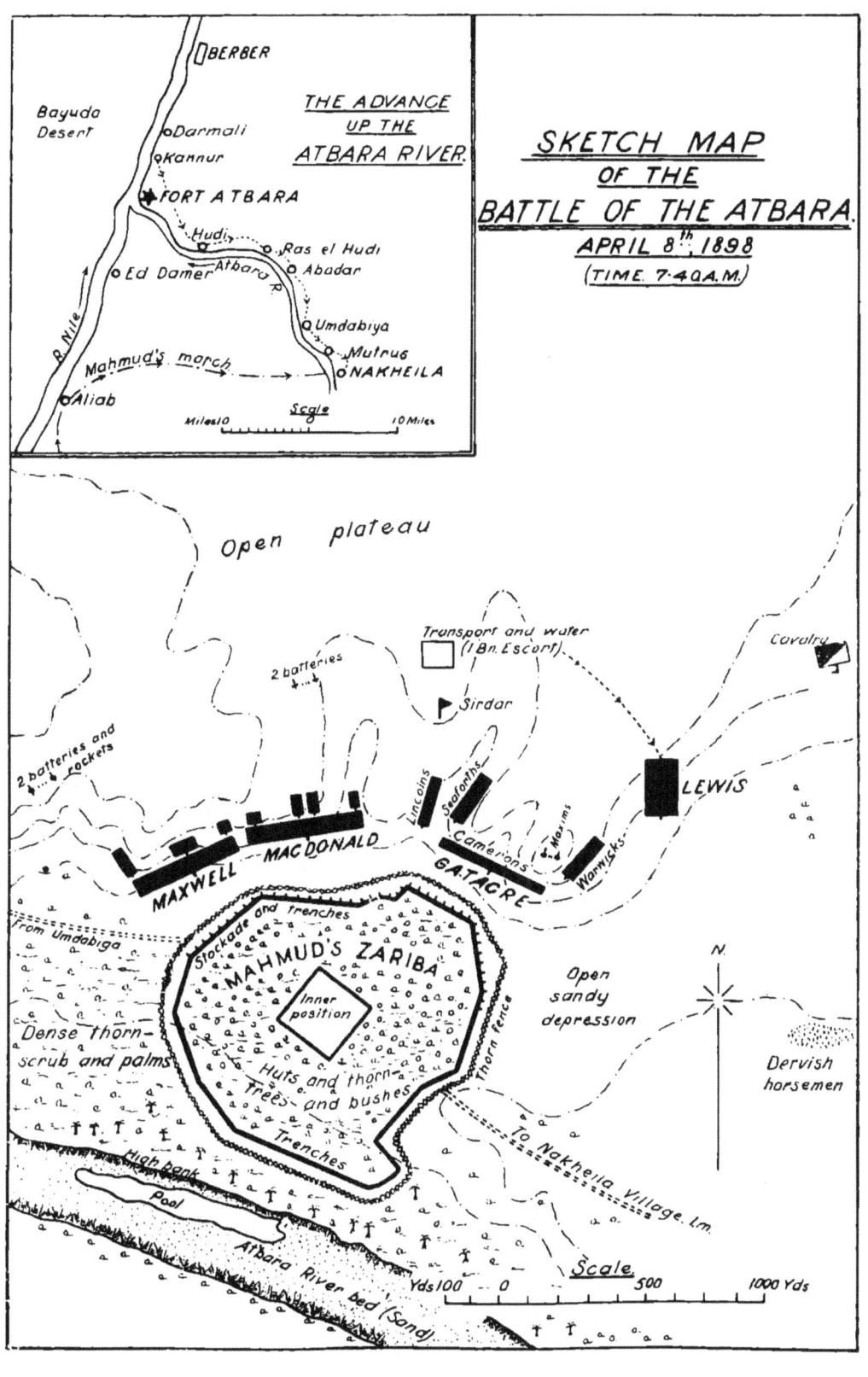

line of companies to the brow of the hill, where they poured in a terrific section volley fire. The enemy opened fire at a range of about 350 yards, and a number of men fell. As soon as the brow of the hill was reached, the *zariba* was seen to be absurdly weak and the appliances for climbing and removing it were dropped. The Camerons ceased their volleys and advanced, the front rank firing independently and the rear rank at the slope. It was a fine sight for us onlookers and a splendid example of discipline. . . . We were with the Maxim Battery, posted on a hill between the Warwicks and the Seaforths, about 300 yards from the *zariba*, and afterwards entered the position with the Warwicks, passing through the left section and coming out at the south-west corner."

Moir continues :— " Having reached the *zariba*, the Camerons proceeded to tear it away, but in most places the companies went straight over it to find themselves confronted by a curious type of stockade. Posts of mimosa or *dom* palm, from three inches to nine inches in diameter, had been driven into the ground until a length of about three feet showed above the surface, and a small gap had been left at every third post. Earth was piled to a height of 18 inches against the posts. Behind this was a trench, three feet deep and said to be narrow at the top and wide at the bottom. In this, the riflemen and spearmen lay during the bombardment, and when the infantry attacked, they were able to stand and fire through the extemporized loopholes. Behind this stockade were two or three lines of similar trenches, in which lay women, donkeys, camels and goats. The trenches were sometimes rifle pits for one man, sometimes continuous, and in them some 8,000 spearmen and riflemen awaited attack.[1] The Camerons, Seaforths and Lincolns (79th, 72nd and 10th) poured through the *zariba* and rushed the stockade, and the Seaforths and Lincolns deployed right and left and swept straight across, killing everyone.[2] The Warwicks (6th) guarded the flank in case of an attack by Dervish horsemen.[3] The attack passed right through to the rear entrenchment, where there was another short struggle, and thence through thick undergrowth to the river, where an awful slaughter took place. The British were wonderfully cool, but among the Sudanese there was intense excitement. The

[1] In January, 1935, the author visited the battlefield. On the open ground to the north is a stone memorial pillar, and near it, among mimosa trees, a small British cemetery with the tombstones of three officers. The entire crater is dotted with thorny trees and bushes, and traces of the dervishes' defences are very hard to find; but three lines of excavation are visible at one place on the southern boundary, and the remains of trenches can be seen in one or two places on the eastern edge. On the high ground to the south are hundreds of Muhammadan graves. The author picked up, on the battlefield, a ·303 expanding bullet.

[2] In the first rush it was almost impossible to take prisoners. With the exception of some hundreds of black slaves, who were chained in the trenches, few of the enemy would surrender. Many of the wounded dervishes shot or stabbed in the back the British soldiers who had passed them as they lay.

[3] Lewis's brigade (less 1 battalion), advancing south of the *zariba*, performed a like office for the whole force.

Sudanese found Mahmud lying wounded, and obtained £50 reward. . . . Mahmud stated afterwards that he was perfectly aware of our advance from the moment we left camp."

Lieutenant M. G. E. Manifold, R.E., who was with MacDonald's 2nd Egyptian Brigade, writes in a letter dated April 9th, 1898 :—
" A bugle sounded the advance and the whole line moved to within 400 yards, rifles firing, bands playing, men shouting, a fearful fusilade. The enemy opened a brisk fire ; shots whizzed everywhere ; men were hit everywhere. In ten minutes, we were right up to the *zariba*. For about two minutes, the opposing forces were five yards apart, blazing at each other ; then our men rushed the fence, got inside, and slew all who remained near it. The scene was almost indescribable : the ground like a sieve, with holes and trenches everywhere, not in any regular order, but all full of men and animals. Gradually the line pushed on, taking holes and pits and pushing back or killing the occupants until, at 8.25 a.m., the infantry came to the edge of the river bank and fired on the fugitives running across the sand to the other side. Then the ' Cease Fire ' sounded. Personally, I never drew sword or revolver, though I kept a wary eye on the wounded. At 8.30 I bade farewell to old 'Mac' and went in search of the Sirdar. The carnage, through which I had to ride back, was horrible. Pits full of hobbled donkeys, alive, dead and wounded ; camels knocked inside out ; dead and wounded men with burning garments ; dead and wounded women, often naked, and shattered by shot and shell. I found the Sirdar, who went to each British regiment in turn to speak a few words and got a tremendous ovation. Then he returned nearly to the place from which we had started, and having put up his flag, sent out for returns of dead and wounded. I had been told to be ready to return quickly to Fort Atbara with his telegrams. Meanwhile, I went back again over our line of advance and on my return to the Sirdar found Mahmud dressed in a beautiful *jibba*, looking very sullen and guarded by Sudanese with fixed bayonets. I hear that Franks[1] saved his life. It is marvellous that the blacks did not kill Mahmud straight away."

Mahmud was captured by the 10th Sudanese while crouching under a bed placed over a hole in the floor of his hut. The hut was situated within an inner stockaded enclosure, the capture of which was attended by heavy casualties, for the stockade was defended desperately by picked men. The Dervish leader, a well-built man about 28 years of age, with the cruel face typical of the Baggara of those days, was brought before the Sirdar and General Hunter.[2] His *jibba* was stained heavily with blood from a bayonet wound in his left leg, but he limped along with a haughty and sullen demeanour

---

[1] Captain (afterwards Major-General Sir) G. McC. K. Franks, R.A.
[2] The scene is depicted in a painting by E. D. Giles, entitled "After the Battle of Atbara. The Emir Mahmoud brought before the Sirdar." A photogravure of this picture can be seen in the R.U.S.I. Museum in London.

and showed no sign of fear. "This is His Excellency the Sirdar," said Hunter. Mahmud ignored both the information and the speaker. The Sirdar then asked, "Why have you come into the Sudan to burn and kill?" to which Mahmud replied with a certain dignity, "As a soldier I have to obey the Khalifa's orders, as you must the Khedive's. I am not a woman to run away." To other questions, he returned evasive answers. He was then removed in custody to Berber and finally to the prison at Rosetta in Egypt, where he remained for many years.

The British Brigade lost five officers and 21 men killed, and 99 officers and men wounded, and the three Egyptian brigades 57 men killed and 386 wounded, including ten British officers. The Dervish losses are unknown; the number of their killed alone was estimated as 40 Emirs (including Wad Bishara of Dongola) and 3,000 men, and no less than 2,500 corpses were counted in and near the *zariba*. The survivors fled southwards as a disorganized rabble, and, of the 12,000 infantry whom Mahmud commanded at Nakheila, scarcely 4,000 reached Gedaref to join the army under the Emir Ahmed Fedil.[1] Needless to say, the prudent Osman Digna was among that number. The Egyptian cavalry attempted a pursuit, but it proved abortive.

The Battle of the Atbara was a striking success, though gained at considerable cost, in less than half an hour of actual fighting, against a horde of half-starved and ill-armed savages. Its effect was greater than that of any event since the fall of Khartoum in 1885, for it destroyed the only army which could hinder an advance on Omdurman and cleared the whole country up to the Sixth Cataract.

The British and Egyptian wounded having been collected from Mahmud's pestilential *zariba* and started on their painful journey to Fort Atbara, the troops marched northwards to go into summer quarters at various places along the Nile. On April 14th, Kitchener made a formal entry into Berber at the head of MacDonald's brigade. The whole town was *en fête*, and the streets lined with cheering crowds, who reviled the captive Mahmud as he walked in rear of the cavalry with his hands bound behind him. This was no relic of the barbarism of ancient Rome, but a very necessary precaution to ensure that the populace should see with their own eyes that the Dervish leader was a prisoner. It seems that Kitchener had given orders in advance that Berber should be properly decorated for his triumphal entry, but that a serious difficulty had arisen when it was found that no flags or bunting could be bought in the town. However, the ladies of Berber came to the rescue of a very harassed Staff Officer, and within a few hours the streets were transformed by festoons of gaudy female garments, fluttering gaily in the breeze.

When military requirements no longer monopolized the transport,

[1] Mahmud himself stated that his strength was 12,000 infantry and 4,000 cavalry, with 10 guns. The cavalry made good their retreat when they saw that the battle was lost.

engineering was resumed with renewed energy, and on May 5th, the railway reached Abidiya, a village on the Nile only 22 miles north of Berber. This place had been selected as a suitable site for an arsenal and for a dockyard in which three new twin-screw gunboats—the *Melik, Sultan* and *Sheikh*—could be put together when they arrived in sections by the Desert Railway. In due course, the sections came to Abidiya, loaded flat on their trucks instead of vertically as on the Dongola Railway,[1] and Kitchener spent his spare time during the heat of the summer in watching their launching and assembly.[2] As a heavy crane intended for lifting the sections from their trucks had failed to arrive, Kitchener ordered Lieutenant G. F. Gorringe, R.E., to unload and launch them, promising him as many fatigue parties of men as he might require. Gorringe set to work with sleepers, rails and rope. One morning, when he was hidden in the middle of a crib-pier of sleepers supporting a section of massive proportions, and was directing the removal of the sleepers so that the section could be lowered on to a slipway of rails, he was horrified to hear Kitchener's voice saying, "Now then, you men. What are you waiting for ? Haul on that rope." The rope in question was arranged for hauling the section on to the slipway, and the men had strict orders not to touch it until the word was given. Strong and unparliamentary language came from the invisible Gorringe, in imminent danger of sudden death, and turning to Wingate, Kitchener remarked, "Perhaps we had better go and have breakfast." Shortly afterwards an invitation reached Gorringe to join the Sirdar at the meal, and thus all ended happily.

After he had completed the launching of the sections of the three gunboats, and the installation of a boiler in the *Melik*, Gorringe was granted a month's leave to England—the first leave he had had since 1894 ! Major W. S. Gordon, R.E., arrived from Wadi Halfa, where he had been superintending the loading and dispatch of the sections, and he and Engineer-Commander E. Bond, R.N., and Captain F. M. B. Hobbs, R.M.L.I., then finished the assembly of the gunboat sections at Abidiya. Great things were expected of the new ships, but unfortunately they failed to give satisfaction. Although they carried a more powerful armament[3] and were better protected than the stern-wheel gunboats of the *Zafir* class, designed by Kitchener, they were useless for towing boats and barges because of their shallow draught,[4] and under a heavy load their speed against the current was only two knots. "Monkey Gordon's Greyhounds," as they were nicknamed, were not a success. They were followed over the railway by eight steel double-decked troop-barges, also in

---

[1] This was possible because there were no deep cuttings.
[2] *The River War*, by the Rt. Hon. Winston Churchill, p. 244.
[3] Two 12½-pounder Maxim-Nordenfeldt guns, one 12-pounder Krupp gun, an Austrian 4-inch howitzer and four Maxims ; also each ship had a searchlight.
[4] The draught was only 18 inches as compared with 30 inches in the *Zafir* class.

MAHMUD, A PRISONER.

In his bloodstained *Jibba* after his capture at the Battle of the Atbara. Escort of 10th Sudanese.

[*By kind permission of General Sir Reginald Wingate, Bt., G.C.B., etc.*]

sections, and these were assembled at Abidiya and proved to be of great value in the subsequent advance.

The conclusion of the Atbara Campaign left Kitchener in a most satisfactory position, though unable to undertake any further operations until the Nile rose. In June, he paid a visit to Cairo, and several of his senior officers proceeded on leave to England. Early in July, 1898, the railway reached Fort Atbara, which was destined to be its terminus until Khartoum was recaptured. Reinforcements were already under orders for the Sudan, and the climax of the war was approaching, a climax which avenged Charles Gordon and freed the country forever from the cruelty, oppression and incompetence of Dervish rule.

THE DEAD CAMEL.
[*from "The Route of the Overland Mail to India."*]

CHAPTER IX.

DESERT RAILWAY AND NILE TELEGRAPH.

THE Battles of the Atbara and Omdurman were won, it is said, in the workshops of Wadi Halfa, for in Halfa was forged the deadliest weapon ever used against Mahdiism—the Sudan Military Railway. Experts vied with each other in declaring that a railway from Halfa across the Nubian Desert to Abu Hamed was an impossibility: they asserted that to attempt to lay it would be not only reckless but mad. Yet Kitchener had such confidence in himself and his men that he took a risk which might have deterred the boldest commander, and launched his rails and sleepers into a waterless desert towards a vigilant, numerous and mobile enemy.

It cannot be too clearly emphasized that the success of the Desert Railway should be attributed primarily to Kitchener himself. He made the preparations for the project: he organized and planned it: he supplied the driving force which carried it through. His assistants were as pawns on a chess-board, moved from square to square as the game demanded. Similarly, throughout the military operations on the Nile from 1896 to 1898, the master mind which foresaw every contingency, planned every move, and inspired every officer and man, was Kitchener's and his alone. He would listen patiently to advice from certain quarters, and sometimes he would act on it; but he did not hesitate to reject it if it ran counter to his personal convictions. He shouldered the full responsibility for both the military and engineering operations, and was allowed ample latitude by Lord Cromer.

" Little was known about the desert route," writes Lieut.-Colonel Longfield,[1] " except what could be gleaned from the Ababda Arabs who patrolled the country from their headquarters at Murrat Wells. They said—and in such a matter the Arab of the desert does not make a mistake—that there was no water; but they added that the ground was good for camels and that there were no high hills lying directly athwart the route. Such was the sum total of the available information. Translated into the language of the engineer, it meant that the building of the railway formation[2] would be easy over most of the distance, and that probably no very deep cuttings would be necessary near the summit of the desert plateau.[3] It was reasonable

---

[1] *The Sudan Railways*, by Lieut.-Colonel W. E. Longfield, R.E. (retd.).
[2] The low embankment necessary to raise the track above normal ground level.
[3] The desert rises 1,600 feet in about 100 miles on the line between Wadi Halfa and Abu Hamed, and then falls gradually during the remaining distance of about 130 miles to Abu Hamed.

to infer that the gradients would not be very severe. Stevenson and Polwhele had mapped the route from Korosko to Murrat Wells, and although the country through which the road ran was broken and rugged, the relative levels taken at different points along the route indicated that there was no sudden change in the general gradient. . . . It was fair to infer that, as the gradients between Korosko and Murrat were easy for a railway, they would probably be still easier between Halfa and the summit of the proposed desert line, which would lie, in all probability, at a lower altitude. It was also fair to assume that since Abu Hamed, according to the old surveys, lay some 400 feet higher than Halfa, the gradients on the southern half of the desert line would be gentler than those between Halfa and the summit. The gravest objection to the undertaking lay in the fact that there was no water, and apparently no prospect of finding any, along the whole route. The need for rapidity in construction, and economy in expenditure, forbade the possibility of taking the railway through Murrat by a long detour. The route from Murrat to Abu Hamed lay through a tangle of rocky hills, where railway construction would have been slow, laborious and expensive. If the desert railway were to be built, it must follow the shortest route, and the water difficulty must be met and overcome."

Preference was given to the direct route from Wadi Halfa to Abu Hamed after very careful consideration of the alternatives. A strategic railway across the Nubian Desert could follow one of three routes—from Korosko through Murrat to Abu Hamed; from Wadi Halfa through Murrat to Abu Hamed; or from Wadi Halfa direct to Abu Hamed[1]—and some months before the occupation of Dongola in the autumn of 1896, Kitchener was considering which route he should adopt if, as he expected, further military operations were undertaken. To begin with, should the railway start from Korosko or from Wadi Halfa? The adoption of the Korosko line would save two days in the river journey upstream from Esh Shallal, the terminus of the Egyptian railway above Aswan, and the railway could follow the caravan route through Murrat, where there was abundant water. On the other hand, there were few facilities for a terminus at Korosko, since the railway construction begun at that place by Lieutenants A. G. Stevenson and R. Polwhele, R.E., in the autumn of 1895, had been abandoned in the following March and the materials removed to Wadi Halfa for use on the Kerma Railway.[2] The workshops and sidings of the Kerma line were at Halfa; and it was advisable not only that the Kerma and Desert lines should be connected, but that, for the rapid transfer of troops, the connection should be as far south as possible. Apart from other considerations, these factors were almost sufficient to rule out Korosko as a possible terminus.

[1] The *Sketch Map of the Sudan Government Military Railways in* 1900, which is included in this chapter, shows the alternative routes and the line as constructed.
[2] See Chapter VII.

Soon after their arrival at Korosko in September, 1895, Stevenson and Polwhele had reconnoitred for a distance of 50 miles towards Murrat Wells as far as the head of a *khor* or valley leading down to Korosko.[1] At this time, although nothing had been decided, there was a possibility that an advance might be made from Korosko, because a railway from that place to Murrat Wells would be covered by the Egyptian and Arab garrison of the oasis, whereas a railway from Wadi Halfa would be exposed to attack. Stevenson made a solitary reconnaissance to Murrat Wells itself, whither Major the Hon. M. G. Talbot, R.E., had proceeded from Wadi Halfa for the same purpose and also to carry out latitude and longitude observations. On arrival at Murrat Wells from Korosko, Stevenson found that Talbot had already left for Wadi Halfa, so he started in hot pursuit, and after covering 126 miles on camel-back in 62 hours, ran him to earth outside Halfa. Talbot was triangulating up the Nile Valley, and was not usually concerned with railway projects; but on this occasion he had been specially deputed to reconnoitre the country for railway routes, and an opportunity to join forces with him was not to be missed.

Lieut.-General Sir George Gorringe remarks :—[2] " Talbot reported fully on the engineering difficulties of the Korosko-Murrat route, but pointed out the advantage of the water available at Murrat. He indicated the advantages of the Halfa-Abu Hamed route as far as he had been able to reconnoitre it with his escort of Ababda Arabs, but added that he had been able to find only one place where there was any sign of water collecting during the periodical rains. This place (afterwards No. 4 Station) had been exploited in the days of Musa Pasha when Governor of the Sudan. Wells had been dug there, and hard rock located some 60 feet down, but no water had been found. I was with Kitchener when Talbot made his report. Indeed, I was with the Sirdar from the time of his arrival at Wadi Halfa until the end of the Dongola Expedition. It was Talbot's report which made Kitchener decide to abandon the Korosko railway."

The Korosko-Murrat Railway scheme was affected also by the needs of the Kerma Railway, which had been begun in April, 1896; but later, partly as a result of the report submitted by Talbot and Stevenson, Kitchener decided to commence the construction of a line from Wadi Halfa leading directly towards Abu Hamed. Although the report in question stated that, with the exception of some difficult country near Murrat, the greater part of the route between that place and Halfa was suitable for a railway, the additional length of line required for a detour from Halfa through Murrat and,

---

[1] Notes by Major-General A. G. Stevenson, C.B., C.M.G., D.S.O., Col. Commandant R.E., sent to the author on January 14th, 1936.
[2] Notes by Lieut.-General Sir George Gorringe, K.C.B., K.C.M.G., D.S.O., Col. Commandant R.E., sent to the author on May 12th, 1936.

according to Arab reports, the broken nature of the tract between Murrat and Abu Hamed, caused the Sirdar to reject the circuitous route. On their way from Murrat to Halfa, both Talbot and Stevenson had noticed that the country on their left was very open and easy for a railway, and during the last 20 miles each had been on the approximate alignment which would be followed by a railway laid between Halfa and Abu Hamed. The general impression derived from their report was that the desert rose to a summit some 100 miles or more from Halfa, and that, for a direct railway to Abu Hamed, it would be necessary to find a valley beyond the summit which the line might follow down to the Nile. No one knew whether such a valley would lead towards Abu Hamed, or trend southwards to the Nile some distance below that place.

The information available after the reconnaissances by Talbot and Stevenson is shown in a map prepared by Lieutenant H. L. Pritchard, R.E.[1] The map indicates by form-lines the configuration of the country within the triangle made by Korosko, Wadi Halfa and Murrat Wells, and the approximate line of the ridge known as the "summit"; but the country between Murrat and Abu Hamed is marked "very vaguely mapped by explorers," and the entire area between Wadi Halfa and Abu Hamed is shown as unmapped.

With no other information than the reports of Talbot, Stevenson, a few explorers and the Ababda Arabs, Kitchener ordered the building of the Desert Railway, and preliminary work was begun at Wadi Halfa on January 1st, 1897. Nevertheless, every effort was made to probe the mysteries of the distant summit and the dangerous country beyond it. Within a few days of the laying of the first points at Wadi Halfa, Lieutenant E. H. S. Cator, R.E., was sent to Murrat Wells to explore southwards, and accompanied by a few Ababda Arabs, set out to ride across the Dervish front.[2] He crossed the direct route between Halfa and Abu Hamed, far beyond the summit, at a point about 150 miles from Halfa, and reached the Nile at Birti in the Fourth Cataract. The route which Cator followed gives the impression that he was looking for a valley leading from the summit down to the Nile, or for an opening in the rough country south of the summit, and that finally, being short of water, he made for the Nile. Unhappily, the hardships of this long and arduous journey sapped his strength, so that he fell a victim to enteric fever and died at Wadi Halfa on February 21st. His gallantry and devotion to duty were not wasted, for his single-handed reconnaissance helped to confirm the opinion that no insuperable difficulties would be encountered up to, and probably beyond, the summit.

[1] The map appears opposite page 77 in *Sudan Campaign, 1896—1899*, by "An Officer" (Lieut. H. L. Pritchard, R.E.)
[2] Cator had been surveying under Pritchard on the Kerma Railway and had been relieved by Lieut. G. C. M. Hall, R.E., who, as recorded later, had joined from England.

There had been some difference of opinion regarding the gauge which should be adopted for the Desert Railway, known officially as the "Sudan Military Railway."[1] Lord Cromer had urged that, for practical and pecuniary reasons, the metre (3 feet 3⅜ inches) gauge should be employed because Egypt had abundant reserves of metre-gauge sleepers and could supply locomotives and rolling stock of that gauge.[2] The Sirdar, however, had other views. The line towards Kerma was on the 3 feet 6 inches gauge, and he objected to a break of gauge at the junction at Wadi Halfa. Also, he hoped that the new Sudan Military Railway would be able to take its proper share in Cecil Rhodes' ambitious scheme for a line from the Cape to Cairo on the South African of 3 feet 6 inches gauge. The new Egyptian extension from Luxor to Aswan was on that gauge, although the remainder of the main line from Luxor to Cairo and Alexandria was on the 4 feet 8½ inches gauge. In the end, the Sirdar prevailed. The 3 feet 6 inches gauge was selected, and Lieutenant E. P. C. Girouard, R.E., the young Director of Railways, was ordered to estimate the requirements.

Kitchener usually asked Girouard for advice on every matter connected with railways; but occasionally his enthusiasm over-ran his good judgment and he acted without consulting his laconic yet outspoken subordinate. For instance, on his return from England after the occupation of Dongola in the autumn of 1896, he informed Girouard gleefully that he had placed an order for six locomotives for the line across the Nubian Desert. He was promptly subjected to a somewhat severe cross-examination which showed that the locomotives were too light and generally unsuitable for their work. "How much money have you got?" asked Girouard bluntly. Kitchener quoted a figure, probably a conservative one. "Then you had better send me to England to order proper material," said the Canadian; and to England he went in February, 1897, soon after the Desert Railway was begun, being seen off by Kitchener with the injunction, "Don't spend too much, Girouard. We are terribly poor."

This warning was well justified, for although Girouard could and did exercise the utmost thrift when occasion demanded, he would never be trammelled by what he considered as false economy. The following story,[3] told by Major-General Sir William Salmond, K.C.B., Col. Commandant R.E., illustrates this trait in his character. Having been appointed in 1899 as Director of Railways for the South African War, Girouard asked the Inspector-General of Fortifications[4] to

[1] It may be noted, however, that, while the Kerma line was in use, the title "Sudan Military Railways" was employed to include both the Kerma and Desert Railways.
[2] *Life of Lord Kitchener*, by Sir George Arthur, Vol. I, p. 207. Metre-gauge material could have been obtained also from India, as it was for the Uganda Railway, which was built between 1896 and 1902.
[3] "K. and Gerry," by Brig.-General R. B. D. Blakeney, C.M.G., D.S.O., late R.E., appearing in *The National Review*, Jan., 1936, pp. 86–94.
[4] General Sir Richard Harrison, K.C.B., C.M.G., Col. Commandant R.E., who dealt with railway requirements for the South African War.

obtain an initial credit of £50,000 for the necessary stores, and a fortnight later received from an unsympathetic Treasury a notification that only £5,000 had been allotted. "Oh!" said he, gazing at the letter through his eye-glass. "I have already placed orders for £300,000 and am asking for another £150,000 to-morrow." And, *mirabile dictu*, he got it.

Before Girouard left Wadi Halfa for England, he and his assistants prepared most elaborate estimates, specifications and indents for everything which might be needed for the proposed railway to Abu Hamed. Locomotives, rolling stock, rails, sleepers, points, fastenings, signals, water-tanks, pumping plant, piping, machinery, tools and hundreds of other items appeared in the lists. Calculations were made for labour and traffic requirements: for fuel, food and water-supplies. Realising that in a waterless desert a considerable part of the train-load must be water for the locomotive, Girouard asked for heavy and powerful engines capable of drawing large loads; and later, while in London, he secured from Cecil Rhodes, Prime Minister in South Africa, permission to borrow a few 70-ton and 80-ton engines intended for the Cape and Natal Government Railways.[1] The results of his labours were truly remarkable. "We were at no time short even of a roll of brass wire," writes Blakeney. Be it remembered that the Desert Railway was no ordinary project. The line had to be laid under military precautions, at the smallest cost, and with the utmost speed; and its progress was threatened by the ever-increasing difficulty of transporting into the desert the supplies for thousands of workers. A breakdown in the supply of water might have entailed consequences which do not bear contemplation, and the greater the distance, the graver the danger of such a catastrophe and also of attack by the enemy.

On one occasion, the disaster of a water famine was averted only by the narrowest margin. Water and food were sent forward to the survey, banking and track-laying parties from rail-head, where a large area was covered by a movable canvas town of some 3,000 inhabitants; but as a precautionary measure, a reserve of 10,000 gallons was maintained at rail-head so that, in the event of a serious breakdown, the workers could survive for a few days. It so happened that, after a series of accidents had disorganized the traffic, Girouard returned from rail-head to Wadi Halfa with all the available water-tanks for refilling. He reached Halfa at 10 p.m. and gave orders for the immediate dispatch of two water-trains, and some permanent way material was added to the second train-load because it was known that the Sirdar would never tolerate any delay in the progress

[1] While in England, Girouard placed orders for 15 locomotives and 200 wagons. Meanwhile, old Egyptian Railway trucks were obtained and the wheels reset on the axles to suit a 3 ft. 6 in. instead of a 4 ft. 8½ in. gauge. These trucks had to be run in sets (because they were side-buffered, whereas the Sudan stock had centre-buffers) and the axles were constantly breaking.

of the line. Under the personal supervision of the Traffic Manager, (Lieutenant R. B. D. Blakeney, R.E.), this material was loaded in the rear trucks of the second train; but before the train started in the early hours of the morning, an enthusiastic Egyptian shunter resorted it without orders and placed the material trucks in front of the water trucks; and, to make matters worse, the station-master dispatched this train in advance of the other. At 1 p.m., a message was received from far up the line that an axle of the leading truck of the train carrying the materials had broken, and that the line was hopelessly blocked. The heat was terrific. No water could pass the obstruction, and it seemed that, within the next few days, thousands of men might perish in the desert.

Girouard promptly got into touch by telegraph with the officer in charge at rail-head. All construction was stopped; the gangs were brought in to rail-head, and an armed guard placed over the precious reserve of water. Lieutenant E. O. A. Newcombe, R.E., with the only serviceable locomotive at Wadi Halfa, and sufficient materials for laying a diversion, was dispatched at express (Desert Railway) speed to the scene of the accident with orders to re-open the line at all costs. Newcombe had already earned a reputation as a remover of wreckage, and on this occasion he accomplished wonders, for within 24 hours he completed a diversion and brought water to many thirsty men; but, before he arrived, the reserve at rail-head had sunk to a perilously low ebb, and at the first intermediate station on the line not a drop remained.

One of the many serious problems of the Sudan Military Railway was the shortage of suitable locomotives, and even after some heavy engines had arrived, the situation was always difficult and sometimes critical.[1] Desert sand and inexperienced drivers play havoc with the best machinery, and most of the Sudan engines had seen better days. In the early morning at Wadi Halfa, Kitchener often strolled in his dressing-gown round the supply yard and workshops; and one day, meeting the Works Manager, Sanderson, he asked him why a certain heavy locomotive was not running. Sanderson replied that the

---

[1] According to information sent to the author by Brig.-General R. B. D. Blakeney, C.M.G., D.S.O., late R.E., on August 17th, 1934, 17 locomotives were available, prior to May, 1897, for both the Kerma and Abu Hamed lines, the two best of which could carry only 100 tons paying load on the Kerma line or 160 tons on the Abu Hamed line; but owing to the heavy strain imposed by the Kosha-Kerma extension, which completed the Kerma line, at least one-half of the locomotives were usually under repair. At the beginning of May, two more heavy locomotives arrived, and late in July, another two. These could carry from 185 to 200 tons on the Abu Hamed line, and the best were 8-wheel coupled Neilsons or Dubs. By the middle of October, 1897, there were seven 8-wheel coupled, and four 6-wheel coupled, engines on the Abu Hamed line. The rapid progress of the line was due largely to these heavy engines. As regards rolling stock, about 90 4-wheel trucks to carry $3\frac{1}{2}$ to 8 tons, and a few saloons, brake-vans and larger trucks were available prior to May, 1897; but early in May, 52 8-wheel 10-ton trucks and about 30 4-wheel $5\frac{1}{2}$-ton trucks arrived. A complete list of the locomotives and rolling stock in use on the Sudan Military Railway a few months later (in March, 1898), appears in the *R.E. Journal*, Vol. 28, 1898, p. 149, in an article entitled "Cairo," by Bt. Colonel A. O. Green, R.E.

boiler had cracked once again and was dangerous. " Oh ! " said Kitchener sadly, " That engine could take a large train-load of supplies across the desert .... *After all, Sanderson, we aren't particular to a man or two."* Needless to say, the suggestion was not taken seriously.[1]

Early in January, 1897, the railway staff of Royal Engineer officers was strengthened by the arrival of Lieutenants G. B. Macauley, G. C. M. Hall and E. O. A. Newcombe; and, at the end of the month, Lieutenant E. C. Midwinter came with a detachment of Royal Engineer mechanics from the 8th Railway Company. In addition, Lieutenant H. A. Micklem joined at the end of February to fill the vacancy caused by the death of Cator. These reinforcements augured well for the progress of the railway; but for a time they helped it very little because the demands of the Kerma line had priority. Not until the completion of that line on May 4th could the Desert Railway receive proper attention. During January, the work consisted chiefly of making arrangements for a terminus at Wadi Halfa and of laying a few miles of track in the correct direction into the desert. At first, this track-laying was supervised by Lieutenant G. F. Gorringe, R.E. (assisted by Lieutenant G. B. Macauley, R.E.), who also superintended the Works Department at Halfa; but afterwards, Lieutenant A. G. Stevenson, R.E., spent much of his time at rail-head, though burdened also with locomotive and traffic duties at Wadi Halfa.[2] The available labourers were 350 Dervish prisoners and 300 Egyptian soldiers. "By the end of February," writes Longfield,[3] " only 17 miles of track had been built. A siding was laid down at rail-end,[4] a ragged tent was pitched, a telephone installed within it, and the first station on the Desert Railway came into being with the obvious, if uninspiring, name of ' Number One '."

The arrival of Midwinter eased the burden of Gorringe, Stevenson and Macauley; and when Girouard returned from England, Gorringe relinquished railway work and devoted his whole attention to the Works Department until he was able to hand it over to Micklem and resume his ordinary Staff duties. Later, when the Kerma line had been completed, the Railway duties were distributed as follows :—Girouard, Director; Macauley, Assistant Director and Chief Engineer of Permanent Way and Stores; Blakeney, Traffic Manager; Stevenson, assisted by Newcombe, Locomotive Superintendent; Pritchard, assisted by Hall, Survey Party; Midwinter

---

[1] The story appears in notes sent to the author by Major-General A. G. Stevenson, C.B., C.M.G., D.S.O., Col. Commandant R.E., on September 22nd, 1934.

[2] Lieut. A. G. Stevenson, R.E., was a Railway officer who had received special training in mechanical engineering.

[3] *The Sudan Railways*, by Lieut.-Colonel W. E. Longfield, R.E. (retd.)

[4] " Rail-end " is the actual end of the completed track. It may be six or seven miles in advance of " rail-head," which is the headquarters and camp of the construction parties.

Rail-head Construction ; Micklem, in charge of Workshops and Buildings. The necessary telegraph and telephone lines were laid alongside the railway by a non-commissioned officer deputed by Lieutenant M. G. E. Manifold, R.E., the Director of Military Telegraphs.[1]

For the first two months, work at rail-head on the Desert Railway was experimental, but increasing gradually in speed. The labour was mostly unskilled : the materials, indifferent or bad. " It was a time of trial, and also of error which, to some extent, yielded to treatment," writes Sir Edward Midwinter.[2] " For instance, between No. 2 and No. 3 Stations, some 20 miles of steel sleepers were laid which proved unsatisfactory because the light desert ballast could not hold them. The track became very rough. Thereafter, wooden sleepers were used and gave a good running line." At this period, two trains ran daily over the Desert Railway—a material train carrying 2,000 yards of track, and a water train with another 500 yards of track. The material train itself was heavily loaded with water, for in addition to five 1,500-gallon tanks of water it had a further 3,000 gallons in the locomotive tender.[3]

As it was known that, for a distance of at least 60 miles from Wadi Halfa, no obstacle would be encountered which would necessitate a radical change in direction, it was safe to push the railway out into the desert for the first 20 miles or so without further reconnaissance. As a matter of fact, no officer was available for such work. In March, 1897, however, after Girouard's return from England, it was considered necessary to gather more precise information as to what lay ahead, and accordingly Stevenson and Pritchard were sent on a distant reconnaissance which proved to be of the utmost importance. They rode southwards until they touched the wilderness of the Batn el Hagar, and then swung eastwards to regain and follow the probable alignment of the railway. Passing over the summit or watershed of the desert, they succeeded in reaching a point two-thirds of the way to Abu Hamed, and returned to rail-head with information of extraordinary value. They had found and followed a suitable alignment for the railway through a gap in some hills by which they entered a convenient valley (the Khor Hagar esh Shema) which seemed to have been designed by Providence to provide a path for a line to the summit ; and, beyond the summit, they

---

[1] Lieut. Manifold, R.E., was in sole charge of the telegraphs throughout the campaign, and his application for an assistant met with no success ; yet, when he resigned at the end of 1898, a Major and two Captains, R.E., were appointed in his place. As regards the railway, it may be remarked that both telegraph and telephone wires were on one line of posts near the line. The telephone service was from station to station. The telegraph service connected only the more important stations, including watering stations.

[2] Notes by Lt.-Col. Sir Edward Midwinter, K.B.E., C.B., C.M.G., D.S.O., R.E. (retd.), sent to the author on April 15th, 1936.

[3] A material train was made up as follows :—water trucks ; locomotive (tender leading) ; rail trucks ; sleeper trucks.

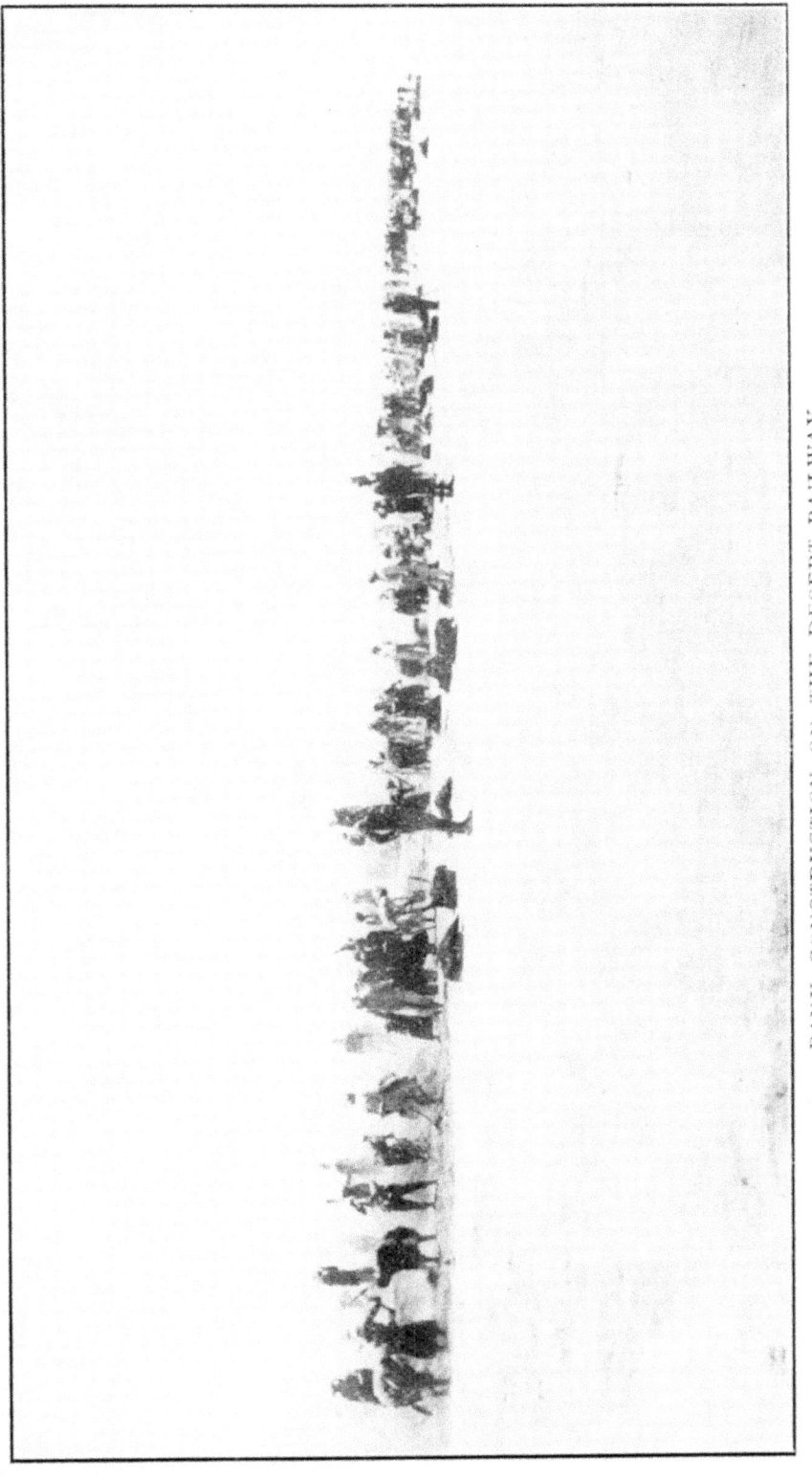

BANK CONSTRUCTION ON THE DESERT RAILWAY.

Railway Battalion working in advance of railhead in the Nubian Desert.

[*By kind permission of Brig.-General R. B. D. Blakeney, C.M.G., D.S.O., late R.E.*]

had discovered another valley (the Wadi Keheli) by which the railway might descend towards the Nile, and had traced it to a point nearly 150 miles from Wadi Halfa. Subsequently, a map was prepared by Pritchard which was a great improvement on any previous one, for it showed not only the possible railway route for two-thirds of the way to Abu Hamed, but indicated by form-lines the main features of the surrounding desert almost as far as the Nile.[1]

More important, however, than the tracing of the railway alignment and the reconnaissance of the country was the remark entered in small letters in two places on the map, referring to localities which were about 77 miles and 126 miles respectively from Wadi Halfa. " Try digging for water here," it ran. Incredible though it may appear, water was found in both these places ; and to this day, in spite of repeated attempts, *not a drop has been discovered at any other point along the desert route.* The wonderful good fortune of Kitchener has never been more clearly exemplified. The success of his daring venture was assured when the first water was drawn to the surface at the nearer locality, which afterwards became the site of Station No. 4 ; but meanwhile, he had to be satisfied with the knowledge that a practicable route existed through and beyond the intricacies of the summit area.

As the work progressed, the distant reconnaissance by Stevenson and Pritchard was followed by other more detailed and local reconnaissances by Pritchard and Hall to fix the alignment close in advance of rail-head. Only 11 miles of track were laid during April, 1897, and there was consequently no need to establish a Survey camp ahead of the railway while the rate of advance was so slow. Indeed, by the end of April, rail-head was no more than 34 miles from Wadi Halfa ; but as more rapid progress was probable when the Kerma line was finished, Pritchard and Hall then moved forward and established a separate Survey camp in order to mark out the centre-line of the track some miles ahead of the embankment gangs. Within the next few days, the Railway Battalion arrived from the Kerma line, with the result that on May 4th about 2,000 yards of track were laid, and during that month, 23 miles. Although the speed of advance was hindered by dust storms, derailments, decrepit locomotives, inexperience of the subordinate staff, an engineering strike in England, lack of sleepers in Egypt owing to a Turkish war, insufficiency of transport on the Lower Nile and a dozen other causes, better progress was made as the gangs became daily more efficient under the able direction of Midwinter. The track-laying organization settled down to a routine which was almost monotonous in its regularity. A mile of track in three hours was the rule ; and in an emergency, as, for instance, if darkness was approaching, this could

---

[1] The map appears opposite p. 79 in *Sudan Campaign, 1896—1899*, by "An Officer" (Lieut. H. L. Pritchard, R.E.).

be improved upon by the rail and sleeper carriers moving at a run. In June, after the arrival of new engines, additional speed was attained, and by the end of that month rail-head was 90 miles from Halfa and rapidly approaching the summit. Pritchard and Hall then carried out a theodolite reconnaissance (using vertical angle) to discover precisely the best route to the highest point, and afterwards reconnoitred in a similar manner for the down-grade beyond the summit.

In the middle of May, when rail-head was about 50 miles from Halfa, it had been decided that an attempt should be made to find water at the nearer point, 77 miles from Halfa, which had been indicated by Talbot and later by Stevenson and Pritchard. At the request of Lord Cromer, Kitchener had proceeded to Aswan with Gorringe in February, 1897, to meet an expert who had proposed that electrically-driven engines should be substituted for steam locomotives on the Desert Railway. The Sirdar had with him Girouard's estimate for the complete line to Abu Hamed, an estimate which made provision for the cost of plant and pipes for pumping water from the Nile at Halfa to a distance of more than 60 miles along the proposed line. The crux of the water problem was that, owing to the heavy demands of the locomotives and the construction parties, it seemed that it might be impossible to move more than 150 miles from the river. After listening to the electrical expert's proposals, which included an elaborate generating plant at Halfa, Kitchener inquired the cost, and received a quotation which effectually disposed of the scheme. Indeed, the estimated cost of the generating plant alone was equal to the total of Girouard's estimate.

A few weeks later, while Gorringe was building a bridge on the Kerma Railway, about two miles inland from the Nile, a well-digging party, working under his orders, encountered hard iron-stone rock, 60 feet below the surface, and could make no impression on it. Gorringe then sent for special stone-quarrying equipment in order to bore through the rock, which seemed to resemble the rock that had frustrated the efforts of Musa Pasha at the spot in the desert visited by Talbot, Stevenson and Pritchard. The *khor* which Gorringe was bridging, brought down storm water from that area, and it was reasonable to infer that if water was found *below* the rock at the bridge site, and the rock proved to be identical with that in the desert, water might be obtainable also at the desert locality from beneath the rock, although none was available above it. Accordingly, he proceeded to test this theory.

"After some weeks of hard work," writes Sir George Gorringe,[1] "my well-digging party, reinforced by convicts from Halfa,

[1] Notes by Lieut.-General Sir George Gorringe, K.C.B., K.C.M.G., D.S.O., Col. Commandant R.E., sent to the author on August 5th, 1936.

penetrated through six feet of hard rock and found water under it. The water was oozing in from a southerly or south-easterly direction and not from the Nile, which was at a lower level, and it was clear and drinkable. Beneath the rock was a thin layer of moist chalk, and below that, sand. We soon had four feet of water in the well. I returned at once to Halfa and suggested to the Sirdar that a well should be sunk at the spot in the desert visited by Talbot. He agreed, so I ordered my well-digging party back from the bridge and left instructions that they should be sent out to rail-head in the desert where camels would meet them." The well-digging party was guided from rail-head by Pritchard, arrangements being made with the Ababda Arabs at Murrat Wells to supply the party with water at Jebel Nahoganet, a large hill to the east of the alignment. The Arabs failed to appear, so Pritchard left some tools to mark the spot, and marched his party back to rail-head after existing for 40 hours on a tin of Bovril.[1]

When news was received later that the Arabs had found the tools, and had deposited sufficient water in skins, Gorringe took the party out again, made a careful reconnaissance of the basin or saucer-shaped depression indicated by Talbot, selected the place where the well was to be sunk, and left an Egyptian officer to begin the work. " After excavating some 50 to 60 feet," continues Sir George, " the party came upon iron-stone rock identical with that we had found at the bridge. We redoubled our efforts, and after nearly three weeks' work reached water, trickling in below the rock from a southerly direction, and noticed beneath the rock the same chalky deposit. I took a bottle of the water to Halfa and showed it to Colonel Maxwell, the Commandant, who remarked, " Don't say a word ! We will have some fun with the Sirdar when he arrives." He poured the water into a sparklet bottle and put the bottle in ice. In came Kitchener, and was invited by Maxwell to have a whisky and soda. The " soda " came from the sparklet bottle, and Kitchener, not liking the taste, asked Maxwell what it was ; to which Maxwell replied that they had wished to give him a surprise and that I had brought the water from the well in the desert. Kitchener was overjoyed. He gave instructions to hold up the order for pumping plant and piping, and I went back to superintend the development of the water-supply at the place which subsequently became No. 4 Station. I was told to press on with the work and report the result. Additional convicts were sent out, and when rail-head reached the site, I handed over the work to the Railway construction party."

Water had been struck at a depth of 72 feet.[2] A steam-pump was erected and an abundant yield obtained. Another well was then

[1] Notes by Major-General H. L. Pritchard, C.B., C.M.G., D.S.O., Col. Commandant R.E., sent to the author on January 14th, 1936.
[2] Paper entitled " Sudan Government Military Railways," read by Major G. B. Macauley, R.E., before the International Engineering Congress at Glasgow in 1901.

sunk about 30 yards from the first, and the two were connected by a tunnel below the rock. Gorringe was asked for advice as to how this tunnel should be driven below water-level. "Quite simple," said he. "Put an Egyptian working party down the first well, cover the top, and tell them to come up the other!" Subsequently a third well was sunk and connected to the first. In an atmosphere of dust, sweat and good-humoured banter, the railway was thrust out slowly into the ever-shifting mirages of the southern desert, screened at first by patrols of friendly Arabs, but afterwards covered also by the pickets of a battalion of Egyptian infantry.[1]

Bereft of humour, the lives of the toilers in the Nubian Desert would have been unendurable. Thousands of men were isolated in a savage desolation of glittering sand with here and there a few huge masses of crumbling rock. They were connected with the outer world only by two thin rails stretching in long perspective as far as the eye could see; and they laboured from dawn to sunset, without relaxation and with machine-like regularity, towards the vague and shimmering horizon beyond which lay Abu Hamed and the Nile. Mirages mocked them on all sides with lakes and rivulets, and often an ocean seemed to stretch in front of them; even the line behind them appeared at times to be submerged in a flood which reflected the telegraph posts as in a mirror. Nevertheless, Rail-head camp was a cheerful place, and its favourite comedian, a Dervish prisoner working on the railway, amused the officers and men with mimicry and comedy of a high order. "He pretended to catch mice," writes a correspondent,[2] "burrowing his fists into the sand and imitating the squeak of the little animal when caught. Then a supposed scorpion stung him on the toe. Next, he imitated numerous Emirs, their truculent walk and their audiences with the people, and finally the hanging of a spy. During the performance, I stood sketching. His quick eye caught the situation, and he finished up his performance with an imitation of the artist at work that fairly brought down the house, or rather the tent."

Only $20\frac{1}{2}$ miles of line were laid during July, 1897, because of a shortage of materials; but this slow progress did not worry Girouard because he dared not approach too close to Abu Hamed until the enemy had been driven from it. On July 23rd, the railway reached the summit, 103 miles from Wadi Halfa, without once overstepping the limits of curve and gradient laid down by Girouard,[3] and also without diverging, except on one occasion, from the general alignment fixed by the reconnaissances. The line was now thoroughly well laid, and carried very heavy trainloads with safety and speed.

[1] The 18th Egyptian Infantry, under Capt. G. H. Ford-Hutchinson, which arrived at rail-head in July, 1897.
[2] Article by the Special Correspondent of *The Standard*, published on September 11th, 1897.
[3] A curve of six degrees and a gradient of 1 in 120.

This was a fine achievement, and brought to a conclusion the most difficult part of the undertaking. The average daily progress during the month was $1\frac{1}{3}$ miles; but on the 27th, 2 miles 80 yards of track were laid, a record which remained unbeaten until close on 3 miles were laid near Abu Hamed on October 25th. The capture of that place by General Hunter on August 7th affected the railway in two ways. The line could now be prolonged without fear of attack; and the utmost speed of advance became essential in order to reach the Nile as quickly as possible, so that the pressure on the precarious lines of supply by the river from Merowe, and by the caravan route through Murrat Wells, might be relieved.

On August 12th, Pritchard and Macauley set out on camels to reconnoitre the last 100 miles which lay between rail-head and Abu Hamed. They reached their destination, and returned to report that easy country continued to within a few miles of the town and that the descent from the summit would not present any serious difficulty. Their estimate of the total length of railway from Wadi Halfa to Abu Hamed proved to be correct to within two miles. It was obtained by recording the times of journeying and by estimating the pace of their camels, which varied according to the time of day or night.

The efforts of the gangs were redoubled, and during the month of August no less than 40 miles of track were laid, in spite of the exasperating but necessary duty of moving camp every four or five days without delaying the work. According to Longfield, the appearance of the rail-head train at such times was that of a refugee train whose passengers had abandoned a threatened area at the last possible moment! Nevertheless, there was order in the apparent chaos. A routine had been established. Every man knew his duty. Stations dotted the line behind the labouring gangs—No. 4 at the first source of water; No. 5 at the summit. At the beginning of September, rail-head was only 80 miles from the Nile; and on September 15th, after a month of strenuous endeavour, water was found near Mile 126 at a depth of 96 feet, and Station No. 6 at that point became an important "half-way house" and depot on the route between Halfa and Abu Hamed.[1]

The country was now open: landmarks there were none. Accordingly, as it was essential to strike direct for Abu Hamed, a couple of Arab guides were called in to verify the alignment fixed by theodolite and compass. "They glared at the sun and scrutinized the range of low hills which bounded the plain to north and south," writes

[1] The stations established on the Wadi Halfa-Abu Hamed line, and their distances in miles from Halfa, were as follows:—No. 1—17; No. 2—35; No. 3—52; No. 4—77 (Water); No. 5—103 (Summit); No. 6—126 (Water); No. 7—149; No. 8—174; No. 9—199; Abu Hamed—230. A siding was laid at every station. The distances are those given by Major G. B. Macauley, R.E., in a paper entitled "Sudan Government Military Railways," which he read before the International Engineering Congress in Glasgow in 1901.

Longfield.[1] "They bent their gaze on the level and featureless horizon to the south-east. The Survey officer showed them how to turn the telescope on its axis and told them to aim it like a gun at Abu Hamed. They consulted together, and then one stepped forward and moved the telescope through a fraction of a point. He drew back, and his companion looked through the sight and nodded his head. The bearing was laid down. On that alignment the railway runs for 45 miles, and the detailed surveys of later years show that the error in direction is less than a degree of arc."

During the last five months, the difficulties of the railway staff were administrative rather than technical. The distance from Wadi Halfa increased daily. The rate of laying had to be accelerated. Engines could only be turned at No. 5 Station. Towards Abu Hamed, when the camp had to be moved every few days—working mostly by night—rail-head would be already a mile in advance of the new camp by the time that the last tent was pitched. Banking parties had to march miles ahead to their work and be watered by camel transport. Every little crossing station was a likely source of derailment. At the beginning of October, only 47 miles of line remained to be completed. It was with a sigh of relief that the Nile was reached at Abu Hamed on October 31st. A material train, half of which was composed of tank-trucks carrying water, had been brought from Wadi Halfa, 230 miles distant. Sufficient material was in hand for only 17 miles of track; but the critics had been confounded by Kitchener's "Band of Boys," who had accomplished what may justly be classed as one of the most remarkable engineering feats of modern times.

An amusing letter from a Special—very Special—Correspondent of the *R.E. Journal*, describing the amenities of Wadi Halfa and a trip over the Desert Railway in October, 1897, may be quoted as an example of the light-hearted spirit which triumphed over the dangers and difficulties of the Sudan. Writing from hospital in Wadi Halfa, the "Special Correspondent" says:—[2]"I have just returned from a visit to rail-head on the Sudan Military Railway, and as the medical officer has ordered me to abstain from alcoholic liquors for a few days, I shall endeavour to describe the progress of this unique undertaking. Halfa has changed beyond all recognition since the Dongola campaign; whereas then it was nasty and noisy, now it is nastier and noisier. The R.E. Staff consists of six officers; but it is unnecessary to repeat their names since this information can be obtained from the *Supplement* to the *R.E. Journal*, which shows them as stationed at Dongola or Cairo. The management of the Sudan Military Railway, under the control of the Sirdar, is in

---

[1] *The Sudan Railways*, by Lieut.-Colonel W. E. Longfield, R.E. (retd.).
[2] Article entitled "The Advance on the Nile," appearing in the *R.E. Journal*, Vol. 27, 1897, p. 241.

SHIFTING CAMP ON THE DESERT RAILWAY.
Rail-head Staff in front.

[*By kind permission of Brig.-General R. B. D. Blakeney, C.M.G., D.S.O., late R.E.*]

the hands of a band of boys, not yet out of their teens. Their keenness is striking; they are typical specimens of what the Britisher is when he is abroad; they never grumble at their food; they never swear; they view with loathing the thought of leave, and they drink nothing but water.[1] This last, strange to say, is found in the River Nile; and it is a true saying that 'They who drink Nile water will never want to drink water again '—for they die of enteric."

The "Special Correspondent" continues:— "We proceeded to rail-head in a first-class saloon, fitted with means for cooling drinks, viz., unglazed earthern jars, supplied by the passenger. Travelling on this line involves fearful hardships. The ice has to be paid for; also, one has to sleep on a camp bed in the saloon instead of reclining on a seat 15 inches wide as at home, and to take a luncheon basket, cooked food, eggs and some fowls for subsistence on the road. Then there are the calculations for liquid refreshment. These are best solved by a formula." [Here the Special Correspondent gives a differential equation in which "dt" figures prominently, and a second equation said to be taken from the *Principles of Internal Structural Design, Part II.*] ... "The train started by the usual signal, *i.e.*, by an Egyptian waving a red flag. The pure dry air of the desert produces a peculiar effect on most people, who at once quote the Arab saying ' There are but two diseases in the desert—hunger and thirst '—and act accordingly. As the journey was performed by night, and as there was no moon, we were fortunate enough to see exquisite mirages on the horizon—cascades, towns, merry-go-rounds, casinos, spires, public-houses and pawn-shops. Can anyone explain this wonderful phenomenon? ... The new towns which are springing up in the desert around the recently discovered wells, are objects of peculiar interest. They consist normally of two tents and an engine-hut, and in the course of time we may see another hut added. Very interesting also are the results of the experiments made here as regards the overturning of trucks round curves, and the passage of rolling stock over split points. Rail-head camp and the working parties are protected by covering parties of infantry, and the camp is further entrenched behind a cordon of broken bottles. Our total expenses for the three days' trip are being scheduled by our creditors."

The unexpected evacuation of Berber on August 24th, 1897, and its subsequent occupation by the Egyptian forces under General Hunter, had rendered it necessary in November to push the railway southwards from Abu Hamed with the utmost speed. The materials in hand were used accordingly for the prolongation of the line through broken country for a distance of about 17 miles to Dagash, while an urgent telegram was sent to England for another 150 miles

---

[1] Needless to say, the "Special Correspondent" is writing in a highly sarcastic vein. The R.E. Staff were normal British officers.

of material for an extension to the Atbara River. The additional material did not arrive until January, 1898, so construction came temporarily to a halt with Dagash as rail-head. However, there was ample work for Girouard and his staff on the line already laid, and the Traffic officers were particularly busy in forwarding the reinforcements and supplies needed for the army.[1] When construction was resumed, it was found that the work was easy and pleasant for the first 35 miles from Dagash. The gangs were expert, the weather was cool, water-trains were no longer needed while the Broad Nile ran close alongside, and rest and shade could be enjoyed beneath the palms which clustered on the bank. During January, the railway was prolonged to Abu Dis, 22 miles from Dagash. Early in March, after traversing some difficult country, it had advanced a further 23 miles to Shereik; and on March 10th, rail-head was at Bashtinab, some 13 miles beyond Shereik and nearly 75 miles from Abu Hamed.[2]

Reconnaissances from Bashtinab showed that the country near the Nile was broken and rocky for the next 50 miles, so Girouard decided to leave the river bank, and having made a wide detour through the level desert, to bring the line back to the Nile above the cataracts near Abidiya.[3] He could afford neither the time nor the money for numerous cuttings, embankments and bridges. From Abidiya, there is a clear waterway at High Nile as far as the Sixth Cataract below Omdurman, hence it was clearly indicated as an ideal spot for the resumption of an alignment along the river bank. When the Battle of the Atbara was fought on April 8th, 1898, rail-head was still in the Abu Sillem Desert, some 20 miles north-east of a place called Gananita, which lies a few miles north of Abidiya; but Abidiya, was reached on May 5th, after traversing a difficult stretch of country in which water-trains were necessary once more. Railhead was then 110 miles from Abu Hamed and only 22 miles short of Berber. Reception sidings for the new gunboats *Melik*, *Sultan* and *Sheikh* were put in hand at Abidiya, and Major W. S. Gordon R.E., arrived to superintend the assembly of the sections of the vessels, which were brought by rail from Wadi Halfa.[4] Meanwhile, construction had been resumed steadily southwards, through easy country near the Nile bank, to Berber; it proceeded thence for another 14 miles to Darmali, and finally to Fort Atbara, 155 miles from Abu Hamed and 385 miles from Wadi Halfa. The railway reached its temporary terminus at the junction of the Nile and the Atbara on July 3rd, 1898; to carry it farther southwards by bridging

[1] Valuable assistance was given to Lieut. R. B. D. Blakeney, R.E., the Traffic Manager, by Muhammad Effendi Fadil (now El Lewa Muhammad Fadil Pasha), an Egyptian Traffic Superintendent with great initiative, whom the author had the pleasure of meeting in Cairo in February, 1935.
[2] See the *Sketch Map of the Sudan Government Military Railways in* 1900, which is included in this chapter.
[3] This detour no longer exists, for in 1911 it was replaced by a direct line along the Nile bank.
[4] See Chapter VIII.

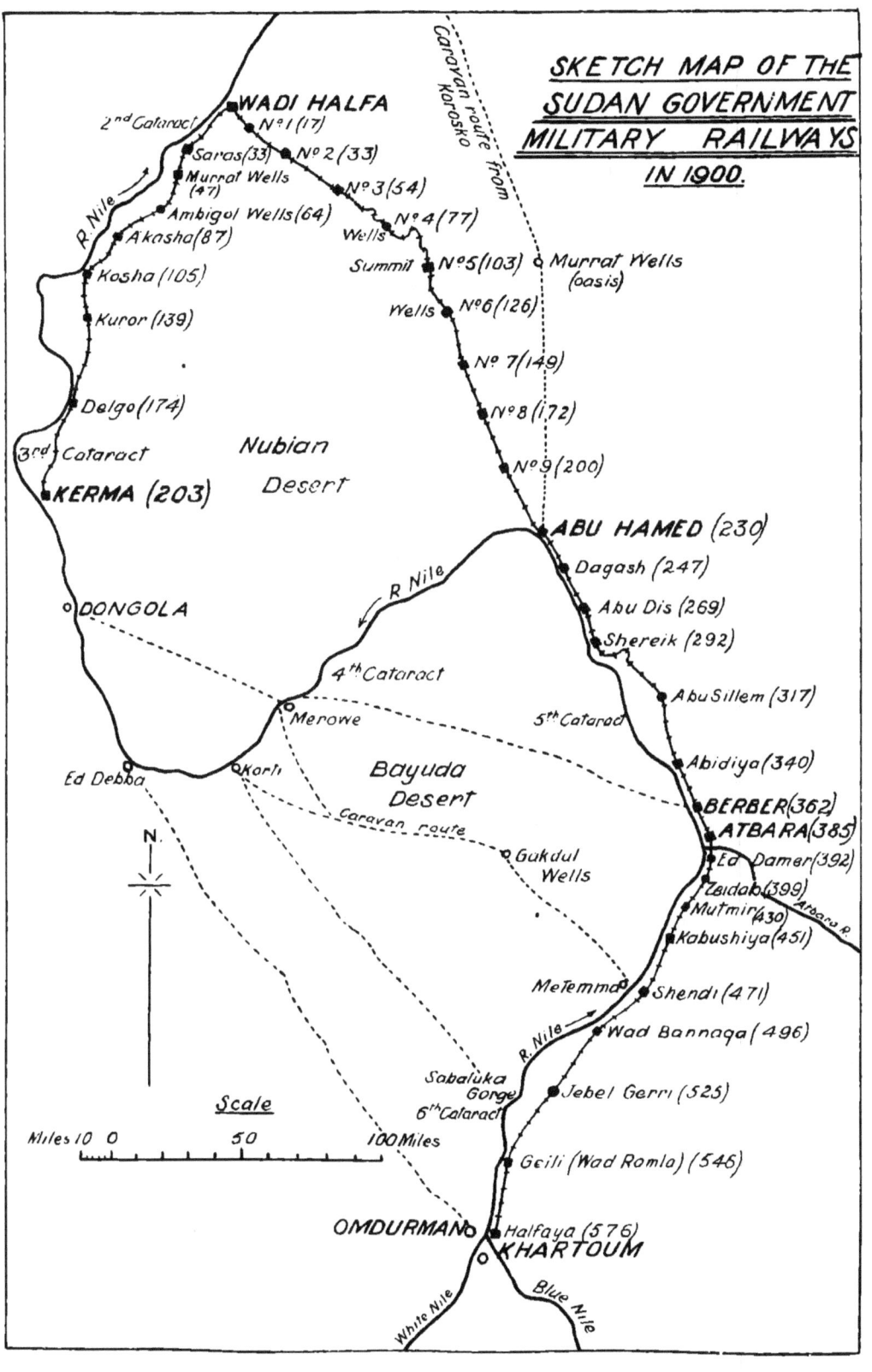

the Atbara was unnecessary and unjustifiable until Khartoum had been recaptured. The site was surveyed, and materials for a temporary bridge were ordered; but otherwise the energies of the railway staff were devoted wholly to the development of the terminus at Fort Atbara, and to the transport of troops, stores and supplies in preparation for an autumn campaign.

The Khalifa had never seen a railway, though his spies had informed him that " it was like a steamer, except that it went on wheels on the land and could not go in the water, and every time it arrived it brought a pile of supplies as high as a mountain."[1] However, the Battle of the Atbara had taught him what railway communication meant, and, as Winston Churchill puts it,[2] " On the day that the first troop train steamed into the fortified camp at the confluence of the Nile and Atbara Rivers, the doom of the dervishes was sealed." The Khalifa, his capital and his army were now within the Sirdar's reach. By means of the railway, troops could be sent into the heart of the Sudan, independent of the season of the year or the level of the river. They could be fully supplied with food and ammunition and properly supported by gunboats operating not only to Khartoum but to the distant waters of the Upper Nile.

Interesting details of a journey from Cairo to rail-head in the Sudan during the spring of 1898, are given by Brevet Colonel A. O. Green, R.E., a most energetic and popular C.R.E. in Egypt. " I felt it a little hard," he writes,[3] " to be left always at the base whilst Major Friend was able to get away as British Staff Officer to Assuan, where he has done right good work in a very onerous and responsible position,[4] and whilst Lieutenant Moir went up to the front with a detachment of the 2nd Company, R.E. However, I was allowed eventually to go as far as rail-head on the Sudan Railway, and starting on the night of February 22nd, I travelled up by rail to Nag Hamadi with Mr. John Aird,[5] who was on his way to inspect the site for the Assuan dam, which had just been sanctioned. At Nag Hamadi, we joined General Sir Francis Grenfell, G.C.M.G., K.C.B., and proceeded to Luxor, where a halt was made for the night. On

---

[1] *Sudan Campaign*, 1896—1899, by " An Officer " (Lieut. H. L. Pritchard, R.E.), p. 137.

[2] *The River War*, by the Rt. Hon. Winston Churchill, M.P., p. 182. Chapter VIII of that book contains an excellent descriptive account of the building of the Desert Railway.

[3] Article entitled " Cairo," by Brevet Colonel A. O. Green, R.E., appearing in the *R.E. Journal*, Vol. 28, 1898, pp. 131–133 and 147–150.

[4] Major (now Major-General Sir Lovick) Friend, R.E., was Staff Officer at Aswan from January to June, 1898, and afterwards Provost Marshal to the Anglo-Egyptian Army in the advance to Omdurman. The maintenance of a proper system of supply through Aswan, during the final stages of the Atbara Campaign, was due largely to his work on the line of communication. Another Royal Engineer who did valuable work on the line of communication was Major (afterwards Major-General) A. E. Sandbach, who was successively A.A.G. Dongola District, Commandant at Wadi Halfa, and A.A.G. Line of Communication, and finally came to the front as A.A.G. Headquarter Staff in time to be present, with Major Friend, at the Battle of Omdurman.

[5] Afterwards Sir John Aird, the famous engineer.

the following morning we started in a special train over the new extension to Assuan. A worse line I never travelled on. It has all the faults it is possible for a line to have. It is badly laid, the work is scamped, the rolling stock is indifferent, and watering arrangements are entirely wanting. The General asked me to write a report on the railway, and I did not spare it. On the 26th, we left Shellal for Halfa in the sternwheeler *Amkeh*. We had a very pleasant party on board, having been joined by Colonel Wingate, C.B., D.S.O., at Assuan, and we reached Halfa on February 28th. It was with great regret that we saw the General and his A.D.C. off on their return journey down the river, and, in company with Colonel Wingate, Surgeon-Captain Adamson and Bimbashi Macauley,[1] started for rail-head."

Colonel Green then gives a concise history of the building of the Desert Railway, and describes the country through which he passed on his way to Abu Hamed. On March 2nd, he visited rail-head near Shereik. "No sooner," he writes, "had our train, of 280 tons' load and carrying about one and a half miles of permanent way, come to a standstill, than it was attacked by an enormous *toulba* (fatigue party) of men from Lieutenant Midwinter's construction companies, who surrounded the trucks like ants. In a few minutes, two long strings of men were passing to the front along the sides of the formation level, each man carrying a sleeper on his shoulder, which he dumped down at a distance of two and a half feet from the preceding one—12 sleepers being allowed to a 30-foot rail, which weighs about 50 pounds per yard. Next came the rails, each carried on the shoulders of eight or nine men, who placed it in its approximate position and doubled back for more. The rails were then adjusted to the three feet six inches gauge-marks on the sleepers, and the ends spiked to the nearest sleepers by the spiking party. Next the fish-plate men came along and fixed each fish-plate temporarily with two bolts only, and the line was straightened to allow the material train to advance over it. Behind the train came other parties to straighten, spike, bolt up fish-plates, and lift the rails into their proper and final places, and finally came the ballasting party.[2] Everybody knew, after months of practice, exactly what to do, and progress was very rapid. In fact, while we had lunch in the train, we advanced about 200 yards over the line as it was laid down in front of us, so that it is easy to understand that, given sufficient material and men, it was no empty boast of Lieutenant Girouard to say that he could lay four miles in one day."

Writing of the staff and personnel of the railway organization in June, 1898, Green remarks:— "The Sudan Railways are worked by a staff of eight or nine officers of the Royal Engineers. They are

[1] Lieutenant G. B. Macauley, R.E., who, in common with all young British officers posted to the Egyptian Army, had joined with the rank of "Bimbashi" or Major.
[2] Stone ballast was not available. Sand or gravel was used.

assisted by a Railway Department Civil Staff of 444 civilians, of whom 59 are on the Kerma line, and by a large military element consisting of 34 R.E. N.C.O's and men, mostly drivers, fitters and platelayers, and an Egyptian Railway Battalion comprising 33 native officers, two quartermasters, and 2,882 N.C.O's and men, of whom 210 are employed on the Kerma line. These men are not clothed in uniform, nor are they armed. The Railway Battalion is organized in ' Base,' ' Traffic,' ' Platelaying,' ' Loco. and Carriage ' and ' Construction ' companies. The total number, all told, is 3,491 officers and men."[1]

The strictures passed by Colonel A. O. Green in February, 1898, on the Egyptian line from Luxor to Aswan had a profound effect, for they resulted, within the next few months, in the departure of Girouard from the Sudan and the severance of his connection with Kitchener until the outbreak of the South African War. Although the Luxor-Aswan line had been guaranteed by the Egyptian State Railways to carry 10,000 tons per diem, the Sirdar, who had travelled over it, entertained grave doubts concerning its reliability. He could not afford to overlook a defective link in his main chain of communication while contemplating important offensive operations. Green's report confirmed his misgivings, and in the spring of 1898, he ordered Girouard to inspect the line and give his opinion.

Girouard went to Luxor with Hall, whom he set forthwith to improve the traffic over the railway to Aswan, and having made a detailed inspection of the line, he reported that it was in a deplorable condition and that, unless drastic steps were taken, its capacity could not exceed 5,000 tons per diem. This was a heavy blow to Kitchener. A conference was called by Lord Cromer, who thus met Girouard for the first time and was much impressed by his knowledge and ability. Girouard was directed to assume charge of the Luxor-Aswan Railway and to remedy its defects within three months, a task which he accomplished successfully and at the same time laid down a programme of further improvements which lasted for a score of years. Cromer now wished to retain Girouard in Egypt, and in June, 1898, he offered the Canadian (who was still a subaltern at the age of 31) the highly-paid appointment of " President of Egyptian State Railways and Alexandria Harbour." Kitchener, with fine generosity, urged Girouard to accept the offer. After all, said he, Girouard's work for the army in the Sudan had been completed when the railway reached the Atbara. Reluctantly, Girouard agreed and departed for Cairo, thus exchanging the camp for the office, and missing the glory and excitement of Omdurman. He was succeeded as Director of Railways by his able assistant, Lieutenant G. B. Macauley, R.E., on whom fell the chief burden of the rapid

[1] Colonel A. O. Green includes a list of the Royal Engineers employed, but omits Lieut. W. R. G. Wollen, R.E., who joined the staff of the Sudan Military Railways in May, 1898, and carried out his duties with marked ability.

extension of the Sudan railway system after the re-occupation of Khartoum. Girouard, however, was inimitable and irreplaceable, and his departure was mourned by the remainder of Kitchener's "Band of Boys," whom he had led with so much skill and energy across the Nubian Desert and up the Nile.

We turn now from Railways to Telegraphs to record some of the extensions of a system which played a most important part, not only in the Dongola Expedition, but in every phase of the subsequent operations on the Nile and the Atbara, and southwards to Khartoum. Telegraphic communication was indispensable to the Sirdar, and he was enjoined by Lord Cromer never to leave the end of the wire. In June, 1897, when Lieutenant M. G. E. Manifold, R.E., returned from sick leave, the telegraph system in the province of Dongola was in good condition, and £2,000 had been allotted for the provision of additional instruments, wire and poles for further extensions. In July, General Hunter began his preparations for an advance up the Nile from Kassinger at the foot of the Fourth Cataract. Thither Manifold proceeded in order to lay a line in the wake of the troops. It was necessary for strategical reasons that Hunter should advance up the right bank, although the existing telegraph line downstream of Kassinger followed the left bank. Hence a cable had to be laid across the river. This was accomplished without difficulty at Kassinger on July 26th, for the Nile was low and only 650 yards wide, and Kitchener had ordered 1,000 yards of cable. He had not forgotten the shortage at Kerma.

Manifold was ordered to prepare at once for the construction of a line along the right bank to Abu Hamed, but was warned that no camel transport could be spared until Hunter had taken that place.[1] "The local Sheikhs will *like*, no doubt, to provide you with donkeys," said Kitchener. A number of decrepit animals having been collected, they were inspected by the Sirdar himself, and when it was pointed out to him that they had no pack saddles, he pushed a donkey over a 110-pound coil of wire, guided its hind legs into the coil, and had the coil hoisted over the animal's rump so that the wire rested on its back and encircled its body. Rough saddle-trees and pads were soon manufactured, and thus the transport problem appeared to have been solved; but Manifold records a few days later "the donkeys are getting rather tired of playing at hoops and have taken to lying down with a flop as soon as loaded!"

Boat transport having been secured for all the poles and some of the wire, Manifold started from Kassinger with 65 donkeys on August 5th, 1897, when Hunter was nearing Abu Hamed, and laid

[1] All the facts in connection with the Telegraph operations, which are recorded in this chapter, are taken from notes sent to the author by Major-General Sir Graham Bowman-Manifold, K.B.E., C.B., C.M.G., D.S.O., late R.E., on Sept. 17th, 1934, and from letters written by the same officer (then Lieut. M. G. E. Manifold) in 1897 and 1898.

COLONEL SIR EDOUARD PERCY CRANWILL GIROUARD, K.C.M.G., D.S.O., LATE ROYAL ENGINEERS.

a line through Mushra el Abiad, Shebabit and Abu Haraz to Hosh el Geref opposite Birti.[1] It has been recorded that the wire was paid out from the backs of the donkeys as they moved along,[2] but unfortunately no such picturesque method could be adopted. Each coil, as it was needed, was unloaded from the animal and unwound off a drum by hand haulage—a slow and wearisome process. No attempt was made to raise the wire on poles, firstly because speed was essential, and secondly because transport was scarce. At Mushra el Abiad, after 18 miles of desert marching, Manifold writes :—" My donkeys are very tired, and I daresay several will die to-night. This place is awful—barren rocks and no shade. The big cataract roars by my bedside."

While the gunboats and other river craft fought their way through the Fourth Cataract, the Telegraph detachment plodded steadily onwards alongside them, laying their bare wire through Salmi, Dakhfili, El Kab and Keheili (Khula) to Abu Hamed, which Hunter had captured on August 7th. Berber had been occupied on September 5th, and orders were received on the 13th for an extension of the telegraph line to that town. This was taken in hand by Corporal Dennett, R.E., while Manifold at Kassinger started Corporal Lewis, R.E., on preparations for poling the line from that place to Abu Hamed. A line was laid also from rail-head in the Nubian Desert to Abu Hamed. The progress of the poling operations depended mainly on the supply of poles, and this in turn on the amount of water-transport available up to Merowe. The poling party was often 150 miles or more in rear of the wire-laying party.

On October 2nd, 1897, when the wire-laying party had almost reached Berber, direct transmission was established with Kassinger through 236 miles of bare wire lying on the ground. No difficulty was experienced between 9 a.m. and 9 p.m.; but at night the insulating property of the sandy desert deteriorated, and distant signalling was uncertain or impossible. In December, the poling party reached Abu Hamed; and in the middle of January, the wire-laying party arrived at Fort Atbara, while the poling party was making rapid progress along the railway south of Abu Hamed.

It will be remembered that Manifold acted as a " galloper " during the Battle of the Atbara on April 8th, 1898.[3] Immediately after the capture of the *zariba*, he was hailed by the Sirdar, who gave him a telegram to Lord Cromer and ordered him to ride as fast as possible to the telegraph office at Fort Atbara, 32 miles distant, and on his way to set the Jaalin Arabs in pursuit of the fleeing dervishes on the other bank. " I left Nakheila at 9.45 a.m.," he writes, " and rode at a canter, with occasional halts to mop my brow. At Abadar, which I reached at 11.20, I had an extraordinary

[1] See the *Sketch Map of the Nile from Kerma to Metemma*, included in Chapter VIII.
[2] *The River War* (original edition), by Winston Churchill, Vol. I, p. 325.
[3] See Chapter VIII.

reception. The Jaalin shouted, "What news?" I replied, "*Mahmud Khalass*" (Mahmud is finished). I told the Arabs that we had caught Mahmud, and ordered the Sheikh to pursue. The Jaalin ran alongside my horse, leaping and shouting. The din was indescribable. Every man fired his rifle into the air, and my horse became almost unmanageable. At 12.15 p.m., I rode into Hudi, and arrived at Fort Atbara at 2 p.m. The dispatch was in Cromer's hands at 2.38, and I had a receipt at 2.50. Then I went to bed. At 4 p.m., the first Press messages came in; at 7 p.m., more Press messages; and at 7.30 p.m., the remainder of the Sirdar's dispatches, which had started by ordinary messenger only one and a half hours after me. . . . I have worked right through the knees of my breeches, and my boots are giving way at the stitching."

The transmission of Press messages bore heavily on the telegraph operators. Although the Sirdar disliked publicity, he had relaxed to some extent the rigid regulations which had governed the movements of Press correspondents, and the result was an ever increasing pile of manuscript. The correspondents met with the greatest courtesy and consideration from Colonel Wingate, who acted as Censor, but they had not the freedom enjoyed by their modern prototypes. In 1896, Kitchener had maintained that, as the Dongola Campaign was purely an Egyptian affair, no British correspondents were necessary. He added that the newspapers often sent out unsuitable men, and that he could not afford to supply transport to those who came. At first, the unfortunate correspondents were forbidden to proceed beyond rail-head; but later they were prohibited only from going out on reconnaissances, joining or preceding the firing line in general actions, or approaching the Sirdar. They were advised that, in the intervals between campaigns, they might, with advantage, return to Cairo. In some of these restrictions, Kitchener was supported by Lord Cromer; but an agitation in Fleet Street brought about a modification of the regulations affecting Press correspondents in the Sudan, and in the end the correspondents came to be tolerated, if not welcomed, by the Sirdar, and proved themselves most agreeable companions in the field.

On at least one occasion, Kitchener made use of the Press correspondents to further his plans. For instance, in November, 1897, the correspondents at Berber, having learnt that no advance on Omdurman was likely to take place until the following year, wished to return to Cairo by the newly opened route to Suakin. This route, through Obak and Sinkat, had been reconnoitred by Lieutenant G. F. Gorringe, R.E., who afterwards made his way to the Atbara and back to Berber.[1] He reported that facilities existed for the construction of a railway leading through Obak and Sinkat to the neighbourhood of Sheikh Barghut, a creek to the north of Suakin,

---

[1] Lieutenant G. F. Gorringe, R.E., was sent to report on the water-supply at Obak.

and finally to Suakin itself. Kitchener listened carefully. Then he said, " Keep that to yourself. Don't say a word to the War Correspondents. We need all our money for the railway from Wadi Halfa to Berber. I have sent the correspondents by the route beyond Sinkat which leads through the Red Sea hills, so that they may report how utterly *impossible* it is to make a railway to Suakin."[1]

Four days after the Battle of the Atbara, Manifold started for Suakin to arrange for the construction of a telegraph line from that port to Berber, and having reached his destination after eleven days on the road, superintended the commencement of the work on May 1st by Sapper May, R.E. Afterwards, he inspected the first few miles of a line through Tokar to Kassala, on which Corporal Lewis, R.E., was employed, and while at Tokar he learnt that Major H. M. Lawson, R.E., had recently passed through that place on his way to Kassala. The work executed by Corporal Lewis and Sapper May deserves the highest praise. Single-handed, and with little experience of the country and its inhabitants, or knowledge of the language, each of these subordinates overcame every difficulty encountered during months of wandering in unmapped deserts. On June 23rd, 77 miles of the Kassala line and 52 miles of the Berber line had been laid; on July 1st, the distances were 100 miles and 73 miles respectively; and by August 3rd, 1898, 167 miles of the Kassala line, and four-fifths of the line to Berber, had been completed. Both telegraph lines were finished after the crisis of the Omdurman Campaign.[2] They afford two instances, among many, of the readiness of non-commissioned officers of the Corps to take responsibility, and the reliance that could be placed on them in the very difficult conditions existing in the Sudan.

Early in June, 1898, Manifold left the Red Sea Littoral and proceeded to Cairo, where he was informed by the Sirdar that the telegraph was to be extended at once from Fort Atbara to Metemma and an additional wire provided between Abu Hamed and Fort Atbara. An extension to Metemma involved the crossing of the Nile, so Manifold next repaired to Suez where, on June 16th, he superintended the loading of 1,200 yards of cable on to a truck. This cable was one of the first consignments to reach Fort Atbara (Dakhila) after the terminus of the railway was established there on July 4th; and by that date, Sergeant Dennett, R.E., shielded by the Jaalin Arabs, had completed a bare-wire extension along the left bank of the Nile to Metemma.[3]

[1] Notes by Lieut.-General Sir George Gorringe, K.C.B., K.C.M.G., D.S.O., Col. Commandant R.E., sent to the author on Jan. 28th, 1936.
[2] The telegraph line from Suakin reached Kassala on September 24th, 1898, but the line to Berber was not completed until November 22nd.
[3] Corporal Dennett, R.E., had been promoted to the rank of Sergeant after the Battle of the Atbara. He wished to lay the wire beyond Metemma, but was forbidden to make the attempt, so he proceeded with the poling of the line as far as Metemma. During the advance on Omdurman in August 1898, he was able to prolong the poling to Wad Hamid.

In order to establish connection with Dennett's line, it was decided that an attempt should be made as soon as possible to lay the cable across the Nile at Fort Atbara, below the confluence of the Nile and Atbara Rivers. Accordingly, it was loaded on to a gunboat, and on July 7th the ship steamed slowly towards the left bank while the cable was paid out from a large coil on her deck. For a time, all went well. Then one turn became entangled in others, a huge knot formed, the anchor was dropped, the anchor-chain broke, and it was necessary to cut the cable with an axe. The gunboat returned to the right bank with only 600 yards of line. Bitterly disappointed though he was, the Sirdar contented himself with remarking that " he couldn't buy new cables *every* day." On the 9th, when the tangled remains of the cable had been unravelled, and additional lengths retrieved from the river, they were repaired and laid successfully from the right bank, upstream of the Atbara, to an island in the Nile, and thence to the left bank. This, however, could only be considered as a temporary expedient, for the cable had been badly damaged in the first attempt.

The situation was further complicated by the arrival of the annual flood in the Atbara River, necessitating the removal of a poled telegraph line which had been laid across the bed, and the substitution of an overhead wire in one span. This work was undertaken in the middle of July by Manifold and his men, who erected two composite poles, each 48 feet high, on the banks of the Atbara and, with the utmost difficulty, spanned the gap with a wire. Within a week, the line was carried away by boats navigating the river. On July 27th, Kitchener withdrew all objections and ordered another cable for the Nile crossing, and on August 9th it arrived by rail at Fort Atbara, where Major W. S. Gordon, R.E. (" Monkey " Gordon), had already manufactured a drum on which it could be wound before laying.

On August 7th, Manifold writes :— " Saat-el (Kitchener) has got ' overhead wire ' on the brain, and to-day I was told by Gordon that I should soon be ordered to build two high towers on the Atbara ; so I said, ' Why not let the 2nd Company do it ? ' and Saat-el was delighted. Major Arkwright[1] is now wrestling with the towers and trying to find some materials for them. Meanwhile, the overhead wire is to be re-established on our 48-foot poles." On the 8th, the letter continues :— " Gordon's gunboat, the *Melik*, anchored this morning in the Atbara. I rode down and got the *Tahra*, and about 3 p.m. had a drum of wire and my men on board her. We were just shoving off when Saat-el and Cecil (Lord Edward) came running down the bank and were taken aboard. We steamed slowly to the *Melik*, paying out the wire and keeping it out of the water. Then

---

[1] Major L. A. Arkwright, R.E., was present with Lieut. J. P. Moir, R.E., in command of a section of the 2nd (Fortress) Company, R.E.

the drum was passed on to the *Melik* and the wire run through a snatch-block at the mast-head. The *Tahra* came up on the other side and took the drum aboard, and off we went again and got safely across. Saat-el was very pleased. We strained the wire taut and worked at once through to Metemma."

At this period the Sirdar spent much of his time in superintending the loading of his ships and barges for the advance towards Omdurman. One day, while he was observing with perfect equanimity the loading of the *Melik* until her Plimsoll mark was submerged, he was approached by the captain of the ship with an objection. The Sirdar eyed him coldly. "*Plimsoll's dead*," said he.

On August 10th, the new cable for the Nile crossing was coiled on to its home-made drum. "I have found on counting the number of turns," writes Manifold, "that the Company has sent us 60 yards short, and I am doubtful whether 1,140 yards is enough. Even 1,200 yards seems too little, but Saat-el insisted on it. The port engine of the *Melik* is still under repair, but is expected to be ready before morning." It appears that the Sirdar had not agreed with Manifold's estimate of the necessary length of cable, and had ordered Pritchard, the Survey officer, to check the demand. "I made theodolite observations from a base," writes General Pritchard,[1] "and then added amounts for the height of the banks and depth of the water, for irregularities of the river-bottom, for the impossibility of laying the cable straight from shore to shore, and finally five per cent. for contingencies. The Sirdar looked at the calculations and said, 'But they *must* lay the cable straight ; and you have included five per cent. for contingencies when you have already allowed for every contingency'—and he struck out the five per cent."

The sequel is interesting. An attempt to lay the cable at a point downstream of the confluence of the Atbara was made on August 11th, 1898. Manifold tells the sad story. "Cecil boarded the *Melik* at 5 a.m. and informed us that Saat-el was not coming, so at 5.15 we began to lay the cable. It paid off beautifully from the drum; but the ship could not steam properly against the swift current, and we went across in a wide curve. When we were below the point of the island, I realized that there was not sufficient cable to complete the crossing, so I shouted to Gordon to drop the anchor. It was overboard within half a minute; but before it could grip, the last turn of the cable had whipped over the side. Then Saat-el appeared in the *Tahra*, furious with 'Monkey' Gordon for starting without him. He had sent an Egyptian orderly to tell us to wait for him, but the orderly had told Gordon to 'start at once.' Saat-el is unapproachable on delicate business this morning.

---

[1] Notes by Major-General H. L. Pritchard, c.b., c.m.g., d.s.o., Col. Commandant R.E., sent to the author on December 22nd, 1935.

It is a pity. More cable should have been ordered, and we should not have tried to cross with only one engine."[1]

The construction of two tripod towers, each 80 feet high, for an improved overhead line across the Atbara, was finished by Arkwright on August 17th, and two wires were slung from top to top. For a time, telegraphic signals could be sent to Metemma over these wires by way of the makeshift cable across the Nile above the mouth of the Atbara, and thence along the line laid by Sergeant Dennett on the left bank; but the cable soon failed in stormy weather, and communication across the Nile had then to be maintained by ferry or, in the case of urgent messages, by heliograph.

Nevertheless, it may be said that the efforts of Manifold and his subordinates to extend and maintain telegraphic communication in the Sudan were attended by remarkable success. Failures occurred from time to time; but these were due, for the most part, to storm, flood, lack of proper material and adequate transport, and the unceasing urge for speed and yet more speed. Never before had messages flashed along more than 230 miles of bare wire in contact with the ground. The Field Telegraph kept the Sirdar in communication with Cairo and every post along the Nile, and in close touch with his railways and river transport. It was thus a most important factor in the organization which enabled him to ensure victory on the field of battle.

---

[1] It may be added that the *Melik*, with her shallow draught, was unfitted for the task and should not have been allotted to it.

CHAPTER X.

OMDURMAN.

> Like the leaves of the forest when summer is green,
> That host with their banners at sunset were seen;
> Like the leaves of the forest when autumn hath blown,
> That host on the morrow lay wither'd and strewn.
> 											BYRON.

AFTER the conclusion of the Atbara Campaign, the Anglo-Egyptian Army lay for several months in summer quarters along the Nile. A programme drawn up early in May, 1898, gave August 20th as the date of the advance southwards from the Atbara; but although the Home Government had agreed to an advance at high Nile, and had promised that more British troops should be sent to the front for that purpose, it seemed that the plan of campaign might be upset by disquieting news which arrived early in July. The Emperor Menelik of Abyssinia was said to have succumbed to intrigues and to be in friendly correspondence with the Khalifa, and it was reported that an Abyssinian force was moving towards Roseires on the upper waters of the Blue Nile. It was rumoured also that a French expedition from Equatorial Africa had traversed the Bahr el Ghazal Province and had appeared on the White Nile far south of Khartoum. Evidently, no time was to be lost.

Arrangements were made to reinforce the Anglo-Egyptian Army by a brigade of British infantry, with some cavalry and artillery; and orders were issued that this brigade (the 2nd) should form, with the brigade already at the front (the 1st), a British Division under Major-General W. F. Gatacre, C.B., D.S.O. Gatacre was directed to hand over the command of the 1st British Brigade (1st Warwicks, 1st Lincolns, 1st Seaforths and 1st Camerons) to Brig.-General A. G. Wauchope, C.B., late Black Watch. The 2nd British Brigade, under Brig.-General the Hon. N. G. Lyttleton, C.B., late Rifle Brigade, was formed by the 1st Battalion, Grenadier Guards, from Gibraltar; the 1st Battalion, Northumberland Fusiliers, and the 2nd Battalion, Lancashire Fusiliers, from Cairo; and the 2nd Battalion, Rifle Brigade, from Malta. The 21st Lancers[1] were sent up from Egypt, together with the 32nd Battery, R.F.A., the 37th Howitzer Battery, R.F.A., a detachment of the 16th Company, R.G.A., a Maxim battery, the remainder of the 2nd (Fortress) Company, R.E. (under

---
[1] Under Brevet Colonel R. H. Martin.

Major L. A. Arkwright, with Lieutenant D. A. Friederichs, R.E.), and certain Medical, Supply and Transport formations.[1]

The Egyptian Division, under Major-General Archibald Hunter, was strengthened by the addition of a fourth brigade. The 1st Brigade was commanded by Lieut.-Colonel H. A. MacDonald, C.B., D.S.O., Royal Fusiliers ; the 2nd Brigade by Lieut.-Colonel J. G. Maxwell, D.S.O., Black Watch ; the 3rd Brigade by Lieut.-Colonel D. F. Lewis, Cheshire Regiment ; and the 4th Brigade by Lieut.-Colonel J. Collinson, Northamptonshire Regiment.[2] The Egyptian artillery, under Lieut.-Colonel C. J. Long, R.A., the Artillery Commander of the entire force, consisted of a horse battery, four field batteries and a Maxim battery.[3] Lieut.-Colonel G. R. Broadwood, 12th Lancers, commanded nine squadrons of Egyptian cavalry ; and Major R. J. Tudway, Essex Regiment, eight companies of the Camel Corps. Under Commander Colin Keppel, D.S.O., R.N., were a flotilla of ten gunboats and five river steamers,[4] and a fleet of barges and boats.

When the reinforcements had arrived, the Anglo-Egyptian Army comprised 8,200 British and 17,600 Egyptian and Sudanese soldiers, with 44 guns and 20 Maxims on land and 36 guns and 24 Maxims on the river. Assisted by Major-General H. M. L. Rundle, C.M.G., D.S.O., as Chief of Staff, and supplied with precise information by the Intelligence Department under Lieut.-Colonel F. R. Wingate, C.B., D.S.O., R.A., the Sirdar could undertake with confidence the task of destroying the Khalifa, capturing Omdurman, and re-opening the waterway to the Equatorial Provinces.

Towards the end of July, 1898, a general concentration of the Egyptian troops was begun, and Kitchener quietly sent forward the 3rd Brigade under Lewis in steamers to Wad Habashi, a village situated upstream of the island of Nasri and a few miles below the foot of the Sixth Cataract.[5] It was announced that the brigade was destined to cut firewood for the steamers ; but in reality its mission was to establish and guard depots of stores in anticipation of a general

---

[1] The 32nd Battery had six 9-pounder Maxim-Nordenfeldt guns. The 37th Battery had six 5-inch howitzers, throwing 50-lb. lyddite shells ; and the detachment of the 16th Company brought two 40-pounder guns. One section of the 2nd Company, R.E., under Lieut. J. P. Moir, R.E., was already at the front.

[2] *1st Brigade*, 2nd Egyptians and 9th, 10th and 11th Sudanese ; *2nd Brigade*, 8th Egyptians and 12th, 13th and 14th Sudanese ; *3rd Brigade*, 3rd, 4th, 7th and 15th Egyptians ; *4th Brigade*, 1st, 5th, 17th and 18th Egyptians.

[3] The Egyptian Horse Battery was armed with six Krupp guns and two Maxims. Each of the Egyptian Field Batteries had six Maxim-Nordenfeldt guns and two Maxims.

[4] *Sultan, Melik* and *Sheikh*, 1898 Class twin-screw gunboats ; *Fateh, Nasir* and *Zafir*, 1896 Class stern-wheel gunboats ; *Tamai, Abu Klea, Metemma* and *Hafir* (formerly *El Teb*), old stern-wheel gunboats ; and *Dal, Akasha, Tahra, Okma* and *Kaibar*, river steamers. Lieut. David Beatty, D.S.O., R.N., commanded the *Fateh*. The *Melik, Metemma* and *Abu Klea* were commanded by R.E. officers during the most critical phase of the operations. The remaining gunboats were commanded by R.N. officers.

[5] See the *Sketch Map of the Nile from Metemma to Khartoum*, which is included in this chapter.

advance, and in order to prevent this movement of troops from becoming known, Kitchener prohibited any mention of it in the dispatches of the War Correspondents. "Shortly after my return from a month's leave," writes General Gorringe,[1] "the Sirdar arrived at Atbara from Berber 'to inspect the troops.' He complimented Major T. E. Hickman, commanding the 15th Egyptians of Lewis' Brigade, on the fine house which he had built, and then told him that he was to proceed upstream to cut firewood at Wad Habashi, where he was to make his battalion comfortable and build another house. Hickman and his battalion soon left for Wad Habashi, and the Sirdar took up his quarters in Atbara Fort—in Hickman's house." The 3rd Egyptian Brigade was followed in due course by the 1st and 2nd Brigades under MacDonald and Maxwell, and later by the 4th Brigade under Collinson. Transport was scarce, and when six battalions of the 1st and 2nd Brigades left Fort Atbara on August 3rd, they were crowded on to four steamers, each towing two double-decked barges and a couple of native boats. On the decks of the ships, barges and boats, the Sudanese and Egyptian soldiers squatted, shoulder to shoulder, toe to back, chin to knee. The steamers swung into the turbid stream and headed ponderously towards the south. Faithful and dusky wives, with babies on their hips, screamed a farewell. The great stern paddle-wheels churned the water to foam, and as the black soldiers disappeared up the Nile, battalions of white soldiers swarmed into Fort Atbara and Darmali and prepared to follow them.

The Embarkation Staff worked at high pressure. The duties of allotting steamers, barges and boats, loading them with troops and supplies, and calculating the river transport needed not only for the advanced troops at Wad Habashi but for a general concentration at Wad Hamid, a short distance farther south, fell to Lieutenant G. F. Gorringe, D.S.O., R.E. On August 13th, the ships carrying Wauchope's 1st British Brigade from Darmali steamed past Fort Atbara towards the new *rendezvous* at Wad Hamid, below the Sixth Cataract. "As soon as the advanced troops had reached that place," writes General Gorringe, "a definite number of complete rations for the whole force, intended for the final advance on Omdurman, had to be accumulated there, and supplies loaded also into barges and boats for use at Omdurman until they could be replenished from Atbara. The carrying capacity of the barges and sailing-boats was a dominant factor, and the calculations were intricate. It was necessary to check carefully the supplies sent forward, the boats or barges in which they were loaded, the places for unloading, and the position on any day of every barge and boat. When the advance took place from Wad Hamid, the Sirdar was annoyed because I had

---

[1] Notes by Lieut.-General Sir George Gorringe, K.C.B., K.C.M.G., D.S.O., Col. Commandant R.E., sent to the author on September 24th, 1936.

two boat-loads of supplies—say 10 tons—in excess of the amount which he wanted, and I had to leave them at Nasri Island."

The Sudan Military Railway had reached Fort Atbara on July 3rd, 1898, and thereafter, under a Railway Staff headed by Lieutenant G. B. Macauley, R.E.,[1] it had poured out troops and supplies. At Fort Atbara also was Lieutenant M. G. E. Manifold, R.E., struggling to maintain telegraphic communication by cable across the Nile and by overhead line across the Atbara. However, when the main body of the troops had passed on towards the front, the pressure on the railway decreased, for Kitchener had already amassed, in Fort Atbara and the adjacent camps, sufficient supplies to last the expedition until the end of October. Consequently, it became possible to employ on military duty the greater part of the Railway Staff of Royal Engineer officers. Ever mindful of the careers of his chosen " Band of Boys," Kitchener sent to the front every young Royal Engineer who could be detached temporarily from technical work.

It is remarkable that, although Kitchener had only one unit of Engineer troops in his army at the front, he arranged that no less than 17 officers of his Corps should be present with him at the Battle of Omdurman. On his Headquarter Staff were Major A. E. Sandbach as A.A.G., Major L. B. Friend as Provost Marshal, Lieutenant G. F. Gorringe, D.S.O., as D.A.A.G.(B), and Major the Hon. M. G. Talbot as an Intelligence Officer working under the orders of Lieut.-Colonel Wingate.[2] The Camel Corps joined the concentration at Wad Hamid, after marching across the Bayuda Desert from Korti to Metemma and thence up the left bank of the Nile; and Talbot, primarily a Surveyor, seized the opportunity of accompanying it in order to fix astronomically the positions of Gakdul Wells, Abu Klea and other points. Major W. F. H. S. Kincaid was A.A.G. to the Egyptian Division; and with the 2nd (Fortress) Company, R.E., were Major L. A. Arkwright and Lieutenants J. P. Moir and D. A. Friederichs. The eight officers already mentioned held appointments which may be considered as normal in a military expedition. But what of the remainder? Here the hand of Kitchener is apparent. Major W. S. (" Monkey ") Gordon—nephew of Charles Gordon, ex-Marine Artilleryman, and energetic assistant of the Sirdar in matters of ordnance supply—was placed in command of the new gunboat *Melik*. Lieutenants A. G. Stevenson and E. O. A. Newcombe, Railway officers with special mechanical training and experience, were given command of the smaller gunboats *Metemma* and *Abu Klea* respectively. Lieutenants G. B. Macauley and

---

[1] On his departure to Egypt in June, 1898, Lieut. E. P. C. Girouard, D.S.O., R.E., had handed over the appointment of Director of Railways to Lieut. G. B. Macauley, R.E.

[2] Lt.-Colonel F. R. Wingate, C.B., D.S.O., R.A., the Director of Military Intelligence, had as his Assistant Director, Lt.-Colonel Slatin Pasha, C.B., the ex-prisoner of the Khalifa.

M. G. E. Manifold were relieved temporarily of their respective duties as Director of Railways and Director of Telegraphs to become Staff Officers with the Egyptian Division. Lieutenants H. L. Pritchard, R. B. D. Blakeney, E. C. Midwinter and H. A. Micklem were taken from their railway work and posted as "gallopers" to the 1st, 2nd, 3rd and 4th Egyptian Brigades. Indeed, with the exception of Lieutenants G. C. M. Hall and W. R. G. Wollen, the Railway service was denuded of Royal Engineers; and it is said that, if Kitchener's instructions had not been disregarded or misunderstood, Hall also would have been at Omdurman.[1] Inclusive of the Sirdar himself, 27 officers of the Corps were serving in Egypt or the Sudan during the period of the Omdurman Campaign, and of these only nine were absent from the decisive battle.[2]

On the morning of August 13th, shortly before the 1st British Brigade passed up the Nile, the Sirdar vanished suddenly from Fort Atbara. At eleven o'clock his troops saw him, grave, inscrutable, courteous and helpful as ever: at noon, he was gone. Such was Kitchener—all patience, to the outward eye, during the time of preparation: all swiftness when the moment for action had arrived. With his usual caution, he had breathed no word of his intention to any but his personal Staff. Then he dictated an official report, boarded a gunboat, and left the local Staff officers to satisfy the inquisitive with any plausible and incorrect explanation of his departure. No one appreciated better than Kitchener the value of secrecy in war.

By August 18th, the last of the British reinforcements had arrived at Fort Atbara. On the same day the advanced troops at Wad Hamid found that the Sabaluka Gorge in the Sixth Cataract, where the enemy was expected to make a stand, had been evacuated. After his arrival at Wad Hamid, Kitchener inspected the Cataract, and also four Dervish forts at its northern entrance, three on the left bank and one on the right. The narrow Sabaluka Gorge, towards the southern end of the Cataract, extends for a distance of about nine miles, its red granite walls rising sheer from the swirling waters to a height of 300 feet. Rocky ridges run east and west from the gorge, and form a natural barrier suitable for defensive purposes, but with the disadvantage that the ends may be turned by forces operating in the desert. Influenced perhaps by this consideration, the Khalifa made no attempt to hold the Sabaluka position and withdrew his outposts towards Omdurman. By August 23rd, the stores

---

[1] Kitchener was very angry when he found that Hall had not been sent to the front. Subsequently, Hall received the D.S.O., for his services during the campaign.

[2] The absentees were Bt. Colonel A. O. Green (C.R.E., Cairo); Lieut.-Colonel R. L. Hippisley (C.R.E., Alexandria); Major H. M. Lawson (on special duty at Kassala); Major E. P. C. Girouard, D.S.O. (President, Railway Board, Cairo); Lieuts. G. C. M. Hall and W. R. G. Wollen (Sudan Military Railway); Lieut. A. H. Crozier, 2nd (Fortress) Company, R.E., Cairo; Major R. H. Brown (Inspector of Irrigation, Cairo); and Capt. H. G. Lyons (Geological Survey, Cairo).

accumulated at Wad Hamid had been transported through the whole length of the Sixth Cataract to Jebel Rowiyan—now, at high Nile, an island—and an advanced post had been established there. Meanwhile, the British infantry continued to voyage up the river in steamers and barges. The mounted troops and artillery, crossing the Nile at Fort Atbara, marched up the left bank ahead of the camel transport, and passing ruined Metemma on their way, rejoined the infantry at Wad Hamid. In this way, a force of about 23,000 men, which on July 27th had been scattered between Cairo and the Atbara, was concentrated by August 23rd below the Sixth Cataract, at a distance of 1,260 miles from the Egyptian capital and within 60 miles of the heart of Dervishdom.

On August 24th, the army began to move southwards by successive divisions to Jebel Rowiyan.[1] Preceded by the cavalry and Camel Corps, the troops marched round the western heights of Sabaluka to a *zariba* camp opposite the Jebel, which all had reached by the 26th. During this and subsequent movements on the left bank, the right bank was swept clear of Dervish patrols by a Camel Corps of 2,500 Arab irregulars under Major the Hon. E. J. Montagu-Stuart-Wortley, C.M.G., 60th Rifles, the same officer who, as a subaltern, had accompanied Charles Wilson to Khartoum in 1885 in the abortive but gallant attempt to rescue Charles Gordon.[2]

It is said that the first person in the Anglo-Egyptian Army to set eyes on Omdurman in 1898 was Major W. S. Gordon, R.E.[3] "Monkey" Gordon, ever ready for any adventure, climbed the heights of Jebel Rowiyan and from this elevated post distinguished through his field-glasses the white dome of the Mahdi's Tomb, the most conspicuous feature in the vast conglomeration of dilapidated mud huts which formed the Khalifa's capital. It was fitting that the first to see Omdurman should be a near relative of the heroic defender of Khartoum.

The Anglo-Egyptian force broke camp opposite Jebel Rowiyan on the 28th, and marching on a broad front up the left bank of the Nile, bivouacked at a place called Wadi el Abid. The formation on the march was now a double line of brigades, the British brigades being nearest to the river. The left flank was protected by the gunboats, and by Stuart-Wortley's irregulars moving on the right bank; the right flank was guarded by the Camel Corps. Each brigade, except Collinson's, was followed by a battery of field artillery; the cavalry and horse artillery covered the front; baggage and supply columns toiled in the rear. At the head of the British infantry rode

[1] Dispatch from Major-General Sir Herbert Kitchener, Sirdar, to Lieut.-General Sir Francis Grenfell, G.C.M.G., K.C.B., Commanding in Egypt, dated Omdurman, September 5th, 1898, quoted in the *R.E. Journal*, Vol. 28, 1898, pp. 233-245. This dispatch gives a clear and concise account of the advance to, and the battle of, Omdurman.
[2] See Chapter IV.
[3] *The Egyptian Campaigns*, 1882—1899, by Charles Royle, p. 555.

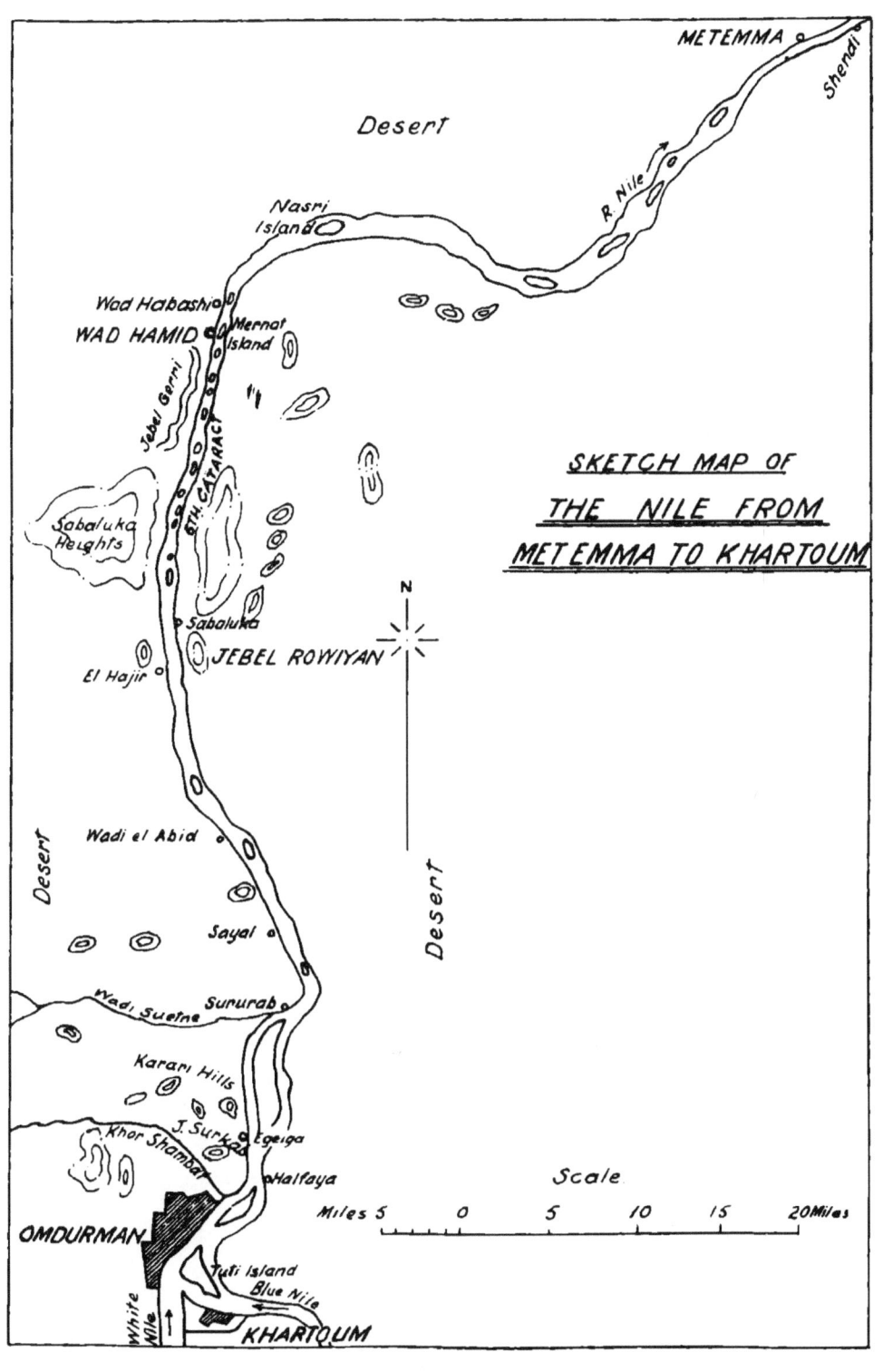

the Sirdar, leading the most powerful army the Sudan has ever seen. It was a spectacle never to be forgotten.

Nevertheless, fate was not too kind. On the 29th, the ill-starred gunboat *Zafir*[1] sprang a leak and sank suddenly near Metemma; and on the same evening a terrific storm broke over the camp at Wadi el Abid, deluging everything and stopping telegraphic communication, which had been maintained—though with occasional interruptions—through a bare wire as far as Wad Hamid and thence by a poled line through Metemma to the Nile crossing at Atbara.[2] On the 30th the army advanced in the same formation to a place called Sayal, whence Kitchener dispatched a letter to the Khalifa warning him to remove his women and children as Omdurman would be bombarded unless it was surrendered. Meanwhile, cavalry patrols penetrated as far as the low range of the Karari (Kerreri) Hills, whence they could look down upon the amphitheatre which was soon to become a bloody battlefield. A few Dervish scouts moved slowly over the dreary landscape, but otherwise there was no sign of the enemy. When the advance was resumed on August 31st, the army marched on a two-brigade front, in a formation well adapted for repelling a sudden assault,[3] and in due course reached a ridge called Sururab, north of the Wadi Suetne and some six miles short of the Karari Hills. At the same time, the gunboats pushed on upstream and bombarded a few Dervish outposts in the hills. The cavalry made a detour south-westwards and saw, from a hill-top, the Khalifa's bodyguard and regular army, perhaps 40,000 men in all, drawn up in five immense masses north-west of Omdurman.

It seems that the Dervish leader had decided to stake all on the issue of a great battle in the amphitheatre south of the Karari Hills. He could muster a host of men. The Mahdi had prophesied that he should succeed. On August 30th, he was told that the enemy was approaching, and accordingly, on the 31st, he paraded his regular troops and harangued his Emirs, and, on September 1st, swept every able-bodied man in the city into the ranks. Although he had hitherto done nothing to hinder the Sirdar's advance on land, he had made some unsuccessful attempts to obstruct the river with mines. Two iron boilers had been filled with black powder, in which were embedded loaded pistols with strings attached to the triggers. An ancient Egyptian prisoner was then detailed to lay one of the mines from the Dervish steamer *Ismailia;* but during the process the string was accidentally pulled, and the mine proved its efficacy by killing the prisoner and sinking the ship. The laying of the second mine devolved on an unfortunate Emir in charge of the Khalifa's arsenal.

[1] The same ship which burst a cylinder at Kosha on September 11th, 1896, during the Dongola Expedition, and was thus put out of action. (See Chapter VI.)

[2] The poling had been extended from Metemma to Wad Hamid after the occupation of the latter place.

[3] Each brigade had three battalions in line, and the fourth at deploying distance in the rear. Square could be formed rapidly by wheeling back the outer battalions.

This astute individual took no risks. He was careful to admit water to the powder before lowering the boiler into the river, and so survived to report to his grateful master that the mine had been duly and properly laid.[1]

On the evening of August 31st another fierce storm broke over the country and raged throughout the night, putting an end to all hope of re-establishing telegraphic communication with the advanced base until the wire could be raised from the ground after hostilities had ceased. In this connection, there is a story which is worth repeating. Queen Victoria, being accustomed to receive daily news regarding the progress of the expedition, became very anxious when the messages ceased to arrive and accordingly telegraphed for information. It is said that from Atbara came the ominous and disturbing reply: " No news of Kitchener's army. Flocks of vultures flying south."

The Sirdar made his final move on the morning of September 1st. With the country to the east of the river cleared by Stuart-Wortley, and the advance screened by gunboats and mounted troops, he marched his army to the village of Egeiga, on the left bank of the Nile, about $1\frac{1}{2}$ miles south of the Karari Hills, and hidden from Omdurman, $6\frac{1}{2}$ miles distant, by the prominent hill and ridge of Jebel Surkab.[2] There, for the moment, we may leave him and proceed to follow the fortunes and misfortunes of other Royal Engineers during the advance from the Atbara.

Two Railway officers, Lieutenants A. G. Stevenson and E. O. A. Newcombe, R.E., voyaged upstream from Fort Atbara on August 21st, 1898, as passengers in the gunboat *Sheikh*, and on arrival at Wad Hamid on the 25th, took command respectively of the gunboats *Metemma* and *Abu Klea*. Newcombe describes the *Abu Klea* as a little stern-wheeler with a very ancient engine and a boiler limited to 60-lb. pressure. She carried a 12-pr. Krupp gun in the bows and two Maxim-Nordenfeldt guns on the upper deck; but the Egyptian gun-crew of the Krupp had not had much practice with their weapon. The ship's crew of Berberine sailors was under an efficient *Reis* (Arab captain), and the engine was tended by a Greek with one or two Sudanese assistants.[3] For several days, both gunboats were employed in towing barges up to Jebel Rowiyan above the Sabaluka Cataract, or in fetching stores from the depot at Nasri Island. Newcombe received " fleet instructions " from Commander Keppel, R.N., and was told that, if in distress, he should hoist a " weft."[4]

---

[1] *The River War*, by the Rt. Hon. Winston Churchill, M.P., p. 253. This book gives a most complete and descriptive account of the Battle of Omdurman and the operations which preceded it. Winston Churchill was an eye-witness of the events described, for he was attached to 21st Lancers and took part in the battle.

[2] Incorrectly alluded to by many historians as " Jebel Surgham."

[3] Notes by Major E. O. A. Newcombe, D.S.O., R.E. (retd.), sent to the author on Feb. 15th, 1936.

[4] A " weft " is a knot tied in a signal flag to indicate " I have something important to communicate." A captain reading this signal, and closing on the ship flying it, would be in a position to afford assistance if needed.

Fortunately he had no occasion to do so, for he had never heard of a "weft" except in its textile significance in relation to a "warp."

Other Railway officers, Lieutenants G. B. Macauley, H. L. Pritchard, R. B. D. Blakeney and E. C. Midwinter, R.E., landed at Wad Hamid on August 25th. The Sirdar found Macauley and Midwinter stranded on the river bank, and with his usual consideration, invited them into his tent and gave them breakfast.[1] There they met Gorringe, one of the busiest officers in the force. After breakfast, the Sirdar detailed the four subalterns to their temporary military appointments in the field—Macauley to the Staff of the Egyptian Division, and the others as "gallopers" to Egyptian brigades. On the following day, all four reported for duty at the camp opposite Jebel Rowiyan.

During the advance to Omdurman, few officers had greater anxieties than Lieutenant M. G. E. Manifold, R.E., the Director of Telegraphs, whose diary may now be quoted : "*August 20th.*—Left Atbara for the south in the gunboat *Hafir* (formerly *Et Teb*). *August 24th.*—At Wad Hamid. Woken by message to say line broken down between east and west banks at Atbara. Then a fearful storm arose. This morning, I started the party detailed to lay the wire southwards. Of course, *all* lines are interrupted by rain. *August 26th.*—There will be great delay in all telegrams as the boat can only cross at Atbara when the wind is moderate. Urgent messages are being sent across by heliograph. *August 28th.*—Have been searching for wire all the morning. Some 25 miles are missing —supposed to be in the *Abu Klea*. *August 29th.*—We are now about 30 miles from Khartoum. I have only $11\frac{1}{2}$ miles of wire with me, but have seen about seven miles in the *Akasha*. At 5.30 a.m., the Sirdar sent for me. I found him shaving. We discussed the wire question, and he decided to send back the *Tahra* to Nasri Island to bring up what remains there. Air very damp this morning, and line has been slow in coming on. *August 30th.*—Twenty miles from Khartoum. Our march to-day was to be eight miles, and I had 12 miles of wire with me ; but we went on and on, and at 2 p.m. the last coil ran out as we reached camp. Have been hunting for wire *everywhere.* None to be had unless the *Tahra* arrives during the night. *September 1st.*—Seven miles from Khartoum. All the wire is done. *Ten miles too short.*"

Telegrams dispatched on the evening of Tuesday, August 30th, were the last to reach England before the Battle of Omdurman (officially known as the "Battle of Khartoum"). No more were received until the afternoon of Saturday, September 3rd,[2] when a message arrived in London which had been carried by steamer to

---

[1] Letter from Lieut. E. C. Midwinter, R.E., published in October, 1898, in the *Parish Magazine*, St. Paul's, Lisson Grove.
[2] *The Egyptian Soudan. Its Loss and Recovery*, by Lieuts. H. S. L. Alford and W. D. Sword, p. 282.

the telegraph station at Wad Hamid below the Sixth Cataract. Manifold was not to blame; but the Sirdar was furious that the news of the victory of September 2nd, so anxiously awaited at home, should have been thus delayed.[1] The poling of the line as far as Wad Hamid had secured a chain of telegraphic communication which was unbroken except at the Atbara crossing of the Nile; and after the concentration at Wad Hamid had been completed, Kitchener did not wish to incur the delay and expense of obtaining insulated ground-cable for the final stages of the advance when it seemed probable that a bare wire might suffice until it could be raised on poles. His calculations were upset by the unexpected and unusual rain. Even along the poled line, transmission was liable to temporary interruption through damage caused by camels or men. Such an accident occurred near Nasri Island during the battle. It was ascribed at first to enemy action, but was found afterwards to have been caused by some Greek sutlers, who had lighted a camp fire too close to a pole and had thus burnt down the line.[2] The telegraph line did not reach Omdurman until September 7th, five days after the decisive battle had been fought.

It may be interesting to record that, until the day preceding the battle, the Khalifa had a small telegraph system operating in Omdurman and Khartoum. From information supplied by Slatin Pasha, it had been known for some time that such a system existed. On entering the northern outskirts of Omdurman after the battle, Sergeant Dennett, R.E., noticed the remains of a poled line, and following it up, discovered a terminal station in a ravine called the Khor Shambat.[3] This station was in the charge of a captive Egyptian telegraph clerk, who had worked the line until it was destroyed by the fire of the gunboats on September 1st.[4] The line ran through the city to the arsenal. It was carried by a cable across the White Nile to Makran Point, and thence to the dockyard in Khartoum.

We turn now to the naval and military operations which immediately preceded the Battle of Omdurman. These operations, and the battle itself, have been described in detail by a number of historians; but a general outline of events may be given in this narrative in connection with the experiences of certain Royal Engineers who were present.

[1] According to Lieut.-General Sir George Gorringe, the first news to reach England was not from the Sirdar but from a War Correspondent who, having tricked the censor, galloped on relays of ponies to Wad Hamid and handed in his telegram before the official dispatch arrived.
[2] Entry in the diary of Lieut. M. G. E. Manifold, R.E., dated October 14th, 1898.
[3] Note entitled "Telegraphic Communications found at Khartoum" (by Lieut. J. P. Moir, R.E.), appearing under the head of "Occasional Notes" in the *R.E. Journal*, Vol. 29, 1899, p. 111.
[4] The original set of instruments (a single current set and graphite wheel recorder) had been supplied by Messrs. Chadburn in 1872. Subsequently, the recorder had been replaced by a relay, supplied by Messrs. Siemens to an order by Charles Gordon in 1878.

SHELLING THE MAHDI'S TOMB.

While Kitchener was marching to his final camp at Egeiga on the morning of September 1st, the five larger gunboats, under Keppel, steamed ahead, followed by the *Tamai*, towing the 37th Howitzer Battery in barges. Meanwhile, the Arab irregulars under Stuart-Wortley co-operated on the right bank by driving back the enemy's patrols. Passing Egeiga on the left bank, the gunboats came under the fire of three Dervish forts on the right bank near Halfaya. These were soon silenced and were occupied by the irregulars. Steaming onwards, the flotilla engaged other riverside forts and batteries in Omdurman and Khartoum and on Tuti Island, smashing embrasures and dismounting guns until the enemy's fire was subdued sufficiently to allow the 5-in. howitzers to be landed on the right bank opposite Omdurman. At 1.30 p.m., the howitzers began to bombard the Mahdi's Tomb with their 50-lb. shells at a range of 3,000 yards, tearing great holes in the dome, bringing down the cupolas, and enveloping the whole structure in a cloud of yellow fumes and dust. This was the first occasion on which Lyddite, the new high-explosive, had been used in actual warfare, and its effect was awe-inspiring.[1] During the course of the afternoon, Keppel led most of his gunboats back to Egeiga, leaving only the *Nasir* and *Tamai* to guard the 37th Howitzer Battery.

"Monkey" Gordon, in the *Melik*, was in the thick of this engagement,[2] though Stevenson and Newcombe in the *Metemma* and *Abu Klea* were prevented from taking part in it. At dawn, they had seen the large gunboats setting off upstream at full speed, and, dropping their barges, had started, together with the little *Hafir*,[3] in hot pursuit; but unhappily the eye of Keppel fell upon them, and a signal followed demanding why the three small boats had advanced without orders. Crestfallen, they returned to their prosaic duties of towing barges and guarding the flanks of the Egeiga Camp. Stevenson, in the *Metemma*, anchored off the upstream or southern flank—that nearest to Omdurman—and Newcombe, in the *Abu Klea*, moored to the river bank at the northern flank. Throughout the afternoon, Stevenson remained ready to take in flank any attack on the camp at Egeiga, but no enemy appeared. The larger gunboats returned before dusk, most of them anchoring near the upstream flank. Only the *Melik*, and one other boat, proceeded to join the *Abu Klea* at the downstream end. At 6 p.m., Stevenson was called to the bank to ship one day's rations for the cavalry in case a pursuit was undertaken. There was little sleep for anyone that night. Word

---

[1] "Novelties in the Soudan Campaign," appearing under the head of "Occasional Notes" in the *R.E. Journal*, Vol. 28, 1898, p. 210.

[2] It has been suggested that the fire of the *Melik* caused most of the damage to the Mahdi's Tomb, but this is unlikely as the *Melik* had only one small howitzer and three small guns. It was due to "Monkey" Gordon that the *Melik*, *Sultan* and *Sheikh* had each been armed with a 4-inch Austrian howitzer, for it was through him that these weapons had been secured.

[3] Commanded by Lieut. C. M. Staveley, R.N.

was passed round Lewis's Brigade that there was some excellent liqueur brandy aboard the *Abu Klea*, and Newcombe had many visitors. With guns loaded and crews alert, the ships' companies awaited the events of the morrow.[1]

Nevertheless, the gunboats had an important duty to perform during the hours of darkness. The Dervish army lay outside Omdurman, and it was evident that its proper strategy was to attack in mass formation before dawn, and to overwhelm the invaders by sheer weight of numbers. Accordingly, the Sirdar ordered that the searchlights of his gunboats should be turned on to the enemy's camp at intervals throughout the night, thus showing any sign of movement and keeping the enemy on tenterhooks. At the same time, he sent forward villagers from Egeiga with instructions to announce themselves as deserters and to inform the enemy that the Anglo-Egyptian army was itself about to launch a night-attack.[2] The ruse succeeded. The Khalifa missed his opportunity. He remained outside Omdurman, awaiting an attack which never came, and with the exception of two false alarms, the night passed without incident.

It is now time to revert to the morning of September 1st to record the operations of the Anglo-Egyptian army while the gunboats were bombarding Omdurman. Shortly before noon, the Sirdar and his Staff reached the rocky summit of Jebel Surkab, the conspicuous hill, about 300 feet in height, which forms, as it were, the southern wall of the wide amphitheatre whose northern boundary is the Karari Hills. Behind them, in that amphitheatre, was the village of Egeiga, where the army was about to camp on the left bank of the Nile. To their right, in the desert, were the Egyptian cavalry, Horse Artillery and Camel Corps; and before them, on the plain stretching southwards to Omdurman, was the entire Dervish army, some three miles distant, advancing in a long line of solid masses under the black banner of the Khalifa and the green or white flags of his Emirs. For the first time, the Sirdar saw the whole of Omdurman laid out before him, with the Mahdi's Tomb rising high in the centre. Almost at the stroke of twelve, the howitzers opened fire on the Tomb, and the third shot blew a great hole in the dome. As it seemed that a Dervish attack was imminent, the Sirdar galloped at once to Egeiga and formed his troops in a defensive line around it; but before 2 p.m., the enemy halted, fired their rifles into the air, and lay down, and as nothing further happened the British and Egyptian troops then proceeded to strengthen their position.

The line around Egeiga was in the shape of an arc, with flattened ends and the Nile for its chord; but the right or downstream end

---

[1] The information relative to the movements of the *Metemma* and *Abu Klea* is taken from a letter written by Lieut. A. G. Stevenson, R.E., on September 8th, 1898, and from notes by Major E. O. A. Newcombe, D.S.O., R.E. (retd.), sent to the author on February 15th, 1936.

[2] *Sudan Campaign*, 1896—1899, by "An Officer" (Lieut. H. L. Pritchard, R.E.), p. 188.

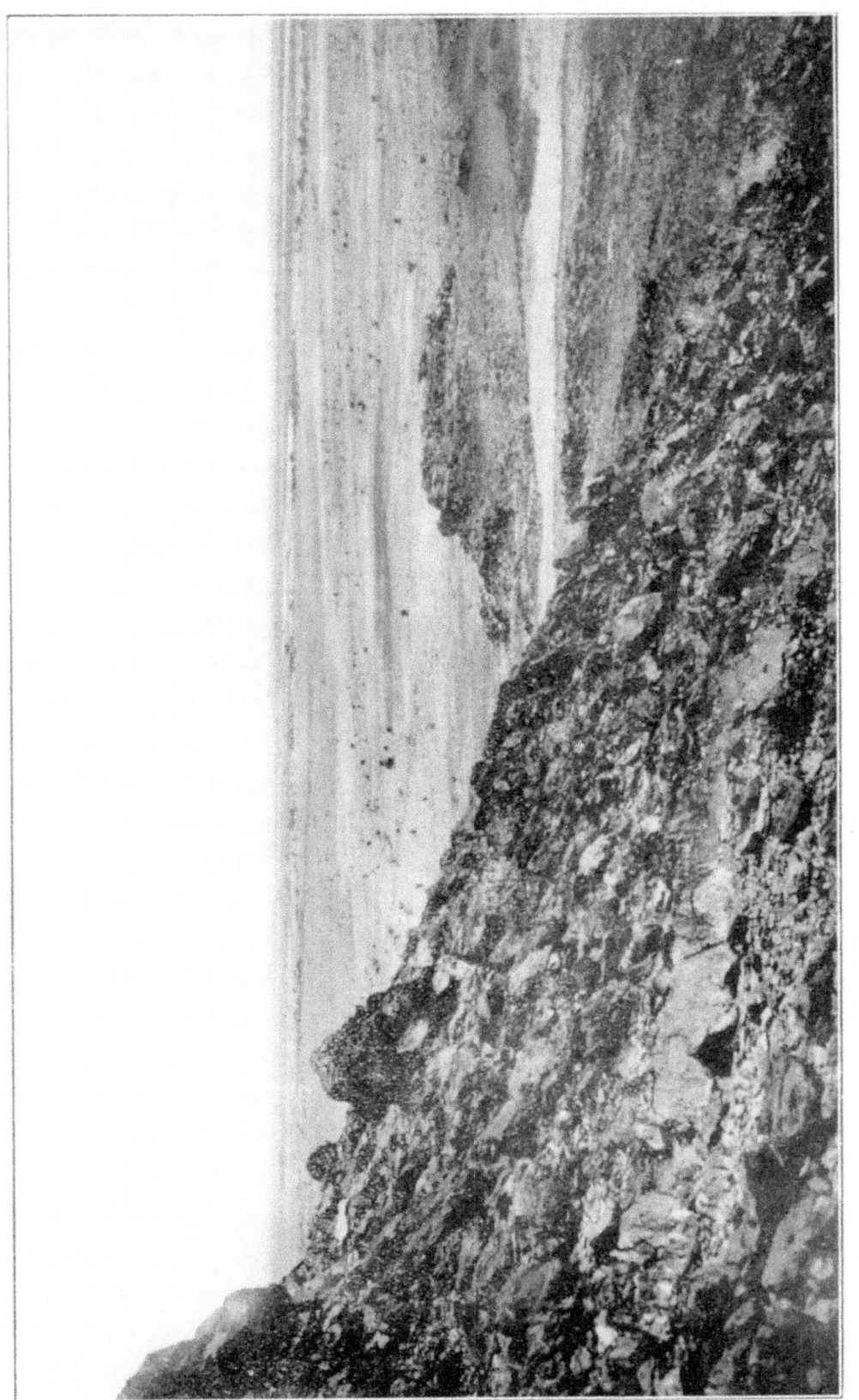

THE BATTLEFIELD OF OMDURMAN FROM JEBEL SURKAB.
Looking towards Egeiga and the Nile.

[*Photo by the Author.*]

did not quite reach the river bank, as the ground on that flank was soft and marshy. The troops were placed as follows: On the left or upstream flank, the 2nd British Brigade (Lyttleton); next to it, the 1st British Brigade (Wauchope); then the 2nd (Fortress) Company, R.E., under Major L. A. Arkwright; next the 2nd Egyptian Brigade (Maxwell), the 1st Egyptian Brigade (MacDonald), and on the right flank, the 3rd Egyptian Brigade (Lewis).[1] In reserve, parallel to the river, was the 4th Egyptian Brigade (Collinson) guarding the supplies, baggage and hospital. The 21st Lancers and 32nd Field Battery were posted on the extreme left. The Egyptian cavalry, Horse Artillery and Camel Corps were on the right, but their outposts were on Jebel Surkab. The Egyptian field artillery and Maxims were between the infantry brigades.[2]

The preparation of the defences was begun about 5 p.m. The two brigades of the British Division were ordered by General Gatacre to build a fence of thorn bushes along their front;[3] while the three Egyptian brigades, under the direction of General Hunter, dug a shallow trench about 5 ft. wide and 1 ft. deep, and raised a small parapet in front of it. The ground occupied by the British Division was certainly harder than that occupied by the Egyptian brigades, and consequently more difficult to excavate; but whereas the Egyptian and Sudanese soldiers could fire from a lying or kneeling position behind some sort of cover, the British were fully exposed, and the rear rank was obliged to stand to fire over the fence. This was a serious mistake, and in due course the British paid the penalty in casualties. At dusk all the mounted troops retreated within the enclosure, the line was strongly picketed and patrolled, and the battalions lay down, fully accoutred. The enclosed area was large and the perimeter long; but Kitchener was prepared to put every man into the front line, and to rely upon the destructive effect of modern rifle fire sweeping over the gently rising plain, which the enemy would have to cross.

Shortly after midnight, Blakeney ("galloper" to Maxwell's 2nd Egyptian Brigade) was present at a conference of brigadiers and regimental commanders, who considered that the situation would be critical if the enemy were to attack before dawn.[4] So long was the perimeter that there was a gap of about 200 yards between two of the brigades, and as Maxwell was obliged to give his two reserve

---

[1] "The Battle of Omdurman," by Major L. B. Friend, R.E., appearing in the *R.E. Journal*, Vol. 28, 1898, pp. 195–196.

[2] The main features of the battlefield, and the positions occupied by the infantry brigades around Egeiga, are shown in the *Sketch Map of the Battle of Omdurman, September 2nd, 1898, First Phase*, which is included in this chapter.

[3] There is no record of the part taken by the 2nd (Fortress) Company, R.E., in the preparation of the defences, but it is presumed that they built a section of the *zariba* and assisted the British Division. During the battle, they acted as infantry. There was no field engineering.

[4] Notes by Brig.-General R. B. D. Blakeney, C.M.G., D.S.O., late R.E., sent to the author on January 26th, 1936.

companies to fill it, he was almost without a reserve during the battle. Although Kitchener has been criticized for not holding the Karari Hills and Jebel Surkab, it is obvious that he could not do so with the force at his disposal. By day, it would have been dangerous : by night, impossible. Troops in occupation of these outlying positions could expect little support from the fire of the gunboats, and the difficulties of water-supply and baggage protection would have been serious.

At 3.30 a.m. on Friday, September 2nd, 1898, the brigades around Egeiga stood to arms, prepared to repel a possible assault before dawn.[1] Lieutenant G. F. Gorringe, R.E., had been employed for several hours in collecting and towing into position the boats carrying supplies and ammunition for the troops, and had reported to the Sirdar that all was ready. "So that is now in order," remarked Kitchener. "We have done our work. If they cannot win the fight, God help them!"[2] Orders had been issued for a general advance at 6 a.m., but it was now decided to await the reports of cavalry patrols before quitting Egeiga. At daylight, the gunboats re-opened the bombardment of Omdurman. The cavalry and Camel Corps moved out in a wide screen to reconnoitre southwards and south-westwards, and sent back messengers at 6 a.m. to say that the entire Dervish army was advancing. Half an hour later, the cavalry were seen on the skyline near Jebel Surkab, and occasional shots could be heard. Then a few flags appeared over the crest, followed by solid masses of spearmen and riflemen, led by horsemen. The muffled roar of a vast multitude reached the ears of the waiting battalions at Egeiga. With ranks well kept, marching behind their Emirs with military regularity, and chanting "*La Illah illa'llah wa Muhammad rasul Allah*,"[3] the enemy spread in a gigantic semi-circle round the front and left of the position. The 21st Lancers, under Colonel R. H. Martin, retreated along the river bank and so regained the shelter of the *zariba*; while the Egyptian cavalry, and the Camel Corps, under Lieut.-Colonel G. R. Broadwood and Major R. J. Tudway respectively, retired northwards with the Horse Artillery towards the Karari Hills, whither they were followed rapidly by 20,000 dervishes under the green flags of the Emirs Osman Wad el Sheikh[4] and Ali Wad Helu. Kitchener had ordered Broadwood and Tudway to retire in this direction to draw the enemy across his

---

[1] Major-General H. L. Pritchard, C.B., C.M.G., D.S.O., Col. Commandant R.E., who was a "galloper" to the 1st Egyptian Brigade, writes :—"On the alarm, both ranks of the brigade fell in standing, the front rank ready to get the order to kneel." In some brigades, however, the order was not given because the ground did not admit of it, and both ranks opened fire standing.

[2] Notes by Lieut.-General Sir George Gorringe, K.C.B., K.C.M.G., D.S.O., Col. Commandant R.E., sent to the author on Sept. 24th, 1936.

[3] "There is but one God, and Muhammad is his Prophet."

[4] Also known as "Osman Sheikh-ed-Din." Osman Wad el Sheikh was a son of the Khalifa. He marched under a dark green flag. Ali Wad Helu had a bright green flag.

front. A force, 8,000 strong, moving northwards under the Emir Osman Azrak, changed direction and bore down upon Egeiga; and another body, of perhaps 6,000 men, under the Khalifa Sherif and the Emir Osman Digna, came over the ridge to the east of Jebel Surkab to attack the extreme left.[1] At 6.50 a.m., the 32nd Field Battery opened fire at a range of 2,700 yards, and was followed in turn by the Egyptian batteries, and by the *Metemma* and other gunboats on the southern flank. The Battle of Omdurman had begun.

Except that the Anglo-Egyptian army was never in squares, the battle was fought, according to Major-General H. L. Pritchard, exactly as Waterloo was fought—close order, line formation, front rank kneeling, rear rank standing;[2] and when, a few years ago, General Pritchard saw the Battle of Waterloo staged at the Aldershot Tattoo, it occurred to him immediately that he had been in just such a fight on the bank of the Nile. Although the British had the ·303 Lee-Metford rifle, the Sudanese and Egyptians had only the old ·450 Martini, and there were few machine-guns. Visual signalling was under battalion control. There were no telephones, nor Divisional nor Brigade Signal Sections. Kitchener, and his Divisional and Brigade Commanders, dispatched their orders by A.D.C's, or by Orderly Officers known as " gallopers," precisely as Wellington and his Generals did on the field of Waterloo.

The Grenadier Guards were the first of the British infantry to engage, opening fire at 2,000 yards' range. Then, as the enemy approached, the other British units began to fire, and later, the Egyptian brigades. Rifles grew so hot that men had to change them for others taken from the supports. The water in the jackets of the Maxims boiled furiously. The yelling dervishes collapsed in heaps under the murderous blizzard. It was slaughter, not battle. " The enemy were divided into masses, each of perhaps 4,000 men," writes Manifold,[3] " and they advanced in a well-defined line. The artillery from all sides opened a hot fire, which did not stop them. On they came steadily, now running, now walking. At about 1,500 yards, they seemed innumerable, covering the whole plain between the hills, and all the ridge from Jebel Surkab to the river. Now the Maxims opened fire with tremendous effect, and the attack began to thin and waver; but many still came on, and at about 800 yards, fire blazed out along the whole line of our infantry, except on the northern flank. The smoke was dense; the noise deafening."

Blakeney, who was with Maxwell's 2nd Egyptian Brigade,

---

[1] See the *Sketch Map of the Battle of Omdurman, September 2nd, 1898. First Phase.*
[2] Notes by Major-General H. L. Pritchard, C.B., C.M.G., D.S.O., Col. Commandant R.E., sent to the author on February 5th, 1936. General Pritchard points out that this was the formation adopted by every brigade, British or Egyptian, after leaving the *zariba* at Egeiga.
[3] Extract from an account of the Battle of Omdurman by Lieut. M. G. E. Manifold, R.E., attached to the Staff of the Egyptian Division under Major-General Archibald Hunter.

takes up the tale:—[1] "The attack was an instance of the futility of gallantry without up-to-date weapons. Led by Emirs, some of whom were in chain mail and carried swords like those of the Crusaders, the dervishes came on under the partial screen of the smoke from the Martini rifles of the Sudanese. Five hundred yards from the position, they broke into a run and charged, gaining a moment's respite while Egyptian subalterns urged their men to keep their muzzles down, and senior officers on horseback stared into the smoke and waited for it to lift. When at last it dispersed there was a notable slackening of the enemy's fire, and only three dervishes—the centre one with a standard—remained to rush to certain death. Great, indeed, was the reward promised to the Faithful! Each warrior who fell would be awaited in Paradise by the wine of Heaven and seventy violet-eyed maidens. Two collapsed, leaving one old man with a white beard to rush forward, crumple and fall. . . . Then behind us we heard a familiar voice, ' Cease fire, please! Cease fire! Cease fire! What a dreadful waste of ammunition,' and the Sirdar rode on."

Some of the enemy's riflemen managed to find cover behind a bank about 300 yards from the British front, and inflicted a number of casualties before they were driven out by shrapnel and shot down by rifles and Maxims. Thus, in a welter of blood, the first phase of the Battle of Omdurman came to an end. At 8 a.m., the survivors of the attack withdrew sullenly towards the west, leaving on the ground some 2,000 dead, among whom was the Emir Osman Azrak.

During this fight, Lieutenant H. A. Micklem, R.E., "galloper" to Collinson's 4th Egyptian Brigade in reserve, was wounded in the foot. "Gunshot wound, toes, slight," ran the entry in dispatches; but the unfortunate Micklem saw no more of the battle. During the South African War, Micklem was again wounded in the foot, a misfortune which is said to have drawn from his friend Maxwell, then a General, the telegram: "Your feet are altogether too big for military purposes!"

While the battle raged around Egeiga, exciting events were taking place in the region of the Karari Hills to which, followed by 20,000 dervishes under Osman Wad el Sheikh and Ali Wad Helu, Colonel Broadwood was withdrawing the Egyptian cavalry, Horse Artillery and Camel Corps. Kitchener sent a message to advise him to close on the main body; but Broadwood continued northwards, and thus enticed a portion of the enemy away from the attack on the Anglo-Egyptian position. Taking up a position in the Karari Hills, he was soon outflanked and in serious difficulty. The Camel Corps proved to be quite unable to contend against a mobile enemy in rocky ground, so Broadwood ordered it to fall back on the right flank of

---

[1] Notes by Brig.-General R. B. D. Blakeney, C.M.G., D.S.O., late R.E., sent to the author on Jan. 26th, 1936.

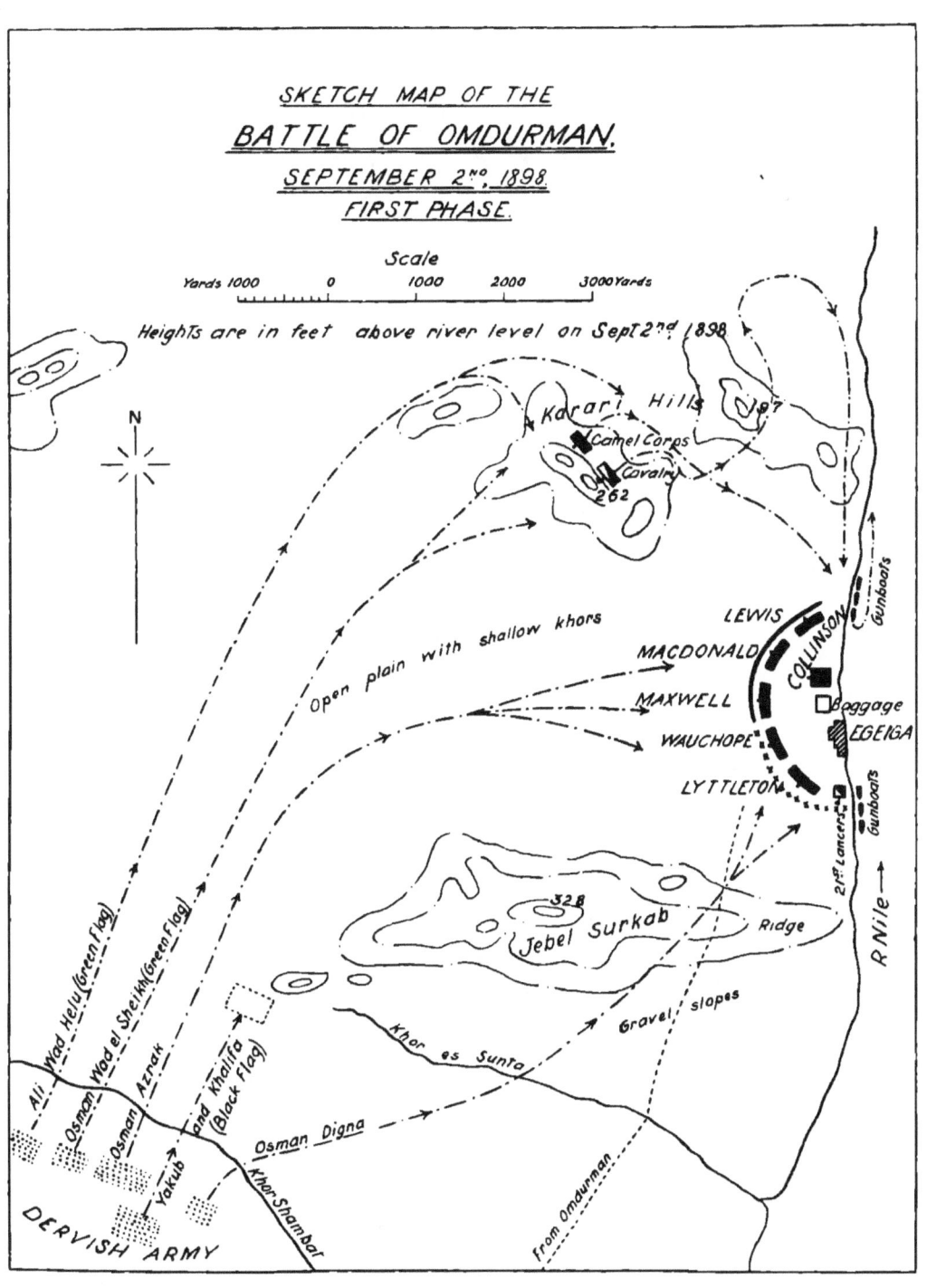

the position at Egeiga, covered by the cavalry and guns. The dervishes pressed the attack. They captured two guns and nearly succeeded in isolating the Camel Corps. However, at a critical moment, the *Melik*, under " Monkey " Gordon, appeared with another gunboat from upstream, and assisted by the fire of the artillery on land, drove the pursuers back with very heavy loss. Kitchener had already sent Major L. B. Friend, R.E., northwards along the river bank to report on the situation and deliver orders to Broadwood; but when Friend reached the scene of the fighting, the gunboats had intervened and the Camel Corps was safe, so he returned to headquarters.[1] Arriving on the bank of the Nile, the Camel Corps marched southwards and entered the entrenched camp, whilst the cavalry, supported by gunfire, hung on the flank of the retreating enemy and moved slowly in the direction of Egeiga.

Newcombe, in the *Abu Klea*, was concerned in these operations. Describing the retreat of the mounted troops towards the Karari Hills, he says :—[2]" The Horse Artillery battery, in perfect order, stopped and fired, then retired, then stopped and fired again. The gunboats lying near me on the northern flank at Egeiga started firing, and estimating the range at about one mile, I ordered my gunners to open with the Krupp; but they were so excited, and so inaccurate in elevation and direction, that after several shots I laid the gun myself. The direction was then correct, but I found that the target was out of range. By this time, the cavalry, artillery and pursuing dervishes had vanished into the folds of the hills, so I ceased fire. In the meantime, the *Melik* and the other gunboat had left me. I found later that they had gone downstream to help the cavalry and Camel Corps, which I saw, afterwards, returning near the river bank towards Egeiga."

The Dervish attack having been repulsed, Kitchener resolved to advance rapidly on Omdurman, in order to interpose his army between the Khalifa and his capital, and to gain possession of the latter without street-fighting. At 8.30 a.m., he sent forward the 21st Lancers to reconnoitre and clear the ground, and issued orders that the army should march in échelon of brigades from the left. Probably, he desired to guard against an attack on his right flank or rear. But did he know that on his right front, hidden behind Jebel Surkab, lay the Army of the Black Flag, 17,000 strong, under the Khalifa himself with his brother Yakub? And if he even suspected the presence of this large force, how did he dare to leave his trenches and execute a flank march between it and the river? Lieut.-General Sir George Gorringe, who was with the Sirdar at the time, states that the latter was fully aware of the presence and

[1] " The Battle of Omdurman " by Major L. B. Friend, R.E., appearing in the *R.E. Journal*, Vol. 28, 1898, pp. 195–196.
[2] Notes by Major E. O. A. Newcombe, D.S.O., R.E. (retd.), sent to the author on Feb. 15th, 1936.

situation of the Army of the Black Flag, and that his plan was to interpose his force between it and Omdurman.[1] On the other hand, when the late Major-General the Hon. E. J. Montagu-Stuart-Wortley revisited the scene of his former exploits, he said that he was convinced that, when Kitchener advanced from Egeiga, he had no knowledge that Ali Wad Helu's army was still behind the Karari Hills, and further that he doubted whether the Sirdar was aware that the Army of the Black Flag lay in wait behind Jebel Surkab. The opinion of Sir George Gorringe, however, may be accepted on this matter. Stuart-Wortley added that, while he was standing on the east bank after the failure of the enemy's attack on Egeiga, a dervish swam the Nile and shouted to him, " Are you the General ? " and when he replied that the Sirdar was on the other side, the dervish shouted, " Then, in the name of Allah, tell him that this attack was delivered only by the sweepings of Omdurman, and that the Khalifa is waiting for him behind Jebel Surkab with the flower of his army and will eat him up if he moves."[2] Stuart-Wortley tried to send a message across the river by heliograph ; but the army was already on the move, and he failed to attract attention. The second phase of the Battle of Omdurman had begun.

The story of the reconnaissance by the 21st Lancers, and the gallant charge against thousands of the enemy in the shallow depression of the Khor es Sunta, south of Jebel Surkab, has been told so graphically by Winston Churchill that it need not be repeated in these pages.[3] Colonel Martin was instructed to reconnoitre and clear the left flank, and to prevent the enemy from re-entering Omdurman. His patrols reported that the way to the open plain beyond Jebel Surkab was barred by some dervishes in a *khor*. Before Martin could advance, and unknown to him, these dervishes were heavily reinforced. He approached the *khor* without further reconnaissance, unaware of its exact position. A few of the enemy were visible on an apparently open plain. They fired on him. The ruse was well known to the Egyptian cavalry, but not to Martin. He wheeled the 21st Lancers to the left and charged. The *khor* came suddenly into view, and the regiment plunged into a dense mass of the enemy concealed in it. The Lancers hacked their way through, but lost 5 officers, 65 men and 119 horses. They were practically out of action for the remainder of the battle, and consequently Kitchener received no immediate confirmation of the menace of the Army of the Black Flag. The heroic charge, which was also a tragic error, is commemorated by a memorial pillar,

---

[1] Notes by Lieut.-General Sir George Gorringe, K.C.B., K.C.M.G., D.S.O., Col. Commandant R.E., sent to the author on September 24th, 1936.

[2] Extract from a letter to the author, dated Jan. 12th, 1936, from Mr. E. G. Sarsfield-Hall, C.M.G., Governor of Khartoum, to whom General Stuart-Wortley related this story.

[3] *The River War*, by the Rt. Hon. Winston Churchill, M.P., pp. 282–287.

surrounded by a high steel fence, on the southern bank of the *khor*.[1]

The march of the main body on Omdurman began about 9 a.m. The infantry wheeled to the left in échelon of brigades, but the formation was soon spoilt. Wauchope's brigade tried to overtake Lyttleton's brigade (which was next to the river) in order that the entire British division under Gatacre should occupy as quickly as possible a ridge running eastwards from Jebel Surkab to the Nile. The result was that Maxwell's 2nd Egyptian Brigade was outdistanced. Normally, MacDonald's 1st Egyptian Brigade would have been behind Maxwell's brigade in the échelon, and Lewis's 3rd Egyptian Brigade would have followed MacDonald's brigade, with Collinson's 4th Egyptian Brigade in rear with the transport; but General Hunter had some misgivings about his right flank and decided to transpose Lewis and MacDonald, placing the latter, supported by three batteries and some Maxims, in the post of honour on the extreme flank of the échelon. Maxwell tried to close the widening gap between him and Wauchope; Lewis hurried to reduce the interval between him and Maxwell; and consequently, MacDonald, having completed his move westwards to the flank, found himself nearly a mile from Lewis.[2]

The progress of the Egyptian brigades was hindered by the Dervish wounded. Midwinter, with Lewis's brigade, records that many of the wounded fired at the troops as they passed,[3] and Manifold confirms this statement. In their ardour for "copy," several of the War Correspondents wandered ahead of the troops, and Manifold watched the hunting of two of them by a burly Baggara armed with a shovel-headed spear.[4] After a time, the Egyptian brigades, far from making up ground, had lost so much distance that Hunter sent Manifold forward to Kitchener, who was with Gatacre near the Jebel Surkab ridge, to request that he would allow time for brigades to regain their proper positions. A desultory, but gradually increasing, fire was coming from enemy snipers on Jebel Surkab. Then, an Egyptian battery unlimbered and began to shell the peak, and Gatacre halted his division as it reached the crest of the ridge between the peak and the river.

Although Kitchener was aware of the presence of the Army of the

[1] When the author visited the Khor es Sunta in 1935, he found that it was invisible from a distance of 100 yards. Near Egeiga, and within the area occupied by the entrenched camp, he saw the tomb of Lieut. R. S. Grenfell, 12th Lancers (attached to the 21st Lancers), who was killed in the charge.

[2] The movements of the brigades are shown in the *Sketch Map of the Battle of Omdurman, September 2nd, 1898. Second Phase*, which is included in this chapter.

[3] Letter from Lieut. E. C. Midwinter, R.E., dated Abidiya, September 6th, 1898, published in the *Parish Magazine*, St. Paul's, Lisson Grove, in October, 1898.

[4] Account of the Battle of Omdurman, written by Lieut. M. G. E. Manifold, R.E. Captain N. M. Smythe, 2nd Dragoon Guards, was afterwards awarded the Victoria Cross for rescuing these correspondents on this occasion.

Black Flag behind Jebel Surkab, MacDonald could see much that was hidden from his chief. At first, from his position on the right flank, MacDonald noticed a few dervishes behind the hill, and turning his brigade slightly towards them, sent Pritchard to Lewis to ask the latter to co-operate in an attack designed to safeguard his flank. Unfortunately, Lewis had just received peremptory orders to make up his distance, and accordingly he refused to stop and fight. His brigade marched on until it was almost out of sight. Left to his own devices, MacDonald advanced unsupported towards the seemingly small body of the enemy in front of him. These men opened fire, and he discovered at last that he was facing a large army, previously hidden from view, which was preparing to overwhelm his isolated brigade.

MacDonald immediately ordered Pritchard to gallop to the Sirdar, who was then on the northern slopes of Jebel Surkab between Maxwell's and Lewis's brigades. " I was to tell him of the mass of dervishes behind the Jebel," writes Major-General Pritchard,[1] " and to inquire whether MacDonald should attack them ; and I was to ask also for the co-operation of Lewis's brigade. The Sirdar's reply was, ' Cannot he see that we are marching on Omdurman ? Tell him to follow on.' I endeavoured to explain MacDonald's dangerous situation, but without effect, so I had to take this cold comfort back to MacDonald. However, shortly after I left him, the Sirdar must have appreciated the situation, for he issued the necessary orders to his subordinate commanders."

The orders issued by Kitchener were that Maxwell's 2nd Egyptian Brigade should change front to the right and storm Jebel Surkab, and that Lewis's 3rd Egyptian Brigade should come into line on Maxwell's right.[2] These messages were entrusted to Major A. E. Sandbach, R.E. The Sirdar then galloped to the British Division, in position on the ridge east of the Jebel, and ordered Lyttleton to form the 2nd Brigade on Maxwell's left facing west, and Wauchope to hurry back with the 1st Brigade to MacDonald's assistance. The 4th Egyptian Brigade under Collinson, and the Camel Corps under Tudway, were instructed to swing round to their right rear. By these movements, the army would be made to face west, with its right flank drawn back to the river. The manœuvres were executed with remarkable quickness and precision. Maxwell, indeed, was already on the move when his orders reached him, for he had turned his brigade to the right as soon as he heard heavy firing to his right rear.[3] He assaulted and captured Jebel Surkab, while Lewis came into action on his right. Wauchope's British troops doubled back in

---

[1] Notes by Major-General H. L. Pritchard, C.B., C.M.G., D.S.O. Col. Commandant R.E., sent to the author on Feb. 5th, 1936.
[2] *The River War*, by the Rt. Hon. Winston Churchill, M.P., p. 293.
[3] Notes by Brig.-General R. B. D. Blakeney, C.M.G., D.S.O., late R.E., sent to the author on Jan. 26th, 1936.

SKETCH MAP OF THE
BATTLE OF OMDURMAN,
SEPTEMBER 2ND, 1898.
SECOND PHASE.

four columns to help MacDonald, and Collinson and Tudway moved westward to guard the new right flank.

While Pritchard was returning to MacDonald with the curt order that the 1st Egyptian Brigade was to march on Omdurman, he passed through the area covered by the Dervish dead and wounded of the first attack. Several of the wounded fired on him as he rode, and a bullet perforated both his reins close to his left hand.[1] On his way, he told Lewis of the critical situation of MacDonald's brigade, and of the order which he was carrying to his brigade commander. The order was cancelled, of course, by the subsequent orders issued by the Sirdar. Meanwhile, General Hunter had sent Manifold to inform the Sirdar of the danger to MacDonald, and the Sirdar replied that he was coming to MacDonald's assistance. Manifold could see the enemy advancing in great numbers and fiercely attacking both MacDonald and Lewis, who were then separated by a gap $\frac{3}{4}$-mile in width. Hunter sent Manifold back again to ask Wauchope to hurry, and in the absence of Kitchener, gave orders that the 1st British Brigade should fill the gap to the left of MacDonald, that is to say, between him and Lewis.[2]

We left MacDonald halted and deployed in front of a Dervish force, which he now realized was an army. Seeing the enemy advancing, his artillery and Sudanese infantry opened fire without orders, wildly and ineffectively. At once, followed by his Brigade Major and by Pritchard and a trumpeter, MacDonald galloped out in front of his men, shouting to them to cease fire and knocking up their rifles. Up and down the blazing line rode the little party, in peril both from friend and foe, until the Sudanese fire died gradually away and only the Dervish bullets flew past. While the enemy took advantage of the lull to approach to within 400 yards, MacDonald harangued his troops in no measured terms, and having done so, ordered fire to be re-opened by company volleys. Discipline was restored. When the enemy, led by 200 mounted Emirs and Sheikhs, charged the Sudanese line, they were met by accurate and well-controlled rifle fire, and by streams of bullets from the machine-guns, and salvos of case-shot from the guns. Nothing could live before the deadly storm.

"So rapid was our fire," writes Pritchard,[3] "that the swish of our bullets was like the swish of water. They swept away the line of charging dervishes. Only one or two horsemen got within 100 yards. The leading Emir was hit twice—one could see him reel in his saddle —but still he came on at full gallop and was lifting his spear when he fell within 40 yards of our line, as if knocked off by a branch of a tree.

---

[1] The bullet was from a modern rifle of small bore. A few of the enemy were armed with such rifles, mostly Italian weapons obtained from Abyssinia.
[2] Account of the Battle of Omdurman by Lieutenant M. G. E. Manifold, R.E.
[3] *Sudan Campaign*, 1896–1899, by "An Officer" (Lieut. H. L. Pritchard, R.E.), p. 208.

The dervishes behind, seeing the slaughter in front, lay down about 400 yards away, whence they kept up a hot fire. At this moment, the movements ordered by the Sirdar began to take effect. Lewis's brigade, although some distance from MacDonald's, could be seen coming up fast, and they soon opened fire on the flank of the Khalifa's force, which was attacking MacDonald's brigade. Maxwell's brigade could also be seen, clearing the enemy from Jebel Surkab and establishing Maxims there. Two batteries arrived to reinforce MacDonald (having been sent by General Hunter), and it seemed as if the moment had come for him to advance and co-operate with Maxwell's and Lewis's brigades, who were converging on the Khalifa's flag."

Yakub and his Army of the Black Flag, checked by MacDonald, were now taken in flank by Maxwell and Lewis, while their communications were threatened by Lyttleton. Their attack wavered. Thousands fell and died. Other thousands streamed terror-stricken towards Omdurman. Yakub himself perished with his face to the foe. Thus ended the second phase of the Battle of Omdurman. It seemed that the battle was finished; and so it would have been had not a new and serious complication arisen.

When Maxwell heard the noise of MacDonald's firing, and turned his brigade to render assistance, he sent his " galloper," Blakeney, to reconnoitre from a col near the peak of Jebel Surkab. " This is what I saw," writes Brigadier-General Blakeney.[1] " MacDonald's brigade was blazing away at a large force of the enemy, above whom fluttered a huge black flag; but away to the north, perhaps unseen by him though clearly visible to me, was another army of about 10,000 dervishes under a green flag. MacDonald was thus in danger of being caught between two forces, and it was evident that a diversion must be made by our brigade. Having heard my report, Maxwell gave me two machine-guns, which I took up to and over the col, and down the farther slope to a position where we were within effective range. We intervened with deadly effect until the old ·450 Maxims jammed, and again after the locks had been changed. The Army of the Black Flag began to wither away under the fire of MacDonald's men, and the valiant dervishes were shot into a shambles of dead and dying."

The whole situation was changed by the threat from the north. Just as MacDonald was about to order an advance against the remnants of the Army of the Black Flag, Captain St. G. C. Henry, Northumberland Fusiliers, arrived from the Camel Corps to inform him that an army under two green flags was coming down from the Karari Hills on to his right rear. Had the attack of this army been simultaneous with that of the Army of the Black Flag, as the Khalifa intended, nothing could have saved MacDonald from destruction;

---

[1] Notes by Brig.-General R. B. D. Blakeney, C.M.G., D.S.O., late R.E., sent to the author on Jan. 26th, 1936.

SKETCH MAP OF THE
BATTLE OF OMDURMAN.
SEPTEMBER 2nd 1898.
THIRD PHASE.

Scale
Yards 1000 0 1000 2000 3,000 Yards

Heights are in feet above river level on Sept. 2nd 1898.

and possibly, after MacDonald, Lewis might have been overwhelmed. If Lewis had gone, who knows what would have happened?

To meet the attack of Osman Wad el Sheikh and Ali Wad Helu from the Karari Hills, MacDonald withdrew his battalions in turn from the line facing west, and formed his brigade into an arrow-head with a gradually lengthening barb facing almost north.[1] Pritchard led one of the battalions (11th Sudanese) to its new position, and each man opened fire as he came into line. As Wauchope's brigade was seen to be approaching rapidly, Pritchard was then sent by MacDonald to ask Wauchope to come up on his right. Wauchope replied, however, that his orders from General Hunter were to come up on MacDonald's left. Nevertheless, after Pritchard had explained the altered situation, Wauchope sent one battalion (Lincolns) to the right and led the remainder to the left. Three batteries of artillery and the Camel Corps had already joined the right face, and when the Lincolns were in position, MacDonald advanced against the Armies of the Green Flags and drove them back towards the hills. The enemy broke, and a charge by the Egyptian cavalry under Broadwood changed their retreat into a rout.

In an imposing array of infantry, artillery, cavalry and camelry, the whole army advanced westwards, driving the dervishes into the desert. At 11.30 a.m. Kitchener shut up his glasses and remarked that the enemy had had " a good dusting." The order was issued to halt, reform and resume the march on the Khalifa's capital. Before noon, the third and final phase of the Battle of Omdurman had come to an end.

A victory had been won which, to use Kitchener's own words, brought about the practical annihilation of the Khalifa's army, the extinction of Mahdiism in the Sudan, and the submission of the whole country formerly ruled under Egyptian authority. Vast territories were thereby re-opened to the benefits of peace, civilization and good government. The death of Charles Gordon was avenged, and British prestige reinstated.

The Dervish losses in the Battle of Omdurman were exceedingly heavy. No less than 10,800 bodies were counted on the field of battle, and it is estimated that the wounded numbered at least 16,000. More than one-half of an army of perhaps 52,000 men had been put out of action. On the other hand, the Anglo-Egyptian losses were remarkably slight, for only 48 officers and men were killed and 382 wounded. Most of the British casualties occurred behind the *zariba* fence at Egeiga, and at the Khor es Sunta during the charge of the 21st Lancers.

Although the Dervish plan for a synchronized attack by the Armies of the Black and Green Flags was well conceived, it failed in

---

[1] See the *Sketch Map of the Battle of Omdurman, September 2nd,* 1898. *Third Phase.*

execution. The Khalifa underestimated the discipline of the Sudanese and Egyptian troops, and the power of modern rifle fire. He committed a fatal error when he missed the opportunity to attack Kitchener under cover of darkness. Alternatively, by remaining in Omdurman he might have inflicted heavy casualties on the Anglo-Egyptian Army in street-fighting. Instead, he fought his enemy under conditions which gave full effect to superior fire-power, discipline and training. As to Kitchener, he solved the tactical problems of the Battle of Omdurman with sound appreciation, and dealt rapidly and effectively with its various situations as they arose. He could not choose his battle-ground. He desired to fight anywhere and at any time, except in the streets of Omdurman or by night, and his chief handicap during the actual battle was the difficulty of transmitting orders, and receiving information, while he himself was with the advanced left wing. He had neither the technical equipment, nor sufficient trained personnel, for the employment of field telephony.

After the Khalifa had been routed, no time was lost in seizing his capital. This task was assigned to Maxwell's 2nd Egyptian Brigade with the intention, no doubt, of emphasizing Egypt's share in the re-occupation of the Sudan. At the head of the 2nd Brigade and the 32nd Field Battery rode the Sirdar, his Staff beside him, behind him the Egyptian flag, and farther in rear, the captured black silk banner of the Khalifa. The column marched at 2 p.m., and halted at the Khor Shambat on the northern boundary of the city, whither it was followed by the British brigades and the other Egyptian brigades, while the mounted troops harried the retreating dervishes in the desert to the west. The heat was terrific, and men and animals drank copiously from the Nile. Midwinter was sent to report the arrival of Lewis's brigade. "The Sirdar looked thoroughly exhausted," he writes,[1] "but I heard him giving his orders with his usual extraordinary mastery of detail. After telling me that the brigade should rest and march into Omdurman in the evening, he turned to Gorringe and began some instructions about the disposal of spare ammunition!"

Maxwell's brigade continued its march and had not moved far from the Khor Shambat when a few unarmed dervishes approached the Sirdar who, in spite of all remonstrances, had insisted on riding at the head of the troops. An old Sheikh came forward, kissed the Sirdar's hand, and appealed for mercy for the inhabitants; to which the Sirdar replied in colloquial Arabic, "Certainly. If you will throw down your arms and not molest us." Turning towards the city, the Sheikh made a signal. Instantly, the tops of the apparently deserted mud walls were lined with black heads, and the

---

[1] Letter from Lieut. E. C. Midwinter, R.E., dated Sept. 6th, 1898, published in the *Parish Magazine*, St. Paul's, Lisson Grove, in October, 1898.

KITCHENER LEADING HIS VICTORIOUS TROOPS FROM THE BATTLEFIELD OF OMDURMAN.
The Sirdar is in white uniform (second from the left). In rear is his flag, and behind it the Khalifa's black banner.

[By kind permission of General Sir Reginald Wingate, Bt., G.C.B., etc.]

shrill, wavering cry of the women spread from hut to hut, and from street to street.

Pressing on for two miles through the suburbs, where deep holes in the roads and alleys were filled with stagnant water in which floated the rotting carcases of men and animals, Maxwell's brigade was confronted by the great wall surrounding the Mahdi's Tomb, the Khalifa's house, the quarters of the bodyguard and a mosque. Blakeney was sent to the Sirdar to ask for orders. "These," he writes,[1] "were exactly what might have been expected. We were to take the place before sunset. There was little time to spare. So on we went. The enclosure was in two halves, of which the first was entered without difficulty; but news came that the second was occupied by the Khalifa and his bodyguard, who intended to fight.[2] On entering the second enclosure, after an ineffective volley had been fired at us, we were faced by two mounted dervishes of the bodyguard who shook their spears and posted themselves behind, and on either side of, the gate at the end of the mosque. A score of Sudanese made a semi-circle in front of it. Suddenly, both horsemen galloped out, killed one soldier and wounded another, and fell at last, riddled by bullets and spitted by bayonets."

While the second enclosure was being cleared of the enemy, the Sirdar had a narrow escape from being killed by a shell from a gunboat, which was bombarding the Khalifa's house. Unfortunately, another shell caused the death of the Hon. Hubert Howard, Correspondent of *The Times* and the *New York Herald*. The bombardment was stopped before further casualties occurred, the Mahdi's Tomb was entered, and Charles Neufeld and other European captives were afterwards released from the prison. Darkness fell over a city foul with unburied corpses. Gradually the noise of desultory street fighting died away as the last resistance was crushed. The gunboats dominated the Nile. The troops held Omdurman. There was much confusion as the brigades and their transport surged through the narrow and evil-smelling streets. A bivouac had been arranged to the west of Omdurman, but the troops had to reach it by traversing the city. Midwinter states that the Mahdi's Tomb was the only landmark, and that artillery, infantry, camels, mules, Generals and officers of all kinds seemed to arrive there simultaneously. Kitchener himself could not find his headquarters' baggage until two hours after dark, and then, after some refreshment, lay on his back dictating orders, by the light of a solitary

[1] Notes by Brig.-General R. B. D. Blakeney, C.M.G., D.S.O., late R.E., sent to the author on Jan. 26th, 1936.
[2] The massive wall was, in some places, 18 feet high. Some units of the 2nd Brigade, turning left, marched along outside it to the river bank, and then advanced southwards between the wall and the river until, at 4.30 p.m., they entered the northern enclosure through a gate which had been demolished by the fire of the gunboats. Three companies then pushed farther along the river bank, and forced an entrance through another gate into the southern enclosure. The Khalifa had already made good his escape.

candle, to Colonel Wingate, who lay in a reverse position beside him.

The Mahdi's Tomb had been erected by the Khalifa as a monument to his predecessor. It was a whitewashed structure of stone, 36 feet square and 30 feet high, surmounted by an hexagonal plinth, 15 feet high, on which rested a dome 40 feet in height.[1] Four small cupolas adorned the corners of the building. The interior of the dome was painted green and chocolate, and all the woodwork was coloured green. Within the building, under a pall of banners, and surrounded by an iron railing taken from the Austrian Mission Church in Khartoum, was a green-painted, wooden sarcophagus containing the Mahdi's remains. Kitchener knew that much of the Dervish fanaticism centred in the Mahdi's Tomb, and that it was a place of pilgrimage, and consequently he decided that it would be politically advisable that the tomb should be destroyed and the body of the Mahdi removed. Lord Cromer himself admitted that these were measures of political necessity.[2] Kitchener pointed out also that the building had been damaged by gunfire to such an extent that it was unsafe. Accordingly, the wrecked dome, the cracked plinth and the cupolas were demolished with charges of explosive by Major W. S. Gordon, R.E., assisted by working parties of Sudanese soldiers. To-day, only four crumbling walls, with a few arched openings, remain as a relic of Dervishdom.[3]

After the occupation of Omdurman, the Egyptian cavalry and Camel Corps started southwards in pursuit of the flying Khalifa, keeping inland from the river bank to avoid flooded country. Some of the gunboats proceeded up the White Nile for a distance of 90 miles, but they were unable to come into touch with the enemy. The *Metemma* had already been loaded with forage and rations for the mounted troops engaged in the pursuit. On the evening of September 2nd, Stevenson moored his ship four miles above Omdurman, and on the following morning exchanged messages with the cavalry. The latter, however, could not approach nearer than 400 yards from the bank because of partially submerged trees, and Stevenson decided to make an attempt to gain contact farther south. He voyaged upstream for a further distance of 16 miles; but being still unable to provision the cavalry, he then returned to Omdurman, reaching it on the 5th, shortly after the mounted troops had arrived in camp after abandoning the pursuit. Thereafter, in

---

[1] *Fire and Sword in the Sudan*, by Rudolf C. Slatin Pasha, C.B. (4th edition), p. 432.

[2] Dispatch from Lord Cromer to the Marquis of Salisbury, dated March 12th, 1899.

[3] Kitchener gave the necessary orders on September 6th, after consulting certain influential inhabitants and several native officers of the Sudanese regiments. These were unanimous in recommending that the tomb should be demolished and the bones of the Mahdi thrown into the Nile. This was done; but, at a later date, the Mahdi's skull was buried, by order of the Sirdar, in the Muhammadan cemetery at Wadi Halfa. (For further particulars see *Letters of Queen Victoria, 1886—1901*, edited by G. E. Buckle, Volume III, pp. 352, 353.)

company with most of the other gunboats, the *Metemma* was employed in towing barges, filled with troops, downstream to Fort Atbara.[1] Almost all the British troops, and a large number of the Sudanese and Egyptian units, were evacuated during September in ships, barges and sailing-boats, and among the earliest to leave the front were the subalterns of the Royal Engineers who had served as " gallopers." Kitchener saw to it that the railway engineers lost not a day in prolonging the line to Khartoum.

An impressive ceremony took place in Khartoum before the troops departed. On September 4th, 1898, representatives of every regiment and corps paraded on the left bank of the Blue Nile in front of Gordon's Palace. The upper storey of the old building had gone ; the windows were blocked with bricks ; the famous staircase had been demolished ; debris was piled high against the walls ; the garden in rear was overgrown with thorn bushes and weeds. W. S. Gordon in the *Melik*, and Newcombe in the *Abu Klea*, brought the troops across from Omdurman, and the *Melik* was moored to the left bank immediately opposite the Palace. Soon afterwards, the *Abu Klea* tied up below the *Melik*, and Newcombe joined Gordon to watch the ceremony. The Sirdar and his staff, with most of the other officers and some of the troops, took up a position in front of the ruined building, the remainder of the troops being formed on either side, facing inwards. On the roof, almost on the spot where Charles Gordon fell, two flagstaffs had been erected. By one, stood two British officers ; by the other, a British and an Egyptian officer. The Sirdar raised his hand. The Union Jack and the Egyptian flag were hoisted. The band of the Grenadier Guards played the National Anthem, and the band of the 11th Sudanese the Khedivial Anthem. A salute of 21 guns was fired by the *Melik*, commanded by Charles Gordon's nephew. The Sirdar then called for three cheers for Her Majesty and three for the Khedive. These demonstrations of loyalty were succeeded by a brief religious service, and by funeral marches played by the two bands. Finally the Sirdar, visibly affected by the solemnity and pathos of the occasion, brought the ceremony to a close with Gordon's favourite hymn " Abide with Me," played by the band of the 11th Sudanese.[2] Thus England and Egypt set their seal forever on Khartoum.

Honours and rewards were showered on the victors of Omdurman, and the Royal Engineers received their full share. Major-General Sir Herbert Kitchener, K.C.B., K.C.M.G., became Baron Kitchener of Khartoum and Aspall, with the award of the G.C.B. and a grant of £30,000. The official notification was delayed for a few days through

[1] The veteran *Bordein*, recaptured from the dervishes, was among the steamers employed in evacuating the troops. Her *Rais* (Arab captain) had been in charge of her for nearly 20 years. As her boiler had lost both safety valve and gauge, the *Rais* used the whistle as a test of suitable steam-pressure !

[2] The tune is now played by the band of the 11th Sudanese after every performance and immediately before the National Anthem. It is known as " Khartoum."

the temporary breakdown of the telegraph, and because of the absence of the Sirdar in the far south, whither he had proceeded, on September 10th, to deal with an urgent and difficult political situation. It was the desire of Her Majesty to inform him of her intention immediately after the battle which restored the Sudan to Egypt, but it was impossible for her to do so until his return from the waters of the Upper Nile. Talbot, Sandbach, Kincaid and W. S. Gordon became Brevet Lieut.-Colonels; Macauley was promised a Brevet Majority on promotion to Captain; and Stevenson, Pritchard, Blakeney, Micklem and Midwinter received the D.S.O.[1]

Outstanding features of this brief campaign are Kitchener's masterly organization for the concentration of his entire force south of the Sixth Cataract and within a few easy marches of Omdurman, and also his general plan for the decisive battle. On these matters Lieut.-General Sir George Gorringe remarks:—[2]" As river transport was limited, the concentration had to be most carefully worked out. Calculations were needed for the supply of rations, complete in every detail, for various formations, for the number of days that each would require them at each camp; and the river transport had to be so arranged that each unit had with it, in separate boats or barges, its rations for multiples of two days, so that it could join a detached force without confusion or delay. As regards the Sirdar's plan for the Battle of Omdurman, his intention, as he had several times mentioned to me, was to manœuvre his force so as to avoid having to fight his way into Omdurman through narrow streets and alleys. He hoped that the Khalifa would give battle close to Omdurman; but he anticipated, nevertheless, that the Dervish leader might choose to do so as far north as the Karari position."

Supported in every crisis by Lord Cromer, Kitchener reconquered the Sudan at an absurdly small financial cost;[3] but like most distinguished military leaders he was assailed by bitter and hostile critics. It was alleged that he had allowed the Dervish wounded to be killed without cause: that Omdurman had been looted: that he had permitted the gunboats to fire on non-combatants, including women and children: that, in fact, he was a ruthless exponent of "frightfulness" in war. Needless to say, every charge was proved to be entirely without foundation. Kitchener could be ruthless when occasion demanded, but he was essentially humane.

[1] Several R.E. officers received Egyptian decorations. In addition, Major H. M. Lawson was promoted to Brevet Lieut.-Colonel for his services at Gedaref, and Lieut. G. C. M. Hall received the D.S.O., although he was not present at Omdurman.

[2] Notes by Lieut.-General Sir George Gorringe, K.C.B., K.C.M.G., D.S.O., Col. Commandant R.E., sent to the author on September 24th, 1936.

[3] According to Lord Cromer's report, dated February 26th, 1899, the total expense from the beginning of the Dongola Expedition in 1896 till the close of the operations in 1898 was only £E.2,354,354. Of this amount, £E.1,181,372 was attributed to the construction of 760 miles of railway, £E.21,825 to the provision of 2,000 miles of telegraph, and £E.154,934 to the building of six gunboats. Thus the military expenditure was only £E.996,223 during nearly three years of campaigning.

THE GORDON MEMORIAL CEREMONY AT KHARTOUM.

Hoisting the British and Egyptian flags over the ruins of the old Palace on September 4th, 1898.

[By kind permission of General Sir Reginald Wingate, Bt., G.C.B., etc.]

He carried the Dongola, Atbara and Omdurman campaigns to a successful conclusion by patience, experience, thrift, natural acumen, careful preparation, engineering knowledge, sound strategy and bold tactics; but transcending all these in value was the force of his personal influence and character, and the genius which enabled him to select and train a staff of officers who understood his methods and could translate into action the plans which he evolved.

A DERVISH PREACHING THE HOLY WAR.

[*from " The War in Egypt and the Sudan."*]

CHAPTER XI.

AFTER OMDURMAN.

ON September 7th, 1898, the Dervish steamer *Tewfikiya*, voyaging unsuspectingly down the White Nile, arrived in Omdurman and was promptly captured. Her crew told a strange story. They stated that, with the steamer *Safiya*, they had been dispatched up the river by the Khalifa to collect grain for the Dervish army, and on approaching a village called Fashoda, about 470 miles from Khartoum, they had been fired upon by a party of black soldiers under European officers. The ships had retreated; and the Emir in command, having disembarked some men at Renk, 300 miles south of Khartoum, had sent the *Tewfikiya* back to Omdurman to ask the Khalifa for reinforcements to enable him to overcome the hated "Turks." The crew of the *Tewfikiya* were positive that their adversaries at Fashoda were disciplined troops under white officers, and in support of their statement produced some nickel-covered bullets, which they had extracted from holes in the ship's side. As no British or Egyptian troops were south of Omdurman, it was evident that some European power had forestalled the Sirdar on the Upper Nile. There was much speculation in camp as to who the strangers might be. The Sirdar, however, had little doubt that they were Commandant Marchand and the officers and men of a small French expedition which, for nearly two years, had been travelling slowly eastwards across Africa from the Atlantic coast. Accordingly, he ordered all the newspaper correspondents back to Cairo, and prepared to carry out certain instructions which he had received through Lord Cromer.

In August, 1898, Lord Salisbury had laid down the line of action to be taken when the Anglo-Egyptian army reached Khartoum.[1] Flotillas were to be sent up the Blue and White Niles. The expedition on the Blue Nile was not to penetrate farther than Roseires, near the Abyssinian border;[2] but that on the White Nile was to proceed, under the leadership of the Sirdar himself, as far south as Fashoda, and was to carry a small body of British troops. The Sirdar was instructed that he should not acknowledge the title of France or Abyssinia to any portion of the Nile Valley, and that he should avoid all collision with the Abyssinians. If necessary, however, he could continue his voyage up the White Nile to beyond the

---

[1] *Life of Lord Kitchener*, by Sir George Arthur, Vol. I, p. 246.
[2] See the *Sketch Map of the Southern Sudan*, which is included in this chapter.

junction of the Sobat River, nearly 60 miles above Fashoda and about 130 miles from the Abyssinian frontier.

It was rumoured that the strangers on the White Nile had established themselves at Fashoda on July 10th, so the utmost haste was necessary. Accordingly, at 6 a.m. on September 10th, Kitchener started southwards in the steamer *Dal*, escorted by the gunboats *Sultan, Fateh*, and *Nasir* under Commander Colin Keppel, R.N.[1] With the Sirdar in the *Dal* were his personal Staff[2] and his chief Intelligence officer, Lieut.-Colonel Wingate, R.A.;[3] and on board the gunboats, or in barges alongside them, were one company of the Cameron Highlanders (under Captain the Hon. A. D. Murray), the 11th and 13th Battalions of Sudanese infantry (under Major H. W. Jackson,[4] Gordon Highlanders, and Lieut.-Colonel H. L. Smith-Dorrien,[5] Derbyshire Regiment, respectively), a battery of Egyptian artillery (under Captain M. Peake, R.A.), and four Maxims.

The only Royal Engineer who accompanied Kitchener to Fashoda was Lieutenant E. O. A. Newcombe. On his arrival in the *Abu Klea* at Fort Atbara with British troops from Omdurman, Newcombe found that no specific railway work had been allotted to him, so he returned to Omdurman with supplies for the garrison. Encumbered by heavily loaded barges, the *Abu Klea* had a most adventurous voyage. The current was so strong that, in order to pass the Sixth Cataract, Newcombe was obliged to raise a dangerous steam-pressure in the ship's boiler by weighting down the safety valve. However, he reached Omdurman on September 11th without disaster, and having cast off his barges, received instructions from Lieutenant G. F. Gorringe, R.E., to follow the Sirdar up the White Nile with supplies and dispatches. Two hours later, the little *Abu Klea* steamed southwards, towing a barge and a native *gyassa* (boat). Wood fuel was piled high on her decks to save her coal. During the first night of her voyage, she collided with a hippopotamus and was blown on to a sand-bank by a violent storm; but she succeeded in gradually overhauling the flotilla, which steamed only by day.

Early on the morning of September 15th, Newcombe saw ahead of him the smoke of the flotilla and began to use his precious coal to increase his speed. When he drew up alongside the *Dal*, he was hailed by Kitchener who shouted, "What! Burning coal! Coal is terribly expensive. I think that I shall be able to give you plenty of wood

---

[1] The *Sultan* was commanded by Lieut. W. H. Cowan, R.N., the *Fateh* by Lieut. David Beatty, R.N., and the *Nasir* by Lieut. the Hon. A. Hood, R.N.

[2] The Sirdar was accompanied by his three A.D.C's—Brevet-Major Lord Edward H. Cecil, Grenadier Guards; Captain J. K. Watson, D.S.O., K.R.R.C.; and Lieut. the Hon. F. H. S. Roberts, K.R.R.C. (a son of Field-Marshal Lord Roberts). Capt. H. E. Hill-Smith, R.A.M.C., accompanied the expedition as Medical Officer.

[3] Colonel Wingate's assistant, Slatin Pasha, was with the cavalry in pursuit of the Khalifa in the swamps south of Omdurman.

[4] With Major Jackson were Capt. E. A. Stanton, Oxf. L.I., and Lieut. G. de H. Smith, Indian Staff Corps.

[5] With Lieut.-Colonel Smith-Dorrien were Major F. I. Maxse, Coldstream Guards, Capt. R. N. Gamble, Lincolnshire Regt., and Capt. T. Capper, E. Lancashire Regt.

in about an hour's time." The flotilla, with the *Sultan* leading and the *Abu Klea* last in the line, then steamed on and came into action against the *Safiya* and the small Dervish garrison at Renk. " My Egyptian gunners opened fire with the Krupp," writes Newcombe[1] "but their shells passed high over the *Safiya;* and when the excited crews of the Nordenfeldts on the upper deck began firing without orders, and did considerable injury to the rigging of the *gyassa* alongside us, I thought it well to cease fire. I dined with the Sirdar that night and he joked about our marksmanship, so I said we had fired at the retreating enemy ashore. He was annoyed because a shell from the *Sultan* had damaged the *Safiya's* boiler.[2] ' Why is it,' said he, ' that the naval people *will* aim at the boiler when they know that we cannot get it repaired here ? " The *Safiya* had plenty of wood aboard her, and each gunboat got her share of it. We then proceeded up the river by easy stages, stopping for the night at places where wood was available. All the troops took their turn in cutting wood. I saw a Sudanese soldier, astride a slender branch, cheerfully cutting it away between himself and the trunk until he and the branch fell together to the ground amid roars of laughter from his friends. Mosquitoes were a terrible nuisance. The unfortunate Camerons, in particular, must have suffered agonies, for their kilts gave them no protection."

Newcombe relates that in the Sudanese units there were a number of Shilluk soldiers, who had come from that region, and that when Kitchener approached Fashoda he sent out some of these men to get into touch with their friends and gather information. One man returned with a local chief, a fine, upstanding fellow, but stark naked. When they came aboard the *Dal*, an orderly gave the chief a cabin-towel to use as a loin-cloth in order that he might present himself, decently clad, before the Sirdar. The Shilluk draped the towel around him ; but on entering the saloon he removed it, and, as a mark of respect, wound it round his head !

On a later occasion, the Sirdar sent a Shilluk sergeant to summon the chiefs of his tribe to an interview, and was much surprised when a series of deputations—always of seven men—waited on him. The sergeant then explained that he had met a large number of Shilluks who wished to see the Sirdar in their national costume of stark nakedness. He had demurred and told them that the great white Pasha would be very angry at such disrespect. To avoid disappointing them, however, he had managed to procure seven loin-cloths to be used in turn by the entire tribe. Hence the deputations of seven. As time was precious, the Sirdar agreed

[1] Notes by Major E. O. A. Newcombe, D.S.O., R.E. (retd.), sent to the author on February 23rd, 1936.

[2] This was not the first occasion on which the *Safiya's* boiler was damaged. When Lord Charles Beresford, in the *Safiya*, rescued Charles Wilson's party above Wad Habashi in January, 1885, the boiler was holed by a Dervish shell In 1898, the plate fixed over that hole was found to be still in position. (See Chapter IV.)

THE GUNBOAT "SULTAN" ON THE WHITE NILE.

[*By kind permission of Colonel E. A. Stanton, C.M.G., late Oxf. L.I.*]

forthwith to receive the remainder of the Shilluks in their national costume.[1]

The interview with the Shilluk chief, who used his loin-cloth as a turban, occurred while the flotilla was moored to the left bank about ten miles below Fashoda on September 18th, and the information then received confirmed Kitchener in the belief that the Europeans at Fashoda were Commandant Marchand and his officers. Desiring, however, to observe a proper formality and to reassure Marchand that the expedition was not a Dervish one, he dispatched a letter to Fashoda,[2] addressed to " The Head of the European Expedition, said to be on the White Nile." In it he announced the victory at Omdurman, the flight of the Khalifa, and the approach of the flotilla carrying British and Egyptian troops. He congratulated the members of the expedition on the completion of their long journey to the White Nile, and promised to escort them safely to Cairo.

At dawn on September 19th, 1898, the flotilla steamed again towards Fashoda. The *Sultan* led the way, with Commander Keppel aboard. Astern of her was the little *Abu Klea*, and then the *Dal*, carrying the Sirdar and his Staff. The *Nasir* and *Fateh* followed some distance in rear. All the ships flew the Egyptian flag alone. When Fashoda came in sight, the four gunboats steamed ahead, the *Nasir* and *Fateh* packed with troops.[3] They drew up before the ruins of an old fort, not far from the left bank of the river, over which floated a large French tricolour. The mud walls were lined with black soldiers, dressed in yellow coats, white zouave trousers, white gaiters and red caps, and here and there were a few white officers with peaked beards. They were Commandant Marchand's expedition of eight Frenchmen and some 120 Senegalese. A landing stage, a *Mudiria* or Governor's House, a few other mud-brick dwellings within the defences, and a number of straw-thatched *tukuls*, sheltering under scattered palm-trees, completed the scene. Beyond the little settlement, the swamps stretched to the horizon. While Commander Keppel and Captain Lord Edward Cecil landed from the *Sultan* to call upon the French commandant, the proceedings were watched with silent interest by hundreds of Dinkas and Shilluks, congregated on the banks of the river.[4]

---

[1] *Sudan Campaign*, 1896–1899, by " An Officer " (Lieut. H. L. Pritchard, R.E.), p. 231.

[2] A Shilluk Sergeant of the 11th Sudanese was the messenger.

[3] The *Nasir* and her barges carried the 11th Sudanese. The *Fateh* and her barges carried the company of Cameron Highlanders and the 13th Sudanese.

[4] The brief account here given of some of the events which took place at Fashoda and elsewhere on the White Nile in 1898 has been compiled from the following sources :— *The River War*, by the Rt. Hon. Winston Churchill, M.P., pp. 312–323 ; *The Egyptian Campaigns*, 1882–1899, by Charles Royle, pp. 584–588 ; *The Egyptian Sudan, Its Loss and Recovery*, by Lieuts. H. S. L. Alford and W. D. Sword, pp. 283–285 ; *Life of Lord Kitchener*, by Sir George Arthur, Vol. I, pp. 246–250 ; an article entitled " Fashoda, 1898," by Sir Herbert W. Jackson, appearing in *Sudan Notes and Records*, Jan. 1920, Vol. III, No 1, pp. 1–11 ; a letter from Colonel F. R. Wingate to Sir Arthur Bigge, dated Sept. 23rd, 1898, quoted in *Letters of Queen*

Meanwhile, when still two miles from Fashoda, the *Dal* had met a steel rowing-boat, paddled by 12 Senegalese and flying a tricolour so large that its end almost trailed in the water. In her were three or four armed Senegalese soldiers under a black sergeant, and also the Sirdar's messenger to Marchand. The boat came alongside and the soldiers climbed aboard. They formed up on deck. The sergeant stepped forward, and saluting smartly, handed to the Sirdar a reply from Marchand. The letter opened with polite congratulations to the Sirdar on his recent victory, and went on to explain that, in accordance with the instructions of his Government, Marchand had occupied the Bahr el Ghazal region and Fashoda and had made a treaty with the local Shilluk chief, who had placed his country under French protection. The sergeant and his men then returned to their boat, and the *Dal* continued on her way to Fashoda, towing the boat alongside her. On arrival, she moored to the bank at the head of the line of ships upstream of the *Sultan* and *Abu Klea*. Commandants Marchand and Germain, Captains Baratier and Mangin,[1] and three other French officers boarded the *Sultan* by a gangway plank at her bows, and, conducted by Commander Keppel, reached the *Dal*, where they were introduced to the Sirdar and Colonel Wingate. Afterwards, all other British and French officers having withdrawn, Kitchener, Wingate, Marchand and Germain sat down at a small table, aft of the cabins, to discuss the situation. " From my position on the *Abu Klea* I could see everything distinctly," writes Newcombe, " although, of course, I could hear nothing. Marchand sat very upright, gesticulating with both hands. Facing him was Kitchener, his legs stretched out, almost lounging, and occasionally waving one hand slowly, as if to emphasize some point."

The course of that momentous discussion is known only to General Sir Reginald Wingate, the sole survivor of the four who met on board the *Dal*. It is unnecessary to describe the negotiations, except to record that in the end the brave and chivalrous Marchand consented to await the orders of the French Government, consequent on the negotiations which would inevitably ensue between the British and French Governments. Meanwhile, no objection was raised to the landing of the Egyptian Expeditionary Force and the occupation of the country. Accordingly, Colonel Wingate went ashore with Commandant Germain and Lord Edward Cecil, and passing

---

Victoria, edited by G. E. Buckle, Vol. III, pp. 285–287 ; notes by Major E. O. A. Newcombe sent to the author on Feb. 23rd, 1936 ; letters written by the same officer in September and October, 1898 ; and correspondence between General Sir Reginald Wingate, Admirals Sir Colin Keppel and Sir Walter Cowan, Colonel E. A. Stanton and the author in March and April, 1936. A good account of the Fashoda incident is given in *Fachoda—Mission Marchand*, 1896–1899, by Médicin-Général J. Emily (2nd Edition, 1935).

[1] Captain Mangin became a distinguished General in the Great War. After being reduced to the command of a Corps on the Western Front from that of an Army, he was promoted to the command of a group of armies and led them in the successful counter-attack launched by the Allies on July 8th, 1918.

MARCHAND'S BOAT APPROACHING THE "DAL" BELOW FASHODA.

The Sirdar is observing her through field-glasses. Beside him is Colonel Wingate.

[*By kind permission of Colonel E. A. Stanton, C.M.G., late Oxf. L.I.*]

through the French defences, proceeded south-westwards for about a quarter of a mile until he reached an embankment carrying a track which led from the river towards the interior. This he selected as a suitable site for the hoisting of the Egyptian flag;[1] and while the *Sultan* and the *Abu Klea* remained at the landing stage near the Fort, the other ships moved a short distance upstream, where the troops disembarked and marched to the place chosen for the ceremony.

" Walter Cowan (from the *Sultan*) having suggested that we should walk along the bank," writes Newcombe, " we found the troops drawn up on ceremonial parade on rather marshy ground. A flagstaff was erected. Peake's battery prepared to fire a salute—with live shell. Kitchener waved his hand and said ' A little more music, please, Jackson,' and the band of the 11th Sudanese played a tune. Then the Egyptian flag was hoisted,[2] the Egyptian National Anthem was played, and a salute of 21 guns fired, Kitchener remarking with sardonic humour that it was well that the guns were pointing across the river." It is possible that the Dinkas on the right bank did not agree with this sentiment, but no casualties were recorded. The ceremony having concluded, the Sirdar and Colonel Wingate called upon Commandant Marchand in his *tukul* near the Fort, where the officers had made themselves a very nice vegetable garden.[3] Marchand produced a bottle of excellent champagne, in which he and Germain drank to the health of Queen Victoria, and the British officers pledged the French Republic. Kitchener and Wingate then returned to the *Dal* to continue their voyage up the White Nile.

The French had accomplished the remarkable feat of bringing with them, across Africa, three steel boats and the sections and machinery of a steam launch—the *Faidherbe*—which they had assembled on the Nile. They had supplies sufficient for several months, but no artillery and few machine-guns. Their stock of ammunition had been severely depleted in beating off the *Tewfikiya* and *Safiya* on August 25th. Marchand had sent the *Faidherbe* southwards in the hope that she might bring help from Abyssinia, or from a small base which he had established at Meshra er Req,

[1] Lord Cromer remarks :—" In order to give an outward and visible sign that, in the eyes of the British Government, the political status of the Sudan differed from that of Egypt, Lord Kitchener was instructed, on the capture of Khartoum, to hoist the British and Egyptian flags side by side. When Lord Kitchener found himself face to face with Commandant Marchand at Fashoda, he very wisely hoisted the Egyptian flag only. . . . " (see *Modern Egypt*, by the Earl of Cromer, Vol. II, p. 115). It was provided in an agreement between the British and Egyptian Governments, signed on January 19th, 1899, that both flags should be used throughout the Sudan, with the exception of the town of Suakin. However, by a later agreement, signed on July 10th, 1899, the status of Suakin was assimilated to that of the remainder of the Sudan.

[2] The flag was hoisted by Captain E. A. Stanton, Oxf. L.I., and Captain T. Capper, E. Lanc. Regt.

[3] The French officers occupied a line of straw-thatched mud huts a short distance from the river. Between the huts and the river was the garden.

far up the Bahr el Ghazal channel beyond the confluence of the Sobat River; but no reinforcements had reached the French at Fashoda, and, in the middle of September, they had heard to their consternation of the approach from the north of five gunboats, which they imagined to be Dervish vessels. Day and night, they laboured at their fortifications; and great was their relief when news came that the flotilla flew the Egyptian flag. There can be little doubt that if Kitchener had not destroyed the Khalifa's army on September 2nd, nothing could have saved Marchand and his small band from annihilation by the Dervish hordes.

Kitchener spent only four hours at Fashoda, for at 3 p.m. on September 19th, he started in the *Dal* for the mouth of the Sobat River to establish an advanced post at that spot and to search for the *Faidherbe*. With him were Colonel Wingate and the remainder of his Staff. On board the gunboats, and in barges alongside them, were a company of Cameron Highlanders and the 13th Sudanese battalion under Maxse, with two guns of Peake's battery and two Maxims. The Egyptian garrison left at Fashoda thus consisted of the 11th Sudanese under Jackson, with four guns and two Maxims. As Commandant, Jackson was given certain instructions regarding his dealings with the French and the neighbouring tribes; and when the smoke of the flotilla had vanished in the south, he established his camp near some empty *tukuls* on drier ground, at a distance of about 500 yards to the south-west of the spot where the flag had been hoisted, and set himself to make the best of a most unpleasant situation.[1]

The French Senegalese troops in Fashoda were in much better case than the Sudanese on their island in the swamps. Each man had an excellent waterproof ground-sheet, a small mosquito net, a waterproof bag for his kit and a waterproof cover for his rifle; his webbing equipment was comfortable and durable, and he was well fed. The Sudanese, on the other hand, had no ground-sheets nor mosquito nets. Each soldier secured what cover he could under a single blanket. The rain fell in torrents, turning biscuits to pulp and flour to dough. The Sudanese sweated and shivered with malaria. To them, Fashoda was a nightmare, and in after years, a place of hideous memory.[2] In 1900, during the administration of Sir Reginald Wingate as Governor-General of the Sudan, the name was wiped off the map. Fashoda became " Kodok," and so it appears to this day.

[1] Major H. W. Jackson was experienced, tactful and capable, and in all respects well fitted for his difficult task. He had seen active service in Egypt and the Sudan in 1882, 1884–85, 1888–89, and 1896–98. After Fashoda, he became Governor of Berber. He was Civil Secretary from 1900 to 1902, and thereafter Governor of the Dongola Province for no less than 20 years. In 1922, he was appointed Inspector-General of the Sudan. He retired at the end of that year as Major-General Sir Herbert Jackson, K.B.E., C.B., after acting on several occasions as Governor-General. He died at Merowe on January 28th, 1931.

[2] At Fashoda, in March, 1899, only 37 men were fit for duty out of a garrison of 317. (See Sir William Garstin's Report: Egypt, No. 5, 1899.)

On September 22nd, Kitchener reached the mouth of the Sobat, where he landed three companies of the 13th Sudanese with two guns (under Captains R. N. Gamble and T. Capper) and hoisted the Egyptian flag. He obtained some valuable political information, but did not see the *Faidherbe* nor any Abyssinians.[1] Newcombe returned to Fashoda in the *Abu Klea* to inform Jackson that the Sirdar would not stop at that place on his voyage northwards, because his ships were short of fuel. It is probable, however, that the Sirdar was actuated also by a desire to reach Omdurman as quickly as possible in order to report to Cairo and London. On the morning of the 23rd, while the troops at Fashoda were drying their clothes and blankets and clearing the ground of rank grass, the *Dal* reappeared from the south, escorted by the gunboats *Sultan*, *Fateh* and *Nasir*. The Sirdar could be seen on her deck, viewing the troops through his field-glasses, and a semaphore signal message was received from him to the effect that he was glad to see that steps were being taken to make the men more comfortable. In due course, he arrived in Omdurman, with the company of Cameron Highlanders, and cabled immediately to the Foreign Office.[2] On October 6th, he was in Cairo.

For several weeks Fashoda was cut off from all communication with the outer world. The *Sultan* and *Abu Klea* under Cowan patrolled the river. Jackson established friendly relations with Marchand, and thus avoided all friction. He sent the *Abu Klea* upstream on several occasions to explore the swampy regions of the Bahr el Ghazal, Bahr el Jebel and Bahr ez Zeraf in the hope of finding the French launch *Faidherbe*, and to explore the navigable channels of the river. On one trip, Peake, Stanton, Newcombe and Hill-Smith (a doctor) succeeded in reaching Lake No, ascending the Bahr el Ghazal and arriving finally at or near Meshra er Req. "There we found traces of the French," writes Newcombe. "We hoisted the Egyptian flag, and having placed at the foot of the flagstaff a bottle containing a piece of paper with an announcement in English and French that the flag had been hoisted by order of the Khedive's Government, we returned to the *Abu Klea*, descended the Bahr el Ghazal, hoisted a second flag near the Bahr el Arab and steamed down to Fashoda." Stanton brought back with him an excellent reconnaissance map of the Bahr el Ghazal.

Capper replaced Stanton in an expedition up the Bahr ez Zeraf. Newcombe and his companions had many exciting adventures with hippopotami and were the victims of myriads of mosquitoes, against which they had little protection. The phantom *Faidherbe* was never seen until she appeared at a later date at Fashoda. These expeditions to the "sudd" regions of the Upper Nile were very

[1] An Abyssinian flag, however, was discovered in a village.
[2] On September 24th, Lieut.-General Sir Francis Grenfell, commanding the British Troops in Egypt, had reached Omdurman from Cairo.

brief, for the *Abu Klea* was not allowed to be absent from Fashoda for more than a fortnight.

Stanton relates that on a difficult trip up the Bahr el Ghazal, the party arrived at the village of Ajwong, whence all the inhabitants had fled with the exception of one old man and his wife. These, being stark naked, were presented tactfully with a roll of calico, and at the same time they were given an Egyptian flag and told to hoist it in the village. The expedition then proceeded farther upstream ; but on their return two days later, they were greatly surprised to see a square yard of calico fluttering on the village flagstaff, and the Egyptian flag draped gracefully round the shoulders of the old lady !

Shortly after Newcombe's return from the Bahr ez Zeraf, the gunboat *Tamai* arrived from the north with orders that he was to hand over the command of the *Abu Klea* and rejoin the Railway Department at Fort Atbara. The same ship brought dispatches for Commandant Marchand from France, and that officer, after reading them, decided to proceed to Cairo, leaving Commandant Germain in charge of the French post at Fashoda. Meanwhile, he arranged that Captain Baratier should be sent to Omdurman, and Newcombe and Baratier quitted Fashoda on October 11th in the *Tamai*. " I found Baratier a most charming companion," writes Newcombe, " although he knew no English and my French was very halting." Within the next fortnight Marchand himself was on his way north. Lieutenant M. G. E. Manifold, R.E., who met him at Wadi Halfa on November 1st, describes him as a small, wiry man with dark hair and a double-peaked beard. Soon afterwards, Manifold travelled over the Desert Railway with Baratier, who was following Marchand with instructions to the latter from his own Government to return to Fashoda. Marchand and Baratier left Cairo for Fashoda during the first week of November. Manifold met them in Wadi Halfa on November 14th, and they were back in Fashoda early in December. Jackson and his second-in-command, Stanton, welcomed the return of the tactful Marchand to Fashoda, where the situation had become so strained that Stanton, in the temporary absence of his chief, had moved the Sudanese camp nearly three miles to the south.

Tranquillity was soon restored ; and as it was known that the French Government had ordered the return of the French expedition to France, Marchand and his men prepared at once for their departure. This was marked by every display of *camaraderie*. Very generously, the French officers presented their supplies of champagne and other wines to the British, whom they entertained at an official dinner. The British, in their turn, invited the French to a luncheon, on which occasion they presented Marchand and his officers with a Dervish flag as a memento of the French victory of August 25th over the *Tewfikiya* and *Safiya*.

Shortly after dawn on December 11th, 1898, the tricolour at Fashoda was lowered with proper ceremony by Marchand, who then divided it into eight pieces, one for each French officer. The *Abu Klea* having been placed at the disposal of the French expedition, that gunboat, and the *Faidherbe* and the steel boats, carried Marchand and his officers and men upstream past the Sudanese camp, where they were received with salutes and cheers, to which they responded most heartily. They proceeded to the Sobat,[1] and marching through Abyssinia to Jibuti, reached Marseilles in a French ship in May, 1899. Thus ended this brief episode—a regrettable, but temporary, difference between friendly nations.[2]

While Kitchener was on the White Nile, a small expedition under Major-General Archibald Hunter ascended the Blue Nile in the gunboats *Sheikh* and *Hafir* as far as Roseires, the extreme limit of navigation. This force, which started from Omdurman on September 19th, consisted of only two companies of the 10th Sudanese and a Maxim battery, but the remainder of the battalion followed as river transport became available. Hunter encountered no resistance. He reached Wad Medani on the 23rd, and Roseires, 400 miles from Khartoum, on the 29th. By October 3rd, he had received the surrender of several Dervish forces and had garrisoned Wad Medani, Sennar, Karkoj and Roseires. Then, having arranged for the patrolling of the river by gunboats, he returned as quickly as possible to Omdurman. No Royal Engineers accompanied in this expedition, which partook of the nature of a triumphal progress.

There was one Dervish leader, however, who refused to submit tamely to the invaders. After the Battle of the Atbara on April 8th, 1898, Ahmed Fedil had been sent by the Khalifa to collect all available reinforcements from the Gedaref and Gallabat Provinces, and to bring them to Omdurman. On September 2nd, he and his army were at Rufaa, within 60 miles of the capital; but the news of his master's defeat, and subsequent flight to the south, induced him to alter his plans and retrace his steps up the right bank of the Blue Nile with the intention of crossing that river at Abu Haraz, and the White Nile near Ed Dueim, and so rejoining the Khalifa in Kordofan. He failed in this project because his passage of the Blue Nile was barred by Egyptian gunboats, and accordingly, he left the river and proceeded to retire in leisurely fashion towards Gedaref.[3]

Meanwhile, the small Egyptian garrison of Kassala, under Lieut-. Colonel C. S. B. Parsons, R.A., had been obliged for several months

[1] Commandant Marchand abandoned the *Faidherbe* a few miles upstream of Gambela on the Baro River, a tributary of the Sobat. (See Chapter XVII.)

[2] It is pleasant to record that most cordial relations persisted after Fashoda between Colonel Marchand and Sir Reginald Wingate, ripening into a close friendship, which was severed only by General Marchand's death in 1934. General Marchand was severely wounded on three occasions during the Great War. These injuries, and the responsibilities of his position in command of a division, may have hastened his end.

[3] Called also Suk Abu Sin.

to content itself with occasional raids and reconnaissances, during one of which—to the Atbara River in May, 1898—Major H. M. Lawson, R.E.,[1] was severely wounded. When August came, and it was obvious that the garrison was not to join in the advance on Omdurman, Parsons determined that, if a suitable opportunity offered, he would attack the Dervish force at Gedaref, 130 miles to the south-west. So long, however, as Ahmed Fedil was at Gedaref with 6,000 men, Parsons dared not advance against him with only 1,350 regulars and irregulars; but on September 7th, after he had learnt that Fedil was far on the road to Omdurman, he started for Gedaref.

The force which Colonel Parsons led from Kassala was composed of 450 men of the 16th Egyptian battalion, 450 men of a local Arab battalion,[2] 80 men of the Egyptian Slavery Department Camel Corps, and 370 Arab irregulars, commanded by Major Lawson, R.E. These irregulars were organized in six tribal bands under their own sheikhs; and although they were undisciplined, their mobility and natural aptitude for desert warfare made them a valuable addition to the force. Two days' marching brought Parsons to El Fasher, at which point he had decided to cross the Atbara. The river was found to be 400 yards wide, with a swift current, and no bridging material was available; but the problem of crossing was solved by Lawson, under whose superintendence the carpenters of the 16th Egyptians built six large canvas boats, and provided them with oars made from pieces of plank nailed to branches of trees. The horses and mules were swum across; the camels were towed across, supported by inflated skins; and within six days, the whole force, with its supplies and baggage, was on the left bank.[3]

On September 22nd, Parsons arrived at Gedaref, and after defeating more than 3,000 Dervishes in a stiff fight in rocky country, succeeded in occupying a group of fortified enclosures on a low hill in the centre of the town. During the battle, the enemy got in amongst the camels of the baggage train, and Lawson and his irregulars were largely instrumental in saving the train from destruction. The Egyptian force suffered casualties amounting to 100 men killed or wounded, but the enemy left more than 500 dead on the field. The Dervish commander, Nur Anga, surrendered after the battle.

---

[1] Afterwards Lieut.-General Sir Henry Lawson, K.C.B., Col. Commandant R.E. Major Lawson had joined the Kassala Garrison in April, 1898.

[2] These men had belonged to a unit raised by the Italians. They were taken over by the Egyptian Government when Kassala was transferred to Egypt.

[3] Article entitled "The Capture of Gedaref," by Major H. M. Lawson, R.E., appearing in the *R.E. Journal*, Vol. 28, 1898, pp. 241–245. This article, which gives a detailed account of the Gedaref operations, is reproduced in *Sudan Campaign, 1896–1899*, by "An Officer" (Lieut. H. L. Pritchard, R.E.), pp. 235–254. A full and descriptive account of all the operations near the Blue Nile, including those at Gedaref, appears in *The River War*, by the Rt. Hon. Winston Churchill, M.P., pp. 327–346.

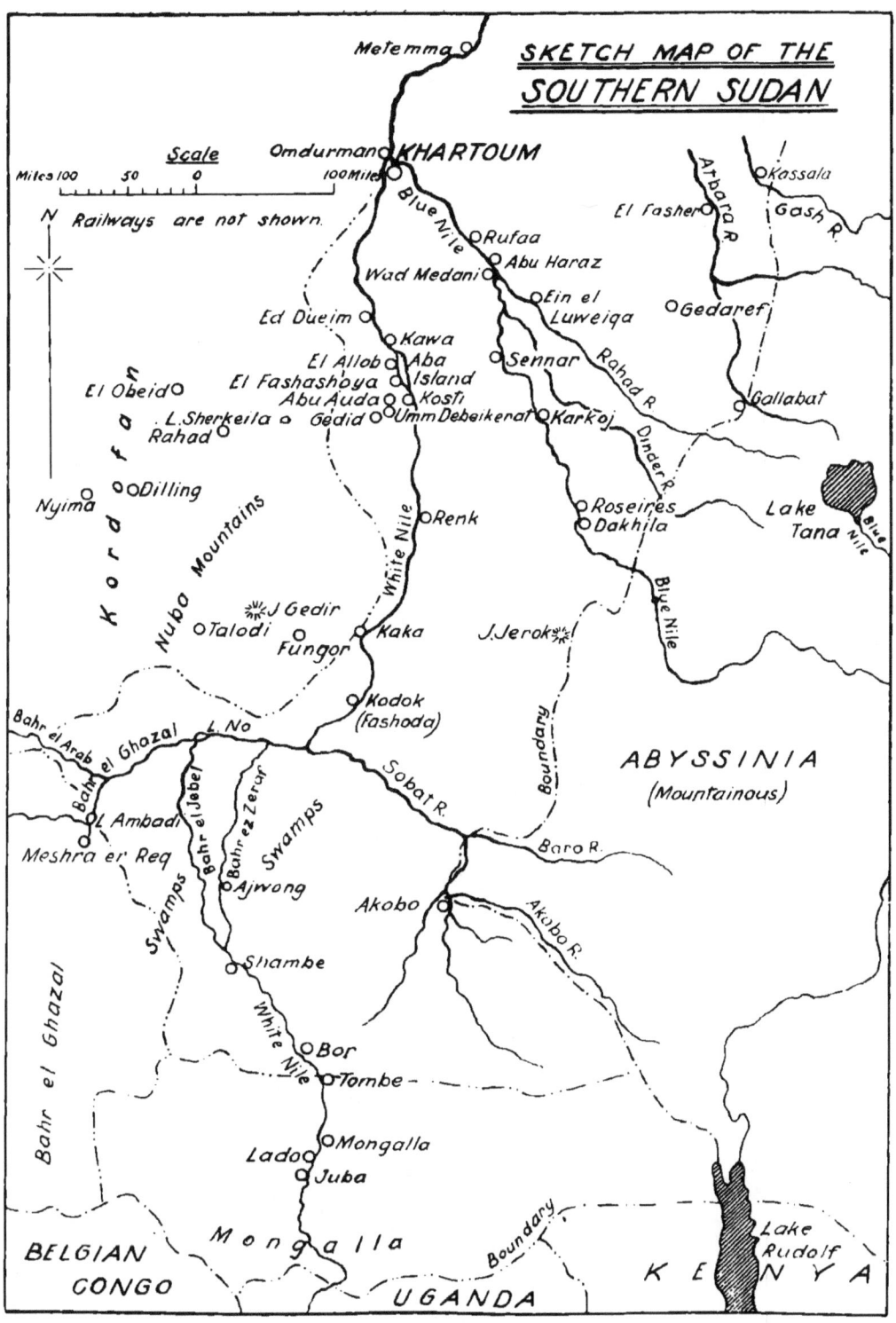

The largest fort at Gedaref, the Beit Zeki, was on the top of the hill and was garrisoned by the 16th Egyptians and the Camel Corps. The Arab battalion held another fort—the Beit el Mal or Treasury—overlooking some wells to the east of the hill. Lawson and his irregulars were in a fortified enclosure north-east of the Beit Zeki, and in a smaller enclosure which flanked it. The troops proceeded to strengthen the defences and clear a field of fire, and succeeded so well that when Ahmed Fedil appeared from the west on September 28th, and launched two attacks against the Beit Zeki, he was repulsed with a loss of 500 killed. The dervishes then withdrew to a camp about two miles to the west, and on October 1st retired still farther westwards. Parsons held his positions on the hill, but could do no more until reinforced.

A relief force under Major-General H. M. L. Rundle, C.M.G., D.S.O., was soon on its way from Omdurman. By October 8th, it was concentrated at Abu Haraz, at the confluence of the Rahad with the Blue Nile. The column comprised the 9th, 12th and half of the 13th Sudanese battalions, and three companies of the Camel Corps. From Abu Haraz, Rundle sent forward the 12th Sudanese and the Camel Corps under Lieut.-Colonel J. Collinson, Northamptonshire Regiment, to march up the Rahad to Ein el Luweiqa and strike thence across the desert for a distance of 100 miles to Gedaref. With this column, as Staff Officer to Collinson, was Lieutenant G. F. Gorringe, D.S.O., R.E.[1] Leaving Ein el Luweiqa on October 17th, Collinson joined Parsons at Gedaref on the 22nd, while Ahmed Fedil made off in a south-westerly direction with the object of escaping across the Blue Nile.

On November 7th, when Ahmed Fedil was on the Dinder,[2] a small mounted column from Omdurman, under Lieut.-Colonel D. F. Lewis, Cheshire Regiment, arrived at Karkoj on the Blue Nile, within 20 miles of him, and headed him off to the south. For the next few weeks, the Dervish leader worked his way through dense forests towards Roseires, seeking for an opportunity to elude the Egyptian gunboats and cross the river. Lewis moved up to Roseires, where he was reinforced by detachments of the 10th Sudanese, and hearing on December 20th that Ahmed Fedil had reached a place called Dakhila, about 20 miles south of Roseires, and that he was engaged in crossing the river, he sent forward some irregulars to operate on the left bank. At midday on December 24th, the gunboat *Melik* and the steamer *Dal* reached him with further reinforcements, so that he then had at his disposal a wing of the 10th Sudanese, 30 men of the 9th Sudanese and 500 irregulars with two Maxims, or about 1,100 officers and men in all. Although malaria was rampant,

[1] Lieut. Gorringe left Omdurman, on October 6th, 1898, four days after the Gedaref Relief Force, which he overtook at Abu Haraz.
[2] A tributary of the Blue Nile. See the *Sketch Map of the Southern Sudan*, included in this chapter.

and the troops were consequently in poor condition, Lewis determined to attack the dervishes at Dakhila before they could complete their crossing of the Blue Nile, and with this object he marched towards them on Christmas Day.

Arriving at Dakhila on December 26th, 1898, Lewis found that about 1,000 Dervishes had crossed to the left bank, while 1,000 more were on an island in midstream. The 10th Sudanese then waded to the island, and charged in most gallant style across open and fire-swept ground against an entrenched position, which they captured, though not without heavy loss. Ahmed Fedil, and the Dervishes who had already gained the left bank, fled westwards to the White Nile at Renk, where most of them surrendered on January 22nd, 1899, to the gunboat *Metemma*;[1] but Fedil himself and a few of his followers managed to cross the river and succeeded in joining the Khalifa in Kordofan. Thus ended a small, but very arduous campaign, which cleared the Eastern Sudan of the enemy and restored it to Egypt. Only three Royal Engineers were concerned in these operations—Major H. M. Lawson and Lieutenant G. F. Gorringe at Gedaref, and Major W. S. Gordon in command of the gunboat *Melik* on the Blue Nile.

It is now time to revert to the movements of Lord Kitchener of Khartoum. Leaving Omdurman early in October, 1898, Kitchener embarked for England after he had completed and submitted the financial statements for the campaign. A great reception awaited him in his native land. He had become the idol of the British public, and his arrival was anticipated with feverish eagerness. Civic bodies vied with each other in preparations to do him honour. Invitations reached him by every mail. When he landed at Dover on October 27th, he was received with military honours, and the enthusiasm of the townsfolk drew from him a speech of unusual length and eloquence. His reception at Charing Cross was even more rapturous. Soon he was accorded a still greater honour. "After luncheon," writes Queen Victoria on October 31st,[2] "I saw the Sirdar, Lord Kitchener, who only arrived in London a few days ago. He looked very well and bronzed. I spoke to him of all that had passed and how well everything had gone off. He was very agreeable and full of information." Banquets and receptions followed in quick succession. He was presented with a Sword of Honour at the Mansion House and received the freedom of the cities of London and Edinburgh. Oxford and Cambridge conferred honorary degrees upon him. He was commanded as a visitor to Balmoral and Windsor. On November 8th, he was the guest of honour at a Corps Dinner in the Royal Engineer Mess at Chatham, under the presidency of the Duke

---

[1] The *Metemma* was commanded by Lieut. Kemble, R.N. Lieut. A. G. Stevenson, R.E., had returned to his duties on the Sudan Military Railway.

[2] Extract from Queen Victoria's Journal, quoted in *Letters of Queen Victoria*, 1886–1901, edited by G. E. Buckle, Vol. III, p. 307.

of Cambridge. A special train carried him to Chatham, where he was received by the Mayor and Corporation. The streets were lined by troops. Triumphal arches spanned the route. The Mess-room in Brompton Barracks was filled to its utmost capacity.[1]

Although ceremonial functions were entirely foreign to Kitchener's inclinations, he submitted with a good grace to live for a time in a blaze of publicity. He accepted the honours heaped upon him, and turned his popularity to good account by appealing for money for the erection of a college at Khartoum in memory of Gordon. A fund was opened by the Lord Mayor at the Mansion House, and with the support of the Prime Minister and Baroness Burdett-Coutts, it soon contained no less than £80,000.[2] The round of festivities and ceremonies then came to an end. The Sudan called insistently for pacification, reconstruction and development. Kitchener's heart was in Khartoum. On December 1st, he was received by Her Majesty, who presented him with a cigarette case bearing the Royal monogram. On December 7th, he left London for the East. On December 28th, he was back in Omdurman in his proper environment at the head of the army.

When the Khalifa fled southwards in September, 1898, he followed the White Nile to Ed Dueim and then struck south-westwards across the desert to the neighbourhood of Lake Sherkeila, where he was joined by the remnants of his followers. News of his raids in the surrounding country was brought from time to time to Colonel Wingate, the Director of Military Intelligence. This information, and the report of the defeat of Ahmed Fedil at Roseires, were laid before the Sirdar on his arrival from England and he determined that an effort should be made forthwith to capture the Khalifa. Accordingly, he sent for his brother, Lieut.-Colonel Frederick Walter Kitchener, West Yorkshire Regiment (Director of Transport), and instructed him to take a small mixed force into Kordofan to reconnoitre that region, and if possible to attack and overwhelm Abdullahi.

The Kordofan Field Force, as it was called, voyaged up the White Nile on January 10th, 1899, disembarked at Ed Dueim, marched southwards, and left the river near Aba Island on the 23rd, making for the oasis of Gedid. The land was a waterless desert, covered with thorn scrub. On the 25th, the troops arrived at Gedid ; but when, four days later, they approached the enemy's camp, they found that the wily Khalifa had evacuated it and retired into the desert beyond. Colonel Walter Kitchener then advanced to within three miles of the Khalifa's new position near Lake Sherkeila, and having placed his force within a *zariba*, sent out his scouts. These men returned with the disconcerting report that the Khalifa had 7,000

[1] An account of Lord Kitchener's visit to Chatham appears in an article entitled " Lord Kitchener at Chatham " in the *R.E. Journal*, Vol. 28, 1898, pp. 239-241. A portrait of the Sirdar appears opposite p. 196 of the same volume.
[2] Before the end of December, 1898, £111,000 had been subscribed.

men with him, instead of 1,000 as had been anticipated. The Kordofan Field Force numbered about 1,200 men[1] with 1,600 camels. It was 125 miles from the Nile. In front, lay a powerful enemy : behind, a cruel wilderness. The alternatives were retreat or destruction. Colonel Kitchener chose to retreat. The force toiled painfully back to the Nile, which it reached on February 5th. The Sherkeila Reconnaissance was a failure, though through no fault of its commander, its officers or its men.[2]

Lord Kitchener had a wide range of military as well as civil matters to occupy his time after his return from England at the end of 1898. The health of the troops was bad. They had suffered to such an extent from malaria contracted on the Blue Nile, and from exposure on the White Nile, that 2,000 men had died, or had been invalided, since the Battle of Omdurman.[3] Military reorganization received full attention, and there were several changes in the Staff. Colonel Wingate became Adjutant-General in place of Major-General Rundle, who had proceeded to England. Lieut.-Colonel the Hon. M. G. Talbot, R.E., was appointed Director of Military Intelligence in succession to Colonel Wingate.[4] Talbot had received, from the Marchand Expedition, topographical information concerning the Southern Sudan which was useful to him in his new appointment. The French expedition had traversed the Congo-Nile watershed and marched through the Bahr el Ghazal, and Marchand had explored many uncharted areas.

Lord Cromer arrived in Omdurman at the beginning of 1899.[5] He addressed the assembled Sheikhs on January 4th, and on the following day, laid the foundation stone of the Gordon Memorial College in Khartoum.[6] On January 19th, under the Anglo-Sudanese agreement, Lord Kitchener became Governor-General of the Sudan, while still retaining the appointment of Sirdar of the Egyptian Army. His responsibilities were heavy and his duties multifarious. "They ranged," says Sir George Arthur,[7] "from the telegraph, land ordinances, general cultivation, the grain supply for starving districts, royalties and the liquor laws, to the building of an hotel and the restoration of the Palace at Khartoum ; from pensions,

---

[1] 2nd Egyptians (450 men), 14th Sudanese (450 men), Egyptian cavalry (two squadrons), Camel Corps (one company), with two guns and two Maxims.

[2] A full account of this small expedition is given in *The River War*, by the Rt. Hon. Winston Churchill, M.P., pp. 347–353. No Royal Engineers took part in the expedition.

[3] Letter from Lord Kitchener to Queen Victoria, dated December 29th, 1898, quoted in *Letters of Queen Victoria*, 1886–1901, edited by G. E. Buckle, Vol. III, p. 325.

[4] Lt.-Colonel Talbot entered the Egyptian Army on January 1st, 1899, with the rank of Miralai (Colonel). He was appointed to the newly created post of Director of Surveys on January 1st, 1900.

[5] Lieut. M. G. E. Manifold, R.E., met Lord Cromer at Wadi Halfa on December 31st, 1898. On the 29th, Manifold had handed over charge of the Sudan Telegraphs to Lieut. J. S. Liddell, R.E., on reversion to the home establishment.

[6] See Chapter XVIII.

[7] *Life of Lord Kitchener*, by Sir George Arthur, Vol. I, p. 258.

indemnities and the bearing of arms, to the appointment of an Anglican bishop; from questions of frontiers and customs with Eritrea, the French, the Congo and Abyssinia, to questions regarding the flag and rights of Egypt as compared with those of England; from superintending a flotilla of steamers on the head-waters of the Nile, to planning the new city of Khartoum, in which he devised a system of radiating streets which met with expert approval."[1] It may be added that, during the winter of 1898-99, Lord Kitchener not only allowed a few tourists to visit Omdurman and Khartoum but went to the trouble of detailing an officer to conduct them on river trips up the White Nile.[2] He gave facilities also to his friend, Mr. William Garstin, the engineer, to proceed to the Bahr el Ghazal, with the result that Garstin produced an exhaustive report on the upper waters of the White Nile which was of infinite value in developing the irrigation of Egypt.

As Governor-General, Kitchener received support and advice from Cromer, who still remained his immediate superior; but the characters and methods of the two men were dissimilar, and they could not always see eye to eye. Cromer was a graphic and descriptive writer. Kitchener detested putting pen to paper. There is a tale that when Kitchener became Sirdar of the Egyptian Army, his Staff drew up a list of maxims for newcomers. It ran as follows:—
" Never write anything. If you want something done, catch the Adjutant-General—he is sure to be here to-morrow. If you want leave, catch the Sirdar. If you *get* leave, go home at once *and take care never to come back.*" Legend goes on to record that the Sirdar found a copy of this facetious document and studied it carefully. " Very sound," said he, and promptly initialled it![3]

The Sirdar's terse style of correspondence was not the only matter which caused some difficulty to the Agent and Consul-General in Egypt. In January, 1899, Lord Cromer complained that Kitchener's methods of civil administration were unusually masterful and peremptory. In February, he added:— " My Sirdar's very drastic method of dealing with civil affairs is a never-ending source of amusement to me. The other day I told him that land speculators were sending money to Greeks in the Sudan in order to make purchases, and that some little care was necessary, as there was at present no legal means for acquiring a valid title. He replied that he abounded in my view—and would I like him to expel every Greek

[1] In appreciation of his planning of Khartoum, Lord Kitchener was elected a Fellow of the Royal Institute of Architects. His design, and the rebuilding of the city, are described in Chapter XVIII.

[2] Three miles up the White Nile the tourists were shown " Gordon's Tree," a large *Haraza* tree marking the site of the tomb of Mahu Bey, the Governor of Khartoum in 1826. It is said that the officer called the tree " Gordon's Tree " to excite the interest of the tourists. (*Sudan Notes and Records*. Vol. VIII, 1925, p. 237.) Among the visitors to Omdurman and Khartoum in December, 1898, were the Duke and Duchess of Connaught.

[3] *Kitchener*, by Brig.-General C. R. Ballard, C.B., C.M.G., p. 59.

from the country who bought or sold anything without his consent ?"[1] It seems that Kitchener favoured a patriarchal and autocratic form of government. Who shall say that, in the circumstances of the Sudan as he found it, he was not justified in his preference ? Cromer advised him to cultivate a sense of the relative importance of events, to recognize the necessity of encouraging his subordinates to express their views fearlessly, and above all to correspond fully and freely with Cairo. The Consul-General undertook, on his part, to avoid interference in the government of the Sudan, except in the most important political or administrative matters. On the whole, it may be said that Kitchener, though often worried by Cromer's suggestions, owed some of his success as Governor-General to the advice which he received.

During the summer and early autumn of 1899, military operations gave place to engineering activities, including not only the rebuilding of Khartoum, but the extension of the Sudan Government Military Railway from Fort Atbara southwards to Halfaya, the terminal station on the Blue Nile opposite the new capital.[2] The route for the railway had been reconnoitred in October, 1898, by Lieutenant A. G. Stevenson, R.E.,[3] assisted by Lieutenant G. C. M. Hall, R.E. The first step, in the autumn of 1898, was to establish communication across the Atbara River as soon as its level had fallen sufficiently for the construction of a temporary bridge, for it would then be possible to accumulate material on the south bank so that, when the next flood came down in June, 1899, and swept away the temporary bridge, the supply to rail-head could be continued without interruption until a permanent bridge was completed. Time was too short, and transport too scarce, to admit of making the depot of material on the south bank sufficiently large to supply the whole extension to Halfaya, and consequently it was evident that, unless the permanent bridge could be finished during the summer of 1899, there would be a long interruption of work during the autumn floods of that year.

The Sirdar had decreed that the railway must be completed by the end of 1899 ; and as the country was easy between the Atbara and Shendi, and there was no danger of interference by the dervishes, the crux of the problem was the Atbara crossing. Accordingly, Lieutenant G. B. Macauley, R.E., the Director of Railways, lost no time in placing contracts for the construction of a permanent bridge across the Atbara and ordering the rails, sleepers and rolling stock for the extension southwards. It is true that some difficulties might

---

[1] *Lord Cromer*, by the Marquess of Zetland, p. 247.

[2] See *Sketch Map of the Sudan Government Military Railways in* 1900, included in Chapter IX ; and *Sketch Map of the Nile from Metemma to Khartoum*, included in Chapter X. The terminal station of Halfaya was upstream of the village of that name.

[3] The original sketch map is in the possession of Major-General A. G. Stevenson, C.B., C.M.G., D.S.O., Col. Commandant R.E. It is entitled " Reconnaissance for a Railway from Khartoum to Atbara. Scale four miles to one inch. Instruments used— sketching and aneroid. Distance by camel-riding."

be encountered beyond Shendi, where it would be necessary to leave the bank of the Nile and strike across the Jebel Gerri Desert to avoid the Sabaluka Gorge, but it was not anticipated that these would be very serious.

The date specified for the completion of the permanent bridge was August 15th, 1899, and the work was divided into two separate contracts, one for the sinking of the steel cylinders, which would form the piers, and the other for the supply and erection of the girder spans.[1] The former contract was placed with an experienced firm of engineers in Alexandria :[2] the latter, with an American firm which specialized in standardized types of bridge construction.[3] By the middle of October, 1898, the Atbara had fallen low enough to allow work to be started on the temporary crossing. At a point about 500 yards upstream from the confluence with the Nile, the track was laid across the dry river-bed and carried over a narrow channel, near the left bank, on a bridge of wooden piles. Connection having been established, work commenced at once on the embankment of the line from Atbara towards Shendi. At this time, Lieutenant E. O. A. Newcombe, R.E., was living in a mud hut on the left or south bank, where he was joined by Lieutenant E. C. Midwinter, R.E., when the latter arrived on November 1st to supervise the arrangements for the formation of a depot of materials on that bank.[4] Forty miles of embankment were completed, through almost uninhabited country, before the sleepers and rails began to arrive in March, 1899.[5] Track-laying was then taken in hand, and in June the railway reached Shendi, which was made the southern headquarters of the line and soon became also the headquarters of the Egyptian cavalry in the Sudan.

The Royal Engineers who were engaged in 1899, under the direction of Lieutenant G. B. Macauley, R.E., on the extension of the Sudan Government Military Railway from the Atbara to Halfaya, were as follows :— Lieutenant E. C. Midwinter, assisted by Lieutenant M. E. Sowerby, in charge of rail-head construction ; Lieutenant A. G. Stevenson, assisted by Lieutenant E. O. A. Newcombe, Locomotive Superintendent ; Lieutenant W. R. G. Wollen, O.C. Survey ; and Lieutenant A. C. Scott, Traffic Manager. Scott and Sowerby joined the Railway cadre in the beginning of 1899. After the line had reached Shendi in June, Midwinter proceeded on leave and did not return until October, when rail-head was within 30 miles of Halfaya. During his absence, Sowerby prolonged the line up the Nile to Wad

---

[1] *The Sudan Railways*, by Lieut.-Colonel W. E. Longfield, R.E. (retd.), Chapter VIII.

[2] Messrs. Successors Impreta Industriale Italiana.

[3] Messrs. A. and P. Roberts, Pencoyd Iron Works, Pa., U.S.A. The contract was given to this firm on the suggestion of Lieut. E. P. C. Girouard, R.E.

[4] Letter from Lt.-Colonel Sir Edward Midwinter, K.B.E., C.B., C.M.G., D.S.O., to the author, dated April 10th, 1936.

[5] Supplies were carried to the banking parties by the old steamer *Bordein* and by camel convoys.

Bannaqa, and through the broken country of the Jebel Gerri Desert, to the neighbourhood of Geili,[1] and finally, on the last day of 1899, Midwinter brought it across an open plain to Halfaya Station, on the bank of the Blue Nile opposite Khartoum. Nearly 200 miles of track had been laid in nine months.[2]

Meanwhile, Lieutenant H. A. Micklem, R.E., had completed the construction of the permanent railway bridge for a single 3 feet 6 inches gauge line across the Atbara. This bridge had seven spans, each 150 feet in length. The steel girders were of pin-truss type, and the superstructure was carried on piers, each consisting of two steel cylinders.[3] The sinking of the cylinders was carried out between February 14th and May 21st. They were then filled with concrete and the piers completed. The erection of the girders began on June 20th and ended on August 17th; and six days later, the bridge was ready for traffic. It was formally opened by Lord Kitchener on August 26th, 1899. The Atbara Bridge still remains one of the finest engineering structures in the Sudan; but it is not in its original form, for it was partially remodelled in 1910 to meet the demands of modern traffic.[4]

As an example of the interest shown by Lord Kitchener in railway development, it may be recorded that, before he left the Sudan in 1899, he made a personal reconnaissance for a railway from the Red Sea littoral to the interior. With Lieutenant G. B. Macauley, R.E., he rode from Kassala down the Wadi Baraka to Tokar and Suakin, and thence through Sinkat to the Atbara, down which he travelled to the Nile. It seems that he had in mind the possibility of building a line to connect Suakin with Kassala by a direct route ; but after this reconnaissance, he informed Lieutenant G. F. Gorringe, R.E., that he was convinced that the Baraka route would not be suitable for a railway, and that he had decided on an alternative route from Suakin towards Sheikh Barghut (now Port Sudan) and thence through Sinkat to the Nile at Fort Atbara. He took steps at once to prepare for the construction of a line along this route, intending to use Suakin as a terminal port until Sheikh Barghut had been suitably developed.[5] However, before the project could

---

[1] See the *Sketch Map of the Sudan Government Military Railways in* 1900, included in Chapter IX.

[2] The line was opened for traffic on February 4th, 1900. There was a weekly service of trains between Wadi Halfa and Halfaya. The journey occupied 55 hours, and the return fares were 1st class £15 7s. 6d., 2nd class £6. Only 18 passengers could be carried. (See *R.E. Journal*, Vol. 30, 1900, p. 66.)

[3] The cylinders were eight feet to ten feet in diameter, and 16 feet apart centre to centre. They were sunk to a maximum depth of 30 feet by men working in a chamber under air pressure. A full account of the construction of the original Atbara Bridge is given in an article entitled " The Atbara Bridge " appearing in the *R.E. Journal*, Vol. 29, 1899, pp. 223–224. This article includes a report by Lieut. H. A. Micklem, R.E., dated August 28th, 1899.

[4] The pin-truss girders were replaced by stronger ones with riveted joints.

[5] Notes by Lieut.-General Sir George Gorringe, K.C.B., K.C.M.G., D.S.O., Col. Commandant R.E., sent to the author on January 28th, 1936.

THE ATBARA BRIDGE.

[*Photo by the Author.*]

take a definite shape, he had relinquished his appointment as Governor-General.

We revert now to the military operations against the Khalifa in Kordofan, which were resumed after the rainy season of 1899. News arrived in September, while Kitchener was in England, that the Khalifa with 10,000 men had established himself near Jebel Gedir in the Nuba Mountains, about 100 miles north-west of Fashoda. The Sirdar hastened back to Egypt, and pushed on at once to Omdurman to make arrangements for the dispatch of an expedition up the White Nile. By October 20th, he had concentrated a mixed force of 8,000 men at the village of Kaka, 50 miles north of Fashoda, and had arrived there in the *Dal* to assume personal command in the field. Screened by cavalry and camelry, Colonel Sir Reginald Wingate led the infantry westwards across a waterless desert for a distance of 50 miles to Fungor in the direction of Jebel Gedir, only to find, on October 23rd, that the wily Khalifa had vanished into the dense jungles towards the north. The mounted troops reconnoitred Jebel Gedir, and shortly afterwards the whole force marched back to Kaka, which it reached on November 1st. The troops then returned to their stations, and Kitchener proceeded to Omdurman, and finally to Cairo. The only Royal Engineers who served under him in this well-planned, but abortive, expedition were Lieut.-Colonel the Hon. M. G. Talbot as Director of Intelligence, and Brevet-Major G. F. Gorringe, D.S.O., as Assistant Adjutant-General.

Although, on this occasion, the Khalifa made good his escape, his end was near. On November 12th, 1899, it became known that, with 3,000 men, he was approaching Aba Island, only 150 miles south of Khartoum, and that his advance guard under Ahmed Fedil had reached the White Nile, and had fired upon the gunboat *Sultan*. In the absence of the Sirdar, Colonel Sir Reginald Wingate was in command at Khartoum, having been sent up from Cairo to act for Colonel J. G. Maxwell. The time had come for another attempt to overwhelm the Khalifa, and as a preliminary, Colonel D. F. Lewis took the 9th and 13th Sudanese battalions up the river in gunboats to Aba Island, and drove Ahmed Fedil away from the bank at a place called El Allob. Kitchener arrived in Khartoum from Cairo on November 18th. " The Commander-in-Chief," writes Sir George Arthur,[1] " might have been expected to administer himself the *coup de grâce;* but Kitchener had foreseen the likelihood of being called to other spheres of labour and—Hunter having gone to India—he was more than anxious that Wingate should be his successor. As Director of Intelligence, the latter had been of inestimable value; but he had so far commanded no troops in the field,[2] and as a test, the Sirdar, with all confidence, entrusted to him the final expedition."

[1] *Life of Lord Kitchener*, by Sir George Arthur, Vol. I, p. 262.
[2] Presumably, Sir George Arthur meant that Sir Reginald Wingate had never commanded a mixed force, acting independently.

Mounted forces having been concentrated at El Fashashoya (Fachi Shoya), on the left bank opposite Aba Island, Sir Reginald Wingate marched from that place on November 1st at the head of a flying column of 3,700 men. The troops comprised a brigade of infantry under Colonel Lewis (9th and 13th Sudanese, one company of 2nd Egyptians and an Irregular Sudanese Battalion), a squadron of Egyptian cavalry, six companies of the Camel Corps, a battery of Egyptian field artillery, a Maxim battery, and the necessary Medical, Supply and Transport formations.

The Irregular Sudanese Battalion was commanded by Brevet Major G. F. Gorringe, D.S.O., R.E., and was composed of *Jehadia*—fanatical ex-soldiers of the Khalifa—of whom 3,000 had been placed at Gorringe's disposal for the rebuilding of Khartoum. On his way down to Cairo with Lord Kitchener after the abortive expedition to Jebel Gedir, Gorringe had suggested to the Sirdar that, when another expedition was sent against the Khalifa, he should be allowed to take a contingent of *Jehadia* off the works at Khartoum to pursue the defeated enemy, and that, if they did well, the men should be suitably rewarded. The *Jehadia* were very mobile and they knew the country. Lord Kitchener considered this suggestion; and when news arrived that the Khalifa was moving north once more, he sent for Gorringe, showed him the telegram, and said that he thought the *Jehadia* might be employed, but that no British officer should accompany them. At this Gorringe demurred, though without immediate result; but after lunch, the Sirdar agreed to his proposal and gave him permission to draw the necessary Remington rifles and ammunition from the Ordnance Store, provided that he could start with them by train that evening. Thanks to Blakeney, who delayed the night express for the purpose, the equipment was loaded into a fish van and left Cairo, with Gorringe in charge of it, within the stipulated time. At Aswan, Gorringe commandeered the Sirdar's steamer; at Halfa, he caught the night train, and at Omdurman, another steamer; and within eleven days after leaving Cairo, he was in action at the head of his irregulars.

It was reported that Ahmed Fedil was at Nafisa, 23 miles from the river; but when that place was reached before daylight on the 22nd, it was found that Fedil had retreated for a distance of five miles to Abu Auda (Abu Aadel), where he lay with about 2,500 men. As the Sudanese and Egyptian infantry could proceed no farther until the water camel-convoy arrived, Colonel Wingate asked Gorringe whether his *Jehadia*, who carried their own water, could continue their march, and being assured that they could do so, sent them forward with a squadron of cavalry and four Maxims as an advanced force under Major B. T. Mahon, D.S.O., 8th Hussars. Mahon was ordered to engage and hold Ahmed Fedil until the infantry could come up. This he accomplished most successfully, and repulsed a counter-attack by the dervishes before the infantry reached the battlefield. " The dervishes charged in most gallant style," writes General Gorringe.[1] " They came on very fast and nearly got in amongst us. Four Marine sergeants were firing the Maxims, and fortunately none of the guns jammed. My men were somewhat wild, and it was difficult to prevent them from charging. After the Dervish attack had failed and the survivors were retiring, I saw, to my amazement, my Sudanese cook ' Jumbo,'[2] with my private camel kneeling behind him, firing rapidly at the enemy with my sporting Martini rifle. He explained that as the Dervish bullets had been falling thickly amongst the transport, and he found that he could not return the fire properly from that position, he had decided to join me in the firing line, where he had enjoyed himself thoroughly." In due course, the infantry came up and assisted in routing the dervishes, who suffered heavy casualties and fled through thick bush and across a grassy plain, pursued by the cavalry. A number of prisoners, and quantities of stores and supplies, fell into Wingate's hands; but Ahmed Fedil escaped to the Khalifa.

Although the exact position of the Khalifa and his main body was uncertain, it was believed that he was moving towards Gedid to join Ahmed Fedil. Accordingly, Wingate resumed his advance and arrived at Gedid at 10 a.m. on November 23rd. Fortunately, a good supply of water was found at that place, for had there been none, the force would have been obliged to retreat at once to the Nile. A Dervish deserter reported that the Khalifa, with 5,000 men, was encamped some seven miles to the north-east at a spot called Umm Debeikerat (Om Dubreikat), and Wingate decided to attack at dawn on the 24th. The Khalifa had no other course open to him but to stand and fight. His route to the north was barred by Wingate; a retreat to the south would lead him through waterless and densely wooded districts; and the bulk of his supplies had already been captured in Ahmed Fedil's camp at Abu Auda.

Covered by the mounted troops, the infantry of the flying column marched from Gedid at 12.30 a.m., making their way with some difficulty through thorny jungle. At 3 a.m., reports were received that the Dervish position lay three miles ahead, and the force deployed into fighting formation. Meanwhile, the cavalry, who were accompanied by Maxim detachments, had halted two miles in advance, at the foot of some rising ground beyond which the enemy's camp was known to lie. Then, very cautiously, the entire force resumed its advance, and at 3.40 a.m. concealed itself in a grassy

[1] Notes by Lieut.-General Sir George Gorringe, K.C.B., K.C.M.G., D.S.O., Col. Commandant R.E., sent to the author on September 24th, 1936.
[2] In January, 1935, the author stayed for a few days at Sennar, the site of the great dam on the Blue Nile above Khartoum, and there he found " Jumbo," whose real name is Muhammad Adriz, in charge of the Government Rest House. When not engaged in culinary operations, the old man was delighted to describe his adventures as Gorringe's servant in Suakin and along the Nile.

hollow to await the dawn, while its pickets occupied the crest.

The battle at Umm Debeikerat began at 5.10 a.m. on November 24th, 1899, when the indistinct forms of dervishes could be seen by the pickets advancing to the attack. Immediately, the Sudanese units rushed up to the crest and opened a heavy fire, to which the enemy replied and at the same time made an unsuccessful attempt to turn the left flank. As the light improved, large bodies of shouting dervishes could be seen advancing; but they made little progress, and soon fell in hundreds, as if mown down by a scythe. Perceiving that the attack had failed, Wingate ordered a general advance. The whole line swept down upon the remnants of the enemy, and with ever-increasing speed, drove them towards their camp, which lay concealed among some trees at a distance of about one and a half miles from the battlefield. "Cease fire," sounded at 6.25 a.m. While the mounted troops continued the pursuit, Wingate received the surrender of a number of dervishes in the camp and took charge of 6,000 women and children, who were huddled in the *tukuls* recently occupied by the enemy.

The battlefield was everywhere a scene of carnage, and in one spot in particular the corpses were piled thickly. "Immediately in front of the line of advance of the 9th Sudanese," writes Sir Reginald Wingate,[1] "a large number of the enemy were seen lying dead, huddled together in a comparatively small space. On examination, these proved to be the bodies of the Khalifa Abdulla et Taaishi, Ali Wad Helu, Ahmed Fedil, the Khalifa's two brothers, the Mahdi's son and a number of other well-known leaders. At a short distance behind them lay their dead horses, and from the few men left alive we learnt that the Khalifa, having failed in his attempt to reach the rising ground, where we had forestalled him, had then endeavoured to make a turning movement, which had been crushed by our fire. Seeing his followers retiring, he made an ineffectual attempt to rally them; but recognizing that the day was lost, he had called on his Emirs to dismount from their horses, and seating himself on his *furwa* or sheepskin—as is the custom of Arab chiefs who disdain surrender—he had placed Ali Wad Helu on his right and Ahmed Fedil on his left, whilst the remaining Emirs seated themselves round him, with their bodyguard in line and some 20 paces to their front. In this position they had unflinchingly met their death. They were given a fitting burial, under our supervision, by the surviving members of their own tribesmen."

The death of the Khalifa was the signal for the wholesale surrender

---

[1] Dispatch, dated Fashashoya, November 25th, 1899, from Colonel Sir Reginald Wingate, Commanding Troops on the White Nile, to H. E. Major-General the Right Hon. the Lord Kitchener of Khartoum, G.C.B., etc., Sirdar, quoted in an article entitled "The Operations against the Khalifa," which appears in the *R.E. Journal*, Vol. 30, 1900, pp. 78–81. This article includes also the dispatch from Lord Kitchener to the Under-Secretary of State for War, forwarding Colonel Wingate's dispatch.

of his followers, amongst the prisoners being his eldest son. Osman Digna alone, of all the important Emirs, remained for a time at liberty. The Sudanese and Egyptian casualties during the expedition were negligible ; but the Dervish losses were estimated at 1,000 killed and wounded, including 27 Emirs killed ; and more than 3,000 fighting men, including two Emirs, were made prisoners. The flying column had covered a distance of 57 miles in 63 hours, during which it had fought two successful battles, so that the praise which it received was well earned.[1] Major G. F. Gorringe, the only Royal Engineer with the force, was mentioned in dispatches. It was stated that the results which he obtained in rapidly organizing his irregulars, and keeping them well in hand during the fighting, were remarkable. As to Sir Reginald himself, no better tribute could be desired than that accorded by Lord Kitchener, who wrote :—[2] " Colonel Sir Reginald Wingate's previous services on the Staff are so notable that I need not allude to them. He has now shown himself to be a capable leader of men. The operations under him were carried out with consummate ability, energy and determination, and he has struck the last blow at Mahdiism. The country has been finally relieved of the military tyranny which started in a movement of wild religious fanaticism upwards of 19 years ago."

A brighter era dawned in the Sudan. El Obeid was occupied in December, 1899, and during the next two years the entire Bahr el Ghazal Province was pacified. Darfur remained unoccupied ; but as this former province of the Khalifa was ruled by a capable if unscrupulous Sultan named Ali Dinar, who had agreed to pay tribute to Egypt, it was decided that no interference was necessary.

A few weeks after the destruction of the Khalifa at Umm Debeikerat, Lord Kitchener left the Sudan. In October, 1899, Great Britain had entered upon the South African War, to which the public attention instantly shifted ; and in December, a series of reverses at Stormberg, Magersfontein and Colenso, and the investment of the force under Lieut.-General Sir George White in Ladysmith, led to the appointment of Field-Marshal Lord Roberts as Commander-in-Chief. The appointment was made, however, on the express stipulation by the Premier, Lord Salisbury, that Lord Kitchener should accompany Lord Roberts to South Africa as Chief of Staff. The Sirdar was at Khartoum when, on December 18th, he received his orders, and three days later he bade a long farewell to the country he had conquered. Never again would the Sudan see that stalwart figure riding at the head of her troops. Kitchener's days of desert warfare were over. On December 21st, urgent

[1] Being obliged to return to Khartoum as quickly as possible, Sir Reginald Wingate handed over charge to Colonel Lewis on the evening after the battle and rode hard for the Nile. He reached it in an exhausted condition, having been without sleep for four nights and days.

[2] Dispatch from Major-General Lord Kitchener of Khartoum, Sirdar, to the Under-Secretary of State for War, dated Khartoum, November 25th, 1899.

telegraphic instructions came to Lieutenant E. C. Midwinter, R.E., at rail-head north of Halfaya, that a special train must be ready that evening at Geili (Wad Ramla) to take the Sirdar to Wadi Halfa. No hint was given as to the Sirdar's final destination. Midwinter directed that the line should be cleared and that engines, with steam up, should be waiting at Abidiya, Abu Hamed and No. 6 Station. Before dusk, a gunboat came downstream. The Sirdar landed, and without a word, entered the waiting train, followed by his Staff. A flag waved, and the train moved out of the siding on its journey of 550 miles to Halfa.[1]

The distance was covered in the record time of 17 hours, and in places at a dangerous speed. Midwinter, who accompanied Kitchener to Abidiya, was unaware until he reached that place that the Sirdar's immediate destination was Cairo and not Wadi Halfa. He had no inkling that he was taking leave of a departing Governor-General. A brief halt outside Cairo to pick up Wingate, and Kitchener was at Alexandria, embarking on H.M.S. *Isis*. At Malta, he transhipped to H.M.S. *Dido*, and after a rough voyage, joined Lord Roberts in the *Dunottar Castle* at Gibraltar on December 27th. Together, they landed at Cape Town on January 10th, 1900, and working in perfect harmony, restored success to the British arms. Lord Kitchener's achievements in South Africa under Lord Roberts, and later in supreme command, have been recorded by many historians. It is enough to say that they added to an already brilliant reputation.

An attempt has been made in these pages to portray Kitchener as a soldier—not the legendary figure imagined by the public, but the actual man as he was known to his friends and subordinates in the Sudan, a man of such outstanding personality and character that he is perhaps without counterpart in history. Of him, Lord Cromer wrote after Omdurman :—[2] " The speedy and successful issue of the campaign depended almost entirely upon the methods adopted for overcoming the very exceptional difficulties connected with the supply and transport of the troops. The main quality required to meet these difficulties was a good head for business. By one of those fortunate accidents which have been frequent in the history of Anglo-Saxon enterprise, a man was found equal to the occasion. Lord Kitchener of Khartoum won his well-deserved peerage because he was an excellent man of business ; he looked carefully after every important detail and enforced economy." This is one point of view. Officers of his own Corps, however, would prefer to think that Kitchener was rewarded, not as an economical and meticulous man of business, but as the organizer and commander of a successful army in the field, who proved, by his subsequent

[1] *The Sudan Railways*, by Lieut.-Colonel W. G. Longfield, R.E. (retd.), Chapter VIII.
[2] *Modern Egypt*, by the Earl of Cromer, Vol. II, p. 107.

initiation of an excellent civil administration in the captured territories, that he could adapt himself readily to new and sometimes irksome duties and responsibilities.

The memory of this great soldier is perpetuated in Khartoum by a statue which stands in front of the War Office facing the Blue Nile. During a tour of the Near East, the Sudan and East Africa in 1910–11, Lord Kitchener revisited Khartoum, where he was welcomed by the Governor-General, Sir Reginald Wingate. The latter happened to remark that the Sudan should certainly possess a monument to its first Governor-General, and Kitchener then asked whether a replica of a bronze equestrian statue of himself would be acceptable, as this could be made from a statue which was being cast by a firm in London for erection on the *maidan* in Calcutta. The offer was accepted with gratitude, and a site was selected near the Law Courts in the main thoroughfare, now called Gordon Avenue.[1] Kitchener said that he would write to the Indian Committee to arrange matters; but within the next few months, an estimate of the cost of the replica, amounting to thousands of pounds, was received from the Committee. This was a sad disappointment, for no funds were available. Sir Reginald, however, was equal to the occasion. He informed the firm in London that, although the Sudan exchequer could not meet the charge, he could send them several tons of ingots of waste brass, made from empty cartridge cases collected from the battle-fields, which, if mixed with tin, would form a suitable bronze. With rare generosity the firm undertook, on these terms, to cast the replica and send it to Khartoum free of cost.[2] Owing, however, to difficulties arising through the Great War, the replica did not reach Port Sudan until November 4th, 1920. After its arrival at Khartoum, the Civil Secretary's office was notified in the usual form that a " parcel " had been received, and consequently an orderly was sent on a bicycle to the Post Office to take delivery of it. The parcel which confronted the astonished man was the enormous statue. In this manner the monument of a great personage made an unobtrusive entry into Khartoum, where it was duly erected in 1921.

After the departure of Lord Kitchener to South Africa, the conduct of affairs fell to Colonel (now General) Sir Reginald Wingate, K.C.M.G., C.B., D.S.O., who was appointed Governor-General of the Sudan and Sirdar of the Egyptian Army on December 23rd, 1899. During the next 17 years,[3] Sir Reginald guided the destinies of the country with skill and diplomacy, and under his control it passed from infancy to manhood, from the meanest poverty to financial stability, if not to actual affluence. The excellent government which

---

[1] The site was subsequently changed.
[2] Actually, the cost to the Sudan Government amounted to £E.680. The value of the statue for Customs purposes was declared as £E.2,232.
[3] Sir Reginald Wingate was Governor-General of the Sudan until December 31st, 1916, when he was transferred to Egypt as High Commissioner.

the Sudan enjoyed enabled reductions to be effected in the strength of the army, and most of the Egyptian units returned to their stations in Egypt, leaving the Sudanese to form the bulk of the garrison. British and Egyptian officers were drawn from the Army to organize and carry on the administration of the country until they could be replaced gradually by carefully selected civilians. Steps were taken also to train young Sudanese as officers for the Sudanese battalions of infantry. For some years, the general characteristics of the military machine remained unchanged; but before the Great War, an Equatorial Battalion was recruited from the pagan tribes of the south for service in that area, and an Eastern Arab Corps was formed on the model of the unit which had done so well at Gedaref in 1898.

Civilization spread its benefits over Khartoum and Omdurman. Khartoum was rebuilt by a Department of Works administered by Royal Engineers.[1] Omdurman was cleansed and improved. The first motor vehicle appeared in 1901, and it is said that a small unit of mechanical transport was formed soon afterwards by Lieutenant B. W. Y. Danford, R.E. No great distances, however, were covered by motor-car until 1909, when Captain H. H. Kelly, R.E., journeyed across the desert from Khartoum to Kassala. At this period, all officers rode about Khartoum on donkeys, but a few pony-carts were making their appearance. Camels were used for long journeys, except in the south, where ponies or donkeys were substituted. It was not until 1914 that officers in Khartoum were forbidden to ride on donkeys when in uniform. Everything was primitive, cheap and effective. Necessity was the mother of invention, and the Sudan was the happy hunting-ground of the ingenious.

Between 1900 and 1914 there were many changes in the cadre of Royal Engineers. Kitchener had seen to it that most of his " Band of Boys " joined him in South Africa, so other officers were sent to replace them in the Sudan. The elaboration of the civil administration was rapid and far reaching, but space does not admit of any attempt to describe its ramifications. Some allusion, however, may be made to a few of the small expeditions or " patrols," to maintain the authority of that administration, in which Royal Engineers took part, and to an embryo unit of Engineers which came into being before the Great War.

At the beginning of 1904, the slave trade in the Eastern Sudan received a severe blow at the hands of Brevet Lieut.-Colonel G. F. Gorringe, C.M.G., D.S.O., R.E., who had been Governor of the Sennar Province since his return from South Africa in December, 1901. A new demarcation of the Sudan-Abyssinia border had placed within the Sudan the stronghold of one Ibrahim Wad Mahmud, a cruel slave-trader. This stronghold was situated at Jebel Jerok in the

[1] The rebuilding of Khartoum is described in Chapter XVIII

country of the Borun negroes, west of the Blue Nile. A column under Gorringe captured the place after three days' fighting. Numbers of slaves were released, the greater part of Mahmud's followers were annihilated, and after a pursuit lasting five days, the ringleader was caught and hanged.[1]

In the summer of 1906, Captain B. W. Y. Danford, R.E., was attached to a small mixed force which was sent from El Obeid to suppress a revolt at Talodi in the turbulent area known as the Nuba Mountains. Three years later, Captain A. E. Coningham, R.E., a Survey officer, accompanied a patrol dispatched to Nyima, west of Dilling in the same area, to deal with insurgents. In 1912, two Survey officers, Major H. D. Pearson and Captain H. H. Kelly, R.E., marched with separate columns operating against the Beirs, who inhabited a part of the Mongalla Province in the far south. In the same year, Captain R. E. M. Russell served in an expedition against the Anuaks, hostile neighbours of the Beirs. From time to time, other Royal Engineers surveyed the country under the protection of armed forces, but they were rarely called upon to perform any military duties. They were fully occupied in technical work, not only as surveyors, but as builders of telegraphs and of structures of every description. They were engaged, in fact, in the general development of the Sudan.

Until 1912, any small engineering works which might be required during military expeditions were carried out by the Egyptian personnel of the Military Works Department, who were supervised by Royal Engineer officers. In that year, however, Major (now Major-General Sir) P. G. Grant, R.E., then Director of Works, received orders from Colonel (now General Sir) J. J. Asser, Adjutant-General of the Egyptian Army, that he should endeavour to form a "Sudanese Sapper Section." With Asser and another officer, Grant went to Omdurman, where there were a number of Nuba boy prisoners. These lads were stark naked and spoke a language which nobody could understand; but nevertheless, a number of them were selected and were handed over to Mr. "Sammy" Hart, an ex-Sergeant, R.E., to be trained in knotting, lashing and simple trades. Grant procured from India a Bengal Sapper and Miner kit, and obtained approval for a similar dress for the Sudanese Sappers, but with a *tarbush*, flash and hackle like the infantry. The original hackle was white above and blue below;[2] but the hackle of the present Engineer Troops of the Sudan Defence Force is of the Corps colours, red and blue.

The Nuba boys grew apace. Within a few years they became armed

[1] *Report on the Finance, Administration and Condition of the Sudan,* 1904.
[2] Notes by Major-General Sir Philip Grant, K.C.B., C.M.G., late R.E., sent to the author on September 4th, 1934. General Grant states that he had a recollection that the old Sapper busby had a white and blue hackle. Hence the selection of these colours.

and disciplined soldiers, though the Sapper Section was not officially recognized as a separate unit. When the Great War broke out, the Section was able to take the field with the infantry, and proved its value on several occasions. The story of its formation and development is typical of a country in which every plant struggles to maturity in an arid soil and under a pitiless sun—a country in which, for many years, the financial strain of recovery from the chaos engendered by Dervish rule was well-nigh insupportable, and was met and finally overcome only by the exercise of the most rigid economy in every department of Government.

THE MUDIRIA SQUARE, KHARTOUM.

CHAPTER XII.

FRONTIER DEFENCE IN THE GREAT WAR, 1914–18.

WHEN Turkey threw in her lot with Germany and Austria on October 30th, 1914, neither Egypt nor the Sudan had the military strength nor financial resources for elaborate offensive action. Egypt had prospered economically since Field-Marshal Viscount Kitchener became Agent and Consul-General in 1911, and the Sudan had been ably administered and developed for many years by General Sir Reginald Wingate; but no military preparation had been possible in either country for a contingency such as the Great War. After the outbreak of hostilities, the safe-guarding of Egypt was entrusted for a short time to the British Army of Occupation, while the small British garrison at Khartoum was made responsible for the security of the Sudan. Any anxiety, however, which may have been felt regarding the political effect of the breach with Turkey on peoples composed principally of Muhammadans, was soon proved to have slender foundation. Both countries stood firmly by Great Britain. Indeed, when Sir Reginald Wingate held a meeting of sheikhs at Khartoum on November 8th, and explained to them the causes of the war, his address was received with enthusiasm, and was followed by spontaneous messages of loyalty. Generally speaking, the war made little impression on the inhabitants of Egypt, and still less on those of the more distant Sudan.

The Egyptian Army rose nobly to the occasion. In the course of the war, its Sudanese and Egyptian soldiers gave active help, not only in their own territories, but in East Africa, Uganda, French Equatorial Africa, Sinai, Palestine, and Arabia. They shared in the defence of the Suez Canal. They fought the Senussi on the Mediterranean coast and among the western oases of Egypt. They took the field in Darfur against Sultan Ali Dinar. A Works Battalion was sent to the Dardanelles. An Egyptian Labour Corps, which numbered in the end more than 100,000 men, toiled ceaselessly on the lines of communication.[1] A Camel Transport Corps, increasing gradually to more than 32,000 animals, fetched and carried in Sinai,

[1] The strength of the Egyptian Labour Corps was as follows:— January, 1916, 39 officers, 2,973 men; August, 1916, 88 officers, 24,838 men; August, 1917, 292 officers, 55,592 men: August 1918, 418 officers, 85,547 men: November, 1918, 504 officers, 100,002 men. In 1916, the Corps sent 10,463 officers and men to France, 8,280 to Mesopotamia and 600 to Salonika. The work executed included the construction and maintenance of railways, roads and pipe-lines; quarrying; stretcher-bearing; loading and discharging ships' cargoes, and stevedoring.

Palestine, and the western deserts.[1] The Stores, Hospital and Ordnance Departments of the Egyptian Army were placed at the disposal of the Expeditionary Forces from Egypt. The Sudan Government Railways provided rolling-stock and permanent way. The Egyptian Survey Department supplied almost all the maps needed for the campaigns in Sinai, Palestine, Syria and Gallipoli, and organized a Field Survey Company. The administrative staffs of every department in Egypt and the Sudan were depleted for war service, and those who remained did double work. As Sir Charles Lucas remarks,[2] it was a great record crowned with success.

In July, 1914, Lord Kitchener was in England, intending to stay there until September. On July 31st, however, all British representatives from abroad were ordered to return to their posts; and on August 3rd, on the eve of the declaration of war against Germany, Kitchener embarked at Dover on his way to Egypt. He then received instructions from Mr. Asquith, the Prime Minister, that he should remain in England, and consequently returned forthwith to London. Three days later, he entered the War Office as Secretary of State for War, and immediately set about the titanic task of creating the armies which eventually brought victory to his country. It is said that in the course of his first morning's work he was handed a pen which refused to function. "Dear me," he murmured, "what a War Office! Not a scrap of Army and not a pen that will write!"[3] His new duties brought him into political contacts which were uncongenial, and an atmosphere which was foreign to him, yet he continued unswervingly on his way. In such a crisis, he was far too valuable to the Empire to be allowed to remain in a civil appointment abroad, and thus Egypt lost his personal direction. Nevertheless, he continued to take the deepest interest in all questions relating to her defence, and secured at the outset the appointment of a commander of his own choosing. Lieutenant-General Sir John Maxwell[4] was deputed to take command of the Force in Egypt in relief of Major-General the Hon. J. Byng, who returned to France to take command of a Cavalry Division. "Conky" Maxwell was the officer who had served Kitchener so well as a brigade leader in the Sudan campaigns. He had commanded the Force in Egypt from 1908 to 1912, and was thoroughly acquainted with the country, its people and its military, political and religious problems. Maxwell landed in Egypt on September 8th, and received a cordial welcome from the inhabitants.

[1] In July, 1917, the Camel Transport Corps consisted of 16 companies and two depots, its total strength of burden camels being 32,712. Of these companies, 11 served in Sinai and Palestine and five in the western deserts. (See *A Brief Record of the Advance of the Egyptian Expeditionary Force, July, 1917 to October, 1918*, p.98.)
[2] *The Empire at War*, by Sir Charles Lucas, Vol. IV, Part VI.
[3] *Life of Lord Kitchener*, by Sir George Arthur, Vol. III, p. 7, footnote.
[4] For the sake of brevity, the decorations held by officers mentioned in this chapter have been omitted.

Kitchener never failed to make full use of his former subordinates. In April, 1915, when the supply of munitions had become a burning question, he summoned to his assistance the builder of the Desert Railway, Sir Percy Girouard, who had been Managing Director of Messrs. Armstrong Whitworth since 1912, and established him in the War Office as Director of the Munitions Department with the local rank of Major-General. Girouard advised Kitchener regarding the capacity of British armament firms, and acted as a link between the War Office and industry. Subsequently, he became Director-General of Munitions under the Coalition Government; but being unable to agree with Mr. Lloyd George, he returned to his post at Armstrongs, where he played a leading part in the war effort of that great firm.

Throughout the Great War, the Sudan was more happily placed than Egypt. She was in no danger of invasion. All that was necessary was to prevent internal trouble, to curtail espionage, to deal with small raids on her frontiers, to subdue Darfur, to counteract enemy propaganda, and to assist Egypt with transport-animals and supplies. The position of Egypt, on the other hand, was highly dangerous during the early stages of the war. Within 130 miles of her eastern frontier lay the Suez Canal, the "throat of England," and it was probable that the forces of Turkey would be sent by Germany against that important thoroughfare. Beyond her western borders were the Senussi, a warlike people who might be instigated to invade with 5,000 men. The Germans were firmly of opinion that the mere appearance of a Turkish force on the Suez Canal would be the signal for a wholesale rising in Egypt. The country was ruled by a pro-Turkish Khedive, Abbas Hilmi, and was still a dependency of Turkey, though controlled by Great Britain.[1] Events proved that the Germans were wrong; but nevertheless, it was recognized that the defence of the Suez Canal against serious attack, or even against raids, was of the utmost importance.

The Royal Navy guarded the ends of the Canal, and its protection against attack by land had been considered most carefully by the Imperial General Staff and the Committee of Imperial Defence. The General Staff had maintained in 1906 that the Sinai Peninsula, about 120 miles in width, formed no impassable obstacle to an invader from Palestine.[2] They believed that a raiding party of 5,000 rifles, supported by a stronger force in rear, could be brought without difficulty within striking distance of the Canal. While admitting that the Canal was the obvious line of defence for the eastern provinces of Egypt, they suggested that a force of camelry should occupy an advanced position at Nekhl to observe and harass the enemy. In pre-war days, it was not contemplated that warships

[1] The suzerainty of Turkey over Egypt was terminated on December 18th, 1914. Abbas Hilmi Pasha was deposed from the Khediviate on December 19th, and replaced by Hussein Kamel Pasha, with the title of Sultan.
[2] *Egypt and the Army*, by Lieut.-Colonel P. G. Elgood, C.M.G., p. 120.

would enter the Canal to assist by gunfire; but in 1914, it was decided that they should do so, and this materially strengthened the case for a defensive position restricted to the Canal itself.[1] " Broadly speaking," writes General Bowman-Manifold,[2] " the British intention was to let the Turks first overcome the desert obstacle, and to use the Suez Canal itself as a second obstacle. The plan was to strike at the enemy only when he arrived at the Suez Canal, where the defenders would have the benefit of ships' guns and armed launches —a purely passive defence." Thus, the Empire's main line of communication was to be employed as an obstacle in front of a fire-trench; and this in spite of the fact that it might be blocked for weeks by a single vessel, mined by the enemy's agents.

As it had been arranged that the garrison of Egypt should conduct a passive defence on the line of the Suez Canal, it was unnecessary to make it mobile in sand desert, and consequently, when war came, it was literally tied to the Canal. Also, its strength did not admit of holding any advanced line in the desert and at the same time guarding the Canal. The first regular reinforcements from the East were small, and were destined for France. Some of the later reinforcements were partially trained colonials or auxiliaries. They were inexperienced in desert warfare, and had no suitable transport. A passive defence of the Canal being forced upon Egypt, she could not escape the consequences. The enemy was able to conceal to the last his points of attack, and accordingly it was necessary to disperse the small defensive force over 100 miles of line until that excessive length could be shortened by suitably placed obstacles. The initiative rested with the enemy.

The Suez or Maritime Canal follows a natural depression, leading through Lake Timsa and the Great and Little Bitter Lakes. Cutting across its centre and southern sections are plateaux, through which the Canal is carried in deep cuttings of the narrowest possible width. These are consequently the easiest points for crossing. They occur north of Ismailia, between that town and El Firdan; south of Ismailia in the region of Tussum and Serapeum, which lie between Lake Timsa and the Great Bitter Lake; and at Esh Shallufa, south of the Little Bitter Lake. In 1914, the width of the Canal at these places was less than 200 feet, while elsewhere it was as much as 300 feet. The maximum depth was about 34 feet. Along the western bank, for the greater part of its length between Port Said in the north[3] and Suez in the south, including the shores of the three lakes, ran branches of the " Sweetwater Canal," carrying fresh Nile

[1] *Military Operations, Egypt and Palestine*, Vol. I, by Lieut.-General Sir George MacMunn, K.C.B., K.C.S.I., D.S.O. and Captain Cyril Falls, late 11th R. Innis. Fusiliers, p. 24. This volume is part of the Official History of the campaign.
[2] *An Outline of the Egyptian and Palestine Campaigns, 1914 to 1918*, by Major-General Sir M. G. E. Bowman-Manifold, K.B.E., C.B., C.M.G., D.S.O., late R.E., p. 10
[3] The Sweetwater Canal does not follow the western bank between Ismailia and El Qantara, but is some four miles to the west of it in this section.

water from Cairo to Ismailia, the central town on the Canal. This canal was about 30 feet wide and 5 feet deep. A single line of standard gauge railway, with a line of telegraph, connected Port Said, Ismailia and Suez. It followed the western bank of the Canal and the shores of the lakes, and was linked with Cairo by a single line, running westwards from Ismailia through Zagazig and, for some distance, close alongside the main supply channel of the Sweetwater Canal. In 1914 the Suez Canal zone was destitute of metalled roads, except in the towns. Such were the means of supply and communication by land for the eastern defensive position.

The question of water-supply dominated both the attack and defence. The target for the attackers was the Sweetwater Canal behind Ismailia, for if installed there, they could render the whole defensive line untenable, and could sever all railway communication with the interior. This was the vital point. The easiest avenue of approach to Egypt from Palestine was by the level and sandy *Darab es Sultani*, or Royal Road, leading from El Arish along the Mediterranean coast and through the Qatiya Oasis, a route which had been followed by the Crusaders and other invaders because of the water available in its shallow wells. It was exposed, however, to interference from the sea, and led, not to the vital point, but to El Qantara, where the Canal was wide, and the country on both sides a dreary waste. A central line of advance was available from Beersheba or El Arish, by various tracks through barren and stony hills, to Bir[1] el Hassana, and thence through Bir el Jifjafa and across a sandy desert to the region of Ismailia.[2] This route could be followed by a large force only when certain wells and rock cisterns had been recently filled by heavy rain, but it had the advantage that it was directed on the vital point. A southern route, by the Pilgrims' Road from Nekhl to Suez, traversed very broken country and offered few strategic attractions. It seemed probable that, weather permitting, the main body of the enemy would advance by the central route against Ismailia. If no rain had fallen, they would be forced to approach by the northern route towards El Qantara.

On his arrival in Egypt in September, 1914, Lieut.-General Sir John Maxwell formed the Suez Canal defences into a separate command under Major-General Alexander Wilson, who had come from India. The 3rd (Lahore) and 7th (Meerut) Divisions landed in Egypt for a few days during their voyage to France. They were followed to Egypt in November by the 10th and 11th Indian Divisions, the Imperial Service Cavalry Brigade and the Bikaner Camel Corps[3]—in all about 30,000 men. Then came several Australian and New Zealand divisions; but it was India who guarded the Canal at the beginning.

[1] *Bir*, a well.
[2] See the *Sketch Map of the Sinai Desert in* 1917.
[3] The Cavalry Brigade and Camel Corps were Native States' troops.

By the end of 1914, there were more than 70,000 British, Dominion and Indian soldiers in the country, though only the regular troops were fully trained. The first danger had then passed. Egypt was firmly held, but the Suez Canal was by no means safe from attack.[1] The defenders were weak in artillery, and consequently relied on British and French warships to supplement their gunfire from the Canal. The Australians and New Zealanders, some Yeomanry and the 42nd Division were being trained and equipped at Cairo, and were in no sense fit to take the field. It was reported that Djemal Pasha, the Turkish commander in Syria, could put 70,000 men into Sinai, though he could not lead such a force across the desert to the Canal. Nevertheless, it was known that he was confident, or wished to appear confident, of success, for he had announced, on his departure from Constantinople, that he would not return until he had entered Cairo.

The first defensive system on the banks of the Suez Canal was simple by comparison with the elaborate one constructed in the Sinai Desert in 1916. It consisted of 18 small redoubts or "bridge-heads" on the east bank, with trenches dug on the west bank at intervals between these posts. North of Ismailia, the posts were located opposite Port Said and at Ras el Esh, El Tina, El Kab, El Qantara, El Balla, El Firdan and a spot known as "Bench Mark." Ismailia Ferry Post was an extensive bridge-head, designed to guard an important crossing. Between Lake Timsa and the Great Bitter Lake, in the region south of Ismailia, posts were established at Tussum, Serapeum and Deversoir. Farther south again, between the Little Bitter Lake and the southern end of the Canal at Port Taufiq (Tewfik), posts were located at Gineifa (Geneffe), Esh Shallufa, "Gurkha Post," El Kubri, "Baluchistan Post," and Esh Shatt.[2] The trenches in these works were revetted with sandbags and protected by barbed wire. The posts were designed to cover temporary ferries and boat bridges, to provide facilities for counter-attack, and to afford mutual support and proper communication on the east bank. A simple plan was evolved to discover traces of the approach of enemy patrols under cover of darkness. Each evening, a brush-barrow, made of sandbags, was dragged over the rough sand between the posts, leaving a smooth corridor which showed the smallest mark.

The Suez Canal Company rendered great assistance in the construction of works of many different kinds, and in the provision of crossings. Its ferries were put at the service of the defence, and a number of new ones added. Three large floating bridges were assembled—the heaviest at Ismailia and others at El Qantara and El Kubri—and 8 small bridges were provided across the Sweetwater Canal. The lack

[1] *The Military Engineer in India*, by Lieut.-Colonel E. W. C. Sandes, D.S.O., M.C., R.E. (retd.), Vol. I. p. 493.
[2] See the *Sketch Map of the Suez Canal Defences in 1915-16*.

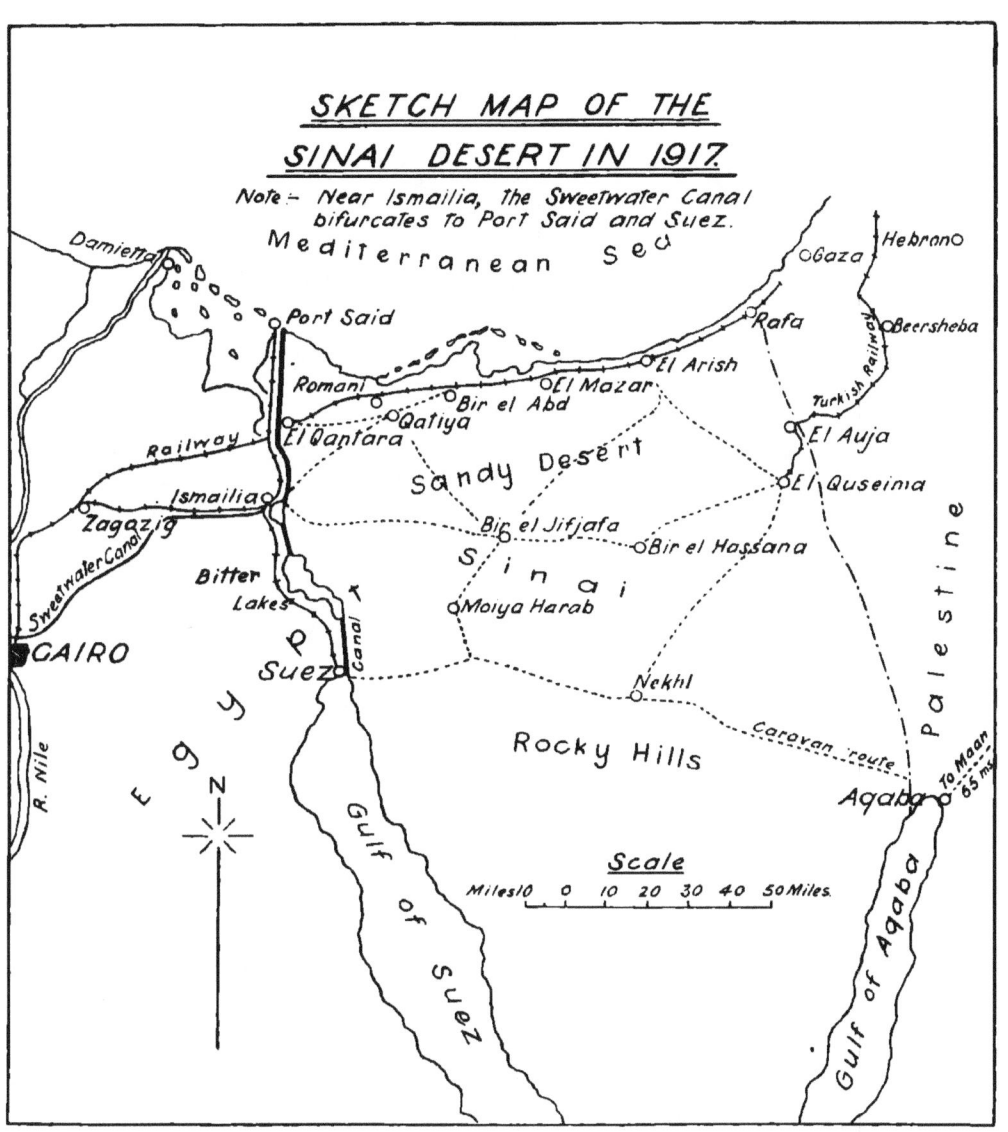

of a metalled road along the west bank of the Maritime Canal was severely felt.[1] In order to reduce the frontage open to attack, a cutting was made in the east bank at Port Said on November 25th, 1914, and the resulting inundation spread over the desert as far as El Kab, north of El Qantara, thus safeguarding 20 miles of the position.[2] On January 2nd, 1915, the bank was cut again a few miles north of El Qantara, and afterwards at one or two points south of it. These inundations, when complete, confined the objective of a serious Turkish offensive to the portion of the Canal between the region of El Balla, 13 miles north of Ismailia, and Deversoir, the same distance south of that town. An attack in force against the southern section, between the Little Bitter Lake and Port Taufiq, was improbable. Deducting the length of Lake Timsa, the threatened section did not exceed 21 miles. This could be defended adequately by the troops assembled on the Canal.

For some months the only regular officer available for military engineering duty was Captain R. E. M. Russell, R.E., who was lent by the Egyptian Army and attached to the headquarters of the G.O.C. Canal Defences. He had served on the Sudan Government Railways from 1905 to 1910, and thereafter chiefly in the Intelligence Department. On November 9th, 1914, he assumed his new appointment of Staff Officer, R.E., for Defence Work, and filled it until June, 1915. Fortunately, the Egyptian State Railways and Telegraph Departments, which included several ex-officers of the Corps—Majors G. B. Macauley and R. B. D. Blakeney, Captain G. C. M. Hall and Major J. S. Liddell—were able to give valuable assistance at the outset. Until the 10th Company, Q.V.O. (Madras) Sappers and Miners, under Captain T. P. Bassett, R.E., arrived from India on December 22nd, 1914, only one field company of Territorial Engineers (East Lancashires) was available; and when the Territorials were withdrawn on January 6th, 1915, the 10th Company was the sole engineering unit for two divisions until No. 3 Field Company, Australian Engineers, arrived from Cairo on January 16th. Excellent work was carried out by the 128th Pioneers from India, and by an unarmed detachment and a small mobile section on camels from the Military Works Department of the Egyptian Army;[3] but it was not until February that another Territorial field company arrived on the scene. Some of these troops came too late to assist in repelling the first Turkish attack. However, during November, December and January, Russell and his available engineer units and formations worked with a will. They advised the infantry in the design and excavation of trenches; they built bridges, constructed

[1] The existing road connecting Port Said, Ismailia and Suez was built in 1916.
[2] This main inundation was completed early in December, 1914. It had been planned by the Chief Engineer, Brig.-General H. B. H. Wright, in consultation with Sir Murdoch MacDonald. The work was executed by the local Egyptian Irrigation Officer.
[3] The Mobile Section was under Lieut. B. T. Wilson, R.E.

aeroplane hangars, stored water, laid water-supplies to camps, cut the canal banks for inundations, installed searchlights, accompanied reconnaissances and performed a hundred other necessary duties. It is not too much to say that they were the backbone of the defence.[1]

Writing of the design of the defensive posts in the early days, Lieut.-Colonel T. P. Bassett says :—[2]" Egypt was the Clapham Junction for other theatres of war. Units and senior officers arrived from all directions and, after brief halts, disappeared in all directions. Consequently, it was difficult for Headquarters to impose their ideas either in the principles or details of defence. Each unit from another theatre brought with it the ideas current in that theatre. No two commanders thought alike. As excavations reveal successive and prehistoric civilizations, so the Canal posts showed the varying ideas of many commanders. The onus of attempting to work to some definite principle fell on the Engineers."

For defensive purposes, the entire line was divided into four sections. The 10th, and part of the 11th, (Indian) Divisions furnished garrisons for the fortified posts on the east bank. The remainder of the 11th (Indian) Division, and the Imperial Service Cavalry Brigade, were retained in reserve at Moascar, near Ismailia.

Shortly after the declaration of war, the enemy had begun to penetrate into the Sinai Peninsula. By November 15th, they were believed to have 5,000 infantry and 3,000 Arab auxiliaries on the Mediterranean coast at El Arish, which, with Nekhl, had been evacuated by Egypt according to plan. On the 19th, they reconnoitred Bir el Abd on the northern route ; and on the 20th, they passed the Qatiya oasis and appeared within 18 miles of El Qantara. Within the next fortnight, the desert in front of the northern section of the Suez Canal was flooded, but the enemy still hovered in the neighbourhood of Qatiya. Owing to exceptionally heavy rain, the rock cisterns and wells of the central route had become filled with sufficient water to open that avenue of advance, and evidence was soon forthcoming that the enemy were approaching from Palestine by all three routes—northern, central and southern. On January 15th, 1915, parties of Turks were located by aeroplane observers on the northern and central routes. Ten days later, Moiya Harab, 25 miles east of the Little Bitter Lake, was reported to be occupied by 6,000 men, and at the same time El Qantara was raided. Warships took post in the Canal, and troops were moved to their positions of defence. On January 27th, the enemy were found to have established themselves five miles east of El Qantara, and to be

---

[1] The duties performed by the engineers are enumerated in a Note entitled, " Engineer Work on the Canal Defences " appearing in *Military Operations, Egypt and Palestine*, Vol. I, by Lieut.-General Sir George MacMunn, K.C.B., K.C.S.I., D.S.O., and Captain Cyril Falls, p. 33.

[2] Notes by Lieut.-Colonel T. P. Bassett, D.S.O., R.E. (retd.), sent to the author on May 28th, 1936. Bassett succeeded Russell on the departure of the latter in June, 1915.

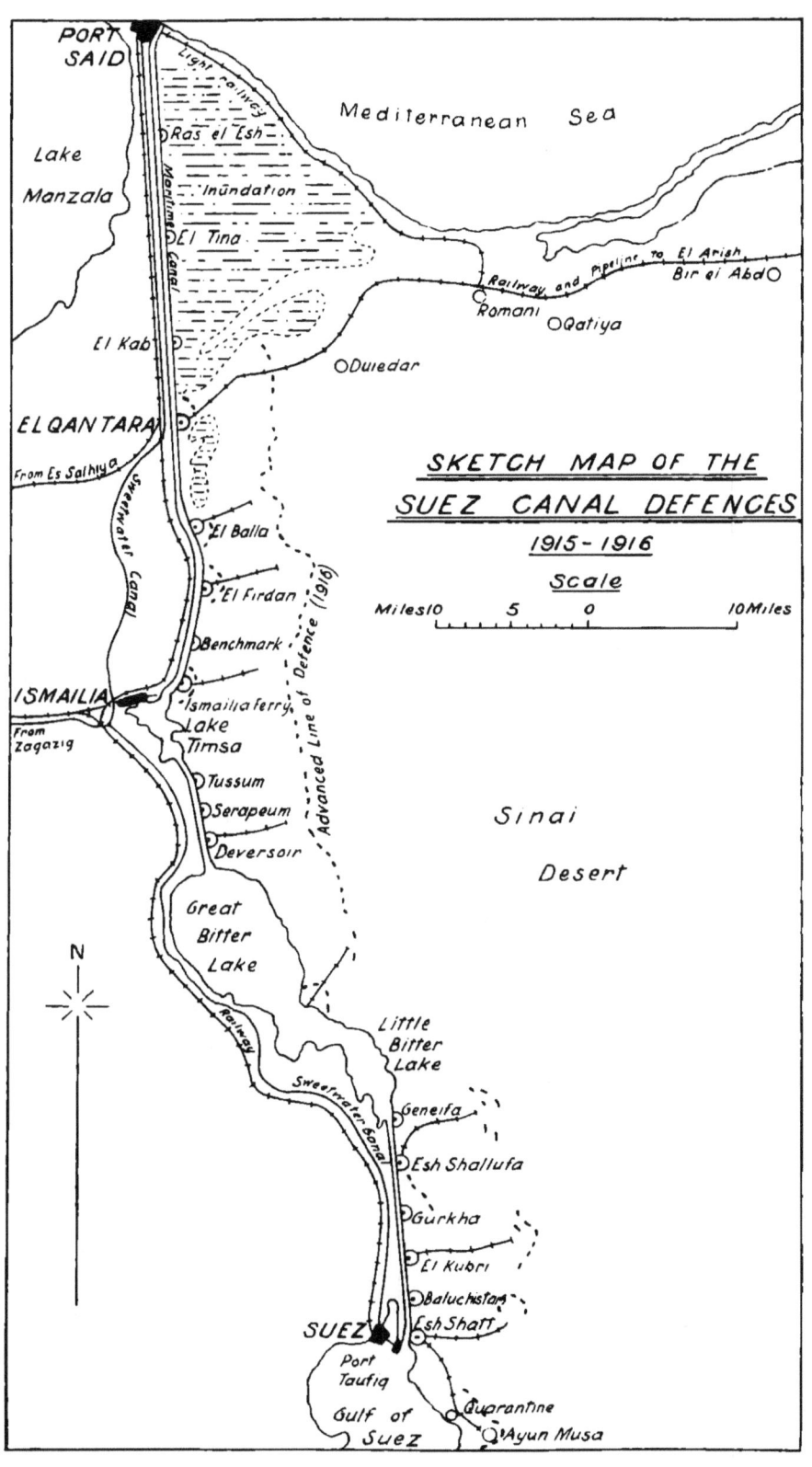

nearing the southern section, where the post at El Kubri was attacked.

The Turkish advance was now in full swing. Djemal Pasha issued a grandiloquent *communiqué* to his troops. " Warriors ! " he wrote. " Behind you lie vast deserts. Before you is the craven enemy, and behind him the rich land of Egypt, which is awaiting you impatiently. If you falter, death will overtake you. Before you, Paradise lies." So the patient Ottoman soldiery, dragging their pontoons and guns, toiled painfully across Sinai in a forlorn attempt to dislodge a disciplined and powerful adversary from an entrenched position on a formidable obstacle, which could be enfiladed by heavy gun-fire from warships. It is difficult to believe that Djemal and his Chief of Staff, the capable and gallant Bavarian, Colonel Kress von Kressenstein, could have been confident of success. However, the Turkish camps continued to multiply in the desert, and on February 2nd, 5,000 infantry with guns were east of Serapeum, a similar body near Ismailia Ferry Post, and 2,000 infantry and guns close to El Qantara. As it was evident that the main attack might be expected shortly in the region of Ismailia, General Wilson reinforced his centre, and his troops stood to arms. His general reserve at Moascar was close at hand.

The Canal defences had been elaborated, and there were now twelve posts on the west bank between Lake Timsa and the Great Bitter Lake, in addition to the posts on the east bank at Tussum, Serapeum and Deversoir. This sector was held by four battalions of Indian infantry, a company of Territorial engineers, a field battery, a pack battery, and some Pioneers. A roaring dust-storm arose on February 2nd, and continued throughout the following night and morning. At 3.25 a.m. on February 3rd, 1915, squads of the enemy could be discerned south of Tussum, carrying pontoon sand rafts[1] down sandy gullies in the east bank towards the water ; and about an hour later, the Egyptian pack battery opened fire on them, and on many other parties who dotted the bank for a distance of $1\frac{1}{2}$ miles. Most of the pontoons and rafts were destroyed before they could be launched. Wreckage strewed the bank. Only three pontoons crossed to the other side, where their occupants were immediately killed or captured, with the exception of a few who held out for many hours under cover of the west bank and bravely kept up a fire on any and every target until obliged to surrender.[2]

The attempt had failed completely; yet the Turkish command did not abandon hope. At 9.30 a.m., they brought up fresh troops against Serapeum and again tried to force a crossing. Traffic in the

---

[1] The pontoons were of German service pattern, of galvanized iron, each capable of holding about 20 men. The rafts consisted of empty kerosene tins, enclosed in a light wooden framework.

[2] A graphic description of the Turkish attack is given in *L'Attaque du Canal de Suez, 3rd Fevrier, 1915,* by Lieutenant de Vaisseau Georges Douin.

Canal was suspended. The shipping in Lake Timsa suffered under accurate artillery fire. The French cruisers *Requin* and *D'Entrecasteaux*, and the British battleships *Ocean* and *Swiftsure*, joined in the engagement, and finally, at 1.30 p.m., the enemy retreated into the desert. No difficulty was experienced in repelling minor attacks against El Qantara, El Firdan and in the southern sector. Covered by weak rearguards, the enemy retired across Sinai. Unfortunately, they were allowed to do so without molestation until the afternoon of February 4th, when the Imperial Service Cavalry Brigade reconnoitred from Ismailia Ferry Post, but did not engage closely.

According to the official history of the campaign,[1] the opportunity for the destruction of the Turkish central force could not be taken because only the Indian infantry, and not all of them, were highly trained, and it was necessary to retain considerable reserves at Cairo and elsewhere. There were no facilities for the rapid crossing of a large body of troops, except at Ismailia. There were no water convoys, and few pack animals for water transport. Accordingly, the force under General Wilson was unsuitable for a counterstroke in the desert. Aerial reconnaissance was difficult and gave scanty information, so there was much uncertainty regarding the enemy's strength and probable intentions.[2] It was not until the middle of February that Lieut.-General Sir John Maxwell was assured that the Turkish attack was not supported by powerful reserves. It may be noted also, that he had been warned by Lord Kitchener not to risk a reverse, which might have far-reaching effects, and he had therefore limited General Wilson to a passive defence, relieved only by local counter-attacks unless an exceptional opportunity offered. Nevertheless, the inaction of the defence, after the failure of the Turkish attack, has been severely criticized. The Turks lost 2,000 men; but the remainder escaped to boast that they had reached the Canal. Indeed, the Germans announced that it had been bridged, that five battalions had crossed, and that the invasion of Egypt would have been accomplished if the attackers had not missed their way in a dust-storm! On the next occasion that the Canal was threatened, 400,000 troops, badly needed by the Allies elsewhere, were massed in Egypt; so it will be seen that the Turkish effort in February, 1915, had important results.

During the spring and summer of 1915, the Turks were too fully occupied by the Allied landings in Gallipoli, and the successful advance in Mesopotamia,[3] to be able to spare any troops for a renewal of the attack on the Suez Canal. The defenders consolidated and improved their position, and kept at a distance the small parties of

---

[1] *Military Operations. Egypt and Palestine*, Vol. I, pp. 48, 49.

[2] The few British aeroplanes and French seaplanes, which were available, were untrustworthy and inadequate for the work.

[3] An account of the advance of the 6th Indian Division and the 30th Indian Brigade under Major-General C. V. F. Townshend is given in *In Kut and Captivity*, by Major E. W. C. Sandes, D.S.O., M.C., R.E.

THE SUEZ CANAL AT TUSSUM.
Near the point of the Turkish crossing in February, 1915.

[*Photo by the Author.*]

the enemy who approached from time to time. After the historic landings in Gallipoli on April 25th, 1915, Egypt was saddled with new responsibilities. The last great offensive of the Gallipoli Campaign—the landing in Suvla Bay—took place on August 6th. It failed, and on October 11th, Lord Kitchener asked General Sir Ian Hamilton for his estimate of the losses which might be incurred if it were decided to evacuate the peninsula. Kitchener arrived at Mudros on November 10th, when Lieut.-General Sir Charles Monro had replaced Sir Ian Hamilton in command, and set himself to consider the highly complicated situation. Sir John Maxwell had come from Egypt to consult with his former chief, for unless an offensive was launched elsewhere, an evacuation of Gallipoli would release an army of Turks for the invasion of Egypt. Kitchener proposed a landing in the Gulf of Alexandretta. He maintained that an attempt to defend Egypt *in* Egypt might entail the loss both of that country and the Sudan. The Alexandretta scheme, however, was not approved, and nothing remained accordingly but to plan an improved defence for the eastern frontier of Egypt. Kitchener decided that the Turks should be engaged in the desert. The orders which reached Brigadier-General H. B. H. Wright on November 16th, were brief and comprehensive. "The defence of the Canal must be taken up seriously and in depth," ran the telegram from Athens. Wright immediately drew up approximate plans for three lines of defence, ordered vast quantities of stores, bought all the timber available in Egypt to the value of £500,000, and secured the mobilization of the Egyptian Public Works Department under Sir Murdoch MacDonald, who was appointed Deputy Director of Works and given the temporary rank of Colonel. A strong line of redoubts and entrenchments was to be prepared about 12,000 yards east of the Suez Canal, so that the latter should be immune from artillery fire. Behind this line would be other lines of supporting positions, metalled roads, railways, pipe-lines and all the other appurtenances of a modern position prepared in depth. The War Office estimate of the force necessary to hold such a position was eight infantry divisions, five mounted divisions and nineteen batteries of heavy or siege artillery, and Kitchener stated that not less than fifteen field companies of Royal Engineers would be required, in addition to those with the Mediterranean Expeditionary Force in Gallipoli and those already in Egypt. On November 24th, he sailed from Mudros for England; and on December 20th, the last British and Dominion soldiers quitted Gallipoli. By February, 1916, 12 infantry divisions and one mounted division were concentrated in Egypt.

The desperate attempt to force a passage to Constantinople does not come within the scope of this history; but it may be remarked that Engineer officers and men from Egypt and the Sudan shared in the enterprise. Among these were Brigadier-General M. G. E. Bowman-Manifold as Director of Army Signals, and Captain M. R. Kennedy, R.E., Director of Public Works in the Sudan, a brilliant engineer whose somewhat stormy career was cut short by his early death in 1924. Kennedy was in charge of much of the engineering work on the lines of communication in Gallipoli, and directed most ably, on the peninsula and at Imbros, the labours of an Egyptian Works Battalion of six companies commanded by Captains P. C. Lord, R. Micklem, Lieutenants W. S. Blunt and B. T. Wilson, R.E., and two temporary officers.[1] These units built piers and breakwaters, made arrangements for water-supply, and helped the army in many other ways. They proved that, as a labourer, the Egyptian *fellah* is invaluable.

When Lord Kitchener returned to England, he sent one of his Staff, Major-General H. S. Horne, to Egypt to reconnoitre the contemplated line of defence east of the Suez Canal, and Horne telegraphed his proposals to the War Office on December 10th, 1915. The selected front line was roughly 11,000 yards from, and parallel to, the Canal. It skirted the main inundation in the north, and terminated in the south near the oasis of Ayun Musa, south-east of Port Taufiq. Horne proposed that there should be a second line of defence about 4,500 yards in rear of the first, and that a series of mutually supporting works, covering bridge-heads and vital points on the east bank of the Suez Canal, should form a third and final line. The second and third lines could be covered by artillery fire from warships in the Canal and lakes.[2] Unfortunately, no additional engineer units were immediately available for the execution of this scheme, though the General Staff sent a number of R.E. officers.[3] The responsibility for the proper execution of the work in its initial stages fell upon Brigadier-General Wright.[4] It was well that Egypt possessed ample labour, supervised by skilled civilian engineers. Sir Murdoch MacDonald, Under-Secretary for Public Works, controlled most of the work, other than planning and constructing defensive positions, and busied himself chiefly with the provision of roads and landing stages and with urgent problems of water-supply to the desert areas. Railway extensions were controlled by Brigadier-General G. B. Macauley, late R.E., Director of Railways, and Telegraph extensions by Major J. S. Liddell, R.E., Director of Army Signals. Both these officers had occupied important posts in Egypt and the Sudan. Military engineering duties, in connection with the new scheme of defence, fell to Major

---

[1] Lieut. W. S. Blunt, R.E., was relieved by another officer in June, 1915. Three of the companies were composed of Railway personnel, and three of Works personnel.
[2] *Military Operations. Egypt and Palestine*, Vol. I, p. 90.
[3] Twenty-seven officers were promised, and 13 arrived in January, 1916.
[4] Letter from Major-General H. B. H. Wright, C.B., C.M.G., late R.E., to the author, dated November 1st, 1934. A committee under Major-General Sir H. V. Cox was appointed to co-ordinate the work and accelerate its progress.

(temp. Brig.-Gen.) P. G. Grant, R.E., who was assisted from November, 1915, to February, 1916, by Lieut.-Colonels G. R. Pridham and H. L. Pritchard, R.E.[1] The latter was placed in command of two field companies of Australian Engineers and a company of New Zealanders, and soon formed a high opinion of them.[2]

In October, 1915, Grant had been ordered suddenly to proceed from France to Egypt, where he was appointed Chief Engineer, Canal Defences, under Brigadier-General Wright and told to report to General Horne. Early in December, he rode out with Horne from various posts along the Suez Canal, and afterwards marked out the advanced line of defence with sand-pillars. In January, 1916, he was directed to commence work. He was told in Cairo that he would be given Egyptian Army reservists as labourers, and was asked whether he could begin at once. Tools were deficient, plans incomplete, materials unknown and the promised labour untrained, but he promptly assented. Subsequently, when the reservists failed to arrive, other labour was obtained, and work was started under conditions which tested to the utmost the ingenuity and persistence of the Chief Engineer.

"We found that no material for revetting the trenches was available on the spot," writes Sir Philip Grant,[3] "so we had to make matting hurdles to prevent the sand from falling in. I secured two ship-loads of timber at Port Said and wired to Sir Reginald Wingate at Khartoum asking him to send all the available matting in the Sudan, which he kindly promised to do. Meeting Hawkins, of the Sudan Railways, in Port Said, I suggested that he should join the Royal Engineers and run a saw-mill in the docks. This he did; and Raikes, another temporary R.E. officer, who knew Egypt well, got the necessary saws. In a short time, Hawkins was sawing up timber and producing hundreds of hurdles which, with the necessary matting, were carried by a fleet of native sailing boats to various stations along the Canal. We made a bridge across the Canal with a number of peculiar native boats from Lake Manzala. It swung on a wooden hinge, and consequently opened and shut most correctly; and as the cables were fixed to a hawser, which lay across the bottom of the Canal when the bridge was open, there was no danger of fouling the propellers of ships. Another bridge was made with casks. On one occasion, the commander of an Army Transport Company asked whether we could supply him with a monkey for his pile-driver. Fortunately, I had noticed some heavy R.M.L. studded shells

---

[1] Lieut.-Colonel H. L. Pritchard, R.E., already well known to readers of this history, came to Egypt from the Dardanelles. From Egypt he was transferred to Salonika, where he was Chief Engineer, 16th Corps, from Feb., 1916 to January, 1919.

[2] As an example of the keenness of these Dominion soldiers, General Pritchard relates that two Australians, who said that they were water-diviners, dug a well three feet in diameter to a depth of 80 feet in soft sandstone in the hope of finding water. Alas, they were disappointed!

[3] Notes by Major-General Sir Philip Grant, K.C.B., C.M.G., late R.E., sent to the author on October 21st, 1934.

lying outside the Coast-guard Office at Port Said. One of these old projectiles was procured without difficulty and made an excellent monkey." The construction of the new eastern defences of Egypt began and continued in this rough and ready fashion; yet it proceeded with remarkable speed in view of the many obstacles to be overcome.

Changes occurred in the higher commands in Egypt after the return of the Mediterranean Expeditionary Force under Lieut.-General Sir Charles Monro from Gallipoli. Lieut.-General Sir John Maxwell was occupied so fully with the internal military administration of the country, and the operations against the Senussi on the western frontier, that he could not supervise the large forces assembling on the Suez Canal. On January 9th, 1916, General Monro relinquished his command to Lieut.-General Sir Archibald Murray, who arrived on that date from England. Sir John Maxwell also vacated his command, which was no longer necessary under the altered circumstances. His departure was greatly regretted, not only by the British officers who had served under him, but by the Egyptian Army as a whole, for he was extremely popular with all ranks. With Maxwell went his staff, and Brigadier-General H. B. H. Wright was succeeded by Major-General Godfrey Williams, late R.E., from Gallipoli.[1] On March 19th, the Mediterranean Expeditionary Force and the Force in Egypt were amalgamated to form an "Egyptian Expeditionary Force," which was strongly reinforced from home and placed under the command of Sir Archibald Murray.

On his arrival in January, General Murray had found that, although the construction of the new Canal defences was proceeding satisfactorily, no part of the advanced line had, as yet, been occupied, owing to the lack of a piped water-supply to it. However, on January 13th, he was able to order his three Army Corps to the Canal to take up their positions according to the revised scheme of defence; and by the end of March, 1916, although the entrenchments were not yet complete, the advanced line was fully occupied. The new Commander-in-Chief looked upon the occupation of this line merely as a temporary expedient. He was convinced that the best method of defending the eastern frontier was to advance across Northern Sinai through Qatiya to El Arish, for it seemed that fewer troops would be needed for such an undertaking than for a passive resistance in front of the Canal. "El Quseima and El Arish wells were the two key points to the Sinai Desert," writes General Bowman-Manifold.[2] "It seemed preferable to guard the 45 miles

[1] Major-General G. Williams was Chief Engineer, Egypt, or Engineer-in-Chief, E.E.F., from January to June, 1916, when he was ordered to India and succeeded by Brig.-General H. B. H. Wright, who returned to Egypt from England.
[2] *Outline of the Egyptian and Palestine Campaigns, 1914–1918*, by Major-General Sir M. G. E. Bowman-Manifold, K.B.E., C.B., C.M.G., D.S.O., late R.E., p. 20. El Quseima (Kossaima) lies south-east of El Arish, near the Sinai-Palestine boundary.

between these two points with mobile troops rather than to anchor some 11 divisions in the Suez Canal fortifications, over 80 miles long." Nevertheless, the possibility of an advance in force rested upon the efforts of the engineers. No large army could cross the wastes of Sinai unless followed step by step not only by a railway, but by a pipe-line carrying fresh water to the front. But whence could such water be obtained? Only from the distant Nile, by way of the Sweetwater Canal running along the western bank of the Suez Canal. The water must be filtered, led *underneath* the wide maritime canal, stored on the east bank and then forced across the desert, mile after mile, by powerful pumps. The engineers assured Sir Archibald Murray that it could be done, so he bought camels and organized large mobile columns for operations in the desert. If he could seize the extensive Qatiya-Romani oasis before a Turkish army released from Gallipoli could descend upon it, there would be little need to hold in strength the elaborate defences in front of the Suez Canal; and after a further advance, with the railway and pipe-line in support, the greater part of the defensive system might be abandoned.

The construction of the front line of defence in the desert needs little comment. The work commenced by the establishment of a series of posts, at varying intervals, at important points. As further labour and material became available, the number of these posts was increased, so that they could be connected later by trenches to form a continuous line. Digging was easy, though it was difficult to keep the trenches clear of sand. Water was supplied to the working parties by camel convoys. The second line of defence, as originally proposed, was never completed. The first line, elaborated in depth in certain areas, and an improved third line along the Suez Canal, connected to the first line by roads, light railways and pipe-lines, sufficed until the entire system was discarded after the offensive towards Palestine had made good progress.

In April, 1916, Sir Archibald Murray occupied Qatiya with a force of Yeomanry. Raiding columns of cavalry and camelry penetrated far into the desert from every Corps area, surprising Turkish posts and destroying wells and rock-cisterns. The Mobile Section of the Egyptian Military Works Department, under Lieutenant B. T. Wilson, R.E., shared in some of these exploits. "Reconnaissance of the Sinai Desert with the Bikaner Camel Corps was a memorable experience," writes Wilson.[1] "I had 30 Egyptians on trotting camels, with some Norton tube wells and an assortment of tools. Sometimes, we rode almost to El Arish, but never encountered the enemy. Our best trip was when we marched, with the Camel Corps, 100 miles eastwards from El Kubri into the Sinai Hills to make a

[1] Notes by Colonel B. T. Wilson, D.S.O., late R.E., sent to the author on February 26th, 1935.

landing-ground for aeroplanes for the bombing of Nekhl. A machine landed, and we found that the observer was A. J. Ross, who had been in the Works Department and was well known to my men. He was one of the most gifted officers I ever met."

Captain A. J. Ross, R.E., was indeed a man of many parts, and his early death in an aeroplane accident was a tragedy. Not only was he an indefatigable worker, a sound engineer, a fine athlete and a most entertaining companion, but a linguist of such attainments that in two years he learned to speak Arabic so well that, when disguised, he could pass as a native. He joined the Intelligence Department, became an observer in the Royal Flying Corps at the end of February, 1915, and served as a pilot in the operations against the Senussi.[1]

The military operations in Sinai during the spring, summer and autumn of 1916 are described fully in the official history for this theatre of the war. In April, a Turkish enterprise against the Yeomanry in the Qatiya area met with considerable success; but on August 4th, in spite of the fact that six divisions had been sent to other fronts, Major-General the Hon. H. A. Lawrence won a decisive victory at Romani over 18,000 Turks under Von Kressenstein, and thus opened the way to El Arish. Egypt was never threatened again. The initiative passed definitely to Sir Archibald Murray, who proceeded to advance by deliberate methods, accompanied by the railway and pipe-line. The troops to the east of the Suez Canal were placed under Lieut.-General Sir Charles Dobell and constituted an "Eastern Force," and the advance to El Arish was entrusted to a Desert Column of four divisions under Lieut.-General Sir Philip Chetwode. No resistance was encountered, and on December 21st, El Arish was occupied. Early in 1917, the Sinai Peninsula was once again in Egyptian hands.

The British failures and final success at Gaza, and Lieut.-General Sir Edmund Allenby's campaign in Palestine and Syria, are outside the scope of this narrative. Many Royal Engineers from Egypt and the Sudan served with the forces. Brigadier-General M. G. E. Bowman-Manifold was Signal Officer in Chief, and with the assistance of Major H. L. Mackworth, Captain R. A. Owen and later of Captain H. C. B. Wemyss, dealt most ably with a vast network of communication;[2] Lieut.-Colonel C. W. Gwynn was on the staff of the Australian and New Zealand Army Corps; Major R. E. M. Russell was Chief Engineer with the Desert Column; and other

---

[1] Lieut. A. J. Ross, R.E., continued to serve with the Royal Flying Corps in Egypt until April 28th, 1917. He was killed in an aeroplane accident in Norfolk on August 2nd, 1917.

[2] On the formation of the Egyptian Expeditionary Force in March, 1916, Brig.-General Bowman-Manifold continued in his appointment of Director of Army Signals. Lieut.-Colonel J. S. Liddell, R.E., then reverted to his office of Inspector-General, Egyptian State Telegraphs, in which he gave all possible assistance to the army.

officers, such as Major A. W. Stokes, were Commanding Royal Engineers or held command of units. Egyptian Sapper Companies, under Lieutenants W. S. Blunt and C. G. Martin, M.C., constructed hospitals and other large buildings as the army advanced. The Railway organization was under Brigadier-General Sir George Macauley. These few names, selected at random, will serve to show that the engineers of Egypt and the Sudan were represented in the operations which crushed Turkey.

The exploits of Lieut.-Colonel S. F. Newcombe, R.E., deserve passing mention. Newcombe had surveyed or built railways in all parts of the Sudan from 1901 until 1913 when, with Lieutenant J. P. S. Greig, R.E., he proceeded to survey in Sinai.[1] With the approval of Lord Kitchener, this survey was extended, during the winter of 1913-14, to cover the region between Beersheba and Aqaba. Newcombe was joined at Beersheba by Leonard Woolley and T. E. Lawrence,[2] archæological explorers who had been working on the Euphrates,[3] and a survey was carried out under the auspices of the Palestine Exploration Fund. While Woolley and Lawrence went south-eastwards to Maan, Newcombe journeyed southwards to survey at Aqaba, where he was joined later by Lawrence. These surveys were valuable during the war. After the outbreak of hostilities, Newcombe worked in the Intelligence Department at Cairo from December, 1914, to August, 1915, assisted by George Lloyd,[4] Aubrey Herbert, Lawrence and Woolley, and then, after serving on several fronts, returned to Arabia in December, 1916, and helped Lawrence in many expeditions. While Lawrence was engaged in the capture of Aqaba in July, 1917, Newcombe and Major W. A. Davenport raided the Hedjaz Railway, 140 miles north of Medina, and destroyed 3 miles of line. In October, Newcombe suggested that he should co-operate in the general offensive by raising the Bedouin, east of Beersheba, against the Turks, and blocking the road to Hebron after Beersheba had been captured. General Allenby assented, and with only 70 British camelry and a few Arabs, Newcombe attempted to bar the enemy's line of retreat by a raid from the east. The exploit ended in disaster, for on November 1st, Newcombe and the survivors among his men were captured after a stiff fight on the Beersheba-Hebron road; but it had the effect of causing the Turks to reinforce their left flank and thus to weaken their centre, through which Allenby forced his way.[5]

Although few officers of the Royal Engineers served in the Arabian

[1] Parts of Sinai had been surveyed by Lieuts. L. N. F. I. King and A. G. Turner, R.E.
[2] "Lawrence of Arabia."
[3] "Explorations and Excavations in Palestine," by Colonel Sir Charles Close, K.B.E., C.B., C.M.G., late R.E., appearing in the *R.E. Journal*, Vol. L, June, 1936, pp. 185-200.
[4] Now Lord Lloyd of Dolobran.
[5] *T. E. Lawrence*, by Liddell Hart, p. 245.

theatre during the Great War, it may be well to give a brief description of some of the events which brought the Arabs of the Hedjaz into active co-operation with the Allies in what became known as the " Arab Revolt," and to record some of the results of that association.

Almost from the outset of the war, General Sir Reginald Wingate, then Governor-General of the Sudan and Sirdar of the Egyptian Army, had foreseen the possibility of weaning Sunnite Islam from the aggressive Pan-Islamism of the Ottoman School, and of creating a balance of power in the central states of the Islamic world ; and early in 1915, with the aid of Sir Sayed Ali el Morghani, a religious notable of the Sudan, he was able to get into touch with the Sherif of Mecca, the guardian of the Holy Places. He was then in a position to report freely to the High Commissioner in Egypt and to Lord Kitchener on the situation in the Hedjaz and other parts of Arabia.[1]

For a time, the Sherif adopted a waiting attitude ; but in the middle of 1915, he asked that Great Britain would guarantee the independence of all Arab lands as the reward of a revolt against Turkey. Prolonged discussions followed ; and in February, 1916, in order to deal with such matters, an " Arab Bureau " was opened in Cairo, to which were attached a number of travellers, archæologists and officials of the Egyptian and Sudan services. As there was a danger that the Turco-German authorities might be able to exploit the Arab cause, the High Commissioner and the Governor-General urged that support should be given to the Sherif, and in the end, Great Britain pledged herself to recognize and maintain the independence of the Arabs within certain boundaries. Consequently, in the spring of 1916, it was decided to assist in expelling the Turks from Arab territory. The Arab Revolt, involving as it did the interests of France in Syria, led to a Pact between the British and French Governments and the interchange of notes between Great Britain, France and Russia. The recognition of Italian interests had already been secured.

Sir Reginald Wingate succeeded in opening direct correspondence with the Sherif, and undertook to send him rifles and munitions. The Sherif's eldest son, Ali, and third son, Feisul, then raised the standard of revolt in Medina. On June 9th, 1916, Sir Reginald heard that the Sherif himself had risen and had occupied one-half of Mecca, where he was under bombardment by the Turks. Without delay, he sent two pack batteries and a machine-gun battery under Egyptian officers to the Hedjaz, and supplemented them later by a few British officers, other native troops and some aircraft. He was appointed General Officer Commanding the Hedjaz Operations, and held that post until March, 1919 ; though at his earnest request, the

---

[1] Notes by General Sir Reginald Wingate, Bt., G.C.B., G.C.V.O., G.B.E., K.C.M.G., D.S.O., sent to the author on August 31st, 1936.

notification of the appointment, and copies of his dispatches, did not appear in the official gazette until the end of December, 1919.

The first British officer sent from the Sudan to the Hedjaz was Lieut.-Colonel C. E. Wilson, Governor of the Red Sea Province, who was appointed by Sir Reginald to act as his representative at Jidda and to advise the Sherif on political and military questions. Wilson was followed by others, such as Lieut.-Colonel Joyce, Captains Lawrence, Ross, Vickery and Davenport, and Major H. D. Pearson, R.E. The Arab forces were divided into three groups under the Sherif's three sons, Ali, Abdulla and Feisul. By June 16th, 1916, both Jidda and Mecca were in the Sherif's hands, and on September 23rd, a Turkish force at Taif, east of Mecca, capitulated to Abdulla. With the exception of Medina, the Hedjaz was soon clear of the enemy; but Medina, though closely invested, held out for a time. It was to Feisul's army that Lawrence, Joyce, Ross and others were attached. They played an important part in destroying the Hedjaz Railway, thus preventing the execution of the original Turco-German plan of withdrawing forces from Arabia to assist in an attack on Egypt, whose British garrison had been denuded in the interests of the Western Front in France. Feisul's army eventually became the flank guard of the British advance into Palestine. All Arab operations north of Maan on the Hedjaz Railway were then directed by General Sir Edmund Allenby; but those south of Maan remained under the direction of General Sir Reginald Wingate, who had succeeded Sir Henry McMahon as High Commissioner for Egypt in January, 1917. It will be seen, accordingly, that the Sudan was closely concerned with the campaign in Arabia.

The construction of the defensive position east of the Suez Canal in 1916, and the subsequent advance into Palestine, would not have been possible without the excellent systems of railways, pipelines and roads provided by the military engineers and their brethren, the civil engineers who joined the forces. It was fortunate that three Royal Engineers—Colonel Sir George Macauley, Major R. B. D. Blakeney and Captain G. C. M. Hall—were serving on the Egyptian State Railways in 1914, for they formed the nucleus of a great railway organization for war. They adapted the traffic systems of peaceful Egypt to the needs of a vast military base, coped with the transport of thousands of troops, and turned their workshops into armament factories. They produced two armoured trains, which patrolled the railway line along the Suez Canal.[1] They tore up track, sent it to the eastern frontier, and relaid it as required for military purposes. Unhappily the decision to construct a position east of the Canal was not reached while the American markets were

[1] The trains were made bullet-proof by means of old steel plates or ballast between planks. They carried mountain guns on field carriages, and a few Maxims.

open and American shipping available, and thus a serious shortage of locomotives, rolling stock and track persisted throughout the war. New supplies could not be obtained, and reserve stocks were soon exhausted.[1] At the end of November, 1915, before the position in the desert was prepared, the existing line from Zagazig to Ismailia (50 miles) was doubled, in order to transport to the Canal zone the enormous numbers of troops and animals arriving from Alexandria. This work was completed by 15,000 men on January 6th, 1916.[2] After the preparation of the desert position had been taken in hand, a network of light railways (2 feet 6 inches gauge) was provided on the east bank of the Canal, to connect the position with the Canal defences and to afford lateral communication. Rails, sleepers and rolling stock for these railways were collected in Egypt; and within a few weeks, more than 100 miles of track were laid by Egyptian army reservists under skilled supervision.

In March, 1916, material began to arrive at El Qantara for the standard (4 feet 8½ inches) gauge line which Sir Archibald Murray needed for his projected advance into Palestine. Screened by the Yeomanry at Qatiya, construction was commenced at El Qantara in April, and 16 miles of track, including sidings, were laid in four weeks. Except for a diversion northwards to avoid sand-dunes near Romani, the railway followed the caravan route. A light railway was laid also from Port Said along the coast. The main line of railway was constructed, operated and maintained by three Railway Companies under Major G. Lubbock, R.E., assisted by personnel of the Egyptian State Railways and by many thousands of men of the Labour Corps. By May 19th, the railway was open for traffic as far as Romani, a distance of 23 miles, and it became possible to establish a strong infantry garrison at that place. After the Battle of Romani in August, rail-head gradually attained a rate of progress of 20 miles a month, so that on November 17th, it was 54 miles, and on December 1st, 64 miles, from El Qantara. The rate was greatly accelerated when the pipe-line reached Romani in November, for the railway was then relieved of the burden of bringing water to the troops. The line reached El Arish on January 4th, 1917, and early in April it was within a few miles of Gaza,[3] where it threw out branch lines and light railways for the second attack on that position. After the fall of Gaza and the continuation of the advance into Palestine, the main line was extended to connect with the Turkish system, which was ultimately converted to standard gauge. Doubling of the line across Sinai was undertaken as material and labour became available. Every officer on Sir George Macauley's staff did well in this rapid

---

[1] *Report on the Finances, Administration and Condition of Egypt and the Sudan*, 1914–1919, p. 85.

[2] Subsequently, a branch line from Zagazig to Es Salhiya was extended to El Qantara.

[3] The distance from rail-head to El Qantara was then about 140 miles.

construction; but in the opinion of many Royal Engineers who served in this theatre, none deserved more credit for the railway extension into Palestine than Major M. E. Sowerby, R.E., whose experience on the Sudan Government Railways was turned to good account in overcoming the obstacles of a peculiarly arid and inhospitable region.[1]

The provision of piped water for the troops stationed in, or advancing across, the Sinai Desert was almost as important as the construction of railways. Indeed, the two projects were interdependent. Experimental borings east of the Suez Canal in 1915 having yielded nothing but salt water, it was evident that the only source of supply for a defensive position in the desert was the so-called Sweetwater Canal on the west bank of the maritime canal. Unfortunately, its water was far from sweet, being infected with *Bilharzia*, a scourge of Egypt, and needing elaborate treatment to render it fit for human consumption. In November, 1915, large orders for piping up to 6-inch diameter, and for storage tanks, were cabled to England and India. The Cairo Waterworks Company erected mechanical filters, settling tanks and engines at six points along the west bank of the Suez Canal—El Qantara, El Balla, El Firdan, Serapeum, Esh Shallufa and El Kubri. Supply channels were dug from the Sweetwater Canal to El Balla and El Firdan. Reinforced concrete reservoirs were built on the east bank of the Suez Canal, and the water was " syphoned " under the canal by the Suez Canal Company.[2] The piping arrived in February, 1916, and 164 miles of it were laid in the desert, though with great difficulty, because some of it was of British and the remainder of American manufacture.[3] Water could then be pumped from the reservoirs on the east bank to others near the front line of defence, whence it was distributed by gravity to the various posts. The whole system, installed under the superintendence of Sir Murdoch MacDonald, was discarded within a few months, for it ceased to serve any useful purpose after El Arish was occupied in December, 1916. It was dismantled during 1917.

When Romani was occupied by the 52nd Division in May, 1916, a 6-inch pipe-line was laid into the desert beside the railway from El Qantara; and although it could not keep pace with rail-head, it

[1] The railway operations in Palestine are described in a Note by Brig.-General Sir George B. Macauley, K.C.M.G., K.B.E., C.B., late R.E., entitled " Military Railways in Palestine during the Great War, July, 1917, to October, 1918."

[2] At certain points this was impracticable. For instance, a reservoir on the east shore of the Great Bitter Lake had to be filled from boats. Another, at Esh Shatt opposite Suez, was supplied by a pipe-line from a reservoir opposite El Kubri.

[3] In notes sent to the author on May 28th, 1936, Lieut.-Colonel T. P. Bassett, D.S.O., R.E. (retd.), remarks:—" Arrangements had been made that the ship carrying the piping should pass along the Canal, unloading at each bridgehead the pipes required at that point; but when unloading began at the first post, it was found that all the big pipes had been loaded at the bottom, and the ship had to return to Port Said for unloading and resorting of her cargo. This mistake caused considerable delay."

began to supply 30,000 gallons daily to Romani at the end of June.[1] This amount was soon found to be inadequate. The brackish water from local wells played havoc with the boilers of locomotives and the interiors of men. It was certain that a 12-inch or 10-inch pipe-line would be needed to supply an army advancing across Sinai. Accordingly, demands for 60 miles of 12-inch piping and 30 miles of 10-inch piping, with the necessary plant for a new system starting from El Qantara and capable of supplying an additional 500,000 gallons daily, were cabled to England on July 12th and passed on to the United States. On September 24th, the first ship-load of 4,500 tons of machinery and piping, chiefly 12-inch, arrived at El Qantara from America. As the railway was already working, the new piping was laid rapidly, although it was necessary to train the "screwing" gangs, alter the threads, and teach the labourers how to handle such heavy sections.[2] By November 17th, the line of 12-inch and 10-inch piping from El Qantara was supplying a reservoir already prepared at Romani. A special railway siding near the reservoir, with 20 high standpipes alongside it, enabled a train of tank-trucks to be filled and sent forward to rail-head, where a line of low canvas storage tanks, replenished from the trucks, supplied camel convoys which carried water to the troops.[3] This system was adopted throughout the advance to Palestine. Through the efforts of many engineer units and labour formations, the pipe-line was laid at an increasing speed when it had passed Bir el Abd beyond Romani; and on February 5th, 1917, 125 days after the first pipe was screwed in, the line reached El Arish, 95 miles from El Qantara. Pumping stations at El Qantara, Romani, Bir el Abd and El Mazar forced the water across the desert. In October, 1917, shortly before Sir Edmund Allenby's advance to Jerusalem, the line was extended to the vicinity of Gaza and Beersheba,[4] thus fulfilling an ancient prophecy that when the waters of the Nile came to Palestine, Jerusalem would be retaken from the Turks.

During 1915-16, some 200 miles of metalled roadway were built

---

[1] *Work of the Royal Engineers in the European War, 1914–19. Water Supply. Egypt and Palestine* (by Major-General H. B. H. Wright, C.B., C.M.G., late R.E., Engineer-in-Chief, E.E.F.), p. 13. This volume gives a concise and comprehensive account of all the water-supply operations on the Suez Canal, and in Sinai and Palestine, during the advance. A general description of the water-supply during the advance appears in *A Brief Record of the Advance of the Egyptian Expeditionary Force, July, 1913 to October, 1918* (Official), p. 83–86.

[2] The organization of the pipe-laying parties was as follows. First, a small party to locate and mark the line. Then, the formation party (1,500 men) to make cuttings and embankments and prepare the surface. Then, the train-loads of pipes, and gangs for unloading. Next, the screwing party divided into 12 gangs. Finally, the covering party to pile sand over the pipe for protection.

[3] Each camel carried two $12\frac{1}{2}$-gallon iron tanks, called *fanatis*. The troops dug many wells, and made use of "Spear points," a variation of the Norton Tube Well, to supplement their water-supply; but the liquid so obtained was suitable only for animals. Every Field Company, R.E., was equipped with extra pumps, canvas troughs and tanks, and tools.

[4] Piping of eight-inch diameter was employed before the line reached El Arish. Afterwards six-inch and four-inch pipes were used.

OPERATIONS AGAINST THE SENUSSI.

under the superintendence of Sir Murdoch MacDonald and his staff, to supplement the light railway communications between the Suez Canal and the position which was being prepared in the desert. In January, 1916, nearly 10,000 men were engaged on this work. Over one million tons of stone, quarried on the shores of the Red Sea, were shipped to various points on the Canal for the construction of parallel roads towards the east, and for lateral thoroughfares. As speed was essential, the work was done by contract and rates were decided later. It may be mentioned that a junior R.E. officer had the unique experience of writing a cheque for £30,000 as an advance to a contractor! "Wire roads" were used extensively in traversing Sinai and parts of Palestine. They had been employed in Gallipoli by Lieut.-Colonel E. M. Paul, R.E.[1] A double layer of wire netting, 12 feet to 16 feet wide, was laid on the sand and tightly pegged down. If grass was available, a mat of this material was placed below the netting. It was found that such roads lasted well, except under horse or heavy motor traffic.

The defence of Egypt was not confined to the eastern frontier. Minor operations were necessary elsewhere. After their failure on the Suez Canal in February, 1915, the Turks sent Nuri Pasha[2] and Jafar Pasha as emissaries to the Senussi with instructions to organize and re-arm them, and to incite them to harass Egypt from the west. The coastal plain, west of the Nile delta, was traversed in 1915 by a standard gauge railway from Alexandria to Daaba, and thence by a cleared track, called the Khedivial Motor Road, to the small ports of Mersa Matruh, El Barrani and Sollum.[3] By the autumn of that year, Sayed Ahmed, leader of the Senussi, who inhabited this region and some of the oases to the west of Egypt, could muster about 5,000 men with a few small guns and machine-guns. In November he proceeded to shell Sollum, raid the coastal plain, and carry off the shipwrecked crew of H.M.S. *Tara*. There was then no alternative but to dispatch an expedition against him.

As Sollum is 280 miles from Alexandria, and El Barrani only 40 miles less, Sir John Maxwell ordered the withdrawal of the Egyptian garrisons of those places to Mersa Matruh, which was within 75 miles of rail-head at Daaba. Early in December, 1915, a small composite force of Yeomanry, British, New Zealand and Indian infantry, a battery and a detachment of artillery, and the Mobile Engineer Section (now called Field Troop) of the Egyptian Military Works Department—in all about 1,400 men—assembled under Major-General A. Wallace at Matruh to cover the western flank of the Nile Delta. The Senussi occupied Sollum and El Barrani. They moved forward to some wells near Matruh and raided eastwards to the Daaba-Alexandria railway.

[1] Now Brig.-General E. M. P. Stewart of Coll, C.B., C.B.E.
[2] Brother of Enver Pasha, the Turkish Minister of War.
[3] See the *Sketch Map of the Western Frontier of Egypt in 1916*.

The campaign against the followers of Sayed Ahmed was in no sense an "Engineer war," except that the troops depended largely on the engineers for their water-supply. Only two regular officers of the Corps—Major D. M. Griffith and Lieutenant W. S. Blunt—took part in the field operations, and another—Captain A. J. Ross—served as a pilot in the Royal Flying Corps. "In November, 1915," writes Blunt,[1] " I happened to visit a cavalry camp near the Pyramids outside Cairo and found great activity there in connection with a proposed expedition against the Senussi, so I went at once to the Engineer-in-Chief and pointed out that my Camel Field Troop on the Suez Canal would be ideal for a desert campaign in which mobility was essential. As a consequence, we soon found ourselves at rail-head at Daaba where, with a company of Sikhs, we were the first troops to arrive. A few days later, two armoured cars took me and a Naval warrant officer to a spot 50 miles from Daaba, where there was reported to be water, and during the following night two other cars picked us up and carried us to Matruh, where we learnt that Sollum had been evacuated. During the next $2\frac{1}{2}$ months, I was Commanding Royal Engineer to the force and had to order one million sandbags to make a fortified perimeter around Matruh, of about 4 miles in length. The Camel Troop arrived by sea from Daaba, and with them came Yuzbashi (Captain) Aref Lebib, M.C., an excellent Egyptian officer, who had served with me in Gallipoli. The camel strength of the unit was doubled by selecting the best trotters from captured stock and equipping them with baggage saddles, so that every Sapper had a trotting transport camel beside him, loaded with equipment. The Camel Troop became the most mobile unit in the force, and always accompanied the leading cavalry in the advance. On the march, we repaired sandy spots with scrub before the transport reached them; and by leap-frogging detachments, and moving at 12 miles an hour, we kept well ahead."

The military operations west of Mersa Matruh are described fully in the official history,[2] and no more than a brief summary can be given in these pages. General Wallace, issuing from Matruh, drove the enemy back on December 13th, 1915, and again on the 25th, but was unable to follow up his advantage. The Senussi withdrew to Hazalin, about 25 miles south-west of Matruh. Reinforcements arrived, and on January 23rd, 1916, Wallace set out in two columns to engage the enemy, who occupied a position about $1\frac{1}{2}$ miles in length. The Senussi retreated for a distance of 3 miles and proceeded to threaten our right flank and mounted troops; but during the afternoon, they drew off, and an indecisive action came to an end.

Brigadier-General H. T. Lukin, commanding a South African

[1] Notes by Lieut.-Colonel W. S. Blunt, M.C., R.E. (retd.), sent to the author on April 15th, 1936.
[2] *Military Operations, Egypt and Palestine*, Vol. I, pp. 101–134.

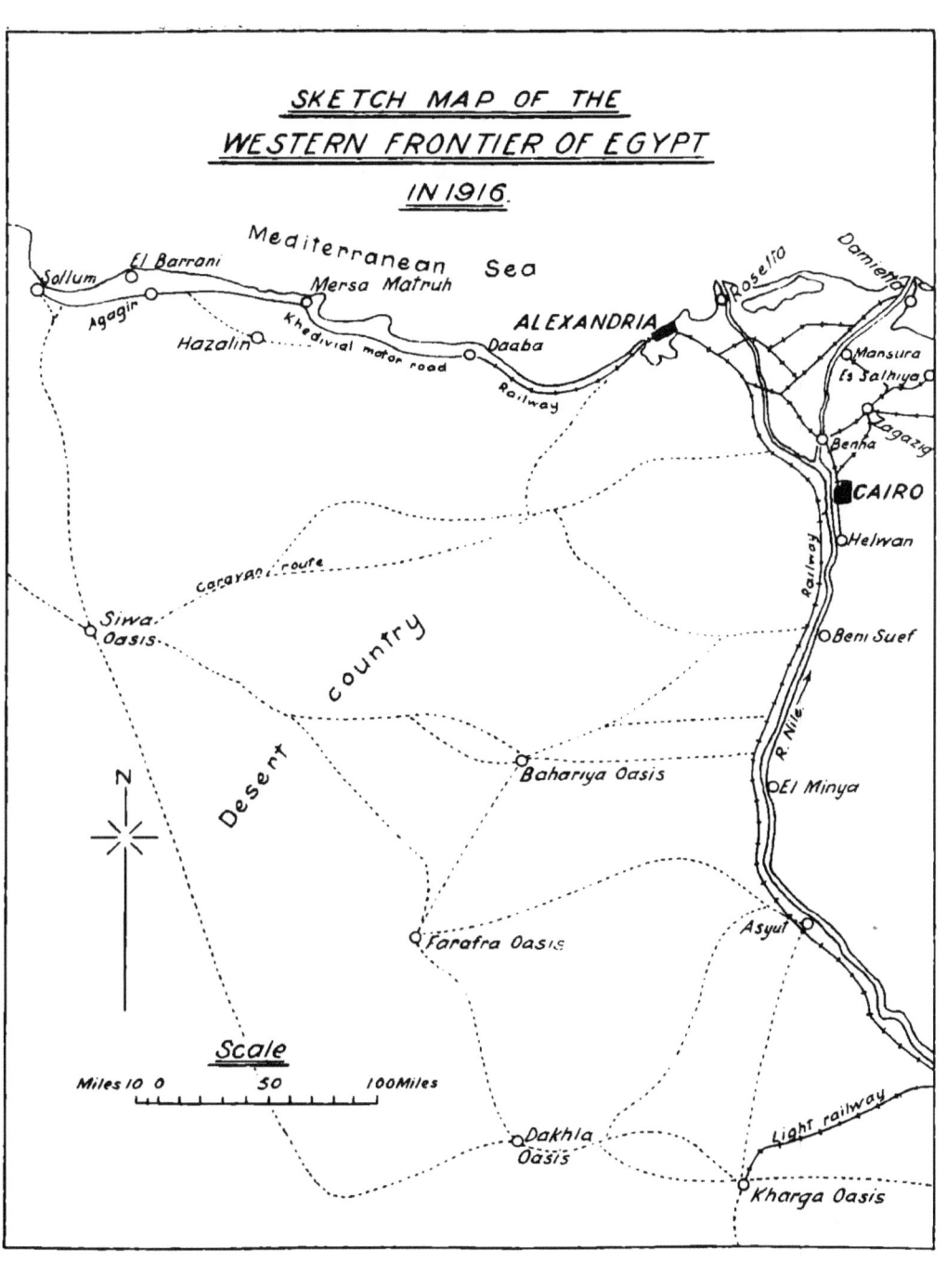

brigade, arrived at Matruh on February 4th, when the enemy's main body was near El Barrani and a smaller force outside Sollum. Obviously, the first step was to defeat the Senussi covering El Barrani, and to establish a depot there for a further advance on Sollum. On February 10th, Major-General W. E. Peyton, a most energetic cavalry leader, succeeded General Wallace in the chief command and brought with him Major D. M. Griffith, R. E., who became Commanding Royal Engineer, with Lieutenant W. S. Blunt, R.E., as his Adjutant. A Kent (Territorial) Field Company, R.E., also joined the force. Further steps were then taken to drive the enemy from the coastal plain by establishing an intermediate supply depot some 50 miles west of Matruh. This brought El Barrani within reach, and on February 20th, Lukin started with a column of four squadrons, three battalions and a battery to defeat the enemy and seize that place. The Senussi were found at Agagir, 14 miles south-east of El Barrani, and on the 26th, Lukin gained a victory which was completed by a gallant charge of Dorset Yeomanry. Jafar Pasha was wounded and captured, but Nuri Pasha escaped.[1] El Barrani was occupied on February 27th. After concentrating his forces, General Peyton advanced westwards in three columns, through country where water was very scarce, and retook Sollum on March 14th. Three days later, Major the Duke of Westminster, Cheshire Yeomanry, made a spectacular dash, 116 miles farther westwards, with a flying column of 45 cars and ambulances, and rescued and brought back within 24 hours, Captain Gwatkin-Williams, R.N., and 90 famished officers and men of H.M.S. *Tara*, who had been prisoners of the Senussi for several months.[2] With the occupation of Sollum, the campaign on the coast came to an end, and most of the troops returned to Alexandria.

According to Major Griffith,[3] the engineering duties during the advance were chiefly the discovery and supply of water and the building of piers; and when Sollum had been re-occupied, the fortification of that place and the installation of a condenser. Blunt became an adept in finding water. On one occasion, having noticed recent traces of sheep, he uncovered five deep wells, cut in solid rock, which had been filled in by the enemy to deprive our troops of a copious supply of good water. " The presence of fresh water on the north littoral of Egypt," he remarks,[4] " is indicated either by

---

[1] Sayed Ahmed had gone to the Siwa Oasis in the interior to direct other operations against Egypt. Jafar Pasha el Askari subsequently joined the British forces and rendered valuable service in Arabia. After the Great War, he was a Minister in Iraq, or represented Iraq in England, for many years. He was murdered in Baghdad on October 31st, 1936.

[2] The thrilling story of the experiences of these prisoners, and of their rescue, is told in *Prisoners of the Red Desert*, by Captain R. S. Gwatkin-Williams, C.M.G., R.N.

[3] Notes by Lieut.-Colonel D. M. Griffith, D.S.O., R.E. (retd.), sent to the author on April 29th, 1936.

[4] Notes by Lieut.-Colonel W. S. Blunt, M.C., R.E. (retd.), sent to the author on April 15th, 1936.

very white sand near the seashore (water soaking from inland and held up by an outcrop of rock), or by a high and apparently artificial mound in the centre of an inland depression (debris from an old Roman rock-cut cistern), or by a well-worn, straight track formed by animals hauling a leather bucket out of a deep well. In this case, the length of the track gives the depth of the well." Blunt and Aref Lebib, when engaged on a water reconnaissance on March 13th, were the first officers to view Sollum before its reoccupation; and on a ceremonial parade on the 14th, they were given the honour of hoisting the British and Egyptian flags over Sollum Fort. On that occasion, a Territorial battery fired a salute with live shell into a hillside and nearly hit General Peyton with a ricochet ! The Camel Troop was then ordered to the Sudan to assist in operations in the Darfur Campaign but arrived too late to take much part in them.

The Senussi Campaign having ended, the British and Italian Governments proceeded to negotiate a peaceful settlement with Sayed Idris, cousin and successor of Sayed Ahmed. As Italian interests were involved, Colonel the Hon. M. G. Talbot, the Royal Engineer who had distinguished himself in the Sudan, was sent from Egypt to Italy in May, 1916, and thence to the Italian colony of Cyrenaica in North Africa; and in July, a joint British and Italian mission, including Talbot, Mr. Francis J. R. Rodd and two Egyptian notables,[1] met Sayed Idris near Benghazi and concluded an Anglo-Italian agreement. Further negotiations, however, were found to be necessary with Sayed Idris, so the " Talbot Mission," after some months in Cairo, returned to Cyrenaica in January, 1917, and met the Italians and Sayed Idris at Tabruk. The conversations which ensued led to agreements on April 12th, 1917, between the British, French, Italians and Senussi, which were agreeable to all; a happy result for which proper credit should be given to Talbot. Sir Reginald Wingate, then High Commissioner in Egypt, wrote in April, 1917[2] " To Colonel Talbot's patience, tact and clear foresight are due not only the signature of our treaty with Sayed Muhammad Idris, but also, in a very considerable degree, the satisfactory arrangements made between the latter and the Italian authorities. His personality and wise counsels have sensibly influenced the attitude of Sayed Idris to the proposals of our Allies." With this fine achievement, Talbot brought to a close a remarkable and varied career in the service of his country.

The Mediterranean Littoral was not the only area through which the Senussi advanced against Egypt in 1916. Over 160 miles south of Sollum is the great oasis of Siwa, whence several caravan routes

[1] One of these was Hassanein Bey, through whose good offices Rosita Forbes was able to penetrate in 1921 to the oasis of Kufara in company with the Bey. Mr. Francis Rodd, now a distinguished banker, was an excellent Italian scholar who entered the Diplomatic Service in 1919.

[2] Dispatch from the High Commissioner in Egypt to the Foreign Office, dated April 28th, 1917.

OPERATIONS AMONG THE WESTERN OASES OF EGYPT.

lead eastwards or south-eastwards to the Nile. The most direct route from Siwa lies through the oasis of Bahariya, and another important line of approach is through the oases of Farafra, Dakhla and Kharga.[1] Siwa being a focus of Senussi influence, which extended from the Mediterranean coast to Darfur in the south-western Sudan, Sayed Ahmed arranged that his northern operations should coincide with an attack on Egypt from the western oases, and another on the Sudan by the Sultan of Darfur. He hoped to create unrest, and thus to secure the retention in Egypt of the greatest possible number of British troops.

In the middle of February, 1916, while General Peyton was preparing to advance from Matruh on Sollum, Sayed Ahmed moved from Siwa and occupied Bahariya, Farafra, Dakhla and Kharga,[2] within striking distance of the Nile. The British garrisons along the river were strengthened, but remained on the defensive. However, on the termination of the coastal operations, the Senussi withdrew from Kharga, which was promptly reoccupied by the British. By the end of October, 1916, an Imperial Camel Corps of British and Dominion troops, and several light car patrols, were in action under Major-General W. A. Watson. The enemy were evicted from Bahariya, and the construction of a narrow-gauge railway was begun to connect that oasis with the Nile. Sayed Ahmed withdrew to the Siwa oasis, near which he was defeated on February 3rd, 1917, by a mechanized force under Brigadier-General H. W. Hodgson. Small detachments of Engineer troops took part in these desert operations, but their experiences call for no particular remark.[3] Events of greater interest had taken place in the Sudan, whither we shall now proceed.

Soon after the outbreak of war, Ali Dinar, Sultan of the huge province of Darfur, had determined to renounce his nominal and almost negligible allegiance to the Sudan and to invade Kordofan, while the followers of Sayed Ahmed advanced through the western oases and northern littoral of Egypt. Sir Reginald Wingate, then Governor-General of the Sudan, had no desire to add to his commitments by undertaking military operations against Ali Dinar, and was content for a time with the establishment of a cordon of posts to prevent intercourse and a traffic in arms between the Senussi and Darfur. In the summer of 1915, however, he sent Lieutenant A. G. Rainsford-Hannay, R.E., to Kordofan to reconnoitre the country between En Nahud and the border of Darfur with a view to finding a suitable line of defence. En Nahud was the most westerly post in Kordofan, lying about 120 miles south-west of El Obeid

---

[1] These oases are shown in the *Sketch Map of the Western Frontier of Egypt in 1916*, which is included in this chapter.
[2] A light railway (2 feet 6 inches gauge) connected Kharga with the Nile.
[3] It may be mentioned that Major R. E. M. Russell, R.E., was concerned in the operations on the Western Frontier, as G.S.O.I., from February to November, 1916.

and 90 miles from the border. Between it and El Fasher, the capital of Darfur, stretched 250 miles of roadless and almost waterless desert.[1]

Rainsford-Hannay reported that the only means of stemming an invasion from Darfur would be to locate a mobile force at En Nahud, with patrols pushed forward towards the frontier. He added that an invading force would probably advance through El Hilla, a small frontier village of Darfur which had a few wells, but that, having passed that place, it might move by any route leading to En Nahud, where the next water would be found. Concealment would be easy in a country of rolling sand-dunes covered with scrub, and the political effect of a raid on En Nahud or El Obeid would be undesirable. He recommended that the initiative should be taken by attacking Ali Dinar in his own territory.

The reconnaissance was executed under peculiarly trying conditions. Scorching heat was interspersed with alarming thunderstorms, in which lightning flashed incessantly from small clouds close to the ground and rain descended in torrents. On one occasion, while resting in the verandah of a bungalow at En Nahud, Rainsford-Hannay and a companion were thrown from their chairs by the concussion following a flash, which set fire to a straw hut (*tukul*) behind the house. As water could be obtained only from wells 80 feet deep, the fire was extinguished successfully with gallons of milk!

At the beginning of 1916, the warlike preparations of Ali Dinar were such that it became necessary to forestall him by offensive action. Sir Reginald Wingate was kept fully informed of Ali Dinar's plans by Mr. H. A. MacMichael,[2] whose work as Political and Intelligence officer with the Darfur Expedition was invaluable. The only Royal Engineer officers available for military duty were Lieutenants A. G. Rainsford-Hannay and G. C. Gowlland,[3] and the only engineer units were the Sudanese Sapper Section of 19 men under Mr. "Sammy" Hart (ex-N.C.O. R.E.) and an unarmed company of Egyptians of the Military Works Department under Egyptian officers. It was arranged accordingly that Rainsford-Hannay should be the Commanding Royal Engineer of the contemplated expedition, and that the Sapper Section should move with the advanced troops. The Egyptian labourers were destined to work on the line of communication from En Nahud onwards. In 1911, the Sudan Government Railway system had been extended westwards from the White Nile as far as El Obeid. The Egyptian company, and the Sapper Section under Saghkolaghasi[4] Hart, were sent by rail to Er Rahad,

[1] See the *Sketch Map of Darfur and Kordofan in 1916.*
[2] Now Sir Harold MacMichael, K.C.M.G., D.S.O., Governor of Tanganyika Mandated Territory.
[3] Lieut. G. C. Gowlland, R.E., had recently returned to Khartoum from France, where he had been seriously wounded.
[4] *Saghkolaghasi* (Adjutant-Major) is an Egyptian Army rank between those of *Yuzbashi* (Captain) and *Bimbashi* (Major). Hart was the first Englishman in the Sudan to be appointed to this rank. Later he became a *Bimbashi*.

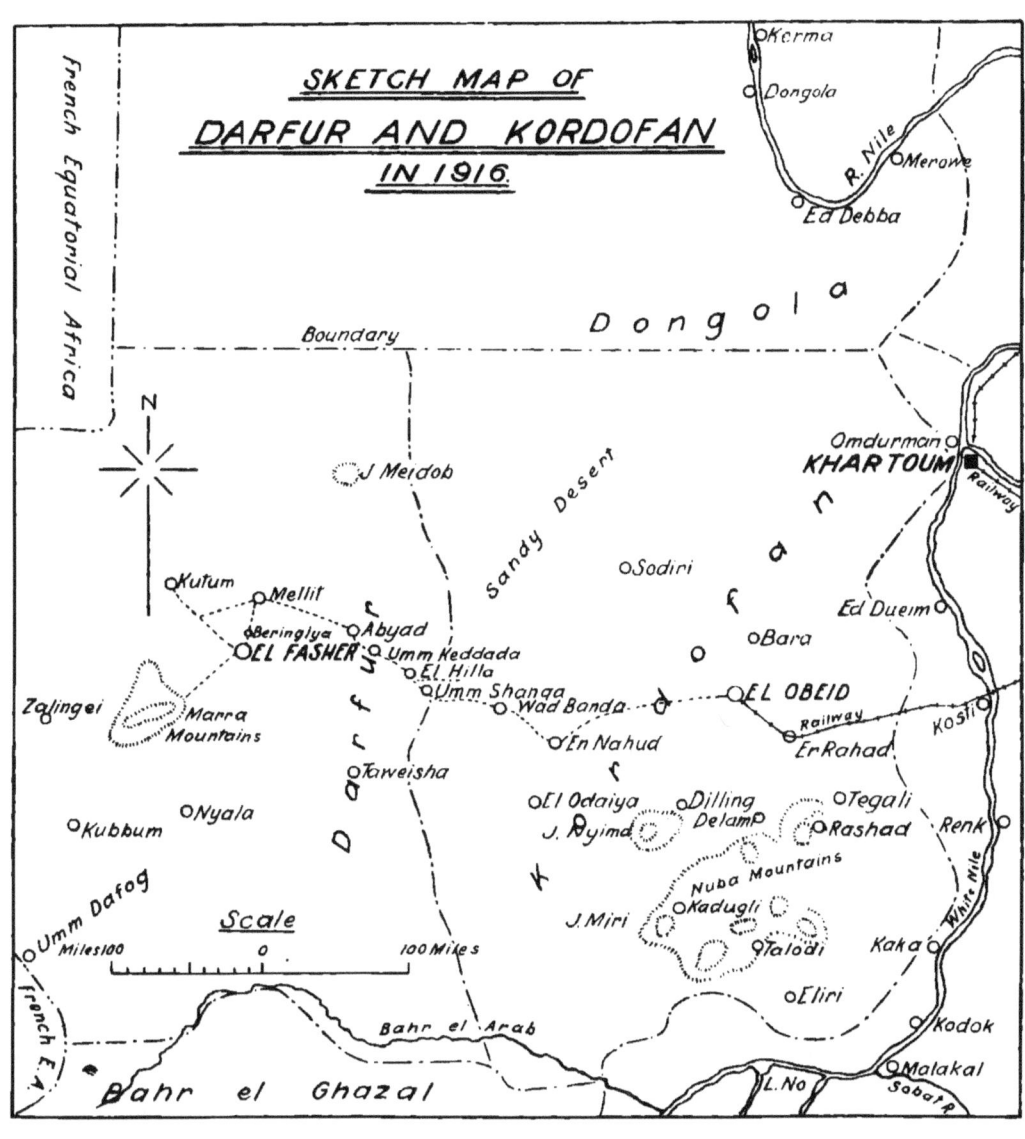

43 miles short of the terminus, and thence they marched to En Nahud, covering 180 miles of desert country in ten days. The Sappers were mounted on camels as they were being trained to act with the Camel Corps. Accompanied by Rainsford-Hannay, the units joined the expeditionary force assembling at En Nahud on February 26th, 1916, and proceeded to build grass huts and fortify a large depot of stores and ammunition. As no better material was available, they were obliged to revet the parapets with mud bricks.

The force at En Nahud was commanded by Lieut.-Colonel P. J. V. Kelly, 3rd Hussars, and comprised 11 companies of infantry (Sudanese, Egyptian and Arab), five companies of the Camel Corps, two companies of Sudanese and Arab mounted infantry, two Egyptian pack batteries,[1] a British machine-gun battery, the engineer units already mentioned, and the usual medical, supply and transport formations—about 4,000 men in all. It will be sufficient to give a brief sketch of the military operations conducted by Colonel Kelly.[2] He advanced on March 16th, 1916, crossed into Darfur, and occupied Umm Shanqa, and then, with a mobile column composed chiefly of the Camel Corps, seized the wells at El Hilla. Meanwhile, Ali Dinar was content to remain inactive at El Fasher with thousands of riflemen and many spear-armed auxiliaries. During April, Kelly occupied Burush, Umm Keddada and Abyad on the only possible route to El Fasher; but in the middle of May, he diverged north-westwards towards Mellit, 40 miles north of the capital, where he knew that he could obtain water, and with the co-operation of a flight of aeroplanes,[3] occupied it on May 18th. The casualties among the transport camels had been very heavy, though the difficulties of supply were eased to some extent by a service of light lorries. On May 22nd, Kelly advanced southwards in an elastic square formation towards El Fasher, and brushing aside the enemy's patrols, halted near the village of Beringiya, 12 miles from the capital. There he was attacked by 4,000 men, who bounded from cover, drove in the Camel Corps, and charged the infantry with a fury reminiscent of the days of Abu Klea. None survived to reach the square. The attack wavered and failed, and finally the enemy

---

[1] A total of six 12½-pounder mountain guns and two Maxims.
[2] An account of these operations is given in *Military Operations, Egypt and Palestine*, Vol. I, pp. 147–153.
[3] The aeroplane service in Darfur was under the energetic command of Major P. R. C. Groves, D.S.O., R.F.C., and contributed greatly towards the success of the operations. This was the first instance of the employment of aircraft in savage warfare. In March, 1916, Sir Reginald Wingate had asked G.H.Q. Egypt for a flight of four aeroplanes, and by May 4th, an air base and landing-ground were ready at Er Rahad and landing-grounds at En Nahud, Wad Banda, El Hilla, Abyad and three intermediate stations. Two machines reached El Hilla on May 13th and reconnoitred to El Fasher on the 14th. Meanwhile, two other machines arrived at En Nahud. Thereafter, air operations continued daily until El Fasher was taken. The work included the protection of columns from ambushes, distant reconnaissances to locate the enemy, the clearing of Mellit by bomb attack, and an attack with bomb and machine-gun at Beringiya during the final engagement. (See *Official Air History*, Vol. V, pp. 170–176.)

retreated, leaving hundreds of dead on the battlefield. Ali Dinar fled south-westwards to the Marra Mountains, beyond which he was killed on November 6th in a skirmish with a small force under Major H. J. Huddleston.[1] Kelly marched into El Fasher on May 23rd, 1916, and thus concluded a brief campaign which led, not only to the subjugation of Darfur, but to an opportunity for co-operating with the French from French Equatorial Africa in an expedition farther north to deal with marauders who had troubled them and the British for some years.

The following description of the engineering operations is given by Lieut.-Colonel Rainsford-Hannay :—[2]

" The defensible depot at En Nahud having been partly finished by March 12th, Hart and his Sudanese Sapper Section started on the 15th for Wad Banda, halfway to the frontier, with pumps, troughs, and rubber hose for syphons, to prepare to water the troops on their arrival there. The Camel Corps and camel-carried artillery reached Wad Banda on the 18th, and the men were supplied with water within five hours of arrival and filled their water-skins for the march to the frontier. The camels could not be watered. From En Nahud in Western Kordofan to El Hilla in Eastern Darfur the scanty population depends for water entirely on the rainfall between June and August. Fortunately, Nature has supplied storage reservoirs in the shape of Tebeldi trees.[3] These trees have massive and hollow trunks, and stout branches rapidly decreasing in diameter. They are grotesque in appearance and often leafless. The natives open a hole in the trunk, usually at the fork of the first branch, and occasionally assist Nature by enlarging the cavity within. Then, they scoop a hollow at the base of the tree to collect all water beneath it, and when a pool has formed, a man climbs into the tree and bails the water into the trunk with a leather bucket attached to a rope. The tree having been filled, the hole is sealed with a grass mat, plastered with mud, to prevent evaporation and pollution by bees. Water which has stood in a Tebeldi tree for a year is unpalatable but sterile. Although the normal capacity of a tree is about 150 gallons, some enormous ones may hold as much as 400 gallons. Ownership, or fractional ownership, of these trees is handed down from father to son, and the water is a source of continual dispute. In 1916, about 4,000 trees on the line of communication were hired by Government to supply the army with water, but the demand was so great that the trees had to be refilled by camel convoys from En Nahud. The quickest way to extract the water is by means of a rubber-hose

[1] Sultan Ali Dinar was killed at a place about 40 miles north of Zalingei and 70 miles from the border of French Equatorial Africa.

[2] Notes by Lieut.-Colonel A. G. Rainsford-Hannay, D.S.O., O.B.E., R.E. (retd.), sent to the author on August 29th, 1934.

[3] Information regarding these trees is given under the head of " Notes " in *Sudan Notes and Records*, Vol. XI, July, 1923, p. 114 ; Vol. VII, July, 1924, p. 135 ; and Vol. VII, December, 1924, p. 117.

TEBELDI TREE, KORDOFAN PROVINCE.

syphon, which works well until the tree is two-thirds empty. Hence the inclusion of syphons among the engineering equipment."

"The first objective of the force," continues Rainsford-Hannay, "was Umm Shanqa, which was reached on March 20th. It consisted of four small villages and four wells. The wells were 230 feet deep in solid rock and gave a very poor yield. We worked all night and the following day, with men at the bottoms of the wells filling the leather buckets, but could only water one-half of the Camel Corps and mounted infantry; consequently, it was decided that a flying column should push on to capture some wells at El Hilla, while the remainder of the force halted at Umm Shanqa. The Sapper Section worked for a week at Umm Shanqa, cleaning the wells and improving the supply, and eventually all the men and animals were watered. The daily ration for officers was $1\frac{1}{2}$ gallons, and for men one gallon; but the camels, poor beasts, could only be given half their normal allowance of nine gallons, although their last drink had been at En Nahud, five days earlier. When the flying column occupied El Hilla, I found that the wells at that place were similar to those at Umm Shanqa. The diameter of the shaft was no greater than the thickness of a man's body! There was ample water, but the yield was limited by the difficulty of raising it to the surface. Accordingly, all animals were sent to an oasis five miles to the north, where there were shallow wells containing brackish water. A few days later, the Sapper Section arrived from Umm Shanqa, and having moved to another well ten miles westwards—an enormous one with a shaft 18 feet in diameter—proceeded to clean and deepen it in spite of the swarms of bees within it. Hart made a large bucket, with a bottom valve, which could be raised by camel traction and held nearly 40 gallons. Troughs and storage tanks were also provided for watering camels and ponies."

While these operations were in progress, Rainsford-Hannay returned to En Nahud to erect three aeroplane hangars, which had been cleverly designed in planking and corrugated iron by Gowlland at Khartoum. The materials were transported to En Nahud in suitable camel loads and assembled at that place. The roof trusses, 40 feet in span, were made of planking, and the columns were built up with planks nailed together and bound with hoop-iron. As no poles were available for use as derricks, the erection of the trusses presented some difficulty; but eventually they were lifted gradually into position by way of a series of platforms, much as the ancient Egyptians manœuvred their enormous stone lintels into place. The hangars were not completed until after the capture of El Fasher, whither Rainsford-Hannay went to prospect for building materials. At El Fasher, the Sapper Section reverted at first to water-supply operations, cleaning and improving a number of small wells on the shores of the shallow lake which forms the only source of water for the town built around it. In these and other ways, a mere handful of engineer soldiers proved their value in the field. The Sudan wages its small wars effectively, but in frugal fashion.

Little remains to be recorded of military engineering in the Sudan during the Great War. In addition to the Darfur expedition, small bodies of troops called "patrols" were dispatched occasionally to outlying districts. Thus, in December, 1914, patrols were sent to restore order in the Mongalla Province, and to punish the Nuers of the Lau District in the Bahr el Ghazal; and early in 1915, more protracted operations were undertaken in the Miri area of the Nuba Mountains. At the beginning of 1916, an Egyptian Field Company was formed at Khartoum by Lieutenant G. C. Gowlland, R.E., from the personnel of the Military Works Department and proceeded later on active service with an expedition to Jebel Nyima in the Nuba Mountains. The unit was organized on the basis of a Field Company, R.E., but its tool carts were drawn by donkeys and its wagons by camels.[1] In the expedition to Nyima, the Military Works Department operated the mechanical transport, and built a road 110 miles in length from rail-head at El Obeid to Dilling. Gowlland was the Commanding Royal Engineer. A patrol sent against the Lau Nuers in the spring of 1917, was accompanied by Lieutenant C. G. Martin, V.C., R.E. The Sudanese Sapper Section under Bimbashi Hart, and men of the Military Works Department under Egyptian officers, shared in some of these and other minor operations, but their work calls for no special notice. Their varied duties were performed in a satisfactory manner.

No account of the events of the war which affected Egypt and the Sudan would be complete without a reference to the tragedy of June 5th, 1916. On that day, Earl Kitchener of Khartoum sailed with his staff from Scapa Flow in H.M.S. *Hampshire* on a mission to Russia; and within three hours, when west of the forbidding Orkney coast, the ship struck a mine laid by the German submarine U 75, and sank almost immediately. Only fourteen of the crew survived. Kitchener was mourned by the entire Empire, and especially by the peoples of Egypt and the Sudan, among whom his name was a household word. A fitting epitaph for this great soldier appears on one of the many monuments erected to his memory. " The unresting giant, who above war's din held his grave course and laboured mightily, now beyond toil and clamour sleeps within the bosom of the eternal sea." So runs the inscription on the memorial in All Saints' Cathedral at Khartoum,[2] the town with which his name will ever be associated.

[1] Notes by Colonel G. C. Gowlland, late R.E., sent to the author on May 15th, 1934.
[2] The memorial is the work of Lady Helena Gleichen, and depicts the recumbent figure of Lord Kitchener borne, as for burial, by British, Indian and Sudanese soldiers. The group is in bronze on a marble plinth, and although it is small, it is finely executed. It was unveiled on February 5th, 1928, by Sir John Maffey, the Governor-General.

CHAPTER XIII.

OPERATIONS SINCE THE GREAT WAR.

THE last prospect of extensive military operations in the Sudan was removed with the occupation of Darfur in 1916. Thereafter, the Government could confine its attention to maintaining order near the Abyssinian frontier and dealing with insurgents in other troubled areas such as the Nuba Mountains and the swamps of the Bahr el Jebel and Bahr ez Zeraf on the Upper Nile. Stiffened by a small British garrison and a few battalions of Sudanese and Egyptian infantry, the Camel Corps, Eastern and Western Arab Corps, Equatorial Corps, and some cavalry, mounted infantry and machine-gun units, were amply sufficient for these purposes.[1] Mobility and strong leadership were the essentials. The leadership was there. Mobility increased with the extension of railways and the improvement of mechanical transport and aircraft. The Sudan became prosperous and happy, disturbed only by the occasional and sporadic outbreaks of certain turbulent, predatory and superstitious tribes.

Egypt was not so fortunate. Sir Charles Gwynn writes:—[2] " The widespread outbreak of disorder in March, 1919, came as a disappointment to people in England who had hoped that the establishment of a definite protectorate over the country would do much to eliminate the unrest which had prevailed in it during the decade preceding the war. Two causes contributed to the outbreak. Firstly, the circumstances under which the protectorate had been declared, coupled with the concessions made to the racial ideals of small nations in post-war settlements, awakened the ambition of the Nationalist Party in Egypt and gave rise to violent agitation for complete independence among the politically minded classes. Secondly, the *fellahin*, to whom independence meant little or nothing, were nursing grievances against British rule arising from measures taken during the war and were in consequence ready to listen to the propaganda of the Nationalist Party."

The meaning of independence to the uneducated *fellah* may be gauged by the following tale. Some villagers, who had burnt down their police station, were asked why they had committed this outrage. They replied that they had voted for independence and had

---

[1] The British garrison included a detachment of the Royal Air Force. The Western Arab Corps was raised in 1917, after the Darfur Campaign.
[2] *Imperial Policing*, by Major-General Sir Charles W. Gwynn, K.C.B., C.M.G., D.S.O., late R.E., p. 65.

worked hard to procure it, and that, having heard that it was in the Police Post, they had politely asked a constable to show them what they had won. His curt refusal had enraged them, and they had retaliated by setting fire to the Post. They were then asked what they thought independence to be. They answered that perhaps it might be something to *eat ;* but that it must certainly be something to see, because people talked so much about it !

The spark which started the conflagration in Egypt was the arrest and deportation of Zaghlul Pasha, and other leaders of the Nationalist Party, on March 8th, 1919. Students incited the people to violence, and the military were called out in aid of the police. Serious rioting occurred at Tanta and Damanhur in Lower Egypt, in the Fayum District west of the Nile, and at Asyut farther south. Europeans were murdered, and railways and telegraphs destroyed ; but Major-General E. S. Bulfin, in command of the British troops in Egypt, was able to restore order by the middle of April. The railways and telegraphs were controlled by Royal Engineers, whose experiences will be dealt with in later chapters. For the present, it is sufficient to remark that the disturbances in 1919 sowed the seeds of trouble which spread gradually to the Sudan, and that the mutiny of certain Egyptian units in Khartoum in 1924 can be traced to the clash of political ideas in Egypt. That mutiny was followed by the formation of the Sudan Defence Force, which included a unit of " Engineer Troops " in replacement of the Sudanese Sapper Section. When the new unit had been properly organized and trained, military engineering ceased to be a matter of hasty improvisation.

Meanwhile, the Sudanese Sapper Section coped successfully with the modest engineering requirements of a few patrols dispatched to outlying districts after the Great War. The men were armed and therefore independent of escort, and they had the support of a permanent working party of Egyptian conscripts of the Military Works Department. Under Lieutenant S. E. Hart, M.C., late R.E.,[1] the Sapper Section constructed blockhouses to protect wells, erected barbed wire defences and was employed at intervals on road work. In 1920, Hart commanded a detachment of the Section which accompanied an expedition to the Bahr el Jebel to punish the Aliab section of the Dinkas for attacking a patrol in 1919 and killing Majors Stigand and White and 25 Sudanese. After his return to Khartoum in 1921, Hart became Assistant Director of Military Works, Khartoum North,[2] and held the position until his retirement from the Egyptian Government Service in 1924. His remarkable

---

[1] " Sammy " Hart, promoted to *Bimbashi* in the Egyptian Army, had been given a temporary commission as a Lieutenant in 1916 and awarded the Military Cross for his services in Darfur.

[2] Khartoum North is the area separated from the remainder of Khartoum by the Blue Nile.

aptitude as a constructional engineer was of great value to the Department.

Several minor operations by patrols were undertaken between 1921 and 1924. The most serious event of the year 1921 was a rising at Nyala, 120 miles south of El Fasher in Darfur, where two British officers and many men were killed by rebels, who attacked a military post on September 26th. A patrol dealt with the insurgents in October. There was trouble also in the eastern Bahr el Ghazal. Early in 1922, it became necessary to check raids into Uganda, and later in that year to deal with minor disturbances in the Tabi Hills of the Fung Province[1] and in the Nuba Mountains of Kordofan. Captain F. E. Fowle, M.C., R.E., commanded two companies of the Eastern Arab Corps in a patrol in the Tabi Hills, acting independently for part of the time.[2] In 1923, small patrols were sent to settle inter-tribal quarrels between the Dinkas and Nuers near Lake No at the junction of the Bahr el Ghazal and Bahr el Jebel, and to restore order in the southern districts of the Nuba Mountains. Action was taken in 1924 against Garluark, the recalcitrant chief of the Nuong section of the Nuers living on the west bank of the Bahr el Jebel, and police posts were established near the Abyssinian frontier, east of Malakal. In many of these minor operations the troops and police were accompanied by small detachments of the Sudanese Sapper Section and conscripts of the Works Department. These men helped them to build and fortify posts, improve the arrangements for water-supply, and clear tracks through the jungle.

Since the disturbances in Lower Egypt in 1919, the efforts of sedition-mongers to spread propaganda in the Sudan had increased steadily. On his return to Egypt in September, 1923, Zaghlul Pasha, the Nationalist leader, proclaimed that he stood for complete independence not only for Egypt, but also for the Sudan. Members of a "White Flag League" made inflammatory speeches and staged demonstrations in the Sudan. On August 9th, 1924, the cadets of the military school in Khartoum broke barracks and marched through the streets. At Atbara, the headquarters of the Sudan Government Railways, the Egyptian Railway Battalion mutinied and committed sabotage in the workshops, and an outbreak on a smaller scale occurred at Port Sudan. These disturbances were suppressed by military and police action, but the respite so obtained was only temporary. On November 19th, the world was shocked by the assassination in Cairo of Major-General Sir Lee O. F. Stack, G.B.E., C.M.G., Governor-General of the Sudan and Sirdar of the Egyptian Army. Lord Allenby, the High Commissioner in Egypt,

[1] The area bounded on the west by the White Nile and on the east by the Blue Nile and the Abyssinian border. The Tabi Hills are about 60 miles south-west of Roseires on the Blue Nile.
[2] Notes by Major F. E. Fowle, M.C., R.E., sent to the author on April 1st, 1936.

then delivered an ultimatum to Zaghlul Pasha, which included among its stringent demands the immediate withdrawal from the Sudan of all Egyptian officers and men of the Egyptian Army. The evacuation of the Egyptian element began on November 24th; but the situation was complicated by the fact that in addition to those in the purely Egyptian units at Khartoum—the 3rd and 4th Egyptian battalions and some Egyptian Artillery—there were many Egyptian officers in Sudanese units at Khartoum and elsewhere, and some of these men had already undermined the loyalty of the Sudanese.

The British troops available at Khartoum for the enforcement of the evacuation were a battalion of the Leicestershire Regiment and another of the Argyll and Sutherland Highlanders. With difficulty, the 4th Egyptian Battalion was induced to entrain for Port Sudan; but the 3rd Battalion and the Artillery refused to leave without a direct order from the Egyptian Government. While this matter was under reference, a serious mutiny occurred in a detachment of the 11th Sudanese Battalion at Khartoum, and the Egyptian officers of the 10th Sudanese Battalion at Talodi in the Nuba Mountains refused to obey orders. A rebellion broke out also among the inmates of the central prison in Khartoum North. On November 27th, the Egyptian units remaining in Khartoum North invited two platoons of the 11th Sudanese, on duty in Khartoum, to join forces with them, promising that the Egyptian artillery would open fire on Khartoum if the British interfered. The platoons left their posts, raided the Musketry School for ammunition, and set forth. They were met by the Officer Commanding Khartoum District, whose orders they ignored, and then by the Acting Sirdar, Brigadier H. J. Huddleston, C.M.G., D.S.O., M.C., who warned them of the results of their disobedience. Again they refused to listen, and fire was opened upon them at 6 p.m. by a cordon of Highlanders in position with machine-guns in Khedive Avenue, now known as Gordon Avenue. The fire was answered by the Sudanese mutineers, but these soon scattered before platoons of the Leicesters and Argylls advancing to outflank them. A party of the mutineers, however, invaded the Military Hospital, next to the R.E. Mess on the river front, where they murdered the Senior Medical Officer, a sergeant and several Syrians and Egyptians, and proceeded to fortify themselves in a building in the Medical Corps Compound, adjoining the hospital.

At dawn on November 28th, the Leicesters and Argylls advanced against the mutineers in the building and suffered some casualties in an unsuccessful attempt to take it. A 4·5-inch howitzer was then brought up, and shelled the building for seven hours at close range, finally destroying it and annihilating the defenders. With the suppression of this mutiny, and of the outbreak at Talodi, peace was restored in the Sudan. By December 4th, 1924, the last Egyptian unit had left the country, and shortly afterwards the evacuation of all Egyptian officers and officials was completed.[1]

Major F. E. Fowle, M.C., R.E., writes as follows :—[2] " The bombardment of the mutineers was closely supervised, from the roof of the R.E. Mess, by Brigadier-General C. W. Singer, C.B., C.M.G., D.S.O., late R.E., at that time Chief Engineer in Egypt. The Sudanese Sapper Section were the only native troops employed during the mutiny. Their work consisted in building prisoners' cages and other accommodation for the mutineers and disaffected population. At the height of the engagement on the evening of the 27th, a Sudanese non-commissioned officer of the Sapper Section, who had been on a course at the Musketry School where the mutineers were quartered, appeared suddenly in the Leicesters' firing line and commenced rapid fire at the enemy. The Leicesters regarded him with some suspicion and tactfully confined him in their Guard Room pending further inquiry. It was then discovered that he was armed with a Mannlicher-Schoenauer rifle, lately the property of the Commandant of the Musketry School ! "

As a result of the evacuation of all Egyptians, the Military Works Department came to an end ; but the Sudanese Sapper Section, now armed, equipped and trained as infantry, remained for a time. The unit had already taken over some of the work of the Department in outlying places, and thus gained further engineering experience. It was suggested that the Public Works Department should become responsible for all Government buildings, and that a reconstituted Military Works Department should be formed and placed under the control of the Director of Public Works, but nothing came of this proposal. The strength of the Sapper Section was only 40 men ; and as it was obvious that a larger Engineer unit was needed, it was decided that the establishment should be increased at first to two platoons, and ultimately to a field company of four platoons, each of 45 other ranks. Skilled artisans, who would also make good soldiers, were difficult to secure ; and although a number of so-called tradesmen were transferred from Sudanese battalions which were in the process of disbandment, the result was not wholly satisfactory. Consequently, it was decided to establish a "Boys' Company and Training School " which might be able, after a few years, to supply suitable men to the Sapper Company.[3] In view of the fact that boy recruits would require four or five years' training to become reasonably efficient, provision was made to recruit only one quarter of the maximum strength in each year.

[1] An interesting account of the mutiny in Khartoum in 1924 is given in *Imperial Policing* by Major-General Sir Charles W. Gwynn, K.C.B., C.M.G., D.S.O., late R.E., pp. 150–180.
[2] Notes by Major F. E. Fowle, M.C., R.E., sent to the author on April 1st, 1936.
[3] An establishment for training military artisans, chiefly for mechanical transport work, had been provided in Khartoum in 1920, but no provision had been made in it for the special technical instruction of Sudanese Sappers.

Throughout the summer of 1925, Major F. E. Fowle, M.C., R.E., assisted by Lieutenant G. R. McMeekan, R.E., was busily engaged in working out the details of the organization and training of the Sapper Company and the Boys' Company, which were to form the Engineer Troops, Sudan Defence Force. It may be explained here that the reconstituted army in the Sudan, known as the Sudan Defence Force, has the characteristics of a powerful body of military police rather than of a regular army. Its organization is on an area basis, and the troops in each area are of the type demanded by the physical features of that area and the nature of the inhabitants. Each of the six areas into which the country is divided has its special corps, consisting of a suitable number of companies of varying types. Each company, of 150 to 200 men under a British officer, is a tactical unit of infantry, or of men mounted on camels, mules or horses, and carries a high proportion of machine-guns. The men provide their own rations[1] and accommodation, though trained and equipped as regulars, and the general result is to produce a highly mobile force, well adapted for operating in detachments and always ready for action. Such was the probable organization which Fowle had to bear in mind when preparing his scheme for an engineer unit. On May 1st, 1925, the Engineer Troops, then comprising 60 men and 12 boys,[2] were moved from unsuitable barracks in Khartoum North to the Wood Pasha Barracks, south of Omdurman, recently vacated by the disbanded 11th Sudanese. There they settled down to a process of gradual expansion, military and technical education, and experiments in training. Fowle was their first Commandant, with the local Sudan Defence Force rank of Kaimakam (Lieut.-Colonel),[3] and under him were four British and seven Sudanese officers; but of these, two British and three Sudanese officers were attached for a time to the Public Works Department to gain experience in local building construction and similar work.

It was laid down that the primary functions of the Sapper Company were to act as fighting troops, or to perform any field engineering duties required on active service, and the training was arranged accordingly. The secondary functions of the unit were to carry out constructional work needed by the Sudan Defence Force in peace time, and if none was required, to execute similar work for the civil

---

[1] When the troops are away from their permanent stations, rations are issued to them. Normally, these consist of grain only; but in special areas, full rations, including meat, are supplied.

[2] Article entitled "Engineer Troops, Sudan Defence Force," by Lieut. A. J. Knott, R.E., appearing in the *R.E. Journal*, Vol. XLVIII, 1934, pp. 121–126. This article gives a concise history of the Engineer Troops and describes their training and their duties.

[3] The appointment of Commandant, Engineer Troops, carries with it the local British Army rank of Major. The other British officers hold the S.D.F. rank of Bimbashi (Major). If they are subalterns, they are made local Captains after about 2 years' service in the Sudan, or on taking command of a company (not of Boys). The badges of rank of a Kaimakam are a crown and two stars; of a Bimbashi, a crown and one star.

WOOD PASHA BARRACKS, OMDURMAN.

Showing the R.E. Officers' Mess and the Boys' Company Barracks of the Engineer Troops, Sudan Defence Force.

[*Photo by the Author.*]

administration, especially in southern stations, where there were few civilian artisans. Accordingly, in the autumn of 1925, a detachment under Captain H. S. Anderson, R.E., was sent to build a house for the District Commissioner at Akobo on the Abyssinian frontier, south-east of Malakal. This was the first constructional work attempted by the unit, and unfortunately the skill of the workers was not equal to the occasion. Not until Anderson reached Akobo did he find that the " trade ratings " of his men had been given for skill in musketry ! Fowle, as Commandant, then decided that no more constructional work should be undertaken by the Engineer Troops until the general standard of proficiency had improved.

By the end of 1925, transfers from other units, and direct enlistment of boys, had raised the strength of the Engineer Troops to 92 men and 83 boys. A minor insurrection at Jebel Gulud, south of Dilling in the Nuba Mountains, supplied a test for the new organization, orders being received that a platoon should join a patrol setting out from El Obeid. The platoon was commanded by Lieutenant G. R. McMeekan, R.E. During the winter of 1925–26 it made roads, blasted rocks and constructed blockhouses, in addition to sharing in the fighting. The road construction consisted, as usual, in clearing the natural surface of trees, undergrowth and rocks, and filling in hollows. The Sudan could not afford metalled roads outside its towns. Shortly after the departure of the platoon from Omdurman, an urgent demand was received from the patrol for a searchlight and a detachment to work it. Accordingly, some old equipment was repaired, and a few men were trained hurriedly in this new branch of engineering, and within a week the searchlight and detachment were on their way southwards. The searchlight was employed to illuminate water-holes so that the enemy could not use them at night —a procedure which proved to be so effective that it is now universally adopted.

Following their customary practice, the rebels of Jebel Gulud took refuge in caves from which the infantry could not evict them, so McMeekan devised a form of " stink-bomb " to render the caves uninhabitable. He was engaged in throwing these bombs into a cave when a sandbag full of them exploded, killing the Sapper carrying the bag and burning McMeekan badly. He was removed to hospital in Khartoum, and replaced at Jebel Gulud by Lieutenant F. C. Nottingham, R.E. A small party of Engineer Troops, who were natives of a neighbouring mountain, finally broke unaided into a cave full of rebel leaders and emerged triumphantly with their heads.[1] This daring exploit ended the disturbance in that area, and after carrying out other work, including clearing the ground for an

[1] In a volume of short stories entitled *People of the Book*, the late Major A. J. Pott, D.C.M., remarks (p. 65) that the bombs were ineffective because the fumes escaped through air-holes. After many grim encounters, the caves were cleared by riflemen carrying electric torches.

aerodrome at Talodi, Nottingham and the Sapper platoon returned to Omdurman.

Serious trouble occurred in 1927, on both sides of the Bahr el Jebel, some 500 miles south of Khartoum, where the primitive negroid tribes, known collectively as Nuers, were incited to rebellion by their witch doctors. The Lau section on the east bank, instigated by the witch doctors Gwek Wonding and Pok, defied the Government and early in December had collected more than 1,000 followers, of whom one half were armed with rifles. On December 15th, the Nuong section on the west bank murdered their District Commissioner, Captain V. H. Fergusson, at Lake Jur, north of Shambe.[1] Two expeditions, based on Malakal and Wau, were then sent against the insurgents. Two companies of the Equatorial Corps, and a detachment of Engineer Troops, proceeded to Shambe to assist in punishing Chief Garluark and the Nuong Nuers by burning their villages and destroying or removing their cattle. A general advance in three columns towards Lake Jur began on January 2nd, 1928. The enemy were driven into swampy country, where they were bombed by aircraft on the 24th and 25th and surrendered on February 3rd.[2] The Engineer Troops were engaged in working a searchlight on a steamer, and in teaching the infantry how to strengthen their positions rapidly with portable wire fencing. Greater interest attaches to the operations of the other expedition against the Lau Nuers under Gwek and Pok, for these involved an engineering work of unusual magnitude, executed by a detachment under Lieutenant G. R. McMeekan, R.E.

" Mr. Gwek had been fortunate in having a particularly successful magic season," writes McMeekan.[3] " He had skilfully claimed the credit for arranging an eclipse in November, and the death of the District Commissioner's best pony in the same month. This greatly increased his prestige; and when he was able to persuade his adherents that the Dengkurs[4] Pyramid had been emitting blue smoke—a sure sign that the days of the foreigner were numbered—he announced his intention of murdering the District Commissioner and advancing on Malakal. Accordingly, a force of one company of mounted infantry, two companies of infantry and half a platoon of engineers (all native troops), with four aeroplanes of the Royal Air Force,[5] were sent to deal with him. The grand finale was to be the destruction of the pyramid, which it was hoped would remove Gwek's last claim to importance and demonstrate the superior magic of the

---

[1] See the *Sketch Map of the Upper Nile*, included in this chapter. An autobiography of Captain Fergusson (entitled *Fergie Bey*) was compiled by General Sir Reginald Wingate, who added an obituary in the form of a Foreword.

[2] *Report on the Finances, Administration and Condition of the Sudan in* 1927, p. 16.

[3] Article entitled " The Demolition of a Pyramid " by Lieut. G. R. McMeekan, R.E., appearing in the *R.E. Journal*, Vol. XLIII, 1929, pp. 285–289.

[4] Dengkurs lies between the Sobat River and the Bahr el Jebel, about 95 miles S.S.E. of Malakal on the White Nile.

[5] One flight from No. 47 (B) Squadron, R.A.F., stationed in Khartoum.

DESTRUCTION OF A PYRAMID.

Sudan Government in general and the Engineer Troops in particular."

Little was known about the Dengkurs Pyramid beyond the facts that, as shown in a photograph by the late Lieut.-Colonel H. D. Pearson, D.S.O., R.E.,[1] it was of mud, about 60 feet in height, and with a base whose diameter was twice the height. Gelignite was the only explosive available in large quantities, and as this high explosive was by no means ideal for the work in prospect, experiments were made in Omdurman before the Engineer Troops started on their journey up the Nile. A mud pyramid, six feet high and with a base 12 feet square, was built up slowly, layer by layer, so that the material should consolidate properly. Careful calculations then led to a decision to experiment on it with nine pounds of gelignite, buried in its vertical axis one foot above ground level. The charge was inserted, tamped and exploded—with the gratifying (?) results that the pyramid subsided into a hole in the ground and a senior spectator was stunned by a lump of mud at a range of 105 yards! However, in order to ensure a still more spectacular effect on the Dengkurs Pyramid itself, a second model was built more slowly and carefully in Omdurman, and demolished with a charge of 18 pounds of gelignite. As the model was one tenth the estimated size of the pyramid, the charge for the latter was then fixed at 1,600 pounds of gelignite and 300 pounds of guncotton.[2] The manufacture of miners' picks, trolleys, an electric lighting set and a ventilating plant was put in hand, so that the Engineer Troops, though untrained in mining, might be able to tunnel into the pyramid. A mile of copper wire and some porcelain insulators completed the special equipment.

On December 15th, 1927, the Lau patrol reached Nyerol, within 35 miles of Dengkurs, and was then in contact with Gwek's followers, who had increased to 4,000 men. On the 19th, 20th and 21st the Royal Air Force carried out air attacks against enemy concentrations at Dengkurs and elsewhere, and on the 30th, the patrol occupied Dengkurs after a sharp fight.[3] The early stages of the advance from Malakal afforded the Engineer Troops many opportunities for the construction of flying bridges in which the collapsible 24-man raft, which forms part of their regular equipment in such country, was supplemented by rafts composed of petrol tins. Road making was undertaken during the later stages of the advance, the operation consisting in clearing the ground of grass and scrub and towing over it an American " grader " at the tail of a lorry.

[1] The photograph had been reproduced in a magazine entitled *Sudan Notes and Records*. Lieut.-Colonel Hugh Pearson, R.E., died at Umm Dafog in Darfur on December 28th, 1922, while engaged on boundary delimitation. His work is alluded to in Chapter XVII.

[2] The opportunity was seized to get rid of this guncotton, which required constant re-wetting in the dry climate of the Sudan.

[3] *Report on the Finances, Administration and Condition of the Sudan*, 1927, p. 15.

The curved blade of the grader soon produced a surface sufficiently level for mechanical transport.

By the beginning of February, 1928, the time had arrived to complete the lesson given to the followers of Gwek and Pok by demolishing the pyramid built by Gwek's grandfather at Dengkurs as a symbol of his magic powers; so the Sappers (McMeekan, a native officer and 20 men) proceeded thither under escort and began to dig with great energy in a temperature of 105 degrees F. They drove a horizontal gallery for a distance of 62 feet into the heart of the structure at a height of 11 feet above ground level, and working in continuous shifts, four hours on and eight hours off, completed the task in 62 working hours. The last shift of seven men, at the extreme end of the gallery, excavated 72 cubic feet in four hours without changing the man working at the face. In an average temperature of 90 degrees F., and on a limited water ration, this was a fine performance. Fortunately, no timber lining was necessary. The chamber intended to hold the charge was dug at right angles to the end of the gallery. Then the enormous mass of explosive was inserted, the leads laid and connected, the gallery tamped, and all was ready.

On the morning of February 8th, the troops, and 34 Nuer chiefs with their followers, assembled three-quarters of a mile from the pyramid. The Nuers were harangued by the District Commissioner, who explained that Gwek and Pok were powerless against the magic of the Government, and that he had only to raise his hand for Gwek's sacred pyramid to dissolve. "The late enemy were extremely subdued and rather nervous," writes McMeekan. "The Sapper officer was also somewhat subdued and *extremely* nervous." At last, the District Commissioner gave the signal, a concealed Sapper trod on the exploder, and the pyramid disappeared in a cloud of dust. But there were some disappointing features in this display. The explosion was almost inaudible to the spectators. No debris was thrown more than 50 yards horizontally, and it was soon apparent that the pyramid was not completely destroyed.[1] The lower portion remained as a crater 25 feet in height,[2] into which much of the debris of the upper portion had fallen. Nevertheless, the Lau Nuers were duly impressed. They swarmed over the ruin, shouting with delight and greeting with derisive laughter any mention of their magicians, Gwek and Pok. Thus law and order were restored among a peculiarly superstitious people.

By 1928, the Sapper Company had attained a fair standard of skill in trades and had been strengthened by a number of boys promoted from the Boys' Company; yet it comprised only two platoons, and

---

[1] Owing to erosion of the upper layers by rain, the diameter at the base was greater than had been calculated. Actually, it was 150 feet.

[2] *Report on the Destruction of the Donkurs Pyramid*, by Bimbashi G. R. McMeekan, dated Malakal, December 12th, 1928.

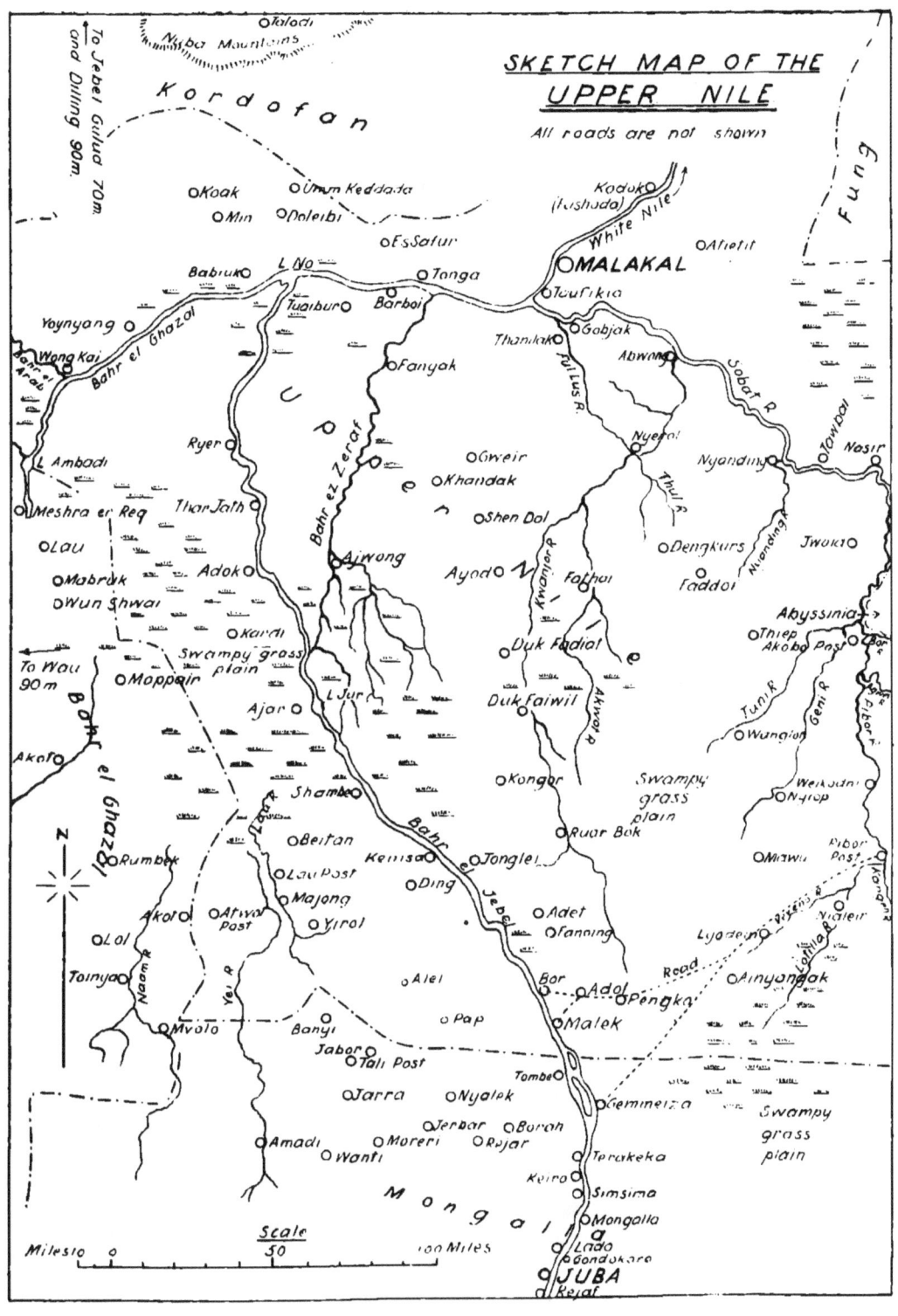

one-quarter of the men were those transferred in 1925 from Sudanese battalions without previous technical training. In addition to four British and four Sudanese officers, the staff included two non-commissioned officers (R.E.), one as Instructor in Field Works and the other as Superintendent of Workshops' Instruction.[1] Boys were enlisted at 12 or 13 years of age to undergo a five years' course of training in the Boys' Company under regular conditions of service. During this period, with the exception of daily physical training, they spent the whole of their time on technical training under civilian instructors directed by the Superintendent of Workshops' Instruction. When promoted as men to the Sapper Company, they engaged to serve nine years with the colours on irregular conditions and with no subsequent liability to join the Reserve. In 1928, the Boys' Company had reached its maximum establishment of 200; but a reduction to 100 was contemplated, as it was estimated that that strength would suffice to replace the annual wastage in the Sapper Company. When Major F. E. Fowle, M.C., R.E., handed over charge of the Engineer Troops to Major C. C. Duchesne, M.C., R.E., in 1929, he left to his successor a small, but well organized command, admirably suited to the modest needs of the country. The men had seen little military service in the field. As will be described later, they were engaged, and are still engaged, chiefly in road-making, water-supply, building, and demolition and clearance operations in outlying districts. Nevertheless, they were ready for field service in case of war, and their existence as Engineer Troops was justified.

A newly created combination of appointments had been filled in January, 1926, by Brevet Lieut.-Colonel (now Brigadier) F. P. Nosworthy, D.S.O., M.C., R.E., who became G.S.O.I. and Second-in-Command of the Sudan Defence Force under Major-General H. J. Huddleston, C.B., C.M.G., D.S.O., M.C., the *Kaid el 'Amm* or General Officer Commanding. Huddleston, a Brigadier, held the local British rank of Major-General and the local Sudan Defence Force rank of *Ferik*. Nosworthy was given the local ranks of Colonel and *Lewa*. Both were therefore "Pashas," *Ferik* being then the equivalent of Lieutenant-General and *Lewa* of Major-General.[2] The two ranks were necessary in each case as the officers had to deal not only with the Sudan Defence Force, but with the British Garrison. Each had to maintain two sets of uniform, including mess kit, into which he changed rapidly as the situation demanded. At short notice, El Lewa Nosworthy Pasha might be replaced by Colonel F. P. Nosworthy; but as the Pasha was always in

---

[1] At this period the Boys' Company and Training School was called the "School of Military Engineering."

[2] A small but very useful Government publication entitled the *Sudan Almanac*, which is produced annually in book form, shows the present equivalent of *Ferik* as Major-General and that of *Lewa* as Brigadier.

complete accord with the Colonel, efficiency and harmony were ensured.

During the summers of 1927, 1928 and 1929, Nosworthy, a Major in the Royal Engineers, acted for several months as General Officer Commanding the Sudan Defence Force (with the local rank of Brigadier) in the absence of Major-General Huddleston. He assisted Huddleston in remodelling the defence scheme of the country. " Our work was peculiarly interesting," he writes,[1] " as it included the entire organization *ab initio* of the new Sudan Defence Force. One of my first duties was to get to know the country, which is as large as British India and practically devoid of communications. A tour of inspection normally occupied about two months, travelling by steamer, six-wheeled lorry, pony, camel, donkey or on foot. Charles Gordon took 21 days on a journey from El Fasher to Khartoum on a fast camel. We could cover the distance by rail and mechanical transport in six days. My successor could do it in eight hours by air. Again, Sir Samuel Baker took three years to reach Juba from Khartoum. We could arrive there by steamer within 12 days. My successor could fly the distance in seven hours. Although the Sudan Defence Force was always in a state of constant readiness, and the danger of Mahdiism was ever present, there were only two ' patrols ' during my tour of office—in the Nuba Mountains in 1926, and in the Nuer country in 1928 when we fought the somewhat historic fight of Dengkurs Pyramid and ended the Nuer rebellion under the witch-doctors Gwek and Pok."

Unfortunately, every section of the Nuers did not settle down quietly after the downfall of Gwek and Pok. In August, 1928, some malcontents of the Lau Nuers assisted the Gaweir section on the Bahr ez Zeraf in attacking the Dinkas. Together, they destroyed the Dinka villages, looted their cattle, and tried to rush a police post at Duk Faiwil, between Dengkurs and Shambe, while it was isolated in the swamps. The police beat them off ; but it was clear that comprehensive measures were needed to restore order, and so the " Nuer Settlement " operations were instituted during the winter of 1928-29. According to Sir Harold MacMichael,[2] extra staff was then posted to the Nuer area and troops were sent to hold focal points ; but the essence of the scheme was to abandon the former procedure of a punitive patrol, followed by evacuation, and to concentrate on more peaceful methods. These were to construct roads passable at all seasons, to create a neutral zone between the Nuers and the Dinkas, to strengthen the authority of the chiefs as against that of the witch-doctors, and to provide civilizing influences, such as dispensaries for the tending of the sick. At the same time, it

---

[1] Notes by Brigadier E. P. Nosworthy, D.S.O., M.C., late R.E., sent to the author on May 29th, 1936.
[2] *The Anglo-Egyptian Sudan*, by Sir Harold A. MacMichael, K.C.M.G., D.S.O., p. 181.

was necessary to round up the recalcitrant element, and to exact reparation for the losses inflicted on the Dinkas. This policy succeeded slowly but surely.

Military operations under Colonel F. P. Nosworthy opened in 1928 with an abortive attack by the rebels on a patrol advancing southwards; but afterwards the work became mere policing. A detachment of Engineer Troops, under Captain G. C. MacM. Kavanagh, R.E., was engaged at first in road-making, rafting, and bridging numerous streams left by the receding floods; subsequently it cleared landing-grounds for aeroplanes and built mosquito-proof houses for a base camp. Work on a Sobat-Bor road, 120 miles in length, between Pibor Post and Bor on the Bahr el Jebel, was one of the principal occupations of the detachment during the spring of 1929 and the winter of 1929-30.

At the end of 1929, authority was received to increase the establishment of the Sapper Company from two to three platoons. This was no mean compliment in view of the drastic reductions which were then being made throughout the remainder of the Sudan Defence Force. The Boys' Company was also expanded so that some boys should be given elementary training as fitters intended for the Mechanical Transport and the Motor Machine-Gun Batteries, before they were transferred as men to the Mechanical Transport establishment in Khartoum North to receive final and more specialized instruction.

In November, 1929, Colonel F. P. Nosworthy was succeeded as "Chief Staff Officer and Assistant Commandant, Sudan Defence Force" by Lieut.-Colonel (local Colonel) B. T. Wilson, D.S.O., R.E., who held the appointment until November, 1933. By the end of 1930, when Major C. C. Duchesne, R.E., handed over charge as Commandant, Engineer Troops, to Major G. C. MacM. Kavanagh, R.E., military operations in the field rarely demanded the services of Sappers, whose energies were directed accordingly to civil engineering pursuits such as building construction, demolition work and water-supply. Military and technical training proceeded as usual in Omdurman. In July, 1931, Kavanagh had four R.E. officers under his command—Captains F. D. Mann, C. L. Fox, G. R. McMeekan, and J. L. H. Chase. The Headquarters and Sapper Company included five native officers, one British non-commissioned officer (R.E.) and 144 other ranks. The Boys' Company was still at its maximum strength of 200.

The first review of the Sudan Defence Force was held in Khartoum in December, 1932, by Major-General S. S. Butler, C.M.G., D.S.O., the General Officer Commanding the Force; and as only those troops who were close at hand could be on parade, the Engineer Troops were the largest unit present. At the close of the review, they staged a display in which the boys, dressed as savages, attacked and burnt down a post office and were driven off by a section of Sappers representing Government troops. The boys showed great ability as actors, and the display was much appreciated. A sure way to appeal to the hearts of a primitive people is to combine pleasure with business. The natives of the Sudan make a happy and carefree audience with a keen sense of humour.

In 1933, Major J. L. H. Chase, R.E., succeeded Major G. C. MacM. Kavanagh, R.E., as Commandant, Engineer Troops. The establishment was then three British officers,[1] one British non-commissioned officer, six native officers, 162 men and 160 boys. The Sapper Company still had only three platoons. In the Boys' Company, 60 boys were destined for transfer to the Mechanical Transport establishment. Although general financial stringency had resulted in the cessation of large building work, the Engineer Troops found employment on small works, and on miscellaneous duties such as sinking wells, blasting rocks in the Nile and clearing landing-grounds for aeroplanes, and underwent military and technical training while at their headquarters in Omdurman.

The author visited the Wood Pasha Barracks in January, 1935. All the necessary buildings were there, well placed and soundly built on the border of a desert that stretched unbroken to the southern horizon. He was shown a small, but comfortable R.E. Mess, the Commandant's quarter, a quarter for two other British officers, a squash court, barracks, a guard-room, a magazine, workshops of all sorts, stores, stables, married quarters, a dispensary, a kitchen and a canteen. An obsolete type of barrack was being demolished and the materials used to build a block of married quarters[2] in sun-dried brick, plastered with mud and camel dung. The new building was roofed with corrugated iron sheets, coated inside and outside with lime-wash. Each quarter for a senior non-commissioned officer had two rooms and a small courtyard. In contrast with the custom in India, the native officers do not live in the lines, but receive lodging allowance and hire suitable accommodation in Omdurman City. The Boys' Company is housed in several brick barracks with pent roofs, clerestory windows and verandahs, each barrack holding one platoon.[3] The boys are cheerful and manly youngsters, up to 17 years of age, and give the impression of being very alert and keen on their profession. They are hardy too, for they sleep at night without pillows on thin straw mats, laid out on low cemented brick platforms which run the length of each barrack room. This is good training for the rigours of desert campaigning. A barelegged squad of these boys, in khaki smocks and shorts, blue-

---

[1] Major J. L. H. Chase, Captain A. J. Knott and Lieut. W. R. G. Walker, R.E.
[2] The married quarters are built and maintained from regimental funds, and are rented to the men, who, as irregular troops, are not entitled to free accommodation.
[3] The boys, though technically "irregular," are provided with excellent government quarters and are fed by regimental contract.

belted and wearing on their heads small khaki-covered straw hats like steel helmets,[1] is a pleasing sight. Soldiering is a highly honoured profession in the Sudan, and the boys are very much in earnest. In the equipment of the Sapper Company the author saw a folding raft of light wooden framing and match-board flooring, encased in a covering of waterproof canvas. Although this raft can be packed and loaded on to four donkeys, it can carry more than 20 men. These few remarks will serve to show the care devoted to the health, welfare, training and equipment of the Engineer Troops.

In 1935–36, after Brigadier H. E. Franklyn, D.S.O., M.C., had succeeded Major-General Butler in command of the Sudan Defence Force, and Major A. J. Knott, R.E., had relieved Major J. L. H. Chase, R.E., as Commandant of the Engineer Troops, it was decided that new Motor Machine-Gun Companies should be formed, and it was proposed that the cost should be met in part by drastic cuts in the establishment of the Engineer Troops. This proposal met with considerable opposition, and in the end a compromise was reached by which a " Motor Machine-Gun Pioneer Company " was formed from two platoons of Engineer Troops and a Machine-Gun Battery, while the third platoon of Engineer Troops (one native officer and 40 other ranks) remained as a Sapper Platoon for specialist engineering duties. The M. M. G. Pioneer Company has three Rifle Platoons, one Machine-Gun Platoon (eight guns) and a Drivers' Platoon[2]—all carried in Ford V-8 motor-cars and trucks—and it is capable of field engineering in addition to fighting.

Owing to the general increase in mechanization, boys are now trained at Omdurman as artisans for the Sudan Defence Force as a whole, instead of for the Engineer Troops and Mechanical Transport alone. A gradual expansion of the Boys' Company up to a total of 300 has been approved, and will be spread over a period of four or five years. The lads are trained in the Engineer Troops' workshops as carpenters, smiths, builders, painters, fitters and drivers, and those who are destined to become armourers, saddlers or tailors receive instruction in the workshops of the Stores Department. All live in the Wood Pasha Barracks. In 1935–36, a Wireless Telegraph Section was added to the Engineer Troops, and 15 youths, of 18 to 23 years of age, were enlisted for training as wireless operators to replace civilians lent by the Posts and Telegraphs Department. The only recent changes in training are those consequent on the introduction of machine-gunners, drivers and wireless signallers. In the summer of 1936, the strength of the reorganized Engineer Troops was four British officers, three British non-

---

[1] In 1935 the men of the Sapper Company wore a similar head-dress. It has now been changed, and it is probable that the Boys' Company will follow suit.

[2] The war (" patrol ") establishment of the Pioneer Company is 2 British officers, 2 native officers, and 143 other ranks.

commissioned officers, five native officers, 229 other ranks and 169 boys.[1]

The native personnel of the Engineer Troops is recruited from all parts of the country. Those who enlist as boys undertake to serve for nine years after transfer as men to the M.M.G. Pioneer Company or Sapper Platoon. Those who enlist as men need serve only for six years. If medically and otherwise fit, all can re-engage for periods of three years up to any limit, and are entitled to a pension after 18 years' service. Native officers have not hitherto been promoted from the ranks. Those now serving were educated in the Gordon Memorial College and the Military School[2] in Khartoum, and as they hold General Service commissions, they are liable to be transferred to other units.

The dress of the Sudanese Sapper consists of a khaki *emma* (turban), a khaki *gibba* (smock), a blue *hizam* (waistband), khaki shorts and puttees, and brown leather sandals. The *emma* has a woollen hackle or fringe, with blue, red and blue stripes, and at the side, a flash or patch of red cloth, with a diamond of blue cloth in its centre and, on the diamond, a brass grenade. The brown leather belt of the equipment[3] is buckled over the *hizam*. Rifle and bayonet are of regulation pattern, and the rifle has a brown leather sling. The pack contains a ground-sheet and blanket. Each man carries a haversack and water-bottle, and sometimes a " food skin " to hold additional rations for long journeys. A canvas kit-bag contains his night-clothes, a spare suit and usually a mosquito-net. The packs and kit-bags are now carried on lorries. The dress and equipment of the Sudanese Sapper is the result of long experience in the deserts of the north and the swamps and jungles of the south, in which he has laboured, fought and died for the maintenance of British rule.

Turning now to Egypt, there is little to record about military engineers and engineering between 1919 and 1934. Barracks, hospitals and other buildings were constructed, altered or repaired; roads extended and improved; and water-supply systems provided or enlarged. Since the Great War, the cantonment of Moascar, near Ismailia on the Suez Canal, has grown in importance and has been the scene of frequent activity. The work in Egypt has been controlled and directed by a succession of Chief Engineers—Colonels C. W. Singer, C.B., C.M.G., D.S.O. (1919–23), G. R. Pridham, C.B.E., D.S.O. (1923–27), B. W. Y. Danford, D.S.O. (1927–30), A. W. Stokes, D.S.O., M.C. (1930–32), H. L. Bingay, D.S.O. (1932–36), and H. W. Tomlinson, now in office. Under their orders have been the

---

[1] The 229 other ranks included 15 N.C.O's and men of the Wireless Telegraph Section and 13 Boys' Instructors. Only three of the four British officers were Royal Engineers. Of the three British N.C.O's, only one was a Royal Engineer.

[2] The Military School was closed after the mutiny of 1924. A new Military School, for the instruction of officers and other ranks, is now under formation in Omdurman. It will absorb the present Musketry School.

[3] The equipment consists of leather belt, pouches, braces and scabbard.

ONBASHI (CORPORAL), ENGINEER TROOPS, SUDAN DEFENCE FORCE.
In Review Order.

[*By kind permission of Major A. J. Knott, R.E.*]

Commanding Royal Engineers of the Cairo District, with headquarters at Abbassia outside Cairo, and of the Canal District, with headquarters at Moascar,[1] each with a staff of Royal Engineer officers as Deputy Commanding Royal Engineers, Garrison Engineers or Surveyors of Works. Several officers of the Corps have held senior General Staff appointments with the British Troops in Egypt since the Great War. For instance, Colonel Commandant C. G. Fuller, C.B., C.M.G., D.S.O., commanded the Canal Infantry Brigade from September, 1925, to July, 1928; Brigadier W. G. S. Dobbie, C.B., C.M.G., D.S.O., commanded the Cairo Infantry Brigade from June, 1928, to July, 1932; Brigadier E. H. Kelly, D.S.O., M.C., was Brigadier, General Staff, from July, 1932, to July, 1936; and Colonel L. E. Barnes, O.B.E., has been Assistant Adjutant General since September, 1933. A complete record of such appointments, however, and of the peacetime organization of the Engineer services in Egypt, is outside the scope of a history devoted primarily to military engineering in war, and to important work executed by military engineers for the civil administration.

Several Royal Engineers stationed in Egypt have been concerned with experiments in mechanical transport, and with desert roads to carry that transport. Writing of his tenure of the post of Chief Engineer, Colonel H. L. Bingay remarks[2] that the conquering of the desert by the motor-car took place in his time, and adds that the 9-inch tyre, with a pressure of 12 lb. to the square inch, has done away with the terrors of soft sand. Lieutenant H. P. Drayson, R.E., describes a desert journey in a motor convoy from Cairo to Darfur and back again during the summer of 1933. "The Morris Van with 15-inch air wheels behind," he writes,[3] "was able to show that, with a large bearing surface, even dunes of soft sand are by no means an insuperable obstacle. With such tyres, the intensity of pressure on the ground is about 8 lb. per square inch compared with a pressure of $12\frac{1}{2}$ lb. per square inch produced by a walking camel." Lieutenant A. W. G. Dobbie, R.E., and three other officers spent a short period of leave in the spring of 1934 in motoring from Cairo through the coastal mountains to Hurghada[4] on the Red Sea in an endeavour to find a new route to the coast. They reached their destination after many adventures in terrible country, and covered 850 miles in 7 days before they arrived once more in the Egyptian capital.[5] Two Field Companies, R.E., have been normally stationed in Egypt, one at

---

[1] Alexandria is included in the Canal District.
[2] Letter from Colonel H. L. Bingay, D.S.O., late R.E., to the author dated July 5th, 1936.
[3] Article entitled "The War Office Experimental Convoy, 1933," by Lieut. H. P. Drayson, R.E., appearing in the *R.E. Journal*, Vol. XLVIII, 1934, pp. 60–73.
[4] Hurghada is about 30 miles south of the entrance to the Gulf of Suez. It is the headquarters of an important oil-field.
[5] The story of this journey is told in an article entitled "A Week's Holiday in the Desert," by Lieut. A. W. G. Dobbie, R.E., appearing in the *R.E. Journal*, Vol. XLVIII, 1934, pp. 442–450.

Abbassia and the other at Moascar. In 1932 and 1933, one of these, the 42nd (Field) Company from Moascar, was engaged in blasting a road, 35 miles in length, along the Red Sea coast from Suez southwards to Zafarana in order to facilitate the patrolling of the coast by the Egyptian Frontier Force.[1] Such diversions afford a welcome change from the routine of garrison duty.

In the autumn of 1935, however, routine duties gave place to emergency measures necessitated by the massing of Italian troops in Lybia, which accompanied the invasion of Abyssinia by General De Bono and the subsequent operations under Marshal Badoglio. It is unnecessary to deal with the steps taken to safeguard Egypt from invasion from the west, except to record that the greater part of the British fleet was concentrated rapidly at Alexandria, and that the 5th Division and other troops occupied and fortified positions stretching southwards for many miles along the frontier from a point west of Sollum on the Mediterranean coast. Mersa Matruh became the advanced base, and Engineer units from Egypt and England were soon at work in that uninviting spot and farther to the west. The 2nd (Field) Company, under Major E. Rait Kerr, M.C., R.E., arrived in Matruh from Cairo (Abbassia) at the beginning of October, 1935, and was followed in the middle of November by the 17th (Field) Company, under Major H. de L. Panet, R.E., from England. Two officers of these companies then carried out a reconnaissance of all water-supplies between Mersa Matruh and Sollum. In January, 1936, the 2nd and 17th Companies were reinforced by the 9th (Field) Company, under Brevet Lieut.-Colonel R. Mac K. Scobie, M.C., R.E., from England, and by a section of the 42nd (Field) Company, under Lieutenant E. C. W. Myers, R.E., from Moascar. Major Rait Kerr acted as Commanding Royal Engineer, 5th Division, until the arrival on January 15th, of Lieut.-Colonel A. Mason, M.C., R.E. Sixteen officers of the Corps were then available for field engineering duties.[2] In April, 1936, when the situation had improved, the 2nd Company and the section of the 42nd Company returned to Cairo and Moascar respectively, and afterwards both companies proceeded to Palestine to repair damaged railways and roads and to demolish buildings at Jaffa during the Arab disturbances.

The most interesting engineering work executed at Mersa Matruh was the provision and extension of a water-supply system. In 1931, a Roman system was discovered by the Governor of the Western Desert Province in an area of oolitic limestone about 5 miles west of

---

[1] Article entitled " Blasting Work on the Suez-Zafarana Road, carried out by the 42nd (Field) Company, R.E., 1933," by Lieut. A. G. White, R.E., appearing in the *R.E. Journal*, Vol. XLVIII, 1934, pp. 99–102.

[2] The other Royal Engineer officers with the units were as follows :—*2nd Company*, Capts. R. H. Maclaren, M.C., E. Croghan and N. A. Armitage ; *17th Company*, Capts. J. S. Howe and E. C. R. Stileman and Lieut. A. F. Bell ; *9th Company*, Capt. M. T. L. Wilkinson and Lieuts. R. R. L. Hutchinson and J. M. Montressor. With the headquarters, 5th Division, were Lieuts. W. F. Anderson and V. R. T. Menage.

Matruh. When cleared and surveyed, this system was found to stretch for 900 yards, and to consist of inclined and flat-bottomed tunnels, about 2½ feet wide and 6 feet high, driven through a water-bearing strata situated only a few feet above sea-level. A square chamber was discovered at the north-east end of the system, from which it is probable that the Romans raised water by Persian wheels to an earthenware pipe-line laid in cement masonry. Traces of this pipe-line were found running eastwards towards the site of the Roman settlement of Praetorium. The source of the water is rain which, after falling on a steep escarpment some miles inland, percolates slowly through the subsoil towards the coast. The quality of the water is satisfactory, though it is slightly brackish. No decision has yet been reached as to the age of the system, but it is commonly known as the " Roman Aqueduct."

" When it was decided to occupy Mersa Matruh," writes Major Rait Kerr,[1] " it was decided also to make use of the Roman water-supply, so the efforts of the 2nd Company, R.E., were devoted at first to the development of that system. We installed pumping machinery at the Roman Aqueduct, and laid a 4-inch pipe-line for a distance of more than 5 miles from the Aqueduct to an existing rock reservoir of 160,000 gallons capacity on a ridge above Matruh. Service mains were laid to the camp areas and provided a daily allowance of 3 gallons per man. Lack of rain, however, and an increased demand, which by Christmas amounted to 30,000 gallons a day, necessitated arrangements being made to bring the bulk of the water by sea from Alexandria, and this involved the installation of additional pumping plant, an extension of the 4-inch main, and alterations in the arrangements for distribution. Concurrently with the above, work was begun on the extension of the gallery system westwards in order to increase the yield. Amateur water-diviners were employed, but with little success. We drove a gallery from the end of the existing system and before long broke into another ancient system, which extended about 500 yards to the south-west. Vertical shafts at frequent intervals rose from the galleries to the original ground level, that is to say the surface of the limestone ; but in the course of time, many of these had become buried in dune sand to a depth of from 20 to 30 feet. Accordingly, it was necessary not only to clear the galleries of sand and to protect them from further falls, but to remove the sand from the rock-shafts and to sink shafts through the superincumbent sand-dunes to connect with them. The positions of the rock-shafts were located by carrying out an underground traverse of the galleries, which was then laid out on the surface by plane-tabling.[2]"

---

[1] Notes by Major (temp. Lt.-Col.) E. Rait Kerr, M.C., R.E., sent to the author on July 7th, 1936.

[2] About 1,100 yards of previously unknown gallery were cleared and brought into use by the R.E. units assisted by Bedouin labour, and nearly 300 yards of new gallery were excavated.

The Field Companies in the western desert executed other useful work in addition to water-supply. In November, 1935, they established an advanced and defended landing-ground for aeroplanes at El Barrani.[1] They supervised native labour employed to build roads in Mersa Matruh and to repair the road from Matruh to El Barrani, which had suffered severely under military traffic.[2] When means became available to improve the accommodation provided for the troops, huts were manufactured at Matruh by civilian carpenters, working under the supervision of the Sappers, and were erected by the latter. The construction of field defences was carried out mainly by the infantry; but the Sappers assisted them by building shelters and blasting rocks and were concerned also in providing coast defences.

The 1st Anti-Aircraft Battalion R.E. was also employed during the emergency on the defence of Alexandria against a possible air attack.

It is impossible to forecast what the future may hold for Egypt and the Sudan. Under the provisions of the Anglo-Egyptian Treaty, signed in London on August 26th, 1936, the British Garrison will be withdrawn from Cairo and concentrated chiefly on the Suez Canal, and units of the Egyptian Army may be readmitted to certain specified garrisons in the Sudan. Time alone will show the effect of these generous concessions to the natural aspirations of an enlightened nation. It is to be hoped that the people of Egypt, and those also of the Sudan, will not forget the debt which they owe to Great Britain for their protection from invasion in the past and for their present prosperity. The protection has been secured by the British Army and Navy, and by native troops led by British officers; the prosperity, by the unremitting efforts of Cromer, Kitchener, Wingate and their military and civilian successors. The outline of the military operations from 1800 to 1936, which has been given in these pages, may serve to emphasize the prominent part taken by Royal Engineers in the protection of Egypt and the Sudan from outside foes and internal disorder, and it remains only to record the extent to which Royal Engineers in civil employment have been responsible for a prosperity which is the envy of many less favoured countries.

[1] Sidi el Barrani.
[2] Excellent metalled and tarred roads now link Cairo with Alexandria and the latter with Sollum *via* Mersa Matruh and El Barrani. Another is under construction through Sinai to Palestine, and a fourth is projected between Alexandria and Port Said or Ismailia.

PART II.—CIVIL

CHAPTER XIV.

IRRIGATION.

FROM the dawn of history, generations of engineers have laboured to control and utilize the waters of the Nile, without which Egypt cannot live. In 4400 B.C., Menes employed thousands of men to dig a new channel for the river, eastward of his city of Memphis near modern Cairo. In 2300 B.C., Amenenhat III, by enlarging an old canal joining the Nile with the Fayum depression, 75 miles south of Cairo, created a vast reservoir, called Lake Moeris, with a surface area of 970 square miles. Seti I (1366 B.C.) devoted much attention to building canals, including one from the Nile to the Red Sea; and at the beginning of the Christian era, the Romans were engaged in schemes for irrigation. Then the science fell into disrepute. The Byzantine and early Muhammadan rulers did little; and not until the advent of Muhammad Ali in 1805 were extensive plans drawn up for irrigation in Egypt.

The Nile is certainly the most famous river in the world, renowned alike for its mystic origin, its length and the political combinations which have centred around it. For about 140 miles after its exit from Lake Albert, its flow is gentle. Then it begins to descend, and in a distance of 100 miles it falls 730 feet, with numerous rapids. Afterwards, it is very flat for about 1150 miles, and navigation would be easy were it not for the presence of masses of floating vegetation, known as "*sudds*," which obstruct several channels, but chiefly the Bahr el Jebel or White Nile in the region south of Lake No. *Sudds* consist of conglomerations of aquatic plants, loosened by wind and flood, and carried downstream until checked by some obstruction. When these floating islands have accumulated into a solid block, sometimes 16 feet in depth, they form a dam which leads to additional flooding of the marshes to right and left. The swamps of the Bahr el Jebel, Bahr ez Zeraf and Bahr el Ghazal cause great loss of precious water by evaporation.

Although the basin of the White Nile and its tributaries is much larger than that of the Blue Nile and the Atbara, the wealth of Egypt is created primarily by the two latter rivers. During August and September, they have a combined flood discharge of nearly 500,000 *cusecs* (cubic feet per second) and come down with a force so impetuous that the waters of the White Nile are held back for a month to let them pass. The Sobat, a tributary of the White Nile, is in high flood in December, when the Blue Nile has a very modest discharge and the Atbara is merely a series of pools. For the next 6 months, Egypt depends for water almost entirely on the supply brought by the White Nile from the lake plateau of Uganda. It is the red floodwater of the Blue Nile and the Atbara, originating in the Abyssinian mountains, that brings the alluvial deposit which is so valuable for agriculture. Egypt depends for her prosperity on securing a share of 85 million tons of silt carried each year for a distance of nearly 2,000 miles from Abyssinia to the Mediterranean, and she is fortunate if one-third of that vast amount finds its way to her fields.

Ancient irrigation, which made Egypt the granary of the world, dealt only with the Nile in flood, a rise in level which must have puzzled the Egyptian engineers because it was as regular as a tide of the sea and accompanied by no rainfall. It is said that they accepted a legend that the flood was due to the tears shed by Isis over the tomb of Osiris, and that philosophers recorded in texts on the Pyramids the dates on which the tear-drops fell. However, the source of this plentiful, if periodic, supply was of small importance to the Egyptians. The problem was to use it. The native engineers and their foreign assistants raised embankments alongside the river, of such a height that they could not be topped even by floods, and at right angles to these built other embankments extending to higher ground. Thus they divided the riparian country into a series of rectangular "basins" of from 3,000 to 60,000 acres in area. Short canals were then cut from the river into these basins, which became flooded to a depth of a few feet when the river rose. The still water deposited its silt, and after the river level fell in October and the basins emptied, the surface of each basin was ploughed and sown with wheat, barley, beans or clover. Any excess of water in a basin could be passed forward to the next in the chain, or discharged back into the river depression through an escape. No further watering was needed. A fine crop was reaped in April, and thereafter the basin lay baking in the sun until the next flood.

As the bed and banks of a river such as the Nile rise year by year with each successive flood, basin irrigation in certain parts of Egypt was easy. Nevertheless, it had a most serious defect in that, as the Nile flooded only during the late summer months, the ground lay fallow and unproductive for the greater part of the year. The climate of Lower Egypt, particularly in the delta region, is singularly favourable to the cultivation of one of the most profitable of the earth's products—cotton. This must be well watered, but it must not be drowned, and it flourishes only during those six months when, under the basin system, most of the country is first waterless and then flooded. Accordingly, during the early years of the last century, Muhammad Ali inaugurated a system of "perennial" irrigation, to be carried out by means of regulating works designed to fill the canals to any desired level at any season of the year, and in the course of time perennial irrigation began to replace basin irrigation in some parts of Egypt. However, for the cultivation of cotton in the Nile Delta it was necessary, under the basin system, to embank the branches of the river for the protection of the crops against inundation during the flood season, and also to dig deep canals to conduct the low level water of the summer Nile to the areas under irrigation. The water had usually to be lifted on to the land by native appliances, such as *shadufs* and *saqiyas*. A prodigious amount of labour brought a very small return, and it was palpable that the system was unsatisfactory.

Muhammad Ali, being a man of remarkable energy and impetuosity, pressed forward schemes for irrigation, especially in the fertile Nile Delta. He called to his aid several French engineers, and with their assistance and advice improved the existing systems of irrigation and excavated some new canals; but it was not until 1833, when he had been Viceroy for 28 years, that he concentrated his attention on the construction of a dam at the bifurcation of the Nile into the Damietta and Rosetta branches, some 14 miles north of Cairo, in order to obviate the appalling difficulties of clearing the deltaic canals to a proper depth. In that year, he boldly commenced operations for increasing the supply in the Damietta or eastern branch by damming the Rosetta or western branch with loose stones to divert all its water into the Damietta channel. The irrigation of the Gharbiya Province between the branches, and of the Daqahliya and Sharqiya Provinces to the east of the Damietta branch, was already carried out mostly from the latter, in which the water levels were always higher than in the Rosetta branch; so Muhammad Ali resolved to sacrifice the Rosetta supply in order to supplement the Damietta supply, regardless of the fact that he would thereby cut off the supply of Alexandria, and of the Beheira Province to the west of the Rosetta channel.

Fortunately, the damming of the Rosetta branch was interrupted by the arrival of M. Linant de Bellefonds, a French engineer in charge of the irrigation of Upper Egypt, who proposed instead that regulating barrages should be constructed across both branches, in order to give command over the distribution of water between the branches in summer and to leave a free passage for the river during the flood season.[1] Muhammad Ali immediately ordered Linant Bey to collect materials for this scheme. He insisted that, rather than incur any delay, Linant should dismantle the Giza Pyramids to obtain the necessary stone! The wise Frenchman made no attempt to oppose the idea and prepared a project for demolishing the most remarkable monuments of all time. He was careful, however, to prove to the

[1] The idea of controlling the distribution of water by barrages located at the heads of both branches, had occurred to Napoleon when in Egypt in 1798, but he proposed that water should be admitted *alternately* into the branches.

head-strong Viceroy that it would be more economical to obtain material from quarries than from the Pyramids, and thus an unparalleled act of vandalism was averted.

While the fate of the Pyramids was still in the balance, Linant suggested that a Commission might be assembled to study the project for barrages at the head of the Delta, and one was formed of members representing a peculiar variety of talent. The Egyptian element consisted of an architect, the Chief Engineer of the Delta, the Director of the School of Engineering, and a retired boatman in the particular confidence of the Viceroy. The European element comprised two British engineers, a foreign engineer who had studied in England, a French mining engineer, and two Commandants of Artillery.[1] As a result of the recommendations of this unwieldy body, a project favoured by Linant and a majority of the members received the Viceroy's approval, and towards the end of 1833, a host of *Corvée* or pressed labourers were set to work upon the construction of barrages across both the Damietta and Rosetta channels. These barrages were widely separated from each other, and situated from 3 to 5 miles downstream of the sites of the present structures in order to obtain good foundations. Work went on fairly well until 1835, when it was checked by plague. Muhammad Ali, once so enthusiastic, became lukewarm. The number of labourers dwindled rapidly, materials ceased to arrive, and in 1837, Linant Bey left the barrages to become Minister of Public Works. Muhammad Ali then appointed another Commission, of no less than 16 members, to examine the whole question of barrage construction, hinting that he thought such works unnecessary. The Commission, however, declared unanimously in favour of barrages, and in the end the Viceroy was obliged to inform the Minister that although the Commission was doubtless quite right, he did not *want* barrages. That pronouncement gave the *coup de grâce* to Linant's scheme.

The *Corvée* was a legalized system of forced and unpaid labour, designed to effect the clearance and repair of Government canals. It was objectionable from an engineering point of view as being a clumsy, wasteful and inefficient instrument. From a philanthropic standpoint it could be regarded only as a deplorable form of slavery. Thousands upon thousands of men were dragged from their villages and sent to work in distant places, unfed, unpaid and unlodged. They supplied even their own tools. " Serf labour had been the custom from the time when Pharaoh suppressed the Jews," remarks Scott-Moncrieff.[2] " The theory had some sort of plausibility. These

[1] *The Delta Barrage of Lower Egypt*, by Major R. Hanbury Brown, C.M.G., R.E., (retd.), p. 6.
[2] Lecture No. 8, entitled " The Nile and its Irrigation," prepared by Colonel Sir Colin C. Scott-Moncrieff, K.C.S.I., K.C.M.G., late R.E., in 1907, and lent to the author by Lady Scott-Moncrieff in March, 1935. From 1893 onwards, Sir Colin often lectured on Egyptian Irrigation in Chatham, London, Edinburgh, Cambridge and other places in Great Britain and overseas.

poor peasants could contribute little to the country's taxation, and their agricultural work did not occupy one half of their time. It would keep them out of mischief to employ them on work which was needed in order that the land should receive its water. But none of the large landowners ever sent a man to the *Corvée*. They kept their tenants and serfs to weed their own cottonfields and do the irrigation. The work had then to be done by the peasants. The village Sheikh was required to find a certain number of men from his village. Those who could afford to do so, bribed him. The poorest were driven off, perhaps 100 miles, to work for several months, while their fields remained untilled and their families were perpetually on the road, taking food to them."

Corrupt officials often permitted landowners to employ the public *Corvée* for private work. Rich Turkish or Egyptian Pashas set their dependents to weed and clear their large estates of fine cotton; but they did not concern themselves in clearing the canals that watered their lands, for that was the duty of their poor neighbours, whose properties suffered accordingly. Although many enlightened Egyptians recognized the mischief wrought by the *Corvée*, they could see no alternative. The country was impoverished and taxation was heavy. The peasants were accustomed to submit tamely to coercion. So the *Corvée*, iniquitous though it was, persisted until a handful of Royal Engineers, and a few civilian assistants, took charge of the irrigation of the country during the period of reorganization and development which followed the Egyptian campaign of 1882.

In 1842, five years after the abandonment of Linant Bey's scheme, another French engineer, named Mougel, arrived in Egypt to construct a graving dock at Alexandria, and offered to rebuild the barrages below Cairo on a new design. Muhammad Ali approved the proposal, and Mougel Bey submitted a project in 1843. His design was bold and ambitious. The Damietta Barrage was to have 45 arched openings: the Rosetta, 39 openings. Each opening, of $26\frac{1}{4}$ feet span, was to be fitted with iron gates, capable of holding up a depth of about 20 feet of water. Mougel considered, quite rightly, that the barrages should be able to divert all the Low Nile water for irrigation. To this, however, the Viceroy's "Council of Bridges and Roads" would not agree, and they returned the project for further study. Muhammad Ali, angry and disappointed, then ordered the immediate construction of the barrages under the direction of Monsieur Mougel.

The fitful energy with which the Viceroy pursued his ideas, and his childish eagerness for their early fulfilment, are surprising. For instance, on one occasion he ordered an Egyptian chief engineer to excavate a canal of certain dimensions, and asked how long he would take to complete it. The man replied that if the proper amount of labour was forthcoming, the canal would be finished within one year.

For this answer he was promptly given 200 strokes with the *bastinado*, and informed that a further 300 would be administered if the canal was not ready for use when the Viceroy returned 4 months later. The work was completed within the specified time.

Throughout the decade following the acceptance of Mougel's project, the construction of the Nile Barrage—a term commonly used to cover both the Damietta and Rosetta works—was carried on in a haphazard manner, but with some success. The Damietta structure was begun first, and no serious difficulties were encountered as the channel was almost dry. Nevertheless, Muhammad Ali was dissatisfied with the rate of progress. When work was started on the Rosetta Barrage in June, 1847, he ordered that 1,000 cubic metres of concrete should be laid daily, whatever the difficulties. Under fear of instant dismissal, Mougel Bey tried to comply. In went the concrete, regardless of the circumstances. At the west end, it fell into the shallowest of foundation trenches; and at the east end, on to a loose mass of rubble stone, over which water was running. The lime in the concrete was carried away, and springs appeared in many places. Under some of the openings, a spongy mixture of concrete and quicksand had to do duty as a floor.

Muhammad Ali died in 1848 and was succeeded by Ibrahim Pasha, who gave place to Abbas Pasha I before the end of the year. The new Viceroy had no faith in the Nile Barrage, and would have abandoned it in 1852 if he had not feared a public outcry. At the same time, Linant Bey, then Minister of Works, declared his preference for elaborate pumping installations. Being dissatisfied with the progress made on the Barrage, Abbas dismissed the unfortunate Mougel Bey in April, 1853, and ordered an Egyptian engineer, Mazhar Bey, to complete the work. The two bridges, each with its road, pathways, parapets and castellated turrets, were finished in 1861 at a total cost of £E.1,880,000. The defects in the foundations had not been remedied. The flooring beneath many of the openings was unsound. In fact, some portions of the Nile Barrage were rotten to the core.

It is unfair to blame the French engineers, Linant and Mougel, for this fiasco. They were mere advisers with little or no executive control, and were powerless to prevent the inconceivable blunders and injustices committed by their employers. Throughout the country, irrigation canals were being made which were faulty in slope, alignment and capacity, and had insufficient or badly placed regulating sluices. The *Corvée* laboured for weeks to clear the silted channels. Outlets to the fields were cut promiscuously from the main canals, so that water was wasted in some areas and unobtainable in others. Pumps were installed where there was insufficient water to feed them. Large tracts were allowed to become waterlogged through neglect of drainage, and the brackish water in the few drainage channels was often pumped back on to the fields. It is not surprising that, in view of the chaotic state of irrigation in Egypt, the Nile Barrage was a deplorable failure.

Mougel Bey had returned to Egypt after the death of Abbas Pasha in 1854, but not to the Barrage. He took up an appointment in the Public Works' Ministry at Cairo and advised the new Viceroy, Said Pasha, on all irrigation matters, including the Barrage. The visit of a body of savants to Egypt in December, 1855, to study the Suez Canal project, gave Mougel an opportunity to obtain their opinion about the Barrage, and at the same time to revive the flagging interest of Said Pasha by playing upon his natural fondness for military display. He suggested to the Viceroy that the Barrage, and its surroundings at the head of the Delta, would provide a favourable position for a fortified military centre, and Said Pasha took up the idea with avidity. "He imagined," writes Hanbury Brown,[1] "that by means of the Barrage and its canals he could raise the water high enough to inundate the whole Delta, and so obliterate all the land routes and endanger the existence of any army which might have disembarked and advanced inland. Further, he thought that, if a fleet made its way up the Nile, he could make short work of it by means of his Barrage and fortifications. Should an enemy come by the land from east or west or south, avoiding the Delta, he reckoned that, with his strongly fortified *têtes de ponts* at either end of the Barrage, he would be strong enough to maintain himself in his citadel, 'Kilat Saidieh,' against any army." So the fortifications—the bait which attracted Said Pasha—were commenced on March 12th, 1856. They comprised masonry bastions, curtains, sallyports, casemates and other works, all on the Vauban system and designed to extend for more than two miles along and between the Damietta and Rosetta channels. Though quite unnecessary and never finished, they served to secure the completion of the Barrage. Some of their lofty and castellated walls can still be seen about ¾ mile north of the beautiful gardens which now adorn the vicinity of the engineering works.

As completed in 1861, the Nile Barrage consisted of two stone bridges of 71 and 61 arches respectively, on approximately the same alignment, and about 1,200 yards apart.[2] It was intended that all the arched openings should be fitted with iron gates, by the lowering of which the water could be held up to a depth of about 15 feet and diverted into three main canals taking off from the river immediately above the bridges. The canal to the east of the Damietta bridge, now known as the Raiya el Taufiqi, was to supply the eastern delta provinces of Daqahliya and Sharqiya; the canal between the bridges—the Raiya el Menufiya—was to serve the fertile central delta province of Gharbiya; and the third canal—the Raiya el Beheira—

---
[1] *The Delta Barrage of Lower Egypt*, by Major R.H. Brown, C.M.G., R.E., (retd.), p.16.
[2] The Damietta bridge was 1,750 feet in length, and the Rosetta, 1,512 feet. Each had two locks. The 71 arches of the Damietta bridge were eventually reduced to 61

to the west of the Rosetta bridge, was to water the Beheira Province down to Alexandria.[1] The central canal passed through the fortifications, and the military advisers of Said Pasha had insisted that it should not be more than 50 feet in width. Accordingly, it was inadequate for the irrigation of the Gharbiya Province. The Barrage was not intended for the storage of water, but merely for its control and diversion. By 1861, the narrow central canal had been excavated throughout most of its length; and the western canal had also been dug, though subsequently it had become choked with sand in a desert section. As regards the eastern canal, only 5 miles had been completed, because an influential Turkish lady refused to allow it to be taken across her land. Gates had been fitted to the Rosetta bridge, but not to the Damietta, and consequently the amount of water which could be held up was negligible.

Commission after Commission was appointed to report on the work. In 1863, the engineers mustered sufficient courage to close the Rosetta gates in an attempt to induce more water to flow into the Damietta branch and the adjacent canal; but although the depth of the impounded water was raised only to $5\frac{1}{2}$ feet, sand was forced out from beneath the concrete floor of the Rosetta bridge, and ominous cracks appeared in it. Four years later, the bridge cracked from top to bottom, and a section of 10 arches towards the west end moved perceptibly downstream. It was saved only by enclosing it in a huge cofferdam. "The Barrage resembles a gangrened body," wrote Linant Bey in 1871. "It is covered with a fine coat, but disease gnaws at its vitals. Palliatives are useless: a major operation is needed." Rather than spend a million pounds on reconstruction, he wished to instal steam pumps throughout the Delta.

Early in 1876, Mr. John Fowler, an eminent engineer, examined the work and proposed that it should not be abandoned, but altered and strengthened at a cost of £E.1,200,000. Other British civil engineers supported Fowler, but their recommendations were rejected by Ismail Pasha, at that time Khedive of Egypt. Reckless as Ismail was in gratifying his own whims, he would not sanction so vast an outlay on a troublesome project bequeathed to him by his predecessors, even if he had possessed the necessary funds.

In the spring of 1876, a Royal Engineer in the person of Major-General (afterwards General) F. H. Rundall, C.S.I., appeared for the first time in the barren field of Egyptian Irrigation. He had been invited by Ismail Pasha to examine the Nile Barrage and submit plans and estimates for improving that work, and for distributing water throughout the Nile Delta. Rundall was an Irrigation expert, who had gained his experience as an assistant to General Sir Arthur Cotton in Southern India from 1844 to 1851, and thereafter in more important appointments under the Madras Government. From 1861

---

[1] See the *Sketch Map of the Nile Barrage in* 1887, included herewith.

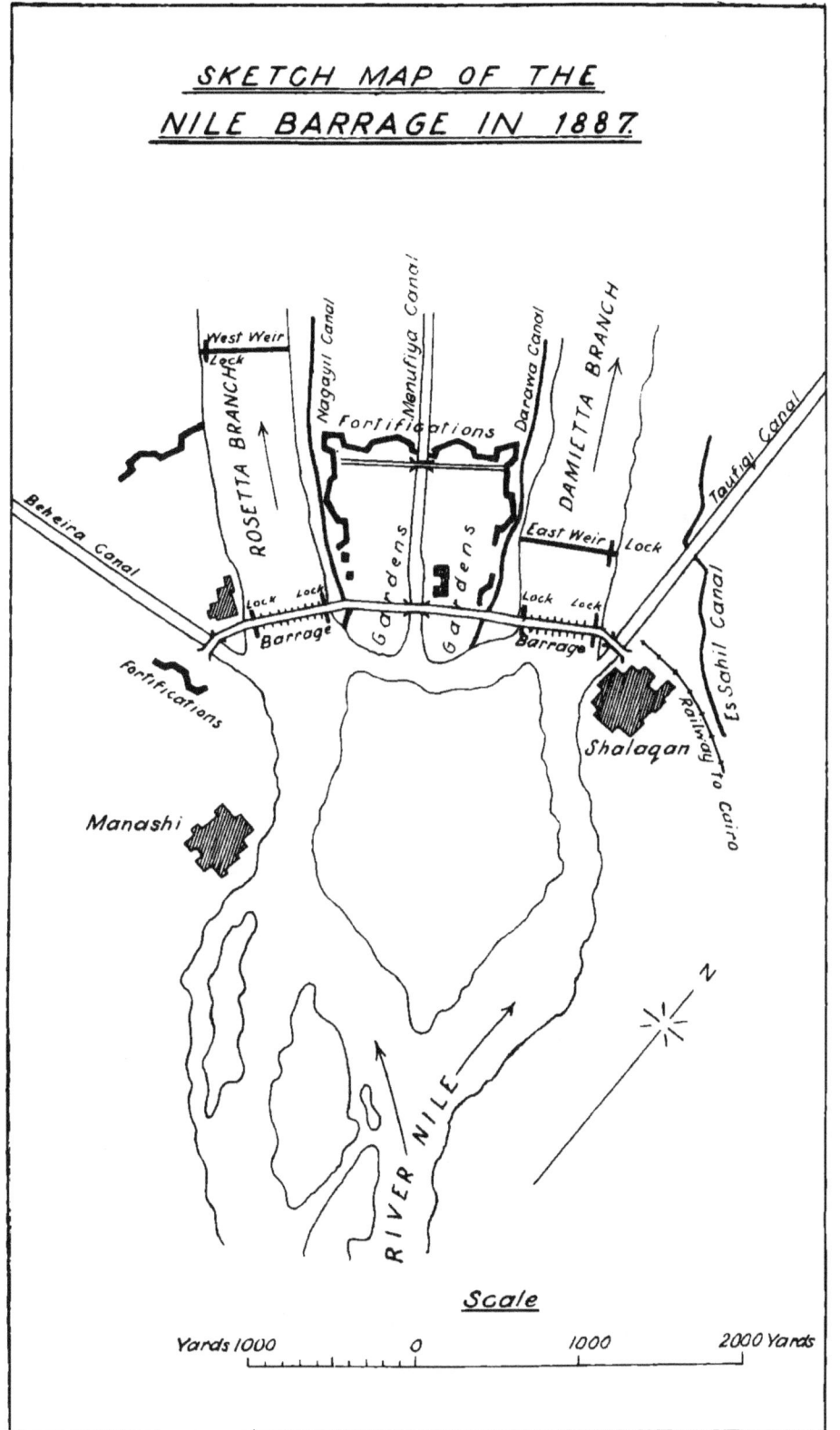

to 1866, he had designed and built large irrigation works in Bihar and Orissa, subsequently becoming Chief Engineer in Bengal, and in 1871, Inspector-General of Irrigation in India.[1] On only one occasion, in the course of 31 years' service in India, did he proceed on leave to England, and that was after he had spent no less than 20 years in the plains. Though not a brilliant engineer like Cotton, Rundall was a sound exponent of his profession, and there can be little doubt that the ability which he displayed as an adviser to the Egyptian Government, helped to secure the recruitment at a later date of Scott-Moncrieff and the other Royal Engineers, who saved Egyptian irrigation from disaster.

After examining the Nile Barrage, Rundall reported in May, 1876, that the substratum of the work seemed to be in a fairly sound condition, as otherwise there would have been more serious settlement than had actually taken place in a portion of the Rosetta bridge. " My own opinion," he wrote,[2] " is that the original foundations of the Barrage were ample as regards *depth*, provided that they had been faithfully built, but that they were deficient as regards *breadth* and the protection given both on the upper and lower sides of the flooring." He recommended the addition of wide rubble aprons and curtains[3] of wells, both upstream and downstream of the flooring, chiefly as a precaution against scour from the rush of water over the floor rather than with the object of preventing excessive seepage below it, and he suggested also the replacement of the existing gates by the " needle " system of closing the openings.[4] He emphasized the necessity of providing river-training works upstream of the Barrage, and estimated that the total cost of his proposals would amount to £E.500,000. As regards new irrigation works in Upper Egypt, he advocated the construction of a mighty dam for the storage of water, not far from the site of the present Aswan dam. However, nothing came of all these recommendations and estimates, because Ismail Pasha and his country were bankrupt. The irrigation works and canal systems of Egypt were allowed to continue on their road to ruin, and Rundall returned sadly to England.

It may be interesting to record that General Rundall was employed once again in an advisory capacity in the Near East, when a powerful syndicate was formed, in 1883, to examine the possibility of constructing a " Palestine Canal " for navigation between the

[1] For further details of the services of General F. H. Rundall, Royal (late Madras) Engineers, in the Indian Irrigation Department, see *The Military Engineer in India*, by Lieut.-Colonel E. W. C. Sandes, D.S.O., M.C., R.E. (retd.), Volume II, pp. 16–19, 23, 24, 27 and 304. A Memoir of General F. H. Rundall appears in the *R.E. Journal*, Vol. VIII, Jan.-Dec., 1908, pp. 383, 384. He died on Sept. 30th, 1908.

[2] Extract from a report, dated May 17th, 1876, from Major-General F. H. Rundall to H.H. the Khedive.

[3] *Apron*. A rough protective floor in prolongation of a masonry floor.

Curtain. A subterranean barrier formed by a masonry wall, or by a line of contiguous piles or wells, usually located at or near the upstream or downstream edge of an apron or a masonry floor.

[4] *Needles*. Vertical baulks lowered between horizontal beams.

Mediterranean and Red Seas. The canal was to tap the trade of Damascus, and to provide for the passage of ships by way of the Jordan Valley and Dead Sea, southwards through prodigious cuttings, to the Gulf of Aqaba. This scheme had to be abandoned. The time was not ripe for such a vast undertaking involving financial, political and engineering difficulties of the first magnitude.

We come now to Colin Scott-Moncrieff, a Royal Engineer who crowned a long career of faithful, though inconspicuous, service in India with a wonderful achievement in Egypt. Colonel C. C. Scott-Moncrieff, C.M.G., C.S.I., though not remarkable as an engineer, possessed courage, energy, sound judgment, common sense, unusual powers of organization, a faculty for the lucid exposition of his views, and a special aptitude for managing men. "He was endowed," remarks Sir Auckland Colvin,[1] "with precisely the qualities which were wanting in some of his contemporaries in Egypt. The term 'soft invincibility,' applied by Thomas Carlyle to his wife, best describes the chief characteristic of Colonel Scott-Moncrieff." Patient, tactful and essentially human, his subordinates found in him an ideal chief. He was deeply religious, and his British superiors recognized him as a man to be relied upon and trusted. Orientals opened their hearts to him. It was a happy day for Egypt when, by a turn of the wheel of Fortune, Scott-Moncrieff set foot on Egyptian soil.

In 1856, after serving in the Oudh Campaign towards the close of the Indian Mutiny, Scott-Moncrieff had joined the Public Works Department as an assistant Engineer on the Western Jumna Canal. From 1861 to 1864, he was on the staff of the Thomason Civil Engineering College at Roorkee, and then reverted to Irrigation employment as an Executive Engineer on the Eastern Jumna Canal, one of his assistants being Lieutenant J. H. Western, R.E., who followed him in later years to Egypt. During a period of furlough in 1867-68, Scott-Moncrieff examined the irrigation systems of Southern Europe, and wrote a book on this subject which brought his name into some prominence. On his return to India in 1869, he succeeded Lieut.-Colonel H. A. Brownlow, R.E., as Superintending Engineer, Northern Division, Ganges Canal, a responsible post which he held for 10 years, with the exception of a few months on famine duty in Madras. After another period of furlough, he became Chief Engineer in Burma, where he was occupied during 1881 and 1882 in constructing roads, buildings, harbour works and light-houses.[2] He retired on January 23rd, 1883, and started from Calcutta for England, his career apparently at an end and his name unassociated with any masterpiece of engineering.

[1] *The Making of Modern Egypt*, by Sir Auckland Colvin, p. 91.
[2] The career of Colonel Sir Colin Scott-Moncrieff is dealt with in *The Life of Sir Colin C. Scott-Moncrieff, K.C.S.I., K.C.M.G., R.E., L.L.D.*, by his niece, Mary Albright Hollings, and in a Memoir by Major Sir Robert Hanbury Brown, K.C.M.G., R.E. (retd.), appearing in the *R.E. Journal*, Vol. XXVI, July-Dec., 1917, pp. 171-178.

At Paricha, he and his wife stayed for a few days with their nephew, a young engineer named William Willcocks,[1] who was building a weir across the Betwa River, and on March 15th they sailed from Bombay. They had often discussed whether they should return to England by America, but had decided in favour of the shorter route. Had they gone by America, Scott-Moncrieff would never have made his reputation in Egypt.

As tourists, homeward bound, the Scott-Moncrieffs landed at Suez on March 26th, 1883, and resolved to take advantage of a last opportunity to visit Cairo. Accordingly, they engaged rooms in the Suez Hotel and prepared to start on the following morning. Late at night, however, a telegram arrived which changed the world for Scott-Moncrieff. It was from Lord Dufferin, Ambassador at Constantinople, who was then in Cairo in connection with the re-organization of the Government, and it invited Scott-Moncrieff to meet him there on official business. The meeting took place on March 31st, when Scott-Moncrieff was offered the appointment of Inspector-General of Irrigation in Egypt on a salary of £E.2,000 per annum, and was advised to continue his journey to England and notify his decision after due consideration. In the latter part of April he accepted the offer; and on May 3rd, 1883, he landed again in Egypt, and at once began to tour the country, in order to learn, not only its irrigation problems, but the manners and customs of its people. He hired a native boat, bought a horse, and refused to issue any orders until 6 months had elapsed.

The reign of the Khedive Ismail had ended with his deposition in 1879, when, by his gross extravagance, he had increased the debt of Egypt from £E.4,000,000 to £E.100,000,000. The unfinished Giza Palace was piled with moth-eaten French hangings and curtains, and in the Government archives was an order for 100 pianos for the ladies of the harem. Corruption and financial confusion were rampant. " Happy is the reformer," wrote Scott-Moncrieff, " who finds things so bad that he cannot make a movement without making an improvement," and in this frame of mind he prepared himself for years of hard work in an employment of his own choosing. Then he received the startling news that Sir Auckland Colvin, on appointment to the Government of India, had recommended him as his successor in the post of Financial Adviser to the Egyptian Government on a salary of £E.3,000 per annum. However, after he had explained to Colvin, and also to Sir Edward Malet, the Consul-General, that his knowledge of finance was limited to the method of drawing his pay at the end of the month, the offer was withdrawn, and Mr. (afterwards Sir) Edgar Vincent was appointed to the vacant post.

Scott-Moncrieff soon realized that he would require able assistants in Egypt, men whom he knew and could trust. The innumerable

[1] William Willcocks had married a niece of Colonel Scott-Moncrieff.

errors of detail in the irrigation system of the country pointed unmistakably to the necessity of constant supervision by expert subordinates. Naturally, he looked to India for help, and consequently entered forthwith into negotiations for the transfer of four Irrigation engineers to Egypt. One day, a letter reached him from an old comrade in India, Major Justin C. Ross, Royal (late Bengal) Engineers, saying that he would like to serve in Egypt; and permission having been obtained, "Justie" Ross joined the Egyptian Government as an Inspector of Irrigation in November, 1883. He was the first of the fine band of assistants who enabled Scott-Moncrieff to raise the irrigation of the Nile Valley from a condition of utter neglect to a state of moderate efficiency, and ultimately almost to perfection. Ross was placed in charge of the irrigation of the Eastern Delta; and William Willcocks, who joined in December, 1883, was stationed at the Nile Barrage.[1]

When Scott-Moncrieff's assistants began to arrive, it was assumed by the Egyptian authorities that they would live in ease and comfort at the headquarters in Cairo. "No," said the Inspector-General, "they shall live in the native towns and villages and rarely come to headquarters; and if they are not allowed to do so, we shall *all* return to India." He won his point, and the Inspectors of Irrigation were enabled, in consequence, to expose and suppress the iniquities of certain officials and landowners, and to secure the fair distribution of water. The Inspectors were ubiquitous. After a time, it was rumoured among the villagers that a *shaitan* (devil), named Moncrieff, had appeared in a certain spot on one day and at another, a hundred miles distant, on the next day, the explanation being that they were unaware that several European Inspectors were already working in different provinces.

Justin Ross was a man of scientific turn of mind, a model of industry and a master of detail. He had not the constructive imagination, amounting perhaps to genius, of William Willcocks, his civilian contemporary, but was always desperately in earnest, whether as an engineer, or as a sportsman, a geologist and an antiquarian, in all of which pursuits he was deeply interested. Beginning his Irrigation career in 1862 as an Assistant Engineer in the Etawah Division of the Ganges Canal, he became in due course an Executive Engineer in the Bulandshahr and Anupshahr Divisions. From 1874, until he arrived in Egypt, he worked in the country served by the Lower Ganges Canal, and earned an excellent reputation for thorough and careful administration and control. Sir Henry Lyons, for many years Director-General of the Egyptian Survey, describes him as the real creator of modern Irrigation in Egypt. " It

---

[1] Scott-Moncrieff divided Egypt into five "Circles" of Irrigation (three in the Delta and two in Upper Egypt) and allotted four of these Circles to his assistants from India.

was Ross," he writes,[1] "who planned the whole new network of canals, drains and regulators. He calculated in metric measures the necessary formulæ for a volume of technical instructions dealing with the canal discharges, sections and velocities most favourable for minimizing the deposit of silt from the Nile flood. Aided by a retentive memory, he could give the proper upstream and downstream level of any regulator in Lower Egypt at any time. Stalking along the canal banks, stick in hand, he was a familiar figure to the cultivators, and was known everywhere as *Abu Nabut* (the man with the staff)." He was unrivalled in the skilful distribution of water, for his eye could judge the slope of a plain when the difference of level was less than one foot in a mile. His linguistic abilities, combined with patience and kindliness of manner, enabled him to obtain great influence among the people. Humorous, musical and addicted to a quaint style in dress, Justin Ross was a man who was the wonder, and at the same time the idol, of the simple cultivators of Egypt. He associated himself with them; he shielded them from oppression; and on occasion he ruled them with a rod of iron.

The proposal made by M. Linant de Bellefonds in 1871, that pumping installations throughout the Nile Delta should be substituted for the unsatisfactory Barrage, was revived in 1883 by Rousseau Pasha, Director-General of Public Works, who stated that the Barrage, in its existing condition, could be employed only to distribute water between the two branches of the river. He added that £E.400,000 would be required for repairs to the Rosetta work, and that the Damietta work was useless except as a bridge. As an alternative, he proposed to irrigate the whole of Lower Egypt by an elaborate system of pumping stations at an initial cost of £E.700,000 and an annual outlay of nearly £E.250,000. In order to supply the Beheira Province in the Western Delta, the Public Works Ministry had already concluded a 33 years' contract with a private Company to pump water from the Rosetta branch of the river into the frequently obstructed and troublesome Beheira Canal at a minimum annual cost of £E.26,000 in addition to payment for the water pumped, making a probable total charge against the Government of some £E.50,000 a year.[2] As regards Rousseau's pumping scheme, Lord Milner remarks[3] that the same object could have been accomplished far more easily and efficiently by holding up the water at the Barrage, if only that work had been put in order instead of being abandoned without adequate trial.

When Scott-Moncrieff landed in Egypt, he was pressed by the

[1] Notes by Colonel Sir Henry G. Lyons, F.R.S., late R.E., sent to the author on December 6th, 1934. Justin Ross spent £E.700,000 on the system of canals between Cairo and Aswan.

[2] As a result of this unfortunate agreement, the Egyptian Government for many years paid £E.26,000 for nothing; for after 1890, when the Barrage became effective, pumping was no longer necessary.

[3] *England in Egypt*, by Alfred Milner (1894), p. 297.

Government to examine the Barrage, but was warned by the local French and Egyptian engineers to have nothing to do with it. The timbers were rotten; the ironwork rusted; the masonry cracked. However, with his Indian experience behind him, he was not satisfied with the advice given to him and felt that, before accepting the extravagant programme of pumping installations, he must be certain that the Barrage was really past repair. Accordingly, in December, 1883, he set William Willcocks to test the work and determine its powers of endurance, while the local engineers expressed their pity for "his ignorance of the country, so natural to a foreigner." The Minister of Public Works, Ali Pasha Mubarek, informed the Consul-General, Sir Evelyn Baring (afterwards Lord Cromer), that he was strongly opposed to any plan for repairing the Barrage and preferred the costly alternative of erecting huge pumps; but he admitted later that he had not visited the work for 27 years![1]

Willcocks found that the closing apparatus of the Rosetta bridge openings was in very bad order, and that there were no gates whatever in the Damietta openings; he reported that the downstream aprons of both bridges were incomplete, the equipment deficient, and the staff incapable of doing anything beyond drawing their pay. Nevertheless, Scott-Moncrieff decided to begin the work of repair, and he and Willcocks placed "tell-tale" patches of cement across every crack, and examined them daily to see whether the cracks were spreading. Then they set to work to remedy the most glaring defects, expending more than £E.25,000 during 1884, and as a result an additional depth of 7 feet of water[2] was successfully held up by the Rosetta bridge or barrage in the month of June when the Nile level was falling, and an additional 3 feet by the Damietta bridge. Water was thus supplied to districts which had not seen it for years except during the flood season. The discharge of the central Menufiya Canal was doubled, small canals between the Barrage and Cairo began to fill, and such enormous savings were effected in canal clearances that the idea of abolishing the *Corvée* was entertained for the first time.[3] The cotton crop, which had never before exceeded 130,000 tons, rose to 160,000 tons, and as each ton was worth about £E.35, the wealth of Egypt was increased by more than £E.1,000,000 or 40 times the expenditure incurred. This result was so encouraging that on July 27th, 1885, Sir Evelyn Baring was able to obtain a loan of a million pounds sterling for Egyptian irrigation works, most of which amount was allotted to the Nile Barrage, and Scott-Moncrieff then knew that he would be able to complete his scheme of improvement and repair. The experiments on the Barrage were continued in 1885 when, by constructing a bar of loose stones across the downstream floor of the

---

[1] *Modern Egypt*, by the Earl of Cromer, Vol. II, p. 459, footnote 2.
[2] Giving a total depth above the floor of about $12\frac{1}{4}$ feet of water.
[3] In 1884, the *Corvée* was equivalent to an army of 165,000 men working for 100 days; in 1885, to only 117,700 men working for the same period.

Rosetta barrage, a " water cushion " was formed which enabled that work to hold up, with moderate safety, a total depth above the floor of 15½ feet of water, while the Damietta barrage supported 11 feet. In this way, the supply to the canals was further increased, at a cost of £E.18,000 including repairs, though some anxiety was caused to the bold experimentors by the partial subsidence of the old cofferdam, which still surrounded the cracked and displaced portion of the Rosetta barrage.

The success of the 1884 operations having persuaded Scott-Moncrieff that he was justified in applying for further help from India, he obtained, in 1884-85, the services of Major J. H. Western, R. (Bengal) E., Captain (afterwards Major Sir Robert) Hanbury Brown, R.E., and Messrs. A. G. W. Reid, E. W. P. Foster, and W. E. Garstin.[1] Western and Reid were sent from India expressly to take charge of the restoration of the Nile Barrage ; the others came for general duty. While it is true that Scott-Moncrieff made the decision that the Barrage should be restored, and subsequently exercised a general supervision over the operations, and that William Willcocks carried out the initial experiments and repairs, the chief credit for the actual work of restoration must be accorded to Western[2] and his assistant, Reid, who designed and executed the additions and alterations.

Major James Halifax Western was an experienced engineer who had gone to India in 1862 and had served afterwards for 3 years as an assistant to Scott-Moncrieff on the Eastern Jumna Canal. From 1870 to 1875, he was Executive Engineer, Northern Division, Ganges Canal, and was then transferred to the Lower Ganges Canal, where he built the weir and headworks at Narora and completed the first reach of the great waterway.[3] Next, he became Superintending Engineer in charge of the new Betwa Canal and constructed the Paricha Dam across the Betwa River near Jhansi. From 1882, until his transfer to Egypt, he was employed on the Sirhind Canal in the Punjab.[4] Thus it will be seen that Western had carried out several important works, and had earned a high reputation as a constructive engineer, before he came to assist Scott-Moncrieff on the Nile Barrage. Captain Robert Hanbury Brown, on the other hand, had yet to make his reputation. He was 10 years junior to Western, and had less than 12 years' experience as an Irrigation engineer in India. Nevertheless, he soon became an expert. During 20 years of faithful service under

[1] Major Western and Captain Hanbury Brown were engaged on salaries of £E.1,500 per annum. The three civilian assistants received salaries of £E.1,000. These officers were supplemented later by others.

[2] Letter from Lady Scott-Moncrieff, dated March 24th, 1918, appearing in the *R.E. Journal*, Vol. XXVIII, Jan.-June, 1918, p. 248.

[3] The designs were prepared by Captain W. Jeffreys, Bengal Engineers (see the *Military Engineer in India*, by Lt.-Col. E. W. C. Sandes, D.S.O., M.C., R.E. (retd.) Vol. II, p. 11).

[4] The services in India and Egypt of Colonel J. H. Western, C.M.G., late Royal (Bengal) Engineers, are given in a Memoir by Major Sir Robert Hanbury Brown, K.C.M.G., R.E. (retd.), appearing in the *R.E. Journal*, Vol. XXV, Jan.-June, 1917, pp. 267-270.

the Egyptian Government, he consolidated the Nile Barrage bequeathed to him by Western, constructed the Zifta Barrage on the Damietta Branch below the Nile Barrage, and executed many other works of less importance. He was awarded the K.C.M.G. in 1902, and retired in 1904 after being Inspector-General of Irrigation in Egypt for several years.[1] " To Mougel Bey," writes Sir William Garstin,[2] " is due the credit of designing and constructing the Nile Barrage ; to Sir Colin Scott-Moncrieff and to Colonel Western that of restoring it and enabling it to fulfil the purpose for which it was originally intended ; and to Major Brown that of developing the work commenced in the second period and thus rendering possible a striking extension of the functions of the structure."

For some time after their arrival in 1885, Western and Reid regarded any attempt to restore the Barrage as so unpromising that they were inclined to favour instead the construction of an entirely new work, and estimates were framed accordingly. However, after some discussion it was decided that the old Barrage should not be abandoned if it were possible to render it fit for service ; but to settle this point, it was necessary to lay bare and examine the floor, which was covered at the moment with $15\frac{1}{2}$ feet of water. The task was complicated by the facts that work was possible only between the beginning of November and the end of June, the period of low Nile, and that the Barrage must continue to hold up water for irrigation while the operations were in progress. Scott-Moncrieff compared the problem with that of mending a watch without stopping the works. In March, 1886, Western and Reid managed to enclose 20 arches at the west end of the Rosetta barrage with a high earthen embankment, and found that they could keep the interior dry by continuous pumping, although it lay 16 feet below the surface of the water. The cracks in the floor and arches were very serious, and borings revealed the fact that no rock foundation was obtainable, even at a depth of 200 feet below the floor ; but it was decided, nevertheless, that it would be worth while to attempt the work of restoration.

" We were required," writes Scott-Moncrieff,[3] " to prevent water passing through the ground under the work, and therefore resolved to adopt the Indian plan of spreading the foundation out very wide. Finding that, from upstream to downstream, the width of the cracked and badly-built flooring was 112 feet, we increased it to 224 feet. We covered the old flooring with a solid mass of concrete and stonework, 3 feet thick, and prolonged it upstream and downstream ; while along

---

[1] A Memoir of Major Sir Robert Hanbury Brown, K.C.M.G., late R.E., appears in the *R.E. Journal*, Vol. XL, March–Dec., 1926, pp. 501–503.

[2] Introduction by Sir William Garstin, K.C.M.G., to *The Delta Barrage of Lower Egypt*, by Major R. H. Brown, C.M.G., R.E., retd. (1902).

[3] Reminiscences quoted in *The Life of Sir Colin C. Scott-Moncrieff, K.C.S.I., K.C.M.G., R.E., L.L.D.*, by his niece Mary Albright Hollings, p. 203. See also an article on Egyptian Irrigation in general by Colonel Scott-Moncrieff, appearing in the *R.E. Journal*, Vol. 21, 1891, pp. 175–177.

the upstream edge we drove a line of sheet-piling, 16 feet deep, so that the water would have to percolate under this wall, and through 224 feet of sand and mud, before it could issue below. During the first working season (1885–86) we finished the flooring of some arches, and placed, just below the bridge, heavy dressed blocks of hard stone from the Alps ; and at the end of November, 1886, we began our preparations for the next season. We could not close the whole of either branch of the river during any one season, so we determined to do one-half at a time, and as there were two branches, that meant 4 years' work. It took us until the middle of February, 1887, to get our embankment round one-half of the Rosetta barrage, and 3 weeks more to get the water out of the enclosed space ; then, in March, we set to work, and laboured day and night until the end of June. On July 1st, when we had finished one-half of the Rosetta barrage, we removed the last of our pumps, reports having arrived daily of the approach of the floods. The embankments, which had taken 3 months to make and had cost about £E.10,000, were soon washed away, and no work was possible until the middle of the following November, when we began new embankments, enclosed another half of the river, and did another season's work. Sometimes, there were as many as 10,000 men on the work. On June 16th, 1890, the English engineers reported at last that all was finished and the embankments could be removed with safety.[1] Since then, no one has seen the dry bed of the Nile. Altogether, about £E.460,000 were spent, and Egypt is yearly the richer by an increase in the cotton crop worth at least 2½ millions sterling. By means of the Barrage, the whole of the water of the Nile, when the river is at its lowest in May and June, is now poured on to the fields, and none whatever escapes to the sea."

It may be remarked that, although Scott-Moncrieff writes as if he were in executive charge of the work of restoration, he was actually Under-Secretary of State for Public Works, an office to which he had been appointed within a few months of his arrival in Egypt, being succeeded as Inspector-General by Major Justin Ross.[2] Until the autumn of 1889, Lieut.-Colonel Western was in immediate charge of the work at the Barrage, with Mr. Reid as his assistant. Then his health failed, and in February, 1890, he was obliged to leave Egypt, so that he did not see the completion of the restoration, which was carried out by Reid and an assistant.[3] Reid then handed over charge to Mr. E. W. P. Foster. In 1892, Foster succeeded Ross as Inspector-General, and Mr. William Garstin followed Scott-Moncrieff as Under-Secretary, changes which occurred on the retirement of the two Royal

---

[1] The repairs and alterations to the Rosetta structure having been completed in June, 1888, work had been begun on the Damietta structure in November, 1888.

[2] As Under-Secretary, Scott-Moncrieff was responsible for railways, roads and buildings in addition to irrigation works.

[3] On his return to England, Lt.-Colonel J. H. Western became Inspecting Engineer to the Egyptian Government, which post he held until 1909. Both Western and Reid received the C.M.G. in recognition of their services on the Nile Barrage.

Engineers in question. Major Hanbury Brown succeeded Foster as Inspector-General in 1894, and thus maintained the connection of the Corps with the Nile Barrage during the process of its final consolidation.

Scott-Moncrieff, while Under-Secretary, was sent to Asia in 1890 to advise the Russian Government regarding the irrigation of Merv. After his retirement, he became Under-Secretary for Scotland and had no further connection with irrigation, except as Chairman of the Indian Irrigation Commission which visited India in 1901–02 and 1902–03, and as a Director of the Aswan Dam. His most notable achievements were the repair and improvement of the Nile Barrage and the abolition of the *Corvée;* but it may be recorded that he also reorganized the Egyptian Irrigation Department, took a hand in the question of the drainage of Lower Egypt and the remodelling of the basin systems of Upper Egypt, directed the preliminary investigations by William Willcocks which led to the construction of the Aswan Dam, and, by persuading landowners to accept a cess on their holdings, endowed the country with many roads between villages. For his services in Egypt, he was awarded the K.C.M.G., and for his chairmanship of the Indian Commission, the K.C.S.I. He died on April 6th, 1916, mourned by many friends, both in Egypt and England.

Egypt nearly lost the services of Scott-Moncrieff at a most critical time in the restoration of the Barrage. On February 5th, 1887, in a fit of exasperation at the apparent failure of British diplomacy to secure the abolition of the *Corvée* against the opposition of certain European Powers and the native Governors of Provinces, he was driven to tender his resignation of the post of Under-Secretary, though he withdrew the application after an interview on February 7th with Sir Evelyn Baring. An arrangement had been in existence for some time by which any man detailed for the *Corvée* was allowed to escape service for one season on payment of $1\frac{1}{2}$ *rials* (dollars), but this was only a half-measure. A sum of £E.400,000 was necessary for the substitution of paid dredging and contract work for the unpaid labour of the *Corvée*, and there seemed to be little hope of securing it. However, Nubar Pasha, a benevolent Minister of Finance, managed to obtain and allot £E.250,000 at once, and his successor found a further £E.150,000, so that, by 1890, serf labour in Egypt had become a thing of the past.

Mr. W. E. Garstin, the Under-Secretary for Irrigation, kept the Nile Barrage under close observation until 1896, when he secured the services of Mr. W. R. Kinipple, a well-known engineer, to experiment on it with his system of "stock-ramming." This consisted in forcing clay down holes bored in the piers, and so to the underside of the floor, in the hope that it would form eventually a continuous and water-tight curtain wall under the centre of the

THE NILE BARRAGE, ROSETTA BRANCH.
Under restoration in 1887.

Barrage. A portion of the Damietta work was selected for the experiment; but it was found that no amount of ramming with a falling weight would make the clay spread laterally from the bottom of the bore. Then Hanbury Brown, after writing to Scott-Moncrieff for his concurrence, suggested the employment of cement grout (cement and water), and the first experiments with this mixture in January, 1897, were so encouraging that it was decided to apply the system to both the Damietta and Rosetta barrages.[1] More than 6,000 barrels of cement were used during 3 seasons' work, and the grouting was finished at a cost of £E.6,000. The process, however, brought to light the dangerous condition of some of the pier foundations; and it was evident that, if it were desired to employ a full head of 6 metres, or nearly 20 feet, of water, as projected by Mougel Bey in 1843—a matter of great importance—some permanent means must be supplied to reduce the strain upon the Barrage during regulation. Accordingly, it was decided to build a permanent supplementary dam or weir in each branch of the river, downstream of the original work, so that the latter would never have to sustain a head greater than 3 metres (9·84 feet) while the weir supported the remainder. Garstin and Hanbury Brown adopted the wide, solid type of rubble stone weir used successfully on the Sone River in India, but substituted a cement-grouted core wall of rubble for the masonry wells or concrete blocks of the prototype. The two weirs, with locks for navigation,[2] were completed in May, 1901, at a cost of £E.434,000, one of the most energetic workers being Corporal (afterwards Lieutenant) "Sammy" Hart, 2nd Company, R.E., whose services were lent to the Public Works Ministry in connection with demolition work. The weirs enabled Hanbury Brown and his civilian assistants to utilize to the full the first rise of the flood in July and August, and by holding up water to a very high level at the main works, to economize still further in silt clearances in the canals.

The Nile Barrage was frequently displayed with justifiable pride to parties of visitors, who were usually greatly impressed by it; but on one occasion, when the novelty and efficacy of cement grouting was being indicated, a lady remarked scornfully that there was nothing new in that operation as her cook had always employed a similar one when he made a pie. The cook, she explained, cut pieces of meat into convenient sizes and placed them in a pie-dish, and having filled the interstices with bisected eggs and livers, covered the dish with a crust and put it in the oven. After it had been withdrawn from the oven, gravy was poured in through a hole in the crust to fill all the spaces between the pieces of meat. The pie was

---

[1] The system of cement grouting was mainly the invention of Major Hanbury Brown. Subsequently, he described it in a Paper read before the Institution of Civil Engineers in 1904, for which he was awarded the Telford Medal.

[2] Hanbury Brown made the locks by a system of cement grouting without the use of cofferdams or pumping. This had never been done before.

then set aside to cool, and when cool its interior was found to be compacted by the congealed gravy into a monolithic mass.

The construction of a new Nile Barrage, downstream of Mougel's work and in replacement of it, at a cost of about 2½ millions sterling, is now being considered. The bridges will be longer and stronger, the gates more efficient, and the river-training works more elaborate. New head regulators will be necessary for the Taufiqi and Beheira Canals, and there will be extensive alterations in the latter.[1] Mougel's Barrage, saved by Scott-Moncrieff and Western and strengthened by Hanbury Brown, may become in time a mere relic of the past. If so, it will match in that respect the connection of Royal Engineers with Egyptian Irrigation, for since the retirement of Major Sir Robert Hanbury Brown, K.C.M.G., in 1904, no officer of the Corps has controlled the water which brings life and prosperity to Egypt.

The irrigation of Lower Egypt having been improved in 1901 by the additions to the Nile Barrage, attention was devoted to the needs of Upper Egypt and the probable future requirements of Lower Egypt. The restoration of the Barrage had placed at the disposal of the Government all the water of the Low Nile; but under British control, the increase in the area requiring irrigation soon outran the increase in the water available, and it became necessary to establish a reserve of water, brought down in the flood season, for use when the river level had fallen. It was estimated that no less than 4,000 millions of tons (or about 4 milliards of cubic metres[2]) of water would be required to allow for the perennial irrigation of all cultivable land throughout the country; but it was decided that this vast amount could not be secured until the finances of Egypt were in a sound condition, and that consequently the country must be content for a time with a smaller storage.

Schemes for storing flood water had often been under consideration in the past. For instance, in 1866 Sir Samuel Baker had suggested that a dam should be built at Aswan below the First Cataract and had made his proposal public by a letter in *The Times*. At a later date, the fame of the ancient Lake Moeris, a natural depression to the west of the Nile in the Fayum district some distance south of Cairo, induced Muhammad Ali to urge M. Linant de Bellefonds to estimate for the use of that basin as a reservoir; but as Linant considered the cost prohibitive, he recommended instead the construction of a weir and canal head at Silsila, north of Aswan. This project was abandoned after the failure of the Nile Barrage. In 1880, Count de la Motte suggested the construction of a dam and reservoir at Silsila, and the

---

[1] A satisfactory head regulator exists on the Central or Menufiya Canal. It was built in 6 months, some 27 years ago, by Mr. (now Sir) Murdoch MacDonald, when Director of Reservoirs. Sir Murdoch states that £10,000,000 worth of crops were saved in consequence during the first year.

[2] 1 cubic metre of water weighs 2,207·25 lb. 1,000 millions = 1 " milliard."

flooding of a depression to the east of the Nile by means of a dam at Kalabsha, south of Aswan; and two years later, an enthusiastic American, named Cope Whitehouse, came forward with a scheme for utilizing the Wadi Rayan basin,[1] south-west of the Fayum, as a reservoir. This basin had been noticed also by Linant Bey, but it was found that the cost of conveying water to it would be excessive.

After the successful repair of the Nile Barrage in 1887, the Government was able to devote attention once again to the question of the storage of water, and Colonel Scott-Moncrieff, as Under-Secretary for Irrigation, deputed Lieut.-Colonel Western to survey the desert between the Wadi Rayan and the Nile; he was to estimate the capacity of the Wadi Rayan depression and to ascertain whether it could be used for storage. Western submitted his plans and estimates in 1888, and supported by Lieut.-Colonel Justin Ross, made a strong recommendation in favour of the scheme. Scott-Moncrieff then deputed William Willcocks to examine the alternative proposals of Count de la Motte, and secured their rejection after Willcocks had stated in 1890 that there was no suitable depression near Kalabsha and no proper rock foundation at Silsila.[2] Willcocks recommended instead the construction of a dam about 6 miles above Aswan, to impound 1,000 millions of tons of water.[3] He negatived a suggestion from Cairo that the Nile might be dammed at Kalabsha, for he had found that there was no suitable rock foundation at the place.[4] Continuing his investigations, he proceeded to survey, bore and level in the deserts stretching from the Fayum southwards as far as Wadi Halfa; and in 1894, he proposed the construction of a dam above Aswan which differed in design from that suggested in 1890[5] and would impound about 2,500 millions of tons of water. The new project met with the approval not only of Sir William Garstin, the Under-Secretary, but also of Sir Benjamin Baker, Monsieur Boulé and Signor Torricelli, members of an International Commission on Egyptian Irrigation. Scott-Moncrieff and Hanbury Brown were consulted with reference to the 1890 project, and Hanbury Brown regarding the 1894 project. Thus, two Royal Engineers took some part in the discussions which preceded the construction of the Aswan Dam by their civilian contemporaries. Every important detail of the 1894 design was submitted to, and approved by, Sir William Garstin, who accepted full responsibility for the scheme.

[1] See the general map of Egypt at the end of this volume.
[2] Report by Mr. William Willcocks, entitled "Nile Reservoirs," published in 1890 with criticisms by Colonel Scott-Moncrieff and Major Hanbury Brown, R.E. Willcocks had become Director-General of Reservoir Studies after the departure from Egypt of Colonel Western. See also *Egyptian Irrigation*, by Mr. W. Willcocks (1889).
[3] This dam was to be about 100 feet high and to contain 60 large under-sluices.
[4] *The Assuan Reservoir and Lake Moeris*, by Sir William Willcocks, K.C.M.G., p. 5.
[5] Report by Mr. William Willcocks entitled "Perennial Irrigation and Flood Protection in Egypt," published in 1894 with an introduction by Sir William Garstin and notes by Major Hanbury Brown, R.E., and Mr. E. W. P. Foster.

The design prepared by Willcocks in 1894 took the form of a series of horizontally arched structures, joining huge abutments of masonry on islands at the head of the First Cataract. The dam was to be provided with 100 under-sluiceways, fitted with Stoney sliding gates. A tortuous alignment was proposed in order that advantage should be taken of the soundest rock for the foundations. The International Commission, however, would not accept this alignment, and in 1895 Willcocks was asked to prepare a design for a straight dam, 1¼ miles in length and about 115 feet in height, to form a reservoir of the same capacity as in the previous design, and provided with 140 lower and 40 upper sluiceways.[1] " The contract was given to Messrs. John Aird and Company," writes Sir Murdoch MacDonald.[2] " It was at this stage that I joined the Government staff, and I remember that the plans had no name on them other than that of a draftsman, and that Willcocks complained to me that his signature, as author of the plans, had been removed or omitted."

Unfortunately, the construction of the Aswan Dam, as designed by Willcocks in 1894 and again in 1895, entailed the partial submergence of a famous group of ancient temples on the Island of Philae, upstream of the dam. Willcocks had recognized this fact, and had allowed £E.250,000 for moving the temples to another island. Sir William Garstin approved the proposal, Signor Torricelli cared little about the fate of the temples, and Sir Benjamin Baker, the expert chosen as Consulting Engineer, advocated the raising of the structures on to a plinth high above the water. Savants and antiquaries joined in the fray. In the face of a storm of protest, not from Egyptians but from European archæologists, Willcocks suggested to his former chief, Scott-Moncrieff, that the cost of the dam might be met by selling the Philae temples to the Americans for removal and re-erection in New York![3] Ultimately, the Government surrendered and ordered that the level of the reservoir, and consequently the height of the dam, should be reduced by 26 feet. Further, they announced that the foundations of the Philae temples would be examined and consolidated, and, as an engineer who had already taken much interest in Egyptian Archæology, they appointed Captain H. G. Lyons, R.E., their Director of Survey, to carry out this work during the winter of 1895-96.[4] Thus, another Royal Engineer became concerned indirectly in the Aswan project. By the reduction in the water level, the storage capacity of the reservoir

---

[1] *The Nile Reservoir Dam at Assuan and After,* by Mr. W. Willcocks, C.M.G., late Director-General of Reservoirs in Egypt (1901), p. 5. The cost of the dam was estimated at about £E.750,000. A straight dam was insisted upon by Sir Benjamin Baker.

[2] Notes by Sir Murdoch MacDonald, K.C.M.G., C.B., M.P., sent to the author on July 31st, 1936.

[3] Lecture No. 8, " The Nile and its Irrigation," by Colonel Sir Colin C. Scott-Moncrieff, K.C.S.I., K.C.M.G., late R.E., dated 1907.

[4] Notes by Colonel Sir Henry G. Lyons, F.R.S., late R.E., sent to the author on December 6th, 1934.

was reduced to 1,000 millions of tons, an action which drew from Mr. Winston Churchill a bitter criticism. "The State must struggle and the people starve," said he, " in order that professors may exult and tourists find some place on which to scratch their names." The foundation stone of the Aswan Dam was laid by H.R.H. The Duke of Connaught on February 12th, 1899, and the work was completed by Sir Benjamin Baker and his staff on December 12th, 1902. The foundations had to be excavated deeper than Willcocks had anticipated, and in the end the project cost about £E.3,000,000; but fortunately, the dam was made so thick that subsequent heightening was rendered possible without extensive alteration to the original structure.

In the spring of 1901, when Sir William Garstin was sent to the upper waters of the White Nile to report on the feasibility of increasing the supply of water to Egypt, he was accompanied by Lyons, who measured the discharges of the White Nile at a number of points between Khartoum and Gondokoro. Lyons assisted Garstin again in 1903 before the latter produced his monumental report entitled "The Basin of the Upper Nile." That report heralded the formation, under Mr. C. E. Dupuis, of the Sudan Branch of the Egyptian Irrigation Service, charged with the preparation of a series of projects for the development of both countries, Lyons' measurements of river discharges in 1901 were so valuable that a party from the Geological Survey continued the measurements on both the Blue and White Niles at Khartoum during 1902 and 1903, and thus laid the foundations of a thorough hydrographical survey of the Nile which was put in hand before the Great War and resumed after it.

On one occasion during the earlier days of his connection with the Nile, Lyons sent an Egyptian subordinate upstream to establish a new river gauge in order that proper warning should be received at Cairo of the approach of a flood. The daily readings from the new gauge soon began to arrive; but when they never varied by a centimetre, in spite of fluctuations at Cairo, Lyons set out to investigate. The subordinate pointed proudly to the gauge. He had screwed it to the side of a boat!

Owing to the apron protection works designed and built by Mr. Murdoch MacDonald after the completion of the original Aswan Dam, and to the massive nature of the structure, it was possible in 1906 to consider the heightening of the dam by 5 metres and the raising of the water level by 7 metres,[1] thus increasing the capacity of the reservoir from 1,000 to 2,700 millions of tons of water. The design was prepared, and the work superintended by, Mr. MacDonald, who increased the thickness of the dam by 5 metres and, at the suggestion

---

[1] The water was to be allowed to rise to within 1 metre of the crest, instead of 3 metres.

of Sir Benjamin Baker, left a space (6 inches in width) between the old and new work, the latter being tied to the old work by steel rods sunk into both structures. Operations for heightening and thickening the dam were begun in 1908[1], and were completed in 1912 at a cost of about £E.2,000,000.

The decision to raise the Aswan Dam, taken on the suggestion of Mr. MacDonald and the recommendation of Sir Benjamin Baker, was rendered possible through the labours of the Egyptian Survey Department under Captain H. G. Lyons, R.E., for during 1905 and 1906, Lyons had superintended the running of a line of levelling from Wadi Halfa to Khartoum for hydrographical purposes, and had prepared contoured plans of all parts of the river that seemed to offer good prospects for the construction of a reservoir. By comparison, it was found that it was preferable to secure the additional water required for Egypt by means of an expansion of the reservoir at Aswan rather than by providing a new reservoir south of Wadi Halfa.

The heightening of the Aswan Dam might well have revived the animosity of the antiquaries, but the Government exercised tact and discretion. "In order to avoid a storm of criticism such as the original submergence of the Philae temples had aroused," writes Sir Henry Lyons,[2] "it was announced that an archæological survey of the area of the valley to be submerged would be made, and that any ancient structure which would be affected would be strengthened. The survey was entrusted to the Survey Department: the strengthening, to the Department of Antiquities. In organizing this survey, I included two anatomists in order that any human remains should be examined by experts, and the result was a notable addition to our knowledge of the diseases of twenty or thirty centuries ago, and of the early inhabitants of the Upper Nile."

A second heightening and strengthening of the Aswan Dam was begun in 1929 and completed in 1934. By adding 9 metres to the height, the capacity of the reservoir was increased to 5,670 millions of tons of water, or more than $5\frac{1}{2}$ times the original amount.[3] Sir Murdoch MacDonald, the Consulting Engineer, was asked to devise a plan for re-heightening the dam, and this necessitated thickening it as well as adding to its height. He adopted the novel principle of making the thickening slide freely over the older structure, thus providing for temperature effects on its mass. This was secured by dressing to a smooth surface the downstream face of the existing structure, so that no bond was given to the new work. The International Commission, which was appointed in view of the magnitude

---

[1] The foundation stone was relaid by H.R.H. The Duke of Connaught on February 29th, 1908.
[2] Notes by Colonel Sir Henry Lyons, F.R.S., late R.E., sent to the author on December 6th, 1934.
[3] *Egyptian Government Almanac*, 1934, p. 299.

THE ASWAN DAM.

[*Photo by the Author.*]

of the undertaking to advise on it before any scheme of heightening could be adopted, recommended the insertion of rustless steel plating between the two works to ensure greater certainty of freedom of movement. The cost of the undertaking, including alterations to locks, the construction of subsidiary works and compensation to landowners, was about £E.4,500,000. The Aswan Reservoir now almost submerges the Philae temples, and raises the level of the Nile as far south as Wadi Halfa, more than 200 miles upstream from the dam. It has repaid its cost many times over, and is a lasting monument to the ability of the eminent civil engineers who were concerned in its design and erection.

In addition to the consolidation of the Nile Barrage and the construction of the Aswan Dam and the Zifta Barrage, the twentieth century has seen the completion of many other irrigation works on the Nile, associated with the names of Sir William Willcocks, Sir Benjamin Baker, Sir Arthur Webb, Sir John Aird, Sir William Garstin, Sir Murdoch MacDonald, Mr. C. E. Dupuis and their successors. In 1902, a barrage was completed at Asyut, halfway between Aswan and Cairo, which was designed to feed the great Ibrahimiya Canal and thus to assist perennial irrigation in the areas served by it. Seven years later, the construction of another barrage was finished at Isna, 110 miles north of Aswan, and by 1930, yet another barrage had been provided at Nag Hammadi between Asyut and Isna, but no Royal Engineers were employed on these works. The Nag Hammadi Barrage in Egypt was one of a series of schemes, recommended by the Nile Projects Commission of 1921, to meet the progressive demands of agriculture at all seasons of the year and to safeguard the country against the effects of an abnormally high flood, the other recommendations being for works in or near the Sudan. The latter included two schemes already in hand, that is to say, a reservoir and dam at Sennar on the Blue Nile to feed a canal system irrigating the fertile and cotton-producing Gezira Plain, south of Khartoum, and to form also an additional reserve for Egypt, and a reservoir and dam at Jebel Auliya on the White Nile, 27 miles south of Khartoum, to increase Egypt's summer supply and afford protection against high floods. The provision of a reservoir and dam at Lake Tsana in Abyssinia was proposed in order to increase the supply to the Sudan and assist flood control on the Blue Nile. Works were advocated at Lake Albert to complete the storage necessary to meet the ultimate demands of Egypt ; and a " short-circuit " channel in the *sudd* region of the Bahr el Jebel was recommended to ensure that the water from the Lake Albert reservoir should flow northwards rapidly and without undue loss from evaporation and absorption.[1]

[1] See " The Nile Control and Irrigation Problems of Egypt," by Capt. F. C. T. Noakes, R.E., appearing in the *R.E. Journal*, Vol. XLVIII, 1934, pp. 528–538.

The Sennar Dam, and the Gezira Canal leading from it, were designed in 1911 by Sir Murdoch MacDonald. Preliminary arrangements were begun in 1914, and after many interruptions caused by the Great War, the work was completed in 1925 at a cost of £E.8,250,000. The dam is of grey granite masonry, about 108 feet high and nearly 2 miles in length, and impounds 781 millions of tons of water. The Gezira canal system has 160 miles of main channel[1] and 2,000 miles of distributary channel, and waters an ever-increasing area of cotton. This is the only large irrigation system in the country.[2] The scheme for a reservoir at Lake Tsana was delayed for many years by difficulties in dealing with the Abyssinian Government, and is now further complicated by the Italian annexation. It is noteworthy that in 1916 Major H. D. Pearson, D.S.O., R.E., led a Mission to Abyssinia to obtain information and data for building a dam at the neck of Lake Tsana, and mapped the shores of the lake. As for the proposed reservoir at Lake Albert and the channel in the *sudd* region, the necessary resources have not yet become available for such difficult undertakings.

The Jebel Auliya Dam is nearing completion and is of particular interest to Royal Engineers because Captain H. S. Francis, R.E., was on the engineering staff of the work for several years and thus revived the past connection of the Corps with Irrigation on the Nile. Owing to the rapid rise of the Blue Nile in flood, the waters of the White Nile, as already explained, are held back until they are released by the subsidence of the Blue Nile. Consequently, a dam was planned at Jebel Auliya, close above Khartoum, in order to take full advantage of the water held temporarily in the White Nile, and by storing it and subsequently releasing it, to protect Egypt and assist the Aswan Reservoir in supplying Egypt during the season of Low Nile. The reservoir so formed will secure the perennial irrigation of hitherto uncultivated areas in Egypt amounting to 1,900,000 acres, and also of 1,200,000 acres under basin irrigation which produce only one crop annually.[3] According to Sir Murdoch MacDonald, the exact site for the dam was not chosen until Lord Kitchener, Sir Reginald Wingate, Sir Arthur Webb, Sir Murdoch MacDonald, Mr. P. M. Tottenham (Inspector-General of Irrigation) and Mr. H. H. McClure (of Messrs. Aird and Company) visited Jebel Auliya in January, 1914. Sir Murdoch MacDonald then advised Lord Kitchener that the most suitable site would be at the Jebel itself, where the flanks of

---

[1] The maximum bed width of the main channel is 40 metres (131 feet), and the maximum discharge is 115 cubic metres per second (4,062 cusecs).

[2] Lieut.-Colonel Sir Edward Midwinter, K.B.E., C.B., C.M.G., D.S.O., R.E. (retd.), General Manager, Sudan Government Railways, was associated with the Gezira Irrigation Scheme from 1917 onwards, and in 1923 became the representative of the Sudan Government for this project.

[3] *Report on the Finances, Administration and Condition of Egypt and the Sudan*, 1914–1919, p. 42.

the work could be properly secured, and Lord Kitchener signified his approval.

The Jebel Auliya Dam consists of two main works—a granite masonry structure across the bed of the river, prolonged westwards by an embankment across a wide area which is flooded only for a few weeks at High Nile. The total length of the gravity dam and embankment is more than 3 miles, and that of the dam itself about 1 mile. Included in the latter is a massive lock, 59 feet wide, and a sluice dam, 497 yards in length, containing 50 openings fitted with gates.[1] The dam will raise the Low Nile level by 21 feet—a small amount in comparison with that at Aswan—but it will form a wide reservoir stretching southwards for 200 miles and holding nearly twice as much water as the Aswan Reservoir.

After undergoing a special course of instruction in England and Scotland, Captain H. S. Francis, R.E., arrived at Jebel Auliya in October, 1933, to find himself the only British Assistant Engineer serving under Mr. F. S. Maconachie, the Chief Engineer of the contractors, Messrs. Gibson and Pauling. Another British engineer had recently been invalided, and Francis was assisted only by a Sudanese engineer and a draughtsman, while a Syrian engineer continued the erection of buildings. However, he took charge at once of the rock excavation, the plotting of rock sections, the marking of lines and levels, the organization of the drawing office and the computations from measurements. In November, he started the triangulation scheme to fix the position of the lock, and from it the line of the sluice dam, taking angles and marking points by day and computing far into the night. Two additional European assistants then arrived, and Francis was able to devote his entire attention to excavation work until March, 1934, when his health suffered and he was obliged to take leave. Afterwards, he was employed on the most difficult part of the whole project, the construction of the massive lock, on which he was engaged when the author visited the work in January, 1935. At mid-day, the heat in the rocky bed of the river was almost insupportable, and gave some indication of what the conditions must have been in the fiery furnace of the previous summer months.

Writing in 1894 of the achievements of Colonel Sir Colin Scott-Moncrieff and his assistants, Lord Milner remarked,[2] " The longer I remained in Egypt and the more I saw of the country, the more clear it became to me that the work of these men had been the basis of all the material improvement of the past ten years. We at the Finance Office have, so to speak, registered that improvement in our easier budgets and growing surpluses. But it is the engineers who have

---

[1] Full details of the project are given in an article entitled " The Gebel Aulia Dam," by Capt. H. S. Francis, R.E., appearing in the *R.E. Journal*, Vol. XLIX, 1935, pp. 169–180.

[2] *England in Egypt*, by Alfred Milner (1894), p. 310.

created it." The same may be said of the Sudan. In Egypt and the Sudan, as in India, engineering works of the greatest magnitude provide a monument to the beneficence of British rule; and perhaps the most remarkable of these are the massive dams and barrages, in the design, building or repair of some of which, a few Royal Engineers have been concerned.

THE MAHMUDIYA CANAL
[*from " The Route of the Overland Mail to India"*

CHAPTER XV.

RAILWAYS.

BY the completion of the railway from Wadi Halfa to Halfaya near Khartoum at the end of 1899, the Northern Sudan was provided with a main line of communication well adapted to the military and administrative needs of a newly conquered territory, while the older line from Wadi Halfa to Kerma sufficed temporarily for the almost depopulated province of Dongola. The Railway staff of Royal Engineers was small but efficient. Brevet Major G. B. Macauley, the Director of Railways, with Lieutenants E. C. Midwinter, D.S.O., W. E. Longfield, M. E. Sowerby and W. R. G. Wollen maintained the reputation earned by Kitchener's " Band of Boys," of whom Macauley and Midwinter alone remained. No less than 778 miles of track had been completed in 3½ years, but the line was of a rough and ready type. " The track had been laid with the utmost speed," writes Longfield,[1] " and nothing had been done save what was absolutely essential for the movement of trains. The only passengers had been soldiers : the only goods traffic, munitions and equipment : the only animal traffic, cavalry horses and transport camels. Two-thirds of the work had been done against time and under war conditions, and the whole had been carried out with the most rigid economy. The light rails, weighing only 50 lb. per yard, were spiked to uncreosoted white-wood sleepers. Sidings had been laid down at intervals of 25 or 30 miles, because trains could not pass each other without them. Pumps and tanks had been installed at two of the desert stations, and at Abu Hamed, Abidiya and Shendi, because engines could not move without water. South of Abu Hamed, a few of the larger watercourses were in the process of being bridged. Shelters for artisans had been erected at some stations, otherwise the European staff would have collapsed from heat-stroke. A telephone had been set up at every station, otherwise collisions would have occurred daily ; and at wayside stations, a ragged bell-tent, which sheltered a telephone fixed to an upright sleeper, housed also the station-master and the telephone clerk. At the more important stations, conditions were slightly better ; but at Halfa alone was there any adequate equipment for the erection and repair of the rolling stock, and for the accommodation of the Railway Battalion and the civilian staff. The headquarters of the railway at that place conformed to the general standard. A mud-walled house of four

[1] *The Sudan Railways*, by Lieut.-Colonel W. E. Longfield, R.E. (retd.)

rooms, with an uneven floor of beaten earth, accommodated the Director of Railways, the Traffic Manager, the Locomotive Superintendent, a Coptic accountant, a Syrian traffic inspector and an Egyptian clerk. A date-palm grew in the Director's office and helped to support a roof of loose boards laid on rails."

The old railway station building at Wadi Halfa had been converted into a hospital, and not a railway platform existed from one end of the line to the other. The number of goods wagons was sufficient; but the passenger accommodation consisted only of two coaches of primitive design, each capable of holding eight persons. The Chief Engineer lived mostly in an antique saloon carriage with shrunken woodwork and 24 loose windows, which excluded neither dust, heat nor cold. British officers and officials travelled in covered goods wagons, 30 feet long, each wagon being divided by a canvas screen into two compartments, in one of which were the servants, cooking pots and other paraphernalia. These "box-trucks," however, were not suitable for the needs of the pampered tourist, and accordingly a small dining car and a bathroom car were designed and built in the Halfa workshops.

The bathroom car was a closed wagon with a lead-covered floor and a water-tank on the roof. "It certainly afforded both hot and cold water," remarks Longfield, "but the choice did not lie with the bather. If he elected to have a bath in the early morning after the train had passed through the Abu Hamed desert, the water was very cold; and if he preferred a bath before dinner after a hot, dusty day, the effect of the sun on the iron roof was to provide water whose temperature would have done credit to a Roman hypocaust." The sleeping and dining cars of the tourist train were electrically lighted from a dynamo driven by a steam engine on wheels which bore a striking resemblance to a threshing machine. The dynamo and steam engine were bolted on to a flat railway wagon and gave a somewhat incongruous appearance to the train, but they added enormously to the comfort of the passengers. These few details will suffice to show that in the year 1900, the Sudan Government Military Railway, though cheap and effective, was but the shadow of the luxurious system over which tourists and officials are now transported from Wadi Halfa or Port Sudan to far beyond Khartoum.

Soon after the railway reached Halfaya, it became obvious that sections of the line were in danger of destruction by floods, or by the depredations of white ants. Between Abu Hamed and the Atbara, except for one diversion inland, the line followed the right bank of the Nile, and in many places the embankment obstructed the natural flow of storm-water descending to the river. Accordingly, it was necessary to provide a great number of bridges and culverts in this section. Serious trouble through flooding was experienced also between the Atbara and Khartoum during the summer of 1900, when

ON THE DESERT RAILWAY AT DAWN.
No. 1 Station near Wadi Halfa.

[*Photo by the Author.*]

long stretches of the line were repeatedly washed away by heavy storms, and the railway south of the engineering headquarters at Shendi was put out of action for 6 weeks. White ants destroyed many miles of the line south of the Atbara. The old pine sleepers laid 15 years earlier on the Batn el Hagar section of the Kerma line, and those on the more recently built Desert Railway, showed no sign of damage; but similar sleepers laid across the alluvial plains between the Atbara and Khartoum, where the rainfall is more regular, fell an easy prey to the destructive termites and had to be replaced by steel sleepers, the creosoted wooden sleeper being then unknown. Fortunately, Lord Cromer paid a second visit to Khartoum at the end of 1900 and noted the difficulties of maintaining the railway. He arranged for a loan of £E.500,000 for bridge construction, the replacement of sleepers, the provision of additional locomotives and rolling stock and other improvements, and enabled Macauley and his staff to repair the line and make it fit to cope with the immediate demands of a steadily increasing traffic.

Nevertheless, it was obvious that a single military line of railway was unsuitable as the main artery for the expanding trade of a vast country, especially when that line had no outlet on the sea-coast but was connected to it by a combined river and railway route nearly 1,000 miles in length. The Sudan demanded a railway terminus at a sea-port for the proper development of her agricultural resources, and that port must be within her own boundaries, that is to say, it must be on the Red Sea coast and not on the Mediterranean. This had been realized by Lord Kitchener long before he reconnoitred in 1899 with Macauley from Kassala down the Wadi Baraka to Tokar and Suakin.[1] In spite of the failure of the short line from Suakin to Otao in 1885, Kitchener was convinced that a satisfactory route could be found through the Red Sea hills to connect the interior plateau with the coast. He reconnoitred by way of Kassala because he believed that a line following that route would be short and would tap the rich grain-producing areas around Gedaref, farther to the south; but he did not overlook the possibility that a better route might exist leading directly to the coast from the Nile at or near Atbara, and consequently he returned from Suakin through Sinkat to Atbara. On his way he noticed, some 30 miles north of Suakin, a fine natural harbour at a spot known as Sheikh Barghut (now Port Sudan) and remarked that it might be used as a terminal port in preference to Suakin, to which a branch line could be run. Finally, after the completion of his journey to Atbara, he informed Lieutenant G. F. Gorringe, R.E., that he had decided in favour of a line from Atbara to the coast, with a terminal port, if possible, at Sheikh Barghut. Then came the South African War, and his departure to new fields of endeavour and

[1] See the *Sketch Map of the Sudan Government Railways in 1930 (south of Abu Hamed)* which is included in this chapter. The reconnaissance by Kitchener and Macauley in 1899 is alluded to in Chapter XI.

conquest. When funds became available, the investigations were resumed by his successor, Sir Reginald Wingate; for whatever linking up of the interior of the Sudan might subsequently be undertaken, the first essential was a line to the Red Sea.

Serious consideration was given to the main caravan route running from Berber, north of Atbara, through Obak and Kokreb to Suakin, for it provided the shortest road to the sea. Water was obtainable at intervals along it, and it had been roughly mapped; but the reconnaissances for the abortive Suakin-Otao Railway had proved that the gradients from the watershed of the Red Sea hills down to the coastal plain would be too severe for a railway unless a valley could be found running north and south, by which a greater length, and consequently a more easily graded line, could be secured. It seems that, at this period, the possible advantages of Sheikh Barghut as a terminal port were overshadowed by the obvious, though mediocre, claims of Suakin, and accordingly all reconnaissances for a Nile-Red Sea Railway were directed on Suakin.

Two Railway officers, Lieutenants W. E. Longfield and S. F. Newcombe, R.E.,[1] began to reconnoitre from the Nile in June, 1901. They did not follow the old caravan route from Berber, but marched up the right bank of the Atbara River towards Adarama and Kassala. At this time, there was an idea that the district around Kassala must be served as soon as possible by the projected railway because it was a centre of the cotton and grain trade, and accordingly the reconnoitring officers were instructed to select a suitable site for the junction of a branch line to Kassala with the main line. Following the track of the old telegraph line built in Gordon's time, they passed through ruined Adarama and reached Goz Regeb, 180 miles up the Atbara. They were unable to recommend a site for a junction; but they decided that Khor el Hilg, 30 miles from the mouth of the Atbara, would be a suitable point from which to make a further examination of the eastern desert.

"The problems to be solved were two," writes Longfield. "First, what water-supply could be counted upon for the first 200 miles of the railway between the Nile and the foothills of the Red Sea range, where the country was open and the gradients easy; and secondly, what constructional difficulties would be encountered in crossing the range itself, where water was at times abundant but the gradients would be severe. The first reconnaissance of the route was made, not by an Engineer officer, but by Abdulla Amran, surnamed Gaharid, one of the two Arab guides who had served under Pritchard and Hall when the railway was being laid to Abu Hamed.[2] Gaharid's instructions were simple. He was told to ride from Khor el Hilg to Sinkat, and onwards by way of the Khor Adit to Suakin; he was then

---

[1] Lieuts. S. F. Newcombe and P. C. Lord, R.E., had joined the Egyptian Army on April 2nd, 1901, and had been posted to the Sudan Government Railways.
[2] See Chapter IX.

to return at once by the caravan road from Suakin to Berber and make his report at the Railway headquarters at Wadi Halfa. With the exception of the Gemilab, the tribes of the Red Sea hills were friendly, and Gaharid's journey seems to have been devoid of incident. The value of his reconnaissance, and the accuracy of his report, are shown by the fact that, of the three " ruling points " on the Nile-Red Sea railway—Tehamiyam Wells, the Summit Ridge and the Kamob Sanha Cutting—he indicated the first two as places through which the line must pass. He stated also that for the greater part of the way the country was open and had good wells, and that there was no steep mountain ridge to be crossed. Macauley then decided that a reconnaissance for the railway should be made along the route followed by the Arab."

In September, 1901, Longfield and S. F. Newcombe set out again from Berber, and having ascended the Atbara to Khor el Hilg, rode eastwards for 70 miles to the Wells of Tendera. Their route lay far to the south of the final trace of the railway line ; but this was of small importance as a railway could be built anywhere across such open desert, provided that water was available. From Tendera, they rode north-eastwards through the oases of Miv and Oi until they debouched into the Tehamiyam Valley below the Wells of Tehamiyam, at a point near the present Haiya Junction of the Kassala Railway. It was then obvious that Gaharid had been justified in maintaining that the railway must pass up the deep-cut Tehamiyam Valley if it were to surmount the main watershed at the " Summit," 7 miles south of Sinkat. Gaharid had ridden from Tehamiyam Wells to the Summit through lateral valleys affording easy passage for his camel, though not for a railway. Longfield and Newcombe noted a suitable railway route to the east on the Barameiyu Plateau, which extends to the Summit. They crossed the Summit at over 3,000 feet above sea-level, passed Sinkat Wells, and followed the downward course of the Khor Adit for 20 miles through bare, rocky and rugged country intersected by narrow valleys. The Khor was very tortuous ; but there was always a shelf, between the bed and the precipitous sides, wide enough for a line of railway.

So far, all had been easy. It seemed probable that the Khor Adit would open into the broad Khor Okwat, which might afford a suitable route to the coastal plain ; but at a place called Kamob Sanha, some 40 miles from the Summit, Longfield and Newcombe found their way northwards barred by a massive saddle of the hardest rock. The Khor Totali, as the Khor Adit was now called, swung sharply to the right and fell at a slope of 1 in 70. It was necessary to leave it and survey for a cutting through the saddle to the Khor Okwat, which lay beyond. Fortunately, the survey showed that a cutting 40 feet deep, and less than ½ mile in length, would suffice to reach the Khor Okwat without exceeding the remarkably flat ruling gradient of 1 in

100 which had hitherto been maintained, and a further survey of the Okwat Valley indicated that, by swinging the line from side to side across the bed, the same ruling gradient could be secured. The last halting place was at the Well of Sallom, whence the party turned southwards round the foothills and reached Suakin on October 15th, 1901. Thus ended a notable reconnaissance, which proved that an easily graded railway could be built from the Nile to the Red Sea without any serious engineering difficulty other than a deep cutting in hard rock at Kamob Sanha.

It seemed so incredible that an Arab camel-man should have discovered the best railway route through the Red Sea hills that Longfield and S. F. Newcombe were directed to examine the Meiz Pass, some 50 miles south of Suakin, before they returned to the Nile. Two days riding brought them to the pass; but a brief reconnaissance was sufficient to show that it was quite unsuitable for a railway. Next, they headed north-westwards along the Barameiyu Plateau and then descended into the Tehamiyam Valley, which they followed to its junction with the great Khor Arab. Afterwards, they marched westwards along the Khor Arab through Shediyeb to Talguharai (Talgwareb), in both of which places were shallow wells. The country was now open and the gradients easy, and a final journey of 140 miles across a waterless desert brought them back once more to the Nile. Although they had found a practicable route for the railway, it was possible that a better one might exist through the unmapped territory south of Sinkat or north of the Khor Okwat, and these tracts came accordingly under close consideration. It was soon evident that the southern area was unsuitable because its rugged valleys led too steeply downwards to the coastal plain, and accordingly, subsequent reconnaissances were confined to the northern area and chiefly to the region lying within 30 miles of Kamob Sanha and the Khor Okwat. The last reconnaissance ended in April, 1902, without the discovery of a better route than that through Tehamiyam, Sinkat and Kamob Sanha.

The detailed survey of the selected route was entrusted also to Longfield and Newcombe. Early in November, 1902, they crossed the desert from Berber to Suakin, accompanied by a small detachment of the Railway Battalion and by a civil engineer, Mr. C. M. Hickley, who was to take charge of the engineering preparations at Suakin, and beginning their survey at Graham's Point, near the entrance to Suakin Harbour, completed it at Atbara on the right bank of the Nile in April, 1903. The only serious difficulty which they encountered was in tracing the alignment up the Khor Okwat to the Kamob Sanha saddle without exceeding a gradient of 1 in 100. Not a tunnel nor a viaduct was needed, and on the western side of the Sinkat summit it was possible to keep the maximum gradient down to 1 in 125. An alignment was selected from Tehamiyam, through Talguharai, direct to the Nile, in spite of the fact no water was obtainable in the 140 miles of desert between Talguharai and Atbara. On the alternative route through Oi, Mib and Tendera to Khor el Hilg on the Atbara and thence down that river to the Nile, it would have been necessary to traverse only 70 miles of waterless country between Tendera and Khor el Hilg ; but as this route would add 30 miles to the length of the line, it was not adopted. Hopes were entertained that borings between Talguharai and Atbara would eventually ease the difficulties of water-supply.

The survey of the Nile-Red Sea Railway having been completed, Lord Cromer and Sir Reginald Wingate invited Mr. Bakewell, an independent expert, to examine the proposed route, which he did from Atbara to Suakin in January, 1904, in company with Macauley and Longfield. He reported that the railway, when constructed would be economical and easy to operate, and Lord Cromer was satisfied. The next question was whether the railway should be built by a contractor, or by the existing railway staff, employing their own labour. Could the railway staff of young Royal Engineers, experienced builders of military lines, realize and cope with the requirements of an essentially commercial venture ? In their favour it was urged that, for the greater part of its length, the line would traverse flat desert country to which they were accustomed ; that the engineering work in the Red Sea hills would not be difficult ; and that the proper organization and management of the base depot at Suakin were within their powers. In the end, Lord Cromer decided that Macauley and his officers should be entrusted with the work, one contract alone—that for the necessary masonry and the erection of steel-work—being given to a contractor, Mr. George Urquhart.[1]

Since his arrival in Suakin in November, 1902, Mr. C. M. Hickley had been occupied in making arrangements for the reception and unloading of large ships, a task in which he was soon joined by Lieutenant Drury, R.N. Unloading was to be done at Graham's Point on to iron pontoons, moored alongside a causeway designed to carry a line of railway, and it was necessary not only to construct the causeway, but to build and launch the pontoons. "The first of the four pontoons," remarks Longfield, " was finished on Quarantine Island in the summer of 1903, and Drury and Hickley were of opinion that its launching should be accompanied by suitable ceremonial. The proceedings opened with an official luncheon, after which the Governor and his staff and all the guests adjourned to the slipway to see the launching. The wedges were knocked out, the tackles manned, a bottle of champagne broken against the iron plating, and Drury gave the order to heave. The pontoon refused to budge ! Headed by the guests, a general rush was made for the ropes, and all

[1] *The Sudan Railways*, by Lieut.-Colonel W. E. Longfield, R.E. (retd.)

pulled and pushed in a vain attempt to move the big iron box. After an hour's strenuous work, the party broke up exhausted, and Drury and his staff sat down to devise new means of moving the pontoon. They succeeded three days later, and the pontoon was towed across to the causeway."

The last of the four pontoons was not launched until April 15th, 1904, by which time Suakin had become a hive of industry. Much trouble had been experienced in increasing the water-supply, for a steamer carrying condensing plant had been wrecked in January, 1904, and it was necessary to improve and use the local system of wells until new plant could be sent out. Two ship-loads of rolling stock, machinery, materials and supplies arrived during February and March, by which time engineering work was already in hand on one section of the line. Macauley had realized that the only undertaking liable to delay the completion of the line was the deep cutting at Kamob Sanha, and with commendable foresight had set 200 men to begin the excavation in the autumn of 1903. This work, which was carried out with jumping-bars and similar tools in the hardest diorite rock, occupied more than a year and was finished only a few weeks before rail-head reached Kamob Sanha in the winter of 1904–05.

In an article written in October, 1903,[1] Macauley described the general alignment of the projected railway between the Nile and the Red Sea and explained the considerations which had influenced the choice of the route. These were that the line as proposed was capable of being connected cheaply with the Kassala District and the Eastern Sudan; that its junction with the main line to Khartoum was within reasonable distance of that place, and yet not too far from the Dongola Province and the mining districts between that province and the Red Sea; and that it had a ruling gradient of 1 in 100 (instead of 1 in 60 by any other route), a maximum curvature of only 5 degrees, wells at certain places, and a minimum of earthwork. " The direct Suakin-Berber caravan road," wrote Macauley, " is considerably shorter than the route chosen; but it has steeper gradients (1 in 60), heavier earthwork, more rock, and a belt of drifting sandhills, 2 miles wide and 100 miles long, near Obak. Also it is not so suitable for administrative reasons as the route selected . . . . The length of the projected line, to the junction near the Atbara, is 332 miles. The gauge is 3 feet 6 inches; the maximum gradient, 1 in 100; the sharpest curve, 5 degrees. There are 64 miles of continuous 1 in 100 gradient between Suakin and Sinkat, and the work in this section is heavy. The country is rocky, there are high banks and steep cuttings, and it is impossible to run a line anywhere, except in the beds of the *khors*, without incurring enormous

---

[1] " The Suakin Nile Railway," by Major G. B. Macauley, R.E., appearing in the *R.E. Journal*, Vol. 33, 1903, pp. 245–246.

expenditure. Many bridges and culverts will be required in this section. Between Sinkat and Atbara, the earthwork is easier; but the soil is like cotton soil and will give considerable trouble in the rainy season. The maximum gradient in this section is 1 in 130,[1] and the sharpest curve, 3 degrees. The chief difficulties in constructing the line are the almost entire absence of water along parts of the route and the heavy work in the Suakin hills. Also, the storms which occur in these hills will wash away the line unless the bridges and culverts are put in as the line advances.[2] Heavy engines will be used on the Suakin–Sinkat section; they will pull the same train over these steeper gradients as the lighter engines will pull over the easier gradients between Sinkat and Atbara. The Suakin-Sinkat section will be laid with 75-lb. rails and heavy sleepers; the remainder of the line with 50-lb. rails and lighter sleepers. The construction is to take 2 years and is to begin in October, 1904, and the cost will be about £6,000 a mile, using Arab labour."

Macauley added that the line would be laid from the Suakin end only—an arrangement which was subsequently altered—and as regards the choice of a terminal sea-port he remarked as follows:—
" When it was decided to adopt the route through Khor Okwat, Sheikh el Barud (Sheikh Barghut) suggested itself as a possible terminus and harbour. On consulting the hydrographer to the Admiralty, the place was found to be unsuitable for a harbour, and so Suakin was chosen as the terminus of the line." Regarding this matter, however, Sir Reginald Wingate wrote subsequently in his official report for the year 1904:[3]—" In the course of the year an important point arose as to the establishment of a new port of entry for the Sudan. Owing to some misunderstanding, which it is now hard to explain, the Government was under the impression that the British naval authorities considered Suakin the most suitable port of entry. Correspondence took place which showed that this was not the case. A Commission was therefore dispatched to investigate the question, and they have reported in favour of establishing the port of entry at Sheikh el Barghut, some 30 miles north of Suakin. It will in future be known as Port Sudan. It has therefore been decided that the construction of the railway should proceed from Suakin as originally determined, and that on its completion, the terminus should be transferred to the new port. Consequent on this decision, the construction or amelioration of the new harbour is being

---

[1] During construction it was found that a gradient of 1 in 125 was needed in some places.

[2] The following girder bridges were erected on the Nile-Red Sea Railway:—35 spans of 105 feet and 54 spans of 55 feet, all being " through " bridges. A great number of small-span bridges and culverts were also built. Full details of the railway are given in Paper No. 35, " Sudan Government Railways and Steamers," by Mr. F. G. A. Pinckney, published by the Institution of Civil Engineers in 1926.

[3] Memorandum, dated March, 1905, by Major-General Sir Reginald Wingate, Governor-General of the Sudan, pp. 18–19, appearing in the *Report on the Finances, Administration and Condition of the Sudan*, 1904.

taken in hand under the direction of Captain M. R. Kennedy, R.E., the Director of Works."

Thus the honour of becoming the main gateway to the Sudan was rightly denied to the ancient but ill-adapted port of Suakin. The foundation and development of Port Sudan will be described in another chapter; but it may be mentioned here that the short alignment from Sallom to Sheikh Barghut was reconnoitred by Captain W. E. Longfield and Lieutenant S. F. Newcombe, R.E., in the autumn of 1904 to ascertain whether there would be any difficulty in bringing the railway down to the new harbour. They found that, with the exception of a few watercourses, the route offered no obstacles to railway construction. The country appeared to be completely uninhabited. Near the entrance to the harbour—a narrow passage between dangerous reefs of coral—stood the white tomb of the patron Sheikh, and on the shore, a fisherman's hut. There was no other habitation nor sign of life.

The building of the railway from the Red Sea to the Nile was begun on September 1st, 1904, but was much delayed during its early stages by labour difficulties and damage caused by heavy rain. Experiments with local labour failed, and men recruited from the Berber District proved to be unsatisfactory. *Saidis* from Northern Egypt were then imported to carry out the earthwork, and were found to be excellent labourers. By the middle of March, 1905, rail-head was 50 miles from Suakin and advancing through the Red Sea hills at the rate of $\frac{1}{2}$-mile a day under the superintendence of Captains W. E. Longfield and M. E. Sowerby, R.E., assisted by Messrs. A. R. Windham, J. E. Montague and C. M. Hickley and four Egyptian officers. The Director of Railways was at Suakin, where he was in close touch with the work and with the organization for the supply of material.[1] The Assistant Director, Captain E. C. Midwinter, D.S.O., R.E., acted for him at the Railway headquarters at Wadi Halfa.

"During the spring and summer of 1905," writes Longfield,[2] "while the Suakin rail-head was being steadily pushed on through the hill-country, another rail-head was advancing eastwards across the desert to meet it. This was an insurance against delays which might prevent the completion of the line in the winter of 1905–06, the date given by Macauley. The loss of the condensers, and the labour difficulties, had threatened to retard the work so seriously that Macauley had decided to build 120 miles of line eastward from the Nile. It was a wise decision; but it threw a heavy burden on the staff of the main line from Wadi Halfa to Khartoum who, in addition to their normal work, were now engaged in pulling up the old railway between Halfa and Kerma and transferring the material to the rail-

---

[1] During the later stages of the work, Lieut. W. E. Longfield was often at Suakin as an assistant to Major Macauley, or acting for him when Macauley visited rail-head.

[2] *The Sudan Railways*, by Lieut.-Colonel W. E. Longfield, R.E. (retd.)

head of a new branch line that was being laid towards Kareima near Merowe. Midwinter and his staff on the Nile side had therefore to organize, equip and maintain two rail-heads, and to arrange for the transport of the necessary stores and material by the long and inconvenient route from Alexandria."

Construction from the Atbara end of the Nile-Red Sea Railway was supervised at first by Lieutenant S. F. Newcombe, R.E., who had previously been digging and improving wells in the desert at places where water was obtainable. Newcombe carried the rail-head forward until he was relieved in the summer of 1905 by Lieutenant R. E. M. Russell, R.E.[1] The extension from Atbara was simple, for it lay through stony and almost featureless desert. Low embanking, and occasional shallow cutting, were sufficient. *Saidi* labourers did the earthwork, and Railway Battalion conscripts the track-work. It was found that the *Saidis* could excavate up to 14 cubic metres a day for banking up to 4 feet in height, and for this herculean task they received 1 piastre (2½d.) per cubic metre. Russell remarks that an excellent feature of Macauley's organization was that the engineers at rail-head were relieved from all accounting and could thus devote their whole attention to engineering.[2] Their chief problems were sickness among the men, correct requisitioning for materials, and occasional difficulties in the supply of water. On one occasion, while Russell was absent at Atbara, a violent dust-storm covered several miles of track with sand, derailed two of the three available locomotives, and left the rail-head gangs of about 1,000 men stranded 80 miles out in the desert. Instructions were telegraphed immediately to rail-head that work should be stopped and the water-reserve guarded and rationed, and thus a catastrophe was averted; but four days elapsed before further supplies reached the marooned workers.

With the end of the rains in September, 1905, the rate of progress of the railway from Suakin increased to ¾-mile a day, and early in October the two rail-heads were only an hour's camel-ride apart. The Atbara rail-head halted at the end of September at its allotted point 120 miles from the Nile, and while it awaited the arrival of the Suakin rail-head, most of its workmen were transferred to the Kareima line. The junction was effected on October 15th, and on the following day the first train from Atbara steamed proudly into the terminus at Graham's Point outside Suakin. Engineers and workmen then proceeded to Sallom to lay the branch line to Port Sudan, which was reached on December 31st. There, on January 27th, 1906, Lord Cromer performed the opening ceremony of the Nile-Red Sea Railway.

[1] Lieut. R. E. M. Russell, R.E., had been posted to the Egyptian Army on April 2nd, 1905.
[2] Notes by Colonel R. E. M. Russell, C.V.O., C.B.E., D.S.O., late R.E., sent to the author on August 30th, 1936. The accounting was done by a separate branch, staffed by native officials.

The Government had excellent reasons for constructing a branch line down the Nile, from No. 10 Station on the Desert Railway to Kareima below the Fourth Cataract, for the service of the Province of Dongola. The old Kerma Railway from Wadi Halfa, which had hitherto answered that purpose after a fashion, was a military line with sharp curves and steep gradients, unsuitable for an expanding commercial traffic. It was badly placed as an artery for trade, for it traversed the unproductive wilderness of the Batn el Hagar, and its southern terminus was isolated from the Central and Southern Sudan by the Bayuda Desert and the Fourth Cataract. On the other hand, a railway less than 140 miles in length, connecting Kareima directly with the main line from Wadi Halfa through Atbara, would allow the valuable date trade of Dongola to reach the Red Sea over the Atbara-Port Sudan line by a route 300 miles shorter than that through Halfa by the Kerma and Desert Railways. Accordingly, it was decided to build the Kareima line with material obtained for the most part by the gradual dismantling of the old Kerma line, over the remaining sections of which a reduced traffic could be maintained until it was no longer needed.[1]

A route for the Kareima Railway was reconnoitred during the winter of 1903–04 by Lieutenant S. F. Newcombe, R.E., and Mr. H. L. V. Hawkins, and again by Newcombe alone, and the latter subsequently made a detailed survey. The alignment was to touch the bank of the Nile only at El Kab and at the terminus at Kareima, whence the river was easily navigable to Kerma and, during the flood season, to Kosha. Construction was begun towards the end of 1904 by a civilian staff under the general control of Captain E. C. Midwinter, D.S.O., R.E.; and in March, 1905, when the track had been laid for a distance of about 50 miles, Captain E. O. A. Newcombe R.E., elder brother of S. F. Newcombe, assumed engineering charge at rail-head.[2] Interrupted only by a period of duty at the Atbara rail-head of the Nile-Red Sea Railway in September and October, 1905, when R. E. M. Russell was on sick leave, E. O. A. Newcombe brought the Kareima line successfully to its terminus above Merowe in February, 1906, and was present when the railway was opened in the following month by Sir Reginald Wingate, the Governor-General of the Sudan.

Life was hard and exacting during the years of intensive development which followed the pacification of the Sudan; yet relaxation was to be found at times in the Railway Mess at Wadi Halfa, where there was always a fund of good stories. It was related, for instance, that on one occasion the Egyptian station-master at No. 6 Station on the Desert Railway reported that a platelayer had died and asked

---

[1] The Kerma Railway was finally closed to all traffic on December 31st, 1904.
[2] Capt. E. O. A. Newcombe, R.E., was assisted by Messrs. G. R. Storrer and J. C. Walker and by a British surveyor. (Letter from Major E. O. A. Newcombe, D.S.O., R.E. (retd.) to the author, dated July 14th, 1936.)

what he should do. " Bury him," was the answer. " But make sure first that he is dead." That seemed to end the matter; but to the surprise of the staff at Wadi Halfa, a second report was received within a few hours from No. 6 Station. "*Buried Muhammad*," it ran, "*and am sure he was dead because I broke his skull with a fish-plate.*"[1]

During the winter of 1905-06, after the completion of the line to Suakin, the headquarters of the Engineering Department of the Sudan Government Railways were transferred to Atbara, and Lieutenant R. E. M. Russell, R.E., was sent there at the end of 1905 to begin the design and construction of a great railway centre. The only building in Atbara was a small station shed, formed by a few sleepers planted vertically in the sand with others laid across them as a roof, and on the river bank were some native huts and the ruins of the old entrenched camp.[2] Amid these dreary surroundings, Russell set to work with planetable and compass and prepared a sketch showing the most favourable sites for a new railway station, offices, workshops, sheds, quarters, a club and a hospital, adding rough designs in pencil for all the buildings. His proposals were approved at Wadi Halfa and he was ordered to commence work. This was no easy task for he had only a smattering of Arabic, and his assistants—a few Egyptian officers—knew little of engineering and could not speak a work of English. However, he taught the local Sudanese to make and burn bricks of the proper size and quality, and to quarry and burn lime for mortar, and he apprenticed gangs of men to a nucleus of Egyptian carpenters and brick-layers to learn their trades. Construction began when the workmen had attained some degree of proficiency, and was well advanced when Russell left Atbara a few months later to survey towards Kassala.

When the engineering headquarters of the railway were moved to Atbara, there was no proper "*suk*" or native bazaar at that place in which the workmen could buy supplies, and the Railway Storekeeper soon noticed that the consumption of axle-grease was going up by leaps and bounds. The matter was reported to the Director of Railways, and after some discussion it was decided that a pint of Croton oil should be added to every barrel of axle-grease in store. The result exceeded all expectations, for a few days later the Senior Medical officer approached the Director after breakfast and announced, with a very grave face, that he feared that a serious outbreak of cholera had started among the employees!

Although an extension of the railway into the fertile Gezira District beyond Khartoum, and thence westwards into Kordofan, had

---

[1] Notes by Major-General Sir Charles W. Gwynn, K.C.B., C.M.G., D.S.O., late R.E., sent to the author on May 25th, 1934.
[2] Notes by Colonel R. E. M. Russell, C.V.O., C.B.E., D.S.O., late R.E., sent to the author on August 30th, 1936.

now become the most urgent demand, it was desirable also that the delta of the River Gash[1] near Kassala should be linked by railway with the Red Sea coast, so that its cotton crop might be exported quickly to foreign markets. The alternatives were a line from Kassala direct to Suakin and Port Sudan—a difficult and costly undertaking —or a line from Kassala to join the Nile-Red Sea Railway near Tehamiyam, and thus to profit by the passage already secured through the Red Sea hills. A line connecting with the Red Sea Railway could be prolonged later to Gedaref, and finally westwards to the Blue Nile at Sennar, where it could join the extension southwards from Khartoum and provide an alternative, though circuitous, route from the capital to the Red Sea. The Kassala-Tehamiyam project being preferred, Lieutenant S. F. Newcombe, R.E., an expert railway surveyor, was sent in the summer of 1906 to reconnoitre a route to Kassala and fixed a preliminary location joining the Red Sea line at Haiya, a few miles west of Tehamiyam Wells.

Shortly afterwards, Russell accompanied Newcombe on camel-back along the alignment to Kassala. Newcombe then started him on the detailed survey from Haiya, which involved placing pegs at 100-foot intervals, laying out curves, drawing cross-sections, and preparing a large-scale map of the ground on each side of the centre line and a small-scale sketch of everything in view beyond it.[2] Fortunately, the ground had already been triangulated by Major C. W. Gwynn, D.S.O., R.E., for an Abyssinian–Eritrean Frontier Commission. Russell had 20 Egyptian conscripts, his servants, and a number of camel-men, but not a soul could read nor write in any language. " During our preliminary reconnaissance, of which I still bear the scars," he writes, " Newcombe and I had selected a suitable point for crossing the River Gash near Aroma north-west of Kassala, and when working towards it, I found no reason for deviating from a true straight line after leaving Ungwatiri. The problem then was to compute the azimuth when the latitude and longitude of the two ends were known. This, however, was beyond my mathematical ability, so I pinned together all the available paper, plotted the alignment carefully several times, took the mean and started off, applying corrections for curvature each day and hoping by these means to obtain a geodetical " straight " as near as a 5-inch theodolite could give it. The pegging occupied a fortnight, and for the last few days we worked through dense bush in the Gash Delta ; but strange to say, the alignment came out absolutely correct, and having finished the detailed survey onwards to Kassala, I reconnoitred for some distance towards Gedaref in view of the possible extension of

---
[1] The Gash, rising in Abyssinia, flows down to Kassala, and then, dividing into several channels, loses itself in the desert sands.
[2] Notes by Colonel R. E. M. Russell, C.V.O., C.B.E., D.S.O., late R.E., sent to the author on August 30th, 1936.

the railway to that place."[1] The length of this remarkable "straight," surveyed on the Kassala line between Ungwatiri and Aroma, was about 76 miles, but many years were to elapse before it could be built. All available money was needed for the development of the railway system beyond Khartoum.

Lieutenant R. Micklem, R.E., joined the Sudan Government Railways in May, 1907, and was the last officer of his Corps to do so.[2] As in India, civil engineers were being recruited in steadily increasing numbers and were filling all vacant posts. Major G. B. Macauley had left the Sudan in October, 1906, to become Director-General of the Egyptian State Railways, and had handed over charge to Captain E. C. Midwinter, under whom were Captains W. E. Longfield, M. E. Sowerby and E. O. A. Newcombe and Lieutenants S. F. Newcombe, R. E. M. Russell and P. C. Lord. Thus, within seven years of the departure of Lord Kitchener, Midwinter was the sole representative of the staff which had built the Kerma and Desert Railways under the leadership of Girouard,

Lieutenants S. F. Newcombe and R. Micklem, R.E., journeyed in 1907 to the upper waters of the Nile to reconnoitre and discuss with the Belgians a possible railway route from the Lado Enclave into the Belgian Congo. The Lado Enclave was a large area around Rejaf[3], which had been leased by Great Britain to King Leopold in 1894, and its northern portion was about to revert to the Sudan under an agreement made in 1906.[4] Newcombe attended negotiations in Brussels during the winter of 1907-08, and revisited the Enclave in May and June, 1910, as a member of a Mission under Captain H. D. Pearson, R.E., which included Lieutenant H. H. Kelly, R.E., Captain C. H. Stigand, R. West Kent Regiment, and Captain T. C. Mackenzie, R.A.M.C. The official transfer of territory was made at Yei, near the Congo and Uganda borders, on June 16th, 1910. From the following November until May, 1911, when he left the Sudan, Newcombe was engaged in exploring railway and transport routes between the Sudan and Abyssinia.[5] He travelled from Gambela, on a tributary of the Sobat River, through Gore to Addis Ababa, and thence westwards to the Wadi Dabus. Afterwards, he followed the latter down to the Blue Nile in Abyssinian territory, and returned to Khartoum through

---

[1] The Kassala Railway was the only line surveyed by Lieut. R. E. M. Russell. He returned to Atbara in October, 1906, to complete his plans and drawings and to resume the building of the railway centre, and in February, 1907, proceeded to Suakin, where he was District Engineer and Railway Agent for a year. Then, he was appointed Agent for the Sudan Government Railways in Alexandria. In June, 1910, he was posted to the Intelligence Department of the Egyptian Army, and thus severed his connection with railway work.

[2] Lieut. R. Micklem, R.E., had been posted to the Egyptian Army on Jan. 24th, 1907.

[3] See the general map of the Anglo-Egyptian Sudan at the end of this volume.

[4] At a later date, the southern portion became part of Uganda.

[5] Notes by Colonel S. F. Newcombe, D.S.O., late R.E., sent to the author on April 23rd, 1936.

Roseires. These distant reconnaissances were valuable, but no railway construction has yet resulted from them.

The Nile-Red Sea Railway having been opened in January, 1906, conferences were held to decide the best positions for a railway station at Khartoum and for a bridge to carry the line across the Blue Nile into the capital. Communication across the river from rail-head at Halfaya Station had been maintained hitherto by a chain-ferry. The Khartoum race-course was chosen as the best locality for a new station, and a site upstream of the Gordon College as the most advantageous for a bridge, and in June, 1907, a contract was given to the Cleveland Bridge and Engineering Company for the construction of a steel girder bridge 1,828 feet in length.[1] Work started in the following autumn, and the permanent bridge was finished at the end of October, 1909, eight months after the first train had crossed the river on a temporary structure.

Railway developments in the Sudan were connected closely with the Gezira irrigation scheme and its corollary, the construction of a dam across the Blue Nile at Sennar. They had been discussed and settled during the construction of the Nile-Red Sea line, when it was decided that an extension southwards from Khartoum should follow the left bank of the Blue Nile through Wad Medani to Sennar and then turn south-westwards across the Gezira plain to Goz Abu Guma on the White Nile near Kosti. The construction of a steel girder bridge, 1,517 feet in length,[2] was begun near Kosti soon after the Blue Nile bridge at Khartoum had been finished, and accordingly the bridge was ready when rail-head reached the White Nile, and there was no delay in carrying on the extension of the railway westwards to El Obeid in Kordofan. A project had been under consideration in 1901 for the construction of a railway west of the Nile from Omdurman to El Obeid, and Lieutenants W. E. Longfield and S. F. Newcombe, R.E., reconnoitred a route in December, 1901, and January, 1902; but several considerations, including the expansion of the cotton industry in the Gezira, put an end to that scheme.

During the winter of 1907–08, S. F. Newcombe made a detailed survey for the projected railway from Khartoum as far as Wad Medani, and afterwards surveyed for the final section from Kosti to El Obeid. He began the construction of the line from Khartoum in April, 1909, and brought rail-head to Wad Medani, through flat and easy country, in the following December. The section from Wad Medani to Sennar was built by Mr. J. C. Walker between April and June, 1910, and on December 28th, 1910, Mr. C. M. Hickley was able to bring rail-head to Kosti, as the White Nile bridge was then

---

[1] The Blue Nile bridge has seven bowstring girder spans, each of 215 feet, one rolling-lift span of 110 feet, and two land spans. It carries a single line of 3 feet 6 inches railway, a roadway with a tram-line, and a wide footway.

[2] The White Nile bridge near Kosti has eight girder spans, each of 146 feet, and a swing-bridge span of 245 feet, pivoted at its centre.

open for traffic.[1] Lieutenant R. Micklem, R.E., next took charge. He laid the track across a flat plain covered with scrub from Kosti to Umm Ruwaba[2] during April, May and June, 1911, and resuming work on October 17th after the rainy season had ended, carried the line to its terminus at El Obeid on December 29th, 1911. This was the last major extension of the Sudan railways in which Royal Engineers took an active part, and it was by a happy chance that when the line was opened at El Obied on February 27th, 1912, the ceremony was performed by Field-Marshal Lord Kitchener, the founder of the Sudan railway system and a Colonel Commandant of the Corps.[3]

After the completion of the line from Khartoum to El Obeid, only one large project awaited further attention. This was for a railway from Haiya on the Red Sea line through Kassala and across the Atbara River to Gedaref, and thence across the Rahad and Dinder tributaries, and the Blue Nile itself, to a junction at Sennar with the El Obeid line. It was arranged that the work should start in the autumn of 1914, but this was prevented by the Great War. Meanwhile, relaying and renewal operations were proceeding steadily. They had been taken in hand between Khartoum and Shendi in 1908, and during the summer of 1910 S. F. Newcombe relaid the line from Shendi to Atbara with 75-lb. rails. Micklem carried out similar work on the desert section of the Nile-Red Sea Railway during the summer of 1911. The Atbara bridge was strengthened in 1910. Long sections of the track were ballasted and many culverts built. The general programme of reconstruction was linked closely with the building of the line to El Obeid, where flat gradients permitted the use of light locomotives and rails. As the distance from Khartoum to El Obeid approximately equalled that from Khartoum through Atbara to the Sinkat Summit on the Red Sea line, the 50-lb. rails removed from the track between Khartoum and the Summit were used for the railway to El Obeid.[4] With the outbreak of war in 1914, relaying was suspended, and little more was done until 1921.[5]

By 1922, the increasing trade and prosperity of the country, and the

[1] The first train crossed the White Nile bridge near Kosti on December 24th, 1910
[2] The alignment deviated southwards to pass through Umm Ruwaba and Er Rahad because water was obtainable at those places, and because the surrounding districts comprised some of the best gum-forests and grazing grounds in the country.
[3] Lord Kitchener was at this time British Agent and Consul General in Egypt.
[4] By 1933, the track from Abu Hamed to Khartoum, and from Atbara to Port Sudan and Suakin, had been relaid with 75-lb. rails on wooden sleepers. Elsewhere, 50-lb. rails on wooden sleepers were in use ; but on the Khartoum-El Obeid line, the Kareima line, and the Kassala line south of Kilometre 190 near Ungwatiri, steel sleepers were employed.
[5] Nevertheless, the responsibilities of the Railway Department were greatly extended during the Great War. By the end of 1917, it had assumed control of all the Government river services, including those from Shellal (above Aswan) to Wadi Halfa, from Khartoum to Rejaf on the White Nile and to the limit of navigation on the Blue Nile, and on the Sobat River to Gambela. It had taken control also of Port Sudan Harbour. The entire transportation system of the Sudan was thus brought under one administration, and it became possible to quote through rates from Port Sudan to Rejaf, and even, by arrangement with the Egyptian State Railways, from Alexandria to Rejaf.

growth of Port Sudan,[1] warranted the building of the long-deferred railway through Kassala for the export of cotton and grain. Consequently, materials and plant were collected, and construction was begun from Haiya Junction on March 31st, 1923, the work being carried out by civil engineers under the general direction of the Chief Engineer, Major P. C. Lord, O.B.E., R.E.[2] The railway reached Kassala through easy country on April 21st, 1924, and construction having been resumed on December 14th, 1926, the line was brought to Gedaref on February 18th, 1928. Another rail-head was then approaching from Sennar to connect with that from Kassala and Gedaref, for the completion of the Sennar Dam in January, 1926, had enabled the engineers to lay a track along it and thus to gain the right bank of the Blue Nile. Large bridges were needed for the crossing of the Upper Atbara between Kassala and Gedaref, and also for crossing the Rahad and Dinder tributaries of the Blue Nile between Gedaref and Sennar; but otherwise few constructional difficulties were encountered, and the Kassala Railway was opened for traffic on February 15th, 1929.

Although no Royal Engineers, other than Major P. C. Lord, were concerned with the building of any part of the loop line of railway through Kassala, the enterprise was controlled, until Kassala was reached, by Lieut.-Colonel (now Sir Edward) Midwinter, C.B., C.M.G., C.B.E., D.S.O., General Manager[3] of the Sudan Government Railways. Lieut.-Colonel E. C. Midwinter retired on March 31st, 1925, after maintaining the Railway Department, for a period of 19 years, in a state of high efficiency which bore testimony to his sound administration and technical ability.[4] Lieut.-Colonel M. E. Sowerby, C.M.G., D.S.O., Chief Engineer from 1906 to 1915, had died while employed on the Egyptian State Railways after the Great War. Lieut.-Colonel R. Micklem, C.M.G., had left the Sudan in May, 1915, and retired in October, 1919; and Lieut.-Colonel W. E. Longfield, after 22 years' railway service, had retired in December, 1922. Many years had elapsed since Captains S. F. Newcombe and R. E. M. Russell had reverted to military employment. The departure of Lieut.-Colonel Midwinter in 1925 was followed in May, 1926, by that of Major P. C. Lord, O.B.E., after 25 years' railway service in the Sudan, exclusive

---

[1] The tonnage carried by the Sudan railway system was as follows :—1903, 46,000; 1907, 134,000; 1911, 186,000; 1915, 223,000; 1919, 232,000; 1920, 357,000; 1921, 552,000; 1924, 733,000. The tonnage of shipping in Port Sudan in 1910 was 431,000. In 1913, it was 692,000; in 1920, 737,000; and in 1922, 1,500,000.

[2] Major P. C. Lord was Chief Engineer, Sudan Government Railways, from April, 1919, to May, 1926.

[3] After the departure of Major G. B. Macauley to the Egyptian State Railways in 1906, Captain E. C. Midwinter became Director of Railways and Captain W. E. Longfield, Assistant Director; but 2 years later, the titles of their appointments were changed to "General Manager" and "Deputy General Manager" respectively.

[4] Memorandum by the Governor-General (p. 9) appearing in the *Report on the Finances, Administration and Condition of the Sudan*, 1925. Lieut.-Colonel Midwinter, who received the Brevet of that rank on January 1st, 1917, was still designated officially as Captain as all officers were ranked according to Egyptian Army seniority and he had retired from the Royal Engineers as a Captain on January 1st, 1907.

of the Great War period ; and finally, in November, 1926, Major E. O. A. Newcombe, D.S.O., after serving on the railways for 21 years, including 19 years as Traffic Manager, bade farewell to the country which he had known since the time of the Dongola Expedition.

Thus, the connection of the Corps of Royal Engineers with the Sudan Government Railways was brought to a close in 1926. Begun when Charles Gordon advised the Egyptian Government to abandon the Wadi Halfa-Saras line in 1877, it was renewed when D. A. Scott, H. W. Clarke and others repaired that line and prolonged it to Akasha in 1884 and 1885. Firmly established by Girouard, Stevenson, Pritchard, Polwhele, Blakeney, Cator, Macauley, Hall, Midwinter, Wollen, H. A. Micklem and E. O. A. Newcombe in and beyond the Nubian Desert during the campaigns of 1896-98, it was maintained by Macauley, Midwinter, the two Newcombes and other officers while the Sudan was making a long recovery from years of Dervish oppression and misrule. Since 1926, the Sudan Railways have prospered under expert civilian control, but no further extension has followed the completion of the Kassala line.[1]

We come now to the connection of the Royal Engineers with the Egyptian State Railways, which may be said to have begun with the arrival of Brevet Major E. P. C. Girouard and Lieutenant G. C. M. Hall in Luxor during the spring of 1898 to remedy the glaring defects noticed by Sir Herbert Kitchener in the Luxor–Aswan line.[2] It is true that some Royal Engineers had been concerned during the Nile, Dongola and Atbara campaigns in arrangements for the transport of troops and supplies over the Egyptian railway system, but they had no control over the maintenance and operation of that system. For a period of 30 years after the completion of the first railway from Alexandria to Cairo in 1856, the Egyptian lines had suffered from unsatisfactory administration. The American Civil War gave an impetus to the cultivation of cotton in Egypt, and consequently to trade and traffic. By 1874, the railway had been extended from Cairo to Asyut, and branch lines were being constructed to the principal towns in the Nile Delta ; but the new lines were badly laid and the traffic inefficiently controlled, and the appointment in 1876 of a cosmopolitan Board to administer the system led to no improvement. The services of Major F. A. Marindin, R.E.,[3] and Mr. (afterwards Lord) Farrer were secured in 1887 for the preparation of a report on the general condition of the Egyptian railways, and the result was a recommendation for drastic reorganization in every department. Nothing seems to have been done, however, until Girouard set Hall to work on the improvement of the Luxor-Aswan

[1] Minor branches, such as the line from Khartoum to Jebel Auliya (28 miles), have been built from time to time during the last 20 years for particular, and occasionally temporary, purposes.
[2] See Chapter IX.
[3] Major Marindin and Mr. Farrer came to Egypt from England, where the former was Chief Inspector of Railways under the Board of Trade.

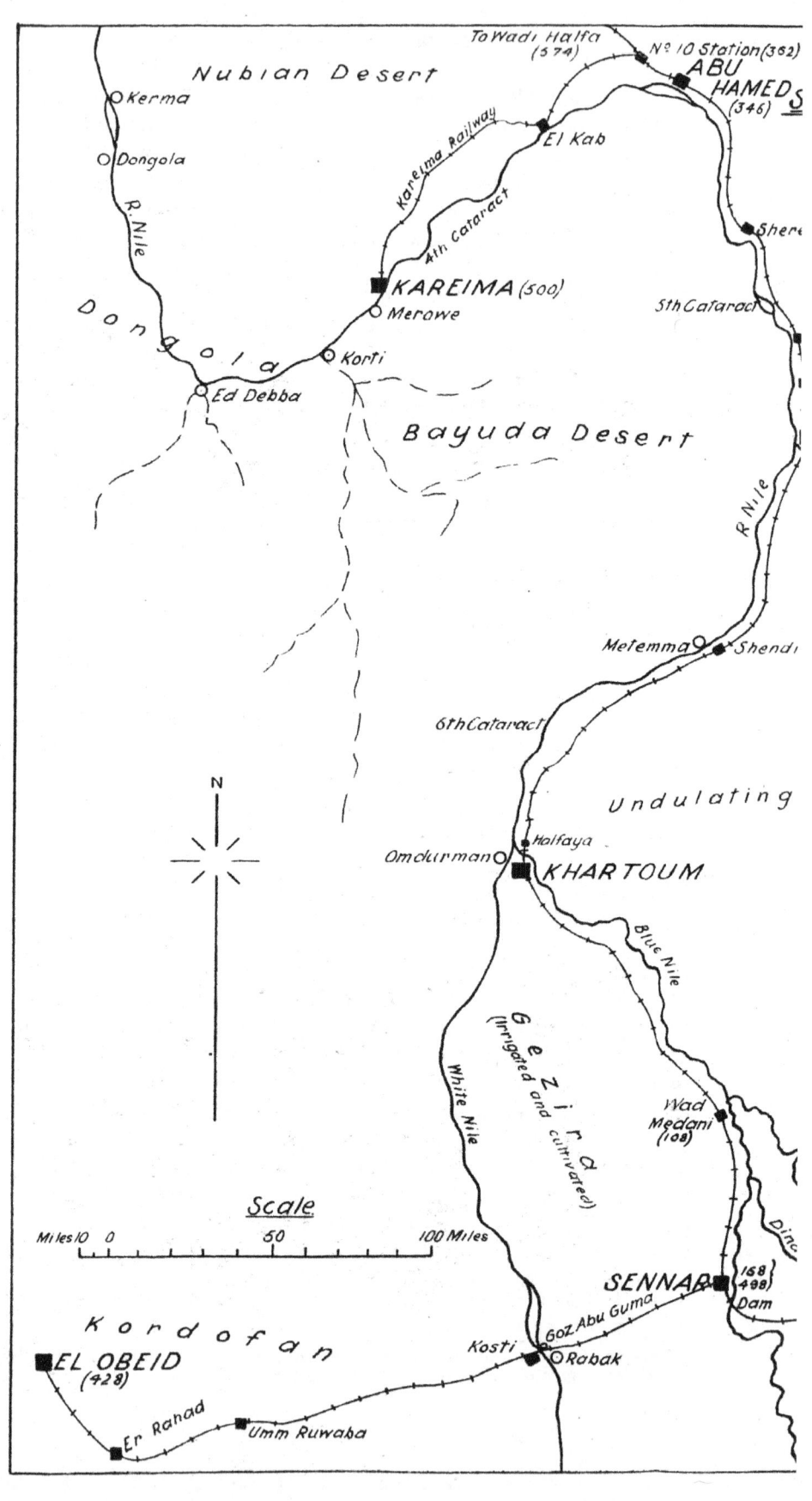

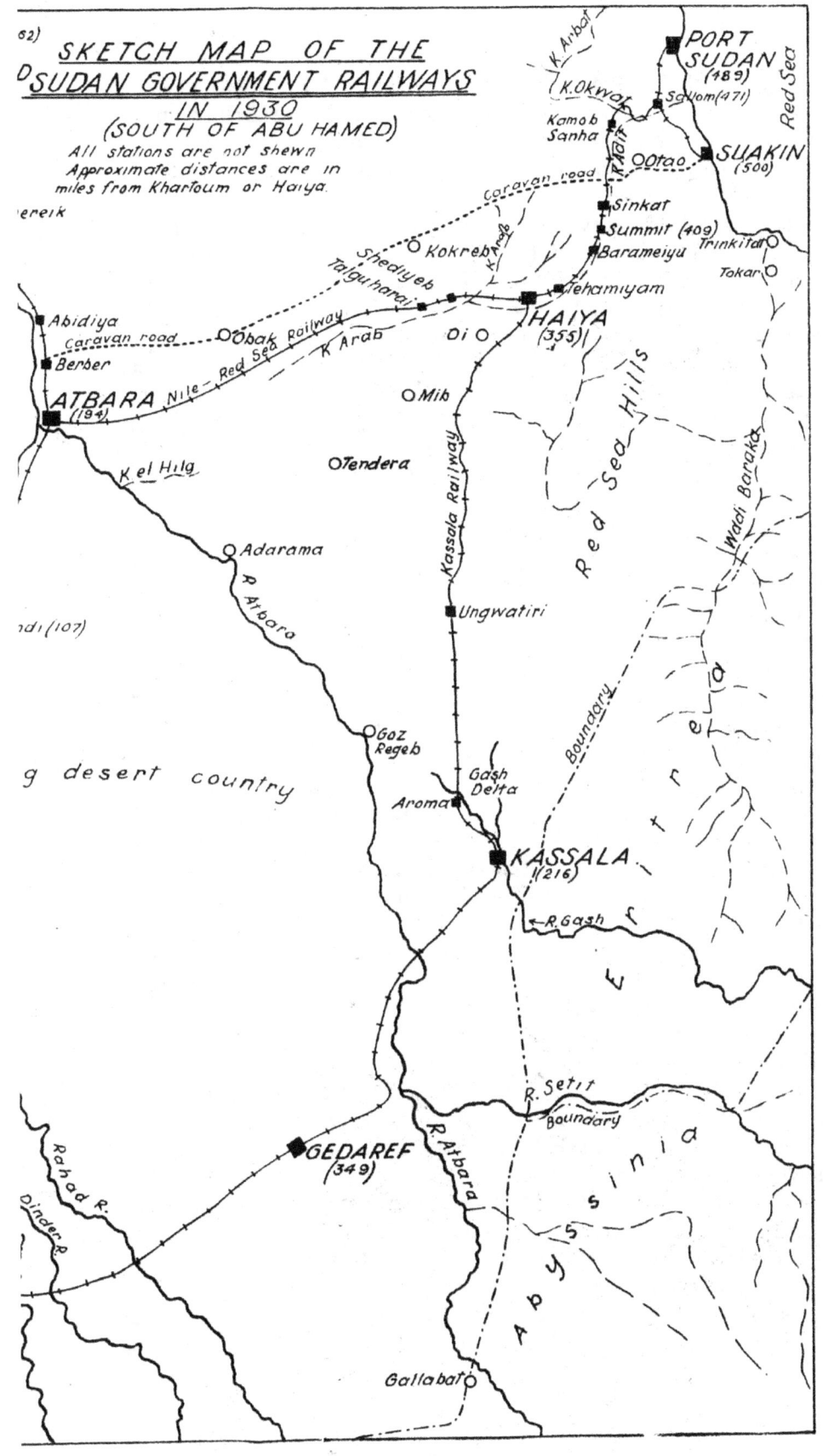

line. In June, 1898, Girouard was appointed as "President of the Egyptian State Railways and Telegraphs and of Alexandria Harbour," and became also the President of the International Board which administered the railways, the other two members being French and Egyptian officials.

The control of the Egyptian railways by Royal Engineers is perhaps one of the most striking features of that remarkable quarter of a century at the close of which British prestige and authority attained their zenith under Lord Kitchener as His Majesty's representative in Cairo. During this period, the complexities and responsibilities of the work increased year by year. The traffic became fast and intense. The employees rose to a total of more than 20,000 men, and the budget to millions of pounds. The Royal Engineers devoted much of their time and energy to the training and welfare of the staff, and thus increased not only its efficiency but also its *esprit de corps*.

Girouard was selected by Lord Cromer at a moment of great emergency, and his arrival in Cairo coincided with a salutary and sweeping change in the composition of the Railway Board. After arranging for the safe passage of reinforcements to Kitchener's army in the region of Berber and Atbara, Girouard ordered a special train and travelled rapidly over all the Egyptian lines. They were in a deplorable condition. The stations were badly designed and congested with dilapidated rolling stock. The signals were not interlocked; and there were no safety appliances, although Egypt was clamouring for express trains. The bridges were weak, the rails worn-out, and 150 miles of track was actually classed as dangerous. The locomotives were not sufficiently powerful. The passenger accommodation was unsatisfactory, and there was a shortage of goods wagons. As to the staff, they were neglected, poorly educated and unreliable. Girouard realized at once that he would need experienced assistants to enforce discipline and cope with increasing traffic, and his first selection was Captain W. A. S. Kincaid, R.E., who was transferred from the post of General Manager of the Egyptian Delta Light Railways and joined the Egyptian State Railways as Traffic Manager early in 1899. The work, however, was so overwhelming that in May, 1899, Girouard secured the transfer of Lieutenants R. B. D. Blakeney and G. C. M. Hall, R.E., from the Sudan to Cairo. Blakeney had been Traffic Manager on the Sudan Government Railways, and Hall was experienced in both traffic work and surveying.

Within a few months of his arrival, Girouard produced a programme of railway work which was faithfully carried out during the next 20 years. It involved not only increases in train-loads and in the weight and power of locomotives, but alterations to all bridges, the re-laying of all permanent way with heavier rails and sleepers, the provision of adequate and modern rolling stock, the reconstruction of the Port of Alexandria, and the development of Port Said and its connection to the railway system. In his blunt yet good-humoured way, he convinced the Egyptian Pashas and officials that whenever they travelled by rail they risked certain death; and thus he paved the way for, and ultimately obtained from the Government, the grant of a large sum of money for the reorganization of the railways and of the ports of Alexandria and Port Said. In May, 1899, he proceeded to England and America to order equipment, and afterwards returned to Egypt to start his great schemes of development; but unfortunately, he was unable to supervise them for more than a few months, for he was called away to South Africa in October, 1899, as Director of Railways in the theatre of war.

Girouard's methods in Cairo were masterful, but highly effective. " It was amazing," writes Brigadier-General Blakeney,[1] " to see him at a Board meeting to which occasionally the Heads of Departments would be summoned. Having started his two foreign colleagues on discussing some comparatively unimportant question, his hand would reach out for the really vital *dossier* among the great pile of untidy papers heaped in front of him; and while intervening occasionally in the play of argument between his colleagues, he would write his decision on the important file and pass it, as if it were a mere question of routine, to the others, both of whom would write " *D'accord* " quite gaily on it and then continue their argument. I saw him do this on a question of the introduction of heavy engines and American freight cars, which involved the relaying of the main lines and rebuilding or strengthening all bridges—a scheme which cost more than £3,000,000 and entailed the entire remodelling of the line."

Though overwhelmed with routine work, Girouard found time to inspect wayside stations and junctions, a rare procedure before his arrival. It seems, that on one occasion, when the International Board had decided to visit a section of the line which it was proposed to extend, their train had been detained at a wayside station. They had noted without surprise the usual accumulation of broken chairs, hen-coops and other paraphernalia on the goods platform, and as time hung heavily on their hands, they had resolved to depart from precedent and inspect the passenger accommodation. Arriving at the Ladies' Waiting-Room, they were about to enter when they were entreated by the Egyptian stationmaster not to do so because, as he said, the room was fully occupied, so they lingered patiently on the platform to allow the ladies time to escape. At last, as the door still remained shut, the French Administrator announced his intention of entering, whatever the consequences. He did so,

---

[1] Notes on the Egyptian State Railways, Telegraphs and Telephones, by Brig.-General R. B. D. Blakeney, C.M.G., D.S.O., late R.E., sent to the author on July 20th 1934.

only to discover that the sole occupant of the room was the station-master's cow!

Girouard found time to prepare a comprehensive programme of harbour and railway improvement for the port of Alexandria. The Egyptian Government offices in Cairo were closed on Friday, that being the Muhammadan holiday, so Girouard was in the habit of proceeding on Thursday afternoon to Alexandria and returning to the capital on Friday evening. He spent the interim in exploring the Alexandria dockyard, planning alterations, estimating for new plant and machinery, and interviewing the leaders of the business community. His schemes were put in hand before he left the country, and some of them are still in the course of execution.

When Girouard returned to England *en route* for South Africa in the autumn of 1899, his appointment as President of the Egyptian State Railways was filled by Major J. H. L'Estrange Johnstone, M.V.O., R.E., who held it until his death in September, 1906. Lieutenant R. B. D. Blakeney, D.S.O., R.E., followed Girouard to South Africa in January, 1900, and did not return to Egypt until June, 1901. Meanwhile, Major Johnstone, Captain W. A. S. Kincaid and Lieutenant G. C. M. Hall, D.S.O., R.E., carried on the administration and operation of the Egyptian railways. In the autumn of 1902, Kincaid reverted to his normal employment on the Indian Establishment and became General Manager of the Burma Railways, being succeeded by Blakeney as Traffic Manager. Four years later, Major G. B. Macauley, R.E., arrived from the Sudan on appointment as General Manager (or President) of the Egyptian State Railways in succession to the late Major Johnstone. Blakeney then became Deputy General Manager, and Hall, Traffic Manager,[1] both being assisted by young civil engineers, who were being recruited annually in increasing numbers.

In 1904, it became evident that heavy outlay must be faced, and Lord Cromer invited a Commission under Lord Farrer to report on the situation and make recommendations. The Farrer Commission was followed by another, under Sir Charles Scotter, at the end of 1905, and as both Commissions advocated large expenditure on railways, Lord Cromer was able to obtain a substantial grant for that purpose. The reforms which were instituted were of lasting benefit to the Egyptian State Railways; and the Scotter Commission accorded such praise to the traffic work of Blakeney and Hall that each received a decoration and an increase of pay from the Egyptian Government.

In the administration, operation and expansion of the Egyptian railways from 1906 until the outbreak of the Great War in 1914, Macauley, Blakeney and Hall worthily upheld the traditions of their Corps, though hampered often by political intrigues and financial

---

[1] From 1902 to 1906, Lieut. G. C. M. Hall, R.E., had been in charge of the Goods Department of the traffic.

stringency. The railways prospered under their guidance and control. New lines were acquired by the Government, heavy engines and modern rolling stock were obtained, the main line from Cairo to Minya was doubled and provided with proper signals, and the quality of the operating staff was improved. The work of Brigadier-General Sir George Macauley and his assistants during the Great War has already been recorded. Early in March, 1919, Macauley handed over to Brigadier-General Blakeney the post of General Manager and became Adviser to the Ministry of Communications; and thus the chief burden of safe-guarding the railways during the political upheaval of that year fell on Blakeney. General Sir Reginald Wingate had recently vacated the office of High Commissioner in Egypt, and his strong and experienced leadership was greatly missed at a most critical period.

The Egyptian railways suffered very severely during the disturbances of March and April, 1919. The lines were cut in about 200 places, and 63 stations were wrecked or damaged.[1] General Blakeney records that all seemed quiet on March 9th, but that on the following day, serious rioting broke out in several places.[2] Armoured trains were dispatched on March 13th and 14th, to patrol the lines; and on the 15th, a general strike took place, which included the employees in the Railway workshop at Bulaq, a suburb of Cairo. Trains started as usual, but could not proceed far, as every junction around the capital had been damaged. An amusing incident occurred when a temporary Royal Engineer officer, on arriving in a car at a goods station outside Cairo, was threatened by strikers, who were engaged in looting the place. It is said that he jumped out of his car, and armed only with a tennis racket, put the crowd to ignominious flight.

When General Sir Edmund Allenby, the newly appointed High Commissioner in Egypt, arrived in Cairo on March 25th, 1919, the situation had improved owing to the energetic action taken by the military forces under Lieut.-General Sir Edward Bulfin; but the subsequent release of Zaghlul Pasha from internment in Malta was followed by further rioting in the streets of Cairo during the first three weeks of April, and by the renewal of strikes in the Railway workshops. These strikes were suppressed eventually by Brigadier-General Blakeney. Lieut.-Colonel M. E. Sowerby, C.M.G., D.S.O., R.E., had been appointed recently as Under-Secretary in the Ministry of Communications,[3] which had taken over the control of

---

[1] *Report on the Finances, Administration and Condition of Egypt and the Sudan,* 1914–1919, p. 85.
[2] Notes on the Egyptian State Railways, Telegraphs and Telephones, by Brig.-General R. B. D. Blakeney, C.M.G., D.S.O., late R.E., sent to the author on July 20th, 1934.
[3] Lieut.-Colonel Sowerby had left the Sudan Government Railways in the summer of 1915 to take part in the Great War. He served in Mudros, Gallipoli, Salonika, Sinai and Palestine, and was awarded the C.M.G. for building the railway across the Sinai Desert into Palestine.

the railways on the abolition of a Supreme Railway Board formed by Lord Cromer; and Lieut.-Colonel G. C. M. Hall, C.M.G., C.B.E., D.S.O., R.E., had retired after refusing an offer of the post filled subsequently by Sowerby. Accordingly, Blakeney was the only Royal Engineer on the staff of the Egyptian State Railways when the strikes occurred.

Worn out by the strain of his many civil duties, and by his work in the Great War, Lieut.-Colonel M. E. Sowerby died in Cairo at the end of January, 1920, and his appointment as Under-Secretary fell to Lieut.-Colonel J. S. Liddell, C.M.G., D.S.O., R.E., the Director of Telegraphs. In February, 1920, Major D. J. McMullen, D.S.O., R.E., joined the Locomotive Department of the Egyptian State Railways, and consequently Brigadier-General Blakeney had the support of an officer of his own Corps in suppressing further strikes among the Railway employees, which occurred during serious rioting in May, 1921, at Cairo, Alexandria, Zagazig, Tanta and other places.

After the independence of Egypt had been proclaimed in February, 1922, it was only natural that the announcement should be followed by a reduction in the number of British officers in the Egyptian service; and among those who retired were Brigadier-Generals Sir George Macauley, K.C.M.G., K.B.E., C.B., and R. B. D. Blakeney, C.M.G., D.S.O. In relinquishing the appointment of General Manager in November, 1923,[1] Blakeney severed a connection with railway work in the Sudan and Egypt extending over a period of more than 27 years. With the departure of Major D. J. McMullen at the beginning of 1930, the last Royal Engineer disappeared from the Egyptian State Railways.[2]

Nevertheless, the connection of the Corps with railway work in the Land of the Pharaohs is still maintained on the miniature system known as the Egyptian Delta Light Railways, a network of 75-centimetre (2 feet 6 inches) gauge lines, with headquarters at Alexandria, which acts as a valuable collector and distributor of produce. The rapid development of irrigation, and the consequent increase of land under cultivation during the latter years of the nineteenth century, demanded an improvement in transport facilities. Till then, the only means for carrying agricultural produce from the villages in the Nile Delta to the larger towns, which were served by the 4 feet 8½ inches gauge lines of the Egyptian State Railways, were camels, carts, donkeys and boats. In 1894, Messrs. John Birch and Company were granted a concession for the construction of a narrow-gauge system in the western and central areas of the delta, and a

---

[1] Brig.-General Blakeney retired from the Egyptian Government Service on March 31st, 1924, after a period of leave.
[2] In 1936, Colonel D. J. Mc.Mullen served as Assistant Director of Transportation in Egypt, and Major P. C. Lord as Transportation Officer, but neither joined the Egyptian State Railways.

MOGHAZI PASHA STATION.
On the Egyptian Delta Light Railways.
[*Photo by the Author.*]

similar concession was given to the Suares Company for the building of a system in the eastern area. Two companies were then formed to operate the lines; but in 1900, their entire property, including 645 kilometres of track, was acquired by a British Company, formed in 1897 under the title of the Egyptian Delta Light Railways. By 1914, the length of the lines had nearly doubled;[1] and by 1930, the tonnage carried annually was 768,000, and the number of passengers, 12,000,000. Under the terms of the original concession, as revised at a later date, the Egyptian Government has the right to acquire the whole system after April 1st, 1938, on payment of the capital expended.

As the system is divided by two branches of the Nile into three districts having no physical connection with each other, workshops and running sheds have to be maintained in each district. In recent years, the Delta Light Railways have had to contend with the keen competition of motor transport; but they have held their own by reducing rates and fares, and by establishing a fleet of motor lorries to collect the cotton, cereals, fruit and building materials, which are the principal commodities carried by them.

Almost all the " Agents and General Managers " of this interesting railway system have been Royal Engineers, and the first Managing Director of the Company was also an officer of the Corps. Lieut.-Colonel E. L. Marryat, R.E., an experienced engineer from the North-Western Railway in India, became Managing Director in 1898, and held that post for 6 years. The first Agent in Egypt was Captain W. A. S. Kincaid, R.E., who was appointed in 1898, but left in the following year to assist Girouard on the Egyptian State Railways. Then came Captain A. Adams, R.E., as Agent from 1899 to 1913; and from 1922 until the present day, Lieut.-Colonel J. R. Marryat, D.S.O., M.C., R.E. (retd.),[2] a son of the original Managing Director, has controlled and administered the system with marked success.

The author had the privilege of touring over a section of the Delta Light Railways, from Damanhur northwards, in February, 1935. The special train, consisting of a diminutive engine and saloon carriage, threaded its way at little more than a walking pace through suburbs and villages, where the whistle was sounded so continuously to clear the line of children, donkeys, fowls and other trespassers that conversation was sometimes impossible. Then, at increased speed, the train ran through flat country covered with luxuriant crops,

---

[1] There are now more than 1,000 kilometres of single-line track and about 135 kilometres of sidings. The rails are flat-footed and supported on pine sleepers. The system has 224 bridges, including 22 swing bridges over navigable canals. There are 128 locomotives, 350 coaching vehicles and 1,471 goods vehicles, and the heaviest type of locomotive is identical with that used on the Simla Railway in India.

[2] Lieut.-Colonels E. L. and J. R. Marryat, R.E., are mentioned on pp. 130 and 139 of *The Military Engineer in India*, Part II, by the present author.

a country utterly unlike the bare wastes of the Sudan. Alongside was a canal on which were heavily laden boats, whose bellying sails seemed almost to overshadow the line. This is Egypt at its richest and fairest—a land of wonderful fertility, reclaimed from swamp and jungle, and brought to prosperity by the admirable system of railways created by British enterprise.

SUAKIN—BERBER RAILWAY, HANDUB.
[*from " The Military Telegraph Bulletin,"* May, 1888

CHAPTER XVI.

TELEGRAPHS.

ON September 2nd, 1898, when Kitchener put his fortune to the test at Omdurman, he was cut off from all communication with the outer world. Between him and the end of the poled telegraph line at Wad Hamid stretched 60 miles of river bank, along which Lieutenant M. G. E. Manifold, R.E., had laid bare wire; but that slender link had failed because of unexpected and torrential rain, and the poled line beyond it had been damaged by careless Greeks. Farther downstream, the cable across the Nile at Atbara was also out of action, and in consequence of these several misfortunes the news of the victory was delayed in transmission to Cairo and England. On September 4th, however, Manifold took in hand the poling of the line from Wad Hamid, and with the assistance of Sergeant Dennett, R.E., brought the telegraph into Omdurman on September 7th, and connected it to the existing cable across the river to Khartoum.[1]

While Kitchener was absent at Fashoda, and afterwards in England, Manifold extended the railway telegraph up the right bank of the Nile from Atbara and completed the line from Suakin to Berber. Christmas Day, 1898, found him at Wadi Halfa, where the Sirdar had just arrived on his return journey to Khartoum. Manifold had sent in his resignation from the Egyptian Army, and was preparing to hand over charge to Lieutenant J. S. Liddell, R.E., the officer appointed to relieve him. The Sirdar gave him copious instructions regarding extensions of the telegraph up the Blue and White Niles south of Khartoum, and left him to explain the situation to Liddell.[2]

The circumstances under which Liddell joined the Egyptian Army are typical of the Kitchener regime. Fresh from his victory at Omdurman, the Sirdar was dining in November, 1898, at the Royal Engineers' Mess at Aldershot, and hearing good reports of "Jock" Liddell of the 17th Field Company, sent for him after dinner and asked him point-blank whether he would like to go to the Sudan for telegraph work.[3] Liddell accepted with great delight, and soon received orders from the War Office to report himself as quickly as possible at the Egyptian Army Headquarters in Cairo. On reaching Cairo, Liddell went to Army Headquarters, where the authorities disclaimed all knowledge of him or his appointment; but when he

---
[1] See Chapter X.
[2] Diary of Lieut. M. G. E. Manifold, R.E., lent to the author by Major-General Sir M. G. E. Bowman-Manifold, K.B.E., C.B., C.M.G., D.S.O., late R.E., in October, 1934.
[3] Notes by the late Major J. S. Liddell, C.M.G., D.S.O., R.E. (retd.), sent to the author by Mrs. Liddell on September 25th, 1934.

explained that he had been posted to the Sudan Telegraphs, he received a pass for Wadi Halfa and set off up the Nile to meet Manifold. Arriving at Halfa on December 29th, he was somewhat perturbed at the prospect before him. " I spent two or three days in taking over from Bimbashi Manifold," he writes, " and he told me that Lord Kitchener had ordered 1,000 miles of wire and the necessary poles, but nothing else, and that we had practically nothing of any kind in store." Manifold added that with the assistance of a detachment of the Telegraph Battalion, R.E., which was expected from home, Liddell might complete the projected lines in two years. Transport, as he explained, was considered as a luxury rather than a necessity, and frequently not an animal was available for the unfortunate Telegraph officer.

Kitchener had planned the construction of a telegraph line from Khartoum up the Blue Nile through Wad Medani and Sennar to Roseires, with a branch line from Sennar to Kassala, a connection from Sennar across the Gezira to the White Nile, and a continuation up that river to Fashoda, afterwards re-named Kodok.[1] Lord Cromer arrived in Wadi Halfa on December 31st, 1898, and questioned Manifold on the subject of these extensions; he also complimented him on the quick transmission of news of the Battle of the Atbara, and condoled with him on the failure of the line before the Battle of Omdurman. On January 1st, 1899, Manifold started for Cairo and shortly afterwards reverted to the Home Establishment, thus severing his connection with the Egyptian Army and with the Sudan, whose system of military telegraphs he had extended so ably from Wadi Halfa to Khartoum and from Berber to the Red Sea.[2]

The Sudan telegraph system at the beginning of 1899 comprised a line of several wires along the railway from Wadi Halfa to railhead south of Atbara, with a loop from Wadi Halfa up the Nile, through Dongola and Merowe, to Abu Hamed on the railway. From Atbara, a line followed the left bank of the Nile to Omdurman and was prolonged by cable to Khartoum; and from Berber, a line extended to Suakin, whence another gave connection with Kassala through Tokar.[3] The telegraph poles were of pine wood imported from Turkey, and were about 18 feet in length, roughly squared, and four inches by four inches at the base. After some experience of the depredations of white ants, it was decided that shorter poles should be used in areas which were free from elephants and giraffes. These

---

[1] See the *Sketch Map of the Sudan Telegraph System in* 1930, which is included in this chapter.

[2] Lieut. M. G. E. Manifold, R.E., reverted to the Home Establishment on January 17th, 1899. From January 1st, 1900, to July 18th, 1901, he served under Lord Kitchener as Superintendent of Telegraphs during the South African War.

[3] At the beginning of 1899, the system of Army Telegraphs was transferred to the Civil Government, and with a Postal Department added to it, was formed into the " Sudan Posts and Telegraphs Department."

poles were bolted into short lengths of channel-iron, which were sunk in the soil so that the bases of the poles were raised a few inches above the ground. The telegraph wire was of galvanized iron.

A few days after Manifold had started for Cairo, Liddell proceeded to Khartoum and reported to the Sirdar. The latter complained at once that the number of mistakes in telegrams had increased since the end of the campaign; but Liddell was able to point out that most of the expert telegraphists, on salaries of £20 a month, had been sent down to Cairo and replaced by novices, who received only £4 a month. Kitchener was well aware of this fact and accepted the explanation without demur, merely remarking that he should expect proper transmission in future. His immediate object had been accomplished. He had wished to test the extent of Liddell's knowledge, and had found that it was satisfactory. By such adroit methods, the Sirdar gained an insight into the characters of his officers and formed his estimate of them.

Before the middle of January, 1899, Liddell was joined by Lieutenants G. B. Roberts[1] and W. S. Douglas, R.E., and by 24 non-commissioned officers and men of the Telegraph Battalion, R.E., under Quarter-Master-Sergeant W. H. Dale, R.E.[2] Kitchener had asked for two officers, but the War Office had insisted on sending also a detachment of other ranks. Liddell then proceeded to beg or borrow materials and stores for the extension of the telegraph from Khartoum to Wad Medani, and being fortunate enough to obtain 20 camels from the Sirdar, he was able to start work. "Lord Kitchener was a magnificent chief," he writes.[3] "We got our orders and were left alone. I often went to see him, and on these occasions he showed a surprising knowledge of my job; but as I usually wanted something, the customary answer was 'No.' One day he inquired when the line would be through to Wad Medani, and I replied that it would reach that place on the following Monday; but afterwards, having some misgivings on the subject, I started a second party to work northwards from Wad Medani to meet the first. They met 15 miles from Wad Medani, and I telegraphed the news to the Sirdar. His reply ran 'Am pleased with progress. What are the prospects towards Sennar?' A few days later, he arrived in Wad Medani by steamer, intending to march through Gedaref and Kassala to Suakin.[4] I lunched with him and he said, 'When I get to Kassala

---

[1] Lieut. G. B. Roberts was a trained Telegraph officer, who had worked on the Post Office Telegraphs during his service of five years in the 2nd Division Telegraph Battalion, R.E., in England.

[2] Lieut. W. S. Douglas was invalided in 1899, and Lieut. G. B. Roberts reverted to the Home Establishment in 1900. Q.M.S. Dale was promoted Quarter-Master and Hon. Lieutenant in November, 1901. Dale began his Army career as a trumpeter in the 1st Division Telegraph Battalion, R.E., and retired in 1921 as an Hon. Major with the O.B.E. and M.C. decorations.

[3] Notes by the late Major J. S. Liddell.

[4] This was the occasion of Lord Kitchener's reconnaissance with Lieut. G. B. Macauley, R.E., for a railway route to the Red Sea (See Chapter XI).

in about ten days' time I shall expect to be able to wire to Sennar.' I told him, however, that he could hardly hope to do so unless he travelled more slowly, as the distance from Wad Medani to Sennar alone was about 60 miles. Having carried the Blue Nile line to Sennar and onwards to Roseires, nearly 300 miles south of Khartoum, I went to meet the Sirdar at Berber on his return from Suakin and heard from his Staff that he had discovered many miles of the Suakin-Berber telegraph line lying on the sand; but as the desert was dry, and he had managed to get a message from Suakin through the line to Berber and thence to Sennar, he said not a word to me about the damage because he knew that, if he did so, I should ask for money to rebuild the line!"

The next undertaking was the construction of a line running westwards across the Gezira from Sennar to the nearest spot on the White Nile, a ridge called Goz Abu Guma.[1] This task was completed by Liddell in September, 1899, shortly before the abortive expedition against the Khalifa at Jebel Gedir;[2] but meanwhile, he had been ordered to run a temporary line northwards from Khartoum to meet the approaching railway, and consequently transferred all his men and tools down the Nile at the earliest opportunity. This new work was still unfinished when he was ordered to build a line southwards from Goz Abu Guma towards Er Renk, and was informed at the same time that the line was to cost nothing and that no transport could be given to him because every animal was needed for the chase of the Khalifa. "The natives around Goz Abu Guma are starving," remarked the Sirdar, "and you can get as many as you like for a handful of *dhurra* a day. As to transport, if I were you I should go a little way up the White Nile and seize the first native boat I met. If you do this, you will have finished the line before the complaint reaches me." By good fortune, however, Liddell was able to obtain the loan of a sailing boat at Khartoum, and having loaded her with *dhurra*, poles and wire scraped together in Omdurman, he dispatched Lieutenant G. B. Roberts, R.E., to Goz Abu Guma to build the line with no other tools than a single pair of pliers. Roberts was met by a non-commissioned officer from Sennar, who brought with him another pair of pliers and an old "buzzer," and so the work began.

The telegraph line from Goz Abu Guma was extended slowly and painfully to Er Renk, and afterwards to Fashoda and Taufikia,[3] and proved to be of some use during the Jebel Gedir expedition. Liddell opened an office at El Jebelein, some 40 miles south of

---

[1] Goz (or Qoz) Abu Guma is the name given to a sand-ridge two miles from the right bank of the White Nile opposite Kosti. It is about two miles north-east of Rabak, where the railway crosses the river.

[2] See Chapter XI.

[3] Taufikia, a station north of the junction of the Sobat River with the White Nile, did not exist in the time of Charles Gordon. It was established later by Sir Samuel Baker.

Goz Abu Guma, and established a Sudanese telegraphist there, with a couple of policemen to protect him. The first message received from the terror-stricken operator ran as follows:—" Am surrounded by lions, leopards and bears. Please send relief at once." Then, after consultation with his guardians, who knew something of the local fauna, he wired: " *My No. 1. Please cancel bears.*"

Many amusing messages and letters have been received by telegraph officers in the Sudan. For instance, a clerk once wrote as follows:—" Sir. Since a few days I am feeling with toothache, and always tormenting me when touches each other when eat, so this frequently cannot be tolerated constantly. When the pain intensed I went to the doctor, and when he saw me said some of them have been eaten by moth and I can take them off, but advise you that it will be a loss to be taken away and it is better to go to Khartoum locally to have them stuffed. There is no tools for stuffing here, so kindly let me have a pass. May God bless you." This man seems to have had more courage than another, who telegraphed :—" Kindly do nothing of any arrangements in my seeing dentest at anywhere. My molars outlook are going successfully now."

The lot of the telegraph operator in an outlying station is not always a happy one. " I am a youngster lying between the paws of danger," writes a despondent individual. Another states that " the office is extremely unhealthy because (a) the lived and dead bats are making a very bad rot with a very bad stench also, which is weakening my eyes by-and-by (b) the bees are buzzing overhead and stinging me (recently) (c) big and strange flies are also doing the same as the bees (also recently)." A third tells of the dire effects of a sudden storm. " The world has never seen or heard of a disaster such as that occurred on the 19th instant," he writes. " At 4.30 p.m. a strong tempest with heavy rains took place and ceased at 9 p.m. I then, having been half-wrecked in waters and muds fallen from the roofs, went to look for the office room and found all the three roofs pulled down into thousands of pieces and formed Heaps. The office and store room were a semi-pool of muds and waters. In short speech, nothing was in order. Clothes destroyed, furniture damaged. No house to live, etc., etc. General health, Extremely Bad."

From the upper waters of the Nile, a pathetic message once came to Khartoum. " Gondokoro dying telegram. Man Shenenda Sonnura. Was seriously ill three days ago. Goodbye. Left you letter explaining case and reason in office. This message written also before I passed away now and dispatched by Postmaster. To be sent if I die, and the receipt issued later by the clerk who may come from Mongalla. Deduct fees from pay please." No better example can be given of the orderly habits and devotion to duty of the humblest servants of the Sudan Government.[1]

At Khartoum, on the evening of November 27th, 1899, Lord Kitchener received Sir Reginald Wingate's report of the destruction of the Dervish force at Umm Debeikerat and promptly went to Liddell. "Now that the Khalifa is dead," said he, "I think we will build a telegraph line from Omdurman to El Obeid. I suppose you won't want anything?"[2] Liddell replied that he would certainly need some wire from Egypt. "But there is a lot of wire lying on the river bank at Omdurman," remonstrated the Sirdar. "Yes, sir," said Liddell, "about 30 miles of it, and the distance to El Obeid is 300 miles." Kitchener then inquired the cost of the extra wire which would be needed in the near future, and after pondering over Liddell's estimate, remarked, "I think we can manage that," and rode away without another word. Rushing to his telegraph office, Liddell dispatched a message to "Monkey" Gordon (Lieut.-Colonel W. S. Gordon, R.E.), the Director of Stores in Cairo. "Sirdar says I can have 100 miles of No. 8 wire," it ran. "Please send immediately." In those days, any demand which was prefaced by the words "Sirdar says" was never open to question, so the wire was soon on its way. Liddell then borrowed some native boats, and having loaded them with all the available telegraph stores and 100 *Jehadia* and their wives, started building the line to El Obeid on the following morning. The line was taken up the left bank of the White Nile to Ed Dueim, whence it ran westwards to Bara, and finally southwards to El Obeid. The episode shows the speed with which decisions were taken, and projects put in hand, under the Kitchener regime.

The *Jehadia*, who were still classed as prisoners of war, drew rations and received an allowance of half-piastre a day for tobacco, and when accompanied by their wives, were perfectly contented. After a time, they were "freed" and given pay at the rate of three piastres a day; but the concession was somewhat marred by the fact that they were then required to feed themselves. Nevertheless, telegraph work was very popular with the natives; and within the next few years, a suburb of Khartoum came to be known as "Telegraph Village" and could always supply as many men as were needed. "Dear Honourable Sir," wrote an applicant for telegraph employment, "I obediently and respectfully beg, with great sighs and many sobs mixed with bloody tears, to bring to your highest well-known kindness that I have become ill of offering many unaccepted poor applications for transferring me from the Posts to the Telegraph School, so would you kindly arrange and save me from being murdered of anger. I think that no poor will burst of hunger

---

[1] The author is indebted to Colonel H. G. Gandy, D.S.O., O.B.E., late R.E., for some of these examples of correspondence.
[2] Notes by the late Major J. S. Liddell.

and thirst while there is a brave, well-trained, educated, honourable knight as Your Excellency to offer smooth hand of help."

Liddell was joined by Lieutenant E. G. Meyricke, R.E., in February, 1901, and during the next three years, with the assistance of Quarter-Master and Honorary Lieutenant W. H. Dale, R.E.,[1] and a few non-commissioned officers, he completed a line of telegraph from Kassala through Gedaref to Sennar, strengthened or repaired many existing lines, and took measures to improve the organization of the Posts and Telegraphs Department and the training of the personnel. The chief difficulty, as ever, was the lack of funds. In the spring of 1904, it was decided that a direct line should be provided for a distance of 190 miles up the White Nile from Khartoum through El Geteina and El Kawa to Goz Abu Guma to connect with the line across the Gezira from Sennar. This project was put in hand on May 4th and finished on October 8th, 1904, and on its completion, the Sudan had 3,242 miles of telegraph line and 38 offices.

During 1904 a decision was reached that the telegraph system should be extended into the swampy region of the Bahr el Ghazal on the Upper Nile, and Liddell was ordered to proceed thither to reconnoitre a route. As no reliable maps could be obtained, Colonel the Hon. M. G. Talbot, the Director of Survey, lent him a theodolite and two watch-chronometers and helped him to revive his knowledge of astronomy. Talbot also insisted that he should take with him two bottles of a concoction which was said to be a sure preventive against the attentions of mosquitoes. " We reached Meshra er Req in safety," writes Liddell, " though our steamer was jammed for several days in floating vegetation called *sudd*, which was solid enough for men to walk on. Some idiot set fire to the reeds on the river bank, and the conflagration spread rapidly towards us, but my men trod the reeds down into the water before the flames could engulf the steamer and barges. Meshra er Req was indeed a desolate spot. We had to struggle on foot through two miles of swamp, often waist-deep in water, to reach dry ground. On the march southwards, I made a rough compass sketch of the route and took nightly observations for latitude, during which the mosquitoes came in clouds and Talbot's preventive proved to be useless. We went through Wau, Tonj and Rumbek to Shambé on the Bahr el Jebel, and there awaited the arrival of a steamer. The traverse proved to be useful when the line was built subsequently from Meshra er Req to Wau."

The late Mr. Abel Chapman, well known as a naturalist and hunter, gives a vivid description of the desolate reaches of the Upper Nile[2] :—" The mental impression left by the *sudd* region is one long memory of the most featureless abomination extant here on earth.

---

[1] As already mentioned, Q.M.S. Dale was promoted to honorary commissioned rank in November, 1901.
[2] *Savage Sudan*, by Abel Chapman, p. 260.

Day after day, as one crawls southward through it, the channel—laboriously kept open for navigation—winds in a ceaseless series of bends, twists and convolutions like the writhings of a wounded snake. Far as the eye can reach, stretch away to either horizon those drear wastes of grey-green papyrus. Rarely, a vision of trees beyond the sky-line, or the distant smoke of a grass fire, may arouse illusory promise of a limit. The slender hope vanishes like a mirage, and soon one is plunged again into the slough of sightless *sudd*. There is nothing to relieve the dead blank of the dismal swamp, unless it be the flop-flop of some heron's flight or the subaquatic activities of darters." Through this wilderness, our telegraph officers and men built their lines, and it says much for their endurance and determination that they always reached their goal.

Liddell proceeded from Shambé, for a distance of 60 miles up the Bahr el Jebel, to Abu Kuka, as he thought that it might be possible to lay a cable across the river at that place for the connection of the projected line from Meshra er Req, through Wau, Tonj and Rumbek, to another projected extension from Taufikia running for some distance along the right or east bank of the Bahr el Jebel. In those days, according to him, no one knew how far the *sudd* extended. In company with a Government pathologist, Dr. S. H. M. Neave, he set out from Abu Kuka with a few men in dugouts and tried to reach firm ground on the right bank; but after paddling for several miles through reeds and *sudd*, and experiencing some narrow escapes from hippopotami and crocodiles, he relinquished the attempt and returned with Neave to the left bank at Abu Kuka, where they indulged in a few days' sport and each shot an elephant. They kept the tusks and gave the carcases to the Dinkas, and within a few hours, nothing was left but the skulls.

When a steamer appeared on her way downstream from Gondokoro, Liddell returned in her to Taufikia after picking up the remainder of his party at Shambé. From Taufikia, he reconnoitred up the right bank of another branch of the Upper Nile, the Bahr ez Zeraf, and penetrated southwards beyond Pabek, a village in the Twi District, situated almost opposite Shambé in the swamps east of the Bahr el Jebel. His farthest point was a water-hole surrounded by a few trees under which elephants were sheltering. Again, his chief object was to select a site for a cable across the Bahr el Jebel; but as no suitable spot could be found, he returned once more to Taufikia.

A few months later, Liddell accompanied Sir William Garstin and Mr. C. G. Crawley up the Bahr el Jebel in connection with a scheme for diverting that channel from Bor to the Sobat River in order to avoid the *sudd*.[1] They came to Shambé, and succeeded in crossing the river and swamps to Pabek, and afterwards explored southwards

---

[1] This project was never put into execution.

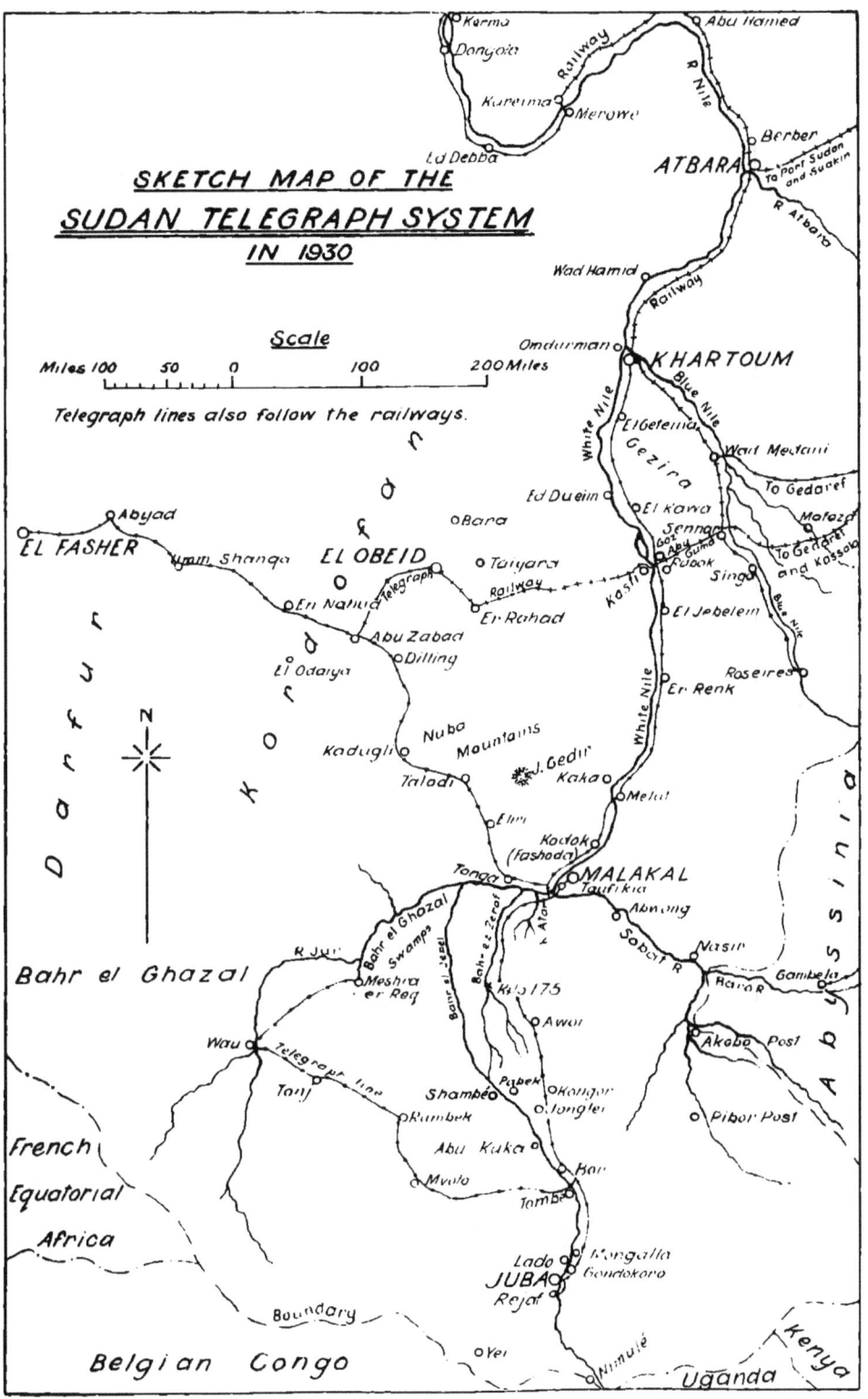

to a point some miles beyond the village of Jonglei. This ended Liddell's adventures on the Upper Nile and also his telegraph work in the Sudan, for in September, 1904, he was appointed Deputy Inspector General of the Egyptian State Telegraphs, under Mr. W. Wallich as Inspector General,[1] and was succeeded as Director of the Sudan Posts and Telegraphs by Captain and Brevet-Major E. V. Turner, R.E. Thus the Sudan lost a most popular officer—a man of great ability and strong, though quiet and unassuming, personality. He was a keen sportsman and a cheerful companion, with a fearless and generous outlook on life. In the course of time, Liddell became Inspector General of the Egyptian State Telegraphs, and as such, played an important part in the improvement and development of that system prior to the Great War and in its operation while hostilities were in progress.[2]

As a result of Liddell's reconnaissances, it was decided in the summer of 1904 that the best method of opening up telegraphic communication in the Bahr el Ghazal Province—known familiarly as " The Bog "—would be to run a line from Meshra er Req on the Bahr el Ghazal, through Wau, Tonj and Rumbek, to Shambé on the Bahr el Jebel, and to link Meshra er Req with Taufikia by a service of motor launches. On December 2nd, 1904, the necessary stores for the construction of the line and its telegraph offices as far as Tonj were dispatched to Meshra er Req, the offices being of a portable wooden type on iron pillars and fitted with mosquito-proof doors and windows. With them went Quarter-Master and Hon. Lieutenant W. H. Dale, R.E., Corporal Stead, R.E., and a working party of 160 *Jehadia*.[3] The party reached Meshra er Req on December 14th, and were engaged, during the next fortnight, in carrying stores across the swamps to dry ground and in building a causeway for the use of 240 camels, which arrived on January 3rd, 1905. Dale had orders to clear a track towards Wau, 18 feet in width, and to place the telegraph line 6 feet from one edge, thus leaving a roadway 12 feet wide. He managed to complete the telegraph line to Wau, a distance of 90 miles, on February 17th, including the laying of a cable across the River Jur. By that date, 90 camels were dead or incapacitated by sickness, accident or exhaustion. The line was unusually heavy as the poles were bolted to iron bases 8 feet in length, and the work was arduous because each pole had to be encircled by a deep trench (as a precaution against the depredations of elephants and giraffes) and the earth piled around its base. On February 24th, Dale was obliged to apply for more transport, and thus reinforced he brought the line to Tonj on April 26th, 1905. Out of a total of 337

[1] Mr. Wallich had recently succeeded Mr. S. A. Floyer as Inspector General. Liddell was appointed to the Egyptian State Telegraphs on the recommendation of Sir William Preece, late Engineer-in-Chief of the General Post Office in London.
[2] Some allusion to Major Liddell's work in Egypt is made later in this chapter.
[3] *Annual Report of the Posts and Telegraphs Department, Sudan Government*, 1904.

camels sent to the Bahr el Ghazal, the survivors then numbered only 35, and of these only 2 lived to reach Khartoum; but 60 out of 85 donkeys returned alive to headquarters. From Tonj, Dale reconnoitred south-eastwards to Rumbek, and then southwards to Mvolo. It was impossible to get through to Bor because no escort had been provided, and consequently Dale marched to Shambé, took ship to Bor to examine that place, and finally followed Stead and the remainder of the party back to Khartoum, where he arrived on June 11th.[1]

At Khartoum, Dale met a new Assistant Director, Lieutenant H. L. Mackworth, D.S.O., R.E., who had replaced Captain E. G. Meyricke, R.E., when the latter reverted to the Home Establishment in January, 1905. At this time, the Posts and Telegraphs Department had a staff of 3 officers and 13 non-commissioned officers, R.E., and 368 clerks, linemen and other employés. Mackworth and Dale were the officers who, under Major E. V. Turner as Director, executed the greater part of the subsequent telegraph extension in the swamps of the Upper Nile.

The construction of the telegraph line to Tonj was not the only work in progress during the early part of 1905. A line was built from Suakin to Port Sudan, and the construction of a permanent line along the Nile-Red Sea Railway was begun from both ends.[2] The reconstruction of the line along the railway from Khartoum northwards to Wadi Halfa was commenced on March 14th,[3] and the provision of a line along the Kareima Railway, then under construction, was begun on June 18th.

After the end of the rainy season, preparations were made for the extension of the Bahr el Ghazal telegraph from Tonj to Rumbek; and on November 16th, 1905, Mackworth and Corporal Walshaw, R.E., reached Shambé from Khartoum with 180 *Jehadia*, 100 camels, 150 donkeys and a large consignment of stores. Transport was already recognized as the ruling factor in all telegraph construction in the Bahr el Ghazal Province, for the chief problem was not the erection of the line, but the carrying of the stores to the proper places. In the case of the section between Tonj and Rumbek, the principal difficulties were the unsuitability of the district for animal transport, the conveyance of 100 tons of material from Shambé to Rumbek (105 miles), and its distribution over 80 miles of forest country to Tonj.[4] The clearing of a track, 15 feet wide, was begun from Rumbek on

[1] *Annual Report of the Posts and Telegraphs Department, Sudan Government*, 1905.
[2] The Suakin-Port Sudan line was built between December 11th, 1904, and February 4th, 1905. The construction of the permanent telegraph line along the Nile-Red Sea Railway was begun from Atbara in December, 1904, and from Suakin in February, 1905. The line had two telegraph and two telephone wires. It was completed on March 1st, 1906.
[3] The Khartoum-Wadi Halfa line was reconstructed to Abu Hamed by January 20th, 1907, and to Wadi Halfa by November 14th, 1907. It had three telegraph and two telephone wires.
[4] *Annual Report of the Posts and Telegraphs Department, Sudan Government*, 1906.

December 1st, 1905, and completed to Tonj on January 16th, 1906. The working party then returned to Rumbek, where it was divided into two parties, one to erect the line to Tonj, and the other to prolong the clearing southwards to Mvolo. The latter party, under Corporal Walshaw, finished the cutting to Mvolo on March 15th.

While Mackworth and his men were thus engaged, Dale was supervising the construction of a line, far up the Bahr el Jebel, from Bor to Gondokoro, in anticipation of the extension of Mackworth's line from Rumbek through Mvolo to Bor. The cutting of a track for the Bor-Gondokoro telegraph was commenced by Corporal Stead on January 1st, 1906, and the erection of the line by Corporal Everitt on February 1st. On March 17th, 1906, the telegraph reached its most southerly point at Gondokoro.[1] Dale and Stead then transferred their attention to the building of a line from El Obeid to En Nahud in Darfur. Dale reconnoitred the route, and Stead began to clear the track on June 23rd, 1906, and the line was completed to En Nahud on August 27th.

During the winter of 1906-07, the extension of the telegraph from Rumbek to Bor was taken in hand. A site for a cable-crossing of the Bahr el Jebel had been selected by Major E. V. Turner, R.E., the Director of Posts and Telegraphs, when on a tour of inspection in January, 1906, and it was decided that the cable should be laid diagonally across the swamps and main channel from Tombé on the left bank, 30 miles south of Bor, to a point on the right bank about 20 miles south of Bor. Mackworth arrived in Tombé on November 21st, 1906, with 20 miles of cable and was able to report on the 27th that he had finished the work and had used only 16 miles of cable.[2] Meanwhile, Dale had begun to erect a land-line from Tombé towards Mvolo, assisted by Corporals Stead and George, with 316 *Jehadia* and 500 donkeys and mules. In spite of heavy casualties among the animals, he reached Mvolo on March 1st, 1907, and Rumbek on April 2nd, thus establishing direct communication between Meshra er Req and Gondokoro. Work then ceased and the parties returned to Khartoum.

The next important link to be forged in the chain of telegraphic communication was a connection between Bor and Taufikia, a project which Turner himself had examined on the Bahr el Jebel in January, 1907.[3] It was decided that the only possible way of traversing this difficult piece of country was to take the line from Taufikia along the right bank of the Bahr el Jebel westwards to Khor Atar, crossing the latter and the Sobat River near their mouths, and then to strike towards the Bahr ez Zeraf and follow the latter southwards as far as the firm bank continued. Afterwards, the line would be diverted

[1] The line was extended later to Rejaf.
[2] Unfortunately this cable was faulty in manufacture, and afterwards gave much trouble.
[3] *Annual Report of the Posts and Telegraphs Department, Sudan Government,* 1907.

inland in a south-easterly direction, and finally it would return to a southerly alignment to meet the Bahr el Jebel at Bor. The problem of finding a route was complicated by the fact that the entire country to the east of the Bahr ez Zeraf is flooded to a depth of two feet during five months of the year. It was realized, accordingly, that the most difficult portion of the undertaking would be the first 50 miles after striking away from the Bahr ez Zeraf.

Mackworth made two reconnaissances in the region between Bor and Taufikia during April, 1907, the first being northwards from Bor. He had no information about the limits of the *sudd*, but he knew the latitude and longitude of a few places fixed by " Jock " Liddell and determined to find the water-hole, about 70 miles north of Bor, which Liddell had marked with the word " elephants." On the voyage from Khartoum to Bor, he made a wooden measuring-wheel and fitted it with a tin revolution-counter, which he tested on arrival at his destination. Starting from Bor with a few *Jehadia* and a couple of Dinka guides, he made good progress northwards through open scrub interspersed with a few trees, and succeeded in keeping on hard ground not far from the edge of the *sudd*. As his mule plodded onwards, he watched the position of his shadow, halting at intervals to take an average bearing from it and to read the distance on the improvised cyclometer. Two or three days' marching brought the little party to the end of the bush country, and climbing a tree, Mackworth gazed across a sea of elephant grass. The green expanse of the *sudd* was clearly visible to his left. It was as if a green sea joined a grey one. On his right, the edge of the bush stretched eastwards to the horizon. The scene was one of unutterable melancholy and loneliness.

After fixing his approximate position on the almost blank map, Mackworth plotted a bearing to Liddell's water-hole, which he estimated to be about 15 miles distant, and then resumed his march. Two days elapsed, however, before he reached the hole. The heat was intense; the ground was honeycombed with elephant holes into which the men fell continually; and the grass was so high that a passage through it could be forced only in single file and with the greatest difficulty. At the rear of the little column trundled the measuring-wheel. Towards sunset, Mackworth decided to set fire to the dry grass in order to clear a site for a camp, and the flames roared down-wind to the edge of the *sudd* two miles away. It was an awe-inspiring sight. The exhausted party then camped for the night on the red-hot ground in a smother of ash. At dawn they toiled onwards through more elephant country, and from the top of a dead tree Mackworth counted fifty huge brown backs. As it would have been madness to advance into the middle of the herd when the limit of vision on the ground was about two yards, the men emitted ear-splitting screams, and the elephants made off at lumbering gallop. At length, when the measuring-wheel showed that 15 miles had been covered, Mackworth climbed another tree and was delighted to see, some two miles to his left front, a clump of green trees which doubtless marked the position of Liddell's water-hole. A nearer approach, however, showed that the site was already occupied by elephants—father, mother and family of four, the mother fondling a baby while two youngsters indulged in a clumsy game of butting and wrestling. Mackworth and his party watched the fun for some time from behind a thicket within fifty yards of the water-hole, until, tired and thirsty, they were obliged to scare the elephants away by screams and whistles. It seems that the natives of this district, when camping at night, produce a similar result by pulling vigorously on a string attached to a tethered hen. After making a number of sketches of the trees around the water-hole, Mackworth finally led his party back towards Bor, and thus brought to an end his first reconnaissance for the Bor-Taufikia telegraph line.[1]

This reconnaissance was followed immediately by another from the north up the Bahr ez Zeraf, along the right bank of which Mackworth proposed to erect a line in such a way that it could be inspected from a launch. He ascended the Zeraf from its junction with the Bahr el Jebel until it petered out in the swamps of the *sudd*. Then he landed, and marching south-eastwards and afterwards southwards, finished his rough traverse by taking a distant bearing on the trees around Liddell's water-hole, which he had already visited from the south. "There was a special interest in this trip," he writes. "I had been told to get into touch with a certain Sheikh Din, who had never yet been encountered. When I landed, I engaged as a guide a weird-looking dwarf of a man, who said that he was a rain-maker, so as the rainy season was imminent, I promised him a reward if we came through without a wetting. To my great surprise, I had to pay that reward. On one occasion, when a heavy rainstorm, which stretched from horizon to horizon, was approaching rapidly, the man caused it to divide shortly before it reached us and to join again after it had passed, so that we were left on a dry strip not more than a quarter of a mile wide. He was called upon several times to 'make his magic,' in which the ritual burning of cow-dung was the chief factor, and greatly to the delight of my men, the oncoming storms seemed to avoid us."

"The nearer we got to Sheikh Din," continues Mackworth, "the more nervous my men became, for he was reported to be a very powerful magician. We camped near his village and I sent forward a messenger. A reply that the Sheikh would see us on the morrow was brought by three charming young ladies carrying a gift of milk. I had with me an assortment of presents—beads, wire, cloth, mirrors and matches—and saw no cause for alarm as the natives had hitherto

[1] The account of these adventures is taken from notes by Colonel H. L. Mackworth, C.M.G., D.S.O., late R.E., sent to the author on October 25th, 1933. During the latter part of his military service, Colonel Mackworth belonged to the Royal Corps of Signals.

been quite friendly. Three empty ·303 cartridges would always buy a small sheep, for these empty cases were the fashionable and only dress of the smartest young women, who wore them as a miniature sporran on a leather thong. Sheikh Din arrived next morning with a retinue of men and women, and after an interminable song by the latter, I told him about the telegraph line that we wished to build and offered him the presents. He stared solemnly into one of the larger mirrors and then passed it to his councillors. Meanwhile, some of the smaller ones had been handed to the women, and the whole crowd became hysterical with laughter. The conference broke up with mutual impressions of good will, and the reconnaissance having been completed, we returned to the north."

Preparations for an expedition were put in hand without delay. As donkey transport alone was to be used, it was necessary to joint the 3 inches by 3 inches wooden poles with iron fish-plates; and as the poles might be attacked by white ants, they required iron bases. Experience had shown that more damage might be expected from giraffes than from elephants, but the latter were known to be no mean performers. On one occasion, an iron base of heavy trough section was found with a complete turn in it, like a piece of twisted paper, while alongside it lay a small fragment of a tusk. An elephant had jammed his tusk between the wood and iron, and when the point of the tusk broke off, he had vented his fury on the iron base.[1] The donkeys for the expedition were secured from Abyssinia by contractors, and any animal which could trot with three men on its back was accepted. About 300 donkey-men were enrolled—one man to five donkeys. They were told to bring their women with them on the following morning, the order being, " One woman to every group of five men, as usual, and the group to select the lady," It may be well to explain at this point that the women were engaged to do the cooking and other camp work and to grind the *dhurra*. At least 300 women appeared next day, and four-fifths of these had to be sent away disconsolate. The groups or messes were an amusing sight. Here you would see an old man squatting with four youths, who had been persuaded that the grey-beard's ugly and rather disreputable wife was an excellent cook and that nothing else mattered. Next to them, five young men, wise in their generation, who had chosen the grandmother of one of them and so ensured a peaceful life. Some groups had perfectly respectable young wives as cooks; but this usually led to domestic trouble and was not encouraged. Occasionally, when in camp, a woman who wished to change her husband would apply to Mackworth for divorce and re-marriage, a process which he performed quite easily—and legally—by giving to each party a copy of a paper for presentation to the proper authority on

---

[1] The iron base lies in the garden of the Post Office at Khartoum, and Colonel Mackworth still has the broken end of the tusk.

PATROLLING THE TELEGRAPH LINE.

[*From a rough sketch by Colonel H. G. Gandy*, D.S.O., O.B.E., *late R.E.*]

return to Khartoum. From this it appears that a telegraph officer's duties in the Sudan are by no means confined to telegraphy.

Turner had arranged that Mackworth should be in general charge of the construction of the line between Bor and Taufikia, and that Dale should supervise the work from the Taufikia end. Accordingly, Mackworth started for Bor on October 15th, 1907, with Corporals Walshaw and Lester, R.E.,[1] 260 *Jehadia* and 425 donkeys, and Dale embarked for Taufikia in November, with Sergeant Gay and Corporal Hobrough, R.E., and a small party of *Jehadia* and animals. During his reconnaissance northwards from Bor in April, Mackworth had noticed, 30 miles from Bor, a hard mound and a clump of trees on the edge of the *sudd*, about 5 miles inland from the Bahr el Jebel, and he determined to reach that spot in order to establish an advanced depot of stores on the line of march from the south. Two very interesting days were spent in forcing the steamer through the *sudd*. "Among these swamps," he writes, "live thousands of hippopotami, millions upon millions of mosquitoes, and a very shy race of men. These people dwell on little mud banks, and their houses consist only of a platform on which they squat and sleep above a smoke-fire. They live entirely on hippopotami and fish, and appear to be the remnant of some lost race, driven into the swamps by invaders. A few Austrian missionaries once tried to get into touch with them, but they fell ill and died. At Kenisa, south of Shambé, there is a small mud-bank on which the missionaries are said to have built a church and some huts."

Having reached the mound and formed a depot, Mackworth proceeded southwards to Bor, where he disembarked his party and the transport and remaining stores. The mosquitoes were ferocious, and every morning the donkeys' legs were streaming with blood, so no time was lost in starting work. While a party of axe-men cleared the track, the holes for the poles were dug and the stores laid out. Another party bolted the jointed poles together, fastened them to the iron bases, and fixed the insulators and lightning wires. Next came the erecting party, then the wiring party, and finally the anti-elephant trench-digging party. The workers spread over 5 miles of country. At the end of the day, they threw their tools on the ground and marched back to camp. The only occasion on which any tools were lost was when a herd of elephants played pitch-and-toss with them.

By the end of 1907, the party working northwards from Bor through bush country had passed Jonglei[2] and Kongor and had completed 88 miles of line, the last 75 miles being absolutely straight. Meanwhile, Mackworth had pushed on ahead to find the southern end of his reconnaissance from the north in April, and after marching for

[1] Corporal Lester, R.E., died on February 10th, 1908, near Bor, when in charge of one of the telegraph construction parties.
[2] Jonglei became the main base for the southern section of the line.

several days through high grass, and finally wading through 1½ miles of swamp, he came to the village where he had met Sheikh Din. Then he retraced his steps, and leaving the southern party in the charge of Corporal Walshaw, returned to Bor. Next, he voyaged down the Bahr el Jebel, and up the Zeraf to a point 175 kilometres from its mouth, where he landed on January 5th, 1908, to select a route to Awoi. The flood still extended for a distance of 3½ miles from the bank, and it was necessary to prepare a track for donkey transport. In the meantime, the southern party under Walshaw had made good progress. On January 13th, it was joined by Mackworth after a subaquatic journey from kilometre 175. The party was then at a point 7 miles south of Awoi and 125 miles from Bor, and had completed its portion of the undertaking. Accordingly, the base was shifted from Bor to kilometre 175 on the Zeraf, whence stores were carried inland for the difficult section of 50 miles to Awoi.

As regards the work of the northern party, it may be recorded that Sergeant Day and Corporal Hobrough began to erect a line from Taufikia on December 1st, 1907, reaching Khor Atar on December 24th, and finishing 69 miles of line, to a point 80 kilometres up the Zeraf, on January 20th, 1908.[1] When the country had dried sufficiently, work was resumed in two parties from kilometre 175, one party reaching Corporal Walshaw's camp near Awoi on February 26th, and the other completing the line to kilometre 80 on March 30th. Direct communication between Khartoum and the Mongalla and Bahr el Ghazal Provinces was opened on March 31st, 1908, an event which marked the conclusion of a notable achievement in telegraph construction. Little trace now remains of this line, for the section between Kongor and Malakal (near Taufikia) was discarded and dismantled in 1935 in favour of wireless transmission.

While Mackworth and his men were floundering in the morasses of the Bahr ez Zeraf, Dale was supervising not only the start of the northern party from Taufikia, but also an extension of the telegraph north-westwards from that place towards Eliri. Work began on November 7th, 1907, from a point on the left bank opposite Taufikia, to which a cable was laid at a later date. On December 16th, the line reached Tonga ; on January 31st, 1908, it was at Eliri ; and on March 8th, at Talodi in the Nuba Mountains. Dale surveyed the route, and Sergeant Stead, R.E., was in charge of the construction. Small extensions of the telegraph system from Gedaref westwards to Mafaza, and from El Obeid eastwards to Taiyara,[2] were made by Corporal George, R.E., during the winter of 1907–08, but these call for no special remark. By the end of 1908, the Sudan system of telegraph was far advanced and comprised nearly 5,000 miles of line.

---

[1] *Annual Report of the Posts and Telegraphs Department, Sudan Government*, 1908.
[2] The El Obeid-Taiyara line (34 miles) was dismantled in 1912.

There remained only the connection of Talodi with El Obeid, and an extension westwards from the latter into Darfur.

The maintenance of telegraphic communication proved to be no easy task, and especially in the lower reaches of the Zeraf. On nine occasions during the spring of 1909, the line was destroyed at a certain spot by elephants, which came to the river to drink. Damage to any pole caused the wire to sag and touch the animals, and widespread havoc followed. In one case, the elephants brought half a mile of line to the ground. Constant patrolling was needed, and it was in the course of one of these tours of inspection that an incident occurred which is worthy of record. Fadl Mulla and Abdulla Atar, Sudanese linemen stationed at Khor Atar, were wading through a channel near the Zeraf when a large crocodile seized Fadl and held him below water until he was unconscious. Then it carried him to the farther bank to eat him. Meanwhile, Abdulla had dashed onwards to the bank, and on the reappearance of the crocodile with its victim, shot it and pulled Fadl ashore. The man's thighs were bitten and torn in a terrible manner, and he had two deep abdominal wounds; but Abdulla rendered first aid, and brought him safely to Khor Atar through 45 miles of swamp and jungle. Fadl was removed to Taufikia, apparently in a dying condition; yet he was able to return to duty after several months in hospital, and when he was offered work elsewhere, he refused and insisted on being sent back to his former post among the crocodiles of the Zeraf!

On January 24th, 1909, Captain H. G. Gandy, R.E., was appointed as Assistant Director in succession to Captain H. L. Mackworth, D.S.O., R.E., whose reversion to the Home Establishment was gazetted on February 25th. Through the departure of Mackworth, the Sudan was deprived of one of its most efficient and popular officers. He served the country well, and left it when the greater part of its telegraph system had been completed, a work in which he had played a most prominent part. Lieutenant F. A. Ferguson, R.E., joined as Deputy Assistant Director on January 10th, 1911, and Quarter-Master and Honorary Lieutenant W. H. Dale, R.E., reverted to the Home Establishment on November 2nd. The Director of Posts and Telegraphs paid a tribute to Dale. " He has served for 13 years in this country," he remarked.[1] " His personality and the nature of his services are known so universally throughout the Sudan that the mention of his name and the fact that he has left us is an ample record of the great loss that the Department has sustained." On September 5th, 1912, the Director himself, Major E. V. Turner, R.E., handed over charge to Major J. P. Moir, D.S.O., R.E., and returned to England. " Not only," wrote Sir Reginald Wingate,[2] " has Turner Bey been responsible for the construction of many

[1] *Annual Report of the Posts and Telegraphs Department, Sudan Government*, 1911.
[2] Farewell Order by H.E. The Sirdar and Governor-General of the Sudan, dated September 1st, 1912.

miles of telegraph[1] in new regions during the past eight years, but he has also had to deal with international postal questions of great importance. In both these duties he has acquitted himself with marked success." Thus within four years of the completion of the Bahr el Ghazal and Bahr el Jebel lines, all the officers concerned in their erection had left the Sudan.

Captain H. G. Gandy, R.E., held the post of Assistant Director for less than two years, for he was invalided on October 23rd, 1912, and never returned to the country. During his brief tour of duty, he was occupied chiefly in surveying under most trying conditions in unhealthy areas. In the spring of 1910, he reconnoitred up the Sobat River for a line to connect Taufikia with Nasir, close to the Abyssinian border; and in the beginning of 1912, he surveyed up the pestilential Bahr el Ghazal from Tonga to Meshra er Req to determine the feasibility of connecting Taufikia by telegraph with Meshra. This project was abandoned, however, after he had reported that 40 miles of cable would be needed. He is remembered in the Sudan, not only as an engineer, but as an artist whose sketches and caricatures have given pleasure to many. The post of Assistant Director vacated by Gandy was filled on February 21st, 1913, by Lieutenant R. Chenevix-Trench, R.E., an officer from the Signal Companies at Aldershot, who arrived in Khartoum on March 7th.

Changes were so frequent in the staff of non-commissioned officers that they cannot be recorded in detail, but two call for special mention. Sergeant Stead, R.E., left the Sudan in September, 1913, after 15 years' service, during which he had participated in the construction of almost every telegraph line in the country; and Sergeant Walshaw, R.E., followed him in October after completing 9 years' service. Like other subordinates of the Posts and Telegraphs Department, these men had shouldered unusual responsibilities and had often lived for months without seeing a white face. The strain was great, but they proved equal to it.

From 1909, until the Great War, there was little alteration or extension of the Sudan telegraph system. In May, 1910, the existing cable across the White Nile between Khartoum and Omdurman was replaced by a larger one; and in October and November, 1911, a cable was laid across the river at Rejaf and the telegraph extended to that place from Gondokoro.[2] The line from kilometre 62 to kilometre 175 on the Bahr ez Zeraf, and also from Awoi to Kongor, was rebuilt, during the spring of 1913, with higher poles on the original iron bases; and the alignment along the Zeraf was altered so that, instead of following the river bank throughout its length, it touched it only at intervals. Ferguson was in charge of some of this work, and afterwards made a compass traverse from Bor through Pibor Post,

[1] Approximately, 1,800 miles of telegraph were built while Major E. V. Turner, R.E., was Director of the Posts and Telegraphs Department.
[2] *Annual Report of the Posts and Telegraphs Department, Sudan Government*, 1911.

Akobo Post and Nasir to Taufikia to examine the possibility of opening up communication by telegraph with the military posts along the Abyssinian frontier, and also to provide an alternative route to the south.[1] This extension, however, was not taken in hand.

The year 1914 saw the introduction of wireless telegraphy into the Sudan. While on leave in England, Lieutenant R. Chenevix-Trench, R.E., received a cypher telegram from Khartoum asking for an estimate of the cost of establishing wireless communication between Malakal on the White Nile and Gambela in Abyssinia, with an intermediate station at Nasir on the Sobat River.[2] Gambela was a trading post on the Baro, a tributary of the Sobat. It was leased to the Sudan, and certain European firms had offices there for the exchange of goods against local produce. A small steamer paid a monthly visit to the place between May and October, at which season there was sufficient water in the Sobat and Baro; but for the remainder of the year, Gambela was cut off from all communication. No reliance could be placed on the single telephone wire that sagged forlornly from tree to tree along the route, 300 miles in length, through Goré to Addis Ababa. In 1914, the only line of telegraphic communication between Abyssinia and the outer world was through the Italian system in Eritrea, and the proposed wireless link with the Sudan was part of a combined agreement to give her an additional outlet. The Abyssinian Government undertook to repair the line from Addis Ababa to Gambela, and the Government of the Sudan agreed to establish wireless connection between Gambela and the important military and telegraph station at Malakal, a distance of 230 miles.

At this time, the wireless industry was in its infancy; but after making extensive inquiries, Chenevix-Trench was able to give a rough estimate of the cost of three wireless sets and was promptly ordered to buy them. This, however, was easier said than done, as sets adapted to the peculiar conditions of the Sudan were not to be found in any catalogue. An extreme and robust simplicity was essential to allow for rough usage by untrained operators and the absence of all facilities for replacement or repair. Happily, the bulk and weight of the apparatus were of small importance. Chenevix-Trench spent the remainder of his leave in designing, calculating, estimating and consulting, and in the end obtained three sets with synchronous rotary sparks. Each set was supplied with power from an 8 h.p. low-speed petrol engine, driving an alternator by means of a belt, and without any intervening dynamo, accumulator or motor. Reception was through a rectifying crystal. The wooden aerial masts were to

---

[1] *Annual Report of the Posts and Telegraphs Department, Sudan Government*, 1913.
[2] Article entitled "Early days of Wireless Communication in the Sudan," by Colonel R. Chenevix-Trench, O.B.E., M.C., late R.E. and Royal Corps of Signals, sent to the author on January 9th, 1936, and published in the *Royal Signals Quarterly Journal*, Vol. IV, No. 14, October, 1936, pp. 183–191.

be 90 feet high, 360 feet apart, and raised from the ground on iron bases.

The supply of the apparatus was so greatly delayed by the outbreak of war that the materials did not begin to arrive in the Sudan until 1915.[1] Meanwhile Chenevix-Trench had erected two model sets in Khartoum, made from toy equipment bought in a London shop, and with these he initiated a number of Sudanese telegraph operators into some of the mysteries of the new system. When the materials for the high frequency circuits reached the capital in 1915, one set was assembled temporarily for the final instruction of the operators and linemen, and afterwards dismantled and sent with the others to Malakal. Chenevix-Trench went also to Malakal with his two assistants, Mr. Sebright of the Public Works Department (formerly a Warrant Officer of the Royal Marines) and Sergeant G. A. Stevens, R.E. (Signals). Sebright was to erect the necessary buildings at Gambela, and Stevens to help Chenevix-Trench in the installation of the wireless. Suitable building accommodation had already been prepared at Malakal and Nasir. The operators were Egyptians or Sudanese, and the fitters, Egyptians or Maltese. No electricians were available.

The erection of the stations at Malakal and Nasir presented no difficulties. Sebright and Stevens went forward to Gambela, while Chenevix-Trench remained at Nasir to instal the instruments and establish communication with Malakal before following the others to Gambela in the next monthly ship. On arrival at Gambela, Chenevix-Trench found that his assistants had met with serious obstruction from one Majid Abood, the local Abyssinian Governor. This man indulged in an illicit trade in ivory and slaves, and being averse to the light which would be thrown on his proceedings by wireless contact with the Sudan, had denied the right of Sebright and Stevens to build a station. He prevented their men from quarrying stone, arrested some of them, and sent soldiers to stop the building. The British engineers, however, continued their work within a fence of barbed wire, and the unwelcome attentions of the Abyssinian officials ceased after Sebright had frightened some intruders at night by waving his arms and moaning sadly in realistic imitation of a lost spirit. He and Stevens were popular with the local inhabitants, whom they treated for small ailments, and consequently Majid's warnings that the Englishmen were the forerunners of an invading army, and that the wireless masts were the implements of witchcraft, fell on deaf ears. On the third day after his arrival, Chenevix-Trench established communication with Malakal. Majid was then invited to witness

[1] While experimenting with wireless in Egypt, Chenevix-Trench overheard a message from German telegraphists in Gaza announcing that they were closing down as the Turks were about to evacuate the place. This information was given at once to General Sir Archibald Murray; but he was unable to transmit it to General Dobell, who was attacking Gaza, as telegraphic communication was temporarily suspended. Unaware that the enemy were about to retreat, General Dobell withdrew his forces, and thus the First Battle of Gaza ended in failure.

TELEGRAPH TRANSPORT CROSSING A CREEK ON THE SOBAT.

the magic concealed in the wireless building, and was so impressed by the leaping spark that he refrained from further interference.

After his return from the south, Chenevix-Trench was required to establish a wireless station at Port Sudan for communication with the ships of the Red Sea Patrol. He managed to secure in Alexandria a "Telefunken" quenched-spark set taken from a captured German ship, and having tested it in Cairo, took it to Port Sudan. The next problem was to find a suitable support for the aerial, and the only solution appeared to be to fix one end to the top of the power station chimney, 170 feet in height. Accordingly, the furnace having been drawn overnight, Chenevix-Trench and a Sudanese lineman proceeded to climb to the top by iron rungs fixed inside the shaft, carrying with them 60 fathoms of light rope. "*Wallahi Effendim*," gasped the lineman. "If she breathe now we are lost." However, no breath came; and after they had hauled up and fastened a block to the top of the chimney and had run a stout rope through it, the two climbers descended to the ground. Black as soot on emerging from the shaft, Chenevix-Trench was welcomed by the other linemen with the remark, "By Allah, you are now indeed our brother!"

A high telegraph pole sufficed for the second support, and the aerial was slung between it and the chimney. The earth connection presented some difficulty as the station stood on non-conducting coral rock; but the problem was solved by blasting a curved trench down to water-level, laying boiler-plates bolted together along the bottom, and connecting them at intervals to the surface by rails projecting above the ground. The trench was then filled in, and the tops of the rails connected by radial wires to a leading-in insulator. By these means, an efficient low-resistance earth was secured. The installation of wireless in Port Sudan furnishes a typical example of the improvisation forced upon telegraph officers in out-lying stations.

Lieut.-Colonel J. P. Moir, D.S.O., R.E., Director of Posts and Telegraphs since 1912, coped successfully with the difficulties inseparable from the abnormal conditions prevailing throughout the period of the Great War. His staff was depleted, and those who remained were overworked. In 1915, he was deprived of the assistance of Captain F. A. Ferguson, R.E., on the reversion of the latter to the Home Establishment. Nevertheless, several new lines were built for military purposes. For instance, during and after the Darfur Expedition of 1916, the existing line from El Obeid to En Nahud was prolonged westwards for a distance of 246 miles to El Fasher. Material was obtained by dismantling less important lines, including the historic desert line from Suakin to Berber[1]. The wireless system expanded steadily. In addition to the stations built

---

[1] *Report on the Finances, Administration and Condition of Egypt and the Sudan,* 1914–1919.

in 1915 at Malakal, Nasir and Gambela, others were provided in 1916 at El Fasher and Kebkabiya[1] in Darfur, and in 1918, at El Kereinik[2] in Darfur and at Mongalla on the Upper Nile. Chenevix-Trench was concerned in the installations at El Fasher and Kebkabiya, and operated portable wireless sets with much success during the Darfur Expedition; but he reverted to the Home Establishment in February, 1917, and consequently took no part in the extension of the wireless to El Kereinik and Mongalla.

There was little alteration in the Sudan telegraph system during 1920 and 1921, except that a few more desert lines, including the Omdurman-El Obeid line through Ed Deuim and Bara, were dismantled and the wire transferred to the railway telegraph lines in order to economize in poles. The wireless system, on the other hand, developed surely and steadily. By the end of 1921, there were 13 wireless stations, many of which had amply justified their existence. During the insurrection among the Aliab Dinkas west of Bor in 1919, the insurgents destroyed 66 miles of telegraph line between Mvolo and Tombé,[3] and had it not been for the new wireless station at Wau, all communication with the Bahr el Ghazal Province would have been severed.[4] The wireless station at Mongalla was also useful when communication by line telegraphy was interrupted by the depredations of elephants and giraffes.

Lieutenant (now Major) R. T. Williams, R. Signals (late R.E.), was appointed Deputy Assistant Director (Wireless), Sudan Posts and Telegraphs Department, on January 12th, 1922. He held this post for the next 10 years, and a large share of the credit for the expansion of wireless communication in the Sudan must be accorded to him.

The chief event in 1922, however, was the departure of Colonel J. P. Moir, D.S.O., late R.E., on September 5th, on reversion to the Home Establishment after 10 years' service as Director. He was succeeded by Mr. H. Wynne, formerly Controller of the Postal Service.[5] Moir's tenure of office was marked not only by the introduction of the wireless service, but by the establishment of a savings bank which was of great benefit to the people. The telephone service in the larger towns was improved and expanded, and at the time of his departure, it had 11 main exchanges, 22 sub-exchanges, 655 miles of open wire and 278 miles of cable.[6]

The years 1923 and 1924 were uneventful; but in February, 1925, the reconstruction of the Port Sudan-Atbara railway telegraph was

---

[1] Kebkabiya is 90 miles west of El Fasher. This station was closed on April 12th, 1921.
[2] El Kereinik is 80 miles west of Kebkabiya.
[3] The Mvolo-Tombé section was rebuilt in March, 1922.
[4] *Annual Report of the Posts and Telegraphs Department, Sudan Government*, **1920**.
[5] Mr. Wynne retired in 1929.
[6] *Annual Report of the Posts and Telegraphs Department, Sudan Government*, 1922

taken in hand, and in November, 1925, the building of a new line southwards from El Obeid.[1] This line was to run through Abu Zabad, Dilling and Kadugli to Talodi to join the line from Taufikia erected by Sergeant Stead, R.E., in 1908. Abu Zabad was reached in January, 1926, and Dilling in the following month; and after some delay caused by an insurrection in the Nuba Mountains, the line was completed to Talodi in 1927, thus providing an alternative route between Khartoum and Malakal.[2] In 1927 also, Abu Zabad was connected with En Nahud; and in 1928, a line was run 48 miles southwards from En Nahud to El Odaiya. The telegraph system then comprised 5,047 miles of line, including 797 miles alongside railways.[3] Since 1928, there has been little change, and consequently a further description of the system is unnecessary.

The connection of Royal Engineers with the Sudan Posts and Telegraphs Department was augmented at the end of 1926, by the appointment of Lieut.-Colonel K. E. Edgeworth, D.S.O., M.C., R.E. (retd.), as Chief Engineer. One of Edgeworth's first tasks was to replace poles on the Port Sudan-Atbara line which had not been properly creosoted, and another was to superimpose telephone circuits on many of the telegraph wires in the Southern Sudan.[4] Subsequently, he turned his attention to improvements in the wireless system and introduced a standard medium-wave[5] set of his own design in gradual replacement of the existing "spark" sets. The working range of the new sets was 300 miles. Several were installed in 1930 for the weekly "Cape to Cairo" Air Service, which was opened in March, 1931, by Imperial Airways.[6] A wireless station for this Service was opened at Wadi Halfa in 1930, and additional transmitters and receivers were installed at Atbara, Khartoum, Malakal and Juba, at which places the machines called.[7] Lieut.-Colonel Edgeworth vacated his post in February, 1931, and was succeeded by Lieut.-Colonel J. L. Tomlin, C.B.E., D.S.O., a Royal Engineer who had recently retired from the Royal Corps of Signals. In December, 1931, Tomlin became Director of Posts and Telegraphs on the abolition of the appointment of Chief Engineer.[8] He was called upon at once to deal with urgent problems of wireless communication. "For air co-operation," he writes,[9] "we used the wireless sets designed and adapted by Edgeworth. The native operators soon learned the simple procedure, and co-operation with

---

[1] *Annual Report of the Posts and Telegraphs Department, Sudan Government*, 1925.
[2] *Ibid*. 1925, 1926 and 1927.
[3] *Ibid*., 1928.
[4] Notes by Lieut.-Colonel K. E. Edgeworth sent to the author on July 13th, 1934.
[5] The wave-length was 900 metres, as adopted for aircraft.
[6] In 1931, the service was chiefly to East Africa.
[7] *Annual Report of the Posts and Telegraphs Department, Sudan Government*, 1930.
[8] The following ex-N.C.O's, R.E., were serving in the Sudan Posts and Telegraphs Department in 1934 :—Messrs. Summerfield (Superintending Engineer) and Prince and Stevens (Assistant Engineers).
[9] Notes by Lieut.-Colonel J. L. Tomlin sent to the author on October 22nd, 1936.

aircraft has since been carried out with marked success. In 1935, the air service became bi-weekly; and in addition to the ordinary navigation messages between the ground and air, a commercial service to and from passengers in the air was introduced. Since 1935, we have been preparing for the Empire Air Scheme—three services each week, with day and night flying. This has entailed the installation of Direction Finding Stations at all the airports, the addition of wireless installations at Kareima and Kosti, and the provision of short-wave apparatus for communication with aircraft. A regular air service has now been introduced through Kano to Lagos on the west coast of Africa, and installations are being erected for this route at El Obeid, El Fasher and El Geneina.[1] These rapid developments have necessitated a large recruitment of skilled Egyptian and Sudanese operators, who are difficult to obtain. Since July, 1935, we have also provided air co-operation for the Italian *Ala Littoria* Air Line, flying between Khartoum, Kassala and Asmara, and now, I believe, to Addis Ababa."

The history of the Sudan telegraph extension, especially in its earlier stages, is a record of human tenacity and endurance which it is hard to equal. Though few of the employés came through unscathed, the result was worth the sacrifice. The country now has a system which is ready for any emergency and constitutes a most valuable link in the chain of Empire communication.

In conclusion, we turn to the connection of Royal Engineers with the Egyptian system of telegraphs. It has been very slender. Indeed, as regards the control of civil telegraphy, it is confined to two officers—Lieutenant E. P. C. Girouard, who was President of the Egyptian State Railways and Telegraphs in 1898, and 1899, and Captain J. S. Liddell, who left the Sudan in 1904 to take up the appointment of Deputy Inspector General of the Egyptian State Telegraphs. A number of Royal Engineers, however, operated some of the dilapidated Egyptian lines under war conditions during the Tel el Kebir and Nile campaigns. Colonel C. E. Webber controlled these lines during both campaigns, ably assisted in 1882 by " C " (Telegraph) Troop, under Major Sir A. W. Mackworth,[2] and in 1884-85 by a detachment of the Telegraph Battalion, R.E., under Captain F. W. Bennet.[3] During the summer of 1885, Lieut.-Colonel H. F. Turner was Director of Army Telegraphs with the Nile Expedition. The Egyptian lines which were used for military purposes in Egypt and the Sudan, were handed back to civil control in 1887,[4] and it is probable that the report of Colonel Webber induced

---

[1] El Geneina is about 190 miles south-west of El Fasher, and near the border of French Equatorial Africa.
[2] See Chapter II.
[3] See Chapter IV.
[4] The Egyptian system extended southwards to Wadi Halfa, and onwards through Dongola to Merowe in the Sudan.

the Board of Administration of the Egyptian Railways and Telegraphs to ask, in 1889, that an expert should be sent to examine the entire system. The request was forwarded to the Postmaster General in London, who suggested that the examination might be conducted by Colonel H. F. Turner, then Commanding Royal Engineer in Egypt.[1] Turner began his inspection in December, 1889, and submitted a devastating report on February 17th, 1890. This was read, discussed, printed and carefully pigeon-holed. No more was ever heard of it.[2]

The report stated that Colonel Turner had visited 99 telegraph offices in Lower Egypt and all the offices in Upper Egypt, and that he had inspected hundreds of instruments and their batteries, tested wires, measured currents, and inquired into methods of working and the number of men employed. He had found that the poles were very old or dangerously weak, and that the wire stays were insecurely fitted and had no swivels. The number of joints in the wires was so prodigious that many of the lines seemed to have been constructed by piecing together short lengths of old wire. In one place there were ten joints in a single span ! The instruments were 20 to 35 years old. Military messages were not entitled to precedence, even in time of war, and an urgent demand for reinforcements might be delayed in favour of a message from a sutler asking for cigarettes. Technical faults, and defects in administration and in the accommodation of the staff, were numerous. Comprehensive reform was needed from top to bottom. This was the gist of the report, which pictures accurately the condition of the Egyptian telegraph system when Liddell arrived in 1904.

From the day of his appointment until the outbreak of the Great War, " Jock " Liddell worked heart and soul to bring order out of confusion, and with such success that, by 1914, he had re-organized the system and was able to meet the sudden demands of an exceptionally heavy military traffic. As Director of Army Signals during the early part of the war, he was invaluable to the Commander-in-Chief in Egypt, and on the Suez Canal ;[3] and after the war, as the first Inspector General of Telegraphs and Telephones,[4] he continued his efficient civil administration. In February, 1920, he became Under-Secretary in the Ministry of Communications,[5] a position in

---

[1] Colonel H. F. Turner succeeded Colonel J. M. H. Maitland as C.R.E. in Cairo in February, 1886, and held the appointment until May, 1890. He was an expert in telegraphy, having served from 1871 to 1885 in command of Telegraph Companies or of the Military Telegraph Establishment under the General Post Office. In 1885, he joined the force under Sir Gerald Graham at Suakin. A Memoir of Colonel H. F. Turner appears in the *R.E. Journal*, Vol. XII, July-December, 1910, pp. 97–104.

[2] A copy of Colonel H. F. Turner's report is in the R.E. Library in London.

[3] See Chapter XII.

[4] Previously he had been Inspector General of Telegraphs. Prior to 1919, the Egyptian telephone system was operated by a Company, but in that year, the Government assumed control.

[5] See Chapter XV.

which he was not happy. His health began to fail; and in 1924, he resigned the appointment to become for a time the agent in London for the Egyptian Government for the purchase of stores. His departure terminated a notable career, which had brought great benefit to Egypt and the Sudan, and it severed one of the last links connecting those countries with the eventful and far distant days when Kitchener ruled in Khartoum.

SUBMARINE CABLE STORE, MEROWE.

[from "*The Military Telegraph Bulletin,*" May, 1888.]

CHAPTER XVII.

SURVEY AND EXPLORATION.

THE first Royal Engineer to survey the Sudan was Colonel Charles Gordon, who landed at Suakin on February 25th, 1874, as the newly appointed "Governor-General of the Equator" in succession to Sir Samuel Baker. Gordon had a natural aptitude for such work. He had shown this in his early reconnaissances in the Crimea, in a subsequent delimitation of the Russian boundaries, and in his surveys around Shanghai, and he now gave another example of his ability in a clear and accurate reconnaissance sketch of his route from Suakin across the desert to Berber, and thence up the Nile to Khartoum.[1] The capital was reached on March 13th in record time; and on April 16th, in company with Lieut.-Colonel Chaillé-Long, he was 1,000 miles farther upstream at Gondokoro, the headquarters of the Equatorial Province. On May 3rd, he was back again in Khartoum and hastening downstream to Berber to meet the remainder of his cosmopolitan staff.[2] Early in June, the complete expedition was on its way southwards from Khartoum, Gordon himself bringing up the rear in the famous *Bordein*. He halted for several weeks at the mouth of the Sobat River, where he established a station, and then ascended the Bahr el Jebel, reaching Shambé on August 25th, and Gondokoro on September 3rd.[3] There he continued his preparations for opening up communication with Lakes Victoria and Albert, and for the suppression of the slave-trade which was conducted by Zubeir and other Arabs with the encouragement of Ismail Ayub Pasha, the Egyptian Governor-General at Khartoum.

Though burdened with political and administrative problems, Gordon had found time during his preliminary journey in March and April, 1874, to map the river route from Khartoum to Gondokoro, and had produced a traverse which formed a valuable addition to the reconnaissances and reports of earlier travellers such as Miami,

---

[1] This sketch, dated February and March, 1874, is in the R.E. Museum at Chatham. It is on squared paper, in ink, with the Nile coloured. A panorama of the Red Sea coast is given, and there are many remarks regarding the route.

[2] Gordon's original staff consisted of two American officers, Lieut.-Colonel C. Chaillé-Long and Major W. Campbell, Romolo Gessi (an Italian), Auguste Linant de Bellefonds (a Frenchman) and three Englishmen, Messrs. J. Kemp, W. Anson and F. J. Russell. Accompanying the expedition were three German naturalists named Witt, Menges and Bohndorff. By the beginning of September, 1874, most of these men were dead, or incapacitated through sickness.

[3] See the *Sketch Map of the Eastern and Southern Frontiers of the Sudan*, which is included in this chapter.

Manuel, Speke, Grant, and Sir Samuel Baker.[1] "I am making a map of the river," he writes on March 23rd,[2] "and find Manuel's map is rather out. I have had to make a log to measure the speed of the steamer. I could not get the triangle to halt in the water at first and then found that I must weight it."

During September and October, 1874, Gordon collected his stores, organized his transport at Gondokoro, and established a new station at Rejaf, 16 miles farther south. In November, he was greatly surprised by the arrival of the two young Royal Engineers, Lieutenants C. M. Watson[3] and W. H. Chippindall, who had been sent from England to assist him. He had asked for their services before he left Cairo in February, but had received no answer. Watson and Chippindall had set out from Suakin on September 10th, and arrived at Berber on the 24th of that month. "On the 30th," writes Chippindall,[4] "we embarked in a small twin-screw steamer put together by Sir Samuel Baker at Gondokoro. She was sadly infested by rats and insects of all descriptions, from the common cockroach to scorpions of various sizes, which have an unpleasant way of secreting themselves in your pockets and in the folds of your clothing. On October 6th, we arrived in Khartoum, where we were met by Mr. Russell, who had been invalided from Gondokoro. One of the American officers, Major Campbell, was also there, very ill; he died a day or two after our arrival. Watson examined our instruments, and we were glad to find none damaged by the journey. Khartoum was left on October 11th, and we steamed up the White Nile. Here we considered our work would fairly be begun. We therefore commenced a map of the river, taking bearings and using our patent log.[5] Whenever we stopped, we found our latitude by circum-meridian altitudes and our longitude by two chronometers. By these means, we have got certain fixed points along the river and a very closely approximating traverse between them. We determined the deviation of the compass by bearings of the pole star. The country is so flat and marshy that at Fashoda I was able to take a meridian altitude of the sun with the grassy marsh as a horizon and obtain a result differing by only one minute from the latitude by the stars."

"On October 25th," continues Chippindall, "we reached the junction of the Sobat with the White Nile. A steamer arrived from Gondokoro having Lieut.-Colonel Long, an American officer, on board. He had been sent by Colonel Gordon on a mission to Mtesa,

---

[1] This survey of the White Nile can be seen in the R.E. Museum at Chatham. It is in pencil, with the river coloured, and shows parallels of latitude and meridians of longitude. The scale is about 60 miles to 1 inch.
[2] *Colonel Gordon in Central Africa*, edited by Dr. G. B. Hill, p. 9.
[3] Afterwards Colonel Sir Charles Watson, K.C.M.G., C.B.
[4] Letter from Lt. W. H. Chippindall, R.E., dated Gondokoro, November 22nd, 1874, appearing in an article entitled "Upper Egypt" in the *R.E. Journal*, Vol. 5, 1875, pp. 9–11.
[5] The nature of this log is not stated. Possibly it may have been the log used by Gordon in March.

King of Uganda, and had just returned after a troublesome journey of eight months. We left the Sobat on the 29th, and on reaching Shambé, were met by a deputation of the Keekah tribe. We had them on board the boat to breakfast, and as soon as they saw the engine they formed up and sang a song in praise of it. This seems to be their custom. They thought that we were white from leprosy, and called our watches " spirits." One man took a tremendous sniff at a bottle of ammonia and fell down, which rather alarmed us ; however, he recovered and laughed till the tears rolled out of his eyes. When we left, they on the shore were still singing about the boat and its excellence. We arrived at Gondokoro on November 14th, and reported ourselves to the Colonel. He proposes sending us on to Ibrahimiya (opposite Dufilé) with an iron sailing boat and a small row boat to be put into the river there above the rapids, and we shall have to explore up to Lake Albert to see whether the river is really navigable for a steamer."

The compass survey of the White Nile and Bahr el Jebel from Khartoum to Rejaf (beyond Gondokoro), made by Watson and Chippindall in the autumn of 1874, has often been compared with later surveys, executed in 1901 and 1903, and has furnished valuable information regarding the permanence of the meandering curves of the river.[1]

After the arrival of Watson and Chippindall, Gordon devoted his whole attention to administration. " I am free from all the science now," he writes on November 23rd.[2] The surveying was to be done by the two subalterns, who spent a fortnight in collecting supplies and on November 29th, started for Rejaf, where they remained for several weeks because they were unable to obtain a suitable escort. Meanwhile, they took observations of the transit of Venus. Both contracted malaria, and in the middle of January, 1875, they were recalled by Gordon to Lado below Gondokoro, where Chippindall regained his strength. On January 29th, however, Watson was obliged to leave for England. " He goes home quite broken down," writes Gordon.[3] " His clothes hang on him as a pole." On the same day, Chippindall set out to explore the river to Dufilé, beyond the present Uganda border, and if possible to reach and survey Lake Albert ; but he got no farther than Dufilé, and on April 15th rejoined Gordon at Rejaf[4] and returned upstream with him to a new station called Kerri, some 40 miles distant. Gordon then went down to Lado to await reinforcements ; but in July, Chippindall

[1] Notes by Colonel Sir Henry G. Lyons, F.R.S., late R.E., sent to the author on December 6th, 1934. This survey was sent to the Royal Geographical Society, and was reproduced in the Journal of that Society in 1876.
[2] *Colonel Gordon in Central Africa*, 1874-79, edited by Dr. G. B. Hill, p. 57.
[3] *Ibid.*, p. 68.
[4] Letter from Lieut. W. H. Chippindall, R.E., in continuation of his letter of November 22nd, 1874, appearing in the *R.E. Journal*, Vol. 5, 1875, pp. 95-96. An interesting article, dated February 7th, 1875, entitled " Colonel Gordon in Central Africa," appears on pp. 40 and 41 of the same volume.

became so seriously ill at Kerri that Gordon found it necessary to send him home. Chippindall had been farther south than any other European except Long, Speke, Grant and Baker. His constitution, however, was unequal to the strain. Thus, within eight months of their arrival, Gordon lost both his Royal Engineer assistants, and was obliged to resume the surveying work which he had delegated to them.

The story of Gordon's explorations in Uganda has been recorded by many writers.[1] At the end of July, 1875, he began an attempt to get a steamer through the rapids above Rejaf, along which he had established a series of posts;[2] but the vessel was wrecked, and he lost his only colleague, the Frenchman, Linant de Bellefonds, in a fight with natives. He waited for some months at Dufilé, and then went down-stream in November to meet his trusted lieutenant, Gessi, who was bringing up reinforcements and the sections of a steamer. Marching south once more, he left the Nile and reached it again at Foweira between Lakes Victoria and Albert, and in January, 1876, followed the river as far southwards as Mrooli. Returning next to Dufilé, he proceeded to survey the cataracts northwards until he reached Lado in March.[3] There he was joined in April by Gessi, who had meanwhile circumnavigated Lake Albert and established a station at Magungo at its northern end.

Gordon was determined to extend his survey of the Nile as far as the Great Lakes, for he and his assistants had already mapped the river as far as Dufilé. Accordingly, on July 20th, 1876, he set out southwards from Dufilé, surveying as he went, and after spending a few days at Magungo on Lake Albert, followed the channel past the Murchison Falls to Foweira, where he arrived on August 11th, having mapped 70 miles of uncharted river in six days. A few extracts from his diary[4] will show what he endured :—" *August 6th.* I am nearly dead. To map the river for eight or ten miles I have had to walk, in pouring rain, some 18 miles through jungle ; but it is done, and I am quite sure that no one will ever do it again. *August 7th.* A weary, hot march of 15 miles. *August 8th.* We got over 15 miles to-day—terrible work. Such a country of ravines and gullies ! I have never had such fatigue. *August 9th.* Got over 18 miles to-day. The path for eight miles was through fearful grass. *August 10th.* After $14\frac{1}{2}$ miles, we reached the deserted *zariba* of the Anfina Station. What with wild vines and convolvuli and other creepers, you sometimes got bound hand and foot. I have had

[1] A concise and clear account is included in *Gordon and the Sudan*, by Dr. Bernard M. Allen, pp. 64–81.
[2] These posts are described by Lieut. W. H. Chippindall, R.E., in an article entitled " Observations on the White Nile between Gondocoro and Affuddo," appearing in the *R.E. Journal*, Vol. 6, 1876, pp. 13, 14.
[3] Article entitled " Colonel C. G. Gordon's Movements in Central Africa " appearing (with a map by Lt. Chippindall) in the *R.E. Journal*, Vol. 6, 1876, pp. 68, 69.
[4] *Colonel Gordon in Central Africa*, 1874–79, edited by Dr. G. B. Hill, pp. 179, 180.

several severe falls." Few men could have won through in the face of such obstacles; yet Gordon continued his march after only four days' rest at Foweira, and on August 17th arrived at Mrooli on the Victoria Nile, west of Lake Kioga. Thence, he marched overland to the village of Niamyongo, within 60 miles of Lake Victoria, and turning north, began to survey down the Nile. Political difficulties had prevented his further progress southward. On October 3rd, he was at Magungo; and on the 11th, at his base at Lado.

Gordon reached Khartoum on October 24th, 1876, and there he met Gessi, with whom he had been in constant correspondence regarding a large-scale map which was being prepared from his route sketches. On November 6th he writes:—[1] " I have been working for the last ten days at the big map of the Sudan; but now it is finished I am again utterly at a loss how to employ my time." He was suffering from the inevitable reaction following on years of intensive effort which had ended in disappointment, for he had been unable to attain his goal at Victoria Nyanza. Yet his maps and sketches of the Nile should have satisfied him, for they extended from the 18th parallel almost to the equator. In addition to those already mentioned, two others can be seen in the R.E. Museum at Chatham—a traverse in pencil, entitled " Survey of the White Nile from Rigaf (Rejaf) to Mrooli," and another of the White Nile from the Sobat to Gondokoro.

From the beginning of 1877, until he left the Sudan in August, 1879, Gordon had little time for surveying. He covered thousands of miles on camel-back, always at high speed and with the minimum of equipment. His work was administrative and military, his responsibilities enormous, his power almost regal. His exploits with the compass and log are overshadowed by his achievements as the ruler of a vast territory; but they should not be disregarded, for they were of great value to the officers of his Corps who resumed the survey of the Southern Sudan after the fall of the Khalifa.

During the military operations of 1884-85, topographical surveys were executed by Lieutenant F. B. Longe, R.E., in the region of Suakin, and by Captain H. G. Kunhardt, R.E., along the alignment of the ill-fated Suakin-Otao Railway;[2] and while with the Nile Expedition, Major D. C. Courtney, R.E., surveyed the country near the river,[3] and Captain H. H. Kitchener, R.E., prepared route sketches of his journeys as an Intelligence Officer. Again, in 1892, Lieutenant H. G. Lyons, R.E., explored and sketched several of the desert roads by which raiding dervishes might advance into Egypt.[4] With these exceptions, however, it seems that, after the

---

[1] *Colonel Gordon in Central Africa*, 1874-79, by Dr. G. B. Hill, p. 323.
[2] See Chapter III.
[3] See Chapter IV.
[4] Notes by Colonel Sir Henry G. Lyons, late R.E. sent to the author on December 6th, 1934.

departure of Charles Gordon, there was little surveying by Royal Engineers in the Sudan until the arrival, in 1893, of Major the Hon. M. G. Talbot, R.E., the most distinguished Survey officer whom the country has ever known. The arid wastes of Nubia and Libya were so over-run by hordes of dervishes that deliberate trigonometrical work could be executed only under the protection of powerful military forces and at great expense, which Egypt could not afford.

Milo Talbot had already earned a great reputation as a trigonometrical surveyor on the North-West Frontier of India.[1] In 1889, he relinquished that employment to enter the Staff College at Camberley, passing in at the top of the list, far ahead of the second candidate. He qualified in December, 1891, and after a few months at Aldershot, was appointed to the Mapping Section of the Intelligence Department at the War Office. In the summer of 1893, he made the acquaintance of Major F. R. Wingate, D.S.O., R.A., then Director of Military Intelligence in Egypt, and on Wingate's recommendation, his services were secured by Kitchener. It was arranged that he should accompany Wingate to Egypt, while still retaining his appointment in Whitehall. On arrival in Egypt in the autumn of 1893, Talbot proceeded at once to the frontier station at Wadi Halfa, and began a small triangulation after fixing his position by telegraphic comparison with Cairo.[2] Subsequently, he accompanied a patrol into the Nubian Desert and determined the position of the oasis known as Murrat Wells, which the Dervishes used in their raids on Egypt. During the winter of 1893-94, he commenced a triangulation from Suakin, based on positions shown on the Admiralty charts, and then returned to his post at the War Office under Colonel Sir John Ardagh, C.B., late R.E. Since the days of the Nile Expedition, when he had been Commandant at the base, Ardagh had never ceased to urge that a topographical survey should be made of Egypt and the occupied portions of the Sudan, and it seemed that at last his representations would meet with proper recognition.

In the spring of 1896, when Kitchener was about to launch the Dongola Expedition, Talbot received permission to return to Egypt as a Special Service Officer, and having proceeded to Wadi Halfa, rode thence to Murrat Wells to reconnoitre for railway routes to the south, and to carry out latitude and longitude observations.[3] After Dongola had been occupied, he completed a survey, based on triangulation, from Halfa to Kerma, and extended it southwards

---

[1] See *The Military Engineer in India*, by Lieut.-Colonel E. W. C. Sandes, D.S.O., M.C., R.E. (retd), Vol. II, pp. 216 and 236–38.
[2] *A Memoir of Colonel the Hon. Milo George Talbot, C.B. (late Royal Engineers)*, by General Sir Reginald Wingate, Bt., G.C.B., G.C.V.O., G.B.E., K.C.M.G., D.S.O., p. 21. This is a most complete memoir of Talbot's career. Another appears in the *R.E. Journal*, Vol. XLVI, 1932, pp. 138–150. Talbot died on September 3rd, 1931.
[3] See Chapter IX.

during the early months of 1897. His survey work then ceased, for he was required to act as Director of Military Intelligence in Cairo from April till September, 1897, in the absence of Major Wingate, who had accompanied the Rodd Mission to Abyssinia. Subsequently, he returned to England. Nevertheless, he was back again in the Sudan in January, 1898, as Intelligence Officer to Major-General H. M. L. Rundle, C.M.G., D.S.O., at Merowe, and found time to fix the position of that place telegraphically and to begin a small triangulation. Points were determined between Merowe and Abu Hamed, and another triangulation was initiated from Korti. After the Battle of the Atbara had cleared the Bayuda Desert of hostile concentrations, Talbot accompanied a column from Korti through Gakdul Wells to Metemma, fixing a number of positions as he went.

There is a story that, shortly before the Battle of Omdurman, Talbot remarked to Major-General Sir Archibald Hunter that he had never yet seen a dervish, and that Hunter afterwards composed the following limerick :—

> " At Kârari said Major Talbot
> No dervish I've seen yet at all, but
> There appeared there and then
> Two thousand times ten,
> Which *quite* satisfied Major Talbot."

On January 1st, 1899, not long after the Fashoda affair, Talbot entered the Egyptian Army with the rank of *Miralai* (Colonel) on appointment as Director of Military Intelligence in succession to Colonel Sir Reginald Wingate, who had become Adjutant-General. His Intelligence work and organization duties prevented him, during this year, from devoting much attention to surveying; but on January 1st, 1900, when Sir Reginald Wingate had succeeded Lord Kitchener as Governor-General,[1] Talbot was appointed to the newly-created post of Director of Surveys, and was then able to resume the mapping of the country. He had wished to follow Kitchener to South Africa, but his services could not be spared.

While Lord Kitchener was Governor-General he had been very anxious that the borders of the newly-conquered Sudan should be properly surveyed, and in particular that a suitable boundary between the Sudan and Abyssinia should be demarcated as far south as the northern end of Lake Rudolf. As this project was beyond the unaided powers of Talbot, who was occupied with Intelligence work, the assistance of the Foreign Office and Sir John Ardagh was invited, and in the autumn of 1899, Major (afterwards Brigadier-General) H. H. Austin, D.S.O., R.E., and Lieutenant (now

---

[1] Sir Reginald Wingate became Governor-General of the Sudan and Sirdar of the Egyptian Army on December 22nd, 1899.

Major-General Sir) Charles W. Gwynn, D.S.O., R.E., were placed under orders to proceed to the Sudan to survey and demarcate the frontier between that country and Abyssinia.

The decision to re-occupy the Sudan had raised many acute boundary problems. Not only were the extent and nature of the territory extremely uncertain, but new neighbours had appeared since the days of the Egyptian occupation. France, Belgium and Italy had all established some sort of claim to areas which were formerly within the Egyptian domains. The Emperor Menelik had organized a kingdom in Abyssinia. Darfur, in the west, was practically an independent state under Sultan Ali Dinar. While Kitchener was advancing southwards, preliminary steps were taken to find solutions for the problems which were foreseen. Italy agreed to hand back Kassala and make a satisfactory delimitation of the Eritrean frontier. The rights of Belgium, and the boundaries of the Congo State, raised no questions of much difficulty, except the leasing to King Leopold of the southern area known as the Lado Enclave. Agreement with France, however, was not so easy, because Commandant Marchand was known to be on his way across Africa to establish a claim to the upper waters of the Nile. Consequently, Major (afterwards Major-General Sir) J. R. L. Macdonald, R.E., was sent to East Africa in June, 1897, to lead a column for Mombasa to the Nile by a route on which no opposition would be encountered, and thus to forestall Marchand. This project was upset by a mutiny of Sudanese troops; but Macdonald was able, nevertheless, to dispatch a small column under Captain H. H. Austin, R.E., to the northern end of Lake Rudolf, where it arrived in the middle of September, 1898, and established a claim to that territory.[1] Considerable privations were experienced by this expedition during its return to Uganda.

As to Darfur, it was decided that no immediate action was necessary. There remained only the problem of Abyssinia; and hence the dispatch of the Rodd Mission to that country in 1897, and the appointment of Captain (afterwards Colonel Sir) John L. Harrington as British Representative at Addis Ababa.

Harrington had long discussions with the Emperor Menelik about the Abyssinian boundaries, for Menelik had advanced claims to territory which had formerly been recognized as part of the Egyptian Sudan. With the exception, however, of the Beni Shangul District, an upland region between the Blue Nile and Sobat Rivers, it was believed that his claims were not supported by effective occupation. Eventually, Harrington induced Menelik to accept, as a sort of

---

[1] Captain Austin, R.E., was accompanied on this occasion by Captain R. G. T. Bright, Rifle Brigade. Austin had served under Macdonald in 1891-92 on the original survey of the Uganda Railway in company with Captain J. W. Pringle and Lieut. P. G. Twining, R.E. (See "Some Royal Engineers and their Work in Africa" by Major-General H. L. Pritchard, C.B., C.M.G., D.S.O., Col. Commandant R.E., appearing in the *R.E. Journal*, Vol. XLI, 1927, pp. 193-216.)

provisional frontier, a blue chalk line drawn on the map in such a way as to divide a few recognized districts in Abyssinia from others in the Sudan; but the line followed neither topographical features nor geographical co-ordinates. It was agreed that the country in the neighbourhood of the blue line must be explored, and a frontier then selected which would be marked as far as possible by natural features, and at the same time would not cut across the territory occupied by any particular tribe. On account of his East African experience, Austin was selected to organize an expedition which was to be split into two parties on arrival in the Sudan. One party, under Austin himself, with Major R. G. T. Bright, was to explore the southern section of the Abyssinian frontier between the Sobat and Lake Rudolf; the other, under Gwynn, accompanied by Lieutenant L. C. Jackson, R.E., was to reconnoitre the northern section between the Blue Nile and the Sobat. The country to the north of the Blue Nile was better known, and its exploration was not immediately necessary. The approximate delimitation of the Sudan-Eritrean boundary still farther to the north, from the Setit River to Kassala, was undertaken by Talbot in conjunction with an Italian delegate.

The expeditions under Austin and Gwynn were delayed for some time in Omdurman because all available river transport had been requisitioned for the hunt of the Khalifa; but on November 19th, 1899, Gwynn and Jackson started up the Blue Nile in three sailing boats with a small party of Sudanese, an escort of *Jehadia* and a few mules, and on December 2nd, Austin and Bright set out with their party by steamer up the White Nile. Sailing, poling and towing up the Blue Nile, which was at a very low level, Gwynn's party reached Roseires on December 14th, having observed for latitude, and made telegraphic comparisons for longitude, at Wad Medani and Sennar. They next proceeded to run a line of latitudes and azimuths southwards to the Sobat, and to carry out a plane-table survey on points fixed from latitude bases.

Gwynn had been instructed by Talbot in Cairo that his main object should be to ascertain, and define on maps, the limits of Abyssinian influence. He was to check the accuracy of Harrington's map, and define the territorial limits of the frontier tribes and the extent of the Abyssinian occupation. These and other general instructions, which were given also to Austin, were written on November 10th, and Talbot supplemented them on November 19th by special instructions to Gwynn, in which he told him to treat the Abyssinians in a friendly manner and gave him much technical information and advice. He ordered him also to examine the country south of Roseires with a view to the subsequent construction of a railway or telegraph line, and to close his traverse at Nasir (Nasser) on the Sobat.

As Gwynn was forbidden to enter any territory occupied by

Abyssinians unless invited to do so, he was unable to ascend to, and march across, the Beni Shangul projection from the main plateau, but was obliged to skirt it through the foothills. The black inhabitants of the villages along his route and in Beni Shangul, were still connected intimately with slave-trading. Tribal organization seemed to have disappeared, and consequently, Harrington's blue line was interpreted as running only on recognizable natural features. Gwynn made it hug the foot of the escarp as far as possible, because water was scarce in the open plain. He wished to ensure that the frontier guards, which might be required to check slave-raiding, should have a succession of water-holes along their patrol routes. The slave-raiders watched his proceedings with much disfavour, but did not interfere, because they believed that his theodolite was a machine-gun ! After passing Kirin, south of the Beni Shangul promontory, Gwynn swung south-eastwards and ascended, through dense belts of bamboo, to high ground inhabited by the prosperous and agricultural Galla race. There he met an Abyssinian officer named Basha Zodi, who had been friendly with Commandant Mangin when the latter was on his way through Abyssinia after separating from Marchand at Fashoda. Basha Zodi was much impressed by the strenuous hill-climbing of Gwynn and Jackson. "What did Commandant Mangin mean," said he, "when he told me that the French were strong on land, but that the British were strong only on the water ; and that the French left Fashoda only because the British could travel on the river ? Are you then web-footed like ducks ?" He was assured that they were not, but was still puzzled.

Abyssinia under native rule was always an easy country to enter, but a most difficult one to leave. The Abyssinians welcomed their guests with smiles, and then held them fast until the Emperor agreed to their departure. "Basha Zodi asked us to come with him to Gidami," writes Sir Charles Gwynn,[1] "and when we got there on February 2nd, 1900, we found that the District Chief, one Dejaj Goti, was absent in Addis Ababa and an old *Wamba* or Minister named Yembo was in charge. I explained my mission, and Wamba Yembo raised no immediate objections. Next morning, however, a letter came from Talbot in which he explained that it would be impossible to send a steamer to meet us on the Sobat, and that consequently, we should return from that river by the Blue Nile. This was awkward, as I had already bought up all the supplies in the villages through which we had passed, and when I explained my change of plans to Wamba Yembo, he became very suspicious. I decided to complete the reconnaissance to the Sobat with only a few men, and Yembo sent some Abyssinians with me ; but when we had been marching for two days, we were overtaken by a large party

[1] Notes by Major-General Sir Charles W. Gwynn, K.C.B., C.M.G., D.S.O., late R.E., sent to the author on May 25th, 1934.

BASHA ZODI, AN ABYSSINIAN OFFICER.

[*From a photo taken by Major C. W. Gwynn*, D.S.O., R.E., *in* 1900.]

with a message that I must return at once to Gidami as an order had come from Menelik that the expedition was to proceed no farther. Accordingly, we retraced our steps to Gidami, where we arrived on February 6th, 1900, only to find that the message from the Emperor was a fiction. As it was obvious that Wamba Yembo was determined to detain us until he had orders from Addis Ababa, I undertook to write to Harrington to procure proper authority, though the messenger might be several weeks on the road; but I stipulated, at the same time, that Yembo should feed our whole party during the enforced halt, and to this he agreed and accepted a daily *menu* which I prepared. Whenever the food was not delivered in full, we made preparations to move, and all deficiencies were immediately made good. At length, on March 8th, the messenger arrived from Addis Ababa with a letter from Harrington enclosing Menelik's permission, and on the following day we started."

" I had decided," continues Sir Charles, " that in spite of Talbot's letter I would not risk returning by the same route, so we surveyed to Nasir, marched down the Sobat, and finally turned northwards, arriving at Fashoda (Kodok) on April 2nd. There we obtained a couple of sailing boats, and reached Omdurman on the 25th, having been picked up by a steamer returning from the *sudd* region with Sir William Garstin's party on board. Garstin gave us our first news of the South African War. The results obtained by the expedition were looked upon as unexpectedly successful. It had been anticipated that we should be able to produce only route traverses; and in consequence, our plane-table sheets, with route traverses added, were very welcome. Neither Jackson nor I spoke Arabic, and we had little experience as surveyors. Our native officer, Farag Effendi, knew no language but Arabic; and as an interpreter, we had a strange creature, one Daniel Desta, an Abyssinian who had been a Bible-seller in Alexandria. Although Daniel's knowledge of Arabic was indifferent, he could write Amharic (the Abyssinian language) and understood some English. He used his Bible to help him in translating English words into Arabic. On one occasion, I ordered him to tell Farag Effendi to have a sentry posted over the cash-chest at night. Now Daniel did not know the word 'sentry,' but his Bible mentioned a 'centurion,' so he told Farag that the order was that a *Ras Miya*, or captain of 100 men, should guard the money, and the unfortunate Farag, though only a 2nd-lieutenant, sat up all night on the cash-chest."

After completing his reports and surveys in Cairo, Gwynn returned to England. In the autumn of 1900, however, he received orders to accompany Harrington to Abyssinia to assist him in securing a more definite boundary settlement with Menelik, and they arrived in Addis Ababa at the end of the year. Menelik was friendly, but extremely suspicious. He kept Gwynn waiting in the capital for more than two months, according occasional interviews to him and Harrington which led to nothing. At length, Lord Cromer wired to Harrington that Gwynn should march westwards without further delay and begin marking out the frontier which he had recommended, so Gwynn left Addis Ababa on March 12th, 1901.[1] While waiting in the capital, he had started a triangulation, which he extended during his journey to join with the triangulation executed in 1900. This was valuable because the existing maps of the routes of former travellers had been violently distorted in compilation, due to the fact that whereas the position of Addis Ababa was approximately correct in longitude, that of Roseires, and indeed of the whole of the Blue Nile, including Khartoum, formerly had errors ranging from about 30 to 50 miles. Gwynn found that a compass was almost useless, as every ridge was highly magnetized. His triangulation was roughly executed; but the plane-table work was correctly oriented by frequent azimuth observations, and the closing error in longitude, on reaching the Sudan, was only two miles. Passing through the district of Beni Shangul, he reached the Blue Nile at Famaka above Roseires on April 13th, and there met Captain N. M. Smyth, V.C.,[2] 2nd Dragoon Guards, with an escort and stores. After a diversion southwards to fix the Beni Shangul boundary, he proceeded to carry the survey northwards along the " blue line " to Gallabat, whence he marched through rain-soaked country to Gedaref. At Doka, 45 miles from Gedaref, the camp was invaded by scorpions, and Smyth and the men suffered severely from their stings. The party arrived in Khartoum, the new headquarters, on June 27th, 1901, and it was then arranged that after returning to England, Gwynn should come out again to the Sudan to work under Talbot in the Survey Department.

It is now time to describe some of the adventures of the southern party under Major H. H. Austin, D.S.O., R.E., who, as already mentioned, left Omdurman on December 2nd, 1899, with Major R. G. T. Bright of the Rifle Brigade, a small escort of Sudanese, a contingent of *Jehadia*, and a large number of transport animals. Precise instructions regarding the exploratory work which he was to carry out had been given to Austin by Lord Kitchener on November 18th, when the Sirdar returned to Omdurman from the Kaka Expedition.[3] The explorers voyaged up the White Nile and the Sobat in barges and boats towed by the gunboat *Tamai*, and disembarked on December 20th at a point on the Sobat, midway between Nasir and the mouth of the river, where the water became

[1] A brief description of Major Gwynn's journey is given under the title of "Anglo-Abyssinian Frontiers," in "Occasional Notes," appearing in the *R.E. Journal*, Vol. 31, 1901, pp. 190, 191.
[2] Now Major-General Sir Nevill Smyth, V.C., K.C.B.
[3] *Among Swamps and Giants in Equatorial Africa*, by Major H. H. Austin, C.M.G., D.S.O., R.E., p. 4. This volume includes a full account of Austin's survey of the Sobat region.

too shallow for further progress. Nasir Post was reached on January 4th, 1900, after a march of eight days up the left bank along the borders of an enormous dried-up swamp, sparsely populated by Dinkas and Nuers. These savages were friendly, though suspicious. The Nuer men, tall and well-made, were stark naked and smeared from head to foot with wood-ash as a protection against cold and the attacks of insects. The elder women wore leather aprons; but the maidens, though as naked as the men, were unadorned with wood-ash, thus exemplifying the hardihood of their sex under the stern dictates of fashion.

Setting out from Nasir on January 7th, and crossing the mouth of the Pibor tributary, Austin and Bright ascended the Baro, or Upper Sobat, through a stretch of most dreary and uninteresting country, and entered Anuak territory, where the banks of the river were wooded and thickly populated. The approach of the expedition was watched with curiosity by men, women and children, perched on lofty wooden stages. The Anuaks proved to be more civilized than the Nuers. All wore aprons of beads or leather, and the men carried wooden spears with heads made from the leg-bones of giraffes. Passing Itang and the site of the present post at Gambela, the expedition came, on January 26th, to the point on the Baro beyond which Marchand had been unable to navigate his launch, the *Faidherbe*. The launch had been hauled on to a wooded island, secured to the trees by chains, and enclosed in a grass hut.[1] Nothing would induce the Anuaks to approach the hut, which, they affirmed, was haunted by evil spirits left to guard the launch. It seems that, some two months after Austin and Bright visited the spot, the Emperor Menelik sent a number of Gallas and Abyssinians to dismantle the *Faidherbe* and carry her in sections to Addis Ababa. They cut her in two, and each section was transported by 100 men to the foot of the precipitous escarp up which a goat-track led to the lofty summit. It is not known whether the sections ever reached the top.

After marching for a few days up the Baro Gorge, the expedition ascended 3,000 feet to the Buré plateau and reached a height of more than 5,000 feet above the sea. All the camels and many of the donkeys fell down the steep slopes, and had it not been for the assistance given by Galla porters, the ascent could never have been made. Austin became seriously ill at Buré; but after a fortnight's rest, he was able to continue to the provincial capital at Goré, which the expedition had been invited by the Abyssinians to visit. The land was picturesque and fertile, and the climate good. Fortunately, the

---

[1] "Survey of the Sobat Region," by Major H. H. Austin, D.S.O., R.E., appearing in *The Geographical Journal*, Vol. XVII, No. 5, May, 1901, pp. 495-512. This article gives a full account of Major Austin's expedition. An abbreviated account is given in an article entitled "Anglo-Abyssinian Frontier," appearing in the *R.E. Journal*, Vol. 30, 1900, pp. 231, 232.

Galla population was friendly. These people used large bars of salt as coinage, ten bars being equivalent to a Maria Theresa dollar. Austin and Bright were virtually held prisoners for nearly a month at Goré, while permission was sought from Addis Ababa for them to leave ; and when the permit arrived, all kinds of difficulties were raised to prevent Austin from replenishing his supplies. The result of this procrastination was that he could not continue his exploration southwards to Lake Rudolf, but had to be content with examining the Sobat catchment area.

On April 24th, 1900, the expedition was back at Itang on the Baro River, and on the 29th, Austin and Bright started southwards to explore the tortuous channels of the swamps between the Baro, Pibor and Akobo. The heat was oppressive, and the mosquitoes voracious. Progress through the swamps was terribly difficult owing to continual rain. Most of the men fell sick, and almost all the transport animals died. A circuitous and nightmare journey ended at last at the junction of the Pibor with the Sobat on May 26th. The expedition reached Omdurman on July 7th, and shortly afterwards Austin and Bright returned to England. Although a visit to Lake Rudolf had not been possible, and consequently a second attempt would be required, the route traverses made by these two officers, during their first exploration from the Sudan, formed a valuable addition to the very incomplete maps of the desolate areas south of the Sobat.

On December 23rd, 1900, Austin and Bright were back in Omdurman to make another attempt to explore the frontier to Lake Rudolf, and on this occasion they were accompanied by a medical officer, Dr. J. Garner. With a small escort of the 10th Sudanese, a number of *Jehadia* and many animals, they voyaged up the White Nile and the Sobat in barges and sailing boats attached to the gunboat *Fateh*, and landing nine miles upstream of Nasir, started their march on January 17th, 1901. They followed the Sobat to the mouth of the Pibor, and then, continuing southwards along the latter, reached the junction of the Pibor and Akobo on February 4th, and swung eastwards to follow the Akobo and skirt some extensive swamps, from which mosquitoes emerged in myriads. This pestilential area gave place in time to wooded country ; and on February 24th, they camped near a peak to the north of the Boma Hills. They had seen many herds of magnificent elephants, and had halted on several occasions to allow the majestic animals to stroll slowly across their path. Leaving the catchment area of the Akobo, the expedition entered the Boma Hills on March 4th. The scenery was now grand, and the climate delightful. Soon, however, the path led downwards to a barren and almost waterless desert.

On March 11th, the scarcity of water became a source of great anxiety. The heat was terrific in the mid-day camp. The men had marched 17 miles during the morning, and no trace of water could be found. There was not a drop, except the small quantity which Austin, Bright and Garner had in their water-bottles. Austin sent forward a party under Mabruk Effendi, his Egyptian officer, to search for water, and when they did not return, sat up all night in an agony of mind, believing that he had sent the men to their death. Happily, they reappeared in the morning with a copious supply from a swamp, and thus a critical situation was averted.

The line of march now swung slowly eastwards, skirting the Abyssinian escarp. On April 8th, 1901, Austin closed his traverse on the Omo River in the Murlé District at the northern end of Lake Rudolf, where he had camped with Bright in September, 1898, when they came from Uganda. He expected to meet an Abyssinian column with supplies from Harrington, and when it failed to arrive, he was confronted with a serious shortage of food. Terrific storms of rain turned parts of the country into a bog. The remainder was a labyrinth of clay cliffs and ravines. Impenetrable forests fringed the Omo River, and beyond lay a formidable escarpment, barring escape into Abyssinia. The rains continued with unabated violence. The animals dropped and died. The men began to fail. As a forlorn hope, Austin decided to march southwards along the western shores of Lake Rudolf to the nearest British post in Uganda, keeping his men alive by slaughtering his transport animals. "I anticipated a loss of perhaps 25 per cent. of the men and 50 per cent. of the animals," he writes,[1] "but in my most pessimistic mood I never imagined the dreadful loss of 75 per cent. of our personnel which we actually suffered."

The march along the shores of Lake Rudolf began on April 25th, 1901. Progress was delayed at first by a vast swamp. Then, on May 5th, three men were murdered by Turkana tribesmen; and during the following night, a furious attack on the camp was repelled by rifle fire. Austin went down with gastritis, and for ten days was compelled to travel on a camel. The men sickened and died for want of cereals. Every movement was watched by the hostile natives. On May 22nd, the column camped for the last time on Lake Rudolf at the mouth of the Turkwell River, along which it afterwards marched westwards and then southwards. The condition of the surviving men and animals grew daily worse. Every article that was not essential was cast away or burnt in order that the sick might ride. By June 2nd, only 41 men remained alive out of an original strength of 62. The column now fought its way through dense and thorny belts of jungle, and on June 13th quitted

[1] "A Journey from Omdurman to Mombasa *via* Lake Rudolf," by Brevet-Major H. H. Austin, C.M.G., D.S.O., R.E., p. 11. This article, which appears in *The Geographical Journal* of June, 1902, gives a good description of the march. A full account appears in a volume by the same author entitled *Among Swamps and Giants in Equatorial Africa*.

the Turkana territory. On the 20th, Austin became seriously ill with scurvy; but nevertheless, the march was continued south-eastwards towards Lake Baringo. At the end of the month, only 20 men were alive, including Austin, Bright and Garner, and between them they had less than 20 pounds of grain. On July 20th, the survivors numbered 17, and had they not been rescued on the western shore of Lake Baringo on August 1st by Mr. Hyde-Baker, the District Collector, it is doubtful whether any would have reached the Uganda Railway. They were escorted to it at Nakuru Station, and arrived at Mombasa on August 26th, and at Suez on September 27th, 1901. The remnant of the 10th Sudanese escort received a great welcome from their comrades on their return to Aswan, and shortly afterwards the British officers sailed for England.

The length of the march from the Sobat to Lake Baringo was about 1,100 miles. With almost unfailing regularity, Austin took nightly observations for latitude with a five-inch theodolite, and used chronometer watches to ascertain his longitude. He mapped the route with thousands of compass bearings, and checked the distances with pedometers. Azimuth observations were taken from points already fixed, and the heights of mountains were determined by the readings of aneroid barometers. As the President of the Royal Geographical Society remarked at a meeting held on April 14th, 1902, it was worthy of admiration that during the attacks of natives, and the terrible sufferings of the latter part of the journey, the three British officers, and especially Austin himself, should have continued to take observations and with such accuracy that they had been able to construct a most valuable map of a region which was partly unknown.

The services of Major C. W. Gwynn, D.S.O., R.E., were lent to the Egyptian Army on October 10th, 1901, and he was appointed as an assistant to Colonel Talbot in the Sudan Survey Department. On arrival in Khartoum in November, he was sent by Talbot to resurvey the Eritrean frontier from Kassala to the Red Sea. This frontier had previously been roughly sketched and beaconed by a joint Anglo-Italian party; but a more accurate map was required to link up Talbot's work in the neighbourhood of Kassala with his triangulation round Suakin. Gwynn was able to close on the Suakin triangulation after extending the Kassala system along the frontier to the sea. He measured a base at Kassala, began his triangulation northwards on December 6th, 1901, and completed it at Suakin on March 12th, 1902. The work involved much strenuous mountaineering. Beyond the Khor Baraka, where the Eritrean frontier trends eastwards, Gwynn had constantly to climb more than 4,000 feet to reach his survey stations on successive spurs of the plateau; and during the final descent of 7,000 feet to the maritime plain, his transport camels had many severe falls. From

SURVEY CAMP NEAR THE ABYSSINIAN FRONTIER.

[From a photo taken by Major C. W. Gwynn, D.S.O., R.E., in 1900.]

Suakin, Gwynn extended Talbot's triangulation towards Berber, which he reached in extremely hot weather on April 27th. In the following November, he started to fix the positions of certain oases in the desert between the Atbara and the Blue Nile, but was soon recalled to demarcate the proposed Abyssinian frontier, north of the Baro, to which Menelik had at last agreed.

It was essential that the local Abyssinian officials should be shown the natural features already selected for the demarcation of the frontier, and the locations of such intermediate beacons as it might be necessary to erect. Accordingly, Gwynn proceeded in December through Gedaref to Gallabat, and reconnoitred northwards for 100 miles to the River Setit while awaiting the arrival of Menelik's officials. Returning to Gallabat, he started northwards again with the Abyssinians on January 1st, 1903, and afterwards followed the proposed boundary southwards. All went well until he reached the Beni Shangul District in the middle of March and found that the Jebel Jerok, an important boundary feature, was occupied by a peculiarly villainous slave-raider named Ibrahim Wad Mahmud, who refused to budge. " I had half an hour's talk with him," writes Sir Charles Gwynn.[1] " My rifle was pointed at his stomach, and behind me stood a Sudanese soldier with orders to shoot at the word. All around lay Ibrahim's followers, covering us with their rifles; and finally, as he refused to take orders from the Abyssinians or myself, I told him that his mountain would be included entirely in the Sudan and that the Government would deal with him in due course."[2] No difficulties were encountered farther south; but in order to avoid passing through Abyssinian territory, Gwynn was obliged to make for Fashoda, which he reached on April 14th. Thence, after some delay, he voyaged up the Sobat to meet another Abyssinian party. After showing the frontier to them, he returned to the junction of the Pibor and Akobo Rivers, where he hoped to meet an expedition under Mr. A. E. Butter, accompanied by Captain (now Brigadier-General) P. Maud, R.E., which was exploring the southern frontier of Abyssinia; but when he heard that the Butter-Maud Expedition proposed to march to Nairobi, he finished his frontier survey and returned to Khartoum.

The main object of the Butter-Maud Expedition was to obtain information which would enable Colonel Sir John Harrington to settle with the Emperor Menelik the frontier between Abyssinia and British East Africa. Mr. Butter and Captain Maud, in company with Sir John, left England in September, 1902, and were joined at Aden by two assistants from the Survey of India, Khan Sahib

---

[1] Notes by Major-General Sir Charles W. Gwynn, K.C.B., C.M.G., D.S.O., late R.E., sent to the author on May 25th, 1934.

[2] Ibrahim Wad Mahmud continued to give trouble; but he was caught and hanged early in 1904, by a column under Lieut.-Col. (now Lieut.-General Sir) G. F. Gorringe, C.M.G., D.S.O., R.E., Governor of the Sennar Province. (See Chapter XI.)

Sher Jung, an excellent plane-tabler, and Jemadar Shahzad Mir of the Bengal Lancers. The instructions received by Maud from the Foreign Office were to survey and report on the country east of Lake Rudolf as far as the Ganalé River,[1] and he was given a copy of a map on which Harrington had marked a possible frontier by a blue line. The expedition proceeded through Jibuti to Addis Ababa, where survey work was begun. Lines of latitudes and azimuths formed the framework of the survey until it became feasible to measure a base, three and one third miles in length, to the east of Lake Rudolf, and to carry a system of triangulation to the northern end of the lake. Brigadier-General Maud records[2] that, owing to the movement of the hot air, it was impossible to use a theodolite to align the base, except for an hour before sunset. At other times, the haze produced extraordinary effects. A man or a flag, at a distance of 1,500 yards, appeared to move from side to side and to take huge leaps in the air. A plane-table survey was made down the eastern side of the lake, and afterwards the system of latitudes and azimuths was resumed to a hill east of Lake Baringo, where the survey ended on July 7th, 1903. Six days later, the expedition reached the Uganda Railway at Nakuru Station. The plane-tabling was done by Sher Jung, and the astronomical and trigonometrical work by Maud, who had great difficulty in finding his longitude because both his chronometers failed. Mr. John L. Baird,[3] Sir John Harrington's assistant at Addis Ababa, accompanied the expedition and learnt to observe for, and to calculate, approximate latitudes. The Butter-Maud Expedition added to the knowledge of the Lake Rudolf region; but as it did not concern the Sudan, it cannot receive further notice in these pages.[4]

Gwynn did no more frontier delimitation in the Sudan after his expedition in the spring of 1903. Large areas of the country remained to be triangulated and surveyed, and only Talbot, Gwynn and four Egyptian officers were available for the work.[5] It was fortunate that time and compass sketches of various areas were being received in increasing numbers from provincial officials, and from Royal Engineers in the Telegraph Department; but many of these sketches could not be incorporated in a general map without correctly fixed positions, and consequently, Talbot and Gwynn had to provide the necessary positions, either by latitude and azimuth or latitude and

---

[1] The Ganalé is a tributary of the Juba River, which flows southwards into the Indian Ocean at Kismayu.

[2] Notes by Brig.-General Philip Maud, C.M.G., C.B.E., late R.E., sent to the author on December 2nd, 1936.

[3] Now Lord Stonehaven of Ury, P.C., G.C.M.G., D.S.O.

[4] A descriptive account of the expedition is given in an article entitled "Exploration in the Southern Borderland of Abyssinia," by Captain Philip Maud, R.E., appearing in *The Geographical Journal*, May, 1904.

[5] The area of the Sudan is approximately 1,007,500 square miles. After deducting the swamp and arid regions, the area to be surveyed was more than 700,000 square miles.

chronometer methods. Talbot suggested certain lines of triangulation, latitudes and azimuths, and astronomical fixings to cover blanks in the maps, and most of these were completed during the next four years. Points were first determined between Kassala and Khartoum and in the Bayuda Desert. During the winter of 1903-04, Gwynn fixed points and supervised the survey work of two Egyptian officers in the Southern Gezira and the country between the Atbara and Blue Nile, including the Rahad and Dinder Valleys. He also carried a flying triangulation from Khartoum to Gedaref.[1] On March 30th, 1904, he finished work at Er Renk on the White Nile, where he was picked up by a launch bringing Captain " Jock " Liddell, R.E., back from a telegraph reconnaissance on the Bahr ez Zeraf. Liddell had observed frequently for latitude and had obtained chronometric longitudes.[2]

While Gwynn was working south of Khartoum, Talbot was supervising the survey operations of two Egyptian officers in the Berber region, and exploring the Bayuda Desert. He marched from Omdurman to Korti, and from Merowe to a point upstream of Ed Damer, and then triangulated from Abu Hamed for some distance up the Nile towards Berber.[3] At Korti, he visited the first cadastral survey party. The need for such detailed surveys of cultivated riverain areas had become apparent, and a commencement had been made in the Dongola Province on a scale of 1 in 2,500. Although Talbot was now one of the most senior officials in the Sudan, and had acted in 1903 as Governor-General in the absence of Sir Reginald Wingate, he found time during the course of his administrative work to pay frequent visits to his subordinates in the field, and to help them by actual surveying ; but the end of his brilliant career in the Sudan was in sight, and looking around for a suitable successor as Director of Surveys, his choice naturally fell on Gwynn, whom he wished to recommend for the post. Gwynn, however, had no liking for cadastral surveying, which was the chief work in prospect, and he wished to compete for entry to the Staff College at Camberley ; so he resigned his appointment in July, 1904, and reverted to the Home Establishment on August 12th, thus severing his connection with a country which had benefited greatly by his frontier delimitations.[4]

[1] *Annual Report, Sudan Survey Department*, 1904, by El Lewa M. G. Talbot Pasha, dated October 19th, 1904, appearing in the *Report on the Finance, Administration and Condition of the Sudan*, 1904.
[2] See Chapter XVI.
[3] *Annual Report, Sudan Survey Department*, 1904.
[4] In 1908, Major Gwynn surveyed again in Abyssinia. With the assistance of Captain R.L. Waller, R.E., and Corporal C. Carter, R.E., he took a triangulation, and a line of latitudes and azimuths, southwards from Addis Ababa to the Ganalé River, whence a compass survey was made westwards. Captain Maud's triangulation near Lake Rudolf was extended and prolonged to the southern extremity of the Sudan. Gwynn's party also triangulated and plane-tabled between Addis Ababa and Harar, and ran lines of plane-table survey from Addis Ababa to the southern frontier. A full account is given in an article entitled " A Journey in Southern Abyssinia,"

Not long afterwards, the Sudan lost the services of Colonel Talbot himself, who, to the profound regret of Sir Reginald Wingate and the Government, resigned the appointment of Director of Surveys on April 18th, 1905, and retired from the Army to devote his energies to the cause of the National Service League. Egypt and the Sudan saw him no more until he returned to Khartoum in 1916 as an Intelligence officer, and afterwards conducted a successful political mission to Cyrenaica.[1] In a farewell order,[2] the Governor-General remarked that the boundary commissions, trigonometrical surveys and astronomical observations, planned and executed by El Lewa the Hon. M. G. Talbot Pasha throughout the Sudan and on its frontiers during a period of nearly five years, were a lasting testimony to the thoroughness and excellence of his work. The Sudan owes much to the genius of Milo Talbot.

On January 5th, 1905, Captain H. D. Pearson, R.E., joined the Egyptian Army, and proceeding to Khartoum, was appointed Director of Surveys on April 19th. Lieutenant A. E. Coningham, R.E., also arrived early in 1905,[3] and became Assistant Director of Surveys. The working season was then far advanced, and the small staff of three Egyptian officers and half a dozen native surveyors was fully occupied with cadastral surveying; so Pearson engaged British surveyors and draftsmen, and started a school for native surveyors in order that topographical surveying might be resumed as soon as possible to provide a framework for the cadastral survey. He instituted a system of rigid traverse in the Halfa and Berber Provinces as a preliminary to cadastral work in those areas, and in the Gezira, a system of " minute of arc " squares, marked by beacons, from which the detailed survey could be filled in.[4] A town-survey of Omdurman, on a scale of 1 in 500, was initiated in 1906, and similar surveys were put in hand later in all the principal cities of the country.

Following in the footsteps of Talbot, Coningham soon became a most efficient triangulator. During the early months of 1905, he worked around Khartoum. In the winter of 1905-06, with a civilian assistant, he connected the Kassala-Suakin chain of triangulation with the system executed by Talbot around Murrat Wells, thus providing fixed points for the demarcation of any mineral concessions which might be granted in the Eastern Nubian

by Major C. W. Gwynn, C.M.G., D.S.O., R.E., appearing in *The Geographical Journal*, August, 1911. (See also *History of the Corps of Royal Engineers*, Vol. III, by Colonel Sir Charles M. Watson, K.C.M.G., late R.E., pp. 184, 185.)

[1] See Chapter XII.
[2] *Sudan Gazette*, No. 75, dated April 19th, 1905.
[3] Lieut. A. E. Coningham, joined the Egyptian Army on the same date as Captain Pearson.
[4] Note on the career of El Lewa H. D. Pearson Pasha, dated January, 1923, by the Assistant Director of Surveys. The author received a copy of this note in April, 1935, from Lt.-Col. S. L. Milligan, C.M.G., D.S.O., R.A. (retd.), Director of Survey, Sudan Government.

Desert. He triangulated no less than 5,000 square miles of broken and arid country during this working season.[1] In February, 1907, he started a triangulation southwards from El Obeid,[2] and resumed it in February, 1908, but was recalled almost immediately to survey with a patrol marching to Natrun Wells in extreme west of the Dongola Province. Thence, he returned to Southern Kordofan, and triangulated for two months before work ceased in the hot weather.[3] In the winter of 1908-09, the triangulation of Southern Kordofan was interrupted by a local insurrection, and Coningham was attached to the Nyima Patrol and mapped the hills while hostilities were in progress. Next, he sketched as far as Talodi; and from that place, past Lake Abyad and across the Bahr el Arab to Meshra er Req. He had intended to survey the course of the Bahr el Arab; but intertribal disputes caused him instead to march westwards to Hofrat en Nahas, near the border of French Equatorial Africa, fixing positions as he went.[4] This ended the season's work.

During the winter of 1909-10, Coningham surveyed in the country south of Roseires. He carried out latitude and azimuth observations from the Tabi Hills southwards to the Sobat, and down that river to the White Nile at Kodok, and succeeded in defining the eastern edge of the vast swamp which lies north of the Lower Sobat.[5] In the following winter, he surveyed towards Yambio along the frontier of the newly-acquired Lado Enclave; but the extent of the country, and the pace at which he was required to work, forced him to relinquish triangulation for latitude and azimuth observations, and occasionally for compass traverses checked by observed latitudes. This was his last survey in the Sudan, for he reverted to the Home Establishment on January 9th, 1912. In bidding him farewell, the Governor-General remarked that in the course of 7 years' service Coningham had visited a very wide area, and that it was mainly due to his efforts that it had been possible to issue provisional maps of all the inhabited portions of the country.[6] In 1905, only 55 sheets had been published; but owing to the framework supplied by Coningham's triangulations and surveys, no less than 126 sheets, compiled from 530 route or area sketches, were ready for issue at the time of his departure.[7]

For the mapping of outlying areas, the Survey Department was dependent to a large extent on the efforts of officers in other

---

[1] *Annual Report, Sudan Survey Department*, 1906.
[2] *Ibid.*, 1907.
[3] *Ibid.*, 1908.
[4] *Ibid.*, 1909. Hofrat en Nahas is 35 miles from the border and about 280 miles north-west of Wau.
[5] *Annual Report, Sudan Survey Department*, 1910.
[6] Memorandum by the Governor-General appearing in the Report on the *Finance, Administration and Condition of the Sudan*, 1911.
[7] *Annual Report, Sudan Survey Department*, 1911. On January 1st, 1921, Major A. E. Coningham, O.B.E., M.C., was transferred from the Royal Engineers to the Army Educational Corps with the rank of Lieut.-Colonel.

employment. These officers supplied the detail, and the Department co-ordinated their work. One of this energetic band of helpers was Captain H. H. Kelly, R.E., who became Director of the Roads and Communications Section of the Public Works Department in 1908, after supervising for several years the building of Port Sudan.[1] Towards the close of 1908, Kelly began to explore in South-Western Abyssinia, marching from Gambela to Goré, and thence south-eastwards to Anderacha. Next, he travelled north-eastwards to Jiran, and then north-westwards for hundreds of miles, through Soddo, Mendi and the Beni Shangul District, until he emerged at Gezan on the Sudan frontier.[2] The greater part of this route had not previously been mapped. In June, 1910, after a commission under Captain H. D. Pearson, R.E., had valued the property in the Lado Enclave on the reversion of that area to the Sudan Government, Kelly marched from Yei and surveyed north-westwards along the frontier to Maridi, thus exploring almost unknown country between the Bahr el Jebel and the upper waters of the Bahr el Ghazal.[3] In the following spring, while Pearson was triangulating in the Nuba Mountains, Kelly penetrated the country east of Malakal and helped to define more closely the limits of the swamp which Coningham had skirted in 1909–10. He also examined the possibility of opening up a route from the White Nile to Gidami in Abyssinia.[4] Early in 1912, he surveyed with one of three columns operating against recalcitrant Beirs in the region of the Pibor River, the surveyors with the other columns being Pearson and Mr. A. A. R. Boyce. Captain R. E. M. Russell, R.E., formerly in the Railway Department and then an Intelligence officer, also assisted with survey work. The resulting sketches and surveys did much to elucidate the complicated Pibor River system.[5]

In company with Captain H. J. Huddleston, Dorsetshire Regiment, Kelly started in December, 1912, to trace a new boundary, east of the Nile, between the Sudan and Uganda, and to reconnoitre the south-western border of Abyssinia for a new military post.[6] They proceeded eastwards from Nimulé to Ikoto, and afterwards with Captain Powell, R.A.M.C., and a small escort, marched to within 50 miles of the northern end of Lake Rudolf, surveying the boundary as they went. They returned to Ikoto by a devious route through uninhabited country, where they ran short of food. From Ikoto, Kelly and Huddleston travelled north-eastwards to Kapoeta, and in April, 1913, set out to reconnoitre the Abyssinian boundary on the Boma Plateau. A march of 10 days brought them to the escarp, and

[1] See Chapter XVIII.
[2] *Annual Report, Sudan Survey Department*, 1908.
[3] *Ibid.*, 1910.
[4] *Annual Report, Sudan Survey Department*, 1911.
[5] *Ibid.*, 1912.
[6] Notes by Major-General H. J. Huddleston, C.B., C.M.G., D.S.O., M.C., sent to the author in June, 1936.

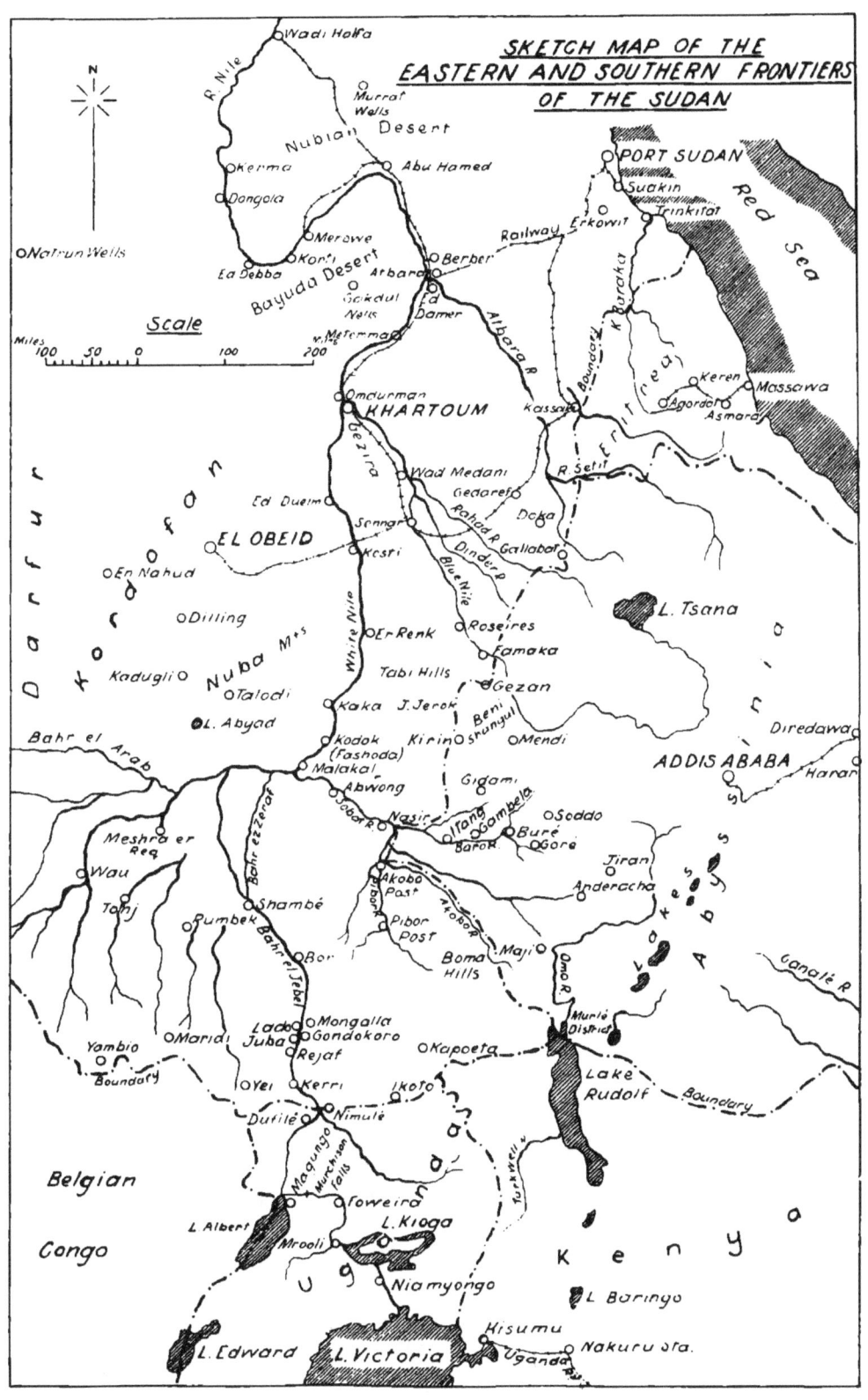

they crossed into Abyssinia in the direction of Maji. Immediately, the Abyssinians began to appear in great numbers, and by nightfall the British officers and their small escort were surrounded by 2,000 warriors. The Abyssinian chiefs were very polite, but would not allow the explorers to proceed unless their permits were ratified by the Emperor Menelik at Addis Ababa. As the chiefs announced a week later that permission had been refused, Kelly and Huddleston retraced their steps, descended the escarp, and struggled through the marshes for seven days to the Pibor Post ; thence they followed the Pibor River northwards to the Akobo Post, and returned by ship to Khartoum.[1] The expedition was not wasted, as Kelly had surveyed hitherto unmapped territory and had connected his work with that of Austin and Gwynn.[2] This was Kelly's last exploration in the Sudan, for he reverted to the Home Establishment on November 8th, 1913. He was killed in action on October 24th, 1914, in France.

By the end of 1911, the greater part of the inhabited Sudan had been explored or mapped in detail ; but much remained to be done in the south-east, and up the Bahr el Arab. The cadastral survey of the Dongola and Berber Provinces had been completed, and that of the Gezira and White Nile Provinces was making good progress. Omdurman City had been surveyed, and similar town-surveys were contemplated for Khartoum North and Khartoum itself. The supervision of these various activities pressed hardly on Major H. D. Pearson, the Director of Surveys, especially after he had lost the services of Captain A. E. Coningham. In the spring of 1913, however, Lieutenant A. G. McNeill, R.E., joined the Survey Department and started topographical work in the Nuba Mountains.[3] During the winter of 1913-14, he and his plane-tablers mapped no less than 5,000 square miles of country. Then came the Great War. First, McNeill, and then Pearson himself, were called away ; and except for triangulation from 1916 onwards in the western province of Darfur, surveying almost ceased.

Hugh Pearson was a keen and energetic officer, an able administrator, an athlete, a sportsman and the life and soul of Khartoum society. He had shown tact and capability as head of the Lado Enclave Commission in 1910 ; and had proved his technical ability in 1911, by fixing more than 100 points in Kordofan, extending over an area of 20,000 square miles, in less than three months. During the Great War, he was employed on a variety of special services. In 1916, he led a mission to Lake Tana in Abyssinia in connection with a proposed dam, and afterwards became a *liaison* officer with

[1] Captain H. H. Kelly described some of his experiences in an article entitled " Some Aspects of Abyssinia with special reference to the Western Frontier," appearing in *The Army Review*, Vol. VI, No. 1, January, 1914, pp. 15-30.
[2] *Annual Report, Sudan Survey Department*, 1913.
[3] *Annual Report, Sudan Survey Department*, 1913. Lieutenant A. G. McNeill served in the Sudan from February 19th, 1913, to January 16th, 1915.

the Arab forces at Jidda. In 1917, he represented the Sudan Government at the coronation of the Empress of Abyssinia at Addis Ababa. Subsequently, he joined the Egyptian Expeditionary Force and was for short periods Military Governor at Jaffa and Jerusalem, and then Commanding Royal Engineer with the Desert Mounted Corps. After the war, he returned to his normal survey work in the Sudan; and from October, 1921, he was employed as the British representative on an Anglo-French Commission for the delimitation of the frontier between the Sudan and the Wadai area of French Equatorial Africa.[1] This was the crowning achievement of 18 years' service in the Sudan, broken only by the Great War. On December 28th, 1922, when the protocol was almost ready for signature, Pearson died at Umm Dafog,[2] in Western Darfur, from blackwater fever complicated by an abscess on the liver. He had insisted on working throughout the rainy season, and this, no doubt, had undermined his constitution. Thus passed one who was the friend of all and the hero of many; and with his passing, the long connection of his Corps with the Sudan Survey Department was brought to an end.[3]

After the death of Lieut.-Colonel H. D. Pearson, the Department was administered by Mr. A. A. R. Boyce as Director. The present holder of the post is Lieut.-Colonel S. L. Milligan, C.M.G., D.S.O., a retired officer of the Royal Artillery, who assumed charge in November, 1927.[4] The developments of the Sudan Survey during the last 15 years, however, are beyond the scope of a history confined to the work of Royal Engineers, and it remains only to describe briefly the connection of the Corps with the Survey of Egypt.

The first surveys by British military engineers in Egypt were made around Alexandria, in 1801–02, by officers serving with the expedition under General Abercromby. An example of their work can be seen in the Alexandria Museum, where there is a large map, drawn by Lieutenant Thomas F. De Havilland of the Madras Engineers, and bearing the discursive title " Plan of that Part of Egypt situated westward of the Nile and northward of Ramanie, with the Peninsula, Canal and Town of Alexandria, Lakes Mareotis, Maudie and Etco, and the Western Branch of the Nile from Ramanie

---

[1] Captain P. K. Boulnois, O.B.E., M.C., R.E., Captain A. C. James (temp. R.E.), Sergeants W. T. Bristow and F. Woolcott, R.E., and Sappers T. W. Gooch and S. J. Morgan, R.E., also served on the Boundary Commission, but were not posted to the Survey Department. Sergeant Woolcott, however, served in the Department from September 25th, 1923, to August 22nd, 1926, and Sergeant A. L. Statham, R.E., from December 26th, 1926, to April 2nd, 1932.

[2] Umm Dafog is about 240 miles south-west of El Fasher and 15 miles from the border of French Equatorial Africa.

[3] A Memoir of Lieut.-Colonel H. D. Pearson, D.S.O., R.E., by Colonel E. V. Turner, C.B., C.M.G., D.S.O., late R.E., appears in the *R.E. Journal*, Vol. XXXVII, 1923, pp. 315–318. Another by General Sir Reginald Wingate, Bt., G.C.B., G.C.V.O., G.B.E., K.C.M.G., D.S.O., Col. Commandant R.A., appears in *The Geographical Journal*, March, 1923.

[4] Mr. A. A. R. Boyce was not gazetted as Director of Survey until August 12th, 1923. He was succeeded by Lieut.-Colonel Milligan on November 30th, 1927.

to its Mouth. February, 1802."[1] De Havilland was assisted by Ensign George Steele (or Steell) of the Bengal Engineers. Other officers who surveyed at this time in the neighbourhood of Alexandria under the direction of Major Alexander Bryce, R.E., the Chief Engineer, were Captain W. H. Ford and Lieutenants G. Kennett and J. Handfield, R.E.[2] In April, 1801, French engineers were engaged in surveying the depression outside Alexandria known as Lake Maryut; but when this land was flooded after Abercromby's death by order of General Hutchinson, they were forced to desist. It is interesting to note that they completed their map subsequently from data acquired by De Havilland during his survey operations.[3] No further mapping of Egypt by British military engineers seems to have occurred until 1882, when reconnaissance sketches were made during the Tel el Kebir Campaign.[4] Palestine, on the other hand, was surveyed in some detail, between 1865 and 1877, by several young Royal Engineers, including Wilson, Warren, Conder and Kitchener, whose names have appeared in these pages.[5]

Various rulers of Egypt had devoted haphazard attention to the survey of their country, but there was much confusion and ineptitude before the British assumed control and regulated and co-ordinated the work. A cadastral survey was instituted in 1813, by Muhammad Ali Pasha. In 1858, Said Ali Pasha ordered elaborate instruments, and caused a topographical survey to be started in 1861, which was remarkable only for its inaccuracy. A cadastral survey begun in 1878, by order of Ismail Pasha, was likewise unsatisfactory.

In 1882, Lieutenant A. M. Mantell, R.E., joined the Egyptian Army after the Tel el Kebir Campaign and was placed in charge of the Meteorological Observatory at Abbassia on the outskirts of Cairo, though, as an Intelligence Officer, he had little concern with its activities.[6] The meteorological work was done by a German, whose duty it was to find the time by astronomical observations and to control the firing of the mid-day gun from the Citadel by transmitting an electrical signal to that place at noon.[7] There is a good story in connection with this time-gun. In 1896, complaints were received that the firing of the gun had become very erratic, and

[1] Ramanie = Rahmaniya. Mareotis = Maryut. Maudie = Maaddiya. Etco = Idku.

[2] A list of the military engineers who served in the Egyptian campaign of 1801–02 is given in Chapter I.

[3] The French map appears in the atlas of a work entitled "*Description de l'Egypte*," published in Paris in 1819. For this and other information, the author is indebted to Mr. A. F. C. de Cosson, the author of *Mareotis*.

[4] It may be remarked, however, that Capt. W. de W. Abney, R.E., visited Thebes in 1874, and observed and photographed the transit of Venus on December 9th. (See the *R.E. Journal*, Vol. 5, 1875, pp. 2–5.)

[5] They worked for the Palestine Exploration Fund. Some allusion to their survey operations appears in Chapter XIX.

[6] He was occupied chiefly in superintending the translation of drill books into Arabic, and in preparing a glossary of Arabic military terms.

[7] Notes by Colonel A. M. Mantell, late R.E., sent to the author on November 21st, 1936.

accordingly, the Surveyor-General proceeded to investigate the cause. Inquiry at the battery in the Citadel showed that the old sergeant in charge preferred to trust his watch rather than the mid-day electrical signal from the Observatory. "But how do you know that your watch is accurate?" he was asked. "I am sure it is, sir," was the reply, "because I compare it two or three times a week with a very fine clock in a watchmaker's shop in the city." The Surveyor-General then went to interview the owner of the clock. "That's a good clock," said he. "Is it reliable?" "I can assure you, sir," replied the watchmaker, "that that clock is *absolutely* accurate, for I set it every day by the time-gun fired from the Citadel."

Lieut.-Colonel H. H. Settle, D.S.O., R.E., was Surveyor-General and Quarter-Master-General, Egyptian Army, from 1886 to 1892.[1] He had more experience, however, as a Staff officer than as a surveyor, and it was not till after his time that the Egyptian Survey was re-organized and extended by a technical expert in the person of Captain H. G. Lyons, R.E.

In January, 1890, Lyons was posted as a subaltern to a Field Company, R.E., in Cairo, and was attached to the Egyptian Army, in the autumn of 1891, for engineering duties at Aswan and Wadi Halfa. He joined Kitchener's staff in 1892, and reconnoitred several desert routes. In 1895, his services were lent to the Ministry of Public Works, and he was employed in examining the Temples of Philae in connection with the proposal to build a dam at Aswan. The Egyptian Government was being pressed at that time to grant mining concessions in the deserts, and Lyons was sent to make geological reconnaissances. In 1896, he retired from the Egyptian Army to become Director of Geological Survey. As no satisfactory maps of the country were in existence, and it was necessary to fix points in Upper Egypt to control the desert traverses of the geological parties, Lyons took charge of the Abbassia Observatory (which had been established and equipped about 1854 by Abbas Pasha I), and by telegraphic interchange of signals, determined the longitude of a number of stations. He found in the corner of a room in the Observatory, an enormous pile of papers. These proved to be meteorological observations, taken daily at 2.30 p.m.; and as this was not a normal observing hour, he made further inquiries. It then transpired that the observations were taken for an unknown gentleman, whose address had been lost. They were part of Egypt's contribution towards the international scheme of observation for 1882–83, and were required for 12 months only. Actually they had been taken for nearly 15 years![2]

[1] From 1892 to 1895, Colonel Settle was Inspector-General, Egyptian Police. A Memoir of Lieut.-General Sir Henry H. Settle, K.C.B., D.S.O., Col. Commandant R.E., appears in the *R.E. Journal*, Vol. XXXVII, 1923, pp. 313, 314.
[2] Notes by Colonel Sir Henry G. Lyons, F.R.S., late R.E., sent to the author on December 6th, 1934.

When the staff of the newly-formed Geological Survey and their topographical assistants had been taught some astronomy and plane-tabling, three parties set out to gain experience in the field, and gradually attained a creditable degree of efficiency. Cadastral survey next demanded attention. By 1891, improved irrigation had brought large tracts of new land under cultivation which were not recorded in the village land-registers, and accordingly a small experimental land-survey was started in 1892, and continued till 1895. An acceleration of work was needed in that year, consequent on the appointment of a Commission to examine the incidence of the land-tax; and in April, 1896, the Egyptian Government secured the services of an officer of the Indian Revenue Survey. Lyons had suggested to Colonel Talbot that the latter might direct the land-survey of Egypt; but Talbot had replied that he had no liking for administrative work and preferred his topographical duties as Director of the Sudan Survey. On the departure of the Indian Revenue officer in October, 1897, Lyons was asked whether he would undertake to complete the geological survey, and also to control the cadastral survey. He agreed to do so provided that topographical survey was included, and formed, with the cadastral survey, into an Egyptian Survey Department under his direction. This was approved, and in July, 1898, he became the first Director-General of Survey in Egypt.

The history of a costly Brunner-Ibanez base-measuring apparatus throws a side-light on Egyptian methods prior to 1898. Talbot visited Cairo in 1897, with instructions from Sir John Ardagh to ascertain the whereabouts and condition of this apparatus, which Said Pasha had ordered from Paris in 1858. Until it was used to measure two short bases near the Giza pyramids in 1876 and 1877, it had lain forgotten in its 15-foot case.[1] A small sum was spent in 1885 on its repair, and again it was returned to its case. Talbot and Lyons went in search of it. In reply to inquiries by Lyons, each Head of Department in Cairo said that he really did not know whether or not he had the Brunner apparatus, but Lyons could search for it in the store-room. The apparatus was discovered at last in the basement of the Abbassia Observatory. Subsequently, it was returned to Paris for overhaul, and was erected in 1904, in a new Observatory at Helwan, south of Cairo, 46 years after it had been ordered from France.

When the Egyptian Survey Department was formed in 1898, the most urgent need was a reliable triangulation to fix points for the control of land measurements, and to prevent the accumulation of

[1] *The Cadastral Survey of Egypt*, 1892–1907, by Captain H. G. Lyons, F.R.S., R.E. (retd.), p. 73. This volume gives a technical description of the development of the survey of Egypt. Topographical and hydrographical information is given also in *The Nile. The Physiography of the River and its Basin*, and *Rains of the Nile Basin and Nile Flood*, by the same author.

small errors in such measurements. This triangulation was taken in hand at once. The Government had decided that a re-assessment of the land taxes must be completed within the next ten years, and consequently the Survey Department had the difficult task of improvising methods, introducing better systems and increasing the output without hindering, for a single week, the progress of the cadastral survey. During the next ten years, 7,000,000 acres of cultivated land were surveyed at a cost of less than £500,000. Cadastral maps were printed and published on a scale of 1 in 2,500, and supplemented by topographical maps on smaller scales.

In 1899, Lyons and his staff began to take meteorological observations at various stations. In 1901, and again in 1903, he accompanied Sir William Garstin up the Nile to Gondokoro in the Southern Sudan and measured discharges of the river, thus paving the way for a thorough hydrographical survey. During 1905 and 1906, a line of levelling was run from Wadi Halfa to Khartoum, and from the information so obtained, a decision was reached to increase the height of the Aswan Dam. In addition, an archæological survey was made of the area to be submerged above Aswan. New Observatory buildings near Cairo had already been provided and taken into use in replacement of the old Abbassia Observatory, which had been adapted, 50 years before, from a guard-house. They were situated on a spur of the limestone desert plateau at Helwan, and were completed in 1904. Lyons was an adept at securing Government support for his schemes, and the Helwan buildings are a record of his foresight and persistence. The Abbassia Observatory was lacking in accommodation, and the electric trams passing near it caused much disturbance to the delicate instruments. The Helwan buildings are essentially modern in type. They include a comparator house in which the standard measurement bars are kept and the wires for base measurement can be verified.

By the end of 1908, the cadastral survey and the re-assessment operations were finished, and Lyons began to revise certain inaccurate maps of parts of the Nile Delta. In 1909, as a Fellow of the Royal Society and the holder of a high Egyptian order, he retired from the post of Director-General of Survey after nearly 18 years' service in the Egyptian Army and the Ministries of Public Works and Finance. During the Great War, he was Commandant of the Army Meteorological Services; and from 1920 to 1934, Director of the Science Museum in London. His departure from Egypt, at a time of great expansion, was a severe loss to the Government.

The last officer of the Royal Engineers to serve in the Egyptian Survey Department was Major (now Brigadier-General) H. G. Joly de Lotbiniere, who joined it under Lyons in 1906, and remained till 1912. He was in charge of the Drawing and Lithographic Printing Office in Cairo, in which maps were prepared for Government departments in Egypt and the Sudan and for the irrigation schemes of Sir William Willcocks in Mesopotamia. The photographic work was supervised by Mr. J. Kearney, a retired Quarter-Master-Sergeant, R.E.

The precise levelling of Egypt having been finished in 1914, attention was concentrated on geodetic triangulation and other scientific pursuits, but these activities were interrupted by the Great War. During that cataclysm, the Egyptian Survey Department furnished the 7th Field Survey Company, R.E., which operated in Sinai, Palestine and elsewhere. The Department supplied the military authorities with thousands of maps of Egypt, the Sudan, Sinai, the Hedjaz, Palestine, Syria and Gallipoli, and issued topographical handbooks to the armies. These achievements, however, and the extensive development of the Department since 1918, lie to the credit of the civilian personnel.

Talbot, Austin, Gwynn, Pearson and Coningham, the leading Royal Engineer surveyors of the Sudan, explored huge tracts of unmapped territory. They travelled fast and far, through areas peopled by savage tribes and offering unique opportunites for bold initiative and adventure. They suffered many hardships in the course of their work. In Egypt, the conditions were very different. The country was partly civilized, but poorly mapped. Expert reform and diplomatic administration were needed for the correction of past errors. These were the tasks which fell to the lot of Colonel Sir Henry Lyons, who may justly be called the founder of scientific surveying in Egypt.

CHAPTER XVIII.

WORKS.

A VISITOR to modern Khartoum, lounging on the wide terrace of the Grand Hotel and listening to a broadcast from England, which he left by air only three days before, may find some difficulty in realizing that the town is a creation of the last forty years, and that, little more than a century ago, a group of fishermen's huts at Makran Point was the only sign of human habitation. It is true that a Christian city called Soba existed on the right bank of the Blue Nile about 13 miles from its confluence with the White Nile; but Soba was destroyed by the Muhammadans in the 15th century, and four centuries later, its ruins were used to supply much of the material required for building the original town of Khartoum.[1]

It is generally accepted that Khartoum was founded in 1822 by Muhammad Osman, a Governor-General appointed by Muhammad Ali, and that afterwards it gradually attained some importance as an administrative and commercial centre, and also as a slave-market. Lord Prudhoe records that in 1829 it still comprised only 30 small mud houses and straw huts, with a larger house for the Governor.[2] In the following year, it became the official headquarters of the province and apparently began to prosper, for in 1834, a French traveller estimated the population at about 15,000.[3] Larger houses had been built, and gardens had appeared, though no trees had yet been planted. The town was allowed to expand promiscuously, without design or plan. A narrow and filthy lane wound through it, parallel to the river, and two others led inwards from the river bank. In fact, the general lay-out was typical of many Arab villages on the banks of the Tigris and Euphrates which became known, only too well, to those who served in Mesopotamia during the Great War.

By 1839, Khartoum had 500 houses, a hospital and a barrack. Malaria was rampant; and two Europeans who spent a year there were disgusted by the dishonesty and corruption of the officials and trading community.[4] Seven years later, the population was

---

[1] In Arabic the word "Khartoum" means "elephant's trunk." The strip of land between the rivers is said to resemble a trunk in shape.
[2] "The Journal of Lord Prudhoe," appearing in the *Journal of the Royal Geographical Society*, Vol. V, 1835.
[3] *Voyage en Egypte et Nubie* (1846), by M. Combes.
[4] *African Wanderings* (1852), by Ferdinand Werne. Translated by J. R. Johnston.

estimated by John Petherick as 60,000, and the town possessed an arsenal or dockyard for the construction and repair of boats.[1] In 1848, the first Roman Catholic missionaries arrived and proceeded to build a chapel.[2] A party of travellers under George Melly came to Khartoum in 1850. They rode to the Governor's whitewashed house, where two companies of infantry were changing guard ; but the dignity of the ceremonial was somewhat spoilt by the fact that each company was preceded by a soldier carrying the Company Commander's bedstead on his bayonet ! The visitors were afterwards shown over the town by the Governor-General's " confidential pipe-bearer," a Frenchman.[3]

Sir Samuel Baker formed a very poor opinion of Khartoum in 1862.[4] " He described it," writes Dr. W. H. McLean,[5] " as a miserable, filthy and unhealthy spot. The houses were chiefly built of mud brick, and the town had a densely crowded population of 30,000." Every man of substance was closely interested in the ivory and slave trades. The reduction in the population may have been due to insanitary conditions, for when Baker returned from the south, he found that an epidemic of typhus was raging and estimated that the population had then shrunk to 15,000. Nevertheless, E. A. de Cosson liked the place when he visited it in 1870. Several European nations had already established Consulates in the town. A busy dockyard existed on the bank of the Blue Nile, and a palace was under construction for the Muhammadan Governor.[6]

Charles Gordon saw Khartoum for the first time in 1874, when on his way southwards as the newly-appointed Governor of the Equatorial Province. " We arrived here on March 13th," he writes.[7] " The Governor-General met me in full uniform, and I landed amid a salute of artillery and a battalion of troops with a band. I have got a good house and am very comfortable. To-day, I visited the hospital and schools. They are very well cared for, and the little blacks were glad to see me. Khartoum is a fine place as far as position goes. The houses are of mud and flat-roofed. I leave on the 20th for Gondokoro."

In 1883, after the disaster to the force under Colonel Hicks, a rich merchant of Khartoum, named Marquet, gave a farewell banquet prior to his departure for France. According to Mr. C.

---

[1] *Egypt, the Sudan and Central Africa* (1861), by John Petherick. In 1936, the population of Khartoum was only 49,741, so Petherick's estimate may have been excessive. The population of Khartoum North was 18,449, and of Omdurman, 110,436.
[2] *The Story of Africa and its Explorers* (1893), by Robert Brown.
[3] *Khartoum and the Blue and White Niles* (1851), by George Melly.
[4] *Albert Nyanza, Great Basin of the Nile* (1866), by Sir Samuel Baker.
[5] *Regional and Town Planning in Principle and Practice* (1930), by Dr. W. H. McLean.
[6] *The Cradle of the Blue Nile* (1873), by E. A. de Cosson.
[7] Extracts from a letter from Colonel Gordon, dated March 14th, 1874, appearing in *Colonel Gordon in Central Africa, 1874-79* (1881), edited by Dr. G. B. Hill.

E. J. Walkey,[1] the Frenchman had a *salon* which was considered superior to many in Paris, with wax-lights, mirrors, servants in livery, cut-glass, silver and flowers. The dinner was thoroughly Parisian, and was prepared by a French *chef*. Champagne, hock and claret were provided for the guests, who were regaled also with green peas, mushrooms, asparagus and strawberries. Old Khartoum before the siege presented the picture of a mass of faded grey houses, above which rose the minaret of a mosque. Between the town and the White Nile was a sterile, sandy plain, without trees or bushes. A narrow street ran through the town from west to east, ending in a market; it was extremely dirty and was bordered mostly by mud houses plastered with cow-dung. Nevertheless, this street, which became an open sewer in the rainy season, was the best in the town and contained the Governor's residence and offices and the houses of the leading Turks, Copts and Arabs. There was no accommodation for European travellers. A Coptic school, a hospital, a prison and some barracks had been built, and near the market-place stood a mosque, coffee-houses and brandy-shops.

Such was the Khartoum which Gordon defended against the Mahdi until the end came on January 26th, 1885. That historic episode has been described in a previous chapter.[2] After the capture of Khartoum, the Mahdi cleared the town of the surviving inhabitants, who were either deported or made to settle on the plain to the south. He allotted the best houses to his relatives, and often stayed in Khartoum himself. On his death in June, he was succeeded by the ambitious and warlike Khalifa, who decided, in 1886, to establish a new capital at Omdurman. Till then, there had been little destruction of house property, except during the days of pillage and massacre which followed the capture. However, in August, 1886, the Khalifa issued a peremptory order that Khartoum was to be evacuated within three days, and on the fourth day, the utter destruction of the town was begun. Houses were demolished by hundreds, and every scrap of ironwork and woodwork was torn ruthlessly from the walls, floors and roofs and transported to Omdurman for use in the Khalifa's house and other new buildings. Khartoum remained for the next twelve years a mournful and deserted wilderness of crumbling walls and thorn bushes, in which lay the mouldering skeletons of those who had perished with Gordon.

When Kitchener entered the town on September 4th, 1898, two days after the Battle of Omdurman, a few palm groves and fruit gardens along the Blue Nile were the only undamaged relics of a once prosperous settlement. Traces could be seen of the main street, and of a few of the larger buildings adjoining it, but nothing of a

---

[1] "The Story of Khartoum," by Mr. C. E. J. Walkey, M.B.E., appearing in *Sudan Notes and Records*, Vol. XVIII, 1935, Part II, pp. 221-241, and Vol. XIX, 1936, Part I, pp. 71-92. This article gives a valuable and concise history of Khartoum.
[2] See Chapter V.

riverside roadway which once existed. Gordon's Palace, and some other prominent structures on the bank of the Blue Nile, had the appearance of buildings which had been gutted by fire. The upper floor of the Palace had gone. Debris was piled high against the walls. The Khartoum Dockyard had been engulfed gradually by the river. There is little need to dwell further upon this hideous scene of desolation. The task before Kitchener and his men was to remove the wreckage, and to replace it by a well-planned town which should form a proper capital for a regenerated country.

The design for a new Khartoum was prepared by Kitchener himself and was intended primarily to satisfy military requirements. In addition, it gave ample space and allowed for easy expansion. It provided for wide main avenues running parallel to the Blue Nile, intersected by others at right angles, and forming with them rectangles about 500 yards square. Each main rectangle was subdivided into small blocks by three longitudinal and three transverse streets. So far, the plan resembled the familiar "gridiron" which Alexander the Great had adopted in building Alexandria more than 2,000 years before. But Kitchener now diverged from common practice. He added diagonal thoroughfares, connecting the intersections of the main avenues, and thus gave to the whole a striking resemblance to a group of Union Jacks or, as some say, to a single Union Jack. There is no foundation for the suggestion that he intended to imitate the national flag. The resemblance was merely fortuitous. The diagonal streets were provided in order that machine-guns, mounted at their points of intersection, should be able to sweep large areas of the town, and also because they would improve the means of access from one part of the town to another; but after a few years, it was found that the diagonal streets gave wedge-shaped plots which were awkward for building purposes, and that the crossings were dangerous for motor traffic. When Lord Kitchener visited Khartoum in 1912, he agreed with Sir Reginald Wingate that the system of diagonal communications might be discontinued.[1] Accordingly, this was done, and the existing diagonals were gradually closed and covered with buildings. To-day, the diagonal streets have almost disappeared from the plan of Khartoum.[2]

The first step towards rebuilding the town was to clear the site, a task which was begun as soon as possible by large gangs of Dervish prisoners. The "Works Battalion," a branch of the Department of Works, was moved up to Omdurman and placed under the control of an energetic and experienced Staff Officer, Lieutenant G. F. Gorringe, D.S.O., R.E. This unit of about 1,000 men, organized in headquarters and three companies, had been formed by Kitchener at Wadi Halfa in 1897, for the eventual rebuilding of Khartoum, and

[1] Letter from Dr. W. H. McLean to the author, dated November 19th, 1936.
[2] See the *Sketch Map of Khartoum in 1935*, which is included in this chapter.

had been employed on railway and other work. " The exact nature of the Department of Works at Khartoum is difficult to describe," remarks Major-General Sir Lovick Friend,[1] " for Kitchener disliked all formal regulations. There were certain materials to hand, such as clay from the banks of the Blue Nile for brick-making, stone from the foreshore of the White Nile at Omdurman, and lime from various pockets up the Blue Nile. About 2,000 Dervish (Baggara) prisoners were employed in roadmaking, and the manufacture of bricks on the bank of the Blue Nile. Parties of *Jehadia* were sent upstream to cut brushwood for the kilns, and a skilled contingent from Suakin was detailed to quarry stone at Omdurman. With the meagre resources at their disposal, it is wonderful that Gorringe and his Staff succeeded in carrying out so much excellent and durable work."

As regards Kitchener's dislike of formal regulations, Lieut.-General Sir George Gorringe relates[2] that at the Atbara Camp an officer once quoted Army regulations to Kitchener as an excuse for the slow progress of some work. " Don't quote regulations to me," said the Sirdar. " They are made for the guidance of fools."

Kitchener decided that the first essential at Khartoum was to commence the rebuilding of the Palace. This was to be the outward and visible sign that the Government intended to remain in the Sudan and complete the reconquest. Almost as important was the provision of a proper system of roads, and hence he devoted early attention also to this project. Labour was secured and organized, and the building of adequate Government offices was taken in hand, so that the headquarters of the administration might be transferred as soon as possible from Omdurman to Khartoum. The personnel of the Department of Works was supervised by Egyptian officers, brought from the Works Department at Cairo and Wadi Halfa, or selected by Gorringe from battalions at Omdurman. The Baggara prisoners were supervised by a few British non-commissioned officers. The *Jehadia* were organized in companies of 400, each under its own headmen, and were employed on brick-making, lime-burning and other duties, as well as wood-cutting. As the local lime was hydraulic and suitable for concrete and mortar, very little cement was needed. Doors and other woodwork were made in local workshops from wood sent up from Alexandria. The Palace windows, however, and steel girders for roofs and floors, were obtained from Cairo.

During the greater part of October and November, 1898, Gorringe was with the Gedaref Relief Force;[3] but he was recalled, on November

---

[1] Notes by Major-General the Rt. Hon. Sir Lovick B. Friend, K.B.E., C.B., late R.E., sent to the author on Sept. 20th, 1934.

[2] Notes by Lieut.-General Sir George F. Gorringe, K.C.B., K.C.M.G., D.S.O., Col. Commandant R.E., sent to the author on April 10th, 1937.

[3] See Chapter XI.

21st, by a telegram from Lord Kitchener which ran, " Proceed at once to Khartoum to start rebuilding. £20,000 available. Commence with Palace." Covering 280 miles of desert in eight days, he reached Omdurman on November 29th and crossed to Khartoum. " There I began to collect tools, materials and artisans from the battalions," he writes,[1] " and I obtained also the services of four Egyptian officers who had been under me at various times as ' Works Officers.' By January 4th, 1899, 2,000 men were brick-making, quarrying and burning lime. Lord Kitchener had returned, and was with me daily at Khartoum, working out plans for the roads. By February 6th, all the roads had been laid out, 7,000 trees had been ordered for avenues, the construction of Government Offices had begun, 5,000 men were at work, and the expenditure was £E.4,000 a month. As regards the Palace, after clearing the rubble from the walls I had prepared a scheme for reconstruction, and had written to England in December for books on Italian and other architecture. These arrived in due course. With the help of the plans, elevations and architectural details which they contained, I designed the first and second floors, the staircase and the verandahs of the new Palace, everything being submitted to, and approved by, Lord Kitchener. The designs for the original Government Offices were also prepared by me. As regards the portion of the Palace facing the river, the ground plan and the shape of the windows on the ground floor differed little from those of Gordon's Palace."

The new Palace at Khartoum was built, as far as possible, on the plinth and foundations of Gordon's Palace. The position of the head of the staircase on which Gordon faced his murderers is marked by a tablet in a corridor wall on the ground floor.[2] The building is in Venetian style, and is a solid and handsome structure which glistens white under the fierce rays of the tropical sun.

Lieutenant M. R. Kennedy, D.S.O., R.E., was posted to the Egyptian Army on July 21st, 1899, and arrived from Malta in August to reinforce Lieutenants[3] Gorringe and Done. In December, he succeeded Gorringe as Director of Works on the departure of the latter to South Africa as Aide-de-Camp to Lord Kitchener. Kennedy was undoubtedly one of the finest engineers the Corps

[1] Notes by Lieut.-General Sir George F. Gorringe, K.C.B., K.C.M.G., D.S.O., Col. Commandant R.E., sent to the author on January 4th, 1937.

[2] See Chapter V.

[3] Lieut. G. F. Gorringe was promoted to the rank of Captain with effect from Feb. 17th, 1899, and his Brevet Majority was dated Feb. 18th; but these promotions were not gazetted until the summer, when they were ante-dated. Promotion was refused in February because Gorringe had not done the necessary " Barrack " and " Active Service " Projects. Eventually, the Commander-in-Chief agreed that the "Active Service" Project alone would suffice, and that this could be done at Khartoum. Well aware that Gorringe was thoroughly fit for promotion, Kitchener then sent for him and, having showed him some previous examination papers, asked him to set one for himself. This Gorringe did, and passed with flying colours ! The episode is an example of Kitchener's resolute refusal to be bound by red-tape.

has ever produced. He made many friends in the Sudan; but as he held strong opinions on various subjects, and did not hesitate to express them, his career was somewhat stormy. Assisted by Done, he continued the work of rebuilding the Palace and extending the town, a task which was complicated by the fact that he knew no Arabic, and Done, only a few words. They kept accounts of the expenditure, and made pencil working drawings or sketches as required. It is remarkable that no detailed drawings of the Palace, or other buildings constructed soon after the re-occupation, can now be found in Khartoum.[1] The construction of the Palace proceeded so rapidly that it was ready for partial occupation in the autumn, 1899, when Lord Kitchener took up his residence in it after his return from England. A house for the Governor of Khartoum was completed in 1900, and the Government Offices were opened at the beginning of 1901.

The methods adopted in rebuilding Khartoum were doubtless approved by Kitchener, and were well suited to the conditions. "Kitchener dominated the whole country," writes Major-General Sir Charles Gwynn.[2] "Some people said that he gave impossible orders; but when objections were raised, it was always found that he had a very clear idea of the best method of carrying out the orders. Kennedy told me that on one occasion Kitchener directed him to make a design for a building, and that, after working all night, he produced a line drawing for approval. Kitchener examined it and asked a few questions. Then he opened a drawer. 'This is my own idea,' said he, and produced a drawing on which he must have worked for many hours. As regards correspondence, Kitchener would read and comment upon the draft of a letter written for him by one of his Staff, but would rarely alter anything. If he disagreed with what was written, he preferred to rewrite the whole letter himself."

The officers who worked under Kitchener in the Sudan had been selected by him with the greatest care. They knew that he trusted them implicitly, that he never gave an impossible order, that every order must be executed with the utmost dispatch, that serious failure probably meant removal, and that no close inquiry would be made into ways and means, provided that the desired end was attained honestly, rapidly, and above all, cheaply. As no contractors

[1] Mr. Basil Burnett, an ex-Director of Public Works, who was in Khartoum in 1906-07, states in a letter to the author, dated April 27th, 1935, that in 1907, when the newly formed Public Works Department assumed control of the maintenance of the Palace and other buildings, no plans or records of these buildings were handed over, nor could any be traced. In 1935, the author was given every assistance by Mr. G. N. Loggin, C.M.G., the Director of Public Works, but was unable to obtain in Khartoum any plan of the Palace as designed in 1899. Lt.-General Sir George Gorringe states, however, that plans and drawings on section paper were prepared by him, and that he handed them over to Kennedy before leaving for South Africa in the winter of 1899–1900.

[2] Notes by Major-General Sir Charles W. Gwynn, K.C.B., C.M.G., D.S.O., late R.E., sent to the author on May 25th, 1934.

THE PALACE, KHARTOUM. [*Photo by the Author.*]

were employed in the early days, there was no necessity for the preparation of detailed plans, specifications and estimates. The engineers could rebuild Khartoum adequately without such aids to precision. They argued probably that as the Sirdar, himself an engineer, saw no immediate necessity for detailed plans, they need not be prepared. Untrammelled by red tape, the reconstruction of Khartoum proceeded at a rapid speed.

In the matter of expenditure, it seems that Kitchener considered that the distribution of the available funds under various heads should rest with him, and not with an official in Cairo. He alone could judge the relative urgency or desirability of the many projects which were under consideration. Simple regulations for financial control by the Egyptian Government were drawn up by Lord Cromer and Lord Kitchener at Omdurman in January, 1899; but it was not until the following year, when Sir Reginald Wingate was Governor-General, that the system of accounts was put on a sound footing, and a financial office established in Khartoum under Major E. E. Bernard.[1] In 1899, the new financial regulations were not always observed. Funds intended for one purpose were sometimes diverted to another, and buildings appeared which had little relation to their official designations. Nevertheless, the money was spent in the best interests of the community, and full value was received for it. Government auditors from Cairo did not visit Khartoum. The occasional camouflage which the system entailed, recalls the story of the British soldier who applied for a pair of spectacles. After much correspondence, they were supplied by the Ordnance Department, not as " Spectacles, pairs, one," but as " Sight-protector," which, being an Ordnance issue for small-arms, was open to no objection. Thus, a stable in Khartoum might appear as a store, or a hospital as a barrack. Necessity is often the mother of a family of innocent inventions.

After his victory at Omdurman, Lord Kitchener devoted his energies not only to the pacification of the Sudan, but also to the development of its resources and the encouragement of its trade; and for these purposes, he wished to found and foster an educative system designed to produce men whose services would be of practical value to the Government. Consequently, on November 30th, 1898, during a brief visit to England, he issued an appeal for funds to erect and endow a college in Khartoum in memory of Charles Gordon. In less than two months, a sum of £100,000 was subscribed. Eventually, the total reached £135,000, of which £30,000 were allotted for the purchase of the land and the construction and equipment of the college, and the remainder was formed into an

[1] Colonel Sir Edgar Bernard, K.B.E., C.M.G., retired from the post of Financial Secretary at the end of 1922. During his 23 years' tenure the revenue increased, from £E.150,000 to £E.4,000,000. He was succeeded by Lieut.-Colonel (afterwards Sir George) Schuster, C.B.E., M.C.

Endowment Fund. A ground plan for a suitable building was prepared by Fabricius Bey, and subsequently, an elevation in Gothic style was drawn by Gorringe.

Thus, the scheme for the Gordon Memorial College was launched; and soon after his return to Omdurman from England on December 28th, 1898, Kitchener selected a suitable site for the institution on the bank of the Blue Nile at the upstream end of Khartoum. On the evening of January 3rd, 1899, Gorringe received a message from the Sirdar that Lord Cromer, who had arrived from Cairo, would lay the foundation stone of the College on January 5th, and that the necessary arrangements were to be made at once. This was a bombshell as the lines of the foundations had not yet been marked on the ground. However, Gorringe set his Department to work overtime. A foundation stone was quarried near Omdurman, roughly dressed, and ferried across to Khartoum. Meanwhile, some trenches were excavated at the site and filled with rubble. On this filling, a few courses of brickwork were laid, and a tripod erected for lowering the foundation stone into position with proper ceremony. In addition, a special trowel was manufactured for Lord Cromer's use. On the evening of January 4th, Gorringe was able to report that all was ready; and on the following morning, the stone was well and truly laid by the British Agent and Consul General in the presence of a large and distinguished gathering. The trowel was sent by Lord Cromer to Queen Victoria. It is hardly necessary to remark that Gorringe had afterwards to uproot the foundation stone with much secrecy, and to let it into a corner of the real building when its correct position had been decided.[1]

The Gordon Memorial College was opened by Lord Kitchener on November 8th, 1902, while on his way to India as Commander-in-Chief. Its history is told in a pamphlet entitled " The Story of the Gordon College and its Work," written by General Sir Reginald Wingate who, as Governor-General, was chiefly responsible for the remarkable results obtained by the institution. Mr. (afterwards Sir James) Currie arrived in November, 1900, as the first Director of Education and Principal-designate of the College, and remained as head of the institution until 1914. At first, its aims were humble—reading, writing and arithmetic for boys, and some elementary instruction for Sudanese sheikhs, who would afterwards become school-teachers. In time, however, as elementary and primary schools multiplied, the Gordon College was advanced to " secondary " status, and promised to attain in time almost to University status.[2] The educa-

[1] Notes by Lieut.-General Sir George F. Gorringe, K.C.B., K.C.M.G., D.S.O., Col. Commandant R.E., sent to the author on September 24th, 1936.

[2] At the opening ceremony in 1902, Lord Kitchener remarked that, when appealing for funds, he had purposely avoided the use of the term " University " because he deprecated haste, but that ultimately he would be content with nothing less than that status. (See *The Educational Experiment in the Anglo-Egyptian Sudan*, 1900–33, by Sir James Currie, K.C.M.G., K.B.E., reprinted from the *Journal of the African Society*.)

tion given is general in nature, with specialization during the last two years of the four years' course for those preparing for the Kitchener School of Medicine, which was founded in 1924 in memory of the first President of the College. Commercial and other courses are given, and there is an Engineering Section for the training of men as overseers and surveyors for employment in the Departments of Public Works, Railways, Irrigation and Survey. In 1933, the College contained 476 students, all living in well-built hostels in the vicinity.[1] There are many ramifications of this educative centre which cannot be dealt with in these pages. The College has repaid in full the care bestowed on it by a succession of able administrators.

The late Sir Henry Wellcome, F.R.S., head of Messrs. Burroughs and Wellcome, manufacturing chemists, was keenly interested not only in the Gordon College, but in the advancement of scientific research. Many Royal Engineers in the Sudan will remember this genial philanthropist. As Mr. H. S. Wellcome, he visited Khartoum in 1900, and became so impressed with the necessity of early research for the improvement of the hygienic conditions and the study of malaria and other tropical diseases that he offered to meet the cost of fully equipped laboratories at Khartoum. His offer was gratefully accepted, and the Wellcome Tropical Research Laboratories were housed in the Gordon College for more than 35 years.[2] One of their earliest achievements was to rid Khartoum of malaria. Sir Henry was a keen archæologist. He discovered several ancient Ethiopian sites in the Sudan, notably one at Jebel Moya, a mountain near Sennar, where he spent a mint of money and built a house known as the "House of the Boulders."[3] It is said—perhaps without adequate foundation—that on the occasion of his first application to Government for permission to make archæological excavations, the official approval was conveyed in the words "Burrow and Welcome!" The story probably originated from Sir Henry himself. His life was a happy blend of science and business, and institutions in many lands benefited by his energy and munificence.[4]

In November, 1900, Lieut.-Colonel L. B. Friend, R.E., arrived from England on appointment as Director of Works, and continued

[1] The maintenance of the College building and hostels has been carried out from the beginning by the Technical Staff of the Education Department, and not by the P.W.D.

[2] Mr. (afterwards Sir Andrew) Balfour was Director until 1913, when he was succeeded by Dr. A. Chalmers. The laboratories have now been closed. Till 1936, they were directed with great energy and skill by Major (now Sir Robert) Archibald, C.M.G., D.S.O., M.D., who succeeded Dr Chalmers.

[3] In 1935, the author visited this remote and extraordinary structure, which is occupied each winter by an archæologist and his family. It is partly rock-hewn, and the remainder is composed of roughly-squared boulders of enormous dimensions. The narrow windows of the main room—a vast and dimly-lit cavern—look out over miles of almost uninhabited desert. The house is perched high on the side of a mountain of black rock.

[4] A Memoir of Sir Henry Wellcome, LL.D., F.R.S., by General Sir Reginald Wingate, Bt., G.C.B., etc., appears in the *Journal of the Royal African Society*, October, 1936.

the building of Khartoum with the assistance of Kennedy and Done. Two years later, he was appointed Director of Works and Stores, which included all military and civil works in the Sudan, all military works in Egypt, and the clothing and equipment of the Egyptian and Sudanese troops.[1] Friend remained as Director until he was transferred to Egypt as C.R.E. (British Army) at the end of March, 1904.[2] His administration of the Department was tactful and efficient, and many works were taken in hand and others completed, both in the capital and in outlying stations. The chief buildings completed in Khartoum were the Palace, the Gordon College as then designed, barracks for the Egyptian troops and a British battalion, the Muhammadan Mosque, and various hospitals, offices and residential quarters. Barracks, quarters and hospitals were built at El Obeid and Kassala, offices and quarters at Wad Medani, and barracks and quarters at Omdurman, Shendi, Berber and other places. The construction of the Gordon College was complicated by the fact that there were many architectural details in the design—such as groined arches over the outside arcades—which were difficult to execute with the scanty material and inexpert workmen available ; but Lord Kitchener had desired that no deviation should be made from the design, and consequently Friend and his Staff had to cope with a number of minor problems.

The construction of a river wall for some distance along the bank of the Blue Nile in front of Khartoum demanded much attention, for it could be carried out only at low Nile, that is to say, during about seven months of the year, and great precautions were needed to prevent damage by floods. Consequently, as suitable stone was scarce, the Director of Works turned envious eyes on the ancient pyramids at Meroë, once the capital of an Ethiopian Empire, which could be seen from the railway about 30 miles north of Shendi. Here was cut stone in profusion, ready for easy transport to the Halfaya terminus. However, his intention was discovered, and a well-known archæologist protested so strongly to the Governor-General that the scheme was abandoned.

Towards the end of his tenure of office, Colonel Friend received a valuable addition to his Staff in the person of Lieutenant H. H. Kelly, R.E., who joined the Egyptian Army on November 13th, 1903. "Long" Kelly, a giant in stature and a heavy-weight Services' Boxing champion, was a fine engineer, well suited to the

---

[1] Notes by Major-General the Rt. Hon. Sir Lovick B. Friend, K.B.E., C.B., late R.E., sent to the author on September 20th, 1934.

[2] Lieut.-Colonel L. B. Friend, R.E., was posted to the Egyptian Army on October 26th, 1900. He was transferred to Egypt on March 31st, 1904, and remained as C.R.E. until he was placed on half-pay on August 12th, 1905. Afterwards, he assisted Sir William Garstin in the Egyptian Irrigation and Public Works Department until January, 1906, when he was appointed Assistant Director of Fortifications and Works at the War Office.

needs of the country. Until he was sent to build Port Sudan, he worked in Khartoum and the outlying stations. Lieutenant A. W. Stokes, R.E., joined the " Works " cadre of the Egyptian Army in April, 1904, Lieutenant K. E. Edgeworth, R.E., in February, 1905, Captain B. W. Y. Danford, R.E., in April, 1905, Lieutenant H. F. O. Thwaites, R.E., in July, 1906, and Lieutenant E. E. B. Mackintosh, R.E., in September, 1906. Edgeworth did not serve in the Sudan until 1908, for he occupied for three years the post of Assistant Director of Military Works in Egypt. Mackintosh assisted Kelly at Port Sudan until his transfer in August, 1907, to the charge of the military works in the Upper Nile, Mongalla and Bahr el Ghazal Districts.[1]

The year 1902 saw a considerable increase in the population of Khartoum, and also in the number of Government and other buildings. Barracks were completed by military labour near the old line of fortification. The finishing touches were put to the Palace. Official residences, and Government offices, were springing up on all sides. The Grand Hotel came into being on the river front. It owed its existence to Lord Kitchener, who had granted mining rights to a London Syndicate in 1900, on condition that they built and maintained an hotel in Khartoum.[2] Four main streets, parallel to the Blue Nile, were partially finished. These were River Avenue (now Kitchener Avenue), Khedive Avenue (now Gordon Avenue), Cromer Avenue (now Sirdar Avenue), and Abbas Pasha Avenue. The town extended southwards as far as the present mosque.[3] By 1904, Khartoum had begun to assume a civilized appearance. The Gordon Statue had been erected, the streets were roughly levelled, and metalling had been laid along River Avenue from the Palace to the Grand Hotel. The Military Hospital, the *Mudiria* and the Works Department Offices were in use. In 1905, as the cuttings planted by Kitchener in the Palace Garden had died, 10,000 young trees were imported and planted along the various avenues. Khedive Avenue was levelled, and Cromer Avenue much improved. A steam tramway was laid towards Makran Point. The river wall was extended, and waterworks and an electric light installation were taken in hand. Mr. O. B. Hatchard, an architect whose services were secured temporarily by Kennedy, designed the Power Station at Khartoum and also the *Mudiria*, the Prison, the Post Office (now the Hotel) and the Schools at Port Sudan. Another architect, Mr. G. B. Bridgman, arrived in 1906, and during a service extending

[1] Notes by Colonel E. E. B. Mackintosh, D.S.O., late R.E., sent to the author in October, 1934. From April, 1908, to October, 1911, Capt. E. E. B. Mackintosh was *A.D.C.* to the Governor-General (Sir Reginald Wingate), and subsequently D.A.A.G. and A.A.G., Egyptian Army, until his reversion to the Home Establishment in May, 1915.
[2] Another hotel, the Victoria, had been established in Khartoum in 1900. It consisted of a group of bungalows at the west end of the town.
[3] " The Story of Khartoum," by Mr. C. E. J. Walkey, M.B.E., appearing in *Sudan Notes and Records*, Vol. XIX, 1936, Part I, p. 88.

over 20 years, designed the Medical School, a new wing for the War Office, and many Government quarters and other buildings in Khartoum.[1]

An elaboration of the original plan of Khartoum was suggested in 1905, by Lieut.-Colonel E. A. Stanton, the Governor of the town. He advocated the establishment of residential areas to the west and south-west, but the scheme was shelved on the score of expense. At about this period, Khartoum began to show a certain lack of symmetry owing to the desirability of utilizing and preserving the remains of the principal buildings and enclosures of the old town on the Government-owned land between Khedive Avenue and the Blue Nile.

After the departure of Colonel Friend, Kennedy continued to control both military and civil works with the assistance of Done, Danford and Stokes, and of Kelly at Port Sudan. By July, 1906, great strides had been made in rebuilding Khartoum. Thwaites records that on the southern perimeter, and some distance from the present town, were the Egyptian Army Barracks, designed to form a defensive ring with the Fort (then under construction) and the British Barracks near the river.[2] The principal buildings and enclosures along the river front were as follows, reading from east to west :— British Barracks, Gordon College (front and one wing), Egyptian Military Hospital, P.M.O.'s House, Legal Secretary's House, Inspector-General's House,[3] Austrian Mission, Sudan Club, British Medical Officers' Mess, Director of Works' House, Department of Works Offices, Workshops' Stores and Barracks, the Palace, the War Office (including the Sudan Government Offices), Post Office, Governor's House, O.C. District's House, Financial Secretary's House, Adjutant-General's House, Irrigation Department Quarters, Grand Hotel and Zoological Gardens. In Khedive Avenue were the Military School, Veterinary Department buildings, Commissariat Department buildings, two Banks, minor Government Offices, A.S.C. Officers' Mess, Law Courts (under construction), the *Mudiria* and the *Zabtia*.[4] The Said Pasha, Ismail Pasha and Abbas Barracks on the southern perimeter accommodated two and a half battalions of Egyptian Infantry. In Khartoum North, across the Blue Nile, were the Artillery Barracks, Egyptian Infantry Barracks (for one battalion), Ordnance Supply Stores, Commissariat Supply Stores and Mill, the Railway Station with sheds and sidings, and the Dockyard. In Omdurman were mud barracks for three Sudanese battalions. The only roads with any metalling were River Avenue

---

[1] Letter from Mr. Basil Burnett to the author, dated April 27th, 1935.

[2] Notes by Lieut.-Colonel H. F. O. Thwaites, M.C., R.E. (retd.), sent to the author on December 28th, 1934.

[3] The Inspector-General was Colonel Sir Rudolf Baron von Slatin, better known as "Slatin Pasha," the ex-prisoner of the Khalifa.

[4] *Mudiria* or *Mudiriya*, the headquarters of the *Mudir* or Governor of a Province. *Zabtia* or *Zabtiya*, District Police Office.

and Khedive Avenue. A few senior officials had dog-carts, but most officers rode on ponies or donkeys. A steam wire-rope ferry plied between Khartoum and Khartoum North; and a river-steamer, with a barge attached, gave a ferry service across the White Nile between Khartoum and Omdurman.

In addition to the Royal Engineer officers, the personnel of the Works Department included 25 Egyptian officers, five British non-commissioned officers as Foremen of Works, and 1,200 military artisans (conscripts). The nucleus of a Public Works Department was under formation, and there were already 12 British Civil Engineers, six civilian Foremen of Works and a civilian Stores and Clerical Staff. A heavy programme of military work was in hand. In Khartoum, a sum of £E.25,000 had been allotted for building the Fort,[1] which was to mount two six-inch howitzers and a five-inch gun, and for the construction also of a defensible Magazine to replace one blown up in 1905. Barracks and workshops were under construction in Khartoum North. On the civil side, there was still greater activity. The works in hand included six double-storeyed houses in Khedive Avenue, and wells and a water-tower for a water-supply scheme. A contractor was installing electric light in many buildings and streets, and a Power House was being built. An extension of the river wall was in progress between the Sudan Club and the Post Office.

The Royal Engineer Mess was situated on the first floor of the Post Office, and when Thwaites arrived in July, 1906, the other occupants were Turner and Dale of the Telegraphs, Pearson of the Survey Department, and Done of the Works Department. Kennedy, Mackworth and Coningham were on leave, Danford was absent with a patrol in the Nuba Mountains, Stokes was in Cairo, and Kelly was Resident Engineer at Port Sudan. Macauley, Midwinter and other Railway engineers were occasional visitors. Ten days after Thwaites joined the Mess, a violent dust-storm struck Khartoum, and he and Mr. Sebright of the Telegraph Department put out in a tug to rescue the crew of a capsized native boat. They picked up five men, and a few minutes later, were surprised to hear loud laughter coming from the dripping group. The survivors then explained to Sebright that the cause of their merriment was the fact that the old woman who cooked for them had not yet appeared on the surface! Sudanese indifference to tragedy may be exemplified further by a scene in the Royal Engineer Mess on the morning of Christmas Day, 1906, when Thwaites was Mess Secretary. He had just come down from his bed on the roof when he heard a knock at his door. " Please, sir," said the Mess butler, " the cook has been murdered, and I want five piastres to buy eggs for breakfast."

It was decided in 1906, that the Department of Works should be

[1] The construction of the Fort was completed in December, 1906.

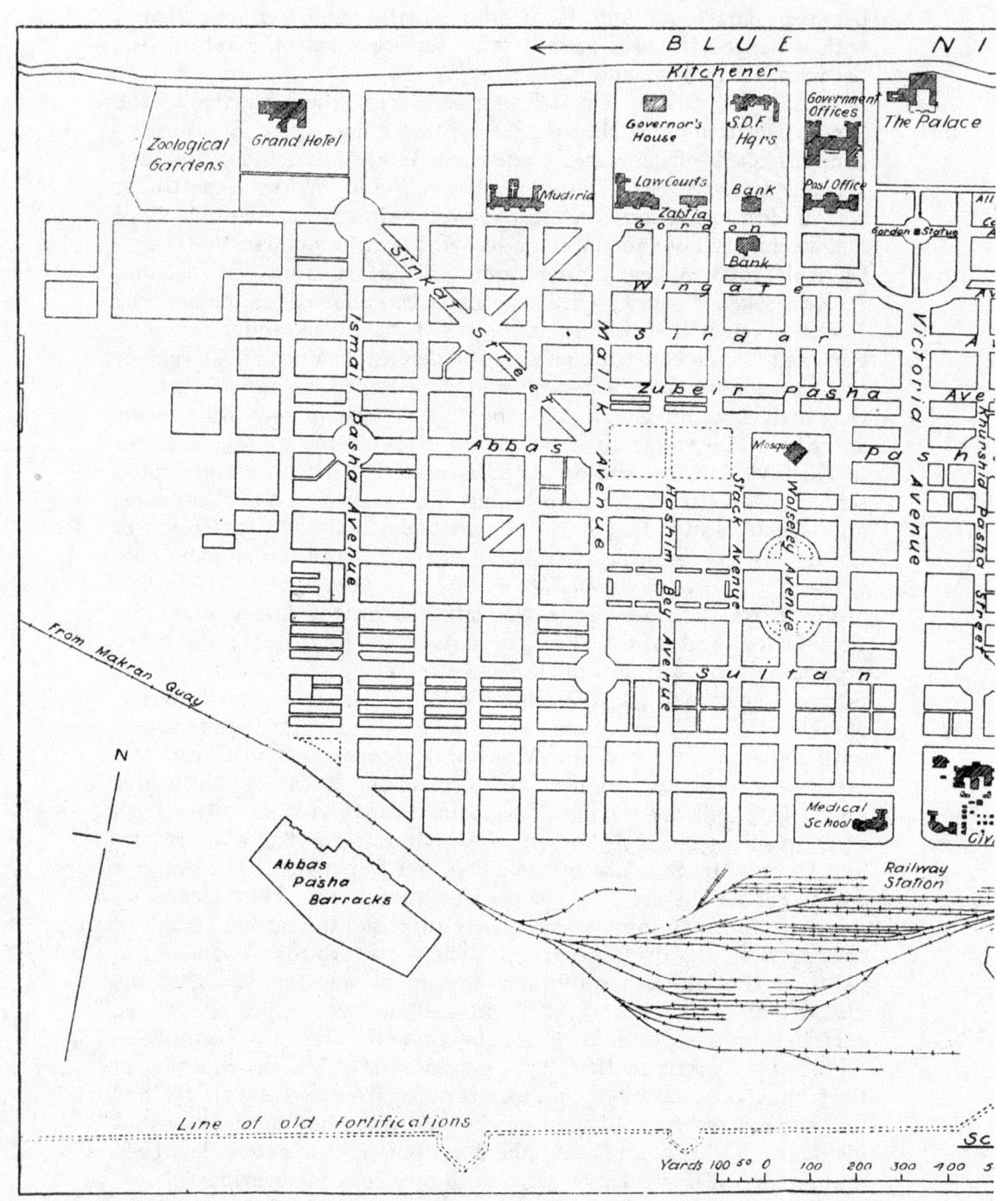

divided into a "Department of Military Works, Egyptian Army," and a "Department of Public Works, Sudan Government." There were many reasons for this decision. The Department of Works had become unwieldy, and the Egyptian Government feared that military labour was being used on civil construction, and that funds allotted for military works were being diverted to civil works, for the line of demarcation between the two classes was thin and easily crossed. Indeed, a Committee of Inquiry was appointed to examine the various aspects of the case; but Kennedy was able to show that all his projects had received official approval, and that his records and statements of expenditure were kept with meticulous care.[1] The division of the Department of Works took place on January 1st, 1907, and thereafter the Military Works were administered by Royal Engineer officers and Egyptian officers of the former Works Department, and the Public Works by Royal Engineer officers or civil engineers with civilian personnel supplied by the Sudan Government. Done was appointed Director of Military Works in Egypt and the Sudan, with Danford, Edgeworth, Stokes and Thwaites as Assistant Directors; while Kennedy became Director of Public Works in the Sudan, with Kelly and Mackintosh as his military assistants. In order to facilitate the separation, Kennedy suggested that he should be allowed to remain in control of both the new Departments until January 1st, 1908, and this was approved by the Government. The Department of Stores, formerly included with Works, was placed under separate administration.

The junior officers of the Military Works Department spent the greater part of each winter in out-stations, where they were visited from time to time by the Director. The annual programme of construction was taken in hand immediately after the close of the rainy season, at which time the young Royal Engineers set out from Khartoum with retinues of Egyptian officers, Egyptian artisans and Sudanese labourers, and a comprehensive assortment of all building materials except bricks.[2] Rapid tours, however, might be necessary at any time. "On February 23rd, 1907," writes Thwaites,[3] "I started from Khartoum for Kassala on camel-back, and accomplished the distance of 262 miles in 8 days. The fort was in good preservation, and the town flourishing. Having spent 6 days at Kassala, I left for Gedaref, and arriving there after a 5 days' journey, selected a site

[1] In his Annual Report for 1907, Kennedy writes:—"Considerable improvement is essential in the strict control of funds by Assistant and District Engineers. These officers have not grasped the necessity of working within the limits of the funds allotted to them for the execution of definite services. In justice, however, I should like to point out some of the difficulties they experience in exercising proper financial control." He then remarks on difficulties such as wastage of labour, delay in supply, changes in plans and the sudden demands of senior officials.

[2] Notes by Colonel A. W. Stokes, D.S.O., M.C., late R.E., sent to the author on September 22nd, 1934.

[3] Notes by Lieut.-Colonel H. F. O. Thwaites, M.C., R.E. (retd.), sent to the author on December 28th, 1934.

for a Military Hospital and set my Egyptian officer to work on it. A British official at Gedaref told me that, in the course of three years, he had shot eleven lions from the verandah of his house. From Gedaref I rode to Gallabat to inspect the buildings and re-design the Fort, which is close to the Abyssinian boundary. I was supposed to return from Gallabat to Wad Medani, but decided instead to strike direct for the Rahad and travel down that river. The journey occupied a week. At a town near Wad Medani, I was given the finest coffee I have ever tasted. The local Sheikh procured it from Abyssinia and kept a special wife to make it, an operation which took her three-quarters of an hour. A very ornate *Mudiria* and other buildings had been erected at Wad Medani, mostly when Gorringe was Governor. After three days, I returned to Khartoum. A room was being built by contract in the Ordnance Workshops at Khartoum North, and as I noticed that the courses were far from horizontal, I ordered the contractor to pull the wall down. Two days later, I found him rubbing the surface of the wall carefully with brick and marking on it new and horizontal lines of pointing!"

Gorringe was responsible for the construction of most of the large buildings in Wad Medani. When he became Governor of the Sennar Province in January, 1902, the health of the Government officers and officials was deplorable. Malaria was rampant. Mud or straw huts were the only habitations available. No roads existed through the bush. Robberies and thefts were everyday occurrences. Lieut.-Colonel L. B. Friend, R.E., the Director of Works, agreed that the new Governor should assume charge of both military and civil works in the Province; and by 1904, when Gorringe left the Sudan, all officers and troops at Wad Medani, Sennar, Singa and Roseires were housed in brick buildings, situated on high ground some distance from the river. Excellent Government offices had been erected at Wad Medani. The Mosque had been rebuilt at the request of the religious leaders, and the town properly laid out at a very small cost. Sanitation had also received attention. Roads were cut through the bush, and rest-houses provided at intervals of 20 miles along them. During the rainy season, wide areas around native quarters were kept clear of vegetation, with the result that malaria was reduced to a minimum. All these activities demanded additional labour, and this was obtained in the following manner. Under a civil ordinance drawn up by Lord Kitchener, any man found wandering without visible means of earning an honest livelihood was arrested and made to work for Government. A labour enclosure accommodated such persons, who were released only if some responsible man would undertake to employ them and produce them on demand. Their footprints were recorded by Police trackers, in order that they might be easily traced if they escaped and reverted to their customary occupation of robbery. While in the labour enclosure, those who were likely to benefit by training received instruction in various trades. By these means, Gorringe reduced crime in his Province, and improved the health and prosperity of the people by his engineering activities.

In April, 1907, Thwaites voyaged up the Blue Nile to inspect works at Roseires and Singa; but on his return journey the steamer which he was to board at Singa failed to arrive, and as Done was anxious to proceed on leave, it was necessary to start for Khartoum without delay. He rode on camel-back throughout the first night and reached Sennar. The next night's journey brought him to Wad Medani. Fresh camels carried him on the third night to El Kamlin, within 60 miles of the capital, and he covered the final stage during the fourth afternoon and night. The total distance exceeded 200 miles. Pending Danford's return from Kordofan, he took over at once from Done, who was able to start for England on the following morning. Thwaites records that Done asked him to supervise the construction of the Anglican Cathedral, which had been commenced some three months before by a Foreman of Works named Latimer, who had been sent out from England by the architect. In July, 1907, Thwaites was transferred to the Public Works Department. By the end of the year, the Law Courts and Irrigation offices in Khartoum had been completed, a new Civil Hospital was being built, and the water-supply system had been almost finished.[1] The town was rapidly becoming a modernized centre of administration and commerce, and the advent of the railway in 1910 completed the first stage of its transformation from the old Khartoum defended by Gordon.

The Anglican place of worship on Gordon Avenue, known as All Saints' Cathedral, owes its existence mainly to the efforts of the Right Reverend Dr. Llewelyn Gwynne, C.M.G., C.B.E., Bishop of Egypt and the Sudan, who arrived in the Sudan as a missionary in 1899. Mr. R. W. Schultz Weir, the architect of the cathedral, records that valuable help and advice was given, during its construction, by Captains Done and Thwaites, R.E.[2] The building was designed to suit the climatic conditions and the materials available, and is composed of red sandstone from quarries at Jebel Auliya. It consists of a chancel, nave and transepts, with a portico at the west end, to which a detached tower is connected by a short passage. The lower part of the tower forms a baptistery, and the upper part contains a clock and a peal of bells. In the north transept is the Gordon Chapel, with stained glass windows, an inscription in bronze letters to the hero of Khartoum,[3] and commemorative tablets to the officers and men who fell during the operations

---
[1] Annual Report, Public Works Department, Sudan Government, 1907.
[2] Notes by Dr. R. W. S. Weir sent to the author on December 7th, 1936.
[3] The inscription is on the wall and runs:—" Praise God for Charles George Gordon, a Servant of Jesus Christ, whose labour was not in vain in the Lord."

GORDON AVENUE, KHARTOUM.
Showing the Gordon Memorial Statue and All Saints' Cathedral.
[*Photo by the Author.*]

between 1884 and 1899. In the south transept is a bronze memorial to Lord Kitchener.[1] Although the foundation stone was laid by H.R.H. Princess Henry of Battenberg on February 7th, 1904, the excavation of the foundations was not begun until December, 1906; and at the time of the consecration of the building by the Bishop of London on January 26th, 1912, the upper part of the west end was still unfinished. This portion was completed in 1913. The construction of the tower was started in 1929. This addition to the cathedral was dedicated on January 26th, 1931, by Bishop Gwynne. Such is the history of a handsome structure, in the building of which, two Royal Engineers were concerned.

In 1906 and 1907, Captain M. R. Kennedy, and Lieutenants H. H. Kelly and E. E. B. Mackintosh, R.E., assisted in the establishment of a hill-station at Erkowit. This picturesque spot is nearly 4,000 feet above sea level and situated in the Red Sea hills some 25 miles east of Sinkat, to which it is connected by a motor road. In February, 1906, Kelly rode southwards from Port Sudan and ascended the Khor Wintri to Erkowit, where he found six wooden huts and some mud buildings, used during the hot weather by officials from Suakin. The site was bare of vegetation, but it had a good supply of water, and Kelly reported that it was suitable for a hill-station provided that permanent bungalows were built and a road constructed to the Nile-Red Sea railway at Sinkat.[2] As a result of this report, a Committee, of which Mackintosh was a member, visited Erkowit on March 18th, 1907, and after examining the surrounding country, proposed a better site on a ridge about two miles north-east of the wooden huts, whence a fine view could be obtained over the plains. The soil was good, the vegetation abundant, the water-supply adequate, and an adjacent grassy hollow gave space for tennis courts and a golf course. A motor road, already under construction from Sinkat, could be prolonged easily to the site.[3] The scheme was approved by Sir Reginald Wingate, and the development of Erkowit was taken in hand forthwith by Kennedy as Director of Public Works.[4] For many years, the place has been a sanatorium and a favourite resort of those who are unable otherwise to escape from the tropical heat of the summer months.

It is necessary, at this juncture, to mention some of the rapid changes which took place, between 1908 and 1916, in the Royal Engineer Staff of the Department of Military Works in the Sudan. Lieutenants B. H. Wilbraham and E. M. Sinauer joined in 1908;

[1] See Chapter XII.
[2] Report by Bimbashi H. H. Kelly to the Director of Works, Khartoum, dated March 3rd, 1906. In October, 1896, a party of the 1st Coy., Madras Sappers and Miners, under Lieut. G. A. F. Sanders, R.E., had dug a well at Erkowit.
[3] Report by Dr. E. S. Crispin, Bimbashi E. E. B. Mackintosh and Mr. E. Pease to the Governor, Red Sea Province, dated March 30th, 1907.
[4] Annual Report, Public Works Department, Sudan Government, 1907.

and in the following year, Major P. G. Grant succeeded Captain R. J. Done as Director, on the reversion of the latter to the Home Establishment, and Captain A.W. Stokes was transferred as Assistant Director to Egypt, where he served for two years before reversion. Lieutenants C. H. Egerton and G. C. Gowlland joined in 1910; and Captains B. W. Y. Danford, K. E. Edgeworth and B. H. Wilbraham reverted in the same year. In 1911, Lieutenants A. J. Ross, A. G. Rainsford-Hannay and W. S. Blunt joined the cadre, Ross replacing Stokes in Egypt, and the others going to the Sudan. In 1912, Lieutenants W. E. Day and B. T. Wilson arrived in Khartoum in replacement of Sinauer and Gowlland, who reverted. Ross was relieved in Egypt by Rainsford-Hannay,[1] and in 1913 was posted to the Intelligence Department. During 1914 and 1915, after the outbreak of the Great War, there was a general exodus. Grant, Egerton, Blunt, Day and Wilson proceeded on active service; and for several months in 1915, until he was rejoined by Gowlland, who had been wounded in France, Rainsford-Hannay was the sole representative of the Corps in Khartoum.

As regards the Public Works Department, it has been recorded already that Captain H. H. Kelly became Director of the Roads and Communications Section in 1908, and in the same year Captain E. E. B. Mackintosh was appointed Aide-de-Camp to the Governor-General. Thus in 1909, Captains M. R. Kennedy and H. F. O. Thwaites were the only Royal Engineers in charge of civil building construction and water-supply in the Sudan. Thwaites reverted to the Home Establishment in 1913; and towards the end of 1915, Kennedy proceeded to the theatre of war in Gallipoli. Prior to the Darfur Expedition in 1916, however, Kennedy returned to his appointment of Director of Public Works, and held it until he was succeeded by Mr. Basil Burnett in March, 1918. He left the Sudan at the end of 1919.[2]

Sweeping reforms were introduced in the Military Works Department when Major P. G. Grant, R.E., became Director in the autumn of 1909. Grant realized at once that the existing primitive, though moderately efficient, methods of constructing and maintaining buildings were no longer suited to the conditions, and accordingly he proceeded to draft regulations modelled to some extent on those of the Military Engineer Services in India. Specifications and schedules of rates were compiled, and instructions issued for the annual preparation of budget proposals. The new system of accurate estimating for work to be executed by military labour, and the introduction of contracts, were highly unpopular in some quarters, but they proved their value during the next few years.

[1] Lieut. A. G. Rainsford-Hannay served in Cairo from the summer of 1912 until October, 1914, when he returned to Khartoum.
[2] Lieut.-Colonel M. Ralston Kennedy, C.M.G., D.S.O., died at St.Servan in France on November 2nd, 1924.

GRANT REORGANIZES THE MILITARY WORKS DEPARTMENT.

Before Grant arrived, the usual practice had been to distribute money and stores to any small construction party sent to an outstation, and to leave the Egyptian officer in charge to execute the work within the sum allotted. Frequently, the estimates were very rough. There were no specifications, and the plans were usually without cross-sections. Buildings were sketched on the sand, and the number of doors and windows was computed on the spot. In Khartoum itself, the methods were similar. On one occasion, Grant found that well-known Foreman of Works, "Sammy" Hart, building a large double-storeyed house without any cross-sectional drawings.[1] He was working out the details as he went, and very well too, being an expert in that line ; but "Sammy" Hart was a law unto himself, and Egyptian officers and subordinates could not emulate his feats of engineering.

In addition to the preparation of plans, estimates, specifications. schedules and budgets, Grant secured the appointment of extra British officers and effected a marked improvement in the training and discipline of the 900 Egyptian officers and men (*Nafars*) of the Department. He introduced steel-frame buildings, pitched roofs in place of flat roofs, and the Indian type of bungalow with verandahs and clerestory windows. In all these schemes for reorganization and improvement, he was supported by the Governor-General, Sir Reginald Wingate, and by Colonel (now General Sir) J. J. Asser, the Adjutant-General, Egyptian Army.

"Some difficulties were overcome by Grant in characteristic manner," writes Rainsford-Hannay.[2] "As there was no glass in any of the Egyptian barracks, the window openings were closed by wooden shutters secured by hooks to prevent damage to the hinges during dust-storms ; but the hooks were rarely used, and continual expense was incurred in repairing the shutters and hinges. Accordingly, Grant instituted a fine of one piastre for every hook found unfastened, and the repair bill was soon reduced to a remarkably low figure. Another innovation dealt with the disposal of date-stones. The Egyptian soldier is very partial to dates, and it is almost impossible to prevent him from chewing them whilst at work. Ordinarily, this is of no great importance ; but when datestones began to appear in newly-set concrete, and caused the formation of pimples which burst with dire results, it was time to take action. Orders were issued that every concrete slab was to bear the number of its maker, and the signature of the Egyptian non-commissioned officer in charge of the party, and after a few cases of disciplinary action, the date-stones were ejected elsewhere."

[1] Notes by Major-General Sir Philip G. Grant, K.C.B., C.M.G., late R.E., sent to the author on September 4th, 1934.
[2] Notes by Lieut.-Colonel A. G. Rainsford-Hannay, D.S.O., O.B.E., R.E. (retd.), sent to the author on August 29th, 1934.

Grant devoted much time and care to the militarization of the men of the Military Works Department, who were popularly known as the "Boys in Blue." Before his arrival, they were dressed in blue blouses (*gallabiyas*), and were indistinguishable from the men of the Commissariat and other Departments. He changed this dress to a khaki uniform, with a turban having a red flash and a brass badge, and instituted Monday morning drills and regular barrack-room inspections. "Sammy" Hart assisted him by instructing the "*Nafars*" in trades. By 1914, they were smart and soldier-like in bearing, and the Egyptian officers prided themselves on being "engineers" and not mere supervisors of fatigue parties. This was in marked contrast to the state of affairs in 1909, when the only Egyptian *Kaimakam* (Lieut.-Colonel) in the Department was employed as a draughtsman! By 1916, the Department had become still more military in character, and included an armed Sapper Section under Hart.[1] In this year, it took charge of the Mechanical Transport during operations in the Nuba Mountains. On the whole, however, it was occupied normally with the construction and maintenance of military buildings in Khartoum, Omdurman and elsewhere.

Meanwhile, the Public Works Department, under Kennedy as Director, continued the development of Khartoum and Port Sudan. For many years, Khartoum had been a Municipality. In 1912, under the direction of Lord Kitchener, Dr. W. H. Maclean, the Municipal Engineer, had prepared a new and elaborate lay-out, providing for the expansion of the town to the south, east and west. Development was resumed after the Great War. In 1927, Khartoum was connected to Omdurman by a steel girder road-bridge across the White Nile.[2] Two years later, when Mr. E. G. Sarsfield-Hall became Governor, a Town Planning Committee was assembled and formulated a comprehensive scheme for the improvement of Khartoum, Khartoum North and Omdurman. Strips of tarred macadam, 15 feet wide, were laid along the principal avenues in Khartoum,[3] the main streets of Omdurman were widened, straightened and partly metalled, and many other works were executed which cannot be described in these pages. No Royal Engineer was concerned in them; but it may be remarked that for several years the Corps has been represented in the Public Works Department at

---

[1] See Chapter XII. The Sapper Section was started in 1913, when some naked orphan Nuba Boys were recruited at the suggestion of Colonel J. J. Asser.

[2] This bridge carries an electric tramway in addition to a roadway. It consists of nine 244 feet spans, and has a total length of 2,196 feet.

[3] Victoria Avenue, running southwards from the Palace, has a width of 150 feet between buildings, a carriage-way (62 feet wide) with a central tarred strip, and two footpaths (each 15 feet wide). Gordon Avenue has a width of 120 feet between buildings, and a carriage-way only 48 feet wide. The dimensions for Sirdar Avenue are 95 feet and 62 feet respectively. Wingate Avenue, between Gordon Avenue and Sirdar Avenue, is tarred to the curbs.

Khartoum by a Garrison Engineer,[1] and that an ex-Royal Engineer, Major H. E. Hebbert, D.S.O., M.C., is now Assistant Director.

Major F. E. Fowle, M.C., R.E., records some of the engineering work executed in the Sudan after the Great War by officers of the Corps.[2] In 1919-20, Captain H. G. Pyne, M.C., reconnoitred for a road from Mongalla to Ikoto, and Captain W. H. Oxley, M.C., started the construction at Omdurman of barracks for two battalions, which were partly occupied at a later date by the Engineer Troops. The building of a military cantonment at Malakal was also taken in hand, and proved to be a matter of some difficulty. The houses had to be founded on reinforced concrete piles, and the stone aggregate brought from quarries 400 miles distant. In 1920-21, Captain H. P. W. Hutson, D.S.O., O.B.E., M.C., started a scheme for battalion barracks at Singa, and the Omdurman scheme was continued. In 1921-22, Captain F. E. Fowle, M.C., began to build barracks at Roseires,[3] and completed the Singa scheme. During this cold weather, Captain R. D. Pank, M.C., met with a serious accident in Khartoum. While sleeping on the upper verandah of the R.E. Mess, he was awakened by a burglar and grappled with the man; but during the struggle which ensued, he was thrown off the verandah and fell 20 feet on to a brick coping, injuring his head. After a period in hospital, he was able to return to duty; but there is little doubt that his death in September, 1926, was accelerated by the fall.

In consequence of the recent mutinies in Khartoum and elsewhere, and the evacuation of Egyptian officers and men, the Military Works Department faded out of existence. It was suggested that the Public Works Department should assume responsibility for all Government buildings, with a reorganized Military Works Department subordinate to the Director of Public Works; but Thwaites, as Director of Military Works, would not agree to this and reverted to the Home Establishment,[4] and the scheme for a Military Works Department as an appendage to the Public Works Department was abandoned. Captain C. G. Martin, V.C., D.S.O., who had joined as Assistant Director in 1920, acted as Director for a few months after Thwaites left, and then he also reverted to the Home Establishment. The remains of the former Military Works Department were absorbed into the Public Works Department; and to cope with the extra work thus thrust upon him, Mr. D. MacFarlane, the civilian Director of Public Works, applied for and obtained the services of 4 officers and

---

[1] In 1935, the Garrison Engineer, P.W.D., was Captain F. D. Mann, R.E. The appointment is now held by Captain A. G. H. Brousson, R.E.

[2] Notes by Major F. E. Fowle, M.C., R.E., sent to the author on April 1st, 1936.

[3] Captain Fowle completed the Roseires scheme during the working season of 1922-23. Building operations in the Sudan are undertaken mostly during the winter and spring. They are impossible in the rainy season, and difficult in the extreme heat.

[4] Major H. F. O. Thwaites, M.C., R.E., was Director of Military Works, Egyptian Army, from September 19th, 1917, to March 31st, 1925.

4 non-commissioned officers of the Royal Engineers.[1] This reinforcement enabled him to carry on the new administration until additional civilian assistant engineers could be recruited and trained.

Some allusion has been made in a previous chapter to the constructional and other work executed in out-stations by the Engineer Troops of the Sudan Defence Force.[2] In 1925, a house was built at the Akobo Post for the District Commissioner, and wells were sunk at Bara in Kordofan. In the following year, the aerodrome at Talodi was cleared of tree-stumps. In 1927, blockhouses were built at El Obeid, the fort at Kassala was repaired, and new barracks and a rifle range were provided at Singa. Buildings were erected at Nyala in Darfur in 1928, and the construction of a road was begun between Bor and the Sobat River. Between 1929 and 1932, military stations were built for the Equatorial Corps at Torit and Kapoeta in the extreme south.[3] This was the largest constructional programme ever undertaken by the company of Engineer Troops. The entire work, from making and burning the bricks to painting the finished houses, was carried out by Sapper labour or under Sapper supervision. The scheme cost £E.16,000 and 23 buildings were erected.[4] In 1934, a detachment of Engineer Troops made 15 miles of road in very hilly country on the Abyssinian frontier, east of Malakal.[5]

Blasting operations in the bed of the Nile were carried out in 1928, at Semna above Wadi Halfa, by a detachment of Engineer Troops under Captain F. D. Mann, R.E., and were repeated at Ambigol in 1931, at Dal in 1932, and at Atbara in 1933. They were necessary because many native boats, sailing downstream to Egypt, were wrecked on hidden rocks. Thousands of cubic metres of rock were removed in and above the Second Cataract, and as a result, only one boat was wrecked in this difficult section during 1932, instead of the usual fifty or more. This improvement was much appreciated by the owners of the boats, and also by the Government, which profited in taxation through the increasing bulk of the date-trade in which the boats were engaged; but the success of the blasting operations was deplored by many patient watchers on the banks of the Nile, whose annual harvest of wreckage dwindled almost to vanishing point.

No history of the connection of the Royal Engineers with Military

---

[1] Notes by Captain F. C. Nottingham, R.E., sent to the author on July 8th, 1935. Of these officers, the only one still serving in the Sudan is Major H. E. Hebbert, D.S.O., M.C., R.E. (retd.).

[2] See Chapter XIII.

[3] Torit is 70 miles south-east of Juba; Kapoeta, 140 miles east of Juba.

[4] Article entitled "Engineer Troops, Sudan Defence Force," by Lieut. A. J. Knott, R.E., appearing in the *R.E. Journal*, Vol. XLVIII, January-June, 1934, pp. 121-126. The buildings comprised seven quarters for British officers, five offices, seven stores, a guardroom and armoury, and three large steel buildings for mechanical transport.

[5] Statement showing the Military Operations, and Civil and Military Works, undertaken by the Engineer Troops, Sudan Defence Force, from 1924 to 1935, by the Commandant, Engineer Troops, dated Omdurman, January 30th, 1935.

and Public Works in the Sudan would be complete without some description of the foundation and development of Port Sudan under the direction of Sir Reginald Wingate as Governor-General. For many centuries before the British occupation, the modest needs of the Red Sea Littoral had been served by Suakin, a port which became, year by year, more heavily obstructed by coral reefs. Lieutenants W. H. Chippindall and C. M. Watson, R.E., spent a week there at the beginning of September, 1874. Subsequently, Chippindall wrote from the Upper Nile,[1] "Whilst waiting at Suakin for the camels to take us across the desert, we had time to look about. One question in particular drew our attention and that was 'Why Suakin was chosen for a harbour?' Nobody knew. The entrance is so blockaded by coral reefs that no ship can attempt to enter at night. Now, farther up the coast to the north is a very good harbour (at least so it seems from the charts, and the captains and pilots all confirm it) at about 30 miles from Suakin, called ' Sheick Barute.' The question naturally presented itself to us why this good harbour should be left utterly unused when, with a couple of lighthouses, it could be entered at any time."

It is probable that this question presented itself again to Watson when he was Governor-General of the Red Sea Littoral in 1886, and also to his brother Engineers, Chermside, Warren and Kitchener, and to other officers who preceded or followed him in that appointment; but it must have been evident to them that no change of base could be contemplated while the coast was a battlefield and the dervishes swarmed along the Nile. When Sir Reginald Wingate became Governor-General of the reconquered Sudan at the end of 1899, he was aware that Suakin was quite unsuitable as the port of entry to so vast a territory,[2] and also undesirable as such for political reasons; but as it was understood that the Hydrographer of the Royal Navy had stated that it was the best port available, no immediate steps were taken to find another. Money was scarce, and the Government was overburdened at the moment with the pacification of the country, the establishment of a proper administration, and the extension of interior communications.

The reconnaissances and surveys executed by Lieutenants W. E. Longfield and S. F. Newcombe, R.E., from 1901 to 1903, confirmed the opinion that the projected Nile-Red Sea Railway should start from Suakin, and accordingly elaborate arrangements were made to

[1] Letter from Lieut. W. H. Chippindall, R.E., dated Gondokoro, November 22nd, 1874, appearing in an article entitled " Upper Egypt," in the *R.E. Journal*, Vol. 5, 1875, p. 5.
[2] According to Lieut.-General Sir George Gorringe, Lord Kitchener was also aware of this fact. He states that, as early as 1896, the Sirdar had in mind two alternative railway routes for the reconquest of the Sudan. These were the Trinkitat-Tokar-Khor Baraka-Kassala route, and the Suakin-Berber route. For the latter, the Sirdar decided on Sheikh Barghut as the eventual terminal port in preference to Suakin. As a temporary measure, however, Suakin was to be utilized as a terminus on account of its buildings, workshops and quays.

convert that port into a suitable terminus.[1] Materials were collected, causeways and jetties built, and sidings laid on the area known as Graham's Point to the south of the narrow entrance to the harbour. It was only natural that Major G. B. Macauley, R.E., the Director of Railways, should be anxious that his plans should not be upset by any sudden change of base, and accordingly, the claims of Suakin were allowed to remain unchallenged; but they were assailed by Captain M. R. Kennedy, R.E., the Director of Works, on April 23rd, 1904, when the preparations for commencing the railway were nearing completion.

Kennedy, having been ordered to examine Suakin Harbour and estimate the cost of straightening the entrance channel, reported that the blasting of the coral reefs would cost £E.48,000 and might occupy his men for two years. " In considering this expenditure," he wrote,[2] " I should like to bring forward the question as to whether Suakin justifies its choice as the port of the Sudan. The harbour is an unsatisfactory one. It can be entered only by day; it can take only a few ships; and it does not lend itself to improvement, except at great expense. As a site for a town, Suakin has little to commend it. The only suitable site is Graham's Point; but a great portion of this is required by the railway, while another large slice is monopolized by a native cemetery, which we cannot touch. I venture to suggest that, if a harbour with greater natural advantages and conveniently situated can be found, we should not be deterred from accepting it because the inferior harbour of Suakin possesses certain traditions, vested interests and a dilapidated town. A glance at the chart naturally causes one to turn to Sheikh Barud (Barghut), about 29 miles north of Suakin. After collecting all the information I could from Captains of coasting vessels, I visited the harbour in the *Mukhbir*. To my mind, there is no comparison between it and Suakin Harbour. It is clear of dangerous reefs, and the entrance is wider and the harbour much larger. With a lighthouse on the Sanganeb Reef and a couple of leading lights, vessels could enter by night as well as day. This harbour, too, lends itself to improvement without excessive expenditure. The ground around is an ideal site for a town, and there is ample space for extension. I am inclined to think that water could be got from deep wells or borings at the feet of the hills inland. I have been unable to obtain a copy of the letter from the Hydrographer on the subject of Sheikh Barud; but I understand that the only objection raised was that the outer harbour was not considered entirely satisfactory during storms from a certain direction. It seems to me that, if Suakin is finally adopted as the port, we shall get a patchwork and restricted town, and an inferior and equally

---

[1] See Chapter XV. A sketch map of Suakin in 1885 appears in Chapter III.
[2] Report dated April 23rd, 1904, from Kaimakam M. Ralston Kennedy, Director of Works, to the Agent General, Sudan Government, Cairo.

PORT SUDAN.
Showing the Hotel and Government Offices.

[*Photo by the Author.*]

restricted harbour. If Sheikh Barud is adopted, we shall have a much larger and better harbour, and a free hand in laying out a town capable of almost any extension. There will be no difficulty in running the railway to Sheikh Barud. As to the work already done by the Railway authorities in improving Suakin Harbour, I take it that they look upon Suakin merely as an existing means of constructing the railway. I have, as instructed, prepared plans for the laying out of Suakin Town and for the new Government buildings required there; but before any expenditure is incurred, I venture to suggest that the question of Sheikh Barud should be gone into by a Committee, of which, say, two of the members should be Naval experts. I would suggest that the Committee should visit Suakin first, and then Sheikh Barud."

Sir Reginald Wingate, with his intimate knowledge of the coast, was fully aware of many of the attractions of Sheikh Barghut before Kennedy drew attention to them. He had already represented to Lord Cromer that the Sudan should have a port entirely its own and better adapted for trade purposes than Suakin. It is probable that Kennedy's estimate of the cost of improving Suakin Harbour weighted the scales in favour of Sheikh Barghut, and caused Sir Reginald to proceed thither at once in the *Mukhbir*. The gangway which was lowered from his steamer must have been almost the first piece of wood to touch those inhospitable and deserted shores. Seeing for himself the wonderful natural harbour and great depth of water at Sheikh Barghut, Sir Reginald came to the conclusion that no better port could be found on the Red Sea coast, and continuing his journey to Cairo, he laid the whole question before Lord Cromer. The British Agent and Consul General then agreed to the appointment of a small Commission to examine Suakin and Sheikh Barghut; and a representative body composed of Captain H. J. Gedge, R.N., Captain R. J. Done, R.E., Mr. F. Ehrlich, P.W.D., and Monsieur B. Malaval, Port Engineer, visited and reported upon both places in August, 1904. Captain M. R. Kennedy, R.E., had been appointed as a member; but as he was obliged to proceed on leave to Europe, his place was taken by Done. At Sheikh Barghut, Done worked with Gedge, using an ancient theodolite borrowed at Suakin.[1] Having measured a base, they planted flags at intervals around the harbour and made a trigonometrical survey of it, a most difficult task owing to the mirage. However, the resulting large-scale map of the inlet was reasonably accurate. Gedge took soundings in the harbour, while Done plane-tabled along the shore. In the meantime, Ehrlich and Malaval had mapped the future Port—quays, wharves, public buildings, roads, railways and quarantine station—and at the conclusion of this operation, met Gedge and Done. It was satisfactory

[1] Letter from Colonel R. J. Done, D.S.O., late R.E., to the author, dated January 24th, 1937.

to find that the work of the two parties combined to produce a suitable lay-out.

The report of the Commission, and some individual reports by the members, were received in September, 1904, and settled the fate of Suakin. Captain Gedge stated that Suakin Harbour was quite unsuitable as the principal port of the Sudan. It was cramped and narrow. The entrance channel had an awkward bend between coral reefs. There was no place for a dry dock, and no space for wharves. The best approach—that from the north, parallel to the shore—led for 25 miles between reefs; and two others were difficult to negotiate by day and positively dangerous by night. Mr. Ehrlich added that Suakin Town was insanitary, badly built, lacking in space for the storage of goods, and too far from any possible railway terminus. He advocated the building of a new town on Graham's Point. As regards Sheikh Barghut, Captain Gedge remarked that the harbour was admirably adapted in every way to be the leading port of the Sudan. It was safe, and the approach to the reef-lined entrance was straight and easy. The coral shores of the harbour lent themselves to the construction of wharves for large ships. A site could be found for a dry dock, and the long north-west arm of the harbour would accommodate small vessels. Mr. Ehrlich stated that the ground around the harbour gave unlimited space for a town and its extensions, and that the only problems were those in connection with water-supply, drainage and materials. The Commission, as a whole, estimated that the improvement of Suakin would cost approximately £E.100,000, and the establishment of a port at Sheikh Barghut about twice that amount; but they recommended most strongly that Sheikh Barghut, rather than Suakin, should be adapted as the port of entry and the terminus of the railway to the Nile.

The reports and recommendations of the Commission were discussed and criticized by Kennedy in a letter addressed to the Governor-General on October 24th, 1904. "Suakin may now be neglected as the future port of the Sudan," he wrote. He deprecated the fact that the Commission had based their estimate of the size of the proposed town at Sheikh Barghut on a density of population similar to that of Alexandria, and he advocated an area at least four times greater than that allowed. He objected to a proposal that water might be obtained from deep wells near the town, and repeated his suggestion that it should be drawn from below the foothills to the west, though at a cost at least double that quoted by the Commission. He estimated that the construction of the town and harbour, exclusive of water-supply, would cost about £E.379,000, and urged that an immediate start should be made in order that the work should be finished simultaneously with the completion of the Nile-Red Sea Railway.

The recommendations of the Commission having been considered and generally approved, Kennedy was ordered to prepare detailed plans and estimates for all the proposed works at Sheikh Barghut. Within a fortnight, they were in the hands of the Governor-General. The estimates amounted now to £E.940,000, and proved, four years later, to be accurate to within £E.17,000.[1] This was a wonderful feat of design and calculation, and it is probable that no officer in the Sudan other than Kennedy could have accomplished it. His extraordinary energy, and meticulous attention to detail, are shown also in the speed with which he started the work of construction, and the clarity and scope of the pencilled instructions given on December 23rd, 1904, to the leader of the first parties of labourers sent to Sheikh Barghut.[2] These parties, under Yuzbashi Muhammad Yusuf, arrived in Suakin from Berber on January 7th, 1905, and reached Sheikh Barghut by sea on the 11th " with everybody in high spirit of anxiety for the coming work," as their leader put it.

So the great undertaking was launched. "As time went on," writes Sir Reginald Wingate,[3] " a correspondence took place between Lord Cromer and myself on the subject of a suitable name for the new port. It was thought that ' Sheikh Barghut,' meaning ' The Sheikh of the Fleas,' was quite unsuitable, and Lord Cromer suggested that the name should be ' Port Wingate.' I replied that as he had been mainly instrumental in obtaining the necessary funds for the railway extension, and for the building of the town and harbour, it would be far more suitable to call the place ' Port Cromer.' He dissented, however, and I then said, ' Why not call it what it is really going to be, that is to say, the port of the Sudan ; in other words, Port Sudan ? ' This was approved, and thus Sheikh Barghut was renamed Port Sudan."

The scheme prepared by Kennedy provided for quays to berth five ships, entrance and leading light towers, dockyard workshops and a slipway, Customs sheds, an electric power station, electrically-operated cranes and coal transporters, an opening-lift bridge to carry the railway over an arm of the harbour, lighting, drainage and water-supply systems, and all the usual staff and administrative buildings required for a town which was to be, not only the chief port of the Sudan, but the headquarters of the Red Sea Province.[4] Burdened as he was with other civil and military work, the supervision of this programme of construction would have been utterly beyond Kennedy's power, had he not been able to secure the appointment of Lieutenant H. H. Kelly, R.E., as Resident Engineer.

[1] Notes by Lieut.-Colonel H. F. O. Thwaites, M.C., R.E. (retd.), sent to the author on December 28th, 1934.
[2] Instructions by Captain M. Ralston Kennedy, D.S.O., R.E., for the Officer in Charge, Sheikh el Barud Parties, dated December 23rd, 1904, appearing in File 123, B. Archaic, P.W.D., Port Sudan.
[3] Letter from General Sir Reginald Wingate, Bt., G.C.B., G.C.V.O., G.B.E., K.C.M.G., D.S.O., to Mr. G. W. Grabham, Gordon College, Khartoum, dated October 24th, 1934.
[4] Notes by Mr. Basil Burnett, sent to the author on December 14th, 1934.

Kelly arrived in Port Sudan at the end of 1904; and thereafter, although a general supervision was exercised by Kennedy, the construction was directed by Kelly, and the survey operations by Captain H. D. Pearson, R.E., the new Director of Surveys. It fell to Kelly, a subaltern of less than five years' service, to spend more than a million pounds in four years, and right well did he do it, showing imagination, foresight, powers of organization and technical ability remarkable in one so young. In September, 1906, he was joined by Lieutenant E. E. B. Mackintosh, R.E. Together, they continued the task, with the help of a staff of civilian specialists in harbour, mechanical, electrical and civil engineering. The office in which they worked is still used by the Resident Engineer, and near it is a small Treasury, the first building erected in Port Sudan by Kelly.

On January 1st, 1906, Sir Reginald Wingate gave the following description of Port Sudan and its surroundings :—[1]" The new port is 30 miles north of Suakin, 800 miles distant from Suez, 497 from Khartoum, 307 from Atbara and 692 from Wadi Halfa. Thus, the route from Khartoum to the sea (at Alexandria) is reduced by upwards of 900 miles. The entrance to the harbour lies open to the south-east, while the port itself consists of an outer basin with two arms, the shorter lying south-west and the other running north-north-west for $2\frac{1}{2}$ miles. Along the coast are fringing reefs, allowing a perfectly clear channel 300 yards wide and 600 yards long into the harbour. . . . The harbour basin is 12 to 15 fathoms deep. There are 237 acres available for large ships up to 5,000 tons, and 70 acres for smaller vessels. The outer reefs break all large waves, and access is easy by day or night in all weathers. There will be beacons and leading lights, and a lighthouse on Sanganeb Reef.[2] The east side of the harbour has been entirely appropriated for commercial wharves, shipping offices, etc., while the town proper has been laid out on the high-lying ground on the west side. Here will be constructed all the Government buildings and offices, the Post and Telegraph office, Hospital, Barracks, Schools and Prison. A Quarantine station is being built on the ground south of the harbour. The main line of railway runs round the end of the harbour. The total quayage, at present under construction, is only 650 metres. . . . An excellent water-supply, ample for all shipping requirements and for any conceivable development of the town, will probably be available. The residential portion of the town has been divided into building lots and lots for business premises. The town is being lighted thoughout by electricity, as will also the harbour and quays.

[1] Extracts from a Memorandum by the Governor-General of the Sudan, dated January 1st, 1906, appearing in the *Report on the Finance, Administration and Condition of the Sudan*, 1905, pp. 52-54. A *Sketch Map of Port Sudan in 1929* is included in this chapter.

[2] Sanganeb Reef is 15 miles north-east of Port Sudan. A description of the reef and lighthouse is given in *The Engineer*, January 24th, 1908, pp. 79, 80.

The central electrical station is being made, large enough to provide power for the cranes and conveyors, and for the pumps of the water-supply station."

Kelly encountered many difficulties in building Port Sudan. The local clay and lime were poor in quality and stone was scarce, so he used coral blocks set in cement. The coral was prone to disintegrate, unless cut and used soon after being exposed to the air. Ironwork corroded with extraordinary rapidity in the damp and salt-laden atmosphere, and even reinforced concrete was unreliable. Nevertheless, good progress was made. By the end of 1907, the schools, Custom House, four warehouses, two quarters for officials, Post and Telegraph offices, the Quarantine station and the *Mudiria* had been completed, and the Prison, Barracks, Electric Power station, Civil Hospital and *Zabtia* were nearly finished. The opening-lift bridge was in position, and could be operated by hand. Four electric cranes had been erected, and the main dockyard buildings were ready.[1] At this time, the last detachment of Military Works Department soldiers returned to Khartoum.

A complete history of the schemes and arrangements for the supply of water to Port Sudan would fill a volume.[2] Early in 1905, under Kennedy's direction, wells were dug in the Khor Mogg within a few miles of the town, but they yielded only brackish water. Better water was obtained from other wells sunk higher up the Khor, and this was brought to the town in tanks by rail. In August, 1905, Kelly discovered a promising site in the more distant Khor Arbaat. This watercourse was visited by a number of experts; and at the end of 1906, Kennedy submitted a scheme for a concrete dam, filters, a pipe-line and reservoirs to cost about £E.250,000. Further investigations and reports by civil engineers and geologists followed. In 1907, Kennedy produced a revised scheme for which funds were not immediately available. Minor improvements were made, but no radical change was attempted until after the Great War. In the summer of 1908, both Kelly and Mackintosh left Port Sudan, Kelly being succeeded as Resident Engineer by a civil engineer, on whom the responsibility for the water-supply then devolved.[3]

April 1st, 1909, saw the formal opening of Port Sudan by H.H. the Khedive, Abbas Pasha Hilmi. On that occasion, the Khedivial Yacht, the *Mahroussa*, broke a ribbon stretched across the harbour entrance,

---

[1] Annual Report, Public Works Department, Sudan Government, 1907, by Captain M. Ralston Kennedy, D.S.O., R.E., Director of Public Works.

[2] A concise, but comprehensive, account is given in an article entitled "The Port Sudan Water Supply," by Major H. E. Hebbert, D.S.O., M.C., R.E. (retd.), appearing in *Sudan Notes and Records*, Vol. XVIII, 1935, Part I, pp. 89-101.

[3] In 1908, the Chief Engineer, Port Sudan Town and Harbour Works, was Mr. Basil Burnett, who was appointed to that post on March 23rd, 1906. Mr. Burnett became Director of Public Works in the Sudan on March 12th, 1918, and retired on May 25th, 1924, when he was succeeded by Mr. D. MacFarlane. Mr. G. N. Loggin was appointed Director of Works on September 29th, 1926, and Mr. B. A. R. Hughes on June 6th, 1936.

and followed by a ship carrying Staff officers and officials, made a stately entry into the new port. The Khedive landed, and the usual formalities of such an occasion were observed. The elaborate decorations of the town and harbour had been ruined on the previous night by heavy rain, but Kennedy had renewed them in time for the ceremonies.

A still more impressive event occurred on January 17th, 1912, when Port Sudan was honoured by a visit from Their Majesties King George V. and Queen Mary. The day has been observed ever since as a public holiday. The King and Queen were returning from their visit to India, and came to Port Sudan in response to a suggestion made to the King by Sir Reginald Wingate when dining at Balmoral in 1911. After their ship, the *Medina*, had moored at 7 a.m., the King and Queen received Lord Kitchener, Sir Reginald and Lady Wingate, Slatin Pasha and other senior Government officials and their wives, and then descended to the quay, where a dais and stands had been erected. The town and harbour were gay with bunting. The Governor-General read an address, and the King replied. At 10 a.m., after several officers, including Captains E. C. Midwinter, E. O. A. Newcombe and M. R. Kennedy, R.E., had been presented, the King and Queen entrained for Sinkat, where they witnessed displays by native horsemen, camel-men and swordsmen. Afterwards, they returned to Port Sudan, and sailed with Lord Kitchener for Suez the same evening. Before leaving the port, His Majesty the King invested Sir Reginald Wingate with the insignia of a Knight Grand Cross of the Victorian Order.

Between 1908 and 1921, several attempts were made to improve the Port Sudan water-supply; but it was not until 1924 that a Khor Arbaat piped system, proposed by Mr. Beeby Thompson, was taken in hand. This was completed at the end of 1930, when the daily consumption of water had increased to 1,500 tons. The two mains which now lead from five wells in the Khor Arbaat, are capable of delivering 2,600 tons daily to high-level tanks in Port Sudan, and to an underground reservoir with a capacity of 5,000 tons. From 1927, the Khor Arbaat scheme was supervised by Major H. E. Hebbert, D.S.O., M.C., R.E., who became District Engineer, P.W.D., at Port Sudan in January of that year, and Divisional Engineer in January, 1931, after retiring from the Army in July, 1929. During a period of nine years as Resident Engineer at Port Sudan,[1] Hebbert constructed the Church, Post office and many less important buildings, and carried on, with efficiency and success, the work begun in 1905 by his brother officers of the Corps.

While the connection of Royal Engineers with public works has

---

[1] Major Hebbert was transferred to Khartoum in January, 1936, and was succeeded at Port Sudan by Mr. W. A. D. Davey.

the driving energy of Gorringe, the genius of Kennedy, the technical ability of Kelly, and the successful efforts of many other Royal Engineers, have contributed in a marked degree towards the establishment of prosperous towns and settlements throughout a country which was once a scene of unspeakable desolation.

CAIRO.

[from "*The Route of the Overland Mail to India*"

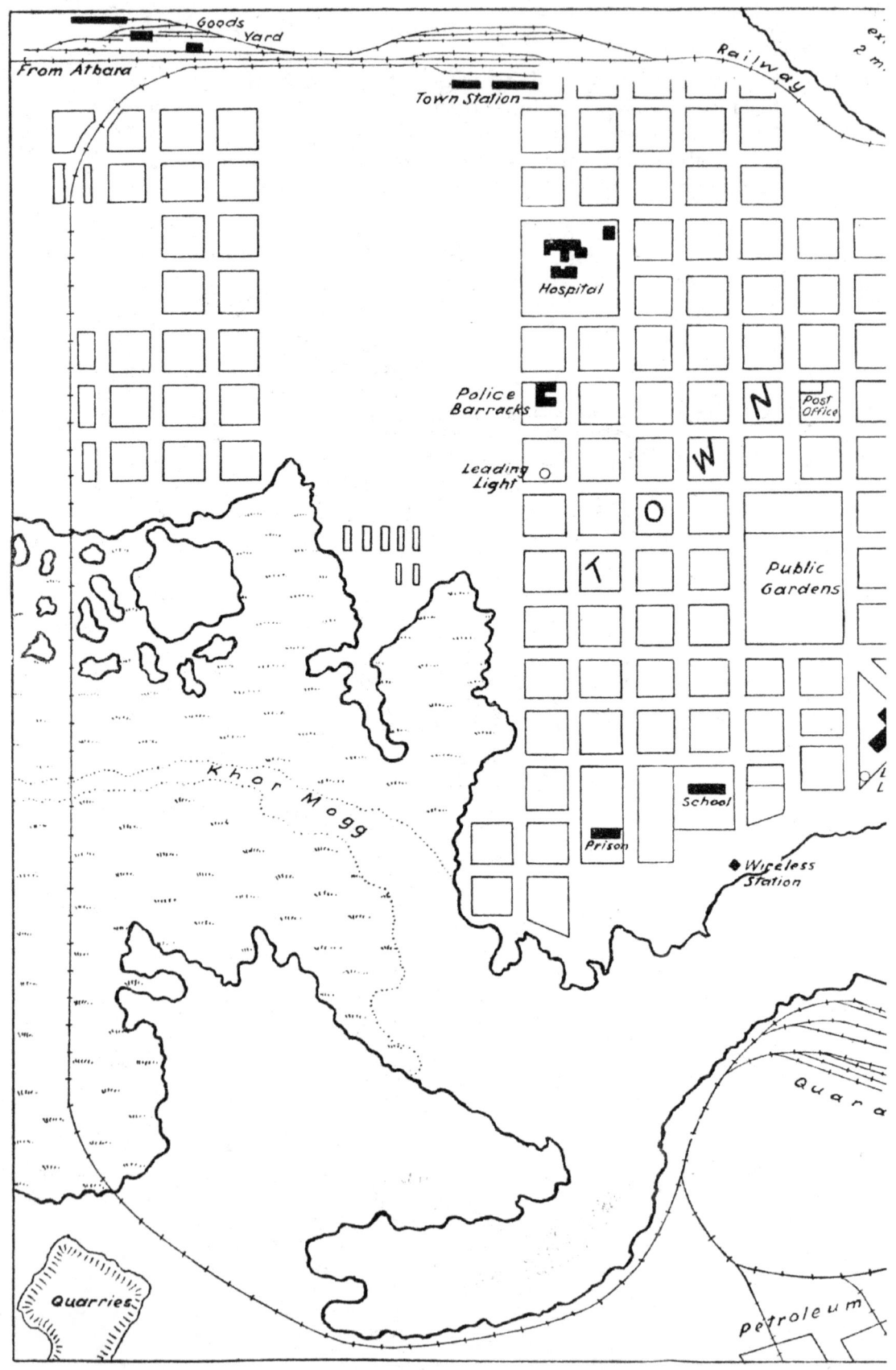

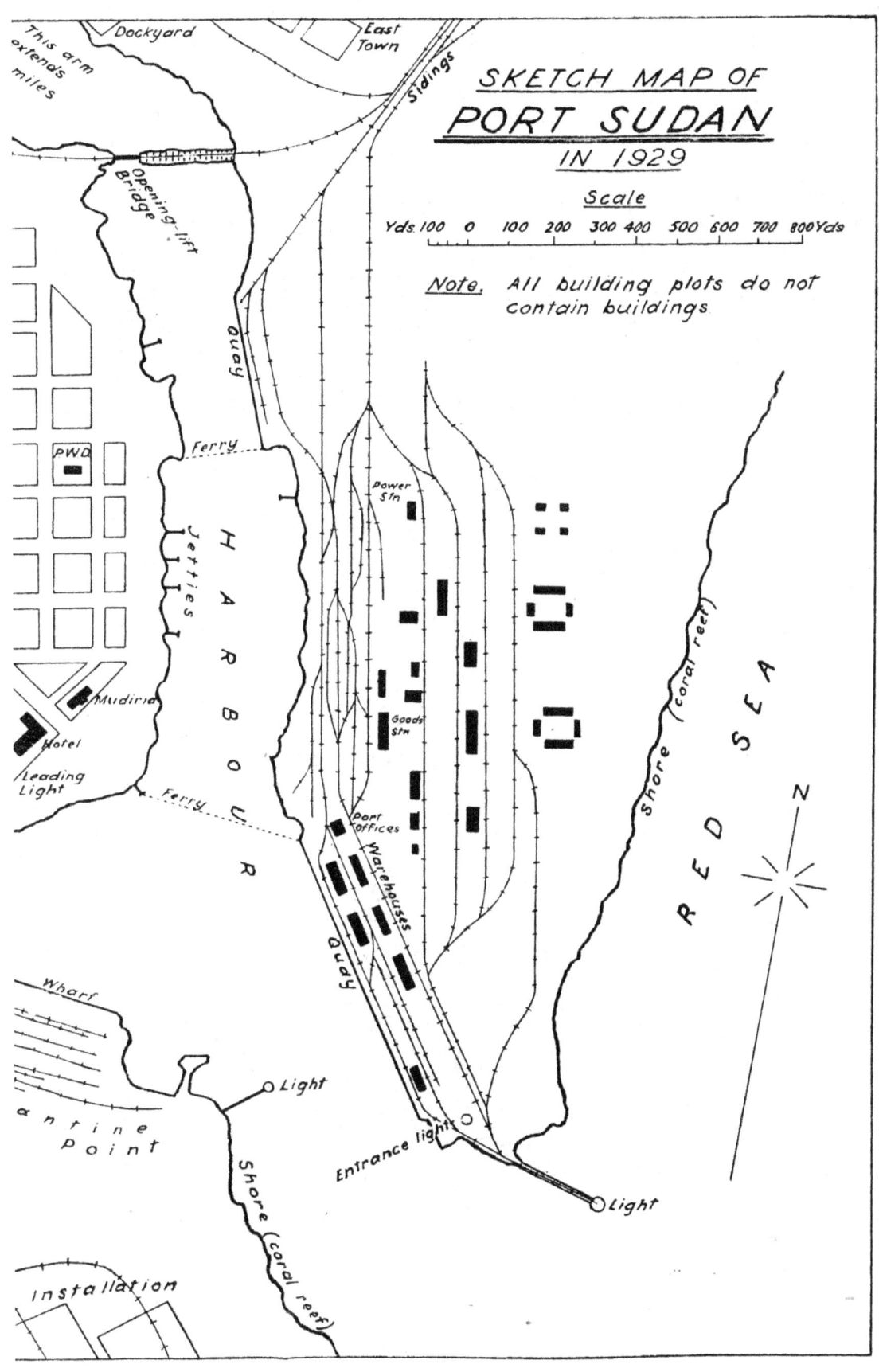

been prominent in the Sudan, it has been very slender in Egypt. Prior to the British occupation, the administration of the Egyptian Department of Irrigation and Public Works was mainly in French hands; but in 1883, it was decided to appoint a British Under-Secretary, and the choice fell upon Colonel Colin Scott-Moncrieff, a retired officer of the Corps, who had taken up the appointment of Inspector-General of Irrigation in Egypt after completing his service in India.[1] As Under-Secretary until 1892, when he was succeeded by Mr. William Garstin, Scott-Moncrieff was intimately concerned with the construction and maintenance of public buildings and roads, and in these duties he was assisted at times by Majors Justin Ross, J. H. Western and Hanbury Brown, R.E., of the Irrigation Branch. It is recorded also that Lieut.-Colonel L. B. Friend, R.E., visited Cairo after he had relinquished the post of Director of Works in the Sudan, and that, while waiting there on half-pay from April, 1904, to August, 1905, he assisted Sir William Garstin in the Public Works Department. Since that day, Royal Engineers have had no concern with public works in Egypt.

On the other hand, military works in Egypt have been controlled for many years by a cadre of officers of the Corps; and until the abolition of the Military Works Department in the Sudan in 1924, an Assistant Director of Military Works was stationed in Cairo. His duties were those normally performed by any divisional officer responsible for the maintenance of barracks, and they call for no particular remark. "I went to Cairo in the summer of 1912, to relieve A. J. Ross," writes Rainsford-Hannay.[2] "Under my orders were 2 Egyptian officers and about 80 men; but any work costing more than £E.100 was done by contract. Although the barracks at Abbassia required little attention, the old Abdin Barracks in Cairo, and the Ras el Tin Barracks at Alexandria, gave much trouble. The Abdin Barracks were lofty and had a roof of lime-concrete, laid on laths and rushes supported by rough wooden beams. This roof was infested with bugs, which we tried to control by painting a tarred frieze on the walls below the ceiling. The bugs which dropped from the ceiling would not cross the frieze when attempting to regain their nests, and could be destroyed with blow-lamps. In addition to these barracks, we maintained a supply depot at Maaddiya, a house for the Sirdar at Gezira, a saluting battery at Port Said, and a recruits' depot at Shellal near Aswan."

Unlike Egypt, the Sudan has offered unique opportunities for the display of originality and resource in the construction and maintenance of buildings. The imagination and foresight of Kitchener,

[1] See Chapter XIV.
[2] Notes by Lieut.-Colonel A. G. Rainsford-Hannay, D.S.O., O.B.E., R.E. (retd.), sent to the author on August 30th, 1934.

CHAPTER XIX.

ARCHÆOLOGY AND GEOLOGY.

ROYAL Engineers in Egypt and the Sudan have not attempted to emulate the archæological and geological achievements of Colonel Colin Mackenzie, Major-General Sir Alexander Cunningham and Lieut.-General Sir Richard Strachey in India.[1] Nevertheless, some of them have found pleasant relaxation from their engineering duties in the study of ancient remains. Others have combined antiquarian and geological research with trigonometrical and topographical surveying in Egypt, Sinai and Palestine. Others again have assisted in the preservation of Egyptian monuments which were threatened with destruction or decay. In many cases, their work has been valuable to Government, and it has helped also towards the elucidation of ancient history.

Visitors to Alexandria may have seen and admired " Pompey's Pillar," a lofty column of red Aswan granite standing in the heart of the city, and may have noticed, on the west side, an inscription in honour of the Emperor Diocletian, placed there in 292 A.D. by a Roman prefect of Egypt. It seems that this inscription attracted the attention of certain officers serving, in 1801, with Sir Ralph Abercromby's expedition. Lieut.-Colonel Robert Wilson wrote in 1803,[2] " The inscription has at length been traced, and this pillar will hereafter be recognized as a monument of British industry and talent. France sent her *savants* to procure the honour of these discoveries ; but their effort to mark the period when this superb column was erected, or to whose fame it was consecrated, proved altogether fruitless. They even pronounced the deciphering impossible. But their veto against further enterprise did not daunt the inquiring genius of two British officers. Captain Dundas, of the Royal Engineers,[3] and Lieutenant Desade, of the Queen's German Regiment, determined on the attempt. For one hour only in each day, whilst the sun cast a shade on the inscription, could they at all discern the characters ; but after a labour of three weeks, success crowned their perseverance, and they traced the inscription, excepting 17 letters."

---

[1] See *The Military Engineer in India*, by Lieut.-Colonel E. W. C. Sandes, D.S.O., M.C., R.E. (retd.), Vol. II., Chapter XIV.

[2] Extract from *History of the British Expedition to Egypt*, by Lieut.-Colonel R. T. Wilson, quoted in *History of the Corps of Royal Engineers*, by Major-General W. Porter, late R.E., Vol. I. p. 234.

[3] Lieutenant the Hon. R. L. Dundas, R.E., was one of the officers serving under Major A. Bryce, R.E., after the latter had succeeded Major W. McKerras, R.E., as C.R.E. (See Chapter I.)

Subsequently, a memoir was presented to the Antiquarian Society by Captain J. Squire, R.E., and Captain Leake, R.A.,[1] in which they also claimed to have deciphered the greater part of the inscription. The obliterations in both readings were filled in by expert archæologists, and a lengthy discussion arose in the *Gentleman's Magazine* regarding certain discrepancies. The main facts, however, were beyond dispute; and accordingly, Squire and Leake shared with Dundas and Desade the honour of being the first British officers to make reliable contributions towards antiquarian research in Egypt.

The next archæological work in Egypt in which Royal Engineers were engaged was the measurement, in 1869, of the base of the Great Pyramid of Kheops (Khufu) at Giza near Cairo. Colonel Sir Henry James, late R.E., a keen archæologist who was then Director-General of the Ordnance Survey of Great Britain,[2] was anxious to ascertain the exact lengths of the cubits, or units of measurement, employed by the Egyptians in setting out the external and internal dimensions of the Pyramid. Accordingly, as a party of Royal Engineers under Captains C. W. Wilson and H. S. Palmer, R.E.,[3] had been sent to survey the Sinai Peninsula during the winter of 1868-69, he directed them on their return through Egypt to measure carefully the four sides of the base of the Pyramid, the original extent of which is shown by rectangular sockets cut in the rock to receive the corner stones. This they did, and found that their measurements agreed closely with those taken in 1865 by Mr. Inglis, a civil engineer.

In July, 1869, Colonel James published a pamphlet entitled *Notes on the Great Pyramid of Egypt and the Cubits used in its Design*, in which he gave the results of his own observations and those of Wilson and Palmer. He deprecated the fantastic theories which had been advanced regarding the significance of the proportions, dimensions and units of measurement of the Pyramid, and the methods employed in its design and construction. " I have inserted diagrams," he wrote, " because I have been desirous of putting the simple geometrical problems, involved in this question, in the clearest possible light. The solution of practical questions of this kind tends to prevent young people being carried away by such crochets about numbers as that, because the number of feet in a degree of longitude at the equator is 365,234, therefore there are as many thousands of feet in a degree of longitude at the equator as there are days in the year, viz., 365·242, and consequently that our English foot is an Earth and Year commensurate unit ; and that as, when our

[1] Captain J. Squire, R.E., had served under Major A. Bryce, R.E., in the siege of Alexandria. Captain Leake, R.A., had been a member of the British Military Mission to Turkey. (See Chapter I.)

[2] A Memoir of Lieut.-General Sir Henry James, K.C.B., late R.E., appears in the *R.E. Journal*, Vol. 7, 1877, p. 54. Sir Henry James was Director General from 1854 to 1874. He was an expert in geodesy and astronomy, and the author of many works dealing with ancient remains in Great Britain and elsewhere. He died in June, 1877.

[3] Afterwards Major-Generals Sir Charles Wilson, K.C.B., K.C.M.G., and H. S. Palmer.

English foot was first used by our Pagan ancestors, no one knew the dimensions of the earth nor the true length of the year, therefore the length of our English foot must have been given us directly from the hand of God! We might add that, as our English foot has thus been proved to be of divine origin, it is a standard by which the truth of the religious beliefs of other nations may be gauged; for those whose standards of length differ most from our 12 inches are the farthest from heaven; and may the Lord have pity on the souls of those who would introduce that utter abomination, the metre of 39·371 inches! This may be taken as a type of the extravagant nonsense to be found in modern works on the Great Pyramid."

The Pyramids of Giza, the oldest monuments of human industry, are too well-known to need any detailed description. The greatest, the Pyramid of Kheops, contains about 2,300,000 blocks of yellowish sandstone, averaging two and a half tons in weight.[1] Herodotus states that 100,000 workmen were employed for three months in each year in building this pyramid, and that after ten years had been occupied in preparing a raised road for the transport of materials from the Nile to the site, the actual construction occupied twenty years. He adds that a sum equivalent to £350,000 was spent on radishes, onions and garlic for the refreshment of the workmen! The pyramid was built in the form of a series of steps, and afterwards covered with a smooth casing of white limestone slabs, well jointed and each at least 30 feet in length. The blocks and slabs were raised from tier to tier by machines made of short wooden beams, and the casing was laid from the apex downwards. Only a few small fragments of this covering now remain. The stupendous structure occupies an area of nearly 13 acres. Its base is now approximately 746 feet square, and its height about 450 feet.

According to Sir Henry James, King Kheops decided that the base should be 500 cubits square, and the rise at its corners, nine in ten. "By this simple order," he writes,[2] "the height of the Pyramid, and consequently the angle of the inclination of the faces, was determined. The architects, having laid out the square base of 500 cubits, could set up, at each corner, profiles having a rise of nine cubits to the horizontal length of ten cubits. Struts to these profiles from the lines of the sides of the base would have the required angle for the inclination of the faces. Such profiles would guide the masons from the base to the apex of the Pyramid. A square pyramid, having a rise of nine in ten at its angles, has this remarkable proportion; its height is to the periphery of the base, approximately, as the

---

[1] *The Pyramids and Temples of Gizeh* (1885), by Professor W. M. Flinders Petrie. A précis of this book appears in a review in the *R.E. Journal*, Vol. 15, 1885, pp. 276–279.

[2] *Notes on the Great Pyramid of Egypt and the Cubits used in its Design*, by Colonel Sir Henry James, F.R.S., late R.E., p. 8.

radius to the circumference of a circle. It is quite possible that King Kheops knew of this proportion."

Access to the Grand Gallery and King's Chamber within the Great Pyramid is obtained by means of a passage ascending steeply from a point a short distance down another passage, which descends at a similar angle from the entrance. Colonel James remarks that the architects used great judgment in making the inclinations of these passages about 26 degrees, that is to say, almost equal to the "angle of rest" of dressed blocks of granite; for after they had placed the dead King in his tomb, they were able to slide three great blocks safely down the passage leading from the Grand Gallery, and thus to close it and conceal its junction with the other passage. The workmen who performed this feat made their exit by a "well" leading almost vertically downwards from the Grand Gallery to the bottom of the descending gallery. Thence, they climbed to the entrance of the Pyramid, which they finally blocked and concealed.

Lieut.-General Sir Charles Warren, G.C.M.G., K.C.B., and Colonel Sir Charles M. Watson, K.C.M.G., C.B., were among other Royal Engineers who were attracted by the problems of the Great Pyramid. In an article published in July, 1899, in the *Quarterly Statement* of the Palestine Exploration Fund, Sir Charles Warren discussed the knowledge possessed by the Egyptians of the properties of circles and squares with reference to the design of the Pyramid. This drew a mathematical thesis from Watson, which appeared in the same periodical in October, 1902.[1] He pointed out that Warren did not seem to have noticed that the dimensions of the Pyramid could be secured by simple geometrical construction, and he recapitulated the objects aimed at by the Egyptian architects. Professor Flinders Petrie had enumerated these objects in 1885. He had stated that the architect had desired a base 440 cubits square,[2] a height equal to the radius of a circle the circumference of which was equal to the periphery of the base, and the location of the King's Chamber at a level where the area of the horizontal section was equal to half the area of the base. Incidentally, Flinders Petrie had remarked that in such a design the diagonal of the square at the level of the King's Chamber was equal to the side of the base, and the side of the square to half the diagonal of the base. Watson proceeded to give the geometrical construction necessary to secure these results, and explained that such a construction could have been laid out easily, on a sufficiently large scale, on a basalt pavement east of the Pyramid.

In April, 1903, Watson discussed the probable length of the Egyptian cubit, and the possible connection between British land measures and the dimensions of the Great Pyramid. " There can

---

[1] This thesis is reproduced in an article entitled "The Construction of the Great Pyramid of Gizeh," appearing in the *R.E. Journal*, Vol. 33, 1903, pp. 32–34.
[2] Apparently Flinders Petrie did not accept the length of the cubit adopted by Colonel James.

be little doubt," he wrote,[1] "that the original cubit represented the length of a man's forearm from the elbow-joint to the end of the middle finger of the hand, usually a little less than 18 inches. This natural cubit was divided into six palms or hand-breadths, and the palm into four digits or finger-breadths. In Egypt, when the cubit was standardized, it was lengthened by the addition of another palm, so that it then consisted of seven palms, and it is fairly correct to say that the length of seven palms was about 20·65 British inches." However, taking Flinders Petrie's estimate of 9,068·8 inches as the exact length of one side of the base of the cased Pyramid, and dividing by 440, he obtained a length of 20·61 inches for the cubit used by the builders. As regards the length of the side, he pointed out that it was almost exactly one eighth part of a geographical mile, and that it was probable that the Egyptians had sufficient astronomical knowledge to fix the length of that unit. At this point, he withdrew from the controversy which has always raged around the Great Pyramid.

Many years ago, several Royal Engineers whose names have appeared in these pages, undertook archæological work in Palestine while engaged in surveying that country. They did not rival the achievements of experts such as Flinders Petrie, Bliss, Macalister and Reisner, and in modern times, Woolley and Starkey; but they made valuable discoveries which are worthy of record, though outside Egypt and the Sudan.

A survey of the Holy Land was started at Jerusalem in 1864, under the patronage of the Baroness Burdett-Coutts. The Baroness required a plan of the Holy City and the surrounding country for the improvement of the water-supply, and Captain C. W. Wilson, R.E., carried out the survey between October, 1864, and May, 1865. "Wilson's excellent survey," remarks Colonel Sir Charles Close,[2] "was the occasion of the first contact of the Corps with the exploration of Palestine; and since that date, officers of the Corps have been engaged almost continuously, in one way or another, in improving and adding to our knowledge of the topography and archæology of this most interesting of all lands." Wilson executed a considerable amount of underground exploration in Jerusalem, especially in the vicinity of the Temple.[3] In addition, he ran a line of levels from the Dead Sea through Jerusalem to Jaffa, and proved that the level of the Dead Sea is 1,292 feet below that of the Mediterranean.

After completing the map of Jerusalem, Wilson returned to

[1] Article entitled "The Great Pyramid," by Colonel C. M. Watson, C.B., C.M.G., late R.E., appearing in the *R.E. Journal*, Vol. 33, 1903, pp. 71–73.
[2] "Explorations and Excavations in Palestine," by Colonel Sir Charles Close, K.B.E., C.B., C.M.G., late R.E., Chairman of the Palestine Exploration Fund, appearing in the *R.E. Journal*, Vol. L, 1936, pp. 185–200.
[3] *The Life of Major-General Sir Charles W. Wilson, K.C.B., K.C.M.G.*, by Colonel Sir Charles M. Watson, K.C.M.G., C.B., late R.E., p. 47.

England, where his services were placed at the disposal of the Palestine Exploration Fund which was formed in June, 1865. In November, 1865, he sailed for Palestine with Lieutenant S. Anderson and Corporal Phillips, R.E., and remained in the field until May, 1866. The party made determinations of time and latitude at 49 points, and ran a line of azimuths from the northern border to Jerusalem. Anderson undertook the greater part of the astronomical and trigonometrical work, while Wilson devoted his energies chiefly to archæological research. Plans and photographs were prepared of 50 churches, synagogues and mosques, and time was found occasionally for excavation.[1]

Stimulated by this admirable preliminary work, the Committee of the Fund decided to initiate a topographical survey of the whole of Western Palestine, and to continue the excavations; and with the approval of the War Office, they selected Lieutenant (afterwards General Sir) Charles Warren and Corporals Birtle, Phillips and Hancock, R.E., to carry out the double task. This party arrived in Palestine in January, 1867. They laboured there for three years, exposed to constant hardship and danger and to frequent obstruction by the local Pashas. Funds were so scarce that Warren was obliged to make large advances from his own resources to meet current expenses. Realizing that a topographical survey would be of little value unless based on a proper trigonometrical framework, which he was unable to supply, he concentrated his attention chiefly on archæological excavation in Jerusalem.[2] At first, the Turkish officials refused to allow him to excavate within 40 feet of the Sanctuary wall; but he met this difficulty by mining to the foundations, which he wished to examine. As regards the walls of the Temple area, he found that the colossal work was covered by debris to a depth of more than 100 feet below ground level, and consequently, it was necessary to lay the foundations bare by means of shafts sunk through this mass. Rocks fell on the unfortunate excavators. Sometimes, they were suffocated by heat: at other times, frozen in the icy waters of a subterranean torrent. Nevertheless, they succeeded in obtaining rock-levels showing the contour of the whole city, except at one point, and in proving that the ancient Temple was probably located on the site now occupied by the Dome of the Rock. Warren explored the underground cisterns within the Haram enclosure, and discovered the shaft up which Joab climbed when David captured the city from the Jebusites. Sir Walter Besant pays

---

[1] See *Golgotha and the Holy Sepulchre* (1906), by Major-General Sir Charles W. Wilson, K.C.B., K.C.M.G., late R.E.

[2] The operations are described in *Underground Jerusalem*, by Captain C. Warren, R.E. (1876), and in a paper read by him before the Royal Historical Society on April 13th, 1876. (See *R.E. Journal*, Vol. 6, 1876, pp. 36, 37.) A description appears also in *Recovery of Jerusalem* by Captains C. W. Wilson and C. Warren, R.E. (1871). Another is given in *History of the Corps of Royal Engineers*, by Major-General W. Porter, late, R.E., Vol. II, pp. 367-371.

the following tribute to his work :—[1] " It is certain that nothing will ever be done in the future to compare with what was done by Warren. It was he who restored the ancient city to the world; he it was who stripped the rubbish from the rocks and showed the glorious Temple standing within its walls, 1,000 feet long and 200 feet high, of mighty masonry; he who opened the secret passages, the ancient aqueducts, the bridge connecting the temple and the town. Whatever else may be done in future, his name will always be associated with the Holy City which he first recovered."

In October, 1868, Captain C. W. Wilson, R.E., sailed from Southampton to explore and survey the Sinai Peninsula. He was accompanied by Captain H. S. Palmer, R.E., Professor E. H. Palmer, the Revd. F. W. Holland, Mr. Wyatt, and four non-commissioned officers of the Royal Engineers.[2] They started from Suez on November 11th and made their way to Jebel Musa, which they identified as the true Mount Sinai.[3] They decided also that the Israelites had crossed the Red Sea at the head of the Gulf of Suez. At the end of April, 1869, after reconnoitring 4,000 square miles of country in Southern Sinai and taking many observations for latitude, the party returned to Egypt, and Captains Wilson and Palmer, as already related, measured the base of the Great Pyramid before embarking for England. Although this expedition was not concerned to any great extent with archæology, its work formed the foundation of subsequent examinations of the area covered by the wanderings of the Israelites, and was thus of some assistance to students of Biblical history.[4]

A trigonometrical survey of Western Palestine was begun in November, 1871, by Captain R. W. Stewart, R.E., assisted by Mr. C. F. Tyrwhitt Drake, an archæologist, and by Sergeants Black and Armstrong, R.E.; but in January, 1872, Stewart was invalided to England, and the work devolved on the two non-commissioned officers under the general superintendence of Drake.[5] In July, 1872, however, Lieutenant C. R. Conder, R.E., arrived from England, and during the next three years, proceeded to carry a network of triangulation gradually over the whole country west of the Jordan. An enormous amount of topographical and archæological information was collected, and a large number of Biblical

[1] *Twenty-one Years' Work in the Holy Land*, by Sir Walter Besant.
[2] Professor Palmer, Captain Gill, R.E., and Lieut. Charrington, R.N., were murdered in the desert in 1882 (See Chapter II). Palmer was a skilled Oriental scholar; Holland, an experienced traveller; and Wyatt, a naturalist.
[3] *History of the Corps of Royal Engineers*, by Major-General W. Porter, late R.E., Vol. II, p. 271. The Survey of Palestine is reviewed from p. 268 to p. 277 of that volume.
[4] *The Life of Major-General Sir Charles Wilson, K.C.B., K.C.M.G.*, by Colonel Sir Charles M. Watson, K.C.M.G., C.B., late R.E., p. 71.
[5] "The Survey of Palestine," appearing in the *R.E. Journal*, Vol. 10, 1880, pp. 171-173.

sites identified.[1] The greater part of the work had been completed by the middle of 1873. "The fatigue of the campaign was very great," writes Conder.[2] "My eyes were quite pink from the effects of the glare of white chalk, my clothes were in rags, my boots had no soles." With the early autumn, the party was again afield, and by Christmas had added Damascus, Baalbek, Hermon and Samson's country to the map. In the spring of 1874, the whole party was prostrated by fever, and Drake died in Jerusalem. Conder was sent to England to save his life, but returned in October and surveyed the districts of Hebron and Beersheba.

In the middle of November, 1874, a new recruit for the Palestine Survey arrived in the person of Lieutenant H. H. Kitchener, R.E., who came to fill the vacancy caused by the death of Drake. His association with Conder was happy and helpful. The survey progressed rapidly until January, 1875, when Kitchener was incapacitated by malaria. In March, he was back at work; and in April, he rescued Conder from drowning while bathing in the sea at Ascalon. On July 10th, 1875, the party was attacked by the people of Safed, a town near the Sea of Galilee. Conder would inevitably have been murdered but for the prompt assistance given by Kitchener, who managed to reach him and cover his retreat by engaging one of the Arabs in single combat. Kitchener, wounded in the arm, is described as "dodging enormous stones, not unfortunately with perfect success."[3] Surveying was abandoned; and on October 1st, Kitchener left Palestine for England, whither Conder followed him after securing the punishment of the offenders. Both were weak with fever, and unfit for further work in the field. Kitchener, however, found pleasurable occupation in the production of his maiden literary effort, *Lieutenant Kitchener's Guinea Book of Photographs of Biblical Sites*.

Conder and Kitchener spent the year 1876 in London preparing the 26 sheets of the great Map of Palestine, and it was not until February, 1877, that Kitchener was able to return to complete the field-work interrupted by the Safed attack. The French archæologist, Clermont Ganneau, gives an interesting description of him at that period. "Tall, slim and vigorous; capable of headstrong acts;

[1] Memoir of Colonel C. R. Conder, late R.E., by Colonel Sir Charles Watson, K.C.M.G., C.B., late R.E., appearing in the *R.E. Journal*, Vol. XI, Jan.–June, 1910, pp. 283–288.

[2] *Tent Work in Palestine* (1878), by Colonel C. R. Conder, late R.E. Conder was the author also of many antiquarian and historical works such as *Heth and Moab* (1883), *Primer of Bible Geography*, *Syrian Stone Lore* (1886), *Altaic Hieroglyphs*, *Palestine* (1891), and *The Tel Amarna Tablets* (1893). While C.R.E. at Weymouth from 1895 to 1900, he wrote *The Bible in the East*, *The Latin Kingdom of Jerusalem*, *The Hittites and their Language*, and *The Jewish Tragedy*; and after leaving Weymouth, *The First Bible* (1902), *Critics and the Law* (1907), *The Rise of Man* (1908), and *The City of Jerusalem* (1909). He died on February 16th, 1910.

[3] Accounts of this incident are given in *Life of Lord Kitchener*, by Sir George Arthur, Vol. I, pp. 17, 18, and in an article entitled "Survey of Palestine," appearing in the *R.E. Journal*, Vol. 6, 1876, pp. 45, 46.

a frank and most outspoken character, with recesses of winsome freshness. His high spirits and cheeriness were in agreeable contrast to the serious, grave characters of some of his comrades. His ardour for his work astonished us." Ganneau wrote also of the young Royal Engineer's marked proficiency in archæological research. Kitchener's reports were lucid, graphic and precise. He was keenly alive to the beauties of the country, describing it as "very lovely, carpeted with flowers and green with growing crops." Could anything be more unlike the popular conception of him as a man of iron, a human machine impervious to the finer sentiments?

In September, 1877, Kitchener brought the survey of Western Palestine to a successful end.[1] This was the most important work on the Holy Land ever given to the world. He handed over to the Committee of the Palestine Exploration Fund the completed Survey, on a one-inch scale, of rather more than 6,000 square miles of country, in addition to 26 volumes of notes and records,[2] a reduced map, a number of photographs, and many plans drawn by Conder and himself. This Survey remained the standard map of Western Palestine until the opening of General Allenby's campaign in the Great War.

September, 1878, found Kitchener surveying in Cyprus, and incidentally, indulging an appetite, which never forsook him, for collecting art treasures. The Cyprus Museum may be regarded as his creation. He transmitted to the Science and Art Department at South Kensington many interesting reports on excavations made by him in the island. As a result, he received an invitation from the British Museum to superintend excavations in Assyria; but this he did not see his way to accept. The survey of Cyprus was almost finished when he joined the Egyptian Army on January 4th, 1883.[3]

Conder returned to Palestine, in 1881, to survey the country east of the Jordan, being accompanied on this occasion by Lieutenant A. M. Mantell and Sergeants Black and Armstrong, R.E. The party landed at Beyrout in March, and in addition to surveying, photographed and sketched the prehistoric stone monuments which abound in that area. The work was stopped by the Turkish Governor of Es Salt; but by interposing as many delays as possible, Conder was able to survey 500 square miles before he was obliged to leave.[4]

Colonel Charles Gordon was once an earnest student of biblical geography and archæology in Palestine. Throughout the greater part of the year 1883, he lived in a small village near Jerusalem, and

---

[1] In a letter dated Beersheba, September 28th, 1877, to the Editor, *R.E. Journal*, Lieut. H. H. Kitchener, R.E., stated that the Survey of Palestine had been finished after 6 years' work. This letter appears in the *R.E. Journal*, Vol. 7, 1877, p. 112.

[2] Twenty volumes were by Conder, and six by Kitchener.

[3] Kitchener secured his appointment through his knowledge of Arabic. (See Chapter II.)

[4] The work accomplished by this expedition is described in an article entitled "Recent Explorations East of the Jordan," by Capt. A. M. Mantell, R.E., appearing in the *R.E. Journal*, Vol. 18, 1888, pp. 222–224.

walked into the city, morning after morning, to work out, with the aid of his Bible, the probable situation of the places named in its pages. He gave prolonged study to the configuration of the city as it was in the days of the early kings and of Herod, and devoted particular attention to the Temple and Golgotha.[1] Though no archæologist, his sketches and diagrams may have encouraged others to undertake biblical research, and his observations, as recorded in a small volume entitled *Reflections in Palestine*, are worthy of perusal.

In 1887, an interesting salvage operation was carried out by Major A. H. Bagnold, R.E., Director of Military Telegraphs in Egypt, near the village of Mitrahina, at the ancient site of Memphis, some 12 miles south of Cairo. Lying face downwards in a flooded depression, with only a portion of the back visible above the muddy water, was a colossal statue of Rameses II. This Colossus had been discovered in 1820 by the explorers Sloane and Caviglia, and presented to the British nation by Muhammad Ali. It was found to be of crystalline limestone; and although the legs were missing below the knees, its weight was estimated as nearly 100 tons. Those who have seen it will admit that it is a fine work of art. The handsome and gentle features of the Egyptian monarch are admirably reproduced. A conventional beard is attached to the chin. In the girdle is a dagger with two falcon's heads; and on the right shoulder, breast and girdle, are the *prænomina* of Rameses II. The workmanship throughout is excellent.

"Long ago," wrote Scott-Moncrieff in February, 1887,[2] "I represented to General Sir Frederick Stephenson[3] that it would be a suitable monument of our British occupation to get old Rameses out of the hole and on his legs on a proper pedestal, and that he, with soldiers at command, might do it." Sir Frederick took up the scheme with avidity, and selected Bagnold to undertake the work of salvage after the failure of two attempts by civil engineers to raise the heavy mass. Bagnold commenced his task on January 20th, 1887. As funds were scarce, it was decided that the colossus should not be erected, but merely lifted above ground level and turned face upwards. The first operation was to remove the water from the hole; and when this had been accomplished, it was found that the colossus measured $38\frac{1}{2}$ feet in length and 27 feet in maximum girth. The head lay at a lower level than the legs, and the centre of the back was $6\frac{3}{4}$ feet below the average inundation level of the Nile. The thickness of the statue from back to chest was $7\frac{1}{2}$ feet. These

---

[1] *Gordon and the Sudan*, by Dr. Bernard M. Allen, p. 187.
[2] Letter from Colonel Colin Scott-Moncrieff, dated Feb. 18th, 1887, quoted in *The Life of Sir Colin-Moncrieff, K.C.S.I., K.C.M.G., R.E., LL.D.*, by M. A. Hollings, pp. 220–221.
[3] Lieut.-General Sir Frederick Stephenson commanded the British Army of Occupation in Egypt.

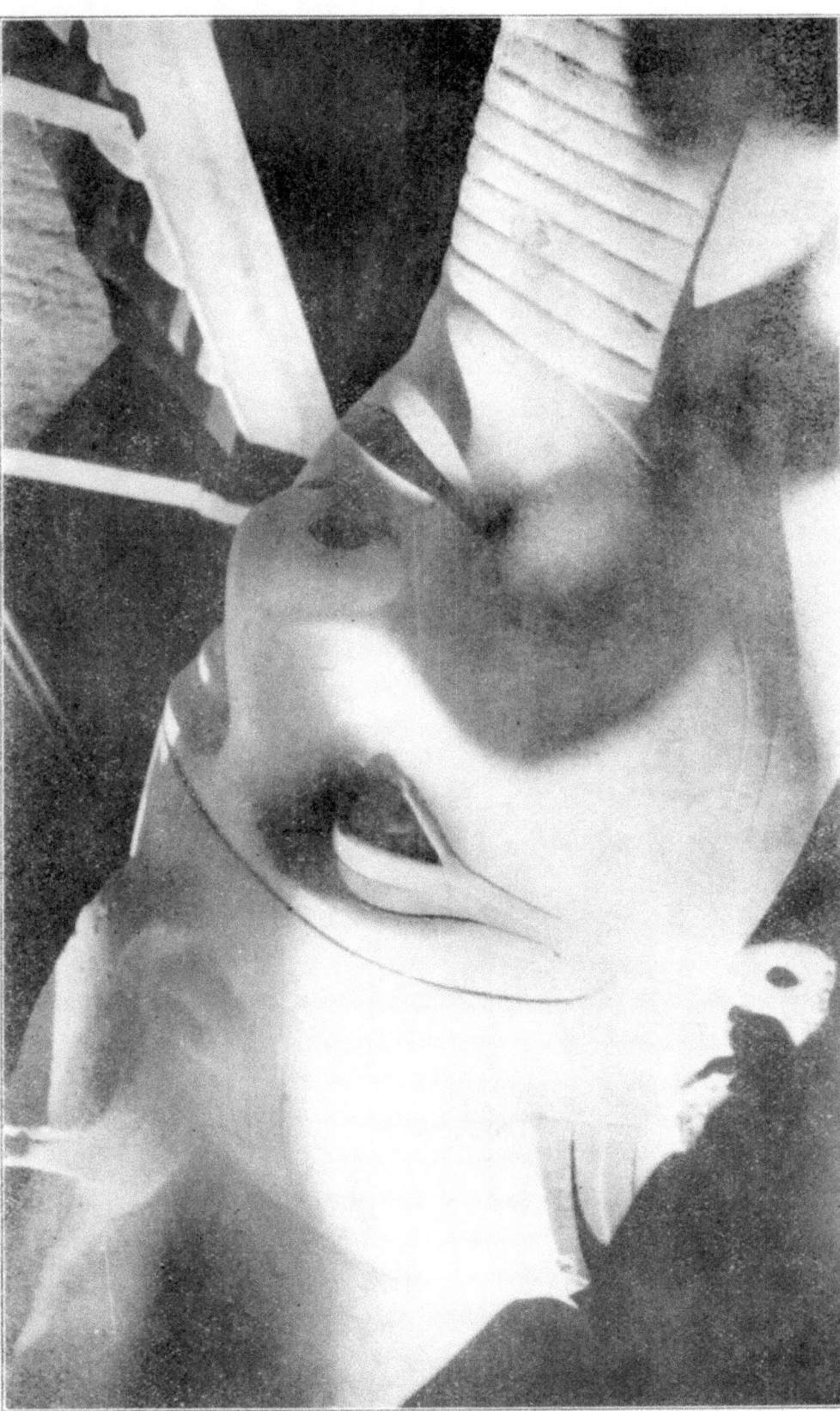

THE COLOSSUS OF RAMESES II AT MEMPHIS.

[*Photo by the Author.*]

dimensions, and the position in which the statue was discovered, will give some idea of the problem which confronted Bagnold.

Rails, sleepers, baulks, blocks of wood, powerful hydraulic jacks, a chain-pump and a variety of other materials and tools were transported to the site from Cairo, and on February 4th, with the assistance of a corporal and two sappers from the Telegraph Section, R.E., and a party of native workmen, Bagnold succeeded in placing a platform of crossed sleepers under the face of the statue and raising the head one inch by driving in wooden wedges. Other platforms were then inserted under the breast and legs; and as a share of the load was transferred to these supports, the earth was excavated gradually from beneath, working from the head towards the legs. Jacks were placed in position, and the lifting of the legs began. On February 19th, Rameses rested horizontally on massive crib piers, bedded in the muddy bottom of the hole.

A search for the missing feet having failed, the next operation was the raising of the whole mass to ground level. As each timber support was removed, the vacant space was filled with broken and rammed fragments of potsherds, collected by Arab boys from the adjacent ruins of Memphis. The first vertical lift of three feet occupied ten days. Lifting was resumed on March 4th, and pumping ceased on the 11th. The usual procedure was to raise the legs and head alternately about two feet at a time. Three supports of timber blocks and sleepers were employed, and were removed in turn to facilitate the packing and ramming of the broken pottery foundation. Four side-struts and one head-strut steadied the statue as it rose. On these struts, rough gantries of rails were erected for the shifting of the 30-ton, 40-ton and 100-ton hydraulic jacks. By April 16th, the total lift was 17 feet. Rameses then rested above ground level, though still face downwards, upon timbering supported by a potsherd foundation, which was surrounded by stone packing and earth filling.

All that remained was to turn the statue face upwards. This operation was begun by lowering the right side gradually until the tilt of the body was 48 degrees. The stumps of both legs were then level, for Rameses had been sculptured with one leg in advance of the other. Greased baulks were next placed under his head and leg-stumps, and on May 6th he was slid 12 feet sideways to allow for the completion of the turning movement. " Pushing at him with jacks on the south side," writes Bagnold,[1] " and with a good bed of sleepers under the right arm, he reached the vertical on May 13th; and struts and jacks having been properly arranged on the north side to take the weight, the statue lay over ten degrees in that direction by the evening. This was a very delicate operation,

[1] *Account of the Manner in which Two Colossal Statues of Rameses II. at Memphis were Raised* (1888), by Major A. H. Bagnold, R.E., p. 5. This pamphlet gives a full account of the work, together with diagrams and illustrations.

but it was performed without a hitch by my able foreman, Corporal Sleigh, R.E., assisted by Sappers Sharpe, Peckham, Christmas and Boswell, R.E. In five more days, Rameses was lowered successfully on to his back, much in the same position as now. Subsequently, two very large stones, bedded in cement concrete, were placed under the statue, and the latter bedded in concrete upon the stones. A strong enclosure wall of sun-dried brick was then built around it, with a small house at the east end for the use of a watchman. Doors with strong locks were provided for this house and the enclosure; and a staging or gallery, easily approached from within by wooden steps, was erected above and across the end of the beard. The magnificent proportions of the statue can be viewed from the gallery. A corrugated iron roof was erected over the head and breast, and a notice painted on the door, fixing a tax of two piastres on all visitors."

Bagnold built the enclosure wall, and secured approval for charging a fee for admission, because he found that the authorities of the Bulac Museum at Cairo would not assume responsibility for the welfare of the rescued monarch. Consequently, it was necessary to make arrangements on the spot to ensure that he was properly cared for. The watchman was most zealous in guarding the statue and in collecting the fee. Shortly after Rameses had been enclosed within his wall, Mr. William Garstin, the Deputy Under-Secretary, P.W.D., arrived to inspect the work and was refused admission unless he produced two piastres! A veil may be drawn over the scene which ensued.[1]

In March, 1889, Mr. (afterwards Sir Ernest) Wallis Budge, the well-known Egyptologist, prepared an inscription in Egyptian hieroglyphics for incisement on a stone tablet within the enclosure. It was intended to record the fact that the colossus had been raised and turned over by Bagnold. Subsequently, the inscription was "engrossed" by Mr. Sidney Smith, of the British Museum, in the following form:—" Year fifty month fourth ploughing season day 29th of majesty her lady of crowns goddess of England lady of seas and countries all divine spouse *Rā-māt-ka* daughter of the Sun Victoria life strength health giver of life like Rā for ever! The soldiers victorious of majesty her were they in Egypt with the General beloved of heart her Stefenson sent he me to Memphis to erect again the image of the king of Upper and Lower Egypt *Rā-user-māt-sotepen-Rā* son of the Sun *Rameses meri Amen* triumphant fallen had he image this upon face his gave *Hafi* water his over him year every. Raised I image this by means of instruments which placed I water in them put I image of majesty his upon back his made I walls his for giving stability to him gave I heart my all to fill the

---

[1] Letter from Colonel A. H. Bagnold, C.B., C.M.G., late R.E., to the author, dated December 23rd, 1934.

heart of the great one Stefenson I the chief of Tligrafia Bagnold." Unfortunately, this unique record of Royal Engineer achievement was never cut in stone, for the proposal was allowed to lapse after Bagnold had left Egypt.[1]

While British Agent and Consul General in Egypt shortly before the Great War, Lord Kitchener raised a fund of £2,500 for the removal of the limestone statue of Rameses II from Memphis and its erection in the Place Ramsés near the Central Railway Station in Cairo. This sum was subscribed by foreign residents in the capital as a species of goodwill offering to the Egyptians, and was deposited in the National Bank of Egypt in the name of Colonel O. A. G. FitzGerald, Lord Kitchener's Military Secretary, who afterwards perished with him in H.M.S. *Hampshire*. Subsequently, the money was transferred to London, and by the end of 1936, the total amounted to £3,500. As, however, it was still insufficient to cover the cost of moving the statue from Memphis, a proposal was made that it should be devoted to some institution of an archæological nature in which Lord Kitchener was interested, and it has been decided that the income from the fund shall be paid to the Egypt Exploration Society. In all probability, Rameses II will never leave his home at Memphis.

During the raising of the great limestone colossus, Bagnold undertook also the raising and moving of a second and smaller colossus[2] of pink granite, lying about 200 yards from the first. This statue of Rameses II was discovered by Hekekyan Bey in 1852. It had been broken off above the ankles, and the nose was mutilated. When Bagnold first saw it, only the left shoulder and a crown, detached from the head, appeared above the surface in a depression in the soil. Many years before, the statue had been thrown down by fanatical Muhammadans, and had crashed on to and through a massive floor of stone. Bagnold excavated beneath it, jacked it over on to its back, and raised it on to oak rollers running on a track of sleepers. It was then pulled and pushed up a long incline to ground level, and finally hauled 130 yards to a small knoll. By June 25th, 1887, it was lying face upwards on this knoll. Afterwards, it was bedded down on three supports so arranged that an inscription on the back could be read from below. The detached crown was placed upright beside it, in company with a double bust of Ptah and Rameses found in the process of excavation. In addition, a *stele* of the 26th Dynasty, weighing ten tons, was dragged from low ground and erected close to the granite colossus. Bagnold and his men then returned to Cairo and relinquished Egyptology for Telegraphy.

The scene now shifts to the great rock-hewn temples of Abu Simbel, on the left bank of the Nile, some 40 miles below Wadi

---

[1] The engrossment, however, is still in the possession of Colonel A. H. Bagnold.
[2] This statue weighed about 600 tons.

Halfa. These were excavated in the time of Rameses II. They are among the most stupendous monuments of ancient Egyptian architecture, and challenge comparison with any remains in Middle or Lower Egypt. The group comprises a Great Temple, a smaller Rock Temple, and a Temple of Hathor in an adjoining valley; but in this narrative, we are concerned only with the Great Temple, where valuable work was executed in 1892 by a small party of Royal Engineers.

The approach by river to Abu Simbel is most impressive. The steamer moors to the sandy bank within a short distance of a rocky precipice, from which has been hewn the façade of the temple and four huge statues of Rameses II. These colossi are arranged in pairs on either side of the entrance, and each is over 65 feet in height. Within the entrance is a series of halls and chambers extending for a distance of 180 feet into the rock, the largest being the Great Hypostyle Hall, whose ceiling is supported by eight square pillars against which stand figures of the Egyptian king, 30 feet high. The ceiling of the " nave " is adorned with flying vultures: those of the aisles, with stars. The coloured reliefs, which cover the walls, are of great historical value. Around and beyond are chambers of absorbing interest to the antiquarian, and of wonder and admiration to the tourist. Yet, had it not been for the engineering operations undertaken in 1892, this remarkable temple might have been buried under a landslide and the four colossi irreparably damaged.

During the autumn of 1890, a survey of the Upper Nile Valley was made by Mr. William Willcocks, the Irrigation engineer, in connection with a scheme for a reservoir to supplement the supply of water to Egypt.[1] Early in 1891, he reported that he had noticed that at Abu Simbel two thick and feebly resistant layers of sandstone above the famous temple were weathering rapidly, and thus leaving an intermediate layer projecting in a dangerous manner. He added that a large fragment from this stratum had already decapitated the second colossus from the left, and that the existence of the first was threatened. The crowns of the first, third and fourth colossi had been damaged by the falling of small fragments, and little remained of the monkey-cornice above the temple façade.[2] The entire cliff above the temple was in urgent need of repair with masonry. Unless this was done, wrote Willcocks, it could not be long before the first colossus on the left would meet the same fate as the second, and the finest production of antiquity in the whole of Egypt would be a ruin. A sum of £E.300, he stated, would suffice to cover the necessary expenditure.

No action seems to have been taken on this representation. On December 5th, 1891, Willcocks reported by telegram that the

---

[1] See Chapter XIV. The site ultimately selected was at Aswan.
[2] The façade is crowned by a concave cornice above which is a row of *cynocephali*, or dog-faced baboons, worshipping the sun.

THE ROCK TEMPLE OF RAMESES II AT ABU SIMBEL.

[*Photo by the Author*]

ledge of rock overhanging the left-hand colossus had moved forwards several feet. He added that the temple was in imminent danger; that if rain fell there might be an accident; and that the cost of the necessary work would be £E.1,000. He supplemented his telegram by a letter and a sketch.

The Egyptian Government now awoke to the urgency of the situation, and the matter was referred to the Director-General of the Department of Antiquities and the Director-General of Irrigation; but as neither of these officials could undertake the work, an application was made to Army Headquarters for the services of a detachment of the 24th (Fortress) Company, R.E. As a result, a party of 12 non-commissioned officers and men, under Lieutenant J. H. L'Estrange Johnstone, R.E., left Cairo by rail on December 27th, 1891, and arrived at Abu Simbel in the gunboat *Et Teb* on February 6th, 1892, with four tons of tools and equipment.

The façade of the Great Temple is 100 feet high and 140 feet wide. Johnstone found that the slope above it was covered with loose debris. A large fragment of rock, above the left-hand statue, was within an inch of toppling over on to it; and a still larger piece, near the other, was cracked all round and overhanging. Many smaller pieces were on the point of slipping. Some 1,400 tons of loose rock required attention; and since much of it was partly buried under drift sand, and the slope was extremely steep, Johnstone had to proceed with the utmost caution.

Native workmen were engaged to make a path up a sand-slope north of the façade and along the hillside above it; and on February 10th, a loose block poised on the cornice immediately over the entrance to the temple was removed by means of tackle attached to a holdfast. "On the 12th," writes Johnstone,[1] " a four-inch steel wire rope arrived from Wadi Halfa, and we set to work to make fast another loose rock to a holdfast of steel bars jumped in the level rock above. This rock weighed 70 tons. Had it slipped, or a loose block behind it fallen on to it, it seemed certain that it must be hurled down on to the finest of the colossi. We got three jacks under the southern portion, and two turns of cable round the northern; and after a week's anxious work, the rock was broken up. On the 23rd, we were able to begin the most serious part of our work—making fast the largest loose rock. After strengthening the holdfast with eight steel drills, we wound five turns of cable round the rock and holdfast, and made all secure with Spanish windlasses, so that by the 26th, we were able to report that all immediate danger was at an end. On this day, thanks to Lyons,[2] who had sent a theodolite down from Halfa, we observed the sunrise on the morning on which the rising sun shines most nearly down the axis

[1] Article entitled "Saving an Egyptian Temple," by Lieut. J. H. L'Estrange Johnstone, R.E., appearing in the *R.E. Journal*, Vol. 23, 1893, pp. 9-12.
[2] Lieut. H. G. Lyons, R.E.

of the temple into the inmost sanctuary, where Rameses the Great sits in state with the three gods Amen, Horus and Ptah. The scene of the bright, level beam striking into the gloomy tunnel, lighting up statue and painting, 3,200 years old, yet graphic and life-like, was one never to be forgotten."

On February 27th, while clearing sand and stones from the rocky face above the cornice, and throwing down fragments of rocks which had been broken up, Johnstone discovered a crack severing from the solid cliff an overhanging mass weighing about 650 tons. The party began to demolish this mass, and for the first ten days made excellent progress. On March 10th, however, they encountered a very hard layer. Although they had no high explosives for blasting, they succeeded in cracking the rock with small charges of gunpowder taken from nine-pounder ammunition in the gunboat *Et Teb*, and by the 18th, most of the hard layer had been removed without damage to the colossi below. A week later, a soft stratum was reached which continued to the bottom of the overhanging mass. As each piece was broken off, it was hauled up the slope by a winch and tackle; and at last the dangerous mass was reduced to a block, of about 100 tons weight, lying well back from the edge of a flat ledge. Great difficulty was experienced in dealing with some fragments of hard rock balanced almost on the edge of the cornice, though in the end, they were broken up and removed without accident. A few of the monkey-figures on the cornice were repaired with cement, and one was furnished with a new leg.

On April 5th, the party began to clear sand away from the entrance to the temple, and to uncover the grave of a British officer on which they had heaped sand to protect it from injury. William Willcocks arrived on the 9th to inspect the work, and expressed his appreciation of what had been accomplished. Johnstone and his men had removed nearly 850 tons of broken and dangerous material, working often in a temperature of 107 degrees in the shade, and the cost of their operations had been less than one-half the estimated amount. Although they had saved the Abu Simbel colossi from destruction, no official record of their achievement was ever placed at the site. Nevertheless, one humble record of their visit remains. On the outside of the right ankle of the third colossus from the left is the inscription "Sapper J. A. W. Beal, R.E., 1892."[1]

Lieutenant H. G. Lyons, R.E., at Wadi Halfa, was much interested in Johnstone's work at Abu Simbel. In the spring of 1890, he had often noticed in the wall of the Kasr el Nil Barracks at Cairo a large and handsome block of stone taken from an ancient tomb at Sakkara near Memphis. It bore the effigy, and votive and dedicatory inscription of one "Zennu," a notable of the 5th Dynasty (about 2500 B.C.). "As I gazed each morning at this inscription," writes Sir

[1] This inscription was discovered by the author on February 10th, 1935.

Henry Lyons,[1] " I wished to know more about the language and people of that time. Accordingly, with the aid of grammars, dictionaries and such other books as were available, and with some help from Lieut.-Colonel Justin Ross, R.E., who had felt a similar urge, I spent my spare time during the hot weather in the study of Egyptology." This interest, much increased during 1892 by excavation work at Wadi Halfa, led at a later date to archæological employment at Philæ above Aswan, and to the superintendence of an Archæological Survey of Nubia.

In the winter of 1895-96, Lyons was deputed to examine and consolidate the foundations of the temples on the Island of Philæ, which at certain seasons might be partially submerged by the water to be impounded by the projected dam at Aswan.[2] Mr. A. H. Atteridge, a Special Correspondent, spent an afternoon at Philæ in April, 1896. " Captain Lyons was completing a thorough survey of the world-famous island and its temples," he writes.[3] " His temporary quarters were on a dismantled steamer, and all who came to Philæ were made welcome on board this craft, which used to be known as ' The Philæ Arms.' After lunch, I was rowed across to the island, and the soldier-archæologist showed me something of the work he had done. The foundations and walls of a small temple, hitherto known only by name, had been laid bare, and the ancient Coptic church at the north end of the island had been cleared out. Lanes had been cut through the mass of debris forming the ruins of the Coptic village, with the result that a fine *stele*, and other interesting objects, had been discovered. The great temple of Isis itself had been thoroughly cleared, and a number of fallen columns, sculptures and stones restored to their original positions, thus adding a great part of a colonnaded court to the beautiful building. Finally, a complete series of accurate plans and record photographs had been prepared. One important result of Captain Lyons' researches has been to show that the foundations of the temples are such that the construction of the proposed Nile reservoir would probably involve their downfall.[4] His work at Philæ, he said, would be completed within the week, with the exception of some observations to fix the latitude and longitude. Then he had to prepare for a greater task—the geological survey of Egypt. As enthusiastic a geologist as an antiquarian, Captain Lyons is singularly well fitted to be the director of this great enterprise."

Until Lyons retired from the Egyptian Service in 1909, he was

---

[1] Notes by Colonel Sir Henry G. Lyons, F.R.S., late R.E., sent to the author on November 21st, 1934.

[2] See Chapter XIV, and also *A Report on the Temples of Philæ* (1896), by Captain H. G. Lyons, R.E.

[3] *Towards Khartoum*, by A. H. Atteridge, Special Correspondent of the *Daily Chronicle* with the Dongola Expeditionary Force, pp. 35–37.

[4] According to Atteridge, Lyons expressed his opinion that, in consequence of this fact, the scheme for a reservoir at Aswan might be abandoned and the reservoir located south of Wadi Halfa. This, however, was not done.

in frequent request in Cairo for showing visitors the great Museum collections. One day, while he was thus engaged, a lady visitor told him that she had seen nine mosques that morning and had thought them " very empty." Subsequently, after passing through many rooms in the Museum, she remarked, " But Captain Lyons, what an extraordinary thing it is that the Egyptians should have kept all these beautiful things hidden away so long in their mosques ! " Lyons made no attempt to explain. The lady talked on, much impressed by what she saw ; and as they passed from the work of the Pyramid builders to the jewellery of the 12th Dynasty, and thence to the curios of the 17th and 18th Dynasties, Lyons rose from " Captain " to " Major," and from " Major " to " Colonel," and by the time they had reached the Royal Mummies he had become a " General ! "

Though Geology is allied to Archæology, few Royal Engineers in Egypt or the Sudan have been able to devote much time to it. Two geological enthusiasts, however, may be mentioned in these pages—Colonels Justin Ross and Sir Henry Lyons. There is little to record of Justin Ross. Whilst on leave from India, where he served from 1862 until he joined the Egyptian Irrigation Department in 1883, he was a regular student of Geology at South Kensington and attained some proficiency in that science. The knowledge so gained was turned to good account in his Irrigation work under Colonel Colin Scott-Moncrieff in Egypt, but he did not undertake any special geological investigations. Lyons, on the other hand, was well known in geological circles in England before he landed in Egypt, and it may be interesting to describe how that occurred.

As a schoolboy, Lyons used to spend his holidays in Dublin where his father, Colonel (afterwards General) T. C. Lyons, C.B., late 87th Foot,[1] was on the Headquarters Staff. There he met a boy who was studying Geology as a subject for the entrance examination to Sandhurst. The lads went fossil-hunting together, and Lyons soon became keenly interested in the pursuit. He read Lyell's *Elements of Geology*, and continued to collect fossils until he joined the Royal Military Academy in February, 1882. By that time, he had made the acquaintance of several leading geologists, including Mr. Etheridge of the Natural History Museum, and had contributed to that institution a small series of Cambrian fossils.

In the summer of 1882, on the recommendation of Mr. Etheridge, he was elected a " Fellow " of the Geological Society. He applied at once for leave of absence from the Royal Military Academy until midnight to attend a meeting of the Society in London, and was promptly summoned to the Orderly Room to explain his reasons for inventing this ingenious but highly improbable excuse. However,

---

[1] T. C. Lyons was commissioned in the 16th Foot. Later in his career, he was posted to the 20th, and finally to the 87th Foot.

when he produced his Certificate of Election, the leave was granted, and thereafter he attended the meetings regularly. In later years, while stationed at Chatham, Gibraltar and Aldershot, he studied Geology and Petrology in his spare time, and at Chatham he arranged the geological collection in the School of Military Engineering.

From 1890 onwards, Lyons found in the Egyptian deserts a perfect field for geological work. His first tours on camel-back were undertaken solely for geological purposes, and geology was combined with military reconnaissance during his subsequent journeys. The experience thus gained, together with his knowledge of engineering and proficiency in Arabic, led to his selection, in 1896, to carry out a geological reconnaissance to assist the Government in dealing with applications for mining concessions, and in consequence, he was transferred from the Egyptian Army Staff to the Ministry of Public Works. He became Director General of the newly formed Geological Survey Department with headquarters in Cairo; and for many years after that Department had been merged into the Survey of Egypt, of which he assumed supreme control, he continued to supervise the training and work of the Geological personnel throughout the length and breadth of the country. It was primarily for Geology, and secondarily for Geodesy and Geo-Physics, that Colonel Lyons gained his election, in 1906, as a Fellow of the Royal Society.

No archæological or geological work of any importance has been executed in the Sudan by Royal Engineers,[1] and the work in Egypt and Palestine has tended more towards the exploration of buried sites, the preservation of monuments, and the mapping of strata, than to the elucidation of historical problems and the discovery and classification of fossils. This, however, is as it should be. In the execution of such work, the engineering and surveying capabilities of officers and men of the Corps have been employed to the best advantage in furthering the general progress of antiquarian research.

---

[1] A concise account of the archæological work executed by civilian experts in the Sudan is given in an article entitled " An Archæological Survey of the Sudan," by Mr. F. Addison, late Conservator of Antiquities, Sudan Government, appearing in *The Anglo-Egyptian Sudan from Within* (1935), edited by Mr. J. A. deC. Hamilton, M.C., Sudan Political Service, pp. 21–39.

CHAPTER XX.

ADMINISTRATION.

IN September, 1873, while Colonel Charles Gordon was acting as British Commissioner on the Danube after several years of regimental duty at Gravesend, he received a letter from the Khedive Ismail offering him the appointment of Governor of the Equatorial Province in the Southern Sudan. The offer was made on the recommendation of Nubar Pasha, the Egyptian Foreign Minister, who had met the celebrated " Chinese " Gordon at Constantinople in 1872, and had learned that he was willing to volunteer his services in a new sphere of action. Gordon was much attracted by the opportunity of opening up the Equatorial Province to legitimate trade, and of suppressing the slave-traffic, and accordingly he applied to the War Office for permission to accept the offer, and having obtained the necessary consent, notified his acceptance and arrived in Cairo in February, 1874. Ismail proposed to pay him a salary of £E.10,000 a year, as received by Sir Samuel Baker, his predecessor as Governor; but Gordon declined to accept more than £E.2,000 a year because he was loath to take money from the pockets of the impoverished Egyptian peasantry and considered that the salary would be an adequate remuneration for his services. Ismail then prepared an elaborate *Firman* appointing him as " Governor-General of the Equator,"[1] and as such, Gordon arrived in Khartoum on March 13th, and in Gondokoro, the capital of his Province, on April 16th.

The duties entrusted to him were to establish a line of posts throughout the enormous territory placed in his charge, to attempt to win the confidence of the tribes and to promote peace amongst them, and above all, to check the horrible traffic in slaves. His own belief was that his mission was a sham designed by Ismail for the deception of Europe, but he determined, nevertheless, to make it a reality.[2] Little was known of the Equatorial Province. Previously, it had been in the hands of traders in ivory and slaves, the most powerful of whom was Zubeir, whom Gordon afterwards nominated for the governorship of Khartoum. At Gondokoro, Gordon discovered that the Egyptian possessions in the Equatorial Province were confined in reality to the forts at that place, Fatiko and

---

[1] This document is in the R.E. Museum at Chatham.
[2] Article entitled " Major-General Charles George Gordon, C.B., R.E.," appearing in the *R.E. Journal*, Vol. 15, 1885, pp. 47-50.

Foweira,[1] the small garrisons of which were virtually besieged. Leaving Lieut.-Colonel Chaillé-Long to represent him at Gondokoro, he returned down the Nile to Berber to fetch the remainder of his cosmopolitan staff, and was back in Gondokoro on September 3rd, after spending several weeks in establishing a station at the mouth of the Sobat.[2] Already, most of his staff were seriously ill; and to add to his troubles, he soon ascertained that one of his Egyptian assistants was a scoundrel. Although his efforts were impeded on every hand by rascally officials, he worked on cheerfully, and established and garrisoned a number of additional stations along the river. With Romolo Gessi[3] as his right-hand man, he laboured so faithfully to fulfil his allotted task that by the end of 1874, when he had been joined by Lieutenants C. M. Watson and W. H. Chippindall, R.E., he had received the submission of many of the native chiefs, opened up communications, restored confidence, and administered a severe check to the slave-trade.

The same year, 1874, saw important developments in the Eastern and Western Sudan.[4] In the west, Zubeir, who had recently been pardoned by the Government and appointed Governor of the Bahr el Ghazal, prepared to invade Darfur from the south, whilst the Government did the same from the east. The plan was duly executed, and Darfur passed under the dominion of the Khedive. Zubeir was made a Pasha, and proceeded forthwith to Cairo to press his claim to be made Governor of Darfur; but he was detained in the capital, and his son Suleiman was left in his place. In the east, the relations with Abyssinia were uncertain and troublesome and led to frequent clashes of arms.

Gordon began his explorations into Uganda in July, 1875, and continued them until his return to Khartoum in October, 1876. Some of his adventures have already been recorded in these pages.[5] On December 2nd, 1876, he arrived in Cairo, worn out and disgusted with the corruption of the Khedive's administration. " I came down in no very good temper with His Highness or any of them," he wrote, " and I went to His Highness with an angry face and heart, determined not to go back." Yet, after an interview in the Abdin Palace, he agreed to return later to the Sudan, provided that the administration

---

[1] Fatiko is about 60 miles north of Foweira in Uganda. Gondokoro and Foweira are shown in the *Sketch Map of the Eastern and Southern Frontiers of the Sudan*, included in Chapter XVII. See also an article entitled " Colonel Gordon in Central Africa " in the *R.E. Journal*, Vol. 5, 1875, pp. 40, 41.

[2] See Chapter XVII.

[3] See Chapter V. Gordon had known the Italian, Romolo Gessi, since the days when the latter was an interpreter in the Crimean War, and had recruited him, in 1874, as one of his staff in the Equatorial Province. Gessi was a born leader and had great ability and energy. Subsequently, he became Governor of the Bahr el Ghazal. He died at Suez in 1881.

[4] *The Anglo-Egyptian Sudan from Within*, edited by J. A. de C. Hamilton, M.C., p. 63.

[5] See Chapter XVII.

was improved, and then sailed for England, where he arrived on Christmas Eve.

During his period as Governor of the Equatorial Province, Gordon had mapped the White Nile to within a short distance of Lake Victoria. He had given a deadly blow to the slave-trade on that river, and had restored confidence and peace among the tribes. He had opened up water-communication between Gondokoro and the Lakes. He had established satisfactory relations with King Mtesa of Uganda. He had formed Government districts, and built secure posts on the river bank; and without the exercise of oppression, he had secured additional revenue for the Khedivial exchequer.[1] All this he had accomplished in the face of constant opposition by Ismail Pasha Ayub, the Egyptian Governor-General of the Sudan, who deliberately encouraged the slave-traders from his headquarters in Khartoum.

On January 31st, 1877, in response to a telegraphic appeal from the Khedive, Gordon set out from England on his return to Egypt. His friends, Colonel Gerald Graham, V.C., and Lieutenant Charles Watson, R.E., urged him not to re-enter the Egyptian service unless he was given control of the entire Sudan, including the Equatorial Province, and to this Ismail Pasha agreed when he interviewed Gordon in Cairo on February 13th.[2] The Khedive undertook also to supersede the Egyptian Governor-General at Khartoum. "He gave me the Sudan," wrote Gordon, and in those few words announced the fact that Ismail had made him ruler over a territory of a million square miles, extending approximately from the Tropic of Cancer to the Equator, and from the shores of the Red Sea to within 450 miles of Lake Tchad.[3]

Armed with supreme authority, Gordon now returned to the Sudan to complete the work interrupted in 1876; but at the request of Ismail, he proceeded thither by way of Abyssinia, hoping to find a *modus vivendi* with King John and his turbulent subjects, and to settle disputes with that monarch concerning territory annexed by Egypt. After landing at Massawa at the end of February, 1877, he made the best arrangements possible with King John, and then prepared to start on a prodigious tour of inspection. "First," writes Dr. Bernard Allen,[4] "he would proceed from the Red Sea through the districts bordering Abyssinia, through Kassala and Sennar to Khartoum. Then, after a short stay there, he would continue his progress through Kordofan to Darfur, where two ugly

---

[1] A tribute to Gordon's early work by Sir Bartle Frere is quoted in the *R.E. Journal*, Vol. 5, 1875, p. 100.

[2] A letter, dated February 16th, 1877, addressed to Her Majesty's Agent and Consul-General in Egypt by Colonel C. G. Gordon in which the latter notifies his appointment as Governor-General of the Sudan, is quoted in the *R.E. Journal*, Vol. 7, 1877, p. 32.

[3] *Gordon and the Sudan*, by Dr. Bernard M. Allen, p. 109.

[4] *Ibid.*, p. 112.

revolts were smouldering. Thence he would work his way northwards to Wadi Halfa and make a personal inspection of the new railway that was eventually to span the strip of country where the Nile route was blocked by the Third and Fourth Cataracts. Thence he would work eastward again to settle finally with the Abyssinians, and afterwards would conclude with revisiting the Equatorial Province, his former seat of Government, and press through to Lake Albert and Lake Victoria. And so he embarked on that wonderful career of camel-riding which made him the supreme pioneer of the mighty spaces of the Sudan and endowed his figure with a romantic grandeur which the humility of his simple letters cannot conceal."

Gordon's introspective and fanatically religious state of mind is shown in a letter written on May 4th, 1877,[1] shortly after his arrival at Khartoum, where he was received with much pomp and circumstance.[2] " I have no easy task before me. . . . First, I have to disband some 6,000 Turks and Bashi-Bazouks, who are the frontier guards, and who must be replaced, for they let the slave-caravans past. . . . Who that had not the Almighty with him would dare to do that ? I will do it, for I value my life as naught, and should only leave much weariness for perfect peace. . . . I have naught to gain in name or riches. I do not care what man may say. I do what I think is pleasing to my God ; and, as far as man goes, I need nothing from anyone. . . . What I have to do is to settle matters that I do not cause a revolution on my own death. Not that I value life. I have done with its comforts in coming here. My work is great, but does not weigh me down. I go as straight as I can. I feel my own weakness and look to Him who is almighty ; and I leave the issue, without inordinate care, to Him. I expect to ride 5,000 miles this year, if I am spared. I am quite alone, and like it. I have become what people call a great fatalist, viz., I trust God will pull me through every difficulty. The solitary grandeur of the desert makes one feel how vain is the effort of man. . . . It is only my firm conviction that I am only an instrument put in use for a time that enables me to bear up ; and in my present state, during my long, long, hot, weary rides, I think my thoughts better and clearer than I should with a companion. . . . I have an enormous province to look after, but it is a great blessing to me to know that God has undertaken the administration of it. If I fail it is His will ; if I succeed it is His work. . . . May I be humbled to the dust and fail, so that He may glorify Himself. The greatness of my position

[1] This letter appears in *Colonel Gordon in Central Africa*, 1874-79, edited by Dr. G. B. Hill, pp. 225-229.

[2] A description, by a native correspondent, of Gordon's arrival, the salute of 21 guns, the public reading of the *Firman* notifying his appointment, and the distribution of gifts to the poor, is given in an article entitled " Gordon Pasha," appearing in the *R.E. Journal*, Vol. 7, 1877, p. 90. A translation of the *Firman* is included.

depresses me, and I cannot help wishing that the time had come when He will lay me aside."

During a few weeks spent in Khartoum, Gordon revolutionized the administration. In three days, he bestowed on the poor and needy upwards of £E.1,000 of his own money. He abolished flogging; he ensured that every opportunity should be given to suppliants for the redress of grievances; he commenced the disbandment of the frontier guards; and he made plans for providing the city with a proper water-supply. Events in Darfur, however, soon claimed his attention for El Fasher, the capital, was besieged, and accordingly he set out from Khartoum on May 19th, 1877, to deal with the insurgents. Riding far and fast, he relieved the garrisons of Dara and El Fasher, and on September 2nd, with only a few men, entered the camp of 3,000 slave-raiders under Suleiman, Zubeir's son, and cowed them into submission. On October 14th, he was back in Khartoum.

Although his campaign in Darfur had met with remarkable success, Gordon had discovered at an early date the hopelessness of attempting to stamp out the slave-trade. Writing from the desert in June, 1877, he explained the circumstances. " I have complete power, military and civil," he remarked.[1] " No one could say a word if I put one or ten men to death. Therefore, I must be considered entirely responsible if the slave trade goes on. But here is my position. Darfur and Kordofan are peopled by huge Bedouin tribes under their own Sheikhs. The country is a vast desert, for the most part with wells few and far between. Some of the tribes can put 2,000 to 6,000 horsemen or camel-men in the field. Now these tribes raid the negro tribes to the south, or else exchange cloth for slaves with the Bedouin tribes beyond even the nominal boundary of Egypt. The slaves then enter Egyptian territory, four or five at a time. The tribes sell the slaves to the little merchants of all kinds, who flock to these lands from all parts of Egypt. These merchants then come down to more populous places with their four or five slaves and sell them to others. . . . It is impossible to prevent slaves passing down in small numbers, and I do not think it will ever be prevented until the frontier of Egypt extends up to the Negro frontier, which it cannot do for 30 years, if then."

Nine days after his return to Khartoum, Gordon set off on a tour through the northern districts, visiting Berber and riding across the desert to Merowe, whence he proceeded beyond Dongola by river. Then came news of serious trouble on the Abyssinian frontier, and fearing an invasion, Gordon hurried back to Khartoum. Four days were spent in the capital, and then he rode eastwards through Kassala and reached Keren, in the country which subsequently became Italian Eritrea. Having induced Walad el Michael, the ruler of that

[1] Letter from Colonel C. G. Gordon, dated June 21st, 1877, quoted in the *R.E. Journal*, Vol. 7, 1877, p. 72.

territory, to come to an agreement, Gordon continued his journey to Massawa and returned to Khartoum by way of Suakin and Berber. His labours were still directed primarily towards the suppression of the slave trade; but they were interrupted in January, 1878, by an appeal from the Khedive urging him to come to Cairo to advise on certain financial problems. He started from Khartoum on February 7th, and was received in Cairo on March 7th, with every mark of distinction. He left the capital, however, on March 30th, with no honours, by an ordinary train, and paying his own fare. His advice had been unpalatable to Ismail, and he was out of his element among the financiers of Cairo. Disgusted with the intrigues of the Egyptian courtiers and officials, he voyaged down the Red Sea, visited the Somaliland coast, returned to Suakin, and reached Khartoum in June, 1878.

During the next nine months, Gordon was occupied in placing the finances of the Sudan on a sound basis. His work helped him to bear the tedium of a life of solitary grandeur in his palace overlooking the Blue Nile, an artificial existence utterly repugnant to his nature and inclinations. By the end of October, 1878, he was able to produce a reliable statement of income and expenditure for the whole country; and as the expenditure far exceeded the income, he proposed a scheme of retrenchment. The unremunerative Somaliland coast was to be excluded from the Sudan; the southern limit of the Egyptian domains was to be fixed at Mrooli, 100 miles north of Lake Victoria;[1] the projected extension of the railway running southwards from Wadi Halfa was to be abandoned. Malaria was prevalent, and accustomed as he was to scouring the desert on a camel, his life at Khartoum was unspeakably dreary. " I am utterly at a loss how to employ my time," he writes on November 6th.[2] " I have pulled another clock to pieces and put it together again "; and on the 13th, " A cuckoo-clock has beaten me to-day. I cannot make it go. The dullness is almost insupportable. From 4.30 p.m. till I go to bed, I have not a single thing to do."

Soon after Gordon's return from Cairo, he had dispatched a force under Gessi to Darfur to deal with Suleiman, who had risen in revolt. In March, 1879, he learned that, after some desperate fighting, Gessi had routed Suleiman and his slavers and liberated 10,000 of their victims, though Suleiman himself had escaped. Gordon then took the field in person. After scouring Southern Darfur and releasing slaves as he went, he met Gessi on June 25th, at Taweisha, 120 miles south-east of El Fasher, and concerted measures with him for the capture of the rebel leader. On July 15th, Suleiman was taken and shot by Gessi, and the news was carried to Gordon in Khartoum. Zubeir, held fast in Cairo, was tried, convicted, and sentenced to

[1] The Equatorial Province was now ruled most ably by " Emin Pasha " (otherwise Edouard Schnitzer), who had assisted Gordon for three years.
[2] *Colonel Gordon in Central Africa*, edited by Dr. G. B. Hill, p. 323.

death; but nevertheless, he was afterwards liberated by the Khedive, and if Gordon had had his way, the slave-trader would have been his right-hand man in the Sudan in 1884.

At the end of June, 1879, the Khedive Ismail was deposed and his son, Tewfik, appointed in his stead. Gordon had already written to his friend Watson that under such circumstances he would not remain in the Sudan, and on July 29th, he left Khartoum, determined never to return. He handed in his resignation to Tewfik Pasha at Cairo, but was persuaded to undertake another mission to Abyssinia before proceeding to England. This duty occupied him for the next four months. It was a thankless task, and the rough travelling in mountainous country taxed his weakened constitution to breaking point. Gordon felt that any terms he might make with King John would be repudiated by Egypt if unpalatable to Tewfik and his ministers. He landed at Massawa on September 5th, and started on his march inland on the 11th; but it was not until October 27th, after covering a distance of more than 300 miles over abominable roads, that he had his first interview with King John at a place called Debra Tabor, east of Lake Tsana. The result was inconclusive, and another interview with the arrogant monarch on November 8th produced no better understanding. Accordingly, Gordon gave up the hopeless task and set out for Khartoum; but after being arrested and detained by the Abyssinians, he changed his plans and made instead for Massawa, where he arrived on December 8th.[1] His efforts to secure a peaceful settlement of the many disputes between Egypt and Abyssinia had failed through no fault of his own. Dejected and worn out, he reached Cairo on January 2nd, 1880, and having placed his resignation once more in the hands of the Khedive, proceeded under medical advice to Switzerland for a period of complete rest.

Gordon's brief experience as Private Secretary to Lord Ripon in India, his visit to China, his service at Mauritius, and his employment at the Cape of Good Hope, which, with a year of biblical research in Palestine, formed the prelude to his return to the Sudan in 1884, do not concern this narrative.[2] Though the benefits resulting from his administration in the Sudan from 1874 to 1879 were destroyed by the tide of Dervishdom which overwhelmed him at Khartoum on January 26th, 1885, his name will remain for ever a household word from end to end of the country and far beyond its borders. The Arabs respected and obeyed him as a ruler whose sublime self-confidence was founded on a religious faith deeper than

[1] Colonel Gordon's adventures in Abyssinia in 1877 and 1879, are described in an article entitled "Colonel C. G. Gordon, C.B., and Abyssinia," by Captain C. M. Watson, R.E., appearing in the *R.E. Journal*, Vol. 10, 1880, pp. 91–95.

[2] Many historians have dealt with these phases of Gordon's career. They are mentioned briefly in the Memoir of Major-General Charles George Gordon included in the *History of the Corps of Royal Engineers*, by Major-General W. Porter, late R.E., Vol. II, pp. 500–529.

their own. This was the secret of his power: this, the source of the trust and devotion which he inspired.

In October, 1884, while General Gordon was besieged in Khartoum,[1] Major H. C. Chermside, C.M.G., was appointed Governor-General of the Red Sea Littoral. He was followed in that office by three other Royal Engineers—Brevet Colonel Sir Charles Warren, G.C.M.G., in February, 1886, Major C.M. Watson in May, 1886, and Lieut.-Colonel H. H. Kitchener, C.M.G., in September, 1886. The firm administration of Chermside and his delicate negotiations with King John of Abyssinia, the milder methods of Warren and Watson, and the combination of prudence and daring shown by Kitchener, have been described in a previous chapter.[2] It may be permissible, however, to add a few remarks on some features of Kitchener's rule at Suakin.

After the conclusion of the Nile Campaign, Kitchener proceeded on leave to England; and at the beginning of November, 1885, he sailed for Zanzibar as British representative on a Commission sent by Great Britain, France and Germany to delimit the East African territory claimed by the Sultan of that island. He was at Suez on his way home from Zanzibar in September, 1886, when he was informed of his appointment as "Governor-General of the Eastern Sudan and Red Sea Littoral" and consequently altered his plans. On arrival at Suakin, his first care was to establish better relations with the surrounding tribes. To the friendly he sent letters of encouragement; to the doubtful he wrote advising them, if they desired peace and prosperity, to come and see him at his headquarters. The tribes were growing tired of Dervish oppression, and the radius of Government authority was extending. Gradually, the news spread that the sheikhs would be received amicably at Suakin and given safe conduct to and from that place, and in consequence, many came to see Kitchener. He told them that they had made a grave mistake in becoming Mahdiists, advised them to discard that creed, and impressed on them the truth of his statements and the sincerity of his aims. After a time, humanitarians in England began to accuse him of adopting a "wicked and wanton policy" and of "attempting to retax and regovern the people against their will." To this he replied, "I have written upon the gate of Suakin 'Peace to those who enter and who leave this place,' and I have strictly carried out these principles. During my administration, no one has been punished for previous acts of hostility, nor for present political opinions."[3]

In January, 1888, Kitchener was severely wounded in a skirmish a few miles from Suakin, and was invalided to Cairo.[4] He returned in March; but as he was still suffering from his injury, he relinquished his post in May, and proceeded to England under medical advice.

---
[1] The story of Gordon's defence of Khartoum is told in Chapter V.
[2] See Chapter III.
[3] *Life of Lord Kitchener*, by Sir George Arthur, Vol. I, p. 154.
[4] See Chapter III.

On his return to Cairo in September, 1888, he was appointed Adjutant-General, Egyptian Army. His tenure of office on the Red Sea Littoral was marked by the constant profession and consistent practice of a friendly policy towards the inhabitants, tempered by strong and aggressive action when occasion demanded the inculcation of a wholesome respect for authority.

Kitchener's next experience of civil administration began when he was invested, on January 19th, 1899, with supreme military and civil command as Governor-General of the reconquered Sudan. Some reference to his work in that capacity has already appeared in this narrative.[1] He was confronted by a stupendous task. " Not only," writes Sir Harold MacMichael,[2] " had the pacification of an immense and almost unknown country to be completed, but a system of administration had to be organized and a budget framed. No time was lost. The re-occupied area was, in the first instance, divided into six provinces, Dongola, Berber, Kassala, Sennar, Fashoda and Khartoum, with Suakin necessarily, for the time being, upon a different footing.[3] The charge of each of these units was entrusted to a senior British officer as *mudir* or governor, assisted by two other British officers as inspectors. Under them, in charge of districts, were Egyptian *mamurs*. The administrative policy ordained from the first for general application was to follow common sense and equity, without undue adherence to ' red tape '."

Kitchener dispatched the following memorandum to his *mudirs* :—
" The necessary Laws and Regulations will be carefully considered and issued as required ; but it is not mainly to the framing and publishing of laws that we must look for the improvement and good government of the country. The task before us all, and especially the *mudirs* and inspectors, is to acquire the confidence of the people, to develop their resources, and to raise them to a higher level. This can only be effected by the district officers being thoroughly in touch with the better class of native, through whom we may hope gradually to influence the whole population. *Mudirs* and inspectors should learn to know personally all the principal men of their district, and show them, by friendly dealings and the interest taken in their individual concerns, that our object is to increase their prosperity. . . . Exhortations, when issued in the shape of proclamations or circulars, effect little ; it is to the individual action of British officers, working independently, but with a common purpose, on the individual natives whose confidence they have gained, that we must look for the moral and industrial regeneration of the Sudan."

[1] See Chapter XI.
[2] *The Anglo-Egyptian Sudan*, by Sir Harold MacMichael, K.C.M.G., D.S.O., p. 72.
[3] Suakin was exempted at first from some of the clauses of an agreement, signed on January 19th, 1899, between the British and Egyptian Governments, relative to the political status of the Sudan. However, by a subsequent agreement, signed on July 10th, 1899, the status of Suakin was assimilated in all respects to that of the remainder of the Sudan.

THE RIVER FRONT AT KHARTOUM.

[*Photo by the Author.*]

During his short tenure of office before he left the Sudan for South Africa in December, 1899, Lord Kitchener, advised by Lord Cromer, dealt with important problems of finance, land-ownership, fiscal and other legislation, education, relations with neighbouring states, town-planning, and the extension of communications, in addition to military measures of reorganization and defence. Much of his success was due to his ready accessibility, and to his minute investigation of all important questions in which he was personally interested. As Sir George Arthur remarks,[1] Kitchener visited as many districts as possible, gave audiences, heard complaints, set going local authorities, rewarded fidelity with honours, and everywhere used his own eyes and ears to learn and assimilate the conditions of the country and study the temper of the people. He profited much by the wise statesmanship and ripe experience of Lord Cromer. Mutual loyalty marked the relations between the two men; but as their outlook on life differed largely, it may have been well that, when Kitchener's task had been accomplished, they were separated by force of circumstances.

Lord Kitchener having been summoned to play his part as Chief of Staff to Lord Roberts, the conduct of affairs devolved on Sir Reginald Wingate. "It would be hard," remarks Sir Harold MacMichael,[2] "to over-estimate the careful skill and diplomacy with which he guided the country's destinies for the next seventeen years. Under his control it passed from infancy to manhood, and from the meanest poverty to stability, if not to affluence." From the time of his assumption of office in December, 1899, until the end of 1909, Sir Reginald continued the system of benevolently autocratic government, wisely organized on military lines for civil purposes, which was so well suited to the needs of the country; but he was careful to modify that system when occasion demanded, and to keep in touch, through his Inspector-General (Slatin Pasha) and the Intelligence Department, with native opinion and political tendencies. On the departure of Lord Kitchener to South Africa, Lord Cromer had contemplated the separation of the appointments of Governor-General of the Sudan and Sirdar of the Egyptian Army; but after Sir Reginald Wingate had represented the drawbacks of that project, Lord Cromer agreed to postpone it, and finally abandoned it. Gradually, as civilization spread and trade expanded, Sir Reginald began to introduce more democratic and representative methods of administration; and at the beginning of 1910, he secured the establishment of a Governor-General's Council to advise on all matters of administrative importance. It is impossible even to outline in these pages the reforms which he carried out prior to his translation on December 31st, 1916, to the office of High Commissioner[3] for Egypt

---

[1] *Life of Lord Kitchener*, by Sir George Arthur, Vol. I, p. 257.
[2] *The Anglo-Egyptian Sudan*, by Sir Harold MacMichael, K.C.M.G., D.S.O., p. 82.
[3] Formerly British Agent and Consul-General.

in succession to Sir Henry MacMahon. The great success which he achieved is an outstanding feature in the history of the Sudan. On January 19th, 1919, he left Egypt for England in answer to a summons by the British Government to a consultation regarding a political crisis in Egypt. Prolonged discussions followed, and as his proposals were not accepted, he resigned the High Commissionership on October 15th, and was succeeded by Lord Allenby. It was a sad day for Egypt when she lost Sir Reginald Wingate.

Lord Kitchener was the last Royal Engineer to hold the combined appointments of Governor-General of the Sudan and Sirdar of the Egyptian Army;[1] but Brevet Colonel the Hon. M. G. Talbot acted in those capacities during the absence of Sir Reginald Wingate on leave during the summer of 1903, and on the termination of this duty, was awarded the 2nd Class *Medjidieh* by H.H. The Khedive.

The only Royal Engineer to hold the appointment of *Mudir* or Provincial Governor after the re-occupation was Brevet Lieut.-Colonel (now Lieut.-General Sir) G. F. Gorringe, C.M.G., D.S.O., who was Governor of the Sennar Province from December, 1901, to December, 1904, after rejoining the Egyptian Army from the South African War.[2] He freed the country of a notorious slave-trader named Ibrahim Wad Mahmud,[3] and brought the southern portion of the Province under control. In addition, he introduced measures for the preservation of forests, devoted particular attention to accounts and the collection of revenue, initiated the cultivation of Egyptian cotton, cut roads through the bush, and constructed a number of buildings at Wad Medani, Sennar, Singa and Roseires.[4] With his departure at the end of 1904, the connection of Royal Engineers with civil administration in the Sudan came to an end.

We turn now to the administrative work performed by officers of the Corps in Egypt. This started several years before Colonel Charles Gordon voyaged up the Nile for the first time to Khartoum and Gondokoro. In 1865, after a period of duty as British Consul-General in Warsaw, Brevet Colonel Edward Stanton, C.B., C.M.G., R.E., was selected by the Foreign office for appointment as British Agent and Consul-General in Egypt, a post which he held until his

---

[1] The list of Governors-General of the Sudan since the reoccupation is as follows :—
Field-Marshal Lord Kitchener of Khartoum, K.C., K.P., P.C., G.C.B., O.M., G.C.S.I., G.C.M.G., G.C.I.E., 19.1.99–22.12.99. General Sir Francis Reginald Wingate, Bt., G.C.B., G.C.V.O., G.B.E., K.C.M.G., D.S.O., 23.12.99–31.12.16. Major-General Sir Lee O. FitzM. Stack, G.B.E., C.M.G., 1.1.17–20.11.24 (murdered in Cairo). Sir Geoffrey F. Archer, K.C.M.G., 4.12.24–17.10.26. Sir John L. Maffey, K.C.M.G., K.C.V.O., C.S.I., C.I.E., 24.10.26–13.11.33. Lieut.-Colonel Sir George Stewart Symes, K.C.M.G., K.B.E., D.S.O., 10.1.34 (in office).

[2] The Sennar Province afterwards became the Fung Province. The latter has recently been absorbed into the Blue Nile, White Nile and Kassala Provinces. Lieut.-Colonel Gorringe arrived in the Sennar Province in January, 1902.

[3] See Chapter XI.

[4] *Report on the Finance, Administration and Condition of the Sudan*, 1904. *Annual Report, Sennar Province*, 1904, pp. 106–118, and *Memorandum* by H.M.'s Agent and Consul-General, 1904, p. 63. As regards engineering work by Lieut.-Colonel Gorringe in the Sennar Province, see Chapter XVIII.

transfer to Bavaria in 1876.[1] In 1856-57, Gordon had been one of Stanton's assistants[2] on an International Commission for the delimitation of a new boundary between Russia, Turkey and Roumania. Consequently, Stanton was greatly interested in Gordon's appointment, in 1874, as Governor of the Equatorial Province, and did all that he could to assist him in opening up that territory. No better man than Stanton could have been sent, in 1865, to control British affairs in Egypt. The Khedive Ismail was commencing the career of extravagance which led to his downfall, and subsequently to the British occupation of his country; but by the exercise of tact and diplomacy, Stanton managed to keep on good terms with him and his ministers, and to further the difficult negotiations in connection with the purchase of his financial interest in the Suez Canal Company.

The names of two other Royal Engineers figure prominently in the history of the Suez Canal, for both Lieut.-General Sir John Stokes, K.C.B., and Lieut.-General Sir Andrew Clarke, G.C.M.G., C.B., C.I.E., were intimately concerned in its administration, management and expansion. The Canal, the construction of which had cost about £14,000,000, was formally opened in November, 1869, by Napoleon III; and in the following January, the Admiralty sent Major Andrew Clarke, R.E., and Captain G. H. Evans, R.N., to examine it.[3] They spent more than a fortnight on this duty, and reported that the Canal was suitable for the transit of all ships, except large ironclads and transports, and that the cost of its maintenance would not be excessive. They suggested, however, that it should be widened. Clarke was so impressed by its advantages that he recommended that it should be purchased outright by an English Company formed for the purpose, and requested that his proposal should be laid before the Cabinet. At that time, the French shareholders, supported by Monsieur Ferdinand de Lesseps, the designer and builder, were ready to sell at a good price, but the outbreak of the Franco-Prussian War interfered with the scheme. There was also considerable opposition to it in England. On August 24th, 1870, Lord Granville, the Foreign Secretary, announced that Mr. Gladstone, the Prime Minister, and Mr. Robert Lowe, the Chancellor of the Exchequer, would have nothing to do with it. This was one of the most serious errors of British policy during the nineteenth century, an error which was only partially remedied at the end of 1875, when Mr. Gladstone had been succeeded by Lord Beaconsfield. The British Government then purchased the Khedive's

---

[1] A Memoir of General Sir Edward Stanton, K.C.B., K.C.M.G., Col. Commandant R.E., appears in *History of the Corps of Royal Engineers*, Vol. III, by Colonel Sir Charles M. Watson, K.C.M.G., C.B., late R.E., pp. 309-312.

[2] The other assistant was Lieut. (afterwards Major-General) E. R. James, R.E.

[3] Major Clarke, R.E., had been Director of Engineering and Architectural Works at the Admiralty since 1864. Captain Evans, R.N., was Hydrographer to the Royal Navy.

shares in the Suez Canal Company—about two-fifths of the entire share capital—and thereby secured the presence of British Directors on the Board of Management. The shares purchased, in 1875, for £4,080,000 are now worth nearly £100,000,000.

Before this transaction had been carried through, Lieut.-Colonel John Stokes, R.E., had become concerned in the administration of the Suez Canal. From 1856 to 1871, Stokes had been engaged in improving the mouths of the Danube as a member of an International Commission appointed for that purpose. In May, 1872, he was appointed by the Foreign office to another International Commission,[1] which was to assemble at Constantinople to solve certain difficulties in regard to the measurement of the tonnage of ships passing through the Suez Canal. He was recognized as an expert in such work because of his experience in tonnage problems on the Danube. The Canal Company, which had formerly charged 10 francs per ton on the net tonnage, had insisted latterly on levying this charge on the gross tonnage, to the consternation of the ship-owners, who appealed to their respective Governments.[2] The Commission assembled in 1873, and thanks to the powers of mediation of Stokes, a compromise was reached, and approved by the Sultan of Turkey, allowing for the addition of a sur-tax in certain circumstances to the normal charge on the net tonnage. Under instructions from the Foreign Office, Stokes next proceeded from Constantinople to Egypt to report on the condition and local administration of the Suez Canal, and having examined the working system of the Canal Company, wrote his report and returned to England in March, 1874. As the Foreign Office desired that he should be available for frequent consultation, he was posted to Chatham. In November, 1875, while Commandant of the School of Military Engineering, he advised the British Government to purchase the Khedive's shares in the Suez Canal Company, which fortunately they decided to do.[3]

Shortly after the purchase of these shares, the Khedive Ismail requested the British Government to send a financial expert to Egypt to help him with advice on Treasury matters. Stokes accompanied this official, and took the opportunity to report on the working of the new tonnage system on the Suez Canal, to which De Lesseps objected. He went into the question with the Frenchman, and sent revised proposals to the Foreign Office. These were then

---

[1] Stokes was succeeded on the Danube Commission by Charles Gordon.

[2] The net tonnage was calculated by deducting the space occupied by machinery, coal bunkers, officers and crew from the gross tonnage, and regarding the difference as the utilizable portion of the vessel for the conveyance of cargo and passengers. The effect of the proposal to levy a charge of 10 francs per ton on the gross, instead of net tonnage, was equivalent to a rate of 15 francs per ton on the latter.

[3] An account of the work of Colonel Stokes in connection with the Suez Canal is given in a Memoir of Lieut.-General Sir John Stokes, K.C.B., late R.E., which appears in the *R.E. Journal*, Vol. 33, 1903, pp. 76–78 and 102–104. See also the Memoir included in the *History of the Corps of Royal Engineers*, Vol. III, by Col. Sir Charles M. Watson, K.C.M.G., C.B., late R.E., pp. 292–298.

submitted to the European powers concerned. With their concurrence, Stokes was empowered to make a formal agreement with De Lesseps, and the matter having been settled amicably, he returned to England, where he received the thanks of Parliament and was created a Knight Commander of the Bath.

When the Khedive's shares were purchased, a stipulation was made that Great Britain should be eligible to nominate three Directors on the Board of Management of the Suez Canal Company, and the first so nominated was Colonel Sir John Stokes. In May, 1879, De Lesseps pressed Stokes to join the Directorate of the Panama Canal Company, which he was then promoting, but Stokes wisely declined to do so. In the following November, Stokes proceeded to Egypt as a member of an International Commission convened for the purposes of examining the works at the port of Alexandria and deciding on the the dues to be levied on shipping. While in Egypt, he again inspected the Suez Canal, and reported favourably on the recent improvements and the proposed rectification of a sharp curve at Timsa.[1]

The Egyptian Campaign of 1882 entailed much difficult work for Sir John Stokes as a Director of the Suez Canal Company. His French colleagues were very irate over the question of British policy in Egypt, but he managed to pacify them. In December, 1886, on the eve of his retirement from the Army as a Lieut.-General, he was sent once more to Egypt to assist Sir Evelyn Baring[2] and the Suez Canal Company in negotiations with the Egyptian Government, and during this visit, he advised the Government on the sanitation of Ismailia and the building of a British Hospital at Port Said.[3] He found that the annual traffic on the Canal already exceeded the 6,000,000 tons envisaged, in 1869, by De Lesseps, and estimated that, after the number of sidings had been increased and some curves rectified, it would amount to 10,000,000 tons. The ship-owners, however, were not satisfied with such improvements; and after Sir John had become Vice-President of the Suez Canal Company in 1887, the Directors decided to widen the Canal along its whole length in order to allow vessels to pass each other without stopping, thus securing a reduction in the time of transit from 34 to 24 hours. Sir John took a prominent part in the arrangements for this enlargement, and continued almost up to the time of his death in November, 1902, to exercise his influence on the Board of Management. Though his greatest services were rendered in a diplomatic rôle, it would be hard to overestimate the value of his administrative ability and experience in questions of engineering, tonnage and finance.

In 1883, a scheme for the duplication of the Suez Canal was under

---

[1] "Occasional Notes," *R.E. Journal*, Vol. 10, 1880, pp. 17 and 135.
[2] British Agent and Consul-General. Afterwards Lord Cromer.
[3] Article entitled "The Suez Canal," appearing in the *R.E. Journal*, Vol. 17, 1887, p. 43. Sir John Stokes became Chairman and Treasurer of the London Committee of the hospital.

consideration as an alternative to its enlargement. Indeed, an agreement for the construction of a second canal was actually prepared, and was the cause of some disparaging comments in the newspapers on the abilities of Sir John Stokes, Sir C. Rivers Wilson and Mr. E. J. S. Standen, the British members of the Suez Canal Council. However, nothing came of this project. Colonel Sir Andrew Clarke, then Inspector General of Fortifications and Works, examined the Suez Canal while on a visit to Egypt in connection with barrack accommodation, and wrote a memorandum in August, 1883, in which he stated that widening the existing canal was preferable to excavating a second canal. As a result, he was nominated a member of an International Consultative Committee appointed to advise the Suez Canal Company on this question, and at the first meeting of the Committee in Paris on June 19th, 1884, he was chosen as Vice-President. It was decided, in the end, that the existing waterway should be widened and deepened. In December, 1884, a technical Commission recommended that the greater portion of the Canal should be widened to 82 metres (90 yards) at the top and 70 metres at the bottom, in order that large ships should be able to pass each other, and that the minimum radius of curvature on the bends should be 2,000 metres.[1] The enlargement scheme, which was estimated to cost about £7,000,000, was sanctioned in February, 1885, and was carried out during the next few years. Since then, the Canal has been further widened and deepened to such an extent that ships of more than 30,000 gross tonnage can now make the transit from Port Said to Suez with ease and rapidity. This happy result may be considered as due in some measure to the advice and guidance so freely given by two Royal Engineers—Colonels Sir John Stokes and Sir Andrew Clarke—more than half a century ago.

The most striking example of successful civil administration by a Royal Engineer in Egypt is furnished by Lord Kitchener's tenure as British Agent and Consul-General before the Great War. Lord Cromer, on the conclusion of a career of unrivalled brilliance, had left Egypt in May, 1907, when he was succeeded by Sir Eldon Gorst, a former Financial Secretary and Adviser to the Egyptian Ministry of the Interior. Sir Eldon was, as his father Sir John had been, a supporter of the slogan "Egypt for the Egyptians"; but his sincere and well-meant efforts to entrust politically-minded Egyptians more and more with the conduct of their own affairs were misinterpreted by them as a sign of weakness. His attempts to demonstrate British sympathy with their legitimate aspirations in the direction of self-government led merely to the lowering of British prestige throughout the country. He was outwitted by the Khedive Abbas Hilmi, and urged, at an ever-increasing speed, along a thorny path which he

---

[1] "Occasional Notes," *R.E. Journal*, Vol. 15, 1885, p. 43. The calculation was made for ships of 15 metres' breadth of beam.

would have preferred to tread slowly and warily. The strain was too great. His health failed, and he died in England in April, 1911.

The British Government, faced with the problem of choosing a strong successor to Sir Eldon Gorst, acceded to the urgent representations of Lord Cromer and selected Lord Kitchener. While Kitchener was available, there could be no other man for the post. The Egyptian appointment demanded special knowledge and experience, and exceptional qualities. "I do not know of anyone," remarked Sir Edward Grey,[1] "who possesses the special knowledge and experience, and those qualities, in so high a degree as Lord Kitchener." So the former Commander-in-Chief in India was called to Egypt and arrived in Cairo as British Agent and Consul-General on September 28th, 1911, only three days before the outbreak of war between Italy and Turkey. This was the appointment on which he had always set his heart. He was now in virtual control of the destinies of Egypt, and in actual control of those of the Sudan through the medium of the Governor-General, his personal friend and former assistant, Sir Reginald Wingate.

Long experience had taught Kitchener that ceremony and display appeal to Eastern peoples. He knew that they are recognized as the hall-mark of the great: that their omission is deplored. Consequently, he set himself to provide them. Brigadier-General R. B. D. Blakeney, then General Manager of the Egyptian State Railways, describes the manner of Lord Kitchener's arrival in Cairo. "It was thought," he writes,[2] "that he would come in a saloon carriage, like Lord Cromer or Sir Eldon Gorst, though the latter sometimes effaced himself still more by travelling in an ordinary reserved compartment. The first indication of a very different policy, and one designed to impress the Oriental mind, was a telegram addressed to the General Manager in the following terms 'Coming in cruiser. Have special train awaiting me on arrival.'" The General Manager, one of his former subordinates in the Sudan, received the message with delight and enthusiasm. Only three months before, he and two brother officers of the Corps had been stoned by strikers. The next order was that the central platform of Cairo Railway Station should be carpeted, and the Royal Entrance thrown open, for the arrival of "His Brittanic Majesty's Representative, Field-Marshal Viscount Kitchener of Khartoum, K.G., K.P., P.C., G.C.B.," etc. All British officials were to attend in top-hats and frock-coats. As the hour of arrival approached, the square outside the station became packed with people, including many of the recent strikers, and the police were in a state of great anxiety. The scene within the station was most impressive. Ministers of Foreign Powers rubbed shoulders with high Officials of State and Members of the Egyptian Cabinet,

[1] Foreign Secretary.
[2] Notes by Brig.-General R. B. D. Blakeney, C.M.G., D.S.O., late R.E., sent to the author on July 20th, 1934.

and the central platform was filled with British, European and Egyptian officials, and the representatives of commercial bodies. Punctually at 7.20 p.m., the train drew up; and soon a tall figure was seen, towering above the heads of the crowd, while arms clashed and the Guards' band played the national anthem. Though dressed in a grey frock-coat and top-hat, Kitchener was martial as ever. He inspected the Guards of Honour, made himself most charming to the officers, was courteous but rather frigid to the high dignitaries, and walked down the ranks, greeting old friends and subordinates. We followed close on his heels until he emerged from the building and paused at the top of the baize-covered steps before descending to the Agency carriage. For a moment, our hearts stood still. Then came a wild yell of delight from the populace. They closed in and followed the carriage, cheering, yelling, and clapping hands, the whole way to the Agency. Kitchener, with his matchless knowledge of Oriental mentality, had struck the right note."

The grandeur of Kitchener's arrival was maintained throughout the period of his administration in Egypt, and for a set purpose. Gorgeously clothed syces ran before his carriage when he drove through the streets. His household attendants were resplendent in gold-decked Turkish costumes. Outwardly, the Kitchener who became His Majesty's Agent and Consul-General in 1911 was different from the Kitchener who left the Sudan in 1899. He entertained lavishly. He added a ballroom to the Agency. The Egyptians were impressed. The foreign community congratulated their British friends on the advent of one who would rule with dignity and power. British prestige was restored to the pinnacle which it had attained under Cromer.

"Lord Kitchener did not pursue his predecessor's policy," writes Lieut.-Colonel P. G. Elgood.[1] "It is doubtful, perhaps, if the new British Agent appreciated immediately that another spirit had overtaken the Egyptians, or that their former calm acceptance of the Occupation had been replaced by a different feeling. In the cordial welcome extended to him by all classes of the population he had every excuse to be blind to the change. The Agency was crowded with callers, anxious to remind the former Sirdar of their existence and past services, for he had that rare quality of remembering humble acquaintances and their work."

When Kitchener had been Sirdar, the rule of Egypt was still patriarchal, though Cromer had begun to secure a greater measure of liberty for the people. With this liberty, however, had come the growth of political parties and the birth of sedition veiled as reform, and early in 1912, Kitchener recorded his realization of the altered state of affairs. "I have been forcibly struck," he wrote, "by the fact that the former homogeneous body of intelligent Muhammadan

[1] *Egypt and the Army*, by Lieut.-Colonel P. G. Elgood, p. 31.

inhabitants is now split up and divided into parties and factions of a political character." Italy had invaded Tripoli and Cyrenaica, and there was, as Kitchener observed,[1] an extremely warm feeling of sympathy in Egypt for the Muhammadan combatants; but Egypt had been declared neutral, and the neutrality was strictly maintained by the Egyptians. The British Agent and Consul-General also used his influence effectively in certain religious differences which threatened to provoke a struggle between the Muhammadans and the Copts. At his bidding, the truculent elements throughout the country turned their swords into ploughshares.

"If it is true to say," remarks Lord Lloyd,[2] "that Kitchener reversed the policy of Gorst, it is true in one sense only. He did not revoke the measures which Government had put in force. He did not even slacken the pace of constitutional reform. But whereas Gorst's main preoccupation had been to demonstrate British sympathy with Egyptian political aspirations, Kitchener naturally regarded political institutions as not in themselves admirable, and in Eastern countries more than likely to be harmful. . . . His policy was to promote the material welfare of the *fellaheen*, and he had his own schemes for that purpose. . . . Those schemes were conceived on far-seeing lines and based upon a clear insight into the needs of the situation. . . . Whatever may have been the defects in his programme, Egypt again achieved a measure of tranquillity, and her prosperous progress was upset by a few political storms. . . . The glamour of Kitchener's past career, and the imposing strength of his personality, were undoubtedly assets of which it is hard to estimate the value, and they enabled him to overcome the danger of the situation created by the Turco-Italian and Balkan Wars and the impending dissolution of the old Ottoman Empire."

Kitchener had a passion for everything connected with agriculture, and one of his first acts as British Agent and Consul-General was to set in motion machinery designed to rescue the impoverished *fellaheen* from the clutches of moneylenders. Whilst he was in India, a law had been passed which had saved the *ryot* from a like situation, and accordingly, he evolved from his own consciousness the famous Five Feddan Law for Egypt and co-operated energetically in its enactment. Five feddans is slightly in excess of five acres, and is approximately the area on which an Egyptian *fellah* can support himself and his family by cultivation. The Five Feddan Law gave protection to the cultivator of any area up to five feddans against expropriation of his land, house or farming utensils for debt, though it did not prevent him from selling his land, should he so desire, or raising money on his crops. It had been the custom of foreign usurers to lend money on mortage to the *fellaheen* at 30%

[1] *Field-Marshal Lord Kitchener*, by E. S. Grew, Vol. III, p. 54.
[2] *Egypt since Cromer*, by Lord Lloyd, Vol. I, pp. 130, 131, 174, 175.

to 40% interest, with the inevitable result that, once the latter were in their clutches, there was no escape. The outcry in the local business world against the Five Feddan Bill was loud and vehement, and the moneylenders rose in wrathful denunciation; but Kitchener was unmoved, and turned a deaf ear to argument and entreaty. The Bill was approved by the Legislative Council on June 14th, 1912, and became law before the end of the year. This was, perhaps, the greatest of Kitchener's reforms in Egypt. As Sir George Arthur remarks,[1] it brought contentment and prosperity into thousands of humble homes.

Other less ambitious reforms, introduced by the British Agent and Consul-General, were the institution of unpaid magistrates in rural areas for the settlement of small cases, and the provision of quays in Cairo, and roadways in the Nile Delta, for convenience in handling and transporting market produce. In these and many other ways, Kitchener showed his care for the poor and needy.

As regards agriculture in general, he secured in 1913 the expansion of a small Department to the status of an independent Ministry, and introduced Government offices where the producer of raw cotton could obtain trustworthy information regarding the weight of his produce and the market prices.[2] He encouraged the oil industry by inducing the Egyptian Government to extend the areas on the Red Sea Coast where boring for oil was permitted, and to broaden the conditions of the licence granted to promoters. He designed model villages and gardens, and insisted on better housing and sanitation for the *fellaheen*. He took a keen interest in educational schemes, not only for the Sudan, but also for Egypt. He set up clinics at dispensing centres, and gave particular attention to hospitals for the treatment of eye diseases. In July, 1913, he brought about the establishment of a single Chamber, called the " Legislative Assembly," in replacement of the Legislative Council and the General Assembly, thus providing more direct representation of the people, though without any pretence of conferring legislative control on them. In the firm belief that Egypt could be made sufficiently productive to meet the cost, he launched out into vast projects of land reclamation, planning improvements on a lordly scale, though himself by nature an economist. He remodelled part of Cairo, and replaced narrow streets and unsavoury slums by spacious avenues and noble squares. In brief, he left his mark on the capital and the country, and in so doing, earned the confidence and affection of all classes except those whose nefarious schemes he frustrated.

The relations between the Khedive Abbas Hilmi and Lord Cromer

---

[1] *Life of Lord Kitchener*, by Sir George Arthur, Vol. II, p. 320.
[2] No one did more towards encouraging the cultivation of cotton in Egypt than Lord Kitchener. Assisted by Sir Arthur Webb, he carried out important improvements in cultivation and went so far as to recommend the expenditure of about £E.20,000,000 to further the project.

CAIRO, FROM THE CITADEL.

[Photo by the Author.

had been bad; but they were far worse between Abbas Hilmi and Lord Kitchener. It is unnecessary and unprofitable to enter into the causes of these estrangements. They were inevitable. Remonstrance and advice having proved unavailing, matters came to a head in 1914. Before Kitchener sailed for England in the early summer of that year, he was resolved that Abbas Hilmi should not remain on the throne; and shortly after the outbreak of the Great War, he secured his deposition, and the installation, as " Sultan of Egypt," of a loyal friend of England in the person of Prince Hussein Kamel.

Thanks to his fluency in Arabic and easy approachability by all and sundry, Kitchener was kept fully informed, not only of intrigues in Cairo, but of many underhand dealings in outlying districts. A village magnate once came to see him and told him in strictest secrecy that a certain influential man had made £E.20,000 through a dishonest transaction. Kitchener listened patiently to the story and then produced a notebook from his breast pocket and turned over a few pages. "Ah!" said he. "I think you are mistaken. The actual amount was £E.23,000."[1]

The determination shown by Kitchener in trying to suppress subversive political activities placed his life in danger, for it earned him the hatred of those against whom he worked. The police endeavoured to induce him to take precautions for his personal safety, but without much success until after an attempt to shoot him had been made in Cairo in July, 1912. On that occasion, he was saved by the courage and resource of Major Fitzgerald, then acting as Military Attaché. Subsequent investigations disclosed the existence of a secret society directed against the Government. In September, 1913, another plot against Kitchener's life was hatched in Egypt. He was to be murdered at Venice while on his return journey from leave in England. News of this design reached the Foreign Office, who conveyed a warning to him in Italy, though they were unable to persuade him to alter his plans. However, owing to the efficiency of the Italian police, his visit to Venice passed without disaster.

The best epitome of Lord Kitchener's administration in Egypt is that written by Sir George Arthur. "The *de facto* ruler of Egypt," he states,[2] "took high honours in the school of statesmanship. His presence served to keep that peace which meant so much for the prosperity of the country; and although he knew trouble was lurking not far below the surface, he could hope that by a long course of wise and just administration, by steady elimination of grievances and alleviation of burdens, and by a liberal and sustained support of

---

[1] Notes by Brig.-General R. B. D. Blakeney, C.M.G., D.S.O., late R.E., sent to the author on July 20th, 1934.
[2] *Life of Lord Kitchener*, by Sir George Arthur, Vol. II, p. 344-346. Sir George Arthur was Private Secretary to Earl Kitchener from 1914 to 1916. He had served on his staff during the South African War, and had taken part with him in the Nile Expedition in 1884-85.

native industry, disaffection would die down and sedition at last find nothing to feed upon. Time was needed, and during his time, at any rate, Kitchener was able and, as it would seem, easily able to obviate any expression of anti-British feeling. . . . The two distracting wars in which Turkey was engaged, the perpetual straining at the leash on the part of the politicians who panted to become legislators, and the ceaseless malfeasances of the Khedive, were superadded to the ordinary complex cares of administration. Over and above the responsibility of damping down these inflammable materials was the duty of devising and carrying out a bevy of constructive measures of legislation. Agriculture, sanitation, education and judicature suggest rather than complete the chapter of subjects dealt with in the course of an Administration to which Kitchener had always looked forward as a prize which might fall to him. Cotton-markets and savings-banks, school buildings and Press supervision, the increase of cattle at home and the control of native students abroad, the overhauling of cantonal justice and the heightening of the Aswan Dam, correspondence alike with the Coptic Archbishop of Sinai and the Anglican Bishop of Jerusalem,[1] were each and all of absorbing interest to him and received equally assiduous attention. . . . The Birthday *Gazette* of June, 1914, announced that the Sovereign had been pleased to confer on Viscount Kitchener the honour of an Earldom, and the telegram announcing his new dignity reached him just as he was starting for England on his annual leave. How little did he think that he would see no more the land he knew and the people he loved, and had cared for, so well!"

The preponderating force in Kitchener's hold over the people of Egypt was his character. It impressed them by its strength, its mystery and its reserve; and the appearance of its owner supported those impressions. Yet, in spite of a somewhat awe-inspiring exterior, Kitchener was essentially human. A childhood spent in Ireland[2] seems to have left behind it an Irish sense of humour which showed itself from time to time. Sir Ronald Storrs gives two instances.[3] On one occasion, when the Khedive Abbas Hilmi had taken a decision as Sovereign and afterwards excused himself for it on the grounds that he was a mere vassal of the Sultan of Turkey, Kitchener remarked bluntly, "My own position here is anomalous enough: we really can't have *two* incomprehensibles!" Again, at a ball which the British Agent and Consul-General gave for the Crown Prince and Princess of Germany, it so happened that Count von Hatzfeldt,

[1] In 1913, Bishop Gwynne was installed at Khartoum as Suffragan to the Bishop of Jerusalem.

[2] Kitchener was born at Gunsborough Lodge, near Listowel in Kerry, on June 24th, 1850. He was christened in the church at Aghavallin, a few miles distant, on September 22nd, 1850, the ceremony being performed by the late Revd. Robert Sandes, a relative of the author.

[3] Articles entitled "Kitchener of Khartoum," by "A Correspondent" (Sir Ronald Storrs, K.C.M.G., C.B.), appearing in *The Times*, June 5th and 8th, 1834.

the German Consul-General, wooed and won a charming lady. Next morning he received from Kitchener a cordial note of congratulation—together with the cushion on which he was presumed to have knelt whilst making his proposal!

Writing in 1916, Lord Esher, an intimate friend, gave the following impressions of Lord Kitchener:—[1] "He possessed all the highest attributes of a constructive administrator; a clear sense of objective, undivergent resolve, flexible methods, and patience. He was said to be ruthless in discarding broken implements; but I found him almost unduly sensitive to giving pain, even to those who served him badly, provided they did so to the best of their powers. For carelessness or neglect of duty he had no pity; but for incompetence he showed extraordinary compassion and unfailing good temper. He would make no scape-goat, and firmly refused to share blame with any of his subordinates. In public, he covered everyone with his authority; and in private, he reproached no one but himself."

Six years later, Lieut.-General Sir Henry Lawson, a brother officer who had known Kitchener since the days of the Nile Expedition, described him as a man who was always imbibing new ideas; always learning, yet never twice the same lesson. "Intellectual courage," remarked Sir Henry,[2] "was perhaps his greatest asset. In the translation of decision into action, his indomitable will and resolution came to his aid. Once he had made up his mind that some end had to be reached, nothing turned him from his purpose. The difficulties in the way of accomplishment seemed so much less to him than to his agents that he was always asking of them more than they thought they could perform, and as a result, they generally achieved, not all he asked, but much more than they had ever thought feasible."

Much nonsense has been written on the subject of Kitchener's attitude towards women. Though shy in the presence of those who were strangers to him, he was in no sense a misogynist. He enjoyed the society of intelligent women whom he had known long and well. With them he would relax into the utmost sociability, laughing, joking and indulging occasionally in quiet repartee. The source of his reputation as a women-hater may have been his refusal, when Sirdar of the Egyptian Army, to allow any of his British officers to marry, or even to become engaged. This restriction, however, was not imposed through any dislike of the fair sex. It was essential, in his opinion, for the efficiency of the Army and its readiness to take the field at a moment's notice. While British Agent and Consul-General in Cairo, he paid frequent visits to the clever and elderly Princess Nazli Fazil, niece of the Khedive Ismail, who lived in a

---

[1] Article entitled "Lord K.," by Viscount Esher, G.C.B., published in *The National Review*, July, 1916, and reprinted in the *R.E. Journal*, Vol. XXIV, July-Dec., 1916, pp. 49-54.
[2] Article entitled "Lord Kitchener," by Lieut.-General Sir Henry M. Lawson, K.C.B., Col. Commandant R.E., published in *The Nineteenth Century and After*, and reprinted in the *R.E. Journal*, Vol. XXXV, Jan.-June, 1922, pp. 32-43.

sumptuous palace behind the Abdin. She had known him since he was a Captain, and treated him with scant respect, pouring forth a torrent of questions, information and advice to which he listened with great good-humour, and from which he often derived valuable knowledge. Kitchener abhorred sycophants and those with axes to grind; and it is thought, by some who knew him well, that he deliberately encouraged the popular belief that he was averse to feminine society in order to protect himself from the advances of women of these types.

In conversation with officers who had constant dealings with Lord Kitchener for many years, the author has gathered a few interesting facts about him. According to these officers, he never blustered and never hurried. His movements were deliberate, and he weighed his words. If unable to accord an interview, he said so at once; but if he agreed to see anyone, he never tried to cut short the conversation. This display of patience made him popular with the Diplomatic Corps. He derived much secret amusement from the periodical visits of a certain foreign Consul-General who, after half an hour's intricate exposition, would exclaim:—" Et maintenant, Monsieur le Maréchal, *je vais vous dire la vérité.*" He was abstemious in the use of wine and alcohol, and during the Great War, followed the example set by his Sovereign in becoming a total abstainer. He detested being "lionized," and would do his utmost to escape from the plaudits of the crowd. On occasion, he was capable of deep emotion, as was evident at the memorial service outside Gordon's ruined palace at Khartoum in September, 1898. His face was usually impassive; but it was possible for some of those who knew him intimately to judge his state of mind by watching his injured eye.[1] If it was steady, all was well; if the normal cast in it had increased, there was trouble in the offing.

Sir George Arthur sums up Kitchener's character in admirable fashion. "Excelling as he did as soldier and statesman," he writes,[2] "as administrator and diplomat, as linguist and archæologist, and proving his worth in other vocations, it is yet arguable whether any single element in his character, or any event in his career, stands out so boldly as to explain a domination which, without effort or intention, he exercised not only over those in close contact with him, but over millions whom he never saw. It is perhaps true that a singularly happy combination of noble qualities, a singularly fine record of notable achievements, made him the least ordinary of men; but behind all these was the man himself. No one could leave his company without the impression of a personality majestically solitary in an inexplicable distinction. . . . Kitchener's mind was as infinitely broad as it was accurately precise. He was

[1] Kitchener's left eye had been injured when he was a small child. This reduced control of its movement, and gave it a slight permanent cast.
[2] *Life of Lord Kitchener*, by Sir George Arthur, Vol. III, pp. 363-372.

above all the mathematician. . . . For this man nothing was too small, nothing too large, nothing too distant. He saw all, not as in a picture with the illusions of perspective, but as in a plan where dimensions and distances figure as they are and not as they seem. The solution of a problem over which others fluttered with many circuits, he was able to seize in a single swoop of intellect ; and while working on that one problem, he discerned with clear-cut certitude the further stages in the argument."

" From his earliest manhood," continues Sir George, " Kitchener seems to have regarded himself as merely the trustee of energies and capacities which were to be improved and spent in the service of his country. . . . For him, everything was dross compared with public duty. . . . Rigorous with himself, he was not inclined to be less exacting with others. . . . Good work never lacked his approval, but it was for the most part silent approval. . . . If there was little praise, there was infinite trust, and to those who served him the Chief gave loyalty as illimitable as he expected from them. . . . Although he disliked most social engagements, he still more disliked being entirely alone. . . . The deep seriousness of his disposition was lightened by a genuine sense of fun and a keen eye for the ridiculous. Wit in others he appreciated keenly, but he had no joy in the thrust of a poisoned weapon or the double meaning of an unseemly jest. . . . Incapable himself of any meanness, viewing all personal questions from the standpoint of public interest, he was ever reluctant to believe that an attack on himself could proceed from malice. Sensitive by nature, he had schooled himself, through long years, to be stoical under criticism. He welcomed all and any criticism from which something could be learned, but mere denunciation broke unavailing on his stately reserve. . . . Devotion to the Sovereign was a fixed point in his scheme of thought. . . . His life was based on religion in the primary sense of the word—the binding himself up with God ; and the sacramental truths in which he had steeped himself in early youth must have instilled in him—not less than the purity of mind—the reverence in which he held all sacred things. . . . It was said—and with perfect truth—of Kitchener that in life he knew no rest and in death he found no grave."

Eternal rest came to Earl Kitchener on June 5th, 1916. He had been Secretary of State for War since August 6th, 1914, and was on his way from Scapa Flow to Archangel in H.M.S. *Hampshire* to examine the situation in Russia. A German submarine had laid mines to the west of the Orkneys and Shetlands, and unhappily the cruiser struck one of these. A tempest was raging, and her escorting destroyers had been ordered back to port. Within a few minutes, she sank to the bottom, carrying with her almost every man on board, and among them the most famous Royal Engineer of all time. A great part of Kitchener's life had been spent in war. It ended in war, as Kitchener would have desired, and in the grandest setting imaginable, a war of the elements.

Looking back down the long vista of years to the far-distant time when Thomas Lacy rode with the Grand Vizier's army across the Sinai Desert to attack the French in Cairo, how many dramatic scenes are called to mind. Gordon in Central Africa ; Graham fighting at Tel el Kebir and on the Red Sea Coast ; Watson taking the Cairo Citadel almost single-handed ; fleets of whalers toiling up the Nile ; Gordon watching for the relief that never came ; Wilson leading a forlorn hope to rescue him ; Kitchener pushing southwards to Dongola ; Girouard building the Desert Railway ; Kitchener again at the Atbara, at Omdurman, and in bitter grief at the memorial service in Khartoum. We see Irrigation engineers controlling mighty floods ; Railway engineers finding a path through the Red Sea Hills ; Telegraph engineers floundering in the swamps of the Upper Nile. Surveyors are scaling the heights of the Abyssinian frontier ; builders are at work in Khartoum and Port Sudan ; administrators are caring for the welfare of the people. It is a picture of sustained and concentrated effort of which the Corps of Royal Engineers may well be proud.

THE END

INDEX.

The rank shown against a person is the highest rank mentioned in this book, not necessarily the highest rank attained by him. As the designation R.E. is inapplicable to an officer of the rank of Colonel or over, in such cases the letters are to be read as implying that the officer has held a commission in the Royal Engineers.

A

Abbasia, *observatory*, **465–7**—*operations at, in* 1882, **49–51**

Abbas Pasha I. *Abbasia* Observatory, **466**—*Viceroy* of Egypt, 1848, **19, 22, 366, 367**

Abbas Pasha Hilmi, *deposition*, **541**—*Khedive* of Egypt, 1892-1914, **19, 309, 536, 540**—*opening* of Port Sudan, **499, 500**—*relations* with Cromer and Kitchener, **541, 542**

Abd el Kadir Pasha, Governor-General of Sudan, fortifies Khartoum, **129, 130, 133, 134**

Abdulla Amran Gaharid, railway reconnaissance, **392, 393**

Abercromby, Major-General Sir Ralph, *commdg.* British Forces in Egypt, 1801, **8–11, 464, 503**—*killed* **12, 465**

Abney, Capt. W. de W., R.E., observes transit of Venus at Thebes, **465**

Abu Hamed, *importance* during Atbara campaign, **201**—*operations* in 1897, **193–5, 197, 198**

Abu Klea, *battle*, **110, 111, 142**—*Buller retires to,* **117**

Abu Kru (Gubat), battle, **113, 115**

Abu Simbel, removal of dangerous rocks, **515–8**

Abu Qir (Aboukir), *feint* landing at, 1882, **31**—*landing* at, 1801, **8–10**—*surrender* to British Force, 1882, **51**

Abyssinia, *British* Mission to, **xi, 448**—*encroachments* in Sudan, **285, 448**—*Gordon's dealings* with, **524, 525, 528**—*inhabitants,* **450**—*Italian* campaign, **356**—*Menelik* intrigues with Khalifa, **249**—*relations* with Government of Sudan, **523**—*surveys,* **459**—*telegraphic* communications, **433**

Adair, Lieut. H. B. N., R.E., Nile expedition, **93**

Adams, Capt. A., R.E., Agent, Delta Light Railways, **413**

Adowa, Italian defeat in 1896 and victory in 1935, **149**

Aeroplanes, *Darfur* operations, **335**—*landing ground* at Sidi el Barrani, **358**

Afafit, action at, 1891, **84, 85**

Agriculture, Kitchener's interest in, **539, 540, 542**

Ahmed Fedil, *death* at Umm Debeikerat, 1899, **300**—*operations against,* **287–9, 291**—*operations* in Kordofan, **297–9,**

Aird, Sir John, *Aswan* dam, **239, 282**—*services to irrigation,* **385**

Air Services, Cape to Cairo, **xiii, 437, 438**

Akasha, *defences,* **161**—*dervish* forces at, **152**—*capture* by Hunter, 1896, **155**—*importance* in Dongola expedition, **160–2**—*railway* at and near, **119, 182**—*temperature,* **160**

Alexandria, *battles* for, 1801, **10, 11**—*blockade* by British, 1801, **13, 17, 26**—*bombardment* by British fleet, **26**—*capture* by Hutchinson, 1801, **17, 18**—*capture* by Napoleon, **3**—*foundation* by Alexander the Great, **473**—*harbour, see* Alexandria, port and harbour—*irrigation,* **360, 367**—*landing* at, 1807, **19**—*massacre* of Christians, **26, 52**—*operations* at, 1807, **20**—*operations* at, 1882, **30–2, 36**—*plan* of, **17, 464**—"*Pompey's pillar,*" **503**—*sea defences,* **30**—*Turkish attack,* **3**

Alexandria, port and harbour, *progress* under Girouard, **365, 408, 410**—*state* in 1882, **22**—*Stokes's report,* 1879, **535**

Alford, Lieut. C. S. L., joint author with Sword of *The Egyptian Soudan, Its Loss and Recovery,* **111, 158, 257, 281**

Ali, son of the Sherif of Mecca, raises revolt against Turks, **324, 325**

Ali Dinar, *defeat and death,* 1916, **336**—*revolt,* **333–6**—*ruler* of Darfur, **301**

Alison, Major-General Sir Archibald, *commdg.* brigade in operations in 1882, **27, 30**—*lands* at Alexandria, **26**—*trial* of Arabi, **51**

Allen, Dr. Bernard M., *Gordon and the Sudan* referred to, **59, 114, 115, 123, 124, 128, 132, 444, 524**—*Gordon in China,* **127**—*help* acknowledged, **xvi, 137, 138**

Allenby, Gen. Lord, *campaign* in Palestine and Syria, **322, 325, 328, 511**—*High Commissioner,* Egypt, **342, 411, 532**

Ambigol Wells, *defence* by Ferrier, **108**—*railway* reaches, **177**

Anderson, Lieut. C. F., R.E., Suakin, 1896, **86, 154**

547

Anderson, Capt. H. S., **R.E.**, builds house at Akobo, **345**
Anderson, Lieut. S. **R.E.**, survey in Palestine, **508**
Anderson, Lieut. W. F., **R.E.**, Western Frontier, 1935-6, **356**
Andrews-Speed, Lieut. H. S., **R.E.**, Egypt, 1882, **29**
Anstruther, Lieut. R. W., **R.E.**, Egypt, 1882, **29, 45**
Arabia, Egyptian troops in, **307**
Arabi Pasha (Ahmed Arabi) Col., Egyptian Army, *defence* of Tel el Kebir, **39, 40, 42, 46**—*flight* to Cairo, **48, 49**—*position* at Kafr el Douwar, **30**—*rebellion* of 1882, **23, 25-7, 31, 34, 38**—*surrender*, **51**—*trial* and condemnation, **51, 52**
Arab revolt, against Turks, **xi, 323, 324**
Archæology, *Egypt*, **503-7, 512-20**—*Palestine*, **507-12**
Ardagh, Major-General Sir John, **R.E.**, *armoured train*, **44**—*at War Office*, **446, 447, 467**—*base* commdt., Nile expedition, **89, 93**—*C.R.E. Alexandria*, **30**—*Egypt*, 1882, **29**—*Red Sea* Littoral, 1884, **60, 65**
Aref Lebib, Yuzbashi, operations against Senussi, **330, 332**
Arish, El, *convention* of, **3-7**—*departure* of Turkish troops for, **7**—*evacuation*, 1914, **314**—*fortification* of, **8**—*railway reaches*, **326**—*reoccupation*, 1916, **327**—*Turkish troops* at, **14**
Arkwright, Major L. A., **R.E.**, Omdurman campaign, **206, 246, 248, 250, 252, 261**
Armitage, Capt. N. A., **R.E.**, Western Frontier, 1935-6, **356**
Armoured trains and trucks, *Egypt*, 1882, **43**—*operations* in 1919, **411**—*Red Sea* Littoral, 1885, **77**—*Suez Canal* defences, **325**
Armstrong, Sergt., **R.E.**, survey in Palestine, **509, 511**
Army, Egyptian, old, *composition* and *strength*, **25**—*disbanded*, 1882, **52, 53**—*operations* in 1882, **25-51**
Army, Egyptian, reconstituted, 1882, *Arab* Battalion, **288, 289**—*artillery*, **162, 169, 195, 214, 250, 261, 264, 271, 279**—*British officers* with, **53**—*camel corps*, **91, 250, 254, 262, 264, 268, 271, 274, 298, 324, 335, 337, 339, 342**—*camel transport* corps, **307, 308**—*clothing* and equipment, **480**—*Eastern Arab* Corps, **304, 339, 341**—*Equatorial battalion*, **304, 339**—*field* company, **308**—*formation*, training and progress, **xi, 52, 147, 324, 339**—*Irregular Sudanese battalion*, **298**—*machine-gun* batteries, **324, 339**—*mounted infantry*, **339**—*part in Great War*, **307, 308**—*railway battalion*, see Railway Battalion—*reduction*, **304**—*sapper* companies, **323**—*Sudanese* Sapper Section, **334-8**—*Western Arab* Corps, **339**—*Works Dept.* companies, **203, 207, 473**—1st Egyptian Battalion, **169, 180, 250**—2nd Egyptian Battalion, **162, 214, 250, 292, 298**—3rd Egyptian Battalion, **162, 195, 214, 250, 342**—4th Egyptian Battalion, **101, 162, 214, 250, 342**—5th Egyptian Battalion, **169, 250**—7th Egyptian Battalion, **162, 176, 179, 187, 199, 214, 250**—8th Egyptian Battalion, **162, 214, 250**—9th Sudanese Battalion, **156, 161, 162, 195, 201, 214, 250, 289, 297, 298**—10th Sudanese Battalion, **161, 162, 195, 197, 214, 218, 250, 287, 289, 290, 342, 454, 456**—11th Sudanese Battalion, **161, 162, 195, 214, 250, 271, 275, 279, 281, 283, 284, 342, 344**—12th Sudanese Battalion, **161-3, 214, 250, 289**—13th Sudanese Battalion, **161, 162, 214, 250, 279, 281, 284, 285, 289, 297, 298, 300**—14th Sudanese Battalion, **214, 250, 292**—15th Egyptian Battalion, **169, 250**—16th Egyptian Battalion, **288**—17th Egyptian Battalion, **250**—18th Egyptian Battalion, **234, 250**
Arnold, Lieut.-General Sir J. R., **R.E.**, Egypt, 1801, **9, 15**
Arthur, Sir George, help acknowledged, **xvi, 297**—*Life of Lord Kitchener* referred to, **54, 94, 148, 151, 203, 213, 215, 226, 270, 281, 292, 308, 510, 529, 531, 540, 541, 542, 544, 545**—*Life of Lord Wolseley*, **89**
Askwith, Lieut. W. B., **R.E.**, killed by accident, Red Sea Littoral, 1884, **68, 71**
Asser, Gen. Sir J. J., *formation* of Sudanese Sapper Section, **305, 490**—*improvements* in works services, **489**
Aswan, *armoured cable*, **104**—dam, see Aswan Dam
Aswan dam, *construction*, **383**—*heightening*, **383-5, 468, 542**—*proposals*, **148, 175, 369, 380, 382, 384**—*submergence* of Philæ, **519**
Atbara, *battle* of, **208-20**—*campaign*, see Atbara campaign—*dervish position*, **208, 212**—*post* and *camp*, see Atbara, post and camp—*river*, see Atbara River
Atbara campaign, 1897-98, *general* situation, **207-21**—*plan* and preparations, **192**—*results*, **221, 447**
Atbara, post and camp, *dockyard*, **205**—*established*, **201**—*headquarters*, *engineering* dept., Sudan Government Railways, **341, 401**—*mutiny*, **341**—*troops* at, **208**
Atbara River, *bridge*, **294, 295**—*description*, **210, 295, 362**—*importance* in irrigation, **361**
Atteridge, Capt. Hilliard, correspondent, *Daily Chronicle*, *Towards Khartoum*, ref. **157, 179, 180, 519**
Attree, Capt. F. W. T., **R.E.**, Suakin, 1886, **79**
Austin, Brig.-General H. H., **R.E.**, *Among Swamps and Giants in Equatorial Africa* referred to, **452, 455**—*expedition* to Lake Rudolf, **448**—*exploration* on Sudan-Abyssinia boundary, **447, 449, 452-6, 463, 469**

Australian and New Zealand troops, *Australian contingent, Red Sea Littoral*, 1885, **70**—*defence* of Suez Canal, **311, 312**—*field companies*, **313, 319**

B

Bagnold, Col. A. H., **R.E.**, *Nile* expedition, **93, 104, 106-8**—*salvage* of Rameses statue, **512-4**

Bahr el Ghazal, *exploration*, **285**—*inhabitants*, **429**—*occupation*, **301**—*swamps*, **361, 421, 422, 429**—*trouble* in 1919, **341**

Baker, Sir Benjamin, *Aswan* dam, **381-4**—*services* to irrigation, **385**

Baker, Sir Samuel, *Albert Nyanza*, referred to, **471**—*brings* out *Ismailia*, **133**—*exploration* in Sudan, **442, 444**—*founds* Taufikia, **418**—*Governor* of Equatorial Province, **58, 99, 125, 129, 350, 441, 522**—*suggests* Aswan dam, **380**—*visits* Khartoum, **471**

Baker, Major-General Valentine, *begins* defences of Suakin, **79, 80**—*defeat* at Et Teb, **58**—*first* Sirdar, 1881, **52**—*head* of Egyptian Gendarmerie, **58**—*second action* of Et Teb, **62**

Baldwin, Lieut. P. B., **R.E.**, Egypt, 1882, **29, 46**

Ballard, Brig.-General C. R., *Kitchener* quoted, **204, 293**

Ballooning, military, Red Sea Littoral, 1885, **74**

Baratier, Capt., French Army, part in Fashoda incident, **282, 286**

Baring, Major, see Cromer, Lord.

Barker, Major-General Sir George, **R.E.**, Egypt, 1882, **28**

Barklie, Capt. R. M., **R.E.**, Nile expedition, **93**

Barnes, Col. L. E., **R.E.**, A.A.G., Egypt, 1933, **355**

Bassett, Lt.-Col. T. P., **R.E.**, Suez Canal defences, **313, 314, 327**

Bate, Capt. C. McG., **R.E.**, Red Sea Littoral, 1885, **71, 79, 81**

Batn el Hagar, *description*, **178**—*penetration*, **91, 165**—*position*, **159**

Bayuda desert, *desert column*, **91, 119**—*exploration and survey*, **459**

Beatty, Admiral of the Fleet Earl, *Atbara* campaign, **198, 214**—*battle* of Hafir, **169**—*Dongola* expedition, **160, 185**—*expedition* to Fashoda, **279**—*Omdurman* campaign, **250**

Bell, Lieut. A. F., **R.E.**, Western Frontier, 1935—36, **356**

Belliard, Gen., French commdr. in Cairo, 1801, **13, 14, 16**

Bennet, Capt. F. W., **R.E.**, *Egypt*, 1882, **29**—*Nile* expedition, **93, 104, 108, 438**—*Report on Army Telegraphs, Nile expedition*, **106**

Berber, *barracks*, **480**—*capture* by dervishes, 1884, **66, 108, 132**—*capture* by Hunter, 1897, **200, 201**—*evacuated* by dervishes, **193, 199**—*Gordon* at, **127**—*military* importance, **200, 205**—*route* to Suakin opened, 1897, **202, 207**—*suggested advance* to, from Suakin, 1884, **65, 129**

Beresford, Capt. Lord Charles, R.N., commdg. Naval brigade, 1884, **92**—*dash* for Khartoum, **115, 116, 280**—*with desert* column, **109, 112, 114**

Beresford, Capt. C. F. C., **R.E.**, Red Sea Littoral, 1885, **70, 77**

Besant, Sir Walter, *Twenty-one Years' Work in the Holy Land*, **508, 509**

Bilbeis, *operations* at, 1801, **3, 5, 7, 14**—*operations* near, 1882, **48, 49**

Bingay, Col. H. L., **R.E.**, *Chief Engineer, Egypt*, 1932–36, **354, 355**—*help* acknowledged, **xvi**

Birch, Gen. J. F., **R.E.**, Egypt, 1801, **9, 15**

Black, Sergt., **R.E.**, *survey* in Palestine, **509, 511**

Blackburn, Capt. J. E., **R.E.**, *battle* of Ginnis, **119**—*Egypt*, 1882, **29**—*Nile* expedition and river column, **109, 118**

Blakeney, Brig.-Gen. R. B. D., **R.E.**, *Atbara* campaign, **211**—*battle* of Hafir, **170**—*battle* of Omdurman, **263, 264, 268, 270, 276**—*Dongola* expedition, **86, 153, 154, 173, 177, 180, 181, 184, 185**—*Egyptian State railways*, **408, 410-12, 537**—*Great War*, **313, 325**—*help* acknowledged, **238**—*notes re* Girouard, **173, 174, 226, 409**—*notes re* vultures, **197**—*Omdurman* campaign, **211, 253, 257, 261, 273**—*Suakin*, 1896, **81, 86**—*Wadi Halfa*-Abu Hamed *railway*, **227, 228**

Blood, Gen. Sir Bindon, **R.E.**, *Egypt*, 1882, **28, 32, 35, 47**—*Foreword* to *The Military Engineer in India*, **vii**

Blue Nile, *bridge* at Khartoum, **404**—*expeditions* up, 278, 287—*importance* in irrigation, **361, 362, 383, 386**—*river wall* at Khartoum, **480**

Blunt, Lieut. W. S., **R.E.**, *Gallipoli* campaign, **318, 330**—*operations* against Senussi, **330-2**—*Sinai* operations, **323**—*works* in Sudan, **488**

Boats, for Nile expedition, **90, 96, 97**

Bond, Maj.-Gen. Sir Francis G., **R.E.**, Egypt, 1882, **29, 45, 46**

Bond, Major R. J., **R.E.**, Egypt, 1882, **28**

Bonham-Carter, Lieut. H., **R.E.**, Red Sea Littoral, 1885, **71**

Borelli Bey, *La Chute de Khartoum*, referred to, **133-6, 138**

Boulnois, Capt. P. K., **R.E.**, Sudan-French Equatorial Africa boundary, **464**

Boundaries, *Kenya*-Abyssinia, **457**—*Sudan*-Abyssinia, **447-51, 457**—*Sudan*-Eritrea, **449, 456**—*Sudan*-French Equatorial Africa, **464**—*Sudan*-Uganda, **462**

Bowles, Lieut. F. G., **R.E.**, Red Sea Littoral, 1885, **71**

Bowman-Manifold, Major-General Sir M. G. E., **R.E.**, *Atbara* campaign, **196,**

199, 209–11, 218, 242, 243—*battle* of Atbara, 218, 243—*battle* of Firket, 162, 164, 165, 189—*battle* of Hafir, 170—*battle* of Omdurman, 263, 267, 269—Dongola expedition, 86, 153–5, 160, 166, 170, 173, 176, 186–8, 191—*help* to railways, 177, 181—*meets* Capt. Baratier, 286—*meets* Cromer, 292—*telegraphs*, Red Sea to Berber and Kassala, 245—*telegraphs*, Wadi Halfa—Abu Hamed railway, 230, 243—Suakin, 1895, 81

Boyce, A. A. R., surveys in Sudan, 462, 464

Boys' Company and Training School, formation and organization, 343, 348, 351–3

Brackenbury, Col. H., *evacuation of Dongola*, 118—*Nile* expedition and river column, 92, 106, 117

Bremner, Lieut. A. G., **R.E.**, Suakin, 1896, 86

Bridges, *Atbara*, 239—*Blue Nile*, at Khartoum, 404—*floating*, Suez Canal, 312, 319—*flying*, Sudan, 347—*White Nile*, at Khartoum, 490—*White Nile*, at Kosti, 404, 405

Bright, Capt. R. G. T., with Austin's expedition, 448, 449, 452–6

British Army of Occupation, *function during Great War*, 307—*reasons* for maintenance, 53—*strength*, 53

British Cavalry, *Egypt*, 1882, and pursuit to Cairo, 36, 45, 48–50—*4th Dragoon Guards*, 50, 51—*10th Hussars*, 59—*19th Hussars*, 59—*21st Lancers*, 249, 261, 262, 265, 271

British garrison, *function during Great War*, 307—*in Egypt*, 358—*in Sudan*, 339, 342—*reasons for maintenance, and strength*, 53

British Infantry, *Argyll and Sutherland Highlanders*, 342—*Berkshires*, 71–3—*Black Watch*, 62, 63—*Cameron Highlanders*, 206, 213, 216, 217, 249, 279–81—*Connaught Rangers*, 284, 285—*Duke of Cornwall's Light Infantry*, 34—*Gordon Highlanders*, 62—*Guards, Brigade of*, 34, 70, 76, 110, 249, 263, 275—*King's Royal Rifle Corps*, 34—*Lancashire Fusiliers*, 249—*Leicesters*, 342, 343—*Lincolns*, 206, 213, 216, 217, 249, 271—*North Staffords*, 149, 153, 156, 158, 165, 168—*Northumberland Fusiliers*, 206, 249—*Rifle Brigade*, 249—*Royal Sussex*, 98, 114—*Royal Warwicks*, 206, 213, 216, 217, 249—*South Staffords*, 95, 98—*York and Lancaster Regiment*, 34

Broadwood, Lt.-Col. R. G., *Atbara campaign and battle of Atbara*, 214, 216—*Omdurman campaign and battle of Omdurman*, 250, 262, 264, 271

Brooke, Major A. de V., **R.E.**, Red Sea Littoral, 1885, 70

Brousson, Capt. A. G. H., **R.E.**, Public Works, Sudan, 491

Brown, Major Sir R. Hanbury, **R.E.**, *Inspector* of Irrigation, Cairo, 253, 501—*memoir*, 376—*memoir on Scott-Moncrieff*, 370—*memoir on Western*, 375—*Nile barrage*, 376, 377, 379, 380—*notes* on Willcocks's perennial irrigation, 381—*service* in Egypt, 375, 376, 381—*The Delta Barrage of Lower Egypt*, referred to, 364, 367, 376

Browne, Lieut.-General Sir James, **R.** (Bengal) **E.**, C.R.E., Indian Contingent, 1882, 28, 42, 43, 47

Brownlow, Lt.-Col. H. A., **R.** (Bengal) **E.**, service in India, 370

Brownrigg, Lieut. H. F., **R.E.**, Egypt, 1801, 9

Bryce, Major-General Sir Alexander, **R.E.**, Egypt, 1801, 9–11, 17, 18, 503, 504—*Plan of the Expedition to Alexandria*, referred to, 10

Buckland, Major-General Sir R. U. H., **R.E.**, battle of Gemmaiza, 84—Red Sea Littoral, 1885, 71

Bucknill, Major J. T., **R.E.**, letter *re* land torpedoes, 138

Bulfin, Major-General E. S., quells disturbances, 1919, 340, 411

Buller, Major-General Sir Redvers, **V.C.**, *Nile expedition and desert column*, 89, 92, 113, 118—*Red Sea Littoral*, 1884, 59, 63, 64—*suggested as comdr.*, Dongola expedition, 150

Burgoyne, Field-Marshal Sir John, **R.E.**, *blockade of Malta*, 9—*Egypt*, 1807, 19

Burleigh, Bennet, correspondent of *Daily Telegraph*, meets Kitchener at Ed Debba, 94—*Sirdar and Khalifa*, referred to, 216

Burnaby, Col. F. G., *killed at Abu Klea*, 111, 113—*Nile expedition and desert column*, 92, 109, 110

Burn-Clerk-Rattray, Col. P. R., **R.E.**, letter from Burn-Murdoch, 48

Burnett, Basil, *help* acknowledged, xvi, 482, 497—*Port Sudan*, 499—*Public Works, Khartoum*, 476, 488

Burn-Murdoch, Major B. F., *battle of Firket*, 162, 163—*design of Zafir*, 167—*skirmish near Akasha*, 161

Burn-Murdoch, Lieut. J., **R.E.**, Egypt, 1882, 29, 43—*capture of Zagazig*, 48, 49—*recommended for* **V.C.**, 42—*Tel el Kebir*, 42

Burton, Lieut. E. M., **R.E.**, Egypt, 1882, 29—*Nile expedition and desert column*, 93, 109, 110, 113—*Red Sea Littoral*, 1884, 60

Butler, Col. W. F., *Charles George Gordon*, 124—*Nile expedition*, 84, 89, 92, 97—*The campaign of the Cataracts*, 95—*Wadi Halfa*, 119

C

Caillard, Lieut. V. H. P., **R.E.**, Egypt, 1882, 29

Cairo, *British advance on*, 1801, 13, 15, 16—*British capture*, 1882, 33, 48–51—*capture by Napoleon*, 3—*citadel*, 49–51—*convention of*, 1801, 16—*military* outbreak, 1879, **24**—*operations* in and near, 1882, **33, 48–51**—*remodelling* by Kitchener, **540**—*R.E. Mess*, **54, 55**

Cambridge, H.R.H. The Duke of, *eulogy* of Kitchener, **94, 291**—*sees Gordon off*, **126**—*unveils* statue of Gordon, **145**

Cameron, Lieut. H. A., **R.E.**, Suakin, 1896, **86, 154**

Campaigns, *see* headings, Atbara campaign, Dongola expedition, Egyptian campaigns of 1801, 1807 and 1882, Great War, Nile expedition, Omdurman campaign. Minor campaigns are included in the heading belonging to the country, etc., in which they took place, *e.g.*, Darfur.

Canals, *Beheira*, **367, 373, 380**—*expenditure* on, **24**—*from* Damietta and Rosetta *barrages*, **367**—*from* Nile to Red Sea, **20, 361**—*Mahmudiya*, **20, 21, 30, 31**—*Menufiya*, **367, 373, 380**—*repair*, by *corvée*, **364, 366**—*Suez, see* Suez Canal—*Sweetwater*, **33–6, 38–42, 46, 48, 310, 321, 327**—*system*, **373**—*Taufikia*, **367, 380**

Capper, Brevet Col. T., *article* in *R.E. Journal*, **10**—*expedition* to Fashoda and Sobat, **279, 283, 285**

Cardew, Lieut. G., **R.E.**, Egypt, 1801, **9**

Carey, Capt. C. de B., **R.E.**, Egypt, 1882, **28, 35**

Cataracts, Nile, *Dongola* expedition, **153, 159, 166**—*fifth*, **200**—*first*, **101, 382**—*fourth*, **198, 199**—*Hannek*, **97**—*Kincaid's* report, **97**—*list* of, **96**—*Nile expedition*, **95, 99, 100, 103**—*second*, **95, 99, 103, 159, 166, 492**—*Semna*, **99**—*Tanjur*, **97, 99**

Cather, Capt. T. P., **R.E.**, Red Sea Littoral, 1885, **70, 76**

Cator, Lieut. E. H. S., **R.E.**, *battle* of Firket, **162**—*battle* of Hafir, **170**—*death* from enteric, **185, 225**—*Dongola* expedition, *railways*, **153, 173, 176, 177, 180, 189, 225**

Cecil, Major Lord Edward H., *Atbara* campaign, **210**—*expedition* to Fashoda, **279, 281, 282**—*Omdurman*, **246, 247**

Chaillé-Long, Lieut.-Col., American Army, with Gordon in Sudan, **441–3, 523**

Chancellor, Lieut.-Col., Sir John R., **R.E.**, *career*, **86**—*Suakin*, 1896, **86, 154**

Chase, Major J. H. L., **R.E.**, Sudan Defence Force, **351–3**

Chenevix-Trench, Lieut. R., **R.E.**, *telegraphs*, Sudan, **432–6**

Chermside, Lieut.-General Sir Herbert C., **R.E.**, *commands* infantry brigade, Egyptian Army, **53**—*defeats* dervishes at Gemai, **119, 120**—*defences* of Suakin, **79, 80**—*Governor-General*, Red Sea Littoral, **66, 67, 70, 72, 79, 493, 529**—*political* service, Egypt, 1882, **28, 29**

Chesney, General Sir G. T., **R.** (Bengal) **E.**, mention, **20**

Childers, Lieut. E. S. E., **R.E.**, *A.D.C.* to Wolseley, **29, 93, 98**

Chippindall, Lieut. W. H., **R.E.**, *joins* Gordon in Equatorial Province, **58, 442**—*surveys* in Sudan, **442–4, 523**—*visit* to Sheikh Barghut, **493**

Churchill, Rt. Hon. Winston S., *battle* of Omdurman, **256, 266, 268**—*remarks* on Aswan dam, **383**—*The River War* referred to, **108, 156, 162, 178, 195, 198, 201, 205, 219, 239, 243, 256, 266, 268, 281, 288, 292**

Clarke, Gen. Sir Andrew, **R.E.**, *organizes* military railway corps, **42**—*Suakin-Berber railway*, **68**—*Suez Canal*, **533, 536**

Clarke, Capt. George Sydenham, **R.E.**, afterwards Lord Sydenham of Combe, Egypt, 1882, **28, 29**—*Red Sea Littoral*, 1885, **70**—*remarks* on sea defences of Alexandria, **30**

Clarke, Major H. W., **R.** (Bengal) **E.**, *see* Wilberforce Clarke.

Clayton, Major A. G., **R.E.**, *battle* of Toski, 1889, **121**

Cleeve, Lieut. S. D., **R.E.**, *article* on Kafr el Dauwar, **31**—Egypt, 1882, **29**

Close, Col. Sir Charles, **R.E.**, *article Explorations and Excavations in Palestine*, **323, 507**

Cockburn, Capt. G. A., **R.E.**, Nile expedition, **93**

Collinson, Lieut.-Col., *commdg.* Egyptian brigade, Omdurman campaign, **250, 251, 261, 264, 267–9**—*relief* of Gedaref, **289**

Colvile, Col. H. E., *History of the Sudan Campaign*, referred to, **90, 92, 96, 110, 112**

Colville, Comdr. Hon. S. C. G., *battle* of Hafir, **169**—*navigation* of Nile, **160, 167, 168**

Colvin, Sir Auckland, *Controller*, 1882, **29**—*offer* to Scott-Moncrieff, **371**—*The Making of Modern Egypt*, **370**

Condenser Island, *see* Quarantine Island.

Conder, Capt. C. R., **R.E.**, *books* by, **510**—*Egypt*, 1882, **29, 38**—*survey* of Palestine, **465, 509–11**

Coningham, Lieut.-Col. A. E., **R.E.**, now A.E.C., *operations* with Nyima patrol, **305, 461**—*surveys* in Sudan, **460–3, 469, 483**

Connaught, Major-General H.R.H. The Duke of, *Aswan* dam, **383, 384**—*commdg.* 1st brigade, Egypt, 1882, **26**—*visits* Khartoum, **293**

Cook and Son, Thomas, transport problems, **90, 91, 156**

Corvée, abolition, **374, 378**—*description*, **364–6**

Cotton, *cultivation in Egypt*, **362, 363, 365, 374, 377, 407, 540, 542**—*cultivation in Sudan*, **402, 404, 532**

Cotton, Gen. Sir Arthur, **R.** (Madras) **E.**, *irrigation* in India, **368, 369**

Courtney, Major D. C., **R.E.**, Nile expedition and river column, **93, 97, 109, 118, 445**

Cowan, Lieut. W. H., R.N., expedition to Fashoda, 279, 282, 283, 285
Croghan, Capt. E., **R.E.**, Western Frontier, 1935-36, 356
Cromer, Lord, *commission* on Egyptian state railways, 410—*conference* on Luxor-Aswan railway, 241—*Consul-General*, 25, 121, 374, 395, 495, 536, 538—*correspondence* with Gordon, 88, 126, 129, 132, 138—*correspondence* with Kitchener, 150, 175, 180, 189, 201, 203, 204, 206, 212, 213, 232, 242-4, 248—*financial* regulations, 477—*Gordon College*, 292, 4.8—*inception* of Dongola expedition, 147, 149, 151—*interview* with Scott-Moncrieff, 378—*letter* to Lord Salisbury, 204—*Modern Egypt*, referred to, 34, 124, 141, 172, 193, 201, 212, 283, 302, 374—*opens* Port Sudan-Atbara railway, 399—*opinion* of Gordon, 124—*opinion* of Kitchener 165, 204, 222, 276, 293, 531, 537—*opinion* of Zubeir, 128—*relations* with Khedive, 541—*selection* of Girouard, 408—*Stokes's help*, 535—*Sudan telegraphs*, 416—*views* on administration of Sudan, 293, 294, 531—*views* on advance from Suakin, 65, 84, 88—*views* on destruction of Mahdi's tomb, 274—*views* on Fashoda incident, 283—*views* on gauge of Sudan railways, 226—*views* on Port Sudan, 495, 497—*views* on reconquest of Sudan, 192—*visits* to Omdurman and Khartoum, 292, 391—*Watson* on Lord Cromer and Sir Charles Wilson, 115
Crozier, Lieut. A. H., **R.E.**, with 2nd Company, Cairo, 253
Cunningham, Maj.-General Sir Alexander, **Bengal Engineers,** archæological research in India, 503
Curtis, Maj.-General Sir R. S., **R.E.**, Suakin, 1890, 81, 84
Cyprus, Kitchener's surveys, 53, 54, 511

D

Dale, Hon. Major W. H., **R.E.**, telegraphs, Sudan, 417, 421, 423-5, 429-31, 483
Damietta *barrage*, 363-7, 369, 373-9, 381—*surrender* of, 51
Danford, Col. B. W. Y., **R.E.**, *C.E.*, Egypt, 1927-30, 354—*M.T. in Sudan*, 304—*with expedition* in Nuba Hills, 305, 483—*works*, Sudan, 481, 482, 484, 486, 488
Darfur, *conquered* by Zubeir, 126—Gordon's expedition, 526—*reconquest*, xi, 307, 309, 333, 436—*Slatin* Governor of, 141—*under* Dinar Ali, 301, 333, 448
Darling, Lieut. C. H., **R.E.**, *Egypt*, 1882, 28, 43, 47—*Red Sea Littoral*, 1885, 71
Davenport, Major W. A., Hedjaz operations, 323, 325
David, Major E. F., R.M.L.I., Dongola expedition, 169, 198

Davis, Maj.-General, Red Sea Littoral, 1884, 59, 63
Day, Lieut. W. E., **R.E.**, works, Sudan, 488
De Coetlogon, Colonel, *commdg.* garrison at Khartoum, 127, 130, 131—*sent* by Gordon to Cairo, 128, 131
De Cosson, A. F. C., help acknowledged, 465
De Havilland, Lieut. T. F., **Madras Engineers,** *captured* by French privateer, 17—*survey* of Alexandria, 464, 465—*with Indian contingent* in Egypt, 1801, 16
De Lesseps, Ferdinand, *administration* of Suez Canal, 533-5—*construction* of Suez Canal, 21, 535—*protest re* use of canal for military purposes, 31
Dengkurs pyramid, demolition of, 346-8, 350
Dennett, Sergt., **R.E.**, telegraphs, Sudan, 189, 243, 245, 246, 248, 258, 415
Department of Military Works, Egyptian Army, *building* of Port Sudan, 497, 499—*company* in Darfur operations, 334—*disbandment*, 343, 491, 501—*field operations*, 305, 340, 341—*mobile section*, Suez Canal defences, 313—*mobile section*, with Senussi operations, 329, 330—*organization*, 484, 489, 490
Department of Public Works, Sudan, *attachment* of B.O's to, 344—*formation* in 1907 and development, 483, 484, 490, 491—*proposals*, 343
Department of Works, Sudan, *division* into Dept. of Mily. Works and Dept. of Public Works, *q.v.* 1907, 483, 484—*organized*, 303, 474—*personnel*, 483—*rebuilding* of Khartoum, 473, 474
Desert column, *battle* of Abu Klea, 111, 112—*battle* of Abu Kru, 113, 115—*plans*, 109, 115—*progress*, 109-11—*retirement*, 117
Dervish army, *distribution*, 1898, 207—*faulty strategy*, 193—*losses* at Omdurman, 271—*manœuvres* before Hafir, 169—*organization*, 1896, 156—*organization*, 1897, 194, 203
Dickie, Lieut. J. E., **R.E.**, Egypt, 1882, 29, 46
Dickinson, Capt. E., **R.E.**, *Egypt*, 1882, 29—*Red Sea Littoral*, 1885, 71
Dinkas, *appetite* for elephants, 422—*attacked* by Nuers, 350—*operations* against, 1919 and 1920, 340, 436
Dobbie, Lieut. A. W. G., **R.E.**, motoring in desert, 355
Dobbie, Brig. W. G. S., **R.E.**, commdg. Cairo infantry brigade, 1928-32, 355
Dobell, Lieut.-General Sir Charles, *attacks* Gaza, 434—*operations* in Sinai, 322
Done, Col. R. J., **R.E.**, *All Saints' Cathedral*, Khartoum, 486—*Director of Mily. Works*, Egyptian Army, 484, 486, 488—*Port Sudan*, 495—*works*, Sudan, 475, 476, 480, 482, 483
Dongola, *condition* in 1896, 171—*expedition, see* Dongola expedition.

Dongola expedition, 1896, *battle* of Firket, *q.v.*—*battle* of Hafir, *q.v.*—*capture* of Dongola, **170, 184**—*cholera,* **165, 166**—*conclusion,* **170, 171**—*dervish forces,* **151**—*Egyptian army* used for, **86, 149, 150**—*finance,* **147, 149**—*inception, progress* and *completion,* **147-72**—*Kitchener's appointment,* **150**—*losses,* **172**—*pause* and *subsequent advance,* **165, 166, 168**—*railways,* **155, 178**—*results,* **171**—*strength* and *composition* of British force, **168**—*telegraphs,* **155**—*transport,* **152, 153**
Dopping-Hepenstal, Lieut. L. J., R.E., Egypt, 1882, **29**
Dorward, Major J. F., R.E., *Egypt,* 1882, **29**—*Nile* expedition and desert column, **93, 97, 98, 109-11, 113**—*Red Sea Littoral,* 1884, **60**
Douglas, Lieut. W. S., R.E., telegraphs, Sudan, **417**
Drake, C. F. Tyrwhitt, *archæology* in Palestine, **509**—*death* at Jerusalem, **510**
Drake, Maj.-General J. M. C., R.E., Egypt, 1882, **28**
Drury Lowe, Maj.-General D. C., *battle* of El Mahuta, **34**—*commdg. cavalry,* 1882, **27**—*first action* of El Qassasin, **36, 37**—*pursuit* to Cairo, **42, 46, 48, 49-51**
Duchesne, Major C. C., R.E., commdt., engineer troops, Sudan Defence Force, 1929-30, **349, 351**
Dumbleton, Lieut. H. N., R.E., Nile expedition, **93**
Dundas, Lieut. Hon. R. L., R.E., *deciphers* "Pompey's pillar," **503, 504**—*Egypt,* 1801, **9, 15, 17**
Dupuis, C. E., *forms* Sudan branch of Egyptian Irrigation Service, **383**—*services* in irrigation, **385**

E

Earle, Maj.-General W., *commdg.* river column, **109, 117, 196**—*commdg.* troops, Nile, **92, 95**—*killed* at El Kirbekan, **117**
Edgeworth, Lieut.-Col. K. E., R.E., *Sudan posts* and *telegraphs,* **437**—*works,* Sudan, **481, 484, 488**
Edwards, Lieut.-General Sir J. Bevan, R.E., *Red Sea Littoral,* 1885, **70**
Egerton, Lieut. C. H., R.E., works, Sudan, **488**
Egypt, bankruptcy in 1879, **369**—*disturbances* in 1919, **339, 411, 412**—*independence,* **412**—*irrigation, q.v.*—*list of rulers,* **19**—*political unrest,* **536, 538, 541**—*survey,* **465-9**—*Turkish suzerainty abolished,* **309**
Egyptian campaign of 1801, *battles* near Alexandria, **10, 11**—*British landing,* **8-10**—*conclusion,* **11-18**—*Turko-French operations,* **3-8**
Egyptian campaign of 1807, narrative, **18-20**

Egyptian campaign of 1882, *battles* of El Qassasin, **36-9**—*battle* of Tel el Kebir, **34, 38-48, 65**—*bombardment* of Alexandria, **26**—*causes* of, **24-6**—*occupation* of Alexandria, **30-2, 36**—*pursuit* to Cairo, **48-51**—*R.E. officers* present, **28, 29**—*Wolseley in command,* **26**
Ehrlich, F., P.W.D., Port Sudan, **495, 496**
Elephants, trouble caused to telegraph lines, **416, 423, 428, 429, 431, 436**
Elgood, Lieut.-Colonel P. G., *Egypt and the Army* referred to, **309, 538**
Elkington, Lieut. G. E., R.E., Dongola expedition, **154, 156, 166, 167, 170, 177, 181**
Elphinstone, Maj.-General Sir Howard, R.E., C.R.E., Indian contingent, 1801, **16**
Elrington (Elrington-Bisset), Lieut. M., R.E., Egypt, 1882, **29**
Equatorial Province, *Emin Pasha* Governor, **527**—*Gordon* Governor, **522-4**
Erkowit, hill station of Suakin, **487**
Ewart, Brig.-General C. B., R.E., Red Sea Littoral, 1885, **70**
Eyre Coote, General, blockade and capture of Alexandria, 1801, **13, 17, 18**

F

Falls, Capt. C., joint author with MacMunn (*q.v.*) of *Military Operations, Egypt and Palestine.*
Farag Pasha, commdg. negro troops, Khartoum, under Gordon, **132, 143**
Farrer, Lord, commission and report on Egyptian state railways, **407, 410**
Fashoda, *bibliography* of incident, **281, 282**—*incident,* 1898, **xi, 278-87**—*name changed* to Kodok, **284**
Fead, Capt., military mission to Turkey, **6**
Feisul, Emir, raises revolt of Arabs against Turks, **324, 325**
Ferguson, Capt. F. A., R.E., telegraphs, Sudan, **431, 432, 435**
Ferrier, Maj.-General J. A., R.E., *defence* of Ambigol wells, **108**—*memoir* on Chermside, **66**—*Nile expedition,* **93, 101**—*railways,* **102, 103**
Firket, *battle* of, 1896, *dervish forces,* **152, 161-3**—*description,* **152, 161-5, 189**
Fitzgerald, Col. O. A. G., Military Secretary to Kitchener, **515, 541**
Fletcher, Lieut.-Col. Sir Richard, R.E., *capture* by French at Alexandria, **9, 18**—*career,* **6**—*military mission* to Turkey, **6, 7, 9**
Flinders Petrie, Prof. W. M., *archæology* in Palestine, **507**—*The Pyramids and Temples of Gizeh,* **505, 506**
Foley, Capt. A. C., R.E., *battle* of Gemmaiza, **84**—*battle* of Toski, **121**
Ford, E. Onslow, statues of Gordon, **144, 145**

Ford, Maj.-General W. H., **R.E.**, *Egypt*, 1801, **9, 15, 17**—*survey* of Alexandria, **465**
Fort Baker, defence, 1884, **61**
Fortescue, Hon. J. W., *History of the British Army* referred to, **10**
Foster, E. W. P., *irrigation*, **375, 377, 378**—*notes* on Willcocks's perennial irrigation, **381**
Foster, Lieut. H. J., **R.E.**, Egypt, 1882, **29, 45**
Fowle, Major F. E., **R.E.**, *action* during mutiny in Khartoum, **343**—*barracks* at Roseires, **491**—*formation* of boys' company, **344**—*operations* in Tabi Hills, 1922, **341**—*Sudan Defence Force*, commdg. engineer troops, **344, 345, 349, 491**
Fowler, J., *report* on Damietta and Rosetta barrages, **368**—*surveys*, Sudan military railways, **100**
Fox, Capt. C. L., **R.E.**, Sudan Defence Force, **351**
Francis, Capt. H. S., **R.E.**, Jebel Auleya dam, **386, 387**
Franklyn, Brig. H. E., commdg. Sudan Defence Force, 1935, **353**
Franklin, Lieut., E.I.Co.'s Army, Military Mission to Turkey, **6**
Fraser, Maj.-General M'Kenzie, commdg. expedition to Egypt, 1807, **19, 20**
Fraser, Maj.-General Sir Thomas, **R.E.**, *Egypt*, 1882, **29, 45**—*Nile expedition*, **93**—*service* in Egyptian Army, **53**
French Equatorial Africa, *Egyptian Army* takes part in operations, **307, 336**—*boundary* commission with Sudan, **464**
Friederichs, Lieut. D. A., **R.E.**, Omdurman campaign, **206, 250, 252**
Friend, Maj.-General Sir Lovick B., **R.E.**, *assists* Garstin, **501**—*battle* of Omdurman, **265**—*Director of Works*, Sudan, **479, 480, 482, 485**—*help* acknowledged, **474**—*later career*, **480**—*Omdurman* campaign, **239, 252**
Fuller, Col. Commdt. C. G., **R.E.**, commdg. Canal infantry brigade, **355**

G

Gakdul wells, *desert column* at, **110**—*Jaalin* rally at, **194**—*retirement* to and evacuation, **117**
Galloway, Alexander, and two sons, John and Thomas Jefferson, *proposal for canal*, Nile to Red Sea, **20**—*survey* of railway, Cairo to Suez, **22**
Gambela, *Austin's visit*, **453**—*description*, **433**—*wireless* station, **433, 434**
Gamble, Capt. R. N., with expedition to Fashoda and Sobat, **279, 285**
Gandy, Col. H. G., **R.E.**, *telegraphs, Sudan*, **431, 432**—*writes* instances of correspondence, **420**
Ganneau, Clermont, description of Kitchener, **510, 511**

Gardiner, Lieut. A., **R.E.**, Suakin, 1896, **81, 86**
Garner, Dr. J., with Austin's expedition, **454-6**
Garstin, Sir William E., *Aswan dam*, **149, 381, 382**—*introduction* to Willcocks's perennial irrigation, **381**—*Nile barrage*, **379**—*report, Egypt No. 5*, **284**—*report, the Basin of the Upper Nile*, **383**—*service* in irrigation, **375, 378, 385, 480**—*Under-Secretary*, **377, 504**—*views* on Mougel Bey, **376**—*visit* to Sudan and White Nile, **293, 383, 422, 451, 468**
Gatacre, Lieut.-General Sir William, *battle* of Atbara, **215, 216**—*commdg.* British brigade, Sudan, **207, 208, 210-3**—*commdg.* British division, Sudan, **249, 261, 267**
Gedaref, *capture* by Parsons, **287, 288**—*relief* by Rundle, **289, 475**—*visited* by Thwaites, **485**
Gedge, Capt. H. J., R.N., Port Sudan, **495, 496**
Gemai, *battle* of, **120**—*boats* assembled, 1884, **95, 96**—*Dongola expedition*, **165**
Geological Survey, *measurements* of Blue and White Niles, **383**—*progress* under Lyons, **154, 466, 467, 519**
George V. H.M. King, visit to Port Sudan, **500**
George, Corpl. R.E., telegraphs, Sudan, **425, 430**
Germain, Commdt., French Army, part in Fashoda incident, **282, 283, 286**
Gessi, Romolo, *assembles* steamship *Ismailia*, **133**—*career*, **523**—*defeats* and kills Suleiman, son of Zubeir, **126, 527**—*on Gordon's staff*, **441, 444, 445, 523**
Gill, Capt. W. J., **R.E.**, *Egypt*, 1882, **29**—*murdered* in Sinai desert, **32, 33, 509**
Ginnis, battle of, **119**
Giraffes, trouble caused to telegraph lines by, **416, 423, 428, 436**
Girouard, Maj.-General Sir. E. Percy C., **R.E.**, *Atbara* campaign, **211**—*battle* of Hafir, **170**—*career*, **173, 174, 403**—*Great War*, **309**—*Nubian desert railway*, **184, 186, 198, 226-30, 232, 234, 238, 240-2**—*Omdurman* campaign, **211**—*President*, Egyptian state railways, **174, 241, 253, 295, 407-10, 413, 438**—*railways*, Dongola expedition, **160, 166, 170, 173, 176, 177, 181, 183, 185, 186, 188**—*South Africa*, **409, 410, 413**
Gladstone, Rt. Hon. W. E., *Egyptian policy*, **26**—*Sudan policy*, **129, 132**—*Suez Canal*, **533**—*suppression of news re* Gordon, **114**
Godby, Brig.-General C., **R.E.**, *battle* of Toski, **121**—*Chief Engineer*, Egyptian Army, **148**—*Red Sea Littoral*, 1885, **71, 73**
Godsal, Lieut. W. C., **R.E.**, Egypt, 1882, **29**

Gondokoro, headquarters, Equatorial Province, **441, 522**
Goodfellow, Lieut.-General Samuel, **Bombay Engineers**, with Indian contingent, Egypt, 1801, **16**
Goodwin, Lieut. H. E., **R.E.**, Egypt, 1882, **29**
Gordon, Maj.-General Charles George, *Abyssinian visit*, **528**—*advises* stopping Egypt-Sudan railway, **100, 101, 407**—*archæological* researches in Palestine, **511, 512, 528**—*arrangements* with relieving force, **91, 128, 129**—*attempts to relieve, see* Nile expedition—*career, earlier*, **441, 533, 534**—*character*, **122-5, 529**—*death*, **116, 117, 143, 144**—*decision to rescue*, **67, 88, 95**—*defence of Khartoum*, **130, 134-9, 529**—*description*, **122, 131**—*dispatches*, **68, 108, 114, 128, 132**—*duties* during siege, **140**—*establishes* dockyard, Khartoum, **133**—*fatalism*, **525**—*Governor of Equatorial province*, 1874-77, **58, 441, 443, 446, 522-4**—*Governor-General of Sudan*, 1877-79, **525-8**—*Governor-General of Sudan*, 1884-85, **57, 59, 65, 125, 126, 128, 141, 442, 443, 529**—*journals*, **125, 127, 136, 138-42**—*land-mines*, **138, 139**—*last journey* to Khartoum, **122, 127**—*memorials*, **144, 475, 481, 486**—*raises force* of negro troops, **132**—*sends* Stewart downstream, **108, 140**—*surveys and travels* in Sudan and Uganda, **125, 350, 441, 442, 444, 445**—*task* in Sudan, **88, 526**—*telegraphs*, **258**—*visits* Ismail, **523, 524, 527**—*work at Suakin*, **80**
Gordon, Capt. C. H., **R.E.**, Egypt, 1882, **29**
Gordon, Lieut.-Col. W. S., **R.E.**, *Atbara campaign*, **211, 220, 238**—*battle* of Toski, **121**—*destruction of Mahdi's tomb*, **274**—*Director* of Stores, Cairo, **147, 167, 420**—*Dongola expedition*, **153**—*first sight of Khartoum*, **254**—*Omdurman campaign*, **211, 246, 247, 252, 259, 265, 275, 276, 290**
Gordon College, *building*, **478, 480**—*education*, **354, 478, 479**—*foundation* laid by Cromer, **292, 478**—*opening*, **478**—*site*, **137, 478, 482**
Gorringe, Lieut.-General Sir George F., **R.E.**, *after Omdurman*, **279, 290, 296, 474**—*Atbara* campaign, **195-7, 200, 201, 204, 211, 220**—*battle* of Firket, **162**—*battle* of Hafir, **170**—*battle* of Omdurman, **262, 265, 266**—*buildings at Wad Medani*, **485**—*builds Atbara fort*, **205**—*builds causeway at Trinkitat*, **85**—*Dongola expedition*, **153, 154, 160, 166, 170, 176, 186**—*Gordon College*, **478**—*Governor, Sennar province*, **485, 532**—*help* acknowledged, **83, 152, 493**—*Omdurman campaign*, **251, 252, 257, 258, 276**—*operations against Ibrahim Wad Mahmud*, **304, 457**—*operations in Kordofan*, **297-9, 301**—*rebuilding of Khartoum*, **473-5**—*reconnoitres Berber-Obak-Sinkat route*, **245, 391**—*service in railways*, **192, 193, 224, 229, 232, 234**—*South Africa*, **475, 532**—*water-supply and works at Suakin*, **81, 86, 206**—*works department* companies, **206, 207, 473**

Gorst, Sir Eldon, British Agent and Consul-General, 1907-11, **536, 537, 539**
Gowlland, Col. G. C., **R.E.**, *Darfur expedition*, **334, 337**—*forms field company*, **338**—*works*, Sudan, **488**
Gracey, Capt. Thomas, **R.E.**, Egypt, 1882, **29**
Graham, Lieut. C., **R.E.**, Egypt, 1801, **9, 15, 17**
Graham, Maj.-General Sir Gerald, V.C., **R.E.**, *action of El Magfar*, **34**—*battle* of Tel el Kebir, **41, 546**—*biographies*, **27**—*career*, **27, 28**—*commdg.* brigade, Egypt, 1882, **26, 27, 29, 32, 34, 41, 42, 45, 54**—*first action of El Qassasin*, **36-8**—*memoirs*, **27**—*Red Sea Littoral*, 1884, **59, 62-6, 88, 92, 93, 129, 546**—*Red Sea Littoral*, 1885, **68-70, 72, 74, 77-9, 546**—*sees Gordon off*, **122, 127**—*views* on advance, Suakin to Berber, **88**
Grant, Maj.-General Sir Philip. G., **R.E.**, *Dir. Mily Works*, **488-90**—*formation of Sudanese sapper section*, **305**—*Suez Canal defences*, **319, 488**
Grant, Lieut.-General Sir Robert, **R.E.**, commdg. Abu Fatima district, **118**
Grant, Major Suene, **R.E.**, Suakin, 1896, **81, 86**
Great War, part played by Egyptian troops, **xi, 307**
Green, Brevet Col. A. O., **R.E.**, *C.R.E.*, Cairo, **253**—*Egypt*, 1882, **28**—*Red Sea Littoral*, 1884, **60**—*reports* on Sudan railways, **228, 239, 240**—*wounded at Et Teb*, **62**
Greig, Lieut. J. P. S., **R.E.**, survey in Sinai, **323**
Grenfell, Maj.-General Sir Francis W., *battle* of Gemmaiza, **84**—*battle* of Toski, **120, 121**—*commdg.* army of occupation, **150, 193, 203, 204, 213, 239, 254**—*Nile* expedition, **92**—*Sirdar, Egyptian army*, **118, 119**—*visit* to Omdurman, **285**
Grew, E. S., *Field-Marshal Lord Kitchener* referred to, **94, 539**
Griffith, Major D. M., **R.E.**, operations against Senussi, **330, 331**
Grover, Major G. E., **R.E.**, Red Sea Littoral, 1885, **70**
Gunboats, *Atbara* campaign, **198, 202, 204, 220, 238**—*Dongola expedition*, **153, 167**—*expedition* to Fashoda and Sobat, **279-85**—*Omdurman* campaign, **250, 252, 255, 259**—*R.E. officers* in command of, **256, 259**
Gwynn, Major-General Sir Charles W., **R.E.**, *Abyssinian-Eritrean* frontier commission, **402**—*anecdote re* dead platelayer, **400, 401**—*asst. supt.*

Survey dept., **456, 458, 459, 469**—*Imperial Policing*, referred to, **339, 343**—*in Abyssinia*, **459**—*notes* on Kitchener, **476**—*Sinai* operations, **322**—*Sudan-Abyssinian* boundary, **448-52, 463**—*Sudan-Eritrean* boundary, **456, 457**

Gwynne, Right Reverend Dr. Llewelyn, *foundation* of All Saints' Cathedral, Khartoum, **486, 487**—*installed* Bishop of Jerusalem, **542**

H

Hafir, *battle* of, **169, 170, 184**

Hake, A. Egmont, *The Journals of Major-General C. G. Gordon at Khartoum*, referred to, **125, 134, 136, 138-42**

Halfaya, *capture* of, Omdurman campaign, **259**—*defeat* of Stewart at, **132**—Gordon's communications cut, **129**—*railway* reaches, **294, 296**

Hall, Lieut.-Col. G. C. M., **R.E.**, *Egyptian state railways*, **241, 407, 408, 412**—*railway extension* to Halfaya, **294, 392**—*railways*, Omdurman campaign, **253, 276**—*Suez Canal* defences, **313, 325, 410**—*Wadi Halfa-Kerma railway*, **225, 229, 231, 232**

Hamilton, General A. F., **R.** (Madras) **E.**, with Indian contingent, Egypt, 1882, **28, 47, 48**

Hamley, Lieut.-General Sir Edward, divisional commr., Egypt, 1882, **26, 32**

Hammill, Comdr. T. F., R.N., accompanies Sir Evelyn Wood up Nile, **95, 96**

Hammuda, Emir, commdg. dervishes opposing Dongola expedition, **156, 161, 162, 164, 165**

Handfield, Lieut. J., **R.E.**, Egypt, 1801, **9, 15, 17**—*survey* of Alexandria, **465**

Handub, *occupation* and subsequent evacuation, 1885, **71, 75-8**—*reoccupation* by Osman Digna, **79, 83**

Harrington, Col. Sir John, British *representative*, Addis Ababa, **448, 451, 452, 457**—*map* of Sudan-Abyssinian boundary, **449, 450, 458**

Harrison, General Sir Richard, **R.E.**, *committee* on telegraph units, **44**—Egypt, 1882, **28, 29**—*Nile* expedition, **93, 97**—*reorganizes* railway service, Sudan railway, **101, 102**—*story* about, **226**

Harrison, Lieut., asst. engineer, Egypt, 1801, **15**

Hart, General Sir Reginald, V.C., **R.E.**, Egypt, 1882, **28, 29**

Hart, Lieut. S. E. (late Sergt., **R.E.**), *career*, **340**—*Darfur* expedition, **334, 336**—*Nile* barrage, **379**—*training* of and operations with Sudan Sapper Section, **305, 338, 340, 390**—*works*, Sudan, **489, 490**

Hashin, *action* at, 1885, **71**—*reoccupation* by Osman Digna, **79**

Hawkins, H. L. V., Sudan railways, *branch* line to Kareima, **400**—*Suez Canal* defences, **319**

Hawkins, Lieut., W. F., **R.E.**, Nile expedition, **93, 103**

Hayes, Lieut. C., **R.E.**, Egypt, 1801, **9, 15, 17**

Haynes, Lieut. A. E., **R.E.**, Egypt, 1882, **29**

Heath-Caldwell, Major-General F. C., **R.E.**, Egypt, 1882, **29**—*Nile* expedition, **67, 71**

Hebbert, Major H. E., **R.E.**, *Dept.* of Public Works, Sudan, **491, 492**—*Port Sudan*, **499, 500**

Hedjaz, revolt in, against Turks, **xi, 324, 325**

Heliopolis, battle of, **4, 5, 7**

Hellard, Lieut. R. C., **R.E.**, Egypt, 1882, **29**

Helwan, observatory, **467, 468**

Hensler, Corpl. **R.E.**, telegraphs, Sudan, **189, 191**

Hepper, Major A. J., **R.E.**, *fortifies* Wadi Halfa, **119**—*Red Sea Littoral*, 1885, **70**

Herbin, Mons., French Consul at Khartoum, *murdered*, **108, 133, 196**—*sent* off by Gordon, **131, 140**

Hickley, C. M., *Khartoum-El Obeid railway*, **404**—*Port Sudan-Atbara railway*, **394, 395, 398**

Hicks Pasha (Col. W. Hicks, retired Indian Army), defeated and killed near El Obeid, **56, 127, 128, 130, 131, 471**

Hickson, Capt. S. A. E., **R.E.**, Red Sea Littoral, 1885, **70**

Hill, Lieut. C., **R.E.**, Nile expedition, **93, 104, 108**

Hill, Dr. G. B., *Col. Gordon in Central Africa* referred to, **443, 444, 471, 527**

Hill-Smith, Capt. H. E., *exploration* of Bahr el Ghazal, **285**—*with expedition* to Fashoda, **279**

Hippisley, Lieut.-Col. R. L., **R.E.**, *C.R.E.*, Alexandria, **253**—*Egypt*, 1882, **29, 45**

Hobrough, Corpl., **R.E.**, Sudan telegraphs, **429, 436**

Holled-Smith, Major-General Sir C., *action* of Afafit, **85**—*brigade comdr.*, battle of Gemmaiza, **84**—*expedition* against Tokar, 1891, **111**—*Governor-General*, Red Sea Littoral, 1888, **83**

Hollings, Mary Albright, *The Life of Sir Colin C. Scott-Moncrieff*, **370, 376, 512**

Holloway, Major-General Sir Charles, **R.E.**, *career*, **6**—*defences* of Jaffa, **7**—*military mission* to Turkey, **4, 6, 7, 9, 13-15**

Hood, Lieut. Hon. A., R.N., *Atbara* campaign, **198**—*with expedition* to Fashoda, **279**

Hope, Capt., military mission to Turkey, **6-8**

Horne, Major-General H. S., report on Suez Canal defences, **318, 319**

Hoste, Lieut. G. C., **R.E.**, Egypt, 1801, **19**
Howe, Capt. J. S., **R.E.**, Western Frontier, 1935-36, **356**
Howell, A. B. B., help acknowledged, **xvi**
Huddleston, Major-General H. J., *action during mutiny in Khartoum*, **342**—*defeat of Ali Dinar*, **336**—*G.O.C., Sudan Defence Force*, **349**—*help acknowledged*, **xvi**—*Sudan-Uganda boundary*, **462**
Hudson, Brig.-General Sir J., commdg. Indian contingent, Red Sea Littoral, 1885, **70, 77, 79**
Huleatt, Lieut. H., **R.E.**, Egypt, 1882, **29, 44, 54**
Hunter, Gen. Sir Archibald, *Atbara campaign*, **194-6, 198, 199, 201, 205, 206, 210-4, 235, 237, 242, 243**—*battle of Atbara*, **217, 218**—*battle of Firket*, **164**—*battle of Hafir*, **170**—*battle of Omdurman*, **261, 263, 267, 269-71**—*Dongola expedition*, **151, 155, 159, 162, 164, 170, 176**—*exploration up Blue Nile*, **287**—*Governor at Suakin*, **81, 86**—*Omdurman campaign, commdg. Egyptian division*, **250, 447**—*reconnoitres Sheikh Barghut*, **85**—*reconnoitres to Adarama*, **202**—*Steevens's opinion*, **194**—*temporary command in Sudan*, **170**
Hunter, C. J., help acknowledged, **xvi**
Hunter-Weston, Lieut.-Gen. Sir A. G., **R.E.**, *battle of Firket*, **162, 163**—*Dongola expedition*, **154, 159, 160, 162, 163**
Hussein Kamel Pasha, Sultan of Egypt, 1914-17, **19, 309, 541**
Hutchinson, Major-General, commdg. British forces in Egypt, 1801, **12-18, 465**
Hutchinson, Lieut. R. R. L., **R.E.**, Western Frontier, 1935-36, **356**
Hutson, Capt. H. P. W., **R.E.**, barracks at Singa, **491**
Hyslop, Capt. R. M., **R.E.**, Egypt, 1882, **29**

I

Ibrahim Pasha, ruler of Egypt, 1848, **19, 366**
Indian Army, *cavalry*, 6th Bengal Cavalry, **48**—*infantry*, 15th Sikhs, **71, 72**—17th Bengal Native Infantry, **71-3**—28th Bombay Native Infantry, **71, 72**—*infantry divisions*, 3rd and 7th, **311**—10th and 11th, **311**—*miscellaneous units*, Bikaner Camel Corps, **311, 321**—Imperial Service cavalry brigade, **311, 314, 315**—*officers of Bengal infantry with Bengal engineers in Egypt*, 1801, **16**—*Pioneers*, Madras, **16**—128th, **313**—*Sappers and Miners*, Q.V.O. Madras, Egypt, 1882, **28, 46, 48**—*Red Sea Littoral*, 1885, **70, 71, 73, 76, 79**—*Red Sea Littoral*, 1886, **79**—*Suakin*, 1896, **86, 87**—*Suez Canal*, **313**
Irrigation, *historical*, **361, 362**—*importance of White Nile*, **293**—*in Egypt*, **361-85, 388**—*in Sudan*, **385-8**
Irvine, Lieut. J. L., **R.E.**, Egypt, 1882, **29, 47**
Ismail Ayub Pasha, Governor-General of Sudan, **441, 524**
Ismailia, operations near, 1882, **31, 32, 43**
Ismail Pasha, *appoints Gordon*, **522, 524**—*construction of Wadi Halfa-Saras railway*, **95, 100**—*deported*, 1879, **25, 126, 371, 528**—*extravagance*, **368, 369**—*Khedive of Egypt*, **19, 23, 24, 104, 368, 369, 527, 534**—*interest in survey*, **465**
Italo-Abyssinian wars, 1895-96, **149**—1935-36, **149**
Italo-Turkish war, 1911-12, effect in Egypt, **537, 539, 542**

J

Jaalin Arabs, *defeat by Mahmud*, **194**—*revolt against Khalifa*, **194, 195, 198, 243, 244**
Jackson, H. C., *Osman Digna referred to*, **57, 66, 80, 85**
Jackson, Major-General Sir Herbert W., *article Fashoda*, 1898, **281**—*career*, **284**—*part in Fashoda incident*, **279, 283-6**
Jackson, Lieut. L. C., **R.E.**, with Gwynn in Sudan, **449-51**
Jafar Pasha, Turkish army, *emissary to Senussi*, **329, 331**—*subsequent career*, **331**
Jaffa, *Turkish advance from*, **13**—*Turkish camp at*, **5, 7**
James, Capt. A. C., temp. **R.E.**, Sudan-French Equatorial Africa boundary, **464**
James, Lieut.-General Sir Henry, **R.E.**, Dir. Gen. Ordnance Survey, *measurement of base of Great Pyramid*, **504, 506**—*notes on the Great Pyramid*, **504, 505**—*Russo-Turkish-Rumanian frontier*, **533**
Jebel Auliya, reservoir and dam, **385, 386**
Jeffreys, Capt. W., **Bengal Engineers**, service in irrigation in India, **375**
Jerusalem, excavations in, **507-9**
John, king of Abyssinia, *Chermside's negotiations with*, **67, 529**—*Gordon's negotiations with*, **524, 528**
Johnstone, Major J. H. L'E., **R.E.**, *Egyptian state railways*, **410**—*work at Abu Simbel*, **517, 518**
Joly de Lotbinière, Brig.-General H. G., **R.E.**, in charge drawing office, Survey Dept., **468**
Jones, Lieut.-Col. H. H., **R.E.**, Egypt, 1882, **29**

K

Kaff, El, *suburb* of Suakin, **61, 80**—*water-supply*, **80, 81**
Kafr el Dauwar, *Arabi takes up position, 1882*, **26, 30, 31**—*operations*, **32**—*surrender*, **51**
Kaka expedition, 1899, indecisive results, **297, 452**
Kamoh Sanha, cutting on Port Sudan-Atbara railway, **393, 394, 396**
Kasr el Nil barracks, Cairo, *captured*, **50, 51**—*R.E. Mess*, **54**
Kassala, *buildings*, **480**—*fort*, **492**—*garrison*, **203, 207**—*Italian force at*, **149, 203, 448**—*railway to*, **85, 392**—*surrender* to dervishes, 1885, **78, 203**
Kavanagh, Major G. C. MacM., **R.E.**, *commdt.*, engineer troops, Sudan Defence Force, **351, 352**—*operations against Nuers*, 1928-29, **351**
Kelly, Brig. E. H., **R.E.**, general staff, Egypt, 1932-36, **355**
Kelly, Capt. H. H., **R.E.**, *director*, roads and communications, Sudan, **462, 480, 488, 502**—*Erkowit*, **487**—*exploration and survey in S.E. Sudan*, **462, 463**—*mission to Lado*, **403**—*operations in Mongalla*, 1912, **305**—*Port Sudan*, **482-4, 497-9**
Kelly, Lieut.-Col. P. J. V., Darfur operations, **335, 336**
Kennedy, Lieut.-Col. M. R., **R.E.**, *death*, **488**—*Dept. of Public Works, Sudan*, **318, 484, 488, 490, 502**—*Erkowit*, **487**—*Gallipoli campaign*, **318**—*Port Sudan*, **398, 490, 494-500**—*rebuilding of Khartoum*, **475, 476, 480, 482, 484, 490**
Kennett, Lieut. G., **R.E.**, *survey of Alexandria*, **465**—*with expedition to Egypt*, 1801, **9, 15, 17**
Kenney, Lieut. A. H., **R.E.**, Nile expedition and river column, **93, 96, 109, 118**
Keppel, Admiral Sir Colin, *Atbara campaign*, **198, 199, 202, 208, 211**—*expedition to Fashoda*, **279, 281, 282**—*Omdurman campaign*, **250, 256, 259**
Kerma, terminus of railway, 1896, **170**
Khalifa Abdullahi, *defeat and death at Umm Debeikerat*, **85, 300, 399, 449**—*escape after Omdurman*, **273, 274, 279**—*news of Dongola expedition*, **156**—*operations in Kordofan*, **291, 292, 297, 418**—*strategy in 1897 and 1898*, **194, 200, 205, 208, 253, 255, 272**—*successor to Mahdi*, **119, 161**—*views on railway*, **239**
Khanka, El, *battle*, **14**—*Ottoman troops at*, **3, 4**
Khartoum, *All Saints' Cathedral*, **338, 486**—*arsenal and dockyard*, **133**—*barracks*, **482**—*British garrison*, **307**—*demolition by Khalifa*, **472**—*fort*, **483**—*Gordon's reforms*, **128**—*history*, **470**—*Kitchener's improvements*, **292, 293**—*Mahdi's occupation*, **472**—*military school rebellion*, **341, 491**—*palace*, **139, 143, 144, 292, 474, 475, 480, 481**—*population in 1936*, **471**—*railway station*, **404**—*rebuilding*, **304, 473-92**—*recapture by Kitchener*, **275, 472**—*siege*, see Khartoum, siege of—*town plan*, **463**—*Wilson's dash for*, **115, 116**
Khartoum, North, *population*, **471**—*schemes for improvement*, **490**
Khartoum, siege of, *capture by Mahdi*, **143, 151**—*defences*, **129-32, 134-9**—*privations of garrison*, **142**—*progress*, **88, 111, 129, 133-44**—*strength of garrison*, **131, 140**
Khor Wintri, Osman Digna *defeated*, 1896, **85**—*road to Erkowit*, **487**
Kincaid, Col. W. F. H. S., **R.E.**, *Atbara campaign*, **196, 200, 211, 214**—*battle of Atbara*, **214**—*battle of Firket*, **162, 164**—*battle of Hafir*, **170**—*Delta light railways*, **408, 413**—*Dongola expedition*, **153, 154, 167, 177**—*Egyptian state railways*, **408, 410, 413**—*Nile expedition and river column*, **93, 97, 98, 109, 118**—*Omdurman campaign*, **252, 276**
King, Lieut. L. N. F. I., **R.E.**, survey of Sinai, **323**
Kirbekan, El, battle, **117**
Kitchener, Lieut.-Col. F. W., *commdg. Kordofan field force*, **291, 292**—*Dongola expedition*, **152**
Kitchener, Field-Marshal Earl, **R.E.**, *Adjutant General, Egyptian Army*, **530**—*adventure as spy*, **94**—*Alexandria riot and bombardment*, **53, 54**—*article on Fall of Khartoum*, **142**—*Atbara campaign*, **192-221**—*" Band of Boys "* **154, 170, 173, 236, 237, 242, 252, 389**—*battle of Atbara*, **208-20**—*battle of Firket*, **161-5**—*battle of Gemmaiza*, **84**—*battle of Hafir*, **169, 170**—*battle of Omdurman*, **258-65**—*battle of Toski*, **120**—*British Agent and Consul General*, **307, 386, 387, 405, 408, 490, 500, 515, 536-42**—*character and achievements*, **121, 212, 302, 542-6**—*death*, **338, 515, 545**—*dispatches*, **193, 211, 254**—*dislike of regulations*, **474**—*Dongola expedition*, **105, 147-72, 493, 546**—*" five feddan law,"* **539, 540**—*Governor-General, Red Sea Littoral*, **67, 82, 83, 86, 493, 529**—*Governor-General, Sudan*, **292, 447, 452, 477, 485, 501, 530-2**—*" Lieut. Kitchener's guinea book of Photographs of Biblical sites "* referred to, **510**—*memorials*, **303, 487**—*Nile expedition and desert column*, **92-4, 98, 106, 108-10, 113**—*Omdurman campaign*, **249-77**—*opens railway to El Obeid*, **405**—*rebuilding of Khartoum*, **475, 476, 481, 490**—*recapture of Khartoum*, **134**—*relations with Khedive*, **541**—*route sketches*, **445**—*Secretary of State for War*, **545**—*selection of and interest in officers*, **154, 160, 174, 415, 446, 476**—*service*

in Egyptian army, **28, 53, 54, 511**—*Sirdar*, Egyptian army, **85, 121, 147, 192**—*South Africa*, **531**—*statue* in Khartoum, **303**—*survey* of Cyprus, **511**—*survey* of Palestine, **465, 510**—*telegraphs*, **420**—*war correspondents*, **244**—*wounded*, **83, 84, 529**—*visit to England*, 1898, **290, 291**—*visit to Khartoum*, 1912, **473**

Kleber, General, *assassinated*, **8**—*commdg*. French troops in Egypt, **3**

Knight, E. F., *Times* correspondent, *Letters from the Sudan* referred to, **157, 160, 167, 168, 175, 176**

Knott, Major A. J., **R.E.**, *article* in *R.E. Journal*, **344, 492**—*Sudan Defence Force*, **352, 353**

Kodok, *name changed* from Fashoda, **284**—*telegraph* reaches, **418**

Koehler, Brig.-General, *commdg*. military mission to Turkey, **5–7**—*death* at Jaffa, **8**

Kordofan, operations of field force, **291, 292**

Korosko, *Gordon's departure* from, **122, 127**—*value* as possible railway terminus, **223**

Korti, *concentration*, **109, 117**—*desert column leaves* Nile at, **91, 110**—*desert column returns* to, **117**

Kosha, *advance* from, **182**—*gunboats arrive at*, **167**—*railway reaches*, **166, 181**

Kressenstein, Col. K. von, *Chief of Staff* to Djemal Pasha, **315**—*defeat at Romani*, **322**

Kunhardt, Capt. H. G., **R.E.**, *Red Sea Littoral*, 1885, **71, 76**—*surveys* Suakin–Otao railway, **445**

L

Lacy, Capt. T., **R.E.**, *accompanies* Turkish force into Egypt, **3–5, 7, 8, 13, 14, 546**—*battle* of El Khanka, **14, 15**—*career*, **6**—*military mission to Turkey*, **6**—*reconnoitres* French position before Cairo, **4**

Lado Enclave, *cession*, **403**—*railway survey*, **403**

Lake Rudolf, *Austin's* march, **455**—*expeditions* to, **448, 458, 459**

Lane-Poole, Stanley, *Watson Pasha* referred to, **38, 58, 67, 79**

Lawrence, Capt. T. E., *archæological exploration in Sinai*, **323**—*compared with Gordon*, **124**—*mission to Hedjaz*, **325**

Lawson, Lieut.-General Sir Henry M., **R.E.**, *article on Kitchener*, **543**—*battle* of Abu Kru, **113**—*battle* of Gedaref, **276, 288–90**—*Kassala*, **245, 253, 288**—*memoir* on R. H. Williams, **54**—Nile expedition and desert column, **93, 97, 98, 109, 111–3**—*Red Sea Littoral*, **60, 61**—*wounded*, **288**

Layard, Lieut. A. A. M., **R.E.**, *Red Sea Littoral*, 1885, **68, 71**

Leach, General Sir E. P., **V.C.**, **R.E.**—*battle* of Tofrik, **73**—*Red Sea Littoral*, 1885, **70, 71**

Leach, Capt. H. P., **R.E.**, Nile expedition and desert column, **93, 97, 109, 110**

Leahy, Lieut. C. A., **R.E.**, Nile expedition, **93**

Leake, Capt., *advance* into Egypt, **14**—*memorandum* on "Pompey's pillar," **504**—*military mission* to Turkey, **6, 13**

Learoyd, Lieut. C. A., **R.E.**, Red Sea Littoral, 1885, **71**

Le Mesurier, Lieut.-Col. F. A., **R.E.**, Red Sea Littoral, 1885, **70**

Lennox, Major-General W. O., **V.C.**, **R.E.**, *career*, **90**—*dispatches* boats for Nile expedition from Alexandria, **90**

Leslie, Capt. F. S., **R.E.**, Nile expedition, **93**

Leverson, Lieut. J. J., **R.E.**, Egypt, 1882, **29**

Lewis, Lieut.-Col. D. F., *Atbara campaign*, **205, 209**—*battle* of Atbara, **214–6**—*battle* of Firket, **162–4**—*Dongola campaign*, **162–4, 168**—*Omdurman campaign*, **250, 251, 260, 261, 267–72**—*operations* after Omdurman, **289, 297, 298, 301**

Lewis, Corpl., **R.E.**, telegraphs, Sudan, **243, 245**

Lewis, Quarter-Master A. T., **R.E.**, Red Sea Littoral, 1885, **71**

Liddell, Lieut.-Col. J. S., **R.E.**, *Egyptian telegraphs*, **423, 438, 439**—*Sinai operations*, **322, 439**—*Sudan telegraphs*, **105, 292, 415, 417, 418, 421–3, 426, 459**—*Suez Canal defences*, **313, 318, 439**—*Under-Secretary*, Ministry of Communications, **412, 439**

Lindley, Lieut. W. D., **R.E.**, *Egypt*, 1882, **28, 47**—*Red Sea Littoral*, 1885, **71**

Lindsay, Lieut. H. E. M., **R.E.**, Red Sea Littoral, 1885, **70, 71, 77**

Linant de Bellefonds, Auguste, *Damietta and Rosetta* barrages, **363–5, 367, 373**—*death*, **444**—*Minister of Public Works*, **364**—*on Gordon's staff*, **441**—*report re dam at Aswan*, **380**—*report re Wadi Rayan basin*, **381**

Littledale, Lieut. R. P., **R.E.**, Nile expedition, **93**

Lloyd, Lord, *Egypt since Cromer* referred to, **539**—*Intelligence* Dept., Cairo, **323**

Loggin, G. N., Dept. of Public Works, Sudan, **476, 499**

Long, Lieut.-Col. C. J., *Atbara campaign*, **214**—*Omdurman campaign*, **250**

Longe, Lieut. F. B., **R.E.**, Red Sea Littoral, 1885, **70, 445**

Longfield, Lieut.-Col. W. E., **R.E.**, *Narrative of The Sudan Railways*, **77, 102, 175, 177, 178, 222, 229, 235, 236, 295, 302, 389, 390, 395, 398, 403, 404, 406, 493**—*reconnoitres* Port Sudan–Atbara railway, **392–5**

Lord, Major P. C., **R.E.**, *Gallipoli* campaign, 318—*Sudan* Government railways, **392, 403, 406**—*transportation* officer, Egypt, **411**

Loxton, Sergt.-Major, **R.E.**, Egypt, 1882, **44**

Luard, Lieut. W. Du C., **R.E.**, Nile expedition, **93, 103**

Lubbock, Major G., **R.E.**, railway, Egypt to Palestine, **326**

Lucas and Aird, contractors for Suakin –Berber railway, **68, 76, 101**

Lukin, Brig.-General H. T., operations against Senussi, **330, 331**

Lybia, Italian massing of troops, 1935–36, **356**

Lyons, Col. Sir Henry G., **R.E.**, *archæological* observation, **518, 519**—*Egyptian* army, **148**—*Geological* survey, **253, 466, 520, 521**—*later career*, **468**—*meteorological* observations, **468**—*opinion* of Ross, **372, 373**—*Philæ*, **382, 466, 519**—*Rains of the Nile Basin*, referred to, **467**—*remarks re* Kitchener, **154, 155**—*Report on Temples of Philæ*, referred to, **519**—*route* sketches, **445**—*surveyor-general*, **384, 466, 467, 469**—*The Cadastral Survey of Egypt*, referred to, **467**—*The Nile* referred to, **467**—*visit* to White Nile, **383, 443**

Lyttleton, Brig.-Gen. Hon. N. G., Omdurman campaign, **249, 261, 267, 268, 278**

M

Macauley, Brig.-General Sir George, **R.E.**, *Atbara* bridge, **294**—*Atbara* campaign, **185, 211, 229**—*Director-General*, Egyptian state railways, **403, 406, 410, 411**—*Director* of railways, Sudan, **389, 391, 483**—*Great War* (railways), **411**—*Omdurman* campaign, **211, 252, 257, 276**—*papers* on Sudan military railways, **178, 233, 235, 397**—*Port Sudan–Atbara* railway, **296, 391, 393, 395–9, 417, 494**—*retirement*, **412**—*Sinai* campaign, **323, 325–7**—*Suez Canal* defences, **313, 318**—*Wadi Halfa–Abu Hamed* railway, **198, 229, 235, 240, 241**

MacCarthy, Lieut. F. D., **R.E.**, Red Sea Littoral, 1885, **71, 73**

Macdonald, Major-General Sir Hector, *Atbara* campaign, **194, 196, 201, 210, 211, 214–6, 218, 219**—*battle* of Atbara, **215, 216, 218**—*battle* of Firket, **162–4**—*battle* of Omdurman, **267–71**—*Dongola* campaign, **162–5, 168, 170, 179, 182, 184**—*Omdurman* campaign, **250, 251, 261, 267–71**

Macdonald, Major-General Sir James R. L., **R.E.**, expedition to Uganda, **448**

MacDonald, Sir Murdoch, *Aswan* dam, **383, 384**—*help* acknowledged, **viii**—*notes re* Aswan dam, **382**—*services* in irrigation, **380, 385**—*Sennar* dam, **386**—*Suez Canal* defences, **313, 317, 318, 327, 329**

MacDonnell, Lieut. A. C., **R.E.**, Red Sea Littoral, 1885, **71**

MacFarlane, D., Dept. of Public Works, Sudan, **491, 499**

Mackenzie, Col. Colin, **R.** (Madras) **E.**, archæological achievements in India, **503**

Mackenzie, Lieut. R. J. H. L., **R.E.**, Red Sea Littoral, 1885, **70, 74, 75**

Mackintosh, Lieut. E. E. B., **R.E.**, *Erkowit*, **487**—*Port Sudan*, **498, 499**—*works*, Sudan, **481, 484, 488**

Mackworth, Major Sir A. W., Bart., **R.E.**, Egypt, 1882, **28, 44–6, 438**

Mackworth, Major H. L., **R.E.**, *Bor-Taufikia* line, **427–30**, *telegraphs*, Sudan, **424–7, 431, 483**—*Sinai* operations, **322**

Maclaren, Capt. R. H., **R.E.**, Western Frontier, 1935–36, **356**

MacMichael, Sir Harold, *political* and intelligence officer, Darfur expedition, **334**—*The Anglo-Egyptian Sudan*, **350, 530, 531**

MacMunn, Lt.-Gen. Sir George, *Military Operations, Egypt and Palestine* referred to, **310, 314, 316, 318, 330, 335**

Macpherson, Major-General Sir Herbert, 𝒱.𝒞., commdg. Indian contingent, Egypt, 1882, **27, 42, 47, 48**

Maffey, Sir John, Governor-General, Sudan, **338, 532**

Magfar, El., *battle*, **34**—*Sweetwater canal* dammed, **32, 35**

Mahdi (Muhammad Ahmed) *closes in* on Khartoum, **140, 142**—*death*, **119**—*defeat* of Hicks, **127, 128**—*height of power*, **117**—*raises* Sudan, **127–9**—*self-proclamation*, **56**—*siege* of Khartoum, **111, 142**—*tomb*, see Mahdi's tomb.

Mahdi's tomb, description, **274**—*shelled*, **259**—*Sirdar's headquarters*, **273**

Mahmud, Emir, *Atbara* campaign, **208–10, 212**—*campaign* against Jaalin, **194, 199**—*commands* dervish army, **194, 203, 204**—*defeat* and capture at Atbara, **214, 216, 218, 219**

Mahuta, El, *advance* to, **34**—*enemy* defences, **33–5**

Maitland, Major-General Sir J. H. M., **R.E.**, Egypt, 1882, **28**

Malakal, *cantonment*, **491**—*wireless station*, **433, 434**

Malet, Sir Edward, Consul-General, Egypt, **29, 371**

Mandara (Mandora) tower, battle of, 1801, **11**

Mangin, General, *career*, **282**—*part* in Fashoda incident, **282, 450**

Manifold, see Bowman-Manifold.

Mann, Capt. F. D., **R.E.**, *blasting* operations in Nile, **492**—*Public Works*, Khartoum, **491**—*Sudan Defence Force*, **351**

Mantell, Col. A. M., **R.E.**, article in

R.E. Journal, 39—*Egypt*, 1882, 29—*in charge* Abbassia observatory, 465—*survey* of Palestine, 511—*with new Egyptian army*, 53, 54
Maps, preparation of, *Bahr el Ghazal*, 285—*dervish*, 199—*Egypt*, 468, 469—*Khartoum*, 133, 135—*Nubian desert*, 225—*Palestine*, 510—*reconnaissances for railway, Atbara to Khartoum*, 294—*Sudan*, 461—*supply* in Great War, 308, 469
Marchand, General, *advance from Ubanghi river*, 192, 249, 278, 292, 448—*Fashoda incident*, 278-81, 285-7, 453
Marindin, Major F. A., R.E., report on Egyptian state railways, 407
Marryat, Lieut.-Col. E. L., R.E., *Delta light railways*, 413
Marryat, Lieut.-Col. J. R., R.E., *Delta light railways*, 413—*help* acknowledged, xvi
Martin, Capt. C. G., V.C., R.E., *A.D. Mily. Works*, Egyptian army, 491—*expedition against Nuers*, 1917, 338—*Sinai operations*, 323
Martin, Brevet Col., R. H., Omdurman campaign, 249, 262, 266
Mason, Lieut.-Col. A., R.E., Western Frontier, 1935-36, 356
Maud, Brig.-General P., R.E., *exploration of southern border of Abyssinia*, 457-9
Maurice, Lieut.-Col. J. F., *Nile expedition*, 92—*The Life of Lord Wolseley* referred to, 89
Maxim batteries, *Atbara campaign*, 206, 216, 217—*Dongola expedition*, 153, 162
Maxse, Major F. I., with expedition to Fashoda and Sobat, 279, 284
Maxwell, Gen. Sir John, *Atbara campaign*, 214-6, 233—*battle of Atbara*, 215, 216—*battle of Firket*, 162, 163—*battle of Omdurman*, 261, 263, 267—*commdg. forces in Egypt*, 308, 311, 316, 317, 320—*Omdurman campaign*, 250, 251, 261, 263, 267, 268, 272, 273, 297
McKerras, Major W., R.E., C.R.E., British force in Egypt, 1801, 8, 9, 503—*killed*, 9, 10
McLean, Dr. W. H., *help* acknowledged, 473—*Regional and Town Planning*, 471
McLeod Innes, General J. J., V.C., R.E. (Bengal), *The Life and Times of General Sir James Browne* referred to, 28
McMeekan, Lieut. G. R., R.E., *destruction of Dengkurs pyramid*, 346, 347—*formation of boys' company*, 344—*operations in Nuba Hills*, 345—*Sudan Defence Force*, 351
McNeill, Lieut. A. G., R.E., survey, Sudan, 463
McNeill, Major-General Sir John C., V.C., "*McNeill's zariba*" (battle of Tofrik), 71-4—*opinion on Nile route*, 89—*Red Sea Littoral*, 70-2

Menage, Lieut. V. R. T., R.E., Western Frontier, 1935-36, 356
Menelik, Negus of Abyssinia, *claims in Sudan*, 448, 451—*Kenya-Abyssinia boundary*, 457—*receives Rodd mission*, 207, 448—*Sudan-Abyssinia boundary*, 451, 453, 457
Menou, General, *commdg.* French forces in Egypt, 8-10, 12, 16-8
Merowe, *base for 1897 operations*, 194—*farthest point reached by Dongola expedition*, 170
Mersa Matruh, *defence of*, 329, 330—*engineer operations*, 358—*massing of troops*, 356—*water-supply*, 356, 357
Meshra er Req, *Egyptian flag hoisted*, 285—*Liddell at*, 421
Metemma, El, *capture by dervishes*, 194—*dervish outpost*, 1897, 193, 202—*desert column reaches Nile at*, 91, 109, 112
Meyricke, Lieut. E. G., R.E., Sudan telegraphs, 421, 424
Micklem, Lieut. H. A., R.E., *Atbara bridge*, 296—*Atbara campaign*, 211—*battle of Omdurman*, 264—*Omdurman campaign*, 211, 253, 264—*railways in Sudan*, 229—*works*, Sudan, 185, 186
Micklem, Lieut. R., R.E., *Gallipoli campaign*, 318—*Sudan railways*, 403, 405, 406
Midwinter, Lieut.-Col. Sir Edward, C. R.E., *Atbara bridge*, 295—*Atbara campaign*, 211—*Jebel Auliya dam*, 386—*Omdurman campaign*, 211, 253, 257, 267, 272, 273—*presented to H.M. the King*, 500—*railways*, Sudan, 185, 186, 229-31, 240, 389, 392, 398, 399, 403, 406, 483—*Wadi Halfa-Abu Hamed railway*, 229-31, 240, 392
Military School, Omdurman, founded, 354
Military Works Department, *see* Department of Military Works, Egyptian army.
Milligan, Lieut.-Col. S. L., *Director of Survey*, 135, 136, 460, 464—*help* acknowledged, xi, xvi, 460
Milner, Sir Alfred, *England in Egypt* referred to, 53, 373, 387—*remarks on Cape to Cairo railway*, xii
Moascar, cantonment near Ismailia, 354
Moeris, Lake, use as reservoir, 380
Moir, Col. J. P., R.E., *Atbara campaign*, 206, 211, 212, 214, 216, 217, 239—*battle of Atbara*, 216, 217—*Director of telegraphs*, Sudan, 431, 435, 436—*Omdurman campaign*, 246, 250, 252
Molony, Lieut. F. A., R.E., Red Sea Littoral, 1885, 70, 76
Mongalla province, *disturbances*, 1912, 305—*disturbances*, 1914, 338—*wireless station*, 436
Monro, Lieut.-Gen. Sir Charles, evacuation of Gallipoli, 317, 320
Montagu-Stuart-Wortley, Major-General Hon. E. J., *accompanies Wilson on dash for Khartoum*, 114-6—*anecdote*

on appointment of Kitchener to Egyptian army, 54—*battle* of Omdurman, 266—*commdg.* Arab corps, 92—*Nile* expedition and desert column, 110—*Omdurman* campaign, 254, 256, 259

Montressor, Lieut. J. M., **R.E.**, Western Frontier, 1935-36, **356**

Motors, *first*, in Sudan, **304**—*in desert*, **355**—*route* Cape Town to Juba, **xiii**

Mougel Bey, *Damietta and Rosetta barrages*, **365, 366, 376, 379, 380**—*dismissal*, **366**—*French* engineer, Wadi Halfa railway, **100**—*Minister* of Works, **366, 367**

Muhammad Ahmed, *see* Mahdi.

Muhammad Ali Pasha, *interest* in irrigation, 361-5—*interest* in survey, **465**—*Viceroy* of Egypt, 1805-48, **19, 20, 22, 470**—*presents* Rameses statue to British nation, **512**

Muhammad Fadil Pasha, el Lewa, *help* acknowledged, **238**—*interview* by author, **100**

Muhammad Tewfik Pasha, *Khedive* of Egypt, 1879-92, **19, 25, 26, 52, 528**—*Prime Minister*, **24**

Mulloy, Major W. H., **R.E.**, *C.R.E.*, Nile expedition, **92**

Murrat Wells, Kerma railway, railway reaches, **177**

Murrat Wells, Nubian desert, *description* by Knight, **175**—*fortified* post, 1896, **152**—*position* fixed by Talbot, **446**—*possible terminus* for Korosko railway, **175, 222-4**

Murray, Lieut.-General Sir Archibald, *commdg*. Mediterranean Expeditionary Force, **320, 434**—*operations* in Sinai, **321, 322, 326**

Mutiny in Khartoum, *origin*, **340**—*progress*, **342**—*quelling*, **342, 343**

Myers, Lieut. E. C. W., **R.E.**, Western Frontier, 1935-36, **356**

N

Nahud, En, post at, **333, 334, 336**

Napier, Field-Marshal Lord, **R.** (Bengal) E., in Abyssinia, **38**

Napoleon the Great, *alliances*, **8, 18, 20**—*calls for report* on canal, Mediterranean to Red Sea, **20**—*campaign* in Egypt and Syria, **3, 5**—*designs* on Egypt, 1807, **19**—*irrigation schemes*, **363**—*opinion* on British occupation of Alexandria, **18**

Nathan, Lieut. M., **R.E.**, Nile expedition, **93, 103**

Naval brigade, *battle* of Tel el Kebir, **41, 42**—*Nile* expedition, **92, 96**—*with desert column*, **109, 114**

Navy, French, defence of Suez canal, **310, 312, 316**

Navy, Royal, *Atbara* campaign, **198**—*bombardment* of Alexandria, **26**—*Dongola* expedition, **169**—*operations* in 1882, **26, 31, 32, 38**—*operations* in 1884, **61**—*operations* in 1885, **71**—*opinion re* boat expedition, **89**—*Suez Canal*, **309, 310, 312, 316**

Nekhl, *bombing*, **322**—*evacuation*, 1914, **314**—*Palmer* dispatched to, **22**

Neufeld, Charles, *prisoner* in Khalifa's hands, **151**—*released*, **273**

Newcombe, Major E. O. A., **R.E.**, *Atbara* bridge, **295**—*commdg*. gunboat *Abu Klea*, **256, 259, 260, 265, 275**—*expedition* to Fashoda and Sobat, **279, 280, 282, 283, 285**—*exploration* of Bahr el Ghazal, **285, 286**—*Omdurman* campaign, **256, 259, 260, 265, 275**—*Sudan* railways, **185, 186, 228, 229, 252, 400, 403, 407**

Newcombe, Lieut.-Col. S. F., **R.E.**, *Port Sudan-Atbara* railway, **392-4, 399, 493**—*raid* on Hedjaz railway, **323**—*Sudan* railways, **392-4, 399, 400, 402-4, 406**—*travels* in S.E. Sudan, **403**

Newman, Lieut. E. M. B., **R.E.**, *killed* at Tofrik, **73**—*Red Sea Littoral*, 1885, **71, 73**

Nicholas, 2nd-Capt. W., **R.E.**, Egypt, 1807, **19**

Nicholson, Field-Marshal Sir William, **R.E.**, afterwards Lord Nicholson, Egypt, 1882, **28**

Nile, *barrage*, **366, 367**, *see also* Damietta and Rosetta barrages—*blasting operations*, **492**—*Blue*, *see* Blue Nile—*British advance* up, 1801, **15**—*crossing* by cable, **190, 191**—*description*, **361**—*floods*, **95, 361, 383, 400**—*hydrographic survey*, **383**—*irrigation*, *see* Irrigation—*measurements*, **468**—*proposed new barrage* near Aswan, **380**—*rise and fall*, **153**—*river transport*, **88, 89, 99, 116, 153, 166, 184, 201**—*route* selected for relief of Gordon, **67, 88, 89, 91**—*voyage* of Indian contingent down, 1801, **17**—*White*, *see* White Nile.

Nile Expedition, 1884-85, *boats* for, **90, 95, 97**—*choice of route*, **67, 88-91**—*conclusion*, **107, 115, 117-9**—*importance* of Dongola in, **93, 95-7**—*plans* for, **88, 91, 101, 108**—*river transport*, **88, 91, 100**—*R.E. officers*, **92, 93**—*strength and composition*, **92**

Nile frontier force, or Egyptian frontier force, *formation*, **118**—*retirement* to Wadi Halfa, **119**

Noakes, Capt. F. C. T., **R.E.**, article on *The Nile Control and Irrigation Problems of Egypt* referred to, **385**

Norris, Lieut. S. L., **R.E.**, Egypt, 1882, **29**

Nosworthy, Brig. F. P., **R.E.**, *general staff*, Sudan defence force, **349-51**—*operations* against Nuers, 1928-29, **351**

Nottingham, Lieut. F. C., **R.E.**, *help* acknowledged, **492**—*operations* in Nuba hills, 1928-29, **345, 346**

Nuba hills, *operations* in 1915-16, **338, 490**—*since Great War*, **339, 341, 345, 350**

Nubar Pasha, *head of cabinet*, 1878–79, **24**—*part* in abolition of *corvée*, **378**
Nubian desert, *description*, **222**—*scouts* in, 1896, **152**—*surveys*, **222-5**
Nuers, *Austin's description*, **453**—*operations* against, 1915, **338**—1927–28, **346, 347, 350**—1928–29, **350**
Nugent, Brig.-General C. B. P. N. H., **R.E.**, commdg. Engineers, Egypt, 1882, **27, 41, 55**
Nuri Pasha, Turkish emissary to Senussi, **329, 331**
Nyima expedition, 1916, **338, 461**

O

Obeid, El, *buildings*, **480, 492**—*capitulates* to Mahdi, **128**—*defeat* of Hicks, **56**—*reoccupation*, **301**
Ohrwalder, Joseph, *opinion* on Gordon's proposals for evacuation, **127**—*opinion* on relief of Khartoum, **115**—*Ten Years' Captivity in the Mahdi's camp* referred to, **127, 142**
Olivier, Capt. H. D., **R.E.**, Sudan railways, **103**
Omdurman, *battle*, see Omdurman, battle of—*barracks*, **480, 482, 491**—*bridge*, **136, 490**—*description*, **273, 274**—*fort*, defence and fall of, **134, 135, 139, 142**—*improvements*, **304**—*Khalifa's capital*, **151, 472**—*Mahdi's camp*, **143**—*population* in 1936, **471**—*schemes* for improvement, 1927, **490**—*town plan*, **460, 463**
Omdurman, battle of, *battlefield*, **255**—*dervish losses*, **271**—*dispatches*, **254**—*effects*, **271**—*operations* preceding, **258-60**—*progress*, **260-74**
Omdurman campaign, British and Egyptian forces, **250**—*dispersal* of forces after, **275**—*programme*, **249**—*progress*, **250-74**
Osman Digna, *acknowledged* emir to Mahdi, **51**—*ancestry*, **57**—*capture* and death, **85**—*movements* after Umm Debeikerat, **300**—*movements* between 1886 and 1900 **84, 85, 155**—*operations* near Suakin, 1884, **58, 59, 63, 66**—1885, **69, 71, 74, 75, 78**—1886, **82-4, 87, 88**—*operations* on Atbara, 1897–98, **202, 209, 219**
Otao, *evacuated*, **77**—*terminus* of Suakin-Berber railway, **75, 76**
Overland route, Alexandria to Suez, *passage* of troops during Indian Mutiny, **21, 22**
Owen, Capt. R. A., **R.E.**, Sinai operations, **322**
Oxley, Capt. W. H., **R.E.**, barracks at Omdurman, **491**

P

Palestine, *Egyptian* troops in, **307**—*exploration* fund, **508, 511**—*operations*, 1936, **356**—*surveys*, **23, 465, 507, 509**
Palmer, Sir Elwin, Dir. General of Finance, presses Kitchener for economy, **203, 204**
Palmer, Prof. E. H., *murdered* in Sinai desert, 1882, **32, 509**—*survey* of Sinai, **509**
Palmer, Major-General H. S., **R.E.**, *measurement* of Pyramid, **504, 509**—*survey* in Sinai, **509**
Panet, Major H. de L., **R.E.**, Western Frontier, 1935–36, **356**
Pank, Capt. R. D., **R.E.**, accident and death in Khartoum, **491**
Paoletti, Mr., *Maltese engineer*, under Manifold, **186, 187**—*returns* to Cairo, **189**
Parker, Lieut. E., **R.E.**, Egypt, 1807, **19**
Parsons, Lieut.-Col. C. S. B., *march* to Kassala, 1897, **203, 207**—*operations* at Gedaref, **287, 288**
Paul, Brig.-General E. M., **R.E.**, see Stewart of Coll.
Peake, Capt. M., *expedition* to Fashoda and Sobat, **279, 283, 284**—*exploration* of Bahr el Ghazal, **285**
Pearson, Lieut.-Col. H. D., **R.E.**, *death* in Darfur, **347, 464**—*Director* of surveys, Sudan, **460, 463, 469, 483**—*expedition* to Lake Tsana, **463**—*Hedjaz* operations, **325, 464**—*mission* to Abyssinia, **386, 464**—*mission* to Lado, **403, 462**—*operations* in Mongalla, 1912, **305**—*operations* in Palestine, **464**—*photo* of Dengkurs pyramid, **347**—*survey* of Port Sudan, **498**
Peck, Major W. E., **R.E.**, Red Sea Littoral, 1885, **70**
Pemberton, Lieut. E. St. C., **R.E.**, Egypt, 1882, **29**
Peyton, Major-General W. E., operations against Senussi, **331-3**
Philæ, submergence of temples, **382, 384, 385, 519**
Pibor river, exploration, **462, 463**
Plunkett, Major G. T., **R.E.**, Nile expedition, **93**
Pollen, Lieut. W. H., **R.E.**, Egypt, 1882, **29**
Polwhele, Lieut. R., **R.E.**, *battle* of Firket, **162, 165**—*death*, **166, 180, 185**—*Dongola* expedition (railways), **153, 156, 159, 173, 176, 177**—*proposed Korosko-Murrat Wells railway*, **175, 222-4**
Porter, Major-General W., **R.E.**, *History of the Corps of Royal Engineers*, Vols. I and II, **6, 9, 75, 96, 98, 127, 503, 508, 509**
Port Said, *British hospital*, **535**—*reorganization* by Girouard, **409**—*water-supply*, **33**
Port Sudan, *building* and growth, **406**—*formal opening*, **499**—*lay-out*, **495, 496, 498**—*mutiny* at, **341**—*naming*, **497**—*railway* terminus, **397**—*site* noticed by Watson, Kitchener, and Wingate, **59, 391, 495**—*water-supply*, **496, 498-500**—*wireless* station, **435**

Posts and telegraph department, Liddell's improvements, **421**
Power, Frank, *British consul* at Khartoum, murdered, **108, 133, 191**—*correspondent* of *Times*, **130, 134**—*defences* of Khartoum, **131**—*Letters from Khartoum*, edited by Arnold Power, **130, 131, 138**—*sent off* by Gordon, **140**
Pridham, Col. G. R., **R.E.**, *Chief Engineer*, Egypt, 1923–27, **354**—*Suez Canal* defences, **319**
Prince, Mr., late **R.E.**, Sudan telegraphs, **437**
Pringle, Capt. J. W., **R.E.**, Uganda railway survey, **448**
Pritchard, Major-General H. L., **R.E.**, *Atbara* campaign, **216**—*battle* of Atbara, **216**—*battle* of Hafir, **170**—*battle* of Omdurman, **262, 263, 268, 269, 271, 272, 276**—*Dongola* expedition, **153, 154, 173, 176, 177, 180, 181, 185, 189, 225**—*notes re* Girouard, **173, 174**—*Omdurman* campaign, **247, 253, 257, 262**—*Sudan Campaign by "an Officer"* referred to, **152, 167, 183, 196, 199, 225, 231, 239, 260, 281, 288**—*Suez Canal* defences, **319**—*Wadi Halfa–Abu Hamed* railway, **198, 230–5, 392**
Public Works Department, *see* Department of Public Works, Sudan.
Pumping installations, for irrigation, **366, 367, 373, 374**
Puzey, Capt. A. R., **R.E.**, Egypt, 1882, **28, 36**
Pyne, Capt. H. G., **R.E.**, road reconnaissance, Mongalla to Ikoto, **491**
Pyramids of Giza, *measurement*, **504–7**—*suggested* demolition, **363**

Q

Qantara, El, Turkish attack, **314**
Qassasin, El, *actions at*, 1882, **36–9**—*advance* from, **40**—*occupation*, **34, 38, 45**—*railway* repaired, **43**
Qatiya, *occupation*, **321**—*operations*, 1916, **322, 326**
Qena, march of Indian contingent, 1801, **16**
Quarantine Island (Suakin) now Condenser Island, *condensers*, **81**—*piers*, **68**—*pontoons*, **395**—*R.E. works*, **68, 79**—*situation*, **61**—*terminus* of Suakin–Berber railway, **75, 76**
Quseir, Indian contingent land at, 1801, **16, 156**

R

Railway battalion, Egyptian army, *Dongola* expedition, **153, 156, 160, 179, 181, 184**—*mutiny*, **341**—*Port Sudan–Atbara* railway, **394, 399**—*recruiting*, **176**—*Wadi Halfa–Abu Hamed* line, **231, 241, 389**

Railways, *Alexandria–Daaba*, **329**—*armoured* trains and trucks, *see that* heading—*Bahariya light*, **22, 31, 33, 311, 326**—*Cairo–Suez* and Port Said, **22, 31, 33, 311, 326**—*Delta*, light, *see* Railways, Delta Light—*Egyptian state*, *see* Railways, Egyptian State—*Egypt–Palestine*, **322, 325, 326**—*expenditure* on, **24**—*first*, in Egypt, **22, 407**—*Hedjaz*, **323, 325**—*in campaign* of 1882, **35, 37, 42–4, 48, 49**—*Great War*, **325, 326**—*Luxor–Aswan*, **174, 176, 207, 226, 240, 241**—*Port Sudan–Atbara*, *see that* heading—*proposed*, to Kassala, **85**—*proposed*, Korosko–Murrat Wells, **174, 222–5**—*Red Sea–Nile*, **58, 59, 67, 68**—*Suakin–Berber*, *see that* heading—*Wadi Halfa–Halfaya*, *see that* heading—*Wadi Halfa–Saras*, *see that* heading.
Railways, Delta Light, *formation* of company, **412, 413**—*system*, **412**
Railways, Egyptian State, *connection* of R.E. with, **407**—*disturbances* of 1919, **411, 412**—*growth*, **407, 411**—*state in* 1898, **408, 409**—*system*, **44, 226**
Railways, Port Sudan–Atbara, *bridges*, **397**—*considerations* as to route, **392**—*construction*, **395, 396, 398, 496**—*Gorringe's reconnaissance*, **244, 245**—*gradient*, **393, 394, 396, 397**—*Kitchener's reconnaissance*, **296, 391, 417**—*line* Sallom to Sheikh Barghut, **398, 399**—*reconnaissance* and survey, **392–5**—*specification*, **396, 397**
Railways, Suakin–Berber, *construction*, **75–7, 80, 101**—*contractors*, **68**—*discontinued*, **77**—*Graham's instructions*, **69**—*Kitchener discards idea*, **192**—*material*, **78**—*proposals re gauge*, **68**—*reaches* Otao, **75–7, 391**—*suggestions* by Kitchener, **85**—*terminus*, **75**—*water* pipes, **81**
Railways, Sudan Government, *see* Sudan Government railways.
Railways, Sudan Military, *see* Sudan Military railways.
Railways, Wadi Halfa–Halfaya, *branch* to Kareima, **399**—*construction* to Abu Hamed, **174, 184, 186, 193, 197, 198, 201, 202, 225, 236, 240**—*continuation* to Atbara, **221, 238, 252**—*continuation* to Berber, **204, 237**—*continuation* to Halfaya, **294, 389**—*floods*, **390**—*gauge*, **226**—*inception*, **192, 194**—*limits* of curve and gradient, **234**—*locomotives*, **228, 232**—*Macauley on*, **185**—*progress*, **207, 208, 219, 231–5, 237**—*reconnaissance*, **222–4, 226**—*"special correspondent"*, **236, 237**—*specification*, **389, 390**
Railways, Wadi Halfa–Saras, *abandonment* proposed by Gordon, **407, 525**—*article on*, **101**—*breached*, **183**—*capacity*, **102**—*construction* to Saras and Kerma, **159, 160, 170, 229**—*Macauley's paper*, **178**—*progress*, **102, 103, 176–81**—*prolonged* to Kerma, **184, 193**—*pulling up*, **186, 398, 400**—

repair by R.E., **91, 407**—*state* in 1884, **95, 99-102**—*state* in 1896, **155, 175, 183**—*state* in 1899, **389**—*surveys* and estimates, **99, 100**—*terminus* at Akasha, **119**—*traffic* staff, training, **178**—*use* of, in 1896, **152, 155, 156, 158, 162, 177, 178**

Rainsford-Hannay, Lieut. A. G., **R.E.**, reconnaissance in Darfur, **333-7**—*works*, Egypt, **501**—*works*, Sudan, **488, 489**

Rait Kerr, Major E., **R.E.**, Western Frontier, 1935-36, **356, 357**

Rameses, statue of, raising, **512-5**

Raouf Pasha, *Governor-General*, Sudan, **129**—*trial* of Arabi, **51**

Rathborne Major W. H., **R.E.**, Red Sea Littoral, 1885, **70, 76**

Red Sea, description of coast, **60**

Red Sea Littoral, *attitude* of tribes, **57, 78**—*campaign* of 1884, **56-66**—1885, **67-77**—1886, **155**—*Governors-General*, **67, 82, 529, 530**

Reid, A. G. W., *irrigation*, **375**—*restoration* of Nile barrage, **376**

Rejaf, established by Gordon, **442**

Renk, Er, defeat of dervishes, **280**

Rhodes, Cecil, *Cape to Cairo* scheme, **xii, 226**—*lends railway stock* to Sudan military railway, **227**

Rich, Capt. H. B., **R.E.**, Egypt, 1882, **28**

River Column, Nile expedition, 1885, *plans for*, **109**—*progress*, **117**—*recalled*, **106, 118**

River transport, *Atbara* campaign, **198, 242**—*Dongola* expedition, **159, 166**—*Omdurman* campaign, **255, 276**

Roads, *Alexandria-Suez* Canal, **358**—*Alexandria-Sollum*, **358**—*Cairo-Alexandria*, **358**—*Dongola* expedition, **160**—*Egypt-Palestine*, **311, 358**—*Khartoum*, **482, 490**—*Khedivial motor* road to Sollum, **329**—*Nyima*, **338**—*Sinai*, **328**—*Sinkat-Erkowit*, **487**—*Sudan*, **345, 347, 351**—*Suez Canal* zone, **313**—*Suez-Zafarana*, **356**—*western desert*, **357**—*wire*, **329**

Roberts, Field-Marshal Lord, Comdr.-in-Chief, South Africa, **301, 302, 531**

Roberts, Lieut. Hon. F. H. S., with expedition to Fashoda, **279**

Roberts, Lieut. G. B., **R.E.**, telegraphs, Sudan, **417, 418**

Rochfort-Boyd, Capt. C. A., **R.E.**, Egypt, 1882, **28**

Rodd, Francis J. R., *mission* to Abyssinia, **448**—*mission* to Sayed Idris, **332**

Romilly, Capt. F. J., **R.E.**, *killed* at Tofrik, **73**—*Red Sea Littoral*, 1885, **70, 73**

Roper, Lieut. A. W., **R.E.**, Nile expedition, **93, 101, 103**

Roseires, *buildings*, **485**—*works*, **486, 491**

Rosetta, *attack* on, 1807, **19**—*barrage*, **363-9, 373-9**—*capture* of, 1801, **12**—*guns* forwarded from, **13**—*surrender* of, 1882, **51**

Ross, Capt. A. J., **R.E.**, *attached R.F.C. Sinai and Senussi operations*, **322**—*works*, Egypt, **488, 501**

Ross, Lieut.-Col. Justin C., **R.** (Bengal) **E.**, *interest* in geology, **520**—*service* in Egypt, **372, 373, 377, 501, 520**—*service* in India, **372, 520**—*study* of Egyptology, **519**—*Wadi Rayan* scheme, **381**

Royal Air Force, detachment in Sudan, **339, 346, 347**

Royal Artillery, *16th Company*, R.G.A., **249**—*32nd Battery*, **249, 261, 263, 272**—*37th Howitzer Battery*, **249, 259**—*R.H.A.*, **34**

Royal Engineers, Companies, *2nd Fortress* (became Field in 1909), **154, 156, 167, 206, 214, 216, 246, 249, 261, 356, 357**—*7th Field Survey*, **356, 357**—*8th Railway*, **28, 29, 38, 42-4, 93, 101-3, 206, 229**—*9th Field*, **356**—*10th Railway*, **70, 71, 76, 77, 101**—*11th Field*, **77, 93, 96, 118, 119**—*17th Field*, **28-30, 35**—*18th Field*, **28, 29, 35**—*21st Field*, **28, 36**—*24th Field*, **28, 29, 35, 38, 70-5, 78, 81, 121, 517**—*26th Field*, **28, 29, 32, 35, 47, 60-4, 81, 93, 96, 98, 118**—*42nd Field*, **356**—*East Lancs* (Territorial), **313**—*Kent* (Territorial), **331**

Royal Engineers, Messes, *Cairo*, **54, 55**—*Khartoum*, **491**

Royal Engineers, Officers, *Atbara* campaign, **211**—*Dongola* expedition, **153, 154**—*Egypt*, 1801, **9**—*Egypt*, 1807, **19**—*Egypt*, 1882, **27-9**—*Egypt*, since Great War, **354, 355**—*Egyptian Army*, **53**—*Egyptian state railways*, **407**—*irrigation*, **380**—*Nile* expedition, **92, 93, 109**—*Omdurman* campaign, **252, 253**—*Red Sea Littoral*, 1884, **59, 60**—*Red Sea Littoral*, 1885, **70**

Royal Engineers, Troops, A Pontoon, **28, 29, 42-6, 47**

Royal Engineers, units, *Balloon Detachment*, **70, 74**—*C Telegraph* Troop and other telegraph units, **28, 29, 42-6, 70, 93, 104, 105, 107, 108, 189, 416, 417, 438**—*Field Parks*, **28, 70**

Royal Marines, *Egypt*, 1882, **34, 36**—*Red Sea Littoral*, 1884, **64**—*Red Sea Littoral*, 1885, **71-3**

Royal Military Artificers, military mission to Turkey, **6, 13**

Royle, Charles, *The Egyptian Campaigns*, 1882-99, **25, 26, 64, 73, 113, 160, 281**

Rundall, Gen. F. H., **R.** (Madras) **E.**, *career*, **368**—*report* on Nile barrage, **368, 369**—*report* on "Palestine Canal," **369**

Rundle, Gen. Sir H. M. Leslie, *Adjutant-General*, Egyptian army, **147, 292**—*battle* of Toski, **121**—*Chief of Staff*, Dongola expedition, **151, 166, 170**—*Chief of Staff*, Omdurman campaign, **250, 447**—*Nile* expedition, **93**—*relief* of Gedaref, **289**

Russell, Col. R. E. M., **R.E.**, *defence* of Suez Canal, **313, 314**—*engineering* headquarters, Sudan Government Railways, Atbara, **401**—*operations* against Anuaks, **305**—*operations* on Western Frontier, **333**—*Port Sudan-Atbara* railway, **399, 400**—*Sinai* operations, **322**—*Sudan Government railways*, **403, 406**—*surveys*, **462**—*Tehamiyam-Kassala* line, **402, 403**—*work* in Intelligence Dept., **403, 462**

S

Said Ali Pasha, *interest* in railways, **99**—*interest* in surveys, **465, 467**—*Viceroy* of Egypt, **19, 99, 367**

St. Clair, Capt. W. A. E., **R.E.**, Red Sea Littoral, 1885, **71, 76**

St. Paul's Cathedral, Gordon Memorial, **122, 145**

Salahieh, *operations* in 1800, **5**—*operations* in 1882, **38**

Salisbury, 3rd Marquess of, *appointment* of Kitchener as Chief of Staff to Roberts, **301**—*comments* on Alexandria massacre, **26**—*dispatches* from Cromer, **274**—*disfavours* Watson, **82**—*favours* Dongola expedition, **149**—*instructions re* action after capture of Khartoum, **278**—*letter* from Cromer *re* Kitchener, **204**

Salmond, Major-General Sir W., **R.E.**, *Egypt*, 1882, **28, 35**—*story* of Girouard, **226**

Sandbach, Major-General A. E., **R.E.**, *battle* of Omdurman, **268**—*Egypt*, 1882, **29, 47**—*Omdurman* campaign, **211, 239, 276**—*Nile* expedition, **93**—*Red Sea Littoral*, 1885, **70, 76**

Sanders, Lieut. G. A. F., **R.E.**, Suakin, 1896, **88, 154, 487**

Sanderson, Mr., Works manager, railways, Wadi Halfa, **228, 230**

Sandes, Lieut.-Col. E. W. C., **R.E.**, *authorship* vii, viii, xii, xv—*career*, ix, x—*In Kut and Captivity* referred to, **x, 161, 316**—*Tales of Turkey*, x—*The Military Engineer in India*, vii, x, xv, **16, 28, 35, 90, 154, 159, 161, 312, 369, 375, 413, 446, 503**—*visits* to various places in Egypt and the Sudan, viii, xv, xvi, **39, 136, 217, 267, 299, 413, 518**

Sankey, Lieut. A. R. M., **R.E.**, with Nile expedition, **93**

Saras, *action* at, **120**—*boats* load up at, **91**—*importance* in Dongola expedition, **158, 159**—*outpost*, **152**—*railway* service to, **95, 100**

Sarsfield-Hall, E. G., *Governor* of Khartoum, **135, 136, 490**—*help* acknowledged, xvi—*letter re* battle of Omdurman, **266**

Sayed Ahmed, leader of Senussi, operations against, **329-33**

Scobie, Lt.-Col. R. McK., **R.E.**, Western frontier, 1935-36, **356**

Scott, Lieut. A. C., **R.E.**, Sudan military railways, **295**

Scott, Major-General D. A., **R.E.**, *Egypt*, 1882, **29, 44, 407**—*Nile* expedition, **93, 101**—*Sudan* railways, **102, 103**

Scott-Moncrieff, Col. Sir Colin C., **R.E.**, Aswan dam, **382**—*career*, **370, 378**—*irrigation* in Egypt, **364, 371-6, 379, 380, 387**—*letter re* Rameses statue, **512**—*Nile* barrage, **374, 380**—*Under-Secretary*, Public Works, **377, 381, 501**

Searchlights, *operations* against Nuers, **346**—*operations* in Nuba hills, **345**

Sebright, Mr., wireless telegraphs, Sudan, **434, 483**

Seggie, Q.M.S., W. F., **R.E.**, *transmission* of telegram, **107**—*wires* Wolseley's dispatch, **46**

Sennar, *buildings*, **485, 532**—*Gorringe governor* of, **532**—*reservoir* and dam, **385, 386, 404, 406**

Senussi, *agreement* with, **332**—*danger* to Egypt, **309**—*operations* against, **320, 329-32**

Settle, Lieut.-General Sir H. H., **R.E.**, *battle* of Afafit, **85**—*battle* of Gemmaiza, **84**—*battle* of Toski, **121**—*Nile* expedition, **93, 118**—*Surveyor-General* and Q.M.G., Egyptian Army, **148, 466**

Seymour, Admiral Sir Beauchamp, Naval comdr., Egypt, 1882, **26, 29, 52, 54**

Shaw, Lieut. T. B., **R.E.**, Nile expedition, **93**

Sheikh Barghut, *description*, **398, 494, 495**—*Gorringe's* railway report, **244**—*market* opened at, **82**—*proposed* railway from, **85, 296, 397**—*renamed* Port Sudan, 1904, **397, 497**—*selection* for terminal port, **492-7**—*Watson's* report, **59**

Shendi, *barracks*, **480**—*engineering* headquarters, Sudan Government railways, **391**—*Keppel's* raid, **212**

Shilluks, *help* to Kitchener on Fashoda expedition, **280**—*Marchand's* dealings with, **282**

Sim, Capt. G. H., **R.E.**, Red Sea Littoral, 1885, **71**

Simmonds, General Sir J. Lintorn, **R.E.**, exoneration of Graham, **37**

Sinai, desert and peninsula, *Egyptian troops* in, **307**—*operations*, 1914-17, **314-22**—*survey*, **23, 509**—*traversed* by Turkish army, 1800, **3**—*value* as military obstacle, **309**—*water-supply*, **321**

Sinauer, Lieut. E. M., **R.E.**, Works, Sudan, **487**

Singa, barracks at, **491, 492**

Singer, Brig.-General C. W., **R.E.**, *action* during mutiny in Khartoum, **343**—*Chief Engineer*, Egypt, 1919-23, **354**

Sinkat, *invested* and captured by Osman Digna, **57-9**—*Mahdi raises tribes* at, **57**—*proposed* railway, **85**

Siwa, operations round, **332, 333**

Slatin Pasha (Major-General Sir Rudolf Baron von), *career*, **140, 141**—*Dongola* expedition, **156**—*escape* from dervishes, **141, 151**—*Fire and Sword in the Sudan* referred to, **133, 135, 141, 274**—*Gordon's head* shown to, **143**—*Inspector-General*, **482, 531**—*Omdurman* campaign, **252, 258**—*opinion re relief*, **115**—*pursuit* of Khalifa, **279**—*received* by H.M. the King at Port Sudan, **500**—*taken prisoner* by dervishes, **140, 141**

Slave trade, Gordon's efforts to suppress, **522, 524, 526, 527**

Smith, Capt. Sydney, **R.E.**, Egypt, 1882, **28, 43**

Smith-Rewse, Major H. W., **R.E.**, Red Sea Littoral, 1885, **70**

Smythe, Major General Sir N. M., **V.C.**, battle of Omdurman, **267**—*Sudan-Abyssinian* boundary, **452**

Sobat River, *exploration*, **452–4**—*importance* in irrigation, **361**—*Marchand's journey* up, **287**—*post* established, **284, 285**

Sollum, *evacuation*, **329**—*reoccupation*, **331, 332**

Sowerby, Lieut.-Col. M. E., **R.E.**, *death*, **406, 407**—*Egypt-Palestine* railway, **327, 411**—*Port Sudan-Atbara* railway, **398**—*Sudan Government* railways, **295, 389**—*Under-Secretary*, Ministry of Communications, **411, 412**

Spaight, Major W. F., **R.E.**, Nile expedition, **93**

Speke, early traveller in Sudan, **442, 444**

Squire, Capt. J., **R.E.**, *memorandum* on " Pompey's pillar," **504**—*with British force* in Egypt, 1801, **9, 15, 504**

Stack, Major-General Sir Lee, Governor-General of Sudan, assassination, **341, 532**

Stanton, Col. E. A., *design* of Sudan stamps, **171**—*elaboration* of design of Khartoum, **482**—*exploration* of Bahr el Ghazal, **285, 286**—*with expedition* to Fashoda, **279, 282, 283, 286**

Stanton, Brevet Col. Edward, **R.E.**, British Agent and Consul General, Egypt, 1865–76, **532, 533**

Stead, Sergt., **R.E.**, Sudan telegraphs, **423–5, 430, 432, 437**

Steamers, *Dongola* expedition, **156**—*ferry* at Khartoum, **483**—*Watson's article*, **99, 114**

Steele, Ensign, George, **Bengal Engineers**, map of Alexandria, **465**

Steevens, G. W., *With Kitchener to Khartoum*, **194, 205**

Stephenson, Lieut.-General Sir Fred., commdg. Army of Occupation, **59, 65, 106, 151, 512, 514**—*defeats* Khalifa at Ginnis, **119**—*views* on advance, Suakin-Berber, **88**

Stevens, Sergt. G. A., **R.E.**, Sudan telegraphs, **437**—*wireless* telegraphs, Sudan, **434**

Stevenson, Major-General A. G., **R.E.**, Atbara campaign, **211**—*battle* of Firket, **162, 165**—*exploits* in gunboat Metemma, **252, 256, 259, 274**—Omdurman campaign, **211, 252, 256, 276**—*proposed Korosko-Murrat Wells railway*, **175, 222–5**—*Wadi Halfa-Abu Hamed railway*, **225, 226, 229–32, 289, 294, 295**—*with Dongola expedition*, railways, **153, 154, 156, 159, 160, 167, 173, 176, 181, 183, 186**

Stewart, Lieut.-Col. J. H. D., *defeated* at Halfaya, **132**—*diary*, **138**—*help* to Gordon in Sudan, **122, 126–8, 130, 131**—*murdered* at El Hebba, **108, 117, 196**—*sent off* by Gordon, **140**

Stewart, Major-General Sir H., *battle* of Abu Klea, **111**—*Egypt*, 1882, **50**—*mortally wounded* at Abu Kru, **113**—*Nile* expedition and desert column, **92, 95, 109–13**—*Red Sea Littoral*, 1884, **66**

Stewart of Coll, Brig.-General E. M. P., **R.E.**, wire roads in Gallipoli, **329**

Stewart, Capt. R. W., **R.E.**, survey of Palestine, **509**

Stigand, Major C. H., *death* at hands of Dinkas, **340**—*deputation* to Lado, **403**

Stileman, Capt. E. C. R., **R.E.**, Western Frontier, 1935–36, **356**

Stokes, Col. A. W., **R.E.**, *Chief Engineer*, Egypt, 1930–32, **354**—*Sinai* operations, **323**—*works*, Egypt, **488**—*works*, Sudan, **481–4, 488**

Stokes, Lieut.-General Sir John, **R.E.**, article on Kitchener's command of Dongola expedition, **150**—*Suez Canal*, **533–6**

Strachey, Lieut.-General Sir Richard, **Bengal Engineers**, archæological researches in India, **503**

Stuart, Major-General Sir Andrew M., **R.E.**, *Nile* expedition, **93, 98, 104, 105, 108**

Stuart-Wortley, *see* Montagu-Stuart-Wortley.

Suakin, *administration*, **530**—*defences*, **79, 80**—*early history*, **60**—*harbour* and port, **61, 68, 395, 396, 493, 494, 496**—*Indian contingents* at, **86, 87, 149, 150**—*operations* near, 1884, **57–67**—*operations* near, 1885, **68–78**—*siege* by Osman Digna, **79**—*water supply*, **80, 81, 86, 396**

Suarda, *capture*, **165**—*dervish forces* at, **152**—*telegraph* extended to, **166**

Sudan, *administration* under Kitchener, **293, 530**—*administration* under Wingate, **303, 531**—*area*, **458**—*book* of loyalty, **ix**—*building* operations, **491**—*Defence Force, see* Sudan Defence Force—*evacuation*, **56, 57, 107, 118**—*Government railways, see* Sudan Government Railways—*irrigation*, **385, 386**—*list* of Governors-General, **532**—*maps* and mapping, **463, 469**—*military railways, see* Sudan Military railways—*mutinies*, 1924, **341, 342**—*operations* since Great War, **339**—*postage stamps*, **171**—*rebellion* under Mahdi, **56**—*reconquest*, **147–277**—*R.E. officers* **ix**

Sudan Defence Force, *clothing,* **305, 353, 354**—*engineer* troops, **352-4, 392**—*Equatorial* Corps, **346, 492**—*formation,* **340**—*functions,* **344**—*motor machine-gun* pioneer corps, **353**—*organization,* **349, 350**—*reduction,* **351**—*review,* **351**—*sapper* company, **344, 346, 348, 351-4**—*sapper* platoon, **353, 354**—*sapper* section, *see* Sudanese Sapper Section—*wireless* telegraph section, **353, 354**

Sudan Government Railways, *administration,* **341**—*branch* to Jebel Auliya, **407**—*branch* to Kareima, **400**—*connection* of R.E. with, **407**—*description* of, in 1900, **390**—*extension* to El Obeid, **334, 401**—*Great War,* **404**—*Haiya*-Kassala-Gedaref-Sennar line, **405, 406**—*paper* by Macauley, **178, 233, 235**—*reaches* Khartoum, **486**—*relaying* lines, **405**—*Tehamiyam-Kassala* line, **402**—*tonnage,* **406**

Sudan Military Railways, *explanation* of title, **226**—*gauge,* **226**—*part played* in Atbara and Omdurman campaigns, **222**—*rolling* stock for Great War, **308.** *See also* Railways, Port Sudan-Atbara, Wadi Halfa-Halfaya and Wadi Halfa-Saras.

Sudanese Sapper Section, *employment* during mutiny, **343**—*field* operations, **341**—*formation,* **305, 306, 340**—*reconstitution,* **343**

Suez, *base* of Indian contingent, 1882, **47**—*British* occupation, 1882, **32**

Suez Canal, *administration,* **23, 533**—*author's* visit, **xvi**—*British* garrison, **358**—*construction* and opening, **21, 367**—*defence,* **307, 309, 310, 312, 315, 316, 318, 320, 321, 325**—*description,* **310, 311**—*International* commission, **22, 535**—*operations* on, 1882, **31, 33, 535**—*strategic* importance, **309, 310**—*Turkish* crossing, **315**—*widening,* **535, 536**

Suez Canal Company, *help* acknowledged, **xvi**—*help* to British forces during Great War, **312**—*sale* of Egyptian shares to Great Britain, **24, 533, 534**—*Stokes* Vice-President, **535**

Suleiman, son of Zubeir, *defeated* and slain by Gessi, **527**—*defeated* by Gordon, **526**—*Governor* of Darfur, **523**

Survey Department, *Aswan* dam, **384**—*Egypt,* **467-9**—*part played* in Great War, **308, 469**—*Sudan,* **458-64**

Surveys, *cadastral,* **459, 466**—*compass* traverse, Bor-Taufikia, **433, 467**—*geological,* *q.v.*—*Nile* basin, **154**—*Palestine,* **507-11**—*Sinai* peninsula, **23, 323**—*Sobat* river, **453**—*Sudan,* **458-61**

Sword, Lieut. W. D., joint author with Alford of *The Egyptian Soudan, Its Loss and Recovery,* see Alford.

Symes, Lieut-Col. Sir George Stewart, Governor-General of Sudan, help acknowledged, **xvi, 532**

Syria, events in 1799-1800, **3, 5, 7, 13, 14**

T

Talbot, Col. Hon. Milo G., **R.E.,** *acting* Governor-General, Sudan, **459, 532**—*Atbara* campaign, **211**—*Director,* Military Intelligence, Egyptian Army, **207, 292, 447**—*Director,* Surveys, **292, 421, 447, 450-2, 456-60, 467, 469**—*Dongola* expedition, **154, 159, 446**—*Kordofan* expedition, **297**—*mission* to Sayed Idris, **332, 460**—*Omdurman* campaign, **211, 252, 276**—*report* on Korosko-Murrat wells railway, **175, 224, 225, 232, 233**—*Sudan-Eritrean* boundary, **449**—*surveys,* **446, 447**

Talodi, aerodrome, **346, 492**

Tamai, *battles,* **63-5, 69, 71**—*operations* round, **75, 78, 79, 82**

Tamanieb, *action* at, **66**—*annihilation* of Egyptian force, **58**

Tanner, Lieut. J. A., **R.E.,** Red Sea Littoral, 1885, **71**

Tara, H.M.S., capture and rescue of crew, **329-31**

Taufikia, telegraph line reaches, **418**

Teb, Et, *battle,* **58**—*second battle,* **61-3**

Telegraphs, *Bor-Gondokoro,* **425**—*Bor-Taufikia,* **425, 426, 429, 430**—*Egypt,* **438-40**—*El Obeid—El Fasher,* **435**—*El Obeid-Talodi,* **431, 437**—*Kassala-Sennar,* **418, 421**—*Khartoum-Roseires,* **416-8**—*Khartoum-Taufikia,* **418**—*Meshra-Tonj* and Rumbek, **421-5**—*military,* Atbara campaign, **242**—*military,* Dongola campaign, **152, 155, 160, 165, 170**—*military,* Egypt, 1882, **45, 46, 48, 438**—*military,* Nile expedition, **98, 99, 103-7, 438**—*military,* Omdurman campaign, **255-7, 415**—*military,* Red Sea Littoral, **104**—*Omdurman-El Obeid,* **420**—*Suakin-Berber,* **415, 416, 418, 435**—*Sudan,* **415-38**—*Taufikia-Talodi,* **430**—*White Nile* line, **415, 416, 418, 421**

Tel el Kebir, *battle,* **41, 44, 45, 47, 48, 165**—*enemy* position, **34, 38-40**—*R.E. officers* at, **30, 36**

Telephones, *Egypt,* **439**—*Sudan,* **436**

Templer, Major J. F. B., Red Sea Littoral, 1885, **70, 74, 75**

Thackeray, General F. R., **R.E.,** Egypt, 1807, **19**

Thomson, Lieut. A. G., **R.E.,** *Egypt,* 1882, **29**—*Red Sea Littoral,* 1884, **67**—*Red Sea Littoral,* 1885, **71**

Thwaites, Lieut. H. F. O., **R.E.,** *All Saints' Cathedral,* Khartoum, **486**—*Director,* Mily. Works, **491**—*help* acknowledged, **497**—*works,* Sudan, **481-4, 486, 488**

Todd, Major K. R., **R.E.,** *Nile* expedition, **93**—*Red Sea Littoral,* 1884, **80**—*starts* R.E. Mess, Cairo, **54**

INDEX.

Tofrik, *action at,* **72, 73, 78**—*balloon employed at,* **74**
Tokar, *attempted relief,* **58**—*besieged by Osman Digna,* **57, 58**—*expedition under Holled-Smith,* **111**—*fall,* **59**—*occupied by Graham,* **62**—*works at, 1896,* **86**
Tomlin, Lieut.-Col. J. L., Royal Signals, late **R.E.**, Sudan posts and telegraphs, **437**
Tomlinson, Col. H. W., **R.E.**, Chief Engineer, Egypt, 1936, **354**
Torricelli, Signor, Aswan dam, **381, 382**
Toski, battle of, **120, 121**
Tower, Capt. G. A., **R.E.**, Nile expedition, **93, 104, 107, 108**
Townshend, Major-General C. V. F., *Dongola expedition,* **161**—*Mesopotamia and defence of Kut,* **x, 316**
Trinkitat, *causeway,* **85**—*works at,* **86**
Tsana, Lake, irrigation schemes, **385, 386**
Tudway, Major R. J., *commdg.* camel corps, Atbara campaign, **214**—*battle of Firket,* **162**—*Bayuda desert,* **198**—*Omdurman campaign,* **250, 262, 268, 269**
Tuke, Lieut. M. L., **R.E.**, *Egypt,* 1882, **29**—*Nile expedition,* **93**—*Red Sea Littoral,* 1884, **60**—*R.E. Mess,* Cairo, **54**
Turkey, *Egypt applies for troops,* **57**—*French proclivities,* 1807, **18**—*in 1882 crisis,* **31**—*military mission,* **5–8**—*Sultan, honours for British officers,* **52**—*suzerainty over Egypt abolished,* **309**
Turko-Egyptian war, operations in 1800, **3–5, 7**
Turner, Lieut. A. G., **R.E.**, survey of Sinai, **323**
Turner, Brevet Major E. V., **R.E.**, *memoir on Pearson,* **464**—*Posts and telegraphs, Sudan,* **423, 425, 429, 431, 432, 483**
Turner, Lieut.-Col. H. F., **R.E.**, *inspection of Egyptian telegraphs,* **439**—*Nile expedition,* **104, 197, 438**—*Red Sea Littoral,* 1885, **70, 71**
Twining, Lieut. P. G., **R.E.**, Uganda railway, **448**
Tyler, Lieut. J. C., **R.E.**, Egypt, 1882, **29**

U

Uganda, *Egyptian troops in,* **307**—*Gordon's travels in,* **523**
Umm Debeikerat, battle of, **85, 299, 300, 420**

V

Vetch, Capt. J., **R.E.**, proposal for Suez Canal, **21**
Vetch, Col. R. H., **R.E.**, *Life, Letters and Diaries of Lieut.-Gen. Sir G. Graham referred to,* **27**—*Life of Lieut.-General Sir Andrew Clarke referred to,* **21, 42**
Victoria, H. M. Queen, *dispatches from Wolseley,* **46**—*inscription on Rameses statue,* **514**—*interest in Kitchener,* **83, 171, 256, 290**
Vidal, Lieut. W. S., **R.E.**, *Egypt,* 1882, **29, 43, 44**—*Nile expedition,* **93, 101, 103**
Vizier, Grand, commdg. Turkish army in Egypt and Syria, **3–8, 13–15**
Von Donop, Capt. P. G., **R.E.**, *Nile expedition,* **93, 101**—*Sudan railways,* **102**
Voyageurs, Nile expedition, **89, 91, 97**
Vultures, flights observed before battles, **197, 256**

W

Wad en Nejumi, Emir, *defeat at Toski,* **120, 121**—*siege of Khartoum,* **142**
Wad Habashi, importance in Omdurman campaign, **250, 251**
Wadi Halfa, *advanced base,* Nile expedition, **95**—*base,* Dongola expedition, **149, 157, 158**—*defences,* **119, 157**—*frontier station,* **56, 119**—*railway base,* **389**—*wireless station,* **437**
Wad Medani, buildings, **480, 485, 532**
Walker, J. C., *branch railway to Kareima,* **400**—*extension to El Obeid,* **404**
Walker, Lieut. W. R. G., **R.E.**, Sudan Defence Force, **352**
Walkey, C. E. J., article on Khartoum, **472, 481**
Wallace, Major-General A., operations against Senussi, **329–31**
Wallace, Major W. A. J., **R.E.**, Egypt, 1882, **29, 43**
Waller, Capt. R. L., **R.E.**, surveying with Gwynn in Abyssinia, **459**
Waller, Capt. S., **R.E.**, Egypt, 1882, **29**
Walshaw, Sergt., **R.E.**, Sudan telegraphs, **424, 425, 429, 430, 432**
Warren, Lieut.-General Sir Charles, **R.E.**, *archæology in Palestine,* **508, 509**—*career,* **32, 75**—*Egypt,* 1882, **28, 29**—*Governor-General, Red Sea Littoral,* **493**—*joint author with Wilson of The Recovery of Jerusalem,* **508**—*notes on Pyramid,* **506**—*sent to investigate murder of Palmer,* **32**—*survey of Palestine,* **465, 508**—*Underground Jerusalem referred to,* **508**
Water-supply, *Darfur expedition,* **336, 337**—*Jerusalem,* **507**—*Khartoum,* **486**—*Mersa Matruh,* **356, 357**—*on Wadi Halfa–Abu Hamed railway,* **227, 228, 231, 232, 235**—*Port Sudan–Atbara railway,* **395, 399**—*Senussi operations,* **331**—*Sinai operations,* **326–8**—*Suakin,* 1884, **61, 80, 81**—*Suez Canal,* **311, 319, 321**
Watson, Col. Sir C. M., **R.E.**, *article on Nile steamers,* **99, 114**—*correspondence with Gordon,* **114, 524, 528**—*detects site for Port Sudan,* **58, 59, 493**—

Egypt, 1882, **29, 48**—*Governor-General, Red Sea Littoral,* **67, 82, 83, 493, 529**—*History of the Corps of Royal Engineers, Vol. III,* referred to, **27, 30, 534**—*Life of Sir Charles Wilson* referred to, **52, 507, 509**—*memoir* on Conder, **510**—*notes* on Pyramid, **506, 507**—*seizure of Cairo,* **48–50, 546**—*survey* in Sudan, **442, 443, 523**—*surveyor-general,* Egyptian army, **53**—*Wilson's defence,* **115**

Watson, Capt. J. K., A.D.C. to Kitchener, Omdurman campaign and expedition to Fashoda, **204, 210, 211, 279**

Wauchope, Brig.-General A. G., Omdurman campaign, **249, 251, 261, 267–9, 271**

Webb, Sir Arthur, *cotton* cultivation, **540**—*irrigation,* **385, 386**

Webber, Major-General C. E., **R.E.,** *Egypt,* 1882, **29, 45, 46, 438**—*Nile* expedition, **92, 104, 106**

Weir, R. W. Schultz, *architect,* All Saints' Cathedral, **486**—*help* acknowledged, **xvi**

Wemyss, Capt. H. C. B., **R.E.,** Sinai operations, **322**

Western, Col. J. H., **R.E.,** *restoration* of Nile barrage, **376, 377, 380**—*service* in Egypt, **375, 376, 501**—*service* in India, **370, 375**—*survey* of Wadi Rayan, **381**

Western Frontier, engineering operations, 1935–36, **356–8**

White, Lieut. A. G., **R.E.,** blasting on Suez–Zafarana road, **356**

White Nile, *bridge* at Kosti, **404, 405**—*difficulties* of navigation, **279**—*expeditions* up, **278**—*importance* in irrigation of Egypt, **293, 361, 362, 383, 386**—*surveys,* **442, 443, 524**

Whitmore, Capt. M. D., **R.E.,** *Egypt,* 1882, **29**

Wilberforce Clarke, Major H., R. (Bengal) E., *Nile* expedition, **93, 101** *Wadi Halfa–Saras* railway, **102, 407**

Wilbraham, Lieut. B. H., **R.E.,** works, Sudan, **487, 488**

Wilkieson, Capt. C. B., **R.E.,** Red Sea Littoral, 1885, **70, 71, 73**

Wilkinson, Capt. M. T. L., **R.E.,** Western Frontier, 1935–36, **356**

Willcocks, Sir William, *Aswan* dam, **381–3**—*Egyptian Irrigation* referred to, **381**—*Mesopotamian* schemes, **469** —*Nile* barrage, **372, 374, 375**—*report* on Abu Simbel, **516, 517**—*report* on Nile reservoirs, **381**—*report* on perennial irrigation in Egypt, **381**—*service* in India, **371, 385**—*The Assouan Reservoir and Lake Moeris* referred to, **381**—*The Nile Reservoir Dam at Assouan and After,* **382**—*Wadi Rayan* scheme, **381**

Williams, Major-General Sir Godfrey, **R.E.,** *Engineer-in-Chief,* Egyptian Expeditionary Force, 1916, **320**— *Red Sea Littoral,* 1885, **71**

Williams, Major R. H., **R.E.,** R.E. Mess, Cairo, **54**

Williams, Major R. T., R. Signals, late **R.E.,** posts and telegraphs, Sudan, **436**

Willis, Lieut.-General G. H. S., divisional commr., Egypt, 1882, **26, 34, 38**

Willock, Lieut. H. B., **R.E.,** Egypt, 1882, **29, 44**

Wilson, Major-General A., Commdg. Suez Canal defences, **311, 315, 316**

Wilson, Col. B. T., **R.E.,** *Gallipoli* campaign, **318**—*operations* in Sinai, **321**—*Sudan Defence Force,* **351**— *Suez Canal* defences, **313**

Wilson, Major-General Sir Charles W., **R.E.,** *attempted relief* of Gordon, **83, 114–7, 254, 546**—*battle* of Abu Klea, **111, 112**—*Egypt,* 1882, **28, 29**—*From Korti to Khartoum* referred to, **110, 113, 115**—*Golgotha and the Holy Sepulchre,* **508**—*measurements* of Pyramid, **504, 509**—*Nile* expedition and desert column, **92, 98, 109, 110, 113**— *Recovery of Jerusalem,* joint author with Warren, **508**—*survey* of Palestine, **465, 507, 508**—*survey* of Sinai, **504, 509**—*trial* of Arabi, **51, 52**

Wilson, Sir C. Rivers, *Minister* of Finance, **24**—*Suez* Canal council, **536**

Wilson, Capt. G. F., **R.E.,** *Nile* expedition, **93, 101**—*Sudan railways,* **102, 103**

Wilson, Lieut.-Col. R. T., *History of the British Expedition to Egypt* referred to, **9, 16–8, 503**

Wingate, General Sir F. Reginald, *Adjutant-General,* Egyptian army, **292, 302, 447**—*arranges* for Slatin's escape, **141**—*Atbara* campaign, **210, 220, 240**— *Darfur* operations, **334, 335**—*defeats* Khalifa at Umm Debeikerat, **85, 148, 151, 158, 161, 188, 244, 297, 301, 446**— *Dongola* expedition, **151**—*foreword,* **vii–xiii**—*friendship* with Marchand, **287**—*Governor-General* of Sudan and Sirdar, Egyptian army, **vii, 140, 284, 303, 307, 319, 333, 334, 400, 431, 447, 459, 481, 487, 489, 493, 531, 537**— *Hedjaz* operations, **324, 325**—*help* acknowledged, **xv, 135**—*High Commissioner,* Egypt, 1917–19, **303, 325, 411, 531, 532**—*Mahdiism and the Egyptian Sudan* referred to, **56, 84, 85, 120, 121, 127, 130, 134–6, 138, 161**—*memoir* on Pearson, **464**—*memoir* on Talbot, **446**—*Nile expedition,* **92**—*Omdurman campaign,* **250, 252, 274, 291**—*planning* of Khartoum, **473**—*Port Sudan,* **59, 495, 497, 498**— *Port Sudan–Atbara railway,* **392, 395, 397**—*The Gordon College and its Work* referred to, **478**—*with expedition* to Fashoda, **279, 281–4**—*with Rodd mission* to Abyssinia, **207, 447**— *views* on agreement with Senussi, **332**—*views* on Arab revolt, **324**— *visit* to Balmoral, **500**

Winn, Lieut. J., **R.E.,** Egypt, 1882, **29**

Wireless telegraphy, Sudan, **430, 433-6**
Wittman, Dr. W., *military mission* to Turkey, **6**—*Travel in Turkey* referred to, **6**
Wollen, Lieut. W. R. G., **R.E.**, *railways*, Omdurman campaign, **241, 253**—*Sudan military railways*, **295, 389**
Wolseley, Field-Marshal Lord, *battle* of Tel el Kebir, **40-2, 165**—*commdg.* expeditionary force to Egypt, 1882, **26-52, 55**—*commdg.* Nile expedition, **68, 88, 92-114**—*confidence* in Graham, **69**—*opinion* of Kitchener, **213**—*The Story of a Soldier's Life* referred to, **89**—*views re* evacuation of Sudan **118**—*visit* to Suakin, **77**
Wood, Capt. C. K., **R.E.**, Nile expedition, **93, 104**
Wood, Major-General Sir Elliott, **R.E.**, *Egypt*, 1882, **28, 30, 35, 47**—*Red Sea Littoral*, 1884, **60, 61, 64, 104**—*Red Sea Littoral*, 1885, **67, 68, 70, 71, 80, 81**
Wood, Major-General Sir Evelyn, V.C., *Egypt*, 1882, **27, 51**—*formation* of new Egyptian army, **52-4**—*Nile* expedition, **90, 92, 95, 117**—*suggested* as comdr., Dongola expedition, **150**—*views re* advance from Suakin, **65**
Woolley, L., archæological exploration in Sinai, **323, 507**
Works, *finance* and regulations, **488**—*Khartoum*, **470-8, 87**
Wright, Brig.-General H. B. H., **R.E.**, Suez Canal defences and Sinai campaign, **313, 317-20, 328**

Y

Yorke, Lieut.-Col. Sir Horatio, **R.E.**, Nile expedition, **93, 101**

Z

Zagazig, *Kitchener's visit* to, **54**—*operations* in 1882, **44, 48**
Zaghlul Pasha, *arrest* and deportation, **340**—*return* to Egypt, **341, 342, 411**
Zubeir Pasha, *British Government* refuse to employ, **128, 129, 132**—*dealings* with Gordon, **126, 128, 441, 522, 527, 528**—*invasion* of Darfur, **523**—*slave trade*, **522**

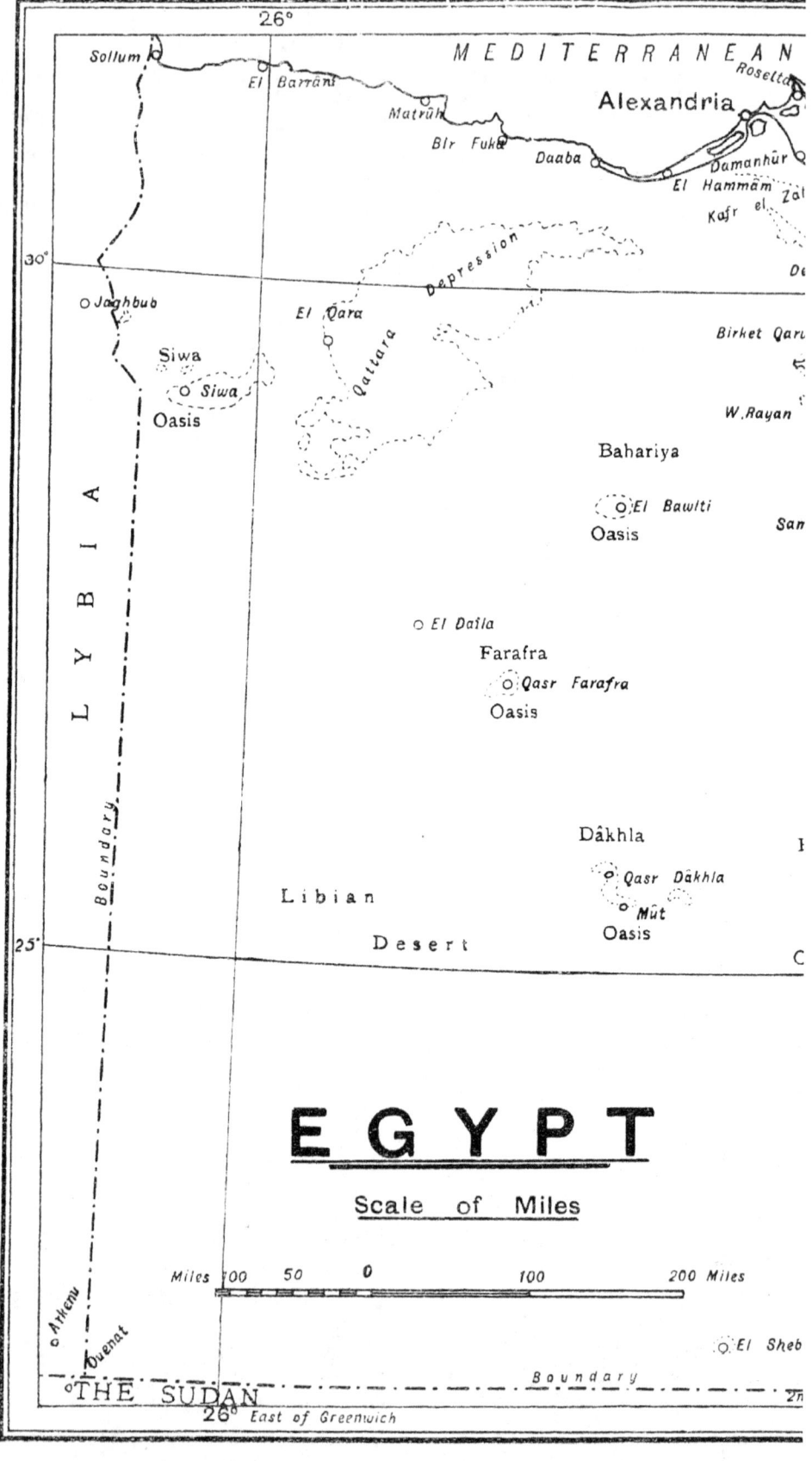

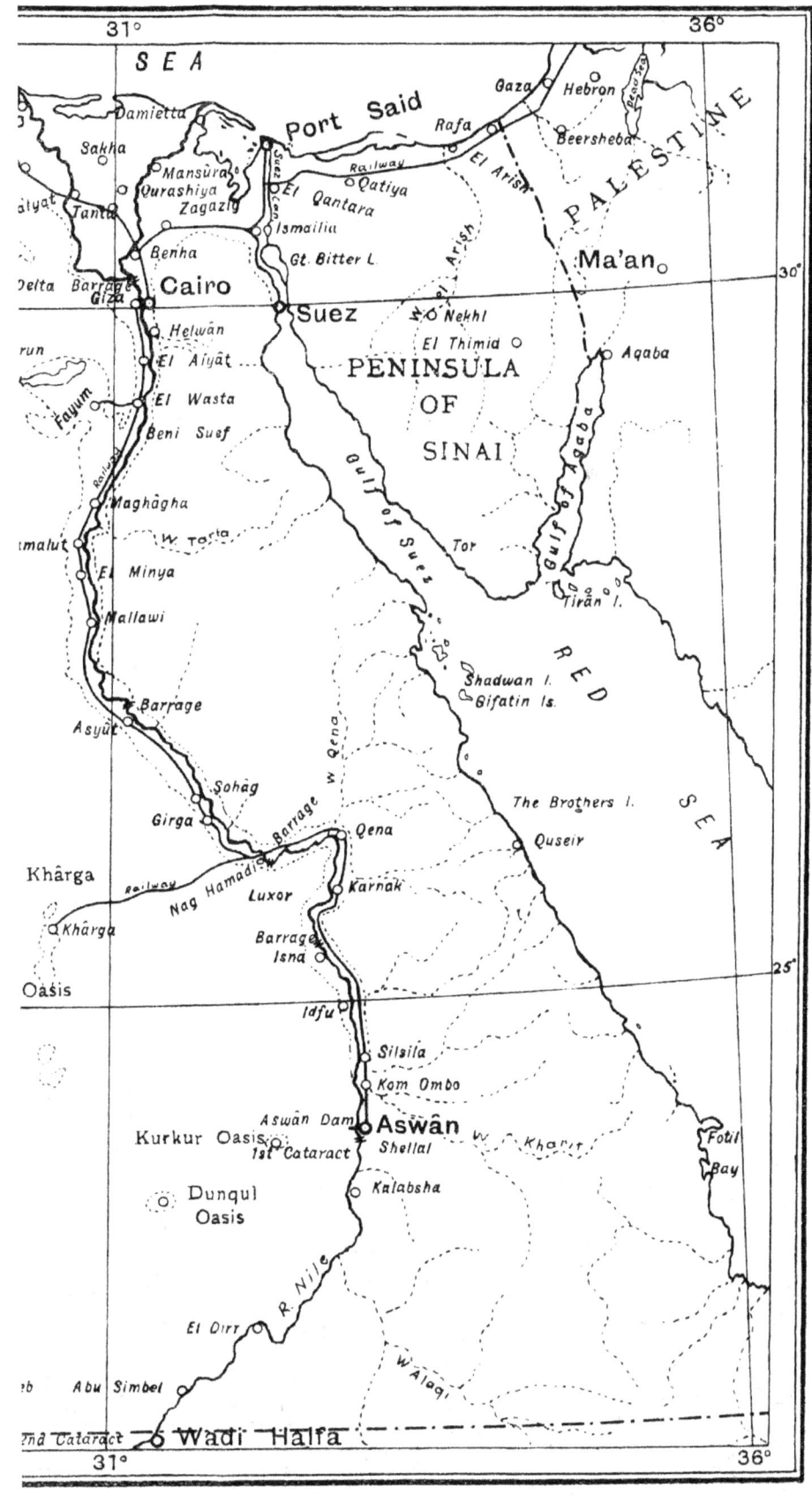

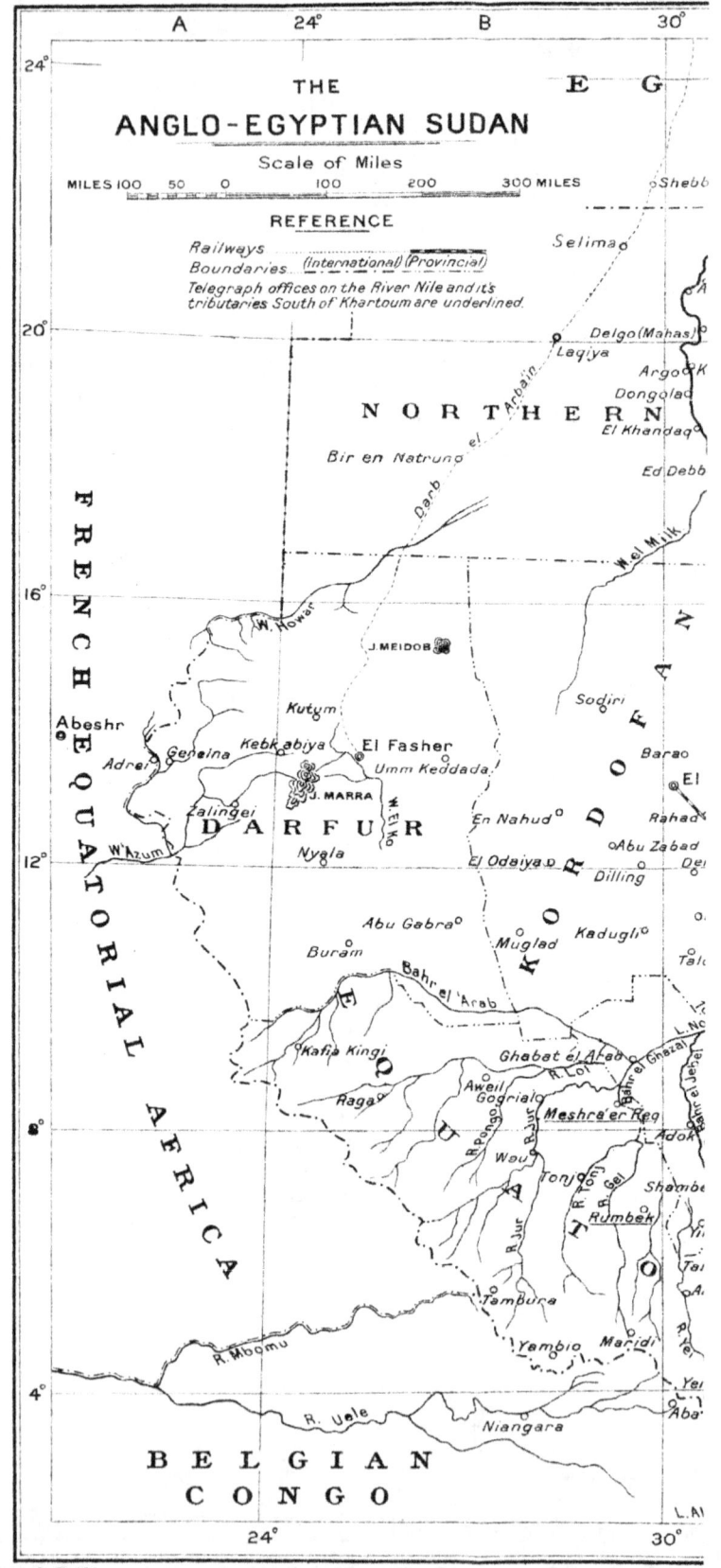

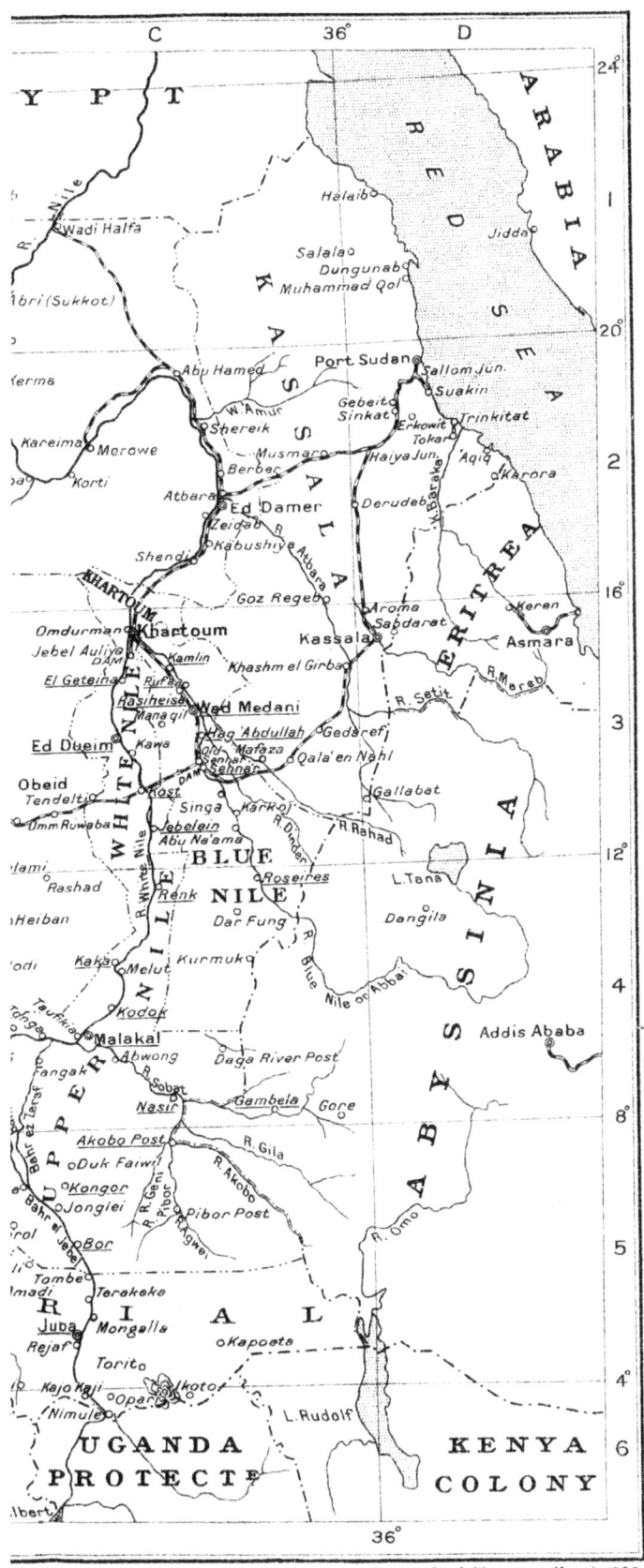

www.ingramcontent.com/pod-product-compliance
Lightning Source LLC
Chambersburg PA
CBHW080750300426
44114CB00020B/2685